Fundamentals of Strategic Management

Fred R. David

Auburn University

MERRILL PUBLISHING COMPANY

A Bell & Howell Company

Columbus   Toronto   London   Sydney

Published by Merrill Publishing Company
A Bell & Howell Company
Columbus, Ohio 43216

This book was set in Goudy Old Style and Palatino.
Production Coordinator: Susan King
Cover Design Coordinator: Cathy Watterson
Text Designer: Rick Chafian

Library of Congress Catalog Card Number: 85-73141
International Standard Book Number: 0-675-20551-4
Printed in the United States of America

2 3 4 5 6 7 8 9—91 90 89 88 87 86

To my family for their love and forbearance

Joy
Forest
Byron
Meredith

Preface

Special Note to Professors

This book is designed to be used as a text for the undergraduate business policy course. Strategic-management techniques are presented in an exciting way that allows students to apply knowledge to actual business situations. An abundance of current, clear examples is used to bring strategic-management concepts to life. This book combines traditional planning concepts with "state-of-the-art" developments in strategic management such as the Quantitative Strategic Planning Matrix (QSPM). A few areas of emphasis include strategic management for small businesses, social responsibility, business ethics, corporate culture, and strategic management in an international environment. The text material is guided by a comprehensive model of the strategic-management process. This text offers some special features, including:

1. A Cohesion Case on Ponderosa, Inc. is presented in Chapter 1. In later chapters, strategic-management concepts are introduced and are applied to the Cohesion Case through experiential exercises, which are provided at the end of each chapter.

2. One full chapter focuses on computer-assisted strategic planning issues and concerns.

3. A separate chapter focuses exclusively on how to write and evaluate a business mission statement.

4. Strategy implementation topics are examined throughout the text; two chapters are devoted entirely to this subject.

5. Current, undisguised cases are provided. No case is older than 1981, and 40 percent of the cases are dated 1984. The cases cover a broad spectrum of organizations and environments, with a special emphasis on smaller businesses.

Special Note to Students

Welcome to business policy. This is a challenging and exciting course that will allow you to function as the chief executive officer in many different organizations. Your major task in business policy will be to make strategic decisions and to justify those decisions through oral and written communication. Strategic decisions determine the future direction and competitive position of an enterprise. A decision to expand geographically or to diversify is an example of a strategic decision. Strategic decision making occurs in all types and sizes of organizations. Many people's lives and jobs are affected by strategic decisions, so the stakes are very high. Often, an organization's very survival is at stake. The primacy of strategic decisions makes this course especially exciting and challenging.

In business policy, you can look forward to making strategic decisions both as an individual and as a member of a team. No matter how hard employees work, an organization is in real trouble if strategic decisions are not made effectively. Doing the right things (effectiveness) is much more important than doing things right (efficiency). For example, Owens-Illinois was an efficient producer of glass containers in the early 1980s, but the company did poorly because plastic containers were capturing the market.

The concepts presented in this text will enable you to develop competitive strategies for all kinds of organizations. In addition, you will learn how an organization can gain competitive advantages through computer technology. Also, you will learn how to integrate into the strategic-management process the knowledge that you have acquired in prior business courses. For this reason, business policy often is called a capstone course. You probably will want to keep this textbook for your personal library.

You will have the opportunity in this course to make actual strategic decisions, perhaps for the first time in your academic career. Do not hesitate to take a stand and defend specific strategies that you determine to be best. The rationale for your strategy decisions will be more important than the actual decision, because no one knows for sure what the "optimal strategy" is for a particular organization at a given point in time. This fact accents the subjective, contingent nature of the strategic-management process. Use the strategic-management techniques and concepts presented in this text to formulate strategies that you can defend as being most appropriate for the organizations that you study.

Acknowledgements

I greatly appreciate the valuable insights and contributions made by many reviewers of this text. I also appreciate the efforts of individuals who contributed cases to this text. Business policy cases are a primary tool for giving students the opportunity to practice strategy formulation, implementation, and evaluation in different types and sizes of organizations. The case contributors to this text are:

Bob Ahuja   Mississippi State University
Larry Alexander   Virginia Polytechnic Institute

Robert Anderson	College of Charleston
Roger Atherton	University of Oklahoma
Jill Austin	Middle Tennessee State University
Terry Avila	Ball State University
Bobby Bizzell	Stephen F. Austin State University
James Chrisman	University of South Carolina
Bruce Coleman	Michigan State University
Fred David	Auburn University
Saul Diamond	University of Northern Iowa
Janet Dolan	Pfeiffer College
Phil Fisher	University of South Dakota at Vermillion
Fred Fry	Bradley University
William Fulmer	University of Alabama
Elmer Gainok	Northern State College
Bob Goddard	Appalachian State University
Lynda Goulet	University of Northern Iowa
Peter Goulet	University of Northern Iowa
Dennis Guthery	American Graduate School of International Management at Glendale, Arizona
Fred Haas	Virginia Commonwealth University
Jim Higgins	Rollins College
Lawrence Jauch	Southern Illinois University—Carbondale
Robert L. Johnson	University of South Dakota
Katie Kemp	Livingston University
Rudolph Koletic	University of Tampa
Mark J. Kroll	Sam Houston State University
Russ LaGrone	University of Alabama
Bob Lonis	University of Alabama
Stephen Lysonski	University of Rhode Island
Miriam Maier	Mississippi State University
Nancy Marlow	Eastern Illinois University
John Matheny	General Electric Corp.
Timothy Miller	University of Wisconsin—Parkside
Jimmy Moss	Sam Houston State University
Ernest Nordtvedt	Loyola University, New Orleans
Raj Padmaraj	Bowling Green State University
Victor Rios	Virginia Polytechnic Institute
Charles Roegiers	University of South Dakota at Vermillion
Arthur Sharplin	Northeast Louisiana University
Matthew Sonfield	Hofstra University
A. J. Strickland III	University of Alabama
James D. Taylor	University of South Dakota

I want to thank my colleagues and friends at Mississippi State University who provided an environment that supported me in this project, especially Dr. Dennis Leyden, Dean of the College of Business and Industry, and Dr. Dennis Ray, Chairman of the Department of Management.

Most of all, I want to express my love and appreciation to my wife, Joy, and my children, Forest, Byron, and Meredith. They sacrificed more than anyone else during the development and writing of this book.

Fred R. David

Contents

PART ONE

Overview of Strategic Management

The Strategic-Management Process

Strategic management is an exciting process that allows an organization to be proactive rather than reactive in shaping its own future. This chapter introduces a strategic-management model and a practical approach for studying and applying strategic-management concepts and techniques. The basic steps and terms that comprise strategic management are defined. They are brought to life with many examples.

WHAT IS STRATEGIC MANAGEMENT?

Once there were two company presidents who competed in the same industry. They decided to go on a camping trip together to discuss a possible joint venture. So they hiked deep into the woods. Suddenly they came upon a grizzly bear that rose on its hind legs and snarled. Almost instantly, the first president began taking off his knapsack and getting out a pair of jogging shoes. The second president said, "Hey, you can't outrun that bear." The first president responded, "Maybe I can't outrun that bear, but I can surely outrun you!" This episode captures the notion of strategic management.

Strategic management can be defined as the *formulation, implementation, and evaluation of actions that will enable an organization to achieve its objectives*. Strategy formulation includes identifying an organization's internal strengths and weaknesses, determining a firm's external opportunities and threats, establishing a company mission, setting objectives, developing alternative strategies, analyzing these alternatives, and deciding which ones to execute. Strategy implementation requires that a firm establish goals, devise policies, motivate employees, and allocate resources in a manner that will allow formulated strategies to be pursued successfully. Strategy evaluation monitors the results of formulation and implementation activities.

Peter Drucker says the prime task of strategic management is thinking through the mission of a business:

> That is, of asking the questions, "What is our business?—and what should it be?" This leads to the setting of objectives, the development of strategies and plans, and the making of today's decisions for tomorrow's results. This clearly must be done only by a part of the organization that can see the entire business; that can make decisions that affect the entire business; that can balance objectives and the needs of today against the needs of tomorrow; and that can allocate resources of men and money to key results.[1]

The strategic-management process can be described as an objective, systematic approach for making major decisions in an organization. Strategic management is not a pure science that lends itself to a nice, neat, one-two-three-type approach. Rather, strategic management is an attempt to organize qualitative and quantitative information in a way that allows effective decisions to be made under conditions of uncertainty. Strategic decisions, compared to purely intuitive decisions, are based more on objective criteria and analysis than on one's past experiences, judgment, and "gut" feelings.

Some managers and owners of businesses profess to have extraordinary abilities for intuitively devising and implementing brilliant strategies. For example, Will Durant, who organized General Motors Corporation, was described by Alfred Sloan as "a

4

man who would proceed on a course of action guided solely, as far as I could tell, by some intuitive flash of brilliance. He never felt obliged to make an engineering hunt for the facts. Yet at times he was astoundingly correct in his judgment."[2] Even Albert Einstein acknowledged the importance of intuition when he said, "I believe in intuition and inspiration. At times I feel certain that I am right while not knowing the reason. Imagination is more important than knowledge, because knowledge is limited, whereas imagination embraces the entire world."[3]

So some organizations today may survive and prosper because they have intuitive geniuses managing them. But not many organizations, if any, have an intuitive psychic as their chief executive officer. Thus, a vast majority of organizations could benefit from a strategic-management approach to decision making. In a recent book, Bruce Henderson describes intuitive decisions more bluntly:

> The accelerating rate of change today is producing a business world in which customary managerial habits in organizations are increasingly inadequate. Experience was an adequate guide when changes could be made in small increments. But intuitive and experience-based management philosophies are grossly inadequate when decisions are strategic and have major, irreversible consequences.[4]

The intuitive-versus-strategic approach to decision making is not really an either-or proposition. In fact, managers at all levels in an organization should inject their intuition and judgment into the strategic-management process. Strategic thinking and intuitive thinking can and should complement each other. A strategic-management approach gives managers more time for creative or intuitive thinking; intuition sometimes reveals special subjective factors that should be considered. In a sense, the strategic-management process is an attempt to duplicate what goes on in the mind of a brilliant intuitive planner.

It is widely acknowledged today that the rate, magnitude, and complexity of changes that impact organizations are accelerating. The strategic-management process is based on the belief that an organization should continually monitor key internal and external events and trends. An enterprise should seek to pursue strategies that capitalize on internal strengths, take advantage of external opportunities, mitigate internal weaknesses, and avoid or mollify the impact of external threats. *This process is the essence of strategic management!* In order to survive in today's marketplace, all sizes and types of firms must be capable of astutely identifying the need for and adapting to changes.

An old adage states, "Anything worth doing isn't easy." This statement is certainly true for the strategic-management process, which requires research, analysis, decision making, commitment, discipline, and a willingness on the part of employees and organizations to make changes. Essentially, a heightened awareness of strategy implementation's importance separates strategic planning of the past from strategic management today. The best-formulated strategies in the world are no good if they cannot be implemented successfully.

Owners, chief executive officers, presidents, and top managers of many profit and nonprofit organizations have concluded that the strategic-management process is vital to success. The importance of strategic management is evidenced in Exhibit 1.1 by the statements of several chief executive officers from well-known corporations. *Business Week* recently concluded that "Strategic management has touched off a revolution among America's 3,100 hard-pressed colleges and universities. All must contend with skyrocketing costs, a drop in federal aid, and decreasing numbers of high school graduates."[5] An increasing number of corporations and institutions are using strategic-management concepts and techniques to make effective decisions.

Exhibit 1.1   Chief executive officers discuss their firm's strategies

Kaiser Aluminum
"We have begun formal implementation of our strategic plan for the decade. Two years in formulation, the plan calls for Kaiser to identify its most promising businesses and to focus its resources on long-term development and profitability. Increased resources will be allocated to business lines where the company believes it has existing strengths, such as superior technology, low costs, or strong market positions." (Cornell Maier, chairman of the board and chief executive officer, in Kaiser's *1982 Annual Report*, p. 6).

Gulf & Western Industries, Inc.
"We are moving swiftly to implement a number of new strategies vital to building on our foundation and designed to solidify Gulf & Western's position as a growth company for the balance of the 1980s and beyond. These strategies include: (1) a major reorganization that is consolidating seven operating groups into three new units geared largely toward the consumer marketplace, each under the direction of a group president, (2) formation of a Corporate Management Board to develop new operating strategies and to review overall operational performance, (3) the sale of virtually all of the company's investment portfolio into a sharply rising stock market and the use of the proceeds to pay down variable rate debt, and (4) a major divestiture program of companies that either do not fit with our core operations, are losing money, are profitable but have a poor return on investment, or have limited growth potential." (Martin S. Davis, vice-chairman and chief executive officer, in Gulf & Western's *1983 Annual Report*, p. 2).

Ogden Corporation
"The best long-run results come from good strategic decisions, which ensure doing the right things (effectiveness), and the combination of design, technology, and automation, which ensures doing things right (efficiency). To predict . . . without the ability to adapt is simply to foresee one's own end! The strategic objectives that Ogden has achieved have enabled the adaptation necessary to cope with the changing economic environment for the balance of this century. We are describing a classic example of evolution; in this case, corporate evolution. To survive, both organisms and corporations must adapt to new circumstances." (Ralph Ablon, chairman of the board, in Ogden's *1982 Annual Report*, pp. 1, 10, 14).

International Multifoods
"In August of 1982, we announced the completion of a major strategic appraisal of alternatives for the future of our business. Fiscal 1983, better than any other year, again demonstrated the validity of our basic strategy of geographic diversification. It also reaffirmed our confidence in product diversification. Fiscal 1983 was our fifteenth consecutive year of improved earnings and our eleventh consecutive year of increased dividends." (William G. Phillips, chairman and chief executive officer, in International Multifood's *1983 Annual Report*, p. 2).

**KEY TERMS IN THE STUDY OF STRATEGIC
MANAGEMENT**

Strategists

Before we go any further in discussing the strategic-management process, we should define and give examples of some key terms. The first key term is *strategists*. Strategists are individuals who are most responsible for the success or failure of an enterprise. Strategists have different job titles, such as chief executive officer, president, owner, chairman of the board, executive director, chancellor, dean, and entrepreneur.

Since strategists are human beings they differ in their attitudes, values, ethics, willingness to take risks, concern for social responsibility, concern for profitability, concern for the short-run versus the long-run, and management style. For example, some strategists have *social responsibility* views similar to those of Ralph Nader, who proclaims that organizations have tremendous social obligations. Other strategists exhibit a philosophy more like that of John Galbraith, an economist who maintains that organizations have no obligation to do any more for society than is legally required. Carroll and Hoy recently suggested that strategists "should be including social policy guidelines in their strategic plans, so that goals and policies can be derived and administered. Ultimately, much of the burden of actually achieving social goals must and should rest on middle- and lower-level managers, but these managers cannot be expected to accomplish broad social objectives."[6]

In the next decade it will become increasingly important for strategists to understand that businesses can fulfill social responsibilities best by converting these obligations into self-interest opportunities. The first social responsibility of any business must be to make enough profit to cover the costs of the future, because if this one is not met, no other social responsibility can be met. Social responsibility issues are addressed throughout this text.

Strategists also differ in their attitudes toward *business ethics*. Laczniak has offered fourteen ethical maxims that enable strategists to deal with the subject of business ethics with confidence; these propositions are presented in Exhibit 1.2. Laczniak emphasizes that a major responsibility of strategists is to develop and communicate a code of business ethics for their organization. IBM, Caterpillar Tractor, Celanese, and the Bank of America are example firms that have formalized their own code of business conduct. The chief executive officers of these and many other firms have spelled out the ethical standards expected of all their employees.

Strategists obviously differ as much as organizations themselves, and these differences must be considered in the formulation, implementation, and evaluation of competitive strategies. Due to their personal philosophies, some strategists simply will not consider some types of strategies. For example, David Wickins, who replaced Colin Chapman as chairman of the board of Lotus, says, "Lotus has never been run with the objective of being a profitable company. Colin Chapman was quite simply interested in making cars go fast. I have a different viewpoint."[7]

Exhibit 1.2   Laczniak's fourteen ethical propositions

- Ethical conflicts and choices are inherent in business decision making.
- Proper ethical behavior exists on a plane above the law. The law merely specifies the lowest common denominator of acceptable behavior.
- There is no single satisfactory standard of ethical action agreeable to everyone that a manager can use to make specific operational decisions.
- Managers should be familiar with a wide variety of ethical standards.
- The discussion of business cases or of situations having ethical implications can make managers more ethically sensitive.
- There are diverse and sometimes conflicting determinants of ethical action. These stem primarily from the individual, from the organization, from professional norms, and from the values of society.
- Individual values are the final standard, although not necessarily the determining reason for ethical behavior.
- Consensus regarding what constitutes proper ethical behavior in a decision-making situation diminishes as the level of analysis proceeds from abstract to specific.
- The moral tone of an organization is set by top management.
- The lower the organizational level of a manager, the greater the perceived pressure to act unethically.
- Individual managers perceive themselves as more ethical than their colleagues.
- Effective codes of ethics should contain meaningful and clearly stated provisions, along with enforced sanctions for noncompliance.
- Employees must have a nonpunitive, fail-safe mechanism for reporting ethical abuses in the organization.
- Every organization should appoint a top-level manager or director to be responsible for acting as an ethical advocate in the organization.

Source: Gene Laczniak, "Business Ethics: A Manager's Primer," *Business*, Georgia State University (January–March, 1983): 23–29.

Mission Statements

A second key term that we should define is *mission statement*. It is an "enduring statement of purpose that distinguishes one business from other similar firms. A mission statement identifies the scope of a firm's operations in product and market terms."[8] A mission statement embodies the philosophy of an organization's strategists. It reveals an organization's self-concept, its principal product or service, and the primary customer needs that the firm is satisfying. In short, a clear and meaningful mission statement describes the values and priorities of an organization. (Chapter 3 is devoted to examining, evaluating, and writing mission statements.) For publicly held firms, a mission statement is often given at the front of the annual report to stockholders. The mission statement that appeared in the *1984 Annual Report of Rohr Industries, Inc.* was:

> Rohr's mission is to maintain the position as the leading aerospace supplier within diversified markets centered around technologically advanced nacelles, reversers and engine components. Rohr will continue to expand its business base by providing system management, design, development, manufacturing and support services to the worldwide aerospace industry.

Internal Strengths

Internal strengths, another key term in strategic management, refers to activities within an organization that are performed especially well. Management, marketing, finance, production, and research and development functions of a business should be audited periodically or examined to identify and evaluate key internal strengths. Successful enterprises pursue strategies that capitalize on internal strengths. Functional area checklists are provided in Chapter 5 to help you identify internal strengths of organizations.

Both profit and nonprofit organizations are striving more and more to capitalize on their internal strengths by instituting a strategic-management approach to decision making. For example, the University of Miami's president, Edward T. Foote II, has developed one of the best strategic plans in the country. An important aspect of the University of Miami's strategy is to take advantage of its strength in marine and atmospheric sciences.

An example internal strength of the Whirlpool Corporation is its reputation for providing outstanding customer service. Whirlpool is the No. 2 maker of major home appliances in the United States behind General Electric. For sixteen years Whirlpool has had a toll-free "Cool-Line" to answer questions about repairs, instructions, parts, warranties, and almost anything else that a customer needs to know. Recently, the company developed and provided a do-it-yourself repair kit for all of its appliances. Whirlpool also surveys customers every year to check on its franchisees' service performances.

Internal Weaknesses

Internal weaknesses is a key term that refers to management, marketing, finance, production, and research and development activities that limit or inhibit an organization's overall success. A firm should strive to pursue strategies that will effectively improve internally weak areas. C.E. Meyer, Jr., president and chief executive officer of Trans World Airlines, reported in 1983 that TWA's three major weaknesses were: labor, capital, and St. Louis. Specifically, TWA had been the least successful of the major U.S. carriers in gaining concessions from its organized workers; its long-term debt of $1.2

billion was more than two and a half times its equity; and with St. Louis as its hub, TWA's U.S. traffic had dropped so much that its rivals have called it the "incredible shrinking airline."[9] TWA has been replaced by Eastern as the third largest U.S. airline, behind United and American.

External Opportunities

Another key term in our study of strategic management is *external opportunities*. This term refers to economic, social, political, technological, and competitive trends and events that could significantly benefit an organization in the future. Massive changes are taking place in our society today on all fronts. The computer revolution, biotechnology, population shifts, changing work values and attitudes, space technology, and increased competition from foreign companies are just some of the major changes. These changes are creating a different type of consumer and consequently a need for different types of products, services, and strategies. In addition to environmental trends, external opportunities include one-time events such as the passage of a new law, a new product decision made by a competitor, or a technological breakthrough.

A basic tenet of strategic management is that firms should formulate strategies to take advantage of external opportunities. For example, an external opportunity that faces the Singer Company is the fact that the aerospace market is expected to expand fourfold between 1984 and 1990. As a result, sewing machines are taking a back seat at Singer, and Joseph B. Flavin, chairman and chief executive officer, is directing Singer's major resources into aerospace.

External Threats

A sixth key term, which is negatively analogous to external opportunities, is *external threats*. External threats consist of economic, social, political, technological, and competitive trends and events that are potentially harmful to an organization's present or future competitive position. For example, specific areas where competitors are strong could be a threat; unrest in the Middle East, rising interest rates, or a new President of the United States could be threatening. A systematic approach for identifying and evaluating potential environmental threats (and opportunities) is presented in Chapter 4. Successful organizations devise strategies that effectively avoid the impact of external threats.

A major external threat that faced Colonial Penn Group Inc. in 1983 was legal action against the company by stockholders and senior citizens. Colonial Penn is one of the nation's largest direct-mail insurers. The company agreed to pay $1.8 million in plaintiffs' legal fees to senior citizens. Another suit by stockholders threatened the company for not fully disclosing its dependence on retirees. The company has faced the threat of other customers withdrawing health care coverage due to this negative publicity.[10]

Objectives

Objectives can be defined as the long-term results that an organization seeks to achieve in pursuing its basic mission. The terms "objectives" and "goals" are used in many different ways in management literature. Some authors use the terms interchangeably; some use the term "objectives" to refer to short-term results and "goals" to refer to long-term results. Other authors reverse these meanings. Still others use "goals" as general organizationwide performance targets and "objectives" as specific targets set by subordinate managers. Therefore, anyone who studies the strategic-management process should be careful to avoid semantic confusion. In this textbook, the term "objectives" refers to long-range (more than one year) results; the term "goals" refers to short-range (one year or less) results. (A number of other writers use the terms this way, including Godiwalla, Meinhart, Warde, Vancil, and Lorange.[11])

Objectives are vital to organizational success because they provide direction, aid in evaluation, create synergy, reveal priorities, allow coordination, and are essential for effective planning, organizing, motivating, and controlling activities. Objectives should be challenging, measurable, consistent, reasonable, and clear. In a diversified conglomerate, objectives should be established for the overall company and for each division.

As an example of company objectives, Fairchild Industries announced that from 1984 to 1987 the firm plans to shrink its military business by 50 percent. It plans to boost commercial aerospace revenues to 38 percent of total company sales from its 1984 level of 18 percent. Fairchild also plans to triple satellite communications revenues to 7 percent by 1987.

Strategies

Another key term that we should define and exemplify is *strategies*. Strategies are the means by which objectives will be achieved. Alternative company strategies include geographic expansion, diversification, acquisition of competitors, gaining of control over suppliers or distributors, product development, market penetration, retrenchment, divestiture, liquidation, joint venture, or a combination of some of these actions. Specific guidelines for understanding when certain types of strategies are most appropriate are given in Chapter 2. Some example strategies being pursued by three different organizations are described in Exhibit 1.3.

Exhibit 1.3   Three organizations' strategies

The B.F. Goodrich Company is a large maker of chemicals, plastics, tires, and rubber products. Between 1980 and 1984, Goodrich pursued a retrenchment, or turnaround, strategy. Goodrich's plan was to dump marginal operations, generate cash from strong, slow-growth businesses, and push expansion in faster-growing businesses. Goodrich has been hampered by sagging employee morale, market miscalculations, and out-of-date management practices. The company's stock in late 1984 was selling for about $27, well below its book value of $47.74. Goodrich's tiremaking division has been the most consistent moneymaker, regularly earning close to $80 million operating profits on sales of $1.4 billion. Goodrich is a distant third among U.S. tire producers, behind Goodyear and Firestone. Chief executive officer John Ong is striving to pursue strategies that will overcome some of the company's internal weaknesses. There exists a drive to give line managers an increasing amount of power and freedom. Operating managers have recently gained more control over their budgets, operating plans, capital-spending plans, and salary administration. B.F. Goodrich's headquarters staff is being trimmed.

The University of Miami in June 1984 formulated a strategy to wipe out its mass-market image by shrinking the undergraduate student enrollment from 10,027 in 1982 to a projected 8,500 in 1985. The university plans to become much more selective, lifting the mean Scholastic Aptitude Test score requirements for applicants from 1,060 in mid-1984 to 1,150 before 1990. It also plans to raise $200 million in capital funds and to increase its applicant pool from 6,000 to 9,000 before 1990. These strategies are in response to some key external threats facing the university, such as a national decrease in the number of eighteen-year-olds and the fact that the Miami area has been suffering race riots and a flood of Cuban refugees. The University of Miami's strategic plan for the late 1980s includes using revenues generated by the business school to support the underendowed marine and atmospheric sciences school, eliminating the degree program in education, and awarding the medical school progressively lower salaries until 1989.

Pacific Power and Light Company has been pursuing a strategy of diversification for the last fifteen years. Headquartered in Portland, Oregon, PP&L is one of the most diversified electric utilities in the United States. In 1983, 45 percent of PP&L's sales and 37 percent of its net income were attributable to nonutility businesses. Some of the external threats that led to Pacific Power's diversificaton strategy were shrinking demand for electricity, disastrously expensive nuclear-construction products, greatly increased operating costs, and lower rate increases. PP&L's Chairman, Don Frisbee, warns other utility strategists that public utility commissions, stockholders, and ratepayers may get up in arms at the idea of "their" utility company diversifying. They simply do not want to subsidize what could become an organization that cannot manage diversified activities. Managing a diversified conglomerate, which PP&L has become, requires excellent management skills. PP&L has interests in cable television, telephones, and natural resources.

Sources: "Behind the Revolving Door at B.F. Goodrich," *Business Week* (October 15, 1984): 150, 153; "How Academia Is Taking a Lesson from Business," *Business Week* (August 27, 1984): 58, 60; "Utilities. Danger! Live Wires!! Diversification Turns up the Juice," *Industry Week* (September 17, 1984): 101–04.

Goals

Goals are short-term (one year or less) milestones or benchmarks that organizations must achieve in order for longer-term objectives to be reached. Goals should be measurable, quantitative, challenging, realistic, consistent, and prioritized. They should be established at the corporate, divisional, and functional levels in a large organization. Goals should be stated in terms of management, marketing, finance, production, and research and development accomplishments. A set of goals is needed for each objective that is established in an organization. Goals are especially important in strategy implementation, whereas objectives are particularly important in strategy formulation. Goals represent the basis for allocating resources. Chapter 8 presents a framework for effectively setting goals, establishing policies, and allocating resources.

An example firm that has clearly established goals is Family Dollar Stores, Inc. This fast-growing discount store chain based in Mathews, North Carolina, opened 106 new stores in the fiscal year ending August 31, 1983, and then set a goal to open 125 new stores before August 31, 1984. Family Dollar Stores' strategy of geographic expansion has led to increased sales and earnings levels for thirty-four consecutive quarters. As of January 24, 1984, the company had 701 stores located in the eastern United States.

Policies

The final key term to be highlighted here is *policies*. Policies can be defined as the means by which stated goals will be achieved, or as guidelines established to support efforts to achieve stated goals. There are two distinguishing characteristics of policies: (1) they are guides to decision making, and (2) they are established for situations that are repetitive or recurring in the life of a strategy. Policies are most often stated in terms of management, marketing, finance, production, and research and development activities. Policies can be established at the corporate level and apply to an entire organization, or they can be established at the divisional level and apply to a single division, or they can be established at the functional level and apply to only certain operational activities or departments. Policies, like goals, are particularly important in the strategy implementation process because they outline the organization's expectations of its people. Policies allow consistency and coordination within and among organizational departments.

Warehousing policies have been a key to L. Luria & Son, Inc.'s success over recent years. L. Luria & Son, a large Miami-based catalog retailer, concentrates merchandise in catalog showrooms and not in central warehouses. L. Luria's delivery policy is to ship within five hours of receipt of an order.

An unfortunate result of a poor policy occurred recently when the Toro Company, a major U.S. producer of snowthrowers and chain saws and a market leader in the premium power lawn mower business, decided to let discounters such as J.C. Penney Co. and K-Mart Corporation sell their machines without having to service them. Thousands of Toro's dealers became outraged and abandoned the company.

STAGES IN THE STRATEGIC-MANAGEMENT PROCESS

The strategic-management process can be viewed as consisting of three stages: strategy formulation, strategy implementation, and strategy evaluation.

Strategy Formulation

Strategy formulation can be defined as the process of establishing a company mission, conducting research to determine internal strengths/weaknesses and external opportunities/threats, performing analyses that match key internal and external factors, and establishing company objectives and strategies. Chosen strategies should effectively capitalize on a firm's strengths, overcome its weaknesses, take advantage of key external opportunities, and avoid external threats. To accomplish the strategy-formulation task, three major activities are required: *research, analysis,* and *decision making.*

Research is the first essential strategy formulation activity. Research must be conducted on two fronts: internal and external. Most organizations refer to the data-gathering activity as an "internal audit" and an "external audit." Internally, research is needed to identify key strengths and weaknesses in areas such as management, marketing, finance, production, and research and development. Key internal factors can be determined in a number of ways that include computing ratios and comparing these to industry averages. Various types of surveys can also be developed and administered to examine internal factors such as employee morale, production efficiency, advertising effectiveness, and customer loyalty.

Externally, research is required to monitor or scan the wealth of strategic information that is published every week. This process of collecting and analyzing external research information is sometimes called "environmental scanning." Published sources of strategic information include periodicals, journals, indexes, newspapers, trade publications, and government reports. Nonpublished sources include suppliers, distributors, customers, creditors, competitors, and shareholders. An excellent way to scan published sources of information effectively is to utilize online, electronically recorded databases.

Access to online databases is a tool of potentially fantastic power. The owner or chief executive of a business can obtain relevant economic, social, demographic, competitive, political, and technological data and forecasts by utilizing a modem and a personal computer. Online databases allow strategists to access market research data from Arthur D. Little or Predicasts, to monitor stock prices, to scan periodicals and newspapers, and to search journals by topic for all kinds of strategic information. Entire libraries, the knowledge of experts, and demographic and economic data are all electronically recorded and are easily accessible with a personal computer. According to the *Directory of Online Databases* (Santa Monica, Calif.: Cuadra Associates, Inc.), there are more than 1600 electronic databases available today.[12]

The second activity required in strategy formulation is *analysis.* Analytical techniques such as the SPACE Matrix, Grand Strategy Portfolio Matrix, and BCG Matrix can be useful in generating and evaluating alternative strategies. These and other important tools are described in Chapter 6. Matching an organization's internal strengths and weaknesses with external opportunities and threats is central to strategy formulation. "Matching" means aligning internal factors with external factors to formulate feasible strategies. For example, aligning an internal strength such as "excess working capital" with an external threat such as "a foreign competitor entering the market" could suggest a strategy such as "increase advertising expenditures 50 percent."

An example of an analytical matching tool is the Threats-Opportunities-Weaknesses-Strengths (TOWS) Matrix. In a recent article, Weihrich illustrates how the TOWS Matrix would have been useful to Winnebago Industries during the early 1970s. Figure 1.1 shows the Winnebago example. Notice in the figure that the alternative

Figure 1.1 Formulating strategy at Winnebago Industries, Inc. (Reprinted with permission from *Long Range Planning*, 15, Heinz Weihrich, "The TOWS Matrix—A Tool for Situational Analysis," Copyright 1982, Pergamon Press, Ltd.

	STRENGTHS	WEAKNESSES
	1. Identifiable corporate name with a good reputation 2. Good service and warranty 3. Established dealer network with good dealer relations 4. Extensive research and development capabilities 5. Automated, economical plant 6. Manufacturing of most parts for the motor home	1. Vulnerability because of one-product company 2. Concentration on higher priced units 3. Heavy investment in toolmaking will raise cost of model changes 4. One-plant location 5. No preparation for transition from family to corporate management
OPPORTUNITIES 1. Demand for smaller RVs 2. Development of international market 3. Demand for low-cost modular housing (FHA subsidy for mortgage loans)	SO STRATEGIES 1. Emphasize smaller, more efficient motor homes (O_1 S_1 S_2 S_3 S_4 S_5 S_6) 2. Expand into foreign markets (O_2 S_1 S_4) 3. Diversify into modular housing (O_3 S_1 S_4 S_6)	WO STRATEGIES 1. Develop and produce smaller RVs (O_1 O_3 W_1 W_2) 2. Build smaller plants in different parts of the country and abroad (O_1 O_2 W_4)
THREATS 1. Gasoline shortage and higher prices of gasoline 2. Slackening demand for RVs 3. "Trade-up" creates secondary market 4. Increased competition (GM, Ford, International Harvester, VW, Toyota) 5. Impending safety regulations	ST STRATEGIES 1. Diversify into farm equipment, railroad cars (T_1 T_2 T_3 S_1 S_3 S_4 S_5) 2. Consider diesel engines for motor homes (T_1 S_4) 3. Make RVs safer in anticipation of safety regulations (e.g. visibility, flame retardant, crash resistant, brakes) (T_5 T_4 S_6)	WT STRATEGIES 1. Sell the company (T_1 T_2 T_4 W_1 W_4 W_5)

strategy, "Expand into Foreign Markets" was feasible for Winnebago because of opportunity number two (O2) being matched with strength number one (S1) and strength number four (S4). The TOWS Matrix is described more fully in Chapter 6.

The third activity required in strategy formulation is *decision making*. Decisions must be made regarding what objectives to establish and which strategies to pursue. No organization has unlimited resources, so top managers must select from a number of alternative strategies that could possibly be beneficial. The Quantitative Strategic Planning Matrix (QSPM), presented in Chapter 6, is an important decision-making tool. Analytical tools, combined with sound business judgment, provide the basis for effective strategy-formulation decisions.

Strategy Implementation

Once strategies have been formulated, the second stage in the strategic-management process is *strategy implementation*. Strategy implementation can be called the action stage of the strategic-management process. Implementing means mobilizing employees and managers to put formulated strategies into action. Like strategy formulation, strategy implementation consists of three essential activities: *establishing goals, establishing policies,* and *allocating resources*. Strategy implementation is often considered to be the most difficult stage in the strategic-management process because it requires personal discipline, commitment, and sacrifice. Successful implementation can hinge upon a manager's ability to motivate employees, and motivating is often considered to be more an art than a science. Strategies formulated but not implemented serve no purpose.

Successful strategy implementation requires that an organization first *establish goals* in areas such as management, marketing, finance, production, and research and development. In large corporations goals are often established at three levels: corporate, divisional, and functional. Goals must be achieved in the short run if objectives are to be accomplished in the long run. The second strategy implementation activity is *establishing policies*. Policies are needed to encourage work toward stated goals, because goal achievement quite simply requires hard work. The third implementation activity involves *allocating resources* in accordance with the priorities indicated by stated goals.

Compared to strategy formulation, strategy implementation is more operational and less intellectual in nature. Subjective, qualitative skills are especially critical for successful strategy implementation. Strategy-implementation activities impact all employees and managers in an organization, whereas strategy formulation may directly involve only a few top managers.

Strategy Evaluation

The third stage in the strategic-management process is strategy evaluation. Three fundamental activities must be performed to evaluate an organization's strategies effectively. First, a firm must *review the internal and external factors that represent the bases for its current strategies*. Key questions to ask include: Are internal strengths still strengths?

Are internal weaknesses still weaknesses? Are external opportunities still opportunities? Are external threats still threats? With the second activity in strategy evaluation, a firm must *measure organizational performance.* Strategists should examine planned versus actual progress being made toward achieving stated goals and objectives. Finally, *corrective actions* should be taken as needed to improve the firm's internal and external strategic position.

Strategy evaluation is a critical stage in the strategic-management process because internal and external factors do change. Successful firms anticipate and adapt to changes quickly and effectively. Major changes in the underlying bases of a strategy may not impact current performance until it is too late to avoid or capitalize upon the event or trend. Therefore, alternative strategies should be considered whenever key internal and external factors change significantly.

Strategy evaluation is needed because success today is no guarantee for success tomorrow! In fact, success generally obsoletes the behavior that brought it about. Success always creates new and different problems. For example, the new (1984) AT&T companies have been making high profits selling about $4.1 billion a year of advertising in the Yellow Pages. But many competitors are now beginning to offer telephone book pages that feature lower prices, more colorful ads, salespersons instead of order takers, and silver pages.[13]

A summary exhibit of the strategic-management activities and stages is provided in Figure 1.2. Strategy formulation, implementation, and evaluation activities occur at three hierarchical levels in a large diversified organization: corporate, divisional, and functional. Managers at these levels have different responsibilities in the strategic-man-

Figure 1.2 The activities and stages in the strategic-management process

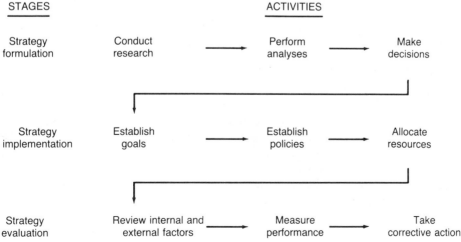

STAGES		ACTIVITIES	
Strategy formulation	Conduct research	Perform analyses	Make decisions
Strategy implementation	Establish goals	Establish policies	Allocate resources
Strategy evaluation	Review internal and external factors	Measure performance	Take corrective action

Figure 1.3   The strategic-management process at three levels (Source: Adapted from Peter Lorange, *Corporate Planning: An Executive Viewpoint* [Englewood Cliffs, N.J., Prentice-Hall, 1980], 61.)

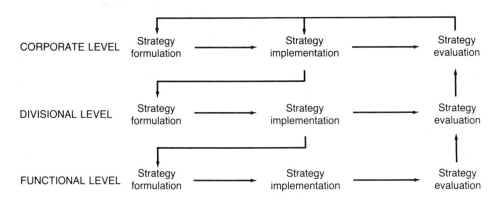

agement process, and they must communicate and interact effectively for strategies to succeed. Figure 1.3 reveals that strategies formulated at the corporate level can be implemented by formulating strategies at the divisional level. Once divisional-level strategies are formulated, they can be implemented by formulating functional-level strategies.

THE STRATEGIC-MANAGEMENT MODEL

Strategic management focuses on the total enterprise. It looks beyond everyday operations, problems, and crises to focus on an organization's overall growth and development. Strategy concerns the nature of the forest, not of the trees! Making effective strategic decisions is the major responsibility of an organization's owner or chief executive officer. Strategic decisions include determining what new businesses to get into, what businesses to abandon, how to allocate resources, whether to expand operations or to diversify, whether to enter other geographic markets, and whether to merge or form a joint venture with another firm.

The strategic-management process can best be studied and applied by using a strategic-management model. The schematic framework exhibited in Figure 1.4 is a comprehensive model of the strategic-management process. This model is certainly not a blueprint for success, but it does represent a clear and practical approach to evaluating strategies in actual situations. Interrelationships among the major components of the strategic-management process are shown in the model. To guide your study of strategic management, a visual display of this model is given in all subsequent chapters of this text. Appropriate areas of the model will be shaded to show the particular focus of each chapter.

Figure 1.4   The strategic-management model

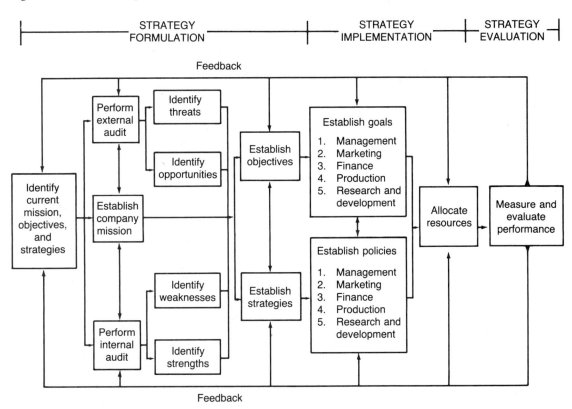

The strategic-management model or process can be summarized in twelve action steps. These steps can help you prepare a business policy case analysis.

1. Determine present mission, objectives, and strategies.
2. Perform external research to identify environmental threats and opportunities.
3. Perform internal research to identify company strengths and weaknesses.
4. Establish company mission.
5. Perform strategy formulation analyses to generate and evaluate feasible alternative strategies.
6. Establish objectives.
7. Establish strategies.

8. Establish goals.
9. Establish policies.
10. Allocate resources.
11. Review internal and external bases for current strategies.
12. Measure performance, and take corrective actions.

The strategic-management process allows an organization to use its strengths effectively to take advantage of external opportunities and to minimize the impact of external threats. Strategy formulation, implementation, and evaluation activities allow an organization to develop offensive as well as defensive strategies.

It is important to realize that the strategic-management process is both dynamic and continuous. A change in any one of the major components in the model can necessitate a change in any or all of the other components at any point. For instance, a shift in the economy could represent a major external threat or opportunity and require a change in company objectives and strategies; a failure to obtain specific divisional or functional goals could require a change in policies or company objectives; a major competitor could announce a change in strategy that poses a significant opportunity or threat. Therefore, internal and external factors and implementation efforts should be evaluated on a continual basis. The strategic-management process never really ends! It is sometimes called a "process of strategic change management." Noel Tichy recently discussed the essentials of strategic change management as follows:

> Organizations today face major, discontinuous change that makes strategic management more difficult and more complex than ever. To succeed in this environment, companies need to look at the technical, political, and cultural systems operative within their organizations. Managers too often focus on small components of the overall change problem, leading to a fixation on tactical concerns. All too often, fad, fashion, or personal proclivity guide decisions about change.[14]

STRATEGIC MANAGEMENT IN SMALL FIRMS

Strategic management is vital for a large firm's success, but what about small firms? The strategic-management process applies to small companies equally as well as to large firms! From their inception, all organizations have a strategy, even if the strategy just evolves out of day-to-day operations.

Dun and Bradstreet and the Small Business Administration report that 1984 was a banner year for new small business incorporations. There were more than 600,000 small business incorporations in that year. SBA's chief counsel for advocacy, Frank Swaim, says the data clearly shows that an ever-increasing number of men and women in the United States are interested in becoming their own bosses.

Numerous academic- and practitioner-oriented articles have focused on applying strategic-management concepts to small businesses, such as those listed in footnote 15 at the end of this chapter. A major conclusion from this research is that a lack of planning knowledge is a serious obstacle for many small businessmen. More exposure to strategic management concepts is vitally needed.

Other problems often encountered in applying strategic-management concepts to small businesses are a lack of sufficient capital to exploit environmental opportunities and a "day-to-day" cognitive frame of reference. Recent research concludes that (1) the strategic-management process in small firms is more informal than in large firms and (2) small firms that engage in strategic planning outperform those that do not.

A summary of research that has specifically examined the value of strategic planning in small firms is presented in Table 1.1. Note that strategic planning offers significant benefits to both manufacturing- and service-oriented small businesses.

STRATEGIC MANAGEMENT IN NONPROFIT AND GOVERNMENTAL ORGANIZATIONS

The strategic-management model can be used effectively by nonprofit and governmental organizations as well as by private sector firms. An increasing number of nonprofit and government organizations have embarked upon the process. For example, the techniques and concepts described in this text are increasingly being utilized with success by educational and medical institutions. Richard Cyert, president of Carnegie-Mellon University, recently said, "I believe we do a far better job of strategic planning than any company I know."[16]

Population shift in the United States away from the Northeast and Midwest to the Southeast and West is but one factor causing trauma for institutions that have not planned ahead for changing enrollments. (An excellent book that focuses on strategic planning in colleges and universities was published in 1983 by the Johns Hopkins Press. The book is entitled *Academic Strategy* and was written by George Keller.)

Medical institutions in this country are facing severe threats from increased costs and regulation. An increasing number of hospitals today are benefiting from a strategic-management approach to decision making. Many private and state-supported medical institutions are in financial trouble as a result of traditionally taking a reactive rather than a proactive approach in dealing with their environment. Declining occupancy rates and an accelerating growth of health maintenance organizations are two major threats facing medical institutions today. Alternative strategies being pursued by many hospitals include creating home health services, establishing nursing homes, developing urgent-care centers, and forming rehabilitation centers.

Other government and nonprofit organizations, such as the Boy Scouts, the Red Cross, chambers of commerce, and public utilities, are also increasingly accepting the strategic-management process as necessary for survival in the late 1980s and 1990s.[17] The Red Cross, for example, is pursuing a strategy of severe retrenchment. Facing growing annual deficits of $2.5 million in 1985 and $6.5 million in 1986, President Richard Schubert of the Red Cross, early in 1985, laid off 248 employees, reduced the organization's clerical staff by 40 percent, and redefined 60 percent of all jobs.[18]

Table 1.1 A summary of research examining the value of strategic planning in small firms

| Study Authors | Sample | | | Methodology | Focus of Study |
	Firms Studied	Type of Business	Definition of Small Business		
Chicha & Julien (1979)	90	Manufacturing	5–199 employees; less than $10 million annual sales	Questionnaire	To study strategic planning, and performance (longitudinal: 1968–1978)

Findings: Identified four types of strategies. Evidence showed significant increases in: (1) number of personnel, (2) sales, and (3) assets for firms having highest degree of strategic planning as evidenced by number of strategy changes.

Study Authors	Firms Studied	Type of Business	Definition of Small Business	Methodology	Focus of Study
Robinson (1979)	42	Service (independent model)	Less than $150,000 in annual sales	Field study intervention	To study the impact of the adoption of strategic planning and the resultant strategy on firm performance

Findings: Strategic planning improved O/M decision making, which led to significant increases in sales and profit and significant decrease in debt/equity ratios.

Study Authors	Firms Studied	Type of Business	Definition of Small Business	Methodology	Focus of Study
Potts (1977)	42	Manufacturing	Established in 1968 and having up to 20 employees; still operating in 1976	Mail questionnaire	To compare the use of outside accounting/financial services between successful and failing small business

Findings: Successful firms used outside accounting services as part of their strategic planning activities more extensively than did unsuccessful firms.

Study	Sample size	Type	Firm size	Method	Purpose
Wyant (1977)	9000	All Types	Not specified	Survey/interview of bankrupted firms and creditor evaluations	To study the causes of business failures

Findings: Business failure was caused by management inexperience, incompetence, and lack of planning.

Robinson (1980, 1982)	101	Service; retail; manufacturers	Up to $3 million in annual sales and up to 50 employees	Interview survey	To assess the impact of outside-based planning on small firm performance

Findings: Small firms engaging in outsider-based strategic planning significantly outperformed control groups in sales, ROS, and employment.

Bracker (1982)	224	Drycleaners	Under $3 million in annual sales	Interview and questionnaire	To assess the relationship among entrepreneurial type, planning sophistication, and performance

Findings: Small drycleaners using "structured" strategic planning performed significantly higher in relation to industry standards than did drycleaners using any other type of planning.

Source: R. Robinson, Jr. and J. Pearce II, "Research Thrusts in Small-Firm Strategic Planning," *Academy of Management Review* 9, no. 1 (January 1984): 133.

To apply strategic-management concepts in nonprofit enterprises, it is important to recognize some of the major differences between profit and nonprofit institutions. Compared to profit firms, nonprofit organizations often function in a monopolistic environment, produce a product or service that offers little or no measurability of performance, and are totally dependent on outside sources of financing. Tim Brady recently suggested a six-step method for applying the strategic-management model to nonprofit organizations:

1. Define the concepts and terminology used in planning.
2. Gather data that helps determine the course of planning.
3. Use simple, concise terms when writing goals, objectives, and action plans.
4. Develop a sound evaluation for positive feedback to the planning effort.
5. Consider contingency planning as the technique for making changes in the process.
6. Remember that planning-committee composition determines the effectiveness of the process.[19]

STRATEGIC MANAGEMENT APPLIED TO INTERNATIONAL CORPORATIONS

For centuries before Columbus discovered America, and surely for centuries to come, businesses searched and will search for new opportunities beyond their national boundaries. There has never been a more internationalized and economically competitive society than today's. Some domestic U.S. industries, such as textiles and consumer electronics, are in complete disarray as a result of the international challenge. Doing business internationally can be both surprising and disastrous to unwary firms.

Strategic Management in a Multinational Corporation (MNC)

The strategic-management process in international corporations is conceptually the same as in purely domestic firms. However, competing in international markets makes strategic management far more complex, because many more variables and interrelationships exist. Political, social, technological, economic, and competitive opportunities and threats that face a multinational corporation are almost limitless. The number and complexity of these factors increase dramatically with the number of products produced and the number of geographic areas served.

More time and effort is required to identify and evaluate effectively key external trends and events in multinational firms. Geographical distance, cultural and national differences, and variations in business practices make communication difficult between domestic headquarters and overseas operations. Strategy implementation can also be more difficult since diverse cultures worldwide have different consumption and production patterns.

In its simplest sense, the international challenge faced by many U.S. businesses is twofold: (1) how to gain and maintain exports to other nations and (2) how to defend domestic markets against imported goods. Few companies can afford to ignore the presence of international competition. Firms that seem insulated and comfortable today may be vulnerable tomorrow. David Garfield, president of Ingersoll-Rand Company, offers three strategy suggestions to make domestic firms more competitive internationally:

1. The best defense is a good offense. Companies need to fight tooth and claw for exports and battle foreign competition on foreign ground wherever possible. This is preferable to competing intensely in domestic markets.

2. Investments that will improve competitive advantage should receive priority attention. Domestic firms should strive to reduce labor costs, lower overhead, compress production cycles, and improve the quality of products and services.

3. Domestic industries and firms need to help one another. They should give preference to U.S. suppliers and distributors; they should encourage one another to take action to improve competitiveness in technology, quality, service, and cost.[20]

The International Challenge of Economic Order

Business strategists should recognize that greater interdependence exists among national economies today than ever before. This interdependence presents enormous benefits as well as severe economic, political, and social risks. Corporations in every corner of the world today are gaining the opportunity to share in the benefits of economic development. Yet markets are shifting so rapidly in tastes, trends, prices, and new products that firms must continually stay abreast of changes. Innovative communication and transport systems are creating an acceleration of technology transfer, shifts in the nature and location of production systems, and a narrowing of response time to changing market conditions. There are immense strategic implications resulting from these changes.

Along with the high degree of global economic interdependence that impacts MNCs, economic nationalism also has a pronounced effect. Governments are playing a larger role in world commerce than ever before, and they do it both by helping their own industries get an upper hand in international competition and by restricting the opportunities open to foreign competitors.

Some United States firms, such as Chrysler and Harley-Davidson, have been successful in persuading the United States Government to aid them directly. For example, when Honda, Kawasaki, Yamaha, and Suzuki shifted their focus from medium-sized motorcycles to the large displacement bikes, Harley-Davidson struggled to defend its domestic market. Harley's market share dropped from 21 percent in 1979 to a meager 9 percent in 1983. After receiving help from the United States Government, Harley-Davidson's market share in mid-1985 was back up to 15 percent.

Perhaps the greatest threat to domestic firms engaged in international operations is the national and international debt situation. When countries become excessively leveraged, they frequently turn to slashing imports and boosting exports in order to generate trade surpluses capable of servicing their debt. In this type of climate, domestic firms producing for export markets often can no longer import essential inputs. When a debtor country is successful in boosting its exports, domestic firms often encounter a protectionist backlash in foreign countries. An example of this today is the U.S. trade deficit with Japan, which is forecasted to exceed $50 billion by the end of 1985. The United States itself is becoming much more protectionist. Separate bills before Congress by the end of 1985 would limit the import of foreign autos to 15 percent of the U.S. market and would impose an across-the-board 20 percent surcharge on all imports. In late 1985, 30 percent of all automobiles sold in the United States were foreign-made.

Multinational business strategists can contribute to the solution of economic trade problems (and improve their firm's competitive position) by maintaining and strengthening communication channels with domestic and foreign governments. Strategists are commonly on the front line of trade and financial crises around the world, so they often have direct knowledge of the gravity and interrelated nature of particular problems. Strategists should relay this knowledge and experience to national leaders. A steady stream of counsel and advice from international business strategists to policymakers and lawmakers can emphasize the deep interdependence that exists in the world economy, and the impossibility of global economic recovery through narrow, nationalist steps that further restrict trade and investment flows.

The Impact of Diverse Industrial Policies

Multinational corporate strategists must gain an understanding of foreign governments' industrial policies. Industrial policies differ in all countries, as governments take different actions to develop their own economies. For example, cooperation between business and government in Japan is so good that some experts doubt whether a clear distinction exists there between government and business. Some analysts use the term Japan, Inc. when referring to the Japanese Government and the Ministry for International Trade and Industry (MITI). Industrial policies include such actions as providing government subsidies, promoting exports, restructuring industries, nationalizing businesses, imposing regulations, changing tax laws, instituting pollution standards, and establishing import quotas. The vicissitudes of foreign affairs make identifying and selecting from alternative strategies a more challenging process for MNCs, as compared to their domestic counterparts.

On December 3, 1984, more than 2,000 residents of Bhopal, India were killed by gas leaking from a Union Carbide pesticide plant. This multinational firm's strategists were faced with a number of problems, such as: How best to aid the victims? How to be sure whatever happened at Bhopal does not happen again somewhere else? How to assure investors about the corporation's financial stability? How to protect the corporation from excessive legal liabilities? Whether to change the firm's strategy of doing business in India?[21]

> Strategic planning has proven to be a valuable tool in the successful firm's repertoire. Firms traveling on the path of international business face more risks than their domestic counterparts, but also may reap greater rewards. Properly done, strategic planning offers these firms a map to guide them on their journey through the perilous paths of international business.[22]

CONCLUSION

All firms have a strategy, even if it is informal, unstructured, and sporadic. All organizations are heading somewhere, but unfortunately some organizations do not know where. There is an old saying, "If you do not know where you are going, then any road will lead you there!" That old saying accents the need for organizations to utilize strategic-management concepts and techniques. The strategic-management process applies equally to small firms, large companies, nonprofit institutions, governmental organizations, and multinational conglomerates.

For approximately 20,000 American companies in 1984, the end of the road was bankruptcy! Too many organizations take a reactive rather than a proactive approach to their environment. The strategic-management process addresses the following basic issues that should be confronted by all organizations:

1. What are we?
2. What do we want to become?
3. How can we best become what we want to become?
4. What are our special strengths and weaknesses?
5. How can we best capitalize on our strengths and overcome our weaknesses?
6. What are the important opportunities and threats in our environment?
7. How can we best take advantage of the opportunities and avoid the threats?
8. What are our competitors doing?
9. What are our competitors' strengths and weaknesses?
10. How will our competitors react to our strategies?
11. How vulnerable are we to our competitors' strategies?
12. How vulnerable are competitors to our strategies?

The strategic-management process represents a logical approach for determining an enterprise's future direction. The stakes are generally too high for strategists to intuitively choose among alternative courses of action without using strategic-management concepts and techniques. Successful top managers take the time to think about their business, where they are with the business, and what they want to be as an organization, and then implement action programs and policies to get from where they are to where they want to be at the end of a reasonable time horizon. It is a known and accepted fact of life that those people and organizations that plan ahead are much more likely to become what they want to become than those who do not plan at all. A "good" strategist plans and controls his plans, while a "bad" strategist never plans and then tries to control people! This textbook is devoted to providing you with the tools necessary to be a "good" strategist.

REVIEW QUESTIONS

1. Explain why business policy is often called a "capstone course."

2. Discuss the stages, activities, and components that comprise the strategic-management process.

3. Define and give an example of strategy formulation, strategy implementation, and strategy evaluation.

4. Why is strategy implementation often considered to be the most difficult stage in the strategic-management process?

5. How would the strategy-formulation process differ for a small versus a large organization? For a profit versus a nonprofit organization?

6. Compare and contrast intuitive versus strategic decision making.

7. For an organization of your choice, write a mission statement.

8. Discuss the relationships among objectives, goals, strategies, and policies.

9. Summarize the results of current research that has examined the value of strategic management in small firms.

10. Which steps in the strategic-management process do you think would take the most time to complete? Why?

11. Discuss the importance of feedback in the strategic-management process.

12. How can strategic managers best assure that strategies formulated will be effectively implemented?

13. Give an example of a recent political development that changed the overall strategy of some organization.

14. Select a publicly held organization of your choice. Go to your college library, and find information regarding that firm's strategy. Who are the firm's major competitors? What are the competitors' strategies? How successful are all of these firms? Why?

FOOTNOTES

1. Peter Drucker, *Management: Tasks, Responsibilities, and Practices* (New York: Harper & Row, 1974), 611.

2. Alfred Sloan, Jr., *Adventures of the White Collar Man* (New York: Doubleday, 1941), 104.

3. Eugene Raudsepp, "Can You Trust Your Hunches?" *Management Review* (April 1960): 7.

4. Bruce Henderson, *Henderson on Corporate Strategy* (Boston: Abt Books, 1979), 6.

5. "How Academia Is Taking a Lesson from Business," *Business Week* (27 August 1984): 58.

6. Archie Carroll and Frank Hoy, "Integrating Corporate Social Policy into Strategic Management," *Journal of Business Strategy* (Winter 1984): 56.

7. Rosemary Brady, "World Class," *Forbes* (18 June 1984): 133.

8. John A. Pearce II, "The Company Mission As a

Strategic Tool," *Sloan Management Review* (Spring 1982): 15.

9. "TWA: The Incredible Shrinking Airline," *Business Week* (25 July 1983): 86, 87.

10. "Colonial Penn: A Bid to Lure Younger Customers with Annuities and Low-Cost Auto Coverage," *Business Week* (8 August 1983): 85, 86.

11. Yedzi Godiwalla, Wayne Meinhart, and William Warde, "General Management and Corporate Strategy," *Managerial Planning* 30, no. 2 (September–October 1981): 18. Also, Richard Vancil and Peter Lorange, "Strategic Planning in Diversified Companies," *Harvard Business Review* 53, no. 1 (January–February 1975): 81.

12. "Plugging Into Online Databases," *Business Marketing* (October 1983): 62–66, 85.

13. Steven Flax, "Whirlwinds Hit the Yellow Pages," *Fortune* (1 October 1984): 113–14.

14. Noel Tichy, "The Essentials of Strategic Change Management," *Journal of Business Strategy* (Spring 1983): 55–57.

15. Some of these articles are: P. H. Thurston, "Should Smaller Companies Make Formal Plans?" *Harvard Business Review* (September–October 1983): 162–88. Also, R. Robinson, J. Pearce, G. Vozikis, and T. Mescon, "The Relationship Between Stage of Development and Small Firm Planning and Performance," *Journal of Small Business Management* 22, no. 2 (April 1984): 45–52. Also, L. Nagel, "Strategy Formulation for the Smaller Firm: A Practical Approach," *Long Range Planning* 14, no. 4 (August 1981): 115–20. Also, P. G. Holland and

W. Boulton, "Balancing the 'Family' and the 'Business' in Family Business," *Business Horizons* (March–April 1984): 16–21. Also, F. David, "Computer Assisted Strategic Planning for Small Businesses," *Journal of Systems Management* 36, no. 7 (July 1985): 24–33.

16. "How Academia Is Taking a Lesson from Business," *Business Week* (27 August 1984): 58.

17. Robert W. Rider, "Making Strategic Planning Work in Local Government," *Long Range Planning* 16, no. 3 (June 1983): 73–81. Also, John Smith, "Strategy—The Key to Planning in the Public Corporation," *Long Range Planning* 14, no. 6 (December 1981): 24–31.

18. Eleanor Tracy, "Radical Surgery at the Red Cross," *Fortune* (21 January 1985): 66.

19. Tim Brady, "Six-Step Method to Long Range Planning for Nonprofit Organizations," *Managerial Planning* 32, no. 4 (January–February 1984): 47.

20. David C. Garfield, "The International Challenge to U.S. Business," *Journal of Business Strategy* 5, no. 4 (Spring 1985): 28, 29.

21. Richard Kirkland, Jr., "Union Carbide Coping with Catastrophe," *Fortune* (7 January 1985): 50.

22. Ellen Fingerhut and Daryl Hatano, "Principles of Strategic Planning Applied to International Corporations," *Managerial Planning* (September–October 1983): 4–14. Another excellent article on this topic is: Narendra Sethi, "Strategic Planning Systems for Multinational Companies," *Long Range Planning* 15, no. 3 (June 1982): 80–89.

SUGGESTED READINGS

"Borg-Warner: Expanding into Services Is Helping to Beat the Recession," *Business Week* (16 August 1983).

Brady, T.S. "Six Step Method to Long Range Planning for Nonprofit Organizations." *Managerial Planning* 32, no. 4 (January–February 1984): 47–50.

Carlucci, F.C. "SMR Forum: Global Economic Order—Facing the Challenge." *Sloan Management Review* (Spring 1985): 65–68.

Carroll, A., and F. Hoy. "Integrating Corporate Social Policy into Strategic Management." *Journal of Business Strategy* (Winter 1984): 48–57.

Dammeyer, R.F. "Developing Information Systems to Meet Top Management's Needs." *AMA Forum* 72, no. 2 (February 1983): 29, 38.

David, F.R. "Computer-Assisted Strategic Planning in Small Businesses." *Journal of Systems Management* 36, no. 7 (July 1985): 24–33.

David, F.R. "QSPM: A Quantitative Approach to Strategy Formulation." *Long Range Planning* (1986) (in press).

Donnelly, R.M. "Strategic Planning for Better Management." *Managerial Planning* 30, no. 3 (November–December 1981): 3, 4, 5, 6, 41.

Drucker, P. *Management: Tasks, Responsibilities, and Practices.* New York: Harper & Row, 1974.

Drucker, P. "The New Meaning of Corporate Social Responsibility." *California Management Review* XXVI, no. 2 (Winter 1984): 53–63.

Fingerhut, Ellen, and Daryl Hatano. "Principles of Strategic Planning Applied to International Corporations." *Managerial Planning* (September–October 1983): 4–14.

Garfield, D.C. "The International Challenge to U.S. Business." *Journal of Business Strategy* 5, no. 4 (Spring 1985): 26–29.

Godiwalla, Y.M., W.A Meinhart, and W.A. Warde. "General Management and Corporate Strategy." *Managerial Planning* 30, no. 2 (September–October 1981): 17–23, 29.

Green, G.L., and E.G. Jones. "Strategic Management Step by Step." *Long Range Planning* 15, no. 3 (June 1982): 61–70.

Henderson, Bruce. *Henderson on Corporate Strategy.* Boston: Abt Books, 1979.

Hofer, C.W., and D. Schendel. *Strategy Formulation: Analytical Concepts.* St. Paul, Minn.: West Publishing, 1978.

Holland, P.G., and W. Boulton. "Balancing the 'Family' and the 'Business' in Family Business." *Business Horizons* (March–April 1984).

Kolbenschlag, M. "Harley-Davidson Takes Lessons from Arch-rivals' Handbook." *International Management* (February 1985): 46–48.

Laczniak, G. "Business Ethics: A Manager's Primer." *Business* (January–March 1983): 23–29.

Lorange, Peter. *Corporate Planning: An Executive Viewpoint.* Englewood Cliffs, N.J.: Prentice-Hall, 1980.

Mintzberg, H. "Strategy Making in Three Modes." *California Management Review* 16, no. 2 (1973): 44–53.

Nagel, L. "Strategy Formulation for the Smaller Firm—

A Practical Approach." *Long Range Planning* 14, no. 4 (August 1981): 115–20.

Pearce, J.A. II. "The Company Mission As a Strategic Tool." *Sloan Management Review* (Spring 1982).

"Plugging into Online Data Bases." *Business Marketing* (October 1983): 62–66, 85.

Raudsepp, E. "Can You Trust Your Hunches?" *Management Review* (April 1960): 4–9.

Rider, Robert W. "Making Strategic Planning Work in Local Government." *Long Range Planning* 16, no. 3 (June 1983): 73–81.

Robinson, R., J. Pearce, G. Vozikis, and T. Mescon. "The Relationship Between Stage of Development and Small Firm Planning and Performance." *Journal of Small Business Management* 22, no. 2 (April 1984): 45–52.

Robinson, R.B., Jr. and J.A. Pearce II. "Research Thrusts in Small Firm Strategic Planning." *Academy of Management Review* 9, no. 1 (January 1984): 128–37.

Sethi, Narendra. "Strategic Planning Systems for Multinational Companies." *Long Range Planning* 15, no. 3 (June 1982): 80–89.

Sloan, A., Jr. *Adventures of the White Collar Man.* New York: Doubleday, 1941.

Smith, John. "Strategy—The Key to Planning in the Public Corporation." *Long Range Planning* 14, no. 6 (December 1981): 24–31.

Steiner, G.A. "The Rise of the Corporate Planner." *Harvard Business Review* (September–October 1970): 133–39.

Thurston, P.H. "Should Smaller Companies Make Formal Plans?" *Harvard Business Review* (September–October 1983): 162–88.

Tichy, N. "The Essentials of Strategic Change Management." *The Journal of Business Strategy* 3, no. 4 (Spring 1983): 55–67.

Vancil, Richard, and Peter Lorange. "Strategic Planning in Diversified Companies." *Harvard Business Review* 53, no. 1 (January–February 1975): 81–90.

Weihrich, H. "The TOWS Matrix—A Tool for Situational Analysis." *Long Range Planning* 15, no. 2 (April 1982): 54–66.

INTRODUCING THE COHESION CASE AND EXPERIENTIAL EXERCISES

Two special features of this text are introduced here: the Cohesion Case and Experiential Exercises. As strategic-management concepts and techniques are introduced in later chapters, they are applied to the Cohesion Case through experiential exercises. At least one experiential exercise at the end of each chapter applies text material to the Cohesion Case. Additional experiential exercises are provided at the end of most chapters to give you a working knowledge of strategic-management concepts and tools.

The Cohesion Case is written on Ponderosa, Inc. Ponderosa is an international operator and franchiser of steakhouses and other types of restaurants. Ponderosa was selected as the Cohesion Case for five major reasons. First, this company is a multidivisional organization, thus allowing strategic-management concepts to be applied at three levels: corporate, divisional, and functional.

Second, Ponderosa is presently undergoing extensive strategic changes. The company is pursuing global market development and concentric diversification into Mexican food. Third, Ponderosa is a relatively small and simple organization with annual sales under $400 million. Fourth, Ponderosa has an international division. Finally, you probably are familiar with Ponderosa and maybe have even patronized its restaurants; therefore, you can focus most of your energy upon actually applying strategic-management concepts and techniques to the case, without having to spend much time "learning this business."

Preparing business policy case analyses is the most widely used approach for applying strategic-management concepts and techniques in the classroom. Part VI of this text provides detailed information on how to prepare a case analysis. The objectives of the case method are:

1. To give you experience applying strategic-management concepts and techniques to different organizations.

2. To give you experience applying and integrating the knowledge you have gained in prior courses and work experiences.

3. To give you decision-making experience in actual organizations.

4. To improve your understanding of interrelationships among the functional areas of business and the strategic-management process.

5. To improve your self-confidence. Since there is no one right answer to a case, you will gain experience justifying and defending your own ideas, analyses, and recommendations.

6. To improve your oral and written communication skills.

7. To give you experience "asking the right questions" when faced with various business problems and situations. A business leader once stated: "Ninety percent of the

task of a top manager is to ask useful questions. Answers are relatively easy to find, but asking good questions—that is the more critical skill."

8. To sharpen your analytical skills. Strategy formulation, implementation, and evaluation decisions should be based on quantitative analyses and qualitative judgments.

The Cohesion Case: Ponderosa, Inc.
FRED DAVID
Auburn University

INTRODUCTION

If you were going out to dinner tonight and could choose any of the following restaurants, which one would you choose: Sizzler, Quincy's, Bonanza, or Ponderosa? Of these four major competitors in the family steakhouse business, only Ponderosa is not affiliated with a large parent corporation. Bonanza, Quincy's, and Sizzler are subsidiaries of USA Cafes, Trans World Corporation, and Collins Foods International, respectively.

After experiencing an 83 percent decline in earnings in 1981, Ponderosa reorganized its structure and installed a strategic-management system. By the end of fiscal 1984, Ponderosa's earnings and revenues were up 16 percent and 7 percent respectively over fiscal 1983. Ponderosa is striving to formulate and successfully implement strategies that will lead to continued growth and profitability in the future. This business policy case describes Ponderosa's internal and external environment and reveals the company's objectives, strategies, goals, policies, problems, and concerns.

HISTORY

The first Ponderosa steakhouse was opened in 1965 in Indiana. In 1969, at the age of 27, Gerald Office was appointed chairman of the board and president of Ponderosa. During the 1970s, Ponderosa reached annual revenues of $322 million and net earnings of $13 million. The company asked for and received the resignation of four top vice-presidents in 1981, as the company's return on average stockholder's equity fell from 20.1 percent to 3.5 percent.

The year 1982 was a turning point in Ponderosa's history, for two major reasons. First, the company began to diversify by acquiring Casa Lupita in April 1982. A Casa Lupita restaurant is a Mexican dinner house serving a broad menu of both Mexican

Note: Copyrighted by Fred David.

and American foods and alcoholic beverages. Ponderosa plans to expand the Casa Lupita concept, but only six of these restaurants were open in 1982. Second, the company began worldwide market development by opening its first international steakhouse in Watford, England on June 26, 1982. Watford has a population of about 800,000 and is located twelve miles from London.

Ponderosa's net income increased 25 percent and earnings per share increased 14 percent in 1983. During 1983, Ponderosa operated 447 company-owned steakhouses in the United States and one in England, 235 licensed steakhouses in the United States and Canada, and two company-operated and four licensed Casa Lupita restaurants in the United States. Ponderosa's 682 steakhouses were very much concentrated in the northeastern United States and Florida. In fact, outside of these areas, there were only seventeen Ponderosa steakhouses.

During fiscal 1984, Ponderosa implemented a number of new programs. The company installed "The World's Biggest, Best Salad Buffet," a striking, thirty-foot-long buffet of over fifty different items. Also introduced in 1984 was "The World's Biggest, Best Breakfast Buffet." New marketing programs were instituted in fiscal 1984 to reduce couponing and discounting. Total advertising expenditures in fiscal 1984 were approximately 4 percent of revenues, with much heavier emphasis being placed on television media. Ponderosa constructed and opened three new Casa Lupita restaurants in fiscal 1984 and purchased four previously licensed units in the Pacific Northwest. This brought the total number of Casa Lupita restaurants to eight. Also during fiscal 1984, Ponderosa began construction of a second restaurant in England and reached a territorial development agreement in the Far East for seven licensed units to be built in Singapore, Malaysia, and Indonesia over the next four years. This strategy of worldwide market development is supported by the fact that most restaurant companies operating overseas are of the fast-food variety, not the family-steakhouse type.

At the beginning of fiscal 1985, Gerald Office still serves as president and chairman of the board of Ponderosa. The company operates in twenty-eight states, seven Canadian provinces, and Great Britain. Ponderosa has 436 company-owned steakhouses in the United States and one in England. There are 221 licensed Ponderosa steakhouses in the United States and Canada, and nine company-owned Casa Lupita restaurants in the United States. The geographic distribution of Ponderosa restaurants is revealed in Table CC1 (Cohesion Case 1). During fiscal 1985, Ponderosa plans to construct eleven new Casa Lupita restaurants in New Jersey, Florida, Pennsylvania, Ohio, Michigan, and Illinois.

Some of Ponderosa's critics say the company should be pursuing domestic market development rather than foreign expansion, since at the end of fiscal 1984 there were only two Ponderosa steakhouses in the southern United States (excluding Florida), no restaurants on the West Coast, only seven restaurants west of Texas, just one Ponderosa steakhouse in Texas, and no Ponderosa restaurants in California or the Carolinas. Critics ask "Why is Ponderosa interested in putting restaurants in Malaysia, Singapore, and Indonesia instead of North Carolina, Louisiana, California, and other states with no Ponderosas?"

Table CC1 The locations of Ponderosa's restaurants at the beginning of fiscal 1985

	Company-Operated Steakhouses	Licensee-Operated Steakhouses	Company-Operated Casa Lupita Restaurants	Total Restaurants
Arizona		2		2
Connecticut	8			8
Florida	22	7	2	31
Georgia	1			1
Illinois	44	11		55
Indiana	20	31		51
Iowa	4			4
Kansas	4			4
Kentucky	9	6		15
Maryland		28		28
Massachusetts	6			6
Michigan	30	22		52
Minnesota	9			9
Missouri	19			19
New Jersey	9	3		12
New York	51	3		54
North Dakota		2		2
Ohio	101	8	2	111
Oregon			1	1
Pennsylvania	52	4		56
Rhode Island	3		1	4
Texas		1		1
Utah		4		4
Vermont		1		1
Virginia	5	5		10
Washington		1	3	4
West Virginia	8			8
Wisconsin	31	4		35
United States Total	436	143	9	588
Alberta		8		8
New Brunswick		2		2
Newfoundland		1		1
Nova Scotia		3		3
Ontario		50		50
Prince Edward Island		1		1
Quebec		13		13
Canada Total		78		78
United Kingdom	1			1
Total Restaurants	437	221	9	667

Source: Ponderosa, Inc., *1984 Annual Report*, 8.

CORPORATE ORGANIZATION

Ponderosa reorganized its operational groups in fiscal 1982 to form four business units or divisions: Ponderosa Steakhouse Division, Specialty Restaurant Group, Ponderosa International Development, Inc., and ESI Meats, Inc. In addition to these four operating divisions, Ponderosa has three functional departments: Human Resources, Corporate Finance, and Corporate Planning. An organizational chart of Ponderosa's operations is provided in Figure CC1.

It is interesting to note that at the beginning of fiscal 1984, Gerald Office personally owned 75,000 shares of Ponderosa's common stock, worth about $642,188. As a group, the directors and officers of Ponderosa owned 145,400 shares of the company's common stock, worth approximately $1,317,558.

Ponderosa Steakhouse Division

The Steakhouse Division is the main operating unit of Ponderosa, Inc. This division has grown remarkably during the company's sixteen-year history. In fiscal 1983, the Steakhouse Division achieved a record market share of 30.9 percent, making Ponderosa

Figure CC1 Ponderosa's Organizational Chart in Fiscal 1985. (Source: Based on information given in Ponderosa's *1984 Annual Report,* p. 38.)

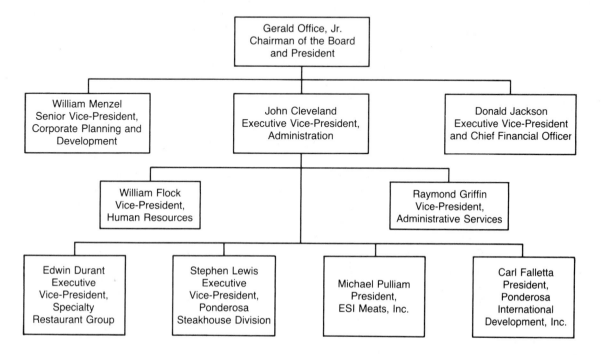

America's favorite family steakhouse chain. The following statistics describe Ponderosa's Steakhouse Division:

	1984	1983	1982	1981
Average weekly customer count	3999	3879	3671	3443
Cost of food sales as a percent of food sales	41.4	39.8	41.7	43.4
Percent of national budget steakhouse market	—	30.9	29.2	26.3
Average check amount	$4.12	$3.82	$3.74	$3.78
Average weekly unit sales	$16,487	$14,803	$13,730	—

Ponderosa maintains tight control over its licensed steakhouses by requiring licensee managers to complete the company's formal training program and to operate their restaurants like a company-operated steakhouse. However, license agreements neither require licensees to purchase any meat or supplies from the company nor require a set of regulated prices. Ponderosa does retain the right to inspect the franchise steakhouse and cancel its license if company standards are not being complied with. The Steakhouse Division's profits have been cyclical and dependent upon the U.S. economy, as shown by a drastic drop in profit during the 1980–81 recession. In an attempt to widen and strengthen its profit margin, Ponderosa is moving away from total dependence on the Steakhouse Division.

Fiscal 1984 was a year of change for the Steakhouse Division. In eight and a half weeks and without customer inconvenience, a new salad buffet was installed throughout the entire system. Installation of the salad bars was performed by fifteen fourteen-man teams that worked between the hours of 10:00 P.M. and 8:00 A.M. Installation of the fifty-item salad bar, which includes soup and fruit, cost about $14.9 million.

Almost immediately after the salad bar was installed, Ponderosa began a roll-out of "The World's Biggest, Best Breakfast Buffet." By the end of fiscal 1985, the breakfast buffet is scheduled to be offered in over 400 company steakhouses and 90 licensed restaurants. It is expected to produce over $60 million of new business annually. During the second quarter of fiscal 1985, prices for the all-you-can-eat breakfast buffet were increased from $2.99 to $3.19 on weekdays and from $3.59 to $3.79 on weekends.

Also during fiscal 1984, Ponderosa expanded its steakhouse menu to include a New York strip steak, a filet mignon, a porterhouse steak, chicken Italian, country-fried steak, and a chicken value meal. To capitalize on these new products, the company changed its marketing strategy to increase television and radio advertising and to reduce the prior emphasis on discounting and couponing. Ponderosa's featured spokesman in its television ads is President Jerry Office. Newspaper advertisements that focus on higher-priced items are being planned for fiscal 1985.

Ponderosa plans to design and test a steakhouse renovation program during fiscal 1985. This renovation will include lighter color schemes, new smallwares, new uniforms, more efficient layouts, and additional seating. Ponderosa also plans to decentralize marketing decision making to allow individual districts and restaurants to respond more quickly to local competitive pressure and customer preferences.

Special Restaurant Group

In April 1982, Ponderosa began implementing a strategy of concentric diversification by acquiring the Casa Lupita concept of Mexican dining. This acquisition and subsequent incorporation of Casa Lupita Restaurants, Inc. is part of long-term diversification strategy to reduce the threat of a bad economy upon Ponderosa revenues. Although Mexican dinner chains are enjoying an average 15 to 20 percent annual growth, Ponderosa has joined a pack of Mexican competitors, many of which have never made a profit. Some of these competitors are El Pacho, El Chico, Monterey House, Taco Villa, Taco Plaza, Taco Bueno, Casa Ole, Ninfu's, and Chi Chi's. Ponderosa does not have a single executive with experience in running Mexican restaurants, unlike its competitors.

Nevertheless, Ponderosa acquired Casa Lupita because it believes Mexican restaurants have a potential of high volume and profits. Tacos and tortillas are much less expensive than beef, so profit margins are higher during bad economic times. Also, Casa Lupita meal tabs on the average run almost double those of a Ponderosa steakhouse. Donald R. Jackson, executive vice-president and chief financial officer, says, "Ten Casa Lupitas would have the same impact on our bottom line as eighty Ponderosas." Several Casa Lupitas are now located in converted Ponderosa steakhouses. The two advantages of converting steakhouses instead of constructing new buildings are price and prime locations.

Casa Lupita Mexican restaurants are designed to attract middle- and upper-income customers. They serve a variety of Mexican foods including chimichangas, enchiladas, burritos, tacos, and a wide variety of beef, seafood, and chicken specialties. Customers enjoy complete bar service with margaritas as the featured drink. The decor is classic Mexican and features stucco, Spanish colonial tiles, and live plants. Casa Lupita restaurants have a distinct physical separation between the bar and the dining areas.

At the end of fiscal 1984, nine company Casa Lupitas were in operation: Florida (2), Ohio (2), Oregon (1), Rhode Island (1), and Washington state (3). During fiscal 1985, Ponderosa plans to open ten more Casa Lupitas in Michigan, Ohio, Pennsylvania, Florida, and New Jersey. By 1990, Ponderosa plans to open approximately 150 Casa Lupita restaurants. Licensed Casa Lupita restaurants are expected to open in fiscal 1985. Long-term development plans call for approximately 50 percent of all Casa Lupitas to be licensed. Once recruited, Casa Lupita franchise licensees undergo a four-month training program that includes both classroom experiences and hands-on exposure.

Ponderosa International Development, Inc.

The international division of Ponderosa is headquartered in London, England, and is responsible for developing business opportunities in international markets. To become less dependent on its domestic Steakhouse Division, Ponderosa launched its first international steakhouse restaurant in Watford, England in June 1982. Ponderosa's international development plan is targeted toward major markets in the free world. Markets currently being developed include the United Kingdom, Australia, West Germany, Singapore, Malaysia, Indonesia, and Puerto Rico.

The Watford restaurant has enjoyed exceptional success. Although the storefront location of this restaurant limits its seating capacity, 50 percent larger customer counts than the average American Ponderosa have been recorded. A second Ponderosa steakhouse opened in Croydon, London, early in fiscal 1985. Ponderosa's long-range international strategy is to find joint venture partners who will develop the Ponderosa concept. Ponderosa estimates that as many as 100 of their steakhouses could operate successfully in Great Britain.

E.S.I. Meats, Inc.

Ponderosa's wholly owned subsidiary, E.S.I. Meats, Inc., operates a meat processing and freezer facility in Bristol, Indiana. Completed in 1980, the Bristol E.S.I. plant is one of the largest freezer facilities under one roof in the world. In addition to supplying all company-owned and most franchised Ponderosa steakhouses with meat products, E.S.I. serves as a distributor for nonmeat items such as french fries, seafood, desserts, and paper products. It also supplies the Mexican restaurants and the Watford, England steakhouse.

While continuing to support Ponderosa operations, E.S.I. plans substantial growth in sales to other restaurant chains, supermarket chains, government agencies, volume wholesalers, and retailers. In fiscal 1983, E.S.I. received product approvals from three multi-unit restaurant chains and also from one of America's largest food service distributors. In addition, E.S.I. began work on a huge contract calling for production in excess of one million pounds of pork in fiscal 1984.

Research and development is a high priority at E.S.I., and constant improvements are being made to upgrade product quality. Its separate research and development function uses the most modern laboratory equipment to insure high-quality beef products. Efficiency in processing is what enables E.S.I. to produce high-quality products at low prices. E.S.I.'s efficient distribution system includes a company-operated fleet of trucks, which helps to keep prices low and profits high.

CORPORATE FINANCE

Ponderosa's income statements and balance sheets for 1982 through 1984 are provided in Exhibit CC1 and Exhibit CC2, respectively. These statements reveal that Ponderosa is financially sound. The company's debt/equity ratio at the end of fiscal 1984 was .56,

Exhibit CC1 Ponderosa's income statements

Statement of Consolidated Income Year ended (in thousands except per share data)	February 23, 1984	February 24, 1983	February 25, 1982
Revenues			
Food sales	$418,039	$376,684	$353,859
Service fees and other income	11,100	8,408	7,004
Total revenues	429,139	385,092	360,863
Cost and expenses			
Cost of food sales	181,711	158,346	157,107
Restaurant operating expenses	193,354	173,700	161,259
Rent expense	15,842	15,084	13,032
General and administrative expenses	11,707	11,160	9,325
Interest expense and other	8,486	9,553	8,763
Total cost and expenses	411,100	367,843	349,486
Income before income taxes	18,039	17,249	11,377
Income taxes			
State and local	1,478	1,325	956
Federal			
Current	531	1,933	679
Deferred	3,899	3,555	1,393
Total income taxes	5,908	6,813	3,028
Net income	$ 12,131	$ 10,436	$ 8,349
Net income per share	$ 1.51	$ 1.50	$ 1.32
Average shares outstanding	8,054	6,972	6,314

Source: Ponderosa, Inc., *1984 Annual Report*, p. 24.

Exhibit CC2   Ponderosa's balance sheets

Consolidated Balance Sheet
(in thousands)

Assets	February 23, 1984	February 24, 1983	February 25, 1982
Current Assets			
Cash	$ 6,221	$ 1,861	$ 997
Short-term investments	2,764	12,314	4,000
Accounts and notes receivable-	5,238	5,297	5,055
Recoverable federal income taxes	1,663	540	9,151
Inventories	16,846	12,831	13,947
Prepaid expenses	3,099	2,616	2,561
Total Current Assets	35,831	35,459	35,711
Property, Plant and Equipment-			
Land and improvements	11,291	9,523	8,662
Buildings, leaseholds and improvements	124,951	116,629	111,583
Equipment	125,156	100,087	95,547
Construction in progress	4,948	1,686	574
Total Property, Plant and Equipment	266,346	227,925	216,366
Less accumulated depreciation and amortization	(100,771)	(88,074)	(74,875)
Net Property, Plant and Equipment	165,575	139,851	141,491
Resources Designated for Construction and Acquisitions	7,053	21,295	—
Other Assets-	18,735	17,128	20,614
Total Assets	$227,194	$213,733	$197,816

Liabilities and Stockholders' Equity	February 23, 1984	February 24, 1983	February 25, 1982
Current Liabilities			
Accounts payable	$ 25,932	$ 21,497	$ 19,119
Accrued payroll and employee benefits	4,537	4,794	4,241
Accrued interest	2,240	2,165	2,246
Accrued expenses	8,503	7,015	5,271
Federal income taxes	—	415	—
Current portion of long-term obligations	4,730	6,824	6,685
Total Current Liabilities	45,942	42,710	37,562
Notes payable	36,248	39,357	57,278
Obligations under Capitalized Leases	25,638	25,215	26,141
Deferred Federal Income Taxes	9,753	6,441	6,090
Stockholders' Equity- Common stock, par value $0.10 per share: authorized 25,000,000 shares (issued 1984—8,871,815; 1983—8,848,897)	887	885	478
Additional paid-in capital	31,718	31,316	10,064
Retained earnings	82,883	73,575	65,432
Foreign currency translation	(403)	(227)	—
Less cost of shares in treasury (shares in 1984—792,918; 1983—803,964)	(5,472)	(5,539)	(5,898)
Total Stockholders' Equity	109,613	100,010	70,076
Total Liabilities and Stockholders' Equity	$227,194	$213,733	$197,816*

Source: Ponderosa, Inc., *1984 Annual Report*, p. 27.

*Note: The 1981 total of $197,816 includes $699 subordinated debentures.

down from 1.20 in fiscal 1982. Both net income and revenues reached all-time highs in fiscal 1984. However, Ponderosa's critics express uneasiness about the company's return-on-equity ratio, which declined from 12.5 percent in 1982 to 11.4 percent in 1984. Also, there is some concern that Ponderosa's capital spending is accelerating too fast, since these totals were $6.6 million in 1982, $14.1 million in 1983, and $41.4 million in 1984. Furthermore, cash provided from operations declined from $42.4 million in fiscal 1983 to $31.7 million in fiscal 1984. Restaurant operating expenses as a percent of revenues were level at 45.1 percent in both fiscal 1983 and fiscal 1984.

During the first quarter of fiscal 1985, Ponderosa successfully negotiated a $60 million revolving credit agreement among five banks. Ponderosa's corporate revenues of $128,945,000 during the second quarter of fiscal 1985 were 34 percent above the revenues for the second quarter of 1984. However, Ponderosa's net income for this quarter was $4,701,000, up less than one percent from the same period in fiscal 1983. Earnings per share were $0.51 for the second quarter of fiscal 1985, compared to $0.58 earned during the second quarter of 1984.

COMPETITION

The family steakhouse industry is intensely competitive. Organizations such as Quincy's, Bonanza, Sizzler, Western Sizzlin, Steak & Ale, Western Steer, Golden Corral, and Family Steakhouse compete directly with Ponderosa, while restaurants such as Shoney's and Denny's also are considered competitors. Since Ponderosa is adding chicken entrees, their competition really includes even more chains of restaurants. Three of Ponderosa's major competitors are examined next.

Quincy's is a chain of family steakhouses that operates in the southeastern United States. As of January 1, 1984, there were 163 Quincy's open. Quincy's is one of the two major divisions of Spartan Food Systems. The other major division is Hardee's. Financially, Spartan had its best year ever in 1983, recording profits of $48 million, up 24 percent over the 1982 total of $39 million. Spartan's revenues were just under $450 million in 1983. Quincy's customers can select from eleven different cuts of meat, ranging from an eighteen-ounce T-bone to a petite sirloin. Quincy's never serves a steak that has been frozen; this dedication to quality results in more than 60 percent of Quincy's business coming from customers who eat there once a week or more. Quincy's salad bar includes more than three dozen items. Quincy's plans to expand aggressively into other areas of the United States.

Sizzler Restaurants International is a 71-percent-owned subsidiary of Collins Foods International, Inc. Collins Foods is one of the largest franchisees of Kentucky Fried Chicken restaurants. At the beginning of fiscal 1984, there were 302 licensed Sizzler steakhouse restaurants and 138 company-owned Sizzler steakhouses. These restaurants were located primarily in the western United States, as indicated in Table CC2. Selected financial information on Sizzler is provided in Table CC3. *Business Week* recently

Table CC2   The locations of the Sizzler Steakhouses

	Licensed	Company-Owned
California	119	59
Oregon	15	6
Washington State	13	3
Nevada	4	4
Utah	13	0
Arizona	6	7
Idaho	5	0
Montana	3	0
Wyoming	2	0
Colorado	2	0
New Mexico	3	0
Texas	17	9
Louisiana	11	0
Oklahoma	2	0
Nebraska	5	0
Minnesota	2	0
Wisconsin	3	0
Michigan	1	0
Missouri	1	0
Illinois	11	7
Indiana	9	3
Kentucky	0	10
Alabama	3	0
Georgia	0	12
Florida	10	9
North Carolina	6	0
New Jersey	1	2
New York	17	7
Alaska	4	0
Hawaii	7	0
Guam	1	0
Japan	3	0
Kuwait	1	0
Saudi Arabia	1	0
United Arab Emirates	1	0
Total	302	138

Table CC3   Selected financial information on Sizzler

	1983	1982	1981
Revenues (millions)			
Company-Owned	118.7	104.5	94.1
Licensed	235.0	219.4	201.6
Net Income Before Taxes (millions)			
Company-Owned	9.2	5.1	3.0
Licensed	3.65	3.83	4.99
Number of Licensed Units	302	315	341
Number of Company-Owned Units	138	133	137
Monthly Average Unit Sales Volume			
Company-Owned	73.6	65.2	59.0
Licensed	64.0	56.1	50.2

reported that Sizzler plans to add 160 stores by 1988, seventy of them company-owned.[1] Sizzler restaurants are currently being "rethemed" into airy, plant-filled restaurants that feature chicken, fish, and salad bars.

The *Bonanza Restaurant Division* is a part of USA Cafes, a large organization that also owns a 36 percent interest in Shakey's Pizza chain. Early in 1984, there were 565 Bonanza steakhouses located throughout the United States, except in the Pacific Northwest. By 1987, Bonanza plans to operate nearly 650 restaurants. States with more than twenty-five Bonanza restaurants included Texas, Arkansas, Tennessee, Illinois, and Michigan.

In 1983, average sales per Bonanza restaurant were up 14 percent from 1982, compared to an average increase of 5.2 percent for the industry. Bonanza is remodeling all of its restaurants to shed its traditional western decor and to introduce a new, lighter, contemporary image. A sixty-item Freshtastiks food bar and new menu items that include broiled chicken and shrimp were introduced. Bonanza restaurants are adding a skylight over the Freshtastiks food bar, replacing tile with carpet, using light-colored wood to replace dark interiors, and replacing wooden doors with glass doors. Bonanza is expected to soon increase its prices, since the company's $4.50 average per-person ticket is significantly below the $6.00 per-person check average of Sizzler.

Bonanza reported profits of about $3 million on gross sales of about $400 million in 1983. Customer traffic during 1983 was up 10 percent over 1982. Between 1981 and 1983, the median age of Bonanza's customers dropped from 39 to 32. From 1982 to 1983, Bonanza's average party size increased from 2.26 to 2.55; the company's share of the budget steak dollars increased from 15.3 percent to 15.9 percent.

FUTURE OUTLOOK

A recent issue of *Restaurant Business* described what is happening in the chain steakhouse industry:

> An upscaling of units is sweeping the chain steakhouse segment, as companies move to shed their budget steakhouse image in order to appeal to a broader range of customers. To this end, there are remodeling programs, expansion of breakfast and lunch menus, and diversification into seafood, chicken, salad, and other non-red-meat items. As business gradually recovers from the debilitating effects of the recent recession, these companies hope to emerge with a larger and stronger share of the dining-out market.[2]

Nearly all of Ponderosa's major competitors are expanding and improving their operations. In response, Ponderosa is expanding into international markets and diversifying into Mexican cuisine. Is this strategy right for Ponderosa? Time will certainly tell.

This business policy case has described the strategies and actions that Ponderosa is taking to position itself in the future. Some special issues that face the company are: Should Ponderosa continue international expansion in lieu of domestic expansion? Should Ponderosa operate more licensed or company-owned restaurants? Is the company expanding too fast? Should Ponderosa diversify further, and if so, in what areas? How is Ponderosa positioned relative to its major competitors? These are critical issues that faced Jerry Office in late 1984. What specific recommendations do you suggest?

FOOTNOTES

1. "Collins Food: Creating Restaurant Chains for Trendier Appetites," *Business Week* (23 April 1984): 110.

2. "Steak," *Business Week* (20 March 1984): 1.

SUGGESTED READINGS

"Bonanza Aims for a 'Lighter, Brighter' New Look." *Nation's Restaurant News* 18, no. 1 (2 January 1984): 46, 50.

"Bonanza's Growth Spurred." *Nation's Restaurant News* 18, no. 3 (30 January 1984): 2, 86.

Kreisman, R. "Ponderosa's Growth Recipe." *Advertising Age* (12 July 1982): 4, 70.

MacDougall, W. and D. Levine. "Restaurants Eaten Alive by Recession." *U.S. News & World Report* (31 January 1983): 48.

"Ponderosa: A Steakhouse Tries to Fatten Profits by Going Mexican." *Business Week* (25 April 1983): 98.

"Ponderosa Showing Gains." *Restaurant Business* (1 July 1983): 44.

"Sizzler Chain Hot." *Barron's/Investment News & Views* (28 February 1983): 53–54.

"Steak Chain Sizzles with Pride." *Restaurant Business* (1 March 1983): 94–98.

EXPERIENTIAL EXERCISE 1A:

Examining Corporate Strategy Articles

PURPOSE

The purpose of this exercise is to familiarize you with corporate strategy articles. Corporate strategy articles can be found weekly in various journals, magazines, and newspapers. By reading and studying such articles, you can gain a better understanding of the strategic-management process. Several of the best journals in which to find corporate strategy articles are *Managerial Planning, Long Range Planning, Planning Review, The Journal of Business Strategy, The Strategic Management Journal,* and *The Journal of Business Policy.* These particular journals regularly report the results of empirical research in strategic management. They apply strategic-management concepts to specific organizations and industries. They introduce new strategic-management techniques and provide short case studies on selected firms.

In addition to journals, magazines regularly publish articles that focus on company strategies. Several of the best magazines in which to find applied corporate strategy articles are *Dun's Business Month, Fortune, Forbes, Business Week,* and *Industry Week.* A corporate strategy article in one of these magazines generally introduces a particular firm's chief executive officer, provides financial data on the company, identifies key competitors in the industry, and presents the company's objectives and strategies. Usually these articles are less than five pages in length.

Various newspapers, such as *USA Today, The Wall Street Journal, The New York Times,* and *Barron's,* consistently publish corporate strategy stories. Articles published in newspapers are exceptionally timely. They generally cover strategy events that occurred the preceding day, such as a joint venture being announced, a bankruptcy being declared, a new advertising campaign starting, a company being acquired, a division being divested, or a chief executive officer being hired or fired.

In combination, journal, magazine, and newspaper articles that examine company strategies can make business policy a more exciting course. Published articles allow strategies of profit and nonprofit organizations to be identified and studied.

YOUR TASK

Your task is to go to your college library and find a recent corporate-strategy article. Copy the article, bring it to class, and give a five minute report summarizing the firm's strategy. What is your personal reaction to the firm's strategy or strategies?

EXPERIENTIAL EXERCISE 1B:

Formulating Individual Strategies

PURPOSE

Individuals and organizations are alike in many ways. They each have competitors and should plan for the future. Every individual and organization has some internal strengths and weaknesses and faces some external opportunities and threats. Both individuals and organizations set goals and allocate resources. These similarities make it possible for individuals to utilize many strategic-management concepts and techniques.

The purpose of this exercise is to demonstrate how the TOWS Matrix, illustrated in Figure 1.1, page 15, can be used by an individual to plan his or her own future. As one nears completion of a college degree and begins to interview for a job, planning can be particularly important.

YOUR TASK

On a separate sheet of paper, construct a TOWS Matrix like the one illustrated in Figure 1.1 for Winnebago. Develop the TOWS Matrix by including what you consider to be your major strengths, your major weaknesses, your major external opportunities, and your major external threats. An external opportunity, for example, may be to go to graduate school; an internal weakness may be a low grade point average. Attempt to match key internal and external factors by recording in the appropriate cell of the matrix the alternative strategies or actions that would allow you to capitalize upon your strengths, overcome your weaknesses, take advantage of your external opportunities, and minimize the impact of external threats. Be sure to use the appropriate matching notation in the strategy cells of the matrix. Since every individual (and organization) is unique, there is no one right answer to this exercise. Similarly, there will be no one right answer when you prepare case analyses. The TOWS Matrix is an important strategy formulation tool and is therefore examined further in Chapter 6.

2

The Nature of Strategic Management

The Benefits of Strategic Management

Examining the Strategic-Management Model

Strategies in Action

Experiential Exercise 2A: Applying the Strategic-Management Process to Ponderosa, Inc.

Experiential Exercise 2B: Strategy Management at the Dynamic Computer Company

The purpose of this chapter is to enhance your understanding of and interest in strategic management. The benefits of good strategic management and probable results of poorly conceived strategies are examined. Alternative strategies are identified, discussed, and exemplified. Some general guidelines are given that suggest when particular strategies are most appropriate. Procedures for conducting an internal and external audit are introduced, as are tools for implementing strategies and criteria for evaluating strategies.

THE BENEFITS OF STRATEGIC MANAGEMENT

Many benefits can be derived from utilizing strategic-management concepts and techniques. First, and perhaps foremost, this process allows an organization to initiate and influence rather than just respond and react to its environment, in controlling its own destiny. William Dearden, chairman of Hershey Foods Corporation, attributes his company's success to strategic management. Dearden says, "There is the strategic-management process. Planning for the long-term future has been entrenched as a way of life at Hershey, and we certainly plan to strengthen and rely on the process going forward."[1]

Strategic-management concepts provide an objective basis for allocating resources and for reducing internal conflicts that can arise when subjectivity alone is the basis for major decisions. The strategic-management process allows an organization to take advantage of key environmental opportunities, to minimize the impact of external threats, to capitalize upon internal strengths, and to overcome internal weaknesses. This approach to decision making can be an effective vehicle for generating synergy and *esprit de corps* among all managers and employees. This benefit alone can make the difference between a successful and an unsuccessful business.

A large number of research studies have concluded that organizations using strategic-management concepts are more profitable and successful than those that do not. A recent longitudinal study of 101 retail, service, and manufacturing firms over a three-year period concluded that businesses using strategic-management concepts show significant improvement in sales, profitability, and productivity compared to firms without systematic planning activities.[2] Another classic study reported that up to 80 percent of the improvement that is possible in a firm's profitability is achieved through changes in a company's strategic direction.[3]

Since 1973, only one major study has found a significant negative relationship between strategic management and organizational performance.[4] This research was conducted by Fulmer and Rue in 1974 and reported in *Managerial Planning*.[5] The Fulmer and Rue study found that nonplanners outperformed planners in service industries. These two authors concluded that strategic management at the time (1974) was in a state of adolescence, which is true.

A major benefit of strategic management is that declining revenues, declining profits, or even bankruptcy are often avoided. Many factors besides ineffective planning can, of course, lead to business failure. But thousands of bankruptcies occur every year across the United States; this fact suggests a need for organizations to more effectively integrate strategic-management concepts and techniques into the decision-making process. A few companies that declared bankruptcy in 1984 were Air Florida, Franklin Computer, Kero-Sun, Air Illinois, and Air Vermont. Other recent petitioners for bankruptcy, Wickes Corporation and Braniff Airlines, left their short-term creditors holding the bag for $2 billion and $1.1 billion respectively.

In some cases, bankruptcy can be the best strategic decision for an organization. Bankruptcy can allow a firm to avoid major debt obligations and to void union contracts. For example, declaring bankruptcy allowed the Manville Corporation and Continental Products to immediately gain protection from liability suits that had been filed over their manufacture of asbestos. Million-dollar judgments against Manville and Continental would have required company liquidation, so bankruptcy was a good strategic decision for both firms. Under Chapter 11 of the U.S. Bankruptcy Code, organizations can reorganize and "come back" after filing a petition for protection. Bobbie Brooks, Inc. is an example firm that filed for Chapter 11 bankruptcy in 1982, reorganized during 1983, and was a profitable company in 1984.

Besides avoiding company demise, other benefits of strategic management include an enhanced awareness of environmental threats, an improved understanding of competitors' strategies, increased employee productivity, reduced resistance to change, and a clearer understanding of performance/reward relationships. Strategic-management activities enhance the problem-prevention capabilities of an organization, because they emphasize interaction among managers at all levels of the firm.

Strategic management is an approach to decision making that can bring order and discipline throughout an enterprise. Organizations of all sizes and types are now using and benefiting from strategic-management concepts and techniques. But this has not always been the case. Prior to the 1980s, the strategic-management process was generally misunderstood and thought to be too sophisticated for all but the largest corporations. Robert Donnelly stresses that effective use of strategic-management techniques may be the only way some companies are going to survive in the late 1980s and 1990s.[6]

A strategic-management approach to decision making is not a guarantee for success, but it can be the beginning of an efficient and effective managerial system. Carter Bayles says the strategic-management process "may renew confidence in the current business strategy, or it may point to the need for action to correct some unsuspected weaknesses, such as an erosion of product superiority and technological edge, or a loss of profitability in some product or customer category."[7]

In many respects, business strategy is like military strategy. An organization tries to use its own strengths to exploit a competitor's weaknesses. If an organization's overall strategy is wrong (ineffective), then all the efficiency in the world may not be enough to succeed. Both business and military success is generally not the happy result of accidental strategies. Rather, success is the product of continuous attention to changing internal and external conditions and the formulation and implementation of insightful adaptations to those conditions. Ginter and Rucks recently concluded that war and business competition are so similar that strategy formulation, implementation, and evaluation techniques apply equally to both areas.[8]

Table 2.1　The Chrysler Corporation: 1979–1984 financial data (in millions of dollars)

	1984	1983	1982	1981	1980	1979
Net Sales	$ 19,572	$ 13,240	$10,045	$ 9,972	$ 8,600	$11,377
Net Income (loss)	2,380	701	170	(476)	(1,710)	(1,097)
Total Assets	9,030	6,772	6,264	6,270	6,618	6,653
Long-term Debt	760	1,104	2,189	2,059	2,483	977
Shares of Common Stock Outstanding	121,472	121,812	79,475	73,133	66,973	66,704
Profit Margin	12.1%	5.3%	1.7%	(4.8%)	(19.9%)	(9.6%)

Source: The Chrysler Corporation, *1984 Annual Report.*

The Chrysler Corporation is a glowing example of an organization that has benefited immensely from strategic-management concepts. Between 1979 and 1983, Lee Iacocca, chief executive officer at Chrysler, formulated and implemented a retrenchment strategy and turned the company around, despite overwhelming internal weaknesses and external threats. Iacocca says: "When I came to Chrysler in 1979, the Michigan State fairgrounds were jammed with thousands of unsold, unwanted, rusting Chryslers, Dodges, and Plymouths. Foreign operations were leeching the lifeblood out of the company. And worst of all, cars were coming off the assembly line with loose doors, chipped paint, and crooked moldings."[9] Iacocca's strategic approach to turning Chrysler around was a major reason for the company receiving federal government loan guarantees. This period of time in Chrysler's history is examined through selected financial data in Table 2.1. Note Chrysler's dramatic recovery since 1980.

EXAMINING THE STRATEGIC-MANAGEMENT MODEL

Identify Current Mission, Objectives, and Strategies

As illustrated in Figure 2.1, the strategic-management process begins with identification of an organization's existing mission, objectives, and strategies. This is a logical starting point because a firm's existing mission, objectives, and strategies may preclude certain strategic alternatives and may even dictate a certain future course of action. Every organization has an existing mission, objectives, and strategy, even if these are not consciously designed, written, or communicated. These three components provide direction for the internal and external audit, provide a basis for revising (if needed) the company mission, and serve as a benchmark for establishing new objectives, strategies, goals, and policies.

Figure 2.1   A model of the strategic-management process

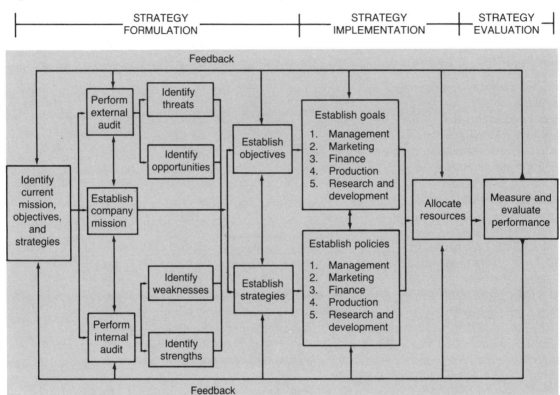

Even in situations where a firm's existing mission, objectives, and strategies change abruptly, a period of several years may elapse before the effects of this occurrence dissipate. The answer to where an organization is going can be largely determined by where the organization has been! Therefore, identification of these three existing elements in a firm is vital to successfully formulating, implementing, and evaluating strategies.

At times, organizations will say one thing publicly and then engage in activities that are at odds with those statements. In some cases a firm cannot communicate its true mission, objectives, and strategy without giving a competitive advantage to other firms or jeopardizing national security. Only by comparing official statements of an organization with actual operations can one identify these elements with confidence.

Perform External Audit

Identifying and evaluating key social, political, economic, technological, and competitive trends and events comprises an external audit. Note from the strategic-management model that the internal and external audit can be conducted simultaneously, because each activity focuses on different variables. External trends and events are generally considered to be factors that an organization cannot control, whereas internal factors can be controlled.

The output of an external strategic-management audit is a finite set of the most important opportunities on which the future of a business should be built, and the most important threats it should assiduously avoid. A task force of managers, using staff support, could be charged with conducting research to determine critical external trends and events that face the firm. This group of individuals should evaluate those factors and develop a critical set of major and minor opportunities and threats. The External Factor Evaluation Matrix, to be introduced in Chapter 4, summarizes the results of the external audit.

Most firms practice some form of environmental analysis as part of their planning process. In a recent study reported in *Long Range Planning,* chief executive officers of the Fortune 500 companies were asked about their company's environmental audit activities. Of the responding chief executive officers, 73 percent reported that their firms perform organized environmental analysis. Another 16 percent reported that they do not have organized environmental analysis, but they probably should. The remaining 11 percent did not conduct an external audit and saw no need for it. The chief executive officers who participated in this research reported numerous benefits of organized environmental analysis. The benefits ranged from "an improved ability to anticipate long-term problems and make adjustments" to "development of additional back-up energy sources."[10]

Corporate strategies should be formulated to take advantage of external opportunities and to minimize the impact of potential threats. Some organizations survive solely because they recognize and take advantage of environmental opportunities. For example, the proliferation of personal computers during the early 1980s was an external opportunity that Dennis Hayes exploited as chief executive officer of Hayes Microcomputer Products (HMP). HMP is a small, private company near Atlanta that controlled 70 percent of the retail market for modems in 1984.[11] (Modems are devices that allow personal computers to communicate with each other over telephone lines.)

An example bit of strategic information that concerns population shifts in the United States is provided in Table 2.2. The dramatic shift away from the Northeast to the West and South affects the production and consumption of products and services in the U.S. Note that Wyoming and Arizona are projected to increase most in population by the year 2000, while the District of Columbia and New York are forecasted to experience the greatest decline. This represents the type of external information that you need to collect when preparing a business policy case analysis.

There are many publications that should be scanned regularly by organizations to obtain strategic information. The most important publications are identified and described in Chapter 4. There are also excellent unpublished sources of information, such as trade association meetings, seminars, and speeches. Surveys or empirical research can be conducted to obtain strategic information on key suppliers, creditors, distributors, customers, stockholders, governments, communities, and investors.

Table 2.2 Population projections by state: 1980 to 2000

Detailed Projections by State

State	Population in 2000	Change From 1980		1980 Rank	2000 Rank
Alabama	4,415,300	Up	13.5%	22	24
Alaska	630,700	Up	57.5%	50	49
Arizona	5,582,500	Up	105.4%	29	15
Arkansas	2,835,400	Up	24.1%	33	32
California	30,613,100	Up	29.3%	1	1
Colorado	4,656,600	Up	61.2%	28	21
Connecticut	3,062,400	Down	1.5%	25	29
Delaware	638,200	Up	7.2%	47	48
Dist. of Columbia	376,500	Down	41.0%	—	—
Florida	17,438,000	Up	79.0%	7	3
Georgia	6,708,200	Up	22.8%	13	11
Hawaii	1,277,700	Up	32.4%	39	42
Idaho	1,512,200	Up	60.2%	41	39
Illinois	11,187,500	Down	2.0%	5	6
Indiana	5,679,200	Up	3.4%	12	14
Iowa	2,972,100	Up	2.0%	27	30
Kansas	2,494,400	Up	5.6%	32	34
Kentucky	4,399,900	Up	20.2%	23	25
Louisiana	5,159,800	Up	22.7%	19	19
Maine	1,308,000	Up	16.3%	38	41
Maryland	4,581,900	Up	8.7%	18	22
Massachusetts	5,490,400	Down	4.3%	11	16
Michigan	9,207,600	Down	0.5%	8	8
Minnesota	4,489,400	Up	10.1%	21	23
Mississippi	2,939,200	Up	16.6%	31	31
Missouri	5,080,000	Up	3.3%	15	20
Montana	963,000	Up	22.4%	44	44
Nebraska	1,661,900	Up	5.9%	35	38
Nevada	1,918,800	Up	140.1%	43	36
New Hampshire	1,363,500	Up	48.1%	42	40
New Jersey	7,427,600	Up	0.9%	9	9
New Mexico	1,727,300	Up	32.9%	37	37
New York	14,990,200	Down	14.6%	2	4
North Carolina	6,867,800	Up	16.9%	10	10
North Dakota	682,000	Up	4.5%	46	47
Ohio	10,356,800	Down	4.1%	6	7
Oklahoma	3,944,500	Up	30.4%	26	27
Oregon	4,025,300	Up	52.9%	30	26
Pennsylvania	11,207,600	Down	5.6%	4	5
Rhode Island	925,800	Down	2.3%	40	45
South Carolina	3,907,100	Up	25.3%	24	28
South Dakota	687,600	Down	0.4%	45	46
Tennessee	5,419,600	Up	18.1%	17	17
Texas	20,739,400	Up	45.8%	3	2
Utah	2,777,400	Up	90.1%	36	33
Vermont	625,000	Up	22.2%	48	50
Virginia	6,389,400	Up	19.5%	14	12
Washington	5,832,500	Up	41.2%	20	13
West Virginia	2,067,700	Up	6.1%	34	35
Wisconsin	5,215,500	Up	10.8%	16	18
Wyoming	1,002,200	Up	112.9%	49	43
U.S.	267,461,600	Up	18.1%	—	—

Reprinted from *U.S. News & World Report* issue of Sept. 19, 1983, 58. Copyright, 1983, U.S. News & World Report, Inc.

One approach to environmental scanning that has proved successful is to assign each source of information to a particular individual and then require periodic scanning reports from those individuals. In addition to providing timely strategic information, a derived benefit of this approach is that it involves many individuals in the strategy-formulation process. Employee and managerial involvement in strategy-formulation activities greatly enhances strategy-implementation efforts. An alternative approach to gathering strategic information is to utilize online databases. The task force of managers charged with performing an external audit should decide what environmental-scanning approach is most appropriate for their organization.

Social, political, economic, technological, and competitive trends and events can determine a firm's success or failure, but perhaps the most important of these areas is competition. Key questions to examine include: Who are the firm's competitors? Where are they located? What strategies are they pursuing? What are their strengths? What are their weaknesses? How vulnerable are they to our strategies? How vulnerable are we to their strategies? Some example social, political, economic, technological, and competitive variables that could be examined during an external audit are given in Exhibit 2.1.

Perform Internal Audit

The strategic-management model illustrates that an internal and external strategic-management audit must be completed before alternative strategies can be chosen. Strategy formulation, implementation, and evaluation depend upon a clear definition of the company mission, an accurate assessment of the external environment, and an internal analysis of the firm. An enterprise will ultimately chart its strategic course with the intention of capitalizing upon its internal strengths and overcoming its weaknesses. Performing an internal audit is an important part of preparing a business policy case analysis.

In an actual organization, an internal audit task force composed of managers from different units of the organization can be charged with developing a concise list of the most important strengths on which a company or division should base its future, and the most significant weaknesses that need to be corrected. According to William King, the team of managers, supported by staff, should be charged with determining a specified number (usually ten to fifteen) of the most important strengths and weaknesses that should influence the future of the organization:

> The development of conclusions on the ten to fifteen most important organizational strengths and weaknesses can be, as any experienced manager knows, a difficult task, when it involves managers representing various organizational interests and points of view. Developing a twenty-page list of strengths and weaknesses could be accomplished relatively easily, but a list of the ten to fifteen most significant ones involves significant analysis and negotiation. This is true because of the judgments that are required and the impact which such a list will inevitably have as it is used in the formulation, implementation, and evaluation of strategy.[12]

Exhibit 2.1   Some example external audit factors

Social Trends
Population changes by age, sex, and geographic area
Delays in marriage and childbearing
Increasing numbers of older adults
Buy-now-and-save-later attitudes
Increased permissiveness
Increased divorce rates
Increased levels of education
Increased numbers of women workers
Political Trends
America's increased dependence on external resources
Tariffs, patents, regulation
Increased unionization
Increased power of interest groups
Economic Trends
Increased global competition and interdependence
Inflation; recession
Decreasing productivity of labor
Rising interest rates
Decreasing value of the dollar
Shift to a service-oriented economy in the U.S.
Exportation of labor and capital from the U.S.
Technological Trends
Increased use of computers and robotics
The information explosion
Increased use of management information systems
Increased automation
Increased need for retraining
Increased scientific breakthroughs
Competitive Trends
Major competitors' strengths
Major competitors' weaknesses
Major competitors' strategies

Once identified, strengths and weaknesses should be evaluated as to their relative magnitude and importance. The Internal Factor Evaluation Matrix, presented in Chapter 5, allows a firm to objectively assign a weight and a rating to each key internal factor. Briefly, the weight indicates the relative importance of each factor to success in a given industry and the rating reveals whether each factor is a major strength, minor strength, minor weakness, or major weakness in the firm. By multiplying each factor's weight times its rating and then summing the resultant weighted scores, a firm can effectively evaluate its internal strategic position.

It is important to note that assumptions, opinions, and judgments are inevitably a part of an internal audit. The Internal Factor Evaluation Matrix is simply a tool that can facilitate the internal audit process. Some example management, marketing, finance, production, and research and development factors that could be examined during an internal strategic-management audit are provided in Exhibit 2.2.

Exhibit 2.2   Some key internal audit questions

Management

1. Does the firm use strategic-management concepts?

2. Are company objectives and goals measurable and well communicated?

3. Do managers at all hierarchical levels plan effectively?

4. Do managers delegate authority well?

5. Is the organization's structure appropriate?

6. Are job descriptions and job specifications clear?

7. Is employee morale high?

8. Is employee turnover and absenteeism low?

9. Are organizational reward and control mechanisms effective?

Marketing

1. Are markets segmented effectively?

2. Is the organization positioned well among competitors?

3. Has the firm's market share been increasing?

4. Are present channels of distribution reliable and cost-effective?

5. Does the firm have an effective sales organization?

6. Does the firm conduct market research?

7. Is product quality and customer service good?

8. Are the firm's products and services priced appropriately?

9. Does the firm have an effective promotion, advertising, and publicity strategy?

10. Is marketing planning and budgeting effective?

11. Do the firm's marketing managers have adequate experience and training?

Finance

1. Where is the firm financially strong and weak as indicated by financial ratio analyses?

2. Can the firm raise needed short-term capital?

3. Can the firm raise needed long-term capital through debt and/or equity?

4. Does the firm have sufficient working capital?

5. Are capital budgeting procedures effective?

6. Are dividend payout policies reasonable?

7. Does the firm have good relations with its investors and stockholders?

8. Are the firm's financial managers experienced and well-trained?

Production

1. Are suppliers of raw materials, parts, and subassemblies reliable and reasonable?

2. Are facilities, equipment, machinery, and offices in good condition?

3. Are inventory control policies and procedures effective?

4. Are quality-control policies and procedures effective?

5. Are facilities, resources, and markets strategically located?

6. Does the firm have technological competencies?

Research and Development

1. Does the firm have R&D facilities? Are they adequate?

2. If outside R&D firms are used, are they cost-effective?

3. Are the organization's R&D personnel well qualified?

4. Are R&D resources allocated effectively?

5. Are management information and computer systems adequate?

6. Is communication between R&D and other organizational units effective?

7. Are present products technologically competitive?

Establish Company Mission

A company mission can perhaps be understood best by focusing on a business when it is first started. In the beginning, a new business is simply a collection of ideas. However, those ideas incorporate the same basic dimensions that comprise a mission statement. Starting a new business rests on a set of beliefs that some organization can offer some product or service, to some customers, in some geographic area, at a profitable price. As a new business grows, it becomes necessary to revise the statement of mission, but the elements of those original entrepreneurial ideas usually are reflected in the revised mission. Mission statements, therefore, can be described as *enduring statements of purpose.*

An effective mission statement answers questions such as: What is the purpose of our organization? Who are our customers? Why do they buy from us? A customer-oriented business mission, rather than a product-oriented statement, is generally the most effective management philosophy to guide the future activities of an organization. This is why American Telephone and Telegraph's business mission is communication and not telephones. The new AT&T's mission statement is given below:

> This new AT&T is in the business of meeting customer needs, worldwide, for the electronic movement and management of information. We will provide modern, nationwide telecommunications facilities, offering a range of services unmatched by other long distance carriers. We will develop and manufacture equipment and systems for our own and other networks, domestically and internationally. We will design, produce and market communications and information products, systems and services for customers whose requirements are large and complex, as well as for those whose needs are relatively few and simple. We will design and produce electronic components, computers and software systems for use within our own organization and outside it. We do not take a narrow view of the opportunities open to us—or of the market we are in. We see that market as a global one, and we will approach the various aspects of our business from a global perspective. We will not try to be all things to all people, but in everything we do we intend to be the best.[13]

Establish Objectives

Objectives are specific, long-range (more than one year) results that an enterprise seeks to achieve in pursuing its mission. As depicted in Figure 2.1, page 52, both objectives and goals are important components in the strategic-management process. Godiwalla, Meinhart, and Warde distinguish between objectives and goals, saying: "Long-range objectives are generally held stable for a considerable period of time because they are very basic to an enterprise. However, goals are far more time-specific and highly quantified. They are like annual targets. Therefore, goals are changed or modified more frequently than objectives in order to correctly reflect changing realities."[14]

Vancil and Lorange differentiate between objectives and goals in a similar way: "Objectives are broad statements describing the nature, scope, and style of a firm for the future. Objectives crystallize the viable ideals and dreams of entrepreneurs. On the other hand, goals are far more specific statements which deal with the conditions of an organization and its environment during a specific time frame, usually one year."[15]

Clearly stated and communicated objectives are vital to success for many reasons. First, objectives provide employees, creditors, suppliers, distributors, and shareholders with an enlightened sense of their role in an organization's future. Objectives provide for consistency in decision making among managers whose values and attitudes differ. By reaching a consensus on objectives during strategy-formulation activities, an organization can minimize potential implementation conflicts later.

Objectives set forth organizational priorities. They provide a basis for choosing strategies. Objectives stimulate exertion and accomplishment. They serve as standards by which individuals, groups, departments, divisions, and organizations themselves are evaluated. Objectives provide the basis for designing jobs and organizing activities to be performed in an organization. Objectives provide direction and allow for organizational synergy. Without objectives, an organization would be aimlessly drifting toward some unknown end!

ConAgra, a diversified food processing company based in Omaha, Nebraska, is an example firm that has clearly stated and communicated objectives. Between 1979 and 1983, ConAgra averaged 24 percent after-tax return on stockholders' equity. ConAgra's well-known products include Banquet Frozen Foods, Singleton Seafoods, Taco Plaza Restaurants, Country Pride Foods, and Country Skillet Poultry. The company's statement of objectives is given as follows:

> ConAgra is committed to major objectives which guide us in fulfilling our responsibility to our stockholders. ConAgra's most important objective is to average in excess of a 20 percent after tax return on common stockholders' equity, and to earn in excess of a 15 percent return in any given year. ConAgra's objective is to increase trend line (five-year average) earnings per share in excess of 14 percent per year. ConAgra's primary financing objective is to maintain a conservative balance sheet. Long-term debt will not exceed 40 percent of total capitalization. ConAgra's objective is to increase dividends consistent with growth in basic trend line earning power. We expect dividends payments to average in the range of 30–35 percent of earnings.[16]

Establish Strategies

Strategies are the means by which an organization attempts to obtain its objectives. Acquisition and merger are two commonly used ways to pursue various strategies, but internal realignment may represent a more economical way to accomplish the same company objective. An acquisition occurs when a large organization takes on (acquires) a smaller firm, whereas a merger occurs when two organizations of about equal size unite to form one enterprise.

Among the mergers and acquisitions made in recent years, same-industry combinations have predominated. That is, organizations are more and more avoiding diversification or conglomeration when acquiring and merging with other firms. Most of the mergers in 1984 were same-industry combinations. Some of the largest of these combinations are shown in Table 2.3.

No organization has unlimited resources. Therefore, strategy decisions have to be made to eliminate some courses of action and to allocate organizational resources among others. Joseph Charyk, CEO of The Communication Satellite Corporation (COMSAT), recently said, "We have to face the cold fact that COMSAT may not be able to do all it wants. By making hard choices on which ventures to keep and which to fold, we hope to boost our sales from $440 million in 1983 to $1 billion by 1989."[17]

Table 2.3 The largest mergers and acquisitions of 1984

Rank	Value of Deal (in $ thousands)	Acquiring Company (Type of Business)	Acquired Company (Type of Business)	Percent of Book Value
1	$13,231,253	Chevron (Oil and gas)	Gulf Oil (Oil and gas)	129.7
2	10,129,245	Texaco (Oil and gas)	Getty Oil (Oil and gas)	102.2
3	5,696,704	Mobil (Oil and gas)	Superior Oil (Oil and gas)	227.0
4	2,699,891	Beatrice Cos. (Food and consumer products)	Esmark (Food and consumer products)	208.3
6	2,555,336	General Motors (Motor vehicles)	Electronic Data Systems	777.8
8	1,827,958	Champion International (Forest products)	St. Regis (Forest products)	138.0
10	1,510,000	Manufacturers Hanover (Financial services)	CIT Financial (Financial services)	106.5

Source: H. J. Steinbreder, "Deals of the Year," *Fortune* (21 January 1985): 126–30.

Strategic decisions require tradeoffs such as long-range versus short-range considerations and maximizing profits versus increasing shareholders' wealth. These types of tradeoffs require subjective judgments and preferences. In many cases, a lack of objectivity in formulating strategy results in a loss of competitive posture and profitability.

A preponderant number of organizations today recognize that strategic management concepts and techniques can enhance the effectiveness of decisions.[18] Subjective factors such as attitudes toward risk, concern for social responsibility, and personal values *will always affect strategy formulation decisions,* but organizations should be as objective as possible in making those decisions. (A strategy-formulation analytical framework is presented in Chapter 6.)

Most organizations can afford to pursue only one or a few strategies at any given time. Organizations obviously do not have to continuously change their strategies. To maintain the current status quo is a viable option often selected. The Carnation Company is an example firm that has not changed its basic strategy in twenty years. Carnation's products are mostly dairy-based items such as evaporated milk and cocoa mix, but also include Friskies pet foods and Contadina tomato paste. *Business Week* has reported that "Carnation's penchant for the status quo does not please everyone. Outsiders criticize the $3.4 billion company for being too cautious. Carnation refuses to borrow money, and earnings have been flat for three years."[19]

There are fourteen alternative strategies that an enterprise could pursue. These strategic options are defined and exemplified in Table 2.4. Exhibit 2.3 reveals situations

Table 2.4   Alternative growth strategies defined and exemplified

Strategy	*Definition*	*Example (Some are hypothetical)*
Forward Integration	Gaining ownership or increased control over distributors or retailers	General Motors buying out its automobile dealers; Wal-Mart purchasing a fleet of trucks
Backward Integration	Seeking ownership or increased control of suppliers	MacDonald's purchasing a cattle ranch; Holiday Inn acquiring a furniture manufacturer
Horizontal Integration	Seeking ownership or increased control over competitors	The acquiring of Getty by Texaco; small banks being acquired by larger banks
Market Penetration	Seeking increased market share for present products in present markets through greater marketing efforts	Wendy's launching a massive advertising campaign based on the slogan "Where's the Beef?"
Market Development	Introducing present products into new geographic areas	The owner of a restaurant building an identical restaurant in a neighboring town
Product Development	Seeking increased sales by improving or modifying (developing) present product	Apple Computer Company introducing the MacIntosh
Concentric Diversification	Adding new, but related, products	Wachovia Bank purchasing an insurance company
Conglomerate Diversification	Adding new, unrelated products	Mary Kay Cosmetics acquiring a food processing company
Horizontal Diversification	Adding new, unrelated products for present customers	Sheraton Inns beginning to sell gasoline
Joint Venture	One company working with another on a special project	Companies working together on the Alaska pipeline project
Retrenchment	A company regrouping through cost and asset reduction in order to reverse declining sales	Braniff Airlines announcing on October 24, 1984 that it is eliminating service at ten major U.S. cities
Divestiture	Selling a division or part of an organization	Holiday Inn selling its Delta Steamship Lines for $96 million
Liquidation	Selling all of a company's assets, in parts, for their tangible worth	DeLorean Motor Company liquidating in 1984
Combination	An organization pursuing two or more strategies simultaneously	K-Mart purchasing Pay Less Drug Stores in 1985 and Waldenbooks in 1984

or conditions under which different strategies are most appropriate. The guidelines presented in Exhibit 2.3 are applicable to all sizes and types of organizations. Alternative strategies can be categorized into four major groups, as follows:

1. Intensive—market penetration, market development, and product development
2. Integrative—forward integration, backward integration, and horizontal integration
3. Diversified—concentric diversification, conglomerate diversification, and horizontal diversification
4. Other—joint venture, retrenchment, divestiture, liquidation, and combination

Exhibit 2.3 Guidelines for situations when particular strategies are most effective

Forward Integration

- When an organization's present distributors are especially expensive, or unreliable, or incapable of meeting the firm's distribution needs
- When the availability of quality distributors is so limited as to offer a competitive advantage to those firms that integrate forward
- When an organization competes in an industry that is growing and is expected to continue to grow markedly; this is a factor because forward integration reduces an organization's ability to diversify if its basic industry falters.
- When an organization has both the capital and human resources needed to manage the new business of distributing its own products
- When the advantages of stable production are particularly high; this is a consideration because an organization can increase the predictability of the demand for its output through forward integration.
- When present distributors or retailers have high profit margins; this situation suggests that a company could profitably distribute its own products and price them more competitively by integrating forward.

Backward Integration

- When an organization's present suppliers are especially expensive, or unreliable, or incapable of meeting the firm's needs for parts, components, assemblies, or raw materials
- When the number of suppliers is few and the number of competitors is many
- When an organization competes in an industry that is growing rapidly; this is a factor because integrative-type strategies (forward, backward, and horizontal) reduce an organization's ability to diversify in a declining industry.
- When an organization has both the capital and human resources needed to manage the new business of supplying its own raw materials
- When the advantages of stable prices are particularly important; this is a factor because an organization can stabilize the cost of its raw materials and the associated price of its products through backward integration.

- When present suppliers have high profit margins, which suggests that the business of supplying products or services in the given industry is a worthwhile venture
- When an organization needs to acquire a needed resource quickly

Horizontal Integration

- When an organization can gain monopolistic characteristics in a particular area or region without being challenged by the federal government for "tending substantially" to reduce competition
- When an organization competes in a growing industry
- When increased economies of scale provide major competitive advantages
- When an organization has both the capital and human talent needed to successfully manage an expanded organization
- When competitors are faltering due to a lack of managerial expertise or a need for particular resources which your organization possesses; note that horizontal integration would not be appropriate if competitors are doing poorly because overall industry sales are declining.

Market Penetration

- When current markets are not saturated with your particular product or service
- When the usage rate of present customers could be significantly increased
- When the market shares of major competitors have been declining while total industry sales have been increasing
- When the correlation between dollar sales and dollar marketing expenditures has historically been high
- When increased economies of scale provide major competitive advantages

Market Development

- When new channels of distribution are available that are reliable, inexpensive, and of good quality
- When an organization is very successful at what it does
- When new untapped or unsaturated markets exist
- When an organization has the needed capital and human resources to manage expanded operations
- When an organization has excess production capacity
- When an organization's basic industry is rapidly becoming global in scope

Product Development

- When an organization has successful products that are in the maturity stage of the product life cycle; the idea here is to attract satisfied customers to try new (improved) products as a result of their positive experience with the organization's present products or services.
- When an organization competes in an industry that is characterized by rapid technological developments

- When major competitors offer better quality products at comparable prices
- When an organization competes in a high-growth industry
- When an organization has especially strong research and development capabilities

Concentric Diversification

- When an organization competes in a no-growth or a slow-growth industry
- When adding new, but related, products would significantly enhance the sales of current products
- When new, but related, products could be offered at highly competitive prices
- When new, but related, products have seasonal sales levels that counterbalance an organization's existing peaks and valleys
- When an organization's products are currently in the decline stage of the product life cycle
- When an organization has a strong management team

Conglomerate Diversification

- When an organization's basic industry is experiencing declining annual sales and profits
- When an organization has the capital and managerial talent needed to compete successfully in a new industry
- When the organization has the opportunity to purchase an unrelated business that is an attractive investment opportunity
- When there exists financial synergy between the acquired and acquiring firm; note that a key difference between concentric and conglomerate diversification is that the former should be based on some commonality in markets, products, or technology; whereas, the latter should be based more on profit considerations.
- When existing markets for an organization's present products are saturated
- When antitrust action could be charged against an organization that has historically concentrated on a single industry

Horizontal Diversification

- When revenues derived from an organization's current products or services would significantly increase by adding the new, unrelated products
- When an organization competes in a highly competitive and/or a no-growth industry, as indicated by low industry profit margins and returns
- When an organization's present channels of distribution can be used to market the new products to current customers
- When the new products have countercyclical sales patterns compared to an organization's present products

Joint Venture

- When a privately owned organization is forming a joint venture with a publicly owned organization; there are some advantages of being privately held, such as close ownership; there are some advantages of being publicly held, such as access to stock issuances as a source of capital. Sometimes, the unique advantages of being privately and publicly held can be synergistically combined in a joint venture.

- When a domestic organization is forming a joint venture with a foreign company; joint venture can provide a domestic company with the opportunity for obtaining local management in a foreign country, thereby reducing risks such as expropriation and harassment by host country officials.
- When the distinctive competencies of two or more firms complement each other especially well
- When some project is potentially very profitable, but requires overwhelming resources and risks; the Alaskan pipeline is an example.
- When two or more smaller firms have trouble competing with a large firm
- When there exists a need to introduce a new technology quickly

Retrenchment

- When an organization has a clearly distinctive competence, but has failed to meet its objectives and goals consistently over time
- When an organization is one of the weakest competitors in a given industry
- When an organization is plagued by inefficiency, low profitability, poor employee morale, and pressure from stockholders to improve performance
- When an organization has failed to capitalize on external opportunities, minimize external threats, take advantage of internal strengths, and overcome internal weaknesses over time; that is, when the organization's strategic managers have failed (and possibly been replaced by more competent individuals)
- When an organization has grown so large so quickly that major internal reorganization is needed

Divestiture

- When an organization has pursued a retrenchment strategy and it failed to accomplish needed improvements
- When a division needs more resources to be competitive than the company can provide
- When a division is responsible for an organization's overall poor performance
- When a division is a misfit with the rest of an organization; this can result from radically different markets, customers, managers, employees, values, or needs.
- When a large amount of cash is needed quickly and cannot be reasonably obtained from other sources
- When government antitrust action threatens an organization

Liquidation

- When an organization has pursued both a retrenchment strategy and a divestiture strategy, and neither has been successful

- When an organization's only alternative is bankruptcy; liquidation represents an orderly and planned means of obtaining the greatest possible cash for an organization's assets. A company can legally declare bankruptcy first and then liquidate various divisions to raise needed capital.

- When the stockholders of a firm can minimize their losses by selling the organization's assets

Source: Adapted from: F.R. David, "How Do We Choose Among Alternative Growth Strategies?" *Managerial Planning* 33, no. 4 (January–February 1985): 14–17, 22.

Strategy Implementation

The strategic-management process does not end when top managers decide which strategy or strategies to pursue. There must be a translation of strategic thought into strategic action. Strategy implementation can be contrasted with strategy formulation in the following ways:

Strategy formulation is the positioning of forces before the action. Strategy implementation is the managing of forces during the action.

Strategy formulation focuses on effectiveness.
Strategy implementation focuses on efficiency.

Strategy formulation is primarily an intellectual process.
Strategy implementation is primarily an operational process.

Strategy implementation is an operationally oriented process because goals and policies must be established and resources allocated throughout the organization. Successful strategy implementation can require the following types of changes: reallocating resources to departments, setting performance standards, installing information systems, establishing reward systems, altering an organization's structure, establishing new sales territories, training new employees and managers, motivating individuals, obtaining new capital, developing new advertising strategies, segmenting new markets, and developing budgets and programs.

As shown in Table 2.5, strategy-implementation changes can be categorized by functional area. Chapter 7 and Chapter 8 examine key strategy-implementation tools in the functional areas of business.[20]

In all but the smallest organizations, the transition from strategy formulation to strategy implementation requires a shift in responsibility from corporate managers to divisional and functional managers. Implementation problems can arise because of this shift in responsibility, especially when strategy-formulation decisions come as a surprise to middle- and lower-level managers. Divisional and functional managers should be involved as much as possible in the strategy-formulation process and corporate managers should be involved as much as possible in the strategy-implementation process.

Strategy Evaluation

In many organizations, strategy evaluation is simply an appraisal of how well an organization performs. Have the firm's assets increased? Has there been an increase in prof-

Table 2.5 Tools for implementing strategy

Management	Marketing	Finance	Production	Research and Development
Goals	Goals	Goals	Goals	Goals
Policies	Policies	Policies	Policies	Policies
Resources	Resources	Resources	Resources	Resources
Budgets	Budgets	Budgets	Budgets	Budgets
Structure	Markets	Capital	Quality Control	R&D facilities
Employees	Distributors	Liquidity	Facilities	R&D personnel
Managers	Customers	Leverage	Transportation	R&D incentives
Employee benefits	Products	Stocks	Technology	R&D equipment
Wages/Salaries	Positioning	Dividends	Shipping	
	Segmentation	Accounting	Cost controls	

itability? Have sales increased? Have productivity levels increased? Have profit margin, return on investment, and earnings-per-share ratios increased? Some firms argue that their strategy must be correct if the answers to these types of questions are affirmative. Well, the strategy or strategies may be correct, but this type of reasoning can be misleading because strategy evaluation must have both a long-run and short-run focus.

Strategies often do not affect short-term operating results until it is too late to make needed changes. Braniff Airlines, for example, did not know that worldwide market development for them would result in bankruptcy until hundreds of new planes had been purchased and extensive resources committed. In addition to the types of questions mentioned above, strategy evaluation requires examination of more difficult issues, such as: Have our key internal strengths and weaknesses changed? Have our key external opportunities and threats changed? Are our objectives and goals being achieved? What corrective actions are needed to improve our competitive position?

It is impossible to demonstrate conclusively that a particular strategy is optimal or even to guarantee that it will work. One can, however, evaluate it for critical flaws. Richard Rumelt offers four criteria that could be used to evaluate strategy: consistency, consonance, advantage, and feasibility. These criteria are adapted for Exhibit 2.4.

Exhibit 2.4 Rumelt's criteria for evaluating strategies

Consistency

A strategy should not present inconsistent goals and policies. Organizational conflict and interdepartmental bickering are often symptoms of a managerial disorder, but these problems may also be a sign of "strategic inconsistency." Rumelt offers three guidelines to help determine if organizational problems are due to inconsistencies in strategy.

- If managerial problems continue despite changes in personnel, and if they tend to be issue-based rather than people-based, then strategies may be inconsistent.

- If success for one organizational department means, or is interpreted to mean, failure for another department, then strategies may be inconsistent.

- If policy problems and issues continue to be brought to the top for resolution, then strategies may be inconsistent.

Consonance

Consonance refers to the need for strategists to examine *sets of trends* as well as individual trends in evaluating strategies. A strategy must represent an adaptive response to the external environment and to the critical changes occurring within it. One difficulty in matching a firm's key internal and external factors in the formulation of strategy is that most trends are the result of interactions among other trends. For example, the daycare explosion came about as a combined result of many trends that included a rise in the average level of education, increased inflation, and an increase in women in the work force. Thus, while single economic or demographic trends might appear steady for many years, there are waves of change going on at the interaction level.

Feasibility

A strategy must neither overtax available resources nor create unsolvable subproblems. The final broad test of strategy is its feasibility; that is, can the strategy be attempted within the physical, human, and financial resources of the enterprise? The financial resources of a business are the easiest to quantify and are normally the first limitation against which strategy is evaluated. It is sometimes forgotten, however, that innovative approaches to financing are often possible. Devices such as captive finance subsidiaries, sale-leaseback arrangements, and tying plant mortgages to long-term contracts have all been used effectively to help win key positions in suddenly expanding industries. A less quantifiable, but actually more rigid limitation on strategic choice is that imposed by individual and organizational capabilities. In evaluating a strategy it is important to examine whether an organization has demonstrated in the past that it possesses the abilities, competencies, skills, and talents needed to carry out a given strategy.

Advantage

A strategy must provide for the creation and/or maintenance of a competitive advantage in a selected area of activity. Competitive advantages normally are the result of superiority in one of three areas: 1) resources, 2) skills, or 3) position. The idea that the positioning of one's resources can enhance their combined effectiveness is familiar to military theorists, chess players, and diplomats. Position can also play a crucial role in an organization's strategy. Once gained, a good position is defensible—meaning so costly to capture that rivals are deterred from full-scale attacks. Positional advantage tends to be self-sustaining, as long as the key internal and environmental factors that underlie it remain stable. This is why entrenched firms can be almost impossible to unseat, even if their raw skill levels are only average. Although not all positional advantages are associated with size, it is true that larger organizations tend to operate in markets and use procedures that turn their size into advantage, while smaller firms seek product/market positions that exploit other types of advantage. The principal characteristic of good position is that it permits the firm to obtain advantage from policies that would not similarly benefit rivals without the same position. Therefore, in evaluating strategy, organizations should examine the nature of positional advantages associated with a given strategy.

Source: Adapted from Richard Rumelt, "The Evaluation of Business Strategy," in W. F. Glueck, ed., *Business Policy and Strategic Management* (New York: McGraw-Hill, 1980), 359–67.

STRATEGIES IN ACTION

This section focuses on strategies being pursued by actual companies. Examples are provided for all fourteen types of strategies. As you study these strategies in action, examine whether or not the companies are following the guidelines given in Exhibit 2.3.

Integrative Strategies

An example of *forward integration* occurred recently when the Fort Howard Paper Company purchased Maryland Cup Corporation for $536 million in cash and stock. At the time, Maryland Cup had twenty-two distribution warehouses across the United States and dominated the paper and plastic cup markets with its Sweetheart brand. There were only a few large distributors of paper cups and Maryland Cup had a 28 percent share of the $2 billion market for cups sold to commercial food service businesses.[21]

Fort Howard, with only two distribution warehouses in the United States, was primarily a producer rather than a distributor of paper tissue, towels, napkins, cups, and placemats. Fort Howard recognized that the paper service industry was expected to grow appreciably in the late 1980s, and it had the financial resources and management skills needed to successfully integrate forward.

Most manufacturers and retailers in the United States purchase needed materials from other companies (suppliers). An example firm that is pursuing *backward integration* is the Transco Energy Company, headquartered in Houston, Texas. This company is one of the most efficient oil and gas pipeline operators in the world. It has an 1,800 mile, eleven-state system that runs from offshore Texas to the Northeast as far as New York, where its customers include Consolidated Edison Co. and Brooklyn Union Gas Co.[22]

Until 1983, suppliers of oil and gas to pipeline operators have always enjoyed "take-or-pay" contracts, which required Transco and other similar firms to buy gas at prices too high to be sold. Transco recently took legal action to create a "spot market" whereby oil and gas could be bought from suppliers at competitive prices. Transco plans to increase its oil exploration and production business after overcoming legal problems with suppliers. Backward integration is an appropriate strategy for Transco, given their poor relationship with suppliers and strong financial position.

American General Corporation (AGC), a multibillion dollar insurance company, has pursued a strategy of *horizontal integration* for thirty-five years. In 1982, AGC purchased a large competitor, NLT Corporation, for a total of $1.7 billion. This was the largest horizontal integration deal ever recorded in the insurance industry. The acquisition pushed American General's assets to over $13.3 billion.

It is interesting to note how AGC arranged this acquisition. The company first acquired 10 percent stock in NLT. Then they optioned those shares to Ashland Oil, Inc. who turned down the offer. AGC garnered the option fee. AGC then gave NLT two alternatives: (1) buy back your shares at 50 percent over the book value to avoid having us sell the shares to a potentially harmful firm, or (2) agree to be acquired by us. Manipulation is not a recommended business tactic, but *Business Week* suggests that American General pursues horizontal integration manipulatively:

> American General's basic technique has been unorthodox, but simple: Instead of investing small bits of its equity portfolio in many companies outside insurance to spread risk, it has bought sizable minority stakes in a limited number of other insurers. Then, by tacitly threatening to sell those stakes to a hostile buyer, American General presents such companies with a choice: Sell out to American General, or buy back the stock and find another buyer, both at a hefty premium for American General. An investment banker for a former American General target compares this to extortion. Others disagree.[23]

Intensive Strategies

Market penetration is a strategy that means increasing the number of salesmen, increasing advertising expenditures, offering extensive sales promotion items, or increasing publicity efforts. Market penetration is widely used as a lone strategy and in conjunction with other strategies. The Pennzoil Company is currently pursuing a market-penetration strategy. Pennzoil has launched a massive campaign to increase market share, spending nearly $25 million per year on advertising. Pennzoil advertisements featurecar racers Jim Hill and Johnny Rutherford. The yellow-canned Pennzoil now enjoys premium shelf space at K-Mart Corporation, Target Stores, and other mass merchandisers. Pennzoil boasts about a 20 percent market share, just behind Quaker State Motor Oil, the leader.

Market development is geographic expansion into new areas. The climate for international market development is becoming much more favorable and rational. Frederick Gluck says, "In many industries, it is going to be very hard to maintain a competitive edge by staying close to home."[24] One firm that is staying at home to pursue market development in domestic markets is Family Dollar Stores, Inc. Based in Matthews, N.C., Family Dollar has become one of the fastest-growing discount store chains in the United States. In 1984 the company operated 635 stores. Family Dollar plans to expand geographically out of the Southeastern United States, increasing the number of stores to 1,100 by 1988. Stores are now operated in a fourteen-state area ranging as far north as Pennsylvania, south to Florida, and west to Arkansas and Louisiana.

Family Dollar provides consumers with good values in low-cost merchandise for family and home needs. The merchandise is sold in a no-frills, low-overhead, self-service environment, with nearly all products being priced at $15.99 or less. Family Dollar's net sales and profits have increased dramatically since the first store was opened in 1959 in Charlotte, North Carolina.[25]

Product development usually entails large research and development expenditures. American Motors is aggressively pursuing a product-development strategy. AMC is moving fast to market a more fuel-efficient Jeep and a hatchback version of the Alliance. The company is betting on an auto industry recovery in the United States between 1985 and 1990. The Renault Alliance and the Jeep Cherokee are successful AMC products. However, GMC, Ford, Toyota, and Chrysler are perceived by many consumers to offer "better products at comparable prices." So product development could be the most effective strategy for AMC to pursue. Paul Tippett, chairman of the board and chief executive officer at AMC, described the firm's product development strategy as follows:

> As we confront the challenges of 1984 and beyond, we have more new and improved products than ever before. New versions of the sporty Renault Fuego and the Renault Sportwagon are being developed. These moves are part of our corporate strategy of bringing to the market a consistent stream of high quality, high technology vehicles. Our overall strategy is to develop products in which we or our partner, Renault, have special expertise, four-wheel-drive and front-wheel-drive vehicles.[26]

Diversification Strategies

In 1984, Pioneer Electronics Corporation pursued a *concentric diversification* strategy, diversifying into laser-equipped videodiscs, two-way cable TV, dictating machines, telephone-answering devices, loudspeakers, and tape recorders. Pioneer is best known for its home stereo equipment, which accounted for nearly 40 percent of total sales in 1984. The reason for this strategic reorientation is declining stereo sales and increasing video equipment sales worldwide. Pioneer has a strong management team that has increased profits from −$12.9 million in 1982 to $32.8 million in 1984.

The Public Service Company of New Mexico (PNM), New Mexico's largest company and only New York Stock Exchange corporation, has announced plans to implement a *conglomerate diversification* strategy. PNM's objective is for nonutility ventures to total 20 percent of profits by 1988. PNM has started a fiberboard manufacturing and a furniture operation. PNM's customers are complaining about the firm's conglomerate diversification strategy:

> When Public Service Co. of New Mexico (PNM) recently began conglomerate diversification, it stirred up a real hornet's nest. Along with the ratepayers' complaints, small businesses charged PNM with unfair competition. However, State Senator Les Houston supports PNM's diversification strategy, saying it will increase the number of jobs in New Mexico. He feels this benefit will eventually convince critics that PNM's strategy is good for the State.[27]

Horizontal diversification is not as risky as conglomerate diversification, because a firm should already be familiar with its present customers. Owens-Illinois, Inc., the world's leading producer of glass containers, recognizes that the demand for glass bottles has declined steadily over recent years, while the demand for plastic containers has increased. The company is therefore pursuing horizontal diversification into high-technology plastic packaging (i.e., a different product for present customers). Owens-Illinois' planned shift from glass into plastic technology was a major factor contributing to the firm's profitability in 1984.

Often it is advantageous for two or more companies to form a temporary partnership or consortium for the purpose of capitalizing on some opportunity. Companies that established *joint ventures* in 1984 include Babcock & Wilcox with Multifuel Boilers, American Cyanamid with Colorim Systems, Diamond Shamrock with Nippon Oil & Fats, Kroger with Foodland Distributors, and General Electric with Rolls-Royce.

The Montedison Group Company formed a joint venture with Hercules Inc. in 1983 to produce polypropylene resin. This joint venture gave Montedison and Hercules a solid 16.5 percent of world polypropylene capacity. The agreement was established because Montedison had developed a new process and catalyst that cut production costs of polypropylene by 20 percent, but the company had no marketing expertise. However, Hercules was an experienced and effective marketer of polypropylene. One Montedison executive explained, "We developed this new technology and we had to use it quickly to beat competitors." The joint venture put Montedison in the huge U.S. market, which it left in 1979 when it sold two U.S. plants to raise capital.[28]

Other Types of Strategies

A *retrenchment* strategy is often called a turnaround or reorganization strategy. It is designed to fortify an organization's basic distinctive competence. During retrenchment, top management has to work with limited resources and face pressure from shareholders, employees, and the media. Retrenchment entails selling off land and buildings to raise needed cash, pruning product lines, closing marginal businesses, closing obsolete factories, automating processes, reducing the number of employees, and instituting expense control systems.

When the market for mobile homes and recreational vehicles collapsed in the mid-1970s, Phillips Industries formulated and implemented a retrenchment strategy. A leading supplier of major components for mobile homes and recreational vehicles, Phillips consolidated manufacturing operations, closed more than ten plants, laid off 27 percent of the work force, and implemented a strict team-study system of cost cutting. Between 1980 and 1984, Phillips rebounded strongly, as sales increased from less than $200 million to over $300 million.

Divestiture is a commonly employed strategy. Ralston Purina Company is divesting (selling) all those divisions that do not complement its basic business or that do not contribute to company profitability. The company has sold its tuna-catching fleet, its mushroom-raising division, and its European-based pet food businesses. As of January 13, 1984, Ralston Purina was the world's largest producer of livestock and poultry feeds, which accounted for 34 percent of company sales and 20 percent of profits. The company is also known for its Jack in the Box chain of restaurants and Chex cereal.

Liquidation is a recognition of defeat and thus can be an emotionally difficult strategy. However, liquidation may be the best strategy to pursue for minimizing shareholders' losses. Five companies that liquidated in 1984 were DeLorean Motors, United Western, Gladstone Shoes, American Equity Invest, and Great Western United.

Quite often, firms will pursue a *combination* of several strategies at the same time. When an organization is financially strong and has exceptional managerial talent, it can afford to pursue opportunities more aggressively and take greater risks than less fortunate firms. Under these conditions, a combination strategy can be particularly effective. Also, when a firm is struggling to survive, it may employ a number of defensive strategies simultaneously, such as divestiture, liquidation, and retrenchment.

In large diversified companies, a combination strategy is usually employed because different divisions may pursue different strategies. An example firm that is pursuing a combination-type strategy is Stone Container Corporation. This company is using forward integration, backward integration, and horizontal integration concurrently. Specifically, Stone Container recently acquired three companies: (1) Samson Paper Bag Co. for $7.4 million (forward integration), (2) Dean-Dempsey Corporation, a wood-chip fiber company (backward integration), for $3 million, and (3) Continental Group Inc.'s containerboard and brown paper operations for $510 million (horizontal integration). The Continental purchase moved Stone Container from being the thirteenth-largest containerboard producer in the United States to the second largest, behind International Paper Company.[29]

CONCLUSION

The main appeal of any managerial approach is the expectation that it will enhance organizational performance. This is especially true of the strategic-management process, which focuses on the formulation, implementation, and evaluation of plans. Strategic-management activities should improve the problem-prevention capabilities of an organization. By making clear productivity/reward relationships, strategic-management activities often improve employee motivation. Through involvement in strategic-management activities, managers and employees alike achieve a better understanding of the priorities and operations of the organization.

The strategic-management process offers many benefits, but not without some costs. Considerable time and effort must be invested by participants. Sometimes top managers do not take an active enough role in strategy implementation. On other occasions, lower-level managers do not have the opportunity to participate in formulating strategy. These situations can be dysfunctional.

The strategic-management process may represent a radical change in philosophy for some organizations, so strategists must be trained to anticipate effectively and respond constructively to questions and issues as they arise during all stages of the strategic-management process. This textbook is designed to give you that training. This chapter has extended your overall knowledge of the strategic-management process, so in subsequent chapters we will examine specific concepts and techniques in greater detail.

1. According to *Fortune* magazine (January 7, 1985), the ten most admired companies in the United States are #1 IBM, #2 Coca-Cola, #3 Dow Jones, #4 3M, #5 Hewlett-Packard, #6 Anheuser-Busch, #7 Boeing, #8 General Electric, #9 Eastman Kodak, and #10 Merck. Select one of these companies. Examine that firm's most recent annual report to determine what strategy or strategies are being pursued. Report your findings to the class.

2. Give some key internal factors that should be examined during an internal strategic-management audit.

3. What are some key environmental trends that organizations should monitor as part of the external audit?

4. Discuss the "matching process" illustrated in the strategic-management model shown in Figure 2.1.

5. Identify and describe five published and five unpublished sources of strategic-management information.

6. Define and give an example of five alternative strategies that organizations could pursue.

7. With regard to cost/riskiness, rank order the following strategies (1 = most costly/risky; 14 = least costly/risky):

	Costly/Risky
Concentric diversification	_____
Market penetration	_____
Forward integration	_____
Product development	_____
Conglomerate diversification	_____
Backward integration	_____
Horizontal diversification	_____
Divestiture	_____
Horizontal integration	_____
Market development	_____
Retrenchment	_____
Joint venture	_____
Liquidation	_____
Combination	_____

8. What are the major advantages and disadvantages of diversification?

9. What are the major advantages and disadvantages of pursuing an integrative type of strategy?

10. Explain five types of changes that may be needed for successful strategy implementation.

11. Discuss the relative importance of consistency, consonance, advantage, and feasibility in strategy evaluation.

12. In your opinion, what are the major benefits of using a strategic-management approach to decision making?

13. How would the strategic-management process differ in profit organizations compared to nonprofit organizations?

14. How could an organization best assure that strategies formulated will be implemented?

FOOTNOTES

1 Hershey Foods Corporation, *1983 Annual Report*, p. 3.

2 Richard Robinson, Jr., "The Importance of Outsiders in Small Firm Strategic Planning," *Academy of Management Journal* 25, no. 1 (March 1982): 80.

3 S. Schoeffler, R. Buzzell, and D. Heany, "Impact of Strategic Planning on Profit Performance," *Harvard Business Review* (March 1974): 137.

4 John Pearce II and Richard Robinson, Jr., *Strategic Management: Strategy Formulation and Implementation* (Homewood, Ill.: Richard D. Irwin, 1982), 18, n. 10.

5 R. Fulmer and L. Rue, "The Practice and Profitability of Long-Range Planning," *Managerial Planning* 22 (1974): 1.

6 Robert Donnelly, "Strategic Planning for Better Management," *Managerial Planning* 30, no. 3 (November–December 1981): 4.

7 Carter Bales, "Strategic Control: The President's Paradox," *Business Horizons* 20, no. 4 (August 1977): 18.

8 Andrew Rucks and Peter Ginter, "War Games and

Business Strategy Formulation," *Managerial Planning* 32, no. 2 (September–October 1983): 15–19, 34.

9 Lee Iacocca, "The Rescue and Resuscitation of Chrysler," *The Journal of Business Strategy* 4, no. 1 (Summer 1983): 67.

10 John Diffenbach, "Corporate Environmental Analysis in Large U.S. Corporations," *Long Range Planning* 16, no. 3 (June 1983): 109.

11 Eleanor Tracy, "When Computers Chat, They Rely on Hayes," *Fortune* (25 June 1984): 48.

12 William King, "Integrating Strength–Weakness Analysis into Strategic Planning," *Journal of Business Research* 11 (1983): 481.

13 The New AT&T, *1983 Annual Report*, p. 2.

14 Yezdi Godiwalla, Wayne Meinhart, and William Warde, "General Management and Corporate Strategy," *Managerial Planning* 30 (September–October 1981): 17–23, 29.

15 Richard Vancil and Peter Lorange, "Strategic Planning in Diversified Companies," *Harvard Business Review* 53, no. 1 (January–February 1975): 81.

16 ConAgra, *1983 Annual Report*, p. 4.

17 "COMSAT: Caught in a Cash Crunch That May Ground Some Ventures," *Business Week* (21 May 1984): 86–87.

18 Fred David, "QSPM: A Quantitative Approach to Strategy Formulation," *Long Range Planning* (1986) (in press).

19 "Carnation: Will a Corporate Recluse Come Out of Its Shell?" *Business Week* (6 August 1984): 86–87.

20 Business policy is often called a capstone course. This is primarily due to the need for students to utilize the knowledge they have acquired in prior courses to successfully *implement strategies.* Whereas strategy-formulation techniques are mostly new for business policy students, strategy-implementation procedures require a working knowledge of all functional business areas.

21 "Fort Howard: New Marketing Muscle from Maryland Cup," *Business Week* (18 July 1983): 132.

22 "Transco Energy: the Natural Gas Pipeliner That's Rewriting the Rules," *Business Week* (18 July 1983): 126.

23 "American General: Gobbling Up Smaller Insurers to Keep Profits Fat," *Business Week* (9 May 1983): 64.

24 Frederick Gluck, "Global Competition in the 1980s," *The Journal of Business Strategy* (Spring 1983): 22.

25 Family Dollar Stores, *1983 Annual Report*, p. 1.

26 American Motors Corporation, *1983 Annual Report*, p. 1.

27 "Public Service of New Mexico: Calming the Critics As It Diversifies," *Business Week* (22 August 1983): 79.

28 "Montedison: Taking a Sharp Ax to an Overgrown Empire," *Business Week* (27 June 1983): 48.

29 "Stone Container: A Risky Purchase Puts It on a Fast-Growth Track," *Business Week* (14 November 1983): 218.

SUGGESTED READINGS

Bales, C.F. "Strategic Control: The President's Paradox." *Business Horizons* 20, no. 4 (August 1977): 17–28.

Bloom, P.N. and P. Kotler. "Strategies for High Market-Share Companies." *Harvard Business Review* 53, no. 6 (November–December 1975): 63–72.

Buzzell, R.D. "Is Vertical Integration Profitable?" *Harvard Business Review* 61, no. 1 (January–February 1983): 92–102.

Collier, D. "Strategic Management in Diversified, Decentralized Companies." *The Journal of Business Strategy* 3, no. 4 (Spring 1983): 85–89.

David, F.R. "How Do We Choose Among Alternative Growth Strategies?" *Managerial Planning* 33, no. 4 (January–February 1985): 14–17, 22.

David, F.R. "QSPM: A Quantitative Approach to Strategy Formulation." *Long Range Planning* (1986) (in press).

Diffenbach, J. "Corporate Environmental Analysis in Large U.S. Corporations." *Long Range Planning* 16, no. 3 (June 1983): 107–116.

Donnelly, R.M. "Strategic Planning for Better Management." *Managerial Planning* 30, no. 3 (November–December 1981): 3–6, 41–42.

Fulmer, R.M. and L.W. Rue. "The Practice and Profitability of Long-Range Planning." *Managerial Planning* 22 (1974): 1–7.

Gallinger, G.W. "Strategic Business Planning." *Managerial Planning* 31, no. 1 (July–August 1982): 41–45.

Gluck, F. "Global Competition in the 1980s." *The Journal of Business Strategy* (Spring 1983): 22–27.

Godiwalla, Y.M., W.A. Meinhart, and W.A. Warde. "General Management and Corporate Strategy." *Managerial Planning* 30, no. 2 (September–October 1981): 17–23, 29.

Harrigan, K.R. "A Framework for Looking at Vertical Integration." *The Journal of Business Strategy* (Winter 1983): 30–37.

Harrigan, K.R. and M.E. Porter. "End-Game Strategies for Declining Industries." *Harvard Business Review* 61, no. 4 (July–August 1983): 111–120.

Iacocca, L.A. "The Rescue and Resuscitation of Chrysler." *The Journal of Business Strategy* 4, no. 1 (Summer 1983): 67–69.

King, W. "Integrating Strength-Weakness Analysis into Strategic Planning." *Journal of Business Research* 11 (1983): 475–487.

"Montedison: Taking a Sharp Ax to an Overgrown Empire." *Business Week* (27 June 1983): 48, 50.

Naylor, T.M. "Effective Use of Strategic Planning, Forecasting, and Modeling in the Executive Suite." *Managerial Planning* 30, no. 4 (January–February 1982): 4–11.

Pearce, J.A. II. "The Company Mission As a Strategic Tool." *Sloan Management Review* (Spring 1982): 15–24.

Pearce, J.A. II and R.B. Robinson, Jr. *Strategic Management: Strategy Formulation and Implementation* (Homewood, Ill.: Richard D. Irwin, Inc., 1982).

Robinson, R.B. Jr. "The Importance of 'Outsiders' in Small Firm Strategic Planning." *Academy of Management Journal* 25, no. 1 (March 1982): 80–93.

Rucks, A. and P. Ginter. "War Games and Business Strategy Formulation." *Managerial Planning* 32, no. 2 (September–October 1983): 15–19, 34.

Schoeffler, S. "How Common Errors in Planning Can Upset Corporate Strategy." *AMA Forum* 72, no. 1 (January 1983): 29, 31.

Schoeffler, S., R.D. Buzzell, and D.F. Heany. "Impact of Strategic Planning on Profit Performance." *Harvard Business Review* (March 1974): 137–145.

Taylor, B. "Turnaround, Recovery, and Growth: The Way Through the Crisis." *Journal of General Management* 8, no. 2 (Winter 1983): 5–13.

Tracy, Eleanor. "When Computers Chat, They Rely on Hayes." *Fortune* (25 June 1984): 48.

Vancil, R.F., and P. Lorange. "Strategic Planning in Diversified Companies." *Harvard Business Review* 53, no. 1 (January–February 1975): 81–90.

Varadarajan, Poondi. "Intensive Growth Opportunities: An Extended Classification." *California Management Review* XXV, no. 3 (Spring 1983): 118–132.

EXPERIENTIAL EXERCISE 2A:

Applying the Strategic Management Process to Ponderosa, Inc.

PURPOSE

The purpose of this exercise is to give you experience identifying some of the components in the strategic-management process.

YOUR TASK

Having read the Cohesion Case, page 32, identify what you consider to be Ponderosa's strengths, weaknesses, opportunities, threats, and strategies. List these key factors on a separate sheet of paper. Be sure to state each factor in specific terms.

Based on the components of the strategic-management process that you have identified, prepare a report for CEO Gerald Office that explains how Ponderosa could benefit from a strategic-management approach to corporate decision making.

EXPERIENTIAL EXERCISE 2B:

Strategy Management at the Dynamic Computer Company

PURPOSE

The purpose of this exercise is to give you experience choosing among alternative growth strategies for a specific company. This exercise focuses on the need to allocate resources effectively to implement strategies once they are formulated. Use the guidelines given in Exhibit 2.3, page 63, to complete this exercise.

THE STRATEGIC SITUATION

Dynamic Computer, Inc. is a highly regarded personal computer manufacturer based in central California. DCI designs, develops, produces, markets, and services microprocessor-based personal computer systems for individuals' needs in business, education, science, engineering, and the home. The company's main product is the Dynamic II personal computer system, complete with optional accessories and software. The company has recently announced a new system, the Dynamic III, which is aimed at large business firms and is much higher priced.

Dynamic's computer systems are distributed in the United States and Canada by 1,000 independent retail stores, and internationally through twenty-one independent distributors that resell to 850 foreign retail outlets. Approximately 700 of the retail outlets in the U.S. and Canada are authorized service centers for Dynamic products, but none of the outlets sells Dynamic products exclusively. Many of the outlets are not marketing Dynamic's products effectively.

The U.S. computer industry grew at an inflation-adjusted, compound annual rate of about 20 percent from 1958 through 1981. Through 1987, the real annual growth in the computer industry is expected to average about 18 percent a year. The outlook for personal computers continues to be very positive. However, this market is highly competitive and is characterized by rapid technological advances in both hardware and software. New firms are entering the industry at an increasing rate and this has resulted in a decline in Dynamic's sales, earnings, and market share in recent years. The company is concerned about its future direction and competitive position. Selected financial information follows.

	1985	1984	1983
Sales	$ 1,000,000	$ 1,200,000	$ 1,300,000
Net Income	50,000	100,000	300,000
Total Assets	25,000,000	20,000,000	18,000,000
Market Share	10%	12%	15%

The owners of DCI have indicated a willingness to explore a number of alternative growth strategies for the future. They have hired you as a consultant to assist them in making strategic decisions regarding the future allocation of resources. The feeling is that to sustain growth, the company is at the point where some critical decisions have to be made. Capital is not a major constraint for DCI. Through retained earnings and a good line of credit, Dynamic is capable of investing in several projects. The owners do, of course, wish to use their resources wisely so as to produce the highest possible return on investment in the future.

YOUR TASK

Based on the strategy guidelines given in Exhibit 2.3, page 63, your task is to offer specific recommendations to the chief executive officer of DCI. Five basic alternative strategies should be considered as follows:

1. Market penetration—establish a nationwide sales force to market Dynamic products to large firms that do not buy through independent retailers.
2. Product development—develop an easier-to-use computer for small business firms.
3. Forward integration—establish a nationwide distribution system of retail stores to sell and service Dynamic products exclusively.
4. Backward integration—purchase a major outside supplier of semiconductor chips.
5. Conglomerate diversification—acquire Toys Unlimited, Inc., a large and successful toy manufacturer.

How would you recommend that DCI allocate its resources among these five alternative strategies? Record your answers in the following blanks. Your only constraint is that the total resources allocated must equal 100 percent. Distribute resources in the manner that you think will offer the greatest future return on investment and profitability. Report your resource allocation percentages to the class and explain your reasoning.

Resource Distribution Summary

Strategic Alternative	Resource Allocation
Market penetration	_____%
Product development	_____%
Forward integration	_____%
Backward integration	_____%
Conglomerate diversification	_____%
	100%

PART TWO

Strategy Formulation

3

The Corporate Mission

The Statement of Mission

A Framework for Writing and Evaluating a Mission Statement

Evaluating Mission Statements

Experiential Exercise 3A: Writing a Business Mission

This chapter focuses on the concepts and tools needed to evaluate and write mission statements successfully. A practical framework for developing mission statements is provided. Actual mission statements from large and small and profit and nonprofit organizations are presented.

THE STATEMENT OF MISSION

The Importance of a Business Mission

One of the major problems for chief executive officers is to allocate the necessary time for strategic-management activities. Too often, top executives spend every day on administrative and tactical concerns. Developing a mission statement is often overlooked as organizations rush too quickly to establish objectives and deal with strategic options. The problem is widespread. Even large organizations often do not develop a clear statement of their business mission.

The corporate mission was defined in Chapter 1 as "an enduring statement of purpose that distinguishes one organization from other similar enterprises." A mission statement is a declaration of an organization's reason for being. The statement is essential to effectively establishing objectives and formulating strategies. A mission statement is sometimes called a creed statement, a statement of purpose, a statement of philosophy, a statement of beliefs, a statement of business principles, or a statement "defining our business." General Mills' mission statement, for example, is called a "statement of corporate beliefs." Gulf Oil's mission statement is called a "statement of business principle."

A surprising number of organizations, such as Jim Walter Corporation, Georgia-Pacific, American Cyanamid, and E–Systems, do not have a written statement of their mission. Other companies, such as General Electric and Northrop, have a mission statement but it is not published. All organizations have a reason for being, even if strategists have not consciously transformed this into writing. A carefully prepared statement of mission is a fundamental component of the strategic-management process.

A mission statement reveals the long-term vision of an organization in terms of what it wants to be and whom it wants to serve. It describes an organization's purpose, customers, products or services, markets, philosophy, and basic technology. In combination, these components of a mission statement answer a key question about an enterprise: "What is our Business?" A good answer to this question makes strategy-formulation, strategy-implementation, and strategy-evaluation activities much easier. According to McGinnis, a mission statement (1) should define what the organization is and what the organization aspires to be; (2) should be limited enough to exclude some ventures and broad enough to allow for creative growth; (3) should distinguish a given organization from all others; (4) should serve as a framework for evaluating both current and prospective activities; and (5) should be stated in terms sufficiently clear to be widely understood throughout the organization.[1]

As illustrated in Figure 3.1, the first step in the strategic-management process is to identify a firm's existing mission. If an organization has no written statement of its mission, then an in-depth examination of the firm's history, customers, products, markets, technology, internal strengths and weaknesses, and external opportunities and threats is needed to establish a mission statement. The strategic-management model illustrates that understanding a firm's mission is needed before objectives and strategies can be established effectively. King and Cleland recommend that organizations carefully develop a written mission statement for the following reasons:

1. To ensure unanimity of purpose within the organization
2. To provide a basis for motivating the use of organizational resources
3. To develop a basis, or standard, for allocating organizational resources
4. To establish a general tone or organizational climate, e.g., to suggest a businesslike operation

Figure 3.1   The model of the strategic-management process

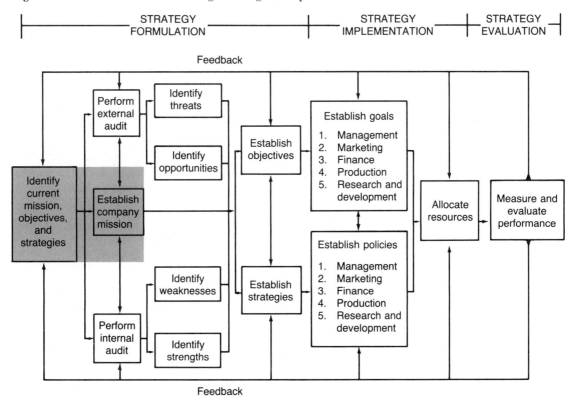

5. To serve as a focal point for those who can identify with the organization's purpose and direction; and to deter those who cannot from participating further in the organization's activities

6. To facilitate the translation of objectives and goals into a work structure involving the assignment of tasks to responsible elements within the organization

7. To specify organizational purposes and the translation of these purposes into goals in such a way that cost, time, and performance parameters can be assessed and controlled[2]

The Nature of a Business Mission

A mission statement is a declaration of attitude and outlook more than a statement of specific details. It is usually broad in scope for at least two major reasons. First, a broad mission statement allows generation and consideration of a range of feasible alternative objectives and strategies without unduly stifling management creativity. Excess specificity would limit the potential of creative growth for the organization. Second, a mission statement must be broad to effectively reconcile differences among an organization's diverse stakeholders.

Stakeholders are individuals and groups of persons who have a special stake or claim on the company. Stakeholders include employees, managers, stockholders, board of directors, customers, suppliers, distributors, creditors, governments (local, state, and federal), unions, competitors, special interest groups, and the general public.[3] Stakeholders provide input to and are affected by an organization's strategic decisions, yet the claims and concerns of diverse constituencies vary and often conflict. For example, the general public is especially interested in social responsibility, whereas stockholders are more interested in profitability.

Claims on any business may literally number in the thousands, and often include clean air, jobs, taxes, investment opportunities, career opportunities, equal employment opportunities, employee benefits, salaries, wages, clean water, and community services. Obviously, all of the stakeholders' claims on an organization cannot be pursued with equal emphasis. A good mission statement indicates the relative attention that an organization will devote to meeting the claims of various stakeholders. George Steiner offers the following insight on the need for a broad mission statement:

> Most business statements of mission are expressed at high levels of abstraction. Vagueness nevertheless has its virtues. Mission statements are not designed to express concrete ends, but rather to provide motivation, general direction, an image, a tone, and a philosophy to guide the enterprise. An excess of detail could prove counterproductive, since concrete specification could be the base for rallying opposition. Precision might stifle creativity in the formulation of an acceptable mission or purpose. Once an aim is cast in concrete it creates a rigidity in an organization and resists change. Vagueness leaves room for other managers to fill in the details, perhaps even to

modify general patterns. Vagueness permits more flexibility in adapting to changing environments and internal operations. It facilitates flexibility in implementation.[4]

Although a mission statement needs to be broad in scope for the reasons described above, care should be taken not to develop an overly general statement that does not exclude any strategic options. Such a statement would be useless. Apple Computer's mission statement, for example, should not open the possibility for diversification into pesticides, or Ford Motor Company's into food processing. Reaching a fine balance between specificity and generality is difficult to achieve, but is well worth the effort.

Current thought on mission statements is largely based on guidelines set forth in the mid-1970s by Peter Drucker. Drucker emphasizes that a major reason for developing a business mission is to create customers. Customers are what give meaning to an organization. A classic description by Drucker of "the purpose of a business" reveals the relative importance of customers in a statement of mission:

> It is the customer who determines what a business is. It is the customer alone whose willingness to pay for a good or for a service converts economic resources into wealth, things into goods. What the business thinks it produces is not of first importance, especially not to the future of the business and to its success. What the customer thinks he is buying, what he considers value, is decisive—it determines what a business is, what it produces, and whether it will prosper. And what the customer buys and considers value is never a product. It is always utility, meaning what a product or service does for him. The customer is the foundation of a business and keeps it in existence.[5]

In his classic work entitled "Marketing Myopia," Theodore Levitt also stresses that firms and industries survive or perish over time based on their ability to define themselves in terms of customer needs.[6]

A good mission statement effectively reflects the anticipations of customers. Rather than develop a product and then try to find a market, the operating philosophy of organizations should be to identify customers' needs and then provide a product or service to fulfill those needs. This is why AT&T's mission statement focuses on communication rather than telephones, Exxon's on energy rather than oil and gas, Union Pacific's on transportation rather than railroads, and Universal Studios' on entertainment, not movies. An anonymous author wrote the following, which is quite valid in developing an organizational mission statement:

Do not offer me things.

Do not offer me clothes. Offer me attractive looks.

Do not offer me shoes. Offer me comfort for my feet and the pleasure of walking.

Do not offer me a house. Offer me security, comfort, and a place that is clean and happy.

Do not offer me books. Offer me hours of pleasure and the benefit of knowledge.

Do not offer me records. Offer me leisure and the sound of music.

Do not offer me tools. Offer me the benefit and the pleasure of making beautiful things.

Do not offer me furniture. Offer me comfort and the quietness of a cozy place.

Do not offer me things. Offer me ideas, emotions, ambience, feelings, and benefits.

Please, do not offer me things.

Statements of mission can and do vary in length, content, format, and specificity. If considerable disagreement exists at the top of an organization over basic purpose and mission, it can cause trouble if not resolved. For example, unresolved disagreement over the company mission was one of the reasons for W.T. Grant's bankruptcy. As one executive reported:

> There was a lot of dissension within the company—whether we should go the K-Mart route or go after the Montgomery Ward and J.C. Penney position. Ed Staley and Lou Lustenberger (two top executives) were at loggerheads over the issue, with the upshot being we took a position between the two and that consequently stood for nothing.[7]

A FRAMEWORK FOR WRITING AND EVALUATING A MISSION STATEMENT

The importance of a mission statement to effective strategic management is well supported in the management literature.[8] A mission statement is often the most visible and public part of a strategic plan. As such, an enterprise should insure that its mission statement includes all of the essential components. A good mission statement communicates feelings that will guide and motivate stakeholders to action.

In preparing a business policy case analysis, you may need to write a mission statement for the organization being studied. Use the framework provided in the next section to develop clear and meaningful mission statements. If a mission statement is given in the particular case being studied, use this framework to evaluate its effectiveness.

Components of a Mission Statement

The components of a mission statement can perhaps best be identified and described by thinking about a firm at its inception. The creation of an enterprise typically rests upon the belief of some entrepreneur that some product or service can be offered profitably to some customers in some market using some type of technology. The entrepreneur typically believes that the management philosophy of the new business will result in a favorable public image and that his or her concept of the business can be communicated to and adopted by key stakeholders.[9]

An effective mission statement arouses one's feelings and emotions for an organization. A good mission statement generates the impression that a firm is successful, knows where it is going, and is worthy of one's time, support, and investment.[10] An entrepreneur's sense of purpose when a business is started offers insight into the desirable components of a mission statement. Specifically, an effective mission statement can be viewed as having ten characteristic components. These components are identified below, along with corresponding questions that a mission statement should answer:

1. **Customers**—Who are the enterprise's customers?

2. **Products or services**—What are the firm's major products or services?

3. **Markets**—Where does the firm compete geographically?

4. **Technology**—What is the firm's basic technology?

5. **Concern for survival, growth, and profitability**—What is the firm's attitude toward economic goals?

6. **Philosophy**—What are the fundamental beliefs, values, aspirations, and philosophical priorities of the firm?

7. **Self-concept**—What are the firm's major strengths and competitive advantages?

8. **Concern for public image**—What is the firm's desired public image?

9. **Reconciliatory effectiveness**—Does the mission statement effectively address the desires of key stakeholders?

10. **Inspiring quality**—Does the mission statement motivate and stimulate its reader to action?

Social Responsibility

Although corporate social policy does not have a clearly accepted definition, it embraces managerial philosophy and thinking at the highest levels of an organization. For this reason, social policy affects the development of a business mission statement. Social policy issues mandate that strategists consider not only what the organization owes its various stakeholders, but also what responsibilities the firm has to consumers, environmentalists, minorities, communities, and other groups. After decades of debate on the topic of social responsibility, firms still wrestle to determine their appropriate social policy.

Social responsibility often becomes a major concern when establishing a business mission. The impact of society on business organizations is becoming more pronounced each year. Social responsibility issues directly affect a firm's customers, products or services, markets, technology, profitability, self-concept, and public image. Such publicized experiences as Dow Chemical's with Agent Orange and Union Carbide's with pesticide leaks are reminders of how social issues can impact the nature of a business mission.

An organization's social policy should be integrated into all strategic-management activities, including development of a mission statement. Carroll and Hoy assert that corporate social policy should be designed and articulated during strategy formulation, should be set and administered during strategy implementation, and should be reaffirmed or changed during strategy evaluation.[11]

The emerging view of social responsibility is that social issues should be attended to both directly and indirectly in determining strategies. Firms should strive to engage in social activities that have economic benefits. An example case where a firm successfully combined social responsibility and economic gains is Kellogg. Headquartered in Battle Creek, Michigan, Kellogg watched during the 1970s and early 1980s, as this city deteriorated. Rather than move its facilities, Kellogg waged an extensive public battle for reforms in the city. The efforts were successful and Kellogg completed in 1984 a new $30-million facility in downtown Battle Creek. Other example cases are Control Data operating inner-city plants in Minneapolis, American Express raising extensive funds for the Atlanta Arts Alliance, and DuPont having a work-related-accident rate twenty-three times below the national average.

The purpose of this section has been to emphasize the need to incorporate social policy into the development of a business mission. Despite differences in approach, most American companies try to assure the public that they conduct business in a socially responsible way. The mission statement is an effective instrument for conveying this message. The Norton Company, for example, concludes its mission statement by saying:

> In order to fulfill this mission, Norton will continue to demonstrate a sense of responsibility to the public interest, and to earn the respect and loyalty of its customers, employees, shareholders, suppliers, and the communities in which it does business.[12]

Actual Mission Statements

Perhaps the best way to develop a skill for writing and evaluating mission statements is to study actual company missions. Therefore, eight mission statements from different organizations are presented in Exhibit 3.1. These statements are then evaluated in Table 3.1, based on the ten criteria: (1) customers, (2) products or services, (3) markets, (4) technology, (5) concern for survival, growth, and profitability, (6) philosophy, (7) self-concept, (8) concern for public image, (9) reconciliatory effectiveness, and (10) inspiring quality. Key parts of Mary Kay Cosmetics' mission statement are italicized for your convenience and study.

Exhibit 3.1   Mission statements of eight companies

Avon Company

Avon's corporate mission is to expand aggressively our new, emerging businesses while continuing our historical growth as the world's leading beauty business. The Company's diverse operations enhance our access to profitable, consistent growth. Our strong financial position will enable us to fund most growth opportunities through internal sources. (Avon Company, *Annual Report, 1982,* p. 1.)

Penn State University

Penn State's fundamental responsibility is to provide programs of instruction, research, and public service, and thus act as an instrument of self-renewal and development for the Commonwealth. As Pennsylvania's land-grant university, Penn State must preserve and enhance its distinctive qualities.

While the modern university maintains links to the past and serves to maintain cultural values, its most extensive task at present is to help people to understand the great changes taking place in our society. People must have the skills and the learning habits that will make it possible for them to educate themselves over a lifetime. The rapid rate of change in contemporary society dictates that the University's programs adjust without undue delay to meet the needs of students and society.

University programs of research and other creative and scholarly activities are essential if the University is to contribute to the solution of the social, scientific, and technical problems of society, and discharge effectively its upper-division and graduate teaching responsibilities. The University must also serve the Commonwealth directly through its programs of extension, continuing education, and other public service programs designed to meet the needs of citizens throughout the state.

By encouraging the enrollment of students from all segments of society and from other states and nations, the University provides the intellectual arena in which the search for rational solutions to societal problems can be nurtured, and in which teaching and learning can be the pivotal function. In performing this function, it is essential that the University foster independent thought and open discussion of alternatives. (Pennsylvania State University, *Baccalaureate Catalog, 1982–1983*)

University of Idaho

In the widest sense, the mission of the University of Idaho, a publicly supported, land-grant institution, is to serve the people of the state and nation as a major center of learning for the advancement, preservation, dissemination, and use of knowledge. Deriving from this multifaceted mission are the functions to be performed and the objectives to be achieved through the interaction of the various components and publics of the university. (University of Idaho, *Bulletin and General Catalog, 1983/1985,* p. 9.)

Nashua Corporation

Nashua Corporation provides products and services in four business segments: office systems and supplies, coated papers and tapes, computer products, and photo products. Most of the product lines in these four areas relate to discrete particle technology. This technology addresses a broad range of market applications in which various substrates are coated with particles that can be activated by light, heat, magnetism, pressure, electrical current and other stimuli. Nashua products are sold internationally by wholly owned foreign subsidiaries and more than 90 distributors. Foreign sales and export sales from the United States totaled $317.7 million and represented 53 percent of the company's total sales in fiscal 1982. (Nashua Corporation, *Annual Report, 1982,* p. 2.)

The General Tire & Rubber Company

Broadly diversified, The General Tire & Rubber Company occupies major business positions in basic, high technology, and service industries, supplying a wide range of products and services to industrial, consumer, and governmental markets. An historic innovator in the rubber industry, the Company is a large domestic tire manufacturer and maintains a full line of passenger and truck tires for the original-equipment and replacement markets. The Company's Chemicals/Plastics/Industrial Products Group furnishes an extensive variety of products to the automotive, construction, appliance, and other industries and is a leader in the production of wallcoverings and athletic products. Aerojet General, through advanced technology, research, and manufacture, is a vital component of the nation's aerospace and defense capability. RKO General, a pioneer in radio and television broadcasting, also has important interests in soft drink bottling, hotel development and management, theatrical productions for pay television and movie production, audio tape and floppy disk reproduction, and airline transportation. Far more than its name implies, General Tire has achieved strength through diversity. (The General Tire & Rubber Company, *Annual Report, 1983*, p. 1.)

Harsco Corporation

The mission of Harsco Corporation is to be a leading international manufacturer, marketer, and distributor of diverse goods and services, principally for industrial, commercial, construction, and defense applications. The Corporation is committed to providing innovative engineering solutions to specialized problems where technology and close attention to customer service can differentiate it from commodity production or job-shop operations. (Harsco Corporation, *Annual Report, 1982*, p. 1.)

Economics Laboratory

Our mission is to establish Economics Laboratory as a leading developer and marketer of chemical specialty products and systems. This mission is dedicated to providing superior products and services, supported by unique technology or marketing, which satisfy the needs of our customers to improve their results and productivity, conserve resources, and preserve the quality of the environment. (Economics Laboratory, *Annual Report, 1982*, p. 1.)

Mary Kay Cosmetics

Choices. A woman's life is filled with them. Her busy world demands choices about how she uses her time, juggles her commitments and reaches her goals. But whatever her lifestyle, Mary Kay is right for the times.

Because we understand a woman's needs and care about meeting them. We do more than just sell a woman cosmetics. We teach a personalized skin-care regimen, help her discover her own glamour look, and provide continuing service to assure that her skin care and beauty programs stay consistent with her changing *needs*.

Our corporate goal for the 1980s is to be the finest teaching-oriented skin-care organization in the world. We're doing that by teaching women about their skin and how to care for it. Our program is based on a personal relationship with an individual Beauty Consultant, who guides, instructs, and counsels each of her clients.

Women appreciate the service and knowledge they get from their Mary Kay Beauty Consultant. Our careful quality assurance and research means we're so confident about our products that we offer a 100-percent satisfaction guarantee.

We can do this because Mary Kay understands the way women want to look and live, offering products and services to meet their needs in the '80s. Equally important, we care about our customers—and make sure they know it. Because customers don't care how much we know until they know how much we care.

It's all part of the Mary Kay philosophy—a philosophy based on the golden rule. A spirit of sharing and caring where people give cheerfully of their time, knowledge, and experience.

Our management believes strongly in human resources. Excellent compensation, recognition, opportunity for growth, and pride motivate our employees, as well as 196,755 independent Beauty Consultants. A key element in the Mary Kay success equation is the Company's organizational structure which stimulates individual and group creativity, communication, and performance. This results in a high level of personal satisfaction, which in turn is reflected in high productivity.

This success-oriented attitude leads everyone to new heights and greater achievements. Achievements which are based on discipline and determination, and mean growth for each individual as well as the Company. (Mary Kay Cosmetics, *Annual Report, 1982,* p. 5.)

Table 3.1   An evaluation matrix of example mission statements

EVALUATIVE CRITERIA

Organizations	Customers	Products or Services	Markets	Technology	Concern for Survival
Avon Company	no	yes	yes	no	yes
Penn State Univ.	yes	yes	yes	yes	no
Univ. of Idaho	yes	yes	yes	no	no
Nashua Corporation	no	yes	yes	yes	no
Economics Lab	yes	yes	no	yes	yes
Harsco Corporation	yes	yes	yes	yes	no
General Tire & Rubber	yes	yes	yes	yes	no
Mary Kay Cosmetics	yes	yes	yes	yes	yes

	Philosophy	Self-Concept	Concern for Public Image	Reconciliatory Effectiveness	Inspiring Quality
Avon Company	no	no	no	no	no
Penn State Univ.	yes	yes	yes	yes	yes
Univ. of Idaho	no	no	no	no	no
Nashua Corporation	no	yes	no	no	no
Economics Lab	yes	yes	yes	no	yes
Harsco Corporation	no	yes	no	no	yes
General Tire & Rubber	no	yes	no	no	yes
Mary Kay Cosmetics	yes	yes	yes	yes	yes

EVALUATING MISSION STATEMENTS

There is no one best mission statement for a particular organization, so good judgment is required in evaluating and writing mission statements. In Table 3.1, a *yes* indicates that the given mission statement answers *satisfactorily* the question posed earlier for the respective evaluative criteria. For example, the *yes* under "customers" for Penn State's mission statement means this statement answers, "Who are Penn State's customers?" Notice that "people of the Commonwealth" are Penn State's customers. A *no* would mean a particular mission statement does not answer or answers *unsatisfactorily* the key question associated with one of the ten evaluative criteria. Note that the Avon mission statement does not identify the company's customers. Table 3.1 indicates that the Mary Kay Cosmetics mission statement is the "best" example and the Nashua mission statement is the "worst" example.

Let's focus specifically on the Mary Kay Cosmetics mission statement to examine why it receives a *yes* on all ten criteria. The Mary Kay mission statement reveals the firm's *customers* to be women. The company's *product* is a "personalized skin care regimen." Mary Kay's *market* or geographic area is the world. Mary Kay's *technology* is based on "quality assurance and research." The company's *concern for survival* is evident, since the statement describes the desire for "high productivity" and "growth of the company." The company's philosophy is "based on the golden rule." Mary Kay's *self-concept* is "to be the finest teaching-oriented skin care organization in the world." The Mary Kay mission statement expands upon this self-concept to reflect a *concern for public image*. The Mary Kay mission statement can be considered to be *reconciliatory* because it acknowledges a special interest in both the firm's customers and employees. Finally, the Mary Kay mission statement is *inspiring* because it is clearly well-written and does arouse emotions.

Mission statements do not have to be lengthy to be effective, as indicated by the Economics Laboratory statement. The example mission statements are weakest in the areas of "philosophy" and "reconciliatory effectiveness"; they are strongest in the areas of "products or services" and "self-concept." Specifically, all of the statements mention the organization's products or services, but only the Penn State and Mary Kay statements effectively reconcile differences among key stakeholders. (An experiential exercise at the end of this chapter gives you practice in evaluating and writing mission statements.)

In a multidivisional organization, the chief executive officer should assure that divisional units perform strategic-management tasks, including the development of a statement of mission. Each division of a firm should utilize strategic-management concepts and techniques and develop its own mission statement, consistent with and supportive of the corporate mission. Divisional mission statements are important for motivating middle- and lower-level managers and employees.

An effective mission statement addresses strategic concerns at the corporate, divisional, and functional levels of an organization. Anchor Hocking is an example of a multinational organization that has developed an overall corporate mission statement and a statement for each of its eight divisions. Anchor Hocking's mission statements are given in Exhibit 3.2.

Exhibit 3.2   Anchor Hocking Corporation strategic plan: mission statements

The Anchor Hocking Corporation
The mission of Anchor Hocking Corporation's management is to profitably provide goods and services to customers in such a way as to enhance shareholder/owner values, as exhibited by the dividends paid and the increase in market valuation of the corporation's stock.

Consumer and Industrial Division
C. & I. Division is committed to becoming a competitive, technically efficient market-focused organization, characterized by distinctive, quality products, either manufactured or acquired, innovativeness, and achievement of financial goals.

Household Products Group
We meet selected consumer, industrial, and foodservice market needs throughout the United States and targeted foreign countries by developing, manufacturing, acquiring, and marketing a focused line of products and services which maximize the group's current and future resources and optimize real growth and profit opportunities.

Plastics, Inc. Division
As the major plastics arm of the Household Products Group of Anchor Hocking Corporation, to be an innovative manufacturer and supplier of high-quality plastics products to the transportation, foodservice, premium, food processor, and consumer markets.

Utilizing broad-based plastics technology and a variety of processes and materials, to supply both customized and standard products to meet the ongoing and developing needs of these domestic and international markets, through its own sales force and distribution and/or those of the parent corporation.

Administrative Services Division
To provide with maximum efficiency, the services required by the operating units of the Company in the areas of
—information systems
—human resources
—facilities management

Foodservice & Trading Company
To provide supplies and services throughout the world for the preparation, storing, and serving of food—away from home. Products provided include glassware, china and ceramicware, metal holloware, plasticware, and related table-top supplies; product sourcing is both self-manufactured and secured from domestic and foreign manufacturers.

Carr-Lowrey Division
The Carr-Lowrey Division's management mission is to promote growth and profitability in markets now being served (toiletries and cosmetics, 75-to-90 percent; other—pharmaceutical, floral, food, lighting, and specialty glassware, 10-to-25 percent) while diversifying into other markets.

All products are designed, engineered, and manufactured in the Baltimore plant and marketed by our own sales forces in Baltimore, New York, Chicago, Los Angeles, and Raleigh, North Carolina.

Our primary tasks are to improve sales growth and profitability through promotion of our manufacturing, technical, and marketing strengths, and quality products that are competitively aggressive.

International Division

Our mission is to build a growing, profitable export business by selling products of Anchor Hocking and related products in world markets, and to license patents, know-how, and technical assistance both from and to Anchor Hocking with industrial organizations throughout the world, excluding the U.S.A. We also investigate possibilities for investing, on a minority basis only, in non-North American manufacturing facilities.

The Closure Group

The mission for the Closure Group is to build a growing, profitable business by designing, producing, and marketing plastic, metal, and combination metal/plastic closures, specialty plastic packages, plastic molds, packaging machinery, and services to meet the known needs of food, toiletries, cosmetics, and household-product packagers. The Closure Group produces products in its own facilities and markets its products through its own organizations in the United States and Canada. Brokers and independent agents are used to sell these products in other countries through our International Division.

Source: Anchor Hocking Corporation, internal reports, 1985.

An organization that fails to develop a comprehensive and inspiring mission statement loses the chance to present itself favorably to current stakeholders, and perhaps more importantly to potential stakeholders. Unquestionably, all organizations need customers, employees, and supporters. The mission statement is an effective vehicle for communicating with important internal and external constituencies. The principal value of a mission statement as a tool of strategic management is derived from its specification of the ultimate aims of a firm:

> It provides managers with a unity of direction that transcends individual, parochial, and transitory needs. It promotes a sense of shared expectations among all levels and generations of employees. It consolidates values over time and across individuals and interest groups. It projects a sense of worth and intent that can be identified and assimilated by company outsiders. Finally, it affirms the company's commitment to responsible action, which is symbiotic with its needs to preserve and protect the essential claims of insiders for sustained survival, growth, and profitability of the firm.[13]

CONCLUSION

Every organization has a unique purpose, philosophy, and social policy. This uniqueness should be reflected in a statement of mission. The nature of an enterprise's mission can represent either a competitive advantage or disadvantage for the firm. An organization achieves a heightened sense of purpose when its top managers develop and communicate a clear business mission. Peter Drucker says this is the "first responsibility of top management."

Mission statements vary in content, length, format, and specificity. However, a good mission statement reveals an organization's customers, products or services, markets, technology, concern for survival, philosophy, self-concept, and concern for public image. In addition, a good mission statement is reconciliatory toward key stakeholders and inspires to action. These ten components can serve as a practical framework for evaluating and writing mission statements.

A well-designed mission statement is essential to effective strategy formulation, strategy implementation, and strategy evaluation. Yet developing a business mission and communicating this in writing is one of the most commonly slighted tasks in strategic management. Without a clear statement of mission, a firm's short-run actions can be counterproductive to its long-run purpose. A mission statement should always be subject to revision in order to meet major environmental changes, but it will require changes only infrequently if carefully prepared. Really effective mission statements stand the test of time.

REVIEW QUESTIONS

1. Explain the principal value of a mission statement.

2. Why is it important for a mission statement to be reconciliatory?

3. In your opinion, what are the three most important criteria for writing and evaluating a company mission statement? Why?

4. Would a mission statement differ for a profit versus a nonprofit organization? Explain your answer.

5. For an organization of your choice, write a company mission statement.

6. Go to your nearest library and look in the annual reports of corporations and in the college catalogs of universities. Find what you consider to be a "good" mission statement and a "bad" mission statement, make a photocopy of each, and report on them in class.

7. Who are the major stakeholders of a bank? What are their major claims?

FOOTNOTES

1 Vern McGinnis, "The Mission Statement: A Key Step in Strategic Planning," *Business* (November–December 1981): 41.

2 W. R. King and D. I. Cleland, *Strategic Planning and Policy* (New York: Van Nostrand Reinhold, 1979): 124.

3 R. Edward Freeman, *Strategic Management: A Stakeholder Approach* (Marshfield, Mass.: Pittman Publishing Inc., 1984).

4 George Steiner, *Strategic Planning: What Every Manager Must Know* (New York: The Free Press, 1979): 160.

5 Peter Drucker, *Management: Tasks, Responsibilities, and Practices* (New York: Harper & Row, 1974): 61.

6 Theodore Levitt, "Marketing Myopia," *Harvard Business Review* (July–August 1960): 24–47.

7 "How W.T. Grant Lost $175 Million Last Year," *Business Week* (25 February 1975): 75.

8 Fred David, D. Cochran, and K. Gibson, "A Framework for Developing an Effective Mission Statement," *Journal of Business Strategies* (Fall 1985): 4.

9 John Pearce II, "The Company Mission As a Strategic Tool," *Sloan Management Review.* (Spring 1982): 17.

10 Patricia Bradley and John Baird, *Communication for Business and the Professions* (Dubuque, Iowa: Wm. C. Brown Co., 1983): 90.

11 Archie Carroll and Frank Hoy, "Integrating Corporate Social Policy into Strategic Management," *Journal of Business Strategy* (Winter 1984): 57.

12 The Norton Company, *1981 Annual Report.*

13 Pearce. "The Company Mission," 74.

SUGGESTED READINGS

Abell, D. F. *Defining the Business: The Starting Point for Strategic Planning.* Englewood Cliffs, N.J.: Prentice–Hall, 1980.

Bradley, P., and P. Baird. *Communication for Business and the Professions.* Dubuque, Iowa: Wm. C. Brown Co., 1983.

Carroll, A., and F. Hoy. "Integrating Corporate Social Policy into Strategic Management." *Journal of Business Strategy* (Winter 1984): 48–57.

Chrisman, J. J., and A. B. Carroll. SMR Forum. "Corporate Responsibility—Reconciling Economic and Social Goals." *Sloan Management Review* (Winter 1984): 59–65.

David, F. R., D. Cochran, and K. Gibson. "A Framework for Developing an Effective Mission Statement." *Journal of Business Strategies* 2, no. 2 (Fall 1985): 4–17.

David, F. R., D. Cochran, J. A. Pearce II, and K. Gibson. "An Empirical Investigation of Mission Statements." Southern Management Assoc. *Proceedings* (1985): 28–30.

Drucker, P. F. *Management: Tasks, Responsibilities, and Practices.* New York: Harper & Row, 1974.

Drucker, P. F. "The New Meaning of Corporate Social Responsibility." *California Management Review* (Winter 1984): 53–63.

Freeman, E. R. *Strategic Management: A Stakeholder Approach.* Marshfield, Mass.: Pittman Publishing Inc., 1984.

Hunter, J. C. "Managers Must Know the Mission: 'If It Ain't Broke Don't Fix It.'" *Managerial Planning* 33, no. 4 (January–February 1985): 18–22.

King, W. R., and D. I. Cleland. *Strategic Planning and Policy.* New York: Van Nostrand Reinhold, 1979.

McGinnis, V. J. "The Mission Statement: A Key Step in Strategic Planning." *Business* (November–December 1981): 39–43.

Pearce, J. A. II. "The Company Mission As a Strategic Tool." *Sloan Management Review* (Spring 1982): 15–24.

Staples, W. A., and K. U. Black. "Defining Your Business Mission: A Strategic Perspective." *Journal of Business Strategies* (Spring 1984): 33–39.

Steiner, G. A. *Strategic Planning.* New York: The Free Press, 1984.

EXPERIENTIAL EXERCISE 3A:

Writing a Business Mission

PURPOSE

An organization's mission statement is an integral part of the strategic-management process. As you know from reading Chapter 3, a statement of mission provides direction for strategy formulation, strategy implementation, and strategy evaluation activities. The purpose of this exercise is to give you practice evaluating and writing mission statements. This skill is essential in preparing written and oral business policy case analyses.

YOUR TASK

Your task is twofold. First, evaluate the mission statements of three organizations: Rockwell International, Mississippi State University, and Anchor Hocking Corporation. On a separate sheet of paper, construct an evaluation matrix like the one presented in Table 3.1. Evaluate the three mission statements based on the ten criteria described in this chapter. You should record a *yes* in all cells of the evaluation matrix where the respective mission statement satisfactorily meets the desired criteria. Record a *no* in all cells where the respective mission statement does not meet the stated criteria.

Second, write a mission statement for Ponderosa, the Cohesion Case. Scan the case for needed details as you prepare this mission statement. Read your written mission statement to the class and ask for evaluative comments.

The Mission Statement of Rockwell International

The leader in diverse markets, we are developing new technologies and applying them to products and systems in our four principal businesses—Aerospace, Electronics, Automotive, and General Industries. Our 103,000 employees, more than 17,000 of them engineers and scientists, are dedicated to excellence in everything they do, from implementing new technologies to managing complex systems, to making products of the highest quality. This effort is serving the needs and meeting the challenges of today's society. It also has given Rockwell International a momentum for continued outstanding financial performance. (Rockwell International, *Annual Report, 1983*, p. 1.)

The Mission Statement of Anchor Hocking Corporation

The mission of Anchor Hocking Corporation's management is to profitably provide goods and services to customers in such a way as to enhance shareholder/owner values, as exhibited by the dividends paid and the increase in market valuation of the corporation's stock. (Anchor Hocking Corporation, internal report.)

The Mission Statement of Mississippi State University

Mississippi State University, a land-grant university, is committed to three broad purposes: (1) instruction, on-campus and off-campus, to enhance the intellectual, cultural, social, and professional development of students; (2) research, to extend current knowledge and to give new insights and interpretations to accumulated knowledge; and (3) service, to apply the fruits of knowledge and research to the lives of people. Fulfilling these purposes is the major responsibility of various educational units, including the academic departments, schools and colleges, Continuing Education, the Mississippi Cooperative Extension Service, and the Mississippi Agricultural and Forestry Experiment Station.

The quality of the University's faculty, staff, and administrators insures that the instruction, research, and service are up-to-date and cost-effective. The quality of the University's programs insures that its students receive a well-designed and comprehensive education which will assist them in achieving their personal and professional goals. Mississippi State University has, from its beginnings, been called "The People's College," and, through its state-wide efforts, it remains that. The main campus in Starkville is augmented by degree-granting centers in Meridian and Jackson, program centers in Vicksburg and at the National Space Technology Laboratory, ten branch stations of the Mississippi Agricultural and Forestry Experiment Station, and offices of the Cooperative Extension Service in all eighty-two counties of the state. Thus, degree and nondegree courses, programs, and services are available to all clients, regardless of race, age, sex, or economic condition. (*Mississippi State Bulletin, 1984-85*, p. 8.)

The Environmental Analysis

This chapter examines the tools and concepts needed to conduct an external strategic-management audit. An external audit involves collecting and evaluating economic, social, cultural, demographic, geographic, political, governmental, legal, technological, and competitive information for the purpose of identifying key opportunities and threats that face an organization. This chapter presents a practical framework for obtaining, organizing, and analyzing environmental information.

A FRAMEWORK FOR CONDUCTING AN EXTERNAL AUDIT

Information has always been a key business asset, but only recently has information become recognized as a powerful strategic tool. The quantity and quality of environmental information available to organizations has increased dramatically in recent years. Advances in computer technology, telecommunications, data access and storage devices, online data bases, graphics equipment, and software have created a wide spectrum of new opportunities and threats for organizations.

Information Technology (IT) is changing the very nature of many industries by altering product life cycles, increasing the speed of distribution, creating new products and services, erasing traditional geographic market limitations, and changing the historical tradeoff between production standardization and flexibility. It is altering economies of scale, changing entry barriers, and changing the relationship between industries and various suppliers, creditors, customers, and competitors. As an example, consider the airline industry's business travel market:

> Given the current rate of development in telecommunications and office technology, video conferences may become a major substitute for some business air travel soon. This would significantly affect the airline industry's business travel market. Strategic managers today must address a crucial question: What impact will IT have on our industry over the next five to ten years in terms of products and services, markets, and production economies?[1]

The existence and magnitude of economic, social, cultural, demographic, geographic, political, governmental, legal, technological, and competitive changes underlie the need for an effective external audit. Recall that the external audit focuses on trends and events that are beyond the control of a single firm, such as increased foreign competition, population shifts to the Sun Belt, a maturing society, information technology, the computer revolution, and the rise of minorities. Increasing levels of education and economic uncertainty are having a major impact upon all products, services, markets, and organizations in the United States. By identifying and evaluating when, where, how, and why relevant trends and events will impact a firm, the external audit can allow an organization to formulate and implement strategies more successfully. The external audit phase of the strategic-management process is illustrated in Figure 4.1.

The increasing complexity of today's business environment is evidenced by more and more countries around the world developing the capacity and the will to compete

Figure 4.1 The strategic-management model

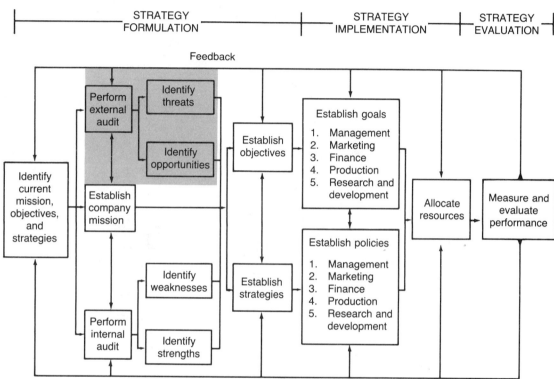

aggressively in world markets. Foreign businesses and countries are eager to improve their economic conditions and are willing to learn, adapt, innovate, and invent to compete successfully in the marketplace. American businesses no longer can beat foreign competitors with ease. A good example of this is the motorcycle industry, where U.S. manufacturers such as Harley-Davidson have been devastated by foreign firms such as Honda, Yamaha, and Suzuki. There are more competitive new technologies in Europe and Japan today than ever before.

Many sudden events that plague organizations from time to time are the result of trends that could have been forecasted. For example, the U.S. auto industry lost $4.2 billion in 1980, mainly because of a failure to anticipate the emerging consumer preference for smaller, more fuel-efficient cars and trucks. Despite such early warning signals as (1) a 20 percent penetration of the U.S. new car market by foreign competition in 1971; (2) the oil embargo of 1973; (3) rapidly climbing fuel prices during the 1970s; (4) an uncertain supply of future crude oil; and (5) declining profitability throughout

Figure 4.2   A framework for conducting an external audit

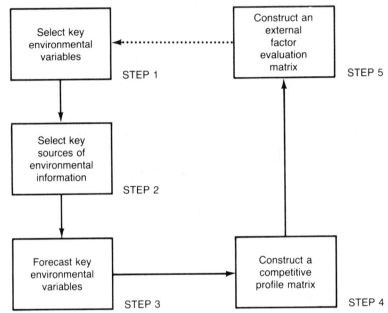

Source: Fred David, "A Framework for Conducting an External Strategic-Management Audit," *Journal of Business Strategies* (Spring 1986). In press.

the 1970s, the U.S. auto makers failed to alter their strategy of producing large cars. Consequently, General Motors, Ford, Chrysler, and American Motors struggled to survive in the early 1980s and still have not recaptured their lost market share. In 1985, AMC had only a 2 percent share of the U.S. passenger car market; Japanese car makers had a 30 percent market share in the United States.

An effective approach for conducting an external audit consists of five steps: (1) select key environmental variables; (2) select key sources of environmental information; (3) use forecasting tools and techniques; (4) construct a Competitive Profile Matrix; and (5) construct an External Factor Evaluation Matrix. This approach is illustrated in Figure 4.2.

KEY ENVIRONMENTAL VARIABLES

An external audit typically begins with selection of key variables in an organization's environment. Selection of key variables to be monitored can vary widely, depending on a company's situation and industry. Environmental variables can be divided into five major categories: (1) economic forces; (2) social, cultural, demographic, and geo-

Figure 4.3 Relationships among key environmental forces and a company

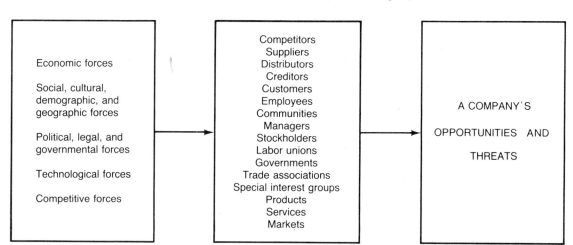

graphic forces; (3) political, governmental, and legal forces; (4) technological forces; and (5) competitive forces. Relationships among key environmental forces and an organization are depicted in Figure 4.3.

Changes in environmental variables translate into changes in consumer demand for both industrial and consumer products and services. Environmental forces affect the types of products developed, the nature of positioning and market segmentation strategies, the types of services offered, and the choice of businesses to acquire or sell. Identifying and evaluating environmental opportunities and threats enables a company to formulate or reformulate its basic mission, to design strategies to achieve its objectives, and to develop policies to achieve its goals. The major categories of environmental variables are now examined more closely.

Economic Forces

Inflation and economic flux have caused sweeping changes in consumer buying patterns during the 1980s. As consumers perceive that more money is buying them less, more and more people are adopting the much-publicized "buy now, save later" motto at the expense of future security.

Economic factors have a direct impact on the potential attractiveness of various company strategies. For example, if monetary policy is tightened, then funds needed for diversification may be too costly or unavailable. As interest rates rise, discretionary income declines, which lowers the demand for discretionary goods. As stock prices fall, the desirability of equity as a source of capital for market development declines. Some important economic variables that often represent opportunities and threats for organizations are provided in Exhibit 4.1.

Exhibit 4.1 Key economic variables to be monitored

Shift to a service economy in the U.S.

Availability of credit

Level of disposable income

Propensity of people to spend

Interest rates

Inflation rates

Economies of scale

Money market rates

Federal government budget deficits

Gross national product trend

Consumption patterns

Unemployment trends

Worker productivity levels

Value of the dollar in world markets

Stock market trends

Foreign countries' economic conditions

Import/export factors

Demand shifts for different categories of goods and services

Income differences by region and consumer groups

Price fluctuations

Exportation of labor and capital from the U.S

Monetary policies

Fiscal policies

Tax rates

European Economic Community (EEC) policies

Organization of Petroleum Exporting Countries (OPEC) policies

Coalitions of Lesser Developed Countries (LDC) policies

Economic facts, trends, issues, and developments that affect organizations are published weekly. Many organizations are capitalizing upon the opportunities that result from various trends in the economy. For example, Control Data Corporation, a large Minneapolis-based computer company, is pouring money into "services" that range from computerizing education to rejuvenating family farms and employing minorities and the handicapped. Control Data has invested in a wind farm in Hawaii and a production facility behind prison bars.[2]

Social, Cultural, Demographic, and Geographic Forces

To sustain growth and profitability, an organization should identify the impact that social, cultural, demographic, and geographic changes are having upon its products, services, markets, and customers. Small and large and profit and nonprofit organizations in all industries are being staggered and challenged by the opportunities and threats arising from changes in social, cultural, demographic, and geographic variables. In virtually every aspect of life, the United States is much different in the 1980s from the way it was in the 1970s, and the 1990s promise even greater changes. Even the toy industry, for example, has changed significantly. Toys like transformers and go-bots are hot-selling items. Greenman Bros., one of the largest and most successful toy wholesalers in the U.S., plans to capitalize on the booming toy industry by increasing the number of its Playland stores from thirty-one in 1984 to 200 by 1990.[3] (A go-bot changes from a go-cart to a robot in seconds.)

Social, cultural, demographic, and geographic variables are shaping the way Americans live, work, produce, and consume. Recent changes in the structure of the nuclear family and the fabric of American society are indisputable. First marriages are being delayed; the divorce rate has increased by 96 percent in the last ten years; the "single head of household" is now recognized as an economic and political entity; the American worker and consumer are becoming more educated and older; narcissism (preoccupation with the self) appears to be replacing the Protestant work ethic; minorities are becoming more influential in business, politics, and community life; people are looking for local rather than federal solutions to problems; and there is less fixation on youth.[4] These types of changes are creating a different type of consumer and consequently a need for different products, different services, and different company strategies.

In 1984 the U.S. population included more individuals of age sixty-five and over than teenagers, for the first time. The number of older citizens in the United States is expected to surpass 31 million by the year 1990, while the teenage population shrinks to 23 million.[5] The trend toward an older America is good news for firms such as home builders, furniture producers, computer manufacturers, travel services, and auto makers, but is bad news for companies that depend on teenage fashions, fads, and foods. Individuals eighty-five and over are increasing in percentage terms faster than any other age group. The maturing American society is resulting in new products, services, markets, and personnel policies, as well as a new look in advertising, a decreased emphasis on schools, an increased emphasis on health care, a growing market for luxury items, and a drop in crime rates. The aging U.S. population affects the strategic orientation of nearly all organizations.

In addition to the trend toward an older society, many social, cultural, demographic, and geographic trends pose opportunities and threats. For example, Americans are on the move in a population shift to the South and West (Sun Belt) and away from the Northeast and Midwest (Frost Belt). While the population shift across the United States is the most pronounced demographic change in the 1980s, the movement of families from cities to suburbs is almost as dramatic. The back-to-the-city movement, talked about so much in the 1970s, has not materialized. The real trend is in the other direction—families moving even farther from cities.[6] There are many strategy formulation implications of population shifts, including where to locate new plants and distribution centers and where to focus marketing efforts.

Organizations should monitor a number of other key social, cultural, demographic, and geographic trends, to identify important opportunities and threats. Examples of these trends are: voter participation in the United States has steadily declined; the American society is becoming much more educated; greater numbers of women are entering the work force. Another trend in America is toward increased affluence, due to a steady growth in *per capita* real income, plus a rapid increase in the number of two-income households. As affluence increases, individuals place a premium on time. Improved customer service, immediate availability, trouble-free operation of products, and dependable maintenance and repair services are becoming more important. Americans today are more willing than ever to pay the price for good service that limits inconvenience.

A steady decline in the view of work as an expression of identity is in evidence in America. There appears to be a weaker commitment to the work environment and ethic, more questioning of corporate values and procedures, more job turnover and absenteeism, and more demand for businesses to assume social functions such as child care and retirement counseling for employees. The 1980s are emerging as a decade in which consumers are preoccupied with personal, rather than social, comfort.[7] It is clear that the work force of the 1980s faces increasing competition for jobs, especially as mandatory retirement moves from age sixty-five to seventy. This means that strategy-implementation problems resulting from frustrated expectations and dissatisfaction among workers may become more prevalent. It is becoming more important for organizations to reward good performance with good compensation.

Some important social, cultural, demographic, and geographic variables are provided in Exhibit 4.2.

Exhibit 4.2   Key social, cultural, demographic, and geographic variables

Childbearing rates

Number of special interest groups

Number of marriages

Number of divorces

Number of births

Number of deaths

Immigration and emigration rates

Social security programs

Life expectancy rates

Per capita income

Location of retailing, manufacturing, and service businesses

Attitudes toward business

Life-styles

Traffic congestion

Inner city environments

Average disposable income

Value placed on leisure time

Trust in government

Attitudes toward government

Attitudes toward work

Buying habits

Ethical concerns

Attitudes toward saving

Sex roles

Attitudes toward investing

Racial equality

Use of birth control

Average level of education

Government regulation

Attitudes toward retirement

Attitudes toward leisure time

Attitudes toward product quality

Attitudes toward customer service

Pollution control

Attitudes toward foreign peoples

Energy conservation

Social programs

Number of churches

Number of church members

Social responsibility

Attitudes toward authority

Attitudes toward careers

Population changes by race, age, sex, and level of affluence

Population changes by city, county, state, region, and country

Regional changes in tastes and preferences

Number of women and minority workers

Number of high school and college graduates by geographic area

Due to trends, events, and changes in these social-related areas, some types of goods and services are expected to be in high demand by 1995. Notice in Exhibit 4.3 that household goods, entertainment activities, and convenience services are example areas that are expected to experience rapid growth in the future.

Many organizations are altering their basic strategies as a result of social, cultural, demographic, and geographic trends, events, and changes. For example, Black and Decker has acquired General Electric Corporation's small-appliance business for $300 million. Chairman Laurence Farley of Black and Decker explains that "demographic and geographic globalization is considered to be a major environmental threat to B&D; the GE purchase will allow Black and Decker to compete effectively in world markets."[8] Black and Decker, and many other organizations, recognize that mass communication and high technology are creating similar patterns of consumption in diverse cultures. Black and Decker is now the No. 1 small-appliance maker in the world.

Exhibit 4.3   High-demand products of the future

- Products that ease drudgery and household maintenance, automate homemaking chores, save time, demonstrate quality, reliability, durability, and luxury
- Products that improve housing, including single-family homes and condominiums, that will appeal to more affluent middle-aged and preretirement husband–wife households: quality furniture, fixtures, appliances, and household services
- Products and services designed to enhance the physical self, particularly those perceived as maintaining and restoring youthfulness: cosmetics, skin care products, health foods, vitamins, cosmetic surgery, spas, hair stylists, clothing consultants, exercise facilities, and diet and health programs
- Products and services that support the psychological self: counseling, education, skills analysis, stress-management training, cultural activities, and self-improvement books and courses.
- Products that permit self-expression and personal statements: personalized products and services, monograms, custom-made items, special orders, modules of all sorts, and participatory sporting and cultural activities
- Products that support mobility and immediate gratification: instant photography, all-night restaurants, portable telephones and computers, emergency health centers, world-wide product services, rentals, "800" telephone numbers, home entertainment centers, automated tellers, and instant credit
- Products and services that will secure and protect individuals' property: sensing devices, home protection systems, security guards, protected residential areas, insurance of various kinds, fire and burglar protection, financial security plans, air and water purifiers, and sanitation products
- Products that promote entertainment and leisure activities, including services as varied as participatory and spectator sports, travel, and gambling
- Products that permit us to differentiate ourselves and that appeal to the snob in all of us: products associated with taste, breeding, graceful life-styles, culture, and the so-called "markets

of the mind": gourmet foods, wines, decorator and designer products and services, paintings, sculpture, and performing arts such as ballet, opera, symphony concerts, and drama.

Source: William Lazer, "Rising Affluence Will Reshape Markets," *American Demographics* (February 1984): 21.

Political, Governmental, and Legal Forces

Federal, state, and local governments are major regulators, deregulators, subsidizers, employers, and customers of organizations in the United States. Political, governmental, and legal factors can therefore represent key opportunities and threats for both small and large organizations. For industries and firms that depend heavily on government contracts or subsidies, political forecasts can be the most important part of an external audit. Changes in patent laws, antitrust legislation, and lobbying activities can significantly impact firms. The increasing global interdependence among economies, markets, governments, and organizations makes it imperative that firms of all sizes consider the possible impact of political variables on the formulation and implementation of competitive strategies.

A number of nationally known firms forecast political, governmental, and legal variables, including Frost & Sullivan, Probe International, and Arthur D. Little. Arthur D. Little forecasts the political environment in foreign countries by examining five criteria: (1) social development, (2) technological advancement, (3) abundance of natural resources, (4) level of domestic tranquility, and (5) type of political system. ADL has found that political unrest follows whenever a country's development in any one of these areas gets too far ahead of the others. Ford, DuPont, Singer, and PepsiCo are among the many companies that use forecasts developed by outside firms to identify key political and governmental opportunities and threats.

Political forecasting can be especially critical and complex for multinational firms that depend on foreign countries for natural resources, use of facilities or lands, distribution of products, special assistance, or customers. In its May issue each year, *Planning Review* publishes an extensive political risk forecast for more than eighty foreign countries. An excerpt from its 1985 political forecast is given in Table 4.1.

Increasing global competition toward the year 2000 accents the need for accurate political and governmental forecasts as an input to the strategic-management process. Many companies will have to become familiar with the capital markets of Europe and Asia and with trading currency futures. East Asian countries have already become world leaders in labor-intensive industries. Frederick Gluck, director of McKinsey & Company, concludes that (1) a world market is emerging from what previously was a multitude of distinct national markets; and (2) the climate for international business in the late 1980s and 1990s is becoming much more favorable than in recent years, due to changes in the oil, currency, and labor markets. This means that many companies may find it difficult to survive by remaining a solely domestic firm.

Table 4.1 The 1985 political forecast for selected countries

Country	Most Likely Regime		Probability of turmoil		Financial Risk	Investment Risk	Exporting Risk
China	Reformers	(80%)	Low	9%	B	B−	C+
Denmark	Liberal Coalition	(65%)	Low	9%	A−	A	A
Iraq	Sassam Hussein	(65%)	High	29%	C	C	B−
USSR	Gorbachev	(85%)	Low	1%	B	C−	B
United States	Reagan	(85%)	Low	15%	A+	A+	A
Zambia	Kaunda	(70%)	Mod.	23%	D+	C	D+

Source: William Coplin and Michael O'Leary, "The 1985 Political Climate for International Business: A Forecast of Risk in 82 Countries," *Planning Review* (May 1985): 36–43.

It is no exaggeration that in an industry that is, or is rapidly becoming, global, the riskiest possible posture is to remain a domestic competitor. The domestic competitor will watch as more aggressive companies use this growth to capture economies of scale and learning. The domestic competitor will then be faced with an attack on domestic markets using different (and possibly superior) technology, product design, manufacturing, marketing approaches, and economies of scale. A few examples suggest how extensive the phenomena of world markets have already become. Hewlett–Packard's manufacturing chain reaches halfway around the globe, from well-paid, skilled engineers in California to low-wage assembly workers in Malaysia. General Electric has survived as a manufacturer of inexpensive audio products by centralizing its world production in Singapore.[9]

Local, state, and federal laws, regulatory agencies, and special interest groups can have a major impact on the strategies of small and large, and profit and nonprofit, organizations. Many companies have abandoned plans or strategies in the past because of political or governmental actions. For example, many nuclear power projects have been halted and many steel plants shut because of pressure from the Environmental Protection Agency (EPA). Other federal regulatory agencies include the Food and Drug Administration (FDA), the National Highway Traffic and Safety Administration (NHTSA), the Occupational Safety and Health Administration (OSHA), the Consumer Product Safety Commission (CPSC), the Federal Trade Commission (FTC), the Securities and Exchange Commission (SEC), the Equal Employment Opportunity Commission (EEOC), the Federal Communications Commission (FCC), the Federal Maritime Commission (FMC), the Interstate Commerce Commission (ICC), the Federal Energy Regulatory Commission (FERC), and the National Labor Relations Board

(NLRB). Local, state, and federal laws, regulations, and political pressures represent significant opportunities and threats for many organizations. Some major political, governmental, and legal variables are provided in Exhibit 4.4.

Exhibit 4.4 Important political, governmental, and legal variables

Government regulations or deregulations
Changes in tax laws
Special tariffs
Political action committees
Voter participation rates
Number, severity, and location of government protests
Number of patents
Changes in patent laws
Environmental protection laws
Level of defense expenditures
Legislation on equal employment
Level of government subsidies
Antitrust legislation
Sino-American relationships
Soviet-American relationships
European-American relationships
African-American relationships
Import-export regulations
Government fiscal and monetary policy changes
Political conditions in foreign countries
Special local, state, and federal laws
Lobbying activities
Size of government budgets
World oil, currency, and labor markets
Location and severity of terrorist activities
Local, state, and national elections

Technological Forces

Revolutionary technological changes such as computer engineering, thinking computers, robotics, unmanned factories, miracle drugs, space communications, lasers, cloning, satellite networks, fiber optics, and electronic funds transfer are having a dramatic impact on organizations. New microprocessor-based equipment and process technologies are burgeoning: computer-aided design and manufacturing (CAD/CAM), direct numerical control (DNC), computer-centralized numerical control (CNC), flexible production centers (FPC), equipment and process technology (EPT), and computer-integrated manufacturing (CIM). Depending on which study is quoted, the annual growth rate of CAD/CAM systems varies from 30 percent to 50 percent, with sales projected to exceed $6.9 billion by 1987.[10]

Technological changes can dramatically affect an organization's products, services, markets, suppliers, distributors, competitors, customers, manufacturing processes, marketing practices, and competitive position. Technological advancements can create new markets, result in a proliferation of new and improved products, change the relative competitive cost positions in an industry, and render existing products and services obsolete.

Technological changes can also collapse or merge previously separate businesses by reducing or eliminating cost barriers; create shorter production runs; create shortages in technical skills; and result in changing values and expectations of employees, managers, and customers. Technological advancements can create new competitive advantages that are more powerful than existing advantages. No company or industry today is insulated against emerging technological developments. In high-tech industries, identification and evaluation of key technological opportunities and threats can be the most important part of the external strategic management audit.

An example of strategic moves to keep up with technological change is General Motors' recent acquisition of Electronic Data Systems and their interests in Automatix, Inc., Teknowledge, Inc., and Robotic Vision Systems, Inc. Another example is Rockwell International Corporation's 1985 purchase of Allen-Bradley Company, a leader in computerized factory automation. A final example of a strategy to exploit technological opportunities was evidenced when Caterpillar Tractor Company purchased a 20 percent interest in Advanced Robotics Corporation. This acquisition helped Caterpillar post a 26 percent increase in sales for calendar 1984 to $6.6 billion, but earnings were a negative $428 million for the year.

A reversal in thinking is urgently needed in organizations that have traditionally limited technological improvement efforts to those that can be funded after marketing and financial requirements are met. The pace of technological change is increasing and the changes are coming from different directions, such as from "unrelated" industries, universities, and foreign competitors.

During 1984 the first generation of electronic greeting cards performed relatively simple feats such as beeping "Jingle Bells" and humming "Joy to the World." For Christmas 1985, a new generaton of cards will play complex melodies, blink lights, and even wish recipients Christmas greetings in a real voice. The new technology for these cards is coming from the Far East. The big three in the industry, Hallmark Cards, American Greetings, and Gibson Greeting Cards, are making substantial investments in new technologies, including laser printing and holography. Hallmark is constructing a $20 million Technology and Innovation Center.

There is an emerging consensus that technology management is one of the key responsibilities of top management. John Harris, Robert Shaw, and William Sommers recently concluded that technology can be leveraged to achieve a sustainable, competitive advantage in the marketplace. The key lies in formulating the right technology strategy and, ultimately, integrating it into the corporate planning process:

In the business environment of the 1980s, we believe that technology-based issues will underlie nearly every important decision that top management makes. Crucial to those decisions will be the ability to approach technology planning analytically and strategically. We also believe that technology can be planned and managed using formal techniques similar to those used in business and capital investment planning. An effective technology strategy is built on a penetrating analysis of technology opportunities and threats, and an assessment of the relative importance of these factors to overall corporate strategy.[11]

In practice, critical technology decisions are too often delegated to lower organizational levels or are made without an understanding of their strategic implications. Strategists spend so many hours analyzing market position, determining market share, positioning products in terms of features and price, forecasting sales and market size, and monitoring and analyzing distribution; yet technology too often does not receive the same respect.

The impact of this oversight is devastating. Firms not managing technology to ensure their futures may eventually find their futures managed by technology. Technology's impact reaches far beyond the "high-tech" companies. Although some industries may appear to be relatively technology-insensitive in terms of products and market requirements, they are not immune from the impact of technology; companies in smokestack as well as service industries must carefully monitor emerging technological opportunities and threats.[12]

Not all sectors of the economy are equally affected by technological developments. For example, the communications industry, electronics industry, aeronautics industry, and pharmaceutical industry are much more volatile than the textile, forestry, and metals industries. Strategists in industries affected by rapid technological change must be particularly sensitive to emerging technological opportunities and threats. Some key technology questions that should be asked during the external audit are provided in Exhibit 4.5.

Exhibit 4.5 Key questions to ask in assessing the technological environment

- What are the technologies within the corporation?
- Which technologies are utilized in the firm's business? products? components and parts?
- How critical is each technology to each of these products and businesses?
- Which of these technologies are shared among different products and businesses?
- Which technologies are contained in purchased parts and material?
- Which of these external technologies might become critical and why? Will they remain available outside the firm?

- What was the evolution of these technologies over time? In which companies were these technological changes initiated?
- What is the likely evolution of these technologies in the future?
- What have been the firm's investments in critical technologies over time?
- What were the investments and investment patterns of its leading technological competitors? Historical? Planned?
- What has been the investment in the product and in the process side of these technologies? For the firm and for its competitors? Design? Production? Implementation and service?
- What is the subjective ranking of different firms in each of these technologies?
- What are the firm's businesses and products?
- What are the parts and components of these products?
- What is the cost and value-added structure of these parts, components, products, and businesses?
- What has been the historical financial and strategic performance of the business, and what are the implications of these trends? In terms of cash generation and earnings characteristics? Investment requirements? Growth? Market position and market share?
- What are the applications of the firm's technologies?
- In which does the firm currently participate and why? In which does the firm not participate and why?
- How attractive is each of these applications as an investment opportunity in terms of its market growth, its potential for profit improvement, and/or its potential for increasing technological leadership?

  —Underlying growth characteristics?

  —Evolution of customer needs and requirements?

  —Current and emerging market segments; segment growth rates?

  —Competitive positioning and likely strategies of key competitors?
- How critical are the firm's technologies to each of these applications?
- What other technologies are critical to the external applications?
- How do the technologies differ in each of these applications?
- What are the competing technologies in each application? What are the determinants of substitution dynamics?
- What is and will be the degree of technological change in each of these technologies?
- What are the applications that the firm should consider entering?
- What should be the priorities of technological resource investment?
- What technological resources are required for the firm to achieve its current business objectives?
- What should be the level and rate of corporate technology investments?

- Which technological investments should be curtailed or eliminated?

- What additional technologies will be required in order to achieve the current corporate business objectives?

- What are the implications of the technology and business portfolios for corporate strategy?

Source: Boris Petrov, "The Advent of the Technology Portfolio." Reprinted by permission from the *Journal of Business Strategy*, Fall 1982. Published by Warren, Gorham & Lamont, Inc. Boston, Mass. Copyright © 1982. All rights reserved.

An example organization that is making significant strategy changes due to technological advancements is Deere & Company. This firm has recently invested millions in radical new equipment and process technology. Deere is making massive technology investments for reasons other than to save on manufacturing costs. Deere is striving to improve quality, reliability, customer service and response, while reducing inventories and lead times. A recent article describes Deere & Company's operations as follows:

> Their facilities are crammed with new manufacturing technology—computer-aided design and computer-aided manufacturing, flexible machining centers, and computer terminals. This technology allows high-school-educated employees to interact with production control and vastly raise the level of employee participation in daily decisions.[13]

Competitive Forces

Analyzing competitors means identifying and evaluating rival firms' strengths, weaknesses, capabilities, opportunities, threats, objectives, goals, and strategies. Collecting and evaluating competitive information is essential to performing an external audit effectively. One of the most important questions that can be asked by any organization is: Who are our major competitors? For some firms, the answer to this question is easy. Apple Computer Company, for example, knows that IBM is its major competitor. According to Future Computing, a Dallas-based research firm, IBM increased its share of the office personal computer market from 18 percent in 1982 to 40 percent at the end of 1984, while Apple's share fell from 22 percent to 11 percent during that period of time.

Determining major competitors is not always easy because many firms have multiple divisions that compete in different industries. Many firms often do not provide sales and profit information on a divisional basis. Furthermore, many firms are privately held and do not publish any financial or marketing information. Despite these factors, financial information on the leading competitors in particular industries can be found in a number of publications. For example, the six top competitors in four different industries are identified in Table 4.2.

When an organization has identified its major competitors, the next step in performing a competitive analysis is to focus on specific questions. The more information and knowledge a firm can obtain on its major competitors, the more likely it will be

Table 4.2 Major competitors in different industries

CHEMICAL INDUSTRY (Figures in Thousands of Dollars)	1984 Revenues	% Change From Year Ago	1984 Net Income	% Change From Year Ago	1983 Profit Margin	1984 Profit Margin
Industry Average		+ 4.8		+ 58.6	4.7	3.1
E.I. du Pont de Nemours & Co.............	$36,218,000	+ 1.3	$1,431,000	+ 27.0	4.0	3.2
Dow Chemical Co........................	11,418,000	+ 4.3	585,000	+ 75.2	5.1	3.1
Allied Corp.	10,734,000	+ 8.4	488,000	+398.0	4.6	1.0
Union Carbide Corp.....................	9,500,000	+ 5.6	341,000	+331.7	3.6	0.9
W. R. Grace & Co.	6,727,823	+ 8.2	195,590	+ 22.5	2.9	2.6
Monsanto Co............................	6,691,000	+ 6.2	439,000	+ 13.1	6.6	6.2
FOREST PRODUCTS INDUSTRY						
Industry Average		+ 13.8		11.4	3.6	3.7
Georgia-Pacific Corp.	$ 6,682,000	+10.6	$119,000	+ 13.3	1.8	1.7
Weyerhaeuser Co.	5,549,738	+13.7	226,187	+ 10.4	4.1	4.2
Champion International Corp.	5,121,089	+20.1	(5,968)	—	—	1.9
International Paper Co....................	4,715,600	+ 8.2	120,100	− 52.9	2.6	5.9
Boise Cascade Corp......................	3,833,320	+11.4	69,610	+ 15.3	1.8	1.8
Kimberly-Clark Corp.....................	3,616,200	+10.4	225,000	+ 19.2	6.2	5.8
OFFICE EQUIPMENT INDUSTRY						
Industry Average		+ 14.4		+ 19.1	9.7	9.3
International Business Machines Corp.......	$45,937,000	+14.3	$6,582,000	+ 20.0	14.3	13.7
Xerox Corp.	8,791,500	+ 3.9	327,400	− 28.7	3.7	5.4
Honeywell Inc...........................	6,073,600	+ 7.2	239,000	+ 3.4	3.9	4.1
Hewlett-Packard Co.	6,044,000	+28.3	665,000	+ 53.9	11.0	9.2
Digital Equipment Corp..................	5,584,426	+30.7	328,779	+ 15.9	5.9	6.6
Control Data Corp.......................	5,026,900	+ 9.7	83,200	− 48.6	1.7	3.5
PETROLEUM INDUSTRY						
Industry Average		+ 3.5		−7.6	4.3	4.9
Exxon Corp.	$97,276,000	+ 2.7	$5,525,000	+ 11.0	5.7	5.3
Mobil Corp.	60,600,000	+ 2.7	1,270,000	− 15.5	2.1	2.6
Texaco Inc..............................	48,100,000	+17.0	306,000	− 75.2	0.6	3.0
Chevron Corp...........................	29,207,000	+ 0.1	1,534,000	− 3.5	5.3	5.5
Standard Oil Co. (Indiana)	28,998,000	− 1.7	2,183,000	+ 16.9	7.5	6.3
Atlantic Richfield Co.	24,654,000	− 1.0	567,000	− 63.4	2.3	6.2

Source: D. W. Sommer, "Industry Week's 1984 Financial Analysis of Industry," *Industry Week*, (18 March 1985): 59–77.

able to formulate and implement effective strategies. Major competitors' weaknesses can represent external opportunities. Similarly, major competitors' strengths could represent key threats. When you prepare a business policy case analysis, study carefully the organization's competitors.

Key Questions About Competitors

1. What are our major competitors' strengths?
2. What are our major competitors' weaknesses?
3. What are our major competitors' goals, objectives, and strategies?
4. How will our major competitors most likely respond to current economic, social, cultural, demographic, geographic, political, governmental, technological, and competitive trends affecting the industry?
5. How vulnerable are our major competitors to our alternative company strategies?
6. How vulnerable are our alternative strategies to successful counterattack by our major competitors?
7. How are our products or services positioned relative to our major competitors?
8. To what extent are new firms entering and old firms leaving the industry?
9. What key factors have resulted in the present competitive position in the industry?
10. How have the sales and profit rankings of major competitors in the industry changed over recent years? Why have these rankings changed that way?
11. What is the nature of supplier and distributor relationships in this industry?
12. To what extent could substitute products or services be a threat to competitors in this industry?

The increasing emphasis on competitive analysis in the United States is evidenced by some corporations putting this function on their organizational charts and appointing a "Director of Competitive Analysis."[14] Other firms have assigned competitive analysis responsibility to an existing staff department. Many other firms have simply expanded the competitive analysis responsibilities of an external-audit task force of managers. Computer-based filing systems are now being used to assimilate newspaper clippings, annual reports, and similar information on competitors.

A recent *Fortune* article describes how many organizations "spy on competitors," using such means as (1) buying competitors' garbage, (2) buying competitors' products and dissecting them, (3) taking plant tours anonymously, (4) counting tractor-trailers leaving competitors' loading bays, (5) studying aerial photographs, (6) analyzing labor contracts, (7) analyzing help-wanted ads, (8) quizzing customers and buyers about the sales of competitors' products, (9) infiltrating customers' and competitors' business operations, (10) grilling suppliers to find out how much competitors are manufacturing, (11) using customers to put out phony bid requests, (12) encouraging key customers to talk, (13) debriefing competitors' former employees, (14) interviewing competitors through consultants, (15) hiring people away from competitors, (16) conducting phony job interviews to get competitors' employees to spill the beans, (17) picking brains at conferences by sending engineers to question competitors' technical people, and (18) milking potential recruits who may have been affiliated with competitors in the past.[15] Some of these activities are illegal and/or unethical, but determining which is a matter of opinion, or a jury in many cases.

Probably the most widely read book on competitive analysis in this decade is Michael Porter's *Competitive Strategy: Techniques for Analyzing Industries and Competitors*. A summary of Porter's ideas is provided in Exhibit 4.6. According to Porter, five competitive forces create vital opportunities and threats to organizations: (1) new entrants, (2) substitute products or services, (3) bargaining power of suppliers, (4) bargaining power of buyers, and (5) rivalry among existing firms. One individual who has utilized Porter's concepts successfully is Jack Tramiel, the CEO of Commodore International between 1980 and 1984. Commodore's sales increased from $126 million to $681 million during that period of time.

Exhibit 4.6   Michael Porter on competitive analysis

The intensity of competition in an industry is neither a matter of coincidence nor bad luck. Rather, competition is rooted in the underlying economic structure of an industry and this goes well beyond the behavior of current competitors. The state of competition in an industry depends on five basic competitive forces: (1) the threat of new entrants, (2) the threat of substitute products or services, (3) the bargaining power of suppliers, (4) the bargaining power of buyers, and (5) the rivalry among existing firms. The collective strength of these forces determines the ultimate profit potential in the industry. Not all industries have the same potential. They differ fundamentally in their ultimate profit potential as the collective strength of the forces differs; the forces range from intense in industries like tires, paper, and steel—where no firm earns spectacular returns—to relatively mild in industries like oil-field equipment and services, cosmetics, and toiletries—where high returns are quite common.

The goal of competitive analysis in an organization or a business unit is to find a position in the industry where the company can best defend itself against these competitive forces or can influence them in its favor. Since the collective strength of the forces may well be painfully apparent to all competitors, the key for developing strategy is to delve below the surface and analyze the sources of each. Knowledge of these underlying sources of competitive pressure highlights the critical strengths and weaknesses of the company, animates its positioning in the industry, clarifies the areas where strategic changes may yield the greatest payoff, and highlights the areas where industry trends promise to hold the greatest significance as either opportunities or threats.

In coping with the five competitive forces, there are three potentially successful generic strategic approaches to outperforming other firms in an industry: (1) overall cost leadership, (2) differentiation, and (3) focus. Sometimes a firm can successfully pursue more than one approach as its primary target, though this is rarely possible. The first strategy, overall cost leadership, requires aggressive construction of efficient-scale facilities, vigorous pursuit of cost reductions from experience, tight cost and overhead control, avoidance of marginal customer accounts, and cost minimization in areas like R&D, service, sales force, advertising, and so on. For example, Briggs and Stratton's success in small horsepower gasoline engines is attributable to an overall cost leadership approach. The second strategy, differentiation, requires creating something unique with the firm's product or service, such as superior customer service, superior technology, or a superior dealer network. For example, Caterpillar is known for dealer network and excellent spare parts availability. The final generic strategy is focusing on a particular buyer group, segment of the product line, or geographic market. The entire focus strategy is built around serving a particular target very well, and each functional policy is developed with this in mind. For example, Fort Howard Paper focuses on a narrow range of industrial-grade papers, avoiding consumer products vulnerable to advertising battles and rapid introductions of new products.

Adapted with permission of the Free Press, a Division of Macmillan, Inc. from *Competitive Strategy: Techniques for Analyzing Industries and Competitors* by Michael E. Porter. Copyright © 1980 by The Free Press.

KEY SOURCES OF ENVIRONMENTAL INFORMATION

Once strategists have selected key environmental variables, the second step in performing an external audit is to select key sources of environmental information. A wealth of strategic information is available to organizations from both published and unpublished sources. Environmental information can be obtained through unpublished sources such as customer surveys, market research, speeches at professional meetings, conversations with stakeholders, interviews, and aerial photographs.

Published sources of strategic information include periodicals, journals, reports, government documents, abstracts, books, directories, and manuals. To access published sources of information effectively, a number of excellent indexes reveal the location of strategic information by subject, topic, source, author, company, and industry. Indexes can save a considerable amount of time and effort in identifying and evaluating environmental opportunities and threats. A description of the major indexes that are available for locating environmental information is provided in Table 4.3.

In addition to indexes, online databases are being used increasingly to locate strategic information. Online databases allow individuals who have no computer programming skills at all to efficiently search hundreds of publications for information by subject, industry, name of organization, SIC code, type of product, geographic area, type of publication, and so forth. The *Directory of Online Databases* gives a description of nearly all available database services. An excellent online database for accessing economic information is *Economics Abstracts International*. For social, cultural, demographic, and geographic information, *Sociological Abstracts* is a good online database.

Table 4.3 Major indexes that reference economic, social, political, technological, and competitive information

Name of Index	Type of Information	Description
Applied Science & Technology Index	Technological	A subject index that covers over 200 selected journals in the fields of aeronautics and space science, automation, chemistry, construction, earth sciences, electricity and electronics, engineering, industrial and mechanical arts, materials, mathematics, metallurgy, physics, telecommunication, transportation, and related subjects. *ASTI* is published monthly.
Business Periodicals Index	Economic Social Political Technological Competitive	This is probably the best known index for its overall subject coverage of selected periodicals in the following fields of business: accounting, advertising and public relations, automation, banking, communications, economics, finance and investments, insurance, labor, management, marketing, taxation, and also specific businesses, industries and trades. This index also includes a review of books appearing in the journals it indexes, listed together under the heading "Book Reviews." *BPI* is published monthly.
F & S Index of Corporations & Industries	Competitive	This is the best index for current information on companies and industries. It covers a wide selection of business, industrial and financial periodicals and also a few brokerage house reports. The yellow pages in the weeklies and the green pages in cumulated issues list articles (or data in articles) on all SIC (Standard Industrial Classification) industries; the white pages list articles on companies. Since many of the entries refer to very brief citations, it is important to note that major articles are designated by a black dot, which precedes the abbreviated title of the journal. *F&S* is published weekly.
F & S Index International	Competitive Political	A companion of the index above, covering articles on foreign companies and industries that have appeared in some 1,000 foreign and domestic periodicals and other documents. It is arranged in three parts: (1) by SIC number or product; (2) by region and country; (3) by company. *F&SI* is published monthly.
Public Affairs Information Service Bulletin	Social[a] Political	This is a selective subject listing in the areas of economic and social conditions, public administration, and international relations, published in English throughout the world. The important differences in this index are: (1) it only selectively indexes journals, to cover those articles

		pertinent to its subject coverage; (2) it covers not only periodical articles but also selected books, pamphlets, government publications, and reports of public and private agencies. There is a companion index called *Public Affairs Information Service: Foreign Language Index.* The *PAIS* is published weekly.
Readers' Guide to Periodical Literature	Economic Social Political Technological Competitive	A very popular author and subject index to periodicals published in the United States. The *RGPL* is published bimonthly.
Social Sciences Index	Social Economic Political	A subject and author index to articles in over 260 journals that cover the fields of anthropology, area studies, economics, environmental science, geography, law and criminology, medical sciences, political science, psychology, public administration, sociology, and related subjects. At the back of each issue is an author listing of book reviews that appear in the indexed journals. The *SSI* is published quarterly.
New York Times Index	Economic Social Political Technological Competitive	This is an excellent and very detailed index of articles published in the *New York Times* newspaper. The index is arranged alphabetically and includes many helpful cross-references. The *NYTI* is published bimonthly.
Wall Street Journal/ Barron's Index	Economic Social Political Technological Competitive	A valuable index of *Wall Street Journal* and *Barron's* articles. Each issue is in two parts, corporate news and general news. The index includes a list of book reviews. The *WSJI* is published monthly.

Source: Adapted from Lorna M. Daniells, *Business Information Sources* (Los Angeles: University of California Press, 1976) 14–17.

a"Social" includes cultural, demographic, and geographic information; "Political" includes governmental and legal information.

One that is widely used for political, governmental, and legal information is the *Public Affairs Information Service (PAIS) International.* The *National Technical Information Service (NTIS)* is an excellent online database for technology-related information. One of the best for locating information on competitors is *PIS Indexes,* which incorporates the *F&S Index of Corporations & Industries.*

Important published sources of environmental information are provided in Exhibits 4.7 through 4.11. Some of the most widely used sources are then described in Table 4.4.

Exhibit 4.7   Sources of economic information

Economic Outlook
American Register of Exporters and Importers
Worldcasts
Federal Reserve Bank of St. Louis, *Rates of Change in Economic Data for Ten Industrial Countries.*
Handbook of Basic Economic Statistics
National Bureau of Economic Research publications
Marketing Economic Guide
U.S. Council of Economic Advisors, *Economic Indicators*
Chase Econometric Associates' publications
U.S. Bureau of Labor Statistics, *Monthly Labor Review*
U.S. Bureau of Labor Statistics, *Handbook of Labor Statistics*
U.S. Bureau of the Census, *Statistical Abstract of the U.S.*
Survey of Business
Business Conditions Digest
Survey of Manufactures
U.S. Department of Commerce, *Survey of Current Business*
U.S. Department of Commerce, *Business Statistics*
U.S. Department of Commerce, *Long-Term Economic Growth*
U.S. Department of Commerce, *Foreign Economic Trends and Their Implications for the United States*
U.S. Industrial Outlook
Securities and Exchange Commission *Survey of Buying Power*
United Nations, *Yearbook of International Trade Statistics*
U.S. Board of Governors of the Federal Reserve System, *Federal Reserve Bulletin*
Kiplinger Washington Letter
Guide to Foreign Trade Statistics
Census of Retail Trade
Census of Wholesale Trade
Index of Economic Articles

Exhibit 4.8   Sources of social, cultural, demographic, and geographic information

American Statistics Index
Demographic Yearbook
Social Indicators and Social Reporting
Brookings Institution Report
Ford Foundation Report
World Bank Atlas
Annals of the American Academy of Political and Social Sciences
Conference Board, *Business Outlook*
Yearbook of International Organizations
County Business Patterns

Great Britain Central Statistical Office, *Social Trends*
Public opinion polls
Census of Population
Census of Housing
Census of Agriculture
Census of Manufactures
Guide to Consumer Markets
County and City Data Book
United Nations Educational, Scientific, and Cultural Organization, *Statistical Yearbook*
Dun & Bradstreet, *Principal International Businesses*
Chamber of Commerce publications
City directories
Telephone directories

Exhibit 4.9 Sources of political and governmental information

Monthly *Catalog of United States Government Publications*
Federal Register
Directory of American Firms Operating In Foreign Countries
Code of Federal Regulations
Congressional Information Service publications
Bureau of National Affairs publications
Chamber of Commerce publications
Kiplinger Washington Letter
Lobbyists
U.S. Congress, *Official Congressional Directory*
Census of Governments
American Statistics Index
Congressional Information Service Annual

Exhibit 4.10 Sources of technological information

Scientific and Technical Information Source
Trade journals and industrial reports
Annual Report of the National Science Foundation
Research and Development Directory
Patent records
World Guide to Trade Associations
University reports
Congressional reports
Department of Defense Annual Reports
Proceedings to professional meetings

Exhibit 4.11   Sources of information on competitors

Annual reports of companies
Directory of Corporate Affiliations
Securities and Exchange Commission, *10K Reports*
U.S. Industrial Outlook
Value Line Investment Survey
Moody's Industrial Manual
Moody's Investors Service
Moody's Handbook of Common Stocks
Moody's Bank and Finance Manual
Moody's Municipal & Government Manual
Moody's Public Utilities Manual
Moody's Transportation Manual
Dun & Bradstreet, *Million Dollar Directory*
Dun & Bradstreet, *Reference Book*
Dun & Bradstreet, *Key Business Ratios*
Standard and Poor's Corp., *Industry Surveys*
Standard and Poor's Corp., *Standard Corporation Records*
Standard and Poor's Corp., *Analyst's Handbook*
Standard and Poor's Corp., *Earnings Forecaster*
Standard and Poor's Corp., *Bond Guide*
Standard and Poor's Corp., *Security Owners Stock Guide*
Standard and Poor's Corp., *The Outlook*
Standard and Poor's *Register of Corporations, Directors, and Executives*
Starch Marketing
U.S. Industrial Directory
U.S. Internal Revenue Service, *Statistics of Income: Corporation Income Tax Returns*
Robert Morris Associates, *Annual Statement Studies*
Troy, Leo, *Almanac of Business and Industrial Financial Ratios*
Fortune 500 Directory
Trade association publications
County Business Patterns
County and City Data Book
Fortune
Dun's Business Month
Industry Week, "Trends and Forecasts"
Industry Week, "Financial Analysis of Industry"
Business Week, "Survey of Capital Requirements of Nonfinancial Corporations"
Business Week, "Annual Survey of International Corporate Performance"
Business Week, "Survey of Corporate Performance"
Business Week, "Investment Outlook"
Business Week, "Annual Survey of Bank Performance"
Barron's
Forbes, "Annual Report on American Industry"
Nation's Business, "Lesson of Leadership"

Census of Manufactures
Encyclopedia of Associations
Facts on File
U.S. Department of Commerce, Overseas Business Reports
U.S. Department of Commerce, International Economic Indicators and Competitive Trends
Barometer of Small Business
Dow Jones & Co., Dow Jones Investor's Handbook
Wall Street Transcript
F & S Index of Corporate Change
Investment Dealers' Digest
Conference Board Record
Conference Board, Business Outlook
U.S. Industrial Outlook
Local newspapers

Table 4.4   Key sources of external information

Source	Brief Description
Statistical Abstract of the U.S. (published annually)	Provides social, demographic, geographic, political, and economic information about the United States.
United States Industrial Outlook (published annually)	Provides industry forecasts, profiles, data, trends, and projections. Industries are classified by type of business and by SIC Code.
Survey of Business (published quarterly)	Provides information concerning the economic outlook of specific industries. Many graphs are given.
Business Conditions Digest (published monthly)	Provides charts and graphs of past, present, and forecasted unemployment rates, productivity and income data, consumption patterns, and prices of products and services.
Survey of Manufacturers (published annually)	Provides manufacturing data for many industries, including the value of inventories, plant and equipment expenditures, book values of assets, rental payments, etc.
Predicasts (published quarterly)	A guide to corporate organization developments, including liquidations, name changes, new companies, joint ventures, bankruptcies, and divestitures
Survey of Buying Power (published annually)	Provides information on households, population shifts, disposable income, and retail sales by geographic area.
Federal Reserve Bulletin (published monthly)	Includes congressional reports, staff studies, announcements, legal developments in the monetary and banking systems.
Forbes (published weekly)	A magazine that focuses on current business issues and topics

Business Week (published weekly)	A magazine that contains current business news, including corporate strategy articles
Fortune (published biweekly)	A popular magazine that reports news and events in the business world
Federal Register (published daily)	Gives all public regulations and legal notices issued by federal agencies.
Trade journals	Provide news, forecasts, changes, and developments in particular industries. Examples are *Hardware Ace* and *The Underwriter.*
Securities and Exchange Commission's *10K Reports* (published annually)	Gives detailed descriptive and financial information on a specific company.
Annual reports (published annually)	Published by corporations for shareholders and interested parties. Reveal company plans, organization, and financial condition.
Moody's Industrial Manual (published annually)	Provides information on firms' capital structure, history, financial condition, and bond ratings.
The Dun & Bradstreet Corporation, Three Century Drive Parsippany, New Jersey 07054	Publishes many reference indexes, including *Market Profile Analysis, Dun's Business Rankings, The Billion Dollar Directory, Who Owns Whom,* and *Principal International Businesses.*
United States Census of Manufactures (published annually)	Presents manufacturing data by state and area within states. Includes data on employment, payroll, number of workers, hours, wages, capital expenditures, and the like.
Value Line (published weekly)	Provides investment information on companies and industries. Evaluates companies and industries on financial criteria.
Guide to Consumer Markets (published annually)	Provides detailed consumer information on the distribution and prices of goods and services, labor force changes, and other key areas.
Chambers of commerce	Provide valuable local business information such as traffic patterns, location of particular businesses, household income levels, etc.
Facts on File (published weekly)	Weekly summaries of world business news are provided.

FORECASTING TOOLS AND TECHNIQUES

Once key environmental variables have been selected and specific sources of information have been located, the third step in performing an external strategic-management audit is to forecast key environmental variables. Forecasts are educated assumptions about future trends and events. Forecasting is a complex activity due to many interrelated factors such as changes in political situations, technological innovations, changes in cultures, new products, improved services, stronger competitors, shifts in government priorities, changing social values, unstable economic conditions, and unforeseen events. Forecasting is so complex that many strategists rely upon published environmental forecasts to effectively identify key environmental opportunities and threats.

Many of the publications cited in Exhibits 4.7 through 4.11 forecast environmental variables. Several examples include *Industry Week's* "Trends and Forecasts," *Business Week's* "Investment Outlook," Standard & Poor's *Earnings Forecaster,* and the *U.S. Industrial Outlook.* The reputation and viability of these publications depends to some extent upon accurate forecasts, so published sources of information can offer the best projections available for some variables.

When published forecasts of key internal or external variables are not available, then organizations must develop their own projections. Most organizations forecast (project) their own revenues and profits annually. Also, organizations sometimes need forecasts that are not provided in published sources, such as market share or customer loyalty information in local areas. Due to the overall importance of forecasting in strategic management and the need to do forecasting as opposed to using a forecast, selected tools are here examined further.

Forecasting tools can be broadly categorized into two groups: quantitative techniques and qualitative techniques. There are three basic types of quantitative forecasting techniques: econometric models, regression, and trend extrapolation. Econometric models are based on simultaneous systems of regression equations. With the advent of sophisticated computers, econometric models have become the most widely used approach for forecasting economic variables. Single and multiple regression is a statistical technique that explains variations in a dependent variable by changes in one or more independent variables. Trend extrapolation is simply projecting past trends into the future.

Perhaps the most powerful and widely used forecasting technique is regression analysis. The basic idea of linear regression is to "fit" a straight line to a set of data points. The equation for a linear regression line is $Y = a + bX$, where Y is the dependent variable (variable that you are forecasting), X is the independent variable (variable being used to predict Y), a is the y-axis intercept, and b is the slope of the line. A linear regression equation allows one to forecast Y based on any value of X; the equation can be determined by calculating the slope and y-axis intercept, using the two formulas given in the example that is provided in Table 4.5.

It is important to note that all quantitative forecasts, regardless of statistical sophistication and complexity, are based on historical relationships among key variables. Linear regression, for example, is based on the assumption that the future will be just like the past—which it never is. Forecasting tools must be used carefully, or the results can be more misleading than helpful. As historical relationships become less stable, quantitative forecasts become less accurate. Quantitative forecasts are most appropriate

Table 4.5   Applying linear regression analysis to forecast sales

The Problem

The Jim Dandy Company would like to forecast its 1987 sales revenues (Y) based on historical advertising expenditures (X). The following information is available: annual sales in 1984, 1985, and 1986 were $10, $15, and $16; annual advertising expenditures in the same years were $1, $3, and $4 respectively.

The Calculations

n	Y Annual Sales	X Advertising Expenditures	X^2	XY
1	10	1	1	10
2	15	3	9	45
3	16	4	16	64
	41 = ΣY	8 = ΣX	26 = ΣX²	119 = ΣXY

$$b = \frac{n\Sigma XY - \Sigma X\Sigma Y}{n\Sigma X^2 - (\Sigma X)^2} = \frac{3\,(119) - 8\,(41)}{3\,(26) - (8)^2} = 2.07$$

$$a = \frac{\Sigma Y - b\Sigma X}{n} = \frac{41 - (2.07)\,(8)}{3} = 8.15$$

Therefore, the forecasting equation is Y = 8.15 + 2.07X. This means you can substitute any value of X into the equation to predict Y.

The Graph

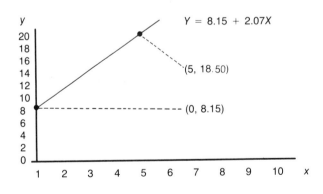

when historical data is available and when the relationships among key variables are expected to continue in the future.

The six fundamental qualitative approaches to forecasting future environmental conditions are: (1) sales-force estimate, (2) juries of executive opinion, (3) anticipatory surveys or market research, (4) scenario forecasts, (5) Delphi forecasts, and (6) brainstorming. Qualitative or judgmental forecasts are particularly useful when historical data is not available or when constituent variables are expected to change significantly in the future.

The first qualitative technique, "sales-force estimate," represents a bottom-up approach to forecasting that consists of aggregating salespersons' forecasts concerning various products, suppliers, distributors, and customers. The "juries of executive opinion" approach involves joint preparation of and/or averaging of forecasts by marketing, production, finance, production, and research and development executives. "Anticipatory surveying or market research" consists of developing and administering telephone or written questionnaires and analyzing respondents' answers. These three qualitative forecasting techniques are commonly used for competitive forecasting.

The fourth type of qualitative forecast, "scenarios," can be described as "alternative sets of possible future occurrences." The impact of various scenarios on an organization is anticipated. Scenario development is probably the most popular of all techniques for social forecasting. In a 1984 article, Reed Moyer advocates more extensive use of scenarios because they are based on the belief that the future cannot be measured, predicted, or controlled.[16]

The "Delphi" and "brainstorming" approaches to qualitative forecasting are widely used to project technological, political, governmental and legal trends, events, and changes. Delphi forecasts require gathering a group of experts together and developing a joint projection. Brainstorming refers to an idea-generation session in which individuals generate possible forecasts in a noncritical group situation.

Due to advancements in computer technology, quantitative forecasting techniques are usually cheaper and faster than qualitative methods. More importantly, some quantitative techniques, such as multiple and linear regression, can generate "measures of error" that allow a manager to estimate the degree of confidence associated with a given forecast. Qualitative techniques require greater intuitive judgment. Too often in qualitative forecasting though, managers are guilty of "forecasting" what they would like to occur. The costs, popularity, and complexity of different forecasting techniques are compared in Table 4.6.

No forecast is perfect and some forecasts are even wildly inaccurate. This fact accents the need for strategists to devote sufficient time and effort to study the underlying bases for published forecasts and to develop internal forecasts of their own. Key external opportunities and threats can be identified effectively only through good forecasts. Accurate forecasts can provide major competitive advantages for organizations. Forecasts are vital to the strategic management process and to the success of organizations.

THE COMPETITIVE PROFILE MATRIX

Of all the environmental trends and events that can affect a firm's strategic position, competitive forces are often considered to have the greatest impact. For this reason, step four in performing an external audit is to develop a Competitive Profile Matrix.

Table 4.6 The costs, popularity, and complexity of quantitative versus qualitative forecasting techniques

Quantitative Techniques	Cost	Popularity	Complexity
Economic Models	High	High	High
Regression	High	High	Medium
Trend Extrapolation	Medium	High	Medium

Qualitative Techniques	Cost	Popularity	Complexity
Sales-force Estimate	Low	High	Low
Juries of Executive Opinion	Low	High	Low
Anticipatory Surveys and Market Research	Medium	Medium	Medium
Scenario	Low	Medium	Low
Delphi	Low	Medium	Medium
Brainstorming	Low	Medium	Medium

Source: Adapted in part from J.A. Pearce II and R.B. Robinson, Jr., "Environmental Forecasting: Key to Strategic Management," *Business* (July–September 1983): 6.

This analytical tool identifies a firm's major competitors and tells where they are particularly strong and weak. The results obtained from a Competitive Profile Matrix are partially dependent upon subjective judgments made in selecting factors, assigning weights, and determining ratings, so this tool should be used carefully as an aid to decision making.

The procedures required to develop a Competitive Profile Matrix are described next. First, strategists need to identify key success factors in the industry. This task can be accomplished by studying the particular industry and, through negotiation, reaching a consensus in terms of the factors most critical to success. The set of key factors can vary over time and by industry. Recall from Porter's framework for competitive analysis that relationship with suppliers or distributors is often a key success factor. Other variables commonly included are market share, breadth of product line, economies of scale, foreign affiliates, proprietary and key account advantages, price competitiveness, advertising and promotion effectiveness, facility location and newness, capacity and productivity, place on the experience curve, financial position, product quality, R & D advantages/position, and caliber of personnel. A set of the five to ten most important key success factors should comprise the Competitive Profile Matrix.

Second, a weight is assigned to each key success factor to indicate the relative importance of that factor to success in the industry. Appropriate weights can be determined by comparing successful competitors with unsuccessful competitors. The weight assigned to each factor must range from 0.0 (not important) to 1.0 (very important). The assigned weights are applicable to all competitors; the weight column must sum to 1.0.

Third, strategists should assign a rating to each competitor to indicate that firm's strength or weakness on each key success factor, where 1 = major weakness, 2 = minor weakness, 3 = minor strength, and 4 = major strength. To the extent possible, the ratings for each competitor should be based on objective information.

Fourth, the weight assigned to each key success factor must be multiplied by the corresponding rating for each competitor to determine a weighted score for each firm. The weighted score indicates the relative strength or weakness of each competitor on each key success factor.

The final task in preparing a Competitive Profile Matrix is to sum the weighted score column for each competitor. This results in a total weighted score for each firm. The total weighted score reveals the relative overall strength of the sample firm compared to each major competitor. The highest total weighted score indicates the strongest competitor while the lowest total weighted score reveals perhaps the weakest firm. The total weighted score could range from 1.0 (lowest) to 4.0 (highest).

A sample Competitive Profile Matrix is provided in Table 4.7. Note that financial position is the most important key success factor, as indicated by a weight of 0.40. The sample company is strongest in product quality as evidenced by a rating of 4. Competitor 1 is strongest on price competitiveness with a rating of 4. Competitor 2 has the best financial position and is the strongest firm overall as indicated by a rating of 4 and

Table 4.7   A Competitive Profile Matrix

Key Success Factors	Weight	Sample Company		Competitor 1		Competitor 2	
		Rating	Weighted Score	Rating	Weighted Score	Rating	Weighted Score
Market Share	0.20	3	0.6	2	0.4	2	0.4
Price Competitiveness	0.20	1	0.2	4	0.8	1	0.2
Financial Position	0.40	2	0.8	1	0.4	4	1.6
Product Quality	0.10	4	0.4	3	0.3	3	0.3
Customer Loyalty	0.10	3	0.3	3	0.3	3	0.3
Total Weighted Score			2.3		2.2		2.8

a total weighted score of 3.13 respectively. Competitor 1 is the weakest firm as evidenced by a total weighted score of 2.2. Competitors' strengths and weaknesses often represent major opportunities and threats for organizations.

THE EXTERNAL FACTOR EVALUATION MATRIX

The final step in conducting an external strategic-management audit is to construct an External Factor Evaluation Matrix. Once key environmental variables have been selected (step 1), key sources of information have been located (step 2), forecasts of key environmental variables have been made (step 3), and the Competitive Profile Matrix has been developed (step 4), then the external factor evaluation analysis allows strategists to summarize and evaluate all of this information. Subjective judgment is again involved in developing an External Factor Evaluation Matrix, so this strategy-formulation tool should not be used indiscriminately. The procedures required to construct an External Factor Evaluation Matrix are:

1. List the firm's key opportunities and threats.
2. Assign a weight that ranges from 0.0 (not important) to 1.0 (very important) to each factor. The weight assigned to a given factor indicates the relative importance of that factor to success in a given industry. The summation of all weights assigned to the factors must total 1.0.
3. Assign a one-to-four rating to each factor to indicate whether that variable represents a major threat (rating = 1), a minor threat (rating = 2), a minor opportunity (rating = 3), or a major opportunity (rating = 4) to the organization.
4. Multiply each factor's weight by its rating to determine a weighted score for each variable.
5. Sum the weighted scores for each variable to determine the total weighted score for an organization.

Regardless of the number of key opportunities and threats that are included in an External Factor Evaluation Matrix, the highest possible total weighted score for an organization is 4.0 and the lowest possible total weighted score is 1.0. The average total weighted score is therefore 2.5. A total weighted score of 4.0 would indicate that an organization competes in an attractive industry and has abundant external opportunities, while a total score of 1.0 would characterize an organization that competes in an unattractive industry and faces severe external threats.

The recommended number of key opportunities and threats to include in the External Factor Evaluation Matrix is from five to twenty. An example is provided in Table 4.8. Note that government deregulation is the most important environmental factor affecting this industry. The sample firm has two major opportunities: the population shift to the American West and the computerized information system. This organization has one major threat, which is rising interest rates. The total weighted score of 2.7 indicates that the sample firm competes in an industry that is just above average in overall attractiveness.

Table 4.8 A sample External Factor Evaluation Matrix

Key External Factor	Weight	Rating	Weighted Score
Rising interest rates	0.20	1	0.20
Population shift to the American West	0.10	4	0.40
Government deregulation	0.30	3	0.90
A major competitor's expansion strategy	0.20	2	0.40
Computerized information system	0.20	4	0.80
Total	1.00		2.70

STRATEGIC CONCERNS OF MULTINATIONAL FIRMS

An increasing number of organizations are seeking to explore business opportunities around the world. David Shanks, manager of the Strategic Management Unit of Arthur D. Little, suggests that three major factors are driving many domestic firms into international operations: (1) Maturation of the economies of industrialized nations, (2) emergence of new geographic markets and business arenas, and (3) globalization of financial systems.[17] The typical evolution of a domestic firm into a multinational corporation (MNC) is illustrated in Figure 4.4.

Special concerns and problems confront a firm involved in international operations. Multinational corporations face unique and diverse environmental risks such as expropriation of assets, currency losses through exchange rate fluctuations and revaluations, unfavorable foreign court interpretations of contracts and agreements, social-political disturbances, import-export restrictions, tariffs, and trade barriers. Strategists

Figure 4.4 The typical evolution of a MNC

Begin Export Operations	Conduct Licensing Activities	Add Foreign Sales Representatives	Build Foreign Manufacturing Facilities	Establish a Foreign Division of the Firm	Establish Several Foreign Business Units	A MNC

Adapted from: C. A. Bartlett, "How Multinational Organizations Evolve," *Journal of Business Strategy* (Summer 1982): 20–32. Also, D. Shanks, "Strategic Planning for Global Competiton," *Journal of Business Strategy* (Winter 1985): 83.

of MNCs are often confronted with the simultaneous need to be globally competitive and nationally responsive. With the rise in world commerce, government and regulatory bodies are more closely monitoring foreign business practices. The United States Foreign Corrupt Practices Act, for example, defines what are "corrupt practices" in many areas of business. A sensitive issue is that some MNCs violate legal and ethical standards of the home, but not the host, country.

A complicating factor for many international firms is the historical propensity of some MNCs to interfere in the internal affairs of less developed countries (LDCs). International Telephone and Telegraph, for example, was implicated in masterminding the overthrow of Allende's socialist government in Chile in 1973. In many foreign countries it is obvious that corporations have in the past removed certain key decisions from the government, forced a floating of the exchange rate by buying foreign exchange, exploited natural resources, and shaped the socioeconomic structures of host countries in a way to enhance their own prospects for further growth. It is important therefore that MNC strategists today be more sensitive to the socioeconomic developmental aspirations of host countries in order to avoid unilateral breaches of contracts by LDCs.

Before entering international markets, firms should scan relevant journals and patent reports, should seek the advice of academic and research organizations, should participate in international trade fairs, and should conduct extensive research to broaden their contacts and diminish the risks of doing business. Firms could also reduce the risks of doing business internationally by obtaining insurance from the U.S. government's Overseas Private Investment Corporation (OPIC).

The Globalization of Industries

Despite the historical social costs of hosting a foreign business, more and more countries around the world are welcoming outside investment and capital. As a result, labor markets have steadily become more international. East Asian countries have become market leaders in labor-intensive industries. Brazil offers abundant natural resources and rapidly developing markets. Germany offers skilled labor and technology. The drive to improve the efficiency of global business operations is leading to greater functional specialization by locations and countries. This is not limited to a search for the familar low cost labor in Latin America or Asia. Other considerations include the cost of energy, availability of resources, existing tax rates, and the nature of trade regulations.

MNCs are increasingly having to monitor different countries' relative strengths and withdraw from areas of relative disadvantage. The People's Republic of China, for example, announced early in 1985 that "Marx's principles are irrelevant to much of what is going on in China today." China is encouraging direct Western investment more and more. Several dozen American corporations already have started business operations in China, including thirteen major oil companies, R.J. Reynolds, Gillette, McDonnell Douglas, 3M, and American Motors.

It is clear that different industries become global for different reasons. Convergence of income levels and standardization made designer clothing a universal product. The need to amortize massive R&D investments over many markets is a major reason why the aircraft industry became global. Knowing when and if one's industry will globalize is an invaluable piece of business intelligence. Knowing how to use that intelligence for one's competitive advantage is even more important. For example, when a MNC chooses a technology, it looks around the world for the best technology and selects one that has the most promise for the largest number of markets. When a MNC designs a product, it designs it to be marketable in a maximum number of countries. When a MNC manufactures a product, it selects the lowest cost source, which may be Japan for semiconductors, Sri Lanka for textiles, Malaysia for simple electronics, and Europe for precision machinery. A MNC designs manufacturing systems to accommodate world markets. These are all reasons why often one of the riskiest strategies for a domestic firm is to remain solely domestic if its industry is rapidly becoming global.

Identification and evaluation of strategic opportunities and threats in an international environment is rapidly becoming a prerequisite competency for strategic managers. There are seemingly myriad and sometimes subtle nuances of competing in international markets. Language, culture, politics, attitudes, and economies are several variables that differ significantly across countries.

The multinational company faces a multiplicity of political, economic, legal, social, and cultural environments as well as a differential rate of change in them. There are complex interactions among these factors. Communications within a MNC can be exceedingly difficult due to time, distance, and cultural barriers between home and host countries. The availability, depth, and reliability of economic, marketing, and bother information varies extensively across countries. Analysis of present and future competition is difficult for the MNC because of differences in industrial structures and business practices across countries. The number and nature of regional organizations and groups vary significantly in different countries. Differences between domestic and multinational operations that affect strategic management are summarized in Table 4.9.

Doing Business in a Foreign Country—Japan

Beyond almost anyone's wildest imagination, Japan has grown into an economic colossus. With a population of 117 million and a gross national product of approximately $1.2 trillion at the end of 1984, Japan represents the second largest market in the free world. Yet, U.S. firms have been largely unsuccessful in entering Japanese markets. Why? Business analysts nearly always cite reasons that are beyond the control of a single firm, such as trade barriers, the undervalued yen, Japan's complex distribution system, nationalistic buying habits, and different business practices. However, many other factors within the control of a single firm account for unsuccessful business entries

Table 4.9 Differences between U.S. and multinational operations that affect strategic management

Factor	U.S. Operations	International Operations
Language	English used almost universally	Local language must be used in many situations
Culture	Relatively homogeneous	Quite diverse, both between countries and within a country
Politics	Stable and relatively unimportant	Often volatile and of decisive importance
Economy	Relatively uniform	Wide variations among countries and between regions within countries
Government interference	Minimal and reasonably predictable	Extensive and subject to rapid change
Labor	Skilled labor available	Skilled labor often scarce, requiring training or redesign of production methods
Financing	Well-developed financial markets	Poorly developed financial markets. Capital flows subject to government control
Market research	Data easy to collect	Data difficult and expensive to collect
Advertising	Many media available; few restrictions	Media limited; many restrictions; low literacy rates rule out print media in some countries
Money	U.S. dollar used universally	Must change from one currency to another; changing exchange rates and government restrictions are problems
Transportation/ communication	Among the best in the world	Often inadequate
Control	Always a problem. Centralized control will work	A worse problem. Centralized control won't work. Must walk a tightrope between overcentralizing and losing control through too much decentralizing
Contracts	Once signed, are binding on both parties, even if one party makes a bad deal	Can be voided and renegotiated if one party becomes dissatisfied
Labor relations	Collective bargaining; can lay off workers easily	Often cannot lay off workers; may have mandatory worker participation in management; workers may seek change through political process rather than collective bargaining
Trade barriers	Nonexistent	Extensive and very important

Source: R. G. Murdick, R. C. Moor, R. H. Eckhouse, and T. W. Zimmerer, *Business Policy: A Framework for Analysis*, 4th ed. (Columbus, Ohio: Grid Publishing Company, 1984), p. 275.

into Japan. Some specific suggestions for MNC strategists who plan to do business in Japan are as follows:

1. Gain an Adequate Understanding of the Japanese Distribution System. Distributorships in Japan take many forms, including large trading companies, nationwide wholesalers, local wholesalers, manufacturers, agents, and family-run centers. (There exists a proliferation of small family-run distribution centers throughout Japan. These distributors assume very little responsibility for marketing; they receive most products from manufacturers on consignment.)

2. Select Distributors Carefully. Each type of distributor has particular strengths and weaknesses. For example, the trading companies are a good choice for industrial products, but they lack expertise in consumer products.

3. Monitor Closely the Timing of Market Entry. The Japanese are often reluctant to admit when the timing of market entry for a particular product is inappropriate, yet there is no substitute for good timing.

4. Use Marginal Pricing. A marginal pricing strategy requires that a company calculate the direct manufacturing costs and then add an appropriate gross margin plus the cost of freight from the U.S. factory to Japan. Too often, American firms use discounting to price products, and discounting implies low quality to the Japanese.

5. Do Not Disregard Critical Success Factors. Companies approaching the Japanese market tend to ignore the critical factors that made them successful in their domestic market. Yet, those critical factors are often the same for a given industry in Japan as for a similar industry in the United States.

One of the few areas where U.S. companies have done well in Japanese markets is the drug industry. U.S. pharmaceutical companies enjoyed a trade surplus with Japan of about $300 million in 1984. To maintain this lead, American manufacturers launched a major drive in 1985 to begin producing drugs in Japan. U.S. pharmaceutical firms' strategy is to become part of the Japanese business climate by establishing their own research, production, and marketing bases in Japan. American drug producers are working for an easing of Japanese rules on testing, licensing, and new-drug applications.

CONCLUSION

Due to increasing turbulence in business environments around the world, the external audit has become an explicit and complex part of the strategic-management process. This chapter describes a five-step approach for collecting and evaluating economic, social, cultural, demographic, geographic, political, governmental, legal, technological, and competitive information. Firms that do not identify, monitor, forecast, and evaluate key environmental variables may fail to anticipate emerging opportunities and threats. This can lead to pursuit of ineffective strategies.

A major responsibility of strategists is to develop an effective external audit system. The external audit approach described in this chapter can be used effectively by any size or type of organization. Analytical tools such as the Competitive Profile Matrix and External Factor Evaluation Matrix can aid in the environmental assessment. Multinational firms especially need a systematic and effective external audit system, since environmental forces vary so greatly among countries worldwide.

REVIEW QUESTIONS

1. Explain the process of conducting an external strategic-management audit.

2. Identify a recent economic, social, political, and technological trend that significantly impacts financial institutions.

3. Discuss the following statement: Major opportunities and threats usually result from an interaction among key environmental trends rather than from a single external event or factor.

4. Identify three industries that are technologically changing rapidly and three industries that are technologically changing slowly. How does the need for technological forecasting differ in these industries? Why?

5. According to the August 19, 1985 issue of *Business Week*, the three largest banks in America are: Citicorp, BankAmerica, and Manufacturers Hanover. Construct a Competitive Profile Matrix on these competitors, based on available information in your college library.

6. What major forecasting techniques would you use to identify (1) economic opportunities and threats and (2) demographic opportunities and threats? Why are these techniques most appropriate?

7. How does the external audit affect other components of the strategic management model?

8. As owner of a small business, explain how you would organize a strategic information scanning system. How would you organize such a system in a large organization?

9. If asked to construct an External Factor Evaluation Matrix for your university, what key success factors would you include? Construct the matrix to show the appropriate weights, ratings, weighted scores, and total weighted score for your university.

10. Make an appointment with a librarian at your university to learn how to access an online database. Report your findings in class.

FOOTNOTES

1 Gregory Parsons, "Information Technology: A New Competitive Weapon," *Sloan Management Review* (Fall 1983): 5.

2 "Control Data: Is There Room for Change?" *Business Week* (17 October 1983): 121.

3 Brian Dumainte, "A Toy Wholesaler Winds up for Retailing," *Fortune* (1 October 1984): 72.

4 Sandra Kresch, "The Impact of Consumer Trends on Corporate Strategy," *Journal of Business Strategy* (Winter 1983): 59.

5 "Ten Forces Reshaping America," *U.S. News & World Report* (19 March 1984): 40.

6 "Ten Forces," 42.

7 Kresch, "Impact of Consumer Trends," 60.

8 Bill Saporito, "Black & Decker's Gamble on 'Globalization,'" *Fortune* (14 May 1984): 40.

9 Frederick Gluck, "Global Competition in the 1990s," *Journal of Business Strategy* (Spring 1983): 22, 24.

10 John Teresko, "All Agree CAD/CAM Sales Will Soar," *Industry Week* (17 September 1984): 111.

11 John Harris, Robert Shaw, Jr., and William Sommers, "The Strategic Management of Technology," *Planning Review* (January 1983): 28, 35.

12 Susan Levine and Michael Yalowitz, "Managing Technology: The Key to Successful Business Growth," *Management Review* (September 1983): 44.

13 Wickham Skinner, "Getting Physical: New Strategic Leverage from Operations," *Journal of Business Strategy* 3, no. 4 (Spring 1983): 75.

14 Robert MacAvoy, "Corporate Strategy and the Power of Competititve Analysis," *Management Review* (July 1983): 9.

15 Steven Flax, "How to Snoop on Your Competitors," *Fortune* (14 May 1984): 29–33.

16 Reed Moyer, "The Futility of Forecasting," *Long Range Planning* 17, no. 1 (February 1984): 71.

17 David Shanks, "Strategic Planning for Global Competition," *Journal of Business Strategy* (Winter 1985): 80.

SUGGESTED READINGS

Aaker, D.A. "Organizing a Strategic Information Scanning System." *California Management Review* XXV, no. 2 (January 1983): 76–83.

"Bankruptcy Scare." *Dun's Business Review* (February 1982): 32–37.

Brown, G.H. "The Impact of Demographic and Societal Changes on U.S. Business." *Planning Review* 11, no. 3 (May 1983): 32–39.

Camillus, J.C., and Venkatraman, N. "Dimensions of Strategic Choice." *Planning Review* (January 1984): 26–31.

"Collision Course: Can the U.S. Avert a Trade War with Japan?" *Business Week* (8 April 1985): 50–55.

Coplin, W.D., and O'Leary, M.K. "Political Forecast for International Business." *Planning Review* 11, no. 3 (May 1983): 14–23.

Dammeyer, R.F. "Developing Information Systems To Meet Top Management's Needs." *AMA Forum* 72, no. 2 (February 1983): 29, 38, 39.

Daniells, L.M. *Business Information Sources.* Los Angeles: University of California Press, 1976.

David, Fred. "A Framework for Conducting an External Strategic-Management Audit." *Journal of Business Strategies* (Spring 1986). In press.

Desta, A. "Assessing Political Risk in Less-Developed Countries." *The Journal of Business Strategy* 5, no. 4 (Spring 1985): 40–53.

Diffenbach, J. "Corporate Environmental Analysis in Large U.S. Corporations." *Long Range Planning* 16, no. 3 (June 1983): 107–16.

Directory of Online Databases, Vol. 5, No. 1. Santa Monica, Calif.: Cuadra Associates, Inc., Fall, 1983.

Fella, J.W. "Capitalizing on Information in the Public Domain." *Planning Review* (March 1984): 34–38, 42.

Filho, P.V. "Environmental Analysis for Strategic Planning." *Managerial Planning* (January/February 1985): 23–30.

Flax, S. "How To Snoop on Your Competitors." *Fortune* (14 May 1984): 28–33.

Fombrun, C. "Environmental Trends Create New Pressures on Human Resources." *Journal of Business Strategy* (Summer 1982): 61–69.

Frohman, A.L., and Bitondo, D. "Coordinating Business Strategy and Technical Planning." *Long Range Planning* 14, no. 6 (December 1981): 58–67.

Gerstein, M., and Reisman, H. "Creating Competitive Advantage with Computer Technology." *Journal of Business Strategy* 3, no. 1 (Summer 1982): 53–60.

"Get the Jump on Tomorrow's Jobs." *Changing Times* 37, no. 8 (August 1983): 26–31.

Gibson, C.F., Singer, C.J., Schnidman, A.A., and Davenport, T.H. "Strategies for Making an Information System Fit Your Organization." *Management Review* (January 1984): 8–14.

Gluck, F. "Global Competition in the 1980s." *Journal of Business Strategy* (Spring 1983): 22–27.

Gould, J.M. "Technological Change and Competition." *Journal of Business Strategy* 4, no. 2 (Fall 1983): 66–71.

Hacker, R.H. "Avoiding Export Failure in Japan." *The Journal of Business Strategy* 5, no. 4 (Spring 1985): 31–34.

Harris, J.M., Shaw, R.W. Jr., and Sommers, W.P. "The Strategic Management of Technology." *Planning Review* (January 1983): 28–35.

Hochstein, M., and Kaagan, L. "New Themes in the Changing Policy-Planning Environment." *Planning Review* (January 1983): 28–35.

Kimmerly, W.C. "R&D Strategic Planning in Turbulent Environments." *Managerial Planning* (March/April 1983): 8–13.

Kresch, S.D. "The Impact of Consumer Trends on Corporate Strategy." *Journal of Business Strategy* (Winter 1983): 58–63.

Lazer, W. "How Rising Affluence Will Reshape Markets." *American Demographics* (February 1984): 20–22.

Levine, S.J., and Yalowitz, M.S. "Managing Technology: The Key to Successful Business Growth." *Management Review* (September 1983): 44–48.

MacAvoy, R.E. "Corporate Strategy and the Power of Competitive Analysis." *Management Review* (July 1983): 9–19.

McFarlan, F.W. "Information Technology Changes the Way You Compete." *Harvard Business Review* (May-June 1984): 98–103.

Mesch, A.H. "Developing an Effective Environmental Assessment Function." *Managerial Planning* 32, no. 5 (March/April 1984): 17–22.

Mesdag, M.V. "Too Much Information, Not Enough Knowledge." *Chief Executive* (May 1983): 38–39.

Mims, R., and Weiss, S. "Profits Keep Falling Back to Earth." *Business Week* (August 19, 1985): 91–107.

Morton, M.R. "Technology and Strategy: Creating a Successful Partnership." *Business Horizons* (January–February 1983): 44–48.

Moyer, R. "The Futility of Forecasting." *Long Range Planning* 17, no. 1 (February 1984): 65–72.

Murdick, R.G., Moor, R.C., Eckhouse, R.H., and Zimmerer, T.W. *Business Policy: A Framework for Analysis.* 4th ed. Columbus, Ohio: Grid Publishing Company, 1984.

Newitt, J. "How To Profit from Demographic Forecasting." *American Demographics* 4, no. 5 (May 1982): 26–31.

Parsons, G.L. "Information Technology: A New Competitive Weapon." *Sloan Management Review* (Fall 1983): 3–14.

Pearce, J.A. II, and Robinson, R.B. Jr. "Environmental Forecasting: Key to Strategic Management." *Business* (July–September 1983): 3–12.

Petrov, B. "The Advent of the Technology Portfolio." *Journal of Business Strategy* (Fall 1982): 70–75.

Pickett, G.C., and Carlson, R.L. "The Crystal Ball." *Management World* (April 1982): 27–28.

Porter, M. *Competitive Strategy: Techniques for Analyzing Industries and Competitors.* New York: The Free Press, 1981.

Porter, M. "Technology and Competitive Advantage." *Journal of Business Strategy* (Winter 1985) 60–79.

Prentice, J. "Competing with the Japanese Approach to Technology." *Long Range Planning* 17, no. 2 (April 1984) 25–32.

Rhyne, L.C. "Strategic Information: The Key to Effective Planning." *Managerial Planning* 32, no. 4 (January–February 1984): 4–10.

Rousseau, S. "Hodgepodge of Pragmatism." *Business and Society Review* 46 (Summer 1983): 15, 16.

Rubin, C. "Touring the Online Databases." *Personal Computing* (January 1984): 82–95, 196.

Schaeffer, R. "A Review of the Book Entitled 'The Next Economy.'" *Business and Society Review* 46 (Summer 1983): 86, 87.

Sethi, N. "Strategic Planning System for Multinational Companies." *Long Range Planning* (June 1982): 80–89.

Shanks, D. "Strategic Planning for Global Competition." *Journal of Business Strategy* (Winter 1985): 80–89.

Skinner, W. "Getting Physical: New Strategic Leverage from Operations." *Journal of Business Strategy* 3, no. 4 (Spring 1983): 74–79.

Sommer, D.W. "Financial Analysis of Industry and a Preview of 1984." *Industry Week* (19 March, 1984): 31–60.

"U.S. Drugmakers Move in for a Bigger Piece of the Action." *Business Week* (22 April 1985): 48–50.

"Where Growth Will Be Fastest, Slowest by 2000." *U.S. News and World Report* 95, no. 12 (19 September 1983): 58.

Wilson, J.O. "Is Economic Theory Hogwash?" *Business and Society Review* 46 (Summer 1983): 17–19.

Wiseman, C., and MacMillan, I.C. "Creating Competitive Weapons from Information Systems." *Journal of Business Strategy* (Fall 1984): 42–50.

Wright, P. "Strategic Management Within a World Parameter." *Managerial Planning* (January/February 1985) 33–36.

Yelsey, A.A. "Multiple Image Forecasting." *Planning Review* (March 1984): 27–29.

EXPERIENTIAL EXERCISE 4A:

The Library Search

PURPOSE

This exercise was written to help you become familiar with important sources of strategic information that are available in your college library. A key part of preparing an external audit is to examine published sources of information for relevant economic, social, cultural, demographic, geographic, political, governmental, technological, and competitive trends and events. Environmental opportunities and threats need to be identified and evaluated before strategies can be formulated effectively.

YOUR TASK

Twenty published sources of information are listed in this exercise. Ten of these sources are then described. Your task is to go to the college library and determine which published sources are described. For the ten sources not described, write a short description. Record all your answers on a separate sheet of paper. That is, number from one to twenty and place the letter of the appropriate description beside the right source. For the ten sources not described here, write your description beside the appropriate source. Bring your answer sheet to class.

TWENTY KEY SOURCES OF STRATEGIC INFORMATION

Twenty key sources of strategic information include

1. *Wall Street Journal*
2. *Census of Retail Trade*
3. *Rand McNally Atlas & Marketing Guide*
4. *Value Line*
5. *Business Periodicals Index*
6. *Survey of Buying Power*
7. *Standard & Poor's Publications*
8. Robert Morris Associates, *Annual Statement Studies*
9. Annual reports of specific companies
10. *Standard Industrial Classification Manual*

11. Moody's publications
12. *Dun & Bradstreet Million Dollar Directory Series*
13. *Survey of Business*
14. *Statistical Abstract of the United States*
15. *Census of Manufactures*
16. *Predicast's F & S Index*
17. *The Wall Street Transcript*
18. *The U.S. Industrial Outlook*
19. *Industry Week*
20. *Barron's*

TEN SHORT DESCRIPTIONS OF KEY STRATEGIC SOURCES

1. This publication contains financial information, divided by industry into six manuals published annually with weekly updates. A monthly *Bond Record* and *Bond Survey* are also published. The six manuals are the *Bank and Finance Manual, International Manual, OTC Industrial Manual, Industrial Manual, Public Utility Manual,* and *The Transportation Manual.* Information is provided on a specific company's history, subsidiaries, product or service, major plants and properties, financial ratios, bond ratings, and stock ratings. Bonds are rated on a scale from AAA (best) to C (worst) and stock is rated from aaa (best) to c (worst).

2. This source of information consists of three quarterly reports, the *OTC, ASE,* and *NYSE,* as well as a monthly *Bond Guide* and *Stock Guide.* The quarterly reports include the following information on each company: (1) earnings and dividend forecasts, (2) a near-term and long-term outlook statement, (3) company stock prices, (4) price-earnings ratios, (5) dividends, (6) bond yields, and (7) stock ratings. In addition, comparative financial information is provided by industry. Stocks are rated A+ (best) to C (worst). The *Bond Guide* lists new offerings, rating changes, and current bond ratings from AAA (best) to D (worst). *Corporation Records* contains company information and *Industry Surveys* contains financial comparisons and projections.

3. This source of information is published yearly by all publicly held corporations. This publication includes a summary of a company's past performance and future plans. It usually includes a discussion of the company's mission, purpose, policies, goals, objectives, strategies, and culture.

4. This source contains financial data on manufacturing, wholesaling, retailing, service, and contracting businesses. Key industry-average financial ratios are given by SIC Code (Standard Industrial Classification) for the four most recent years.

5. This source of information provides detailed statistics on social, political, and economic trends in the United States. An example of the type of information contained in this publication is:

Women-owned firms—number and receipts by industry in 1982

Industry	All Firms	Number Women-Owned	% of All Firms
All	9833	702	7.1
Building	1107	21	1.9
Manufacturing	287	19	6.6

6. This is a monthly index of articles published in magazines. The articles are indexed by subject, which includes industries, corporations, and individuals.

7. This publication contains detailed information, in five volumes, on 450 manufacturing industries in every state, including for each: number of establishments, value of shipments, cost of materials, capital expenditures, assets, rents, inventories, employment, and payrolls.

8. This source of information is divided into four volumes that include all companies with a net worth over $500,000. Companies are listed alphabetically by business name. Volume I includes businesses with net worth over $1,670,000; Volume II includes businesses with net worth from $847,000 to $1,670,000; and Volume III covers businesses with $500,000 to $847,000 net worth. Each entry gives a specific company's name, address, type of business, top executives' names and titles, annual sales, number of employees, principal bank, and SIC code. The listings are also cross-referenced geographically, alphabetically, and by industry.

9. This source is published five days a week and is devoted to businessmen and businesswomen. Regular features include: "What's New," "Special Reports," "The Outlook," and detailed results of the previous day's NYSE, ASE, and commodities markets. An index for the articles appearing in this publication is available. The front section of the index lists articles on companies and the back section lists articles by industry or subject.

10. This publication provides statistics by state, Standard Metropolitan Statistical Areas (SMSA), and areas outside SMSAs for about 100 different kinds of retail enterprises. The data includes number of establishments, sales, payroll, and employment. This publication is updated and reprinted every five years.

Note: This exercise was edited by Kelly Janousek, Social Sciences Librarian at Mississippi State University.

EXPERIENTIAL EXERCISE 4B:

Developing an External Factor Evaluation Matrix for Ponderosa, Inc.

PURPOSE

This exercise is designed to give you practice in constructing an External Factor Evaluation Matrix. This analytical tool summarizes the results of an external audit. It is an important technique often used in preparing a business policy case analysis.

YOUR TASK

Five steps were outlined in this chapter for constructing an External Factor Evaluation Matrix. Your task here is to prepare this matrix for the Cohesion Case on Ponderosa, Inc. Utilize the information actually provided in this case, along with other information that you can find in your college library, to identify the key external opportunities and threats that face Ponderosa. Come to class prepared to present and discuss your analysis.

5

The Internal Assessment

This chapter provides a framework for conducting an internal audit. The purpose of an internal audit is to identify and evaluate organizational strengths and weaknesses in the functional areas of business: management, marketing, finance, production, and research and development. Strategic implications of important functional area concepts are examined.

INTERRELATIONSHIPS AMONG THE FUNCTIONAL AREAS OF BUSINESS

The strategic-management process is sometimes misperceived as a unidirectional flow of strategies, objectives, goals, policies, and decisions from corporate- to divisional- to functional-level managers. However, this process is actually highly interactive and requires effective coordination among all the functional areas of business. There are an infinite number of critical interrelationships among management, marketing, finance, production, and research and development activities. For example, financial problems could restrict the number of feasible options available to marketing and production managers. A strong research and development team could invent products so successful that all the other functional areas could set higher goals. Although the strategic-management process is overseen by top managers, success requires that managers from all functional areas work together to provide inputs, ideas, and information.

A failure to recognize important interrelationships among the functional areas of business contributes to an increasing number of business failures each year in the United States. Small business owners and entrepreneurs, in particular, often have special expertise in one or two business functions, but lack sufficient knowledge in other vital areas. For larger domestic and multinational firms, coordination and communication among functional, divisional, and corporate managers becomes more difficult. The number of interrelationships that must be managed among the functional areas of business increases dramatically with a firm's size, diversity, geographic dispersion, and number of products or services offered. Governmental and nonprofit enterprises have traditionally not placed sufficient emphasis on interrelationships among the business functions. For example, some state governments, utilities, universities, and hospitals have only recently begun to establish marketing goals and policies that are consistent with their financial capabilities and limitations.

A failure to identify and understand interrelationships among the functional areas of business is often detrimental to the strategic-management process. Evaluating financial ratios is an activity that exemplifies the complexity of interrelationships among the functional areas of business. A declining return on investment or profit margin ratio could be the result of ineffective marketing, poor management policies, research and development errors, or other factors. Planning is another activity that reveals the interrelatedness of major business functions. Most plans are based on achieving coordinated effort among all the functional areas of business.

We may, of course, conceptually separate planning for the purpose of theoretical discussion and analysis, but in practice, neither is it a distinct entity nor is it capable of being separated. The planning function is mixed with all other business functions and, like ink once mixed with water, it cannot be set apart. It is spread throughout and is a part of the whole of managing an organization.[1]

The internal audit focuses on interrelationships among the functional areas of business. This phase of the strategic-management process is highlighted in Figure 5.1. Internal strengths and weaknesses, coupled with the key external factors and a clear statement of mission, provide the bases for establishing company objectives and strategies. This chapter describes how to conduct functional area audits and how to consolidate this information so that important interrelationships are identified and evaluated.

Figure 5.1   The strategic-management model

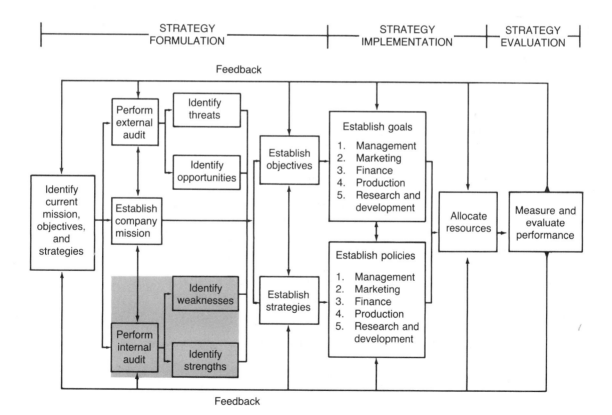

THE MANAGEMENT AUDIT

Planning

Managers perform five basic activities: planning, organizing, motivating, staffing, and controlling. Although planning is often considered to be the foundation of management, it is commonly the most neglected task of a manager's job. The only thing certain about the future of any organization is change, and planning is the essential bridge between the present and the future. Planning increases the likelihood that desired results will be achieved. As indicated in Table 5.1, planning is the cornerstone of effective strategy formulation. Planning is also essential for successful strategy imple-

Table 5.1   The basic functions of management

Function	Description	Most Important at What Stage of the Strategic-Management Process
Planning	Planning consists of all those managerial activities related to preparing for the future. Specific tasks include forecasting, establishing objectives, devising strategies, developing policies, and setting goals.	Strategy Formulation
Organizing	Organizing includes all those managerial activities that result in a structure of task and authority relationships. Specific areas include organizational design, job specialization, job descriptions, job specifications, span of the control, unity of command, coordination, job design, and job analysis.	Strategy Implementation
Motivating	Motivating involves efforts directed towards shaping human behavior. Specific topics include leadership, communication, work groups, behavior modification, delegation of authority, job enrichment, job satisfaction, needs fulfillment, organizational change, employee morale, and managers' morale.	Strategy Implementation
Staffing	Staffing activities are centered on personnel or human resource management. Included are wage and salary administration, employee benefits, interviewing, hiring, firing, training, management development, employee safety, affirmative action, equal employment opportunity, union relations, career development, personnel research, discipline policies, grievance procedures, and public relations.	Strategy Implementation
Controlling	Controlling refers to all those managerial activities directed towards assuring that actual results are consistent with planned results. Key areas of concern include quality control, financial control, sales control, inventory control, expense control, analysis of variances, rewards, and sanctions.	Strategy Evaluation

mentation and strategy evaluation, because organizing, motivating, staffing, and controlling activities are dependent upon good planning.

To be effective, planning must begin at the top of an organization and filter down. The major reason for beginning at the corporate level is that top management must establish a firm's mission, strategies, and objectives before divisional and functional managers can effectively set goals and institute policies. The three levels of planning, shown in Figure 5.2, are analogous to the three levels of strategic management: corporate, divisional, and functional.

Firms that use formal planning approaches are generally more profitable than those that do not.[2] There are some important reasons why planning has a positive impact on organizational and individual performance. First, planning allows an organization to identify and take advantage of environmental opportunities; it allows an organization to minimize the impact of environmental threats. Planning is more than extrapolating from the past and present into the future. It is also determining the likelihood that future events and trends could be harmful or beneficial to an enterprise.

Second, an organization can develop synergy through planning. Synergy exists when everyone pulls together like a team that knows what it wants to achieve. Synergy

Figure 5.2   The three levels of planning

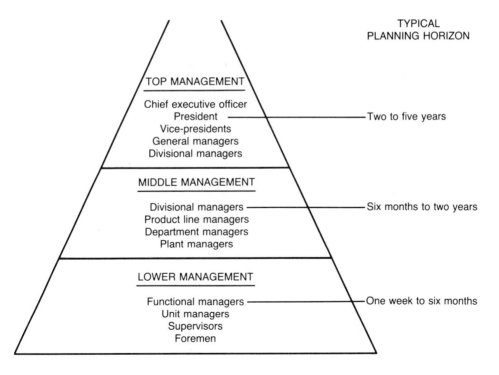

is the $2 + 2 = 5$ effect. By establishing and communicating clear objectives and goals, all employees and managers can work together toward desired results. Synergy can result in powerful competitive advantages.

Third, planning allows a firm to adapt to changing environments, and thus to shape its own destiny. The strategic-management process can be viewed as a formal planning process that allows an organization to pursue proactive rather than reactive strategies. Successful organizations strive to control their own future, rather than merely reacting to external forces and events as they occur. Historically, organisms and organizations that have not adapted to changing environments have become extinct. As indicated in the previous chapter, global business environments are changing and the speed of these changes is accelerating.

Organizing

The purpose of organizing is to achieve coordinated effort by defining task and authority relationships. Organizing means determining who does what and who reports to whom. A well-organized firm can formulate, implement, and evaluate strategies much more effectively than a disorganized firm. The organizing function of management can be viewed as consisting of three sequential activities: breaking tasks down into jobs, combining jobs to form departments, and delegating authority to individuals in departments.

Breaking tasks down into jobs requires development of job descriptions and job specifications. These tools enable managers to effectively match people to jobs. They also clarify for both employee and supervisor what a given job entails, and they are essential components in the performance evaluation process.

Combining jobs to form departments results in an organizational structure. Organizational structure is a major concern when implementing strategy, so this topic is discussed further in Chapter 7. Changes in strategy often require changes in structure. For example, General Motors recently announced a major reorganization to support the company's strategic shift to small cars. Specifically, GM created two new "super groups" that divide and encompass all operations along small-car/large-car lines. The two groups are each about equal in size to Ford Motor Company. Under the new organization, Chevrolet, Pontiac Motor, and GM of Canada are being merged to form a small-car division. Buick, Oldsmobile, and Cadillac will comprise the large-car segment. GM expects this structural reorganization to be fully implemented by 1989.

Delegating authority to subordinates provides managers with more time to do important chores, such as planning. Delegation can be a valuable training and development tool. There is an old saying in management that "you can tell how good a manager is by observing how his department functions when he is not there." This saying accents the fact that employees today are more educated and more capable of participating in organizational decision making than ever before. In many cases, they expect to be delegated authority and responsibility. As an example, delegation of authority is embedded in the strategic-management process at Johnson & Johnson. J&J was recently described as a prime example of good organizing and delegating:

> The people running Johnson & Johnson's divisions enjoy autonomy unheard of in most corporations. Most divisions have their own boards. J&J's corporate headquarters staff is a scant 750 people. And only one management layer separates division presidents from the 14-member executive committee to whom they report. J&J's earnings growth in the last 10 years has averaged 13% annually.[3]

Motivating

Motivating can be defined as the process of influencing people to act. Motivation explains why some people work hard and others do not. Objectives, goals, strategies, and policies have little chance of succeeding if employees and managers are not motivated to implement strategies once they are formulated. The motivating function of management includes at least four major components: leadership, group dynamics, communication flows, and organizational change.

Individuals can be particularly effective leaders when they set a good example, are knowledgeable in the area that they are leading, have self-confidence, and are personable. There are some basic characteristics that are important for being an effective leader. Specifically, a leader must be willing to negotiate, must have a heightened sense of corporate social responsibility, must be willing to give up some authority, and must take great responsibility for the career development of employees.[4] Good leaders motivate employees to achieve high levels of productivity.

Group dynamics plays a major role in employee morale and satisfaction. Informal groups or coalitions form in every organization. Work-group norms can range from being very positive to very negative toward management. It is important therefore that strategists try to identify how many informal groups exist, how large is each group, how cohesive is each group, who are the groups' members, who are the groups' leaders, and what are the groups' norms? Information about the composition and nature of informal groups in a department can facilitate managers' efforts to implement strategy, to gain support for department goals and policies, and to manage political relationships.[5]

Communication is a third major component in motivating others. A poor communication system can derail the strategic-managment process. An organization's system of communication can alone determine whether strategies will be implemented successfully. Good two-way communication is vital for gaining employees' support for departmental goals and policies. Top-down communication encourages bottom up communication. The strategic-management process becomes a whole lot easier when subordinates are encouraged to discuss their concerns, reveal their problems, provide recommendations, and give suggestions.

A firm that exemplifies an excellent communication system is Citicorp, one of the largest and most successful banks in the United States. An important element of Citicorp's strategic-management philosophy is that good two-way communication offers major competitive advantages:

> Citi is an open society that encourages people to speak their minds, in sharp contrast to such banks as Chase and First Chicago where chief executives have installed electronic voting machines so managers can voice their opinions anonymously. Moreover, at Citi, the belief is sacred that anyone with a good idea should have the chance to try it out. The philosophy at Citi is to "let a thousand flowers bloom." This may explain why Citi, whose electronic network connects with 6,500 corporate offices around the world, is far ahead of competitors.[6]

A final key factor in motivating subordinates is the need to manage change. Due to diverse internal and external forces, change is a fact of life in organizations. The rate, speed, magnitude, and direction of changes vary over time by type of industry and organization. Managers should strive to create a work environment where change is recognized as necessary and beneficial, so that individuals can adapt to change more easily. Adopting a strategic-management approach to decision making can itself entail major changes in the philosophy and operations of a firm.

There are a number of positive actions that managers can take to minimize employees' resistance to change. For example, get employees that are going to be affected by a change involved in the decision to make the change. Involve employees in decisions regarding how to implement changes. Plan for and anticipate changes. Develop and offer training and development workshops so that employees can adapt to changes. Communicate effectively the need for changes.

Change guidelines become particularly vital when making strategic changes. In order for strategies to be successfully implemented, middle and lower level managers must be involved in strategy-formulation decisions. The strategic-management process can be described as a process of managing change.

Stability is so crucial to success in some organizations that a strategy of no change at all can sometimes be feasible for long periods of time. The RCA Corporation has recently experienced anything but stability. RCA's year-end profit margin on sales was below 3 percent in 1982, 1983, and again in 1984. Massive changes have nearly crippled the company:

> Few companies have been battered as badly by their own managements as the RCA Corp. Under its last four chief executives, each of whom pursued a different strategy, the company has been diversified, divested, directed toward long-term goals, redirected toward short-term goals, nearly done in by a massive acquisition, and finally drawn back to its roots—all in the space of 10 years. That the company survived such trauma is remarkable.[7]

Staffing

The management function of staffing is oftentimes called personnel management or human resource management. Human resource managers assist line managers in performing staffing activities such as recruiting, interviewing, testing, selecting, orienting, training, developing, caring for, evaluating, rewarding, disciplining, promoting, transferring, demoting, and dismissing employees. Staffing activities play a major role in strategy implementation efforts. For this reason, human resource managers are becoming more actively involved in the strategy-formulation process.

The complexity and importance of human resource activities has increased to such a degree that all but the smallest organizations often need a full-time human resource manager. Line managers simply cannot stay abreast of all the legal developments and requirements regarding staffing. There exists a need to effectively coordinate line managers' actions in the staffing area, so that an organization as a whole meets legal requirements. A human resource department provides needed consistency in company rules, wages, practices, and policies. Legislation such as the Civil Rights Act, the Occupational Safety and Health Act, and the Privacy Act, as well as government regulatory agencies such as the National Labor Relations Board (NLRB), the Equal Employment Opportunity Commission (EEOC), and the Occupational Safety and Health Administration (OSHA) outline in detail what organizations can and cannot do in meeting staffing needs. Numerous court cases that directly impact staffing activities are decided each day. Organizations and individuals can be penalized severely for not following federal, state, and local laws and guidelines related to the management function of staffing.

A recent study of firms in eleven different industries revealed five staffing characteristics that distinguish America's leading enterprises.[8] First, staffing is a joint effort between human resource managers and line management. Second, people-related programs are consistent with strategic business plans. Third, leader companies solve people problems with current resources before seeking additional sources. Fourth, leading companies have staffing departments that are more proactive in initiating focused programs and in communicating with line management. Finally, corporate and divisional staffing departments in leader firms share responsibilities for policy development and program administration.

Chief executive officers are becoming increasingly aware of how important human resources are to effective strategic management. For example, a large aerospace company about to undertake the development of a major new product for the federal government recently asked its human resource managers to first put together a comprehensive human resources plan. It had become obvious that unless the company could change its recruitment, selection, compensation, and training practices, the needed engineering and professional staff could not be obtained.[9] In the future, the human resource or staffing function of management is expected to become even more proactive—anticipating and initiating rather than responding.

Controlling

The controlling function of management includes all those activities undertaken to assure that actual operations conform to planned operations. All managers in an orga-

nization have controlling responsibilities, which include conducting performance evaluations and taking necessary actions to minimize inefficiencies. The controlling function of management is particularly important for effective strategy evaluation.
Controlling consists of four basic steps:

1. Establish performance standards.
2. Measure actual performance.
3. Compare actual performance to planned performance standards.
4. Take corrective actions.

Establishing performance standards is an activity that commonly follows goal setting. Most organizations divide goals into subgoals called standards. Performance standards such as "units produced per hour" or "sales generated per month" are widely used.
Standards, like goals, should be measurable, quantitative, challenging, reasonable, consistent, and clearly stated.

The measuring of actual performance is often conducted ineffectively or not at all
in organizations. Some reasons for this shortcoming is that the evaluation process can
create confrontation that most managers prefer to avoid, can take more time than most
managers are willing to give, and can require skills that most managers lack.[10] No single
approach to measuring individual performance is without limitations. Therefore, an
organization should examine various methods such as the graphic rating scale, the be-
haviorally anchored rating scale, or the critical incident method, and then develop or
select a performance appraisal instrument that best suits the firm's needs.

The third step in the controlling function of management is comparing actual
performance to standard performance. This activity results in the generation of favorable and unfavorable variances. Unfavorable variances indicate weak areas that should
be analyzed to determine underlying problem areas.

Taking corrective actions, the final step in the controlling process, sometimes includes changing standards, but this action should come only after careful study suggests
that original standards are inappropriate. Management controls are essential for monitoring the success or failure of an organization's strategies. Table 5.2 gives an example
of sales control for Food Distributors, Inc.

A Management Audit Questionnaire

The checklist of questions provided in Exhibit 5.1 can be helpful in determining specific strengths and weaknesses in management. An answer of NO to any one of the
audit questions could indicate a potential management weakness. The strategic significance and implications of negative answers will of course vary by organization, industry,
and severity of the weakness. Positive or YES answers to the audit questions suggest
potential areas of strength. The audit checklists are not all-inclusive and should not be
blindly applied to all organizations without recognition of individual organizational differences. They are not a global panacea that will identify all internal organizational
ills. Audit checklists for all the major functional areas of business are provided in this

chapter to aid strategists in identifying key internal factors and interrelationships. The audit checklists can help you in preparing business policy case analyses, because effective strategies capitalize on strengths and overcome weaknesses.

Table 5.2 Sales control for Food Distributors, Inc.

	Standard Performance	Actual Performance	Variance
Territory A			
Total sales	6,000	7,000	+ 1,000
Total expenses	3,000	3,500	+ 500
Net revenue	3,000	3,500	+ 500
Miles traveled per salesman	600	550	− 50
Units sold per salesman	60	70	+ 10
Dollars sold per salesman	800	900	+ 100
New accounts opened	30	50	+ 20
Territory B			
Total sales	8,000	7,000	− 1,000
Total expenses	4,500	5,000	+ 500
Net revenue	3,500	3,000	− 500
Miles traveled per salesman	500	500	0
Units sold per salesman	50	40	− 10
Dollars sold per salesman	1,000	900	− 100
New accounts opened	20	30	+ 10

Exhibit 5.1 A management audit checklist

Planning

1. Does the organization have clearly stated goals and objectives?

2. Does the organization have an overall strategy for competing in its basic industry?

3. Does the organization monitor and forecast relevant trends in the economic, political, social, and technological environments?

4. Does the organization monitor and anticipate competitors' actions and reactions in the marketplace?

5. Does the organization monitor and anticipate the needs of key customers, suppliers, distributors, creditors, shareholders, and employees?

6. Does the organization have an effective budgeting process?

7. Does the organization use a strategic-management approach to corporate decision making?

8. Does the organization have a written mission statement?

9. Does the organization have contingency plans?

10. Does the organization have synergy?

11. Does the organization allocate resources based on stated goals?

12. Does the organization have objectives, strategies, goals, and policies that are mutually consistent, supportive, and clearly communicated?

Organizing

1. Does the enterprise have a clear organizational structure as evidenced by a formal organizational chart?

2. Does the organizational chart reflect the most desirable structure for the firm?

3. Does the organizational chart exhibit acceptable spans of control?

4. Are similar activities appropriately grouped together in the organizational chart?

5. Are staff functions, such as personnel, shown appropriately in the organizational chart?

6. Is the unity of command principle adhered to in the organizational chart?

7. Do the organization's managers delegate authority well?

8. Does the organization have and use written job descriptions?

9. Does the organization have and use written job specifications?

10. Are the organization's jobs meaningful, rewarding, and challenging?

Motivating

1. Is employee morale high?

2. Is managerial morale high?

3. Is job satisfaction high?

4. Is a participative management style used?

5. Is creativity encouraged?

6. Are absenteeism rates in the organization low?

7. Are turnover rates in the organization low?

8. Have managers identified the number and composition of informal groups in the organization?

9. Are the norms of informal groups in the organization favorable to management?

10. Does a good system for two-way communication exist in the organization?

11. Are managers in the organization good leaders?

12. Does the organization have a good system of rewards and sanctions?

13. Does the organization and its employees adapt well to changes?

14. Are employees able to satisfy individual needs through the organization?

15. Are department policies reasonable and supportive of stated goals?

Staffing

1. Does the organization have a personnel manager or human resource department?

2. Does the organization hire employees only after careful recruiting, interviewing, testing, and selecting?

3. Does the organization provide employee training and management-development programs?

4. Does the organization provide reasonable employee benefits?

5. Does the organization have an effective performance evaluation system?

6. Does the organization have a good wage and salary administration system?

7. Does the organization have stated grievance procedures?

8. Does the organization have stated disciplinary policies?

9. Does the organization have a career planning system for its employees?

10. Does mutual trust and respect exist between line managers and personnel managers in the organization?

11. Are working conditions in the organization clean and safe?

12. Does the organization have equal employment opportunities?

13. Does the organization have an affirmative action program?

14. Does the organization promote employees from within?

15. Does the organization provide employee counseling?

16. Are union-management relations good in the organization?

17. Does the organization have a code of ethics?

Controlling

1. Does the organization have an effective financial control system?

2. Does it have an effective sales control system?

3. Does it have an effective inventory control system?

4. Does it have an effective expense control system?

5. Does it have an effective production control system?

6. Does it have an effective management control system?

7. Does it have an effective quality control system?

8. Does it have computer-assisted control systems?

9. Have productivity standards been established in all departments of the organization?

10. Does the organization regularly monitor favorable and unfavorable variances in the control process?

11. Are corrective actions taken promptly to improve unfavorable variances?

12. Are rewards and sanctions in the organization supportive of established control systems?

13. Is unethical behavior effectively controlled in the organization?

14. Are the organization's control systems prompt, accurate, and thorough?

THE MARKETING AUDIT

Marketing can be described as the process of defining, anticipating, creating, and fulfilling customers' needs and wants for products and services. Joel Evans and Barry Berman suggest that there are nine basic functions of marketing: (1) Customer analysis, (2) Buying, (3) Selling, (4) Product and service planning, (5) Price planning, (6) Distribution, (7) Marketing research, (8) Opportunity analysis, and (9) Social responsibility.[11] These functions of marketing are examined next to help you identify and evaluate marketing strengths and weaknesses when preparing business policy case analyses.

Customer Analysis

Examination and evaluation of consumer needs, desires, and wants is called customer analysis. Customer analysis involves administering customer surveys, analyzing consumer information, evaluating market positioning strategies, developing customer profiles, and determining optimal market segmentation strategies. Customer analysis information can be essential in developing an effective mission statement. Profiles, for example, can reveal the demographic characteristics of an organization's customers. Customer profile information about the readers of *USA Today* and *Wall Street Journal,* the two most widely read newspapers in the United States, indicates that: (1) 69 percent of *USA Today* readers have attended college, compared to 73 percent for the *Wall Street Journal,* (2) 43 percent of *USA Today* readers have household incomes of $35,000 or more, compared to 57 percent for the *Wall Street Journal,* and (3) 56 percent of *USA Today* readers are in the 18–39 age group, compared to 46 percent for the *Wall Street Journal.*[12]

Buyers, sellers, distributors, salesmen, managers, wholesalers, retailers, suppliers, and creditors can all participate in gathering information to successfully identify customers' needs and wants. Successful organizations continually monitor present and potential customers' buying patterns, as emphasized in the following statements:

> Instead of trying to market what is easiest for us to make, we (General Foods) must find out much more about what the consumer is willing to buy. In other words, we must apply our creativeness more intelligently to people and their needs, rather than to products.[13]
>
> What a business thinks it produces is not of first importance, especially not to the future of the business or to its success. What the customer thinks he is buying, what he considers "value" is decisive. It determines what a business is, what it produces, and whether it will prosper.[14]

Buying

The second function of marketing is buying. Buying means obtaining the goods and services needed to produce and sell a product or service. Buying consists of evaluating alternative suppliers, selecting the best suppliers, arranging acceptable terms with suppliers, and procurement. The buying process can be complicated by a number of factors that include price controls, recession, foreign trade restrictions, strikes, walkouts, and machine breakdowns. Even the weather can significantly disrupt the procurement of needed supplies. Quite often, the question arises whether to "make or buy" needed supplies and services. As you know, backward integration involves gaining control over suppliers. This strategy is particularly attractive when suppliers are unreliable, costly, or incapable of meeting company needs.

Selling

Selling includes many marketing activities, such as advertising, sales promotion, publicity, personal selling, sales force management, customer relations, and dealer relations. These activities are especially critical when a firm pursues a market penetration strategy. The effectiveness of various selling tools varies between consumer products and industrial products. For industrial-goods companies, personal selling is most important, and for consumer-goods companies, advertising is most important. Successful strategy implementation generally rests on the ability of an organization to sell some product or service. In the case of cigarettes, companies like Philip Morris and R. J. Reynolds are having to use elaborate sales techniques that include massive discounting and couponing. (The total number of cigarettes consumed in the United States declined annually between 1981 and 1985, with Marlboro, Winston, Salem, and Kool being the top-selling brands.)

Advertising often plays an important role in the strategy-implementation process. Advertising can be described as a five-step procedure: (1) set goals, (2) make budget decisions, (3) make message decisions, (4) make media decisions, and (5) evaluate the advertising process. Clear goals are needed, stipulating whether specific ads are supposed to inform, persuade, or remind buyers. An advertising budget could be established based on specific criteria or objectives, such as what is affordable, a percentage of sales, or competitors' expenditures. The message decision calls for developing ads, evaluating and selecting among them, and finally executing them effectively. The media decision calls for identifying the reach and frequency of various media such as radio, television, magazines, and newspapers, selecting specific media, and scheduling the media. Finally, evaluation of the advertising process can require measuring sales effects before, during, and after specific ads are used.[15]

Product and Service Planning

This function of marketing includes activities such as new product development, test marketing, product and brand positioning, warranties, packaging, product options, product features, product style, product quality, deleting old products, and customer service. Product and service planning is particularly important when product development or diversification is pursued.

One of the most effective product and service planning techniques is test marketing. Test markets allow an organization to pretest alternative marketing plans and to forecast the future sales of a new product. In conducting a test market, an organization must decide how many test cities to include, which cities to include, how long to run the test, what information to collect during the test, and what action to take after the test has been completed.

Test marketing is more frequently used by consumer goods companies than industrial companies. Strategically, test marketing can allow an organization to avoid great losses by revealing weak products and ineffective marketing approaches before large scale production begins. Joseph Seagram & Sons recently test-marketed a new low-alcohol wine called St. Regis California Blanc. Also, K-Mart test-marketed in Texas and Florida the idea of adding insurance centers in its stores. (K-Mart plans to sell insurance in 100 stores.)

Price Planning

Four major factors affect pricing decisions: consumers, governments, channel members, and competitors. Sometimes an organization will pursue a forward-integration strategy primarily to gain better control over prices charged to consumers. Federal, state, and local governments can impose various pricing limitations that include: price fixing, price discrimination, minimum prices, unit pricing, price advertising, and price controls. For example, the Robinson–Patman Act prohibits manufacturers and wholesalers from discriminating in price among channel-member purchasers if competition is injured.

To avoid price-fixing litigation, a company must be careful not to coordinate discounts, credit terms, or conditions of sale. Firms must not discuss prices, markups, and costs at trade association meetings, or arrange with competitors to issue new price lists on the same date. It is illegal to arrange with competitors to rotate low bids on contracts, or to agree with competitors to uniformly restrict production to maintain high prices.

Different channel members such as manufacturers, wholesalers, and retailers often set different prices for identical products due to different costs, profit requirements, and other factors. Therefore, conflicts sometimes arise among various channel members regarding pricing. To minimize potential conflicts, manufacturers could first determine the final selling price that consumers should pay for a given product or service, and then work backwards to determine the profit margins and prices appropriate for wholesalers and retailers.

Competitors have a major impact on the pricing of products and services. Firms may compete in (1) a market-controlled pricing environment in which no single firm has significant control over prices, (2) a company-controlled pricing environment in which a few firms exert strong control of prices, or (3) a government-controlled pricing environment where prices are set by the government. Organizations should view price from both a short-run and long-run perspective, because competitors can copy price strategies relatively easily. Oftentimes, a dominant firm in an industry will aggressively match all price cuts by competitors.

Distribution

The distribution function of marketing includes warehousing, physical distribution channels, distribution coverage, retail site locations, sales territories, inventory levels and location, transportation carriers, wholesaling, and retailing. Most producers today do not sell their goods directly to consumers. Between producers and consumers, many marketing entities act as intermediaries and provide a variety of functions. They bear a variety of names such as wholesalers, retailers, brokers, facilitators, agents, middlemen, vendors, and simply distributors. This area of marketing becomes especially important when a firm is striving to implement a market development or forward integration strategy.

Major competitive advantages can be gained by increasing a firm's control over lines of distribution. Intermediaries flourish in our economy today because many producers lack the financial resources and expertise to carry out direct marketing. Manufacturers who could afford to sell directly to the public often could gain greater returns by expanding and improving their current operations. But General Motors, for example, would find it very difficult to buy out its more than 18,000 independent dealers.

Successful organizations identify and evaluate alternative ways to reach their ultimate market. Possible approaches vary from direct selling, to using just one wholesaler and retailer, to using many levels and numbers of intermediaries. Each channel alternative should be evaluated according to economic, control, and adaptive criteria. That is, organizations should consider the costs versus benefits of various wholesaling and retailing options. They must consider the need to motivate and control channel members, and the need to adapt to environmental changes in the future. Once a marketing channel is chosen, an organization usually must adhere to it for a substantial period of time. Some of the most complex and challenging decisions facing a firm concern the distribution function of marketing. According to McGinnis and LaLonde, the job of physical distribution managers has become so demanding that these individuals need to be actively involved in the strategic-management process.[16]

Marketing Research

Marketing research is the systematic gathering, recording, and analyzing of data about problems relating to the marketing of goods and services. Marketing research can uncover critical strengths and weaknesses. For example, recent marketing research regarding the three television networks, ABC, NBC, and CBS, reveals that NBC leads substantially in prime time ratings, while CBS leads in daytime programming.[17]

Marketing research activities obviously support all the other basic marketing functions and all the other major business functions of a company. Effective marketing research is particularly important during the strategy-formulation stage of the strategic-management process. Marketing research may be undertaken by impartial agencies or internally by businesses themselves. The marketing-research process can be viewed as consisting of five basic steps:

1. Defining the problem through exploratory research
2. Examining secondary data that is available within and external to the firm
3. Generating primary data through research design and data collection
4. Analyzing data
5. Making recommendations

Numerous scales, instruments, procedures, concepts, and techniques are employed by marketing researchers. A discussion of all of these concepts is not possible or appropriate in this text. However, the semantic differential scale is examined further here because it is commonly used in determining internal strengths and weaknesses and analyzing competitors.

The semantic differential is a research technique that consists of a list of bipolar (opposite) adjective scales, each of which is evaluated by respondents. Average ratings for all respondents are computed. An overall company or product profile emerges. This profile can be compared with competitors' profiles or to other products' ratings to reveal strategic information. An example semantic differential for the motel industry is given in Figure 5.3.

Opportunity Analysis

The eighth function of marketing is opportunity analysis, an appraisal of the costs, benefits, and risks associated with marketing-related and/or strategic decisions. Three steps are required to perform a cost/benefit analysis: (1) compute the total costs associated with a given strategy, (2) estimate the total benefits from the strategy, and (3) compare the total costs with the total benefits. As expected benefits exceed total costs, an opportunity becomes more attractive. Sometimes the variables included in a cost/benefit analysis cannot be quantified or even measured, but usually reasonable estimates can be made to allow the analysis to be performed. A key factor that must be considered in cost/benefit analyses is risk.

Social Responsibility

The final function of marketing, according to Evans and Berman, is social responsibility. Social responsibility includes a company's obligation to offer products and services that are safe, ethical, and reasonably priced. Recall from Chapter 3 that corporate social policy was described as essential for developing an effective mission statement. A clear social policy also facilitates efforts to perform a marketing audit. According to Chrisman and Carroll, the major problem with the contemporary view of social responsibility is that it is based on a mistaken notion:

Figure 5.3   A semantic differential scale

Please check the blanks that best indicate your feelings about Holiday Inn, Hilton Hotels, and Days Inn.

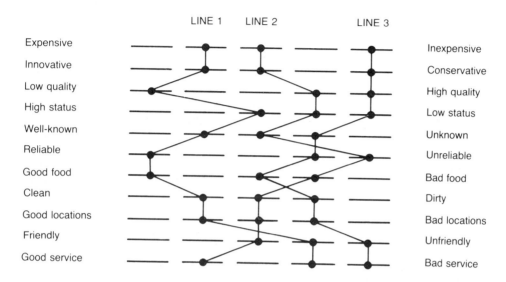

Legend:

Line 1 = Motel chain 1
Line 2 = Motel chain 2
Line 3 = Motel chain 3

What is especially unfortunate is how many business people have misinterpreted or misunderstood the concept of social responsibility. Many of them have viewed social responsibility as a focus which detracts from or is counter to their profit-minded pursuits. Although there may be some clearly distinct economic versus social concerns, there is a rather broad area in which economic and social concerns are consistent with one another. It is corporate activities which fall into this area that provide the more realistic view of social responsibility, that is, activities that are profitable but at the same time are socially responsible. When a firm engages in social activities, it must do so in a way that receives economic advantages. The net effect is that the firm simultaneously achieves social and economic objectives. This concept also recognizes that social activity can lead to economic rewards and that business should attempt to create such a favorable situation.[18]

Demands by special interest groups on business organizations have greatly increased since World War II. Arguments still rage today about how socially responsible a firm should be. Chief executive officers themselves exhibit a wide range of attitudes on this subject. Some side with the economist Milton Friedman who proclaims that organizations have no inherent obligation to society, yet others agree with Ralph Nader that organizations have immense social responsibility.

A classic article in the *Academy of Management Review* concludes that there is only a small relationship between social responsibility and organizational performance.[19] A description of social responsibility activities at Levi Strauss & Company is given in Exhibit 5.2. Although Levi Strauss is clearly committed to social responsibility, the company posted a 78 percent plunge in net income for 1984 over 1983. Levi Strauss closed fourteen domestic plants and five foreign plants in 1984, eliminating a total of 5,000 jobs. The expenses in closing plants were absorbed in 1984, and losses reflect this.

Exhibit 5.2   Levi Strauss on social responsibility

Social Responsibility

In the midst of this year's business difficulties, Levi Strauss & Co.'s long-standing emphasis on social responsibility was nationally recognized; the company became the first to receive in a single year two of the most prestigious awards for corporate philanthropy and volunteerism.

In ceremonies at the White House, the company received the President's Volunteer Action Award for Corporate Volunteerism on behalf of the employees and retirees who are members of the company's 90 Community Involvement Teams. In November, the company was named the winner of the Lawrence A. Wien prize in Corporate Social Responsibility for "its pioneering accomplishments in corporate philanthropy . . . and its profound commitment to its employees and to the communities in which they live."

That commitment was reflected in the assistance the company provided this year to employees and communities affected by plant closings. In addition to severance benefits, extended medical coverage and help in finding employment, affected employees were offered job-retraining and placement programs developed by the Community Affairs Department in conjunction with state and federal agencies.

Furthermore, the Levi Strauss Foundation will provide continuing funding for up to three years to select local organizations that had been supported by Community Involvement Teams or that served communities adversely affected by the closing of a company facility.

Community Affairs

Despite a difficult year, the company continued its charitable contributions programs. During 1984, Levi Strauss & Co. donations included more than $2 million to the Levi Strauss Foundation and nearly $1 million in direct contributions. Although these contributions are lower than in the past, the Foundation was able to continue its charitable work at a comparable level with last year by drawing on reserves that had been accumulated for this purpose during more prosperous periods. The grants last year again emphasized strengthening the family, the neighborhood and the community.

The company's expanded Employee Social Benefits Programs continued in 1984, with the Levi Strauss Foundation contributing increased funds to human service agencies, arts organizations and institutions of higher education to which employees made personal donations or served as volunteers or board members.

Minority Purchasing Program

Company policy encourages business transactions with minority-owned vendors. Under the program, such purchases last year increased to $23 million.

Equal Employment Opportunity

The relative positions of minorities and women in the company's work force increased in several job categories during 1984. After many years of steady improvement, however, there was a decline in the percentage of women and minorities in sales positions and in the percentage of women officials and managers; this was largely due to the 1984 reduction in force. The company is committed to reversing these declines and increasing representation of women and minorities in other job categories, specifically production and management.

The following table, a regular feature of this report, shows the percentage representation of minorities and women by employment classification in the company's domestic work force.

EEO comparative data

	%Women		%Minorities	
	1984	1983	1984	1983
Officials and Managers	32.4	33.0	21.6	18.0
Professionals	52.2	51.1	30.2	29.5
Technicians	46.4	40.0	40.0	36.5
Sales	19.9	21.0	10.7	11.2
Office and Clerical	84.0	83.7	46.6	41.7
Craftpersons	44.3	46.1	48.5	45.6
Operatives	87.5	87.8	57.9	56.9
Service Workers	34.6	34.1	59.6	53.5
Total	78.2	77.5	52.4	50.4

Source: Levi Strauss and Company, *1984 Annual Report,* pp. 11, 12.

A Marketing Audit Questionnaire

Organizations can identify marketing strengths and weaknesses by undertaking a comprehensive study called a marketing audit. Philip Kotler defines the marketing audit as a comprehensive, systematic, independent, and periodic examination of a company's marketing environment, objectives, strategies, and activities.[20] In both his graduate and undergraduate marketing textbooks, Kotler provides the most widely used marketing audit in the United States. Kotler's checklist of key marketing questions is given in Exhibit 5.3. These questions could be adapted to fit the marketing audit needs of almost any type or size of organization. The checklist of questions is not, of course, an exhaustive list of questions applicable to all organizations.

Exhibit 5.3   A marketing audit checklist

A Marketing Systems Audit

1. Is the marketing intelligence system producing accurate, sufficient, and timely information about marketplace developments with respect to customers, prospects, distributors and dealers, competitors, suppliers, and various publics?

2. Are company decision makers asking for enough marketing research, and are they using the results?

3. Is the company employing the best methods for market and sales forecasting?

4. Is the marketing planning system well conceived and effective?

5. Is sales forecasting and market potential measurement soundly carried out?

6. Are sales quotas set on a proper basis?

7. Are the control procedures adequate to ensure that the annual goals are being achieved?

8. Does management periodically analyze the profitability of products, markets, territories, and channels of distribution?

9. Are marketing costs periodically examined?

10. Is the company well organized to gather, generate, and screen new-product ideas?

11. Does the company do adequate concept research and business analysis before investing in new ideas?

12. Does the company carry out adequate product and market testing before launching new products?

A Marketing Productivity Audit

1. What is the profitability of the company's different products, markets, territories, and channels of distribution?

2. Should the company enter, expand, contract, or withdraw from any business segments and what would be the short- and long-run profit consequences?

3. Do any marketing activities seem to have excessive costs? Can cost-reducing steps be taken?

A Marketing Function Audit

1. What are the product-line objectives? Are these objectives sound? Is the current product line meeting the objectives?

2. Should the product line be stretched or contracted upward, downward, or both ways?

3. Which products should be phased out? Which products should be added?

4. What is the buyers' knowledge and attitudes toward the company's and competitors' product quality, features, styling, brand names, etc.? What areas of product strategy need improvement?

5. What are the pricing objectives, policies, strategies, and procedures? To what extent are prices set on cost, demand, and competitive criteria?

6. Do the customers see the company's prices as being in line with the value of its offer?

7. What does management know about the price elasticity of demand, experience curve effects, and competitors' prices and pricing policies?

8. To what extent are price policies compatible with the needs of distributors and dealers, suppliers, and government regulation?

9. What are the distribution objectives and strategies?

10. Is there adequate market coverage and service?

11. How effective are the following channel members: distributors, dealers, manufacturers' representatives, brokers, agents, etc.?

12. Should the company consider changing its distribution channels?

13. What are the organization's advertising objectives? Are they sound?

14. Is the right amount being spent on advertising? How is the budget determined?

15. Are the ad themes and copy effective? What do customers and the public think about the advertising?

16. Are the advertising media well chosen?

17. Is the internal advertising staff adequate?

18. Is the sales promotion budget adequate? Is there effective and sufficient use of sales promotion tools such as samples, coupons, displays, sales contests?

19. Is the publicity budget adequate? Is the public relations staff competent and creative?

20. What are the organization's sales-force objectives?

21. Is the sales force large enough to accomplish the company's objectives?

22. Is the sales force organized along the proper principles of specialization (territory, market, product)? Are there enough (or too many) sales managers to guide the field sales representatives?

23. Does the sales-compensation level and structure provide adequate incentive and reward?

24. Does the sales force show high morale, ability, and effort?

25. Are the procedures adequate for setting quotas and evaluating performances?

26. How does the company's sales force compare to competitors' sales forces?

Source: Philip Kotler, *Marketing Management: Analysis, Planning and Control,* © 1984, pp. 767–70. Adapted by permission of Prentice-Hall, Inc., Englewood Cliffs, New Jersey.

THE FINANCIAL AUDIT

Financial condition is often considered the single best measure of a firm's competitive position and overall attractiveness to investors. Determining an organization's financial strengths and weaknesses is essential to formulating strategies effectively. A firm's liquidity, leverage, working capital, profitability, asset utilization, cash flow, and equity position can eliminate some strategies as feasible alternatives. Financial factors often result in existing strategies being altered and implementation plans being changed.

The Functions of Finance

According to James Van Horne, three areas comprise the functions, or basic decision areas of finance: the investment decision, the financing decision, and the dividend decision.[21] Financial ratio analysis is the most widely used method for determining an organization's strengths and weaknesses in the investment, financing, and dividend areas. Since the functional areas of business are so interrelated, financial ratios can also signal strengths or weaknesses in management, marketing, production, and research and development activities.

The investment decision is sometimes called capital budgeting, which is the allocation and reallocation of capital to projects, products, assets, and divisions of an organization. Once strategies are formulated, capital budgeting decisions are required for successful strategy implementation. The investment decision determines how a firm's resources will be allocated, so this activity is examined further in Chapter 8.

The financing decision is concerned with determining the best financing mix or capital structure for the firm. This decision includes examination of the various methods by which a firm can raise capital—by issuing stock, increasing debt, selling assets, or using some combination of these approaches. The financing decision requires consideration of short-term versus long-term financing and working capital needs. Two key financial ratios that indicate whether a firm's financing decisions have been effective are the debt-to-equity ratio and the debt-to-total-assets ratio.

The third important function of finance is the dividend policy. Dividend decisions involve such issues as the percentage of earnings paid to stockholders, the stability of dividends paid over time, and the repurchase or issuance of stock. Dividend decisions determine the amount of funds that are retained in a firm compared to the amount paid out to stockholders. The benefits of paying dividends to investors must be balanced against the opportunity cost of retaining funds internally. There is no set formula on how to balance this tradeoff.

Three financial ratios that are helpful in evaluating a firm's dividend decisions are the earnings-per-share ratio, the dividends-per-share ratio, and the price-earnings ratio. For the following reasons, dividends are sometimes paid out even when funds could be better reinvested in the business or when the firm has to tap outside sources for the funds:

1. Paying cash dividends is customary. Failure to do so could be thought of as a stigma. A dividend change is considered a signal about the future.

2. Dividends represent a sales point for investment bankers. Some institutional investors can buy only dividend-paying stocks.

3. Shareholders often demand dividends, even in companies with great opportunities for reinvesting all available funds.

4. There exists a myth that paying dividends will result in a higher stock price.

Basic Types of Financial Ratios

Financial ratios are computed from an organization's income statement and balance sheet. Financial ratios are meaningful only when comparisons are made over time and to industry averages. Computing financial ratios is like taking a picture, because they reflect a situation at just one point in time. Comparing ratios over time and to industry averages is essential for uncovering positive and negative trends. Trend analysis, illustrated in Figure 5.4, is an excellent way to identify internal strengths and weaknesses in the functional areas of business. Trend analysis incorporates both the time and industry average dimensions of financial ratio analysis.

Financial ratios can be classified into five fundamental types:

1. Liquidity ratios. They measure a firm's ability to meet maturing short-term obligations.

   - Current ratio
   - Quick or acid-test ratio

Figure 5.4   A financial ratio trend analysis

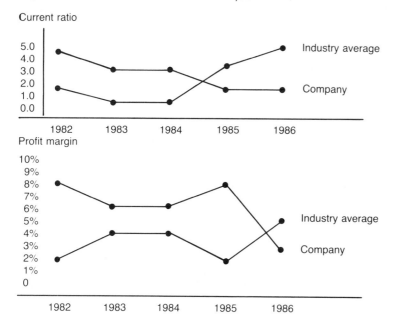

2. Leverage ratios. They measure the extent to which a firm has been financed by debt.
   - Debt-to-total-assets ratio
   - Debt-to-equity ratio
   - Long-term debt-to-equity ratio
   - Times-interest-earned (or coverage) ratio

3. Activity ratios. They measure how effectively a firm is using its resources.
   - Inventory turnover ratio
   - Total assets turnover
   - Fixed assets turnover
   - Average collection period

4. Profitability ratios. They measure management's overall effectiveness as shown by the returns generated on sales and investment.
   - Gross profit margin
   - Operating profit margin
   - Net profit margin
   - Return on total assets (ROA)
   - Return on stockholders' equity (ROE)
   - Earnings per share

5. Growth ratios. They measure a firm's ability to maintain its economic position in the growth of the economy and industry.
   - Sales
   - Net income
   - Earnings per share
   - Dividends per share
   - Price-earnings ratio

Table 5.3 provides a summary of the key financial ratios, showing how each ratio is calculated and what each ratio measures. Income statements and balance sheets for L. Luria & Son are given in Table 5.4. L. Luria is a rapidly expanding chain of retail stores based in Miami, Florida. Actual financial ratios, computed from L. Luria's income statements and balance sheets, are provided in Table 5.5. along with appropriate comparisons to the industry average.

There are four major sources of industry-average financial ratios. These sources are identified and described as follows:

1. Dun & Bradstreet's *Industry Norms and Key Business Ratios*—Fourteen different ratios are calculated in an industry-average format for 800 different types of businesses. The ratios are presented by Standard Industrial Classification (SIC) number and are grouped by annual sales into three size categories.

Table 5.3 A summary of key financial ratios

Ratio	How Calculated	What It Measures
Liquidity Ratios		
Current ratio	$\dfrac{\text{Current assets}}{\text{Current liabilities}}$	The extent to which a firm can meet its short-term obligations
Quick ratio	$\dfrac{\text{Current assets—inventory}}{\text{Current liabilities}}$	The extent to which a firm can meet its short-term obligations without relying upon the sale of its inventories
Leverage Ratios		
Debt-to-total-assets ratio	$\dfrac{\text{Total debt}}{\text{Total assets}}$	The percentage of total funds that are provided by creditors
Debt-to-equity ratio	$\dfrac{\text{Total debt}}{\text{Total stockholders' equity}}$	The percentage of total funds provided by creditors versus by owners
Long-term-debt-to-equity ratio	$\dfrac{\text{Long-term debt}}{\text{Total stockholders' equity}}$	The balance between debt and equity in a firm's long-term capital structure
Times-interest-earned ratio	$\dfrac{\text{Profits before interest and taxes}}{\text{Total interest charges}}$	The extent to which earnings can decline without the firm becoming unable to meet its annual interest costs.
Activity Ratios		
Inventory turnover	$\dfrac{\text{Sales}}{\text{Inventory of finished goods}}$	Whether a firm holds excessive stocks of inventories and whether a firm is selling its inventories slowly compared to the industry average
Fixed-assets turnover	$\dfrac{\text{Sales}}{\text{Fixed assets}}$	Sales productivity and plant and equipment utilization
Total-assets turnover	$\dfrac{\text{Sales}}{\text{Total assets}}$	Whether a firm is generating a sufficient volume of business for the size of its assest investment
Accounts-receivable turnover	$\dfrac{\text{Annual credit sales}}{\text{Accounts receivable}}$	(In percentage terms) the average length of time it takes a firm to collect credit sales
Average collection period	$\dfrac{\text{Accounts receivable}}{\text{Total sales/365 days}}$	(In days) the average length of time it takes a firm to collect on credit sales
Profitability Ratios		
Gross profit margin	$\dfrac{\text{Sales minus cost of goods sold}}{\text{Sales}}$	The total margin available to cover operating expenses and yield a profit
Operating profit margin	$\dfrac{\text{Earnings before interest and taxes (EBIT)}}{\text{Sales}}$	Profitability without concern for taxes and interest
Net profit margin	$\dfrac{\text{Net income}}{\text{Sales}}$	After-tax profits per dollar of sales
Return on total assets (ROA)	$\dfrac{\text{Net income}}{\text{Total assets}}$	After-tax profits per dollar of assets; this ratio is also called return on investment (ROI).
Return on stockholders' equity (ROE)	$\dfrac{\text{Net income}}{\text{Total stockholders' equity}}$	After-tax profits per dollar of stockholders' investment in the firm
Earnings per share (EPS)	$\dfrac{\text{Net income}}{\text{Number of shares of common stock outstanding}}$	Earnings available to the owners of common stock
Growth Ratios		
Sales	Annual percentage growth in total sales	Firm's growth rate in sales
Income	Annual percentage growth in profits	Firm's growth rate in profits
Earnings per share	Annual percentage growth in EPS	Firm's growth rate in EPS
Dividends per share	Annual percentage growth in dividends per share	Firm's growth rate in dividends per share
Price-earning ratio	$\dfrac{\text{Market price per share}}{\text{Earnings per share}}$	Faster-growing and less risky firms tend to have higher price-earnings ratios

Table 5.4 L. Luria & Son's income statements and balance sheets

	Income Statements	
	1983	*1982*
OPERATING INCOME		
Net sales	$123,836,350	$108,906,993
Cost of sales	83,861,108	74,001,486
Gross margin	39,975,242	34,905,507
OPERATING EXPENSES		
Selling, general, and		
administrative expenses	30,182,244	25,715,157
INCOME FROM OPERATIONS	9,792,998	9,190,350
INTEREST EXPENSE (INCOME)—NET	(187,831)	372,974
INCOME BEFORE TAXES	9,980,829	8,817,376
TAXES	4,425,000	4,195,000
NET INCOME	$ 5,555,829	$ 4,622,376
EARNINGS PER COMMON SHARE	$1.10	$1.03

	Balance Sheets	
	1983	*1982*
CURRENT ASSETS		
Cash and short-term investment	$ 3,866,645	$ 2,379,214
Accounts receivable	301,139	396,737
Inventories	49,594,357	35,412,048
Prepaid expenses	448,135	358,892
Total current assets	54,210,276	38,546,891
Land	1,335,072	1,335,072
Buildings	3,131,903	1,710,860
Furniture and equipment	5,968,936	4,654,652
Leasehold improvements	7,538,917	6,350,851
Construction in progress	993,790	153,828
Total	18,968,618	14,205,263
Less accumulated depreciation	5,213,185	4,000,288
Property—Net	13,755,433	10,204,975
Other Assets	354,585	322,161
TOTAL	$68,320,294	$49,074,027

	1983	1982
CURRENT LIABILITIES		
Notes payable:		
Bank	$ 10,000	$ 10,000
Suppliers, non-interest-bearing	659,817	1,648,801
Accounts payable:		
Trade	22,881,483	14,928,561
Other	1,079,417	950,795
Accrued liabilities:		
Income taxes	211,837	1,448,611
Other	972,691	896,823
Current portion of long-term debt	25,135	22,922
Total current liabilities	25,840,380	19,906,513
LONG-TERM DEBT		
9.25% Mortgage note payable	1,353,733	1,378,868
Note payable—bank	—	1,500,000
DEFERRED CREDITS	1,251,981	887,057
STOCKHOLDERS' EQUITY		
Common and preferred stock	52,800	45,000
Warrants	—	500
Additional paid-in capital	15,541,815	6,632,333
Retained earnings	24,279,585	18,723,756
Total stockholders' equity	39,874,200	25,401,589
TOTAL	$ 68,320,294	$ 49,074,027

Table 5.5   Financial ratio calculations for L. Luria & Son

	1983	1982	*Dun & Bradstreet 1983 Industry Avg. Catalog Retailers (SIC 5961)*
Liquidity Ratios			
Current Ratio	2.0979	1.9364	2.200
Quick Ratio	.1786	1.1575	.800
Leverage Ratios			
Debt-to-Total Assets	.4164	.4824	.372
Debt-to-Equity	.7134	.9319	.665
Long-Term-Debt-to-Equity	.0340	.0543	.592
Times Interest Earned	—	—	—
Activity Ratios			
Inventory Turnover	2.4970	3.0754	7.000
Fixed-Asset Turnover	9.0027	10.6720	11.780
Total-Asset Turnover	1.8126	2.2192	2.286
Accounts-Receivable Turnover	—	—	—
Avg. Collection Period	.8876	1.3297	14.600
Profitability Ratios			
Gross Profit Margin	32.28%	32.05%	33.8%
Operating Profit Margin	7.91%	8.44%	5.5%
Net Profit Margin	4.49%	4.24%	6.3%
Return on Total Assets	8.13%	9.42%	9.9%
Return on Stockholders' Equity	13.93%	18.20%	19.3%
Earnings Per Share	1.10	1.03	—
Growth Ratios (One-Year Growth)			
Sales	13.71%	20.21%	—
Income	20.19%	44.38%	—
EPS	6.80%	35.52%	—
Dividends per Share			
Price Earning Ratio			

Source: L. Luria & Son, *Annual Report*, 1983.

2. Robert Morris Associates, *Annual Statement Studies*—Sixteen different ratios are calculated in an industry-average format. Industries are referenced by Standard Industrial Classification (SIC) numbers, which are published by the U.S. Bureau of the Census. The ratios are presented in four size categories by annual sales and "for all firms" in the industry.

3. Troy Leo, *Almanac of Business and Industrial Financial Ratios*—Twenty-two financial ratios and percentages are provided in an industry-average format for all major in-

dustries. The ratios and percentages are given for twelve different company-size categories and for all firms in a given industry.

4. Federal Trade Commission Reports—The FTC publishes quarterly financial data including ratios on manufacturing companies. FTC reports include analyses by industry group and asset size.

Financial ratios analysis is not without some limitations. First of all, financial ratios are based on accounting data, and firms differ in their treatment of such items as depreciation, inventory valuation, research and development expenditures, pension plan costs, mergers, and taxes. Also, seasonal factors can influence comparative ratios when firms use different fiscal years. Therefore, conformity to industry composite ratios does not establish with certainty that a firm is performing normally or that it is well managed. Likewise, departures from industry averages do not always indicate that a firm is doing especially well or badly. For example, a high inventory-turnover ratio could indicate efficient inventory management and a strong working capital position, but it could also indicate a serious inventory shortage and a weak working capital position.

It is important to recognize that a firm's financial condition depends not only on the three functions of finance investment, financing, and dividend decisions, but also on many other factors that include (1) management, marketing, production, and research and development decisions, (2) actions by competitors, suppliers, distributors, creditors, customers, and shareholders, and (3) economic, social, demographic, political, governmental, and technological trends. So financial ratio analysis, like other analytical tools, should be used wisely with judgment and caution.

The McDonald's Corporation is an example firm that has many financial strengths. McDonald's sales in 1984 were up 11.5 percent from 1983; net income was up 13.5 percent to $389 million. McDonald's market share increased from 40 percent to 45 percent of the domestic burger market between 1981 and 1984. There were 8,304 McDonald's restaurants open on January 1, 1985. The company plans to open 500 new restaurants worldwide in 1985. Although McDonald's two major competitors, Burger King (#2) and Wendy's International (#3), are exceedingly aggressive, they have not weakened McDonald's financial position. According to McDonald's top management, almost 17 million people a day worldwide suffer Big Mac attacks or a sudden craving for Chicken McNuggets.[22]

The Sources and Uses of Funds Statement

A statement of changes in financial position, commonly called the *sources and uses of funds statement,* indicates where cash comes from and how it is used. The sources and uses of funds statement requires examination of a firm's balance sheet to determine changes in each asset and liability account from one period to the next. This examination provides useful information regarding a firm's past strategies. It contributes to a better understanding of the internal environment of a company and can reveal possible strengths and weaknesses. Changes in the balance sheet items from one year to the next must be tabulated and then classified as either sources or uses of funds. There are four essential uses of funds and four sources of funds, as follows:

USES OF FUNDS	SOURCES OF FUNDS
Increase in an asset account	Increase in a liability account
Decrease in a liability account	Decrease in an asset account
Decrease in an equity account	Increase in an equity account
Loss from operations	Profit from operations

A Financial Audit Questionnaire

Financial ratio analysis is the primary tool used to audit a firm's financial position. By calculating the twenty-two ratios described earlier and comparing them over time and to industry averages, a firm can identify particular strengths and weaknesses. A useful financial audit checklist of key questions follows in Exhibit 5.4. Negative answers signal possible financial weaknesses and positive answers indicate areas of strength. Strategic implications of these responses will again vary by organization and type of industry.

Exhibit 5.4 A financial audit checklist

Liquidity

1. Have the firm's liquidity ratios been increasing over time?

2. Are the firm's liquidity ratios above industry averages?

Leverage

1. Have the firm's leverage ratios been increasing over time?

2. Are the firm's leverage ratios below industry averages?

Activity

1. Have the firm's activity ratios been moving favorably over time?

2. Do the firm's activity ratios compare favorably with industry averages?

Profitability

1. Have the firm's profitability ratios been increasing over time?

2. Are the firm's profitability ratios above industry averages?

Growth

1. Have the firm's growth ratios been increasing over time?

2. Are the firm's growth ratios above industry averages?

THE PRODUCTION AUDIT

The production or operations function of a business consists of all those activities that transform inputs into goods and services. The types of inputs, transformations, and outputs that comprise production management vary across industries and environments. A manufacturing operation, for example, transforms or converts inputs such as raw materials, labor, capital, machines, and facilities into finished goods. Service operations transform inputs into needed services. A restaurant uses inputs such as meat, potatoes, vegetables, dairy products, and chefs to produce breakfasts, lunches, and dinners.

The Production Functions

Roger Schroeder suggests that production management consists of five functions or decision areas: process, capacity, inventory, work force, and quality. These functions of production or operations management are described in Exhibit 5.5.

Exhibit 5.5   The basic functions of production management

Function	Description
1. Process	Process decisions concern the design of the physical production system. Specific decisions include choice of technology, facility layout, process flow analysis, facility location, line balancing, process control, and transportation analysis.
2. Capacity	Capacity decisions concern determination of optimal output levels for the organization—not too much and not too little. Specific decisions include forecasting, facilities planning, aggregate planning, scheduling, capacity planning, and queuing analysis.
3. Inventory	Inventory decisions involve managing the level of raw materials, work in process, and finished goods. Specific decisions include what to order, when to order, how much to order, and materials handling.
4. Work Force	Work force decisions are concerned with managing the skilled, unskilled, clerical, and managerial employees. Specific decisions include job design, work measurement, job enrichment, work standards, and motivation techniques.
5. Quality	Quality decisions are aimed at assuring that high-quality goods and services are produced. Specific decisions include quality control, sampling, testing, quality assurance, and cost control.

Source: R. Schroeder, *Operations Management* (New York: McGraw-Hill Book Co., 1981): 12.

Production or operations activities often represent the largest part of a company's human and capital assets. In most industries, the major costs of producing a product or service are incurred within operations, so production management can have great value as a competitive weapon in a company's overall strategy. Strengths and weaknesses in the five functions of production can mean the success or failure of an enterprise. For example, the Goodyear Company's outstanding production facilities and procedures have resulted in the firm having a secure grip on one-third of the U.S. tire business and nearly one-fifth of the world market. *Fortune* summarized Goodyear's emphasis on production as follows:

> After a ten-year battle to hold its position as the world's largest tiremaker, Goodyear sits high atop the rubber heap these days. The Akron-based company has overwhelmed traditional U.S. competitors and faced down formidable foreigners—France's Michelin, Japan's Bridgestone—with production methods generally conceded to be the most efficient in the industry. Over the last ten years the company spent $3.2 billion to upgrade plant and equipment around the world, $2 billion of it tied directly to radials. Goodyear streamlined its production to offset the lower labor costs enjoyed by foreign competitors.[23]

Many professors, consultants, and top managers have recently expressed concern that organizations have not taken sufficient account of the capabilities and limitations of the operations part of a business. They contend that this neglect has had unfavorable consequences on corporate performance in America.[24] Production capabilities and policies can actually dictate corporate strategies:

> Given today's decision-making environment with shortages, inflation, technological booms, and government intervention, a company's manufacturing capabilities and operating policies may not be able to fulfill the demands dictated by strategic plans. As a matter of fact, manufacturing capabilities and policies may dictate corporate strategies. It is hard to imagine that an organization can formulate a strategic plan today before first considering the constraints and limitations imposed by its existing manufacturing structure. An integrative mechanism between strategic planning and manufacturing policy is essential.[25]

The functions of operations management should be harnessed in the pursuit of company objectives and goals. In Table 5.6, James Dillworth outlines several types of strategic decisions that a company might make and considers the implications for production management. A recent study of the best managed, most efficient factories in the United States revealed ten plants that exemplify superior American production management. These ten plants are identified and described in Table 5.7.

Table 5.6 Impact of strategy elements on production management

Possible Elements of Strategy	Concomitant Conditions That May Affect the Operations Function and Advantages and Disadvantages
1. Compete as low-cost provider of goods or services	Discourages competition. Broadens market. Requires longer production runs and fewer product changes. Requires special-purpose equipment and facilities.
2. Compete as high-quality provider	Often possible to obtain more profit per unit, and perhaps more total profit from a smaller volume of sales. Requires more quality-assurance effort and higher operating cost. Requires more precise equipment, which is more expensive. Requires highly skilled workers, necessitating higher wages and greater training efforts.
3. Stress customer service	Requires broader development of service people and service parts and equipment. Requires rapid response to customer needs or changes in customer tastes, rapid and accurate information system, careful coordination. Requires a higher inventory investment.
4. Provide rapid and frequent introduction of new products	Requires versatile equipment and people. Has higher research and development costs. Has high retraining costs and high tooling and changeover in manufacturing. Provides lower volumes for each product and fewer opportunities for improvements due to the learning curve.
5. Strive for absolute growth	Requires accepting some projects or products with lower marginal value, which reduces ROI. Diverts talents to areas of weakness instead of concentrating on strengths.
6. Seek vertical integration	Enables company to control more of the process. May not have economies of scale at some stages of process. May require high capital investment as well as technology and skills beyond those currently available within the organization.
7. Maintain reserve capacity for flexibility	Provides ability to meet peak demands and quickly implement some contingency plans if forecasts are too low. Requires capital investment in idle capacity. Provides capability to grow during the lead time normally required for expansion.
8. Consolidate processing (Centralize)	Can result in economies of scale. Can locate near one major customer or supplier. Vulnerability: one strike, fire, or flood can halt the entire operation.
9. Disperse processing of service (Decentralize)	Can be near several market territories. Requires more complex coordination network: perhaps expensive data transmission and duplication of some personnel and equipment at each location. If each location produces one product in the line, then other products still must be transported to be available at all locations. If each location specializes in a type of component for all products, the company is vulnerable to strike, fire, flood, etc. If each location provides total product line, then economies of scale may not be realized.
10. Stress the use of mechanization, automation, robots	Requires high capital investment. Reduces flexibility. May affect labor relations. Makes maintenance more crucial.
11. Stress stability of employment	Serves the security needs of employees and may develop employee loyalty. Helps to attract and retain highly skilled employees. May require revisions of make-or-buy decisions, use of idle time, inventory, and subcontractors as demand fluctuates.

From *Production and Operations Management: Manufacturing and Nonmanufacturing, Second Edition,* by J. Dilworth. Copyright © 1983 by Random House, Inc. Reprinted by permission of the publisher.

Table 5.7   America's best-managed factories

Company	Location	Product
AT&T Technologies	Richmond, Virginia	Circuit boards
Chaparral Steel	Midlothian, Texas	Steel products
Dana Corp.'s Spicer Division	Auburn, Indiana	Truck clutches
E.T. Wright & Co.	Rockland, Massachusetts	Men's shoes
General Electric	Erie, Pennsylvania	Locomotives
General Electric	Louisville, Kentucky	Dishwashers
Hewlett–Packard	Waltham, Massachusetts	Medical electronics
IBM	East Fishkill, New York	Semiconductors
Lincoln Electric	Cleveland, Ohio	Welding equipment
Nissan Motor	Smyrna, Tennessee	Pickup trucks

Source: "America's Best-Managed Factories," *Fortune* (28 May 1984): 16–24.

The *Fortune* article also said the following:

> The best-run factories don't look alike when you first walk into them. Stepping into GE's spanking new dishwasher plant is like stepping into the Hyatt Regency. By comparison, stepping into Lincoln Electric's thirty-three-year-old, cavernous, dimly lit factory is like stumbling into a dingy big-city gymnasium. It's only when one starts looking at how these factories do things that similarities become apparent.
>
> The best plants are merging design with manufacturing into a continuous, smoothly flowing process. This represents a radical improvement over the more conventional practice of inspecting a product at the end of the line and then fusing over what may be wrong.
>
> Managers of the best-run plants convince workers that the factory's survival, and everyone's job, depends on being tops in quality. To this end, they often display the products of rival manufacturers right on the factory floor to show just how good the competition is.
>
> Managers of the best plants think they have found the key to quality and productivity in flexible automation. This kind of automation makes it possible to use the same machines to process different parts; they don't have to be retooled or set up anew each time.
>
> Managers of the best plants have convinced workers that their enemy is not management, but rather it's the competition, and that they must pull together to survive. In fact, managers and workers at the best plants have merged into a single team. These shops aren't holding worker-management love-ins, nor have workers' complaints stopped, but in general, trust has

replaced strife, and communication has been substituted for confrontation. In most well-managed plants, workers now get frequent reports on plant profits, product quality and cost, the competitive situation, and other subjects—information not normally released in less efficient plants.[26]

A Production Audit Questionnaire

An audit instrument is provided in Exhibit 5.6 to aid strategists in identifying strengths and weaknesses in the functional areas of production. This set of questions does not, of course, apply to all types of production systems, but it can aid in identifying strengths and weaknesses for many firms. General Motors recently completed a production audit of its manufacturing facilities and determined a need to redesign and overhaul its basic production system and processes. GM is converting assembly-line operations to modular production processes, as described recently in a *Wall Street Journal* article:

> Picture how a typical American auto-assembly plant now builds a car. Workers are strung out along miles of assembly lines. Cars are assembled one task at a time out of 10,000 or so parts. Modular assembly, as GM envisions it, would change much of that. Under modular construction, parts are first subassembled into a few fairly large components called "modules." Workers or teams of workers posted at stationary work stations put the modules together, and instead of having one or only a few tasks to do, they perform a cluster of tasks, such as building a whole fender or front end. Trolleys carrying the partly completed cars move at command from station to station.[27]

Exhibit 5.6   A production audit checklist

Process

1. Are facilities located effectively?

2. Are facilities designed effectively?

3. Should the organization be integrated backward or forward to a greater extent?

4. Are transportation costs for receiving and shipping excessive?

5. Is the process technology that is being used appropriate?

6. Is an effective and efficient flow or sequence of operations being used to convert inputs into outputs?

   - Line flow—characterized by a linear sequence of operations used to make the product or service; extremely efficient but also extremely inflexible. Examples are cafeterias and automobile assembly lines.

   - Intermittent flow—characterized by production in batches at intermittent intervals; equipment and labor are organized into work centers by similar types of skill or equipment. Examples are the flow operations used by fast-food restaurants and hospitals.

- Project flow—characterized by a sequence of operations used to produce a unique product; no real product flow; used when there is a great need for creativity and uniqueness. Examples are developing a new product or building a ship.

7. Is the product or service being made to order, made to stock, or both? Is this activity most effective and efficient?

- Made to order—processing activities are keyed to individual customer orders; process consists of customer placing an order, firm responding with a price and delivery date, and customer accepting or rejecting the offer. Delivery time and control of order flow are critical. Examples are a restaurant operation and painting a portrait.

- Made to stock—process consists of producing a standardized product line; inventories are maintained to meet, say, a 95 percent service level of orders. Forecasting, inventory management, and capacity planning are critical. Examples are a furniture plant and oil refinery.

Capacity

1. Is overall demand for the product or service regularly and effectively forecasted?
2. Are appropriate economies of scale achieved?
3. Are factories, warehouses, and stores located effectively?
4. Are there an appropriate number of factories, warehouses, and stores?
5. Are factories, warehouses, and stores of an appropriate size?
6. Have aggregate planning costs been determined and minimized?
   - Hiring and firing costs
   - Overtime and undertime costs
   - Inventory-carrying costs
   - Subcontracting costs
   - Part-time labor costs
   - Cost of stockout or back order
7. Are loading, scheduling, and dispatching activities performed effectively?
8. Have strategies been developed for dealing with nonuniform demand?
9. Does the firm have an effective and efficient production control system?

Inventory

1. Have the costs of producing or buying needed inventories been examined?
2. Have inventory carrying costs been determined?
3. Have inventory ordering costs been determined?
4. Have purchasing, receiving, and shipping costs been determined?
5. Have stockout costs been determined?
6. Have service level versus inventory level considerations been examined?
7. Have appropriate production lot sizes been determined?

8. Does the firm have an effective inventory control system?
   - Single-bin system
   - Two-bin system
   - Card-file system
   - Computerized system
   - Economic Order Quantity (EOQ) system
   - Materials Requirements Planning (MRP) system
   - Order-point systems

Work Force

1. Have time and motion studies been completed on all operations-related jobs?
2. Have production jobs been designed effectively and efficiently?
3. Are production management employees competent, efficient, and motivated?
4. Are production standards clear, reasonable, and effective?
5. Have productivity rewards and sanctions been established?
6. Have reasonable and effective operations policies been established?
7. Are absenteeism and turnover rates low among production employees?
8. Is employee morale high among production employees?
9. Are the firm's operations managers effective leaders?

Quality

1. Does the organization have an effective and efficient quality control system?
2. Have the following quality control costs been determined and evaluated?
   - Prevention costs, such as the cost of training and development programs, and marketing studies to determine customers' quality needs and desires?
   - Appraisal costs, such as the cost of determining the quality of incoming raw materials, sampling procedures, finished goods inspections and tests, and operating laboratories?
   - Internal failure costs, such as the cost of scrap material, downtime, retesting, and inspections?
   - External failure costs, such as the cost of refunds, repairing products, replacing products, and settling customer complaints?[28]

THE RESEARCH AND DEVELOPMENT AUDIT

The fifth major area of internal operations that needs to be examined for specific strengths and weaknesses is research and development. There are many firms today that conduct no research and development, and yet there are many other companies that depend on successful research and development activities for survival. Firms pursuing a product development strategy especially need to have a strong R&D orientation. Re-

Table 5.8   Research and development expenditures at the Grumman Corporation

Year	Internal R&D	External R&D	Total R&D
1981	$31,567,000	$52,000,000	$ 83,567,000
1982	38,267,000	57,600,000	95,867,000
1983	53,531,000	64,200,000	117,731,000
1984	78,125,000	76,000,000	154,125,000

Source: Grumman Corporation, Form 10K, 1984, p. 6.

search and development expenditures by American companies increased at an average annual rate of 16 percent in the early 1980s. Total R&D expenditures by U.S. industry and the federal government exceeded $100 billion in 1984. Energy firms, high-technology industries, and the Reagan administration have led the growth in R&D expenditures.

A recent survey of over 700 companies by Booz, Allen & Hamilton suggests that companies expect 31 percent of their profits over the next five years to come from new products.[29] A new-product development strategy in organizations can take two basic forms: (1) internal product development where the firm operates its own research and development department, and (2) contract product development in which the firm hires independent researchers or independent agencies to develop specific products. Many companies now utilize both of these approaches to develop new products. For example, see the internal/external breakdown of R&D expenditures by the Grumman Corporation, provided in Table 5.8.

The costs and risks associated with research and development activities can be excessive. Most firms have no choice but to continually develop new and improved products, because of changing consumer needs and tastes, new technologies, shortened product life cycles, and increased domestic and foreign competition. Studies indicate that the new-product failure rates for consumer products, industrial products, and service-related products are about 40 percent, 20 percent, and 18 percent, respectively.[30]

Research and Development Functions

Research and development can be viewed as consisting of three major decision areas or functions: basic and applied research, new-product development, and pilot plant or prototype testing. Cost distributions among the three major R&D activities can vary by company and industry, but total R&D costs generally do not exceed the resultant manufacturing and marketing start-up costs. Four approaches to determining R&D budget allocations have been used successfully: (1) financing as many project proposals as possible, (2) using a percentage-of-sales method, (3) budgeting for R&D about what competitors spend, or (4) deciding how many successful new products are needed and working backwards to estimate the required R&D investment.

Basic research can be described as investigating physical phenomena without any predetermined use for the knowledge. Applied research, in contrast, consists of undertaking studies to determine specific applications of general knowledge. Both basic and applied research can be conducted in either laboratory or field settings. Research ideas can be gained from many sources that include customers, salespeople, wholesalers, retailers, competitors, trade shows, patent offices, the Library of Congress, inventors, consultants, trade associations, and advertising agencies.

Whenever a potentially successful idea is discovered through basic or applied research, R&D managers must then develop the idea into a marketable product or service. Developmental activities can include both concept and design modifications, as well as improvements and testing. Some firms have neither the financial nor human resources to conduct basic and applied research, so they monitor the research efforts of other firms and then strive to develop others' ideas into successful products and services of their own.

Developing successful new products can take R&D departments days, weeks, months, or even years. According to company spokesmen, General Foods' R&D managers spent four months developing a brand of coffee that was "bold, vigorous, and deep tasting." It can take several years to develop products such as computers and commercial aircraft.

A number of factors suggest that successful new-product development is becoming more difficult, more costly, and more risky. A shortage of new-product ideas, increased global competition, increased market segmentation, strong special-interest groups, and increased government regulation have reduced successful new-product development in many industries. In the pharmaceutical industry, for example, only one out of every 10,000 drugs created in the laboratory ends up on pharmacists' shelves.

Before manufacturing and marketing start-up can begin, R&D managers must perform pilot plant or prototype tests. These tests involve rigorous examinations of the product or service, both in laboratory settings and field trials. A firm must make sure that its new product or service performs safely, cleanly, and efficiently. In one recent case of equipment testing, the Bissell Company's prototype tests of a combination electric vacuum cleaner and floor scrubber revealed that their product was too heavy, did not glide easily, and left residue on the floor.[31]

R&D by Outsiders

Research and development does not have to be carried on in-house, but can be purchased outside the company, mainly from two sources—independent research laboratories and universities. In some industries, separate companies have formed solely to do basic and applied research for other firms. Specialized research companies offer the needed scientists, technicians, information, raw materials, and facilities to successfully research, develop, and test various products and services. When a firm uses a university as a vehicle for obtaining needed research and development work, individual faculty members usually will be hired to conduct research in their own areas of expertise. Sometimes a research and development contract will be made with a university itself.

Another widely used approach for obtaining outside research and development assistance is to pursue a joint-venture strategy with another firm. Joint ventures in R&D are particularly effective when the research project will be of value to several companies or to an entire industry. In these arrangements, all research, development, and testing costs are shared, and of course the results are also shared. For example, Abbott Laboratories recently formed an R&D venture with a Japanese firm. The new joint venture produced six new drug applications in a short period of time.[32] (On occasion, the potential for antitrust action by the Justice Department has kept some firms from forming joint ventures.)

Regardless of whether a company employs its own research and development staff, hires outside sources, or uses a combination of these two approaches, new product research, development, and testing has become vital for success in many organizations. Research and development strengths and weaknesses can play a major role in the strategy-formulation process.

A Research and Development Audit Questionnaire

A research and development audit questionnaire is provided to help you identify areas where an organization is particularly strong or weak in its R&D activities. Like the preceding audit questionnaires, this checklist of questions is not an exhaustive list for all organizations. *NO* answers to the key questions simply indicate potential internal weaknesses, and *YES* answers simply suggest areas of strength.

Exhibit 5.7   A research and development audit checklist

1. Has the organization examined the research and development practices in its basic industry?
2. Does the organization have the personnel needed to conduct successful research and development?
3. Does the organization have the facilities and equipment needed to conduct successful research and development?
4. Does the organization have the information flows and resources needed to conduct successful research and development?
5. Has the organization investigated the relative benefits of focusing R&D efforts on existing versus new products?
6. Has the organization examined the tradeoffs between developing new and improved products on the one hand, and developing new and improved production processes on the other?
7. Has the organization established a research and development department?

8. Does the organization allocate sufficient human and capital resources to conduct successful research and development?

9. Does the organization capitalize on available sources of new product ideas?

10. Is the organization prepared to take the risk of instituting long periods of research without discovering ideas that have commercial value?

11. Is the organization prepared to take the risk of financing long periods of product development and testing without eventual successful marketing of the product?

12. Does the organization have, or can it obtain, needed capital to exploit discoveries if and when they are made?

13. Has the organization examined the potential benefits of using outside agencies or individuals to conduct basic and applied research for the firm?

14. Has the organization established clear research and development goals and policies?

15. Does the organization understand the research and development strategies of its major competitors?

16. Has the organization considered joint ventures in research and development?

17. Is the organization knowledgeable about domestic and foreign licenses, royalty fees, patents, trademarks, and other regulatory concerns applicable to research and development activities in its basic industry?

18. Does the organization have an overall research and development strategy?

THE INTERNAL FACTOR EVALUATION MATRIX

The final step in conducting an internal strategic-management audit is to construct an Internal Factor Evaluation Matrix. This strategy-formulation analytical tool summarizes and evaluates the major strengths and weaknesses in management, marketing, finance, production, and research and development. It provides a basis for examining interrelationships among the functional areas of business.

Subjective judgments are required in developing an Internal Factor Evaluation Matrix, so the appearance of a scientific approach should not mislead strategists into thinking that this is an all-powerful technique. All analytical tools can be abused if applied indiscriminately without good judgment.[33] Five steps are required to develop the Internal Factor Evaluation Matrix:

1. Identify the organization's key strengths and weaknesses.

2. Assign a weight that ranges from 0.0 (not important) to 1.0 (all-important) to each factor. The weight indicates the relative importance of each factor in being successful within a given industry. Regardless of whether key factors are internal strengths or weaknesses, those factors considered to have the greatest impact on performance should be assigned high weights. The summation of all weights assigned to the factors must total 1.0.

3. Assign a 1 to 4 rating to each factor, to indicate whether that variable represents a major weakness (rating = 1), a minor weakness (rating = 2), a minor strength (rating = 3), or a major strength (rating = 4).

4. Multiply each factor's weight by its rating to determine a weighted score for each variable.

5. Sum the weighted scores for each variable to determine the total weighted score for an organization.

Regardless of how many factors are included in an Internal Factor Evaluation Matrix, the total weighted score can range from a low of 1.0 to a high of 4.0, with the average score being 2.5. Total weighted scores well below 2.5 characterize organizations that are weak internally, whereas scores significantly above 2.5 indicate organizations with a strong internal position. The Internal Factor Evaluation Matrix should include from five to twenty key factors, but the number of factors has no effect upon the range of total weighted scores.

An example Internal Factor Evaluation Matrix is provided in Table 5.9. Note that the firm's major weakness is the absence of an organizational structure, as indicated by a rating of 1, whereas the firm's major strength is product quality, which received a rating of 4. Organizational structure and employee morale have the greatest impact on organizational performance in this industry, as indicated by assigned weights of .30 and .22 respectively. The total weighted score of 2.31 indicates that the firm is just below average in its overall internal strategic position.

In multidivisional firms, each autonomous division or strategic business unit should construct an Internal Factor Evaluation Matrix. Divisional matrices can then be integrated to develop an overall corporate matrix. The Internal Factor Evaluation Matrix, coupled with the External Factor Evaluation Matrix, the Competitive Profile Matrix, and a clear statement of mission, provide the input information needed to successfully formulate competitive strategies.

Table 5.9 A sample Internal Factor Evaluation Matrix

Key Internal Factor	Weight	Rating	Weighted Score
Employee morale is low.	0.22	2	0.44
Product quality is excellent.	0.18	4	0.72
Profit margins exceed industry average.	0.10	3	0.30
Excess working capital is available.	0.15	3	0.45
No organizational structure exists.	0.30	1	0.30
No research and development staff is employed.	0.05	2	0.10
Total	1.00		2.31

CONCLUSION

The notion that periodic audits of a firm's internal operations are vital to corporate health continues to be discussed in board rooms across America. Many companies still prefer to be judged solely on their bottom-line performance. However, an ever-increasing number of successful organizations are using the internal audit to gain a competitive advantage over firms that do not utilize a strategic-management approach to decision making. This chapter has described important tools and concepts needed to conduct an internal audit effectively.

Systematic methodologies for performing strength–weakness assessments are not well developed in the strategic-management literature, but it is clear that important internal and external factors must be identified, evaluated, and matched to formulate competitive strategies effectively. This chapter offers a practical framework for conducting an internal strength–weakness analysis that is applicable to all types of organizations. Audit-question checklists are provided to facilitate your internal audit efforts when analyzing a business policy case.

REVIEW QUESTIONS

1. How would the time allocated to long-run versus short-run planning differ for top-, middle-, and lower-level managers?

2. How would clear job descriptions and job specifications for jet airline pilots aid in the strategy-implementation efforts of United Airlines?

3. How can delegation of authority contribute to an effective strategic-management process?

4. Diagram a formal organizational chart that reflects the following positions: a president, two executive officers, four middle managers, and eighteen lower-level managers. Now diagram three overlying and hypothetical informal group structures. How can this information be helpful to a chief executive officer in formulating and implementing strategy?

5. There are several approaches that can be used to measure an individual's performance. Which method do you prefer? Why? Discuss the advantages and disadvantages of tying wage increases directly to performance-evaluation measures.

6. Which of the fundamental functions of marketing would be most important to the success of a market-development strategy for the following institutions:

A bank

A hospital

A university

A fast food restaurant

7. When a percentage change in price results in an even greater percentage change in quantity purchased, this is called elastic demand. When a percentage change in price results in an equal percentage change in quantity, we speak of unitary elasticity of demand. Inelastic demand refers to the situation where a percentage change in price results in a corresponding smaller percentage change in quantity. How would you describe the demand for the following products, and what are the strategic implications of this demand for manufacturers of these products?

Luxury cars

Economy cars

Personal computers

Furniture

8. Construct a five-item semantic differential scale that could be used by Mary Kay Cosmetics to assess consumer

attitudes in the cosmetic industry. Compare Avon and Mary Kay products on the five items.

9. On the following ten-point scale, describe your attitude toward social responsibility.

Ralph Nader's position								Milton Friedman's position	
1	2	3	4	5	6	7	8	9	10

How could a chief executive officer's attitude toward social responsibility affect a firm's strategy?

10. Which of the three major functions of finance do you feel is most important in a small electronics manufacturing concern? Justify your position.

11. Looking at Table 5.5, identify L. Luria's key financial strengths and weaknesses.

12. Describe the production system in a police department. How could strengths and weaknesses in production affect a police department's strategy?

13. From a strategic viewpoint, what are the overall costs versus benefits of conducting research and development internally versus externally in an organization?

14. After conducting an internal audit, a firm discovers a total of 100 strengths and 100 weaknesses. What procedures could then be used to determine the most important factors? Why is it important to reduce the total number of key factors?

FOOTNOTES

1 Claude George, Jr, *The History of Management Thought,* 2nd ed. (Englewood Cliffs, N.J.: Prentice-Hall, 1972): 174.

2 Z. Malik and D. Karger, "Does LR Planning Improve Company Performance?" *Management Review* (September 1975): 27–31.

3 "Changing a Corporate Culture," *Business Week* (May 14, 1984): 130, 131.

4 M. Bisesi, "Strategies for Successful Leadership in Changing Times," *Sloan Management Review* (Fall 1983): 62.

5 John A. Pearce, II and Fred David, "A Social Network Approach to Organizational Design–Performance," *Academy of Management Review* 8, no. 3 (July 1983): 436–44.

6 "The New Shape of Banking," *Business Week* (June 18, 1984): 108.

7 "RCA: Will It Ever Be a Top Performer?" *Business Week* (April 2, 1984): 52.

8 C. Gitzendanner, K. Misa, and R. Stein, "Management's Involvement in Human Resources," *Management Review* (October 1983): 13.

9 Stello Nkomo, "Stage Three in Personnel Administration: Strategic Human Resources Management," *Personnel* (July–August 1980): 75.

10 Stephen Harper, "A Developmental Approach to Performance Appraisal," *Business Horizons* (September–October 1983): 69.

11 J. Evans and B. Berman, *Marketing* (New York: Macmillan, 1982): 17.

12 "Simmons Data Profiles Buyers of USA Today," *Editor and Publisher* (May 7, 1983): 10.

13 C. Mortimer, "The Creative Factor in Marketing" (Lecture, Philadelphia Chapter, American Marketing Association, May 13, 1959).

14 Peter Drucker, *The Practice of Management* (New York: Harper & Row, 1954): 37.

15 P. Kotler, *Marketing Management* 5th ed. (Englewood Cliffs, N.J.: Prentice-Hall, 1984): 658.

16 M. McGinnis and B. Lalonde, "The Physical Distribution Manager and Strategic Planning," *Managerial Planning* 31, no. 5 (March–April 1983): 39.

17 "NBC's Emmy Showing," *Broadcasting* (August 12, 1985): 54.

18 James Chrisman and Archie Carroll, "Corporate Responsibility—Reconciling Economic and Social Goals," *Sloan Management Review* (Winter 1984): 61. Also, Philip Cochran and Robert Wood, "Corporate Social Responsibility and Financial Performance," *Academy of Management Journal* 22, no. 1 (March 1984): 42–56.

Also, an excellent discussion of current social-responsibility thought is provided in Peter Drucker, "The Meaning of Corporate Social Responsibility," *California Management Review* XXVI, no. 2 (Winter 1984): 53–63.

19 P. Arlow and M. Gannon, "Social Responsiveness, Corporate Structure, and Economic Performance," *Academy of Management Review* 7, no. 2 (1982): 239.

20 P. Kotler, W. Gregor, and W. Rodgers, "The Marketing Audit Comes of Age," *Sloan Management Review* (Winter 1977): 25–43.

21 J. V. Horne. *Financial Management and Policy*, (Englewood Cliffs, N.J.: Prentice-Hall, 1974), 10.

22 Stephen Kindel, "Where's the Growth?" *Forbes* (April 23, 1984): 80.

23 Kenneth Labich, "The King of Tires Is Discontented," *Fortune* (May 28, 1984): 64.

24 R. Lubar, "Rediscovering the Factory," *Fortune* (July 13, 1981): 54. Also, "New Breed of Strategic Planner: Number-Crunching Professionals Are Giving Way to Line Managers," *Business Week* (September 17, 1984): 62–68.

25 W. Bouldon and B. Saladin, "Let's Make Production-Operations Management Top Priority for Strategic Planning in the 1980s," *Managerial Planning* 32, no. 1 (July–August 1983): 19.

26 "America's Best-Managed Factories," *Fortune* (May 28, 1984): 16–24.

27 Amal Nag, "Gearing Down: To Build a Small Car, GM Tries to Redesign Its Production System," *Wall Street Journal* (May 14, 1984): 1, 12.

28 R. Schroeder, *Operations Management* (New York: McGraw-Hill, 1981), 528.

29 *New Products Management for the 1980s* (New York: Booz, Allen & Hamilton, 1982).

30 D. Hopkins and E. Bailey, "New Product Pressures," *Conference Board Record* (June 1971): 16–24.

31 R. Westfall and H. Boyd, Jr., *Cases in Marketing Management* (Homewood, Ill.: Richard Irwin, 1961): 365.

32 "Abbott: Profiting from Products That Cut Costs," *Business Week* (June 18, 1984): 60.

33 "New Breed of Strategic Planner: Number-Crunching Professionals Are Giving Way to Line Managers," *Business Week* (September 17, 1984): 62–68.

SUGGESTED READINGS

Alexander, R. *Marketing Definitions: A Glossary of Marketing Terms.* Chicago, I11.: American Marketing Association, 1960, 16.

Arlow, P., and M. Gannon. "Social Responsiveness, Corporate Structure, and Economic Performance." *Academy of Management Review* 7, no. 2 (1982): 235–41.

Bisesi, M. "SMR Forum: Strategies for Successful Leadership in Changing Times." *Sloan Management Review* (Fall 1983): 61–64.

Boulton, W.R., and B.A. Saladin. "Let's Make Production/Operations Management Top Priority for Strategic Planning in the 1980s." *Managerial Planning* 32, no. 1 (July–August 1983): 14–21.

Carleton, W., and J. Davis. "Financing of Strategic Action." In *From Strategic Planning to Strategic Action.* Manchester, England: John Wiley and Sons, 1976.

"Changing a Corporate Culture." *Business Week* (May 14, 1983): 130–38.

Cravens, D.W. "Strategic Marketing's New Challenge." *Business Horizons* (March–April 1983): 18–24.

Cushing, B., and C.R. Cushing. "Periodic Audits Hold a Mirror Up to Management." *Management Review* (March 1982): 57–61.

David, F.R. "Formulating Strategies Objectively: Analytical Tools." *Handbook of Business Strategy—1985/1986 Yearbook* (November 1985).

Dillsworth, J. *Production and Operations Management.* 2nd ed. New York: Random House, 1983.

Doz, Y.L., and C.K. Prahalad. "Headquarters Influence and Strategic Control in MNCs." *Sloan Management Review* 23, no. 1 (Fall 1981): 15–29.

Drucker, P. *The Practice of Management.* New York: Harper & Row, 1954.

Edwards, M.R., M. Wolfe, and J.R. Sproull. "Improving Comparability in Performance Appraisal." *Business Horizons* (September–October 1983): 75–83.

Evans, J. R., and B. Berman. *Marketing*. New York: Macmillan, 1982.

Gitzendanner, C., K.F. Misa, and R.T. Stein. "Management's Involvement in the Strategic Utilization of the Human Resource." *Management Review* (October 1983): 13–17.

Goretsky, M.E. "Frameworks of Strategic Marketing Information Needs." *Industrial Marketing Management* 12 (1983): 7–11.

Greenley, G.E. "Where Marketing Planning Fails." *Long Range Planning* 16 (February 1983): 106–15.

Harper, S.C. "A Developmental Approach to Performance Appraisal." *Business Horizons* (September–October 1983): 68–74.

Harris, J.M., R.W. Shaw Jr., and W.P. Sommers. "The Strategic Management of Technology." *Planning Review* (January 1983): 28–35.

Horne, J.V. *Financial Management and Policy*. 3rd ed. Englewood Cliffs, N.J.: Prentice–Hall, 1974.

Kahalas, H. "Planning for Organizational Design." *Managerial Planning* 31, no. 6 (May–June 1983): 4–8, 45.

Kelley, C.A. "Auditing the Planning Process." *Managerial Planning* 32, no. 4 (January–February 1984): 12–14.

Kimmerly, W.C. "R&D Strategic Planning in Turbulent Environments." *Managerial Planning* 31, no. 5 (March–April 1983): 8–13.

King, W.R. "Integrating Strength-Weakness Analysis Into Strategic Planning." *Journal of Business Research* 11 (1983): 475–87.

Kotler, P. *Marketing Management*. 5th ed. Englewood Cliffs, N.J.: Prentice–Hall, 1984.

Kotler, P., W. Gregor, and W. Rodgers. "The Marketing Audit Comes of Age." *Sloan Management Review* (Winter 1977): 25–43.

Kuczmarski, T.D., and S.J. Silver. "Strategy: The Key to Successful New-Product Development." *Management Review* (July 1982): 26–41.

Leontiades, M. "The Importance of Integrating Marketing Planning with Corporate Planning." *Journal of Business Research* 11 (1983): 457–73.

Malernee, J.K. Jr., and G. Jaffe. "An Integrative Approach to Strategic and Financial Planning." *Managerial Planning* (January–February 1982): 35–43.

Malik, Z., and D. Karger. "Does LR Planning Improve Company Performance?" *Management Review* (September 1975): 27–31.

Mansfield, E. *The Production and Application of New Industrial Technology*. New York: W.W. Norton, 1977, 71.

McGinnis, M.A., and B.J. LaLonde. "The Physical Distribution Manager and Strategic Planning." *Managerial Planning* 31, no. 5 (March–April 1983): 39–42, 48.

Nag, A. "Gearing Down: To Build a Small Car, GM Tries to Redesign Its Production System." *Wall Street Journal* (May 14, 1984): 1, 12.

Naylor, T.H., and K. Neva. "The Planning Audit." *Managerial Planning* (September–October 1979): 31–37.

Newman, W.H., and J.P. Logan. *Strategy, Policy, and Central Management*. 9th ed. Cincinnati, Ohio: South–Western Publishing Co., 1985.

Nkomo, S.M. "Stage Three in Personnel Administration: Strategic Human Resources Management." *Personnel* (July–August 1980): 69–77.

Pearce, J.A. II, and F.R. David. "A Social Network Approach to Organizational Design–Performance." *Academy of Management Review* 8, no. 3 (July 1983): 436–44.

Porter, M.E. "The Contributions of Industrial Organization to Strategic Management." *Academy of Management Review* 6, no. 4 (1981): 609–20.

Robertson, T.S., and Y. Wind. "Marketing Strategy: New Directions for Theory and Research." *Journal of Marketing* (Spring 1983): 12–24.

Schroeder, R. *Operations Management*. New York: McGraw–Hill, 1981.

Smith, E.C. "How To Tie Human Resource Planning to Strategic Business Planning." *Managerial Planning* (September–October 1983): 29–34.

Smith, M.J. "Job Evaluation Systems Fail To Meet Current Needs." *Managerial Planning* 32, no. 4 (January–February 1984): 36–43.

Sommers, D.E. "Industrial Marketing Research Helps Develop Product/Market Strategies." *Industrial Marketing Management* 12 (1983): 1–6.

Stobaugh R., and P. Telesio. "Match Manufacturing Policies and Product Strategy." *Harvard Business Review* 61, no. 2 (March–April 1983): 113–20.

Stybel, L.J. "Linking Strategic Planning and Management Manpower Planning." *California Management Review* 25, no. 1 (Fall 1982): 48–56.

Tichy, N. "The Essentials of Strategic Change Management." *The Journal of Business Strategy* (Spring 1983): 55–67.

Treleaven, C. "Documenting the Financial Planning Model—An Overlooked Problem." *Managerial Planning* 31, no. 5 (March–April 1983): 18–23.

Wood, D.R., Jr. "The Impact of Comprehensive Planning on Financial Performance." *Academy of Management Journal* 22, no. 3 (1979): 516–26.

Zand, D. "Reviewing the Policy Process." *California Management Review* XXI, no. 1 (Fall 1978): 35–46.

EXPERIENTIAL EXERCISE 5A:

Constructing an Internal Factor Evaluation Matrix for Ponderosa, Inc.

PURPOSE

The purpose of this exercise is to give you experience in developing an Internal Factor Evaluation Matrix.

YOUR TASK

Your task is to perform an internal strategic-management audit for Ponderosa, Inc. Use the concepts and audit questionnaires presented in Chapter 5 to identify Ponderosa's key strengths and weaknesses in management, marketing, finance, production, and research and development. Prepare an Internal Factor Evaluation Matrix to summarize and evaluate the key internal factors. Present your internal analysis of Ponderosa to the class. During your presentation, be sure to answer the following questions:

1. Is Ponderosa's total weighted score above or below 2.5 in your evaluation matrix? What does this suggest?

2. How many key factors were included in your matrix? Why did you include those particular factors?

3. Are your key factors stated in specific terms?

4. Which factors have the greatest effect upon organizational performance in the fast food industry? Why? Which factors have the least effect? Why?

5. How could Ponderosa best capitalize on its major strengths? What strategies would allow Ponderosa to overcome its major weaknesses?

6. Why might other students in this class develop an Internal Factor Evaluation Matrix that is not the same as yours?

6

Strategic Analysis and Choice

Figure 6.1 The strategic-management model

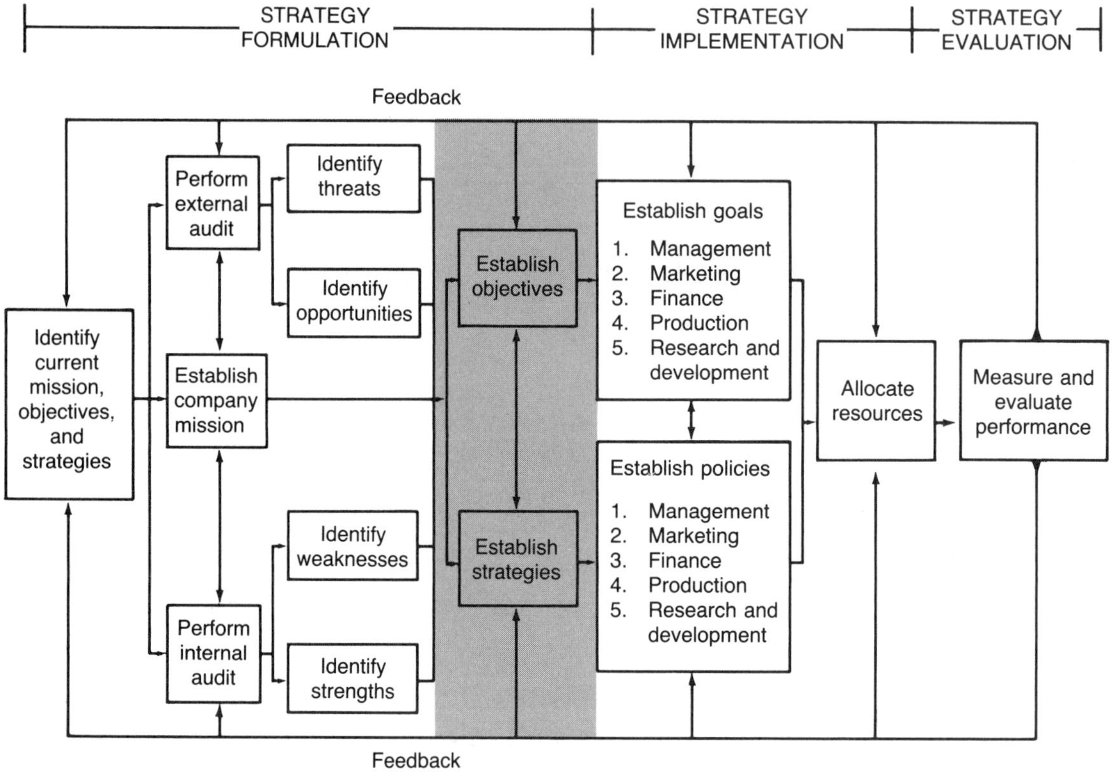

The strategic-management model illustrates that strategy formulation requires developing a company mission, performing an internal and external audit, and establishing objectives and strategies. This chapter introduces important tools and concepts that can aid strategists in generating feasible alternative strategies, evaluating those options, and finally selecting a specific course of action.

The process of establishing objectives and selecting strategies always involves subjective judgment, but analytical tools described in this chapter can aid in this strategic decision-making process. Numerous examples of important techniques are provided. The appropriate role of a board of directors is also discussed. The specific focus of this chapter is shaded in Figure 6.1.

ESTABLISHING OBJECTIVES

Some executives and academicians combine objectives and strategies under the heading of *grand strategy*. However, the distinction between objectives and strategies has merit.

196

Objectives represent the results that are expected from pursuit of certain strategies. Conversely, strategies represent the actions that will be taken to accomplish objectives. The time frame for objectives and strategies should be consistent, usually from two to five years.

An increasing number of successful top managers recognize that establishing objectives and strategies must be a give and take process. Like an objective, a strategy can be an "end" in the sense that an organization often cannot recover from a "wrong" strategy. In actual practice, organizations generally establish objectives and strategies concurrently. Therefore, the strategic-management model reveals an interrelationship between establishing objectives and establishing strategies.

Recall from Chapter 1 that objectives were defined as "the long-term (more than one year) results that an organization seeks to achieve in pursuing its basic mission."[1] Objectives should be quantitative, measurable, realistic, understandable, challenging, hierarchical, obtainable, and congruent among organizational units. There should be a time deadline associated with each objective. Objectives are commonly stated in terms such as growth in assets, growth in sales, profitability, market share, degree and nature of diversification, degree and nature of vertical integration, earnings per share, and social responsibility.

Clearly established objectives offer many benefits. They provide direction, allow synergy, aid in evaluation, establish priorities, reduce uncertainty, minimize conflicts, stimulate exertion, and aid in both the allocation of resources and the design of jobs. Without objectives, an organization is similar to a ship without a rudder, drifting aimlessly in the sea.

As you know, the strategic-management process impacts three hierarchical levels in an organization: corporate, divisional, and functional. Objectives are needed at all three levels; they are an important measure of managerial performance. Many practitioners and academicians attribute a significant part of American industry's competitive decline in world markets to the short-term, rather than long-term, strategic orientation of U.S. managers. Arthur D. Little, a well-known strategic-management consulting firm based in Cambridge, Mass., argues that management compensation practices today must be realigned to support corporate long-term objectives and strategies.

A general framework for relating objectives to performance evaluation results is provided in Table 6.1. A particular organization could tailor these guidelines to meet its own needs. Note that incentives should be attached to both long-term and short-term results.

Establishing objectives is an essential component of the strategic-management process. Objectives become crystallized as feasible strategies are formulated and selected. An educator once said: "If you think education is expensive, try ignorance." The idea behind this saying also applies to establishing objectives, when you consider the following alternatives of not managing by objectives:

Managing by Extrapolation—adheres to the principle, "If it ain't broke, don't fix it." The idea is to keep on doing about the same things in the same ways, because things are going well.

Table 6.1   Varying performance measures by organizational level

Organizational Level	Basis for Annual Bonus or Merit Pay
Corporate	75% based on objectives (long-term) 25% based on goals (short-term)
Divisional	50% based on objectives 50% based on goals
Functional	25% based on objectives 75% based on goals

Managing by Crisis—relies upon the belief that the true measure of a really good manager is one's ability to solve problems. Since there are plenty of crises and problems to go around for every person and every organization, managers ought to bring their time and creative energy to bear on solving the most pressing problems of the day. Managing by crisis is actually a form of reacting rather than acting, and of letting events dictate the whats and whens of management decisions.

Managing by Subjectives—built on the idea that there is no general plan for which way to go and what to do, so you just do the best you can to accomplish what you think should be done. In short, "do your own thing, the best way you know how" (sometimes referred to as "the mystery approach to decision making" because subordinates are left to figure out what is happening and why).

Managing by Hope—based on the fact that the future is laden with great uncertainty and that if we try and do not succeed, then we hope our second (or third) attempt will succeed. Decisions are predicated on the hope that they will work and that good times are just around the corner, especially if luck and good fortune are on our side.[2]

A STRATEGY-FORMULATION ANALYTICAL FRAMEWORK

Important strategy-formulation analytical techniques can be integrated into a three-stage decision-making framework, as shown in Figure 6.2. The tools presented in the strategy-formulation framework are all described, explained, and exemplified in this chapter. They all are applicable to various sizes and types of organizations.

It is important to know that some business policy cases do not provide sufficient information to use all of the tools represented in the decision-making framework. Additional information about a particular case can usually be obtained in a college library, but all of the tools do not have to be used all of the time. For most business policy case analyses, and certainly for organizations in general, the strategy-formulation analytical framework is useful in identifying, evaluating, and selecting strategies.

Figure 6.2 The strategy-formulation analytical framework

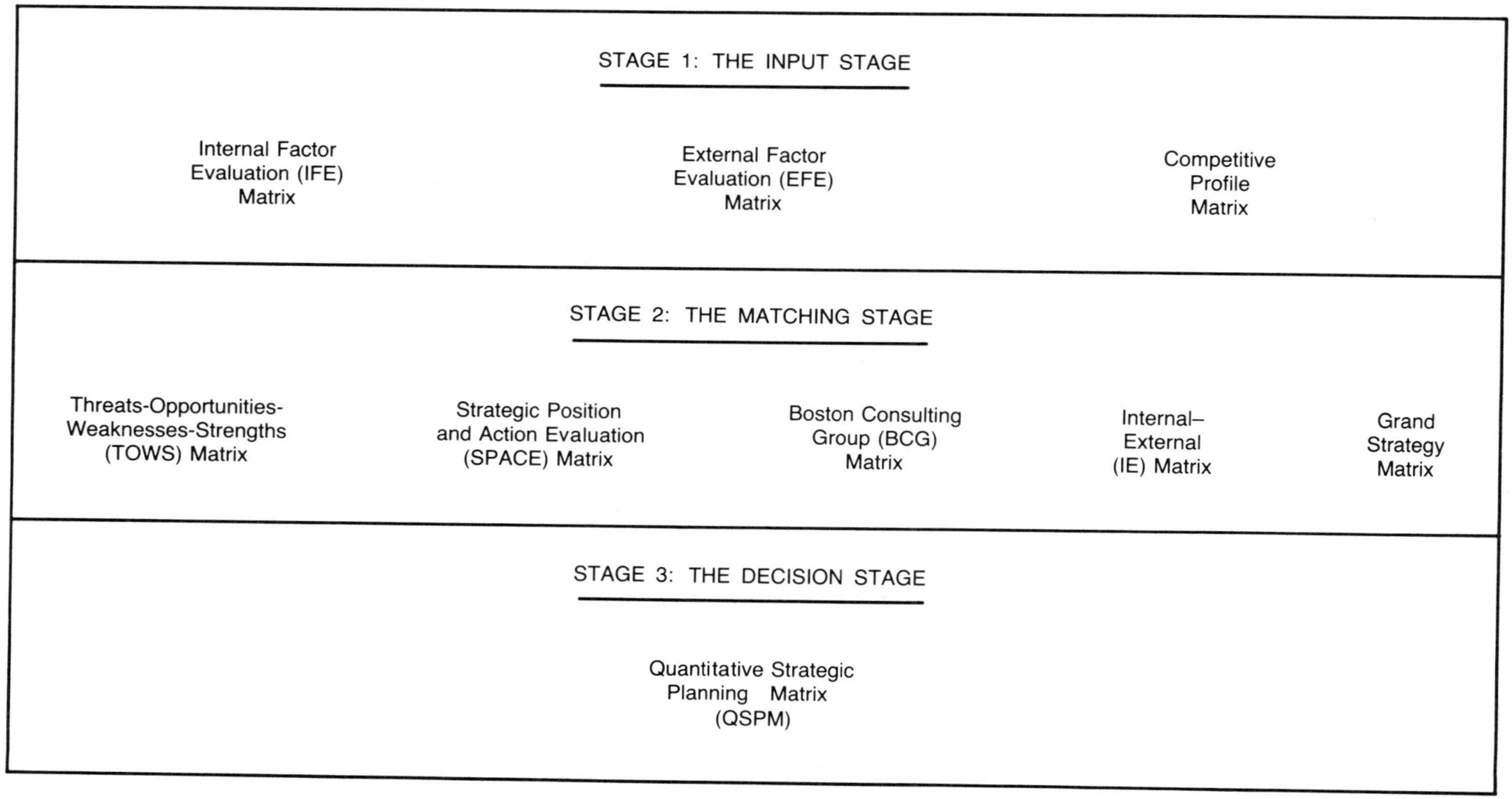

STAGE 1: THE INPUT STAGE

| Internal Factor Evaluation (IFE) Matrix | External Factor Evaluation (EFE) Matrix | Competitive Profile Matrix |

STAGE 2: THE MATCHING STAGE

| Threats-Opportunities-Weaknesses-Strengths (TOWS) Matrix | Strategic Position and Action Evaluation (SPACE) Matrix | Boston Consulting Group (BCG) Matrix | Internal–External (IE) Matrix | Grand Strategy Matrix |

STAGE 3: THE DECISION STAGE

Quantitative Strategic Planning Matrix (QSPM)

The first stage of the analytical framework consists of the IFE Matrix, the EFE Matrix, and the Competitive Profile Matrix. Stage 1 is called the "input" stage because the three tools summarize the basic input information needed to generate feasible alternative strategies.

Stage 2 of the strategy-formulation analytical framework focuses on generating feasible alternative strategies. Stage 2 is called the "matching" stage because key internal and external factors are matched. Techniques include the TOWS Matrix, the SPACE Matrix, the BCG Matrix, the IE Matrix, and the GS Matrix. These tools suggest feasible alternative strategies that should be considered by an organization.

Stage 3 of the analytical framework is the "decision" stage, composed of a single technique—the Quantitative Strategic Planning Matrix (QSPM). QSPM uses input information derived from Stage 1 to evaluate feasible alternative strategies identified in Stage 2. QSPM reveals the relative attractiveness of alternative strategies, thus providing an objective basis for selecting specific strategies.

Before we begin to examine the strategy-formulation analytical framework in more detail, a word of caution is needed about analytical tools. *The results obtained from quantitative techniques can be only as good as the qualitative judgments that were made in deriving the results.* Although analytical tools can significantly enhance the strategic decision-making process, they should not be used indiscriminately.

THE INPUT STAGE

The Internal Factor Evaluation (IFE) Matrix

The IFE Matrix summarizes an organization's key management, marketing, finance, production, and research and development strengths and weaknesses. Recall that specific steps required to develop an IFE Matrix were presented in the previous chapter. This tool is now examined further because it is an essential part of the strategy-formulation analytical framework, answering four major questions about a firm's internal strategic position:

1. What are the organization's key strengths and weaknesses?
2. What is the relative importance of each strength and weakness to the firm's overall performance?
3. Does each factor represent a major weakness (rating = 1), a minor weakness (rating = 2), a minor strength (rating = 3), or a major strength (rating = 4)?
4. What is the firm's total weighted score resulting from the IFE analysis? Is the score above or below the average of 2.50?

To the extent possible, key internal factors should be stated in objective terms. The particular factors selected for inclusion are important because they represent the internal bases from which an organization's strategies and objectives will be established.

Appropriate weights and ratings should be assigned by strategists or the group of managers charged with performing the internal audit.

Sometimes a key internal factor can be both a strength and a weakness. When this situation occurs, the factor should be included twice in the IFE Matrix, with the appropriate weight and rating assigned to each statement. For example, the Playboy name, logo, and image both *help and hurt* Playboy Enterprises. They attracted business to the London casinos, but helped lose the casino licensees. They keep the cable show out of many markets, because Americans are ambivalent about sex and pornography.[3] So the Playboy name can be viewed as both a strength and weakness for the company.

An example IFE Matrix for Reichhold Chemicals, headquartered in White Plains, N.Y., is provided in Table 6.2. Among Reichhold's key strengths and weaknesses, note that level of productivity and technical competence are considered the most important factors, as indicated by weights of .25 and .20 respectively. The analysis indicates that Reichhold's major strength is an established reputation for technical excellence (rating = 4). The firm's major internal weakness is its low level of productivity. The total weighted score of 2.60 suggests that Reichhold is just above average in terms of its overall internal strategic position. Reichhold's 1984 sales and profits were $801 million and $26 million respectively.

Table 6.2   An IFE matrix for Reichhold Chemicals, Inc.

Key Internal Factor	Weight	Rating	Weighted Score
1. The firm's level of productivity has dropped to 65%.	.20	1	.20
2. The firm's organizational structure is being totally revamped.	.05	2	.10
3. The firm's EPS was only $.25 in 1982, second lowest in the industry.	.10	2	.20
4. The firm's ROI was only 2.2% in 1982, second lowest in the industry.	.10	2	.20
5. The firm is boosting R & D expenditures to 20% of sales in 1983.	.15	3	.45
6. Through 34 plant locations, the firm offers excellent customer service.	.15	3	.45
7. The firm has established a reputation for technical excellence.	.25	4	1.00
TOTAL WEIGHTED SCORE	1.00		2.60

Source: Based on Reichhold's *1984 Annual Report* and an article entitled, "Reichhold Chemicals: Now the Emphasis Is on Profits Rather Than Volume," *Business Week* (June 20, 1983): 178–79.

The External Factor Evaluation (EFE) Matrix

The second tool included in the "input" stage of the strategy-formulation analytical framework is the EFE Matrix. This technique is analogous to the IFE Matrix, except that the focus is on economic, social, cultural, demographic, geographic, political, governmental, legal, technological, and competitive opportunities and threats, rather than internal strengths and weaknesses. The specific steps required to construct an EFE Matrix were presented in Chapter 4. The EFE Matrix answers four incisive questions:

1. What are the firm's environmental opportunities and threats?
2. What is the relative importance of each opportunity and threat to the firm's overall performance?
3. Does each factor represent a major threat (rating = 1), a minor threat (rating = 2), a minor opportunity (rating = 3), or a major opportunity (rating = 4)?
4. What is the firm's total weighted score resulting from the EFE analysis? Is the score above or below the average of 2.50?

An example EFE Matrix is provided in Table 6.3 for Dresser Industries. Dresser Industries is a $3 billion energy company with over 40,000 employees. Such a large

Table 6.3 An EFE matrix for Dresser Industries, Inc.

Key External Factor	Weighting	Rating	Weighted Score
1. U.S. trade sanctions barring Dresser from supplying the Soviet Union and other foreign countries; 79% of Dresser's net profit in 1983 had come from operations in Europe.	.35	1	.35
2. In the petroleum industry, drilling expenditures declined nearly 50% between 1981 and 1983; 45% of Dresser's revenues had come from petroleum operations.	.15	2	.30
3. Oil prices are declining. They fell from $34 per barrel to $29 per barrel in 1983.	.10	2	.20
4. Turmoil in the Middle East. Threats from Iran and Iraq to disrupt oil shipments from the Persian Gulf.	.25	2	.50
5. The U.S. coal market, which accounted for 50% of Dresser's mining sales in 1983, is booming.	.15	3	.45
TOTAL WEIGHTED SCORE	1.00		1.80

Source: Based on Dresser's *1984 Annual Report* and an article entitled, "Dresser Industries: A Leaner Look As It Waits Out a Lingering Slump," *Business Week* (September 26, 1983): 78–79.

firm obviously faces many external opportunities and threats, but a finite set (five to twenty) of the most important external factors should be included in the EFE Matrix.

Note in the Dresser example that four key external threats and one key opportunity faced the company in 1984. Among the key factors included in the EFE Matrix, U.S. trade sanctions are most important to the firm's success, as indicated by a weighting of .35; this factor also represents Dresser's major threat as evidenced by a rating of 1. A minor opportunity (rating = 3) that Dresser could take advantage of in the future is large U.S. coal reserves. Note that each factor in the EFE Matrix is (and should be) stated in specific terms. The total weighted score of 1.80 indicates that Dresser has a weak external strategic position, which could be a major reason why sales and profits declined from a high of $4.6 billion and $317 million respectively in 1981, to $3.7 billion and $97 million in 1984.

The IFE Matrix and EFE Matrix require strategists to quantify subjectivity during the early stages of the strategy-formulation process. Making many "small" decisions in the input and matching matrices allows top managers to make final strategy decisions more effectively. Good intuitive judgment is always needed in determining appropriate weights and ratings. The input matrices provide a basis for objectively identifying and evaluating feasible alternative strategies. An absence of objective input information too often results in biases, politics, and halo error playing a dominant role in the strategy-formulation process. (*Halo error* refers to the tendency to put too much weight on a single factor.)

Autonomous divisions in an organization should use strategy-formulation analytical tools to develop their own strategies and objectives. These lower-level analyses provide a basis for identifying, evaluating, and selecting among alternative corporate-level strategies.

The Competitive Profile Matrix

Identifying and evaluating competitors' strengths, weaknesses, strategies, and objectives is often considered to be the most important part of the strategy-formulation process. The Competitive Profile Matrix is therefore an important "input" tool that summarizes vital information about competitors. In developing a Competitive Profile Matrix, strategists should use factual information as much as possible in choosing key factors, deciding on appropriate weights, and assigning ratings. A Competitive Profile Matrix answers the following questions:

1. Who are our major competitors?
2. What key factors are most important to being successful in the industry?
3. What is the relative importance of each key factor to success in the industry?
4. To what extent is each competitor strong or weak on each key success factor (where 1 = major weakness, 2 = minor weakness, 3 = minor strength, and 4 = major strength)?
5. Overall, how strong or weak is each major competitor?

An example Competitive Profile Matrix is given in Table 6.4 for three firms in the personal computer industry. The analysis includes seven key success factors in the personal computer industry. The rating scores of 4 suggest that Company 1 is strongest in customer service, dealer relations, and advertising effectiveness, Company 2 is strongest in price competitiveness, and Company 3 is strongest in technological superiority and financial strength. Company 3 is weak in price competitiveness and dealer relations (rating = 2), while Company 2 is weak in financial strength and advertising effectiveness. In this example, Company 1 is the strongest competitor in the personal computer industry, with a total weighted score of 3.41, followed by Company 2 and Company 3 with scores of 3.01 and 2.91 respectively.

Nearly all industries have become increasingly competitive in the 1980s. This fact accents the need for the Competitive Profile Matrix to be developed carefully and updated regularly. In the soft drink industry for example, Coke and Pepsi battle it out for the No. 1 position. Seven–Up recently mounted an aggressive anticaffeine marketing campaign: "Never had it. Never will." A soft drink that does have caffeine, Diet Coke, recently toppled 7–Up and usurped third place. Diet Coke sold about 375 mil-

Table 6.4 A sample Competitive Profile Matrix

Key Success Factors	Weight	Company 1		Company 2		Company 3	
		Rating	Weighted Score	Rating	Weighted Score	Rating	Weighted Score
Customer Service	.22	4	.88	3	.66	3	.66
Price	.20	3	.60	4	.80	2	.40
Product Quality	.18	3	.54	3	.54	3	.54
Technological Superiority	.11	3	.33	3	.33	4	.44
Dealer Relations	.10	4	.40	3	.30	2	.20
Financial Strength	.10	3	.30	2	.20	4	.40
Advertising Effectiveness	.09	4	.36	2	.18	3	.27
TOTAL WEIGHTED SCORES	1.00		3.41		3.01		2.91

Note: The weight is always the same for all firms in a given industry.

lion cases in 1984, a gain of nearly 50 percent over 1983, compared to 7–Up's 350 million cases, a mere 5 percent increase. Coca-Cola Company's introduction of Coca-Cola Classic, New Coke, and Cherry Coke in 1985 further exemplifies how competitive the beverage industry has become.[4]

THE MATCHING STAGE

The Threats-Opportunities-Weaknesses-Strengths (TOWS) Matrix

The matching stage of the analytical framework for strategy formulation includes the TOWS Matrix, the SPACE Matrix, the BCG Matrix, the IE Matrix, and the Grand Strategy Matrix. These matching tools rely upon input information derived from the IFE Matrix, EFE Matrix, and Competitive Profile Matrix. Matching internal strengths/weaknesses with external opportunities/threats suggests feasible alternative strategies.

Although the concept of "matching" was introduced in Chapter 1, more detail is provided now. Matching means aligning internal factors with external factors to generate alternative strategies. For example, a firm with excess working capital (an internal strength) could take advantage of the aerospace industry's growing 40 percent annually (an external opportunity) by acquiring a firm in the aerospace industry. This example portrays simple one-to-one matching. In most situations, internal and external relationships are more complex and the matching process requires more thought. The basic concept of matching is further exemplified in Table 6.5.

Any organization, whether military, product-oriented, service-oriented, governmental, or even athletic, must devise and execute good strategies to win. A good

Table 6.5   Matching key internal and external factors to formulate alternative strategies

Key Internal Factor		Key External Factor		Resultant Strategy
Excess working capital (an internal strength)	+	40% annual growth of the aerospace industry (an external opportunity)	=	Acquire Aerospace, Inc.
Insufficient capacity (an internal weakness)	+	Exit of two major foreign competitors from the industry (an external opportunity)	=	Pursue horizontal integration by buying competitors' facilities
Strong R&D expertise (an internal strength)	+	Decreasing numbers of young adults (an external threat)	=	Develop new products for older adults
Poor employee morale (an internal weakness)	+	Strong union activity (an external threat)	=	Develop a new employee-benefits package

offense without a good defense, or vice versa, most often leads to defeat. Every organization has some internal strengths and weaknesses and external opportunities and threats. A firm can use its internal strengths to take advantage of external opportunities or to overcome external threats. Alternatively, a firm could pursue defensive-type strategies aimed at overcoming weaknesses and avoiding external threats.

External threats can be disastrous to firms that additionally have major internal weaknesses. An organization could pursue strategies that improve on its internal weaknesses by taking advantage of external opportunities. Matching key internal and external factors is more an art than a science! Strategic analysis and choice largely involve making subjective judgments based on objective information.

The TOWS Matrix is an important strategy-formulation matching tool that results in the development of four types of strategies: **SO** Strategies, **WO** Strategies, **ST** Strategies, and **WT** Strategies.[5] The letters **S, O, W,** and **T** stand for *strengths, opportunities, weaknesses,* and *threats.* **SO** Strategies are based on using a firm's internal strengths to take advantage of external opportunities.

Any company would like to be in a position where it can use its strengths to exploit external opportunities. Such an enterprise can lead from strengths, utilizing resources to take advantage of the market for its products and services. For example, Mercedes Benz, with its technical know-how and quality image (internal strengths), could take advantage of the increasing demand for luxury cars (external opportunity) by expanding production.

Organizations generally will pursue **WO, ST,** or **WT** in order to get into a situation where they can then apply an **SO** strategy. When a firm has major weaknesses, it will strive to overcome them, making them strengths. When a company faces major threats, it will seek to avoid them, in order to concentrate more on opportunities.

WO Strategies aim at improving internal weaknesses by taking advantage of external opportunities. Sometimes key external opportunities exist, but a firm has internal weaknesses that prevent those opportunities from being exploited. For example, there may be a great demand for electronic devices to control the amount and timing of fuel injection in automobile engines (opportunity), but a certain auto parts manufacturer may lack the technology required for producing these devices (weakness). One possible **WO** strategy would be to acquire this technology by forming a joint venture with a firm having competency in this field. Another **WO** strategy would be to hire and train people with the required technical capabilities.

ST Strategies are based on using a firm's strengths to avoid or reduce the impact of external threats. The aim is to capitalize on the firm's strengths by minimizing external threats. This does not mean that a strong company should always meet threats in the external environment head-on. General Motors found this out in the 1960s when Ralph Nader (an external threat) exposed safety hazards of the Corvair automobile. GM used its strengths (size and influence) to ridicule Nader, and the direct confrontation caused more problems than expected. In retrospect, this **ST** Strategy was probably inappropriate for GM at the time.

WT Strategies are directed at overcoming internal weaknesses and avoiding environmental threats. The attempt is to minimize both weaknesses and threats. **WT** strategies are defensive. A company faced with many external threats and internal weaknesses may indeed be in a precarious position. In fact, such a firm may have to fight for its survival, merge, retrench, declare bankruptcy, or choose liquidation.

A schematic representation of the TOWS Matrix is provided in Figure 6.3. Note that a TOWS Matrix is composed of nine cells. As shown, there are four key factor cells, four strategy cells, and one cell that is always left blank (the upper left cell). The four strategy cells, labeled **SO, WO, ST,** and **WT,** are developed after the four key factor cells, labeled **S, W, O,** and **T** are completed.

Figure 6.3   The TOWS Matrix

	STRENGTHS—S	WEAKNESSES—W
Always leave blank	1. 2. 3. 4. 5. 6. List 7. strengths 8. 9. 10.	1. 2. 3. 4. 5. 6. List 7. weaknesses 8. 9. 10.
OPPORTUNITIES—O 1. 2. 3. 4. List 5. opportunities 6. 7. 8. 9. 10.	SO STRATEGIES 1. 2. 3. 4. Use strengths 5. to take 6. advantage of 7. opportunities 8. 9. 10.	WO STRATEGIES 1. 2. 3. 4. Overcome 5. weaknesses 6. by taking 7. advantage of 8. opportunities 9. 10.
THREATS—T 1. 2. List 3. threats 4. 5. 6. 7. 8. 9. 10.	ST STRATEGIES 1. 2. Use 3. strengths 4. to avoid 5. threats 6. 7. 8. 9. 10.	WT STRATEGIES 1. 2. Minimize 3. weaknesses 4. and 5. avoid 6. threats 7. 8. 9. 10.

The steps involved in constructing a TOWS Matrix are:

1. List the firm's key internal strengths.
2. List the firm's key internal weaknesses.
3. List the firm's key external opportunities.
4. List the firm's key external threats.
5. Match internal strengths with external opportunities and record the resultant **SO** Strategies in the appropriate cell.
6. Match internal weaknesses with external opportunities and record the resultant **WO** strategies.
7. Match internal strengths with external threats and record the resultant **ST** strategies.
8. Match internal weaknesses with external threats and record the resultant **WT** strategies.

Matching key internal and external factors is the most difficult part of developing a TOWS Matrix. The matching process requires good judgment and there is no one best answer. Note in Table 6.5, presented earlier, that the first, second, third, and fourth strategies were **SO, WO, ST,** and **WT** strategies respectively. Some other examples of how to match key factors to generate feasible strategies are given as follows:

1. A strong financial position (internal strength) coupled with unsaturated foreign markets (external opportunity) could suggest that market development would be an appropriate **SO**-type strategy.
2. A lack of technical expertise (internal weakness) coupled with a strong demand for computer services (external opportunity) could suggest the **WO** strategy of acquiring a high-tech computer company.
3. A strong distribution system (internal strength) coupled with intense government deregulation (external threat) could suggest that concentric diversification would be a desirable strategy.
4. Poor product quality (internal weakness) coupled with unreliable suppliers (external threat) could suggest that backward integration would be a feasible strategy.

The purpose of each Stage 2 matching tool is to generate feasible alternative strategies, not to select or determine which strategies are best. Therefore, not all of the strategies developed in the TOWS Matrix and the other Stage 2 tools will be selected for implementation.

An example TOWS Matrix is provided in Figure 6.4 for Levi Strauss & Company. Levi Strauss is headquartered in San Francisco and has been the leader in the $1.7 billion-per-year United States jeans business. Some of Levi's key strengths, weaknesses, opportunities, threats, and strategies are identified. The notation "S2, O3" indicates

Figure 6.4   The TOWS Matrix applied to Levi Strauss & Company

	STRENGTHS 1. Levi Strauss has excess working capital. 2. Advertising effectiveness is excellent. 3. David Hunter has become a successful fashion brand.	WEAKNESSES 1. Customer loyalty has declined. 2. Retail sales of Levi's Jeans are declining. 3. Nine plants have been shut since 1982.
OPPORTUNITIES 1. The consumer is becoming more leisure-oriented and wearing jeans more often. 2. Levi Strauss commands 43% of the market share in jeans. 3. K-Mart, Wal-Mart, and other retailers do not currently sell Levi's jeans.	**SO** STRATEGIES 1. Product development (Add "Davy Hunter" line of jeans). **S**1, **S**3, **O**1. 2. Forward integration (Attract K-Mart and Wal-Mart as distributors). **S**2, **O**3.	**WO** STRATEGIES
THREATS 1. Both Blue Bell and VF Corp.'s jeans are gaining market share. 2. Sears and J. C. Penney's may withdraw their orders from Levi Strauss. 3. Levi Strauss' traditional distributors are angered by Levi's policy of selling to mass retailers such as Sears. 4. 1980–1982 were financially disastrous years for Levi's.	**ST** STRATEGIES	**WT** STRATEGIES 1. Retrenchment (close more plants). **W**2, **W**3, **T**3, **T**4. 2. Market penetration (offer small retailers special incentives). **W**2, **T**3.

Source: Based on Levi Strauss' *1984 Annual Report* and an article entitled "Levi Strauss: A Touch of Fashion—and a Dash of Humility," *Business Week* (October 24, 1983): 85–88.

that the justification for Levi Strauss considering forward integration is "strength number two (advertising effectiveness)" matched with "opportunity number three (mass retailers do not carry Levi's jeans)." Similarly, the notation "**W**2, **T**3" indicates that Levi Strauss should consider offering small retailers special incentives due to "weakness number two (declining retail sales)" coupled with "threat number three (present distributors are angered)." This type of notation should always be used in constructing a TOWS Matrix to reveal the bases for specific strategies. Sometimes several internal factors will be matched with several external factors to generate a feasible alternative strategy. As indicated in the Levi example, strategies do not necessarily have to be developed for all four strategy cells.

When an organization has both the capital and human resources needed to distribute its own products (internal strength), and distributors are unreliable, costly, or incapable of meeting the firm's needs (external threat), then forward integration can be an attractive ST type strategy. Similarly, when a firm has excess production capacity (internal weakness), and its basic industry is experiencing declining annual sales and profits (external threat), then concentric diversification can be an effective **WT**-type strategy. The strategy-formulation guidelines provided in Chapter 2 can enhance strategists' efforts to match key internal and external factors effectively.

It is important, in developing the TOWS Matrix, that one tailor specific strategies to the given organization. That is, do not just conclude that "an organization should consider pursuing concentric diversification." Rather, be more specific, saying, perhaps, "The organization should consider diversifying concentrically by adding motor homes to its product line."

An article entitled, "Mobil Wants To Be Your Milkman," suggests that Mobil is planning to pursue a major **ST** Strategy. Mobil's strength, 12,000 stations nationwide, and an external threat, 50,000+ convenience stores in the United States now selling gasoline, combine to make the following **ST** strategy potentially attractive: Mobil intends to turn as many as possible of its full-service stations into self-service gas islands in combination with convenience stores. (Mobil calls them "snack shops.")[6] Mobil's yearly sales and profits declined from a high of $69 billion and $2.4 billion respectively in 1981 to $60 billion and $1.3 billion in 1984.

The Strategic Position and Action Evaluation (SPACE) Matrix

The SPACE Matrix is a second important Stage 2 "matching" tool. The format for the SPACE Matrix is illustrated in Figure 6.5. As shown, the SPACE Matrix is a four-

Figure 6.5   The SPACE Matrix[7]

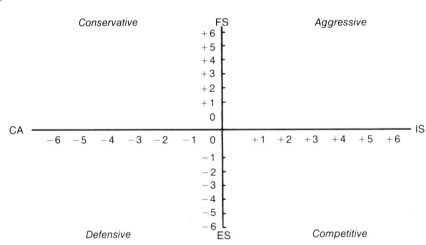

quadrant framework that suggests whether aggressive, conservative, defensive, or competitive-type strategies are most appropriate for a given organization. The SPACE Matrix axes are: financial strength **(FS)**, competitive advantage **(CA)**, environmental stability **(ES)**, and industry strength **(IS).** The two internal dimensions, financial strength **(FS)** and competitive advantage **(CA)**, and two external dimensions, industry strength **(IS)** and environmental stability **(ES),** can be considered the most important determinants of an organization's overall strategic position.[8]

Depending upon the type of organization, there are numerous variables that could comprise each of the dimensions represented on the axes of the SPACE Matrix. Some example variables often included are given in Exhibit 6.1. For example, return on investment, leverage, liquidity, working capital, and cash flow are commonly considered determining factors of an organization's financial strength. Like the TOWS Matrix, the SPACE Matrix should be tailored for a particular organization being studied, and based on factual information to the extent possible.

Exhibit 6.1   Some example factors that comprise the SPACE Matrix axes

INTERNAL STRATEGIC POSITION	EXTERNAL STRATEGIC POSITION
Financial Strength (FS)	**Environmental Stability (ES)** *
Return on investment	Technological changes
Leverage	Rate of inflation
Liquidity	Demand variability
Working capital	Price range of competing products
Cash flow	Barriers to entry into market
Ease of exit from market	Competitive pressure
Risk involved in business	Price elasticity of demand
Competitive Advantage (CA)	**Industry Strength (IS)**
Market share	Growth potential
Product quality	Profit potential
Product life cycle	Financial stability
Customer loyalty	Technological know-how
Competition's capacity utilization	Resource utilization
Technological know-how	Capital intensity
Control over suppliers and distributors	Ease of entry into market
	Productivity, capacity utilization

Source: H. Rowe, R. Mason, and K. Dickel, *Strategic Management & Business Policy: A Methodological Approach* (Reading, Mass.: Addison–Wesley Publishing Company, Inc., 1982), 155–156.

*A stable environment represents a better strategic position than an unstable environment.

The steps required in developing a SPACE Matrix are:

1. For financial strength **(FS)** and industry strength **(IS),** assign a numerical value ranging from +1 (worst) to +6 (best) to each of the variables that comprise these dimensions. For environmental stability **(ES)** and competitive advantage **(CA),** assign a numerical value ranging from −1 (best) to −6 (worst) to each of the variables that comprise these dimensions.

2. Compute an average score for **FS, CA, IS,** and **ES** by summing each dimension's factor ratings and dividing by the number of variables included in the respective dimension.

3. Plot the average scores for **FS, IS, ES,** and **CA** on the appropriate axis in the SPACE Matrix.

4. Add the two scores on the (horizontal) x-axis and plot the resultant point on x. Add the two scores on the (vertical) y-axis and plot the resultant point on y. Plot the intersection of the new xy point.

5. Draw a directional vector from the origin of the SPACE Matrix through the new intersection point. This vector reveals the type of strategies—aggressive, competitive, defensive, or conservative—most appropriate for the company.

Some example strategy profiles that can emerge from a SPACE analysis are shown in Figure 6.6. The directional vector associated with each profile suggests the type of strategies to pursue: aggressive, conservative, defensive, or competitive. When a firm's directional vector is located in the aggressive quadrant of the SPACE Matrix, this means the organization is in an excellent position to use its internal strengths to (1) take advantage of external opportunities, (2) overcome internal weaknesses, and (3) avoid external threats. Therefore, market penetration, market development, product development, backward integration, forward integration, horizontal integration, conglomerate diversification, concentric diversification, horizontal diversification, or a combination-type strategy can all be feasible, depending on the specific circumstances that face the firm.

The directional vector may point into the conservative, or upper left quadrant of the SPACE Matrix, which implies staying close to the firm's basic competencies and not taking excessive risks. Conservative-type strategies most often include market penetration, market development, product development, and concentric diversification.

Third, the directional vector may be located in the lower left quadrant of the SPACE Matrix, suggesting that defensive strategies are most appropriate. The firm should focus on improving internal weaknesses and avoiding external threats. Defensive-type strategies include retrenchment, divestiture, liquidation, and concentric diversification.

Finally, the directional vector may point into the lower right quadrant of the SPACE Matrix, indicating competitive-type strategies. Competitive strategies include backward, forward, and horizontal integration, market penetration, market development, product development, and joint venture.

Figure 6.6 Some example strategy profiles

Aggressive Profiles

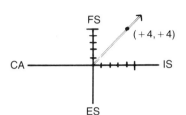

A financially strong firm that
has achieved major
competitive advantages in a
growing and stable industry

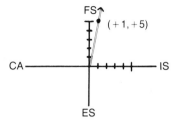

A firm whose financial
strength is a dominating
factor in the industry

Conservative Profiles

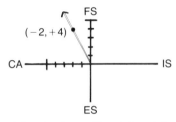

A firm that has achieved financial
strength in a stable industry that is
not growing; the firm has no major
competitive advantages.

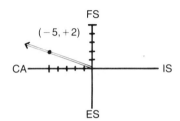

A firm that suffers from major
competitive disadvantages in an
industry that is technologically
stable but declining in sales

Competitive Profiles

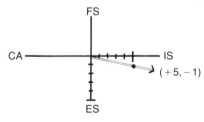

A firm with major competitive
advantages in a high-growth
industry

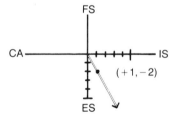

An organization that is competing
fairly well in an unstable
industry

Defensive Profiles

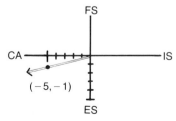

A firm that has a very weak
competitive position in a negative
growth, stable industry

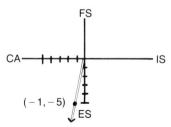

A financially troubled firm in a very
unstable industry

An example SPACE Matrix analysis for Uniroyal, Inc. is provided in Exhibit 6.2. Uniroyal is a $2 billion tire, chemicals, and plastics maker in the United States. Uniroyal rebounded strongly in 1983 and 1984 after disastrous years in 1980 and 1981. The $(+2, +1)$ coordinates for the directional vector indicate that Uniroyal should pursue aggressive-type strategies. The company's aggressive posture was evidenced in 1985 by its leveraged buyout of Clayton & Dubilier, Inc., for $836 million.

Another firm that is pursuing aggressive-type strategies is Canon, Inc. Canon is the world's largest manufacturer of copying units and is one of the largest producers of

Exhibit 6.2   An example SPACE analysis for Uniroyal, Inc.

INTERNAL STRATEGIC POSITION		EXTERNAL STRATEGIC POSITION	
Financial Strength (FS)	Rating	**Environmental Stability**	Rating
Debt/Equity ratio is down from 1.54 in 1980 to 0.75 in 1983.	+5	Uniroyal's sales depend largely on automobile sales.	−5
Net income after taxes tripled from 1982 to 1983.	+5	The chemical industry is technologically unstable.	−3
FS average	+5	ES Average	−4
Competitive Advantage (CA)		**Industry Strength (IS)**	
Uniroyal is now second behind Goodyear Tire & Rubber in total sales in the industry.	−1	The market for tires is growing.	+4
Uniroyal has only a 7% share of the large replacement-tire market.	−5	The agricultural services industry is booming.	+6
CA Average	−3	IS Average	+5

x-axis: −3 + (+5) = +2
y-axis: +5 + (−4) = +1

Coordinates: (+2, +1)

Source: Based on Uniroyal's *1984 Annual Report* and an article entitled "Uniroyal: Back from the Brink and Ready To Put a Bigger Bet on Chemicals," *Business Week* (October 10, 1983): 114, 116.

cameras. As part of an aggressive effort to become a diversified giant, Canon is selling Apple, Burroughs, and Hewlett-Packard computers in Japan.[9]

The Boston Consulting Group (BCG) Matrix

Autonomous divisions (or profit centers) of an organization comprise what is called a "business portfolio." When a firm's divisions compete in different industries, a separate strategy often must be developed for each business. The BCG Matrix and the IE Matrix that follow are designed specifically to enhance a multidivisional firm's efforts to formulate strategies.

The BCG Matrix graphically portrays differences among divisions in terms of relative market share and industry growth rate, and is an important matching tool in Stage 2 of the strategy-formulation analytical framework.[10] The BCG Matrix allows a multidivisional organization to manage its "portfolio of businesses" by examining the relative market share position and the industry growth rate of each division relative to all other divisions.

Relative market share position can be defined as the ratio of a division's own market share of the industry to the market share held by the largest rival firm. Relative market share position is given on the x-axis of the BCG Matrix. Typically, the midpoint on the x-axis is set at .50, which corresponds to a division that has half the market share of the leading firm in the industry. The y-axis represents the industry growth rate in sales, measured in percentage terms. The growth rate percentages on the y-axis could range from -20 to $+20$ percent, with 0.0 being the midpoint. These numerical ranges on the x and y axes are often used, but other numerical values could be established as deemed appropriate for particular organizations.[11]

A sample BCG Matrix is illustrated in Figure 6.7. Each circle represents a separate division. The size of the circle corresponds to the proportion of corporate revenue generated by that business unit. The pie slice indicates the proportion of corporate profits generated by that division. For reasons to be discussed in a moment, divisions located in Quadrant I of the BCG Matrix are called Question Marks, those located in Quadrant II are called Stars, those located in Quadrant III are called Cash Cows, and finally, those divisions located in Quadrant IV are called Dogs. The BCG Matrix allows top managers to examine, in one schematic representation, relationships among all its divisions. This comparative analysis, combined with the TOWS Matrix and SPACE Matrix, provides a basis for identifying feasible alternative strategies.

Question Marks Quadrant I divisions in the BCG Matrix have a low relative market share, yet compete in high-growth-rate industries. Generally, these firms' cash needs are high and their cash generation is low. Quadrant I divisions should be significantly strengthened through increased allocation of company resources, or alternatively, they should be divested. This is why these businesses are called Question Marks, because the organization must decide whether to pursue an intensive strategy (market penetration, market development, or product development) or divest the division.

Figure 6.7   The BCG Matrix

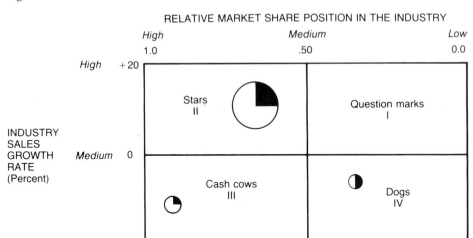

Stars   Quadrant II businesses represent the organization's best long-run opportunities for growth and profitability. Divisions with a high relative market share and a high industry growth rate should receive substantial investment to maintain or strengthen their dominant position. Quadrant II businesses are often called Stars. Forward integration, backward integration, horizontal integration, market penetration, market development, and product development are all appropriate strategies for these divisions to consider.

Cash Cows   Divisions that are positioned in Quadrant III have a high relative market share but compete in a low-growth industry. They are called Cash Cows. Many of today's Cash Cows were yesterday's Stars. Due to their dominant position and minimal need for additional resources, these businesses generate cash in excess of their needs. Therefore, they are often "milked." Cash Cow divisions should be managed to maintain their strong position for as long as possible. Product development or concentric diversification may be attractive strategies for strong Cash Cows. However, as a Cash Cow division becomes weak, retrenchment and divestiture can become more appropriate. Today's Cash Cows often become tomorrow's Dogs.

Dogs   Quadrant IV divisions of the organization have a low relative market share and compete in a slow- or no-market-growth industry; they are the Dogs in the firm's portfolio. Because of their weak internal and external position, these businesses often are liquidated, divested, or trimmed down (retrenched). When a division first becomes a Dog, retrenchment can be the best strategy to pursue, because many Dogs have historically bounced back, after strenuous asset and cost reduction, to be viable, profitable divisions. For example, AMF's marine products division was considered a DOG in 1982, when it lost nearly $5 million. However, after a 50 percent decline in capital expenditures in 1983, AMF's marine products division made nearly $2 million in operating profit. (In 1985, AMF was the target of a $276 million hostile bid by investor Irwin L. Jacobs, who plans to offer $23 a share for 12 million AMF shares. This would bring Mr. Jacobs' holdings to 50.5 percent of AMF's total number of shares outstanding.)

Overall, the major benefit of the BCG Matrix is that it draws attention to the cash flow, investment characteristics, and needs of an organization's various divisions. Historically, the divisions of many firms evolve over time as follows: Dogs become Question Marks, Question Marks become Stars, Stars become Cash Cows, and Cash Cows become Dogs, in an ongoing counterclockwise motion. Less frequently, Stars become Question Marks, Question Marks become Dogs, Dogs become Cash Cows, and Cash Cows become Stars, in a clockwise motion. In some organizations, no cyclical motion is apparent. Over time, organizations should strive to achieve a portfolio of divisions that are Stars.

An example BCG Matrix is provided in Figure 6.8. The example organization is composed of five divisions that have annual sales ranging from $5,000 to $60,000.

Figure 6.8   An example BCG Matrix

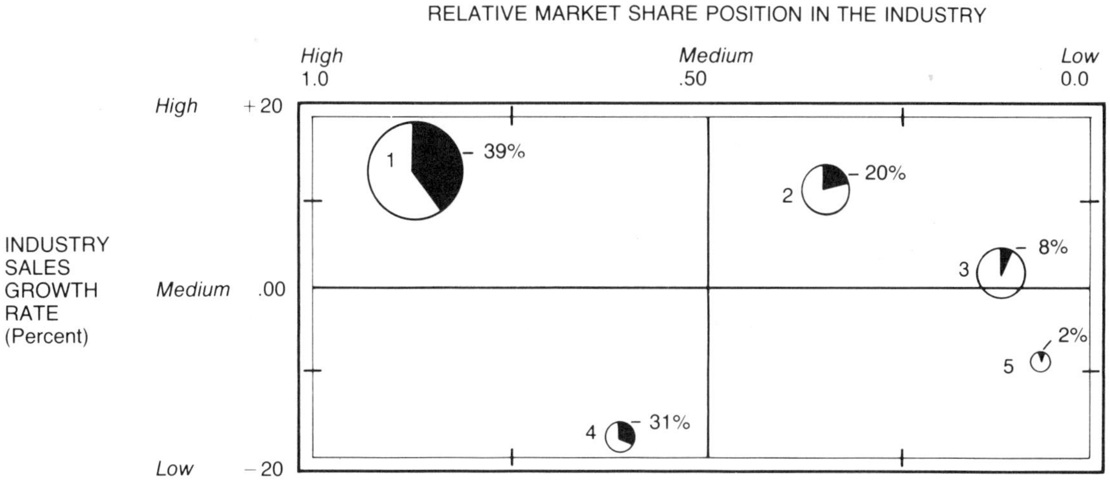

Division	Revenues	%Revenues	Profits	%Profits	%Market share	%Growth rate
1	$60,000	37	$10,000	39	80	+15
2	40,000	24	5,000	20	40	+10
3	40,000	24	2,000	8	10	1
4	20,000	12	8,000	31	60	−20
5	5,000	3	500	2	5	−10
Total	$165,000	100	$25,500	100		

Division 1 has the greatest sales volume, so the circle representing that division is largest in the Matrix. The circle corresponding to Division 5 is the smallest, since its sales volume of $5,000 is least among all the divisions. The pie slices within the circles reveal the relative percent of corporate profits contributed by each division. As shown, Division 1 contributes the highest profit percentage, 39 percent. Notice in the diagram that Division 1 is considered a Star, Division 2 is a Question Mark, Division 3 is also a Question Mark, Division 4 is a Cash Cow, and Division 5 is a Dog.

The BCG Matrix, like all analytical techniques, has some limitations. For example, viewing all businesses as either a Star, Cash Cow, Dog, or Question Mark is oversimplified. Some businesses fall right in the middle of the BCG Matrix and are thus not easily classified. Also, the BCG Matrix does not reflect whether or not various divisions or their industries are growing over time. That is, the matrix has no temporal qualities, but rather is a snapshot of an organization at a given point in time. Another limitation is that there are other variables besides relative market share position and industry growth rate in sales, such as size of the market and competitive advantages, that are important in making strategic decisions about various divisions.

Successfully managing a multidivisional firm has become more and more difficult in the 1980s. This is evidenced in recent actions by two of the largest multidivisional firms in America, General Mills and Procter & Gamble. First, General Mills announced on January 28, 1985 that it was putting three of its nonfood divisions up for sale: (1) Izod, an apparel maker, (2) Parker Bros., a video game business, and (3) Kenner Products, a toy business. Although it was one of America's largest food companies, in calendar 1984 General Mills' profits were off 4.8 percent to $233.4 million, and sales were up 1 percent to $5.6 billion.

Second, Procter & Gamble, the colossal multidivisional firm based in Cincinnati, is having trouble managing its product-based divisions. For example, Kimberly–Clark's Huggies have recently overtaken Procter & Gamble's Luvs as leader in the high-priced disposable diaper market; Lever Brothers' Dove beauty soap has replaced P&G's 105-year-old Ivory as No. 1 in sales. Furthermore, Lever's laundry detergent, Wisk, recently replaced P&G's Cheer as the second-largest-selling detergent. P&G's Tide is still the biggest clothes washer, but its market share has fallen from a peak of 27 percent in 1975 to about 20 percent in 1985. P&G is also struggling in coffee, where its Folger's brand is still trying to topple General Foods' Maxwell House.[12] The GM and P&G examples portray the increasing complexity of managing many divisions at once.

The Internal-External (IE) Matrix

The IE Matrix positions an organization's various divisions in a nine-cell display.[13] The IE Matrix is similar to the BCG Matrix in several respects. First, both tools involve plotting organizational divisions in a schematic diagram; this is why they are both called portfolio matrices. Second, the size of each circle represents the percentage sales contribution of each division. Finally, the pie slices reveal the percentage profit contribution of each division.

There are also some important differences between the BCG Matrix and the IE Matrix. The axes are different. The IE Matrix requires more information about the divisions than the BCG Matrix. The strategic implications of each matrix are different. For these reasons, strategists in multidivisional firms often develop both the BCG and IE Matrices in the strategy-generation process.

The IE Matrix is based on two key dimensions: (1) IFE total weighted scores on the x-axis and (2) EFE total weighted scores on the y-axis. Recall that each division of a firm should construct an IFE Matrix and an EFE Matrix for its part of the organization. The total weighted scores derived from the divisions allow construction of a corporate-level IE Matrix.

On the x-axis of the IE Matrix, an IFE total weighted score of 1.0 to 1.99 represents a weak internal position, a score of 2.0 to 2.99 is considered average, and a score of 3.0 to 4.0 is strong. Similarly, on the y-axis, an EFE total weighted score of 1.0 to 1.99 is considered low, a score of 2.0 to 2.99 is medium, and a score of 3.0 to 4.00 high. A schematic diagram of the IE Matrix is provided in Figure 6.9.

The IE Matrix can be divided into three major regions that have different strategy implications. First, the prescription for divisions that fall into cells I, II, or IV can be "Grow and Build." Intensive (market penetration, market development, and product

Figure 6.9   The Internal-External (IE) Matrix

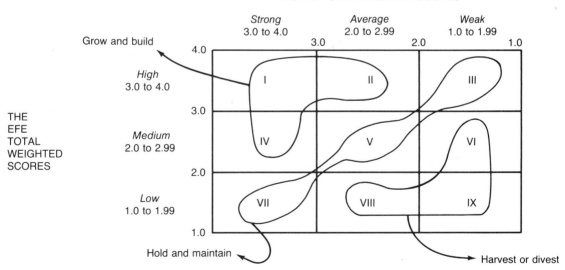

Note: The IE was developed from the General Electric (GE) Business Screen Matrix. For a description of the GE Matrix, see: Michael Allen, "Diagramming GE's Planning for What's WATT," in *Corporate Planning: Techniques and Applications,* ed. R. Allio and M. Pennington (New York: AMACOM, 1979).

development) or integrative (backward integration, forward integration, and horizontal integration) strategies can be most appropriate for these divisions. Second, divisions that fall into cells III, V, or VII can best be managed with "Hold and Maintain" strategies. Market penetration and product development are two commonly employed strategies for these types of divisions. Third, a common prescription for divisions that fall into cells VI, VIII, or IX is "Harvest or Divest." Successful organizations are able to achieve a portfolio of businesses that are positioned in or around cell I in the IE Matrix.

An example IE Matrix is given in Figure 6.10. This organization is composed of four divisions. As indicated by the positioning of the circles, "Grow and Build" strategies are appropriate for Division 1, Division 2, and Division 3. Division 4 is a candidate for "Harvest or Divest." Division 2 contributes the greatest percentage of company sales and thus is represented by the largest circle. Division 1 contributes the greatest proportion of total profits, since it has the largest percentage pie slice.

Two companies that are struggling to "Hold and Maintain" a number of their divisions are Anheuser–Busch and R.J. Reynolds Tobacco. Hikes in state and federal

Figure 6.10   An example IE Matrix

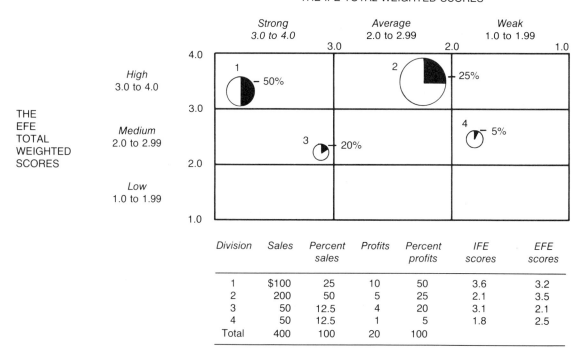

Division	Sales	Percent sales	Profits	Percent profits	IFE scores	EFE scores
1	$100	25	10	50	3.6	3.2
2	200	50	5	25	2.1	3.5
3	50	12.5	4	20	3.1	2.1
4	50	12.5	1	5	1.8	2.5
Total	400	100	20	100		

excise taxes on cigarettes, coupled with the "End Smoking by the Year 2000" campaign, have resulted in an annual 6 percent decline in U.S. cigarette consumption. This is bad news for RJR. Between 1980 and 1984 seventeen states raised their legal drinking age, which has resulted in a yearly decline in the total amount of beer consumed in the United States. This is bad news for Anheuser. To combat these trends, RJR is spending $7 million on a new campaign to promote cigarettes; Anheuser–Busch is marketing a new 2.2 percent-alcohol-content beer called LA (light in alcohol).[14]

The Grand Strategy Matrix

In addition to the TOWS Matrix, SPACE Matrix, BCG Matrix, and IE Matrix, the Grand Strategy Matrix has become a popular tool for formulating company strategy. All organizations can be positioned in one of four strategy quadrants of the Grand Strategy Matrix. The divisions of a firm could likewise be positioned. As illustrated in Figure 6.11, the Grand Strategy Matrix is based on two evaluative dimensions: competitive position and market growth. Appropriate strategies for an organization to consider are listed in order of attractiveness in each quadrant of the matrix.

Figure 6.11   The Grand Strategy Matrix

Source: Adapted from Roland Christensen, Norman Berg, and Malcolm Sulter, *Policy Formulation and Administration* (Homewood, Ill.: Richard D. Irwin, 1976), 16–18.

Firms located in Quadrant I of the Grand Strategy Matrix are in an excellent strategic position. For these firms, continued concentration on current markets (market penetration and market development) and products (product development) are appropriate strategies. It is unwise for a Quadrant I firm to shift notably from its established competitive advantages. When a Quadrant I organization has excessive resources, then backward, forward, or horizontal integration may be effective strategies. When a Quadrant I firm is too heavily committed to a single product, then concentric diversification may reduce the risks associated with a narrow product line. Quadrant I firms can afford to take advantage of external opportunities in many areas; they can aggressively take risks as judged necessary.

Firms positioned in Quadrant II need to evaluate seriously their present approach to the marketplace. Although their industry is growing, they are unable to compete effectively. There is a need to determine why the firm's current approach is ineffectual, and how the company can best change to improve its competitive position. As shown in The Grand Strategy Matrix, Figure 6.11, market penetration, market development, product development, horizontal integration, divestiture, and finally liquidation are appropriate strategies to be considered by Quadrant II firms.

Since Quadrant II firms are in a rapid-market-growth industry, an intensive strategy (as opposed to integration or diversification) is usually the first option that should be considered. However, if the firm is lacking a distinctive competence or competitive advantage, then horizontal integration is often a desirable alternative. As a last resort, divestiture or liquidation should be considered. Divestiture can provide funds needed to develop alternative business activities. Liquidation is an undeniable admission of failure, but often this strategy is a viable alternative to bankruptcy.

Quadrant III organizations compete in a slow-growth industry and have a weak competitive position. These firms must make some drastic changes quickly to avoid further loss and possible extinction. Extensive cost and asset reduction (retrenchment) should be pursued first. An alternative strategy is to shift resources away from the current business into different areas. If all else fails, the final options for Quadrant III businesses are divestiture or liquidation.

Finally, Quadrant IV businesses have a strong competitive position but are in a slow-growth industry. These firms have the strength to launch diversified programs into more promising growth areas. Quadrant IV firms have characteristically high cash flow levels and limited internal growth needs, and often can successfully pursue concentric, horizontal, or conglomerate diversification. Another viable option for the Quadrant IV firm is to form a joint venture.

The Grand Strategy Matrix can be a useful strategy formulation tool for any organization. The original authors of this matching technique did not offer a range of numerical values for the x and y axes. Understandably, there is no "one best set" of numerical values that should be engraved on the Grand Strategy Matrix. Good subjective judgment is required, and appropriate numerical values may differ by type and size of organization. However, a reasonable process for actually establishing numerical values on the Grand Strategy Matrix is given as follows:

The *x*-Axis   The "Competitive Position" axis of the Grand Strategy Matrix is analogous to the "Competitive Advantage" (CA) axis of the SPACE Matrix. The 0 to -6 CA scale described earlier for the SPACE Matrix could be used with the Grand Strategy Matrix. Recall that 0 = strong competitive position and -6 = weak competitive position. A numerical value of -3 could represent an average competitive position on the Grand Strategy Matrix, as it did on the SPACE Matrix. The *x*-axis intersection point on the Grand Strategy Matrix could therefore be -3.

The *y*-Axis   The "Market Growth" axis of the Grand Strategy Matrix is analogous to the "Industry Sales Growth" axis on the BCG Business Portfolio Matrix. The -20 to $+20$ percent scale described earlier for the BCG Matrix could be used for the Grand Strategy Matrix. Recall that $+20$ percent equals rapid market growth and -20 percent equals rapid market decline, with 0 percent growth being the intersection point. A numerical value of 0 could therefore represent the *y*-axis intersection point on the Grand Strategy Matrix.

THE DECISION STAGE

The Quantitative Strategic Planning Matrix (QSPM)

QSPM comprises Stage 3 of the strategy-formulation analytical framework. This matrix objectively suggests which alternative strategies are best. QSPM is the most current of the strategy-formulation analytical techniques.[15] QSPM utilizes "input" information from the Stage 1 analyses and "matching" results from the Stage 2 analyses to objectively "decide" among alternative strategies. That is, the IFE Matrix, EFE Matrix, and the Competitive Profile Matrix (all Stage 1), coupled with the TOWS Matrix, SPACE Analysis, BCG Matrix, IE Matrix, and the Grand Strategy Matrix (all Stage 2), provide the needed information for setting up the Quantitative Strategic Planning Matrix (Stage 3). QSPM is a technique that allows strategists to evaluate alternative strategies quantitatively, based on specific organizational capabilities and limitations. Like other strategy-formulation analytical tools, QSPM requires subjective decisions in assigning weights and ratings. Therefore, it too should be used wisely, not indiscriminately.

The basic format of the Quantitative Strategic Planning Matrix is illustrated in Table 6.6. Note that the left column of QSPM consists of key internal and external factors, and the top row consists of feasible alternative strategies. Specifically, the left column of a QSPM consists of information obtained directly from the IFE Matrix and the EFE Matrix. In a column adjacent to these key factors, the respective ratings received by each factor are recorded. The ratings are the same as those in the IFE and EFE Matrices. The top row of a QSPM consists of alternative strategies that are derived from the TOWS Matrix, SPACE Matrix, BCG Matrix, IE Matrix, and Grand Strategy Matrix. Generally, these "matching" tools generate feasible alternatives that are similar. Every strategy suggested by the matching techniques does not have to be eval-

Table 6.6   The Quantitative Strategic Planning Matrix—QSPM

		STRATEGIC ALTERNATIVES		
Key Factors	*Ratings*	*Strategy 1*	*Strategy 2*	*Strategy 3*
Internal Factors				
Management				
Marketing				
Finance				
Production				
Research and Development				
External Factors				
Economy				
Political				
Social				
Technological				
Competitive				

Internal Factors: 1 = major weakness; 2 = minor weakness; 3 = minor strength; 4 = major strength
External Factors: 1 = major threat; 2 = minor threat; 3 = minor opportunity; 4 = major opportunity

uated in the QSPM. Strategists should use common sense in making this determination.

Conceptually, QSPM determines the relative attractiveness of various strategies based on key internal and external factors. The relative attractiveness of each strategy within a set of alternatives is computed by determining the cumulative impact of each key internal and external factor. Any number of sets of alternative strategies can be included in a QSPM, and any number of strategies can comprise a given set. But only strategies within a given set are evaluated relative to each other. For example, one set of strategies may include concentric, horizontal, and conglomerate diversification, whereas another set may include issuing stock versus divesting of a division to raise needed capital. Recognize that these two sets of strategies are totally different, so the QSPM evaluates strategies only within sets. Note in Table 6.6 that three strategies were included and they comprised just one set.

A more detailed example of QSPM is provided in Table 6.7. This example illustrates all of the components of the QSPM: Key Factors, Strategic Alternatives, Ratings, Attractiveness Scores, Total Attractiveness Scores, and Sum Total Attractiveness Score. The three new terms just introduced, (1) Attractiveness Scores, (2) Total Attractiveness Scores, and (3) Sum Total Attractiveness Score, are defined and explained as the six steps required to develop a QSPM are discussed.

Table 6.7 A sample Quantitative Strategic Planning Matrix

Key Factors	Rating	Acquire Financial Services, Inc.		Acquire Food Services, Inc.		Rationale for Attractiveness Score
		AS*	TAS*	AS*	TAS*	
Internal Factors						
Top management team has fifteen years' experience.	3	4	12	2	6	Fifteen years' experience is in financial services
We have excess working capital of $2 million.	4	2	8	3	12	Food Services is valued at $2 million.
All of our twenty plants are located in the Northeast United States.	1	2	2	4	4	Food Services is located in the Sunbelt.
Our R&D department is outstanding.	3	—	—	—	—	This item does not affect the strategy choice.
Our Return on Investment (ROI) ratio of .12 is lowest in the industry.	1	2	2	3	3	ROI at Food Services is higher than at Financial Services.
External Factors						
Interest rates are expected to rise to 15 percent in 1987.	2	3	6	4	8	Rising rates will hurt the financial services business.
Population of the South is expected to grow by 15.3 million between 1980 and 2000.	3	4	12	2	6	Many new houses and apartments will be built and financed.
The financial services industry is expected to grow by 40 percent in 1986.	4	4	16	2	8	This 40 percent growth is in financial services.
Two major foreign competitors are entering the industry.	1	1	1	3	3	Food Services, Inc. is not affected by this entry.
President Reagan is expected to deregulate the industry.	2	—	—	—	—	This item does not affect the strategy choice.
SUM TOTAL ATTRACTIVENESS SCORE			59		50	

*AS = Attractiveness Score; TAS = Total Attractiveness Score

Attractiveness Score: 1 = not acceptable; 2 = possibly acceptable; 3 = probably acceptable; 4 = most acceptable

Internal Ratings: 1 = major weakness; 2 = minor weakness; 3 = minor strength; 4 = major strength

External Ratings: 1 = major threat; 2 = minor threat; 3 = minor opportunity; 4 = major opportunity

Note: Multiplying the rating times the attractiveness score is based upon the premise that to capitalize on strengths and take advantage of opportunities is more important for firms than improving weaknesses and avoiding threats. Some strategists do not agree with this premise and therefore do not compute the total attractiveness scores. They simply sum the attractiveness scores to determine the relative attractiveness of strategies using the QSPM.

Step One—List the firm's key internal strengths/weaknesses and external opportunities/threats in the left column of the QSPM. This information should be taken directly from the IFE Matrix and the EFE Matrix. A minimum of five key internal factors and five key external factors should be included in the QSPM. Remember that each factor should be stated in specific terms.

Step Two—Assign Ratings to each key internal and external factor. These Ratings are identical to those in the IFE Matrix and the EFE Matrix. The Ratings are presented in a straight column just to the right of the key internal and external factor statements, as shown in Table 6.7.

Step Three—Examine the Stage 2 (matching) matrices and identify alternative strategies that the organization should consider implementing. Record these strategies in the top row of the QSPM. Group the strategies into sets if appropriate.

Step Four—Determine the Attractiveness Scores. They are defined as numerical values that indicate the relative attractiveness of each strategy in a given set of alternatives. Attractiveness Scores are determined by examining each internal or external factor, one at a time, and asking the question "Does this key factor have an effect on the choice of the strategies being evaluated?" If the answer to this question is YES, then the strategy should be evaluated relative to that key factor. Specifically, Attractiveness Scores should be assigned to each strategy in the given set of alternatives, where 1 = the strategy is not acceptable, 2 = the strategy is possibly acceptable, 3 = the strategy is probably acceptable, and 4 = the strategy is most acceptable. However, if the answer to the above question is NO, indicating that the respective key factor has no effect upon the specific choice being made, then do not assign Attractiveness Scores to the strategies in that set. Note in Table 6.7 that the "outstanding R&D Department" (an internal strength) has no significant effect upon the choice being made between acquiring the finance service versus the food company, so "blank" lines are placed in that row of the QSPM. "Two major foreign competitors are entering the industry" is a major external threat that results in an Attractiveness Score of "1" for "Acquire Financial Services," compared to an Attractiveness Score of "3" for the "Acquire Food Services" strategy. These scores indicate that acquiring Financial Services, Inc. is "not an acceptable strategy" whereas acquiring Food Services, Inc. is "probably an acceptable strategy," considering this single external threat.

Step Five—Compute the Total Attractiveness Scores. Total Attractiveness Scores are defined as the product of multiplying the Ratings (Step Two) by the Attractiveness Scores (Step Four) in each row. The Total Attractiveness Scores indicate the relative attractiveness of each alternative strategy, considering only the impact of the adjacent internal or external factor. Total Attractiveness Scores for each alternative are provided in Table 6.7. The higher the Total Attractiveness Score, the more attractive the strategic alternative (considering only the respective internal or external factor).

Step Six—Compute the Sum Total Attractiveness Score. It is the summation of the Total Attractiveness Scores in a strategy column of the QSPM. Sum Total Attractiveness Scores reveal which strategy is most attractive in each set of alternatives. Higher scores indicate more attractive strategies, considering all the relevant internal and external factors that could impact the strategic decisions. The magnitude of the difference between the Sum Total Attractiveness Scores in a given set of strategic alternatives indicates the relative desirability of one strategy over another. (In the example, the Sum Total Attractiveness Score of 59, compared to 50, indicates that Financial Services, Inc. should be acquired).

Applying the QSPM

A direct application of QSPM to Wendy's International, Inc. is provided in Table 6.8, to further illustrate the major steps in applying the Quantitative Strategic Planning Matrix. Wendy's has grown to a position of being the third-largest fast-food hamburger chain in the United States, ranking behind only MacDonald's and Burger King. During the decade of the 1970s, Wendy's grew explosively from a single store in Columbus, Ohio, to over 1800 stores. The average sales per Wendy's restaurant climbed steadily from $230,000 in 1970 to over $600,000 by the end of 1979. In 1979, Wendy's signed franchise agreements with eight European countries and Japan, and opened its first European restaurant in Munich, West Germany. Fully 82 percent of all Wendy's business comes from customers over age 25, an unusually old market for any fast-food chain. By contrast, MacDonald's generates 35 percent of its revenue from youngsters under age 19.

The QSPM illustrated in Table 6.8 reveals that Wendy's top managers recently faced three important strategy decisions: (1) Should we expand into foreign markets or concentrate on the U.S. market? (2) Should we cater to children or continue our practice of appealing to older adults? (3) Should we utilize stock or debt to finance our new restaurant construction?

According to the Sum Total Attractiveness Scores computed in Table 6.8, Wendy's should concentrate on domestic markets, continue targeting on the over-age-25 segment, and use common stock to finance expansion. For example, the Sum Total Attractiveness Score of 57 suggests that domestic markets should be exploited before further development into foreign markets (sum = 35), even though a corporate goal is to open 300 new restaurants yearly. Wendy's revenues, net income, and number of restaurants increased throughout the early 1980s. Wendy's added 201 restaurants in 1982, 243 in 1983, 275 in 1984, and 350 in 1985.

Positive Features and Limitations of QSPM

The positive features of QSPM should be noted. First, sets of strategies can be examined sequentially or simultaneously. For example, corporate-level strategies could be evaluated first, followed by divisional-level strategies, and then functional-level strategies. Second, there is no limit to the number of strategies that can be evaluated or the number of sets of strategies that can be examined at once.

Table 6.8 The application of QSPM to Wendy's International, Inc.

Key Factors	Ratings	Management / Growth Strategy		Strategic Alternatives / Marketing / Market Segmentation		Finance / Capital Expansion Financing	
		1. Concentrate on domestic markets	2. Develop foreign markets	1. Target for the under-age-25 segment	2. Continue targeting on the over-age-25 segment	1. Debt	2. Common Stock
Internal Factors							
Management							
Transaction time is the lowest in the industry at 1 minute.	4	—	—	3 |12	4 |16	—	—
Company goals and objectives are clearly stated as indicated by plan to open 300 new restaurants in 1980.	3	4 |12	3 |9	—	—	—	—
Franchise owners are discontented: 84 sold out to company in 1979.	1	4 |4	2 |2	4 |4	2 |2	—	—
Marketing							
Restaurant decor is not designed for children.	2	—	—	1 |2	4 |8	—	—
Company advertising theme "There ain't no reason to go anywhere else" has been effective.	2	2 |4	1 |2	3 |6	2 |4	—	—
Company is currently test marketing a children's breakfast menu.	4	—	—	3 |12	2 |8	—	—

Internal / External Factors	Weight						
Finance							
Current ratio fell from 1.23 (1978) to .82 (1979).	2	3 | 6	2 | 4	—	—	2 | 4	4 | 8
Profit margins, ROA, and ROE all declined from 1978–79 (11.7 to 8.4; 17 to 13.4; 29.4 to 23 respectively).	1	4 | 4	1 | 1	2 | 2	4 | 4	1 | 1	4 | 4
External Factors							
Economy							
Rising energy costs and high inflation are reducing individuals' disposable income by 20% in 1980.	2	2 | 4	3 | 6	4 | 8	2 | 4	—	—
Political							
Social							
The over-age-25 group is growing 5% yearly while the under-age-25 group is declining.	4	4 | 16	2 | 8	2 | 8	4 | 16	—	—
Technology	—	—	—	—	—	—	—
Competition							
MacDonald's is the largest hamburger chain in the world.	1	4 | 4	1 | 1	2 | 2	3 | 3	2 | 2	4 | 4
MacDonald's P/E ratio (9.74) and EPS (3.12) in 1979 far exceeds Wendy's ratios of 4.6 and 1.45 in 1979.	1	3 | 3	2 | 2	2 | 2	3 | 3	3 | 3	2 | 2
SUM TOTAL		37	22	22	30	10	18

Note: This example based on Wendy's situation in 1980.

Third, a personal computer or mainframe computer can be utilized effectively to develop, expand, and update the QSPM. Visicalc, or some other spreadsheet type of software, can be used to facilitate the QSPM process, especially when numerous sets of strategies are being evaluated. A menu-driven computer program specifically for QSPM is now available.[16] (This program is given in Experiential Exercise 10B).

A fourth positive feature of QSPM is that it requires top managers to integrate pertinent internal and external factors into each strategic decision being made. The QSPM process makes it less likely that key factors will be overlooked or weighted inappropriately. QSPM also draws attention to important interrelationships that impact strategy decisions. (Failure to consider interrelationships among the functional areas of business can lead to ineffective strategic decisions.) Although developing a QSPM requires a number of subjective decisions, making small decisions along the way again enhances the probability that the final strategic decisions will be best for the organization.

A final positive feature is that QSPM can be adapted for use by profit or nonprofit organizations, and can be applied to virtually any type of firm. QSPM can especially enhance the strategic decision-making process in multinational firms, because many key factors and strategies can be considered at once. The matrix also has been applied successfully by a number of small businesses.[17] QSPM has been used with success by many scores of business-policy students in preparing case analyses.

The Quantitative Strategic Planning Matrix is not without some limitations. First, subjective judgments and educated guesses are always required. The 4-point numerical values that are assigned as Ratings and Attractiveness Scores are judgmental decisions even though they should be based on objective information. For example, one individual may assign a 3 (probably acceptable) to Strategy 1 and another manager may assign a 4 (most acceptable) to the same strategy. However, negotiation among managers throughout the strategy-formulation process, including development of the QSPM, is constructive and needed for effective strategic decisions or outcomes. Constructive discussion among managers is common because of genuine differences of interpretation of information and varying opinions of what is really the appropriate strategy. Another limitation of QSPM is that it can be only as good as the input information and matching analyses upon which it is based.

Sometimes political biases and personal preferences get unduly embedded in strategy-formulation analytical matrices. The politics of strategy formulation is therefore discussed next.

THE POLITICS OF STRATEGY FORMULATION

Internal politics affect the choice of strategies in all organizations. The hierarchy of command in an organization, combined with career aspirations of different individuals and the need to allocate scarce resources, guarantee the formation of coalitions of individuals who strive to take care of themselves first and the organization second, third, or fourth.

Coalitions of individuals often form around key strategy issues that face an enterprise. A major responsibility of strategists is to guide the development of coalitions, to nurture an overall team concept, and to gain the support of key individuals and groups of individuals. Internal support for a firm's strategies and objectives is particularly important when the going gets tough, because an organization, and a strategist, can fight only so many losing battles.

Unfortunately, strategy decisions in organizations are too often based on the politics of the moment. Why? Because when major groups of individuals do not support the "best" strategy, then that strategy cannot be implemented effectively. Fortunately, with the development of improved strategy-formulation analytical procedures, political factors can be used less as the primary basis of strategic decisions. In the absence of objectivity, political factors sometimes dictate strategies, and this is unfortunate.

Managing political relationships is an integral part of building enthusiasm and *esprit de corps* in an organization. In a classic study of strategic management in nine large corporations, the political tactics of successful versus unsuccessful executives were examined.[18] According to this study, successful top managers let weakly supported ideas and proposals die through inaction. They establish additional hurdles or tests for strongly supported ideas that are considered unacceptable but are best not opposed openly. Successful chief executive officers keep a low political profile on unacceptable proposals. They strive to let most negative decisions come from subordinates or a group consensus, thereby reserving their own personal vetoes for big issues and crucial moments. Successful strategists do a lot of chatting and informal questioning to stay abreast of how things are progressing and to know when to step in to intervene. They lead strategy, but do not dictate it. They give few orders, announce few decisions, depend heavily on informal questioning, and seek to probe and clarify until a consensus emerges.

This classic study found that successful executives generously and visibly reward key thrusts that succeed; they assign responsibility for major new thrusts to "champions," who are individuals most strongly identified with the idea or product and whose future is linked to its success. Successful chief executive officers stay alert to the symbolic impact of their own actions and statements, so as not to send a false signal that could stimulate proposals and movements in unwanted directions.

Successful top managers ensure that all major power bases within an organization have representation in or access to top management. They interject new faces and new views into considerations of major changes. (This is important because new employees generally have more enthusiasm and drive than employees who have been with the firm a long time. New employees do not "see the world the same old way" and act as systematic screens against changes. Successful strategists minimize their own political exposure on issues that are highly controversial and in circumstances where opposition from major power centers can trigger a "shootout."

In combination, these guidelines provide a basis for managing political relationships in an organization. Experiential Exercise 6A at the end of this chapter focuses on a political issue, the use of power in formulating strategies.

THE ROLE OF A BOARD OF DIRECTORS

Boards of directors usually have not attempted to second-guess chief executive officers, even on strategic issues. It has been generally understood that those responsible for implementing strategy should formulate it. Chief executive officers have often avoided discussions of overall strategy with directors because the results could restrict their freedom of action. The judgments of board members have seldom been used even on acquisitions, divestitures, large capital investments, and other strategic matters. Often the board will meet only annually to fulfill its minimum legal requirements. Members just serve a traditional legitimizing role in many organizations. This widespread lack of involvement by boards of directors in the strategic-management process is rapidly changing in America!

There are a number of reasons for the expanded role of boards of directors in formulating, implementing, and evaluating corporate strategies. Stockholders, government agencies, and interest groups are more and more filing legal suits against directors for fraud, omissions, inaccurate disclosures, lack of due diligence, and for not knowing what is going on in sufficient detail. Example legal cases where directors were held liable or charged with negligence are *Gould* v. *American Hawaiian Steamship Co.* (1972), *Lanze* v. *Drezel & Company* (1974), *SEC* v. *Penn Central* (1974), and *SEC* v. *Gulf Oil Corporation* (1975).

More recently, two particular rulings have affected the role of a board of directors in the strategy-formulation process. The Supreme Court of Delaware in 1985 ruled that the directors of the Trans Union Corporation violated the interests of shareholders when they hastily accepted a takeover bid from the Marmon Group. Some legal experts say the ruling erodes the broad discretion directors have always enjoyed under the so-called business judgment rule, which protects directors from liability as long as their decisions represent a good-faith effort to serve the best interests of the corporation. One clear signal from the Trans Union case is that haste can be costly for board members. In the second ruling, the Federal Deposit Insurance Corporation, in 1985, forced Continental Illinois to accept the resignations of ten of the troubled bank's outside directors. This case illustrates that boards of directors are increasingly being held responsible for the overall performance of corporations.

The impact of increasing legal pressures on board members is that directors are demanding to have access to more financial performance information on a regular basis. Directors are beginning to place more emphasis on staying informed about the corporation's health and operations; they are taking a more active role in assuring that publicly issued documents are accurate representations of the firm's status. It is becoming widely recognized that a board of directors has legal responsibilities to stockholders and society for all company activities, for corporate performance, and for seeing to it that a firm has an effective strategy. Failure to accept responsibility for auditing or evaluating a firm's strategy is a serious breach of a director's duties.

A direct response of increased pressures on directors to stay informed and execute their responsibilities is that audit committees are becoming commonplace. Milton Lauenstein proposes that a board of directors should conduct an annual strategy audit in much the same fashion that it reviews the annual financial audit.[19] In performing such an audit, a board could work jointly with operating management and/or seek outside counsel. The questions provided in Exhibit 6.3 are illustrative of the areas that a strategy audit might encompass. Not all of these questions, of course, apply to every situation and organization.

The trend among corporations toward increased diversification, multidivisional structures, and multinational operations, the rapid changes in the environment, and increased legal pressures, augment the problem of keeping directors informed. Boulton stresses that boards should play a role beyond that of performing a strategic audit. They should provide greater input and advice in the strategy-formulation process to assure that top management is providing for the strategic needs of the firm.[20]

Exhibit 6.3   A board of directors strategy audit framework

- Is the company adequately informed about its markets? What further information would be worth the cost of getting? How should it be obtained?

- How well informed is the company about its competitors? How well is it able to forecast what competitors will do under various circumstances? Is there a sound basis for such competitive appraisals? Is the company underestimating or overestimating its competitors?

- Has management adequately explored various ways of segmenting its market? To what extent is it addressing market segments in which the company's strengths provide meaningful advantages?

- Are the products and services the company proposes to sell ones that it can provide more effectively than competitors? What is the basis for such a belief?

- Do the various activities proposed in the strategy provide synergistic advantages? Are they compatible?

- Does the proposed strategy adequately address questions of corporate objectives, financial policy, scope of operations, organization, and integration?

- What specific resources (personnel, skills, information, facilities, technology, finances, relationships) will be needed to execute the strategy? Does the company already possess these resources? Has management established programs for building these resources and overall competence which will provide telling competitive advantages over the long run?

- To what extent does the strategy define a unique and appropriate economic role for the company? How different is it from the competitors' strategy?

- Has the issue of growth rate been raised? Are there good reasons to believe that investment in growth will pay off? Does the company's track record support such a conclusion?

- Does the proposed dividend policy reflect the company's growth policy, based on a demonstrated ability or inability to reinvest cash flow advantageously? Or is it just a "safe" compromise, conforming to what others usually do?

- Is management capable of implementing the strategy effectively? What leads to this conclusion?

- How and to what extent is the strategy to be communicated to the organization? Is it to be distributed in written form? If competitors are aware of the company's strategy, will that help or hurt?

- What provision is to be made for employing the strategy as a guide to operating decisions? To what extent is it to be used by the board? How?

- How is it to be kept up-to-date? Are there to be regular reviews? How often and by whom?

- Has a set of long-range projections of operations following the strategy been prepared? Have the possible results of following alternative strategies been prepared?

- Does the strategy focus on the few really important key issues? Is it too detailed? Does it address genuine business questions (as opposed to "motherhood" statements)?

- In its strategic thinking, has management avoided the lure of simplistic approaches such as:

  Growth for growth's sake?

  Diversification for diversification's sake?

  Aping the industry leader?

  Broadening the scope in order to secure "incremental" earnings?

  Assuming it can execute better than competitors without objective evidence that such is the case?

- Are there other issues, trends, or potential events that should have been taken into account?

Source: Milton Lauenstein, "Boards of Directors: The Strategy Audit," *Journal of Business Strategy* 4, no. 3 (Winter 1984): 90, 91.

CONCLUSION

The essence of strategy formulation is an assessment of whether an organization is doing the right things and how it can be more effective in what it does. Every organization should be wary of becoming a prisoner of its own strategy, because even the best strategies become obsolete sooner or later. A strategic plan should never be cast in stone. Regular reappraisal of strategy helps management avoid complacency.

Objectives and strategies should be developed consciously and coordinated rather than just evolved out of day-to-day operating decisions. Remember that organizations with no sense of direction and no coherent strategy precipitate their own demise. When an organization does not know where it wants to go, it usually ends up someplace it does not want to be. Every organization should establish and communicate clear objectives and strategies.

Important strategy-formulation tools and concepts are described in this chapter. An effective strategy-formulation analytical framework is presented. Analytical tools such as the SPACE Matrix, BCG Matrix, IE Matrix, and QSPM can significantly enhance the quality of strategy decisions, but they should never be used blindly to dictate the choice of strategies.

Due to increased legal pressure from outside groups, boards of directors are assuming a more active role in the strategy-formulation process. The trend toward director activity, providing input to and auditing strategic-management activities, should benefit corporate performance in the future.

REVIEW QUESTIONS

1. How would application of the strategy-formulation analytical framework differ in a small versus a large organization?

2. What types of strategies would you recommend for a division that scores 3.6 on its IFE total weighted score and 1.2 on its EFE total weighted score?

3. Given the following information, construct a SPACE Matrix for the XYZ Corporation.
FS = +2   ES = -6   CA = -2   IS = +4

4. Go to your college library and find a recent Annual Report on a multidivisional organization. Diagram a BCG Matrix for the company, based on information provided in the organization's *Annual Report, Moody's Industrial Manual,* and the *Stock Reports.*

5. Explain the steps involved in applying QSPM.

6. Describe how you would develop a set of objectives for your School of Business.

7. Identify five major subjective variables that could impact the selection of specific strategies and objectives. Could these variables be quantified? How?

8. How are the TOWS Matrix, SPACE Matrix, BCG Matrix, IE Matrix, and Grand Strategy Matrix similar? How are they different?

9. How would profit versus nonprofit organizations differ in their application of the strategy-formulation analytical framework?

10. Select one of the articles given in the suggested readings at the end of this chapter. Prepare a report to the class on that article.

FOOTNOTES

1 In this text, goals refer to short-term (one year or less) results that an organization strives to achieve, whereas objectives refer to long-term (more than one year) aims. Although there exists some inconsistency among authors in the use of these terms, this text is consistent with a number of writers, including Godiwalla, Meinhart, Warde, Vancil, Lorange, and others mentioned in Chapter 2.

2 These four alternatives were first presented in Steven C. Brandt, *Strategic Planning in Emerging Companies,* © 1981, Addison–Wesley, Reading, Massachusetts. Excerpted material from Chapter 2. Reprinted with permission.

3 Jill Bettner, "After the Centerfold," *Forbes* (March 26, 1984): 44.

4 Eleanor Tracy, "Knocked from Third Place, 7–Up Is Going Flat," *Fortune* (May 14, 1984): 96. Also, "Coke's

Man on the Spot," *Business Week* (July 29, 1985): 56–61.

5 Heinz Weihrich, "The TOWS Matrix: A Tool for Situational Analysis," *Long Range Planning* 15, no. 2 (April 1982): 61.

6 Carol Curtis, "Mobil Wants To Be Your Milkman," *Forbes* (February 13, 1984): 44.

7 A. Rowe, R. Mason, and K. Dickel, *Strategic Management and Business Policy: A Methodological Approach"* (*Reading, Mass.:* Addison–Wesley Publishing Co., 1982): 155.

8 Ibid., *155–64.*

9 *Michael Cieply, "And Then We Will Attack," Forbes* (March 26, 1984): 42.

10 Boston Consulting Group, *Perspectives on Experience* (Boston: The Boston Consulting Group, 1974). Also,

Barry Hedley, "Strategy and the Business Portfolio," *Long Range Planning* 10, no. 1 (February 1977): 9.

11 A. A. Thompson, Jr. and A. J. Strickland III, *Strategic Management: Concepts and Cases* (Plano, Texas: Business Publications, Inc., 1984), 122.

12 Faye Rice, "Trouble at Procter & Gamble," *Fortune* (March 5, 1984): 70.

13 The IE Matrix was developed especially for this text. This technique is similar to the General Electric Business Screen, but the axes are labeled more clearly and the scoring procedure is improved.

14 Tom Post, "Preserving Endangered Products," *Fortune* (March 5, 1984): 70.

15 Fred David, "Evaluating Alternative Growth Strategies—An Analytical Approach," *Long Range Planning* (Spring 1986). In press.

16 Fred David, "Computer-Assisted Strategic Planning in Small Businesses," *Journal of Systems Management* 36, no. 7 (July 1985): 24–34.

17 Ibid.

18 James Brian Quinn, *Strategies for Change: Logical Incrementalism* (Homewood, Ill.: Richard D. Irwin, 1980), 128–145. These political tactics are listed in A. Thompson and A. Strickland, *Strategic Management: Concepts and Cases* (Plano, Texas: Business Publications, Inc., 1984), 261.

19 Milton Lauenstein, "Boards of Directors: The Strategic Audit," *Journal of Business Strategy* (Winter 1984): 87–91.

20 William Boulton, "Effective Board Development: Five Areas for Concern," *Journal of Business Strategy* (Spring 1983): 94–100.

SUGGESTED READINGS

Allen, Michael. "Diagramming GE's Planning for What's WATT." In *Corporate Planning: Techniques and Applications,* edited by R. Allio and M. Pennington. New York: AMACOM, 1979.

Bloom, P.N., and P. Kotler. "Strategies for High Market-Share Companies." *Harvard Business Review* 53, no. 6 (November–December 1975): 63–72.

Boston Consulting Group. *Perspectives on Experience.* Boston: The Boston Consulting Group, 1974.

Boulton, William. "Effective Board Development: Five Areas for Concern." *Journal of Business Strategy* (Spring 1983): 94–100.

Brandt, S.C. *Strategic Planning in Emerging Companies.* Reading, Mass.: Addison–Wesley Publishing Co., 1981.

Buzzell, R.D. "Is Vertical Integration Profitable?" *Harvard Business Review* 61, no. 1 (January–February 1983): 92–102.

Christenson, C.R. "The Dog Business: Strategy Development for Low Market Share Businesses." *Business Horizons* (November–December 1982): 12–18.

Collier, D. "Strategic Management in Diversified, Decentralized Companies." *Journal of Business Strategy* 3, no. 1 (Summer 1982): 85–89.

David, F.R. "Computer-Assisted Strategic Planning in Small Businesses." *Journal of Systems Management* 36, no. 7 (July 1985): 24–34.

David, F.R. "Evaluating Alternative Growth Strategies—An Analytical Approach." *Long Range Planning* (Spring 1986). In press.

David, F.R. "Formulating Strategies Objectively: Analytical Tools." In *Handbook of Business Strategy—1985/1986 Yearbook.* New York: Warren, Gorham & Lamont, Inc., November 1985. Also, David, Fred R. "A Framework for Evaluating Strategies Objectively." In Southern Management Association *Proceedings,* 1985: 31–33.

"Dresser Industries: A Leaner Look As It Waits Out a Lingering Slump." *Business Week* (September 26, 1983): 78–79.

Ebeling, H.W. and T.L. Doorley III. "A Strategic Approach to Acquisitions." *Journal of Business Strategy* (Winter 1983): 44–54.

Harrigan, K.R. "A Framework for Looking at Vertical Integration." *Journal of Business Strategy* (Winter 1983): 30–37.

Harrigan, K.R. and M.E. Porter. "End-Game Strategies

for Declining Industries." *Harvard Business Review* 61, no. 4 (July–August 1983): 111–20.

Haspeslagh, P. "Portfolio Planning: Uses and Limits." *Harvard Business Review* 60, no. 1 (January–February 1982): 17–25.

Hedley, B. "Strategy and the Business Portfolio." *Long Range Planning* 10, no. 1 (February 1977): 9–15.

Hofer, C.W. and D. Schendel. *Strategy Formulation: Analytical Concepts.* St. Paul, Minn.: West Publishing Co., 1978.

Lauenstein, Milton. "Boards of Directors: The Strategic Audit." *Journal of Business Strategy* (Winter 1984): 87–91.

Machiavelli, N. *The Prince.* New York: The Washington Press, 1963.

Miesing, P. "Limitations of Matrix Models As a Strategic Planning Tool." *Managerial Planning* (May–June 1983): 42–45.

Migliore, R.H. "Linking Strategy, Performance, and Pay." *Journal of Business Strategy* 3, no. 1 (Summer 1982): 90–94.

Napper, W.C. "Tools for Managing in Mature Operations." *The Journal of Business Strategy* (Summer 1983): 90–96.

Norburn, D. "The British Boardroom: Time for a Revolution." *Long Range Planning* (October 1984): 35–44.

Pearce, J.A. II. "Selecting Among Alternative Grand Strategies." *California Management Review* (Spring 1982): 23–31.

Porter, M.E. "How Competitive Forces Shape Strategy." *Harvard Business Review* (April 1979): 141–45.

Rowe, A., R. Mason, and K. Dickel. *Strategic Management and Business Policy: A Methodological Approach.* Reading, Mass.: Addison–Wesley Publishing Company, 1982.

Rumelt, R. "Diversification Strategy and Profitability." *Strategic Management Journal* (October–December 1982): 359–69.

South, S.E. "Competitive Advantage: The Cornerstone of Strategic Thinking." *Journal of Business Strategy* (Spring 1981): 15–25.

Tomasko, R.M. "Focusing Company Reward Systems To Help Achieve Business Objectives." *Management Review* (October 1982): 8–12.

Vancil, R.F. and P. Lorange. "Strategic Planning in Diversified Companies." *Harvard Business Review* 53, no. 1 (January–February 1975): 81–90.

Weihrich, Heinz. "The TOWS Matrix—A Tool for Situational Analysis." *Long Range Planning* 15, no. 2 (April 1982): 54–66.

Wind, Y., and V. Mahajan. "Designing Product and Business Portfolios." *Harvard Business Review* (January–February 1981): 155–65.

EXPERIENTIAL EXERCISE 6A:

The Mach Test

PURPOSE

The purpose of this exercise is to enhance your understanding of the impact that internal political factors can have on the strategy-formulation process. Recall from Chapter 6 that successful strategists ensure that all major power bases within an organization have representation in, or access to, top management.

INSTRUCTIONS

For each of the following statements, circle the number that most closely resembles your attitude. Then add the number you have circled on questions 1, 3, 4, 5, 9, and 10. For the other four questions, reverse the numbers you circled, so a 5 becomes a 1, 4 becomes 2, 2 becomes 4, 1 becomes 5, and 3 remains 3. Add those four numbers. Finally, add your two subtotal scores together to get a Final Score.

Statement	Disagree			Agree	
	A lot	A little	Neutral	A little	A lot
1. The best way to handle people is to tell them what they want to hear.	1	2	3	4	5
2. When you ask someone to do something for you, it is best to give the real reason for wanting it, rather than giving a reason that might carry more weight.	1	2	3	4	5
3. Anyone who completely trusts anyone else is asking for trouble.	1	2	3	4	5
4. It is hard to get ahead without cutting corners here and there.	1	2	3	4	5
5. It is safest to assume that all people have a vicious streak, and it will come out when they are given a chance.	1	2	3	4	5
6. One should take action only when it is morally right.	1	2	3	4	5
7. Most people are basically good and kind.	1	2	3	4	5
8. There is no excuse for lying to someone else.	1	2	3	4	5
9. Most men forget more easily the death of their father than the loss of their property.	1	2	3	4	5
10. Generally speaking, men won't work hard unless they're forced to do so.	1	2	3	4	5

YOUR FINAL SCORE

Your Final Score is actually your Machiavellian Score. The National Opinion Research Center, which used this short form in a random sample of American adults, found the national average Final Score to be 25.[1] The higher your score, the more Machiavellian (manipulative) you tend to be. The following scale is representative of individual scores on this test:

below 16: Never uses manipulation as a tool.

16 to 20: Rarely uses manipulation as a tool.

21 to 25: Sometimes uses manipulation as a tool.

26 to 30: Often uses manipulation as a tool.

over 30: Always uses manipulation as a tool.

A classic book on power relationships, *The Prince,* was written by Niccolo Machiavelli. Machiavellian principles are defined in a dictionary as "manipulative, dishonest, deceiving, and favoring political expediency over morality." *Machiavellian tactics are not desirable or recommended in the strategic-management process.* Several excerpts from *The Prince* are given below:

> Men must either be cajoled or crushed, for they will revenge themselves for slight wrongs, while for grave ones they cannot. The injury therefore that you do to a man should be such that you need not fear his revenge.
>
> We must bear in mind . . . that there is nothing more difficult and dangerous, or more doubtful of success, than an attempt to introduce a new order of things in any state. The innovator has for enemies all those who derived advantages from the old order of things, while those who expect to be benefited by the new institution will be but lukewarm defenders.
>
> A wise prince, therefore, will steadily pursue such a course that the citizens of his state will always and under all circumstances feel the need for his authority, and will therefore always prove faithful to him.
>
> A prince should seem to be merciful, faithful, humane, religious, and upright, and should even be so in reality; but he should have his mind so trained that, when occasion requires it, he may know how to change to the opposite.[2]

TEST DEVELOPMENT

The Mach (Machiavellian) test was developed by Dr. Richard Christie because of his interest in individuals who were effective in manipulating others. A good example of someone who is a high Mach (score over 30) is the role J. R. Ewing plays on the television show, *Dallas.* Dr. Christie's research suggests the following tendencies:

1. Men are generally more Machiavellian than women.

2. There is no significant difference between high Machs and low Machs on measures of intelligence or ability.

3. Although high Machs are detached from others, they are not detached in a pathological sense.

4. Machiavellian scores are not statistically related to authoritarian scores.

5. High Machs tend to be professionals that emphasize the control and manipulation of individuals; for example, lawyers, psychiatrists, and behavioral scientists.

6. Machiavellianism is not significantly related to the major demographic characteristics such as educational level or marital status.

7. High Machs tend to come from a city or urban background.

8. Older adults tend to have lower Mach scores than younger adults.[3]

FOOTNOTES

1 Richard Christie and Florence L. Geis, *Studies in Machiavellianism* (Academic Press, 1970).

2 Nicholas Machiavelli, *The Prince* (New York: The Washington Press, 1963).

3 Op cit. 82–83.

EXPERIENTIAL EXERCISE 6B:

Developing a Quantitative Strategic Planning Matrix (QSPM) for Ponderosa, Inc.

PURPOSE

The purpose of this exercise is to give you practice developing a Quantitative Strategic Planning Matrix. This technique comprises Stage 3 of the strategy-formulation analytical framework. The QSPM can help you determine the relative attractiveness of various strategic alternatives when analyzing a business policy case.

YOUR TASK

In Chapter 6, six steps were described for developing a QSPM. Your task here is to follow those steps and develop a QSPM for the Cohesion Case on Ponderosa. To accomplish this task, use information provided in the case as well as any other relevant materials you can find in your college library. Come to class prepared to present and discuss the Quantitative Strategic Planning Matrix that you develop.

PART THREE

Strategy Implementation

7

Implementing Strategies

243

Strategy implementation involves restructuring and reorganizing internal activities in a way that encourages and rewards efforts to achieve stated objectives. This chapter presents a framework for accomplishing the strategy-implementation task. Functional business concepts central to successful strategy implementation are examined. (The next chapter examines goals setting, policy making, and resource allocation activities. Together, these two chapters describe the strategy-implementation process.)

THE STRATEGY-IMPLEMENTATION PROCESS

A Framework for Strategy Implementation

The strategy implementation stage of the strategic-management process is shown in Figure 7.1. Note that the strategic-management process does not end when top management decides how the firm is going to achieve its objectives. There is still a need to

Figure 7.1 The strategic-management model

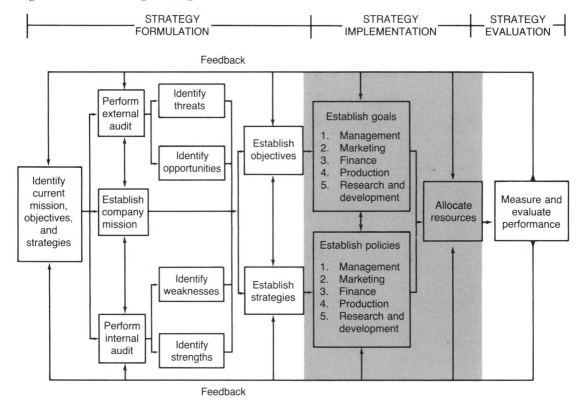

set goals, establish policies, and allocate resources. Successful strategy formulation does not guarantee successful strategy implementation. Formulation and implementation activities are fundamentally different. Strategy formulation is largely an intellectual process, whereas strategy implementation is more operational in character. Strategy formulation requires good conceptual, integrative, and analytical skills, but strategy implementation requires special skills in motivating and managing others. Strategy formulation occurs primarily at the corporate level of an organization, while strategy implementation permeates all hierarchical levels. Strategy formulation requires coordination among a few individuals, but strategy implementation requires coordination among many. It is always more difficult to do something (strategy implementation) than to say you are going to do it (strategy formulation)!

The basic activities required for effective strategy formulation (conduct research, perform analysis, and make decisions) do not differ greatly for small or large, profit or nonprofit organizations. However, the strategy-implementation process can vary considerably among different types and sizes of organizations. Implementing strategy includes such actions as altering sales territories, adding new departments, closing facilities, hiring new employees, changing an organization's pricing strategy, developing financial budgets, developing new employee benefits, establishing cost control procedures, changing advertising strategies, building new facilities, training new employees, and transferring managers among divisions. These activities obviously differ significantly, depending on the type and size of organization. Recall from Chapter 1 that there are three fundamental strategy-implementation activities: establish goals, establish policies, and allocate resources.

Implementing strategy affects an organization from top to bottom; it impacts all the functional areas of business. It is beyond the purpose and scope of this text to examine all of the functional business concepts and tools that are important in the strategy-implementation process. However, this chapter focuses on management, marketing, finance, production, and research and development issues that are central to strategy implementation; that is, functional business techniques most commonly required to successfully implement strategies are examined. The next chapter focuses on the fundamental implementation activities: goal setting, policy making, and resource allocation. The concepts examined in these two chapters are summarized in the framework shown in Figure 7.2.

The strategy-implementation framework reflects the need for functional-area business changes in implementing new strategies. These changes will be more extensive when strategies to be implemented move a firm in a major new direction or intensify efforts to achieve current objectives. Changes commonly needed include altering the existing organizational structure, revising reward and incentive plans, implementing change, managing new political relationships, developing a strategy-supportive corporate culture, segmenting new markets, positioning new products, preparing *pro forma* financial statements, devising financial budgets, measuring the worth of a business, improving production operations, and shifting areas of emphasis in research and development.

Figure 7.2   A strategy-implementation framework

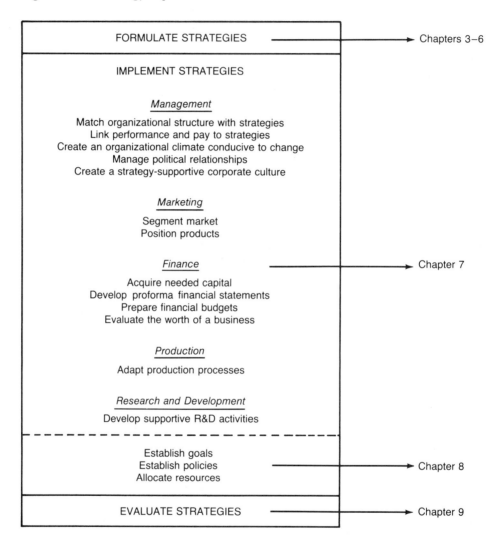

Strategy implementation directly impacts the working lives of marketing managers, finance managers, production managers, research and development managers, plant managers, division managers, department managers, sales managers, product managers, project managers, personnel managers, staff managers, and all other employees. Many of these individuals may not have participated in the strategy-formulation process at all. Therefore, they may not appreciate, understand, or even accept the research, analysis, and decision making that went into the strategy-formulation process. There may be some foot-dragging or resistance on their part. In some cases, managers and employees may even attempt to sabotage the strategy-implementation process in hopes that the organization will return to its old ways.

Guidelines for Implementing Strategies

Before we examine functional business concepts and techniques that can facilitate the implementation process, some overall guidelines are presented that commonly enhance strategy-implementation efforts. First, mechanisms are needed to assure that managers throughout an organization participate early and directly in the strategy-implementation process. Successful strategy implementation requires commitment and support from lower-level managers. Managers' involvement in strategy-implementation decisions and activities should build upon prior involvement in the strategy-formulation process.

In addition to lower- and middle-level managers' support, top management's encouragement and enthusiasm is essential for implementation activities to succeed. Top management's expressed personal commitment to strategy implementation is a necessary and powerful motivational force for middle- and lower-level managers. Too often top managers are "too busy" to actively support implementation efforts, and this can be detrimental to the entire strategic-management process.

When company objectives are established and strategies are chosen, top managers should communicate clearly the primary reasons why the enterprise needs to move in the chosen direction. The rationale for objectives and strategies should be explained. Major competitors' accomplishments, products, plans, actions, and performance should be discussed. Major external opportunities and threats should be communicated, and managers' and employees' questions should be answered. This top-down flow of communication is essential for developing bottom-up support.

To implement strategies successfully, an organization's reward system should be studied and perhaps revamped to encourage and support the work needed to achieve stated objectives. Incentives such as bonuses and profit sharing can effectively be tied to accomplishment of desired results. The skills and special competencies of particular managers and employees should be nurtured.

New strategies often mean new markets and new products. Existing market segmentation and positioning should be examined and perhaps altered to support strategy-implementation efforts. Market segmentation and market positioning are often considered the two most important marketing concepts that affect the success of strategy-implementation efforts.[1]

Pro forma financial statements should be prepared on a companywide, divisional, and departmental basis. Projected financial statements provide the basis for financial budgets and controls that are needed to insure that resources are used effectively during the implementation process. When strategy implementation requires additional capital, Earnings Per Share/Earnings Before Interest and Taxes (EPS/EBIT) analysis is needed to determine whether stock, debt, or some combination of stock and debt should be used as the source of capital. Production and research and development operations, too, can enhance, restrict, or constrain strategy-implementation efforts.

The guidelines offered above for implementing strategies are developed more extensively in this chapter so that you will have a working knowledge of central strategy-implementation tools and concepts. Let's first focus attention on some central management issues that arise when implementing strategies.

MANAGEMENT PERSPECTIVES ON STRATEGY IMPLEMENTATION

Matching Organizational Structure with Strategy

There are two major reasons why changes in company strategy often require changes in the way an organization is structured. The first reason is that structure dictates how goals and policies will be established. For example, the format for goals and policies that are established under a geographic organizational structure will be couched in geographic terms, whereas goals and policies established in a structure based on customer groups will be stated in terms of major customers. This difference in the way goals and policies are devised can have a significant impact on the strategy-implementation process.

The second reason why changes in company strategy often require changes in an organization's structure is that structure dictates how resources will be allocated. If an organization's structure is based on customer groups, then resources will be allocated in that manner. Similarly, if an organization's structure is set up along functional business lines, then resources are allocated by functional areas. So, an organization's structure dictates not only how goals and policies will be established, but also how resources will be allocated. Unless new or revised strategies place emphasis in the same areas as old strategies, structural reorientation is commonly a part of strategy-implementation efforts.

In a classic study of seventy large American corporations, Alfred Chandler concluded that changes in company strategy lead to changes in organizational structure.[2] Structure, he says, should be designed to facilitate the strategic pursuit of a firm. Structure, therefore, follows strategy. Chandler found a particular sequence to be often repeated as organizations grow and change strategy over time. This sequence is depicted in Figure 7.3.

There is no one optimal organizational design or structure for a given type or size of organization. What is appropriate for one organization may not be appropriate for a similar firm, although successful firms in a given industry do tend to organize themselves in a similar way. For example, consumer-goods companies tend to emulate the divisional-structure-by-product form of organization. Small firms tend to be functionally structured (centralized). Medium-size firms tend to be divisionally structured (decentralized). Large firms tend to use an SBU (strategic business unit) or matrix-type structure. As organizations grow from small to large, their structures generally must change

Figure 7.3   Chandler's strategy–structure relationship

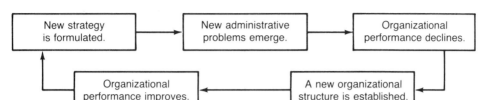

from simple to complex, "as the result of concatenation, or the linking together of several basic strategies."[3]

Although the strategic-management literature stresses the need to match structure with strategy, it is undeniable that structure can and does influence strategy.[4] As emphasized throughout this text, strategies formulated must be workable. Therefore, if a certain new strategy would require massive structural changes, that fact would make the strategy less attractive. In this way, structure can shape the choice of strategies. The more important concern in this chapter is what types of structural changes are needed to implement new strategies, and how can these changes best be accomplished? This issue is examined by focusing on the seven basic types of organizational structure: functional, divisional by geographic area, divisional by product, divisional by customer, divisional by process, strategic business unit (SBU), and matrix.

Peter Drucker describes the difficulties in choosing an appropriate organizational structure by saying: "The simplest organization structure that will do the job is the best one. What makes an organization structure 'good' are the problems it does not create. The simpler the structure, the less that can go wrong."[5] It is important to recognize that various organizational designs are tools, and tools are neither good nor bad in themselves. The architect of an organization should start out with a clear focus on key activities needed to produce key results.

The Functional Structure   The most widely used type of structure is the functional or centralized design, primarily because this structure is the simplest and least expensive of the seven alternatives. A functional design groups tasks and activities together by business function such as production/operations, marketing, finance/accounting, research and development, and personnel. A university may structure its activities by major functions that include academic affairs, student services, alumni relations, athletics, maintenance, and accounting. A functional organizational structure is illustrated in Figure 7.4.

Besides being simple and inexpensive, other advantages of a functional structure are that it promotes specialization of labor, encourages efficiency, minimizes the need for an elaborate control system, and allows rapid decision making. Some disadvantages of a functional structure are that it forces accountability to the top, minimizes career-development opportunities, and is sometimes characterized by low employee morale,

Figure 7.4   A functional organizational structure

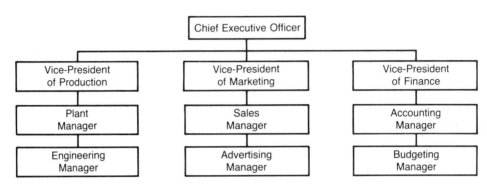

line–staff conflicts, poor delegation of authority, and inadequate planning for products and markets.

In July 1984, Hewlett–Packard revamped its organizational structure to be more functional.[6] A primary reason for H–P's reorganization was to increase the firm's emphasis on marketing. Among other changes, a new corporate marketing department was established. Hewlett–Packard is the largest and most diversified producer of electronic instruments in the world; HWP's 1984 sales of $6 billion and profits of $665 million were the highest in the firm's history.

The Divisional Structure   The divisional or decentralized structure is the second most common type used by American businesses. In order to more fully understand the nature and benefits of decentralization, recall from Chapter 5 the importance of delegation of authority. As a small organization grows, it becomes increasingly difficult for top managers to manage different products and services in different markets. Some form of divisional structure generally becomes necessary to motivate employees effectively, control operations, and compete successfully in diverse locations. The divisional structure can be organized in one of four basic ways: by geographic area, by product or service, by customer, or by process. Within a divisional structure, functional activities are performed centrally and in each separate division.

A divisional structure has some clear advantages. First, and perhaps foremost, accountability is clear. That is, divisional managers can be held responsible for sales and profit levels. Since this design is based on extensive delegation of authority, managers and employees can easily see the results of their good or bad performances. As a result, employee morale is generally higher in a divisional structure than in a centralized design. Other advantages of the divisional design are that it creates career development opportunities for managers, allows local control of local situations, leads to a competitive climate within an organization, and allows new businesses and products to be added easily.

The divisional design is not without some limitations. Perhaps most important is that a divisional structure is costly, for a number of reasons. First, there exists a need for functional specialists in each division, and these individuals' salaries must be paid. Second, there exists some duplication of staff services, facilities, and personnel. For instance, functional specialists are also needed centrally (at headquarters) to coordinate divisional activities. Third, managers must be well-qualified since the divisional design forces delegation of authority. Better-qualified individuals require higher salaries. Finally, a divisional structure can be costly because it requires an elaborate, head-quarters-driven control system.

Other limitations of a divisional structure include special treatment sometimes given to certain regions, products, or customers, and a difficulty in maintaining consistent company-wide practices. However, for most large organizations and many small firms, the advantages of a divisional structure more than offset the potential limitations.

An example firm that is radically decentralized is 3M. This company has 39 divisions selling a staggering 50,000 types and sizes of products. "3M has built one of the most enviable long-term-growth records in the country by relying on small entrepreneurial teams to develop new products that are spun off into separate businesses as they grow."[7]

Diagrams of a divisional structure by geographic area, product, customer, and process are provided in Figure 7.5. A divisional structure by geographic area is appropriate for organizations where strategies need to be tailored to fit the particular needs and characteristics of customers in different geographic areas. This type of structure can be most appropriate for organizations that have similar branch facilities located in widely dispersed areas. A divisional structure by geographic area allows local participation in decision making and improved coordination within a region. Example organizations that use the geographic type of divisional structure include the Internal Revenue Service, the American Red Cross, the Small Business Administration, Sears and Roebuck, and A & P.

The divisional structure by product is most effective for implementing company strategies when special emphasis needs to be placed on specific products or services, or when an organization offers only a limited number of products or services, or when an organization's products differ substantially, or when different marketing approaches are required for the organization's various products. The divisional structure allows strict control and attention to product lines, but its advantages can be offset by the requirement of a more greatly skilled management force and reduced top-management control. General Motors, DuPont, and Procter and Gamble use the product type of divisional structure to implement company strategies.

When a few major customers are of paramount importance and many different services are provided to these customers, then a divisional structure by customer can be the most effective way to implement company strategies. This type of structure allows an organization to cater effectively to the requirements of clearly defined customer groups. For example, book publishing companies often organize their activities around customer groups such as colleges, secondary schools, and private commercial schools. Some airline companies have two major customer divisions: passengers and freight or cargo services.

Figure 7.5 Alternative divisional structures

A. A divisional structure by geographic area

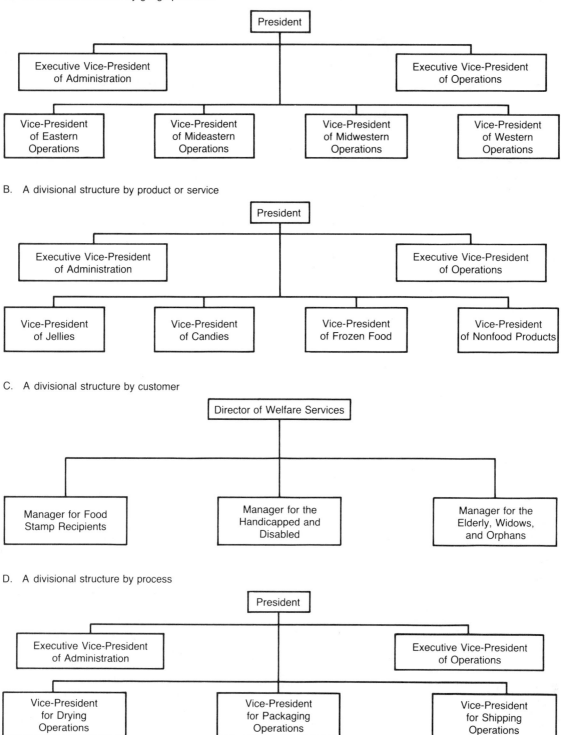

B. A divisional structure by product or service

C. A divisional structure by customer

D. A divisional structure by process

Possible underemployment of facilities may result from this structure by customer if the importance of customer groups decreases. Merrill Lynch in mid-1984 reorganized its operations into fifteen new business units, each of which caters to a specific group of customers, including wealthy individuals, institutional investors, and small corporations.[8] Prior to this reorganization, Merrill Lynch's divisional structure was based on products. For the first quarter of 1985, Merrill Lynch's net income was $55.6 million on revenues of $1.56 billion. For the same period in 1984, net income was $18.6 million on revenues of $1.39 billion. Merrill Lynch attributes the company's higher performance to the corporate reorganization and to lower interest rates.

A divisional structure by process is similar to the functional structure, since company activities are organized according to the way work is actually performed. However, the key difference between these two designs is that functional departments are not accountable for profits or revenues, whereas divisional process departments are evaluated on these criteria. An example divisional structure by process could be a manufacturing business that is organized into six divisions: electrical work, glass cutting, welding, grinding, painting, and foundry work. In this case, all operations related to these specific processes would be grouped under the separate divisions. Each process (division) would be responsible for generating revenues and profits. The divisional structure by process can be particularly effective in achieving company objectives when distinct production processes represent the thrust of competitiveness in an industry.

The Strategic Business Unit (SBU) Structure As decentralized organizations grow, the number, size, and diversity of their divisions increases. As a result, it becomes increasingly difficult for corporate management to control and evaluate divisional operations. Increases in sales often are not accompanied by similar increases in profitability, and the span of management becomes too great for a single chief executive officer. Imagine a large conglomerate organization composed of ninety divisions. The chief executive officer of this firm could have difficulty remembering even the first names of each of his divisional presidents. When this is the case, an SBU structure can greatly facilitate strategy-implementation efforts.

The SBU structure groups similar divisions into strategic business units and delegates authority and responsibility for each unit to a senior executive who reports directly to the chief executive officer. This change in structure can facilitate the strategy-implementation process by improving the coordination between similar divisions and channeling accountability to distinct business units. In the example mentioned above, the ninety divisions could perhaps be regrouped into fifteen Strategic Business Units that have homogeneous characteristics. This restructuring would reduce the chief executive officer's span of control from ninety to six fifteen-unit divisions. Divisions that comprise a single SBU could be homogeneous in a number of different ways—they could all compete in the same industry, or they could all be located in the same area, or they could all have the same customers.

Two disadvantages of the SBU structure are that an additional layer of management is needed, which increases salary expenses. Also, the role of the group vice-president is often ambiguous. However, these limitations often do not outweigh the

Figure 7.6   The SBU-type structure

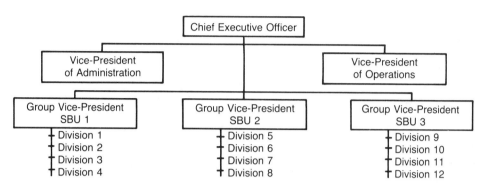

advantages of improved coordination and accountability. A general diagram of the SBU type of organizational structure is provided in Figure 7.6. AMF, the large sporting equipment manufacturer, has established an SBU structure, as illustrated in Figure 7.7.

The Matrix Structure   A matrix-type organizational structure is the most complex of the seven alternative designs. The complexity of the matrix structure stems from its dependence upon both vertical and horizontal flows of authority and communication (hence the term "matrix"). In contrast, the functional and divisional structures depend primarily on vertical flows of authority and communication.

Other characteristics of the matrix structure that contribute to overall complexity include dual lines of budget authority (a violation of the unity-of-command principle), dual sources of reward and punishment, shared authority, dual reporting channels, and a need for an extensive and effective communication system. In order for a matrix structure to be successfully put in place, great attention should be paid to such things as thorough participative planning, training, clear mutual understanding of roles and responsibilities, excellent internal communication, and mutual trust and confidence.

Despite its overall complexity, the matrix structure is being used more and more by American businesses. Why? Because firms are turning more and more to strategies that add new products, customer groups, and technology to their range of activities. Out of these changes are coming product managers, functional managers, geographic-area managers, business-level managers, and SBU managers, all of whom have important strategic responsibilities.[9] When several variables such as product, customer, technology, geography, functional area, and line of business have roughly equal strategic priorities, a matrix organization can be an effective structural form.

Organizations that typically use a matrix structure include hospitals, construction companies, research and development organizations, accounting firms, colleges and universities, and large organizations. Shell Oil, Bechtel, Texas Instruments, and Gen-

Figure 7.7   AMF's organizational structure

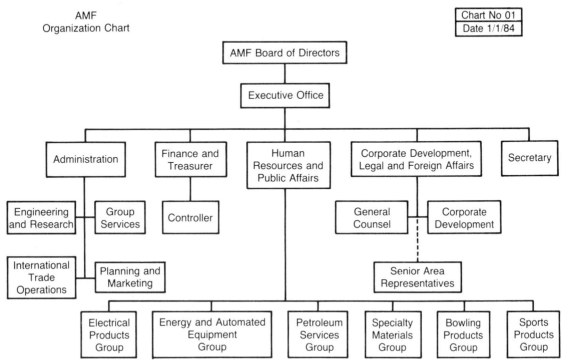

eral Electric all use a matrix-type organizational structure. An example matrix structure for a college of business administration is illustrated in Figure 7.8.

As you know, there are numerous internal and external forces that affect an organization. A firm could not change its structure every time one of these forces changes, because this would lead to chaos. However, when a firm changes its strategy in response to one or more of these forces, the existing organizational structure may become ineffective. Symptoms of an ineffective organizational structure include too many management levels, too many meetings attended by too many people, too much attention being directed toward solving interdepartmental conflicts, too large a span of management, and too many objectives not being achieved. Changes in structure can facilitate strategy-implementation efforts, but changes in an organization's structure should not be expected to make a bad strategy good, or to make bad managers good, or to make bad products sell.

Ineffective performance incentives, rather than a poor organizational structure, could be the root cause of strategy-implementation problems. This topic is discussed next.

Figure 7.8   A matrix organizational structure

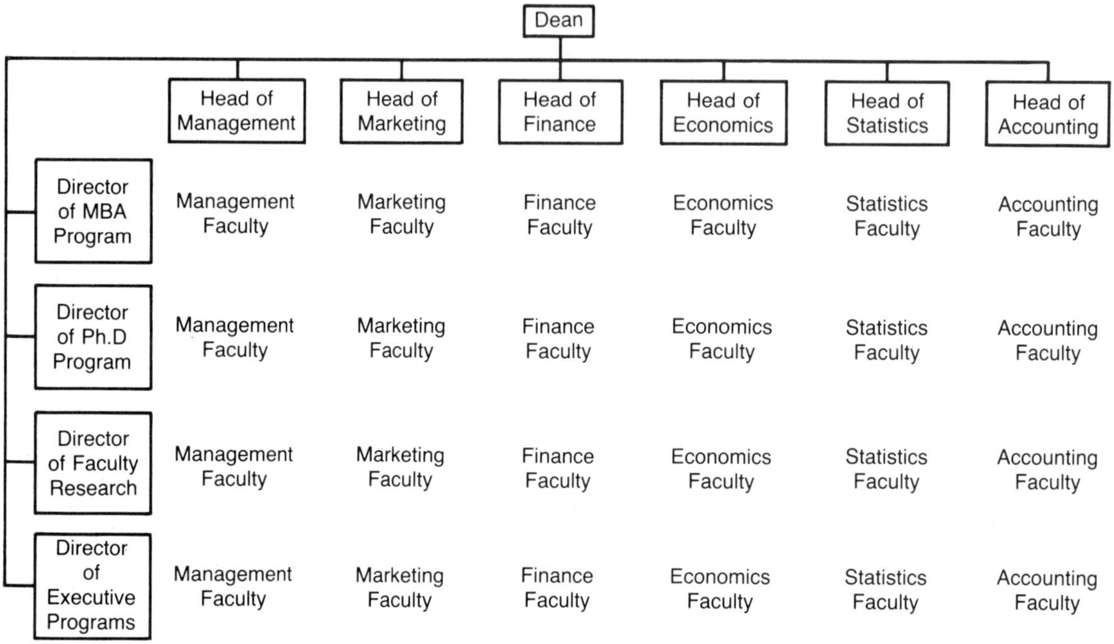

	Head of Management	Head of Marketing	Head of Finance	Head of Economics	Head of Statistics	Head of Accounting
				Dean		
Director of MBA Program	Management Faculty	Marketing Faculty	Finance Faculty	Economics Faculty	Statistics Faculty	Accounting Faculty
Director of Ph.D Program	Management Faculty	Marketing Faculty	Finance Faculty	Economics Faculty	Statistics Faculty	Accounting Faculty
Director of Faculty Research	Management Faculty	Marketing Faculty	Finance Faculty	Economics Faculty	Statistics Faculty	Accounting Faculty
Director of Executive Programs	Management Faculty	Marketing Faculty	Finance Faculty	Economics Faculty	Statistics Faculty	Accounting Faculty

Linking Performance and Pay to Strategies

There exists a need for American companies to align more closely strategy, performance, and pay. Executive compensation programs in too many U.S. corporations have rewarded executives handsomely for performances that have not benefited shareholders equally.[10] A low correlation between corporate performance and executives' pay generally characterizes American businesses, for a number of reasons. First, there exists an "increased pay for increased size" phenomenon. Second, too much reliance is placed on short-term performance. Third, staff control of pay systems too often prevents line managers from using financial compensation as a strategic tool. Flexibility regarding managerial and employee compensation is needed to allow short-term tactical shifts in compensation that can stimulate efforts to achieve long-term objectives.

How can an organization's reward system be more closely linked to strategic performance? How can decisions on salary increases, promotions, merit pay, and bonuses be more closely aligned to support the long-term strategic objectives of the organization? There are no widely accepted answers to these questions, but an annual bonus system for managers can be an effective motivating tool to implement strategies.

An effective bonus system could be based on two key factors: annual results (goals) and long-term results (objectives). The percentage of managers' annual bonus attributable to short-term versus long-term results should vary by the hierarchical level in the organization. A chief executive officer's annual bonus could, for example, be determined on a 75 percent short-term and 25 percent long-term basis. It is important that bonuses not be based solely on short-term results, because such a system ignores long-term company strategies and objectives.

According to *Fortune*, performance-based long-term incentives have been adopted by roughly 40 percent of the Fortune 500, including General Motors, General Electric, and Dart & Kraft.[11] The most important and commonly used criterion is earnings per share. Bristol-Myers, General Electric, Gulf Resources & Chemical, and Honeywell all use EPS as the gauge in determining bonuses. At Honeywell, for example, the fifty-one senior executives covered by the plan receive long-term performance awards only if earnings per share grow at least 9 percent annually over four years, as calculated by the company's own esoteric formula:

> If the earnings per share grow by 17 percent or more, the executives receive the maximum awards. From 1978 through 1981, Honeywell easily surpassed the 17 percent figure. However, in 1980 through 1983, Honeywell's earnings per share declined slightly, so no awards were made.[12]

Criteria such as sales, profit, production efficiency, quality, and safety could serve as bases for an effective bonus system. If an organization meets certain understood, agreed-upon profit objectives, every member should share in the harvest. A bonus system can be an effective tool for motivating individuals to support strategy-implementation efforts.

In addition to an annual bonus system, a combination of reward-strategy-incentives including salary raises, stock options, fringe benefits, promotions, praise, recognition, criticism, fear, increased job autonomy, awards, and profit sharing can be utilized to encourage managers and employees to push hard for successful strategy implementation. Recognize that the range of options for getting people, departments, and divisions to actively support strategy-implementation goals in a particular organization are almost limitless. Motivational incentives can be positive, negative, intrinsic, or extrinsic. In the final analysis, a successful reward-performance system allows for blended fulfillment of both organizational and personal objectives.

Proposed strategy-implementation changes in an organization often meet resistance, a topic that is discussed next.

Creating an Organizational Climate Conducive to Change

No organization or individual can escape change. But the thought of change raises anxieties because people fear economic loss, inconvenience, uncertainty, and a break in normal social patterns. Almost any change in structure, technology, persons, or processes has the potential to disrupt comfortable interaction patterns. For this reason, it is understandable that people innately resist change. The strategic-management process itself can impose tremendous changes on individuals and processes. Reorienting an organization to get people to think and act strategically is not an easy turnaround.

> The level of familiarity with strategic thinking in the U.S. is high, but acceptance is low. U.S. management has to undergo a cultural change, and it's difficult to force people to change their thinking; it's like ordering them to use personal computers. One obstacle is that top executives are often too busy fighting fires to devote time to developing managers who can think strategically. Yet, the best-run companies recognize the need to develop managers who can fashion and implement strategy.[13]

Resistance to change can be considered the single greatest threat to successful strategy implementation, because implementation is basically a change process. Resistance, in the form of sabotaged production machines, absenteeism, filing of unfounded grievances, and an unwillingness to cooperate, regularly occurs in organizations. People often resist strategy-implementation changes because they do not understand what is happening or why changes are taking place. In this case, employees may simply need accurate information. Successful strategy implementation hinges upon managers' ability to develop an organizational climate conducive to change.

Resistance to change can emerge at any stage or level of the strategy-implementation process. Although there are various approaches for implementing changes, three commonly used strategies are: a force change strategy, an educative change strategy, and a rational or self-interest change strategy. A force change strategy means giving orders and enforcing those orders. This type of change strategy has the advantage of being fast, but it is plagued by low commitment and high resistance. The educative change strategy is one whereby information is presented to convince people of the need for change. The disadvantage of an educative change strategy is that the implementation process is slow and difficult. However, the level of commitment is higher and resistance is lower than with the force strategy. Finally, a rational or self-interest change strategy is one in which efforts are made to convince individuals that the change is to their personal advantage. When this appeal is successful, strategy implementation can be relatively easy. However, implementation changes are seldom to everyone's advantage.

The rational change strategy is the most desirable, so this approach is examined a bit further. Managers can improve the likelihood of successfully implementing change by carefully designing change efforts. Jack Duncan describes a rational or self-interest change strategy as consisting of four steps. First, employees are invited to participate in the process of change and the details of transition. This allows everyone to give opinions, to feel a part of the change process, and to identify their own self-interests regarding the recommended change. Second, some motivation or incentive to change is required. Self-interest can be the most important motivator. Third, communication is needed so that people can understand the purpose for the alterations. Giving and receiving feedback is the fourth step. Everyone enjoys knowing how things are going and how much progress is being made.[14]

Managing Political Relationships

Effectively managing political relationships can enhance change processes. All organizations are political. In the previous chapter, political relationships relating to strategy formulation were discussed. Managing political relationships is equally, and perhaps even more important to successful strategy implementation. Employees and managers often do not get alarmed as strategy-formulation processes proceed, but when it comes time to implement new strategies, hidden hostilities can rise to the surface quickly.

Successful strategy implementation can depend on having good leaders in the right jobs. Fortunately, recent research has examined the need to "choose the right managers to fit the strategy."[15] The major problem in accomplishing this task appears to be that most jobs have specific and relatively static responsibilities, while people are dynamic in their personal development. This problem can be overcome in various ways that include frequent promotions, job enlargement (adding duties to the job), and job enrichment (adding responsibilities to the job). (Experiential Exercise 7A at the end of this chapter focuses on the need to match individuals to the strategy being implemented.)

Managing political relationships for effective strategy implementation can be achieved by changing leaders at appropriate levels, developing appropriate leadership styles and climates, and getting involved in the career development of managers. The following questions should be addressed:

1. Do current managers have the right education, abilities, experience, temperament, and personality to implement the new strategy?
2. Do current managers understand and support the new strategy?
3. Can current managers change their leadership style if that is needed to make the new strategy work?

In addition to having supportive leaders in the right positions, a number of other guidelines can help ensure that political relationships facilitate rather than disrupt strategy-implementation efforts. Specifically, managers should do a lot of chatting and informal questioning to stay abreast of how things are progressing and to know when to intervene. Managers can build support for strategy-implementation efforts by giving few orders, announcing few decisions, depending heavily on informal questioning, and seeking to probe and clarify until a consensus emerges. Key thrusts that succeed should be rewarded generously and visibly.

Managers should ensure that all major power bases have representation in key strategy-implementation decisions. They should interject new faces and new views into considerations of major changes, rather than rely on those who primarily strive to "keep the world the same old way." When implementing strategies, nothing is gained by "knocking" the views of those who argue for opposing implementation approaches. Managers should strive to understand the unique political relationships that exist in their work environment and use this information to facilitate strategy-implementation processes.

Sometimes political relationships are embedded in an organization's culture, so this is the next central strategy implementation topic.

Creating a Strategy-Supportive Corporate Culture

All organizations have a corporate culture. Although there is no clear consensus on how to define *culture*, this concept includes the set of shared values, beliefs, attitudes, customs, norms, personalities, and heroes that describe a firm. More simply, culture is the unique way an organization does business. Strategists are beginning to realize that an organization's culture can represent a major obstacle or contributor to successful strategy implementation. The corporate culture in two organizations is evidenced below:

1. All employees at Hewlett-Packard work in shirt sleeves. This company's corporate culture is called "the HP Way." It is described as "the policies and actions that flow from the belief that men and women want to do a good job, a creative job, and that if they are provided with the proper environment they will do so." It is the tradition of treating every individual with consideration and respect and recognizing personal achievement.

2. The 3M Company acts as a community cultural center for employees, as opposed to just a place to work. They have employee clubs, intramural sports, travel clubs, and a choral group. With the breakdown of traditional social-family structures in some parts of America, 3M has been described as a mother institution. It maintains a spirit of entrepreneurship.

Although interest in corporate culture has increased dramatically in recent years, cultural change is still a black art, difficult to pin down, nearly impossible to quantify or measure, and remarkably resistant to change.[16] However, ensuring that an organization's culture is a positive force in the strategy-implementation process is one of top management's key concerns. Techniques used by some companies to develop an effective corporate culture include tolerating mistakes, relocating employees as needed, encouraging informality, acting as community cultural centers, locating in noncosmopolitan settings, treating employees with trust and respect, including employees families in the corporate family, and having executives make frequent field visits. The following steps are commonly used as a guide to managing a corporate culture:

1. Identify the kind of culture that is needed.
2. Determine the existing culture within the organization.
3. Identify any gaps between current and needed culture.
4. Describe what methods are to be used to close the gaps.
5. Implement the choices.
6. Repeat this entire process on a regular basis.[17]

The American Telephone and Telegraph (AT&T) Company represents a current example of strategy-implementation problems resulting from organizational culture. Incorporated in 1885, AT&T divested itself of the local operations of its twenty-two wholly owned local telephone companies effective January 1, 1984. The "old" corporate culture at AT&T could be described as consisting of lifetime careers, intense loyalty to the company, up-from-the-ranks management succession, dedication to the service ethos, and a consensus management style. As AT&T moves from a regulated monopoly to a highly competitive environment, these elements of its culture significantly affect strategy-implementation processes. In a recent article entitled "Cultural Transition at AT&T," Brooke Tunstall reveals six major guidelines that AT&T is following to create a new strategy-supportive culture.

1. Set an example—Ensure that managers' behavior is consistent with the norms and values articulated for the company.

2. Revamp the system of management—Reorient the organizational structure, reward patterns, and resource-allocation processes.

3. Articulate the value system explicitly—Communicate to all employees in specific terms precisely what the corporate value system is. This is especially important in periods of change.

4. Gear training to support cultural values—Provide management training to modify behavior in support of new corporate values.

5. Revise recruiting aims and methods—Alter recruiting aims and methods to ensure that new managers and employees have value systems, personalities, and educational backgrounds that are in harmony with the corporation's aims.

6. Modify the symbols—Change the logo, name, and other symbols of the "old" organization so that the "new" culture can facilitate strategy-implementation processes.[18]

AT&T has abandoned its familiar logo (a bell with a circle) and adopted a new logo (a globe circled by electronic communications). This new logo is symbolic of AT&T's new competitive strategies. In a similar vein, many observers were shocked recently when the Sperry Rand Corporation abandoned its famous Univac name. But Gerald Probst, Sperry's chairman, explained that dropping the Univac name was a necessary part of the company's strategy to redeploy its assets into new electronic defense systems.[19]

MARKETING ISSUES AND STRATEGY IMPLEMENTATION

Segmenting Markets

The strategy-implementation process is becoming more and more dependent upon a close working relationship between corporate strategists and marketing managers. Understanding the needs and wants of consumers in diverse markets is critical to both strategy formulation and implementation. Although there are many marketing variables that impact the success or failure of strategy-implementation efforts, two variables are central to the process—market segmentation and product positioning. Ralph Biggadike asserts that "market segmentation and its counterpart, positioning, must rank as mar-

Table 7.1   The marketing mix component factors

Product	*Place*	*Promotion*	*Price*
Quality	Distribution channels	Advertising	Level
Features and options	Distribution coverage	Personal selling	Discounts and allowances
Style	Outlet locations	Sales promotion	Payment terms
Brand name	Sales territories	Publicity	
Packaging	Inventory levels and locations		
Product line	Transportation carriers		
Warranty			
Service level			
Other services			

Source: E. Jerome McCarthy, *Basic Marketing: A Managerial Approach,* 4th ed. (Homewood, Ill.: Richard D. Irwin, Inc., 1971) p. 44 (1st ed., 1960).

keting's most important contributions to strategic management."[20] Market segmentation can be defined as "the subdividing of a market into distinct subsets of customers, according to their needs and the way they buy and use a product or service."[21]

Market segmentation has become an increasingly popular technique for implementing strategies in the 1980s, especially for small and specialized firms. There are three major reasons why market segmentation is an important variable in the strategy-implementation process. First, many company strategies, including market development, product development, market penetration, and diversification, require increased sales through new markets and products. To implement these strategies successfully, new or improved market segmentation approaches are required.

Second, market segmentation is a key implementation concept because it allows a firm to pursue strategies with limited resources and specialization, since mass production, mass distribution, and mass advertising are not required. Market segmentation often enables a smaller firm to compete successfully with a larger firm by maximizing per-unit profits and per-segment sales. Finally, market segmentation is a central strategy-implementation issue because decisions regarding the marketing-mix variables, product, place, promotion, and price, depend on how the market is segmented. Specific marketing-mix factors that are affected by segmentation decisions are shown in Table 7.1.

The common bases for segmenting a market are given in Table 7.2. As shown, market segmentation variables can be categorized in four groups: geographic, demographic, psychographic, and behavioral. Geographic and demographic bases are the most commonly employed.

Table 7.2 Alternative bases for market segmentation

Variable	Typical Breakdowns
Geographic	
Region	Pacific, Mountain, West North Central, West South Central, East North Central, East South Central, South Atlantic, Middle Atlantic, New England
County Size	A, B, C, D
City or SMSA size	Under 5,000; 5,000–20,000; 20,000–50,000; 50,000–100,000; 100,000–250,000; 250,000–500,000; 500,000–1,000,000; 1,000,000–4,000,000; 4,000,000 or over
Density	Urban, suburban, rural
Climate	Northern, southern
Demographic	
Age	Under 6, 6–11, 12–19, 20–34, 35–49, 50–64, 65+
Sex	Male, female
Family size	1–2, 3–4, 5+
Family life cycle	Young, single; young, married, no children; young, married, youngest child under 6; young, married, youngest child 6 or over; older, married, with children; older, married, no children under 18; older, single; other
Income	Under $2,500; $2,500–$5,000; $5,000–$7,500; $7,500–$10,000; $10,000–$15,000; $15,000–$20,000; $20,000–$30,000; $30,000–$50,000; $50,000 and over
Occupation	Professional and technical; managers, officials, and proprietors; clerical, sales; craftsmen, foremen; operatives; farmers; retired; students; housewives; unemployed
Education	Grade school or less; some high school; high school graduate; some college; college graduate
Religion	Catholic, Protestant, Jewish, other
Race	White, black, Oriental
Nationality	American, British, French, German, Scandinavian, Italian, Latin American, Middle Eastern, Japanese
Psychographic	
Social class	Lower lowers, upper lowers, lower middles, upper middles, lower uppers, upper uppers
Lifestyle	Straights, swingers, longhairs
Personality	Compulsive, gregarious, authoritarian, ambitious
Behavioral	
Use occasion	Regular occasion, special occasion
Benefits sought	Quality, service, economy
User status	Nonuser, ex-user, potential user, first-time user, regular user
Usage rate	Light user, medium user, heavy user
Loyalty status	None, medium, strong, absolute
Readiness stage	Unaware, aware, informed, interested, desirous, intending to buy
Attitude toward product	Enthusiastic, positive, indifferent, negative, hostile

Source: Philip Kotler, *Marketing Management: Analysis, Planning and Control*, © 1984, p. 256. Reprinted by permission of Prentice-Hall, Inc., Englewood Cliffs, New Jersey.

An example of the behavioral approach to segmenting a market with the "user occasion" variable exists in the beer industry. As described below, beer producers have generally divided the light beer market into three segments:

> The light beer market can be meaningfully separated into three motivation segments: those who are calorie-conscious, those who prefer less alcohol, and those who prefer a lighter taste. In fact, it is possible for one person to consume light beer on three separate occasions for three different reasons. The situation may therefore dictate the segment the consumer falls into.[22]

Market segmentation errors have recently been blamed for Izod, Ltd. experiencing hard times. The alligator-brand shirtmaker in 1984 experienced a 10 percent decline in sales and a 30 percent decline in profits. Some analysts attribute Izod's decline to their market segmentation strategy that focuses primarily on children and not teenagers. Izod is turning out what salespeople often call "Grandma bait."[23]

Recognizing the value of market segmentation in implementing company strategy is important, but actually choosing the most appropriate segmentation variable is even more important. Evaluating potential market segments requires determination of the characteristics and needs of consumers, analysis of consumer similarities and differences, and development of consumer group profiles. Segmenting consumer markets is generally much simpler and easier than segmenting industrial markets. The major reason is that industrial products, such as electronic circuits, have multiple applications and appeal to diverse customer groups.

Market segmentation matrices and decision trees have recently been developed to facilitate implementing strategies effectively. An example matrix for segmenting the lawn fertilizer market is provided in Figure 7.9. Similar types of matrices could be developed for almost any market, product, or service.

To qualify as an attractive market segment, six criteria must be satisfied. First, the segment must be "measurable." That is, information must be obtainable on the buyer characteristic chosen to segment the market. Second, the market segment must be "accessible," meaning that a firm must be able to focus its efforts effectively on the chosen segment. Third, the segment must be "substantial," i.e., large and/or profitable enough to justify the marketing costs. Fourth, the segment must be "defensible" against mass market competitors. Fifth, the market segment must be "durable," that is, the unique characteristics of the segment should be expected to endure over time. Lastly, the segment must "allow the organization to capitalize on its distinctive competencies"; this means that, compared to major competitors, a firm should have a relative advantage in the types of skills required to serve the particular segment that is chosen.

As you analyze a business policy case, decide on an appropriate market segmentation approach for implementing chosen strategies.

Positioning Products Effectively

Deciding what market segments to go after sets the stage for deciding how to meet the needs and wants of particular consumer groups. Meeting special consumer needs and wants is accomplished through effective product positioning. Product positioning is a

Figure 7.9   Tools for segmenting the lawn fertilizer market

Lawn Fertilizer Usage: a Demographic Segmentation Plan

Heavy users	High income	Central city
		Suburban
		Rural
	Low income	Central city
		Suburban
		Rural
Light users	High income	Central city
		Suburban
		Rural
	Low income	Central city
		Suburban
		Rural
Nonusers	High income	Central city
		Suburban
		Rural
	Low income	Central city
		Suburban
		Rural

Source: Fred Winter, "Market Segmentation: A Tactical Approach," *Business Horizons* (January–February 1984): 60, 61.

key strategy-implementation technique because it focuses on analyzing competitors' products or services in terms of how they are perceived by the chosen target market, and then developing a marketing program to effectively "position" the organization's product or service. The following steps are required in product positioning:

1. Select key criteria that effectively differentiate the products or services in the industry.

2. Diagram a two-dimensional product positioning map with specified criteria on each axis.

3. Plot major competitors' products or services in the resultant four-quadrant matrix.

4. Identify areas in the positioning map where the company's products or services could be most competitive in the given target market. Look for vacant areas (niches).

5. Develop a marketing plan to position the company's products or services appropriately.

   Since only two criteria are usually examined on a single product positioning map, multiple maps should be developed to best determine the most effective marketing plan for a company's products or services. Multidimensional scaling could be used to examine three or more criteria simultaneously, but this technique requires computer assistance and is beyond the scope of this text. Some example product positioning maps are illustrated in Figure 7.10.

Figure 7.10   Example product positioning maps

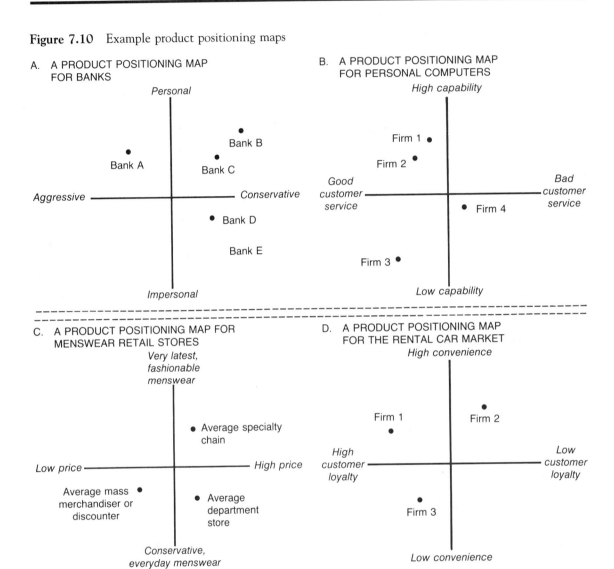

A.   A PRODUCT POSITIONING MAP
     FOR BANKS

B.   A PRODUCT POSITIONING MAP
     FOR PERSONAL COMPUTERS

C.   A PRODUCT POSITIONING MAP FOR
     MENSWEAR RETAIL STORES

D.   A PRODUCT POSITIONING MAP
     FOR THE RENTAL CAR MARKET

The following rules of thumb are recommended for using product positioning as a strategy-implementation tool:

1. Look for the hole or vacant niche. The best strategic opportunity might be an unserved segment.

2. Don't squat between segments. Any advantage from squatting (such as a larger target market) is offset by a failure to satisfy one segment. In decision-theory terms,

the intent here is to avoid suboptimization by trying to serve more than one objective function.

3. Don't serve two segments with the same strategy. Usually, a successful strategy with one segment cannot be directly transferred to another segment.

4. Don't position yourself in the middle of the map. The middle usually means a strategy that is not clearly perceived to have any distinguishing characteristics. This rule can vary with the number of competitors. For example, when there are only two competitors, as in U.S. presidential elections, the middle becomes the preferred strategic position.[24]

An example firm that has successfully developed a vacant niche is Redken Laboratories. Unlike its competitors, Jhirmack, Sassoon, L'Oreal, and Wella, Redken is not found in drugstores and supermarkets, but rather is sold exclusively by beauty salons and barber shops.[25] Such marketing is called salon retailing and is the fastest-growing segment of the $13 billion salon business.

FINANCIAL CONCERNS WHEN IMPLEMENTING STRATEGIES

Acquiring Needed Capital

Successful strategy implementation often requires the procurement of additional capital. For example, acquiring competitors (horizontal integration), gaining control over distributors (forward integration), purchasing suppliers (backward integration), and diversification can take large amounts of extra capital. There are two basic sources of funds for an ongoing enterprise: debt and equity. Determining an appropriate mix of debt and equity in a firm's capital structure can be vital to successful strategy implementation. This section examines capital acquisition techniques and concepts that are used to finance the implementation of company strategies.

Earnings Per Share/Earnings Before Interest and Taxes (EPS/EBIT) analysis is the most widely used technique for determining whether debt or stock, or a combination of debt and stock, is the best alternative for raising capital to implement strategies. Essentially, the technique involves an examination of the impact that debt versus stock financing has on earnings per share, under various assumptions as to EBIT.

Theoretically, an enterprise should have enough debt in its capital structure to boost its return on investment by applying debt to products and projects earning more than the cost of the debt. However, in low earnings periods, too much debt in the capital structure of an organization can endanger stockholders' return and jeopardize company survival. Fixed debt obligations generally must be met, regardless of circumstances. This does not mean that stock issuances are always better than debt for raising capital. Some special concerns with stock issuances are dilution of ownerships, effect on stock price, and the fact that the firm may have to share future earnings with those new shareholders until eternity.

Table 7.3   EPS/EBIT analysis for The Brown Company (in millions)

	Common Stock Financing			Debt Financing			Combination Financing		
	Recession	*Normal*	*Boom*	*Recession*	*Normal*	*Boom*	*Recession*	*Normal*	*Boom*
EBIT	$2.0	$ 4.0	$ 8.0	$2.0	$ 4.0	$ 8.0	$2.0	$ 4.0	$ 8.0
Interest[a]	0.0	0.0	0.0	.10	.10	.10	.05	.05	.05
EBT	2.0	4.0	8.0	1.9	3.9	7.9	1.95	3.95	7.95
Taxes	1.0	2.0	4.0	.95	1.95	3.95	.975	1.975	3.975
EAT	1.0	2.0	4.0	.95	1.95	3.95	.975	1.975	3.975
# Shares[b]	.12	.12	.12	.10	.10	.10	.11	.11	.11
EPS[c]	8.33	16.66	33.33	9.5	19.50	39.50	8.86	17.95	36.14

Notes:

[a]The annual interest charge on $1 million at 10% is $100,000 and on $0.5 million is $50,000.

[b]To raise all of the needed $1 million with stock, 20,000 new shares must be issued, raising the total to 120,000 shares outstanding. To raise one half of the needed $1 million with stock, 10,000 new shares must be issued, raising the total to 110,000 shares outstanding.

[c]EPS = Earnings After Taxes (EAT) divided by (Number of shares outstanding)

Without going into detail on other institutional and legal issues related to the debt versus stock decision, EPS/EBIT is explained by working through an example. Let's say the Brown Company needs to raise $1 million to finance implementation of a market-development strategy. The company's common stock currently sells for $50 per share and 100,000 shares are outstanding. The prime interest rate is 10 percent and the company's tax rate is 50 percent. The company's earnings before interest and taxes (EBIT) next year are expected to be $2 million, if a recession occurs, $4 million if the economy stays as is, and $8 million if the economy significantly improves. EPS/EBIT analysis can be used to determine if all stock, all debt, or some combination of stock and debt is the best capital financing alternative. The EPS/EBIT analysis for this example is provided in Table 7.3.

As indicated by the EPS values of 9.5, 19.50, and 39.50 in Table 7.3, debt is the best financing alternative for the Brown Company if a recession, boom, or normal year is expected. An EPS/EBIT chart can be constructed to determine the break-even point where one financing alternative becomes more attractive than another. Figure 7.11 indicates that an issuance of common stock is the least attractive financing alternative for the Brown Company.

EPS/EBIT analysis is a valuable tool for making capital financing decisions needed to implement strategies. However, there are some complicating factors that must be

Figure 7.11 An EPS/EBIT chart for the Brown Company

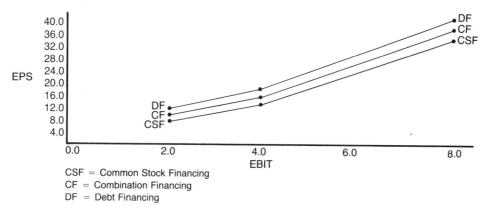

CSF = Common Stock Financing
CF = Combination Financing
DF = Debt Financing

considered in using this technique. First, profit levels may be higher for stock or debt alternatives when EPS levels are lower. For example, looking only at the earnings after taxes (EAT) values in Table 7.3, the common stock option is the best alternative, regardless of economic conditions. If the Brown Company's mission is strictly profit maximization, as opposed to the maximization of stockholder's wealth or some other criteria, then profitability alone may dictate the choice of financing.

A second concern with EPS/EBIT analysis is flexibility. As an organization's capital structure changes, so does its flexibility for considering future capital needs. Using all debt or all stock to raise capital in the present may impose fixed obligations, restrictive covenants, or other constraints that could severely reduce a firm's ability to raise additional capital in the future.

Third, there is a question of control. When additional stock is issued to finance the implementation of company strategy, ownership and control of the enterprise is diluted. Dilution of ownership can be an overriding concern in closely held corporations, because stock issuances affect the decision-making power of majority stockholders. For example, the Smucker family owns 30 percent of the stock in Smucker's, a well-known jam and jelly company.[26] When Smucker's recently acquired Dickson Family, Inc., the company used mostly debt rather than stock in order not to dilute the family's ownership. (In mid-1985, Smucker's has the largest share of the preserve and jelly market in the United States.)

Finally, there is a question of timing in relation to the movements of prices in the securities markets. In times of depressed stock prices, debt may prove to be the most suitable alternative from both a cost and a demand standpoint. However, when the costs of capital (interest rates) are high, stock issuances become more attractive. In conclusion, EPS/EBIT analysis, like all quantitative techniques, should be used with sound business judgment.

Developing *Pro Forma* Financial Statements

Pro forma (projected) financial statement analysis is a central strategy-implementation technique because it allows an organization to examine the expected results of various strategy-implementation approaches. *Pro forma* analysis is also useful in analyzing feasible alternative strategies. This type of analysis can be used to forecast the impact of implementation decisions, such as to increase promotion expenditures by 50 percent to support a market-development strategy, or to increase the salaries by 25 percent to support a market-penetration strategy, or to increase research and development expenditures by 70 percent to support product development, or to sell $1 million of common stock to raise capital for diversification. The *pro forma* income statement and balance sheet analysis also allows an organization to compute projected financial ratios under various strategy-implementation scenarios. When compared to prior years and to industry averages, financial ratios provide valuable insight into the feasibility of various strategy-implementation actions.

A *pro forma* income statement and balance sheet for the Litten Company is provided in Exhibit 7.1. The example *pro forma* statements for Litten are based on five assumptions: (1) the company needs to raise $45 million to finance expansion into foreign markets, (2) $30 million of this total will be raised through increased debt and $15 million through common stock, (3) sales are expected to increase 50 percent, (4) three new facilities, costing a total of $30 million, will be constructed in foreign markets, and (5) land for the new facilities is already owned by the company. Note in Exhibit 7.1 that Litten's strategies and their implementation are expected to result in a sales increase from $100 million to $150 million and a net income increase from $6 million to $9.75 million in the forecasted year.

Six Steps in Performing Pro Forma *Analysis*

1. Prepare the *pro forma* income statement first, i.e. before the balance sheet. Start by forecasting sales as accurately as possible. Use one or more of the forecasting techniques discussed in Chapter 4. Incorporate your recommendations and implementation plans into this forecast.

2. Use the percentage-of-sales method to project cost-of-goods-sold (CGS) and the expense items in the income statement. For example, if CGS is 70 percent of sales in the prior year (as it is in Exhibit 7.1), then use that same percentage to calculate CGS in the future year—unless there is reason to use a different percentage. Items such as "interest," "dividends," and "taxes" must be treated independently and cannot be forecasted using the percentage-of-sales method.

3. Calculate the projected net income.

4. Subtract from the net income any dividends to be paid and add the remaining net income to "retained earnings." Reflect the "retained earnings" total on both the income statement and balance sheet, because this item is the key link between the two projected statements.

Exhibit 7.1 A *pro forma* income statement and balance sheet for the Litten Company (in millions)

Pro Forma **Income Statement**

	Prior Year 1985	Projected Year 1986	Remarks
Sales	100	150.00	50% increase
Cost of goods sold	70	105.00	70% of sales
Gross margin	30	45.00	
Selling expense	10	15.00	10% of sales
Administrative expense	5	7.50	5% of sales
Earnings before interest and taxes	15	22.50	
Interest	3	3.00	
Earnings before taxes	12	19.50	
Taxes	6	9.75	50% rate
Net income	6	9.75	
Dividends	2	5.00	
Retained earnings	4	4.75	

Pro Forma **Balance Sheet**

Assets			
Cash	5	7.75	Plug figure
Accounts receivable	2	4.00	Incr. 50% with sales
Inventory	20	45.00	
Total current assets	27	56.75	
Land	15	15.00	
Plant and equipment	50	80.00	Add 3 new @ $10
Less: depreciation	10	20.00	million each
Net plant and equipment	40	60.00	
Total fixed assets	55	75.00	
Total assets	82	131.75	
Liabilities			
Accounts payable	10	10.00	
Notes payable	10	10.00	
Total current liabilities	20	20.00	
Long-term debt	40	70.00	Borrowed $30 million
Common stock	20	35.00	Issued 100000 shares @ $150 each
Retained earnings	2	6.75	2 + 4.75
Total liabilities and new worth	82	131.75	

5. Project the balance sheet items beginning with retained earnings and proceeding to forecast stockholders' equity, long-term liabilities, current liabilities, total liabilities, total assets, fixed assets, and current assets, in that sequential order. Use the "cash" account as the plug figure; that is, use the cash account to make the assets total the liabilities. Then make appropriate adjustments. For example, if the "cash" needed to balance the statements is too small (or too large), make some appropriate changes such as to borrow more (or less) money than planned.

6. List comments (remarks) on the projected statements. Any time a significant change is made in an item from a prior year to the projected year, an explanation (remark) should be provided. Remarks are essential because otherwise *pro formas* are meaningless.

Preparing Financial Budgets

Financial budgets are a part of the total planning and control process. A financial budget is actually a plan that details how funds will be obtained and spent for a specified period of time. Annual budgets are the most common type employed, although the period of time for a budget can range from a day to over ten years. Fundamentally, the budgeting process is a method for specifying what must be done to get the strategy-implementation job completed successfully. Financial budgeting should not be thought of as merely a tool for limiting expenditures, but instead is a method for obtaining the most productive and profitable use of the organization's resources. Budgets can be viewed as the planned allocation of a firm's resources, based on forecasts of the future.

There are almost as many different types of financial budgets as there are types of organizations. Some common types of budgets include cash budgets, operating budgets, sales budgets, profit budgets, factory budgets, capital budgets, expense budgets, divisional budgets, variable budgets, flexible budgets, and fixed budgets. Whenever an organization is experiencing financial difficulties, budgets are particularly needed to guide the strategy-implementation process. Perhaps the most commonly employed budget is the cash budget. An example cash budget for the Toddler Toy Company is provided in Table 7.4. Note that Toddler is not expecting to have surplus cash until November of 1986.

There are some limitations regarding the use of financial budgets. First, budgetary programs can become so detailed that they are cumbersome and overly expensive. Overbudgeting and underbudgeting alike can cause problems. Second, financial budgets can become a substitute for company goals and objectives. A budget is a tool and is not an end in itself. Third, budgets can hide inefficiencies when they are based solely on precedent rather than periodic evaluation of circumstances and standards. Finally, budgets are sometimes used as instruments of tyranny that result in frustration, resentment, absenteeism, and high turnover. To minimize the effect of this last limitation, managers should increase the participation level of subordinates in preparing budgets.

Table 7.4 A six-month cash budget for the Toddler Toy Company in 1986

Cash Budget (in thousands)	July	Aug.	Sept.	Oct.	Nov.	Dec.	Jan.
Receipts:							
Collections	$12,000	$21,000	$31,000	$35,000	$22,000	$18,000	$11,000
Payments:							
Purchases	$14,000	$21,000	$28,000	$14,000	$14,000	$ 7,000	
Wages and salaries	1,500	2,000	2,500	1,500	1,500	1,000	
Rent	500	500	500	500	500	500	
Other expenses	200	300	400	200	200	100	
Taxes	—	—	—	—	—	—	
Payment on machine	—	8,000	10,000	—	—	—	
Total payments	$16,200	$31,800	$41,400	$16,200	$16,200	$ 8,600	
Net cash gain (loss) during month	-$4,200	-$10,800	-$10,400	$18,800	$ 5,800	$ 9,400	
Cash at start of month if no borrowing is done	6,000	1,800	-9,000	-19,400	-600	5,200	
Cumulative cash (cash at start plus gains or minus losses)	$ 1,800	-$ 9,000	-$19,400	-$ 600	$ 5,200	$14,600	
Less: Desired level of cash	-5,000	-5,000	-5,000	-5,000	-5,000	-5,000	
Total loans outstanding to maintain $5,000 cash balance	$ 3,200	$14,000	$24,400	$ 5,600	—	—	
Surplus cash	—	—	—	—	$ 200	$ 9,600	

Evaluating the Worth of a Business

Evaluating the worth of a business is a central strategy-implementation issue because integrative, intensive, and diversification strategies are often implemented by acquiring other firms. Other strategies, such as retrenchment and divestiture, result in a division of an organization being sold, or in the firm itself being sold. In all of these cases it is necessary to establish the financial worth of a business in order to successfully implement the chosen strategies. Evaluating the worth of a business is a commonly used technique in preparing business policy case analyses.

The two largest corporate acquisitions in U.S. history are the Texaco purchase of Getty for $9.9 billion in January 1984, and the DuPont purchase of Conoco for $8 billion in 1981. Approximately 12,000 transactions occur each year in which businesses are bought or sold in the United States.[27]

There are various methods for determining a business's worth, but all the methods can be grouped into three main approaches: what a firm owns, what a firm earns, or what a firm will bring in the market. These three approaches are described in a moment, but it is important initially to realize that valuation is not an exact science. The valuation of a firm's worth is based on financial facts, but common sense and informed judgment must enter into the process. It is difficult to assign a monetary value to factors such as a loyal customer base, a history of growth, legal suits pending, dedicated employees, a favorable lease and credit rating, and good patents. These factors may not be reflected in a firm's financial statements. Also, different valuation methods will yield different totals for a firm's worth, and there is no prescribed approach that is best for a certain situation. Evaluating the worth of a business requires both qualitative judgment and quantitative analysis.

The first approach to evaluating the worth of a business is determining the firm's net worth or stockholders' equity. Net worth represents the sum of common stock, additional paid-in capital, and retained earnings. After this calculation, add or subtract an appropriate amount for goodwill (such as high customer loyalty) and overvalued or undervalued assets. This total provides a reasonable estimate of a firm's monetary value.

The second approach to measuring the value of a firm grows out of the belief that the worth of any business should be based largely on the future benefits its owners may derive through net profits. A conservative rule of thumb is to establish a business's worth to be five times the firm's current annual profit. A five-year average profit level could also be used. In this approach, consider that firms normally have done everything possible in their financial statements to suppress earnings in order to minimize taxes.

The third approach, letting the market determine a company's worth, is comprised of two methods. First, base the firm's worth on what a similar company recently sold for by finding comparable facts and figures. A problem with this method is that sometimes comparable figures are not easy to locate, even though substantial information is available in major libraries on firms that buy or sell to other firms. The alternative under this approach is called the price-earnings ratio method. With this method, divide the market price of the firm's common stock by the annual earnings per share and multiply this number by the firm's average net income for the past five years.

Business evaluations are becoming routine in many situations. In addition to buying or selling a business, there are other strategy-implementation reasons why a firm should determine its business worth. Employee plans, taxes, retirements, mergers, acquisitions, expansion plans, banking relationships, death of a principal, divorce, partnership agreements, and IRS audits are other reasons for a periodic valuation.[28] It is just good business to have a reasonable understanding of what your firm is worth. This knowledge protects the interests of all parties involved.

ADAPTING PRODUCTION PROCESSES TO FACILITATE STRATEGY IMPLEMENTATION

The degree of development of production and manufacturing policies to support the implementation of company strategy can significantly enhance or inhibit the attainment of a company's objectives. Remember from Chapter 5 that production processes exist in all organizations and typically constitute more than 70 percent of a firm's total assets. A major part of the strategy-implementation process takes place at the production site.

Production-related decisions such as plant size, plant location, product design, choice of equipment, kind of tooling, size of inventory, inventory control, quality control, cost control, use of standards, job specialization, employee training, equipment utilization, resource utilization, shipping and packaging, and technological innovation can have a dramatic impact on the success or failure of strategy-implementation efforts. Decisions in these areas affect decisions in management, marketing, finance, and research and development areas. For example, a large canned soup manufacturer routinely adjusts recipes to the tastes of local markets, and then adapts manufacturing processes to make use of locally available ingredients. The risk of not adapting production processes to changes in strategy often outweighs any cost benefits of centralizing production in one facility to serve diverse markets.

Some example production system adjustments that could be required to implement various company strategies for both profit and nonprofit organizations are provided in Table 7.5. For instance, note that when a bank formulates and selects a strategy to add ten new branches, a production-related implementation concern is site location.

A recent development in production processing is the "Just in Time" (JIT) concept, whereby parts and materials are delivered to the production line just as they are needed, rather than being stockpiled as a hedge against late deliveries. JIT manufacturing schemes have been found to significantly reduce the costs of implementing strategies. *Industry Week* gives the following observation about JIT:

> Most of the nation's 1000 largest industrial companies are experimenting with, or preparing to implement, "Just in Time" manufacturing schemes. Suppliers who can't, or won't, play by the new rules are finding themselves on the sidelines. "Just in Case" just isn't good enough any more.[29]

Table 7.5   Production management and strategy implementation

Type of Organization	Strategy Being Implemented	Production System Adjustments
Hospital	Adding a cancer center (Product Development)	Purchase specialized equipment and add specialized people.
Bank	Adding ten new branches (Market Development)	Perform site location analysis.
Beer brewery	Purchasing a barley farm operation (Backward Integration)	Revise the inventory control system.
Steel manufacturer	Acquiring a fast-food chain (Conglomerate Diversification)	Improve the quality control system.
Computer company	Purchase a retail distribution chain (Forward Integration)	Alter the shipping, packaging, and transportation systems.

Failure to match production and manufacturing policies with company strategy can have disastrous results. For example, Babcock and Wilcox (B&W) not too long ago located a manufacturing facility for nuclear pressure containers in a cornfield in southwestern Indiana. The reason was to tap an unspoiled labor market. In spite of a massive training program to turn farmers into technicians, poor quality, slow delivery, and discipline problems plagued this B&W facility from its inception. Factors that should be studied before locating production facilities include the availability of major resources, the prevailing wage rates in the area, transportation costs related to shipping and receiving, the location of major markets, political risks in the area or country, and the availability of trainable employees.

For high-technology companies, production costs may not be as important as production flexibility, because major product changes can be needed often. Industries like biogenetics and plastics, for example, rely on manufacturing systems that are flexible enough to allow frequent changes and rapid introduction to the market. On the other hand, for marketing-oriented products, production costs are often more important than production flexibility, since marketing, rather than production, provides the competitive edge for these products. Production resources that are carefully and purposefully deployed to support the strategy-implementation process can effectively serve as a fulcrum for competitive leverage.

Companies that fail to match manufacturing policies and product strategy effectively get into trouble. For example, Warwick Electronics at one time was the only supplier of color televisions to Sears, Roebuck and Company. Warwick depended on Sears for almost 75 percent of its sales. As technology changed and price competition increased, Warwick failed to adjust its manufacturing operations appropriately. Warwick was soon forced to sell its television business to Sanyo, a Japanese manufacturer. An article in the *Harvard Business Review* recently explained why companies like Warwick get into trouble:

> They get into trouble because they too slowly realize that a change in product strategy alters the tasks of a manufacturing system. These tasks, which can be stated in terms of requirements for cost, product flexibility, volume flexibility, product performance, and product consistency, determine which manufacturing policies are appropriate. As strategies shift over time, so must production policies covering the location and scale of manufacturing facilities, the choice of manufacturing process, the degree of vertical integration of each manufacturing facility, the use of R&D units, the control of the production system, and the licensing of technology.[30]

Whirlpool is an example company that spent $90 million in 1984 to modernize production, upgrading its computer-assisted design and robotics systems. Whirlpool spent another $150 million to develop a lighter washing machine with one-third fewer parts.[31] Sales to Sears, Roebuck accounted for 45 percent of Whirlpool's revenues in 1985.

DEVELOPING SUPPORTIVE RESEARCH AND DEVELOPMENT ACTIVITIES

Research and development personnel can play an integral part in the strategy-implementation process. These individuals are generally charged with developing new products and improving old products in a way that will allow company strategies to be implemented effectively. R&D units commonly perform tasks such as the transfer of complex technology, the adjustment of processes to local raw materials, the adaptation of processes to local markets, and the altering of products to local tastes and specifications. Strategies such as product development, market penetration, concentric diversification, and others require that new products be successfully developed and/or that old products be significantly improved. Research and development staffs play a key role in performing implementation tasks.

According to William Kimmerly, an effective approach to improving the strategy-implementation process of research-intensive organizations is threefold:

1. Improving the information-processing capabilities of such organizations.
2. Putting constraints on the activities of research scientists without excessively detracting from a creative environment.
3. Achieving a high degree of compatibility in the goals of managers and researchers, thereby facilitating coordination and communication.[32]

Two major developments in American society have led to a rapid growth in the number and size of research and development departments. First, technological improvements that impact consumer and industrial products and services are occurring at an increasing rate. Second, companies in virtually every industry are relying more and

Exhibit 7.2   Three measures of the top 15 in R&D spending

Three Ways to Rank the Top R&D Spenders		
In Total Dollars (millions)	In Percent of Sales	In Dollars per Employee
1. IBM................\$3,148	1. Dysan.................27.3%	1. Xonics.............\$92,347
2. General Motors........ 3,076	2. ADAC Laboratories....26.4	2. MicroPro International.........27,203
3. AT&T................. 2,368	3. Hogan Systems.........22.9	3. Ultimate 26,667
4. Ford Motor............ 1,915	4. VLSI Technology 21.8	4. VLSI Technology 24,175
5. Du Pont.............. 1,097	5. Xicor.................21.4	5. Applied Materials.....21,180
6. General Electric........ 1,038	6. Policy Management Systems 20.1	6. Hogan Systems........21,154
7. United Technologies ... 1,012	7. Management Science Amer.................18.8	7. ADAC Laboratories...20,879
8. Eastman Kodak 838	8. Applied Materials......18.5	8. Lotus Development....19,908
9. Exxon.................. 736	9. Advanced Micro Devices...............17.4	9. Fortune Systems.......19,469
10. Digital Equipment........ 631	10. TeleSciences...........17.2	10. Amdahl 18,663
11. Hewlett-Packard 592	11. GenRad 16.5	11. Dysan 17,214
12. Xerox 561	12. Computer Consoles 16.4	12. Marion Laboratories...17,160
13. ITT.................... 520	13. Cray Research 16.4	13. Eagle Computer.......17,157
14. Dow Chemical.......... 507	14. Amdahl 16.3	14. Ungermann-Bass......17,150
15. Boeing 506	15. Applied Data Research 16.2	15. Cray Research 17,038

DATA: STANDARD & POOR'S COMPUSTAT SERVICES INC.

Source: Reprinted from the July 8, 1985 issue of *Business Week* (p. 87) by special permission. © 1984 by McGraw-Hill, Inc.

more upon the development of new products and services to fuel profitability and growth. Exhibit 7.2 provides a breakdown of R&D expenditures in 1984 for the fifteen American companies that spent the most on R&D. According to *Business Week*, American companies in 1984 increased their expenditures to develop new products and processes at a rate that outran inflation by 10 percent, and this represented a 14 percent increase over 1983's total R&D expenditures. The increasing R&D expenditures reflect a deepening concern among American companies that foreign competitors are becoming more technologically advanced.[33] Figure 7.12 indicates that the corporate profit contribution from new products was expected to increase from 22 percent (1976-1981)

Figure 7.12   Corporate profit contribution from new products: past versus present

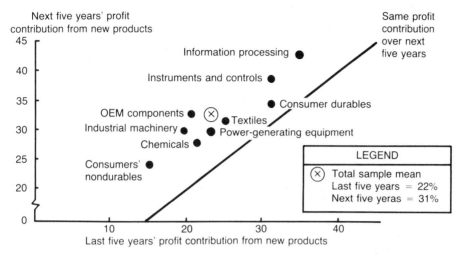

to 31 percent (1982-1986). Statistics like this suggest that research and development staffs are playing an increasingly important role in the strategy-implementation process.

Recent surveys suggest that "the most successful new-product companies (those with a new-product success rate of better than 90 percent) use a research and development strategy that ties internal strengths to external opportunities and is linked with corporate objectives."[34] Well-formulated research and development policies effectively match market opportunities with internal capabilities and provide an initial screen to all ideas generated.

The R&D function is more important in manufacturing industries than service industries. Table 7.6 gives some example R&D activities that could be required for successful implementation of various company strategies.

An example company that effectively uses research and development to implement its strategy of market penetration is L'Oreal, the world's third largest toiletries and cosmetics company. L'Oreal spends 3.3 percent of cosmetics sales on research and development, which in dollars is double that spent by Revlon and triple that of Avon.

> While Revlon was built on marketing savvy, L'Oreal's roots are in research. During the last five years, L'Oreal posted annual compound revenue growth of 20.8%, more than triple the 6% growth rate of number one Avon ($3 billion sales) and better than double the 9% rate of number two Revlon (about $2.4 billion sales).[35]

Table 7.6 Research and development involvement in selected strategy-implementation situations

Type of Organization	Strategy Being Implemented	R & D Activity
Pharmaceutical company	Product development	Develop a procedure for testing the effects of a new drug on different subgroups.
Boat manufacturer	Concentric diversification	Develop a procedure to test the performance of various keel designs under various conditions.
Plastic container manufacturer	Market penetration	Develop a more durable container.
Electronics company	Market development	Develop a telecommunications system.

CONCLUSION

In a single word, strategy implementation means "change." *Successful strategy formulation does not at all guarantee successful strategy implementation.* Although inextricably interdependent, strategy formulation and strategy implementation are characteristically different. It is widely agreed that "the real work begins after strategies are formulated." Successful strategy implementation requires support, discipline, motivation, and much hard work from all managers and employees. It is sometimes frightening to think that a sole individual can sabotage strategy-implementation efforts irreparably. The difference between strategic planning and strategic management is strategy implementation!

This chapter and the next are structured around a comprehensive strategy-implementation framework. The framework incorporates functional-area business changes that are commonly required to implement strategies successfully. Key functional-area changes discussed in this chapter included matching organizational structure with strategy, linking performance and pay to strategies, creating an organizational climate conducive to change, managing political relationships, creating a strategy-supportive culture, segmenting markets effectively, positioning products effectively, acquiring needed capital, developing *pro forma* financial statements, preparing financial budgets, evaluating the worth of a business, adapting production processes, and developing supportive research and development activities.

Techniques and concepts in the areas listed span all the divisions and functional departments of an organization. Although not an all-inclusive list of tools that can facilitate the strategy-implementation process, the techniques examined in this chapter do provide a critical link between strategy formulation and successful strategy implementation. They provide the basis for setting goals, establishing policies, and allocating resources, which are examined in the next chapter.

REVIEW QUESTIONS

1. Identify some key interrelationships among management, marketing, finance, production, and research and development. How could these interrelationships affect the strategy-implementation process?

2. Compare the strategy-formulation process with the strategy-implementation process in terms of each being an "art" or a "science."

3. Explain why organizational structure is so important in the strategy-implementation process.

4. In your opinion, how many separate divisions could an organization reasonably have without using an SBU type of organizational structure? Why?

5. What criteria would you use to decide whether a divisional structure by geographic area, product, customer, or process would be best for a given organization?

6. What are the major advantages and disadvantages of decentralizing the wage and salary function of an organization? How could this be accomplished?

7. Think of a high school or college organization of which you were a member. How did internal politics affect the strategy-implementation process in that organization?

8. Suppose your company has just acquired a firm that produces battery-operated lawn mowers and top management wants to implement a market-penetration strategy. How would you segment the market for this product? Justify your answer.

9. Diagram and label clearly a product-positioning map that includes the five major colleges and universities in your state.

10. Explain why EPS/EBIT analysis is a key strategy-implementation technique.

11. As the production manager of a local newspaper, what problems would you anticipate in implementing a company strategy to increase the average number of pages in the paper by 40 percent?

12. How would the R&D role in strategy implementation differ in small versus large organizations?

FOOTNOTES

1 Yoram Wind and Thomas Robertson, "Marketing Strategy: New Directions for Theory and Research," *Journal of Marketing* 47 (Spring 1983): 18.

2 Alfred Chandler, *Strategy and Structure* (Cambridge, Mass: MIT Press, 1962).

3 Ibid., 14.

4 A. Hax and N. Majluf, "Organization Design: A Case Study on Matching Strategy and Structure," *Journal of Business Strategy* 4, no. 2 (Fall 1983): 72–86.

5 Peter Drucker, *Management: Tasks, Responsibilities, and Practices* (New York: Harper & Row, 1974): 601–02.

6 "Hewlett Packard Discovers Marketing," *Fortune* (October 1, 1984): 51.

7 "3M's Aggressive New Consumer Drive," *Business Week* (July 16, 1984): 114.

8 "Merrill Lynch's Not-So-Thundering Recovery Plan," *Fortune* (August 6, 1984): 81.

9 Arthur Thompson, Jr. and Art Strickland III, *Strategy Formulation and Implementation* (Plano, Texas: Business Publications, Inc., 1983), 335.

10 Alfred Rappaport, "How To Design Value-Contributing Executive Incentives," *Journal of Business Strategy* (Fall 1983): 49. Also, L. Rappaport, "Corporate Performance Standards and Shareholder Value," *Journal of Business Strategy.* For a criticism of executive compensation programs, see L. Brindisi, Jr., "Why Executive Compensation Programs Go Wrong," *The Wall Street Journal, Manager's Journal* (June 14, 1982). Also see H. Platt and D. McCarthy, "Executive Compensation: Performance and Patience," *Business Horizons* (January–February 1985): 48–53.

11 Arthur Louis, "Business Is Bungling Long-Term Compensation," *Fortune* (July 23, 1984): 65. Also see H. Platt and D. McCarthy, "Executive Compensation: Performance and Patience," *Business Horizons* (January–February, 1985): 18–24.

12 Ibid., 66.

13 Perry Pascarella, "The Toughest Turnaround of All," *Industry Week* (April 2, 1984): 33.

14 Jack Duncan, *Management* (New York: Random House 1983), 381–90.

15 Anil Gupta and V. Govindarajan, "Business Unit Strategy, Managerial Characteristics, and Business Unit Effectiveness at Strategy Implementation," *Academy of Management Journal* 27, no. 1 (March 1984): 25–41. Other good references on this subject are: Milton Leontiades, "Choosing the Right Manager To Fit the Strategy," *Journal of Business Strategy* 3, no. 2 (Fall 1982): 58 Michael Bisesi, "Strategies for Successful Leadership in Changing Times," *Sloan Management Review* (Fall 1983): 61–64 M. Gerstein and H. Reisman, "Strategic Selection: Matching Executives to Business Conditions," *Sloan Management Review* (Winter 1983): 33–47.

16 W. Brooke Tunstall, "Cultural Transition at AT&T," *Sloan Management Review* (Fall 1983): 17.

17 Edwin Baker, "Managing Organizational Culture," *Management Review* 69 (July 1980): 13. Also see Meryl Gardner, "Creating a Corporate Culture for the Eighties," *Business Horizons* (January–February 1985): 59–63.

18 Tunstall, "AT&T," 22–24.

19 "Sperry: Out of an Identity Crisis: A New Dedication to Electronics," *Business Week* (April 30, 1984): 69.

20 E. Ralph Biggadike, "The Contributions of Marketing to Strategic Management," *Academy of Management Review* 6, no. 4 (October 1981): 624.

21 Philip Kotler, *Marketing Management* (Englewood Cliffs, N.J.: Prentice–Hall, 1976), 144.

22 Fred Winter, "Market Segmentation: A Tactical Approach," *Business Horizons* (January–February 1984): 59.

23 Bill Saporito, "When Business Got So Good It Got Dangerous," *Fortune* (April 2, 1984): 61.

24 Biggadike, "Contributions of Marketing," 627.

25 Ellen Paris, "Snip, Snip, Sell, Sell," *Forbes* (September 24, 1984): 178.

26 Paul Brown, "A Bread-and-Butter Business," *Forbes* (January 30, 1984): 77.

27 Alan Johnson, "How To Measure Your Company's Value," *Nation's Business* (April 1983): 68.

28 Richard Rodnick, "Getting the Right Price for Your Firm," *Nation's Business* (March 1984): 70.

29 "Just in Time: Putting the Squeeze on Suppliers," *Industry Week* (July 9, 1984): 59.

30 Robert Stobaugh and Piero Telesio, "Match Manufacturing Policies and Product Strategy," *Harvard Business Review* 61, no. 2 (March–April 1983): 113.

31 Jeff Blyskal, "Diversification Is for the Birds," *Forbes* (November 7, 1983): 132.

32 William Kimmerly, "R&D Planning in Turbulent Environments," *Managerial Planning* 31, no. 5 (March–April 1983): 11.

33 "Reagan and Foreign Rivalry Light a Fire Under Spending," *Business Week* (July 8, 1985): 86–104.

34 T. Kuczmarski and S. Silver, "Strategy: The Key to Successful New Product Development," *Management Review* (July 1982): 27.

35 Marcia Berss, "On the Scent," *Forbes* (March 12, 1984): 88.

SUGGESTED READINGS

Arthur Louis. "Business Is Bungling Longterm Compensation." *Fortune* (July 23, 1984): 65.

Assael, H., and A.M. Roscoe, Jr. "Approaches to Market Segmentation Analysis." *Journal of Marketing* 40 (October 1976): 67–76.

Baker, E. "Managing Organizational Culture." *Management Review* 69 (July 1980): 13–16.

Biggadike, E.R. "The Contributions of Marketing to Strategic Management." *Academy of Management Review* 6, no. 4 (October 1981): 621–32.

Bisesi, M. "Strategies for Successful Leadership in Changing Times." *Sloan Management Review* (Fall 1983): 61–64.

Brunton, G.C. "Implementing Corporate Strategy." *Journal of Business Strategy* (Fall 1984): 6–15.

Chandler, A.D. *Strategy and Structure*. Cambridge, Mass.: M.I.T. Press, 1962.

Chase, R.B., and N.J. Aquilano. *Production and Operations Management*. Homewood, Ill.: Richard D. Irwin, 1981.

Cook, V.F. Jr. "Marketing Strategy and Differential Advantage." *Journal of Marketing* 47, (Spring, 1983): 68–75.

Davis, S.M. and P.R. Lawrence. "Problems of Matrix Organizations." *Harvard Business Review* 56, no. 3 (May–June 1978): 131–42.

Duncan, Jack. *Management.* New York: Random House, 1983.

Drucker, Peter. *Management: Tasks, Responsibilities, and Practices.* New York: Harper & Row, 1974.

Finkin, E.F. "Developing and Managing New Products." *Journal of Business Strategy* (Spring 1983): 39–46.

Galbraith, J. and D. Nathanson. *Strategy Implementation: The Role of Structure and Process.* St. Paul, Minn.: West Publishing Company, 1978.

Gardner, M.P. "Creating a Corporate Culture for the Eighties." *Business Horizons* (January–February 1985): 59–63.

Gerstein, M. and H. Reisman. "Strategic Selection: Matching Executives to Business Conditions." *Sloan Management Review* (Winter 1983): 33–47.

Greenley, G.E. "Where Marketing Planning Fails." *Long Range Planning.* 16 (February 1983): 106–15.

Gupta, A. and V. Govindarajan. "Business Unit Strategy, Managerial Characteristics, and Business Unit Effectiveness at Strategy Implementation." *Academy of Management Journal* 27, no. 1 (March 1984): 25–41.

Hall, W.K. "SBU's: Hot New Topic in the Management of Diversification." *Business Horizons* 21, no. 1 (February 1978): 15–20.

Hax, A.C. and N.S. Majluf. "Organization Design: A Case Study on Matching Strategy and Structure." *The Journal of Business Strategy* 4, no. 2 (Fall 1983): 72–86.

Hobbs, J. and D. Heany. "Coupling Strategy to Operating Plans." *Harvard Business Review* (May–June 1977): 119–26.

Hrebiniak, L.G. and W.F. Joyce. *Implementing Strategy.* New York: Macmillan, 1984.

Johnson, A. "How To Measure Your Company's Value." *Nation's Business* (April 1983): 68, 70.

Kahalas, H. "Planning for Organizational Design." *Managerial Planning* (May–June 1983): 4–8, 45.

Kimmerly, W. "R&D Planning in Turbulent Environments." *Managerial Planning* 31, no. 5 (March–April 1983): 11–13.

Kotler, P. *Marketing Management.* Englewood Cliffs, N.J.: Prentice-Hall, 1976.

Kuczmarski, T.D. and S.J. Silver. "Strategy: The Key to Successful New Product Development." *Management Review* (July 1982): 26–40.

Laufer, A.C. *Production and Operations Management.* Cincinnati: South–Western Publishing Co., 1984.

Leontiades, M. "Choosing the Right Manager to Fit the Strategy." *Journal of Business Strategy* 3, no. 2 (Fall 1982): 58–69.

Lorange, P. *Implementation of Strategic Planning.* Englewood Cliffs, N.J.: Prentice-Hall, 1982.

Lorsch, J.W. and A.H. Walker. "Organizational Choice: Product vs. Function." *Harvard Business Review* 46, no. 6 (November–December 1968): 129–38.

Morton, M.R. "Technology and Strategy: Creating a Successful Partnership." *Business Horizons* (January–February 1983): 44–48.

Platt, H.D. and D.J. McCarthy. "Executive Compensation: Performance and Patience." *Business Horizons* (January–February 1985): 18–24.

Rappaport, A. "Executive Incentives versus Corporate Growth." *Harvard Business Review* (July–August 1978): 81–88.

Rodnick, R. "Getting the Right Price for Your Firm." *Nation's Business* (March 1984): 70, 71.

Salter, M.S. "Stages of Corporate Development." *Journal of Business Policy* 1, no. 1 (Spring 1970): 23–27.

Shapiro, B. and B. Thomas. "How To Segment Industrial Markets." *Harvard Business Review* (May–June 1984): 104–10.

Sheth, J.N. and G.L. Frazier. "A Margin-Return Model for Strategic Market Planning." *Journal of Marketing* 47 (Spring 1983): 100–09.

Slocum, J.W. Jr. and D. Hellriegel. "Using Organizational Designs to Cope with Change." *Business Horizons* 22, no. 6 (December 1979): 65–76.

Stobaugh, R. and P. Telesio. "Match Manufacturing Policies and Product Strategy." *Harvard Business Review* (March–April 1983): 113–20.

Stybel, L.J. "Linking Strategic Planning and Management Manpower Planning." *California Management Review* 25, no. 1 (Fall 1982): 48–56.

Tomasko, R.M. "Focusing Company Reward Systems To Help Achieve Business Objectives." *Management Review* (October 1982): 8–12.

Tunstall, W.B. "Cultural Transition at AT&T." *Sloan Management Review* (Fall 1983): 15–26.

Wind, J. and T.S. Robertson. "Marketing Strategy: New Directions for Theory and Research." *Journal of Marketing* 47 (Spring 1983): 12–25.

Wheelwright, S.C. "Reflecting Corporate Strategy in Manufacturing Decisions." *Business Horizons* (February 1978): 57–66.

Winter, F. "Market Segmentation: A Tactical Approach." *Business Horizons* (January–February 1984): 57–63.

Zalenik, A. "Power and Politics in Organizational Life." *Harvard Business Review* 48, no. 3 (May–June 1970): 47–60.

EXPERIENTIAL EXERCISE 7A:

Matching Managers with Strategy

PURPOSE

For many years, executives believed that good managers could adapt to the handling of any situation. Consequently, executives rarely replaced or transferred managers as the need arose to implement new strategies. Today, this situation is changing. Research supports the notion that certain management characteristics are needed for certain strategic situations.[1] Chase Manhattan Bank, Heublein, Texas Instruments, Corning Glass, and General Electric are example companies engaged in matching managers to strategic requirements.

The purpose of this exercise is to improve your awareness and understanding of particular managerial characteristics that have been found to be most desirable for implementing certain types of strategies. As discussed in Chapter 7, having the right managers in the right jobs can determine the success or failure of strategy-implementation efforts. This exercise is based on a recently published framework that has proved to be useful in "matching managers to strategy."[2]

YOUR TASK

Your task in this exercise is to match specific managerial characteristics with particular strategies. Four broad types of strategies are examined:

1. Retrenchment/Turnaround
2. Intensive (market penetration, market development, and product development)

3. Liquidation/divestiture

4. Integration (backward, forward, and horizontal)

Five managerial characteristics have been found to be associated with each of these strategies. On a separate sheet of paper, write down the four types of strategy. Beside each strategy, record the appropriate letter of the five managerial characteristics which you believe are most needed to successfully implement those strategies. Each of the managerial characteristics that is listed should be used only once in completing this exercise:

a. Is technically knowledgeable—"knows the business."

b. Is "callous"—tough-minded, determined, willing to be the bad guy.

c. Is "Take Charge"-oriented—strong leader.

d. Is good negotiator.

e. Wants to be respected, not necessarily liked.

f. Has good analytical ability.

g. Is low in glory seeking—willing to do dirty jobs; does not want glamour.

h. Has excellent staffing skills.

i. Handles pressure well.

j. Is risk taker.

k. Has good relationship-building skills.

l. Has good organizational and team-building skills.

m. Is oriented to getting out the most efficiency, not growth.

n. Anticipates problems—"Problem Finder."

o. Has strong analytical and diagnostic skills, especially financial.

p. Is excellent business strategist.

q. Has good communication skills.

r. Has personal magnetism.

s. Is highly analytical—focuses on costs/benefits; does not easily accept current ways of doing things.

t. Has good interpersonal influence.

FOOTNOTES

1 Marc Gerstein and Heather Reisman, "Strategic Selection: Matching Executives to Business Conditions," *Sloan Management Review* (Winter 1983): 33–47.

2 Gerstein and Reisman, "Strategic Selection," 37.

EXPERIENTIAL EXERCISE 7B:

Matching Organizational Structure with Strategy

PURPOSE

Now that you have read Chapter 7, you are knowledgeable about the concept of matching organizational structure with strategy. However, you have not yet had much opportunity to integrate and apply this new knowledge base. The purpose of this exercise is to give you experience evaluating the appropriateness of a firm's structure. A short description of three firms is provided in this exercise along with information regarding each organization's strategy. The sample firms are actual organizations: Atlantic Richfield Company (ARCO), Fairchild Industries, Inc., and L. Luria & Son, Inc. At the time of the information furnished in Tables 1, 2, and 3, ARCO and Fairchild were experiencing declining sales and net income, while L. Luria was doing well. The organizational structures of ARCO, Fairchild, and L. Luria are illustrated in Figure 1, Figure 2, and Figure 3 respectively.

YOUR TASK

Your task in this exercise is to study the short description of each firm and its strategy, then examine each firm's organizational chart. Finally, discuss whether or not you feel the firm's structure is most appropriate for implementing its strategy. Focus on answering the following questions:

1. What type of structure does each firm have?
2. Why is that type of structure most appropriate or inappropriate for the firm?
3. What are the advantages and disadvantages of each firm's structure?
4. If you were going to recommend structural changes for each firm, what would they be?

Atlantic Richfield Company

ARCO ranks seventh in sales among U.S. oil companies. The company is currently pursuing a market penetration strategy by pouring money into advertising, allowing discounts for cash, lowering the price of gas, accepting a variety of bank credit cards,

Table 1 ARCO's sales by segment information for 1983, 1982, and 1981

	1983	*1982*	*1981*
Sales and other operating revenues (in millions of dollars):			
Oil and gas	$ 6,686	$ 6,569	$ 6,587
Fuels:			
Refining and marketing	20,600	22,135	23,726
Transportation	1,223	1,187	1,130
Minerals	396	549	501
Materials:			
Chemicals	2,550	2,242	2,739
Metals	1,146	1,030	1,319
Other operations	167	154	131
Elimination of intersegment amounts	(6,831)	(6,875)	(7,925)
Total	$25,937	$26,991	$28,208

Source: ARCO's *1983 Annual Report,* p. 41.

and turning many of its service stations into mini-marts. ARCO obtains over 50 percent of its oil from Alaskan North Slope, which is expected possibly to run dry by the year 1995. ARCO's total revenues and net income in 1983 were $26.2 billion and $1.1 billion respectively. The company's total revenues and net income in 1982 were $27.5 billion and $1.7 billion. A three-year summary of ARCO's sales by industry segment is provided in Table 1.

Fairchild Industries, Inc.

About half of Fairchild's revenues come from military work, with the remaining sales coming from commercial aerospace, industrial products, and communications businesses. By 1987, Fairchild plans to reduce its military business from 50 to 25 percent of sales, to increase its commercial aerospace business from 18 percent now to 38 percent, and to triple its satellite communications business to 7 percent of sales. In 1983, Fairchild's total revenues and net income were $891.6 million and $28.4 million respectively. Comparatively, Fairchild's 1982 revenues and net income were $1.1 billion and $35.3 million. A five-year summary of Fairchild's sales by business segment is provided in Table 2.

Figure 1 Atlantic Richfield's (ARCO's) organizational chart

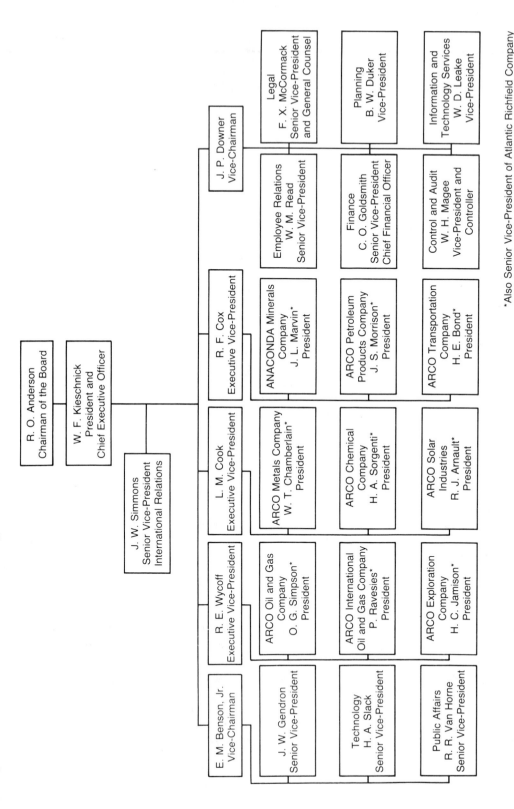

Source: Atlantic Richfield Company, *Supplement to the 1982 Annual Report,* Los Angeles, Calif.: Atlantic Richfield Company, 1983.

Table 2 Fairchild's sales by segment information for the period 1979–1983

Sales by Business Segment (in thousands of dollars)	1983	1982	1981	1980	1979
Government aerospace.............	$330,913	$ 490,722	$ 593,909	$542,930	$460,712
Commercial aerospace.............	157,194	199,718	255,417	253,808	193,964
Communications, electronics & space...........................	71,720	64,268	54,648	46,983	41,259
Aerospace fasteners................	90,514	106,850	177,754	25,330	—
Tooling for plastics................	88,508	91,242	105,231	15,153	—
General industry	156,075	147,131	164,264	32,065	12,924
Intersegment sales included in communications, electronics & space...........................	(3,332)	(6,670)	(12,318)	(10,039)	(7,056)
Total	$891,592	$1,093,261	$1,338,905	$906,230	$701,803

Source: Fairchild's *1983 Annual Report,* p. 14.

L. Luria & Son

L. Luria is a retail catalog company in Florida that offers cameras, jewelry, silverware, toasters, and brand name goods at nearly wholesale prices. L. Luria has grown at a 31 percent annual rate over five years and plans to open twelve to fifteen new stores by 1986. By that time, L. Luria will have saturated Florida. Company plans are to continue its market development strategy after 1986 by building a showroom in New Orleans, Dallas, and Washington, D.C. In 1983, L. Luria's sales and net income were $123.8 million and $5.5 million respectively. In 1982, the company's sales and net income were $108.9 million and $4.5 million. L. Luria's inventories at the end of fiscal 1983 and 1982 are summarized in Table 3.

Table 3 L. Luria's inventories at fiscal year end 1983 and 1982

	1983	1982
Diamonds	$ 1,900,188	$ 1,161,467
Jewelry	25,441,345	17,054,387
Other Merchandise	22,252,824	17,196,194
Total	$49,594,357	$35,412,048

Source: L. Luria's *1983 Annual Report,* p. 17.

Figure 2 Fairchild Industries' organizational chart

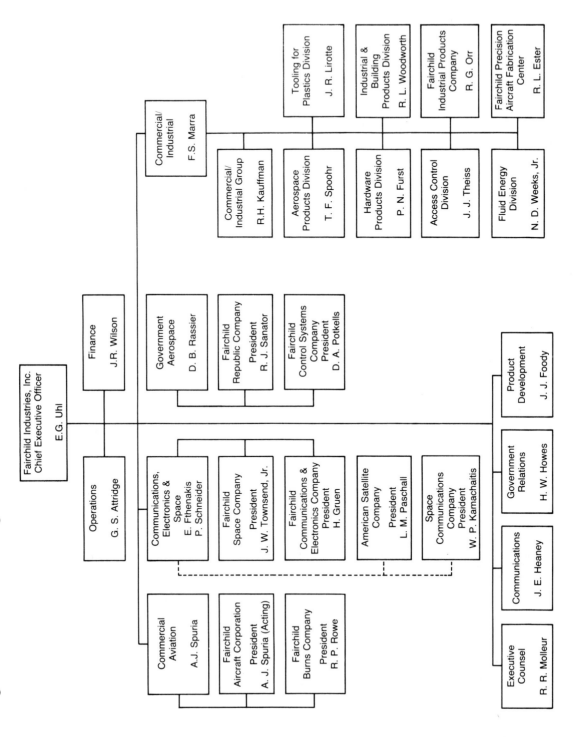

Figure 3 L. Luria & Sons' organizational chart

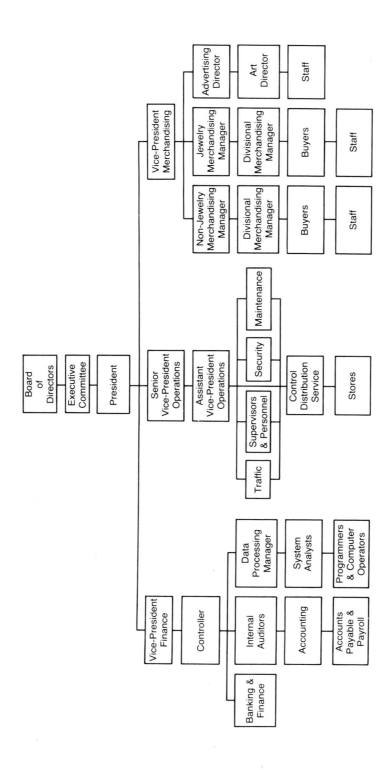

REFERENCES

"Atlantic Richfield: Marketing Muscle Has the Competition Reeling." *Business Week* (September 12, 1983): 86, 88.

"Fairchild Industries: Looking to Aerospace As It Braces for a Lag in Defense." *Business Week* (May 23, 1983): 134, 137.

"L. Luria & Son: A Cataloger Whose Profits Match Its Classy Image." *Business Week* (July 11, 1983): 98.

EXPERIENTIAL EXERCISE 7C:

Preparing Pro Forma *Statements for Ponderosa, Inc.*

PURPOSE

The purpose of this exercise is to give you experience preparing *pro forma* financial statements. *Pro forma* analysis is a central strategy-implementation technique because it allows managers to anticipate and evaluate the results of various implementation actions.

YOUR TASK

Recall that Ponderosa's 1984 income statement and balance sheet are provided in the Cohesion Case. Your task in this exercise is to determine what strategies and implementation actions are best for Ponderosa, and incorporate those recommendations into a forecasted (1985) income statement and balance sheet for the company. Prepare your *pro forma* statements by following the steps outlined on pages 270–72.

What impact do your recommendations have on Ponderosa's 1985 sales and net income? Are your projections optimistic, realistic, or pessimistic in preparing *pro formas*? Why? Do the financial ratios computed from your projected statements compare favorably with Ponderosa's 1984 and 1983 ratios? Explain any significant deviations in these ratios.

8

Setting Goals, Establishing Policies, and Allocating Resources

This chapter examines the three basic strategy-implementation activities: setting goals, establishing policies, and allocating financial, physical, human, and technological resources. Goals are essential for motivating and evaluating employees. Policies are needed to guide, direct, limit, encourage, and constrain behavior. Allocating resources appropriately supports key areas of strategic emphasis. Performing these activities effectively is both challenging and critical to successful strategic management.

IMPLEMENTING STRATEGIES SUCCESSFULLY

The quarterback of a football team can call the best play possible in the huddle, but that does not mean the play will go for a touchdown. In fact, the team may lose yardage unless the play is executed (implemented) well. It has been estimated that less than 10 percent of business strategies that are formulated are successfully implemented. There are many reasons for this low success rate. Individuals' resistance to change, lack of an effective organizational structure, failure to segment markets appropriately, and paying too much for a new acquisition are a few reasons that were examined in the last chapter. However, if goal setting, policy making, and resource-allocation activities are not performed well, strategy-implementation efforts have little chance of succeeding. The basic strategy-implementation activities are appropriately shaded in the strategic-management model illustrated in Figure 8.1.

A checklist of questions that comprise a framework for setting goals, establishing policies, and allocating resources is presented in Exhibit 8.1. These questions correspond to problem areas that often prevent objectives from being accomplished. Problems that commonly inhibit goal setting, policy making, and resource-allocation efforts are examined in this chapter. The checklist of questions can guide managers' efforts to develop clear goals, devise effective policies, and allocate resources appropriately. The set of questions is not, of course, an exhaustive list, nor applicable to all organizations and environments.

ESTABLISHING GOALS

Establishing goals is a decentralized activity that directly involves all managers in an organization. When you prepare a business policy case analysis, a necessary task is to develop specific goals for the firm being studied. (Recall from Chapter 1 that some authors use the terms goals and objectives interchangeably, some authors use a single term to refer to both short-range and long-range aims, and still other writers refer to goals as long-term results and objectives as short-term aims. In this textbook, "goals" are short-range [annual] results and "objectives" are long-range [more than 1 year] accomplishments.)

Active participation in goal-setting activities can lead to acceptance and commitment. Goals are essential for successful strategy implementation because they represent the basis for allocating resources, they are the primary mechanism for evaluating managers, they are the major instrument for monitoring progress towards achieving stated

Figure 8.1 The strategic-management model

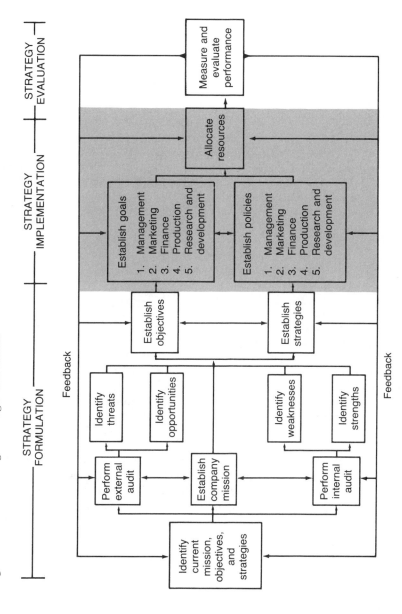

Exhibit 8.1   A framework for setting goals, establishing policies, and allocating resources

Establish Objectives and Strategies
Are objectives and strategies clearly communicated?

Establish Goals

Are goals clear, specific, measurable, challenging, obtainable, timely, consistent, and prioritized?

Is there an appropriate number of goals?

Are goals established in all key areas?

Do stated goals allow accomplishment of company objectives?

Are stated goals compatible with employees' and managers' values?

Are stated goals supported by reasonable and effective policies?

Do stated goals provide a basis for effective resource allocation?

Is there a reasonable link between stated goals and the organization's reward system?

Are goals communicated to all who need to be informed?

Are the strategies, objectives, goals, and policies all consistent and mutually supporting?

Establish Policies

Have policies been established that are reasonable, fair, consistent, clear, timely, and enforceable?

Is there an appropriate number of policies?

Are policies established in all key areas?

Are stated policies compatible with employees' and managers' values?

Do stated policies appropriately limit and constrain employees' and managers' activities?

Do stated policies support the organization's goals by encouraging work, commitment, and sacrifice?

Have appropriate disciplinary measures been established for noncompliance with stated policies?

Allocate Resources

Has a resource inventory been developed for the entire organization?

Has a resource inventory been developed for each division?

Has a resource inventory been developed for each department?

Have resource requests been prepared by all divisions and departments?

Are resource requests consistent with established goals?

Are resource requests feasible considering the total resources available?

objectives, and they establish organizational, divisional, and departmental priorities. For all of these reasons, considerable time and effort should be devoted to assuring that goals are well-conceived, consistent with stated objectives, and supportive of strategies to be implemented. Managers should involve their subordinates in the goal-setting process because lower-level employees' productivity and motivation are critical to organizational success. Two well-known writers have described the purpose of goals as follows:

> Goals serve as guidelines for action, directing and channeling efforts and activities of organization members. Goals provide a source of legitimacy for an enterprise by justifying its activities, and, indeed, its very existence to such groups as customers, politicians, employees, stockholders, and society at large. Goals serve as standards of performance. To the extent that goals

are clearly stated and understood, they offer direct standards for evaluating performance. Goals serve as an important source of employee motivation and identification. Goals give incentives for employees to perform. Goals provide a basis for organizational design. Enterprise goals and structure interact in that the actions necessary for goal accomplishment may impose unavoidable restrictions on employee activities and resource utilization patterns, necessitating implementation of a variety of organization design elements.[1]

Goals vary by type and size of organization. Large firms generally give considerable attention to socially oriented goals, while small companies focus more on economic goals. Organizations that use extensive environmental resources, such as Georgia Pacific and Shell Oil, give more attention to efficiency- and conservation-related goals. Firms that compete in dynamic technological environments, such as Apple Computer and General Electric, stress research and development goals more than firms competing in stable environments. In summary, the goal structure of corporations may vary depending upon the time, the strategic issues facing a given industry, the economic situation, environmental uncertainty, the values of top management, and the size of the firm.[2] However, clearly stated and communicated goals are critical to success in all types and sizes of firms.

A statement of Gold Kist's goals is given in Exhibit 8.2. Gold Kist, headquartered in Atlanta, Georgia, is a diversified farm products company with 10,000 employees.

Exhibit 8.2   Gold Kist's statement of goals

Specific goals are quantified levels of performance which are to be accomplished within a given future time period. Each specific goal must be contributory to a continuing objective and consistent with corporate policies. Specific goals are developed at all levels within Gold Kist. The major items for which specific goals are developed include:

1. Sales volume expressed in dollars and units for all Plants, Divisions, Groups, and the Corporation as a whole.
2. Net profit margins for each of the above.
3. Net returns per dollar of capital utilized.
4. Operating cost reductions.
5. Product yields from processing facilities.
6. Feed conversions for poultry and livestock.

Source: Gold Kist, Inc., *Internal Report,* 1984.

The traditional goals of profitability, growth, and market share are still the dominant types in most organizations. Goals in these three areas are commonly established by business segment, by geographic area, by customer groups, and by product. General Mills has established two overriding financial goals: (1) to have an annual return on equity of at least 19 percent and (2) to average growing 6 percent per year plus the rate of inflation. The Ferro Company, based in Cleveland, Ohio, recently established the following annual goals:

Return on equity:	15%
Return on net assets:	8%
Earnings growth:	12%
Net earnings on sales:	5%
Debt to equity:	30–35%
Dividend payout:	30–35%
Earnings:	33% domestic / 66% international

The information seen in Table 8.1 provided a basis for the Chrysler Corporation to establish 1985 goals in terms of the total number of cars and trucks it would sell in the U.S., Canada, and foreign countries. Note that Chrysler sold nearly as many cars and trucks worldwide in 1984 as it did in 1978.

Figure 8.2 illustrates how another firm, the Stamus Company, could break down its revenue objectives into annual goals. Table 8.2 reveals the associated revenue figures that correspond to the objectives and goals outlined in Figure 8.2. Note that, according to plan, the Stamus Company will slightly exceed its planned objective of doubling company revenues in two years, since 4.065 is greater than twice 2.0.

As indicated in Figure 8.2, production goals could be subdivided into related areas such as purchasing, shipping, and quality control. Similarly, marketing goals could be subdivided into areas such as advertising, sales promotion, marketing research, and public relations. Finance goals could be subdivided into auditing, accounting, investments, collections, working capital, liquidity, leverage, profitability, and other areas. Personnel and research and development functions could similarly be subdivided into lower-level goals.

It should be clear that a hierarchy of goals can be established based on the way an organization is structured. Each goal contributes to the goals of the next higher organizational level. Goals should be consistent across hierarchical levels, forming a network of supportive aims. Horizontal consistency of goals is as important as vertical consistency. For example, it would not be effective for manufacturing to achieve more than its goal of units produced if marketing could not sell the additional units.

Table 8.1 Unit sales of Chrysler cars and trucks by geographic area

	1984	1983	1982	1981	1980	1979	1978
United States							
Passenger Cars	1,163,221	968,647	737,350	834,155	721,868	1,021,826	1,229,548
Trucks	573,248	294,703	231,756	184,011	213,516	329,212	502,594
TOTAL UNITED STATES	1,736,469	1,263,350	969,106	1,018,166	935,384	1,351,038	1,732,142
Canada							
Passenger Cars	176,220	149,242	105,264	103,031	112,692	158,020	180,575
Trucks	53,338	29,330	21,328	29,463	31,489	42,702	43,856
TOTAL U.S. AND CANADA	1,966,027	1,441,922	1,095,698	1,150,660	1,079,565	1,551,760	1,956,573
Outside U.S. and Canada							
Passenger Cars	39,885	32,560	46,231	69,172	82,285	165,587	166,526
Trucks	28,436	19,479	39,797	63,181	63,073	79,118	88,436
TOTAL OUTSIDE U.S. AND CANADA	68,321	52,039	86,028	132,353	145,358	244,705	254,962
TOTAL WORLDWIDE	2,034,348	1,493,961	1,181,726	1,283,013	1,224,923	1,796,465	2,211,535

Source: Chrysler Corporation, *Annual Report*, 1984, p. 42.

Figure 8.2   The Stamus Company's hierarchy of aims

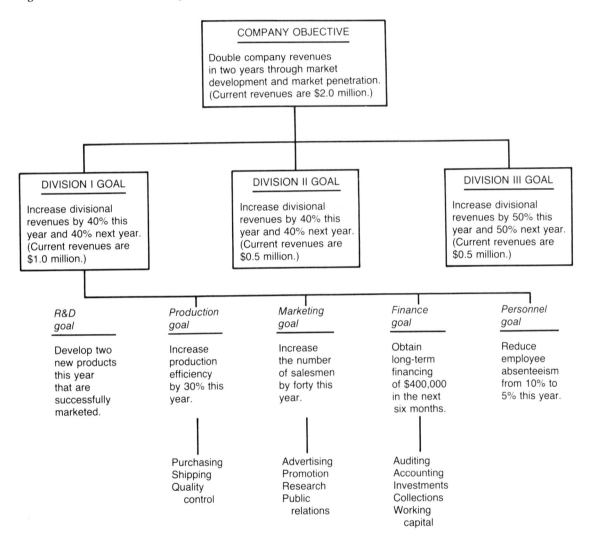

Guidelines for Setting Goals

Goals should be measurable, consistent, reasonable, challenging, clear, communicated throughout the organization, and characterized by an appropriate time dimension. Commensurate rewards and sanctions should be established for all major goals. Too

Table 8.2   The Stamus Company's revenue expectations (in millions of dollars)

	1986	1987	1988
Division I Revenues	1.0	1.400	1.960
Division II Revenues	0.5	0.700	.980
Division III Revenues	0.5	0.750	1.125
Total Company Revenues	2.0	2.950	4.065

often, goals are stated in generalities, with little operational usefulness. For example, goals such as "to improve communication" or "to maximize profits" are not clear, specific, or measurable. Goals should state quantity, quality, cost, time, and be verifiable. Terms such as "maximize," "minimize," "as soon as possible," and "adequate" should be avoided.

Goals should be challenging yet reasonable, and require some effort for achievement. Unrealistic goals can be demoralizing to both managers and employees. Goals should relate not only to business operations, but should also include personal and professional development accomplishments. There should be an appropriate number of goals associated with each stated objective. Too many goals detract from the really important objectives. Sometimes several goals can be combined into one. The number of goals should be manageable. "Often, employees are assigned twenty or thirty goals, not realizing how difficult it is to keep track of so many key result areas. Some management experts believe that an individual cannot pursue more than two to five goals effectively."[3]

Goals should be compatible with employees' and managers' values and should be supported by clearly stated policies. In setting goals, more of something is not always better. Improved quality or reduced cost may, for example, be more important than quantity. It is important to tie rewards and sanctions to stated goals, so that employees and managers will understand that goal attainment is critical to the success of strategy-implementation efforts. Clearly stated goals do not guarantee successful strategy implementation, but they do increase the likelihood that personal and organizational aims will be accomplished.

Overemphasis on goal attainment can result in undesirable conduct, such as faking the numbers, distorting the records, and letting goals become ends in themselves. Managers must be alert to detect and prevent undesirable activities.

An example firm that has communicated its mission, objectives, and goals is CF Industries, Inc. However, note in Exhibit 8.3 that this firm's objectives and goals are stated in terms that are too general. Based in Long Grove, Illinois, CF Industries employs about 2,000 persons and has annual sales of nearly $1 billion in chemical fertilizers.

Exhibit 8.3 CF Industries, Inc.—mission statement and objectives

Corporate Mission

The purpose of the Corporation is to provide dependable, long-term supplies of high-quality fertilizers and related products and services at competitive prices to the member cooperatives which own CF Industries and to generate a return on investment which will assure the continued viability of the Corporation and the provision of dependable product supplies for the members.

Objective No. 1: Supply the Contractual Product Supply Commitments to the Members.

The primary objective of CF Industries is to economically supply the annual volumes of nitrogen, phosphate, and potash specified in the long-term Member Product Purchase Agreements with the individual members. To avoid liquidated damages for failure to perform, the member must purchase 90 percent and CF must supply 96 percent of the annual contract quantities.

Corporate goals supporting this objective include the following:

1. Make available, on a best-efforts basis, the quantity of nitrogen, phosphate, and potash agreed to be provided to members each year.

2. Supply, on a cost-justified basis, the nitrogen, phosphate, and potash in the product forms as specified yearly by members.

3. Sell products to the members at prices competitive with other comparable sources of product and levels of service for the respective market areas.

4. Supply products with quality specifications generally accepted in the industry or as established by CF and the members, based upon economic and technical feasibility.

5. Provide services equal to, or better than (when cost-justified), that provided by competitors.

6. Provide products and services on a timely basis in desirable locations.

Source: CF Industries, Inc., Excerpt from an *Internal Report,* 1984.

Managing Conflict

Unfortunately, the interdependency of goals often leads to conflict. Conflict can be defined as a disagreement between two or more parties on one or more issues. The goal-setting process can lead to conflict due to competition over scarce resources, different goal expectations among individuals, different perceptions among individuals, miscommunication, time pressure, personality incompatibility, and line and staff misunderstanding. For example, a collection manager's goal of reducing bad debts by 50 percent in a given year may conflict with a divisional goal to increase sales by 20 percent.

Establishing goals also can lead to conflict due to common tradeoffs faced by managers. Some of these tradeoffs are short-term profits versus long-term growth, profit margin versus market share, direct sales effort versus developmental effort, market penetration versus market development, growth versus stability, high risk versus low risk, and social responsiveness versus profit maximization. Conflict is unavoidable in organizations, so it is important that managers develop the ability to manage and resolve conflict before dysfunctional consequences affect organizational performance.

Various approaches for minimizing and resolving conflict can be classified into three categories: avoidance, defusion, and confrontation. The strategy of avoidance includes such actions as ignoring the problem situation in hopes that the conflict will resolve itself, or physically separating the conflicting individuals (or groups) from each other. A defusion strategy can include playing down the differences between conflicting parties while accenting their similarities and common interests, or compromising so that there is neither a clear winner nor loser, or resorting to majority rule, or appealing to a higher authority, or redesigning present positions. A confrontation approach is exemplified by exchanging members of conflicting parties so that each can gain an appreciation of the other's point of view, or focusing on superordinate goals such as company survival, or holding a meeting whereby conflicting parties present their views and work through their differences.

Conflict is not always detrimental to the strategy-implementation process. In most cases, conflict will result in both positive and negative consequences. The presence of conflict can indicate that employees and managers are taking goals seriously, which is desirable. An absence of conflict sometimes signals indifference and apathy. Conflict can serve to "energize" opposing groups into action and can facilitate identification of problem areas.

ESTABLISHING POLICIES

The Role of Policies

Changes in a firm's strategic direction do not occur automatically. On a day-to-day basis, policies are needed to make a strategy work. Once a strategy is formulated, managers should attempt to determine in advance the most frequent implementation problems that might occur. Then, policies should be established to facilitate solving those repetitive or recurring problems. The role of policies is to guide the implementation of strategy.

The term "policy" refers to specific guidelines, methods, procedures, rules, forms, and administrative practices that are established to support and encourage work toward stated goals.[4] Policies can be viewed as instruments for strategy implementation. Policies set boundaries, constraints, and limits on the kinds of administrative actions that can be taken to reward and sanction behavior. Policies clarify what can and cannot be done in pursuit of an organization's goals and objectives.

Policies let both employees and managers know what is expected of them, thereby increasing the likelihood that strategies will be implemented successfully. Policies provide a basis for management control, allow coordination across organizational units, and reduce the amount of time managers spend making decisions. Policies also clarify what work is to be done by whom and promote delegation of decision making to the managerial level that must face the problem when it arises. An organization could develop hundreds of policies to cover the important areas of business.

Policies can be simple, such as, "Coffee breaks can last up to ten minutes in length"; policies can be complex, such as, "We must standardize component parts in producing our products." Policies can apply to all divisions and departments. An example of this is, "We are an equal opportunity employer." Some policies apply only to a single department, such as "Employees in this department must take at least one training and development course each year." Whatever the scope and form of policies, they serve as mechanisms for implementing strategies and obtaining goals. Policies should be stated in writing whenever possible, but in some cases they may consist of unwritten understandings derived from past actions. Policies represent the means for carrying out strategic decisions. Example policies that could be established to support a company strategy, a divisional goal, and a departmental goal are given in Exhibit 8.4.

There are three types of policies that correspond to the hierarchical levels in an organization: corporate, divisional, and functional. Corporate policies apply throughout an organization, divisional policies apply to a given division, and departmental policies apply only within a given department. Corporate, divisional, and departmental policies are commonly stated in terms of the functional areas of business. Some example management, marketing, finance, production, and research and development policies are given on pages 305–307.

Exhibit 8.4   A hierarchy of policies

Company Strategy: Acquire a chain of retail stores to meet our sales growth and profitability objectives.

Supporting policies:

1. "All stores will be open from 8:00 AM to 8:00 PM Monday through Saturday." (This policy could increase retail sales if stores currently are open only forty hours a week.)

2. "All stores must submit a Monthly Control Data Report." (This policy could reduce expense-to-sales ratios.)

3. "All stores must support company advertising by contributing 5 percent of their total monthly revenues for this purpose." (This policy could allow the company to establish a national reputation.)

4. "All stores must adhere to the uniform pricing guidelines set forth in the Company Handbook." (This policy could help assure customers that the company offers a consistent product in terms of price and quality in all its stores.)

Divisional Goal: Increase the division's revenues from $10 million in 1986 to $15 million in 1987.

Supporting policies:

1. "Beginning in January 1987, this division's salespersons must file a weekly activity report that includes the number of calls made, the number of miles traveled, the number of units sold, the dollar volume sold, and the number of new accounts opened." (This policy could assure that salespersons do not place too great an emphasis in certain areas.)

2. "Beginning in January 1987, this division will return to its employees 5 percent of its gross revenues in the form of a Christmas bonus." (This policy could increase employee productivity.)

3. "Beginning in January 1987, inventory levels carried in warehouses will be decreased by 30 percent in accordance with a Just-In-Time manufacturing approach." (This policy could reduce production expenses and thus free funds for increased marketing efforts.)

Production Department Goal: Increase production from 20,000 units in 1986 to 30,000 units in 1987.

Supporting policies:

1. "Beginning in January 1987, employees will have the option of working up to twenty hours of overtime per week." (This policy could minimize the need to hire additional employees.)

2. "Beginning in January 1987, perfect attendance awards in the amount of $100 will be given to all employees who do not miss a workday in a given year." (This policy could decrease absenteeism and increase productivity.)

3. "Beginning in January 1987, new equipment must be leased rather than purchased." (This policy could reduce tax liabilities and thus allow more funds to be invested in modernizing production processes.)

Some Decision Areas Where Policies Are Employed

Management

- To offer extensive or limited management-development workshops and seminars?
- To centralize or decentralize employee-training activities?
- To recruit through employment agencies, college campuses, or newspaper?
- To promote from within or hire from the outside?
- To promote on the basis of merit or on the basis of seniority?
- How to tie executive compensation to strategic objectives?

- To offer what type and amount of employee benefits?
- How to deal with labor union issues?
- To delegate authority for large expenditures or to retain this authority centrally?

Marketing

- To use exclusive dealerships or multiple channels of distribution?
- To use heavy, light, or no TV advertising?
- To limit (or not) the share of business done with a single customer?
- To be a price leader or a price follower?
- To offer a complete or limited warranty?
- To reward salespeople based on a straight commission or a combination salary/commission?

Finance

- The desired proportion of short-term debt, long-term debt, and preferred and common equity?
- To lease or buy fixed assets?
- The regularity and amount of dividend payouts?
- The use of a LIFO, FIFO, or market-value accounting approach?
- To extend the time of accounts receivable?
- To establish a percentage discount on accounts paid within a certain period of time?
- To determine the amount of cash that should be kept on hand?

Production

- To allow much, some, or no overtime work?
- To establish a high- or low-safety stock of inventory?
- To use one or more suppliers?
- To buy, lease, or rent new production equipment?
- To stress quality control immensely or lightly?
- To establish many or only a few production standards?
- To operate one, two, or three shifts?

Research and Development

- To emphasize product or process improvements?
- To stress basic or applied research?
- To be leaders or followers in R&D?
- To develop a robotics or manual-type process?

- To spend a high, average, or low amount on R&D?
- To perform R&D within the firm or to contract R&D out to specialized firms?
- To use university researchers or private-sector researchers?

Some Example Policies

The Singer Company's net income increased dramatically from $16.2 million in 1983 to $50.3 million in 1984. As of August 1985, Singer had a $1 billion backlog of orders in marine and aerospace equipment. Part of Singer Company's outstanding performance could be attributed to the firm's policy on "probationary periods" which is stated as follows:

> If you are classified as a regular full-time employee, the first two calendar months of employment at Singer is your Probationary Period. During this time, your overall job performance will be carefully evaluated by your supervisor. Upon successful completion of your Probationary Period, you become a regular full-time employee and your date of hire then becomes your service base date or seniority date.[5]

Headquartered in New York City, the Pfizer Company has spent close to $300 million on R&D in 1985. Visine eye drops and Ben Gay ointment are two of Pfizer's many drug-related products. An example policy on "using inside information" at Pfizer is as follows:

> Pfizer policy forbids its employees from using, for personal advantage, corporate information that they learn during the course of their employment with the Company. This type of inside information could be used for personal advantage in a number of ways. One way is associated with trading in Company stock. The purchase or sale of Company stock based upon inside information by an employee or by others who have acquired inside information from the employee, besides raising obvious ethical considerations, subjects the user of such information to legal risks and could prove to be embarrassing to the individual and to the Company. All employees must exercise caution not to disclose secret information to outsiders, either intentionally or inadvertently, under any circumstances, whether at meetings held as part of the business day, or at informal after-hour discussions.[6]

Some example policies that have been established by the A.H. Robins Company, a major U.S. manufacturer of pharmaceutical products, are provided in Exhibit 8.5. A. H. Robins' net income declined from $58 million in 1983 to minus $461 million in 1984, primarily due to failure of an intrauterine birth control device.

Family Dollar Stores, a retail chain of merchandise stores based in Matthews, N.C., has established the policies stated in Exhibit 8.6.

Exhibit 8.5   A.H. Robins' policies in four areas

Accounting and Financial Information
All business records produced by the Company must be factual, timely, reliable and accurate. This requirement is equally applicable to sales orders, invoices, purchase orders, receiving reports, checks, financial statements, expense reports, or any other form of accounting or financial information which employees or officials of the Company initiate, process, or approve. Every reasonable effort must be made to avoid misleading persons using these documents, either within the Company or outside. Employees are cautioned that unauthorized disclosure of information may involve violations of laws and regulations as well as departures from Company policy.

Company Funds
Each employee is personally accountable for Company funds over which he or she has control. This accountability applies to cash as well as to the authority to sign checks and approve invoices. Anyone who spends Company funds or approves Company expenditures has the responsibility to ensure that the Company receives merchandise and services of appropriate value. Any employee responsible for receiving or handling company revenue must exercise proper care in safeguarding these funds. In addition, each employee who either receives or disburses Company funds is required to keep accurate and adequate records to account for those transactions.

Company Property
During the normal course of business, all employees use Company property. This property may consist of supplies, equipment, machinery, furniture, raw materials, or finished products. It is the responsibility of every employee to safeguard these assets and to prevent their abuse, misuse, or misappropriation. Company property represents an investment made by the Company for current and future use. Company assets should not be used for personal benefit or for any other unauthorized purpose. They should not be sold, loaned, given away, or otherwise disposed of, regardless of condition or value, except with proper authorization. All employees have an obligation to report any wrongful use of Company property to their supervisor or the Company's internal Auditing Department.

Employee Policies
It is the policy of the Company to extend equal opportunity in employment, job placement, transfer, promotion and compensation to all individuals. Discrimination on the basis of race, religion, sex, national origin, age, or handicaps will not be tolerated. In addition, the Company is committed to provide progressive personnel policies, procedures, and programs which will maximize the opportunity for development of each employee and will enable employees to utilize their skills to contribute to the betterment of the Company. Most questions concerning employee relations are addressed in the Company's *Personnel Policies and Procedures Manual,* which is revised from time to time as needed. Each supervisor should have a copy of this manual and should be prepared to assist other employees in understanding it. Employees are encouraged to discuss problems or questions relating to personnel relations or practices with their supervisor or the Personnel Department.

Source: A.H. Robins' *Policy Guide for Employees,* 1984.

Exhibit 8.6   Family Dollar Stores' policies in six areas

Position Toward Union Affiliation

It is our policy to provide competitive wages and benefits; to provide the best possible working conditions; to deal with our employees fairly and honestly; and to consider, respect, and trust each employee as an individual. We want to keep our organization free from artificially created tensions that can be brought on by the intervention of outsiders such as a union. We feel that a union would be of no advantage to any of us and only hurt the business upon which we all depend for our livelihood. To this end, the Company wishes to inform all employees that union representation is not necessary and that the Company is opposed to any attempt to intrude upon the fine relationship which currently exists between management and employees.

Sexual Harassment

Family Dollar's policy has been, and continues to be, to maintain a working environment free from all forms of sexual harassment or intimidation. Unwelcome sexual advances, requests for sexual favors, and other verbal or physical conduct of a sexual nature are serious violations of our policy and will not be condoned or permitted. Not only is sexual harassment a violation of our policy, but it could also violate the law. Any employee who is subjected to sexual harassment or intimidation should immediately contact the Personnel Manager. All complaints of sexual harassment will be promptly and confidentially investigated. Any employee who violates this policy will be subject to appropriate disciplinary action up to and including discharge.

Polygraph Examinations

It is the policy of Family Dollar to use a polygraph test as part of its regular pre-employment application procedures as well as from time to time thereafter.

Identification Badges

The Company has established a policy that all employees wear their identification badges while on the job. It is very important that badges are worn and visible at all times since it is a necessary factor for us to maintain security in our Company.

Employee Performance

Employees are expected to devote their full time, attention, ability, and best effort to the performance of their duties for Family Dollar Stores. An employee may not "moonlight," i.e., work off hours with another company, if such activity adversely affects the employee's job performance. A review of each employee's job performance and progress is conducted at least once each year by the employee's immediate supervisor.

Resignation or Termination

It is Company policy that an employee give at least two weeks notice to his/her supervisor, in writing, prior to resigning his/her employment with Family Dollar. This requirement may be waived at the option of the Company. An employee or the Company may terminate the employee's employment with Family Dollar at any time for any reason with or without cause.

Source: Family Dollar Stores' *Employee Handbook*, 1984.

ALLOCATING RESOURCES

Types of Resources

Once goals and policies have been established and approved by top management, an organization's resources must be allocated. Resources should be allocated according to the priorities established by approved goals. For example, if top management approves a certain division's goal to increase revenues by 40 percent next year, then there should be a corresponding substantial increase in the amount of resources allocated to that division. Nothing could be more detrimental to the strategic-management process than for management to fail to support approved goals by not allocating resources according to the priorities indicated by those goals. This is a major reason why establishing appropriate goals is such an important activity in the strategy-implementation process. Approving, revising, or rejecting goals is much more than a rubber stamp managerial activity because goals dictate how resources are to be allocated.

All organizations have at least four types of resources that can be used to achieve desired goals: financial resources, physical resources, human resources, and technological resources. These types of resources are described in Table 8.3.

Strategies are not implemented by just allocating resources in the right direction. For example, various nonprofit organizations send extensive financial aid to Ethiopia, but this does not assure that Ethiopian children are better nourished. Similarly, allocating resources to particular divisions and departments does not mean that strategies will be successfully implemented.

There are five major factors that commonly prohibit effective resource allocation: an overprotection of resources, too great an emphasis on short-run financial criteria, company politics, vague strategy targets, and a reluctance to take risks.[7] In addition to

Table 8.3   Types of resources available in an organization

Type of Resource	Description
Financial	Includes all of an organization's liquid assets, liabilities, and equity. This includes cash, receivables, marketable securities, bonds, stock, bank notes working capital, retained earnings, and net income.
Physical	Includes all of an organization's tangible assets. This includes plants, equipment, land, inventory, raw materials, facilities, and machinery.
Human	Includes all of an organization's people, such as top managers, divisional managers, department managers, engineers, scientists, lawyers, accountants, skilled employees, and unskilled employees.
Technological	Includes all the knowledge, skills, methods, and tools that enable a firm to carry on its chosen activities. This includes the firm's quality control systems, computer systems, accounting systems, management information systems, engineering, R&D, and communication systems.

these factors, there are two other reasons why resources are commonly not deployed effectively. First, top managers only rarely possess enough knowledge about diversified operations to make specific resource allocation decisions. The larger an organization, the greater is the risk that senior managers lack sufficient knowledge to allocate resources when, where, and how they are most needed. Second, lower- and middle-level managers rarely possess enough knowledge about the ramifications of new strategies to make appropriate resource requests.

By far the largest number of resource requests that originate with lower- and middle-level managers are triggered by a need related to existing operations, such as a faulty elevator. The world of lower- and middle-level managers is filled with current and local problems, and rewards are typically tied to short-run solutions of those problems. Below the top management level, there often exists an absence of systematic linking between resources requested and strategic plans. Yavitz and Newman explain why:

> Managers normally have many more tasks than they can do. They must allocate their own time and the resources at their disposal among these tasks. And then, pressure builds up. Total expenses are too high. The CEO wants a good financial report for the third quarter. Or incoming orders take an unexpected spurt. The allocation is hard to make; some things must be squeezed down. Over and over, it is the strategic activities that are deferred. Today's problems soak up available energies and resources. The scrambled accounts and budgets fail to reveal the shift in allocations away from strategic actions to currently squeaking wheels.[8]

Neither a top-down nor a bottom-up approach to allocating resources is desirable. Rather, a combination of the two is recommended. Two actions that can enhance the resource-allocation process are especially important. First, formal resource requests should be prepared by middle- and lower-level managers. Resource requests should be accompanied by a written statement of the impact that the proposed allocation would have on current strategy.[9] Unless a clear strategic purpose can be shown, the resource request should be rejected. Second, as new strategies are formulated, top managers should develop strategy programs that show what, when, and where new resources are needed to achieve the desired results. Together, these two activities can enhance the resource-allocation phase of the strategy-implementation process. They are incorporated into the resource-allocation framework presented next.

A Framework for Allocating Resources

Most organizations frequently find that the demand for resources is greater than the total resources available. It is therefore necessary that organizations use a systematic approach to allocate resources. Resource allocation can be viewed to consist of four basic steps, as follows:

1. Develop an inventory of the total resources available to the firm.
2. Develop an inventory of each division's resources and each department's resources.

3. Develop division and departmental resource requests.

4. Allocate resources appropriately to each division and department.

As indicated above, the first step in the process of allocating resources is to develop an inventory of what resources an organization has available. This inventory should include all of the firm's financial, physical, human, and technological resources. A total resource inventory is provided in Exhibit 8.7 for a small cement business. Victor Weintraub describes this first step in the resource-allocation process as follows:

> The first step is to determine what resources an organization has at its disposal. The list should include items other than those contained on the balance sheet. This means that, in addition to cash, plant, equipment, and inventory, the list should include people, suppliers, marketing organizations, customers, trade names, technology, management skills, raw materials supplies, and so forth. Obviously, resources vary greatly in their value to a corporation. Additionally, it must be recognized that the value of resources will change with the business environment. The objective is to generate an honest and thoughtful evaluation of the resources at hand, their present value, and an assessment of their future worth. Bear in mind that many resources are convertible. Cash can be converted into technology by licensing agreements or R&D expenditures. Plants can be converted into cash by sale. And so on.[10]

The second step in the resource-allocation process is to develop resource inventories for each division and department. This activity signals where an organization's existing resources are currently deployed. Such knowledge is essential for the third step, which requires that each department and division prepare resource requests. Resource requests should be consistent with approved goals.

Exhibit 8.7 A total resource inventory for Thurston's Cement Company

	Financial
Cash:	$10,000 in the bank
Accounts Receivable:	$5,000 of credit sales
	Physical
Inventory:	$50,000 worth of merchandise
Buildings:	Two retail stores, one garage
Land:	One cement mill, two three-acre lots
Equipment:	Ten cement mixers, four small trucks
	Human
Employees:	Fifteen truck drivers, five salespeople, five clerical employees
Managers:	Six managers
	Technological
Computers:	Seven Apple IIe personal computers

The final step in the resource allocation process is to compare current resource requests with approved goals and with existing resource levels. This provides a basis for allocating available resources appropriately. The real value of any resource-allocation program lies in the resulting accomplishment of an organization's goals and objectives. Allocating resources makes strategy execution possible, but does not guarantee success. "Programs, organization, key personnel, controls, and commitment must breathe life into the resources provided."[11] Strategic management itself is sometimes referred to as a "resource-allocation process."

CONCLUSION

This chapter presents a framework for establishing goals and policies and allocating resources. These activities represent the major thrusts of strategy implementation. Goals are key components in the strategic-management process because they dictate how resources will be allocated, they serve as standards by which managers are evaluated, they provide organizational direction, and they serve as milestones that must be achieved before objectives can be accomplished. Since goals directly affect the lives and work of all employees and managers, they sometimes result in conflicts. Three basic approaches for conflict resolution have been discussed: avoidance, defusion, and confrontation. Managers can use these conflict-resolution approaches to minimize potentially dysfunctional effects associated with goal setting.

Like goals, policies are a vital component of effective strategic management. Policies are needed to guide day-to-day administrative actions. Policies should encourage and support individual efforts to achieve stated goals. Examples of policies from Singer, Pfizer, Family Dollar Store, and A. H. Robins have been provided.

No organization has unlimited resources. It is imperative therefore that resources be allocated in accordance with established goals. This chapter describes the basic types of resources: financial, physical, human, and technological. A four-step procedure for allocating resources has been examined: (1) developing a total resource inventory, (2) preparing divisional and departmental resource inventories, (3) preparing resource requests, and (4) allocating resources appropriately.

In summary, the strategy-implementation process is often called the action phase of the strategic-management process. It is not enough to formulate the right strategies, because managers and employees must then be motivated to work towards implementing those strategies. Furthermore, it is not sufficient to successfully set goals, establish policies, and allocate resources, because strategies must then be evaluated and controlled. Strategy evaluation and control is the subject of the next chapter.

REVIEW QUESTIONS

1. Explain the interrelationships among organizational objectives, strategies, goals, and policies.

2. For an organization that you are familiar with, list a major objective and two supporting goals.

3. Identify and discuss three policies that apply to your present business policy class.

4. Explain the following statement: Horizontal consistency of goals is as important as vertical consistency.

5. Discuss three major reasons why conflict may occur during goal-setting activities.

6. In your opinion, what approach to conflict resolution would be best for resolving a disagreement between a personnel manager and a sales manager over the firing of a particular salesperson? Why?

7. How would market penetration and market development differ in terms of the resources that could be required to implement those strategies?

FOOTNOTES

1 A.G. Bedeian and W.F. Glueck, *Management*, 3rd ed. (Chicago: The Dryden Press, 1983), 212.

2 Y.K. Shetty, "New Look at Corporate Goals," *California Management Review* XXII, no. 2 (Winter 1979): 71–79.

3 Heinz Weihrich, "How To Set Goals That Work for Your Company and Improve the Bottom Line," *Management Review* (February 1982): 63.

4 Most authors consider procedures and rules to be policies that offer little flexibility in interpretation. Procedures can be defined as chronological steps that must be followed to complete a particular action, such as completing an application form. Rules can be defined as actions that can or cannot be taken, such as "No Smoking." Neither a procedure nor a rule provides much latitude in decision making, so some writers do not consider either to be a policy.

5 Singer Company, *You and Singer: Sharing Success* (September 1, 1983): 14. (Internal report)

6 Pfizer Company, *Summary of Pfizer Policies on Business Conduct* (June 1982): 8. (Internal report)

7 Boris Yavitz and William Newman, *Strategy in Action: The Execution, Politics, and Payoff of Business Planning* (New York: The Free Press, 1982), 195.

8 Ibid., 200.

9 Ibid., 196.

10 Victor Weintraub, "Strategic Planning Approach to Resource Allocation," *S.A.M. Advanced Management Journal* (Summer 1979): 53.

11 Yavitz and Newman, *Strategy in Action*, 205.

SUGGESTED READINGS

Adams, R.H. "Goalstorming," *S.A.M. Advanced Management Journal.* (Summer 1979): 55–61.

Bedeian, A.G. and W. F. Glueck. *Management.* 3rd ed. Chicago: The Dryden Press, 1983.

Bower, J.L. *Managing the Resource Allocation Process: A Study of Corporate Planning and Investment.* Homewood, Ill.: Richard D. Irwin, 1972.

Giasi, R.W. "Finding Suitable Objectives." *Managerial Planning* (November–December 1983): 43–45.

Granger, C.H. "The Hierarchy of Objectives." *Harvard Business Review* 42, no. 3 (May–June 1964): 63–74.

Hofer, C.W. and D. Schendel. *Strategy Formulation: Analytical Concepts.* St. Paul, Minn.: West Publishing Company, 1978.

Lee, S.M. and J. P. Shim. "Zero Base Budgeting—Dealing with Conflicting Objectives." *Long Range Planning* (October 1984): 103–10.

Lorange, P. and D. Murphy. "Considerations in Implementing Strategic Control." *Journal of Business Strategy* (Spring 1984): 27–35.

Simon, H.A. "On the Concept of Organizational Goals." *Administrative Science Quarterly* (1964): 1–22.

Stonich, P.J. "How To Use Strategic Funds Programming." *The Journal of Business Strategy* (Fall 1980).

Szilagyi, A.D. Jr. *Management and Performance.* Santa Monica, Calif.: Goodyear Publishing Company, Inc., 1981.

Usry, M.F. "Organizing Capital Expenditure Resource Allocation and Control Systems." *Managerial Planning* (May–June 1983): 10, 18–21.

Vancil, R. and P. Lorange. "Strategic Planning in Diversified Companies." *Harvard Business Review* 50 (September 1972): 81–90

Weihrich, H. "How To Set Goals That Work for Your Company—And Improve the Bottom Line!" *Management Review* (February 1982): 60–65.

Weihrich, H. "A Hierarchy and Network of Aims." *Management Review* (January 1982): 47–54.

Weintraub, V. "Strategic Planning Approach to Resource Allocation." *S.A.M. Advanced Management Journal* (Summer 1979): 47–53.

Winer, L. "How To Add Goal-Directed Creativity to Planning." *Managerial Planning* (November–December 1983): 30–37.

Yavitz, B. and W. Newman. *Strategy in Action.* New York: The Free Press, 1982.

EXPERIENTIAL EXERCISE 8A:

Establishing Goals at IBM

PURPOSE

Having read Chapter 8, you should more fully understand the process of establishing goals. Recall that revenue and profitability goals are commonly established by business segment and geographic area. The purpose of this exercise is to give you experience establishing goals for an organization that has recently formulated new strategies and established new long-range objectives.

YOUR TASK

Your task is to read and study the information provided on International Business Machines, the well-known corporation that dominates the computer industry. Then, establish 1985 and 1986 goals for IBM. Finally, explain to your classmates and instructor why you feel those goals are reasonable and effective.

INFORMATION ON IBM

IBM's worldwide revenues and profits in 1984 were $45.9 billion and $6.6 billion, up 14.3 percent and 20.0 percent respectively from the company's 1983 figures of $40.2 billion and $5.5 billion. (See Exhibit 8A.) Barring global economic crises, IBM plans to more than double its revenues to $100 billion annually by 1990.

A new chief executive officer of IBM took office on February 1, 1985. His name is John F. Akers, a former top executive with IBM. Akers is committed to making sure

Exhibit 8A   Worldwide revenues and profits for 1983 and 1984

	1986	1985	(in millions) 1984	1983
Revenues			$ 45,937	$ 40,180
Net earnings			6,582	5,485
Total assets			42,808	37,461
Long-term debt			3,269	2,674
Stockholders' equity			26,489	23,219
Number of employees*			394,930	369,545
Number of stockholders*			792,506	769,979
Return on stockholders' equity*			26.5%	25.4%

*Amounts for these items are in thousands

IBM's growth by segment exceeds the information processing industry's growth by segment, which ranges from 12 percent per year for large mainframe computers to 40 percent for personal computers and software. Since 1980, IBM has met this annual goal in each segment.

IBM is currently setting goals for 1985 and 1986.

IBM's STRATEGY

IBM's emphasis is beginning to shift dramatically from hardware to software. While software accounted for about 10 percent of IBM's sales in 1984, management is aiming for a 35 percent growth rate in the years ahead. By the 1990s, software is expected to represent up to one-third of IBM's business. The biggest technical challenge for IBM is developing communications software that is compatible with the firm's hardware and software systems and with the outside world. Even though IBM employed over 395,000 employees in 1985, only about six of these individuals were familiar with all of the company's computer systems.

The merger of computers and communications has long proven elusive for IBM. It was primarily for this reason that the company acquired Rohm Corporation in November 1984 for $1.26 billion. By aligning Rohm with the Satellite Business Systems Division, IBM is positioned to compete with American Telephone & Telegraph Company in such promising new markets as voice- and data-communications networks.

If IBM has any major problems, it is in foreign markets. IBM's rigid policies, such as 100 percent ownership of its foreign factories, are running head on into economic nationalism. IBM was forced to leave India in 1979. In 1985, Mexico refused to let IBM build a wholly owned personal computer plant. Equity policies in Brazil and Malaysia are hampering IBM's plans to expand. Europeans are taking an especially cynical view of IBM's recent advances, forcing the company to create joint ventures and the like to expand in Europe. The Japanese have become IBM's major competitor in the world. In foreign countries and at home, IBM's overpowering size is blamed by many for everything from slowing innovation to putting companies out of business.

Source: Based on the cover story article in *Business Week* entitled "IBM: More Worlds To Conquer" (February 18, 1985): 84–98. Also, see IBM's 1984 *Annual Report*.

EXPERIENTIAL EXERCISE 8B:

Establishing Policies at Ponderosa, Inc.

PURPOSE

The purpose of this exercise is to give you experience establishing policies that are supportive of an organization's philosophy.

YOUR TASK

Think of yourself as the manager of a Ponderosa steakhouse restaurant. Suppose you have just read Ponderosa's *Statement of Organization Philosophy*. One section of this document is entitled "Recognizing Individual Qualities." This section is provided in Exhibit 8B. Read this information and develop some policies that you feel would be supportive of that philosophy.

Exhibit 8B   Ponderosa's philosophy on recognizing individual qualities

---

We value individuality. We will not try to make everyone fit into the same mold. By allowing people to be themselves, we expect to bring fresh ideas and increased productivity to our business. We will maintain a working environment, both physical and mental, that supports a high level of employee performance and energy.

In this environment, there still will be the basic requirements of discipline and policy adherence, in order to maintain consistency and order.

Beyond these basic elements, we expect to create an environment that fosters development of the following human qualities:

- Pride, one of the essential forces that moves us
- Self-reliance and the ability to handle delegated authority independently

- Courage to be open with one another and to change our minds as we receive new facts and new insights from each other
- Self-determination—With the knowledge that people grow at different rates and have varying needs, we will create an attitude of trying to bring out the best in people, giving them the opportunity to shape their own lives and careers.

Source: Ponderosa, Inc., *Statement of Organization Philosophy,* 1983, p. 11.

PART FOUR

Strategy Evaluation

9

Strategy Review, Evaluation, and Control

The Strategy-Evaluation Process

A Strategy-Evaluation Framework

Requirements of an Effective Evaluation System

Contingency Planning

Auditing

Using Computers to Evaluate Strategies

Experiential Exercise 9A: Preparing a Strategy-Evaluation Report

Experiential Exercise 9B: Analyzing the Strategy-Evaluation Model Used by Ponderosa, Inc.

The best formulated and implemented strategies become obsolete as a firm's internal and external environment changes. It is essential, therefore, that top managers systematically review, evaluate, and control the execution of strategies. This chapter presents a framework that can guide managers' efforts to evaluate strategic-management activities, to make sure they are working, and to make timely changes.

THE STRATEGY-EVALUATION PROCESS

The strategic-management process results in decisions that can have significant, long-lasting consequences. Strategic decisions can inflict severe penalties if erroneous, and can be exceedingly difficult, if not impossible, to reverse. Most top managers agree therefore that evaluation of the strategic-management process is vital to an organization's well-being; the idea is to alert management to problems or potential problems before a situation becomes critical. The strategy-evaluation process includes examining the underlying bases of a firm's strategy, comparing expected results with actual results, and taking corrective actions to assure that performance conforms to plans. Taking corrective actions could include revising objectives, strategies, goals, policies, or the organization's mission. It could involve making personnel or production changes. The strategy-evaluation stage of the strategic-management process is illustrated in Figure 9.1.

Adequate and timely feedback information is the cornerstone of effective strategy evaluation. Strategy evaluation can be no better than the information on which it operates. Too much pressure from the top may result in lower managers contriving numbers they think will be satisfactory. Senior managers have a responsibility not only to develop evaluation systems, but to operate them in such a manner that the pressures to report falsely are minimal and procedures to detect such activity are enforced.

The Boy Scouts of America organization recently revealed that membership figures coming in from the field had been falsified. To their chagrin, the leaders found that evaluation and control systems can produce unintended consequences: the drive to increase membership had motivated people to increase the number of new members reported, but had not motivated them to increase the number of Boy Scouts actually enrolled.[1]

Strategy evaluation can be a complex and sensitive undertaking. Too much emphasis on evaluating strategies may be expensive and counterproductive. No one likes to be evaluated too closely. Dalton and Lawrence emphasize that, often, the more managers attempt to evaluate the behavior of others, the less control they have. Yet too little or no evaluation can create even worse problems.[2] Strategy evaluation is necessary to assure that strategy formulation and implementation activities are meeting stated goals and objectives.

Recall from Chapter 1 that strategy evaluation consists of three activities: (1) reviewing the underlying internal and external factors that represent the bases of current strategies, (2) measuring organizational performance, and (3) taking corrective actions. These activities review the conclusions reached during strategy formulation,

Figure 9.1 A model of the strategic-management process

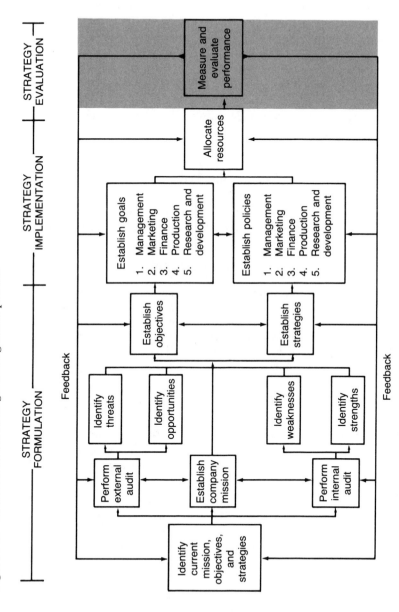

examine the actions taken during strategy implementation, compare planned results to actual results, and make needed changes to control operations.

The three activities that comprise strategy evaluation are appropriate for all sizes and kinds of organizations. According to Dale Zand, strategy evaluation should initiate managerial questioning of expectations and assumptions, should trigger a review of goals and values, and should stimulate creativity in generating alternatives and formulating criteria of evaluation.[3] Regardless of the size of the organization, a certain amount of "management by wandering around" at all levels is essential to effective strategy evaluation. Strategy-evaluation activities should be performed on a continuing basis, rather than at the end of specified periods of time or just after problems occur. Waiting until the end of the year, for example, could result in a firm "closing the barn door after the horses have already escaped."

An enterprise can react quickly and appropriately to changing circumstances by obtaining feedback through mechanisms such as a board of director's strategy audit, an environmental assessment, and an internal audit. Information gathered during the strategy-evaluation process affects future strategy-formulation and strategy-implementation decisions. William Glueck has said that strategy evaluation is like going to a medical doctor:

> Successful strategists are like physicians when they treat an illness. They look at symptoms and make the most probable diagnosis. Then they prescribe the best procedure or medicine for their diagnosis. The diagnosis results from the analysis and choice stages of the strategic management process. The prescription for medicine is the implementation. If the prescription does not work, the physicians may believe that they made the wrong diagnosis (strategic choice), and then they may make another diagnosis. Just as physicians do not give up if the first choice does not work, strategists also then make another choice. They are ready, no doubt, with an alternative choice, a contingency plan.[4]

Evaluating strategies on a continuous rather than a periodic basis allows benchmarks of progress to be established and more effectively monitored. Some strategies take years to implement and consequently associated results may not become apparent for years. Successful strategists combine patience with a willingness to take corrective actions promptly when necessary.

In a recent study that examined the timing of strategy evaluation in many organizationss, Lindsay and Rue hypothesized that strategy-evaluation activities would be conducted more frequently as environmental complexity and instability increased.[5] However, the researchers found a surprising inverse relationship between "planning review frequency" and organizational environment. Specifically, top managers in dynamic environments performed strategy-evaluation activities less frequently than those in stable environments. The authors concluded that forecasting is more difficult under complex and unstable environmental conditions, so managers may see less need for frequent evaluation of their long-range plans. Evidence for this conclusion was stronger for large firms than for small ones.

A STRATEGY-EVALUATION FRAMEWORK

A number of internal and/or external problems commonly prohibit a firm from achieving stated goals and objectives. Internally, the wrong strategies may be formulated, or the right strategies may be formulated but not effectively implemented, or goals and objectives may be set too high. Externally, actions by competitors, changes in demand, changes in technology, economic changes, demographic shifts, and governmental actions may prohibit goals and objectives from being accomplished.

Strategy-evaluation activities focus on potential internal and external problem areas. First, internal strengths/weaknesses and external opportunities/threats that represent the bases of current strategies are reexamined. Some initial questions to address in evaluating strategies are:

1. Are our internal strengths still strengths?
2. Have we added other internal strengths? If so, what are they?
3. Are our internal weaknesses still weaknesses?
4. Do we now have other internal weaknesses? If so, what are they?
5. Are our external opportunities still opportunities?
6. Are there now other external opportunities? If so, what are they?
7. Are our external threats still threats?
8. Are there now other external threats? If so, what are they?

The second strategy-evaluation activity is to measure organizational performance. This activity includes comparing expected versus actual results of strategy-implementation efforts, investigating deviations from plans, evaluating individual performances, and examining progress being made toward meeting stated goals and objectives.

Goals and objectives are criteria commonly used to evaluate strategies. Criteria for evaluating strategies need to be measurable and easily verifiable. Criteria that predict results may be more important than those that reveal what already has happened. For example, managers do not want to find out that sales the last quarter were 20 percent under what was desired. More importantly, they need to know today that sales next quarter may be 20 percent under standard unless some action is taken to counter the trend. Really effective control requires accurate forecasting.[6]

The third strategy-evaluation activity, taking corrective actions, requires making changes to reposition a firm competitively for the future. Some example changes that could be appropriate are altering an organization's structure, replacing one or more key individuals, selling a division, or revising a company mission. Other changes could include establishing additional goals and objectives, devising new policies, issuing stock to raise capital, adding additional salespeople to a marketing department, allocating resources differently, or developing new performance incentives. "Taking corrective actions" does not necessarily mean that existing strategies will be abandoned or even that new strategies must be formulated. But it does mean that revised strategies and implementation approaches should be considered. Claude George describes the need to take corrective actions as follows:

> The best laid plans of mice and men sometimes go astray. This seems to be particularly true in managerial endeavors involving multiple individuals. In fact, the probabilities and possibilities for incorrect or inappropriate action seem to increase geometrically with an arithmetic increase in personnel. As a result, any person directing an overall undertaking must check on the actions of the participants as well as the results which they have achieved. If either the actions or results do not comply with preconceived or planned achievements, then planned and needed action must be communicated to the participants for them either to correct what they have done or to take remedial action during subsequent events.[7]

Table 9.1 summarizes the three strategy-evaluation activities in terms of key questions that should be addressed, alternative answers to those questions, and appropriate actions for a firm to take. Notice that corrective actions are almost always needed, except when internal and external factors have not significantly changed *and* a firm is progressing satisfactorily toward achieving its stated goals and objectives.

Strategy evaluation is important because organizations face dynamic environments in which key internal and external factors often change quickly and dramatically. *Success today is no guarantee for success tomorrow. An enterprise should never be lulled into complacency by success!* There are countless examples of firms that were thriving in one

Table 9.1   A strategy-evaluation assessment matrix

Have Major Changes Occurred in the Firm's Internal Strategic Position?	Have Major Changes Occurred in the Firm's External Strategic Position?	Has the Firm Progressed Satisfactorily Toward Achieving Its Stated Goals and Objectives?	Result
no	no	no	Take corrective actions
yes	yes	yes	Take corrective actions
yes	yes	no	Take corrective actions
yes	no	yes	Take corrective actions
yes	no	no	Take corrective actions
no	yes	yes	Take corrective actions
no	yes	no	Take corrective actions
no	no	yes	Continue present strategic course

year and then struggling to survive the next year. Organizational demise can come swiftly, as evidenced by the following examples:

Only yesterday, it seems, Georgia–Pacific Corp. was considered the best run of the forest products companies. Fueled by the decades-long housing boom, G–P's earnings doubled every five years for a quarter-century, until the late 1970s. Those days are gone. The housing slump and the high interest on borrowed expansion money were a double whammy, says T. Marshall Hahn Jr., 57, chairman and chief executive. Of twenty-four good-size companies in forest products, G–P now ranks twenty-first on return on total capital over five years. The company spent $3.2 billion between 1977 and 1982 to expand and upgrade facilities, including a corporate move from Portland, Oregon to Atlanta to be closer to its trees, but there's not much to show for it yet, except a tripling in long-term debt, now totaling $1.45 billion.[8]

Like a battle-scarred starship in some nightmarish video game, Atari, Inc. is wobbling in space. After Pac-Man became a national rage, Atari reported 1982 sales of $2 billion and profits of $323 million, both records. Yet before year-end, the boom fizzled. Atari's 1982 sales included millions of video game cartridges that never found their way to consumers. In 1983, those cartridges came streaming back from retailers, and sales fell to $1 billion. Unfortunately for Atari, 1984 results made 1983 look good.[9]

Interrelationships among the three strategy-evaluation activities are illustrated in Figure 9.2. This framework is examined in the next three sections of this chapter. The strategy-evaluation framework is not a magic key for all organizations, but it is an effective way to approach the strategy-evaluation task.   .

Review Underlying Bases of Strategy

It is appropriate for strategy evaluation to begin with a review of the existing bases of an organization's current strategy, because internal and external factors do change. As illustrated in Figure 9.2, reviewing the underlying bases of an organization's strategy could be approached by developing revised internal and external factor evaluation matrices.

Following the steps described earlier in Chapter 4, a revised External Factor Evaluation Matrix can be developed and compared to an existing External Factor Evaluation Matrix. If these two evaluations are similar, then a firm can conclude at this point in the process that corrective actions are not needed. This conclusion is tentative, because a firm's internal strategic position and its progress toward accomplishing stated goals and objectives must also be examined before a final decision can be made regarding the need for corrective measures.

If a revised EFE Matrix reveals major changes in a firm's external opportunities and threats, then current strategies should be reconsidered by proceeding through the strategy-formulation process. It is important to note here that strategic reorientation can be appropriate even when an organization's current performance and progress

Figure 9.2   A strategy-evaluation framework

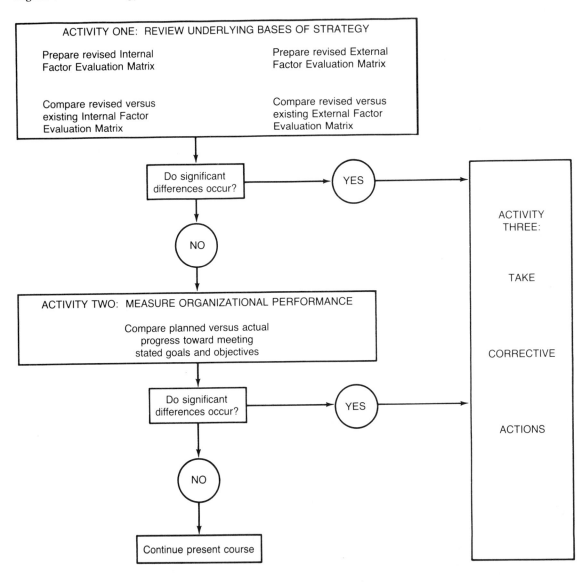

towards stated goals is satisfactory. This is true because significant changes in the internal and external bases of an existing strategy may not be reflected in short-term operating results, yet still can have a detrimental impact on an organization's long-term performance and competitive position. One of the major benefits of strategy evaluation is that it allows an organization to monitor external trends and to astutely anticipate environmental changes.

Perhaps the most important part of preparing a revised EFE Matrix is to determine how a firm's position has changed relative to major competitors. This analysis should address questions like the following:

1. How have competitors reacted to our strategies?

2. How have competitors' strategies changed?

3. Have major competitors' strengths and weaknesses changed?

4. Why are competitors making certain strategic changes?

5. Why are some competitors' strategies more successful than others?

6. How satisfied are our competitors with their present market position and profitability?

7. How far can our major competitors be pushed before retaliating?

Figure 9.2 also illustrates that examination of the internal bases for a firm's strategy is a critical part of the first evaluation activity. A revised Internal Factor Evaluation Matrix could be developed and compared to a firm's existing Internal Factor Evaluation Matrix. This comparison process is analogous to the revised versus existing EFE Matrix analysis described earlier. An example revised versus existing IFE Matrix is given in Table 9.2 for the Reichhold Chemicals Corporation. This analysis indicates that Reichhold was internally weak in 1982, but became stronger in 1983. For instance, note that problems associated with internal reorganization were considered a major weakness (rating = 1) in 1982, but became a major strength (rating = 4) in 1983. The relative importance of Reichhold's key internal success factors did not change during this period of time, as indicated by identical weights assigned to the key factors in 1982 and 1983. Reichhold's annual sales exceeded $800 million for the first time in 1984, and the firm plans to acquire Eschem in 1985. (Eschem is a worldwide adhesives and coating business.)

Measure Organizational Performance

As shown in Figure 9.2, the second strategy-evaluation activity is determining whether goals and objectives are being achieved. Organizational objectives and goals are key components of an effective strategic-management system. Failure to achieve stated goals or to make satisfactory progress toward accomplishing company objectives signals a need for corrective actions. A myriad of factors can result in unsatisfactory progress toward meeting goals and objectives, such as unreasonable policies, unexpected turns in the economy, unreliable suppliers or distributors, or ineffective strategies.

Whenever goals and objectives are not being met, top managers must determine what corrective actions are needed. Are problems resulting from ineffectiveness (not doing the right things) or inefficiency (not doing things right)? Are problems resulting

Table 9.2 A revised versus existing internal factor evaluation—Reichhold Chemicals Corp.

Key Factor	1982 Evaluation			1983 Evaluation		
	Weight	Rating	Weighted Score	Weight	Rating	Weighted Score
Productivity	.10	1	.10	.10	2	.20
Management changes	.20	1	.20	.20	4	.80
EPS stock market value	.10	2	.20	.10	2	.20
Return on investment	.05	2	.10	.05	3	.15
Rate of return on equity	.10	2	.20	.10	2	.20
Research & development	.15	4	.60	.15	4	.60
Customer service	.05	4	.20	.05	4	.20
Technical excellence	.10	4	.40	.10	3	.30
Product quality	.05	3	.15	.05	3	.15
Dividend policy	.05	3	.15	.05	2	.10
Debt/equity ratio	.05	3	.15	.05	4	.20
Total	1.00		2.45	1.00		3.10

Notes: In 1982, Reichhold's level of productivity was 65 percent, earnings per share were low at $.25, the company's stock price was only 40 percent of book value, return on investment and return on equity were low at 2.2 percent and 8.4 percent respectively, and the company's debt-to-equity ratio was 35 compared to an industry average of 49. Reichhold had thirty-four plant locations and offered special customer services in 1982. The company was strong in technical competence and product quality. Reichhold Chemicals made significant improvements in 1983, as indicated by the internal factor evaluation score increasing from 2.45 to 3.10.

from pursuit of the wrong strategies or from poor implementation practices? An effective strategy-evaluation system signals when performance starts to falter or to exceed expectations. This knowledge allows management to investigate the cause and either take early remedial action or capitalize on unexpected favorable conditions.[10]

Determining which goals and objectives are most important in the evaluation of company strategies can be difficult. Strategy evaluation is based on both objective and subjective factors. George Steiner suggests that goals and objectives in three areas are most important in evaluating strategy: management quality and development, environmental analysis and diagnosis, and financial return.[11] Charles Hofer suggests three other areas as most important in evaluating strategy: (1) growth as measured in dollar sales, unit sales, dollar assets, (2) efficiency as measured in gross margin, net profits, net profits/dollar sales, and (3) asset utilization as measured by return on investment, return on equity, and earnings per share.[12]

Richard Rumelt identifies four special characteristics of organizational goals and objectives as being particularly important in evaluating strategy: consistency, consonance, advantage, and feasibility.[13] Recall that Rumelt's characteristics were examined earlier in Chapter 2. Selecting the exact set of criteria for evaluating strategies is dependent on a particular organization's size, industry, strategies, and management philosophy. An organization pursuing a retrenchment strategy, for example, could have an entirely different set of evaluative criteria from those of an organization pursuing a market-development strategy.

Perhaps the most commonly used criteria to evaluate strategies are financial ratios. As you know, financial ratios often serve as goals and objectives. Top managers make three critical comparisons in using ratios to evaluate strategy: (1) compare the firm's performance over different time periods, (2) compare the firm's performance to that of competitors, and (3) compare the firm's performance to industry averages. Some key financial ratios widely used as criteria for strategy evaluation include the following:

1. Return on investment
2. Return on equity
3. Profit margin
4. Market share
5. Debt to equity
6. Earnings per share
7. Sales growth
8. Asset growth

There are some problems associated with using quantitative criteria for evaluating strategies. First, most quantitative criteria are geared to short-term goals rather than long-term objectives. Second, different accounting methods can provide different results on many quantitative criteria. Third, subjective judgments are almost always involved in deriving quantitative criteria. Finally, the relative emphasis on particular quantitative criteria often changes during the strategy-implementation process.

Although critically important, financial and quantitative criteria comprise only part of the strategy-evaluation process. Much of the activity that determines the success or failure of a firm's strategies is nonfinancial in nature. Human factors such as absenteeism and turnover rates, production quality and quantity rates, and employee satisfaction measures can be underlying causes of poor company performance. Marketing, production, or research and development factors can also cause financial problems. Top management must recognize the importance of nonfinancial goals and objectives. Seymour Tilles identifies six qualitative-type questions that are commonly used to evaluate strategies:

1. Is the strategy internally consistent?
2. Is the strategy consistent with the environment?
3. Is the strategy appropriate in view of available resources?

4. Does the strategy involve an acceptable degree of risk?

5. Does the strategy have an appropriate time framework?

6. Is the strategy workable?[14]

Some additional key questions that reveal the need for subjective judgments in the strategy-evaluation process are:

1. How good is the firm's balance of investments between high-risk and low-risk projects?

2. How good is the firm's balance of investments between long-term and short-term projects?

3. How good is the firm's balance of investments between slow-growing markets and fast-growing markets?

4. How good is the firm's balance of investments among different divisions?

5. To what extent are the firm's alternative strategies socially responsible?

6. What are the interrelationships among the firm's key internal and external strategic factors?

7. How are major competitors likely to respond to particular strategies?

A number of publications can be helpful in evaluating a firm's strategies. For example, in its May and June issues each year, *Fortune* identifies and evaluates the Fortune 1000 largest manufacturers and the Fortune 50s, which are the fifty largest retailers, transportation companies, utilities, banks, insurance companies, and diversified financial corporations in the United States. In these issues, *Fortune* ranks the best and worst performers on various factors such as return on investment, sales volume, and profitability. In its January issue each year, *Fortune* evaluates organizations in twenty-five industries. Eight key attributes serve as evaluative criteria: quality of management; innovativeness; quality of products or services; long-term investment value; financial soundness; community and environmental stability; ability to attract, develop, and keep talented people; and use of corporate assets. *Fortune's* 1985 evaluations of firms in four industries are revealed in Exhibit 9.1. (This information is not a *Fortune* ranking; it is the result of a survey done for *Fortune*. The survey polled 8000 executives, outside directors, and financial analysts and asked them to rate the top ten companies in their industry on a scale from one (poor) to ten (excellent) on eight key attributes. Fifty-two percent of those surveyed responded, yielding the results in Exhibit 9.1.)

Another excellent evaluation of corporations in America is published annually in the January issue of *Forbes*, called "The Annual Report on American Industry." It provides a detailed and comprehensive evaluation of hundreds of American companies in many different industries. *Business Week, Industry Week,* and *Dun's Business Month* also periodically publish detailed evaluations of American businesses and industries. Although *Fortune, Forbes, Business Week, Industry Week,* and *Dun's Business Month* evaluations focus primarily on large, publicly held businesses, the comparative ratios and related information are widely used to evaluate small businesses and privately owned firms as well.

Exhibit 9.1 Fortune's 1985 ranking of companies in four industries

Apparel

Levi Strauss, which hasn't had much luck diversifying away from a fading jeans market, tumbles from the top apparel spot for the first time. The new champ is VF, the maker of Lee jeans and Vanity Fair intimate apparel. VF got particularly high marks from security analysts. Hartmarx rates tops for product quality.

Rank	Last Year	Company	Score
1	2	VF	7.30
2	3	Hartmarx	7.13
3	—	Oxford Industries[1]	6.68
4	4	Interco	6.63[2]
4	1	Levi Strauss	6.63[2]
6	5	Warnaco	6.62
7	6	Cluett Peabody	6.42
8	9	Gulf & Western Industries	6.04
9	10	Kellwood	5.75
10	8	Blue Bell[3]	5.65

Chemicals

FORTUNE's survey was completed before Union Carbide's catastrophic gas leak in India, but among the 250 companies, it is only No. 195. The one category in which it ranks in the top half of its industry group: community and environmental responsibility. Du Pont scores highest except for use of assets.

Rank	Last Year	Company	Score
1	1	Du Pont	7.47
2	2	Monsanto	6.88
3	3	Dow Chemical	6.71
4	4	Hercules	6.39
5	6	American Cyanamid	6.18
6	7	W.R. Grace	5.78
7	5	Union Carbide	5.68
8	—	Williams Cos.[1]	5.39
9	10	Celanese	5.33
10	—	National Distillers & Chemical[1]	5.18

Beverages

Coke is it. The world's largest beverage company replaces Anheuser-Busch as the group's most admired. Coca-Cola leads for every attribute except management quality, for which it ranks second to Anheuser-Busch. PepsiCo improved its score but remains a distant third. General Cinema is a Pepsi bottler.

Rank	Last Year	Company	Score
1	2	Coca-Cola	8.34
2	1	Anheuser-Busch	7.96
3	3	PepsiCo	7.37
4	—	MEI[1]	7.06
5	7	General Cinema	7.02
6	5	Joseph E. Seagram & Sons	6.78
7	6	Brown-Forman	6.47
8	4	G. Heileman Brewing	6.45
9	9	Adolph Coors	5.87
10	10	Pabst Brewing	4.59

Commercial Banking

J.P. Morgan, the most profitable of the major banking companies, rates first in its group for every attribute except innovativeness and community responsibility. Citicorp leads the 250 for innovativeness but ranks fifth in the banking group for financial soundness. BankAmerica gets the nod for responsibility.

Rank	Last Year	Company	Score
1	1	J.P. Morgan	7.49
2	2	Citicorp	7.29
3	3	Security Pacific	7.04
4	4	Bankers Trust New York	6.65
5	5	First Interstate Bancorp	6.07
6	8	Chemical New York	5.90
7	6	BankAmerica	5.46
8	7	Manufacturers Hanover	5.39[4]
9	9	Chase Manhattan	5.39[4]
10	10	Continental Illinois	2.58

Source: Patricia Sellers, "America's Most Admired Corporations," *Fortune* (January 7, 1985): 25. Used with permission.

[1]Not ranked last year.

[2]Tie. Each scores higher than the other on four of eight attributes.

[3]Taken private November 1984.

[4]Tie. Manufacturers Hanover scores higher than Chase Manhattan on five of eight attributes.

Take Corrective Actions

No organization can survive as an island; no organization can escape change. The third activity in the strategy-evaluation process, taking corrective actions, is needed to keep an organization on track toward achieving its goals and objectives. The internal and external environments in which organizations operate today are more complex and dynamic than ever before. In his thought-provoking books, *Future Shock* and *The Third Wave*, Alvin Toffler argues that environments are in fact becoming so dynamic and complex that they threaten people and organizations with "future shock."

Future shock occurs when the nature, types, and speed of changes overpower an individual or organization's ability and capacity to adapt. Strategy evaluation enhances an organization's ability to adapt successfully to changing circumstances. Brown and Agnew refer to this notion as "corporate agility."[15]

Taking corrective actions raises employees' and managers' anxieties. Research suggests that participation in strategy-evaluation activities is one of the best ways to overcome individuals' resistance to change. According to Erez and Kanfer, individuals accept change best when they have a cognitive understanding of the changes, a sense of control over the situation, and an awareness that necessary actions will be taken to implement the changes.[16]

Strategy evaluation can lead to strategy-formulation changes, strategy-implementation changes, or both formulation and implementation changes. Top managers cannot escape being faced with revising strategies and implementation approaches. Hussey and Langham offer the following insight on taking corrective actions:

> Resistance to change is often emotionally based and is not easily overcome by rational argument. The resistance may be based on such feelings as: loss of status, implied criticism of present competence, fear of failure in the new situation, annoyance at not being consulted, lack of understanding of the need for the change, or insecurity in changing from well-known and fixed methods. It is necessary, therefore, to overcome such resistance by creating situations of participation and full explanation (with two-way dialogue) when changes are envisaged.[17]

Corrective actions should place an organization in a better position to capitalize on internal strengths, to take advantage of key external opportunities, to avoid, reduce or mitigate external threats, and to overcome internal weaknesses. Strategic changes should have a proper time horizon and an appropriate amount of risk. They should be internally consistent and socially responsible. Perhaps most importantly, strategic changes should improve an organization's competitive position in its basic industry. Continuous strategy evaluation keeps top management close to the pulse of an organization and provides information needed for an effective strategic-management system. Carter Bayles describes the benefits of strategy evaluation as follows:

> Evaluation activities may renew confidence in the current business strategy, or may point to the need for action to correct some unsuspected weaknesses—erosion of product superiority or technological edge, or loss of prof-

itability in some product or customer category. But in many cases, the benefits are much more far-reaching, for the outcome of the process may be a fundamentally new strategy that will lead, even in a business that is already turning a respectable profit, to substantially increased earnings. It is this possibility that justifies all formal strategy work, for the payoff can be very large.[18]

REQUIREMENTS OF AN EFFECTIVE EVALUATION SYSTEM

In the world of business today, strategy evaluation must meet several requirements to be effective. First, strategy-evaluation activities must be economical. Too much information can be just as bad as too little information, and too many controls can do more harm than good. Second, strategy-evaluation activities should be meaningful. They should be related to a firm's goals and objectives. They should provide managers with useful information about tasks over which they have control and influence.

Third, strategy-evaluation activities should provide timely information. A key question is "Do our strategy-evaluation activities provide information in time to be of use to the management team?" On occasion and in some areas, information may be needed on a daily basis. For example, when a firm has diversified by acquiring another firm, evaluative information may be needed frequently. However, in a research and development department, daily or even weekly evaluative information could be dysfunctional. Approximate information that is timely is generally more desirable as a basis for evaluation and decisions than accurate information that does not depict the present.

Fourth, evaluation activities should be designed to provide a true picture of what is happening. For example, in a severe economic downturn, productivity and profitability ratios may drop alarmingly, while employees and managers are actually working harder. Strategy-evaluation reports should portray this type of situation fairly. Fifth, information derived from the strategy-evaluation process should facilitate action. Evaluation information should be directed to those individuals in the organization who need to take action based on it. Managers commonly ignore evaluative reports that are provided for informational purposes only. All managers do not need to receive all reports.

Sixth, the strategy-evaluation process should not dominate decisions. Strategy-evaluation activities should foster mutual understanding, trust, and common sense. No department should fail to cooperate with another for solely evaluative reasons. Seventh, strategy reports should be simple, not too cumbersome or too restrictive. Complex strategy-evaluation systems often confuse people and accomplish little. The test of an effective evaluation system is its usefulness, not its complexity.[19]

Eighth, it is worthwhile to note differences in strategy evaluation in large and small companies. For large organizations, a more elaborate and detailed system is needed due to increased difficulties in coordinating efforts among different divisions and functional areas. In small companies, managers are often in daily communication with each other and their employees, so extensive evaluative reporting systems are not needed. Familiarity with local environments usually makes gathering and evaluating information much easier for the small business than for the large business.[20]

Ninth, the key to an effective strategy-evaluation system can be convincing participants that failure to accomplish certain objectives and goals within a prescribed time is not necessarily a reflection of their performance.[21] This guideline is particularly important during the early stages of the strategy-evaluation process. Finally, managers should recognize that there is no one ideal strategy-evaluation system. The activities described in this chapter can be applied to any large or small, profit or nonprofit organization. However, the unique characteristics of an organization, including its size, management style, purpose, problems, and strengths, can determine an evaluation system's final design.

CONTINGENCY PLANNING

Regardless of how carefully strategies are formulated, implemented, and evaluated, unforeseen events such as strikes, boycotts, natural disasters, foreign competitors, and government actions can make a company's strategy obsolete. To minimize the impact of potential threats, organizations should develop contingency plans as part of the strategy-evaluation process. Contingency plans can be defined as "alternative plans that can be put into effect if certain key events do not occur as expected." Only high-priority areas require the insurance of contingency plans. Top managers cannot and should not try to cover all bases by planning for all possible contingencies.

Contingency plans should be developed as part of the formal planning process so that when strategy evaluation activities reveal the need for a major change quickly, an appropriate contingency plan can be executed in a timely way. Predeveloped contingency plans can hasten top management's ability to respond quickly to key changes in the internal and external bases of an organization's current strategy. For example, if underlying assumptions about the economy turn out to be wrong, then appropriate changes can be made promptly if contingency plans are ready.

In some cases, internal or external conditions present unexpected opportunities. In those situations, too, contingency plans allow an organization to capitalize quickly on the opportunity. Contingency plans should be as simple as possible.

Linneman and Chandran have found in their research that contingency planning gives users such as DuPont, Dow Chemical, Consolidated Foods, and Emerson Electric three major benefits: it permits quick response to change, it prevents panic in crisis situations, and it makes managers more adaptable by encouraging them to appreciate just how variable the future can be. Linneman and Chandran suggest that effective contingency planning involves a seven-step process as follows:

1. Identify both beneficial and unfavorable events that could possibly derail company strategy.

2. Specify trigger points. Calculate about when the various contingency plans would

have to go into effect. In other words, determine when contingent events are likely to occur.

3. Assess the impact of each contingent event. Estimate the potential benefit or harm of each contingent event.

4. Develop contingency plans. Be sure that contingency plans are compatible with current strategy and are economically feasible.

5. Assess the counterimpact of each contingency plan. That is, estimate how much each contingency plan will capitalize on or cancel out its associated contingent event. Doing this will quantify the potential value of each contingency plan.

6. Determine early warning signals for key contingent events. Monitor the early warning signals.

7. For contingent events with reliable early warning signals, develop advance action plans to take advantage of the available lead time.[22]

AUDITING

A frequently used tool in the strategy-evaluation process is the audit. Auditing is defined by the American Accounting Association (AAA) as "a systematic process of objectively obtaining and evaluating evidence regarding assertions about economic actions and events, to ascertain the degree of correspondence between those assertions and established criteria, and communicating the results to interested users."[23] People who perform audits can be divided into three groups: independent auditors, government auditors, and internal auditors. Independent auditors usually are certified public accountants (CPAs) who provide their services to organizations for a fee. Independent auditors examine the financial statements of an organization to determine whether they have been prepared according to generally accepted accounting principles (GAAP) and whether they fairly represent the activities of the firm. Independent auditors use a set of standards called generally accepted auditing standards (GAAS). Public accounting firms often have a consulting arm that provides strategy-evaluation services.

Two government agencies, the General Accounting Office (GAO) and the Internal Revenue Service (IRS), employ government auditors who are responsible for making sure that organizations comply with federal laws, statutes, and policies. GAO and IRS auditors can audit any public or private organization.

The third group of auditors are those employees within an organization who are responsible for safeguarding the assets of the company, for assessing the efficiency of company operations, and for assuring that generally accepted business procedures are practiced.

The idea of applying an auditing philosophy to the strategy-evaluation process is not new. To evaluate the effectiveness of an organization's strategic-management system, internal auditors often seek answers to the questions posed in Exhibit 9.2 (1978). Naylor and Neva described a specific audit questionnaire in 1979 in *Managerial Plan-*

Exhibit 9.2   Key strategy-evaluation questions

1. Do you feel that the strategic-management system exists to provide service to you in your day-to-day work? How has it helped you in this respect?

2. Has the strategic-management system provided the service that you feel was promised at the start of its design and implementation? In which areas has it failed and excelled, in your opinion?

3. Do you consider that the strategic-management system has been implemented with due regard to costs and benefits? Are there any areas in which you consider the costs to be excessive?

4. Do you feel comfortable using the system? Could more attention have been paid to matching the output of the system to your needs and if so, in what areas?

5. Is the system flexible enough in your opinion? If not, where should changes be made?

6. Do you still keep a personal store of information in a notebook or elsewhere? If so, will you share that information with the system? Do you see any benefits in so doing?

7. Do you think that the strategic-management system is still evolving? Can you influence this evolution and, if not, why not?

8. Does the system provide you with timely, relevant, and accurate information? Are there any areas of deficiency in this respect?

9. Do you think that the strategic-management system makes too much use of complex procedures and models? Can you suggest areas in which less complicated techniques might be used to advantage?

10. Do you consider that there has been sufficient attention paid to the confidentiality and security of the information in the system? Can you suggest areas for improvement of these aspects of its operation?

Source: K.J. Radford, *Information Systems for Strategic Decisions,* © 1978, pp. 220–21. Reprinted by permission of Prentice-Hall, Inc., Englewood Cliffs, N.J. Also, Lloyd Byars, *Strategic Management* (New York: Harper & Row, 1984), 237.

ning.[24] More recently, Aaron Kelly developed an instrument that he calls a Planning Process Audit (PPA). Kelly's PPA is provided in Exhibit 9.3.

USING COMPUTERS TO EVALUATE STRATEGIES

The power of computers in facilitating the strategy-evaluation process should be mentioned. When properly designed, installed, and operated, the computer can be an extremely efficient method by which to acquire information promptly and accurately. Recall from earlier chapters that computers can facilitate the strategy-formulation process in a number of ways, such as by using online databases to gather strategic information.

Exhibit 9.3   The Planning Process Audit

1. To what extent do you feel top management has been committed to the pursuit of stated corporate strategy?

2. To what extent do you feel committed to the pursuit of stated corporate strategy?

3. Has top management's decision making been consistent with stated corporate strategy?

4. Has decision making been more or less centralized than anticipated?

5. Do you feel you have received sufficient resource support (financial and human) to pursue your stated plans?

6. Do everyday, operational plans seem to support the overall corporate strategy?

7. How would you rate the extent and quality of the coordination of plans among functional areas/departments/divisions?

8. How would you rate the extent and quality of the communication of plans to lower organizational levels?

9. Does the reward system (pay, promotions, etc.) seem to be tied to your planning efforts?

10. Do the written plans seem to adequately represent the actual goals toward which managers seem to be working?

11. How complex is the present planning process?

12. How formal is the present planning process?

13. Do you feel you have the right types and amounts of external information to fulfill your planning responsibilities?

14. Do you feel you have the right types and amounts of internal information to fulfill your planning responsibilities? If not, what other internal information do you feel you need?

15. Would any other training help you do a better job of planning? If Yes, what other specific training would help?

16. What are the major problems of the current planning systems?

17. How might the planning process be improved upon?

Source: C. Aaron Kelly, "Auditing the Planning Process," *Managerial Planning* 32, no. 4 (January–February 1984): 13. Used with permission.

Computers can allow diverse strategy-evaluation reports to be generated for different levels and types of managers. For example, top managers need reports concerned with whether the mission, objectives, and strategies of the enterprise are still adequate. Middle managers require strategy-implementation information reports, such as whether construction of a new facility is on schedule or a product's development is proceeding as expected. Lower level managers could need evaluation reports that focus on more operational concerns, such as absenteeism and turnover rates, productivity rates, and the number and nature of grievances. Computers are being used more and more to facilitate the strategy-evaluation process at all levels in organizations. The final chapter of this text focuses specifically on computer-assisted strategic planning.

CONCLUSION

This chapter presents and examines a strategy-evaluation framework which can facilitate managers' assuring that strategy formulation and implementation activities lead to accomplishment of organizational objectives and goals. Effective strategy evaluation allows an organization to capitalize on internal strengths as they develop, to expeditiously exploit external opportunities as they emerge, to recognize and defend against environmental threats, and to improve internal weaknesses before they become detrimental.

In successful organizations, it seems that top managers take the time to deliberately and systematically formulate, implement, and evaluate strategies. A good top manager moves the enterprise forward with purpose and direction, continually evaluating and improving the firm's internal and external strategic position. Strategy evaluation allows an organization to take a proactive stance towards shaping its own future, rather than constantly being shaped by remote forces that have little or no vested interest in the well-being of the enterprise.

The key to effective strategy evaluation and successful strategic management could be an integration of intuition and analysis. Throughout this text, intuition and analytical tools are noted as being essential to successful strategic management. Intuition allows strategists to better understand the insights developed from analyses; analytical tools aid strategists in organizing and evaluating intuitive information.

A recent article in the *Sloan Management Review* accents the need for strategy-evaluation activities to effectively integrate intuition and analysis:

> A potentially fatal problem is the tendency for analytical and intuitive issues to polarize. This polarization leads to strategy evaluation that is dominated by either analysis or intuition, or to strategy evaluation that is discontinuous, with a lack of coordination among analytical and intuitive issues.[25]

REVIEW QUESTIONS

1. Why is strategy evaluation so important in today's business environment?

2. Discuss the three major steps involved in evaluating the strategy of a fast-food restaurant.

3. Under what conditions would corrective actions not be required in the strategy-evaluation process?

4. Identify some organizations that need to evaluate strategy more frequently than others. Justify your choices.

5. Identify five key financial ratios that would be particularly important in evaluating strategy in a banking institution.

6. Develop a set of contingency plans for the school of business administration in your college or university.

7. Strategy evaluation allows an organization to take a proactive (rather than a reactive) stance towards shaping its own future. Discuss the meaning of this statement.

FOOTNOTES

1 Cortlandt Cammann and David Nadler, *Fit Control Systems to Your Managerial Style,"* *Harvard Business Review* 54 (January–February 1976): 65.

2 Gene Dalton and Paul Lawrence, *Motivation and Control in Organizations* (Homewood, Ill.: Richard D. Irwin, 1971), 5.

3 Dale Zand, "Reviewing the Policy Process," *California Management Review* XXI, no. 1 (Fall 1978): 37.

4 William Glueck and Lawrence Jauch, *Business Policy and Strategic Management,* 4th ed. (New York: McGraw–Hill, 1984), 392.

5 W. Lindsay and L. Rue, "Impact of the Organization Environment on the Long-Range Planning Process: A Contingency View," *Academy of Management Journal* 23, no. 3 (September 1980): 402.

6 George Steiner, *Strategic Planning: What Every Manager Must Know* (New York: The Free Press, 1979), 269.

7 Claude S. George, Jr., *The History of Management Thought* (Englewood Cliffs, N.J.: Prentice-Hall, 1968), 165–66.

8 Barry Stavro, "Trying To Get Out of the Woods," *Forbes* (May 7, 1984): 172.

9 Gary Hector, "The Big Shrink Is on at Atari," *Fortune* (July 9, 1984): 23.

10 Ross Weber, *Management* (Homewood, Ill.: Richard D. Irwin, 1975), 321.

11 George Steiner, *Strategic Factors in Business Success* (New York: Financial Executives Research Foundation, 1969).

12 Charles Hofer, "ROVA: A New Measure for Assessing Organizational Effectiveness" (Graduate School of Business, New York University, 1979, Mimeographed).

13 Richard Rumelt, "The Evaluation of Business Strategy," In *Business Policy and Strategic Management,* ed. William Glueck (New York: McGraw-Hill, 1980), 360.

14 Seymour Tilles, "How to Evaluate Corporate Strategy," *Harvard Business Review* 41 (July–August 1963): 111–21.

15 John Brown and Neil Agnew, "Corporate Agility," *Business Horizons* (March–April 1982): 29.

16 M. Erez and F. Kanfer, "The Role of Goal Acceptance in Goal Setting and Task Performance," *Academy of Management Review* 8, no. 3 (July 1983): 457.

17 D. Hussey and M. Langham, *Corporate Planning: The Human Factor* (Oxford, England: Pergamon Press, 1979), 138.

18 Carter Bayles, "Strategic Control: The President's Paradox," *Business Horizons* (August 1977): 18.

19 Peter Drucker, *Management Tasks, Responsibilities and Practices* (New York: Harper & Row, 1974), 498–504. Also, William Sihler, "Toward Better Management Control Systems," *California Management Review* 14, no. 2 (Winter 1971): 33–39.

20 George Rice, Jr., "Strategic Decision Making in Small Business," *Journal of General Management* 9, no. 1 (Autumn 1983): 64.

21 Timothy Brady, "Six-Step Method to Long-Range Planning for Nonprofit Organizations," *Managerial Planning* 32, no. 4 (January–February 1984): 49.

22 Robert Linneman and Rajan Chandran, "Contingency Planning: A Key to Swift Managerial Action in the Uncertain Tomorrow," *Managerial Planning* 29 (January–February 1981): 23–27.

23 American Accounting Association, *Report of Committee on Basic Auditing Concepts* (1971).

24 Thomas Naylor and Kristin Neva, "The Planning Audit," *Managerial Planning* (September–October 1979): 36–37.

25 Michael McGinnis, "The Key to Strategic Planning: Integrating Analysis and Intuition," *Sloan Management Review* (Fall 1984): 49.

SUGGESTED READINGS

Bales, C.F. "Strategic Control: The President's Paradox." *Business Horizons* 20, no. 4 (August 1977): 17–28.

Brady, T. "Six-Step Method to Long-Range Planning for Nonprofit Organizations." *Managerial Planning* 32, no. 4 (January–February 1984): 47–49.

Brown, J.L. and N.M. Agnew. "Corporate Agility." *Business Horizons* (March–April 1982): 29–33.

Buchele, R.B. "How To Evaluate a Firm." *California Management Review* 4, no. 1 (Fall 1962): 5–17.

Cammann, C. and D. Nadler. "Fit Control Systems to Your Managerial Style." *Harvard Business Review* 54 (January–February 1976): 65–72.

Christopher, W. "Achievement Reporting—Controlling Performance Against Objectives." *Long-Range Planning* (October 1977): 14–24.

Cunningham, J. "Approaches to the Evaluation of Organizational Effectiveness." *Academy of Management Review* (July 1977): 463–74.

Cushing, B. and C. Cushing. "Periodic Audits Hold a Mirror Up to Management." *Management Review* (March 1982): 57–61.

Dalton, G. and P. Lawrence. *Motivation and Control in Organizations* Homewood, Ill.: Richard D. Irwin, 1971.

de Noya, L. "How To Evaluate a Long-Range Plan." *Long Range Planning* 11 (June 1978): 36–40.

Doz, J.L. and C.K. Prahalad. "Headquarters Influence and Strategic Control in MNCs." *Sloan Management Review* 23, no. 1 (Fall 1981): 15–29.

Drucker, P. *Management Tasks, Responsibilities, and Practices.* New York: Harper & Row, 1974.

Erez, M. and F.H. Kanfer. "The Role of Goal Acceptance in Goal Setting and Task Performance." *Academy of Management Review* 8, no. 3 (July 1983): 454–63.

George, C.S. Jr. *The History of Management Thought.* Englewood Cliffs, N.J.: Prentice–Hall, 1968.

Greenley, Gordon. "Effectiveness in Planning: Problems of Definition." *Managerial Planning* 33, no. 2 (September–October 1984): 27–29, 34.

Gupta, A. and V. Govindarajan. "Build, Hold, Harvest: Converting Strategic Intentions Into Reality." *Journal of Business Strategy* 4, no. 3 (Winter 1984): 34–45.

Henry, H.W. "Appraising a Company's Strengths and Weaknesses." *Managerial Planning* (July–August 1980): 31–36.

Holmberg, S. "Monitoring Long-Range Plans." *Long Range Planning* 7, no. 3 (June 1974): 63–69.

Horovitz, J.N. "Strategic Control: A New Task for Top Management." *Long Range Planning* (June 1979): 2–7.

Hussey, D.E. and M.J. Langham. *Corporate Planning: The Human Factor.* Oxford, England: Pergamon Press, 1979.

Kelley, C.A. "Auditing the Planning Process." *Managerial Planning* 32, no. 4 (January–February 1984): 12–14.

King, William. "Evaluating the Effectiveness of Your Planning." *Managerial Planning* 33, no. 2 (September–October 1984): 4–8, 26.

Lindsay, W.M. and L.W. Rue. "Impact of the Organization Environment on the Long-Range Planning Process: A Contingency View." *Academy of Management Journal* 23, no. 3 (September 1980): 385–404.

Linneman, R.E. and R. Chandran. "Contingency Planning: A Key to Swift Managerial Action in the Uncertain Tomorrow." *Managerial Planning* 29 (January–February 1981): 23–27.

Lorange, P. and D. Murphy. "Considerations in Implementing Strategic Control." *Journal of Business Strategy* (Spring 1984): 27–35.

Machin, J.L. and L.S. Wilson. "Closing the Gap Between Planning and Control." *Long Range Planning* (April 1979): 16–32.

McGinnis, M.A. "The Key to Strategic Planning: Integrating Analysis and Intuition." *Sloan Management Review* (Fall 1984): 45–52.

Mendelow, A.L. "Setting Corporate Goals and Measuring Organizational Effectiveness—A Practical Approach." *Long Range Planning* 16, no. 1 (February 1983): 70–76.

Naylor, T. and K. Neva. "The Planning Audit." *Managerial Planning* (September–October 1979): 31–37.

Pomeranz, F. and J.C. Gale. "Is This Strategy Working? A New Role for Accountants." *Management Review* (March 1980): 14–18.

Quinn, J.B. "Strategic Goals: Process and Politics." *Sloan Management Review* (Fall 1978): 7–21.

Radford, K.J. *Information Systems for Strategic Decisions.* Reston, Va.: Reston Publishing Company, 1978.

Rappaport, A. "Corporate Performance Standards and Shareholder Value." *Journal of Business Strategy* 3, no. 4 (Spring 1983): 28–38.

Rice, G. Jr. "Strategic Decision Making in Small Business." *Journal of General Management* 9, no. 1 (Autumn 1983): 58–65.

Schoeffler, S., R.D. Buzzell, and D.F. Heany. "Impact of Strategic Planning on Profit Performance." *Harvard Business Review* (March–April 1974): 137–145.

Siegel, J.G. and M.S. Rubin. "Corporate Planning and Control Through Variance Analysis." *Managerial Planning* 33, no. 2 (September–October 1984): 35–39, 49.

Stavro, B. "Trying To Get Out of the Woods." *Forbes* (May 7, 1984): 172–74.

Steiner, G. *Strategic Factors in Business Success.* New York: Financial Executives Research Foundation, 1969.

Steiner, G. *Strategic Planning: What Every Manager Must Know.* New York: The Free Press, 1979.

Tichy, N. "The Essentials of Strategic Change Management." *Journal of Business Strategy* (Spring 1983): 55–67.

Tilles, S. "How To Evaluate Corporate Strategy." *Harvard Business Review* 41, no. 4 (1963): 111–21.

Toffler, A. *Future Shock.* New York: Random House, 1970.

Tosi, H.L., F.R. Rizzo, and S.J. Carroll. "Setting Goals in Management by Objectives." *California Management Review* 12, no. 4 (Summer 1970): 70–78.

Zand, D. "Reviewing the Policy Process." *California Management Review* XXI, no. 1 (Fall 1978): 35–46.

EXPERIENTIAL EXERCISE 9A:

Preparing a Strategy-Evaluation Report

PURPOSE

The purpose of this exercise is to give you experience in locating and utilizing strategy evaluation information in a college library. As you know, various publications periodically evaluate companies and publish their findings. This information can significantly enhance the strategy-evaluation process.

YOUR TASK

Your task is to locate in your college library strategy-evaluation information on Ponderosa, Inc. Begin your search by going to the *F & S Index of Corporations and Industries*, Standard and Poor's *Corporation Records*, and *Business Periodicals Index*. Based on your findings, prepare a strategy-evaluation report for Ponderosa's chief executive officer, Gerald Office, Jr. Include the following items in your report:

1. A summary of Ponderosa's strategies in 1985
2. A revised IFEM for Ponderosa
3. A revised EFEM for Ponderosa
4. A summary of Ponderosa's performance in 1985
5. A summary of your conclusions regarding Ponderosa's strategies

EXPERIENTIAL EXERCISE 9B:

Analyzing the Strategy-Evaluation Model Used by Ponderosa, Inc.

PURPOSE

This exercise was developed to give you the opportunity to evaluate Ponderosa's strategy-evaluation procedures, as described in an article published in the May 1984 issue of *Planning Review*. Mark Lawless, vice president and director of corporate planning at Ponderosa, wrote the article to describe Ponderosa's strategy-evaluation system. The article, entitled "Investment and Strategy Evaluation: A Personal Computer Model," is presented in Exhibit 9B.

YOUR TASK

Your task is to read Mr. Lawless's strategy-evaluation article. Then write a letter to Gerald Office to give your assessment of the evaluation procedures described in the article.

Exhibit 9B   Investment and strategy evaluation: a personal computer model

A standard chore for most planning departments in strategically managed companies is evaluating capital spending strategies and alternatives. To make these evaluations, planners need to consider both financial and nonfinancial criteria since there are minimum financial requirements that have to be met before a potential investment can be taken seriously. No matter how attractive an opportunity may seem, it will fall by the wayside unless specific financial conditions—such as investment hurdle rates—can be satisfied.

The investment hurdle rate is simply the minimum acceptable return on investment—based on the degree of risk, expected inflation, and the return on riskless investments (such as Treasury Bills). Return on investment (ROI) usually sets the basic criteria for evaluating an investment, and the most widely accepted measure of ROI is now the internal rate of return.

In order to make the best possible evaluation of an investment opportunity, management usually requests a variety of detailed scenarios. But putting these scenarios together can be a lengthy business. Even worse, the exercise can muddle the investment criteria and dull the judgment of the analysts.

This article offers an analysis tool that quickly screens the investment performance and permits an objective view of the requirements. The technique is based on my investment analysis model for investment and strategy screening, with a case study of its application for Ponderosa, Inc. The model can be used by any business and is quite easy to alter to fit particular business considerations, although it's not essential to do this to benefit from the model's simulation capabilities in "generic form."

Strategy Analysis

Ponderosa, Inc. is a major diversified company in the food service industry. Its dominant business is a chain of family steakhouses concentrated in the heartland area of the United States. The company owns a meat-processing plant that sells most of its products to the Ponderosa Steakhouses, and it recently acquired and is expanding a Mexican specialty restaurant business. This portfolio of businesses was designed to provide the basic synergies essential to developing restaurant chains, to balancing market opportunities and risks, and to providing a level of vertical integration that would strengthen the businesses' cost-value equation. Given this portfolio, a major strategic issue is how to grow the business through unit addition.

Ponderosa has been considering several expansion alternatives: first of all, building and operating the units, its primary vehicle for growth up to now; second, licensing the concept on a market or individual unit basis, Ponderosa's secondary source of previous expansion. A third, and extremely interesting option would be a joint venture with some other investor.

The present case concerns the feasibility of Ponderosa's expanding in United Kingdom markets. One U.K. company-owned-and-operated steakhouse has provided a good learning base. The specific requirements of a joint-venture arrangement were considered to determine what variable cost and profit structures were required, considering the operating characteristics of the steakhouse and the potential for change.

Information obtained from several different banking institutions indicated that Ponderosa would need a 15–20 percent return over a five-year time horizon. The specific evaluations were:

Investment:	$1.1 million with $.5 million residual value at the end of five years
Fixed Cost:	$180 thousand plus $20 thousand per year
Customer Traffic:	305 thousand per year (5,865 per week)
Average Check:	$4.75 plus $.25 annually
Cash Flow Pattern:	.1 .2 .3 .2 .2
Variable Costs (% of sales):	
Food:	43–47%
Labor:	17–19%
Advertising:	3–4%
Licensing Fee:	4%
Other Variables:	5–7%
Total Variable Cost:	72–81%
Variable Profit:	19–28%

Although the 19–28 percent range for variable profit was considered achievable, these are relatively thin margins, considering:

- The five-year time horizon for return.
- The investment requirement.
- The fixed cost structure.

- The uniqueness of the asset as reflected in the relatively low residual value at the end of the period.

  The residual value estimate was very conservative, taking into account only the worth of the furniture and equipment in a sale of the assets, not the sale of the restaurant or the goodwill value of its name. A long hard look at these factors cast considerable doubt on the unit's ability to achieve the necessary return on investment.

  Another concern was the estimated volume of customer traffic and the average expenditure per customer. The average check is essentially determined by the market positioning of the concept, the target customer, prevailing economic conditions, and the product mix. The level of customer traffic is affected by the same factors—the average check, alternatives facing the consumer, and the capacity limits of the restaurant. Average check and customer traffic tend to vary inversely with one another, so the most desirable combinations of check size and volume were a significant consideration. Using all available economic and demographic data, as well as site and size considerations, we estimated customer volumes between 286,000 and 315,000 per year. These volumes were consistent with an average check of $4.75 in the initial year, sustainable with check increases of 5 percent annually (that is, averaging between $4.75 and $5.75 over the five-year period).

  We studied a series of simulations to determine the requisite operating features, given the business parameters we'd outlined. These simulations (Table 1) used a model adapted to the food service industry from a generic model.

TABLE 1 [*]

1. Desired ROI:	15%	18%	20%
2. Required Variable Profit ($000)	635	705	753
Expected Level	368	368	368
3. Required Sales Level ($000)	2760	3062	3274
Expected Level	1600	1600	1600
4. Required Variable Profit % of Sales	39%	44%	47%
Expected Level	19–28% (23%)	19–28% (23%)	19–28% (23%)

[*] Values shown are average annual values (specific values vary by year).

Table 1 shows that the expected business performance fell short of what we needed to satisfy the requirements for a successful joint venture. Nevertheless, this option still had several clear advantages that made it a desirable long-term strategy. It permitted risk sharing, a more timely expansion of the business into new markets, and the integration of domestic and U.K. businesses.

We then set out to find alternatives that could eventually make the joint venture a viable approach. We determined that we needed to:

- Reduce investor requirements for return and timing.
- Reduce initial investment through unit design changes.

- Modify menu and service systems to increase operating margins.
- Institute additional cost controls to improve efficiency.
- Develop marketing programs to increase the level of achievable sales.
- Various combinations of the above.

Management chose the last alternative since it was the approach most likely to produce favorable conditions for a joint venture, and Ponderosa's International Development subsidiary is currently acting on this program.

How sensitive are the results to the areas of potential action? Using the 15 percent ROI level scenario, the following changes were evaluated. A $200,000 reduction in the initial investment reduces the required variable profit by $86,000 and 5 percentage points. A $30,000 reduction in annual fixed costs reduces the required variable profit by an additional $30,000 and 2 percentage points. These two actions alone could lower the required variable profit from 39 percent of sales to 32 percent of sales. An increase of 1 percentage point in advertising expenditures, leading to a 10 percent increase in the average check, would give an additional 3-percentage-point reduction in the required variable profit percentage (although it wouldn't reduce the required dollar amount of variable profit). This would reduce the percentage of required variable profit to 29 percent.

As you can see, relatively small changes in some of the business parameters result in significant changes in what is needed to produce the desired ROI.

Source: Mark Lawless, "Investment and Strategy Evaluation: A Personal Computer Model," *Planning Review* (May 1984): 24–27. Used with permission.

PART FIVE

Computers and Strategic Planning

10

Computer-Assisted Strategic Planning

This chapter examines computer-assisted strategic planning (CASP) concepts and tools. Computer software now offers top executives integration, uniformity, analysis, and economy in performing strategic-management activities. An examination of the benefits and limitations of strategic-decision support systems (SDSSs) is provided in this chapter. Specific steps and guidelines are described for developing an effective computer-based strategic-planning system. This is an exciting new area in the field of strategic management.

INFORMATION MANAGEMENT AS A STRATEGIC WEAPON

For over a decade, we have been reading about the senior executive "war room" and what more recently has been termed "the office of the future." The idea is a room consisting of a number of computer terminals with graphical displays. In this room the chief executive officer of an organization spends most of the day monitoring the firm's internal and external environment and formulating, implementing, and evaluating competitive strategies.

The corporate war room may never become a reality, but computers are rapidly becoming an integral part of strategic-management systems. In March, 1985, *Fortune* reported that one in eight chief executive officers of large corporations is a computer buff, including Mack Truck's C.E.O. John Curcio, Duke Power's Chairman William Lee, C.E.O. J. Tylee Wilson of R.J. Reynolds, Quaker Oats' Chairman William Smithburg, Procter & Gamble's Chairman Owen Butler, Hewlett-Packard's C.E.O. John Young, and NCR's C.E.O. Charles Exley, Jr.[1]

Today's business environment has become so competitive that top managers are being forced to extend planning horizons and to make decisions under greater and greater degrees of uncertainty. As a result, more and more information has to be manipulated and evaluated to make effective decisions. In most industries, the availability of scarce resources is decreasing while the number of competitors is increasing.

The strategic-management process requires an ongoing search for and analysis of large amounts of internal and external data which must be assembled, evaluated, and stored. Information management is constantly becoming recognized as the cornerstone of effective strategic management. The advent and proliferation of computer technology has resulted in information systems of all varieties becoming prominent in organizations. A computer can allow managers to obtain, analyze, and evaluate vast amounts of information quickly and accurately. Most strategy-formulation analytical tools can be programmed on a computer to facilitate the transformation of data from many sources into useful strategic information.

Due to powerful information-management capabilities, computers can provide a strategic advantage for many organizations. It is important that strategists afford computer technology the time and importance it deserves, instead of viewing computers merely as a more economical way to do the same old things. Computers can significantly enhance the process of effectively integrating intuition and analysis. The United

States General Accounting Office offers the following conclusions regarding the appropriate role of computers in the strategic-management process:

> The aim is to enhance and extend judgment. Computers should be looked upon not as a provider of solutions, but rather as a framework which permits science and judgment to be brought together and made explicit. It is the explicitness of this structure, the decision-maker's ability to probe, modify, and examine "What if?" alternatives, that is of value in extending judgment.[2]

The computer revolution is upon us and is being compared in magnitude to the industrial revolution. Computer-based technology is penetrating all sectors and areas of American society. Word processing systems, electronic mail and filing, electronic communications networks, desk-top computers, robotics, electronic funds transfer, electronic spreadsheets, and strategic-decision support systems are just some of the many successful business applications of computers. Organizations that fail to utilize computer-assisted strategic planning in the decades ahead are expected to become less and less competitive in all industries. A Fall 1984 article in the *Sloan Management Review* concluded that computers will soon be common "at the desks of almost every professional and administrative employee of industry, government, and academia. In college dormitories, computers will be part of the furniture. An ever-improving price/performance relationship will continue to spur the advance."[3]

CYBERPHOBIA

An estimated 90 percent of the roughly ten million executives and professional managers in the United States today are computer illiterates.[4] It has also been suggested that between 20 and 30 percent of computer users develop cyberphobia: a fear of computers.[5] Cyberphobia manifests itself in a fear of working with computers, a fear of failing to use computers properly, a fear of not understanding computers, and a fear of being replaced by computers. Reasons for cyberphobia include an unfamiliarity with computer hardware and software, previous bad experiences, the "mystery" of the computer, and the belief that computers will undermine one's status within the organization. Simple tasks like inputing information into a computer can be met with much resistance.

Faced with the seriousness of cyberphobia, organizations need to build internal support before, during, and after the introduction of computer systems. All employees and managers could be encouraged to participate in the purchasing decision, to make suggestions, and to discuss the organizational changes brought about by computers. Actions can be taken to make computers more acceptable. For example, one firm found that it was necessary to insert a ten-second delay in their programs, because an instantaneous response from the computer raised employees' defense mechanisms.[6] Users were happier with a machine that had to "think" before answering.

DOONESBURY. Copyright 1982, G. B. Trudeau. Reprinted with permission of Universal Press Syndicate.

Cyberphobia commonly is the result of inadequate training. Training does not just mean learning how to input information into a computer system; it also means educating users about the system: why it is needed, what it is supposed to do, how it performs its functions, who is involved, what is each individual's role, and how these elements of the system are interrelated. In Exhibit 10.1, Robert Rector describes the nature and importance of training in the implementation and operation of a computer-assisted strategic-planning system.

Exhibit 10.1   How to introduce CASP in an organization

The training should be done in a formal classroom situation. The classroom may be a lunchroom, a boardroom, a library, a conference room, or any other available room, as long as it affords the appearance and the atmosphere of a classroom-type environment.

There are a few props needed—all of which can be portable; a chalkboard, flip chart, and in many cases, a projection screen for the slides or Vu-graph transparencies. The key is to remember that everything presented verbally or visually must be said three times, then reinforced with cases and examples.

Remember the importance of developing structured cases or example problems that are realistic and in terms the user or management understands. These exercises need to be carefully structured to guarantee that they are understandable and fully utilize the system. Normally the exercises go from fairly simple to very complex problems, or from the routine to the exceptions.

The trainee needs a good training document and a notebook, as well as appropriate reference material. The documentation normally considered User Documentation is in fact User Reference Material. Encyclopedias are excellent to use in the preparation of academic reports or for other reference work, but hardly appropriate for the classroom instruction: The same applies to User or Management Training—too much User Documentation is kin to an encyclopedia. Often the trainees come from the first session laden down with two and one-half inch thick bound copies of "instruction." They immediately become so frustrated that learning is blocked. Pediatricians tell us not to pile the child's plate too full, or he will not eat.

Training manuals need to be in a sequence the reader understands, which is generally a different sequence from that of the newly designed system. Typically the training materials should go from a broad overview, examples, then input requirements, system codes, procedures, and all other details that need to be explained to make the system work.

The documentation should describe what needs to be done and the uses of the models, rather than how it was constructed. The trainer must explain what the user or manager needs to do to make the system generate the reports or outputs that can be created.

The training documents need to be written below the perceived comprehension level of the reader. The old proverb, "if you can't dazzle them, then baffle them" is hardly appropriate. Too much user documentation looks like unadulterated baffle. Throughout the teaching process, training examples are needed—simple examples which will lead to complex understanding.

The emphasis in the manuals as well as the classroom, needs to be on what the manager has to do to make the DSS work. Do not give them the theory of data processing nor the history or evaluation of the computer, nor the application being implemented. Tell them how to operate the system, and what to do when error conditions arise; relate it to their areas of decision. The emphasis needs to be on what needs to be done, and at all costs avoid computer theory and jargon.

Finally, training needs to be brought together by practice. Often practice can be combined. The practice needs to be controlled, controlled by using cases and problems designed for simple presentation of management, again below their perceived comprehension level. The trainer should start with simple problems that utilize the basic features of the DSS and work toward very complex cases that use the exception routines.

Problems should introduce data that will cause errors, to force results into the exception status. All cases need to be structured like the real environment the manager works in. The trainer should try to make the case problems as realistic as possible. Practice, practice, practice is the rule—this means many cases!

What traditionally takes a week to learn can be compressed into a day with properly planned techniques. Work under controlled conditions, (the classroom) on problems you know the answers to (cases); build from the individual's reference point (management perception) without the typical interruptions. The manager is motivated; he/she understands and will realize personal gain.

Source: Robert Rector, "Decision Support Systems—Strategic Planning Tool," *Managerial Planning* 31, no. 6 (May–June 1983): 39, 40. Used with permission.

STRATEGIC-DECISION SUPPORT SYSTEMS (SDSSs)

Since 1970, computer-assisted strategic planning has evolved from Management Information Systems (MISs) to Decision Support Systems (DSSs) and finally to Strategic-Decision Support Systems (SDSSs). A DSS is a computer-based approach to obtaining and evaluating large amounts of information that can aid in decision making. Exhibit 10.2 summarizes some important differences between MISs and DSSs. Note for example that DSSs focus more on improving unstructured decisions such as those made by top managers, whereas MISs primarily are applicable to the more structured situations that commonly face middle- and lower-level managers.

Exhibit 10.2   MIS versus DSS

MIS Is Characterized By	DSS Is Characterized By
Use of internal, historic data	Use of internal and external data
Focus on repetitive tasks	Focus on the future (planning) rather than the past (control)
Focus on the information requirements of middle- and lower-level management	Focus on the information requirements of top management
Absence of a modeling language (generally)	Use of a modeling language (generally)
Focus on problem solving or finding the cause of a set of symptoms	Focus on decision making or selecting among alternatives

Source: Adapted from Birgit Norgaard, "Pitfalls To Avoid with Modeling Languages," *Management Decisions* 22, no. 2 (1984): 25.

A decision support system designed specifically to support strategic-management activities is called a strategic-decision support system (SDSS). Strategic-decision support systems obtain and analyze information needed to evaluate alternative business strategies. At the present time, a number of SDSSs have been developed by different organizations, including FACETS, DESIGN MANAGER, DATA REQUIREMENTS MODEL, CUFFS, EMPIRE, EXPRESS, FCS, IFPS, REVEAL, SIMPLAN, XSIM, CAUSE, GADS, COSMOS, and STRATPAC.[7] Reports of many other SDSSs have appeared in the public literature, and even more are under development and consideration. A description of STRATPAC that appears regularly in leading strategic-management journals is shown in Exhibit 10.3.

IBM's research division has recently developed GADS (Geodata Analysis and Display System), an effective system for analyzing configurations of census tracts for polit-

Exhibit 10.3   STRATPAC: A new SDSS

Stratpac®
A NEW TOOL TO IMPROVE YOUR STRATEGIC PLANNING
Corporate bankruptcies are now running at the highest level since the Great Depression. Business today is full of uncertainties. To survive, it is imperative that a company should have fast, sophisticated but flexible strategic planning.

STRATPAC IS FAST, FLEXIBLE AND SOPHISTICATED
STRATPAC is not another spread sheet package. It is a Micro computer assisted strategic planning system. It helps you make and test strategic plans fast. It includes almost all the latest strategic and financial planning techniques.

STRATPAC is very flexible. You can do forecasting, financial modelling, strategic analysis at business unit and corporate levels. Separately or as a fully integrated system.

STRATPAC incorporates sophisticated color graphics for forecasting financial and strategic analysis. Financial modelling is comprehensive and includes imaginative "What if" routines.

STRATPAC HAS MANY APPLICATIONS
STRATPAC will help you prepare:

- Product planning
- Sales forecasts
- Financial projections
- Business unit models
- Corporate and divisional consolidations
- Corporate and business unit financial analysis
- Corporate models
- Acquisition studies
- Divestment studies
- Competitor analysis
- Growth share portfolio plans
- Business unit competitive position reports
- Strategic investment portfolio
- Industry business unit growth analysis
- Investment intensity market dominance portfolios

PLUS MANY MORE

STRATPAC IS EASY TO USE—IMMEDIATELY
STRATPAC has been written for planners and line managers to use. Immediately. There is absolutely no programming required. Just input your data and start planning. Hard copy printout of tables and graphics is also available in black and white or colour with an Epson or Integrex CX 80 printer.

STRATPAC has been developed by leading world experts in financial planning and strategic management. The comprehensive manual doesn't just tell you how to use STRATPAC, it is written in management language and helps you interpret your business plans.

STRATPAC RUNS ON READILY AVAILABLE MICROCOMPUTERS
STRATPAC runs on micros with good graphics facilities. Versions are currently available for Apple II and Apple III. IBM Personal Computer and ACT Sirius versions will be available shortly. A minimum of 48K of RAM and two disc drives are required. For color graphics a colour card is needed.

STRATPAC COSTS LESS THAN A DAY'S CONSULTANCY
STRATPAC costs $795. Yet it has features more advanced than many mainframe based planning packages costing up to 100 times more.

Don't delay—complete the coupon and send for your copy of STRATPAC today.

Source: Used with permission of Stratpac Ltd.

ical redistricting, conducting police department planning, and selecting strategies that involve spatial configurations as alternatives. Other companies such as RCA, Citibank, Louisiana National Bank, American Airlines, the First National Bank of Chicago, and the *New York Times* have reported the successful development and implementation of an SDSS.[8] Top executives are increasingly becoming involved in computer-assisted strategic planning systems. A recent *Industry Week* survey offers the following conclusion:

> The top executive who is too busy, too old-fashioned, or too intimidated to use a computer may be a vanishing breed. Roughly two-thirds of the executives responding to our survey have used a computer or word processor for business purposes. "I can't believe the computer revolution has reached this level!" says Peter Finn, chairman of Research & Forecasts. "It's astonishing! It runs contrary to the expectations of a lot of people who see the computer as a tool used by middle levels of management but not at the top levels."[9]

Several SDSSs are now available that effectively analyze competitors' strategies. For example, SICIS (Strategy Issue Competitive Information System) uses the concept of strategic issue analysis and allows a user to gain access to a complex database consisting of information about competitors. Another system, called COSMOS (Competitive Scenario Modeling System), allows a user to test proposed strategies by anticipating competitors' likely responses. This system permits many combinations of factors to be considered simultaneously in an attempt to "outthink" competitors.

Strategic decision-support systems vary considerably in format, price, flexibility, and degree of sophistication, partly because many of the programs have been developed for a single organization. However, SDSSs applicable to diverse organizations are increasingly being developed by firms such as Information Systems of America, Inc., Ferox Microsystems, Inc., Boeing Computer Services, and IBM.

Ginter and Rucks recently conducted a survey of the 4,000 members of the Planning Executives Institute (PEI) to determine the extent of use and application of strategic-decision support systems. The results of their extensive survey are summarized below:

> Strategic models and simulations are being widely used. Four hundred and seventy-nine or 50.8 percent of the respondents reported that computer-based models and simulations are used in the strategic planning process. In addition, almost 93.6 percent of those using mathematical models and simulations reported that they are computer-based. These figures suggest that strategy modeling has advanced considerably in the fifteen years since Gershefski studied the use of computer-assisted strategic planning in American industry.[10]

One of the major advantages of computer-assisted strategic planning is that it allows rapid evaluation of the financial consequences of many alternative assumptions about the economy, competition, the gross national product, and other key internal and external factors. Computer-based planning systems allow organizations to examine the potential impact of various alternative strategies and to answer "What if" questions such as the following:

1. What should we do if government regulations are relaxed?
2. What should we do if our competitors introduce a new, improved product?
3. What should we do if interest rates rise to 18 percent next year?
4. What should we do if our present suppliers fail to meet our needs next year?
5. What will happen if we allocate 40 percent of our resources to forward integration over the next three years?
6. What will happen if we diversify into related businesses by acquiring Cromwell, Incorporated?

Positive Factors Influencing SDSS Development

A number of positive trends are leading to increased efforts to develop and implement strategic-decision support systems. For example, there is a dramatic increase in innovative computer hardware and software designed for specialized business purposes. Computer systems are becoming more efficient, less costly, and more powerful. Also, there is a growing acceptance and use of computer-based systems to perform many varied business and nonbusiness functions.

An estimated 800,000 personal computers were in use by 1984 and more than half of these were being used in businesses. Dozens of monthly newsletters and magazines are now devoted entirely to computers. Computer systems are becoming increasingly interactive and compatible with each other. By linking up with other computerized systems and sources of information, an SDSS represents a valuable strategic decision-making tool.

A very positive trend is the development of analytical strategy-formulation techniques that lend themselves to computer-based strategic planning. (Experiential Exercise 10B at the end of this chapter focuses upon a recently published computer program for QSPM.)[11] Trade publications, academic journals, and professional meetings are reporting that organizations using computer-assisted strategic planning are more successful than similar organizations not utilizing this resource.

Holloway and Pearce recently studied the strategic-management process in hundreds of organizations and came to the following conclusion:

> The emerging computer-assisted planning models help to provide a more comprehensive, meaningful, and quantified basis for the corporate strategic process. By so doing, they broaden the scope of planning activities and enhance the quality of strategic choice.[12]

Another positive trend leading to increased use of SDSSs is in the prices of computer hardware and software, which are rapidly falling as more and more competitors enter the market. An Apple IIe starter system, for example, cost over $2,000 at the beginning of 1984, but this system could be purchased for under $1,000 in 1985.

Finally, the physical size of computer hardware is decreasing dramatically. The IBM 360/20 computer introduced in 1964 weighed 2.5 tons and was larger than a car. A similarly capable computer today weighs about 45 pounds. Lightweight, portable, highly advanced, and relatively inexpensive microcomputers are now available.

Some Limitations of SDSSs

The almost limitless benefits of computer-assisted strategic planning systems should be qualified by some limitations. First of all, any quantitative approach to decision making that involves qualitative judgments is bound to be incomplete. This limitation is not peculiar to strategic-decision support systems but applies equally to model building in general. Personal values, attitudes, morals, preferences, politics, personalities, and emotions are not programmable into an SDSS. Such factors are more important in some strategic decisions than others. This limitation of an SDSS accents the need to view computer-assisted strategic planning as a tool for integrating intuition and analysis, rather than as "the" strategy decision-making device. Recall from earlier chapters that subjective judgment is an integral part of all strategy-formulation analytical tools; this is also true of computer-based models.

A second limitation of SDSSs is the actual cost of development, operation, and maintenance. A recent article in *Managerial Planning* estimates average developmental costs to be $375,000, plus yearly maintenance costs of $45,000.[13] Third, security can be a problem. Computer fraud and computer crime are terms that appear with increasing frequency in the mass media. According to a recent study, security and privacy violations (44 percent) and loss of control (34 percent) are the two biggest fears that have emerged from the advent of computers.[14] The FBI reports that the average bank robbery grosses $3,200 and the average bank fraud grosses $23,000. This is small change compared to the average computer-related theft, which is $500,000. A checklist of questions to insure computer security is provided in Exhibit 10.4. A number of specific measures that can be taken to maintain computer security are provided in Exhibit 10.5. Note that effective use of passwords is a major factor in maintaining the security of an SDSS.

Martin and Winch recently identified four other limitations of contemporary strategic-decision support systems. First, top management too often does not generate or evaluate alternative plans, but rather simply approves (or rejects) plans pushed up from below. Hence, top management is sometimes only interested in computer-based decision aids insofar as they assist lower levels.

Second, plans are commonly developed by managers performing multiple tasks under time pressure. There is frequently limited ability, incentive, or time to explore alternative future environments. Additionally, managers are generally evaluated or judged by the results of their decisions, rather than by the quality of their decision

Exhibit 10.4   A checklist for computer security

For data security:

- Are terminals that access confidential data sufficiently secured?
- Are materials containing confidential data properly protected until destroyed?
- Are confidential printouts sufficiently protected from unauthorized disclosure?
- Does the user department destroy its own confidential trash?

For computer equipment analysis (the facility and peripherals):

- Are facility entry authorization and access mechanisms immediately revoked for terminated or suspended employees?
- Are access control devices changed or recorded on either a regular or unscheduled program?
- Are external facility windows and doors protected against intruder entry and damage?
- Are data entry personnel required to log in?
- Are all supervisory personnel aware of potential security weaknesses?
- Do computer facility personnel wear identification?
- Are building maintenance or cleaning personnel permitted in the facility when facility personnel are not present?

For systems operations security:

- Are operators or supervisors allowed to run shifts by themselves?
- Are batch data deliveries logged?
- Do operators maintain trouble logs?
- Are trouble logs reviewed regularly by supervisory personnel?
- Are equipment use meters logged and reviewed by supervisory personnel?
- Are all exceptions to standard operating procedures promptly investigated and corrective measures taken?
- Are modifications to operational programs and cataloged procedures reviewed by qualified and trusted personnel?
- Are cataloged procedures and operational programs protected by access and modification protection software?

Source: Robert Vichas, "Locking out Computer Crime," *Management World* (July 1982): 14. Used with permission.

Exhibit 10.5 Maintaining the security of an SDSS

The security system should be refined over time to tighten the controls over access. It should be under constant evaluation to limit its exposure to misuse. Some general measures which should be considered are:

- The system should not be available for access during nonbusiness hours. Any noncritical data communication lines should be brought down.

- The system should terminate access capabilities of an operator after "N" minutes of no activity. Normally, an operator will sign-on to the system, perform the necessary work, and sign-off the terminal. Inactivity indicates that the operator failed to sign-off the system, and thus an entry point for system access is left open.

- The password access levels assigned must take into consideration the compatibility of functions and must enforce separation of duties. By restricting transactions activity through the use of a password, the security system can perform this necessary function.

- The updating and maintenance of the security file which controls the passwords must be convenient and preferably real time. If the system is difficult to update, then it will encourage noncompliance.

- The system must enforce password changes. In order to reduce the risk of a password being compromised, it should be periodically changed. However, manual follow-up can be prohibitive, so the system should require the password to be changed as specified by company policy.

- Training on the use and purpose of the password and the online controls is imperative. Ignorance breeds noncompliance and probable security violations.

- The system should deactivate a terminal after "N" number of security violations. Hopefully, the security system will prohibit a true security leak, but any condition that is rejected as an "attempted" security violation should be logged. If a significant number of "attempted" security violations occur, it would indicate that possibly someone is trying to compromise the controls. Thus, the terminal should be systematically deactivated to prohibit further activity.

- Passwords keyed into the terminal should not be displayed. Secured video should be utilized.

- The confidential portion of a password should not be printed on output reports. Only the nonconfidential portion of the password should be viewed.

- Where required, a tiered approach should be established for password authorization. Under this concept, the password would allow a clerk to perform certain transactions and a supervisor to perform other more restricted transactions. In some cases, dual control requires two different operator passwords.

Source: Charles Holley and Keith Reynolds, "Audit Concerns in an Online Distributed Computer Network," *Journal of Systems Management* (June 1984): 34, 35. Used with permission.

analysis. Third, when misconception and misunderstanding of the strategic-management process exists in a firm, introduction of computer-assisted strategic planning can aggravate the situation. Finally, there is often an oversimplification of causal relationships in planning models. In too many firms, model development activities are isolated from actual strategy-formulation activities.[15]

Guidelines for Implementing an SDSS

An excellent way for a company to gain the support of managers and employees is to aid in their personal acquisition of a computer that is compatible with or identical to equipment purchased by the organization. Shearson–American Express, for example, has inaugurated a discount-buying program for the company's 4,500 brokers. During 1984, orders from employees were received at the rate of three a day.

In addition to providing incentives for purchasing a personal computer, some companies are supporting the establishment of personal computer clubs and providing meeting space for these user groups. As an organization integrates a strategic-decision support system into its culture and work ethic, it must realize that the technology of hardware and software is only the surface. Professor Rosabeth Kanter of Yale University recommends six actions to help ensure successful implementation of an SDSS:

1. Long in advance of implementation, send up trial balloons on ideas and plans to make sure that all employees "buy in."

2. Form a steering committee to manage the entire effort, and provide members of the group with special training in people-sensitive consulting.

3. Encourage involvement by soliciting suggestions and holding management briefings. Use this input to help shape purchasing decisions.

4. At installation time, start dialogs between users and vendors and ensure that vendors are willing to modify their plans to accommodate the needs of a particular office.

5. Offer open-ended, people-oriented training sessions that are self-paced, problem-centered, and based on real-life situations.

6. Establish monthly user meetings on a permanent basis to provide encouragement and support.[16]

An Example SDSS in Operation

One of the most advanced SDSSs in the United States is being used by Northwest Industries in Chicago. The company instituted a formal strategic-planning system in 1968, and it developed and began using a strategic-decision support system in 1977. Since 1968, Northwest has had the most impressive growth rate in earnings of any diversified conglomerate in the United States.[17] The company's compounded annual growth rate in earnings per share between 1968 and 1980 was 20.6 percent. Northwest Industries' net income jumped from $7.3 million in 1983 to $77.5 million in 1984. On

April 10, 1985, Northwest Industries announced an agreement to be acquired by Chicago investor W.F. Farley for $1 billion.

The Chief Executive Officer of Northwest Industries, Ben Heineman, attributes much of the firm's success to its strategic-decision support system. As a diversified conglomerate, Northwest Industries consists of nine operating companies that include Lone Star Steel, Acme Boot, Union Underwear, Coca-Cola of Los Angeles, and General Battery. The SDSS developed by Northwest Industries is used primarily to evaluate the strategic plans of the operating companies.

Two specific cases where Northwest Industries' SDSS proved helpful are noted here. First, senior executives at the company recently considered an $800 million capital expenditure project to expand the production capacity of Lone Star Steel. The results generated by the SDSS were a key element in causing corporate management to reject the project and to consider alternatives. Second, both General Battery and Union Underwear in 1980 were projecting continued expansion of their sales and profits based on recent trends. However, the corporate SDSS projected a serious recession in 1980 with significant negative effects on the profitability of these two businesses. The SDSS was correct and significant inventory losses were avoided.

The degree of commitment of senior management to computer-based planning and modeling at Northwest Industries is exceptional. Ben Heineman uses his own computer terminals on a daily basis for planning, forecasting, and monitoring the performance of each of the nine operating divisions and the company as a whole. Northwest Industries is a glowing example of what is possible if an organization is really committed to computer-assisted strategic planning.

COMPUTER-ASSISTED STRATEGIC PLANNING (CASP)

CASP in Large Businesses

In large organizations, a Strategic-Decision Support Center (SDSC) could be established for managing CASP activities. An SDSC director may be responsible for coordinating strategic-management activities and for making strategy formulation recommendations to the chief executive officer. An example organizational structure for an SDSC is depicted in Figure 10.1. Note that the structure could include an SDSC director, an internal environment coordinator, an external environment coordinator, and individual monitors. All of these individuals could be managers who have other primary responsibilities in the organization; an SDSC should not become a centralized, insulated planning department. Coordinators and monitors could be changed annually so that more and more individuals may be actively involved in the planning process.

The SDSC director should evaluate both the internal and external information received, input this information into a computer-based SDSS model, formulate competitive strategies, and communicate specific recommendations to the firm's chief executive officer. The internal logic of the SDSS could follow the strategy-formulation analytical framework that was provided in Figure 7.2.

Figure 10.1   A proposed organizational structure for a Strategic Decision Support Center

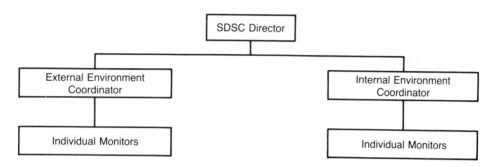

Computer-assisted strategic planning in large businesses is largely "computer-assisted strategy formulation," for two major reasons. First, CASP concepts and software are relatively new. Second, strategy-implementation efforts vary markedly from one organization to another. In the future, strategy-implementation concerns will undoubtedly become more and more a part of strategic-decision support systems.

Computer-assisted strategic planning can contribute to reducing the hierarchical levels of management in an organization. For example, at Hercules, Inc., a sophisticated combination of word processing, electronic mail, videoconferencing, and high-speed communications has permitted Chairman Alexander Giacco to cut the levels of management between himself and plant managers from a dozen to six or seven. Every top manager at Hercules has a computer terminal in his office.[18] Hercules' strategic plan to divest itself of commodity petrochemicals and to concentrate on specialty products has been successful. Hercules expects profits from its specialty business to double to $200 million by 1989.

Thomas Naylor, a nationally recognized leader in the area of computer-assisted strategic planning, recommends a number of guidelines for developing an SDSS for large businesses such as Hercules. According to Naylor, an SDSS ideally should be developed internally by a corporate planning staff and used by senior management to evaluate the effects of alternative corporate strategies under different scenarios. Second, Naylor says an SDSS should be a "What if?" model. It should be designed to include a separate sub-model for each of the company's major divisions or strategic business units. Third, two types of output should be generated from an SDSS: a strategic plan for the overall organization and a strategic plan for each operating division. The output reports could include a *pro forma* income statement, a *pro forma* balance sheet, and a Quantitative Strategic Planning Matrix. Fourth, an SDSS should be an annual forecasted model with a three- to five-year time horizon. It should be interactive, well-documented, and user-oriented. The internal logic of the model should not be viewed as a black box, but rather should be understood by all senior corporate executives. Finally, Naylor emphasizes that an SDSS should not make any decisions, but rather should be used by senior management to evaluate alternative strategies.[19]

CASP in Small Businesses

Computers have begun to proliferate even into the smallest businesses. Compared to managers in large organizations, small business owners and managers generally have less sophistication and experience with computers, less capital to hire computer specialists, and less of a need for extensive computer-based controls. Also, small business owners often flinch at the thought of spending more for computer software than hardware. They often cannot even find the application software that suits their needs, because software companies have not yet focused on the small business market.[20] For these reasons, most small businesses that engage in strategic planning use a spreadsheet approach.

Electronic spreadsheets designed for strategic planning in small firms were recently described in the article that is reprinted in Exhibit 10.6. A spreadsheet approach to

Exhibit 10.6   A spreadsheet approach to strategic planning

The development of "electronic spreadsheets" has done two things for business users. First, it has made computerized planning affordable. Second, it has made it easier—so easy, in fact, that the executive who has to live with the plan can do the job himself instead of relying on DP specialists who have only an indirect interest in its success or failure.

Ten years ago, those advances would not have made much of an impact. Planning was then an esoteric function, done only by big corporations which could afford to fork out thousands of pounds on sophisticated modelling systems. The average management was content to fly by the seat of its pants. It wasn't only the High Street entrepreneur who boasted that he did his planning on the back of an envelope.

Attitudes have been changed by the recession. Even the diehards now recognize that those who don't try to peer into the future may not have a future to peer into.

All that really remains of the old antipathy to planning is the inborn desire to keep things simple. That, no doubt, is why software supplier, Sapphire Systems, advertises that it "has computerized the back of an envelope."

Spreadsheet technology is founded on the fact that a change in any one of a number of variables will affect the end-result of a business activity. The name of the game is to anticipate changes and, where necessary, take corrective action.

In a process company, for example, management needs to know what will happen to margins if the price of a prime material shoots up by 50 per cent; or if, more cheerfully, a major competitor has to pull out of the market.

The construction of a realistic, yet flexible, plan depends on asking "what if" questions about a large number of variables.

In the old days (which, for most businesses, means before the advent of low-cost micros), projections were done on large sheets of paper ruled into rows and columns. There were obviously limits to the size of the sheet and, even when electronic calculators came into use, on the number of what-ifs which could be worked through.

The situation changed dramatically a few years ago when it became feasible to transfer this operation to the inexpensive, VDU-based desktop computer that had recently appeared on the market.

A matrix of columns and rows is displayed on the VDU screen and "labelled" to meet the requirements of a specific planning operation. The user then sets a relation between these rows and columns, so that a single change will automatically change the information in every other row or column affected by it.

The limitation on the size of the screen is overcome by scrolling the display up or down or moving it sideways. In theory, at least, the matrix can be made up of as many rows and columns as needed.

The spreadsheet technique was pioneered by the American VisiCorp company with its VisiCalc software package. This proved so successful that, before long, many other suppliers were either marketing "own-label" versions of VisiCalc or had developed look-alikes.

Competition has brought two predictable results: considerable enhancement of the basic concept, and a steady fall in prices. Today, you can buy a rudimentary spreadsheet program for less than £50 ($75) and a pretty sophisticated one for around £150 ($225).

This combination can, however, do a very useful job for the head of a profit or cost centre who wishes to achieve tighter control of such things as cash flow or return on capital employed. Typical applications are monthly budgeting, re-forecasting, job-costing, and profit and loss accounting. There are scores more, some of them highly specialized.

Probably the most important advance in this field is that, because of low hardware/software costs and the high degree of user-friendliness, the manager whose performance benefits from such information has become self-reliant. He does not have to queue up at the door of a centralized DP department, who may put his request for assistance a long way down its list of priorities.

Though spreadsheets are now being used by very small businesses, the main activity is still within substantial companies. Some companies have a policy of encouraging this kind of departmental initiative. Others have put an embargo on the introduction of dedicated micros while a corps of specialists tries to map out the whole organization's DP future. The latter may be foregoing immediate opportunities to improve operating efficiency, when the outlay would not need to be much more than petty-cash amounts.

A major drawback of the early spreadsheet systems was that the planning data had to be laboriously re-entered on each occasion. This was quickly overcome. All of the current systems enable information to be retained on disk for subsequent use. More sophisticated systems have facilities for merging spreadsheets produced by different users or for different purposes.

The essence of the simpler systems is that they show what happens to the bottom-line if any variable is changed. More sophisticated packages take the user further into modelling by working "in reverse" and showing what changes have to be made in order to produce a certain result—for instance, the sales volume required to produce a specified net profit. Such packages cost up to £750 ($1050) and sometimes more, and of course they can only be used on appropriate hardware.

Micro-based spreadsheets cannot match the capabilities of large-scale planning systems based on "procedural modelling languages." These are much more costly, are designed for mainframe computers, and generally demand the expertise of DP specialists. Nevertheless the gap between the two concepts is closing.

One notable example is the Mapper system behind which Sperry is putting a great deal of its marketing muscle. This is described as "a real-time, general purpose applications development tool which enables end-users to organize and manipulate their own data without the intervention of the computer department."

Another significant sign of things to come is that VisiCorp, the pioneer, has under development a product which will enable a micro user to extract information from a very large company database and then produce plans in a typical spreadsheet operation.

Source: Michael Mellor, "Spreadsheet Route to Planning," *Chief Executive* (April 1984): 55. Used with permission.

strategic planning is more affordable and easier to use than a more elaborate SDSS. Perhaps the most widely used spreadsheet software today is VisiCalc, which is available on the IBM, Apple, Radio Shack, and Commodore personal computers.

Although small business owners do not generally have a strategic-decision support system, they are not immune from potential problems such as computer fraud, breech of privacy, and computer theft. Many small businesses use computer hardware and software in areas other than electronic spreadsheet planning, such as for inventory control and wage and salary administration. The trend is toward integrating these systems and having access points at various locations in an organization. A direct computer application of QSPM to small businesses was published in July 1985 in the *Journal of Systems Management.* [21]

Campbell and Cermak have developed a checklist of questions to aid small business owners in evaluating, developing, implementing, and operating a computer-based strategic planning system. Their checklist of questions, provided in Exhibit 10.7, focuses on seven critical areas where small businesses often go astray in devising and

Exhibit 10.7   Systems control checklist for small business

SYSTEMS PLAN

- has an overall systems plan been developed?
- was an installation schedule with target dates for each application used to keep the project on schedule?
- was the success or failure of the plan evaluated and were guidelines established for future and more effective installations based on the evaluation?

APPLICATION CONTROLS

- were application controls considered when software was being selected?
- is a control book maintained so that each batch or application cycle can be accounted for and balanced to each preceding computer run?
- do application programs utilize reasonableness tests, check digits, or provide for one-to-one checking of input data?
- are forms prenumbered and accounted for in the control book?
- has a clearly defined and documented procedure been established for correcting or removing erroneous transactions?
- when a "unique" error occurs is it handled by carefully documenting the process by which it is corrected?
- are all error conditions recorded in the control book?
- have specific procedures been established for the checking, posting in the control book, and distribution of computer output?

PERSONNEL

- are crosstraining, job rotation, or mandatory vacations used to assure that segregation of function occurs?
- are background checks used to verify the records of prospective employees?

DOCUMENTATION

- has a procedure manual been established and is the manual kept up to date?
- if programs are vulnerable to unauthorized changes, is a comparison program used on a periodic, but random basis, to check for unknown software changes?
- are procedures in effect for the authorization, testing, documenting, and evaluation of program changes?

ACCESS

- is program documentation stored in a safe place both on and off site?
- is access to documentation regulated and recorded?
- are data files backed up regularly and stored both on and off site?
- is password protection used to protect application programs from unauthorized use?
- is computer hardware safe from theft, or misuse?

PROCESSING

- is an operations log maintained by all those using the computer?
- is a processing schedule, which may be part of the procedure manual, followed and periodically compared with the operations log?

PHYSICAL CONTROLS

- are smoke detectors, fire drills and other fire prevention measures used to minimize disruption to business due to fire?
- has the entire information system been evaluated for vulnerability to water damage and has corrective action been taken?
- have precautions been taken to minimize loss due to power failure?
- is hardware covered by a maintenance contract with a reliable firm?
- have provisions been made for hardware backup in the event of extended down time?
- has this source of hardware backup been tested to assure it will work?
- is insurance coverage adequate to compensate for losses due to disaster, error, or criminal activity?

Source: Mary Campbell and Margaret Cermak, "Practical DP Controls for the Small Business," *Journal of Systems Management* (August 1984): 21.

operating a computer-based system: systems plan, application controls, personnel, documentation, access, processing, and physical controls. Campbell and Cermak describe the benefits of their checklist as follows:

> A small business owner who follows the checklist of questions can feel assured that he has taken steps to protect the information assets of his business and that transactions, reports, and inquiries will be processed accurately, when needed, without disrupting the flow of business.[22]

BASICS OF ONLINE DATABASES

An online database service is a collection of reference information or data that can be accessed with a personal computer and retrieved, for a reasonable fee. Online databases allow managers to scan voluminous libraries of strategic information by subject, industry, topic, customer, source, or keyword. Besides a personal computer, a modem is required to access online databases. A modem is simply a communication device that lets a computer receive and transmit data over a telephone line. The fee for most online services is determined based on the amount of information retrieved and the amount of time the service is used.

Link Resources Corporation, a New York-based market research and consulting firm, puts gross distribution revenues for the use of online databases in the North American market at $1,047 million in 1982 and predicts an overall industry growth rate averaging 22.8 percent for the next five years, with the total market expected to exceed $2.9 billion in 1987.[23] The percentage distribution of online database revenues shown in Figure 10.2 reveals that business information represents more than 70 percent of total revenues.

Selection of a database depends on the type of information needed. Online databases are particularly good for obtaining economic, cultural, social, demographic, governmental, political, legal, technological, and competitive information. Several other databases are widely used, including ABI/Inform which is the largest reference business database providing information for top managers. ABI/Inform has 650 business and management publications online. Information can be obtained in many areas that include finance, economics, manufacturing, technology, human resources, and data processing. Most of the data accessible by ABI/Inform is updated weekly. Disclosure II is another online database that includes financial and statistical information on about 8,500 publicly owned companies. Disclosure II also is updated weekly.

PTS U.S. Time Series and PTS International Time Series are databases that monitor over 150,000 time series. Time series are measurements over time of variables such as productivity rates, consumption patterns, prices, foreign trade, population statistics, income levels, and agricultural factors. The PTS U.S. Time Series is updated three times a year and the PTS International Time Series is updated monthly. Graphical displays of this information are available.

Figure 10.2   Percentage distribution of online database revenues by major category

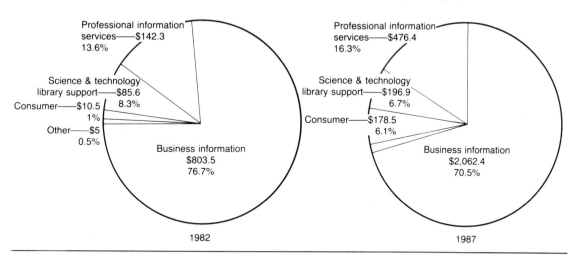

Source: "Plugging into Online Databases," *Business Marketing* (October 1983): 64. Used with permission.

Another commonly used database is the *Harvard Business Review*/Online, often called the *HBR*/Online. It covers a wide range of subjects that include accounting, organizational behavior, marketing, industry analysis, international trade, business ethics, computers, time management, and strategic management. The subscriber can print a full text of every article, citation, or abstract from 1976 to the present.

Three excellent databases that are tailored specifically for home users are: Compuserve, The Source, and Dow Jones On-Line. All three of these services have grown over 100 percent per year since 1980. Some individuals and businesses are buying computers with no particular use in mind, and then find out that tapping into an online database is one of the simplest and most beneficial things to do. The growth of home computers has tremendous implications for strategic decision support systems because home usage reduces cyberphobia.

Usually, answers to online database queries are received within a few seconds or at most within several minutes. The exact amount of time can depend on the extent of the search, the size of the database, and how many other persons are accessing the information at the same time. Database users should identify the precise words that the computer should use to conduct its search for the right articles or statistics. This will save time and money.

The *Directory of Online Databases* is an excellent reference book on databases. This Directory, published twice a year, describes about 1,800 online databases offered by 900 organizations. It can be ordered from Caudra Associates, Inc. for $75 per year (2001 Wilshire Blvd., Suite 305, Santa Monica, California, 90403).

There are two good newsletters devoted to database information:

1. *Database Update* ($97 a year). Address: 10076 Boca Entrada Blvd., Boca Raton, Florida 33433.

2. *Database Alert* ($48 a year). Address: Knowledge Industry Publications, Inc., 701 Westchester Avenue, White Plains, New York 10604.

It is estimated that more than 150,000 personal computer owners were tapping into online databases in 1985, and their numbers were growing rapidly. Online databases can significantly enhance a strategic-decision support system. Increasingly, top managers are coming to recognize that the volume and complexity of strategic information relevant to their business is so immense that computer-assisted strategic planning offers major competitive advantages.

MANAGING WITH MICROCOMPUTERS

Personal computers, or microcomputers, are appealing to top managers more and more because they can be used quickly, inexpensively, and flexibly. They can be taken home or carried on a business trip. Dollar sales of personal computers to corporations were $680 million in 1980 and are expected bo be $4.2 billion in 1985.[24]

STRATPAC and most other SDSSs can be used on a microcomputer. Whereas mainframe or minicomputer versions of an SDSS program could cost in excess of $4,000, microcomputer versions can often be purchased for less than $500. Goode, Harmon, and Jenkins give the following conclusions on the use of microcomputers in strategic planning:

> The use of microcomputers by managers may cause definite shifts in the way users conceptualize and practice the art of management. The role of the manager as a decision maker will expand to include the manager as a developer of white collar tools, including computer program applications and specialized data bases. Some of these tools, such as SDSSs, have the potential to help overcome the short-term bias for which American business has been criticized. The microcomputer can remove much of the computational burden of doing analyses that stretch many years into the future. Thus, the long-range implications of current decisions can be more easily assessed.[25]

In 1984, 250 personal computer manufacturers were offering about 800 different types of computers. There were about 2,400 software vendors, with over 150 of these offering local-area networking (LAN) technology. (Networking involves connecting the personal computers (PCs) in an organization so they can "talk" to each other.) It is estimated that 20 percent of all PCs will be hooked into networks by 1988. A recent development in the growth of local networks is the prospect of merging voice, text, data, and graphics communications. Convergence of these technologies has the potential to significantly improve the strategic decision-making process.

ARTIFICIAL INTELLIGENCE

An SDSS is a type of "expert system." Expert systems evolved out of "artificial intelligence" research. Artificial intelligence researchers have been trying for thirty years to develop computer software that can "think and learn" the way human beings do. These efforts were largely unsuccessful throughout the 1960s and 1970s. However, major advancements in the development of expert systems and SDSSs have been made in the 1980s. More than thirty of the largest U.S. corporations, including Hughes Aircraft, AT&T, General Electric, Digital Equipment, ITT, and Litton have hefty artificial intelligence efforts underway.

A massive drive by the Japanese to build a new generation of "thinking" computers by 1992 has accented the need for urgency in U.S. efforts. In the United States, the federal government is spending over $60 million annually on artificial intelligence research. In 1983, the United States launched an effort called Strategic Computing Program to develop "superintelligent" computers. U.S. industry has responded to Japan's artificial intelligence consortium, Fifth Generation, by forming Microelectronics and Computer Technology Corporation, a Texas-based cooperative comprised of eighteen corporate giants including Lockheed, Gould, and Eastman Kodak. Many universities are also working to develop more effective and efficient expert systems, as indicated in the article that is reprinted in Exhibit 10.8.

Exhibit 10.8   The academics are cashing in at Carnegie-Mellon University

THE ACADEMICS CASHING IN AT CARNEGIE GROUP
The idea of starting a new company to market artificial intelligence systems did not occur to four professors working in the field at Carnegie-Mellon University until two venture capital firms descended on them. Yet when the professors decided to found Carnegie Group Inc., they discovered they did not need venture capital after all.

Clamoring to invest in the AI venture was a flock of industrial companies including the two high-tech giants that ended up financing the deal: Digital Equipment Corp. and General Electric Co. They were lured to Pittsburgh by the reputations the professors had built in AI.

"Corporations see AI as a new star in the heavens," explains Larry K. Geisel, a computer industry veteran recruited to manage the company. "There's such a tremendous rush to own a piece of AI," Geisel says, "that we were a multimillion-dollar company before we opened our doors."

The 18-month-old company expects revenues of $2 million this year from research for its backers and other companies, including Westinghouse, Litton Industries, General Motors, and Rand. By 1985 it plans to push revenues to more than $6 million with AI applications in robotics and manufacturing.

FIREMAN'S HELPER. The first products will be introduced later this year—a software package making it easier to build expert systems and a program that will allow users to communicate with computers in "natural" language. Other products in the works include an AI system that monitors buildings for fires, activates sprinklers, closes fire doors, directs firemen to the fire, and guides occupants out of a building.

With its staff now totaling 18, Carnegie Group has cornered most of the AI talent at Carnegie-Mellon. And, while they all continue their work at the university, they find the commercial potential irresistible. "If someone is going to get rich out of the technology developed here, it ought to be the people who developed it," declares Reddy, a Carnegie Group founder who is also director of the university's Robotics Institute.

Reprinted from the July 9, 1984 issue of *Business Week* by special permission, © 1984 by McGraw-Hill, Inc.

Despite their origins in artificial intelligence, SDSSs are not (and perhaps never will be) totally effective in simulating the actual thought process of strategists.[26] However, by serving as a bridge between intuition and analysis, SDSSs can be a valuable decision-making tool.

CONCLUSION

Information has always been one of the primary components of strategic decision making in a business, personal, military, and even an athletic context. In any competitive situation, the side with the best intelligence (information) usually wins. Computers are becoming widely recognized as the most effective and efficient way to manage information.

This chapter focuses on the use and development of strategic-decision support systems as a tool for obtaining, analyzing, and utilizing strategic information. The advantages and disadvantages of computer-assisted strategic planning are addressed. Specific steps and guidelines for designing and using a strategic-decision support system are provided. Some example SDSSs currently being used in various organizations are described.

Strategic-decision support systems have the potential to improve significantly the quality of strategic decision making. Although many firms are not currently taking full advantage of computer technology, there are positive forces of change operating in organizations and their environments. Improved computer-assisted strategic planning models are being developed. These systems promise to improve the effectiveness of planning activities and to enhance the quality of strategy formulation, implementation, and evaluation decisions in the future. All sizes and kinds of organizations can reap these benefits.

REVIEW QUESTIONS

1. Explain how computers are expected to impact the strategic-planning process in the next decade.

2. Explain why SDSSs today "vary considerably in format, price, flexibility, and sophistication."

3. Conduct library research to identify three major SDSSs that are currently available. Discuss how you would go about deciding which of the SDSSs to implement in your business.

4. For your university, diagram an organizational structure for a SDSC.

5. Discuss the internal logic of a SDSS.

6. Discuss the limitations of strategic-decision support systems.

7. Find, bring to class, and report on a current computer-assisted strategic planning article in *Managerial Planning, Long Range Planning, Planning Review,* the *Journal of Business Strategy,* or the *Journal of Systems Management.*

8. Are computer-based strategic decisions necessarily less socially responsible and more Machiavellian than non-computer-based decisions?

9. Discuss how you can maintain the security of a strategic decision support system.

10. Go to your college library and identify several online databases that focus specifically on providing information about the following industries: banking, food retailing, and hotel management.

FOOTNOTES

1 "C.E.O.s at the PC," *Fortune* (March 4, 1985): 30.

2 *GAO Report PAD-80-21,* p. 17.

3 John Akers, "SMR Forum: A Responsible Future—An Address to the Computer Industry," *Sloan Management Review* (Fall 1984): 53.

4 M. Bralove, "Computer Anxiety Hits Middle Management," *Wall Street Journal* (March 7, 1983): 4.

5 Phillip Wright, "Computers, Change and Fear: An Unholy Trio," *Management Decisions* 22, no. 2 (1984): 32.

6 Ibid.

7 Thomas Naylor, "Effective Use of Strategic Planning, Forecasting, and Modeling in the Executive Suite," *Managerial Planning* 30, no. 4 (1982): 11.

8 William King, "Achieving the Potential of Decision Support Systems," *Journal of Business Strategy* 3, no. 3 (Winter 1983): 85.

9 Perry Pascarella, "Computer Arrives in Executive Suite," *Industry Week* (August 6, 1984): 15.

10 Peter Ginter and Andrew Rucks, "Strategic Models and Simulations: An Emerging Decision-Making Aid," *Journal of Systems Management* (June 1984): 15.

11 Fred David, "Computer-Assisted Strategic Planning in Small Businesses," *Journal of Systems Management* (July 1985): 24–34.

12 Clark Holloway and John Pearce II, "Computer-Assisted Strategic Planning," *Long Range Planning* 15, no. 4 (August 1982): 62.

13 Peter Ginter and Andrew Rucks, "War Games and Business Strategy Formulation," *Managerial Planning* (September–October 1983): 18.

14 William Patterson, "Surviving the Micro Attack," *Industry Week.* (June 11, 1984): 46.

15 C. Martin and G. Winch, "Senior Managers and Computers," *Management Decisions* 22, no. 2 (1984): 20–21.

16 William Patterson, "Surviving the Micro Attack," 46.

17 Thomas Naylor, "Effective Use of Strategic Planning," 9–10.

18 "Office Automation Restructures Business," *Business Week* (October 8, 1984): 118, 125.

19 Thomas Naylor, "Effective Use," 8–9.

20 "Small Business Stumbles into the Computer Age," *Business Week* (October 8, 1984): 126.

21 Fred David, "Computer-Assisted Strategic Planning."

22 Mary Campbell and Margaret Cermak, "Practical DP Controls for the Small Business," *Journal of Systems Management* (August 1984): 20–21.

23 "Plugging into Online Databases," *Business Marketing* (October 1983): 62–66, 85.

24 "The Fortune 500 Microcomputers," *Popular Computing* (September 1982): 62.

25 Robert Good, Robert Harmon, and Kenneth Jenkins, "Managing with Microcomputers," *Business* (January–March 1983): 40.

26 Tom Alexander, "Why Computers Can't Outthink the Experts," *Fortune* (August 20, 1984): 10.

SUGGESTED READINGS

Akers, J. "SMR Forum: A Responsible Future—An Address to the Computer Industry." *Sloan Management Review* (Fall 1984): 53–57.

"Artificial Intelligence Is Here." *Business Week* (July 9, 1984): 54–62.

"Basics of Online Databases." *Office Administration and Automation* (August 1984): 57–59.

Bazoian, H.M. "How New Software Makes Managing Easier." *Nation's Business* (October 1983): 66–68.

Bellack, P.M. "Dofasco's Microcomputer Decision Support System." *Planning Review* (July 1984): 21–23.

Campbell, M.V., and M.M. Cermak. "Practical DP Controls for the Small Business." *Journal of Systems Management* (August 1984): 16–22.

Comptroller General of the United States, General Accounting Office. "Models, Data, and War: A Critique of the Foundation of Defense Analysis." *GAO Report PAD-80-21* (1980): 17.

David, F. "Computer Assisted Strategic Planning in Small Businesses." *Journal of Systems Management* (July 1985): 24–34.

Davis, R.K. "New Tools and Techniques to Make Data Base Professionals More Productive." *Journal of Systems Management* (June 1984): 20–25.

Dearden, J. "SMR Forum: Will the Computer Change the Job of Top Management?" *Sloan Management Review* (Fall 1983): 57–60.

Galitz, W.O. and D.J. Cirillo. "The Electronic Office: How To Make It User Friendly." *Management Review* (April 1983): 24–28, 37–38.

Gatty, B. "Personal Computers Are Coming of Age." *Nation's Business* (September 1983): 46–50.

Gerstein, M. and H. Reisman. "Creating Competitive Advantage with Computer Technology." *Journal of Business Strategy* 3, no. 1 (Summer 1982): 53–60.

Ginter, P.M. and A.C. Rucks. "War Games and Business Strategy Formulation." *Managerial Planning* (September–October 1983): 15–19, 34.

Ginter, P.M. and A.C. Rucks. "Strategic Models and Simulations: An Emerging Decision-Making Aid." *Journal of Systems Management* (June 1984): 12–16.

Good, R.E., R.R. Harmon, and K.M. Jenkins. "Managing with Microcomputers." *Business* (January–March 1983): 37–43.

Haeckel, D.A. and B.B. Johnson. "The Importance of Management Input in the Development of Information Systems Security." *Management Review* (August 1983): 26–28, 38–42.

Harrison, F.L. "Microcomputers—The Breakthrough in Computer Modelling." *Long Range Planning* 16, no. 5 (October 1983): 94–99.

Hayen, R.L. "How To Design a Financial Planning Model." *Long Range Planning* 16, no. 5 (October 1983): 111–22.

Hirschheim, R.A. "Database—A Neglected Corporate Resource." *Long Range Planning* 16, no. 5 (October 1983): 79–88.

Holloway, C. "Strategic Management and Artificial Intelligence." *Long Range Planning* 16, no. 5 (October 1983): 89–93.

Holloway, C. and J.A. Pearce. II. "Computer Assisted Strategic Planning." *Long Range Planning* 15, no. 4 (August 1982): 56–63.

Holley, C. and K. Reynolds. "Audit Concerns in an Online Distributed Computer Network." *Journal of Systems Management* (June 1984): 32–36.

Jugoslav, Multinovich S., and V. Vlahovich. "A Strategy for a Successful MIS/DSS Implementation." *Journal of Systems Management* (August 1984): 8–15.

King, W.R. "Achieving the Potential of Decision Support Systems." *Journal of Business Strategy* 3, no. 3 (Winter 1983): 84–90.

King, W.R. "Integrating Computerized Planning Systems into the Organization." *Managerial Planning* 32, no. 1 (July–August 1983): 10–13, 21.

King, W.R. "Planning for Strategic Decision Support Systems." *Long Range Planning* 16, no. 5 (October 1983): 73–78.

Long, J.E. "The Office of 1990: Management." *Management World* (January 1982): 11–13, 41.

MacGregor, J.M. "What Users Think About Computer Models." *Long Range Planning* 16, no. 5 (October 1983): 45–57.

Maas, M. "In Offices of the Future: The Productivity Value of Environment." *Management Review* (March 1983): 16–20.

Martin, C.J. and G.W. Winch. "Senior Managers and Computers." *Management Decision* 22, no. 2 (1984): 12–24.

Mellor, M. "Spreadsheet Route to Planning." *Chief Executive* (April 1984): 55.

Naylor, T.H. "Effective Use of Strategic Planning, Forecasting, and Modeling in the Executive Suite." *Managerial Planning* 30, no. 4 (January–February 1982): 4–11.

Norgaard, B. "Pitfalls To Avoid with Modelling Languages." *Management Decision* 22, no. 2 (1984): 25–30.

"Plugging into Online Databases." *Business Marketing* (October 1983): 62–66, 85.

Rand, T. "Power Moves from Centre." *Chief Executive* (April 1984): 37–38.

Rector, R.L. "Decision Support Systems—Strategic Planning Tool." *Managerial Planning* 31, no. 6 (May–June 1983): 36–40.

Roberts, R.C. and L.E. Boone. "MIS Development in American Industry." *Journal of Business Strategy* 3, no. 4 (Spring 1983): 106–11.

Seiler, R.E. and J.L. Boockholdt. "Creative Development Of Computerized Information Systems." *Long Range Planning* 16, no. 5 (October 1983): 100–06.

Sethi, N.K. "M.I.S. and the Planning Process." *Managerial Planning* 32, no. 3 (November–December 1983): 46–51.

Shrivastava, P. "Strategic Planning for MIS." *Long Range Planning.* 16, no. 5 (October 1983): 19–28.

Sizer, R. "Key Issues in Managing Information." *Long Range Planning* 16, no. 5 (October 1983): 10–18.

Spooner, P. "Coaching Top Management To Catch up with the Computer." *Chief Executive* (April 1983): 40–48.

"The Fortune 500 Microcomputers." *Popular Computing* (September 1982): 62.

"The Office Takes Off." *Nation's Business* (May 1983): 62–72.

Thomas, H. and C.R. Schwenk. "Decision Analysis as an Aid to Strategy." *Management Decision.* 22, no. 2, 1984, 50–60.

Vichas, R.P. "Locking Out Computer Crime." *Management World* (July 1982): 14–16.

White, K.B. "Dynamic Decision Support Teams." *Journal of Systems Management* (June 1984): 26–31.

Wright, C.R. "Decision Trees: Computer Modeling Facilitates Their Use To Improve Managerial Planning." *Managerial Planning* 31, no. 2 (September–October 1982): 30–34.

Wright, P. "Computers, Change, and Fear: An Unholy Trio." *Management Decision* 22, no. 2 (1984): 31–35.

EXPERIENTIAL EXERCISE 10A:

Your Computer IQ

PURPOSE

Now that you are aware of the computer's basic capabilities and how it can enhance the strategic-management process, it is time to find out how knowledgeable you are of certain key computer concepts.

YOUR TASK

Your task in this exercise is to match some key computer terms with their appropriate definitions and to record your answers on a separate sheet of paper. Each correct answer is worth five points, so your total possible score is 100.

Key Computer Terms

1. Minicomputer
2. Microcomputer
3. Information Resource Management (IRM)
4. FORTRAN
5. COBOL
6. Data Base Management Systems
7. Application Software Package
8. Data Base Administrator (DBA)
9. Modem (Modulator–Demodulator)
10. Compatibility
11. Back-End Processor
12. Floppy Disk
13. Data Description Language (DDL)
14. Mainframe
15. Console
16. Boot Up
17. Documentation
18. Hard Copy
19. Soft Copy
20. User-Friendly

Key Definitions

a. A concept advocating that information be treated as a corporate resource.

b. A small computer with limited capability.

c. A medium-size computer with considerable power.

d. A high-level programming language designed primarily for scientific applications.

e. The individual responsible for the physical and logical maintenance of the database.

f. A device used to convert computer-compatible electrical signals to signals suitable for transmission.

g. Pertaining to the ability of one computer to execute the programs of, access the database of, and communicate with another computer.

h. The unit of a computer system that allows operator and computer to communicate.

i. A programming language used primarily for administrative information systems.

j. A thin flexible disk upon which data are stored.

k. A prewritten set of computer programs designed for a specific application.

l. A host subordinate processor that handles administrative tasks associated with retrieval and manipulation of data.

m. Central processing unit.

n. All the software necessary for the creation and maintenance of the database.

o. That portion of the database management system (DBMS) software that describes the logical relationships of the data.

p. Indicates that hardware and software are designed for use by ordinary people as well as computer professionals.

q. The results of computer processing being displayed on a screen.

r. Start the computer and make it ready for work.

s. The printed material customarily supplied with programs and equipment; includes instruction manuals and technical guides for maintenance.

t. Anything processed by a computer and printed on paper.

EXPERIENTIAL EXERCISE 10B:

Using a Computer Program for QSPM

PURPOSE

This exercise introduces you to the idea of developing and using computer programs for strategy-formulation analytical tools. A computer program for QSPM is provided. This program is written in the BASIC computer language that you probably learned in your Introduction to Computers course.

YOUR TASK

Your task is to become familiar with the QSPM program that follows in Exhibit 1. Use the program to generate the QSPM that you developed for Ponderosa in Experiential Exercise 6B, page 240. Revise the QSPM program, tailoring it to your particular needs.

Attempt to write a similar computer program for another strategy-formulation analytical tool. In performing business policy case analyses, try to use your computer programs to generate the matrices you need.

Exhibit 1   The QSPM computer program

```
]( IST

10   PRINT "QUANTITATIVE STRATEGIC
     PLANNING MATRIX"
20   PRINT
30   PRINT "WHAT IS THE NAME OF TH
     E COMPANY"
40   INPUT N$
50   T = 40 - LEN (N$)
60   PRINT "HOW MANY FACTORS WILL
     BE CONSIDERED UNDERING MARKE
     TING"
70   INPUT C1
74   IF C1 = 0 THEN Z = 1
75   IF Z = 1 THEN 180
80   FOR I = 1 TO C1
90   LET A1 = A1 + 1
100  PRINT "WHAT IS THE NAME OF F
     ACTOR ";A1;" UNDER MARKETING
     "
110  INPUT MA$(I)
120  T1(I) = 30 - LEN (MA$(I))
130  NEXT I
140  FOR I = 1 TO C1
150  PRINT "WHAT IS THE RATING FO
     R THE FACTOR ";MA$(I);" UNDE
     R MARKETING"
160  INPUT MA(I)
170  NEXT I
180  PRINT "HOW MANY FACTORS WILL
     BE CONSIDERED UNDER FINANCE
     "

190  INPUT C2
194  IF C2 = 0 THEN Z1 = 1
195  IF Z1 = 1 THEN 310
200  FOR I = 1 TO C2
210  A2 = A2 + 1
220  PRINT "WHAT IS THE NAME OF F
     ACTOR ";A2;" UNDER FINANCE"
230  INPUT FA$(I)
240  T2(I) = 30 - LEN (FA$(I))
250  NEXT I
260  FOR I = 1 TO C2
270  PRINT "WHAT IS THE RATING FO
     R THE FACTOR ";FA$(I);" UNDE
     R FINANCE"
280  INPUT FA(I)
290  NEXT I
310  PRINT "HOW MANY FACTORS WILL
     BE CONSIDERED UNDER MANAGEM
     ENT"
320  INPUT C3
324  IF C3 = 0 THEN Z2 = 1
325  IF Z2 = 1 THEN 430
330  FOR I = 1 TO C3
340  LET A3 = A3 + 1
350  PRINT "WHAT IS THE NAME OF F
     ACTOR ";A3;" UNDER MANAGEMEN
     T"
360  INPUT MB$(I)
370  T3(I) = 30 - LEN (MB$(I))
380  NEXT I
390  FOR I = 1 TO C3
400  PRINT "WHAT IS THE RATING FO

     R THE FACTOR ";MB$(I);" UNDE
     R MANAGEMENT"
410  INPUT MB(I)
420  NEXT I
430  PRINT "HOW MANY FACTORS WILL
     BE CONSIDERED RESEARCH AND
     DEVELOPMENT"
440  INPUT C4
444  IF C4 = 0 THEN Z3 = 1
445  IF Z3 = 1 THEN 550
450  FOR I = 1 TO C4
460  A4 = A4 + 1
470  PRINT "WHAT IS THE NAME OF F
     ACTOR ";A4;" UNDER RESEARCH
     AND DEVELOPMENT"
480  INPUT RD$(I)
490  T4(I) = 30 - LEN (RD$(I))
500  NEXT I
510  FOR I = 1 TO C4
520  PRINT "WHAT IS THE RATING FO
     R THE FACTOR ";RD$(I);" UNDE
     R RESEARCH AND ";
525  PRINT "DEVELOPMENT"
530  INPUT RD(I)
540  NEXT I
550  PRINT "HOW MANY FACTORS WILL
     BE CONSIDERED UNDER PRODUCT
     ION"
560  INPUT C5
564  IF C5 = 0 THEN Z4 = 1
565  IF Z4 = 1 THEN 670
570  FOR I = 1 TO C5
```

```
580  A5 = A5 + 1
590  PRINT "WHAT IS THE NAME OF F
     ACTOR ";A5;" UNDER PRODUCTIO
     N"
600  INPUT PA$(I)
610  T5(I) = 30 - LEN (PA$(I))
620  NEXT I
630  FOR I = 1 TO C5
640  PRINT "WHAT IS THE RATING FO
     R THE FACTOR ";PA$(I);" UNDE
     R PRODUCTION"
650  INPUT PA(I)
660  NEXT I
670  PRINT "HOW MANY FACTORS WILL
      BE CONSIDERED UNDER ECONOMY
     "
680  INPUT C6
684  IF C6 = 0 THEN Z5 = 1
685  IF Z5 = 1 THEN 790
690  FOR I = 1 TO C6
700  A6 = A6 + 1
710  PRINT "WHAT IS THE NAME OF F
     ACTOR ";C6;" UNDER ECONOMY"
720  INPUT EA$(I)
730  T6(I) = 30 - LEN (EA$(I))
740  NEXT I
750  FOR I = 1 TO C6
760  PRINT "WHAT IS THE FOR THE F
     ACTOR ";EA$(I);" UNDER ECONOM
     Y"
770  INPUT EA(I)
780  NEXT I
790  PRINT "HOW MANY FACTORS WILL
      BE CONSIDERED UNDER POLITIC
     AL"
800  INPUT C7
804  IF C7 = 0 THEN Z6 = 1
805  IF Z6 = 1 THEN 910
810  FOR I = 1 TO C7
820  LET A7 = A7 + 1
830  PRINT "WHAT IS THE NAME OF F
     ACTOR ";A7;" UNDER POLITICAL
     "
840  INPUT GA$(I)
850  T7(I) = 30 - LEN (GA$(I))
860  NEXT I
870  FOR I = 1 TO C7
880  PRINT "WHAT IS THE RATING FO
     R THE FACTOR ";GA$(I);" UNDE
     R POLITICAL"
890  INPUT GA(I)
900  NEXT I
910  PRINT "HOW MANY FACTORS WILL
      BE CONSIDERED UNDER SOCIAL"
920  INPUT C8
924  IF C8 = 0 THEN Z7 = 1
925  IF Z7 = 1 THEN 1030
930  FOR I = 1 TO C8
940  A8 = A8 + 1
950  PRINT "WHAT IS THE NAME OF F
     ACTOR ";A8;" UNDER SOCIAL"
960  INPUT SA$(I)
970  T8(I) = 30 - LEN (SA$(I))
980  NEXT I
990  FOR I = 1 TO C8
1000 PRINT "WHAT IS THE RATING F
     OR THE FACTOR ";SA$(I);" UND
     ER SOCIAL"
1010 INPUT SA(I)
1020 NEXT I
1030 PRINT "HOW MANY FACTORS WIL
     L BE CONSIDERED UNDER TECHNO
     LOGY"
1040 INPUT C9
1044 IF C9 = 0 THEN Z8 = 1
1045 IF Z8 = 1 THEN 1150
1050 FOR I = 1 TO C9
1060 A9 = A9 + 1
1070 PRINT "WHAT IS THE NAME OF
     FACTOR ";A9;" UNDER TECHNOLO
     GY"
1080 INPUT TA$(I)
1090 T9(I) = 30 - LEN (TA$(I))
1100 NEXT I

1110 FOR I = 1 TO C9
1120 PRINT "WHAT IS THE RATING F
     OR THE FACTOR ";TA$(I);" UND
     ER TECHNOLOGY"
1130 INPUT TA(I)
1140 NEXT I
1150 PRINT "HOW MANY FACTORS WIL
     L BE CONSIDERED UNDER COMPET
     ITION"
1160 INPUT CB
1164 IF CB = 0 THEN Z9 = 1
1165 IF Z9 = 1 THEN 1270
1170 FOR I = 1 TO CB
1180 LET AB = AB + 1
1190 PRINT "WHAT IS THE NAME OF
     FACTOR ";AB;" UNDER COMPETIT
     ION"
1200 INPUT CA$(I)
1210 TB(I) = 30 - LEN (CA$(I))
1220 NEXT I
1230 FOR I = 1 TO CB
1240 PRINT "WHAT IS THE RATING F
     OR THE FACTOR ";CA$(I);" UND
     ER COMPETITION"
1250 INPUT CA(I)
1260 NEXT I
1270 PRINT "HOW MANY ALTERNATIVE
     S WILL BE COMPARED"
1280 INPUT CC
1290 FOR H = 1 TO CC
1300 LET AB1 = AB1 + 1
1310 PRINT "WHAT IS ALTERNATIVE
     ";AB1
1320 INPUT AL$(H)
1340 NEXT H
1350 FOR H = 1 TO CC
1360 P = 0
1365 IF Z = 1 THEN 1425
1370 FOR I = 1 TO C1
1380 PRINT "WHAT IS THE RATING F
     OR ";AL$(H);" FOR THE FACTOR
      ";MA$(I);
1385 PRINT "UNDER MARKETING"
1390 INPUT R1(H,I)
1400 D1(H,I) = R1(H,I) * MA(I)
1410 P = P + D1(H,I)
1420 NEXT I
1425 IF Z1 = 1 THEN 1485
1430 FOR I = 1 TO C2
1440 PRINT "WHAT IS THE RATING F
     OR ";AL$(H);" FOR THE FACTOR
      ";FA$(I);
1445 PRINT "UNDER FINANCE"
1450 INPUT R2(H,I)
1460 D2(H,I) = R2(H,I) * FA(I)
1470 P = P + D2(H,I)
1480 NEXT I
1485 IF Z2 = 1 THEN 1545
1490 FOR I = 1 TO C3
1500 PRINT "WHAT IS THE RATING F
     OR ";AL$(H);" FOR THE FACTOR
      ";MB$(I);
1505 PRINT " UNDER MANAGEMENT"
1510 INPUT R3(H,I)
1520 D3(H,I) = R3(H,I) * MB(I)
1530 P = P + D3(H,I)
1540 NEXT I
1545 IF Z3 = 1 THEN 1605
1550 FOR I = 1 TO C4
1560 PRINT "WHAT IS THE RATING F
     OR ";AL$(H);" FOR THE FACTOR
      ";RD$(I);
1565 PRINT " UNDER RESEARCH AND
     DEVELOPMENT"
1570 INPUT R4(H,I)
1580 D4(H,I) = R4(H,I) * RD(I)
1590 P = P + D4(H,I)
1600 NEXT I
1605 IF Z4 = 1 THEN 1665
1610 FOR I = 1 TO C5
1620 PRINT "WHAT IS THE RATING F
     OR ";AL$(H);" FOR THE FACTOR
      ";PA$(I);
1625 PRINT " UNDER PRODUCTION"

1630 INPUT R5(H,I)
1640 D5(H,I) = R5(H,I) * PA(I)
1650 P = P + D5(H,I)
1660 NEXT I
1665 IF Z5 = 1 THEN 1725
1670 FOR I = 1 TO C6
1680 PRINT "WHAT IS THE RATING F
     OR ";AL$(H);" FOR THE FACTOR
      ";EA$(I);
1685 PRINT " UNDER ECONOMY"
1690 INPUT R6(H,I)
1700 D6(H,I) = R6(H,I) * EA(I)
1710 P = P + D6(H,I)
1720 NEXT I
1725 IF Z6 = 1 THEN 1785
1730 FOR I = 1 TO C7
1740 PRINT "WHAT IS THE RATING F
     OR ";AL$(I);" FOR THE FACTOR
      ";GA$(I);
1745 PRINT " UNDER POLITICAL"
1750 INPUT R7(H,I)
1760 D7(H,I) = R7(H,I) * GA(I)
1770 P = P + D7(H,I)
1780 NEXT I
1785 IF Z7 = 1 THEN 1845
1790 FOR I = 1 TO C8
1800 PRINT "WHAT IS THE RATING F
     OR ";AL$(H);" FOR THE FACTOR
      ";SA$(I);
1805 PRINT " UNDER SOCIAL"
1810 INPUT R8(H,I)
1820 D8(H,I) = R8(H,I) * SA(I)
1830 P = P + D8(H,I)
1840 NEXT I
1845 IF Z8 = 1 THEN 1905
1850 FOR I = 1 TO C9
1860 PRINT "WHAT IS THE RATING F
     OR ";AL$(H);" FOR THE FACTOR
      ";TA$(I);
1865 PRINT "UNDER TECHNOLOGY"
1870 INPUT R9(H,I)
1880 D9(H,I) = R9(H,I) * TA(I)
1890 P = P + D9(H,I)
1900 NEXT I
1905 IF Z9 = 1 THEN 1955
1910 FOR I = 1 TO CB
1920 PRINT "WHAT IS THE RATING F
     OR ";AL$(H);" FOR THE FACTOR
      ";CA$(I);
1925 PRINT " UNDER COMPETITION"
1930 INPUT RB(H,I)
1940 DB(H,I) = RB(H,I) * CA(I)
1950 NEXT I
1955 P1(H) = P
1960 NEXT H
1963 PR# 1
1965 PRINT  TAB( T);N$
1970 PRINT  TAB( 21);"QUANTITATI
     VE STRATEGIC PLANNING MATRIX
     "
1975 PRINT
1980 PRINT  TAB( 24);"STATEMENT"
     ;"        ";"ALTERNATIVES"
1990 PRINT "KEY SUCCESS FACTORS"
     ;"      ";"EVALUATION";"
     ;
2000 FOR H = 1 TO CC
2010 X = X + 1
2020 PRINT X;"      ";
2030 NEXT H
2040 PRINT ""
2045 IF Z = 1 THEN 2125
2050 PRINT "MARKETING"
2060 FOR I = 1 TO C1
2070 PRINT MA$(I),MA(I);"   ";
2080 FOR H = 1 TO CC
2090 PRINT R1(H,I);"(";D1(H,I);"
     )";"  ";
2100 NEXT H
2110 PRINT ""
2120 NEXT I
2125 IF Z1 = 1 THEN 2205
2130 PRINT "FINANCE"
2140 FOR I = 1 TO C2
```

```
2150  PRINT FA$(I),FA(I);"  ";
2160  FOR H = 1 TO CC
2170  PRINT R2(H,I);"(";D2(H,I);"
      )";"  ";
2180  NEXT H
2190  PRINT ""
2200  NEXT I
2205  IF Z2 = 1 THEN 2285
2210  PRINT "MANAGEMENT"
2220  FOR I = 1 TO C3
2230  PRINT MB$(I),MB(I);"  ";
2240  FOR H = 1 TO CC
2250  PRINT R3(H,I);"(";D3(H,I);"
      )";"  ";
2260  NEXT H
2270  PRINT ""
2280  NEXT I
2285  IF Z3 = 1 THEN 2365
2290  PRINT "RESEARCH AND DEVELOP
      MENT"
2300  FOR I = 1 TO C4
2310  PRINT RD$(I),RD(I);"  ";
2320  FOR H = 1 TO CC
2330  PRINT R4(H,I);"(";D4(H,I);"
      )";"  ";
2340  NEXT H
2350  PRINT ""
2360  NEXT I
2365  IF Z4 = 1 THEN 2445
2370  PRINT "PRODUCTION"
2380  FOR I = 1 TO C5
2390  PRINT PA$(I),PA(I);"  ";
2400  FOR H = 1 TO CC
2410  PRINT R5(H,I);"(";D5(H,I);"
      )";"  ";

2420  NEXT H
2430  PRINT ""
2440  NEXT I
2445  IF Z5 = 1 THEN 2535
2450  PRINT "ECONOMY"
2470  FOR I = 1 TO C6
2480  PRINT EA$(I),EA(I);"  ";
2490  FOR H = 1 TO CC
2500  PRINT R6(H,I);"(";D6(H,I);"
      )";"  ";
2510  NEXT H
2520  PRINT "
2530  NEXT I
2535  IF Z6 = 1 THEN 2615
2540  PRINT "POLITICAL"
2550  FOR I = 1 TO C7
2560  PRINT GA$(I),GA(I);"  ";
2570  FOR H = 1 TO CC
2580  PRINT R7(H,I);"(";D7(H,I);"
      )";"  ";
2590  NEXT H
2600  PRINT ""
2610  NEXT I
2615  IF Z7 = 1 THEN 2695
2620  PRINT "SOCIAL"
2630  FOR I = 1 TO C8
2640  PRINT SA$(I),SA(I);"  ";
2650  FOR H = 1 TO CC
2660  PRINT R8(H,I);"(";D8(H,I);"
      )";"  ";
2670  NEXT H
2680  PRINT ""
2690  NEXT I
2695  IF Z8 = 1 THEN 2775
2700  PRINT "TECHNOLOGY"

2710  FOR I = 1 TO C9
2720  PRINT TA$(I),TA(I);"  ";
2730  FOR H = 1 TO CC
2740  PRINT R9(H,I);"(";D9(H,I);"
      )";"  ";
2750  NEXT H
2760  PRINT ""
2770  NEXT I
2775  IF Z9 = 1 THEN 2860
2780  PRINT "COMPETITION"
2790  FOR I = 1 TO CB
2800  PRINT CA$(I),CA(I);"  ";
2810  FOR H = 1 TO CC
2820  PRINT RB(H,I);"(";DB(H,I);"
      )";"  ";
2830  NEXT H
2840  PRINT ""
2850  NEXT I
2860  PRINT  TAB( 40);
2870  FOR H = 1 TO CC
2880  PRINT P1(H);"      ";
2890  NEXT H
2900  PRINT ""
2910  PRINT
2920  FOR H = 1 TO CC
2930  LET W = W + 1
2940  PRINT "ALTERNATIVE ";W;" IS
      ";AL$(H);"."
2950  PRINT "ITS TOTAL ATTRACTIVE
      NESS SCORE IS ";P1(H);"."
2960  NEXT H
2970  END
```

Business Policy Cases

How to Analyze a Business Policy Case

Preparing a Case for Class Discussion
Preparing a Written Case Analysis
Guidelines for Preparing Case Analyses
A Sample Case Analysis Outline
A Description of the Cases in This Text

The purpose of Part Six is to provide students with some guidelines on how to prepare oral and written case analyses. Specific steps for preparing a case analysis are described. A sample case analysis outline is provided.

PREPARING A CASE FOR CLASS DISCUSSION

Your professor on occasion will ask you to prepare a business policy case for class discussion. This assignment means that you need to read the case before class, make notes regarding the organization's internal strengths/weaknesses and external opportunities/ threats, perform appropriate analyses, and come to class prepared to offer and defend some specific recommendations.

The case method of teaching and learning involves a classroom situation where *students do most of the talking.* Your professor's role is mainly to ask questions and encourage student interaction regarding ideas, analyses, and recommendations. Chances are, you will become involved in each class discussion, so be prepared. Expect your professor to ask questions such as:

1. What are the company's internal strengths?
2. What are the firm's internal weaknesses?
3. How would you describe the organization's financial condition?
4. What are the firm's external opportunities?
5. What are the firm's external threats?
6. What is the firm's existing strategy or strategies?
7. What are the company's objectives?
8. Who are the firm's competitors? What are the major competitors' strategies?
9. What objectives and strategies would you recommend for this organization?
10. How could the company best implement your recommendations? What implementation problems do you envision? How could the firm avoid or solve those problems?

Be prepared to justify your answers to the above types of questions. Since there is no one right answer in solving a case, be prepared for a discussion along the lines of, "What do you think, what would you do, why would you do it, when would you do it, how would you do it, and what do you feel is most important?"

When discussing a case in class, do not hesitate to take a stand on the issues and to support your position with objective analyses and outside research. Apply the strategic-management model, concepts, and matrices in preparing your case for class discussion. Strive for defensible arguments and positions. Support your opinions and judgments with facts and analyses. Be willing to submit your recommendations to the class without fear of disapproval. Respect the views of others, but be willing to "go against the grain" of majority opinion when you can justify a "better" position.

The case method approach is an opportunity for you to learn more about yourself, your colleagues, strategic management, and the decision-making process in organizations. The rewards of this experience will be dependent upon the effort you put forth, so do the best you can. Discussing business policy cases in class is an exciting and challenging experience.

PREPARING A WRITTEN CASE ANALYSIS

In addition to preparing a case for class discussion, your professor sometimes will ask you to prepare a written case analysis. Preparing a written case analysis is similar to preparing a case for class discussion, except written reports are generally more structured and more detailed. There is no ironclad procedure for preparing a written case analysis, because cases differ in focus, type of organization, size of organization, and complexity. Your professor may ask you to focus your written analysis on a particular part of the strategic-management model, such as "to identify and evaluate the company's existing mission, objectives, and strategies" or "to propose and defend specific recommendations for the company."

For selected cases, your professor may ask you to prepare a "comprehensive written case analysis." This assignment requires that you apply the entire strategic-management process to the particular organization. In preparing a comprehensive written case analysis, picture yourself as a consultant who has been asked by a company to "conduct a study of our internal and external environment and make specific recommendations for our future." In performing a comprehensive written case analysis, you could follow the steps outlined in Exhibit A. Note that the steps in preparing a comprehensive written case analysis follow the stages in the strategic-management model and the chapters in this text.

Exhibit A Steps in preparing a comprehensive written case analysis

---

1. Identify and evaluate the organization's existing mission, objectives, and strategies.

2. Write a mission statement for the organization. If a mission statement is given in the case, determine whether you can improve the statement. Follow the guidelines in Chapter 3 for writing a mission statement.

3. Identify the organization's external opportunities and threats that are described in the case. Then go to the library and search for other social, economic, political, technological, and competitive information that also could represent environmental opportunities or threats to the firm. Determine the *most significant opportunities and threats* that face the company. Construct an External Factor Evaluation Matrix and a Competitive Profile Matrix as described in Chapter 4.

4. Identify the organization's internal strengths and weaknesses in management, marketing, finance, production, and research and development. Study the tables, exhibits, and financial statements given in the case. Use the functional area checklists that are provided in Chapter 5. Determine the *most significant strengths and weaknesses* that characterize the firm. Construct an Internal Factor Evaluation Matrix as described in Chapter 5.

5. Prepare appropriate strategy-formulation matrices as discussed in Chapter 6. The TOWS Matrix, SPACE Matrix, BCG Matrix, IE Matrix, Grand Strategy Matrix, and the QSPM are commonly used.

6. Recommend specific company objectives and strategies.

7. Perform appropriate strategy-implementation analyses, using the information presented and described in Chapter 7.

8. Recommend specific goals and policies for the firm. Recommend how the organization should allocate resources. Use Chapter 8 as a guide.

9. Recommend procedures for strategy review and evaluation. Chapter 9 can serve as a guide.

10. Recommend procedures for improving the firm's computer-assisted strategic planning attitudes and processes. Use Chapter 10 as a guide.

GUIDELINES FOR PREPARING CASE ANALYSES

There are some important guidelines to follow in preparing oral and written case analyses. First, recognize that most of the information in a case is established fact, but some information may be opinions, judgments, and beliefs. For example, the owner of a small business may say in a case that "technological change does not affect my business." This may be an opinion that in actuality is not true. Therefore, do not accept all statements in a case as established fact.

Second, do not prepare an analysis that omits all arguments not supportive of your recommendations. Present the major advantages and disadvantages of several feasible alternatives. Try not to exaggerate, stereotype, prejudge, or overdramatize. Rather, strive to demonstrate that your interpretation of the evidence is reasonable and objective.

Do not make broad generalizations, such as, "The company should pursue a market penetration strategy." Tell what, when, why, how, and where. *Be specific!* A failure to use specifics is the single major shortcoming of students' case analyses! In the internal audit, for example, instead of saying, "The firm's liquidity is bad," say, "The firm's current ratio fell from 2.2 in 1985 to 1.3 in 1986; this is a major weakness." Instead of concluding from a SPACE Matrix that a firm should be defensive, be more specific by describing some defensive strategies that could be appropriate for that particular firm. Be specific throughout your analysis, especially in making recommendations.

Recognize that there is no such thing as a complete case. That is, all of the information that you need to conduct analyses and make recommendations is never given in a case. In the business world, too, managers never have all of the information that they need to make decisions. Needed information may not be availabile, or it may be too costly, or it can take too much time to obtain. Therefore, in preparing cases, you should do exactly what managers do—make reasonable assumptions about unknowns, state the assumptions clearly, perform the needed analyses, and make the necessary decisions. For example, break-even analysis assumes one price and product, but most companies have many products. Generally, you can calculate an average price, state your assumptions, and still perform break-even analysis. Similarly, in performing *pro forma* financial analysis, make reasonable assumptions, state them appropriately, and proceed to show what impact your recommendations should have on the organization's financial position. In preparing case analyses, avoid saying, "I don't have enough information." Also, avoid recommending a course of action beyond a company's means. *Be realistic.*

Evaluate the values and attitudes of the company's top managers, particularly the chief executive officer. Personal values and attitudes can eliminate some strategic alternatives and make others especially attractive. Values, culture, and attitudes are often the major strategy consideration in small, privately held organizations.

Search for and delineate alternatives. Follow closely the steps given in Exhibit A. Be especially careful to match internal strengths and weaknesses with external opportunities and threats. Remember that the most important part of analyzing cases is not what strategies you recommend, but rather how you support your decisions and how you propose that they be implemented. Since there is no single best solution to a case, the justification for recommendations is of paramount importance. In the business world, managers usually do not know if their strategic decisions are "right" until resources have been allocated and used, and then it is often too late to reverse the decisions. This cold fact accents the need for careful integration of analysis and intuition in preparing a business policy case analysis.

Strategy-formulation, implementation, and evaluation decisions are commonly made by a group of individuals rather than by a single person. Therefore, your professor may divide the class into three- or four-person teams to write and discuss cases. Members of a strategic-management team, whether in the classroom or in the business world, differ in their aversion to risk, their concern for the short-run versus long-run, their attitudes toward social responsibility, and other key factors. There are no perfect people, so there are no perfect strategists. Use facts, figures, analyses, and charts to support your ideas. Be open-minded to others' views. Be both a good listener and a good contributor.

A SAMPLE CASE ANALYSIS OUTLINE

As indicated earlier, there is no one best way to prepare a comprehensive written case analysis. Cases differ in focus and professors differ in preferred format. The outline provided in Exhibit B is offered as a general structure for organizing a comprehensive written case analysis. Components of the proposed outline could represent headings and subheading in your written analysis.

Exhibit B   A suggested outline for your comprehensive written case analysis

A. **Introduction**
  1. Background
  2. Mission
B. **Internal Audit**
  1. Strengths
  2. Weaknesses
  3. Internal Factor Evaluation Matrix (IFEM)
C. **External Audit**
  1. Opportunities
  2. Threats
  3. Competitive Profile Matrix (CPM)
  4. External Factor Evaluation Matrix (EFEM)
D. **Strategy Analyses**
  1. TOWS Matrix
  2. SPACE Matrix
  3. Grand Strategy Matrix
  4. BCG Matrix
  5. IE Matrix
  6. QSPM
E. **Recommendations**
  1. Strategy Formulation
  2. Strategy Implementation
  3. *Pro forma* Financial Statements
F. **Epilogue**

A DESCRIPTION OF THE CASES IN THIS TEXT

The cases in this text are described in Table A and Table B. Note that a good mixture of different sizes and types of organizations is included. The cases focus on many different strategic-management issues, in many different situations. The cases are current, exciting, and challenging.

Table A A summary matrix of the cases in this text

Date of Case	Size, Type, Complexity of Business	Firm's Performance	International Business?	Case
1981	Large, automobile, highly complex	Poor	Yes	1. The New Chrysler Corporation
1981	Medium, publishing, moderately complex	Poor	Yes	2. Playboy Enterprises, Inc.
1981	Small, food, lightly complex	Poor	No	3. Kitchen Made Pies
1981	Medium, restaurant, moderately complex	Poor	No	4. Sambo's Restaurants
1981	Small, plant nursery, lightly complex	Poor	No	5. Cottage Gardens, Inc.
1981	Large, computers, highly complex	Good	Yes	6. Hewlett–Packard, Inc.
1982	Large, computers, highly complex	Good	Yes	7. Apple Computer, Inc..
1982	Medium, beer, moderately complex	Poor	No	8. Pabst Brewing Co.
1982	Medium, airlines, moderately complex	Poor	Yes	9. Braniff Airlines
1982	Medium, child care, moderately complex	Good	No	10. Kinder-Care Learning Centers, Inc..
1982	Medium, welding, lightly complex	Good	No	11. The Lincoln Electric Company
1982	Medium, airlines, moderately complex	Poor	No	12. New York Air
1982	Small, diversified, lightly complex	Poor	No	13. Jefferson Enterprises: Small Business Conglomerate Style
1983	Small, tourist, lightly complex	Good	No	14. Wall Drug Store, 1983
1983	Small, education, lightly complex	Poor	No	15. Wallace Women's College
1983	Medium, economy lodging, moderately complex	Poor	No	16. Super 8 Motels
1983	Small, publishing, lightly complex	Poor	No	17. The Classic Car Club of America
1983	Small, hardware store, lightly complex	Good	No	18. Bevell's True Value Hardware, Inc.
1983	Small, tires, lightly complex	Good	No	19. Dick's Place, Inc..
1983	Small, plant nursery, moderately complex	Good	No	20. Western Nursery, Inc.
1983	Small, oil/gas, moderately complex	Poor	No	21. Jensen Oil
1983	Large, housing products, highly complex	Good	No	22. Star Manufacturing, Inc.
1983	Small, craft shop, lightly complex	Poor	No	23. Kitty's Knitting & Fabric Shoppe
1984	Large, air cargo, highly complex	Poor	Yes	24. The Flying Tiger Airline
1984	Medium, airplanes, highly complex	Poor	Yes	25. Cessna Aircraft Corporation
1984	Small, bicycle shop, lightly complex	Poor	No	26. Bicycles Unlimited
1984	Medium, motorcycles, moderately complex	Poor	No	27. Harley–Davidson Motor Company, Inc.
1984	Large, drugs, highly complex	Good	Yes	28. Bristol–Myers
1984	Medium, financial services, highly complex	Good	Yes	29. Lomas & Nettleton Financial Corporation
1984	Large, women's clothing, moderately complex	Good	No	30. The Limited, Inc.
1984	Small, hospital, moderately complex	Good	No	31. Tri-City Area Scanner Cooperative, Inc.
1984	Medium, cosmetics, moderately complex	Poor	Yes	32. Mary Kay Cosmetics, Inc.
1984	Medium, motor homes, moderately complex	Good	No	33. Winnebago Industries, Inc.
1984	Small, electronics, moderately complex	Good	No	34. Daktronics, Inc.

Table B A description of the cases in this text

Case	Income Statements and Balance Sheets Provided?	A Description of the Case
1. The New Chrysler Corporation	Yes	As Chrysler enters 1982, Lee Iacocca faces severe short-term operating problems. He is trying to implement a retrenchment strategy. The case examines Chrysler's marketing, management, finance, production, and research and development activities.
2. Playboy Enterprises, Inc.	Yes	Christie Hefner struggles to stop the red ink at Playboy. The firm lost $120 million during the first half of 1982.
3. Kitchen Made Pies	Yes	This small business is struggling to survive by automating the production of pies, lengthening production runs, and working longer hours. New marketing strategies are needed.
4. Sambo's Restaurants	Yes	Sambo's faces bankruptcy, retrenchment, and major internal reorganization.
5. Cottage Gardens, Inc.	Yes	Severe price cutting by competitors, internal organizational changes, and overcapacity have resulted in a loss of $6,000 on sales of $6 million in 1981.
6. Hewlett–Packard, Inc.	Yes	This is a strategy-evaluation case. H-P has recenty completed major reorganization. Sales growth has slowed. An internal reassessment is underway.
7. Apple Computer, Inc.	Yes	Apple is having problems with counterfeit Apples, poor marketing practices, and intense competition from IBM. A major concern is how to introduce the Lisa and MacIntosh.
8. Pabst Brewing Company	Yes	Pabst struggles to beat back seven takeover attempts. The firm succeeds, but only at great cost. New strategies and implementation plans are required.
9. Braniff Airlines	Yes	Braniff has just lost $160 million for the year 1981 and is struggling to survive. The case describes the history of Braniff and focuses on the need to devise an effective retrenchment strategy.
10. Kinder-Care Learning Centers, Inc.	Yes	This organization is considering expansion into foreign markets and/or diversifying into retail merchandising. Kinder-Care is financially strong.
11. The Lincoln Electric Company	Yes	This is a classic case on a Cleveland-based welding firm that has thrived since 1906, using unorthodox management strategies that may or may not be effective in the future.

12. New York Air	Yes	New York Air's challenge to Eastern has resulted in a net loss of $7.2 million. What should New York Air do now?
13. Jefferson Enterprises: Small Business Conglomerate Style	Yes	This small business conglomerate has just lost $11,947 for 1982. Six specific retrenchment strategies are being considered and must be evaluated.
14. Wall Drug Store	Yes	This classic case focuses on Wall's financial condition and environmental threats, such as gasoline price hikes, rising power costs, and the Highway Beautification Act.
15. Wallace Women's College	Yes	Declining enrollments, reduced federal assistance, and increased costs are a few reasons why Wallace should implement a strategic-management system.
16. Super 8 Motels	Yes	Super 8's long-range plan is to become the first economy lodging chain in all fifty states. Despite a five-fold increase in assets in 1983, net income fell 50 percent.
17. The Classic Car Club of America	Yes	Rising costs and declining membership are creating trauma for this club. The board of directors is considering raising dues, reducing services, etc. as strategies for the future.
18. Bevell's True Value Hardware, Inc.	Yes	Bevell's is faced with expanding some product lines and discontinuing others. Limited growth potential in the area makes relocation a feasible alternative strategy for this small business.
19. Dick's Place, Inc.	Yes	This small business sells new and recapped tires. Possible strategies are to build a new recapping facility, add a new line of products, and/or add a fourth franchise.
20. Western Nursery, Inc.	Yes	Western's management, marketing, finance, and production policies are described, providing a basis for allocating resources in the coming year.
21. Jensen Oil	Yes	Jensen is operating as a Subchapter S company. Horizontal integration and market development are being considered. Profits have declined to nearly zero in 1983.
22. Star Manufacturing, Inc.	Yes	Star is implementing a strategic-planning process. It is establishing a mission, studying its environment, and setting objectives.
23. Kitty's Knitting & Fabric Shoppe	Yes	Kitty's is in serious financial trouble. The owner is considering Chapter 7, 11, or 13 bankruptcy. However, she would prefer to revamp marketing practices and relocate.
24. The Flying Tiger Airline	Yes	Airline deregulation and intense competition from Emery and Lufthansa have resulted in Flying Tiger losing over $200 million in 1983.

25. Cessna Aircraft Corporation	Yes	Cessna is struggling to survive. Numerous strategies and implementation approaches have been proposed.
26. Bicycles Unlimited	No	This bicycle shop is having trouble due to falling demand, a poor location, a lack of bookkeeping records, and intense competition.
27. Harley–Davidson Motor Company, Inc.	No	Japanese firms such as Honda and Yamaha have reduced Harley's market share to 3.2 percent in 1983. The ITC has imposed tariffs against the import of foreign made motorcycles, but these regulations end in 1987.
28. Bristol-Myers	Yes	Special concerns of BM are the prices of prescription drugs, the change in Medicare reimbursement rules, foreign competitors, strengthening OTC drugs, and the value of the dollar in world markets.
29. Lomas & Nettleton Financial Corporation	Yes	Although L&N is the largest mortgage banking firm in the U.S., the financial services industry is changing dramatically. Firms like Sears, Xerox, and Citicorp are diversifying into L&N's markets.
30. The Limited, Inc.	Yes	The Limited is trying to acquire Carter Hawley Hale Stores, Inc. The environment surrounding this takeover attempt is described.
31. Tri-City Area Scanner Cooperative, Inc.	No	Three hospitals are considering forming a joint venture to purchase and use computerized tomography (CT) equipment.
32. Mary Kay Cosmetics, Inc.	Yes	Mary Kay's sales and profits are down dramatically in 1984. Internal problems coupled with intense competition from Avon and Revlon make it imperative that Mary Kay formulate new strategies.
33. Winnebago Industries, Inc.	Yes	Winnebago is having problems with its dealers. The firm is highly dependent on the price and availability of gas. Fleetwood and Coachman have relegated Winnebago to third place in an industry it once dominated.
34. Daktronics, Inc.	Yes	This small business is having inventory and management problems. Shifting from an engineering- to a marketing-oriented company has created other problems as well.

The (New?) Chrysler Corporation

ERNEST R. NORDTVEDT

Loyola University, New Orleans

INTRODUCTION

". . . I am happy to tell you today that in the second quarter of this year (1981), just completed, Chrysler earned a net profit of $12 million. . . . Now if we had returned to profitability in a booming car market it would have been a remarkable achievement. But to do it against all the odds, in spite of double-digit inflation and a 20 percent prime rate, in the most depressed market in 50 years, is maybe a little miracle . . . We've been accused of adjusting the books just a little. Let me say this is a genuine operating profit. . . . Chrysler has fought its way back to profitability, and everyone associated with this company has reason to be proud."
—Lee Iacocca, Chairman and Chief Executive Officer, Chrysler Corporation, at The National Press Club, Washington, D.C., July 22, 1981.

Much white water has passed under the bridge since Lee Iacocca was elected Chairman of the Board and Chief Executive Officer of the Chrysler Corporation on September 20, 1979, after John Riccardo's sudden retirement amid the rising crescendo of Chrysler's financial problems. A quarterly net profit of $12 million on sales of $3 billion is not usually an event which sees a CEO proclaiming it as something of which "everyone associated with this company has reason to be proud." The excitement is placed in perspective, however, when Chrysler's record of the last seven years is examined: American market share declining from 16 percent to 8.8 percent, net losses exceeding net profit by $2.7 billion, and lost per share of common stock totaling $46.72 in 1978 through 1980 alone.

Much has changed at Chrysler during Mr. Iacocca's short tenure and many of the changes have been beyond his control. The single overriding control mechanism in Chrysler's management picture was the Chrysler Corporation Loan Guarantee Act of 1979 (the Act), a statute which provided loan guarantees by the federal government up to a total of $1.5 billion, and was the centerpiece of a massive effort to ward off Chrysler's bankruptcy. Along with the guarantees, however, came a variety of preconditions which in themselves produced some far-reaching changes. Relationships between the company and the federal, state and other jurisdictions where Chrysler does business, between the company and its suppliers, banks and other lenders, its shareholders, and its major union, have all changed substantively as a result of the Act's provisions. Spillovers could impact on other firms of the auto industry, on attempts to revitalize the industry and even on the total reindustrialization of the U.S. industrial base.

At Chrysler, divestiture of several operations had occurred and more could come. Survival as a full-line manufacturer of autos was the goal. Cost reductions, increased production efficiency, new smaller efficient cars, intense marketing efforts, concessions from Chrysler stakeholders and government loan guarantees were the tools to be used in attaining the goal.

The case first will examine briefly Chrysler's history including the stages of product and product line strategy and development. The focus will then narrow to the circumstances and conditions which led to crisis at Chrysler. Discussion of the survival plan will center on the terms and implementation of the Act and indicators of progress toward recovery as of July, 1981. Finally, current and future problems and challenges facing Chrysler in its pursuit of long-term viability will be indicated. Little reference will be made to competitors or other environmental elements found within the industry.

HISTORICAL PERSPECTIVE

The Chrysler Corporation grew out of the efforts and talents of Walter P. Chrysler, truly one of the giants of the U.S. auto industry. He left General Motors in 1920 and assumed control of Maxwell-Chalmers, an ailing manufacturer of autos. He incorporated the new company, giving it his name in 1925. The Dodge Company was absorbed in 1928. The third major nameplate, Plymouth, was also added in 1928 as an entrant in the low price field to compete with Ford and Chevrolet, the latter the General Motors entrant. The Chrysler Corporation enjoyed solid success throughout the 1930s and when Walter died in 1940, the company held a quarter of the domestic market and was the number two auto manufacturer in the world behind General Motors.

After World War II, Plymouth and Dodge autos were downsized in an effort to lock onto the small car market. However, Chrysler's smaller cars did not achieve widespread market acceptance and its place in the market began to slip. In 1948, Ford assumed second place among the domestic manufacturers, a position Chrysler has never regained. By 1954, Chrysler's market share dropped to 12 percent from over 20 percent, and has not risen above 18 percent since.

In 1958, American Motors introduced the Rambler, a compact similar in size to the ones Chrysler had manufactured for several years, but with much greater market penetration and product acceptance. Under pressure from the large cars of General Motors and Ford, Chrysler again began to emphasize large cars in the late 1950s. The company also continued in the small car market with the Dodge Dart and the Plymouth Valiant competing with the Rambler. Compacts comprised about a quarter of Chrysler's production throughout the 1960s compared to Ford's 18 percent and General Motors' 13 percent. Although the decade of the 1960s was a period of modest market share growth and profitability was consistent, Chrysler's relatively heavier concentration on lower margin smaller cars made the company less profitable than its market share and volume would indicate, and also less profitable than its two competitors.

CURRENT BACKGROUND

Management Decisions

In 1969, Chevrolet and Ford introduced new subcompact models, the Vega and the Pinto, respectively. Chrysler, long a champion of the compact, had a choice to make. It could follow the other two manufacturers into the subcompact market or it could push for a bigger share of the more profitable larger car market. Due to limited resources the company could not afford the investment in tooling and facilities required to do both. The decision was to increase emphasis on larger cars. That decision set in motion a series of events which has found Chrysler out of step with the economy, the market, or its competitors—or all three—for the past thirteen years. Examples of those events are found below.

- Chrysler's investment program for 1968–70 was increased based on optimistic projections of population growth and improved highways. The decision coincided with the 1969–70 recession.

- Intermediate size models were restyled in 1971 as the economy emerged from the recession and the demand swung back to full-size cars.

- New full-size cars were introduced in 1974 just in time to join the gas lines brought about by the Arab oil embargo, and to face the demand shift to smaller cars. The $450 million Chrysler invested in this series of large cars represents a costly decision from which Chrysler seems not to have recovered yet.

- Tentative down-sizing of cars began with the new intermediate in 1975 as the memory of the gas lines dimmed and consumer preference shifted back toward larger cars. Government control of gasoline prices gave the consumer little incentive to buy smaller, more efficient cars.

- The 1975 enactment of the Energy Policy and Conservation Act introduced the Corporate Average Fuel Economy (CAFE), a government mandated goal for the average fuel economy for the entire corporate auto production. The subcompact, which was missing from the Chrysler line, would have contributed to meeting the mandate.

Foreign Operations

Chrysler's unprofitable forays into the European market were late and its acquisitions unfortunate. Its intent was to supplement small car offerings in the U.S. market while gaining entry to the European market. In 1957, Chrysler acquired a major stake in Simca, a French auto maker, followed in 1963 by an additional 38 percent and the remainder in 1971. In 1964–65, it acquired two-thirds of the voting and non-voting stock of the Rootes Group in Great Britain. Neither investment was successful. The primary products, the Simca and the Hillman autos, did not achieve market acceptance in the U.S. and suffered steady declines in local markets as well. The British government provided $329 million to Chrysler-UK in 1976, but its market share continued to dwindle. Both operations were subsequently disposed of and Chrysler finds itself in 1981 as largely a North American firm, essentially without overseas operations. Ford and General Motors, by contrast, share almost 21 percent of the European market.

The company's agreement with Mitsubishi, a Japanese firm, has been much more successful. Mitsubishi manufactures autos for sale in the U.S. under the Dodge and Plymouth nameplates. While these captive imports have helped Chrysler financially, the Energy and Conservation Act permitted inclusion of imports in the computation of the CAFE for 1978 and 1979 only.

Recent Performance

Chrysler's current decline appears to have begun in earnest in 1976 when the last big car boom started. Chrysler's resources were inadequate to cover the wide product spectrum indicated by rapidly changing economic conditions and the confusing and contradictory signals sent out by consumers and government alike. The consumer had been greatly influenced in 1974 by shortages and increases in the cost of gasoline, increases which, however, were limited by government control of oil prices. The alarm sounded by the oil embargo of 1973–74 was forgotten by 1976. Sales of full-size and intermediate cars were brisk that year and General Motors had a six-month supply of Vega subcompacts on hand. Sales of American subcompacts declined from 12.3 percent of the 1975 market to 7.4 percent in 1976. Imports were down to 14.8 percent, their lowest share of the U.S. market in five years. Chrysler was unable to satisfy its big car demand. Its strength was in compact cars, a market segment which was declining. Chrysler lost money in 1974 and 1975, and again 1978, losses which turned into a hemorrhage in 1979 and 1980.

General Motors began marketing downsized Chevrolet Chevettes and Cadillac Sevilles in 1976 as part of a $15 billion investment directed at the ultimate downsizing of its entire fleet by 1985. Consumer resistance to the downsizing was experienced. Ford and Chrysler began marketing downsized cars in 1978 in an effort to avoid federal penalties to be assessed if CAFE standards were not met. Both brought out new subcompacts which sold well, although Chrysler had to source the needed four-cylinder engines for its Omni and Horizon autos. Chrysler's subcompacts were badly hurt, however, by a Consumer Reports story that reported the steering to be unsafe. And the public was still buying large cars.

Image

Chrysler's image as a producer of quality products was also becoming tarnished in the eyes of the consumer. Ralph Nader, in a statement before the Senate Committee on Banking, Housing and Urban Affairs on November 20, 1979, gave lack of consumer confidence as a key to Chrysler's problems.

The company is not selling the volume of vehicles it must in order to be profitable. Year after year, Chrysler has been acting in ways to diminish or shatter consumer confidence in its products. Recent years have been vintage for Chrysler lemons—and lemons of the most unsettling kind. Volares and Aspens for instance . . .. Judging by letters which we receive, owners of Chrysler cars are among the most bitter . . ..

In a study of 1975–77 consumer complaints, the Center for Auto Safety reported in a letter to the Chrysler Board Chairman on August 26, 1977, findings which "reflect disturbing safety and consumer problems as well as poor quality control with Chrysler Corporation." The report detailed carburetor, brake, transmission and steering problems of the Volare and Aspen, as well as Cordoba autos. Other minor problems encountered by consumers with other Chrysler products were also described. A general perception held by the American consumer was that U.S. made autos in general and Chrysler autos in particular were inferior products, especially when compared to foreign makes. Whether statistically supportable or not, the perception helped import sales at the expense of Chrysler and other U.S. auto manufacturers.

THE CRISIS

A Rosy Picture

Despite a 1978 loss of $204.6 million, Chrysler's management was optimistic in its outlook as expressed to shareholders as it entered 1979. A fourth quarter, 1978, profit of $43.2 million had been registered. Although its annual production and unit sales were down in 1978, production of the Omni and Horizon autos had begun, thus filling the gap in the subcompact part of the product line. These new cars were selling well, although limited in number by the availability of sourced four-cylinder engines. New full-size and luxury cars also entered production. Passenger vans and recreational vehicles, a market segment at which Chrysler directed substantial emphasis and resources, were moving well after recovery from a slowdown in 1973–74. A new line of subcompact trucks manufactured by Mitsubishi was introduced to the U.S. market. For the first time in many years, Chrysler seemed to have all of the bases in the market covered. Although economists were predicting a slowdown in the economy and its growth rate, early 1979 sales were strong. Industry forecasts indicated a good year was at hand.

Deterioration

It was not to happen. The Shah of Iran was overthrown in January and the revolution resulted in interruption of oil supplies from that country. The image of 1973–74 gas lines became all too vivid in the minds of consumers again. The demand for large cars diminished sharply and inventories grew. This was accompanied by an increase in small car demand and long waiting lists quickly developed. All manufacturers were caught short and Chrysler with availability of subcompacts limited by supply of its purchased four-cylinder engines was again unable to satisfy demand, this time at the end of the product spectrum which had been its strength—the small car segment. Overall, for

1979, sales by U.S. manufacturers declined by more than 10 percent from 1978 while the imports claimed a market share larger by 4.2 percent. Chrysler's sales declined by more than 200,000 units and its share of a shrinking market decreased by a full point to 11.3 percent. The market for inefficient trucks, vans and recreational vehicles, which had been a profitable part of Chrysler's market, virtually disappeared as spot gasoline shortages began to appear.

Many of the factors which came together to damage the U.S. auto manufacturers in general and Chrysler in particular were beyond management's control. These included increasing interest rates, inflation, fear of recession and decreasing consumer confidence in the economy. However, one Chrysler management practice contributed substantially to company problems. Most auto manufacturers matched production with dealer order levels thereby minimizing or at least controlling the level of finished goods inventory. This practice resulted in more variation in production levels but minimized the enormous cost of carrying the inventory. Chrysler had adopted a policy of leveling the production numbers, producing for inventory in the face of declining demand. In late 1979, Chrysler had an unsold backlog of autos totaling more than 80,000 units worth $750 million, many of which were large cars and vans for which little demand existed or could be generated. The storage, handling and interest charges approached $2 million per week. The marketing effort to eliminate this inventory before and even after 1980 model introduction saw the use of factory rebates and many other costly marketing innovations. Not only did the company suffer due to inventory costs but it also sold the units at or below cost simply to move them.

By early 1979, it became apparent that Chrysler faced a serious cash flow problem which limited its ability to finance its programs fully and perhaps threatened its survival. Despite a reduction in costs, improvements to internal operations and a new planning system which matched production with dealer orders, deterioration of the company's position continued. In July, 1979, Chrysler approached the federal government with a request for financial assistance.

THE RECOVERY PLAN

General

On July 24, 1979, The Chrysler Corporation made its initial request to the Treasury Department for $1 billion in cash loans or tax concessions over the ensuing eighteen months. Secretary William Miller quickly rejected the request but did indicate a willingness to explore loan guarantees as a means of helping Chrysler. In its October 17 revision, Chrysler asked for up to $750 million in loan guarantees and on November 1, the Treasury Department sent a preliminary draft of the Chrysler Corporation Loan Guarantee Act of 1979 to the Congress. The measure passed the Congress on December 21 and was signed into law by President Carter on January 7, 1980. A chronology of associated events is included as Exhibit 1. As might be expected, rhetoric revolved around the free-enterprise capitalistic system and government's proper role therein. Major considerations which were raised are indicated below.

Exhibit 1 Chronology of events: Passage and implementation of the Chrysler Corporation Loan Guarantee Act of 1979

1979

July 24	Chrysler outlined proposal for financial aid (loans, tax concessions to Treasury Department)
October 17	Chrysler submitted revised request for up to $750 million in federal loan guarantees
November 1	Treasury sent draft bill to Congress
December 21	Congress passed the bill
December 31	Chrysler reported net loss for 1979 of $1,097 million

1980

January 7	President Carter signed the bill into Law
April 29	Chrysler Loan Guarantee Board meets to begin consideration of issuing commitments for $1.5 billion in loan guarantees
April 29	Chrysler submitted plan in justification of First Takedown
May 10	Chrysler submitted plan revisions
June 24	First Takedown of $500 million approved by the Board
July 10	Chrysler submitted plan in justification of Second Takedown
July 31	Second Takedown of $300 million approved by the Board
December 31	Chrysler reported 1980 loss of $1,710 million

1981

January 15	Chrysler submitted plan in justification of Third Takedown
February 2	Third Takedown of $400 million approved by the Board
March 31	Chrysler reported a First Quarter 1981 loss of $298.4 million
June 30	Chrysler reported Second Quarter 1981 profit of $11.6 million. Year to date: $286.8 million loss

Debate: For Assistance

Cost to the Federal Government Chrysler's demise would produce losses of revenue, additional unemployment payments and welfare costs, and costs to the Pension Guarantee Corporation. These totaled an estimated $3 billion. State and Local governments would incur substantial additional costs of a similar nature.

Employment Secretary Miller estimated that unemployment would increase by about 100,000 during the 1980–81 time frame, primarily among the 400,000 Chrysler, Chrysler dealer and supplier employees. The impact would be especially hard in the Detroit area where unemployment, already above 7 percent, would increase to about 11 percent. Other pockets of Chrysler activity throughout the midwest and northeast would suffer locally heavy impact.

Industry Concentration With a Chrysler failure, only General Motors and Ford would remain as major producers of domestic make autos, representing a narrow competitive base. With high entry barriers already limiting new competition, concern about the effectiveness of the competitive process arises. Chrysler's efforts in the compact market in recent years were cited as providing added competition to General Motors and Ford, and added choice to the consumer.

Balance of Payments   Current import penetration of the U.S. car market would be expected to increase and partially fill the vacuum left by a Chrysler failure. The impact on U.S. balance of payments would be negative.

Lowered Economic Activity   Congressional testimony estimated that a Chrysler collapse would lower real economic growth by 0.5 to 1.0 percent in 1980, together with an increase in unemployment. This would only deepen the recession already in process at the time.

Precedent   The Lockheed loan guarantee was cited as the most applicable precedent, although loan guarantees provided for homes, rural electrification, shipbuilding, medical facilities, railroads, steel, and by the Small Business Administration were also cited. The total of outstanding government loan guarantees was estimated at about $240 billion in October 1979.

Debate: Against Assistance

Intervention in Capital Markets   Government loan guarantees would alter the pattern of resource allocation to the most efficient use, a pattern which theoretically occurs in the free capital markets. Loan guarantees would upset the private market requirement for management discipline and strategy adjustments from firms unsuccessful in selling their products and competing in the market.

Rewarding Failure   A free marketplace rewards failure not with additional capital through loan guarantees but through liquidation or bankruptcy. Chrysler's management decisions have not reflected a sensitivity to consumers or the marketplace, and should not be rewarded with support to avoid bankruptcy.

Impact on Auto Demand   Retail sales of autos would not be appreciably changed by Chrysler's failure. Its sales would in part be picked up by the other domestic manufacturers and in part by the imports. But the same number of jobs would be available in the long term because the auto demand would remain unchanged.

Government Aid Historically Has Been Unsuccessful   The British experience with auto manufacturers, British Leyland and Chrysler-UK, had shown that cash infusions by government did not produce long term viability. Conditions which led to the initial difficulties were not corrected with the provision of financial aid because the pressures of the marketplace were missing in such 'bailouts'.

THE CHRYSLER CORPORATION LOAN GUARANTEE ACT

Provisions

The Act created a Loan Guarantee Board with authority to issue $1.5 billion in federal loan guarantees prior to December 31, 1983, to be repaid by the end of 1990. An outline of the Act's provisions will be found in Exhibit 2, but some provisions are

Exhibit 2   Major provisions of the Chrysler Corporation Loan Guarantee Act of 1979

Loan Guarantee Board

Secretary of the Treasury, Comptroller General and Chairman of the Federal Reserve Board. Non-Voting Members: Secretaries of Labor and Transportation.

Authority

Authorized $1.5 billion in loan guarantees for Chrysler Corporation.
Authority terminated December 31, 1983, loans to be repaid by end 1990.
Requires security (collateral) for loan.

Fees

Requires 0.5 percent per year on daily balance.

Conditions of Loan

Satisfactory energy savings plan.
Certification by Board that failure to secure funds would adversely affect economy or employment in any region of the country.
Requires satisfactory operating and financial plans.
Non-federally guaranteed assistance in amount of $1.43 billion from Chrysler stakeholders, sale of assets, and issuance of $1 billion in common stock for sale to its employees.

Loan Guarantee Requirements

Credit not otherwise available to company on reasonable terms.
No substantial likelihood of merger or sale of company to foreign entity.
No stock dividends paid while guaranteed loans are outstanding.

Non-federally Guaranteed Assistance

At least $500 million from domestic banks, financial institutions or other creditors; $400 million must be new loans or credits and $100 million concessions on outstanding debt.
At least $150 million from foreign banks, financial institutions and other creditors in the form of new loans or credits.
At least $300 million from the sale of corporate assets.
At least $250 million from state, local and other governments.
At least $180 million from suppliers and dealers, with at least $50 million in the form of capital.
At least $50 million from additional sale of stock.
Board may modify as long as total reaches $1.43 billion.

Employee Contributions

Unionized employees reduce current wage contract with company by $462.5 million. (Effective date of contract: 9/14/79 to 9/14/82.) Non-union employees make at least $125 million in wage concessions over the same three-year period.

Exhibit 3   Chrysler consolidated balance sheet, 1976–1981 ($ millions)

	1976	1977	1978	1979	1980	1981[a]
Cash	478	409	523	474	297	358
Accounts Receivable	798	897	848	610	476	605
Inventories	2,354	2,623	1,981	1,874	1,916	1,563
Other	248	225	210	162	172	176
Total Current Assets	3,878	4,154	3,562	3,120	2,861	2,702
Investments, Other Assets	—	1,089	1,396	1,184	1,237	1,240
Net Property, Plant, Equipment	3,196	2,425	2,023	2,349	2,520	2,455
Total Assets	7,074	7,668	6,981	6,653	6,618	6,397
Accounts Payable	2,522	2,685	2,424	2,338	2,700	2,261
Short-Term Debt	172	250	49	601	151	156
Payments Due Within One Year on Long-Term Debt	69	91	12	276	166	143
Other	63	64	1	17	12	27
Total Current Liabilities	2,826	3,090	2,486	3,232	3,029	2,587
Other Liabilities	385	382	361	621	646	787
Long-Term Debt	1,048	1,240	1,189	977	2,483	2,304
Net Worth	2,815	2,956	2,945	1,824	460	719
Total Liabilities/Net Worth	7,074	7,668	6,981	6,653	6,618	6,397

[a]Through June

Source: Company Annual Reports

mentioned here as pertinent to the discussion of Chrysler's performance in the period since the implementation of the Act.

Loan guarantees were to be made available if credit was unavailable to the company elsewhere on reasonable terms; if there was reasonable assurance of repayment; and if failure of the company to secure such funds would adversely affect the economy or employment in any region of the country. Annual submission of satisfactory operating and financial plans covering four fiscal years was required. Actual and forecast Balance Sheet, Operating Statement and Market Penetration data are found in Exhibits 3 through 7.

In a major provision, the Act made obtaining the federal loan guarantees contin-

Exhibit 4 Chrysler forecast consolidated balance sheet, 1981–1985 ($ millions)

	1981	**1982**	**1983**	**1984**	**1985**
Cash	162	180	150	156	165
Accounts Receivable	653	698	750	850	950
Inventories	1,871	2,158	2,254	2,480	2,737
Other[a]	428	180	180	180	180
Total Current Assets	3,114	3,216	3,334	3,666	4,032
Investments, Other Assets	871	872	893	925	965
Net Property, Plant, Equipment	2,146	2,431	2,758	2,869	3,162
Total Assets	6,131	6,519	6,985	7,460	8,159
Accounts Payable	2,536	2,608	2,789	3,135	3,462
Short-Term Debt	35	37	40	25	20
Payments Due Within One Year on Long-Term Debt	20	34	135	186	128
Other	9	13	13	13	13
Total Current Liab.	2,600	2,692	2,977	3,359	3,623
Other Liabilities	682	727	825	874	940
Long Term Debt	1,204	1,044	1,100	927	800
Net Worth	795	1,256	1,883	3,050	4,396
Financing Contingency[b]	(850)	(800)	(200)	750	600
Total Liabilities/Net Worth	6,131	6,519	6,985	7,460	8,159

[a]Includes $250 million receivable from anticipated Chrysler Financial Corporation Sale in 1981.
[b]If forecasts are fully attained in all years, the amounts shown as financial contingency would be available to fund short term peak seasonal needs and to fund additional capital expenditures.

Source: Findings of the Chrysler Corporation Loan Guarantee Board (January 19, 1981)

gent on the provision of $1.43 billion in non-federally guaranteed assistance by stakeholders in Chrysler's continued existence. The Act also specified that there had to be reasonable assurance of corporate viability beyond December 31, 1983, without additional federal loan guarantees.

Non-Federally Guaranteed Assistance

The Act specifies that there must be "$1 of non-federally guaranteed assistance in place for each dollar of guarantee." Although not specified, the implication is that assistance

Exhibit 5   Chrysler statement of operations, 1976–1981[a] ($ millions)

	1976	**1977**	**1978**	**1979**	**1980**	**1981**[a]
Total Revenues	12,240	13,051	13,670	12,004	9,169	5,503
Costs other than items below	11,759[b]	12,185	13,213	12,229	9,694	5,236
Depreciation & Amortization	—	320	352	401	567	231
Pension Plans	—	274	262	261	302	166
Interest Expenses — Net	—	75	129	215	276	139
Earnings Before Taxes & Minority Interest	481	197	(286)	(1,102)	(1,670)	(269)
Taxes on Income (Credit) & Minority Interest	153	34	(81)	(5)	40	18
Net Earnings/(Loss)	328	163	(205)	(1,097)	(1,710)	(287)

[a]Through June
[b]Total Costs, 1976
Source: Company Annual Reports

Exhibit 6   Chrysler forecast statement of operations, 1981–1985 ($ millions)

	1981	**1982**	**1983**	**1984**	**1985**
Total Revenues	12,476	14,931	18,360	21,019	23,265
Costs other than items below.	11,506	13,257	16,288	18,302	20,336
Depreciation & Amortiz.	501	541	616	732	761
Pension Plans	343	401	475	526	568
Interest Expenses — Net	350	383	360	318	165
Earnings Before Taxes & Minority Interest	(224)	349	621	1,141	1,435
Taxes on Income (Credit) and Minority Interest	29	30	34	52	162
Net Earnings/(Loss)	(253)	319	587	1,089	1,273

Source: Findings of the Chrysler Corporation Loan Guarantee Board (January 19, 1981).

was to be accrued against the amount of guarantees outstanding at any one time. Chrysler obtained concessions from a variety of stakeholders and also sold a portion of corporate assets to achieve the levels of non-federally guaranteed assistance specified by the Act. Although included initially, a requirement for sale of new equity to the public was modified by the Loan Guarantee Board as unrealistic in light of Chrysler's current financial condition.

Exhibit 7 Chrysler market penetration and net income (Actual: 1974–June 1981; Forecast: 1981–1984)

Year	Industry Sales/Units (Millions)	Chrysler Mkt Share (Percent)	Chrysler Net Income ($ Million)
1974	8.9	13.6	(52)
1975	8.6	11.5	(260)
1976	10.1	11.7	328
1977	11.2	10.9	163
1978	11.3	10.1	(205)
1979	10.7	8.9	(1,097)
1980	9.0	8.8	(1,710)
1981[a]	4.6	10.0	(287)
1981	9.6	9.1	(253)
1982	10.6	9.7	319
1983	11.4	9.7	587
1984	11.6	9.5	1,089

[a]Actual through June

Source: Wards Automotive Report, July 13, 1981 (Actual 1981 Sales data)
Company Report for Six Months Ended June 30, 1981 (Actual 1981 Income data)
Findings of the Chrysler Corporation Loan Guarantee Board, January 19, 1981 (Forecast Data)
Company Annual Reports
Wards Automotive Yearbooks
Standard & Poor's Industry Surveys, January 1981

Labor Both union and non-union labor agreed to forego raises or other monetary related employment benefits, such as cost of living allowances. This was particularly difficult in the case of the UAW which had completed negotiations with Chrysler on a new three year contract in the Fall, 1979. The Union did, however, forego certain of the benefits contained in that contract to achieve the targeted contribution.

Pension Deferral Although not an original funding source, Chrysler deferred pension contributions for one year until the succeeding year. The financing benefit of the deferral was allowed as a contribution in meeting the total requirements of the Act.

State and Local Governments Four states (Michigan, Indiana, Delaware and Illinois) approved loans to the company. The government of Canada and the province of Ontario contributed assistance to sustain Chrysler's Canadian operations.

Summary Exhibit 8 summarizes non-federally guaranteed assistance Chrysler received from its stakeholders along with the accruals through the time of the Third Takedown (January, 1981).

Exhibit 8   Non-federally guaranteed assistance ($ millions)

Assistance Category	Target	Approved			Accrued[a]	
		5/15/80	*7/10/80*	*1/15/81*	*7/80*	*1/81*
Lender	650	642	655	911	51	112
State/Local Gov't.	250	357	357	357	186	186
Suppliers	180	63	150	195	19	32
Asset Sales	300	628	730	730	224	333
Pension Deferral	0	342	342	342	182	271
Additional Equity	50	0	0	0	0	0
Other	227	0	0	0	0	0
Labor (Union)	463	463	463	1,370	139	245
Labor (Non-Union)	125	125	125			

[a]Section 8(b) of the Act limits the principal amount of loans guaranteed to the amount of non-federally guaranteed assistance which has actually accrued to the corporation through the date of the takedown.

Source: Findings of the Chrysler Corporation Loan Guarantee Board
(May 12, 1980 and January 19, 1981).
Report of the Chrysler Corporation Loan Guarantee Board (July 15, 1980).

The January, 1981, Financing Plan   Because sales were lower than had been expected when the initial loan guarantees were issued in June and July, 1980, a significant portion of the planned financial margin had been used or was expected to be used when the Third Takedown request was prepared in January 1981. The new operating plan provided details of additional non-federally guaranteed financing which had been obtained above the July plan and were not anticipated in any of the previous submissions. This financing is outlined in Exhibit 9, but the detail of the institutional lenders' concessions are of sufficient import to Chrysler to be presented below.

In accordance with an override agreement in effect with most of its institutional lenders, Chrysler restructured $1,109 million in debt on February 1, 1981. The terms of those agreements allowed conversion of $685.9 million in debt in two installments (February 27 and June 12, 1981) into Preferred Stock, with a redemption value of $1,097.4 million. Chrysler had an option to redeem most of the remainder ($623.1 million) at 30 cents cash on the dollar. This option was exercised on March 31 when $233.8 million was redeemed for $71.3 million. The debt restructure helped the cash flow situation substantially by eliminating fixed charges and converting debt to equity.

The new non-federally guaranteed assistance in Exhibit 9 also shows additional concessions from both union and non-union labor. The impact of all new assistance was spread through years 1981–85.

Exhibit 9   Non-federally guaranteed assistance (cash impact of actions in January 1981 plan not previously anticipated—$ millions)

Year	Reduced Planned Expenditures	Lender[a] Interest Concessions	Supplier Concessions	Employee Concessions	Fixed Manpower Other Reductions	Total New Concessions
1981	670	25	45	293	97	1,130
1982	603	58	—	490	35	1,186
1983	441	61	—	—	41	543
1984	354	56	—	—	44	454
1985	(180)	56	—	—	48	(76)

[a]The low end of the range estimating the cash impact of Lender interest concessions is indicated. In addition to the cash interest savings, Chrysler will avoid additional interest charges paid in notes instead of in cash 1981–85.

Source: Findings of the Chrysler Corporation Loan Guarantee Board (January 19, 1981)

PERFORMANCE SINCE LOAN GUARANTEE ISSUE

Critical Assumptions

Certain of the underlying assumptions were most critical to success of the recovery plan. All impacted on net profit.

Product Strategy   Chrysler stated an intention to remain a full-line producer of automobiles in the U.S. market, and resisted suggestions that it should specialize or find a particular product or market niche in which it could excel. The argument against specialization maintained that profit margins in a highly competitive small car market and the volume associated with specialty products were insufficient to sustain a major competitor. Additionally, increased industry concentration would accompany Chrysler's withdrawal from markets shared with General Motors and Ford. Chrysler later modified this position publicly but published product plans seemed to leave doubt that anything but full-line competition was intended.

Volume, Mix and Market Penetration   Volume is essential to achieve break-even and to recover the high capital investment characteristic of the auto industry. Chrysler's break-even volume for its entire North American operations was estimated at 2.61 million units in 1979 by the staff of the Chrysler Loan Guarantee Board. The break-even goal for 1983 in the same market was set at 1.65 million units. The criticalness of Chrysler's market penetration can be illustrated by the fact that a one percentage point variation in market share was estimated to produce a $200 million variation in annual income before taxes, based on 1980 volume and unit margins. The continued market acceptance of an increasingly heavier mix of fuel efficient autos accompanied by a switch to consumer buying of U.S. autos were important factors in Chrysler's plans to regain the market share levels lost in recent years. Maintenance of the existing dealer network as a sales and service outlet and contact with the consumer was also essential.

Variable Margin Improvement   Programmed efforts to increase the variable margin included better targeting of standard options and design of new ones taking advantage of technology (trip computers, electronic/digital instrumentation), product action (new styling, design, front-wheel drive), design cost reduction (value engineering), manufacturing efficiency through new production techniques and facilities (paint processes, robots), making rather than purchasing more components, improved warranty and quality control programs to decrease the incidence and necessity of recalls, purchasing programs to reduce material costs, and a better reading of market, consumer and environmental changes. Exhibit 10 indicates the desired Variable Margin Improvement in monetary terms per unit for these programs.

Fixed Cost Reduction   Reductions in manufacturing burden, general, administrative and sales expenses were targeted for completion by the end of 1981.

Cash Flow   The ability to fund operations and future programs involved increasing the revenue and accompanying profit margins, obtaining concessions from stakeholders and loan guarantees from the federal government.

Performance Measures

It was apparent from the critical assumptions that if Chrysler was to return to long term viability, its sales, income and market share would have to increase while capital ex-

Exhibit 10   Variable margin improvements by type of program (per unit, 1980–1984 model years)

Program	Amount per Unit
Product Action	$ 112
Options and Equipment Changes	91
Design Cost Reductions	126
Manufacturing Improvements	204
Component Insourcing	41
Warranty Improvements	67
Purchasing Programs	125
Market Demand Changes	(112)
Total Variable Margin Improvement	$ 654

Source: Report of the Chrysler Corporation Loan Guarantee Board (July 15, 1980).

penditures for new products and facilities were maintained at high levels. The company was required to periodically submit detailed operating and financial plans to the Loan Guarantee Board, and specific submissions were required to support requests to receive loan guarantees against the $1.5 billion authorized by the Act.

The following sections examine critical area forecasts made by the company in its plans submitted in support of its loan guarantee takedown requests of April and July, 1980, and January 1981. Forecasts of these performance indicators were the basis for the recovery plan.

Industry Sales Forecasts In each instance except the July/April, 1980 forecasts for 1983, Chrysler's forecasts were more optimistic than those of the independent forecasters. Another pattern shows the 1981 and 1982 forecasts made by both sources decreasing substantially as the year (1980) progressed due to the fact that performance did not live up to expectations.

Industry sales volume was of great significance to Chrysler and its forecasts were of central import to the recovery plan. In a shrinking or level sales volume market, the company could improve its share only at the expense of an industry competitor, most of whom were stronger than Chrysler. In an expanding market, concurrent growth for all, including Chrysler, was a possibility. (See Exhibit 11.)

Market Penetration An optimistic pattern of forecast market penetration similar to that found in the industry sales forecast was apparent. (See Exhibit 12.) The optimism was based on significant quality improvements, emphasis on front-wheel drive autos and a steady stream of new products. The K-car was the first of these and was to be followed by larger derivatives for entry in the basic middle market segment. A station wagon and a new sport specialty car were planned for 1982 and 1983, respectively.

Exhibit 11 U.S. car sales forecast (million units)

Date of Forecast	1980	1981	1982	1983	1984
April 1980					
Chrysler	9.8	11.0	12.1	10.8	—
Independent (Ave.)	9.7	10.1	10.9	11.4	—
July 1980					
Chrysler	8.8	11.0	12.1	10.8	11.7
Independent (Ave.)	8.8	9.4	10.4	11.4	11.5
January 1981					
Chrysler	9.0[a]	9.6	10.6	11.4	11.6
Independent (Ave.)	—	9.4	10.4	11.0	11.3

[a]Actual Note: Independent (Ave.) is a composite of several independent forecasts.

Source: Chrysler Corporation Loan Guarantee Board

Exhibit 12   Chrysler market share projection (percent)

Date of Forecast	1980	1981	1982	1983	1984
October 1979	10.2	11.1	11.6	11.9	—
April 1980	9.5	11.1	11.1	12.4	—
July 1980	10.1	11.1	11.1	12.4	11.3
January 1981	8.8[a]	9.1	9.7	9.7	9.5

[a]Actual

Source: Chrysler Corporation Loan Guarantee Board

Exhibit 13   Chrysler net income forecast ($ millions)

Date of Forecast	1980	1981	1982	1983	1984
April 1980	(781)	304	642	368	890
July 1980	(1,225)	78	508	21	482
January 1981	(1,710)[a]	(253)	320	587	1,089

[a]Actual

Source: Chrysler Coporation Loan Guarantee Board

Chrysler suggested that by the mid-1980s, fuel economy would no longer be the primary tool for product differentiation, as only small differences in economy would then exist among competing products. Instead, the passenger capacity would become more important to the consumer.

As can be seen, Chrysler's product and market penetration strategies depended heavily on introduction of new products which in turn depended on a steady stream of reliable financing. Again, growth in industry sales volume was extremely important to the recovery plan.

Net Income   The non-attainment of planned sales volume showed clearly in the revised net income forecasts prepared for successive loan guarantee takedown applications. (See Exhibit 13.) For reasons of unfavorable economic conditions and product non-acceptance, Chrysler's future outlook became progressively less favorable as 1980 progressed. This deterioration was a major factor in the company's decision to ask for a third takedown in December 1980. Actions taken by Chrysler to improve its cash flow and financial condition included the following:

- Decreased planned expenditures by $1,888 million between 1981 and 1985.
- Obtained an additional $622 million in concessions from the UAW.
- Negotiated $72 million in price and other concessions from suppliers.

- Reduced fixed manpower by 3,000.
- Sought infusion of capital through merger, joint venture or other means.

The impact of these actions on future product plans becomes apparent in the planned expenditure reductions outlined below.

Planned Expenditures In addition to the actions taken above, the company's situation required a critical analysis of new product development plans and programs. Cancellation and/or deferral of the following were under consideration to achieve the decreased levels of expenditure required in Exhibit 14.

- Cancel the 1985 A-body subcompact scheduled to replace the current L-body cars.
- Defer the 1982 K-premium 2-door to model year 1982 1/2.
- Defer the K-24 "sport model" introduction until 1983 1/2.
- Defer the 4-speed automatic transaxle from 1984 to 1988.
- Defer all capacity expansion plans involved with an additional front-wheel drive plant.

The questions of long-term competitive viability and market acceptance of its product line required the simultaneous evaluation of the impact of deferral/cancellation of product changes and new product introduction.

Booz, Allen, Hamilton, Management Consultants, stated in an Attachment to Chrysler's Third Takedown application that results of actions in the new plan gave the company a reasonable prospect of recovery. The Consultant cautioned that a basic assumption underlying that opinion was that unforeseen outside factors (e.g., abnormally high interest rates, disruption of oil supplies) would not hold back the recovery of the industry. Booz, Allen also commented that the major cash shortfall would occur in the First Quarter, 1981. (Chrysler successfully passed that milestone.) Nevertheless, another major caveat in the Consultant's opinion was that the company faced a major long term risk that its competitive position in the worldwide automotive industry might be impaired and that alternatives such as merger and joint venture should be examined.

Exhibit 14 Planned product and capital expenditures ($ millions)

Date of Forecast	1981	1982	1983	1984	1985	Total
October 1979	1,812	2,102	2,168	2,191	2,145	10,418
April 1980	1,459	1,896	2,006	1,658	1,314	8,333
July 1980	1,459	1,896	2,006	1,658	1,314	8,333
January 1981	789	1,293	1,565	1,304	1,494	6,445

Source: Chrysler Corporation Loan Guarantee Board

Exhibit 15   U.S. car dealers, 1979–1980

Dealer	**1979**	**1980**
Chrysler	4,434	3,834
Ford	6,582	6,053
General Motors	11,425	11,060
American Motors	2,317	2,154
Volkswagen of America	1,015	1,018

Source: Wards Automotive Yearbook, 1981

Dealer Network   Although not a specific forecast area, the retention of a healthy dealer network was essential to the revitalization of the company and was implicit in its recovery plans. Survival of the dealer network was contingent on the basic strength of the individual dealership, consumer acceptance of Chrysler products, support provided by the manufacturer and, in some instances, assistance provided by the Small Business Administration. In 1980, Chrysler lost 600 dealers. This loss was larger than that of any other U.S. auto maker as shown in Exhibit 15.

THE FUTURE

Thus, as 1981 enters its last months, Mr. Iacocca must solve not only the short term operating problems which threaten survival of the Chrysler Corporation, but must also plan for long term viability without additional federal loan guarantees after December 31, 1983. He must do so in an environment which finds Chrysler as the weakest of the full line manufacturers in an increasingly competitive industry. Issues of public policy, corporate strategy, financing, markets and marketing, product lines and labor relations are among the issues which must be addressed. Specifically:

- Chrysler has reduced its planned capital expenditures but survival and long term viability depend on new product introduction which requires enormous capital investment.

- The consumer image of Chrysler (and the entire industry) is largely negative, while the image of major foreign competitors is much more positive.

- Strong sentiment exists for the erection of trade barriers to protect the U.S. auto industry. Can the domestic automakers recover without such protection? Are the implications the same for Chrysler as they are for other domestic automakers?

- A continuing conflict will exist between the environmentalists and industries such as the auto industry. Both have socially acceptable goals but different perceptions of how they should be brought into consonance.

- A major responsibility of government is to ensure some certainty in the business environment. Regulation on one hand and assistance such as that provided Chrysler seem to present a basic conflict. What is the role of government in business? Protector? Helper? Decision-maker? Owner?

- A study of Economics points out many ills attendant to high industry concentration. Government's role is to regulate monopolies or near monopolies as a substitute for competition. In Chrysler's case, government kept the company in business, thereby keeping the auto industry concentration from increasing. Should the industry be allowed to become a monopoly and then regulated as a utility?

- Chrysler is a major defense contractor and the only large manufacturer of tanks for the U.S. Army in the country. Its non-automotive operations, which are mostly defense operations, produced an average of $700 million in annual revenue over the three-year period 1978–80. Merger with a foreign company is a possibility.

- Chrysler has rejected the partial line product niche which American Motors used as a successful survival strategy in the late 1950s.

- Labor was given a seat on Chrysler's Board of Directors in return for concessions. The future will require a changing definition of labor-management relations.

Participation of labor, government and management is essential to the satisfactory resolution of these and other issues contained in the Chrysler situation. How the players interact will determine the shape of the company and the structure of the industry of the future.

CASE 2

Playboy "C": The New PEI

JAMES M. HIGGINS
Rollins College

In May, 1982, Playboy Enterprises Incorporated, PEI, finds itself at a major crossroads in its history. PEI has been a conglomerate for over 15 years. It had profits of $14.4 million on $389 million in sales for the fiscal year ending June 30, 1981. At that time it held strategic interests in publishing, clubs, hotels, gambling, entertainment and

This case was written by James M. Higgins, Associate Professor of Management, The Roy E. Crummer Graduate School of Business, Rollins College, Winter Park, Florida, with the aid of graduate assistant, Cid Stoll. This case does not indicate effective or ineffective handling of an administrative situation. Rather, it is to be used for class discussion purposes. All rights reserved to the contributor. Reprinted by permission.

other areas. It now finds itself a restructured company, essentially a magazine publishing company. Perhaps most importantly, PEI finds itself with a new chief operating officer and president, Christie Hefner, 29, daughter of PEI founder Hugh Hefner. What happened to cause these tremendous changes?

During FY 1982 PEI was confronted with several major problems which resulted in significant changes. Due to legal difficulties, it was forced in the fall of 1981 to withdraw ownership from its major profitable operation, its casinos and betting shops in England. Another profitable operation, its flagship magazine *Playboy*, experienced both a decline in sales volume and a decline in the number of advertising pages at various times during calendar year 1981 continuing earlier trends. Its clubs were experiencing continued financial difficulties. The company had recently divested or closed nearly all of its hotels. And in April, 1982, the company found that its hoped for big profits from its new casino in Atlantic City, New Jersey, were not likely to materialize. The state of New Jersey had refused to grant Playboy a permanent gambling license in April of 1982, forcing PEI to sell its interest to its joint venture partner, Elsinore. The rest of 1982 promised to be a period of decision at PEI.

PLAYBOY—HEFNER'S INFLUENCE

In 1976 Hugh Hefner, primary owner and then chief executive officer (CEO) and chief operating office (COO), made what many consider to be his last major decision at Playboy Enterprises, Inc., that of placing Derick Daniels in charge of PEI as president and COO. Since then Hefner, who owns 70% of Playboy's stock and was still technically considered "the boss," became difficult to reach and all but retired. While he still personally oversaw the magazine operations, most notably the centerfold and cartoon pages, he had very little to do with the business end of PEI. Hefner's detachment led to some disgruntlement among certain top managers. Despite continued losses in several of its major divisions, Hefner managed to hold his empire together, even improving profits in the period of 1977–1981. As can be seen, earnings improved substantially from the rocky period of the early 1970s. Exhibits 1 and 2 to 4 contain major financial information for FY 1977–1981 and for FY 1979–1981 respectively.

THE PLAYBOY EMPIRE CHANGES

The principal components of the Playboy empire changed dramatically in FY 1982. At the end of FY 1981, the SBU's were magazine publishing, gaming, clubs and hotels, and other business. As of April 1982, hotels and gaming had disappeared as major components.

Magazine Publishing

The Playboy Magazine Publishing Group has had its problems. The principal money-maker of this group, *Playboy* magazine, dropped in circulation from about 6 million

Exhibit 1   Selected financial data for the years ended June 30 (in thousands except per-share amounts)

	1981	1980	1979	1978	1977
Net sales and revenues	$388,870	$363,190	$297,486	$246,746	$223,402
Net earnings	14,341	13,078	9,104	6,269	4,167
Total assets	291,895	320,481	255,668	218,258	181,815
Long-term financing obligations	18,806	19,633	21,244	16,185	16,271
Net earnings per common share					
Primary	1.45	1.31	.90	.65	.45
Fully diluted	1.45	1.31	.90	.62	.44
Cash dividends declared per common share	.12	.12	.12	.12	.12

Exhibit 2   Financial information relating to industry segments for years ended June 30 (in thousands)

	1981	1980	1979
Sales to Non-Affiliates			
Magazine publishing			
PLAYBOY magazine	$136,603	$144,145	$126,596
Other	19,845	17,803	14,150
Subtotal	156,448	161,948	140,746
Gaming			
Casinos	110,683	90,562	70,879
Betting shops	10,088	10,103	1,364
Subtotal	120,771	100,665	72,243
Clubs and hotels	60,331	62,582	60,161
Other businesses[3]	51,320	37,995	24,336
Total	$388,870	$363,190	$297,486
Earnings Before Income Taxes			
Magazine publishing[1]	$ 6,017	$ 14,744	$ 11,304
Gaming	39,793	31,196	34,926
Clubs and hotels[1,2]	(5,153)	(4,937)	(479)
Other businesses[3,4]	964	2,743	(6,311)
Equity in Atlantic City venture's undistributed loss	(1,024)	—	—
Gain on sale of OUI magazine	621	—	—
Corporate administration and promotion[1]	(18,948)	(18,458)	(15,743)
Interest, net	2,494	6,112	2,990
Foreign exchange gain (loss)	(332)	441	1,149
Other, net[4]	1,009	237	—
Total	$ 25,441	$ 32,078	$ 27,836

Exhibit 2 (continued)   Financial information relating to industry segments

	1981	1980	1979
Identifiable Assets			
Magazine publishing	$ 40,839	$ 38,680	$ 37,165
Gaming	47,201	54,106	23,548
Clubs and hotels	77,107	77,101	86,646
Other businesses	26,257	17,979	14,618
Corporate administration and promotion	64,245	107,896	82,010
Investment in Atlantic City venture	36,246	24,719	11,681
Total	$291,895	$320,481	$255,668
Depreciation and Amortization of Property, Plant and Equipment			
Magazine publishing	$ 306	$ 468	$ 532
Gaming	1,564	1,326	894
Clubs and hotels	3,695	3,867	3,419
Other businesses	627	237	265
Corporate administration and promotion	985	1,065	1,117
Total	$ 7,177	$ 6,963	$ 6,227
Capital Expenditures			
Magazine publishing	$ 501	$ 342	$ 424
Gaming	1,914	5,690	1,579
Clubs and hotels	3,894	4,497	1,805
Other businesses	4,169	2,636	428
Corporate administration and promotion	948	641	1,827
Total	$ 11,426	$ 13,806	$ 6,063

[1] During fiscal 1981, a more comprehensive method of allocating costs and expenses incurred for the benefit of operating segments was developed to upgrade the company's reporting system. The effect of the revised allocation in fiscal 1981 was to decrease corporate administration and promotion expense by approximately $1,100,000, decrease Clubs and Hotels earnings before income taxes by $1,800,000, and increase Magazine Publishing's earnings before income taxes by $700,000. The effect of the revised allocation method on the other industry segments was not significant.

[2] In February 1980, the company ceased operating the Towers Hotel in Chicago. The figures shown on the previous page for Clubs and Hotels include the operating losses of the hotel which approximated $884,000 and $1,222,000 for fiscal years 1980 and 1979, respectively.

[3] Sales to non-affiliates and earnings before income taxes include write-downs relating to estimates made in the company's book publishing operations of $3,100,000 and $5,700,000, respectively, for fiscal 1979. In fiscal 1981, $2,116,000 of these write-downs were reversed, increasing sales and earnings before income taxes by that amount.

[4] During fiscal 1980, as a result of a change in the estimated future benefits of costs related to the promotion of Book Club memberships, the company changed its method of accounting for such costs from the deferral method to the expense-as-incurred method. The amount of such costs that was deferred at June 30, 1979, and subsequently expensed in fiscal 1980, was $1,351,000.

copies per month in 1975 to 5.2 million copies per month in 1981. Operating earnings from magazine publishing fell more than 50% during fiscal 1981 to $6 million. *Games* magazine acquired in 1978, has yet to live up to its promise. *Oui* magazine, Playboy's foreign counterpart, was sold in June, 1981, due to continuing poor performance.

To combat the falling revenues, new magazine ventures have been and are being initiated. PEI has published a men's fashion guide that will probably become a monthly

Exhibit 2 (continued)   Financial information by geographic area for years ended June 30 (in thousands)

	1981	1980	1979
Sales to Non-Affiliates			
United States[1]	$266,627	$262,014	$225,025
United Kingdom	112,370	89,109	64,768
Other geographic areas	9,873	12,067	7,693
Total	$388,870	$363,190	$297,486
Earnings Before Income Taxes			
United States[1]	$ 890	$ 15,309	$ 4,535
United Kingdom	40,357	30,756	35,275
Other geographic areas	374	(2,319)	(370)
Equity in Atlantic City venture's undistributed loss	(1,024)	—	—
Gain on sale of OUI magazine	621	—	—
Corporate administration and promotion	(18,948)	(18,458)	(15,743)
Interest, net	2,494	6,112	2,990
Foreign exchange gain (loss)	(332)	441	1,149
Other, net[3]	1,009	237	—
Total	$ 25,441	$ 32,078	$ 27,836
Identifiable Assets[2]			
United States	$143,509	$133,607	$133,997
United Kingdom	46,345	52,427	22,655
Other geographic areas	1,550	1,832	5,325
Corporate administration and promotion	64,245	107,896	82,010
Investment in Atlantic City venture	36,246	24,719	11,681
Total	$291,895	$320,481	$255,668

[1] Sales to non-affiliates and earnings before income taxes include write-downs relating to estimates made in the company's book publishing operations of $3,100,000 and $5,700,000, respectively, for 1979. In fiscal 1981, $2,116,000 of these write-downs were reversed, increasing sales and earnings before income taxes by that amount.

[2] Cash and short-term interest-bearing deposits, working capital and total assets held in areas outside of the United States were $40,982,000, $12,802,000 and $94,515,000, respectively, at June 30, 1981; $62,831,000, $1,944,000 and $108,658,000, respectively, at June 30, 1980; and $64,272,000, $27,691,000, and $86,519,000, respectively, at June 30, 1979.

[3] During fiscal 1980, as a result of a change in the estimated future benefits of costs related to the promotion of Book Club memberships, the company changed its method of accounting for such costs from the deferral method to the expense-as-incurred method. The amount of such costs that were deferred at June 30, 1979, and subsequently expensed in fiscal 1980, was $1,351,000.

offering based on the popularity of the first issues. In addition, several other guides are in the works, including issues devoted to travel, food, wine, and photography.

Clubs and Hotels

At the end of FY 1981, PEI maintained 10 clubs in various population centers of the U.S., such as Chicago, St. Petersburg, and L.A.; 5 foreign clubs, such as in Tokyo; and two hotels. Ten of the 15 clubs are franchised. This division of PEI has been unprofitable for years and clubs have been closed and hotels sold or closed to reduce their losses. The Jamaica hotel was closed in 1979. The Chicago hotel was closed in 1980. The clubs and hotels division lost $5 million during FY 1981 due largely to a drop in the number of keyholders and lower club usage rates and the losses sustained by its remaining company-owned resorts. On November 20, 1981, an agreement was reached in principle to sell the Lake Geneva (Wisconsin), and Great Gorge (New Jersey) hotels to a joint venture for $42,000,000.

Gaming

While the domestic clubs and resorts were losing money, the foreign gaming clubs in Manchester, Portsmouth and London, England, had become quite successful. In FY 1981, the company's gaming operations were responsible for 87% of the company's operating income.

PEI's gaming operation had been successful from the start and PEI expanded their Playboy Club operations in England in 1972 acquiring the Clermont Club and in 1979, acquiring Norwich Company and its associated gaming interests. They also leased and then ran a casino operation in the Bahamas beginning in 1978. But in FY 1982, a crisis struck the gaming SBU.

In early 1981, legal problems occurred in the London Casinos. Playboy was alleged to have engaged in several credit irregularities, including illegally discounting debts and extending credit to gamblers who had "stiffed" other London casinos with bad checks. Eventually Playboy lost its operating license in England and the casinos had to be sold. Agreement was reached on November 3, 1981 to sell British gaming interests to Trident Television, Ltd. for $31,400,000. Based on certain asset transfers, as much as $50 million in cash may flow to PEI from this sale.

Worse though, Playboy's casino in Atlantic City, a hoped-for money maker, ran into serious difficulties in the fall of 1981.

For a while it looked as if Playboy might lose its gambling license in New Jersey strictly because of its problems in England. These problems resulted in the termination of PEI's long-time gambling operations chief executive, Victor Lownes, and later resulted in the "leaves of absence" of four Playboy executives involved with Playboy's New Jersey venture. Finally, after many hours of discussion and several major changes in operations by Playboy, New Jersey allowed PEI to keep its temporary gambling license with another review due in April 1982. A discussion of the New Jersey situation occurs in much greater detail later in the case.

Other Businesses

This PEI SBU includes the movie and television, and records divisions.

Playboy's recording studios have all but closed except to produce special projects for Hefner. The future of Playboy Productions (movies and TV) is uncertain although TV seems to be the central focus. Costly movies were being avoided in order to focus efforts on producing TV scripts and pilot series for consideration by the TV networks.

Exhibit 3 Playboy Enterprises, Inc., and subsidiaries consolidated balance sheets as of June 30, 1981 and 1980 (in thousands)

	1981	1980
Assets		
Cash	$ 12,174	$ 7,529
Short-term investments at cost, which approximates market	28,677	63,830
Receivables	29,390	31,055
Inventories	26,284	24,550
Recoverable income taxes	12,666	27,264
Prepaid Expenses	8,639	5,152
Total current assets	117,830	159,380
Property, plant and equipment		
Land	4,836	4,836
Buildings and improvements	73,357	73,076
Furniture and equipment	41,004	35,104
Leasehold improvements	14,391	11,501
Capitalized leases	5,510	5,473
	139,098	129,990
Less accumulated depreciation and amortization	52,620	46,429
	86,478	83,561
Investment in Atlantic City	36,246	24,719
Excess cost over net assets of acquired subsidiaries	19,525	19,508
Deferred charges	20,413	21,483
Other assets	11,403	11,830
Total Assets	$291,895	$320,481
Liabilities		
Current financing obligations	$ 13,010	$ 14,792
Accounts payable	24,546	25,958
Accrued expenses	19,933	18,062
Income taxes		
Currently payable	22,581	45,384
Deferred	88	9,430
Total current liabilities	80,158	113,626
Long-term financing obligations	18,806	19,633
Deferred income	47,973	52,516
Non-current and deferred income taxes	17,883	22,749
Commitments and contingencies		
Shareholders' Equity		
Common stock, $1 par value, 15,000,000 shares authorized, 10,063,799 and 9,601,769 issued at June 30, 1981 and 1980, respectively	10,064	9,602
Capital in excess of par value	14,616	13,042
Retained earnings	103,798	90,618
	128,478	113,262
Less cost of 201,701 and 195,000 shares in treasury at June 30, 1981 and 1980, respectively	1,403	1,305
	127,075	111,957
Total Liabilities and Shareholders' Equity	$291,895	$320,481

In addition, PEI has been investigating the cable TV and pay TV fields hoping to produce a late night "Playboy Magazine of the Air." Such a series would include nude photo sessions, in-depth interviews and other features that would parallel the printed magazine. PEI is investing heavily in this joint venture.

Keeping with the diversification preferred by Hefner, PEI has several other divisions. There is the Playboy Foundation; the Sales Division which handles a multitude of items carrying the bunny emblem; and other subsidiaries ranging from modeling agencies to insurance marketing. Recently PEI licensed a Pillsbury Co. unit to market cake pans shaped like the rabbit head mascot of the company.

PUBLICITY PROBLEMS

Problems seemed to compound in 1980, 1981 and 1982 as the company experienced a siege of additional bad publicity. In early 1980 the Securities and Exchange Commission charged Hefner with violating federal securities laws by failing to disclose use of the Chicago and Los Angeles Playboy mansions for personal entertainment. Later in the year, an audit committee of Playboy's Board of Directors prompted Hefner to return almost $1 million to Playboy as payment for use of the mansions and other company "perquisites." In 1981, Dorothy Stratten, 1980's Playmate of the Year, was murdered by her manager and husband.

THE PLAYBOY CASINO, ATLANTIC CITY, N.J.

Atlantic City is one of the largest seaside resorts in the world. It lies on the southeast coast of New Jersey, approximately 140 miles south of New York City. Atlantic City is a fairly small town, run down in parts, and populated mostly by those people who operate the establishments on its boardwalk.

The famous boardwalk stretches for about seven miles along the ocean. It is 60 feet wide and on either side can be found a multitude of different shops, theatres, restaurants, and hotels. The boardwalk is open year round. With over 16 million people visiting Atlantic City each year, tourism is the major industry.

In 1976 the officers of the city passed legislation to allow gambling along its boardwalk. A building boom started as Vegas clubs and companies raced to capture the East Coast gambling market. However, land was, and still is, very scarce and expensive. Most of the real estate along the boardwalk is in small, privately owned parcels, making it necessary for prospective casino owners to make several purchases, often with ten or more land owners, in order to secure enough land on which to build their club. Once the land was purchased, a race began. Each company wanted to have the first completed casino to establish a dominant share of the market. This "race to the finish" caused construction companies to raise their prices as deadlines were shortened. Even though many of the casinos are complete in 1982 and in operation, there have been recent reports stating that runaway construction costs are still prevalent.

Market Potential

From reports given by Bally, Caesars, and Resorts International, the companies which opened the first three casinos on the boardwalk in 1978, the East Coast apparently has a large and unsatisfied appetite for casino gambling. In March 1980, the average gross per day was $600,000, almost double that of the Las Vegas gambling strip. While any casino opening after 1981 will have smaller sales figures than the original three, there is substantial evidence that new casinos could eventually do quite well. The eastern gambling market is developing slowly but surely as more and more people from the nearby population centers of New York and Philadelphia begin to discover that they can get the same thrill of gambling and the same good service in New Jersey that they can in Nevada.

However, there could be a problem if too many developers try to take advantage of the eastern casino market. While initial demand was heavy, a single casino's share of the market will drop as competition increases. In fact, some sources reported that over half of the casinos in Atlantic City lost money in 1981. There are geographical problems. Atlantic City has far less room to grow than its western counterpart, Las Vegas. It remains to be seen whether the city, with its limited accommodations, will attract as many visitors to the East Coast as Las Vegas has attracted tourists to Nevada. And, Atlantic City is somewhat geographically remote from major cities.

Another consideration in the New Jersey market is that so far most of the gamblers frequenting the casinos in Atlantic City are from blue collar occupations. There have been far fewer of the rich, sophisticated gamers than had been expected.

Playboy Casino—Site and Building

Seeing the tremendous potential in Atlantic City and given their successes in casinos in England, PEI decided to move swiftly into this market. Buying property in Atlantic City was the first priority in the Playboy Casino venture, and PEI executives began looking for a suitable building site in November 1976. The company made an unusual choice, purchasing a small parcel of land that lay between the Boardwalk, the Atlantic City Convention Center and the street. The parcel was unusually small, only three-fourths of an acre of land, compared with up to eight acre lots used by other casino developers. However, the site was near the convention center and there was only one owner with which to contend.

After the sale was complete, the search for the "perfect building" began. Because of a New Jersey law requiring that even a small casino be attached to a 500 room hotel, some creative designing was needed. PEI's architect, Martin Stern & Associates, came up with a unique, 3-tiered casino that was to be part of a towering 30-story structure. This casino/hotel was the first completely new hotel on the Boardwalk in 30 years, and Playboy wanted it to be spectacular.

However, several governmental approvals were necessary before the construction of the building could begin. The Atlantic City Planning Board had to give its approval, and since the site was located on beachfront property, the state environmental agency also had to give its approval. In addition, the New Jersey Casino Control Commission had books full of regulations that had to be met. Playboy seemed to have everyone's approval by mid-1977, when the Federal Aviation Agency closed down the project saying it was too close to the airport to erect a 30-story building. The plans had to be revamped and a mad rush was on to acquire additional land. A one acre parcel of land was found that would allow Playboy to build an adjacent structure that would connect itself to the first parcel by a ramp. This violated a Commission rule and Playboy had to obtain special permission to construct a 2-structure hotel/casino.

The new plans were approved and Playboy began dealing for the land. This new parcel was not as easy to buy as the first had been because it had nine separate owners. Playboy needed extra funds to secure the land, but a state loan was blocked because one of the titleholders of the acre was the state of New Jersey itself. A private investor was finally located and the land deal was closed just one day before the option on the land ended. The construction of the casino finally began in early 1980.

Financing the New Jersey Operation

When PEI began the Atlantic City venture, the casino was given a $50 million budget estimate. Due to delays, soaring costs and additional needs, however, this estimate more than doubled. A total of $7 million was spent for land, including $2 million for additional land that had to be purchased to appease the FAA. Not included in this amount is another $1.1 million that Playboy had to pay to the state of New Jersey in order to gain clear title to its extra acre.

The initial and redrawn plans added a cost of $2 million, and staff and legal expenses added over $300,000 per month to the total; all in addition to the actual construction costs of the building itself.

It became obvious Playboy would need help financing this project, but loans for casinos were difficult to obtain. Lenders are generally reluctant to get involved in casinos, with only 29% of all financial institutions willing to lend money for this purpose. When PEI needed additional funds for its revamped and larger casino it began looking for private investors. What it found was Elsinore Corporation.

Elsinore is a subsidiary of the Hyatt Corporation, and was spun off as a part of an action under which Hyatt went private. The company is a gaming company, 27.5% owned by the Chicago Pritzaker family. Elsinore has its own casino in Las Vegas and management was looking for a link that would get them into the Atlantic City casino business. The price and location of the Playboy casino was attractive and in December 1978 the two companies agreed on a joint venture. In March 1979, a $45 million loan agreement was secured with a Chicago bank and Playboy was able to keep the casino project alive.

The final total for the Atlantic City project has been cited as $135 million, over 2-1/2 times the original estimate. Playboy reportedly invested perhaps as much as $60 million by early 1982 in this venture, almost half of its total equity. (See Exhibits for other information.)

Exhibit 4 Playboy Enterprises, Inc., and subsidiaries consolidated statements of changes in financial position for the years ended June 30 (in thousands)

	1981	1980	1979
Source of Working Capital			
Operations:			
Net earnings	$ 14,341	$13,078	$ 9,104
Add (deduct) items not affecting working capital:			
Deferred income, net of deferred charges	(842)	6,264	10,506
Depreciation and amortization	8,923	8,542	7,327
Noncurrent and deferred income taxes	(4,866)	11,407	95
Equity in Atlantic City Venture's undistributed loss	1,024		
Gain on sale of OUI magazine	(621)		
Other	(1,733)	259	404
Working capital provided from operations	16,226	39,550	27,436
Issuance of stock	1,938	382	493
Sale of time-sharing receivables		4,231	6,000
Decrease in time-sharing receivables	103	996	—
Sale of leasehold interest and other property, plant and equipment	1,114	8,070	—
Additional long-term financing	15,196	13,183	—
Other	872	1,030	1,102
Total sources of working capital	35,449	67,442	35,031
Application of Working Capital			
Additions to property, plant and equipment	11,426	9,777	6,063
Additions to the Atlantic City project	12,840	12,894	7,219
Acquisition of Norwich Enterprises, Ltd., net of working capital	—	23,057	—
Increase in time-sharing receivables	—	—	4,292
Acquisition of GAMES magazine, net of working capital	—	—	2,369
Reduction of long-term financing	14,884	12,857	605
Payment of cash dividends	1,161	1,124	1,113
Other	3,220	3,462	2,632
Total uses of working capital	43,531	63,171	24,293
Increase (decrease) in working capital	$(8,082)	$ 4,271	$10,738
Changes in Working Capital Components			
Cash and short-term investments	$(30,508)	$ 6,950	$16,115
Receivables	(1,665)	6,469	4,803
Inventories	1,734	3,932	(1,168)
Recoverable income taxes	(14,598)	27,264	—
Prepaid expenses	3,487	(1,227)	(1,905)
Current financing obligations	1,782	(8,470)	13,243
Accounts payable and accrued expenses	(459)	(5,129)	(8,944)
Income taxes payable	32,145	(25,518)	(11,406)
Increase (decrease) in working capital	$ (8,082)	$ 4,271	$10,738

Regulation in Atlantic City

The New Jersey Casino Control Commission (CCC) coordinates and enforces the state's gambling regulations, and is known as a very strict agency. Dozens of requirements are centered around the layout of the gambling rooms and the types of equipment used throughout the casino. There are strict licensing procedures on agents arranging travel packages to the casino, restrictions on gaming advertising, and a ban on extending credit lines to guests before arrival and clearance in Atlantic City. Adding to the already strict regulations in 1981 and 1982 was the Abscam incident which implicated eight Congressmen as possible bribe takers. The CCC was also linked to the scandal and this has caused the Commission to become extremely thorough in its duties, in an attempt to reclaim a "tough but honest" reputation.

A casino opening night ritual is run by the CCC in order to test security, dealer proficiency and credit control. During this ritual gamblers with fake money descend upon the casino's dealers and other staff, confronting them with more "sticky situations" in one night than they are likely to encounter in a year.

As noted before, PEI's early problems with the CCC were due largely to the procedural questions regarding credit regulations which had been raised in the London casinos. These troubles in England led to problems in New Jersey. In April 1981 the CCC granted Playboy a temporary license for its casino provided four top executives involved in the London scandal took leaves of absence. This trade-off was agreed to by PEI, and a senior vice-president, the vice-president of Atlantic City casino operations, the executive vice-president in charge of resorts and casinos, and the director of casino operations in Atlantic City took temporary but indefinite leaves. Problems in England continued and by November 1981, the British casinos had been sold. This crisis with the London casinos had a direct effect on the Atlantic City operation both in terms of strict United States regulation and close monitoring by the CCC, and in terms of the increasingly desperate need for Atlantic City to be profitable.

Competition

Playboy's casino (officially opened for business on April 14, 1981) was the seventh casino to open on the Boardwalk since May 1978, and two more followed closely behind. Resorts International was the first casino to open and thus has the most loyal following, and the Golden Nugget with its aggressive marketing techniques and unique decor has shown the highest profitability.

Profit margins for all casinos in general have been weak, however, and some casino projects have been dropped by their investors. Two major factors contributed to these low profits: too much competition and too few employees. Since the opening of the first three casinos in 1978, all of the establishments have been trying to hook the "jet set" crowd, and there just are not enough high stakes gamblers to go around. Even the rich only have so much time and money to spend gambling. A secondary problem is staffing. In order to find high quality dealers and other employees, each new casino makes its bid to try and lure employees away from jobs with established clubs. This hurts both the casino losing the employee and the casino gaining the employee. The "loser" is minus one or more experienced people and must "make do" until new employees can be found or trained, giving customers less than top-notch service during the interim. The "winner," on the other hand, must present an irresistible salary and benefits package in order to lure the employee away, and this leads to increased operating expenses with no sure guarantee of increased revenue.

Playboy held one distinct advantage over the competition—its notoriety. After the Coca-Cola trademark, the bunny symbol is the best-known logo in the world. A bunny sign can be put on a casino roof and give the establishment instant market identification. Also notable are the "real" Bunnies—those women acting as dealers, bartenders, waitresses, and coat checkers. More than one competitor has remarked that casino Bunnies will be hard to beat. Apparently it is felt that anyone who seriously gambles is going to enjoy it more with Bunnies as dealers.

PEI not only had external competitors to watch out for; Playboy was also originally competing against itself. The company-owned club in Great Gorge, New Jersey would lose customers to the casino.

Strategies

PEI counted heavily on a profit in Atlantic City in order to keep the other facets of the company operating. Hefner wished to keep Playboy a diversified company, with interests in several different industries. Without a casino operation, however, President and former COO Daniels (resigned May, 1982) remarked that PEI could, once again, turn into nothing but a privately owned magazine.

Initial Playboy Strategies

In order to attain the high profits needed from Atlantic City, PEI put almost everything else on a "back burner" and concentrated on the operation and promotion of the New Jersey casino. Daniels' initial strategy was to aim for the international high rollers, those professional gamblers with a lot of money and time to gamble. Daniels wanted to stake out the high end of the market by appealing to the "jet set." This approach had worked to Playboy's advantage in England and Daniels felt it would work in Atlantic City as well.

Daniels also tried to put together air package deals in order to better attract gamblers from distant U.S. and foreign cities. The Casino Control Commission of New Jersey has put a damper on this idea by banning air junkets unless they can see and approve passenger lists 15 days in advance.

Another initial strategy was that of promoting the New Jersey casino to *Playboy* subscribers and club keyholders. This, too, was controlled by commission regulations regarding such things as advance credit to keyholders or special deals for subscribers.

Later Strategies (late 1981—early 1982)

After the first few months of Playboy's casino operations in Atlantic City, their profits seemed to call for a re-evaluation of the initial operating and marketing strategies used. Derek Daniels called for the following strategy updates:

1. Broaden Playboy casino's advertising approach to reach more of the mass market and take away the impression that the casino caters only to the upper income brackets. This plan seems to be working well at the more profitable casinos such as Golden Nugget.
2. Redesign the layout of the casino so it becomes a little more traditional and a little less unique.
3. Increase transportation programs (such as bus shuttles) to encourage blue collar and middle class gamblers to come to Atlantic City from New York City and Philadelphia.
4. Capitalize more on the Playboy name and mystique.

Misfortune Strikes Again

But Playboy may not have been meant to own a casino in New Jersey. Citing a 20-year-old incident involving Hefner's efforts to obtain a New York liquor license, the New Jersey CCC refused PEI a permanent gambling license in April, 1982 for its Atlantic City project. The only alternative to losing the license was for Hefner to divert his 70% stock interest in PEI. According to provisions in the joint venture agreement, Elsinore must purchase PEI's share of the joint venture if the license is refused. Exhibit 5 contains information on the pertinent provisions.

THE FUTURE AT PEI

Christie Hefner joined Playboy in 1975, after graduating summa cum laude from Brandeis University. She moved to the vice-president level of the firm in 1980, where she developed the highly successful guide series. Derick J. Daniels, who trained Christie for her eventual presidency, declares, "She's ready." Christie and PEI have some $100 million to spend on restructuring PEI as the result of recent divestments. One of her first purchases may be *Savvy*, a two-year-old feminist magazine devoted to the young career woman. First, she has to stop a flow of red ink. PEI lost $7.7 million on operations on sales of $120 million for the first half of 1982.

Exhibit 5 Portion of Note D from 1981 annual statement: Atlantic City project

The company, through various intermediate entities, holds a 45.74 percent interest in a Venture to construct, own and operate a 500-room hotel/casino on the Boardwalk in Atlantic City. The Venture is a general partnership known as Playboy-Elsinore Associates. The other principal partner in the Venture, who also holds a 45.74 percent interest, is Elsub Corporation ("Elsub"), which is a wholly owned subsidiary of Elsinore Corporation ("Elsinore").

The Venture's total assets at June 30, 1981 are $159,305,000 and its net loss for the period from opening through June 30, 1981 was $4,152,000. The company's investment in the Venture at June 30 is comprised of the following (in thousands):

	1981	1980
Partner's equity account	$ 10	$ 10
Loans to the Venture and interest accrued thereon	30,960	20,211
Capitalization of other company costs	6,300	4,498
Equity in Venture's undistributed loss	(1,024)	—
	$36,246	$24,719

Although Elsinore would be required to purchase the company's interest in the hotel/casino in the event that the company does not obtain a permanent license, the company could nevertheless incur substantial losses. In addition to possible losses from the sale of its investment in the joint venture, the company could be required to write off the approximately $6,300,000 of other capitalized costs related to the hotel/casino. However, if the company were determined to be eligible for licensing in New Jersey within three years after an initial denial of a permanent license, the company would have the right to repurchase its interest from Elsinore on terms that would substantially restore it to the position it would have had if it had not been declared ineligible.

Total Project Costs of the Venture, including construction, furnishings, and financing costs, are now budgeted to be $135,000,000 or more. An additional budget of $15,000,000 has been provisionally established for working capital to cover items including pre-opening and opening expenses. A final tabulation of project costs will be made as soon as the remaining minor portion of construction activities is completed, and the related litigation discussed in Note L is concluded.

REFERENCES

Alsop, R. "Reckless Gamblers Who Know Fear of Mob Playboy Casino." *Wall Street Journal.* April 10, 1981.

———. "Boss's Daughter." *Fortune.* May 31, 1982, p. 11.

Blum, D. "Pajama Game: Playboy Chief Hefner Devotes Little Time to His Company Now." *Wall Street Journal.* April 7, 1981.

Kornbluth, J. "The Education of Christie Hefner." *Savvy* (March 1980) pp. 15–22.

———. "Licenses Lifted: Playboy's Threatened Profits." *Fortune.* November 2, 1981: p. 8.

Minsky. T. "Playboy Could Meet Only Fraction of Costs If It Loses Profitable Casino Operations." *Wall Street Journal.* October 7, 1981, p. 8.

———. "Playboy Casino Gets Permit; Test Gaming May Begin Tomorrow." *Wall Street Journal.* April 9, 1981.

————. "Playboy Casino in Atlantic City Receives Permit As 4 Officers Agree To Take Leaves." *Wall Street Journal.* April 6, 1981.

————. "Playboy's Risky Bet on Atlantic City Gambling." *Business Week.* March 16, 1981, pp. 154, 157.

————. "Playboy's Wider Net in Atlantic City." *Business Week.* August 24, 1981; p. 32.

Rout, L. "High-Stakes Race: Playboy's Work on Atlantic City Casino Is More Hurdle Race than Sprint to Gold." *Wall Street Journal.* April 15, 1980, p. 48.

"Playboy Agrees to Shed Its Stake in Casino, Asks New Jersey to Accept Escrow Proposal." *Wall Street Journal.* April 14, 1982, p. 4.

CASE 3

Kitchen Made Pies

JAMES J. CHRISMAN
University of South Carolina

FRED L. FRY
Bradley University

As 1982 approached, Paul Dubicki, owner and president of Kitchen Made Pies, realized something needed to be done to strengthen his company's competitive market position. Company sales had stagnated since 1975, and the firm was about to suffer its fourth straight year of losses. Competitive forces were strong, the local economy was in bad shape, and Kitchen Made was experiencing a number of difficulties with a big customer and with its bank financing. To further compound things, the firm's financial condition had deteriorated to the point where options for turning the situation around were limited. Nonetheless, Mr. Dubicki was dedicated to returning his business to profitability and, in fact, was confident that the task could be accomplished if he could only get enough relief from the press of day-to-day decision making to attend to the company's future direction and strategy.

In commenting on the current situation at Kitchen Made, Mr. Dubicki emphasized volume as the key to the company's success: "We must increase our customer base, and we must somehow encourage our present distributors to provide the promotional support retailers need to sell our products. One well-publicized special can sell more pies in one day than can be sold in a normal week without one. That's what I'd like to concentrate on, but every day something else comes up around here."

COMPANY HISTORY

Kitchen Made Pies produced a wide variety of pies and other bakery products for distribution in the Midwest. Its offices and baking facilities were all located at a single site in Peoria, Illinois. The firm was founded in the 1950s by Frank Dubicki, Paul's father, and was run like most family businesses.

As a youngster, Paul Dubicki often worked at odd jobs in the plant, but he was not really very interested in the family's baking enterprise. After leaving the business for a while to pursue other activities, Paul returned to the company in 1968 and later became, along with David Dubicki, a minority stockholder. During this time, he often found himself frustrated by the never-ending details associated with the operational and administrative aspects of the business. In 1981, however, Paul became owner-manager of the business. Earlier that year, the elder Dubicki had been persuaded to sell out, though he did retain ownership of the company's land and facilities. The sale took the form of a redemption of Frank Dubicki's stock by the corporation and an elimination of his debt to the corporation. During the same period, David exited from the business leaving Paul as the sole owner.

Upon assuming control, Paul immediately set about changing and updating the firm's operations and, for the first time in the firm's recent history, made a commitment to devote top-management time (mainly his) to charting a course and strategy for the company. Unfortunately, at the same time, problems building up over a long period of time began to surface, and Paul's commitment to his role as chief entrepreneur took a backseat to wrestling with daily operations.

Exhibit 1   Pie categories at Kitchen Made Pies

4-Inch	*8-Inch*	*9-Inch*	*Other*
Apple	Apple	Apple	Shortcake
Pineapple	Applecrumb	Applecrumb	10-inch cakes
Cherry	Peach	Peach	
Blackberry	Pineapple	Pineapple	8-inch cakes
Lemon	Lemon	Blackberry	Sheet cakes
Coconut	Coconut	Black Raspberry	
Chocolate	Chocolate	Walnut	
Peach	Black Raspberry	Cherry	
	Pumpkin	Lemon Meringue	
	Cherry	Coconut Meringue	
	High-Top Meringues	Chocolate Meringue	
	Regular Meringues	Banana Meringue	
		Pumpkin	
		Chocolate Boston	
		Boston	
		Lemon Whip	
		Coconut Whip	
		Chocolate Whip	
		Banana Whip	
		Pumpkin Whip	

PRODUCT LINE

Kitchen Made Pies makes a full line of pies, some on a regular basis, some seasonally, and a much more limited variety of cakes. Exhibit 1 lists all major sizes and flavors of pies currently produced by Kitchen Made, as well as the cake products which the firm makes.

Kitchen Made sells both fresh and frozen pies, though the former is preferred due to better turnover and more predictable ordering on the part of the customers. Another problem restricting frozen pie sales is limited freezer space. Kitchen Made can currently freeze and store only 3,500 pies per day.

Kitchen Made takes pride in its long-standing use of only the highest-quality ingredients in its products. Many customers have reported that Kitchen Made pies are better than competitors' products. However, Kitchen Made's emphasis on quality results in its pies being priced above competitors' products. Mr. Dubicki views the quality of Kitchen Made's pies as a major strength, especially to maintain repeat business. Still, he concedes that many buyers are price conscious and select lower-priced pies over Kitchen Made's products. On balance, though, Mr. Dubicki believes quality counts for more than lower price insofar as his company's business is concerned.

MARKETS/CUSTOMERS

The majority of Kitchen Made's sales are to food/baker distributors who basically supply two major market segments. The first is the institutional segment which consists of restaurants, as well as university, hospital, corporate, and government cafeterias. The second is the retail segment which includes supermarkets and convenience food store outlets. The institutional segment accounts for the majority of Kitchen Made's cake and 9-inch pie sales, while sales to the retail segment are mainly comprised of 4-inch and 8-inch pies. Most distributors concentrate on one market segment or the other, thus determining the type of products they buy. Buying motives for both markets vary depending upon the customer and market area involved. Kitchen Made's distributors report that some of their institutional customers are very price conscious in their selection among pies and brands. However, restaurant users are usually quality conscious, and many grocers, while price and quality conscious, are quite concerned about having strong promotional support for the brands they choose to stock (to help achieve high turnover and shelf space productivity).

Most of the Kitchen Made's products are sold in the Peoria and St. Louis areas, but the firm also services customers in other parts of Missouri and Illinois, as well as in Iowa and Wisconsin. Major distributors of Kitchen Made products, as well as their served markets, are included in Exhibit 2.

Besides the differences in buying motives and the type of products purchased by the two end markets, there are several other distinguishing features which differentiate them from each other. Institutional users frequently prefer frozen pies, partly because of their tendency to buy supplies on a monthly basis and partly because of the lower risk of spoilage. On the other hand, in the grocery business, where purchases are made weekly or bi-monthly, the economics favors fresh pies because they can be put directly on the shelf, they do not require more expensive freezer storage, and handling costs are lower—although there is greater risk that the products will lose their freshness before they are sold to shoppers. Generally, fresh pies sell best in the those supermarkets with in-store bakeries because of the "freshness" connotation perceived by shoppers.

Unlike institutional users, grocery retailers depend heavily upon promotional assistance for sales. One reason Dean's Distributing has become a less important customer for Kitchen Made is because of its policy of not offering grocers promotional support. As a result, Dean's and Kitchen Made (as Dean's supplier) have lost much of the retail grocer business in recent years in the Peoria areas. Today, most of Dean's pie distribution business done in the Peoria vicinity, as well as in other markets, is institutional.

Some distributors sell to grocers on a guaranteed basis, with unsold products returned to the dealer at no charge. Others sell products unguaranteed, where grocers take full responsibility for all products they buy. Naturally, profit margins for the methods differ. Grocers usually make about 23 to 25 percent on guaranteed sales, while unguaranteed sales yield margins of approximately 35 to 40 percent. However, because of the inherent risks involved in unguaranteed purchases, most grocers prefer the lower-but-safer profit margins of guaranteed arrangements when dealing with "door-to-store" distributors such as Dean's. Nonguaranteed sales work well through efficient drop shipment techniques customarily used by bread bakers.

Door-to-store distributors accumulate individual orders on a daily basis, pick up what they need from the pie baker, and deliver merchandise direct from the pie baker to the grocer. On the other hand, drop shipment distributors order large supplies of pies from the pie baker, take them to warehouses, and fill individual customer orders from their warehouse inventories. In some cases, drop shipment distributors, such as Eisner's, sell direct to their own or an affiliated grocery chain and, thus, enjoy profits on both the wholesale and retail end. This can be an important competitive advantage since 40–50 percent of the product cost is in distribution.

Exhibit 2 Distributors of Kitchen Made Pies

Distributor	Type of Segment Served	Percent of Kitchen Made's Sales
Dean's Distributing	Institutional/Retail	40%
McCormick Distributing	Institutional	10
Lowenberg	Retail	11
Eisner's	Retail	8
Master Snack & New Process	Retail	13
Edward's	Retail	4
Other (including Schnuck's)	Retail	16

Mr. Dubicki has expressed a desire to expand Kitchen Made's sales to drop shipment distributors because they operate on a lower margin of markup than door-to-store distributors, thus helping to hold down the prices retailers charge for Kitchen Made pies. This, he feels, could help circumvent the higher prices Kitchen Made charges distributors. Furthermore, since drop shippers order larger quantities, longer production runs and, therefore, lower pie-baking costs are possible.

In addition to sales to bakery wholesalers, Kitchen Made also operates its own delivery truck to handle specialty or rush orders. No plans have been made to expand this portion of Kitchen Made's operations

THE BAKING INDUSTRY

Though the outlook for the baking industry has been helped by scalebacks in flour and sugar prices, overall prospects have been unfavorable and should continue to be so until economic conditions pick up. The baking industry, and particularly the pie and cake segment, is more susceptible to cyclical economic variabilities than other foodstuffs due to the discretionary nature of purchases. Pies and cakes are more or less luxury foods and are readily cut from household shopping lists when times are hard.

Further dampening the outlook for the industry is the national swing toward nutrition. Sweets and sugar intake have decreased because too much is considered unhealthy, besides, of course, being very fattening. Additionally, because of demographic changes, the average age of the population is higher. Historically, younger individuals account for a large portion of the consumption of pies, cakes, and other desserts.

The frozen segment of the bakery industry currently is in even worse condition, owing to the higher prices of frozen food items, including pies. Frozen food items, given the effects of recession and consumer budget tightening, are not expected to assume a bigger role in grocery budgets until shoppers are in a mood to spend more money on more expensive types of food items.

In addition to the conditions previously cited, other developments were changing in the industry's makeup. Between 1972 and 1977 the number of firms included under SIC code 2051 (Bread, cake, and related products) dropped from 3,323 to 3,062, but at the same time, the number of establishments employing less than 20 workers increased. A major contributor to this trend was the economic impact of higher gasoline prices; the industry's transportation costs, already high due to the perishable nature of bakery products, became a big distribution factor. The transportation cost advantage went to the large-volume, national-brand firms with internal delivery capabilities and to the smaller firms which emphasized local business. Medium-sized firms which did not have the volume to support their own delivery function and which depended on a more diffuse range of customers were hurt most by rising distribution and shipping costs.

Other factors likely to affect the performance of the industry in the future were recent trends toward eating out and the emerging popularity of pre-prepared foods. With more women in the work force and more working couples, the food away from home segment was expected to grow. Dessert sales to restaurants and fast food outlets

Exhibit 3 Comparative changes in price levels of cereal and bakery products

	1975	*1976*	*1977*	*1978*	*1979*	*1980*
Retail:						
Cereal and bakery products	11.3%	−2.2%	1.6%	8.9%	10.1%	11.9%
All foods	8.5	3.1	6.3	10.0	10.9	8.6
Consumer price index	9.1	5.8	6.5	7.7	11.3	13.5
Wholesale:						
Cereal and bakery products	4.0	3.3	0.1	9.8	10.5	12.2
All foods	6.7	3.8	4.4	10.5	9.6	8.2

Source: U. S. Department of Labor.

were viewed as having growth potential. However, many fast food chains had a policy of using standard desserts supplied from central sources rather than each unit making its selections and purchases from local dessert manufacturers. As of yet, Mr. Dubicki had not investigated the opportunities of Kitchen Made making desserts to meet the specifications of area fast food chains.

Overall, the bakery industry was giving every sign of being very mature. There had been little real growth in sales over the past few years. However, prices and costs had risen substantially, reflecting inflationary conditions and shortages of certain ingredients. Since ingredient costs represented a major expense (approximately 50 percent of the manufacturer's selling price), recent declines in the prices of baking ingredients (e.g., sugar prices fell from $.55 per pound in November 1980 to $.26 per pound in October 1981) had given bakers the opportunity to improve profit margins. Changes in cereal and bakery prices, both wholesale and retail, as well as the consumer price index for the past six years, are provided in Exhibit 3.

THE LOCAL ECONOMY

Changes in the local retail market, prompted by changing demographics and a fluctuating economy, were threatening to have a dramatic effect on Kitchen Made's pie sales. Even though the Peoria area, like most midwestern cities, had shown little or no population growth in the past decade, the economy in Peoria had traditionally been solid due to the dominant impact of Caterpillar Tractor Co., a Pabst Brewing plant, a Hiram-Walker distillery, a number of other medium-sized manufacturing facilities, and a host of small plants—many of which are suppliers of Caterpillar. Peoria wage rates had consistently ranked in the top 20 cities in the nation, and local people were fond of saying, "Peoria doesn't have recessions." But this was changing rapidly.

Caterpillar endured a 12-week strike in the fall of 1979 that idled many of the 30,000 Peoria-area Caterpillar workers and did far more damage to the many suppliers and other businesses that depended either directly or indirectly on the firm. In addition, the Hiram-Walker plant closed in 1981, and the Pabst plant was scheduled to close in March 1982. Caterpillar, for the first time in 20 years, laid off substantial numbers of workers in 1981 and 1982. These events posed a significant threat to the sale of pies and other desserts in the Peoria area. For instance, Caterpillar's cafeteria was now using less than half as many pies compared to 10 years ago.

COMPETITION

Kitchen Made was the only pie manufacturer located in the Peoria area, although it did face competition from food service firms which had their own in-house baking capabilities. The biggest competitors were other regional and national firms which sold their products in the same areas as did Kitchen Made (see Exhibit 4).

Some of Kitchen Made's rivals made a full line of pies, and several were diversified into breads and other bakery products. Some of the smaller rivals concentrated on specific sizes or types of pies to allow longer production runs, permit lower inventories, and help contain production costs. Mr. Dubicki felt, however, that Kitchen Made's full line of pies gave the firm an advantage over competitors in attracting new customers and protected sales from changes in customer taste.

PRODUCTION

Baking and production techniques at Kitchen Made are relatively simple, though not without their own special problems. In most instances, pie crusts and fillings are made via the assembly line method. One person operates the dough machine which flattens the dough and rolls enough out to make one crust. The dough is passed to a second person who places it into a pie pan. The machine then presses the dough into the pan. Afterward, the crust passes under a filling machine which is set according to the size of pie being made. After the crust is filled with the desired ingredients, the pie passes

Exhibit 4 Kitchen Made's major rivals in the Peoria-St. Louis market area

Company	Headquarters Location	Geographic Area Served	Product Lines	Market Segments Served
Lloyd Harris (Div. of Fasano)	Chicago	East of Rockies	Fresh 9-inch pies	Institutional and retail
Chef Pierre		Nationwide	8-inch and 10-inch frozen	Institutional and retail
Mrs. Smith	Pottstown, PA.	Nationwide	8-inch and 10-inch frozen	Institutional and retail
Bluebird Baking	Dayton	Midwest	4-inch and 8-inch fresh	Retail
Shenandoah Pie	St. Louis	St. Louis	Full line fresh	Institutional and retail

under another station where the top crust is molded onto the sides of the pie pan and the excess dough removed. This excess is transported by conveyor back to the dough machine. Once the pies are assembled, they are placed on racks and wheeled over to the ovens for baking. All fresh pies are baked; frozen pies may or may not be baked, depending on the type of pie and filling.

A major problem associated with production is the frequent conversions required each time the size or the flavor is changed. It takes approximately 15–20 minutes to change over pie size and 4–5 minutes to change the type of ingredient. Size changes usually occur twice a day (from 4-inch to 8-inch to 9-inch), but ingredients must be changed from 20 to 25 times per day depending upon the production schedule.

All fruit pies are put together by the method described above, but currently cream pies are filled by hand. Mr. Dubicki intends to go to automated pie assembly for both fruit and cream pies in the near future. He is also studying the purchase of a more efficient pie machine; the drawbacks are the $150,000 purchase price and the long production runs needed to maintain peak efficiency with this type of machine.

One way to cut production costs is to limit the numbers of different types of pies made. Substantial savings in change-over time and production efficiency are available by limiting pie varieties. For example, with full crews, Kitchen Made currently bakes about $30,000 worth of pies and cakes per week. Yet, on those occasions where the firm has received a large order for one type of pie, a half crew has been able to produce $10,000 worth of pies on a single eight-hour shift. However, Mr. Dubicki is concerned that a move to few varieties could hurt sales since many retail and institutional buyers prefer to buy full lines of products from the same supplier.

Recently, Mr. Dubicki hired a production manager to allow him more time away from the pie assembly operation. The production manager is still in the process of learning all the requirements of the job and Mr. Dubicki has been spending a lot of time giving the new manager on-the-job training. Mr. Dubicki has so far been reluctant to delegate full authority to the new manager even though he is pleased with the progress she is making in taking over the supervision of pie making activities. The transfer of authority has been hindered by the fact that all aspects of the pie making

Exhibit 5   Sales/operating profits by product lines, last 12 months

	Sales Revenues		Gross Profits		
Product	**Dollars**	**Percent of Total**	**Dollars**	**Percent**	**Gross Profit Margin**
4-inch pie	$ 536,000	33.5%	$147,600	61.5%	27.5%
8-inch pie	296,000	18.5	24,700	10.3	8.3
9-inch pie	704,000	44.0	50,400	21.0	7.2
Cakes	64,000	4.0	17,300	7.2	27.0
Total	$1,600,000	100.0%	$240,000	100.0%	15.0%

operation have not been smoothly worked out and some are in the midst of being changed.

One positive development has been the progress made to reduce inventory. Though done as much out of necessity as out of design, the move has nonetheless helped in many respects. In the past, ingredients were often bought in six-month quantities. Today, the firm tries to buy only what it needs for one or two weeks, except in special cases when supplies are hard to find or favorable price breaks can be obtained.

FINANCIAL SITUATION

Mr. Dubicki believes that with Kitchen Made's current product mix, sales of approximately $35,000 per week ($1,820,000 per year) are needed to break even. Variable expenses are estimated to be about 85 percent of sales revenue. Exhibit 5 provides a breakdown of Kitchen Made's sales and gross profits by product line in percentages and dollar amounts. Margins on the 4-inch pies and the cakes are the biggest, with margins on the 8-inch pie and 9-inch pie varieties substantially lower.

The prices of Kitchen Made's pie and cake products have not been changed for approximately 12 months. Exhibit 6 shows the prices for the various types of pies made by Kitchen Made.

Kitchen Made's management is particularly pleased with the company's high-top meringue pie. Because of its superior looks and acceptance by consumers, the high-top pies command a 50 cent premium over the price of regular meringue pies, yet they cost only a few pennies more to make.

Because of stagnant sales and rising costs over the past several years, the financial condition of Kitchen Made has deteriorated. Exhibit 7 provides condensed operating results for the years 1971 through 1981. Exhibit 8 shows a condensed balance sheet for 1981. Exhibit 9 presents the computable financial ratios for Kitchen Made as compared to industry averages for SIC code 2051 businesses (i.e., Bread, Cake, and Related Products) with sales of under $50 million.

The most immediate financial problem relates to the unsecured $70,000 bank note which has currently come due. Kitchen Made has had an agreement with a local financial institution which allowed the firm to borrow $70,000 on a program resembling revolving credit. Kitchen Made pays only interest on this loan, with the principal due

Exhibit 6   Wholesale pie prices for Kitchen Made Pies

4-inch pies	$.25	8-inch regular meringue	$.90	9-inch fruit pies	$1.30
		8-inch high-top meringue	$1.40	9-inch whips	$1.30
		8-inch fruit pies	$1.00	9-inch meringue	$1.25
				9-inch specialty	$1.60
				9-inch walnut	$2.00
				9-inch cherry	$2.25

Exhibit 7 Kitchen Made Pies' condensed operating results, 1971–1981

| | | Net Income (Loss) | | Costs as a Percent of Sales Revenues* | | | | |
Year	Sales Revenues	Dollars	As a Percent of Sales	Materials	Labor	Selling	Administration	Facilities, Equipment, and Other
1971	$ 844,000	$14,000	1.7%	51.2%	30.0%	2.9%	9.9%	7.6%
1972	955,000	8,000	.8	50.5	29.3	2.8	9.5	7.1
1973	1,246,000	24,000	1.9	52.7	24.6	2.8	9.2	8.9
1974	1,453,000	18,000	1.2	57.0	22.3	2.5	7.7	9.3
1975	1,604,000	110,000	6.9	53.9	20.7	2.2	6.9	9.4
1976	1,580,000	109,000	6.9	48.8	23.0	2.6	7.4	11.3
1977	1,642,000	7,000	.4	48.9	26.0	2.7	8.5	13.5
1978	1,608,000	−24,000	(1.5)	50.9	26.3	2.2	9.4	12.7
1979	1,601,000	−58,000	(3.6)	50.6	27.0	2.8	10.0	13.1
1980	1,506,000	−91,000	(6.0)	51.3	28.3	3.3	10.3	12.8
1981	1,635,000	−178,000	(10.9)	54.3	27.7	4.1	11.2	13.5

*All of the cost percentages are not completely comparable from year to year due to several changes in how costs were allocated between categories of expenses.

Exhibit 8 Kitchen Made Pies' balance sheet, 1981

Assets		Liabilities and Equity	
Current Assets:		Current Liabilities:	
Cash	$ 2,000	Accounts payable	$291,000
Accounts receivable	163,000	Unsecured bank note	70,000
Inventory	137,000	Accrued payroll and taxes	25,000
Prepaid expenses	17,000	Note—F. Dubicki	8,000
Total current assets	319,000	Total current liabilities	394,000
Fixed assets:		Long term liabilities:	
(After depreciation)			
Leasehold improvements	1,000	Note on truck	15,000
Machinery and equipment	48,000	Note on equipment	12,000
Autos and trucks	28,000		
Total fixed assets	77,000	Total long-term	27,000
		Total liabilities	421,000
		Owner's equity	(25,000)
Total assets	$396,000	Total liabilities and equity	$396,000

Exhibit 9   Selected company and industry financial ratios, 1981

	Industry SIC Code 2051	Kitchen Made Pies
Current ratio	.76	.81 (without Dean's .66)
Net profit/sales	3.8%	Negative
Net profit/total assets	6.5%	Negative
Net profit/equity	19.5%	Negative
Sales/equity	7.6x	Negative
Sales/total assets	2.5x	4.1x
Collection period	14 days	36 (without Dean's 23)
Sales/working capital	8.8x	Negative
Sales/inventory	53.3x	11.9x
Fixed assets/equity	131.6%	Negative
Total debt/equity	201.7%	Negative

Source: *Key Business Ratios 1981*, Dun & Bradstreet.

in lump sum at the end of the borrowing period. One option Mr. Dubicki is considering involves trying to refinance the loan and get the borrowing period extended. But he is also considering whether to switch his business to another bank. Mr. Dubicki feels that because Kitchen Made often has a $20,000 to $30,000 balance in its bank account, it is entitled to some relief on the interest rate being paid. Furthermore, in discussions with the bank's loan officers over the possibility of refinancing the loan, Mr. Dubicki has been informed that the bank will insist on a secured note. Since Mr. Dubicki's father holds title to Kitchen Made's property, the bank has mentioned the use of a second mortgage on Mr. Dubicki's personal home as possible security for the loan. This is not attractive to Mr. Dubicki, and he is hopeful that other Peoria banks will be interested in giving Kitchen Made an unsecured loan in the amount of $70,000. Mr. Dubicki is quite willing to establish a business relationship with a different bank in the event satisfactory terms can be worked out. If not, he sees little option but to agree to the second mortgage condition for a secured note at Kitchen Made's present bank.

Another problem causing concern is slow payments by some customers. While such customers as Lowenberg and Eisner's consistently take advantage of discounts for early payment (usual terms are 2%/10 days net/30 days), Dean's Distributing currently owes over six months back payments amounting to $60,000. Mr. Dubicki feels most of this account is uncollectible but has not, as of yet, written the amount off as bad debt expense. Mr. Dubicki has expressed a desire to eliminate or substantially cut back on the business done with Dean's Distributing but in an effort to maintain sales levels has continued to supply its pies to Dean's on a strictly cash basis.

In spite of these financial difficulties, Kitchen Made has been able to generate enough cash flow to meet its current obligations and also to make small payments on the amounts owed to creditors of longer standing. Thus, while the situation is far from ideal and the firm is very vulnerable to unforeseen events, liquidity is probably not a life-or-death concern at the moment. However, Mr. Dubicki realizes that any further decline in sales and cash flows could be extremely hazardous and potentially fatal.

PERSONNEL

Most of the managerial activities at Kitchen Made Pies are handled directly by Mr. Dubicki. Besides the production manager, Ms. Barbara Britt, the only other management personnel are Ms. Charolette Watson, office manager, and Mr. Lonnie Beard, the sales promotion manager. Mr. Beard is responsible for making sure products are stocked and advertised properly at local retail outlets, which he visits periodically. Mr. Dubicki, besides being president and owner, acts as sales and distribution manager, prepares cash flow projections, searches for new accounts, and, of course, oversees all day-to-day activities. He also is really the only person who completely understands all aspects of the business. About the only activity he is not directly involved with is the actual assembly of the pies.

Kitchen Made currently employs about 30 production workers, 6 office workers, several maintenance workers, and a truck driver. The shop is unionized and pays wages comparable to other like-sized area firms.

FUTURE PROSPECTS AND OUTLOOK

Though the current situation at Kitchen Made Pies is far from ideal, Mr. Dubicki believes the situation is not hopeless and that a turnaround in his company's fortunes is manageable. As he put it, "I'm optimistic about our future, but then again, isn't that the only way I can feel?" He thinks good progress is being made in solving internal operating problems, and he has established good rapport with his work force; he feels the latter will facilitate making many of the internal changes he is considering. Yet, Mr. Dubicki recognizes the need to address several nagging issues:

- Would lengthening production runs reduce costs enough to justify a move to narrow Kitchen Made's product line?

- How important to Kitchen Made's competitive position is a broad product line? What product mix really makes the most sense?

- Would it be economical for Kitchen Made to purchase more equipment to automate its pie assembly operations, and how could such equipment be financed in the event it would improve Kitchen Made's efficiency?

- Should Kitchen Made continue to position itself at the high end of the price/quality range?

Mr. Dubicki also realizes that plain old hard work and dedication on his part, while helpful and necessary, will not be sufficient—improved operating results and a workable strategy are, of necessity, high on his agenda.

CASE 4

Sambo's Restaurants

A. J. STRICKLAND
The University of Alabama

BOB LONIS
The University of Alabama

In the latter part of 1979, Sambo's, a family restaurant chain, which by anyone's standard had a phenomenal growth story, found itself installing a new management team. The new executives were chosen by City Investing Corp., a large conglomerate, which had acquired a 16 percent interest in Sambo's after Sambo's had slid into technical default on its long-term debt. In its investment in Sambo's, City Investing acquired a company that was facing numerous lawsuits from previous owners and managers as well as boycott threats from certain minority groups. The chain's name was still the target of activists who proclaimed that it was a racial slur against blacks emanating from the children's story "Little Black Sambo." Manager turnover was high and profits were on a rapid decline.

Despite all these problems, the "Kings of Turnaround" said the investment in Sambo's was a gift toward the future.

LINE OF BUSINESS

Sambo's was founded in 1957 by Sam D. Battistone and F. Newell Bohnett with one coffee shop on the beach in Santa Barbara, California. In 1967, Sam D. Battistone, Jr., at the age of 27, took charge of the small chain of restaurants his father had founded. Under the young Battistone's management, within a mere five years the fledgling chain of Sambo's blossomed from a privately held $3 million-a-year, regional and returns at least 50 percent interest in each of most cases.

As managing agent, the company provides the restaurants with most of the food and related products used by the restaurants. The company charges the restaurants for all of the actual expenses incurred at the restaurant level, with the company providing operational, accounting, advertising, and management-related services on a proportionate share basis.

In addition to its restaurant operations, Sambo's is involved in equipment leasing, real estate, insurance, and product distribution. Their primary purpose in having these

The research and written case information were presented at a Case Research Symposium and were evaluated by the Case Research Association's Editorial Board. All rights reserved to the authors and the Case Research Association. Copyright © 1982, the Case Research Association.

supplemental operations is to complement their restaurant operations and create for themselves a competitive edge over others. These supplemental operations allow Sambo's to take advantage of substantial volume discounts and cost efficiencies.

COMPANY BACKGROUND

Sambo's was founded in 1957 by Sam D. Battistone and F. Newell Bohnett with one coffee shop on the beach in Santa Barbara, California. In 1967, Sam D. Battistone, Jr., at the age of 27, took charge of the small chain of restaurants his father had founded. Under the young Battistone's management, within a mere five years the fledgling chain of Sambo's blossomed from a privately held $3 million-a-year, regional operation primarily in California to become a $68 million, publicly held enterprise with units across the western United States.

At the age of 33, Sam D. Battistone, Jr., had what most men work for all their lives. As president of Sambo's Restaurants, Inc., he was successful and rich with almost $10 million in Sambo's stock. The May 1, 1976, issue of *Forbes* referred to Battistone as a "prodigal son."

In 1973, the young Battistone left Sambo's to try to venture out on his own. He still was active in the company even after leaving the post of president, in that he was still a member of the board of directors and still managed the family's extensive California real estate holdings. On his own, Battistone formed a new company, Invest West Sports, which soon owned, among other operations, 50 percent of a World Football team, an interest in the New Orleans franchise of the National Basketball Association, and a rather large group of sports camps. Venturing out on his own, though, wasn't as fruitful as the young Battistone had envisioned. By 1975, he was looking at million-dollar losses, rather than the million-dollar gains he had been accustomed to at the helm of Sambo's.

During Battistone's leave of absence, however, Sambo's continued to grow under his successor, Wayne Kees. By 1975, the chain had 526 restaurants with earnings increasing at a phenomenal rate of 46 percent *each year* since 1965. During 1975, earnings were up over 37 percent to $17.6 million while sales increased $138 million. (See Exhibit 1.)

In January 1976, Wayne Kees, at the age of 53, suddenly decided to retire at the same time Battistone returned to take over Sambo's active management. Company executives insisted that it was only coincidental that Kees decided to retire at the same time Battistone was to return.

Battistone, upon returning to the presidency of Sambo's, commented to a *Forbes* writer, "When I left to do other things, that was something I had to do. I love the restaurant business. Those three years gave me a chance to look at Sambo's objectives of wanting to do in our segment of the industry what McDonald's did in theirs."

During 1976, Sambo's stock was listed on the New York Stock exchange and the chain had approximately 750 restaurant units located in 40 states. (See Exhibit 2.)

Exhibit 1   Sambo's Restaurants' consolidated statements of earnings

| | Year Ended December 31 | | | |
	1977	1976	1975	1974
Revenues				
Restaurant sales	$453,058,000	$348,443,000	$118,401,821	$ 84,242,374
Food and restaurant supply sales (nonowned)	19,299,000	19,344,000	11,957,804	8,692,157
Sales of interests in restaurant joint ventures	15,962,000	7,700,000	6,460,000	5,092,000
Other income	3,434,000	4,831,000	2,124,042	2,845,190
Total revenues	491,753,000	380,318,000	138,943,667	100,871,721
Costs and expenses				
Cost of sales				
Restaurant sales	284,864,000	212,757,000		
Food and restaurant supply sales	18,453,000	18,571,000		
Operating, general, and administrative	111,608,000	81,968,000		
Minority interests in income-restaurant joint ventures	20,237,000	20,719,000		
Depreciation and amortization	12,527,000	7,625,000	4,753,383	3,414,359
Interest	4,388,000	722,000	655,059	320,225
Total costs and expenses	452,077,000	342,362,000	108,263,089	77,333,669
Earnings before income taxes	39,676,000	37,956,000	30,680,578	23,538,052
Income taxes	15,330,000	14,890,000	13,040,000	10,692,000
Net earnings	$ 24,346,000	$ 23,066,000	$17,640,578	$ 12,846,052
Earnings per common share	$1.90	$1.80	$1.48	$1.09

Although Sambo's was having remarkable earnings growth, Battistone was concerned about the level of traffic growth at the chains units. Battistone commented:

> We have been a volume control oriented company all along. Since our founding, we always felt that the basic way to run a restaurant is to control food costs, and by the word of mouth advertising, you'll continue to grow. But we also realize that as you become larger and the competition becomes greater, you have to market your product. I like the opportunity of moving from a cost-controlled company to being a marketing one. The way we've

Exhibit 2 Growth of units, 1974–1979

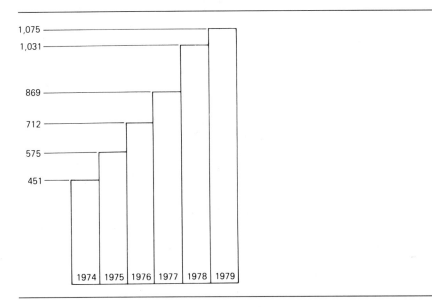

organized any additional volume we had really makes a difference because it comes right down to the bottom line. It's much better than being a volume-oriented company looking for controls.

In 1976, Battistone increased the marketing expenditure rate to 2.75 percent of gross revenues, up a full percentage point from the 1.75 percent being spent previously. In addition, he hired Arthur G. Gunther, a marketing expert from McDonald's, to help booster Sambo's marketing effort. Battistone felt that the increased advertising would lead to an annual growth of the restaurants' sales volume of 5 percent.

As Sambo's continued to prosper, Battistone became more and more concerned about trying to maintain such an impressive growth record as had been experienced in the past. The earnings growth record led the entire restaurant industry and served as a model for others to follow.

SAMBO'S "FRACTION-OF-THE-ACTION" BLUEPRINT

Sambo's strategy for growth was concentration with limited backward vertical integration. Sambo's objective was straightforward; they simply wanted to be the nation's fastest-growing restaurant chain. The strategy for growth was developed by Battistone, Sr., and was termed "Fraction of the Action."

In late 1957, the two cofounders sold 20 percent of the original Santa Barbara Sambo's to the first manager/partner for $20,000. They believed that there must be a sharing of profits as an intrinsic feature of the organization if they were eventually to grow into a major chain. With the opening of the second unit, the new manager purchased 20 percent for $20,000. The first manager was also given the opportunity to invest again, this time in the new unit. This concept remained intact through the early years—the operating manager/partner purchasing 20 percent for $20,000, the corporation usually retaining 50 percent, and other managers and field supervisors having the opportunity to purchase shares in the remaining 30 percent. This remaining 30 percent was put into a pool, which included similar 30 percent interests in the other restaurants, and then "investment units" from this pool were sold for $5,000 apiece.

The manager's 20 percent stake, together with his investment units, made him more than just an employee by giving him a share in the restaurant's profits. By 1974, the return on "investments" were averaging 50 percent a year. According to Wayne Kees, "Our boys know they can make it big and retire after a few years if they want. They promote themselves, each other, the chain; and they work like dogs." Kees cited four territorial managers, each with a salary of $850 per month, who were making more than $100,000 a year from their investments.

During 1976, the average store was showing a 66 percent annual return on investment. This percent of profit was unheard of in the restaurant business but was accomplished, in part, by Sambo's keeping the manager's salary very low. Battistone commented about the salaries:

> The original salary of a partner/manager was only $500 a month, and after 20 years that salary was still only $750 a month. We eliminated entirely a certain segment of the population from even wanting to come into our management because the salaries were so low.
>
> A person who invests in his own business, who has a chance to participate in the profit of his own restaurant, who has his own capital involved, who can build an estate and invest in his own future is better off than a salaried or bonus person.
>
> However, we also had to pay a livable wage along with those benefits for everyday living.

This unique management incentive program virtually eliminated turnover. In addition, the program has received credit for holding marketing costs down to 1.75 percent of total sales, compared to 3 percent to 5 percent as an industry average. The 50 percent interest that Sambo's kept gave management control over its restaurants. No less important was the initial $20,000 from each manager and the $5,000 that each investment unit generated as these contributions provided substantial capital for expansion purposes of its company.

The incentive plan, though, did have some drawbacks. The primary one was the need to keep growing at an increasing rate. Unless more restaurants were added, there could be no investment units to reward managers. The growth situation was compounded because sales and profits tend to reach a certain level and then plateau. For

Sambo's, each unit was expected to reach a net profit level of $50,000 a year and then remain at that level.

One new restaurant manager made the following comment shortly after he left Sambo's: "They run a lot of people through this (hiring and training) program compared to the number they get out of it. They are getting a lot of cheap labor, if you ask me, and they seem to be looking for people with money to buy investment units, not people with management ability."

Restaurant managers were recruited from many occupations, from gas station operators to teachers. The majority of personnel recruited were, according to a Sambo's executive, willing to work hard to achieve financial independence.

After a detailed training program covering everything from dishwashing to management, the new manager was ready to begin work in the field under the watchful eye of a "veteran manager."

Each new manager tended to have a common style when he or she completed the training program. Regardless of the age of the manager, each was led to believe that they would not manage a restaurant more than 10 years. The training classes also heard many stories about managers who worked for only a few years and then "retired" at $40,000 a year. This incentive made the "promote from within" policy work extremely well.

Obtaining the $20,000 down payment required to purchase the 20 percent interest seemed to deter some prospective managers from joining Sambo's, but most banks were willing to loan the money, on an unsecured basis, since the rate of return on investment track record for Sambo's was so sound. In many cases the veteran managers assisted in arranging the loans.

A CHANGING COURSE

1977 arrived and was projected to be another banner year for Sambo's. But instead of being a record-breaking year, 1977 proved to be one of the darkest periods for Sambo's. Top management and Battistone realized that the Fraction-of-the-Action and the company's continued success were on a collision course. When Battistone, Sr., started the unique incentive plan, he misjudged how successful the plan would be. The continuance of capitalizing each store at $100,000 over the years resulted in a powerful leveraging situation, also partly brought on due to the unrealistic low overhead charges that were being made. The results were that in 1976 the average store was showing a $66,000 profit, or 66 percent, return on their investment. As the managers purchased additional investment units, they grew to expect the same 66 percent return. It was not long before top management realized that it could not keep the high rate of return going on into the future. Owen Johnson, senior vice president and treasurer, commented to Madelin Schnider in a leading trade journal: "It was unfair to employees, stockholders, and customers to offer this kind of motivation to managers. We were hesitant to tamper with something that was working, and yet it was an unreasonable return on investment. It had to be changed." And change, it did.

NEW COMPENSATION PROGRAM

In August 1977, Sambo's introduced a new compensation package for managers which substantially changed the 20-year-old Fraction-of-the-Action program. The plan was to give Sambo's a leading edge for managerial talent in an industry that competition for such talent had heightened. The new plan was to (1) provide more immediate benefits for the restaurant manager and their families; (2) retain the opportunity for ownership participation for the individual managers; and (3) be more consistent with a fair return to Sambo's shareholders. The program consisted of upgrading manager base salaries from the original $9,000 annual amount to a new range of $15,000 to $21,600 annual salaries. Quarterly bonuses were also granted for superior profit performance. The combined salary and bonus packaged aids nearly doubled the direct compensation that managers received under the old program.

The "new deal" also included greater life insurance coverage as well as extended medical coverage for all members of the manager's family.

The managers were still allowed to purchase interests in their restaurants, but some significant changes were made in the program. Under this new program managers were entitled to purchase only a 1 percent interest in their restaurant, although they did retain the right to invest in units of other restaurants. The interest purchasing price was increased from the old $1,000 per 1 percent to $3,000 for a 1 percent interest investment.

Managers who were employed at the time of the change were given the choice of continuing under the old plan or selling part of their interests back to the company and participating in the new compensation program. The new system was considered one of the best in the industry but, compared to the old program, it was not seen as desirable by many.

Nearly 250 managers left the company upon hearing of the proposed changes. Management was concerned what effect such a large turnover rate among its managers might have on the company's operation. After much debate, they decided to keep the new program.

The old program was seen as too risky, due to an informal investigation by the Securities and Exchange Commission (SEC) into the income-recording procedures for the capital contributed by the managers in obtaining their interest shares. The SEC concluded that the company could no longer record this cash flow as income if Sambo's wished to maintain the option to repurchase the interests of those managers who left. Based largely on the ruling, as well as the need to make appropriate changes for the future, Sambo's elected to stay with their new program. The abandonment of the old plan, which had been the keystone to their growth success, led to a chain of events that was to plague the company for many years to come.

EFFECT OF THE CHANGE

Fiscal Year 1978 was looked upon with great enthusiasm by company officials. They felt that their new compensation program would stop the manager turnover problem and get the company back on its path of profits, but the financial picture for 1978 would be dampened by rumors of pending mergers and litigation from former managers/ investors in the old programs. To help combat the sluggishness of the firm's profits, Battistone formed an advisory board made up of selected unit managers and made several significant alterations to the company's operations.

Menu selection was greatly enlarged in order to better meet the wants and demands of the American public. Children's dishes and many regional specialty dishes were added. The changes were heavily promoted, mostly through television. Sambo's commercials were run in over 150 separate market areas covering all the states in which the company operated. The Sambo's theme, "Just what the family ordered," was effectively distributed through the use of all mass media channels. The new expanded regular menu had over 180 separate items, and an entirely new dessert menu was introduced.

Complementing the menu expansion program, several of the Sambo's units underwent major renovation, while others incorporated minor changes in an attempt to create a more relaxed environment and dining pleasure. The more extensive remodeling incorporated the latest design and decor concepts of Sambo's newest and most successful restaurant. Such changes as new lighting, carpeting, and color schemes created a relaxing mood, while layout changes and installation of state of the art equipment were aimed at increasing production efficiency in order to reduce operating costs. In 1978 alone, over $10 million was spent on leasehold improvements.

Worsening Conditions

Despite the valiant efforts put forth by the company's management, 1978 was a poor financial year with Sambo's net earnings dropping more than $15 million from the previous year to a low of $7.56 million. (See Exhibits 3 and 4.) The manager turnover

Exhibit 3 Net earnings, 1974–1979

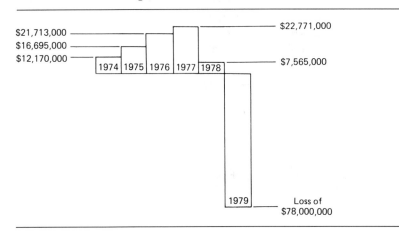

Exhibit 4   Stock price profile, 1971–1979

problem was a major contribution to the poor financial showing. It was estimated that during the year, more than half of the company's restaurants were staffed by inexperienced managers which led to a particularly high level of operating costs. The decision to retain a larger percentage ownership in new restaurants led to a rather drastic reduction in revenue and profits from sales of restaurant interests in the latter half of the year. Due to liquidity problems, the board of directors voted not to declare dividends in the first half of 1979 and to reevaluate the dividend policy at that time for future periods.

Litigation Proceedings

During 1978 and 1979, the number of legal proceedings against Sambo's rose significantly, most of them relating to the disposing of the Fraction-of-the-Action compensation program. Former restaurant managers contended that (1) changes in the compensation program had adverse effects on the managers' retirement plans; (2) certain charges by the company to the restaurant joint ventures were excessive; (3) unreasonable restraints of trade were in effect under the company's distribution procedures; and (4) there was improper accounting by the company regarding the financial interests of the subject restaurants.

In addition to these suits, pending legal action was evident in some states as to whether the company could continue to use its name in its restaurant business. Many racial advocates claimed the name was a direct racial slur against blacks. The company denied these allegations, claiming "Sambo's" was a combination of the names of its two founders. Sam Battistone, Sr., and F. Newell Bohnett. In the very near future, Sambo's would have to decide whether to "fight or switch" in its attempt to keep the name.

TROUBLES LEAD TO NEW MANAGEMENT

The first half of 1979 was disastrous for Sambo's as its losses were well over $20 million and its liquidity position was suspect at best. In June of 1979, the company was unable to meet the financial coverage requirements and other conditions that were set forth in the long-term debt covenants. The result was that long-term liabilities of approximately $100 million dollars had to be reclassified as current liabilities. The default led to the unseating of Battistone as chief executive officer. His successor, Karl V. Willig, was appointed in July but he would hold the post only for a very brief time, just five months, before he too would be replaced.

In November 1979, Sambo's sold 593,875 shares of a new series of cumulative, convertible, voting preferred stock to GDV, Inc., an 80 percent owned subsidiary of City Investing Corp. The preferred stock represented an approximate ownership interest of 16 percent of the common stock outstanding. Along with the ownership interest came the right to name new management. City Investing installed the "Kings of Turnaround" as Sambo's new management. This group of turnaround experts was spearheaded by Daniel E. Shanghnessy who, with his crew, had worked a managerial miracle while at Motel 6, a budget motel operation.

The new management team found a formidable task. The 1979 loss figure was $77.8 million dollars, which in Shanghnessy's words was "an abominable performance." Knowing that time was of utmost importance in turning the performance of a floundering company around, the new team embarked on a strategy to reduce company losses and get Sambo's back on its feet financially.

Key elements of their strategy included slashing of general and administrative expenses; severely cutting marketing, training, and headquarters support personnel; revisions of menus in order to emphasize higher-margin items, enabling the units to increase their selling prices; and the development of local marketing programs to aid in increasing sales volume in low-volume restaurant units.

The administrative cuts led to the disappearance of district managers. In altering its structure to meet the new situation, the chain was divided up territorially with regional vice presidents responsible for groups of 100 or more restaurants. Disgusted unit managers left the chain and were replaced primarily by lower-paid high school graduates. The estimated savings from the employment of their cost-cutting strategy amounted to approximately $40 million for 1980.

FURTHER ALTERATIONS

In early spring of 1980, Sambo's again revised the compensation program. The new package significantly reduced the amount of monetary compensation available to unit management. The plan, now based on sales volume rather than profit level, was again greeted unfavorably by managers.

In July Sambo's received another cash infusion from City Investing, via its GDV Inc. subsidiary, of just over $15 million in exchange for 1,034,483 shares of convertible preferred stock. This investment raised GDV's interest level to approximately 34 percent.

Another cost-cutting procedure was instated in 1980 by Shanghnessy and his "cost bandits" as they raised the administrative overhead charge to the individual units from 1.6 percent to 5.1 percent of sales, an increase of 225 percent, in an attempt to meet the family restaurant image that new management wished to communicate. Sambo's recruited the former advertising chief at Walt Disney Productions to lead its promotional efforts and hired a foreign-trained chef to aid in upgrading its menu.

IMPROVING RESULTS AND OPTIMISM

The results of Shanghnessy's first six months of 1980 were very commendable. (See Exhibits 5 through 8.) The Company reported a loss figure of only $7 million dollars, and it estimated that the total loss for 1980 would be around only $12 million dollars, compared to nearly $78 million in 1979. Though happy with the results of his efforts, Shanghnessy was concerned with overall sales volume. Sales volume had for the first time dipped below $500,000 on a unit basis. The industry norm at that time was nearly $640,000 per unit. Thus, Shanghnessy embarked on a profit analysis by units to determine where the sales volume problem led. As suspected, there were numerous poorly performing units, but in spite of this problem, Shanghnessy and his management team were optimistic about future operations.

Exhibit 5   Sambo's Restaurants, Inc., and subsidiaries' consolidated statements of operations ($000)

	Year Ended		
	January 1, 1981	December 31, 1979	December 31, 1978
Revenues			
Restaurant sales	$489,170	$543,817	$538,629
Food and restaurant supply sales		25,165	22,189
Sales of interests in restaurant joint ventures			13,209
Other income	927	5,411	3,416
	490,097	574,393	577,443
Costs and expenses			
Cost of sales			
Restaurant sales	321,485	345,468	338,097
Food and restaurant supply sales		24,117	20,442
Operating	91,879	94,475	77,432
Selling, general, and administrative	31,121	105,967	69,950
Minority interests in income (losses) of restaurant joint ventures	(3,484)	6,601	12,054
Depreciation and amortization	31,485	30,352	25,617
Interest, net	29,232	31,981	24,544
Write-downs of assets and provisions for losses		35,211	
	501,718	674,172	568,136
Earnings (loss) before income taxes	(11,621)	(99,779)	9,307
Income taxes (credit)		(22,000)	1,742
Net earnings (loss)	$(11,621)	$(77,779)	$ 7,565
Earnings (loss) per common share	$(1.05)	$(6.06)	$0.59

Exhibit 6   Sambo's Restaurants, Inc.'s consolidated balance sheets ($000)

Assets	January 1, 1981	December 31, 1979
Current assets		
Cash, including temporary cash investments of $51,845 and $25,703	$ 49,204	$ 47,870
Accounts receivable, less allowance for doubtful accounts of $10,087 and $5,819	3,700	5,810
Refundable income taxes		8,996
Inventories	19,623	18,495
Prepaid expenses and other	4,127	1,860
Total current assets	76,654	83,031
Property and equipment, partially pledged		
Land	27,637	27,586
Buildings and improvements	47,992	53,890
Leasehold improvements	36,636	27,922
Furniture, fixtures, and equipment	166,854	162,591
	279,119	271,989
Less: Accumulated depreciation	84,514	64,798
Net property and equipment	194,605	207,191
Leased property under capital leases		
Land	406	406
Buildings	198,718	187,786
Furniture, fixtures, and equipment	8,570	9,734
	207,694	197,926
Less: Accumulated amortization	46,998	37,623
Net leased property under capital leases	160,696	160,303
Other assets		
Investments in repurchased restaurant joint venture interests, at cost, less accumulated amortization of $885 and $401	4,588	2,583
Deposits and miscellaneous assets	5,355	5,506
Total other assets	9,943	8,089
	$441,898	$458,614

Liabilities and Shareholders' Equity	January 1, 1981	December 31, 1979
Current liabilities		
Notes payable to banks		$ 17,846
Long-term debt reclassified		97,400
Accounts payable	$ 20,015	59,494
Accrued expenses	33,360	31,598
Current maturities of long-term debt and obligations under capital leases	12,933	6,963
Total current liabilities	66,308	213,301
Long-term debt	115,691	5,426
Obligations under capital leases	191,749	188,116
Deferred income taxes	1,389	1,389
Other long-term liabilities	13,000	
Commitments and contingencies		
Shareholders' equity		
Preferred stock	28,659	13,659
Common stock, issued and outstanding 12,841,518 shares	7,063	7,063
Additional paid-in capital	28,931	28,931
Retained earnings (deficit)	(10,892)	729
Total shareholders' equity	53,761	50,382
	$441,898	$458,614

Exhibit 7 Sambo's Restaurants, Inc.'s consolidated statements of changes in financial position ($000)

	Year Ended		
	January 1, 1981	December 31, 1979	December 31, 1978
Sources of working capital			
Net earnings (loss)	$ (11,621)	$ (77,779)	$ 7,565
Items which do not use working capital:			
Depreciation and amortization of property and equipment	20,290	19,217	16,331
Net capitalized lease expense	3,542	3,327	1,257
Deferred income taxes		(9,201)	4,880
Write-downs of assets		29,184	
Other, net	575	1,692	1,790
Working capital provided by (used in) operations	12,786	(33,560)	31,823
Effect of debt restructuring	115,246		
Proceeds from sale of property and equipment	532	6,146	5,879
Proceeds from term loans			5,000
Proceeds from mortgage financing		876	5,822
Mortgage assumptions	2,547		
Net change in revolving credit loans		1,300	21,300
Proceeds from sales of preferred stock	15,000	13,659	
Other, net	16,119	7,313	(8,425)
Total sources	162,230	(4,266)	61,399
Applications of working capital			
Reclassification of long-term debt		92,150	
New properties	2,814	15,879	79,205
Replacements and rehabilitations	11,784	10,295	6,000
Current installments of restructured debt	4,000		
Current installments and repayments of mortgage obligations	3,016	4,366	2,703
Cash dividends declared			7,705
Total applications	21,614	122,690	95,613
Increase (decrease) in working capital	$140,616	$(126,956)	$(34,214)
Changes in components of working capital			
Increase (decrease) in current assets:			
Cash	$ 1,334	$ 36,709	$(32,434)
Accounts receivable	(2,110)	(5,056)	(4,344)
Refundable income taxes	(8,996)	(810)	9,096
Inventories	1,128	(14,796)	13,983
Prepaid expenses and other	2,267	183	18
(Increase) decrease in current liabilities:			
Notes payable	17,846	(5,846)	(8,725)
Long-term debt reclassified	97,400	(97,400)	
Accounts payable	39,479	(33,174)	(7,321)
Accrued expenses	(1,762)	(8,325)	(2,656)
Current maturities of long-term obligations	(5,970)	1,559	(1,831)
Increase (decrease) in working capital	$140,616	$(126,956)	$(34,214)

Exhibit 8 Sambo's Restaurants, Inc.'s consolidated statements of shareholders' equity ($000)

	Year Ended		
	January 1, 1981	December 31, 1979	December 31, 1978
Preferred stock, no par value, authorized 2,000,000 shares:			
$1.84 cumulative convertible (on a four-for-one basis into common stock) voting; liquidation preference $23 per share; 593,875 shares issued (during fiscal 1979) and outstanding	$ 13,659	$13,659	
$1.45 cumulative convertible (on a four-for-one basis into common stock) voting; liquidation preference $14.50 per share; 1,034,483 shares issued (during fiscal 1980) and outstanding	15,000		
Total preferred stock at end of year	28,659	13,659	
Common stock no par value (stated value, $.55 a share); authorized 43,000,000 shares; issued and outstanding, 12,841,518 shares at beginning and end of each year	7,063	7,063	$ 7,063
Additional paid-in capital, balance at beginning and end of each year	28,931	28,931	28,931
Retained earnings (deficit):			
Balance at beginning of year	729	78,508	78,648
Net earnings (loss) for the year	(11,621)	(77,779)	7,565
Cash dividends—$.60 per share			(7,705)
Balance at end of year (deficit)	(10,892)	729	78,508
Total shareholders' equity at end of year	$53,761	$50,382	$114,502

Cottage Gardens, Inc. (Revised)

BRUCE P. COLEMAN
Michigan State University

For Cottage Gardens, Inc., the fiscal year ending January 31, 1981, showed a net loss of $6,000 on sales of $3.2 million, on the heels of a four-year decline in net income. It also showed a sales decline of $65,800 from the prior year following a 41 percent sales growth since 1977 and 140 percent since 1973.

Despite the 1980 performance, William Hicks, executive vice president and general manager, approached the end of 1981 with confidence and enthusiasm, believing that 1981–82 would "be the best year in 10." He indicated that they "took their lumps" in 1980–81 expecting 1981–82 to be a good year as a result of cost-cutting measures and an increase in salable inventory.

Cottage Gardens, with headquarters in Lansing, Michigan, was a wholesale grower and distributor of shade and ornamental trees and evergreen and deciduous shrubs. It also sold landscaping supplies such as small tools, fertilizer weed sprays, burlap, and plastic edging. Although its farms were located in Michigan and Ohio, it sold throughout the United States with emphasis on the Midwest.

According to a 1981 study by *Nursery Business*, Cottage Gardens ranked 57th among the top 100 wholesale nurseries in the United States. Those 100 represented about .3 percent of the 27,000 U.S. wholesale growers. Cottage Gardens was the second largest in the state of Michigan (Zelenka was the largest with sales of $14 million on 1,800 acres) among the 1,354 Michigan nurseries representing $105 million in total sales.

COMPANY HISTORY

The Cottage Gardens nursery was founded in 1923 by Nick I. W. Kriek, a former Dutch-bulb broker, who took over a neglected nursery and developed it into a viable business. At first he operated as a landscape nurseryman but gradually constructed propagation houses and sold liners as well as landscape material. As the firm grew, valuable expertise was gained in the propagation of trees and evergreens, and by the 1940s the company had developed a reputation for quality plant material. It was among the first (if not the first) to introduce yews into Michigan landscapes. Its 1930 catalog listed: "New to trade; 'Hicks Yews' 1 1/2 foot plants at $8.00 each." Nick Kriek's basic policy was: "If you can make a profit on an item, sell. Don't hold it for a possible higher price. You may not get it."

Company data provided by William N. Hicks. All rights reserved by the author.

In 1946, Harold Hicks, Nick Kriek's son-in-law, joined the firm. Under the influence of Harold Hicks, who was heavily sales- and volume-oriented, the firm gradually changed from a landscape business to a wholesale grower, or production-agency nursery. It grew in Michigan only those species that could be produced economically there. Most of the plant material was in containers and was "jobbed" to large retail outlets. The company supplied other landscape garden centers with its own plant material as well as plant stock bought and shipped from other areas of the country.

William N. Hicks, Harold's son, joined the company permanently in 1972 with the title of shipping and office manager, following his graduation from Michigan State University with a degree in business administration. As William gained experience and authority within the firm, he brought about internal changes resulting in more formal operations in planning, inventory control, cost accounting, budgeting, and organization.

The firm continued to prosper. The product line expanded, growing capacity increased, and sales blossomed. Cottage Gardens serviced its customers by providing "the right plants, at the right time, in the right quantities, and at the right place."

PRODUCT LINE

The product line of Cottage Gardens consisted of liners (a name given to any small plant that is grown to a larger one) and general nursery stock—shade and ornamental trees and shrubs. The fall 1981–spring 1982 wholesale price list contained approximately 140 different types and varieties of plants. The shade and ornamental trees consisted of maple, birch, hawthorne, ash, locust, pine, oak, crabapple, cherry, linden, mountain ash, Russian olive, peach, pear, and plum. Shrubs included juniper, yew, privet, arborvitae, euonymus, japonica, lilacs, cottoneaster, rhododendron, azalea, and burning bush. Within types of plants, numerous varieties were offered. For example, there were 12 varieties of azaleas; 11 of junipers; 15 of maples; 9 of rhododendron; 8 of yews; 9 of crabapple; 4 of linden, ash, hawthorne, and locust; and 3 of oak. Most trees and many shrubs were available in varying sizes. A limited line of roses (not grown by Cottage Gardens) was also offered.

The types and varieties of plants offered were continually changing as a result of sales and profitability analysis. Several changes between the 1981–82 and 1980–81 price lists included fewer varieties of azalea and rhododendron, the dropping of holly and ground cover, and the addition of one yew and cottoneaster.

Cottage Gardens obtained a patent on a new variety of azalea in 1981. The "Azalea Silver Sword," having a pink blossom and a unique silver and green variegated leaf color, was the result of more than five years' development.

LAND AND FACILITIES

Cottage Gardens leased or owned approximately 700 acres of land. The location and amount of land were as follows:

Location	Acres
Lansing, Michigan	210
Okemos, Michigan	30
Copemish, Michigan	260
Perry, Ohio	<u>205</u>
Total	705

As late as 1975, Cottage Gardens had leased 120 acres in Okemos. However, because of the poor soil conditions and high taxes, the company had been moving off of the land on a planned basis. In 1981, all but 30 acres had been sold by the owners, but 50 acres could be considered under cultivation since the rights to the plants were retained by Cottage Gardens for three years from the date of sale of a parcel of land.

Cultivation of leased land was managed at what was considered an optimum level. In no location was 100 percent of the acreage planted. Some contained lakes. All required a program of scheduled rotation of cover crops for soil enrichment and that could account for 25 to 50 percent of the acreage at any time.

Ownership of the leased land lay in a number of sources. Thirty-five acres in Ohio and 120 in Lansing were leased from individuals not associated with the company or with the Hicks family. The remainder of the leased land was owned by members of the Hicks family or by employees of the company. For example, Ted Myers and Tony Pulido owned portions of the Copemish farms; and Jim Sabo and Dick Hart, portions of the Ohio farm. Cottage Gardens acquired ownership of 15 acres in Perry, Ohio, on October 1, 1981, from an uncle of William Hicks and was negotiating for 46 acres in Lansing in December 1981. Efforts to acquire additional land in Ohio had not borne fruit.

Facilities owned by Cottage Gardens consisted solely of warehousing and office space. In Lansing were the main office building, two warehouses, and eight poly houses. (A poly house is a greenhouse using polyethylene rather than glass. Cottage Gardens used pipe as a frame and stretched polyethylene sheet over it. Not only did the poly house protect plans from cold weather but it also permitted heat and humidity control.) In Copemish was a warehouse (60 feet by 180 feet) which also contained an office. In Ohio there were two warehouses (60 feet by 180 feet and 50 feet by 100 feet) and 248 poly houses (each poly house measured 15 feet by 200 feet). Office space in Ohio was also in a warehouse.

PRODUCTION

Production operations consisted of planting, growing, and harvesting. Growing involved repotting (of container grown material), watering or irrigating, spraying, fertilizing, and trimming. Harvesting, in preparation for shipping, could take several forms. One was in potted form in which the plant was shipped in the container in which it was grown. Another was bare root where the plant was taken to a warehouse area and held for shipping. A third was balled and burlapped (B&B) in which the plant was packed in soil and the "ball" wrapped and tied for shipping. Here again there was some warehousing prior to shipping.

The growing season was from April to October, and plants were harvested from late March to May and from October through December or January.

The lead time for planting was one to seven or more years—a short time for evergreens and shrubs, longer for various types and sizes of trees. The production (planting) schedule each year was based upon a projection of plant material for several years, consisting of not only the type of plant material to be grown but also the number of each for different size requirements. These projections were extrapolations of current sales levels, available inventory, and expected plant growth rates adjusted on the basis of a judgment of salability or demand and of profitability. Weeping birch trees, for example, were withdrawn from the 1982 production schedule because of low sales volume.

In general, shade and ornamental trees were grown in Michigan and shrubs in Ohio. Virtually all plant material was grown by Cottage Gardens with the exception of liners. This position had been achieved through a program of increased planting and shrub propagation. Ten years earlier the company had purchased 40 percent of its trees and 70 percent of its nonevergreen shrubs. It had an excellent shrub propagation capability, and earlier efforts to develop a tree propagator had been abandoned.

During the past six years planting had been increased significantly, and in 1979 and 1980, purchases for growing material had increased dramatically, tripling and quadrupling in those years respectively. The result was a much larger total inventory of salable stock. The large increase in planting in 1979 was also prompted by a loss of $400,000 worth of stock in Ohio resulting from a combination of severe winter weather and a probable weak crop caused by a poor balance of soil mix.

The company was also in the final stages of obtaining a trademark for "Root-Kare," a name given to the way it grew trees in Copemish. The production and harvesting process consisted of a program for managing the soil and the root system growth of the tree, specially designed digging equipment, a mist system on the trailer during transportation, and packing the trees in sawdust prior to shipping to the customer. The process was not patentable, but the trademark identified it as being unique and would serve as a sales tool, especially to municipals.

Cottage Gardens was essentially self-sufficient in its production operations. It was necessary only to lease additional trucks during harvesting. A machine had been developed for mechanically packing soil and wrapping the "ball" around a bare root tree, thus saving costly hand operations. A bare-root digging machine made possible the digging of 11 trees per minute with a crew of 6 where formerly the rate had been 1 tree per minute with a crew of 12. In addition, equipment available throughout the industry was used, such as a "canning" machine for transplanting container-grown plants, for example, from a one-gallon to a three-gallon container.

Efforts to increase capacity and output were continuous. Total acreage leased had increased by 100 acres in the past four years. In order to obtain a greater yield, rows were planted as closely as possible in Ohio. An increasing number of plants were container grown in poly houses. Experimentation with accelerated plant growth had been undertaken utilizing a system developed by a Michigan State University forestry professor.

Beginning in 1979, a small amount of land (less than an acre) was leased from a nursery in Venice, Florida, and planting begun on an experimental basis. The experimentation was with the early growing of plant material in Florida and then transfer to Michigan and Ohio for further growth. The intent was to take advantage of the much more rapid growth rate of plants in warmer climates. Problems of high temperature were creating difficulties in this experimentation. There was also under consideration the growing in Florida and sale there and in Michigan of indoor foliage plants. In 1981 there was approximately $15,000 worth of plants in inventory, and Cottage Gardens was looking for land to purchase in Venice.

Weed and insect problems were well controlled through new technology. Two other problems associated with production operations persisted. The first was personnel requirements. These fluctuated from 60 workers in the winter to 175 in spring, 50 in summer, and 150 in fall. The peak demand for personnel occurred during harvesting. The second problem was weather and its effect on harvesting. If there was too much snow, rain, or cold in the spring, digging was difficult or impossible. Very warm weather might come early and stop harvesting because trees could not be dug after buds began sprouting leaves.

MARKETING

The market of Cottage Gardens was defined by William Hicks as the "upper Midwest"—Denver to Philadelphia and Louisville north. Approximately 50 percent of sales were in Michigan, 30 percent in Ohio, Indiana, and Illinois, with the remainder spread throughout the other Midwest states.

There were three major types of customers: garden centers (including chain stores) constituting 55 percent of sales—mostly shrubs but some trees; landscapers, 35 percent of sales—mainly trees but some shrubs; and municipalities, 10 percent of sales—only trees.

Cottage Gardens had approximately 1,000 customers. (The actual number was less but the above figure included individual stores of chains if they were billed separately.) Among its major customers were Frank's Nursery & Crafts (Detroit), K-mart (Detroit), Meijer Thrifty Acres (Grand Rapids, Michigan), Richter's Gardens (Lansing), and Anderson's (Maumee, Ohio). The company sold to all of Frank's garden centers (76). A $133 million firm, Frank's planned eight new stores in 1982—three in Michigan, four in Chicago, and one in Ohio. It was estimated that Cottage Gardens sold to 80 percent of the stores in the K-mart Midwest region. No customer constituted more than 30 percent of any product line. Furthermore, dealing with the large customers enabled the firm to grow with the customer's growth. The company also stressed sales to local and regional chains (3–10 stores) and garden centers and discount operations.

The primary municipal customers were Chicago, Milwaukee, Minneapolis, and the smaller Michigan cities of Flint, Troy, and Livonia. The municipal market had been shrinking because of a squeeze on money and a slower population growth. There were, however, in many communities, pressures for more street tree programs, resulting in demand for replacement trees which were larger trees and for which demand had been smaller.

In Lansing, the company operated CG Associates (CG-Lansing), a cash-and-carry distribution operation for small orders (above the minimum order size but too small for shipment). Cottage Gardens had operated a CG Associates in Columbus, Ohio, for two years but closed it in June 1980 upon expiration of its lease there. Although the CG had achieved profitability on sales of almost $400,000, the decision to close it was based upon lower sales projections and higher costs.

Cottage Gardens served as the exclusive representative, in a specified geographic area, for several other nurseries. Although the companies changed over time, in 1982 they included Warren County Nursery in Tennessee, Lone Star Rose in Texas, Speer & Sons in Oregon, and Rhode Island Nursery and Boulevard Nursery in Rhode Island. As the representative, Cottage Gardens received a 10 percent commission, half of which went to the salesmen and half to the company. Cottage Gardens made the sale, but the grower shipped and invoiced the plants to the customer. In the case of Rhode Island Nursery, however, Cottage Gardens booked the order, the grower shipped the plants to the customer, and Cottage Gardens invoiced the customer.

There were five salesmen. The sales territories for individuals were as follows: (1) greater Detroit and selected customers having an office in Detroit (Chicago firms, for example); 2) Ohio; (3) Michigan and selected outside accounts; (4) municipalities and major cities in Illinois, Wisconsin, Minnesota, Iowa, Nebraska, and Missouri; and (5) Indiana and missionary work for large new accounts.

In addition, in late November 1981, Cottage Gardens hired a sales group of six people that had been employed by a competitive nursery in Michigan which decided to utilize only in-house sales representatives. This group, headquartered in Louisville, Kentucky, functioned as brokers and covered a territory including Indiana, Kentucky, Tennessee, Illinois, Missouri, Iowa, Nebraska, and Kansas. Two of the salespeople were in Chicago. The head of the group set a goal of $500,000 in sales of Cottage Gardens' stock for 1982.

Prices were set by adjusting current year's prices by whatever change was believed needed to cover projected expenses and still be supported by the market. A close watch was kept over competitors' prices. In some instances, price adjustments were made based upon knowledge of costs of specific types of plants. Furthermore, management was beginning to learn break-even points on certain lines.

Minimum order size for delivery from each farm was $850, and prices were FOB point of origin. Potted and container grown plants were available from Perry, Ohio; container-grown plants from Lansing; pro-ball (bare-root which were balled and burlapped in a special mix) and bare root trees from Copemish; and B&B trees and shrubs from Lansing. Terms of sale were net 30 days to customers with established credit and cash for all others. A VIP (Volume Incentive Purchase) plan provided discounts or rebates to qualified volume purchasers.

A Lansing advertising and consumer survey company assisted Cottage Gardens with its advertising. All copy which the company wanted associated with itself contained the logo of the Dutch girl picking tulips, a logo which was well known in the trade. Often the Dutch girl was used alone but in some cases was combined with other copy. (See Exhibit 1.) The advertising theme was changed at least annually. In 1981, the phrase, "If you like profits, you'll love Cottage Gardens," was used in all major advertisements. Other phrases used in recent years were "Quality trimmed. A degree of excellence" and "Cottage Gardens. Fifty-five years and over 5 million trees."

In the latter part of the 1970s, advertising had been increased both in dollars and scope. Advertising was expanded to such trade journals as *Weeds Trees & Turf, Land-*

Exhibit 1   Advertising logo

Cottage Gardens inc.
SOUTH WAVERLY & BISHOP ROADS
LANSING, MI 48910
PHONE (517) 882-5728

scape Architecture, Nursery Business, Lawn & Garden Marketing, and *Trees.* In 1981, however, advertising expenditures were cut back and advertising limited to *American Nurseryman* and regional nursery publications. Plans were being discussed to advertise in such journals as *Chain Store Age* and to conduct consumer surveys.

COMPETITION

The nursery wholesale business was composed of a few large growers and many small ones. In the 1981 *Nursery Business* survey, of the 27,000 nurseries, only 15 companies had sales of $10 million or more and 20 firms had sales of $5–$10 million.

William Hicks indicated that the competition of Cottage Gardens consisted of a few large companies and hundreds of small growers who raised plants for their local areas. The large competitors were AMFAC American Gardens Products Division ($31.5 million in sales); Zelenka Nursery ($14 million) and Northland Evergreen Nursery of Grand Haven, Michigan; and Bork Nursery ($3.5 million) of Illinois. Several of the more formidable competitors 10 years ago were no longer competitive.

MANAGEMENT, ORGANIZATION, AND PERSONNEL

Cottage Gardens was managed by the president, Harold Hicks, and the executive vice president and general manager, William Hicks. Harold Hicks was involved in major decisions such as acquisitions, personnel, and long-range plans, while William managed the firm on a day-to-day basis. They operated as a team with close communications and shared decision making. The position of chairman of the board had been left vacant since the death of Nick Kriek in 1978. William Hicks also filled the position of Corporate Secretary.

Although the organization and staffing of the company was in a state of transition, Exhibit 2 illustrates the organization in December 1981.

Both Jim Sabo and Ted Myers had the title of vice president. Each had been with the company some 17 years and had managed the Ohio and Michigan farms until recently. Younger men had been moved into the management of operations in order to provide a more businesslike orientation as well as continuity to the firm.

In Ohio, Jim Sabo concentrated on propagation and advising on growing. While not a technically educated person, he had a fine ability to sense what a plant needed for healthy growth. Further, he was reputed to be one of the best propagation experts in the nation. He had developed new methods of propagation; new and hardier strains of evergreens, rhododendron, and azaleas; and new methods for growing and protecting plants. A propagator and assistant worked with him.

In Michigan and Ohio, Ted Myers was used as a technical advisor on all aspects of operations for all farms, e.g., soil testing and composition, diseases, fertilizers, test plots, machinery, and new products and marketing developments. Skilled in the technical aspects of the business, his was primarily a research and development role.

Each farm was headed by a manager. All were highly experienced and skilled in farm operations. Tony Pulido in Copemish had been with Cottage Gardens for about 25 years, Mike Bell in Lansing, 4 years, and Dick Hart in Perry, 10 years. In late 1981, Tom Varcak, who had been with the firm since 1977 and was a former manager of the Lansing farms, was moved to Ohio as operations manager for a three-to five-year trial period. He served primarily as a coordinator for all Ohio operations. The Manager of CG Associates (Lansing) was Jane Hargreaves who had a degree in business and had been with the company for two years. Two workers performing warehouse-type jobs reported to Jane, and their jobs served as a training ground for field work.

The Venice operation was operated by Harold Hicks, Jr., with the aid of part-time student help. Harold, a high school science teacher, worked with the operation part-time and had no plans for devoting more time to it. His father planned to spend an increasing amount of time there as the operation was expanded.

Eugene Hopp was corporate treasurer and spent full time on financial and accounting matters. His activities are described in some detail in the Accounting and Finance section. Jim Macy was in charge of the Customer Service Office. A former intern from Michigan State University and a graduate in horticulture and sales and marketing, his tasks included soliciting and taking orders, including some house accounts, traffic, expediting, and customer complaints. Most of his sales efforts were missionary. He obtained the account of Meijer Thrifty Acres, a rapidly growing regional discount chain in Michigan, and was pursuing A&P and Murphy Mart. Jim Macy organized and ran the sales meetings and was being groomed for sales manager.

The salesmen were highly skilled professionals—competent and independent. Most had been with the company for many years, two of them for over 22 years.

The reporting and coordinating relationships among company personnel were quite varied and, in some instances, multiple, as Exhibit 2 suggests. For example, sales representatives, as skilled professionals, dealt with William Hicks on some matters and Jim Macy on others. The Lansing Farms manager reported to William Hicks but also to Ted Myers and Eugene Hopp on certain matters. Some of the older people, such as Bill Poleo (Detroit area salesman) and Jim Sabo, tended to deal more directly with Harold Hicks. Harold Hicks, Jr., who managed the Venice operation, dealt with his father and brother on an informal but business-like basis.

A continuing effort was made to provide fair and adequate compensation but also to provide incentives. The field force was paid the prevailing wage for agricultural workers. Sales personnel were paid a straight commission of 10 percent of sales, except for Jim Macy who was paid a salary. Jim Sabo and Ted Myers were paid a straight salary, although a salary plus percentage of division sales had been tried several years before. Other means for trying to tie key personnel to the company were through the ownership of land leased to Cottage Gardens, an employee health insurance program, an employee retirement program, and a volunteer life insurance program funded by the company.

The company also cooperated with the internship program of the Michigan State University Horticulture Department. These students performed field operations and proved to be dependable workers.

Exhibit 2   Organization chart, December 1981

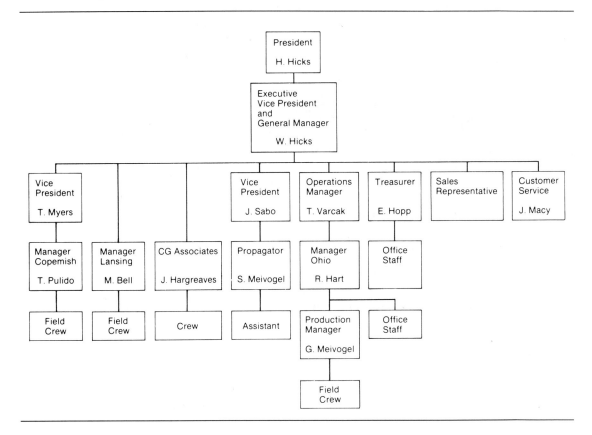

The total permanent work force of Cottage Gardens was about 60 people, and seasonal labor doubled the size of the work force. Effort was being made to reduce the need for seasonal workers in several ways. One was shifting work to the off-season or slower parts of the season. For example, rather than picture tag plants as they were loaded for shipping, tags were attached while the plants were in the poly houses. Another was the move to more container grown material versus ground grown. Still another was the use of more or new machinery. Through the use of new machinery the size of the Lansing work crews had been cut in half.

ACCOUNTING AND FINANCE

A local CPA firm drew up financial statements for the company for income tax purposes. Exhibits 3 through 6 contain consolidated financial statements for the years 1976–1980 based on a year-end date of January 31. Exhibit 7 reflects monthly and

Exhibit 3 Cottage Gardens, Inc.'s consolidated balance sheets, years ending January 31, 1977–1981

	1977	1978	1979	1980	1981
Assets					
Current assets:					
Cash	$ 21,331	$ 14,186	$ 12,105	$ (3,655)	$ 7,226
Accounts receivable—customers	67,714	92,005	104,964	83,629	187,915
Less: allowance for doubtful accounts	(1,693)	(2,081)	(2,306)	(1,226)	(1,884)
Accounts receivable—other			1,679	979	
Inventory—supplies	23,200	33,007	60,652	38,943	77,779
Notes receivable	6,280	8,280	8,280		
Commission advances	7,709	502			7,712
Employee advances		241		1,400	1,626
Deposits—machinery and equipment		2,000	445	645	445
Bid deposits	1,191	10,393	15,320		14,278
Refund receivable		4,600			
Investment	10	10	10	10	10
Total current assets	125,742	163,143	201,149	120,725	295,106
Fixed assets:					
Machinery and equipment	370,145	491,327	596,548	657,008	665,384
Furniture and fixtures	4,103	10,664	10,880	11,221	11,315
Transportation equipment	72,923	82,474	92,795	106,411	126,070
Building and land	44,322	84,908	87,167	167,307	169,766
Less: Accumulated depreciation	(222,185)	(269,114)	(368,953)	(465,587)	(521,288)
Total fixed assets	269,308	400,259	418,437	476,360	451,247
Total assets	$395,050	$563,402	$619,586	$597,085	$746,353

	1977	1978	1979	1980	1981
Liabilities and Stockholders' Equity					
Current liabilities:					
Accounts payable—trade	$158,990	$192,244	$ 50,780	$ 37,924	$ 18,298
Accounts payable—other		182	11,776	5,321	336
Employee insurance	4,374			378	382
Employee savings		2,584	2,818	5,339	9,108
Notes payable—bank	100,000	250,000	371,734	342,074	350,000
Notes payable—other	39,694	40,592	111,202	111,476	74,704
Current portion long-term debt					53,384
Accrued payroll withholding taxes	577		765	120	1,003
Accrued interest	1,342	2,453	3,848	4,220	9,115
Accrued single business tax	4,645				
Total current liabilities	309,622	488,045	552,923	506,852	516,330
Long-term liabilities:					
Mortgage payable				33,225	32,335
Notes payable (less current portion)					153,673
Total long-term liabilities				33,225	186,008
Stockholders' equity:					
Common stock—par value $10.00 per share					
Issued and outstanding 5,000 shares	50,000	50,000	50,000	50,000	50,000
Undistributed taxable income	35,428	25,347	16,663	7,009	(5,986)
Total stockholders' equity	85,428	75,347	66,663	57,009	44,014
Total liabilities and stockholders' equity	$395,050	$563,402	$619,586	$597,085	$746,353

Source: Company annual reports.

Exhibit 4 Cottage Gardens, Inc.'s consolidated statements of income, years ending January 31, 1977–1981

	1977		1978		1979		1980		1981	
	Dollars	Percent of Sales	Dollars	Percent of Sales	Dollars	Percent of Sales	Dollars	Percent of Sales	Dollars	Percent of Sales
Sales:										
Grown	$1,595,015	70.6%	$1,591,292	63.9%	$1,845,980	60.8%	$2,363,166	72.5%	$2,774,121	86.8 %
Resale	513,788	22.7	763,698	30.7	1,100,149	36.2	798,323	24.5	355,897	11.1
Commissions	150,722	6.7	135,186	5.4	90,012	3.0	100,136	3.0	65,771	2.1
Total sales	2,259,525	100.0	2,490,176	100.0	3,036,141	100.0	3,261,625	100.0	3,195,789	100.0
Cost of sales	2,033,251	90.0	2,259,961	90.8	2,734,785	90.1	2,935,141	90.0	2,822,375	88.3
Gross income	226,274	10.0	230,215	9.2	301,356	9.9	326,484	10.0	373,414	11.7
General and administrative expenses	200,951	8.9	217,086	8.7	297,691	9.8	355,617	10.9	420,654	13.2
Net income from operations	25,323	1.1	13,129	.5	3,665	.1	(29,133)	(.9)	(47,240)	(1.5)
Other income:										
Interest	2,002	.1	3,825	.2	4,063	.1	6,987	.2	7,506	.2
Miscellaneous	2,130	.1	1,043	.0	4,587	.2	17,985	.5	1,254	.0
Rents	5,973	.3	8,428	.3	4,417	.1	11,151	.4	18,168	.6
Gain on equipment sales			(1,078)	.0	(69)	.0	19	.0	14,326	.5
Total other income	10,105	.5	12,218	.5	12,998	.4	36,142	1.1	41,254	1.3
Net income	$ 35,428	1.6%	$ 25,347	1.0%	$ 16,663	.5%	$ 7,009	.2%	$ (5,986)	(.2)%

Source: Company records.

Exhibit 5 Cottage Gardens, Inc.'s consolidated schedules of cost of sales, years ending January 31, 1977–1981

	1977		1978		1979		1980		1981	
	Dollars	Percent of Sales	Dollars	Percent of Sales	Dollars	Percent of Sales	Dollars	Percent of Sales	Dollars	Percent of Sales
Salaries—administrative	$ 86,420	3.8%	$ 84,300	3.4%	$114,169	3.8%	$117,250	3.6%	$124,350	4.0%
Salaries and wages	30,689	1.4	42,710	1.7	51,185	1.7	49,728	1.5	65,044	2.0
Advertising	138	.0	62	.0	192	.0	10,258	.3	7,776	.3
Bad debts	1,909	.1	612	.0	(225)	.0	754	.0	658	.0
Collection costs	531	.0	1,134	.1	1,219	.0	252	.0	821	.0
Customer relations	1,051	.0	411	.0	301	.0	586	.0	71	.0
Contract work					410	.0	540	.0	895	.0
Depreciation	11,035	.5	14,550	.6	17,707	.6	13,187	.5	15,763	.5
Donations	56	.0		.0	50	.0	595	.0	340	.0
Dues and subscriptions	2,272	.1	215	.0	2,167	.1	3,914	.1	2,141	.1
Electricity and water	794	.0	871	.0	807	.0	1,683	.1	1,278	.0
Gasoline and oil	1,796	.1	2,057	.1	2,454	.1	4,048	.1	4,897	.1
Heat	928	.1	793	.0	874	.0	955	.0	1,173	.0
Insurance	5,301	.2	6,645	.3	8,953	.3	13,972	.4	15,807	.5
Interest	9,366	.4	14,454	.6	40,502	1.4	60,219	1.8	95,903	3.1
Legal and audit	3,221	.1	1,909	.1	6,694	.2	4,472	.1	8,519	.3
Maintenance and repair	4,916	.2	8,107	.3	3,756	.1	7,746	.2	8,831	.3
Mileage expense	1,148	.1	1,589	.1	1,858	.1	3,032	.1	4,156	.1
Miscellaneous expense	1,985	.1	5,338	.2	1,752	.1	3,558	.1	1,833	.0
Rents	5,710	.3	5,864	.2	8,429	.3	8,439	.3	8,601	.3
Supplies—office	7,075	.3	7,862	.3			8,619	.3	15,144	.5
Small tools					8,593	.3		.0		.0
Taxes	20,471	.9	15,892	.6	22,064	.7	19,988	.7	16,659	.5
Telephone	1,392	.1	1,101	.0	1,105	.0	6,124	.2	6,993	.2
Travel and entertainment	2,747	.1	610	.0	2,675	.1	15,698	.5	13,001	.4
Total general and administrative	$200,951	8.9%	$217,086	8.7%	$297,691	9.8%	$355,617	10.9%	$420,654	13.2%

Source: Company records.

Exhibit 6 Cottage Gardens, Inc.'s consolidated schedules of general and administrative expenses, years ending January 31, 1977–1981

	1977		1978		1979		1980		1981	
	Dollars	Percent of Sales	Dollars	Percent of Sales	Dollars	Percent of Sales	Dollars	Percent of Sales	Dollars	Percent of Sales
Salaries—administrative	$ 86,420	3.8%	$ 84,300	3.4%	$114,169	3.8%	$117,250	3.6%	$124,350	4.0%
Salaries and wages	30,689	1.4	42,710	1.7	51,185	1.7	49,728	1.5	65,044	2.0
Advertising	138	.0	62	.0	192	.0	10,258	.3	7,776	.3
Bad debts	1,909	.1	612	.0	(225)	.0	754	.0	658	.0
Collection costs	531	.0	1,134	.1	1,219	.0	252	.0	821	.0
Customer relations	1,051	.0	411	.0	301	.0	586	.0	71	.0
Contract work					410	.0	540	.0	895	.0
Depreciation	11,035	.5	14,550	.6	17,707	.6	13,187	.5	15,763	.5
Donations	56	.0			50	.0	595	.0	340	.0
Dues and subscriptions	2,272	.1	215	.0	2,167	.1	3,914	.1	2,141	.1
Electricity and water	794	.0	871	.0	807	.0	1,683	.1	1,278	.0
Gasoline and oil	1,796	.1	2,057	.1	2,454	.1	4,048	.1	4,897	.1
Heat	928	.1	793	.0	874	.0	955	.0	1,173	.0
Insurance	5,301	.2	6,645	.3	8,953	.3	13,972	.4	15,807	.5
Interest	9,366	.4	14,454	.6	40,502	1.4	60,219	1.8	95,903	3.1
Legal and audit	3,221	.1	1,909	.1	6,694	.2	4,472	.1	8,519	.3
Maintenance and repair	4,916	.2	8,107	.3	3,756	.1	7,746	.2	8,831	.3
Mileage expense	1,148	.1	1,589	.1	1,858	.1	3,032	.1	4,156	.1
Miscellaneous expense	1,985	.1	5,338	.2	1,752	.1	3,558	.1	1,833	.0
Rents	5,710	.3	5,864	.2	8,429	.3	8,439	.3	8,601	.3
Supplies—office	7,075	.3	7,862	.3			8,619	.3	15,144	.5
Small tools					8,593	.3				.0
Taxes	20,471	.9	15,892	.6	22,064	.7	19,988	.7	16,659	.5
Telephone	1,392	.1	1,101	.0	1,105	.0	6,124	.2	6,993	.2
Travel and entertainment	2,747	.1	610	.0	2,675	.1	15,698	.5	13,001	.4
Total general and administrative	$200,951	8.9%	$217,086	8.7%	$297,691	9.8%	$355,617	10.9%	$420,654	13.2%

Source: Company records.

Exhibit 7 Selected financial data, monthly and cumulative, February 1981–January 1982

	February	March	April	May	June	July	August	September	October	November	December	January
For the month:												
Total revenues	$ 78,994	$550,151	$1,216,244	$ 431,320	$ 192,601	$ 83,647	$ 73,439	$ 168,728	$ 63,345	$ 218,291	$ 22,510	$ 71,918
Total cost of revenues	91,073	108,843	326,081	667,546	276,439	166,365	127,159	130,167	146,056	152,380	191,948	210,478
Gross income	(12,079)	441,308	890,162	(236,226)	(83,837)	(82,717)	(53,720)	38,561	(82,712)	65,911	(169,438)	(132,560)
Operating expenses	29,047	30,986	61,152	45,665	31,526	42,689	34,224	47,226	31,447	36,821	51,386	101,429
Net operating income	(41,125)	410,322	829,010	(281,891)	(115,364)	(125,402)	(87,944)	(8,665)	(114,159)	29,090	(220,823)	(233,989)
Other income	794	726	1,265	541	3,366	2,708	1,191	2,350	4,814	(1,626)	1,216	3,490
Net income	$ (40,331)	$411,048	$ 830,275	$ (281,350)	$ (111,997)	$ (122,695)	$ (86,754)	$ (6,315)	$ (109,345)	$ 27,464	$ (219,607)	(230,499)
Cumulative:												
Total revenues		$629,146	$1,845,389	$2,276,709	$2,469,310	$2,552,958	$2,626,397	$2,795,125	$2,858,469	$3,076,760	$3,099,270	3,177,188
Total cost of revenues		199,916	525,997	1,193,543	1,469,981	1,636,346	1,763,505	1,893,672	2,043,812	2,196,192	2,388,140	2,598,618
Gross income		429,230	1,319,392	1,083,166	999,329	916,612	862,892	901,453	814,657	880,568	711,130	578,570
Operating expenses		60,033	121,185	166,850	198,377	241,062	275,286	322,512	356,070	392,892	444,277	545,706
Net operating income		369,197	1,198,207	916,316	800,952	675,550	587,606	578,941	458,587	487,676	266,853	32,864
Other income		1,520	2,785	3,326	6,693	9,400	10,591	12,940	17,755	16,128	17,344	20,834
Net income		$370,717	$1,200,992	$ 919,642	$ 807,645	$ 684,950	$ 598,196	$ 591,881	$ 476,341	$ 503,805	$ 284,197	53,698
End of Month:												
Bank Cash	$ 2,773	$ (573)	$ 125,745	$ 162,565	$ 129,469	$ 62,931	$ 23,720	$ 2,234	$ 28,068	$ 28,841	$ (2,068)	(5,563)
Accounts receivable—trade	207,440	727,509	1,409,393	1,129,876	583,078	412,956	318,754	403,155	317,055	329,425	212,948	137,203
Accounts payable	40,839	39,617	20,213	248,747	103,483	42,897	36,319	68,366	33,779	32,408	85,279	112,715
Notes payable—bank	604,609	714,160	693,711	464,263	191,114	186,665	182,217	177,768	268,319	253,871	259,422	354,973

Source: Company records.

cumulative figures for selected accounts for the period of February, 1981 through January, 1982.

Cottage Gardens was a Subchapter S agriculture firm. Accounting statements conformed to reporting requirements for companies so classified, and earnings were taxed as personal income to the owners. The agricultural classification permitted certain tax benefits for the company but also placed some restrictions on operations, e.g., the company had to grow at least 50 percent of what it sold.

Inventories stated in the accounting statements were exclusive of nursery stock because the company elected, for both accounting and tax purposes, to expense costs as they were incurred in the raising of stock. The nursery stock inventory was measured and valued at an average current market value before harvesting and marketing expenses. While the total inventory was taken annually, inventory of salable stock was taken twice a year (June and September) and updated monthly. The year-end valuations of total inventory for 1976–81 were as follows:

Year	Inventory ($ millions)
1976	3.5
1977	3.7
1978	4.1
1979	4.5
1980	5.2
1981	6.1

Fixed assets were valued at cost; and the total fixed asset figures, at cost less depreciation. As of January 31, 1981, total assets were shown as 54 percent depreciated, but machinery and equipment was 64 percent depreciated; furniture and fixtures, 60 percent; transportation equipment, 56 percent; and buildings, 10 percent.

A line of credit of $750,000 was maintained with the Michigan National Bank and was secured by corporate accounts receivable, inventory, equipment, and assignment of land leases of real estate which held plant inventory. Notes payable—other consisted of demand notes for commissions, rents, and loans to stockholders. In September 1979, Cottage Gardens acquired a warehouse and 28 acres of land in payment of an account. The mortgage payable was that property. In July 1980, long-term debt was employed for the first time and consisted of long-term equipment obligations on a total line of credit of $250,000.

Sales were classified as grown, resold, and commission. Grown sales consisted of plant material, except sales of other growers' plants. Resold sales consisted of supplies (internally called wholesale) and of plants of other growers which were handled by Cottage Gardens and invoiced as its own stock. Commissions were from sales which were shipped directly to the customer by the grower, invoiced by the grower, and a commission paid to Cottage Gardens. CG Associates sales of plants were classified as grown and sales of supplies as resold. (In 1980 all of CG-Lansing sales had been classified as grown and all of CG-Columbus sales had been classified as resold. Prior to 1980 all CG sales were classified as resold.)

Purchases were for growing and for resale. Purchases for growing included plant material and growing supplies, such as dirt, fertilizer, and insecticide, for the current year's and future years' stock. Purchases for resale consisted of supplies sold and plant material bought from other growers and resold. Of the total purchases in 1981, 12 percent was for resale, a drastic change from 78 percent two years earlier. However, purchases relating to CG operations were classified for growing and for resale in 1980 and earlier, consistent with the classification of sales in those years.

The company allocated revenues and expenses to particular production and selling functions which were called divisions. Overhead costs were allocated on the basis of dollar sales volume. The divisions were as follows:

Lansing (balled and burlapped)

Lansing (container grown)

CG-Lansing

Lansing propagation

Copemish

Ohio

Direct shipment (from other growers)

Venice

Planned changes included moving Lansing container-grown material to Ohio and Michigan propagation to Ohio. The changes were expected to improve operations and control, as well as simplify divisions for accounting purposes.

Cottage Gardens owned an NCR 399 computer. All accounting functions except inventory were on the computer, including payroll, invoicing, accounts receivable and payable, and general ledger. Monthly performance data were generated for each division.

Beginning in 1981, budgets were prepared for each division as well as consolidated operations; and in October, budgeted-versus-actual results were integrated into the monthly computer printouts of operations. In addition, effort was directed toward cash flow analysis and planning and longer-range planning of equipment requirements.

Ownership of the corporation was held by Harold Hicks (87.6 percent) and William Hicks (12.4 percent). William was acquiring shares from his father on a planned basis.

ASSOCIATION ACTIVITIES

The company maintained memberships in the American Association of Nurserymen (AAN), the Michigan Association of Nurserymen (MAN), the Central Michigan Landscape & Nurserymen Association, and others, including associations in Ohio, Indiana, and Illinois. The AAN was very active in lobbying, conducting research, spon-

soring management seminars, monitoring legislation and other activities related to nursery operation, and in disseminating information through pamphlets, research reports,
and its bi-monthly publication, *American Nurseryman.* This latter publication contained
a wealth of information related to association activities, research, marketing, advertising, pricing, and production.

The MAN served as a vehicle for uniting Michigan nurserymen for their mutual
benefit and protection. It was a means for interaction among members, exchange of
information, and cooperation with governmental agencies. Nick Kriek had been secretary—treasurer in 1932-33 and Harold Hicks had been president in 1959–60. In
1981–82, William Hicks was president, and other Cottage Gardens personnel were on
MAN committees.

The AAN national convention and trade show was held annually in July, and the
state trade shows were in January. At least two people from Cottage Gardens attended
the AAN convention as well as those for Michigan, Ohio, Indiana, Iowa, and the
Mid-Am Convention, which included Illinois, Wisconsin, and Minnesota.

REFLECTIONS AND A VIEW TOWARD THE FUTURE

In reflecting on the status of Cottage Gardens, William Hicks was looking to the 1981–
82 season with optimism. He was quite pleased with the quality of the initial budgeting
efforts and believed that the organizational changes, while creating some upheaval,
would greatly strengthen Cottage Gardens and provide growth and development opportunities for the younger people in the company. He also indicated that he felt good
progress was being made in knowing the costs of operations and in getting all divisions
profitable. Efforts to obtain cost data on individual plant types were being conducted
on a side-study basis.

William's principal concern was over continued high interest rates, inflation, and
the health of the economy as they affected the nursery business. He explained that
short-term recessions have relatively small effect on the nursery business, but the sustained recessionary conditions were not only squeezing the municipals market but also
were being reflected in the landscaping business. To aggravate that condition, some
competing nurseries were engaging in severe price cutting because of overcapacity and
the need to service the debt which financed their large inventories. Furthermore, there
was an overcapacity of products in the industry largely created by the larger growers,
such as Zelenka, American Garden Products of AMFAC, and Weyerhauser. Some of
these growers were flooding the market with plant material at prices, according to
William Hicks, below harvesting costs.

A related factor which caused concern and over which he had no control was
spring weather. A late spring delayed orders and shipping, thus curtailing sales. Often
very warm weather then followed quickly, thereby shortening the selling season and
creating shipping difficulties. Two additional problems he identified were his desire to
reduce bank debt and keep it at a manageable level and the continuing challenge of
finding the right place for individuals within the firm.

When asked for an identification of objectives, William responded that they seemed to change continually as he thought about them. However, he defined the objectives of the company as sustained internal growth of 10 percent per year above inflation and increased profitability through improved internal efficiency. He felt that his father wanted to live comfortably and enjoy what he had built. He own personal objectives revolved around a desire to reach a position where he could have more leisure time, especially to spend with his family.

CASE 6

Hewlett-Packard, 1978–1981: The Evolution of Leadership

ROGER M. ATHERTON
University of Oklahoma

In May 1978, one day before his 65th birthday, Bill Hewlett resigned from his position as Chief Executive Officer of Hewlett-Packard, the company he had helped found in 1939. He was appointed Chairman of the Executive Committee and joined David Packard, Chairman of the Board of Directors, in semi-retirement. John Young, who had succeeded Bill Hewlett as President and Chief Operating Officer in November 1977, was promoted to the vacated C.E.O. position. For the first time in its 39-year history, H-P was to be directed by an executive who had been developed from within the organization rather than being led by its original, almost legendary founders. It had become John Young's responsibility to manage the rapidly growing company as it headed deeper and deeper into the unfriendly territory of computational technology, where the competition was both bigger and tougher than in H-P's traditional businesses—electronic test and measurement, medical electronic equipment, and analytical instrumentation. The question raised by the trade press, Wall Street analysts, and some employees was whether John Young could provide the needed strategies and leadership in this more hostile environment for continued successful growth. [See "Hewlett-Packard (A)"[1] for a description of the industry and HP's objectives, strategies, policies, structure, and performance from 1972 to 1975. See "Hewlett-Packard: A 1975–1978

[1]ICCH 9–376–754.

Review"[2] for a description of the company's growth, structure, strategies and policies, organization and leadership, early moves into computational technology, and performance from 1975 to 1978.]

STRATEGIC CHANGES[3]

Electronic Office Systems

By 1981 H-P had become the world's third-largest minicomputer manufacturer, exceeded only by IBM and Digital Equipment Corporation. In October 1981, the *Wall Street Journal*[4] reported that H-P had decided to expand from their traditional base of data-processing equipment for business, factory, and scientific purposes into the word-processing and office terminal field dominated by IBM and Wang Laboratories. John Young indicated that H-P's strategy would be to place computer power in the form of interactive, information-processing networks directly into the hands of all office professionals, specialists, and managers, as well as secretaries and the data-processing staff. To implement this strategy, H-P introduced 27 new office products, including two new minicomputers, new word-processing terminals, improved computer terminals for creating graphic representations of numbers, new low-cost disc memories, and four new data communications products to tie all these elements together. Electronic mail and electronic filing packages were due to be introduced within a year. Combined with its previously announced products, such as laser printers and a low-cost personal computer, these new products gave H-P a fully integrated office system. For the first time, H-P had the potential to penetrate the full spectrum of business computer uses.

Although in 1979 and 1980 Hewlett-Packard had enjoyed an average annual growth rate of 45% in electronic data products revenues, that growth rate dropped in 1981 to 17%. According to *Business Week*,[5] a growing number of their data processing customers had begun to purchase equipment from such companies as Wang Laboratories, Datapoint, and Lanier Business Products, which offered systems aimed directly at the automated office. Growth in the market for conventional minicomputers had slowed to 25%, so that H-P needed to tap into the market for the larger so-called superminis and the market for office systems, since both were expanding at about 40% a year, if it wanted to continue its healthy growth rate.

A major target for H-P's thrust into office systems would be manufacturing companies. H-P had focused its efforts in minicomputers on this market segment, which accounted for 40% of the company's business computer sales. H-P wanted to offer these same customers systems that integrated everything from measurement instruments and data collection terminals on the factory floor to word processors in the front office in a single data-processing network.

[2]ICCH 9–380–749.

[3]1972–1981.

[4]*Wall Street Journal*, "Digital Equipment and Hewlett-Packard Enter Electronic Office Systems Market," October 30, 1981, p. 48.

[5]*Business Week*, "Two Giants Bid for Office Sales," November 9, 1981, pp. 86–96.

The office market presented H-P with new marketing challenges. Minicomputer makers traditionally sold to data processing departments, but to sell office equipment they would have to identify a whole new set of buyers among their large corporate customers. H-P had developed plans to expand its business computer marketing force by 25% and service force by one-third. It also intended to go after new customers in financial services, retailing, and other non-manufacturing sectors. John Young had indicated that H-P would not aggressively go after new customers in these other areas except as there were spare resources to do so. These markets were seen as highly opportunistic sectors of the market, where perhaps some additional business could be picked up, but they were not seen as part of the basic strategic program.

Whether H-P could win sales outside its own manufacturing customer base remained to be seen. But few industry watchers doubted the company's new products would appeal to a large proportion of their regular customers. One competitor believed that if they could execute their strategies and follow them up with service and support, there was no question that H-P would gain market share at the expense of word processor vendors with narrower offerings. Conversely, a Wang Laboratories vice president indicated that H-P didn't concern them that much because H-P's strength was selling to data processing managers. Wang and IBM had much more experience selling directly into the office.

The office automation market was expected to triple to $36 billion by 1990, according to a market research report released in October 1981 by International Resource Development, Inc. No doubt the major contenders would compete fiercely to dominate the market while the multitude of small firms, which had just entered the new market, would have to scramble to survive. But in 1981, no single company had managed to secure for itself a corner on the market. *Electronics*,[6] a major trade journal, predicted that the main contenders would be IBM, AT&T, Xerox, and very possibly Wang and Datapoint. It also indicated that DEC and H-P had the background for especially good chances of success. The unanswered question was whether Hewlett-Packard could manage this new growth and whether the company could manage to remain technologically competitive in this new business and their traditional businesses at the same time.

Electronic Calculators

In sharp contrast to the rapid-growth market in electronic office equipment, the market for electronic hand-held calculators was largely saturated. Texas Instruments had been the pioneer in inexpensive hand-held calculators and dominated the market for years, until low-priced Japanese models had taken over the lower end of the market. In 1981–82 the different calculator makers were attempting to develop specific market niches that they believed would provide opportunities for further growth. The big Japanese producers had added gimmicks like solar calculators and games such as boxing matches and electronic cube puzzles. Casio was trying to get more business by driving prices still lower. It was also offering low-cost printer calculators that could fit in a shirt pocket.

[6]*Electronics*, "H-P: A drive into office automation," November 3, 1981, pp. 106–110.

At the high-priced end of the market, companies were developing—or were already producing—products that could compete in the newly formed hand-held computer market. This market had only developed recently when Tandy (Radio Shack), Casio, and others introduced their pocket computers. In fact, *Business Week*[7] even questioned whether there was still a market for calculators with $300 price tags, since the Japanese and Radio Shack had begun to sell hand-held computers that cost less. One consultant asserted that hand-held computers would replace programmable calculators in the following three to five years. Other experts felt that the market might flatten out, but that the market for programmable calculators would die slowly and hard.

The essential difference between hand-held calculators and computers is the way the units are programmed. On advanced calculators, programs are written by pressing a series of fixed-function keys in the order needed to step through calculations. Hand-held computers, however, use a conventional programming language which consists of short statements that tell the machine what to do. Both TI and H-P were working to reposition their products in this developing market segment.

Hewlett-Packard had dominated the top end of the market from the beginning with its highly successful scientific calculator, the HP-35, introduced in 1972. With its late 1981 introduction of several new products, H-P put its calculator somewhere in the increasingly gray border between programmable calculators and hand-held computers. For example, the Hewlett-Packard Interface Loop (HP-IL) provided a link that let the HP-41 calculator control and communicate with other machines and computers, including the company's HP-80 personal computer. Complementary products included a battery-operated printer, a digital cassette drive, cassettes that significantly expanded the calculator's memory, and a device that other companies could build into their computers to make them compatible with the system. The company aimed the new system at its favorite customers: engineers and scientists. The products would allow H-P to sell accessory products to people who already owned the popular HP-41 series calculators, and to attract new customers who would prefer to pay $325 and add components later, instead of paying $2,000 or more for a personal computer.

Analysts expected that both Texas Instruments and Tandy Corporation (Radio Shack) would be strong competitors, especially at the high-priced end of the market. However, as *Business Week*[8] and the *Wall Street Journal*[9] were quick to point out, the Japanese producers were not limiting their horizons to the high end of the calculator market. They were clearly working on strategies and products that would expand pocket computers to the mass market. One of Casio's vice-presidents eventually expected to have a pocket computer low enough in price to do away with all the scientific calculators in the market. It seemed clear that H-P would have to be both technologically innovative and cost effective if it intended to be competitive in this market.

[7]*Business Week,* "When Calculator Is a Dirty Word," June 14, 1982, p. 62.

[8]Op. cit.

[9]*Wall Street Journal,* "Calculator Makers Add Features and Cut Prices to Find a Niche in a Crowded Market," December 21, 1981, p. 23.

Business Segment Performance (1978–1981)

Hewlett-Packard reported data by business segment, with both electronic office systems and hand-held calculators and computers included in electronic data products. The other business segments were electronic test and measurement, medical electronic equipment, and analytical instrumentation. Exhibit 1 provides data on net sales, earn-

Exhibit 1 Selected data on business segments (millions)

	1978	1979	1980	1981	Percent Average Annual Growth 1978–81
Net Sales					
Electronic data products	$715	$1,060	$1,510	$1,771	36
Electronic test and measurement	731	986	1,200	1,349	23
Medical electronic equipment	163	193	230	273	19
Analytical instrumentation	98	122	159	185	24
Earnings Before Taxes					
Electronic data products	$124	$ 183	$ 285	$ 319	38
Electronic test and measurement	180	242	271	284	17
Medical electronic equipment	26	27	37	50	25
Analytical instrumentation	16	16	24	32	28
Identifiable Assets					
Electronic data products	$587	$ 767	$1,000	$1,169	26
Electronic test and measurement	452	594	709	817	22
Medical electronic equipment	120	131	146	175	14
Analytical instrumentation	71	83	94	99	16
Capital Expenditures					
Electronic data products	$ 90	$ 115	$ 148	$ 174	25
Electronic test and measurement	49	46	85	89	28
Medical electronic equipment	7	5	11	18	52
Analytical instrumentation	7	6	11	9	17

Source: Hewlett-Packard *Annual Reports*

ings before taxes, identifiable assets, and capital expenditures for these four business segments. Exhibit 2 compares electronic data products with the other business segments combined together to provide a summary comparison of their comparatively newer, more competitive, and higher-risk line of business with their basic and more traditional business activities. The electronic data products appeared to have provided greater growth in profit margins (ebt/sales), asset turnover (sales/assets), and return on assets (ebt/assets), although the level of returns was higher in the more traditional businesses.

STRATEGIC IMPLEMENTATION

Structural Changes

The January 1982 Hewlett-Packard Corporate Organization Chart (Exhibits 3 and 4) shows that a number of changes have been made since Mr. Young became Chief Executive Officer. Ralph Lee, Executive Vice President—Operations, retired in 1980 after 35 years with H-P. Paul Ely, Vice President and General Manager—Computer Systems, and Bill Terry, Vice President and General Manager—Instruments, were subsequently made Executive Vice Presidents—Operations.

Bill Doolittle had been promoted from Vice President—International to Senior Vice President—International. Al Oliverio had been promoted from Vice President—Marketing to Senior Vice President—Marketing. Ed van Bronkhorst had been promoted from Vice President to Senior Vice President, Corporate Treasurer, and Chief Financial Officer. Franco Mariotti had been promoted from Managing Director—Europe to Vice President—Europe. Dick Alberding had been promoted from General Manager—Medical Group to Vice President—Medical Group. Dr. Bernard Oliver retired as an officer and director of the company in May 1981. He had been with H-P for 29 years as head of corporate research and development activities, John Doyle, Vice President of Personnel, replaced Oliver as Vice President—Research and Development. Appointed Director of Personnel, succeeding Doyle, was Bill Craven, General Manager of the McMinnville Division (Medical Group) since 1976. Exhibit 5 provides background information on these executive officers.

Corporate Manufacturing Services had been shifted from being part of corporate staff, reporting to administration, to having a direct reporting relationship to operations. An Internal Audit department had been set up and reported directly to John Young. The Computer Systems Group had been split into four separate entities—the Technical Computer Group, the Business Computer Group, the Computer Peripherals Group, and the Computer Terminals Group. The products of these four groups continued to be marketed through one organization, the Computer Marketing Group. The Instruments Group had been divided into the Microwave and Communication Instrument Group and the Electronic Measurements Group. The products of these two groups continued to be marketed through one organization, Instrument Marketing. The handheld calculator and personal computer activities had been elevated to product group status, the Personal Computation Group. As a result, there were ten product groups

Exhibit 2 Comparison of electronic data products and other business segments combined*

Summary Data	1978	1979	1980	1981	Percent Average Annual Growth 1978–81
Net Sales (millions)					
Electronic Data Products	$ 715	$1,060	$1,510	$1,771	36
Other Segments Combined	992	1,301	1,589	1,807	22
Earnings Before Taxes (millions)					
Electronic Data Products	$ 124	$ 183	$ 285	$ 319	38
Other Segments Combined	222	285	332	366	18
Identifiable Assets (millions)					
Electronic Data Products	$ 587	$ 767	$1,000	$1,169	26
Other Segments Combined	643	808	949	1,091	19
Capital Expenditures (millions)					
Electronic Data Products	$ 90	$ 115	$ 148	$ 174	25
Other Segments Combined	63	57	107	106	26
Strategic Ratio Analysis					
EBT/Sales (percent)					
Electronic Data Products	17.3	17.3	18.9	18.0	2
Other Segments Combined	22.4	21.9	20.9	20.3	–3
Sales/Identifiable Assets (times)					
Electronic Data Products	1.22	1.38	1.51	1.51	8
Other Segments Combined	1.54	1.61	1.67	1.66	3
EBT/Identifiable Assets (percent)					
Electronic Data Products	21.1	23.9	28.5	27.3	9
Other Segments Combined	34.5	35.3	35.0	33.5	–1

*Electronic Test and Measurement, Medical Electronic Equipment, and Analytical Instrumentation.

Exhibit 3 Hewlett-Packard corporate organization, January 1982

Viewed broadly, Hewlett-Packard Company is a rather complex organization made up of many business units that offer a wide range of advanced electronic products to a variety of markets around the world. Giving it common direction and cohesion are shared philosophies, practices and goals as well as technologies.

Within this broad context, the individual business units—called product divisions—are relatively small and self-sufficient so that decisions can be made at the level of the organization most responsible for putting them into action. Consistent with this approach, it has always been a practice at Hewlett-Packard to give each individual employee considerable freedom to implement methods and ideas that meet specific local organizational goals and broad corporate objectives.

Since its start in 1939, the HP organization has grown to more than 40 product divisions. To provide for effective overall management and coordination, the company has aligned these divisions into product groups characterized by product and/or market focus. Today there are ten such groups or segments. Six sales-and-service forces, organized around broad product categories, represent the product groups in the field.

HP's corporate structure is designed to foster a small-business flexibility within its many individual operating units while supporting them with the strengths of a larger organization. The accompanying chart provides a graphic view of the relationship of the various groups and other organizational elements. The organization has been structured to allow the groups and their divisions to concentrate on their product-development, manufacturing and marketing activities without having to perform all the administrative tasks required of a company doing business worldwide. Normal and functional lines of responsibility and communication are indicated on the chart; however, direct and informal communication across lines and between levels is encouraged.

Here is a closer look at the company's basic organizational units:

PRODUCT DIVISIONS

An HP product division is a vertically integrated organization that conducts itself very much like an independent business. Its fundamental responsibilities are to develop, manufacture and market products that are profitable and which make contributions in the market place by virtue of technological or economic advantage.

Each division has its own distinct family of products, for which it has worldwide marketing responsibility. A division also is responsible for its own accounting, personnel activities, quality assurance, and support of its products in the field. In addition, it has important social and economic responsibilities in its local community.

PRODUCT GROUPS

Product groups, which are composed of divisions having closely related product lines, are responsible for coordinating the activities of their respective divisions. The management of each group has overall responsibility for the operations and financial performance of its members. Further; each group has worldwide responsibility for its manufacturing operations and sales/service forces. Management staffs of the four U.S. sales regions and two international headquarters (European and Intercontinental Operations) assist the groups in coordinating the sales/service functions.

The group management structure provides a primary channel of communication between the divisions and corporate departments.

CORPORATE OPERATIONS

Corporate Operations management has responsibility for the day-to-day operation of the company. The executive vice presidents in charge of Corporate Operations are directly responsible to HP's president for the performance of their assigned product groups; they also provide a primary channel of communication between the groups and the president.

CORPORATE ADMINISTRATION

The principal responsibility of Corporate Administration is to insure that the corporate staff offices provide the specialized policies, expertise and resources to adequately support the divisions and groups on a worldwide basis. The executive vice president in charge of Corporate Administration also reports to the president, providing an important upward channel of communication for the corporate staff activities.

The Marketing and International offices, through the U.S. sales regions and two international headquarters, insure that—on a worldwide basis—all corporate policies and practices are followed and that local legal and fiscal requirements are met.

CORPORATE RESEARCH AND DEVELOPMENT

HP Laboratories is the corporate research and development organization that provides a central source of technical support for the product-development efforts of HP product divisions. In these efforts, the divisions make important use of the advanced technologies, materials, components, and theoretical analyses researched or developed by HP Labs. Through their endeavors in areas of science and technology, the corporate laboratories also help the company evaluate promising new areas of business.

BOARD OF DIRECTORS

The Board of Directors and its chairman have ultimate responsibility for the legal and ethical conduct of the company and its officers. It is the board's duty to protect and advance the interests of the stockholders, to foster a continuing concern for fairness in the company's relations with employees, and to fulfill all requirements of the law with regard to the board's stewardship. The board counsels management on general business matters and also reviews and evaluates the performance of management. To assist in discharging these responsibilities, the board has formed various committees to oversee the company's activities and programs in such areas as employee benefits, compensation, financial auditing and investment.

PRESIDENT

The president has operating responsibility for the overall performance and direction of the company, subject to the authority of the Board of Directors. Also, the president is directly responsible for corporate development and planning functions, and for HP Labs.

EXECUTIVE COMMITTEE

This committee meets weekly for the purpose of setting and reviewing corporate policies, and making coordinated decisions on a wide range of current operations and activities. Members include the Executive Committee chairman, the chairman of the Board, the president and the executive vice presidents for Operations and Administration. All are members of the Board of Directors.

OPERATIONS COUNCIL

Primary responsibilities of this body are to review operating policies on a broad basis and to turn policy decisions into corporate action. Members include the executive vice presidents, product group general managers, the senior vice presidents of Marketing and International, the vice president—Europe, and the managing director of Intercontinental.

Exhibit 4 Hewlett-Packard corporate organization as of January 1982

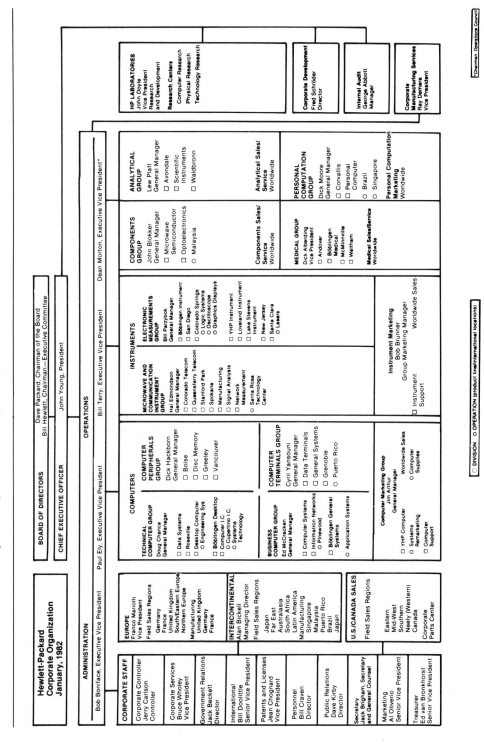

Source: Public document, Hewlett-Packard Corp.

Exhibit 5   Executive officers of the Hewlett-Packard Company

David Packard; age 69; Chairman, H-P. Mr. Packard is a co-founder of the Company and has been a director since 1947.[1] He has served as Chairman of the Board of Directors since 1972 and was the Company's President from 1947 to 1964. Mr. Packard also served as Chairman of the Board and Chief Executive Officer from 1964 to 1968 when he was appointed U.S. Deputy Secretary of Defense. Mr. Packard is a Director of Caterpillar Tractor Company; Standard Oil Company of California; The Boeing Company; and Genentech, Inc.

William R. Hewlett; age 68; Chairman of the Executive Committee, H-P. Mr. Hewlett is a co-founder of the Company and has served on its Board of Directors since 1947. Mr. Hewlett served as Executive Vice President of the Company from 1947 to 1964 when he was appointed President. He served as President and Chief Executive Officer from 1969 to 1977 and was Chief Executive Officer and Chairman of the Executive Committee from November, 1977 to May, 1978 when he retired as Chief Executive Officer. Mr. Hewlett remains the Chairman of the Company's Executive Committee. He also is a Director of Chrysler Corporation and Utah International, Inc., a mining company.

John A. Young; age 49; President and Chief Executive Officer, H-P. Mr. Young has served as President and Chief Executive Officer of the Company since May, 1978. He was named President and Chief Operating Officer of the Company as of November 1, 1977 and has been a member of the Company's Board of Directors since 1974. Prior to his appointment as President and Chief Operating Officer, Mr. Young served as Executive Vice President from 1974. Mr. Young is a Director of Wells Fargo & Company; Wells Fargo Bank, N.A.; Dillingham Corporation; and SRI International. He also serves on the Board of Trustees of Stanford University.

Robert L. Boniface; age 57; Executive Vice President, H-P. Mr. Boniface has been a Director of the Company since 1974. He has served as an Executive Vice President of the Company since 1975 and was Vice President, Administration from 1974 to 1975. Mr. Boniface served as Vice President, Marketing from 1970 to 1974.

Paul C. Ely, Jr.; age 49; Executive Vice President, H-P. Mr. Ely was named an Executive Vice President of the Company in July, 1980 and was elected to the Board of Directors effective September, 1980. Mr. Ely is responsible for the Company's Computer Groups. Prior to his appointment as Executive Vice President, Mr. Ely served as Computer Group General Manager from 1974 and as Vice President from 1976.

Dean O. Morton; age 49; Executive Vice President, H-P. Mr. Morton was elected a Director of the Company in September, 1977. He was appointed a Vice President of the Company in 1973 and was also appointed General Manager of the Company's Medical Products Group in 1974. Mr. Morton served in those dual capacities until he assumed his present position in November, 1977. Mr. Morton is also a Director of State Street Investment Corporation and Cobe Laboratories, Inc.

William E. Terry; age 48; Executive Vice President, H-P. Mr. Terry was named an Executive Vice President of the Company in July, 1980 and was elected to the Board of Directors effective September, 1980. Mr. Terry is responsible for the Company's Instrument Groups. Prior to his appointment as Executive Vice President, Mr. Terry served as Vice President and General Manager of the Company's Instrument Group from 1974. Mr. Terry served as General Manager of the Company's Data Products Group from 1971 to 1974. Mr. Terry is a Director of Applied Magnetics Corporation; Altus Corporation, a manufacturer of lithium batteries; and Kevex Corporation, a manufacturer of x-ray spectrometers.

William P. Doolittle; age 63; Senior Vice President, International, H-P. Mr. Doolittle has been a Director of the Company since 1971 and served as Vice President, International from 1963 until he assumed his present position in July, 1981. Mr. Doolittle is also a director of Machine Intelligence Corp. and Creative Strategies International.

Alfred P. Oliverio; age 54; Senior Vice President, Marketing, H-P. Mr. Oliverio served as Vice President, Marketing from 1974 until he assumed his present position in July, 1981.

Edwin E. van Bronkhorst; age 57; Senior Vice President, Treasurer, H-P. Mr. van Bronkhorst served as Vice President and Treasurer of the Company from 1963 until his appointment as Senior Vice President and Treasurer in July, 1981. He also serves as the Company's Chief Financial Officer. He was named a Director of the Company in 1962 and currently serves as a Director of ROLM Corporation, a manufacturer of computerized communication systems; Northern California Savings and Loan Association; and TRIAD Systems Corporation, a manufacturer of microcomputer-based data processing systems primarily for the auto parts distribution industry.

Richard C. Alberding; age 50; Vice President, Medical Products Group, H-P. Mr. Alberding was appointed to his present position in July, 1981, and has served as general manager of the Company's Medical Products Group since 1977. Mr. Alberding was director of the Company's European operations from 1970 until 1977.

Jean C. Chognard; age 57; Vice President, Patents and Licenses, H-P. Mr. Chognard has been Patent Counsel for the Company since 1958 and has been a Vice President of the Company since May, 1976.

Raymond M. Demere, Jr.; age 60; Vice President, Manufacturing Services, H-P. Mr. Demere has been a Vice President of the Company since 1971 and served as operations manager of the Instrument Group of the Company from 1974 until September, 1977 when he was appointed Vice President, Manufacturing Services.

John L. Doyle; age 48; Vice President, Research and Development, H-P. Mr. Doyle was appointed Corporate Director of Personnel in June, 1976 and thereafter elected Vice President, Personnel in July, 1976. In June, 1981 Mr. Doyle assumed his present position as Vice President, Research and Development.

Franco Mariotti; age 46; Vice President, Europe, H-P. Mr. Mariotti was appointed to his present position in July, 1981 and has served as managing director of the Company's European operations since 1977. From 1976 to 1977 Mr. Mariotti served as marketing manager for Europe.

W. Bruce Wholey; age 60; Vice President, Corporate Services, H-P. Mr. Wholey has been Vice President, Corporate Services since January, 1973.

S. T. Jack Brigham III; age 42; Secretary and General Counsel, H-P. Mr. Brigham was elected Assistant Secretary of the Company in May, 1974. He served in that capacity as well as General Attorney of the Company until May, 1976 when he was elected Secretary and General Counsel of the Company.

[1]Mr. Packard did not serve as a Director during his service as United States Deputy Secretary of Defense from January, 1969 to December, 1971.

Source: Hewlett-Packard 1981 Form 10-K.

instead of the six in 1978. There remained, however, the same six marketing organizations.

Leadership

According to the *San Jose Mercury*,[10] John Young's team of employees was learning to play the electronics game by Young's rules, which demanded diligent planning, close attention to cost effectiveness, and no last-minute surprises. Although many had originally doubted that he could fill the shoes of the two founders, these critics have since admitted they like the way Young has changed and redirected the firm. He has placed added emphasis on manufacturing and marketing, dropped technological programs

[10]*San Jose Mercury*, "H-P—now it's the house that Young built," August 24, 1981, pp. 1D and 7D.

when they weren't cost effective, and monitored day-to-day details to correct problems before they snowballed. At the same time, he has balanced his approach by stimulating efforts on new products and technologies, such as electronic office systems and hand-held computers with the associated H-P Integrated Loop. Young has not emphasized formal planning done by corporate planners. Instead, he has pushed a pragmatic system, with the operating people doing the planning. Young believed his contribution consisted of putting emphasis on having a lot more time spent in thoughtful consideration of what the company was doing, but not in a formal planning regime.

John Young was reported to be a serious chief executive with a dry sense of humor, a logical thinker who often asked leading questions to get his managers to come around to his way of thinking, and an efficient worker who did not tolerate incompetence. Associates saw him as a "numbers man" with a top priority of profits. Despite his devotion to numbers and planning, Young also followed two basic and more subtle tenets of the H-P way of life: managing by wandering around and showing respect and empathy for employees. Exhibit 6 provides a brief outline of "The HP Way." For all his formal position power, Young has relied heavily on consensus-style management. He has met often with his executive committee, and few major decisions have been made without the agreement of everyone around the table. Members of the committee were expected to be independent thinkers, but Young has used a subtle approach based on logic to bring people around to his point of view. When Young has not agreed with a colleague's opinion, he has asked questions. These were not confrontational kinds of questions, but they were penetrating. Young would then go along with whatever course the executive eventually recommended. Young saw himself as being good at the non-directive approach and worked hard at being a good coach.

High on Young's list of priorities for the 1980s was for H-P to become a low-cost manufacturer. Young admitted this had not been one of H-P's strengths. His concern for cost effectiveness was almost legendary. When he initially assumed the presidency, he put a lot of effort into convincing his management team that the company could do a better job of managing assets, particularly inventory and accounts receivable. One of the first things he axed was research for research's sake. Yet about 70% of total company product orders in 1981 resulted from products developed after 1977. Under Young, technology has received more of a profit-and-loss kind of consideration and evaluation. In 1981, research and development was increased to 9.7% of sales, an increase of 1.1% over the previous year. Further, John Young has restructured H-P laboratories entirely. He has also created over the last three years a computer and semi-conductor research facility staffed with 100 professionals. He thought this would become one of the top such facilities in the United States.

In September 1979, an attitude survey was taken in which 7,966 employees were asked to evaluate more than 100 topics at H-P, including pay, benefits, supervision, management, job satisfaction, and many other items. Exhibit 7 provides results on major items and a comparison to national norms. With a 67% favorable response, employees rated H-P management well above the national norm of 46%. The rating covered such questions as the fairness of management decisions and the concern of

Exhibit 6   The H-P way

___

Business Practices

Pay As We Go — No Long-Term Borrowing
- Helps to maintain a stable financial environment during depressed business times.
- Serves as an excellent self-regulating mechanism for H-P managers.

Market Expansion and Leadership Based on New Product Contributions
- Engineering excellence determines market recognition of new H-P products.
- Novel new-product ideas and implementations serve as the basis for expansion of existing markets or diversification into new markets.

Customer Satisfaction Second to None
- Sell only what has been thoroughly designed, tested, and specified.
- Products must have lasting value, having high reliability (quality) and customers discover additional benefits while using them.
- Offer best after-sales service and support in the industry.

Honesty and Integrity in All Matters
- Dishonest dealings with vendors or customers (such as bribes and kickbacks) not tolerated.
- Open and honest communication with employees and stockholders alike. Conservative financial reporting.

People Practices

Belief in Our People
- Confidence in, and respect for, H-P people as opposed to dependence on extensive rules, procedures, etc.
- Trust people to do their job right (individual freedom) without constant directives.
- Opportunity for meaningful participation (job dignity).
- Emphasis on working together and sharing rewards (teamwork and partnership).
- Share responsibilities; help each other; learn from each other; provide chance to make mistakes.
- Recognition based on contribution to results — sense of achievement and self-esteem.
- Profit sharing; stock purchase plan; retirement program, etc., aimed at employees and company sharing in each other's success.
- Company financial management emphasis on protecting employees' job security.

A Superior Working Environment
- Informality — open, honest communications; no artificial distinctions between employees (first-name basis); management by wandering around; and open-door communication policy.
- Develop and promote from within — lifetime training, education, career counseling to give employees maximum opportunities to grow and develop with the company.
- Decentralization — emphasis on keeping work groups as small as possible for maximum employee identification with our businesses and customers.
- Management-By-Objectives (MBO) — provides a sound basis for measuring performance of employees as well as managers; is objective, not political.

Management Style

Management by Wandering Around
- To have a well-managed operation, managers and supervisors must be aware of what happens in their areas — at several levels above and below their immediate level.
- Since people are our most important resource, managers have direct responsibility for employee training, performance and general well being. To do this, managers must move around to find out how people feel about their jobs — what they think will make their work more productive and meaningful.

Open Door Policy
- Managers and supervisors are expected to foster a work environment in which employees feel free and comfortable to seek individual counsel or express general concerns.
- Therefore, if employees feel such steps are necessary, they have the right to discuss their concerns with higher-level managers. Any effort through intimidation or other means to prevent an employee from going 'up the line' is absolutely contrary to company policy — and will be dealt with accordingly.
- Also, use of the Open Door policy must not in any way influence evaluations of employees or produce any other adverse consequences.
- Employees also have responsibilities — particularly in keeping their discussions with upper-level managers to the point and focused on concerns of significance.

___

Source: Measure, September-October, 1981, p. 14.

Exhibit 7 H-P attitude survey

	Percent Favorable Responses	
	H-P Employees	*National Sample*[*]
Work organization	70	65
Work efficiency	67	63
Management	67	46
Job training and information	61	56
Work associates	81	78
Supervision	70	61
Overall communications	58	41
Performance and advancement	75	58
Pay	52	39
Benefits	70	53
Job satisfaction	76	66
Organizational identification	84	59
Organization change	28	25
Working conditions	59	44
Job stability	56	60
Policies and practices	81	69
Reactions to the survey	77	55

[*]200 Top U.S. Companies.

Source: Measure, "Open Line," March-April 1981, p. 12b.

managers for the well-being of the people they managed. As reported in the March-April issue of *Measure*[11] (H-P's magazine), four of the top 22 issues generated by the survey analysis showed concern about top management and the application of management philosophy. The quality of some managers was questioned; management-by-objective and management-by-wandering-around were criticized for not being used widely enough; and the use of the Open Door Policy was sometimes frustrated by a feeling of threat of retribution. The fundamental responses to these concerns were seen by top management as chiefly matters of local responsibility and action, although corporate support in the form of training, communication, and management evaluation was believed to be important. The startup of more than 300 quality teams at many locations was believed to improve both productivity and the practice of MBO. The Open Door Policy as well as MBWA were topics of messages by Young in various issues of *Measure*. Both of these policies were seen by John Young as important to the creation of a feeling of openness and providing informal opportunities for everyone to hear and be heard.

[11]*Measure*, "Open-Line," March-April, 1981, pp. 12a–h.

He believed the desired result was to achieve mutual trust and respect for both the people and the process involved. He has tried to make it clear both in his communications and his actions that the H-P manager has no greater responsibility.

Performance (1978–1981)

Since 1978, when John Young became CEO, Hewlett-Packard has grown rapidly. The annual growth rate of net sales has averaged 27.4% and that of net earnings has averaged 26.9%. The growth rates for 1980–81, however, were substantially lower than previous years, 15.5% and 16.0%, respectively. The 1981 *Annual Report*[12] indicated

Exhibit 8   Four-year consolidated summary* for the years ended October 31 (millions except for employee and per share amounts)

	1978	**1979**	**1980**	**1981**
Net Sales	$1,737	$2,361	$3,099	$3,578
Costs and expenses				
Cost of goods sold	808	1,106	1,475	1,703
Research and development	154	204	272	347
Marketing	264	362	459	526
Administration and general	215	291	370	422
	1,441	1,963	2,576	2,998
Earnings before taxes	296	398	523	580
Provision for taxes	143	195	254	268
Net earnings	$ 153	$ 203	$ 269	$ 312
Per share *				
Net earnings	$ 1.32	$ 1.72	$ 2.23	$ 2.55
Cash dividends	$ .12	$ .17	$ .20	$ .22
At year-end				
Total assets	$1,462	$1,900	$2,337	$2,758
Long-term debt	$ 10	$ 15	$ 29	$ 26
Common shares outstanding*	116	118	120	123
Thousands of employees	42	52	57	64

*Reflects the 2-for-1 stock splits in 1979 and 1981.

Source: Hewlett-Packard *Annual Reports.*

[12]Hewlett-Packard Company, *1981 Annual Report,* pp. 2–4.

that the major cause of the reduced growth was the adverse economic conditions in the United States and abroad. Net sales were somewhat below projections, and incoming orders were considerably lower than expectations. These shortfalls, coupled with a high level of committed expenses for new product development and product introductions, put heavy pressure on operating profit. Two changes were made in 1981 that somewhat modified earnings. The first was a $14 million reduction in accrued pension expense for the year, which increased net earnings by $7 million. This change resulted from a scheduled five-year review of the initial funding assumptions used for the U.S. Supplemental Pension Plan begun in 1976. The second was an $8 million reduction in income taxes, resulting from the Economic Recovery Tax Act of 1981. Without these two adjustments, the company's net earnings would have been $297 million, up only 10.4% from 1980. Exhibit 8 provides a four-year consolidated summary of various measures of performance. Exhibit 9 provides an analysis of operating results. Exhibit 10 is a consolidated balance sheet. Exhibit 11 is a consolidated statement of changes in financial position, showing how funds were provided and how they were used. Exhibit 12 provides a strategic ratio analysis of H-P's performance during this period. Exhibit 13 includes information on sales, profits, and research and development expenses for selected companies and industries.

A TIME FOR EVALUATION

John Young had just reviewed the changes made in strategy and strategic implementation while he had served as chief executive officer. He wondered whether the strategic changes made had been the right ones and whether any additional changes might be needed. He believed the performance of the various business segments might offer a

Exhibit 9 Analysis of operating results

	Percent Increase from Prior Year				Percent of Net Sales			
	1978	*1979*	*1980*	*1981*	*1978*	*1979*	*1980*	*1981*
Net Sales	27.0	35.9	31.3	15.5	100.0	100.0	100.0	100.0
Cost of goods sold	29.3	36.9	33.4	15.5	45.7	46.8	47.6	47.6
Research and development	23.2	32.5	33.3	27.6	8.9	8.6	8.8	9.7
Marketing	26.9	37.1	26.8	14.6	15.2	15.3	14.8	14.7
Administrative and general	18.8	35.3	27.1	14.1	12.4	12.3	11.9	11.8
Earnings before taxes	29.3	34.5	31.4	10.9	17.0	16.9	16.9	16.2
Provision for taxes	32.4	36.4	30.3	5.5	8.2	8.3	8.2	7.5
Net earnings	26.4	32.7	32.5	16.0	8.8	8.6	8.7	8.7

Exhibit 10 Consolidated balance sheet*

Assets	1978	1979	1980	1981
Current assets				
Cash and temporary cash investments	$ 189	$ 248	$ 247	$ 290
Accounts and notes receivable	371	491	622	682
Inventories				
Finished goods	99	120	148	186
Purchased parts and fabricated assemblies	257	358	397	456
Other current assets:	36	52	77	91
Total current assets	952	1,269	1,491	1,705
Property, plant, and equipment				
Land	44	53	69	78
Buildings and leasehold improvements	405	491	645	789
Machinery and equipment	272	348	447	581
	721	892	1,161	1,448
Accumulated depreciation	245	301	372	469
	476	591	789	979
Other assets	34	40	57	74
	$1,462	$1,900	$2,337	$2,758

Liabilities and Shareholder's Equity	1978	1979	1980	1981
Current liabilities				
Notes payable and commercial paper	$ 85	$ 147	$ 143	$ 144
Accounts payable	71	109	104	143
Employee compensation, benefits, and accruals	171	237	297	308
Accrued taxes on income	88	106	147	109
Total current liabilities	415	599	691	704
Long term debt	10	15	29	26
Deferred taxes on earnings	35	51	70	108
Shareholders' equity				
Common stock	29	59	60	123
Capital in excess of par	247	267	333	358
Retained earnings	727	909	1,154	1,439
Total shareholders' equity	1,002	1,235	1,547	1,920
	$1,462	$1,900	$2,337	$2,758

*In millions; for fiscal years ending October 31.

Source: Hewlett-Packard *Annual Reports.*

Exhibit 11   Consolidated statement of changes in financial position*

	1978	1979	1980	1981
Funds provided				
Net earnings	$153	$203	$269	$312
Items not affecting funds:				
Depreciation and amortization	56	72	93	120
Other, net	11	27	27	53
Total from operations	220	302	389	485
Proceeds from sale of stock	29	37	50	67
Increase in accounts payable and accrued liabilities	59	104	55	50
Total funds provided	308	443	494	602
Funds used				
Investment in property, plant and equipment	159	191	297	318
Increase in accounts and notes receivable	99	120	131	60
Increase in inventories	77	122	67	97
Increase in other current assets	8	16	25	14
Decrease (increase) in accrued taxes	(26)	(18)	(41)	38
Dividends to shareholders	14	20	24	27
Other, net	(1)	(5)	(12)	6
Total funds used	330	446	491	560
Increase (decrease) in cash and temporary cash investment, net of notes payable and commercial paper	$ (22)	$ (3)	$ 3	$ 42
Net cash at beginning of year	126	104	101	104
Net cash at end of year	$104	$101	$104	$146

*In millions; for fiscal years ending October 31.

Source: Hewlett-Packard *Annual Reports.*

Exhibit 12   Strategic ratio analysis

Fiscal Year	Profit Margin *Earnings* *Sales*	Asset Turnover *Sales* *Assets*	Return on Assets *Earnings* *Assets*	Financial Leverage *Assets* *Net Worth*	Return on Net Worth *Earnings* *Net Worth*
	(Percent)	*(Times)*	*(Percent)*	*(Times)*	*(Percent)*
1978	8.81	1.19	10.5	1.46	15.3
1979	8.60	1.24	10.7	1.54	16.4
1980	8.68	1.33	11.5	1.51	17.4
1981	8.72	1.30	11.3	1.44	16.3

valuable point of departure for his analysis. He also felt that this seemed like an appropriate time to review the changes made in organization structure, his management and leadership of the company, and the organization's overall corporate performance during these recent years of growth and strategic change. He believed that enough time had passed that a reasonably objective assessment could be made as to whether he had provided the necessary strategies and leadership to the Hewlett-Packard Company during this difficult transition period.

Exhibit 13   Sales, profits, and R&D data on selected companies and industries

	Sales		Profits		R & D Expense			
	1981 Millions of Dollars	Percent Annual Change (1977–81)	1981 Millions of Dollars	Percent Annual Change (1977–81)	1981 Millions of Dollars	Percent of Sales	Percent of Profit	Dollars per Employee
Selected Companies								
AT&T	58214	12.2	6888	10.6	507.2	0.9	7.4	594
Datapoint	396	40.1	49	53.8	34.7	8.8	71.2	5091
Digital Equipment	3198	31.1	343	33.2	251.2	7.9	73.2	3987
Hewlett-Packard	3578	28.4	312	27.9	347.0	9.7	111.2	5422
Lanier Business Products	303	35.9	26	39.4	4.7	1.5	18.4	1163
IBM	29070	12.3	3308	5.4	1612.0	5.5	48.7	4542
Texas Instruments	4206	21.0	109	2.7	219.4	5.2	202.2	2621
Wang Laboratories	856	60.2	78	73.3	66.9	7.8	85.7	4240
Xerox	8691	14.3	598	8.4	526.3	6.1	88.0	4350
Industry Composites								
Instruments	14106	18.6	740	17.4	647.5	4.6	87.5	2571
Information Processing								
Computers	60057	15.5	5311	9.4	3845.5	6.4	72.4	4231
Office Equipment	14716	17.9	771	13.2	729.2	5.0	94.6	3324
Peripherals & Services	5800	29.3	365	35.7	344.1	5.9	94.2	3284

Source: Business Week, "R & D Scoreboard," July 5, 1982, pp. 54–72.

CASE 7

Apple Computer, Inc.
WILLIAM E. FULMER
The University of Alabama

RUSS LaGRONE
The University of Alabama

In early 1983, Steven Jobs was reflecting on how much his life had changed in six years. Although he still liked to wear frayed jeans, suede boots and a cowboy shirt and he still used a small office with only a steel desk and two chairs and had no reserved parking place, he was now chairman of the board of a company which had in 1982 broken into the *Fortune 500* with a 411 ranking and whose stock had a market value of over $1.7 billion.

In spite of his incredible success and wealth (personal worth in excess of $210 million), his life was much more complicated than it had been just a few years before. Although his company had broken the $100 million sales mark ($133.6 million) in the first fiscal quarter of 1982 and he had made good on his promise to give all 3,391 employees an extra week of vacation, he had little time to vacation himself. In fact, he had been able to take only a few days off in the last few years to go backpacking in Yosemite National Park. Except for some Japanese wood prints and a Maxfield Parrish painting, his unpretentious home was largely bare. *Time* described his home in Los Gatos as "nothing that would interest *Architectural Digest:* freshly laundered shirts lie on the floor of an unfurnished second bedroom, a love letter is magneted to the kitchen fridge, the master bedroom holds a dresser, a few framed photos (Einstein, Jobs with his buddy Governor Jerry Brown, a guru), a mattress, an Apple II."

In recent months Apple Computer had been hit with a host of unexpected problems, ranging from counterfeit Apples to an antitrust suit to the likely resignation of its president. In addition, expected problems such as the effect of the recession on sales, increased competition (especially from IBM), and the introduction of Apple's new Lisa and MacIntosh models were serious concerns. The challenges facing Jobs were enough to keep any 28-year-old occupied.

Prepared by William E. Fulmer and Russ LaGrone, The University of Alabama. Copyright © 1983 by William E. Fulmer.

THE PERSONAL COMPUTER[1]

The manufacture of the personal computer became possible with the development by Intel Corporation in 1971 of the microprocessor, a tiny electronic computer engraved on a silicon chip. Today it is used in an immense variety of smart machines, from microwave ovens to video games and sophisticated military weapons.

Soon after microprocessors became commercially available, electronic tinkerers in the back shops and garages in California's Silicon Valley and elsewhere began building crude personal computers. The early hand-soldered machines were inelegant, barely functional, and almost incomprehensible to anyone without a degree in electrical engineering.

By 1982 the typical personal computer consisted of a computer with a standard typewriter keyboard, at least 32,000 (32K) bytes[2] of working memory, one floppy disk drive or computer-controlled tape drive, a video monitor, and an inexpensive printer. However, peripheral products, such as color display screens, additional memory storage, and an immense variety of software, could turn even the most simple personal computer into a powerful machine. Most of the computers utilized an 8-bit[3] microprocessor, but many of the newer models used 16-bit microprocessors, and 32-bit machines were expected on the market soon.

The power of the new personal computers can be understood by comparing them to the mainframe computers of years past. The IBM 360 model 30 mainframe introduced in the early 1960s required special handling—an air-conditioned room about 18 feet square, which housed the central processing unit (CPU), the control console, a printer, and a desk for a keypunch operator. The CPU alone was 5 feet high and 6 feet wide and had to be water cooled to prevent overheating. The CPU of IBM's new desktop Personal Computer (PC) was inscribed on a silicon chip smaller than a fingernail. The 360 model 30 could do 33,000 additions a second at full speed. The personal computer could do 700,000 a second. In 1960 dollars the model 30 had a cost of $280,000. The personal computer, fully equipped, retailed for $4,000 to $5,000.

---

[1]Much of the material in this section is based on "To Each His Own Computer," *Newsweek*, February 22, 1982, pp. 50–56.

[2]A byte refers to a character of memory. A computer with 64K (or "kilobytes") of memory can store about 64,000 characters, roughly the same as 35 typewritten pages. Computers have a set amount of working memory, i.e., directly accessible memory, but an almost unlimited amount of mass storage can be added.

[3]A bit refers to a basic unit of information. Everything the computer does, whether it sends a space ship streaking across a color video screen or takes dictation, is represented in numbers, counted out in a binary code the way people would count if endowed with only two fingers: 0, 1, 10, 11, 100, 101, and on and on. A 16-bit microprocessor can process 16 basic units of computer information at one time, compared with the 8-bit processor which can handle only 8 units. Thus the 16-bit processor is much faster and more powerful than the 8-bit processor.

INDUSTRY BACKGROUND

In 1981 approximately 500,000 personal computers were sold. For the first time over $1 billion of U.S. sales were achieved, with total worldwide sales eclipsing the $2 billion mark. Growth estimates for the market for the next five years ranged from 50 percent to 100 percent annually with estimates of total sales ranging anywhere from $4 billion to $15 billion by 1986.

By 1982 at least 150 firms were battling for position in the exploding market. Competitors included such companies as tiny Sinclair Electronics and giants of the business computer and electronics industries—IBM, Digital Equipment (DEC), and Hewlett-Packard (HP). The competition also included firms from Japan, Britain, and Italy (Exhibits 1 and 2). U.S. market share for 1980–82 was estimated by *Business Week* to be divided as shown in the following table:

	1980	1982
Apple	27%	26%
IBM	—	17
Commodore	20	12
Nippon Electric	5	11
Radio Shack (Tandy)	21	10
Hewlett-Packard	9	7
Others	18	17

The growth of the personal computer market was not only hard to predict in total but especially difficult by segment (Exhibits 3 and 4). Although the upper-end segment, designed primarily for business application and typified by the Apple II and Apple III and IBM's PC, accounted for 90% of the total sales in 1981, both the home and portable segments were expected to realize tremendous growth over the next five years. The basic price of an upper-segment model was about $1,500 but additions of sophisticated peripherals frequently drove the price over $6,000. Sophistication in the upper end ranged as far as Xerox's $16,000 Star Work Stations which featured a personal computer and an array of products tied together by a coaxial cable network.

The most significant development of 1981 in the upper-end market was the introduction of the IBM PC in August. Utilizing a 16-bit microprocessor, the IBM computer achieved third place in industry revenues within six months. Sales for the first year were 150,000 units. This success prompted rumors that other IBM personal computer models would follow as early as 1983. Some industry analysts were predicting that the industry was "now in a market driven by IBM, not Apple." Even Apple executives conceded that their biggest rivals were "IBM, IBM, and IBM."

Although the home computer segment achieved sales of $120 million and 160,000 units in 1981, in 1982 all four of the segment's leaders—Atari, Tandy, Texas Instruments, and Commodore—were expected to exceed 160,000 units of sales, with total

Exhibit 1   Product comparisons, 1981

Computer/ Price Range	Where to Buy It	Primary Applications	Advantages/ Disadvantages
Apple II $1,330–$7,000	Computer stores	Home, schools, small business, professionals	Lots of software, but not enough power for some business uses
Apple III $4,240–5,810	Computer stores	Professionals	Not much software
Atari 400 $399–$720	Computer, department, and electronics stores	Home	Low cost and excellent graphics, but keyboard difficult to use
Atari 800 $1,080–$2,000	Computer department, and electronics stores	Home, schools, professionals	Excellent graphics, but cannot expand into a large system
Commodore VIC $299–$550	Computer and department stores	Home, schools	Low cost, but not much software
Commodore PET $995–$2,885	Computer stores	Home, schools	Not supported well in field
Commodore CBM $1,495–$4,000	Computer stores	Small business, professionals	Not supported well in field
Hewlett-Packard 85 $3,250–$6,000	Computer stores, direct sales	Scientific/technical, professionals	Special features for technical users, but small screen
IBM $1,565–$6,000	Computer stores, direct sales	Home, schools, small business, professionals	Good field support, but availability could be limited
Osborne Computer $1,795	Computer stores	Professionals	Portable, but small screen
Radio Shack Model 2 $3,000–$8,000	Radio Shack stores	Professionals, small business	Lots of software, but no color
Radio Shack Model 3 $699–$4,000	Radio Shack stores	Home, schools, small business, professionals	Low price, but no color
Texas Instruments 99/4 $525–$4,000	Department stores, catalogs	Home, schools	Low price, but limited software
Xerox 820 $3,195–$6,400	Computer stores, direct sales	Small business, professionals	Good support, but no color
Zenith Z89 $2,895–$9,000	Computer stores, Heath Electronic centers	Small business, professionals	Very reliable, but no color

Source: *Business Week,* September 28, 1981, p. 80. Data from Datapro Research Corp., Future Computing, Inc., and Gnostic Concepts, Inc.

units reaching 2.2 million. Many industry experts predicted that by 1985 home computer sales alone would top the $3 billion mark, with such companies as Mattel and Coleco entering the market. The four leaders used a wide combination of price reductions, rebates, and dealer discounts to hold or increase their market shares. Tandy's

Exhibit 2 Product comparisons, 1982

IBM Personal Computer

1.	Computer	IBM Personal Computer	$1,268
2.	Working memory	64K (with expansion modules)	415
3.	Mass storage	160K/disk (with interface)	790
4.	Video display	11½-inch B/W (with interface, 25 rows, 79 characters)	680
5.	Printer	Dot matrix (with interface)	755
6.	Operating system	IBM DOS	40
	System total		$3,948

Software: Good selection available now, including VisiCalc and word processing, and IBM is working on developing an extensive selection.

Other comments: The IBM Personal Computer is a competitively priced unit backed by IBM's extensive service network. It is the only computer in this collection built around a 16-bit microprocessor, which allows it to process information with the speed of a minicomputer. It is available with color graphics plus the cost of a color TV monitor.

Osborne I

1.	Computer	Osborne I	$ 795
2.	Working memory	64K	Included
3.	Mass storage	102K/disk	Included
4.	Video display	5-inch B/W (24 rows, 52 characters)	Included
5.	Printer	User supplied	500
6.	Operating system	CP/M	Included
	System total		$2,295

Software: An almost unlimited selection with CP/M operating system. The computer comes standard with software that if purchased separately would cost about $1,500.

Other comments: The Osborne I is a new portable computer that weighs about 24 pounds. Supply is limited with a four-to-six month waiting time.

Xerox 820-III

1.	Computer	Model 820	$2,995
2.	Working memory	64K	Included
3.	Mass storage	81K/disk	Included
4.	Video display	12-inch B/W (24 rows, 80 characters)	Included
5.	Printer	User supplied	400
6.	Operating system	CP/M-80	200
	System total		$3,595

Software: An almost unlimited selection with CP/M operating system.

Other comments: The Model 820 is a high-quality, low-priced machine, backed by Xerox's use of CP/M for the 820 in many ways made CP/M the de facto operating system for personal business computers.

TRS-80 Model III

1.	Computer	TRS-80 Model III	$2,495
2.	Working memory	48K	Included
3.	Mass storage	175K/disk	Included
4.	Video display	12-inch B/W (16 rows, characters)	Included
5.	Printer	TRS Line Printer VII (dot matrix)	399
6.	Operating system	TRSDOS	Included
	System total		$2,894

Software: Like Apple, Radio Shack has developed extensive software for both models of the TRS-80, including VisiCalc.

Other comments: Radio Shack has the largest unit-volume market share in personal computers. The Model II's price-performance ratio is competitive with just about any personal business computer on the market, while the Model II is able to run more complex software packages.

Apple II +

1.	Computer	Apple II Plus	$1,530
2.	Working memory	48K	Included
3.	Mass storage	143K/disk	645
4.	Video display	12-inch B/W (24 rows, 40 characters)	320
5.	Printer	Silentype (thermal)	395
6.	Operating system	Apple DOS	Included
	System total		$2,890

Software: While the Apple doesn't use the CP/M operating system, the company and independent publishers have developed extensive software for the Apple II Plus. VisiCalc, for instance, was first written for the Apple and is widely credited with pushing Apple Computer Inc. into first place in dollar sales in the personal computer market.

Other comments: With 2,500 independent dealers around the world selling Apples, the machine is easy to get serviced. It is also expandable in ways its designers never dreamed of and can create good color graphics with the appropriate peripherals. (The Apple III system, which is slightly more expensive than $5,000, offers color graphics standard and is more powerful than the II Plus.)

NEC APC

1.	Computer	PC 8012A with 8012A	$2,090
2.	Working memory	64K	Included
3.	Mass storage	160K/disk	1,295
4.	Video display	12-inch B/W (25 rows, 80 characters)	285
5.	Printer	High-speed dot matrix	795
6.	Operating system	CP/M	150
	System total		$4,615

Software: Almost unlimited selection with CP/M operating system.

Other comments: The NEC PC-8000 is a new system.

Sources: *Money*, November 1982, pp. 102–115, and *Inc.*, October 1981.

Exhibit 3   Personal computer market projections, 1980–85

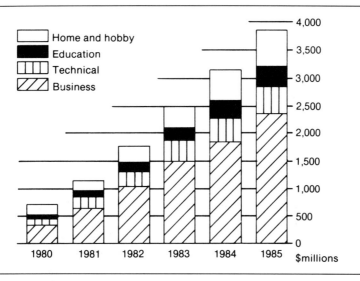

Source: *Business Week,* September 28, 1981, p. 78.

Exhibit 4   U.S. market for personal computers, 1981–1983

	1981	*1982**	*1983**
Home (less than $1,000)			
Sales (units)	235,000	1.05 million	2.05 million
Value of market	$165 million	$630 million	$1.13 billion
Leaders: Atari, Texas Instruments, and Commodore			
Professional (less than $3,000)			
Sales (units)	440,000	670,000	895,000
Values of market	$1.2 billion	$1.9 billion	$2.6 billion
Leaders: Apple, Radio Shack, IBM, Osborne, and Hewlett-Packard			
Small Business (less than $10,000)			
Sales (units)	80,000	140,000	200,000
Value of market	$768 million	$1.3 billion	$1.8 billion
Leaders: Radio Shack, Apple, Vector Graphic, Cromemco, and Altas			

*Estimates

Source: *Business Week,* October 25, 1982, p. 31.

price reductions lagged behind the other three, causing a serious erosion of market share.

A newer segment of the personal computer market was the portable computer, such as a hand-held or fold-up model. In 1981, 55,000 units were sold and estimates were that it would be a $1.25 billion industry by 1986. Models ranged from the $79.99 build-it-yourself portable up to a deluxe $8,150 model. The early star was the Osborne I ($1,795)—a complete system with disk memories, 2.6-inch by 3.6-inch video screen that displayed 24 lines, powerful enough to do word processing and accounting programs, and yet it could be folded up and placed under an airplane seat. Although a portable unit, the Osborne contained memory comparable to the Apple II. It took only 40 screws and 68 minutes to assemble. In 1982, approximately 130,000 Osborne units were sold.

A major problem facing the personal computer industry was how to reach the customer. Three basic approaches existed for a computer manufacturer to market its product—independent specialty chains, mass merchandisers, or the computer manufacturer's own sales force.

The specialty chains were the hottest segment of distribution. The first "mom and pop" stores opened in the mid 1970s and were primarily aimed at technicians and engineers. Little attention was given to developing skills of retailing. With the arrival of the fully assembled personal computers, requests poured in for standardized programs to fit the new computers. Many of the computer stores did not adjust to meet the new demands and, even though the market was expanding, many stores were only marginally profitable; in 1981 over 100 stores went out of business.

By the late 1970s the large specialty chains were a major force in the distribution system. In 1981 ComputerLand was the largest chain, with approximately 300 units, and was opening new stores at the rate of one a day. Each store averaged $1 million in sales. Its chief rivals included Compushop, Microage, and Computer Store. The strategy of the specialty chain was to carry a broad range of products from various manufacturers (at least four makers), price them competitively, and offer the expertise of store personnel to assist in training and in the utilization of the computers. Store owners estimated that customers needed four visits, totaling up to seven hours, before they bought.

Established mass retailers concentrated primarily on the low priced compact machines that needed little explanation or support. Sears, J. C. Penney, and Montgomery Ward all had entered the personal computer distribution market by the early 1980s. In 1981 Sears took a broad step from long-standing policy by establishing five computer stores separate from its department stores. They stocked personal computers, copiers, word processors and other products made by IBM, Hewlett-Packard, and Exxon. Most industry experts expected department stores ultimately to sell millions of computers, most likely for use in the home.

Discount stores such as Toys "R" US and K mart began to carry the Commodore home computer designed to compete with video games. Texas Instruments and Atari also tried to sell their wares through mass merchandisers.

Opening up mass merchandising channels was expected to allow other competitors to enter the personal computer competition. General Electric, RCA, and Zenith all reportedly had begun planning the introduction of a personal computer as part of a home entertainment system. AT&T had the freedom to enter the data processing field and could become a major force.

Japanese firms also would benefit from a larger distribution system. Early efforts to enter the American market by Nippon Electric, which held 40% of the $362 million Japanese personal computer market, and Sony were largely unsuccessful. Part of the failure was the result of a lack of understanding of the distribution system where many brands competed for shelf space in dealerships. A large system would make room for a renewed Japanese invasion. According to Mike Markkula, Apple's president, "The Japanese will continue to study what is required to succeed in the personal computer business and will invest heavily in doing these things. Over a five- to eight-year period, the Japanese will become one of the major factors in the marketplace."

Several of the established computer makers such as IBM, DEC, and Xerox used their sales force to aid in the introduction of a personal computer. The advantage of the established sales force was that it was well equipped to deal with corporations in making large batch sales. However, many independent dealers looked upon the sales forces as undermining their market.

Several manufacturers chose to establish their own stores. The success of Tandy's 6,000 Radio Shack electronic stores (with 641 computer departments) prompted such manufacturers as IBM, Xerox, and DEC to establish retail stores to sell business equipment. Some of the stores carried other manufacturers' equipment. Even Tandy had begun operating a chain devoted to computers (466 stores in 1982 and opening 12 each month) and had agreed to sell a line of home computers through independent distributors and retailers.

STEVEN WOZNIAK

Steven Wozniak, "Woz" to his friends, began learning about computers in the fourth grade when, with the help of his father, an electronics engineer at Lockheed Corporation's Missile and Space Company in Sunnyvale, California, he began designing logic circuits. By the eighth grade, he was building entire computers.

One of his best friends at Homestead High School in Los Altos was Steven Jobs. Pooling their talents, the two Steves built and sold so-called blue boxes, illegal electronic attachments for telephones that allowed users to make long-distance calls for free. *Time* reported that on one occasion Wozniak called the Vatican, pretending to be Henry Kissinger and asked for Pope Paul VI. It was only after the Pontiff was summoned and a Bishop came on the line to act as translator that Vatican officials caught on to the ruse. Although he claimed never to have used the box to defraud AT&T, Woz acknowledged that he would "get on the phone all night long and try to figure out how to work my way through the labyrinth of the worldwide phone system."

After high school Wozniak attended the University of Colorado where he became interested in minicomputers but then transferred to DeAnza College in Cupertino, where he came close to designing what he thought was the first low-cost hobby computer. After a year of designing software for a small West Coast firm, he enrolled at the University of California in Berkeley but then left in 1972 to take a design position with Hewlett-Packard in Palo Alto, California. In that job, he proposed a personal computer for HP but, according to an associate, "He couldn't get anybody to listen."

STEPHEN JOBS

Time recounted Stephen Jobs's background thusly:[4]

His parents, Paul and Clara Jobs, adopted Steven in February, 1955 and later moved from Mountain View on the peninsula south of San Francisco, to Los Altos after their son complained of rough times at the junior high school. "He came home one day from the seventh grade," Paul Jobs remembers, "and said if he had to go back to school there again he just wouldn't go. So we decided we'd better move."

Jobs made his way through Homestead High, recalls electronics teacher John McCollum, "as something of a loner. He always had a different way of looking at things." Solitude may, however, have bred ambition. McCollum was stunned to learn that the young loner, needing parts for class projects, picked up the phone and called Burroughs collect in Detroit and Bill Hewlett, co-founder of Hewlett-Packard, over in Palo Alto.

Hewlett wound up supplying Jobs with parts for a frequency counter, a device that measures the speed of electronic impulses. This introduced Jobs to the concept of timing, critical for understanding a computer, and furnished him with a cornerstone that, according to Wozniak, he never bothered to build on. Says Wozniak: "I doubt Steve was careful down to the last detail, which is really the key to high-level engineering." Shape, not subtlety, was more in Jobs's line, foreshadowing what one Apple manager calls the "technical ignorance he's not willing to admit." It was the practical applications of technology that excited Jobs, whether it was getting together with Wozniak to use "blue boxes" to make free long-distance calls or helping to design for the graduating class of '71 a mechanical sign that showed a huge hand making a time-honored gesture of rudeness.

Despite such spirited eruptions, Jobs was still uncertain, displaced, curious. He graduated, dropped acid for the first time ("All of a sudden the wheat field was playing Bach") and lived with his first serious girlfriend in a small wooden house along the Santa Cruz Mountains. As the summer ended, he headed for Reed College in Oregon. His father recalls what must have been a familiar litany: "He said if he didn't go there he didn't want to go anywhere." Jobs lasted only a semester but hung around the campus wandering the labyrinths of postadolescent mysticism and post-Woodstock

[4]Jay Cocks, "The Updated Books of Jobs," *Time*, January 3, 1983, p. 26.

culture. He tried pre-philosophy, meditation, the *I Ching,* LSD and the excellent vegetarian curries at the Hare Krishna house in Portland. He swore off meat about this time and took up vegetarianism "in my typically nutso way." One temporary result, say friends, was skin tinted by an excess of carotene to the color of an early sunset.

Cutting loose from Reed in 1974, Jobs journeyed back toward home and, answering a help-wanted ad in a local newspaper, landed a job at a video-game outfit called Atari, then in its second year of business. Jobs became the 40th employee of the small and idiosyncratic company founded by Nolan Bushnell and fueled by the success of Pong, the first of a long line of video recreations that turned simple games into eye-glazing national obsessions. Atari was a pretty loose place—staff brainstorming sessions were fueled with generous quantities of grass—but even there Jobs did not quite fit in. "His mind kept going a mile a minute," says Al Alcorn, Atari's chief engineer at the time. "The engineers in the lab didn't like him. They thought he was arrogant and brash. Finally, we made an agreement that he come to work late at night."

His Atari salary helped stake Jobs to a trip to India, where he met up with a Reed buddy, Don Kottke. "It was kind of an escetic pilgrimage," says Kottke, "except we didn't know where we were going." Seeking spiritual solace and enlightenment with a shaved head and a backpack did not distract Jobs from stubbornly haggling over prices in the marketplace and dressing down a Hindu woman for apparently watering their milk. An erratic Siddhartha at best, Jobs came home in the fall of 1974 with more questions than answers. He tried primal therapy, went in search of his real parents and on a friend's farm bumped his head on one of the last vestiges of '60s idealism: communal living. "Once I spent a night sleeping under a table in the kitchen," Jobs says. "In the middle of the night everybody came in and ripped off each other's food."

Jobs turned from life science to applied technology. Wozniak and some other friends gravitated toward an outfit called the Homebrew Computer Club in 1975, and Jobs would occasionally drop by. Wozniak was the computer zealot, the kind of guy who can see a sonnet in a circuit. What Jobs saw was profit. At convocations of the Homebrew, Jobs showed scant interest in the fine points of design, but he was enthusiastic about selling the machines Wozniak was making.

"I was nowhere as good an engineer as Woz," Jobs freely admits. "He was always the better designer." No one in the neighborhood, however, could match Jobs's entrepreneurial flair and his instincts for the big score.

COMPANY BACKGROUND

During this period, Jobs and Wozniak met often while tinkering with various electronic devices. They began serious collaboration in 1976 when over a six-month period they designed their first machine, a circuit board, in Jobs's bedroom; built it in his parents' garage in approximately 40 hours from scrounged parts; and showed it to a local computer store owner who promptly ordered 50 boards, fully assembled and tested. Jobs' response was "hot damn, we're in business." By June they made the first shipment on the order for $666.66 per board.

Whereas Wozniak saw the new machine as a gadget to show his fellow computer buffs, Jobs saw the commercial potential of the machine and urged that they form a company to market the computer. According to Wozniak,

> Steve didn't do one circuit, design, or piece of code. He's not really been into computers and . . . has never gone through a computer manual. But it never crossed my mind to sell computers. It was Steve who said, "Let's hold them up in the air and sell a few."

By selling Jobs's Volkswagen microbus and Wozniak's Hewlett-Packard scientific calculator, they raised $1,300 and opened a makeshift product line in Jobs's parents' garage. They obtained $10,000 worth of parts on credit from several sources. According to Jobs, "They'd say, 'Well, how's 30 days net?' We said, 'Sign us up.' We didn't know what 30 days net was." They made 200 more boards and quickly sold 75. Eventually they built 600 units. Jobs, recalling a pleasant summer that he had spent working in the orchards of Oregon, named the new company Apple. According to Jobs, "One day I just told everyone that unless they came up with a better name by 5 P.M. we would go with Apple."

They quickly started designing a new machine, Apple II, that would be fully programmable. They also placed a technical article in a leading trade journal, established a distribution agreement with several computer retailers, and persuaded an attorney to provide legal services on a pay-later plan.

When demand for the personal computer, which came mainly from hobbyists, quickly outstripped their ability to produce they began looking for help. According to Jobs, "We didn't know what the hell we were doing, but we were very careful observers and learned quickly." First they called Itel Corporation and asked who did their advertisements. When told that the agency was Regis McKenna, Inc., of Palo Alto, Jobs pestered Regis McKenna to take on Apple as a client. After refusing twice, McKenna finally agreed. Again, the arrangement was a pay-later basis. All during this time and until 1977 the company's receipts were kept in a desk drawer.

For advice on how to raise money, Jobs consulted both McKenna and Nolan Bushnell of Atari. They suggested that he call Don Valentine, an investor who frequently put money into new firms. When Valentine came around to inspect the new computer, he found Jobs wearing cut-off jeans and sandals while sporting shoulder-length hair and a Ho Chi Minh beard. Valentine later asked McKenna, "Why did you send me this renegade from the human race?"

Valentine mentioned the company to Mike Markkula, a 35 year-old marketing manager at Itel. In exchange for his expertise and $250,000, he was made an equal partner. According to Jobs, "He has sensitivity and knew we were not just two guys in a garage. And the chemistry clicked." By February 1977 Markkula had helped arrange a credit line with the Bank of America and had persuaded venture capitalist Arthur

Rock and Teledyne Chairman Henry Singleton to invest $57,600 and $320,000, respectively. In March 1977 Apple incorporated and moved out of the garage.

As a *Time* article reported, Jobs had a tough time making the transition:[5]

> Jobs, hyper and overwrought from the flush of such success, would occasionally burst into tears at meetings and would have to be cooled out with a slow walk around the parking lot. His personal life was also precarious. He again met the woman with whom he spent the summer in the mountains, and she became pregnant before they finally broke up anew. The baby, a girl, was born in the summer of 1978, with Jobs denying his fatherhood and refusing to pay child support. A voluntary blood test performed the following year said "the probability of paternity for Jobs, Steven . . . is 94.1%." Jobs insists that "28% of the male population of the United States could be the father." Nonetheless, the court ordered Jobs to begin paying $385 a month for child support.

As more individuals became involved in the company, the question arose, "Who wants to be president?" Neither Jobs nor Wozniak wanted the day-to-day operating job, so they chose Markkula as chairman and at his suggestion persuaded Michael Scott to join them as president. Scott, who at 33 was director of manufacturing at National Semiconductor Corporation, was willing to take a 50 percent pay cut to join Apple. At the time Jobs claimed that Scott's selection was "one of the best moves we've made." Jobs became vice chairman; Wozniak, vice president of research and development; and Markkula, vice president of marketing.

One of the first tasks of the new management team was to redesign the prototype of the Apple II. Jobs insisted that the cases for the keyboard and the video display be made of light, attractive plastic instead of metal. They also wrote clear, concise instruction manuals that made the machine easy for customers to use. The basic Apple II consisted of a typewriter keyboard, about the size of an attaché case, that plugged into any TV set and flashed information on the screen. It was designed with 136 standard integrated circuits and had a feature that included eight slots inside the Apple II into which the additional parts could be plugged. The product was assembled with semiconductors, plastic and metal parts, and certain electromechanical subassemblies purchased from independent suppliers. Most of the parts were standard, but a few (such as circuit boards) were built to Apple specifications. Certain components (power supplies and integrated circuits) were obtained from a single source, although the company believed there were other sources available. In time, Apple began to manufacture such components as disk drives and keyboards, but the company's operations consisted mainly of testing materials and components and assembling purchased parts into computer products.

Sales increased from $200,000 in 1976 to $2.7 million in 1977, and pretax profits increased from 20 percent to 30 percent. The management team concluded that Apple, in order not to be acquired or run out of business, had to grow rapidly and become one

---

[5]Ibid., p. 27.

of the dominant firms in the new industry. They set high goals ($18 million sales in 1978 and $50–75 million for 1979) and hired overqualified personnel. According to one industry observer, even without Markkula, Jobs and Wozniak would have been successful. Both had "the smarts to find out what they didn't know. Many others were doing the same thing, but the others let their egos get in the way."

The rapid growth was hard to control. According to Markkula, the problem became how to "keep the racecar on the track." They did keep it on the track by managing on a consensus basis. According to Jobs, "basically if we have a hard decision to make, we get everyone to agree. There is a sort of balance and the chemistry works well." The management philosophy was described by Jobs as "just common sense."

By 1978 the company had grown to 150 employees and had sold 25,000 Apple IIs at prices ranging from $1,195 for the basic model to $3,000 for a model with all the trimmings such as two floppy disks, a graphics tablet, and a printer. Total sales were reported to be approximately $17.5 million. At the time Jobs was predicting, "We will sell more computers this year than IBM has in five."

In 1979 total employment had grown to 400 and sales had reached $70 million. In reflecting on the growing demand for personal computers, Jobs observed that "people are hungry for more data—from the date of Don Larson's perfect game to an instant glance at a diet program—and we're trying to satisfy that hunger."

The Apple II could be programmed by anyone familiar with BASIC, the simplistic computer language, to do income tax, balance a worksheet, record recipes, update the Christmas card list, and play chess and backgammon. Some people used their Apple II for evaluating security portfolios and doing cash flow projections. A belly dancer used her Apple to keep track of her inventory of exotic costumes and records. An oil company depended on one to operate a rig off California, and others kept track of statistics for politicians, controlled lights in theaters, and synthesized music for rock stars. The Rolling Stones used an Apple to help their official biographer store information to write the group's history. Even children were using them in elementary schools. According to Jobs, "Here comes 1984, and instead of huge monolithic computers, you have seven-year-olds playing with computers. Things aren't turning out the way people had feared."

As for Apple's role in the industry, Jobs claimed:

> We're trying to move into the big leagues in a hurry and 1979 will be our pivotal year. If we survive, we'll be the DEC of the personal computer industry. Every dollar we make we're plowing back into the company. Sure, we'll be up against the biggies, but we're defining the right product for the market. And the reason we have a chance is that it is a totally brand new market. And nobody knows how it will go.

At the time, Jobs's opinion was that if his company were to be sold, it could bring a purchase price of over $10,000,000.

By 1979, although there were 50 firms in the $300 million personal computer field, it was dominated by Apple, Radio Shack, and Commodore. However, Texas Instruments had just introduced a model and as many as a dozen large companies were expected to join the market for personal computers costing less than $10,000. IBM, Xerox, and Digital Equipment were all reportedly working on personal computers and some Japanese firms were preparing to enter the U.S. market.

There was no question that many of these companies were aiming to take away Apple's business. At Xerox, members of the personal computer development team referred to their machine as "the worm." Other manufacturers were elbowing in on Apple's distribution network. For example, shortly before the end of 1980 Commodore signed a deal with ComputerLand, the independent chain of retail computer stores that was selling 14 percent of all Apple computers. Apple executives publicly welcomed the new entrants, claiming that the newcomers would help expand the market for all by advertising heavily. They predicted that Apple would hit the billion-dollar mark in annual revenue by 1990 and set as their goal to be a quarter-billion-dollar company by 1982.

In May 1980 the Apple III was introduced at the National Computer Show. Jobs described it as the first microcomputer designed specifically for professional and small business users. Priced from $4,340 to $7,800, the new product began to be shipped in November and was eventually supported by some 30-odd hardware and software products, each designed for the needs of a particular market. Actually there were two versions of the Apple III. The first was priced at about $4,400, had a 96,000 character memory, and included software. The second was a word processor costing approximately $5,400 and included such accessories as a printer. Already there were rumors of an Apple IV, expected to come out within the next 18 months.

In 1980 Apple management decided it needed to increase its recognition factor. A six-week radio campaign boosted its awareness level from 8 percent of the population to 39 percent and after six weeks of TV ads, it was known by 80 percent of those polled. By late 1980, industry observers were saying that Apple had developed an "IBM-like reputation for quality. When people think of personal computers they think of Apple."

Although Apple's growth was 100 percent in 1980, a big concern for the cofounders was the possibility of boredom. In reflecting on where the company had been and where it was headed, Jobs remarked that "we have made our mistakes but we strive for the little ones. We've never made big glaring mistakes, the kind that would be large enough to kill the company." He explained that Apple managers made 4 to 10 times as many daily decisions as most other managers make, even in the fast-paced Silicon Valley. "You can't slow that process down. There is no time to research each decision." In reflecting on business, he called it "the best-kept secret. It is incredible as a practice and a concept. Most of the bright minds I know didn't go into business. It's really sad." He felt that they were wasting their lives pursuing nonproductive pursuits.

He described the management of creative employees as a "most important problem. If we have 18 ideas and can go with only two, we will have 16 unhappy people." On the other hand, the "bean counters" in the company "go crazy" when individuals "enamored by technology" are granted funding for a pet project.

To develop an atmosphere that pampered creative employees, an incentive program was begun to develop computer literacy. Any employee demonstrating proficiency with two programs was loaned an Apple II for use at home, and after one year title was given to the employee. Jobs described this "loan-to-own" program "as part of an overall desire to institute a more humane workplace." He claimed that it gave employees "the chance to get involved in solving problems that can ultimately affect the success of the entire company."

In a 1980 memo, Mike Scott announced:

> EFFECTIVE IMMEDIATELY!! NO MORE TYPEWRITERS ARE TO BE PURCHASED, LEASED, ETC., ETC. Apple is an innovative company. We must believe and lead in all areas. If word processing is so neat, then let's all use it! Goal: By 1-1-81, NO typewriters at Apple . . . We believe the typewriter is obsolete. Let's prove it inside before we try and convince our customers.

By late 1981, there were only 20 typewriters for 2,200 employees. The Apple II was being used to compose and disseminate letters, memos, documents and reports, catalogue the more than 1,500 resumes received each month, create graphs and charts, and perform various financial, marketing, and production functions.

Another decision was to drop the term *secretary* and replace it with *area associate* to reflect the more varied responsibilities made possible by personal computers. According to Ann Bowers, vice president of human resources, "we felt we needed a different term because 'secretary' was loaded with connotations of typist, errand-runner, and phone answerer. We wanted to expand the area associates' functions so they could use their brains, in addition to their clerical skills." As a result of "working smarter," Bowers felt there was greater job satisfaction and

> virtually no job turnover. Our middle-management people have more time to do what they're best at—coaching their employees instead of shuffling paper. There's also a wonderful thing that happens in terms of relationship with your support staff. I feel it when I ask my area associate to do more responsible things than just type letters.

There were, however, other motivators for employees at Apple. The private company in 1980 was 78 percent owned by the employees with the balance owned by a few outsiders. According to Jobs, "We like it that way because it contributes to people working hard. They know that if Apple is successful, that it would change their life-style." Although only nonhourly employees owned stock in the company, management's goal was to have all the employees as shareholders. If that was to happen, management felt that the firm would have to go public, something the officers did not want. They felt that going public would cause the loss of 20 percent of the time of Apple's top officers as they would have to devote time to SEC paper work, annual and interim reports, and appearances before and interviews with financial analysts. "We're frustrated, and there is no solution. The problem is taking up a lot of time," according to Jobs.

In 1980 the company had a key employee bonus plan, a profit participation plan and a stock option plan. The bonus plan was primarily for management and provided for a bonus pool ($554,000 in fiscal 1980) determined by a formula based on annual sales and pretax profit margins. Ninety percent of the pool was available to individuals in specific job categories (70 percent was automatically awarded, and 30 percent was awarded at the discretion of the president), and 10 percent was available for award at the discretion of the president to individuals not in the specific job categories. The profit participation plan distributed up to 3 percent of pretax earnings for each calendar quarter ($379,000 in fiscal 1980) to all employees working at least 30 hours per week and who had a minimum of six months' company service, except officers and directors. The 1980 stock option plan reserved 3.2 million shares of common stock for issuance.

In a 1980 interview with *Industry Week,* Steve Wozniak explained some of the less-material rewards of working at Apple. "We are making the emerging industry grow correctly, without getting it all screwed up. We will have the right products, at the right price, at the right time. We want to be a major contributor."

Wozniak and Jobs were convinced that from their industry would come some of the major societal contributions of the next five years. They cited as an example the Minnesota Educational Consortium selecting the Apple II for Minnesota's schools. "There is not one child in the elementary school system that is not affected," according to Jobs. Another project underway was a special outreach project in which schools in the San Francisco Bay area were visited with a van full of Apple IIs, bringing classes in programming to elementary and high school students in their classroom.

On December 12, 1980, Apple Computer went public with 4,600,000 shares of stock at $22 a share. *Fortune* reported that Arthur Rock ended up with stock worth $14 million, Henry Singleton with $26 million, Mike Markkula with $154 million, and Scott with $62 million. Jobs instantly became worth $165 million, and Wozniak became worth $88 million, plus his parents and siblings owned nearly $3 million in Apple stock, and his first wife owned $27 million. The top four officials owned 40 percent of the company.

Some observers believed that the stock market had overreacted to Apple's offering. At its opening price of $22 per share Apple was selling at 100 times its per share earnings of 24 cents for the year ending September 26. By contrast, Tandem Computers, Inc., one of the industry's hottest companies, with nearly a 100 percent earning growth rate, was selling at about 60 times earnings over the same period. Nevertheless, Apple's stock jumped to $29 per share on the first day of trading. As a result, Apple officers were already referring to IBM as "the other computer company."

1981—A PROBLEM YEAR

Although 1980 ended on a positive financial note, (Exhibits 5, 6, and 7), bad news was to follow. In early 1981 Steven Wozniak crashed a Beechcraft Bonanza airplane on take-off at a small California Airport. Not only did it nearly kill him but he hit his

Exhibit 5   Apple Computer, Inc.'s consolidated income statement 1977–82 ($000, except per share amounts)

	1982	1981	1980	1979	1978	1977
Net sales	$583,061	$334,783	$117,126	$47,867	$7,856	$744
Cost and expenses:						
Cost of sales	288,001	170,124	66,490	27,450		
Research and development	37,979	20,956	7,282	3,601		
Marketing	119,945	55,369	12,619	4,097		
General and administration	34,927	22,191	7,150	2,617		
	480,852	268,640	93,541	37,765		
Operating income	102,209	66,143	23,585	10,102		
Interest, net	14,563	10,400	567	3		
Income before taxes	116,772	76,543	24,152	10,105		
Provision for taxes	55,466	37,123	12,454	5,032		
Net income	$ 61,306	$39,420	$11,698	$ 5,073	$ 793	$ 42
Earnings per common and						
common equivilent share	$1.06	$.70	$.24	$.12	$.03	$.01
Common and common equivalent						
shares used in the calculation						
of earnings per share	57,798	56,161	48,412			

head so hard that he still cannot remember the accident. After the accident, he announced his plans to leave Apple and return to Berkeley to finish his bachelor's degree in computer science. He also married for the second time and bought a mansion in the hills above Santa Cruz. Described by *Newsweek* as a "brilliant—if somewhat erratic—engineer," whose passion was designing electronic gizmos, Woz was considered Apple's "creative force." Wealthy beyond his wildest dream and the acknowledged dean of Apple's freewheeling cadre of computer crazies, he had a taste for rich men's toys but talked about going back to Apple at the bottom, as a rank-and-file engineer. His real goal would be "to fix a lot of motivational problems" in a company that had grown rapidly since the garage days. He also hoped to stage rock concerts and to that end formed a corporation, Unuson (Unite Us in Song), to promote rock concerts and a "new kind of unity." The for-profit corporation's goal was to eliminate what he saw as a distressing national tendency to ask, "What's in it for me?" Instead, he wanted young Americans to ask "What's in it for us?" In addition, he hoped to pursue his interest in the mechanisms of human, rather than electronic, memory. "I've got enough money to sit back in the pool and watch it all go by. But I want to be in life."

Shortly after the Apple III hit the market, observers were calling the introduction a "fiasco." The new machines were plagued by technical and mechanical problems.

Exhibit 6 Apple Computer, Inc.'s consolidated balance sheets 1979–82 ($000)

	1982	*1981*	*1980*	*1979*
Assets				
Current assets:..................................				
Cash and temporary cash investments........	$153,056	$72,834	$ 363	$ 563
Accounts receivable	71,478	42,330	15,814	9,178
Inventories.................................	81,229	103,873	34,191	10,103
Other current assets	11,312	8,067	3,738	
Total current assets....................	317,075	227,104	54,106	19,844
Property, plant, and equipment:				
Land and buildings	7,220	4,815	243	
Machinery and equipment	26,136	14,688	3,669	404
Office furniture and equipment	13,423	6,192	1,673	322
Leasehold improvements	10,515	5,129	710	384
	57,294	30,824	6,295	1,110
Accumulated depreciation and amortization......	(22,811)	(8,453)	(1,516)	(210)
Net property, plant, and equipment	34,483	22,371	4,779	900
Reacquired distribution rights			5,311	
Other assets	6,229	5,363	1,154	427
Total assets................................	$357,787	$254,838	$65,350	$21,171
Liabilities and Shareholders' Equity				
Current liabilities:				
Notes payable to banks	$ 4,185	$ 10,745	$ 7,850	
Accounts payable..........................	25,125	26,613	14,495	$ 5,411
Accured compensation and employee benefits	11,774	7,759	2,553	1,720
Income taxes payable......................	15,307	8,621	8,135	1,879
Accrued advertising........................	8,815	3,540		
Other current liabilities	20,550	13,002	4,747	22
Total current liabilities	85,756	70,280	37,780	9,032
Noncurrent obligations under capital leases	2,052	1,909	671	203
Deferred taxes on income	12,887	5,262	951	2,255
Shareholders' equity				
Common stock, no par value, 160,000,000 shares authorized	141,070	123,317	12,348	4,298
Retained earnings	118,332	57,027	17,606	5,908
	259,402	180,343	29,954	10,206
Notes receivable from shareholders	(2,310)	(2,956)	(4,006)	(525)
Total shareholders' equity	257,092	177,387	25,948	9,681
Total liabilities and shareholders' equity	$357,787	$254,838	$65,350	$21,171

Exhibit 7   Apple Computer, Inc.'s consolidated statements of changes in financial position 1980–82 ($000)

	1982	1981	1980
Working capital was provided by:.....................			
Operations:			
Net income	$ 61,306	$ 39,420	$11,698
Charges to operations not affecting................			
Working capital:			
Depreciation and amortization.................	16,556	8,590	1,377
Deferred taxes on income (noncurrent)	7,625	4,311	747
Total working capital provided by operations...........	85,487	52,321	13,822
Increases in common stock and related tax			
Benefits, net of changes in notes receivable from			
shareholders	18,399	112,019	4,569
Increases in noncurrent obligations under capital			
leases..	1,172	1,747	752
Total working capital provided..............	105,058	166,087	19,143
Working capital was applied to:			
Purchase of property, plant, and equipment,...........			
Net of retirements	26,470	24,529	4,878
Reacquisition of distribution rights			5,401
Other	4,093	1,060	1,298
Total working capital applied	30,563	25,589	11,577
Increase in working capital	$74,495	$140,498	$ 7,566
Increase (decrease) in working capital by component:			
Cash and temporary cash investments................	$80,222	$ 72,471	$ (200)
Accounts receivable	29,148	26,516	6,688
Inventories.......................................	(22,644)	69,682	24,089
Other current assets	3,245	4,329	3,685
Notes payable to banks	6,560	(2,895)	(7,850)
Accounts payable.................................	1,488	(12,118)	(9,084)
Accured compensation and employee benefits	(4,015)	(5,206)	(1,727)
Income taxes payable.............................	(6,686)	(486)	(4,205)
Accrued advertising and other current liabilities	(12,823)	(11,795)	(3,830)
Increase in working capital	$74,495	$140,498	$ 7,566

The following excerpt from *The Wall Street Journal,*[6] indicated the extent of the problem:

> It is the first group of 1,000 or so Apple IIIs that has given the most trouble. Lawrence Shephard bought one of these in February, and though he considers himself an Apple loyalist, four failures in two months have turned him sour on the product.
>
> Mr. Shephard planned to use his $5,000 machine to track tax accounts and store data for the agricultural economics class he teaches at the University of California at Davis. "A week after purchase, the words 'system error' lit up on the screen," Prof. Shephard recalls. He brought the computer back to the store, where a serviceman removed a loose screw and reinserted some chips.
>
> "It worked about 10 hours before the same error recurred," Mr. Shephard continues. This time, the machine went back to the factory, and he got another one on loan.
>
> Then, "within 20 hours my loaner failed, too," he says, his anger flashing as the memory returns.
>
> Prof. Shephard soon got his original back, outfitted free of charge with new memory chips. But, "15 hours after I got it home it started to crackle and threw some jibberish on the screen."
>
> If this sounds like the Woody Allen routine, in which the comic is driven mad by a gang of rebellious kitchen appliances, Mr. Shephard isn't laughing. "I know computers, and I've used the big ones, IBM and Burroughs machines," he says, "It isn't as if I took my Apple III home and tried to make toast on it."

Apple adopted a policy of outright exchange to placate users like Mr. Shephard. Getting the faulty machines back also helped in diagnosing the trouble. Among the problems found were: (1) Chip sockets often were too loose so that chips slipped out during shipment. This problem rendered 20 percent of the first computers dead on arrival. (2) A clock/calendar chip, purchased from National Semiconductor Corporation, turned out not to meet specifications. Apple gave customers a $50 rebate and stopped using the chip. (3) Cables to the computer keyboard were too short. (4) Connectors, the metal slots attaching the printed circuit board to the computer, had a variety of mechanical problems. In at least one case, Apple's solution gave rise to new problems. When assembly workers tightened chip sockets they had to push in the chip carriers with such force that some pins were bent. This defect was discovered only after shipment. In responding to the problems with the Apple III, the company strengthened test and inspection procedures and eased out the general manager of personal computer operations. Eventually 14,000 IIIs had to be recalled.

To some dealers the most damaging problem with the Apple III was the delay in supplying special Apple III software, especially a word processing program. This program, called the Word Painter, was originally promised for May 1981, but its scheduled

[6]*The Wall Street Journal,* April 15, 1981.

availability was postponed for seven or eight months. According to Markkula, "one of our key guys on the project was in the hospital." Consequently, the Apple III was unsupported by any of the special programs that would place it beyond the Apple II.

As a result of the problems with Apple III, the company was restructured, and in March 1981 a major reorganization occurred. In the management shake-up, a top-level team of vice presidents took over the running of the company from Michael Scott who was demoted from president to vice chairman soon after he fired 40 employees. Scott's management style was described as "decisive, but also authoritarian and insensitive." His demotion (he later resigned), according to Ann S. Bowers, "was a clear signal that we were not pleased with the way he dealt with the problems." Markkula became president and Jobs became chairman.

One Apple manager, a veteran of the semiconductor industry, described the company during this period as "Camp Run Amok." Another manager, who joined the company in 1981 when the company doubled its size to nearly 2,500 employees, observed that "there seems to be so little control and so much chaos that I can't believe the company isn't flying off into space in a thousand pieces. On the other hand it does seem to keep pulling off its plans."

Markkula has been described as "pragmatic," and his "wryly humorous approach" is seen as an "essential counterweight to Jobs's creative temperament and sometimes arrogant demeanor."

> Yet Jobs's qualities, which engender a certain nervousness in the financial community, are to some degree mirrored in Apple's corporate culture and make the company attractive to bright young engineers and business school graduates. "Apple is seen as a dynamic and creative place to work, where you get a chance to make a contribution," says product manager Kristen A. Olson, who joined Apple after she got her M.B.A. in 1981.
>
> Jobs himself characterizes the Apple corporate culture as one in which "we have what you might call an eccentric passion for what we are doing."[7]
>
> Employees and friends describe Jobs in a variety of ways:
>
> "He (Jobs) can con you into believing his dream," says Bill Atkinson, who by some estimates is the most gifted programmer at Apple. A company consultant, Guy Tribble, says that Jobs sets up what he calls "A reality-distortion field. He has the ability to make people around him believe in his perception of reality through a combination of very fast comeback, catch phrases and the occasional very original insight, which he throws in to keep you off balance . . .
>
> As a boss, Jobs is admired for courting long chances, but adds a friend, "Something is happening to Steve that's sad and not pretty, something related to money and power and loneliness. He's less sensitive to people's feelings. He runs over them, snowballs them." Adds Jeff King, a former Apple publications manager: "He would have made an excellent King of France." . . .

[7]"Apple Takes on Its Biggest Test Yet," *Business Week,* January 31, 1983, p. 79.

Jobs drives the staff hard, expecting long hours, high productivity and infinite patience with his scattershot ideas. "He should be running Walt Disney," says a longtime Apple manager. "That way, every day when he's got some new idea, he can contribute to something different."

Taking care of business means, for Jobs, not just lighting fires under the staff and gladhanding the media. It also involves—crucially—keeping the lines open to the young. His planned donation of 10,000 Apples to California schools gets him good will, a generous tax break and an even stronger foothold in what Hollywood likes to call "the youth market." He makes periodic campus appearances, where he is likely as not to sit, shoes off, in the lotus position atop a dormitory coffee table and engagingly field questions. Nothing too specific, mind. The students will not press for details on "Supersite," a hazy combination of Disneyland and industrial park that Jobs has been formulating. They may not even know that Jobs, an independent, has at times mulled over some vague political plans, perhaps following in the unorthodox footsteps of Jerry Brown.[8]

Although volume sales finally began for the Apple III in March 1981, the company had to turn its attention to a rumor that it had a new product under development that was intended to supplant Apple III. According to Markkula, "it's untrue. The Apple III is designed to have a 10-year life span."

Some software suppliers were growing concerned that unless Apple positioned the II against Apple III very carefully, competition was going to hurt the III. In spite of such concerns, Jobs predicted that the Apple III would outsell the new IBM machine in 1982. Some industry sources reported, however, that they would be surprised if Apple III sales exceeded 50,000 units in 1982 while they expected IBM to sell at least 200,000, provided the company could make that many.

Another issue confronting the company was the possibility of vertical integration. The company was beginning to do more of its own software development and not just for the new products in the pipeline. Although Markkula denied these products indicated a move toward vertical integration in software, Apple was entering into a head on competition with the independent software vendors on which it had depended for most of its business applications software. The software business was expected to grow from $400 million in 1981 to $4.2 billion in 1986, as over 100 new programs hit the market every month. By late 1982 approximately 16,000 software programs had been written exclusively for the 700,000 buyers of Apple II.

Another problem area concerned product distribution. Although Apple did acquire a wholesale distributor in 1980 to sell its machines, it depended on independent dealers. According to Markkula, "We believe that customers want stores carrying more than one personal computer, and we do not think it would be practical for Apple to own that store." He also had ruled out a direct sales force.

---

[8]Cocks, "Updated Book of Jobs," pp. 25–27.

To develop strong ties with its retail outlets Apple used such tools as sales and product training, toll free software hotlines manned by applications specialists, monthly newsletters and a handsome magazine that focused on a particular application area in each issue. Also they used a co-op ad program in which dealers were reimbursed up to 3 percent of their dollar purchases.

In March of 1981 Apple scrapped its arrangement of marketing through five independent distributors, who purchased products for resale to retailers, and began to sell to the stores through its own regional support centers. Four were in existence in 1980 and three more planned for 1981 (Exhibit 8). Apple's objectives were to gain tighter inventory control, enhance direct training of dealers, and gain better access to end users.

To reinforce its new strategy, Apple launched the *Apple Means Business* (AMB) program, designed to help dealers go after targeted markets. AMB gave dealers a series of objectives and such help as sales seminars for 6–20 prospects at a time built around a single application, and structured presentations the dealers could use, along with a kit of 172 color slides for illustrating the various applications. Dealers were taught how to organize the seminars and execute the post-meeting follow-up, and were even told how many computers they could sell in a given period of time.

In the service area, Apple trained and certified 650 dealers to provide same-day, walk-in repairs. Dealers were also trained to provide service at a profit for equipment not under warranty.

In August 1981 Apple asked its 1,100 retail dealers in the United States and Canada to sign amended contracts promising not to engage in telephone or mail-order sales. In a letter accompanying the contract Apple's vice president of sales, Jean Carter, explained that "mail-order sales are neither suited to providing the consumer education that emerging markets require, nor are they structured to providing the consumer satisfaction that has become associated with the Apple name." The company's policy was quickly challenged in court on antitrust grounds.

Apple's chief antagonist was Francis Ravel, who owned Olympic Sales Company in Los Angeles. On December 3, 1981, Mr. Ravel and his attorney asked for a temporary restraining order to block Apple from enforcing its new policy on the grounds that it constituted restraint of trade. Describing this as a temporary step, Ravel said he would seek a formal hearing on the issues and seek a preliminary injunction. According to Ravel, "there are about 150 (Apple claimed there were only 75) black sheep like us. All we want is to buy and sell and be left alone. Fair trade laws have been abolished. They can't tell us not to ship from our store. Hewlett-Packard wouldn't dare do that." According to Jobs, "It's not discounting that bothers us. It's the smile—or rather, the lack of it—on our customer's face when service is inadequate. What we're doing is the state-of-the-art in antitrust law. We could go all the way to the Supreme Court."

One owner of a computer store claimed that 75 percent of his company's $6 million in annual sales came from mail order sales and that if Apple cut him off, "we'll go out of business." Even if Apple cut off its authorized dealers, it was not clear if they could stop unauthorized dealers. One such New York store expected to sell approxi-

Exhibit 8 Plant and office facilities

	Square Feet	Lease Expiration
Manufacturing:		
Cupertino, California (2 locations)	54,000	11/83 to 6/89
San Jose, California	35,000	5/86
Sunnyvale, California	92,000	4/86
Garden Grove, California (2 locations)	43,000	8/84 to 9/86
Newbury Park, California	6,000	8/83
Carrollton, Texas	282,000	7/85
County Cork, Ireland	83,000	Owned
Singapore	75,000	6/84
	670,000	
Distribution:		
Sunnyvale, California (2 locations)	82,000	12/82 to 6/85
Irvine, California	32,000	8/86
Charlotte, North Carolina	29,000	9/85
Carrollton, Texas	39,000	7/85
Zeiat, Netherlands	29,000	5/85
Munich, Germany	15,000	3/86
Toronto, Canada	15,000	3/86
	241,000	
Administration and Research and Development:		
Cupertino, California (11 locations)	166,000	12/81 to 12/90
Cupertino, California	3,000	Owned
Slough, England	7,000	12/82
	176,000	
Expansion—committed but not yet occupied:		
Cupertino, California (Adm. and R&D)	99,000	12/91
Ireland (3 locations) (Mfg.)	175,000	Owned
Singapore (Mfg.)	58,000	6/84
	332,000	

mately 3,000 Apples in 1981. A source familiar with unauthorized dealerships said they generally get their stock from dealers who order more Apples than they can sell. A typical New York dealer's contract yielded 38 percent profit on resale if 80 or more units were bought and only 29 percent if a few were purchased. According to one West Coast store owner, "Mail-order sales have increased Apple's market share quite a bit. They're cutting off their nose to spite their face."

Apple's policy change reportedly encouraged its network of full service dealers. According to ComputerLand president, Edward Faber, it cost $150,000 to open a store with the service centers, test equipment, and the technicians that Apple required.

> If the dealer makes that kind of investment, he must get a return on the sale of the product. If the retail pricing is being watered down, by mail order discounting, then it becomes difficult. It's discouraging to do all the presale education and support of a prospective customer and then have him buy the equipment somewhere else.

As an example of the concern, 47th Street Photo in New York, with estimated annual sales of $100 million (one quarter in computer goods), was selling Apple IIs for $1,095 when the authorized dealer price was $1,330. To meet competition, some New York dealers had only an 8 percent margin.

Apple officials said that their intent was to go after big-volume mail houses but there would be no exception to its policy. ComputerLand claimed it would continue mailing to long-standing or geographically remote customers.

1982—ANOTHER PROBLEM YEAR

In early 1982 Apple executives were considering plans to cut off sales of its personal computers to ComputerLand's corporate purchasing department. ComputerLand accounted for approximately 10 percent of Apple's 1981 sales (down from 14 percent in 1980) yet Apple had become concerned about the growing competition between ComputerLand stores and its other dealers. It was considering insisting that they sign a new contract giving Apple the right to decide which ComputerLand stores could sell Apple computers.

Early reports of counterfeit Apples were written off by Apple executives as insignificant, but by early 1982 Apple's legal counsel, Albert Eisenstat, returned from an eight-day swing through Taiwan and Southeast Asia and reported finding at least a half-dozen "garage type" operations turning out counterfeit copies of the Apple II. According to Eisenstat, "Our fear is that, if we do nothing, it might encourage larger, better-financed operations to follow suit." One example of the alleged counterfeits was a machine stamped with the Apple logo, identical down to the crescent shaped bit, and labeled with a name similar to Apple, in identical type.

The proliferation of personal computer manufacturers in Asia began when video game sales began to slip and manufacturers with inventories of electronic parts and personnel skilled in assembling and copying electronic machines looked for new products. A local trade magazine printed the main electronic schematics for the Apple II, and before long there were 20 good-size manufacturers making minicomputers, not counting the students and retired people who assembled them to earn pocket money.

At first Apple counterfeiters passed off their machines as the real thing but soon came to realize that fake Apples could be almost as good as the real thing. Computer vendors merely showed that their machines could use Apple programming. To advertise that fact, the machines frequently had names like "Ap It," "Apcom," and even the Chinese name for "Green Apple."

Lin Hsiao-chi, general manager of a Taiwan computer company, while acknowledging that he copied the Apple II "to gain experience," said he might stop production of his Apollo II, which he sold for $400, and introduce his Apollo III at under $600. He claimed the Apollo III was not a carbon copy of the Apple III but was similar and could use the same programs.

By the end of the summer observers estimated that anywhere from 2,000 to 4,500 counterfeit Apple IIs were being turned out each month in Taiwan alone. Apple distributors in the area, however, were selling only 300 to 400 authentic Apples a month. According to the general manager of an Apple regional distributor, for every genuine Apple II sold in Hong Kong, there were five fakes sold.

By August the problem had spread to other areas of the world. In New Zealand the "Orange" was one of the hottest-selling computers. In Italy, the "Lemon" was selling well. The impact could be seen in Australia, where in 1978 Apple's share of the market was 90 percent but by mid-1982 had dropped to below 30 percent.

Even in the United States at least one company was making a machine that could run all Apple II software, and by mid-1982 approximately 60 companies, mostly in the United States, had sprung up to sell Apple II attachments for replacements for many of its major parts. Even its brain could be changed so that the Apple II could act like another brand of computer. For example, a California company had begun making a plug-in that raised Apple memory above the IBM memory level. Another plug-in from a Michigan firm allowed the Apple to create financial planning models with VisiCalc, the most popular modeling program, that were several times larger than the IBM computer could handle. A Colorado firm announced an attachment that opened the Apple owner's door to IBM personal computer programs.

By 1982 Apple was under pressure to bring out new products since it was lagging behind IBM and Tandy in bringing out a 16-bit machine. Apple planned to outpace the competition by maintaining an innovative edge. Spending on research and development increased from $3.6 million in 1979 to $7.3 million in 1980 and $20.9 million in 1981. The budget for 1982 was forecast at approximately $30 million. Such expenditures were expected to pay off in new products. According to John D. Couch, general manager of Apple's personal office systems division, "We're driven by the desire to build products that combine ideas already out there at low enough cost to make them useful. We're not really a technology-driven company."

LISA

In early 1983 the company hoped to unveil a new machine, code-named Lisa, after one of Jobs's ex-girlfriends. According to Jobs, it will "reduce the time it takes a new user to get up to speed on a personal computer from 20–40 hours to 20 minutes." To provide such innovative features would take a major investment in software. More than 200 man-years of basic software development ($20 million) will have gone into Lisa when it is introduced. This compared with 25 man-years for the Apple III and 2 man-years for the Apple II.

The development of a Lisa began in 1978 when Jobs decided to go after the market of 15 million managers, professionals, and administrative assistants. He recruited 30-year-old John Couch from Hewlett-Packard, who not only agreed with Jobs that the key to success would be good software that was easy to use but also was willing to take a cut in salary from $55,000 to $40,000 and a cut in responsibilities, from 141 people to none.

Jobs and Couch had no trouble convincing others of the promise of an easy-to-use computer:

> Eighteen programmers followed Couch from Hewlett-Packard. Lisa's chief engineer, Wayne Rosing, 36, came from Digital Equipment Corp. One day in 1980, Rosing was on a quick trip to California when he stopped in to see Couch on the recommendation of a friend. Within minutes he knew he wanted to work for Apple. By the next day he had a deal with Couch and phoned Digital to resign. Four colleagues from Digital joined him at Apple. Lawrence G. Tesler, 37, who was the software manager for Lisa, was formerly a computer researcher for Xerox. In December 1979 he was demonstrating some techniques in computer friendliness Xerox had developed to a troupe of Apple engineers and marketing executives led by Jobs and Couch. "I was expecting a bunch of hobbyists," Tesler recalls, "and was impressed to find people sophisticated in computer science." Tesler decided on the spot to join Apple. (Eventually more than 15 Xerox engineers joined the project).
>
> That day of briefings at Xerox was the turning point in Lisa's development. Although Jobs and Couch had been brainstorming about the project, occasionally while sipping brandy in the hot tub at Couch's house in Los Gatos, and company engineers had been busy building prototypes of a new machine, the critical software remained only a vague concept. The Xerox researchers demonstrated a programming language called Smalltalk that worked with a mouse.[9] Suddenly the possibilities became apparent.
>
> Xerox has since incorporated some features of Smalltalk into a product called Star. While a technological marvel, Star has not sold well since its introduction in April 1981. Each Star computer costs $16,600 and won't work well unless hooked up to a large disk drive costing $55,000 or more. According to industry rumors, Xerox is working on a smaller, less expensive version of Star. E. David Crockett, senior vice president of Dataquest, a market research firm in Cupertino, California, says Xerox is selling about 100 to 200 Stars per month. "It's a product looking for a home," he says. In one sense, it has found a home at Apple.

---

[9]The mouse is a cigarette pack-size plastic box with a button on top and a cable connected to the computer. When the mouse is moved on the surface of a desk, an arrow moves on Lisa's TV-like monitor screen. This permits the user to juggle words or statistics around.

The Apple group resolved to create on Lisa's screen the look and procedures of an everyday office. To do this, they have used pictures to represent certain procedures—a wastebasket for the disposal of information, a clipboard for temporary storage, a folder for filing data. But they soon discovered that even the simplest improvement demanded much more software. The mouse on Xerox's Star for example, has two different command buttons. It took the Apple team six months to reduce their mouse's buttons from two to one.[10]

Keeping the Lisa project moving at Apple took several forms. First there were rambling late-night rap sessions between Jobs and Couch, then the installation of a 40-man team in quarters behind the Good Earth health food restaurant in Cupertino, California. Finally, in 1982, a 400-man force, many in their 20s, was established in three one-story beige- and red-tile buildings near Apple's antiseptic headquarters in Cupertino. Couch fired up the workers with what he called the "Outward Bound School of Business," stressing the virtues of originality and sweat. New workers were employed as pristine users, and psychologists tested new features for what the industry called "user friendliness."[11]

Peter Nulty in a feature article in a 1983 issue of *Fortune* magazine described some of the obstacles of developing Lisa:

> The greatest mystery of all in the Lisa development was how to integrate the different computer applications, such as word processing, statistical and graphics programs, so that the user could easily swap material. Tesler says he estimated in 1980 it would take anywhere from two months to two years to accomplish that. Years was closer to the mark. By last summer, however, the programs were beginning to come together. One July afternoon, Tesler recalls, the programmers succeeded in getting all six application programs on the screen at the same time. Lisa was expertly pulling the budget report, for instance, out of the middle of the pile of documents and then putting it in full view on top.
>
> To celebrate their achievement, the programmers broke out bottles of Stanford, a California champagne (price: $4.29 per bottle). Soon feeling giddy, some people decided to work on the next project: moving the data from within one program to another. The schedule allotted two weeks for this development, but with their champagne-induced confidence, the programmers had it working within hours. So they had a second champagne party that night—this time uncorking Korbel, which is twice as expensive as Stanford. "Since then, there have been a lot of parties," says Tesler. "But we really knew we had done well when the marketing department started paying for the bubbly."

[10]Peter Nulty, "Apple's Bid to Stay in the Big Time," *Fortune,* February 7, 1983, p. 40.

[11]Philip Faflick, "The Year of the Mouse," *Time,* January 31, 1983, p. 51.

Basically the 50-pound, $9,995 Lisa uses a graphic list of functions and data file arrays called "menus," including pictures of a file folder, a document, a wastebasket or other familiar office tools (Exhibit 9). This format enables a user to select a piece of data or initiate a task without typing coded commands. It includes a 12-inch black-and-white screen with high-resolution imaging, one million bits of main memory storage, a profile hard disk supplying 40 million bits of data storage, electric typewriter style, expanded keyboard with a separate 10-key-pad for numerical calculations, and a mouse which can be used to select data files or functions illustrated on the screen.

Included in the Lisa system are six integrated software applications: LisaCalc, an electronic spreadsheet; LisaGraph, for plotting spreadsheet data in bar, line, pie, or other graphic formats; LisaDraw, a freehand graphics package; LisaList, an electronic file folder, and LisaProject, a project-management tool for tracking progress of industrial or financial projects. Further, it can be infinitely expanded.

Lisa systems will run BASIC, COBOL, and Pascal, and there are plans for equipment that will allow Lisa to talk to IBM mainframe computers.

Although Jobs claimed that "with Lisa's technology we have set the direction for the computer industry for the next 5 to 10 years," and that he did not "think we will have any trouble selling all the Lisas we can build," Markkula concedes, "It's going to take time to get the message of what Lisa's all about across," and Couch acknowledges, "If we had known how big Lisa would get, I'm not sure we would have begun at all. It turned out to have a $50 million start-up cost." Even Jobs acknowledges that "Lisa was just bigger than we anticipated. Scheduling is an art. Most of Lisa's software was created from scratch and that's very hard to predict."

Although Lisa has a balky printer, a sluggish word processor, no color, is relatively slow in retrieving information, and its software can only run on Lisa machines, Apple expected more than one third of its sales in 1983 to be to the 2300 U.S. companies with over $120 million in annual revenues. Published estimates of first year sales ranged from 2,000 to 50,000 units.

MACINTOSH

Another new product, the MacIntosh, with an estimated price of $2,000 to $5,000, was to be introduced in 1983. Although using the Lisa technology, it was incompatible with Lisa. It was priced lower because of hardware innovations and because it initially would run only a few fixed programs, including word processing and financial modeling. The MacIntosh project was personally headed by Jobs. Reportedly Michael Scott refused to let Jobs run the Lisa team because he was too inexperienced; according to one insider, "Steve was furious and went off and started the Mac project. He was determined to prove that Mac could be a bigger success." Some of Jobs's team put in seven-day 90-hour weeks trying to make the Mac project a success.

The company also planned to announce another new product in 1983, Apple IIE, to capitalize on the popularity in Apple II, which it contended had the largest-installed base of any personal computer (more than 700,000 units had been purchased by the

Exhibit 9 Lisa—business graphics and monitor screen

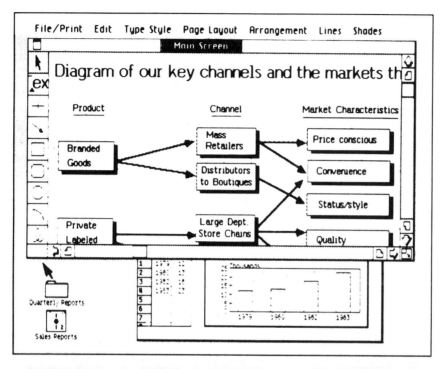

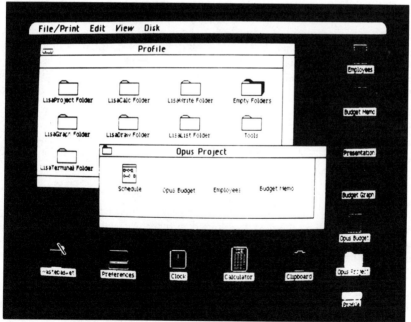

Sources: *Newsweek*, January 31, 1983, and *Fortune*, February 7, 1983.

end of 1982). Apple was even more secretive about IIE than about Lisa, but it was reported to be a revised Apple II with full upper- and lowercase keyboard, video display, 80-column screen, 64 kilobytes of memory and ability to run all Apple II programs without modification. The major expected change was to be in the manufacturing approach. Functionally it was said to be not much more capable than what a customer willing to add a few parts to an Apple II could have. But while the Apple II had 136 standard integrated circuits, the IIE was scheduled to have 11, 1 for the microprocessor, 8 for 64,000 characters of main memory and 2 for all the other electronics. If speculation about the Apple IIE proved correct, industry experts thought that the new machine, priced at $1,395, could be made profitable for perhaps five years, giving Apple's basic computer design a decade or more of life.

1983—A NEW EPOCH?

In early 1983, a California market research firm reported that personal computers shipped in 1982 had reached 2.8 million and predicted unit shipments of 10.5 million in 1985. Also, it was estimated that 300 new machines were being prepared for introduction in 1984–85 that would reflect three emerging trends:

- *Less Expensive.* Although the price of microcomputers had tended to fall 25 percent a year, increased competition, especially from Japan, was expected to push prices down even faster. Some experts believed a dozen Japanese products in the $100 range were being prepared for introduction into the United States and that ultimately home computers would sell for $50. The pressure on prices was also coming from technological breakthroughs. Whereas machines had been made chiefly with standard off-the-shelf components designed for other uses, manufacturers had begun designing components especially for personal computers. For example, by using very large-scale integration (VLSI) techniques some companies were reducing the number of chips in a computer from more than 100 to 1 or 2 and cutting chip costs by 90 percent.

- *Easier to Use.* Integrated software was expected to be standard on most desk-top computers by 1985. Commodore had announced plans to launch a Lisa-like product by 1984 at 60 percent of the price. Texas Instrument's Pegasus, designed so that it could use the same files and data as IBM's PC, was expected to combine 64K bytes of memory and a 320K byte floppy disk with the capability to respond to a limited number of spoken commands and accept certain commands in English sentences at a price of $2,595. VisiCorp soon was expected to introduce a program, costing less than $1,000, that would work with IBM's PC and do most of what Lisa could do. Furthermore, sales of small computers, weighing 15 pounds or less, were expected to grow more quickly during the next two years than other segments. Nippon Electric had recently unveiled a $550 computer the size of a loose-leaf binder with a flatpanel display that would run on batteries for 18 hours, yet with the computing power of an Apple II and a full-size keyboard.

- *More Powerful.* Machines were being designed with 32-bit microprocessors and with the capability of being upgraded with higher-capacity memory in just five minutes without using tools.

As Stephen Jobs evaluated the myriad problems facing his company in 1983, he knew that Apple needed to establish a clear direction to remain the leader in the industry. Sales of Apple II had hit a plateau of 30,000 a month in late 1982, a price war was developing, and sales of Apple III were only 3,000–3,500 per month even at the reduced $2,995 price.

Even Lisa and MacIntosh raised new problems for him, not the least of which was how to introduce and market them. For example, should Lisa be sold through a small sales force, or should Apple rely on selected local dealers? How should service and support be provided? The full-service dealers were already unhappy with recently announced plans to discount Apple II and cut dealer margins in half.

The IBM challenge was growing. Not only was IBM selling 20,000 units per month and approaching 20 percent market share but it was rumored to be readying a new 16-bit machine, "Peanut," that would sell for less than $1,000, and an executive work station, "Popcorn," that might take Lisa head on.

As Jobs glanced through the materials on his desk, his attention was caught by an article in a major business publication, "The Coming Shakeout in Personal Computers." He could not help but wonder how his company with its young management team (Exhibit 10) would fare over the next few years and if a suitable replacement could be found for Mike Markkula, who for months had been talking about his plans to resign as president and take life a little easier. What Apple needs, he thought to himself, is a "heart transplant."

Exhibit 10   Management team, 1983

A. C. Markkula, Jr.*   President and Chief Executive Officer (age 39)

> Mr. Markkula has been a director of the Company since March 1977 and has served as President and Chief Executive Officer since March 1981. In addition, he served as Chairman of the Board from May 1977 to March 1981, as Vice President—Marketing from May 1977 through June 1980, and as Executive Vice President from June 1980 to March 1981. From 1971 to December 1976, he was Marketing Manager at Intel Corporation, a manufacturer of integrated circuits.

Steven P. Jobs*   Chairman of the Board and Vice President (age 26)

> Mr. Jobs, a cofounder of the Company, has served as Chairman of the Board since March 1981 and as Vice President since May 1977 and has been a director since March 1977. He served as Vice Chairman of the Board from August 1979 to March 1981. Prior to March 1977 he worked as an engineer for two years with Atari, Inc., a computer games manufacturer.

Kenneth R. Zerbe   Executive Vice President—Finance and Administration (age 46)

> Mr. Zerbe joined the Company in April 1979 as Vice President—Finance and Administration and served in that position until June 1980, at which time he was promoted to Executive Vice President—Finance and Administration. From April 1976 to April 1979, he was Senior Vice President of Finance and Administration for American Microsystems, Inc., a manufacturer of semiconductors. Prior to that time, he was Senior Vice President of Finance at Fisher and Porter Co., a manufacturer of electronic process instrumentation.

Ann S. Bowers   Vice President—Human Resources (age 44)

Ms. Bowers joined the Company in July 1980 as Vice President—Human Resources. From October 1976 through June 1980, she served as an independent personnel management consultant to high technology growth firms. Prior to that time she served as Director of Personnel at Intel Corporation for over six years.

Gene P. Carter   Vice President—Sales (age 47)

Mr. Carter joined the Company in August 1977 as National Sales Manager and in December 1978 was promoted to Vice President—Sales. Prior to that time he was Director of Microprocessor Marketing at National Semiconductor Corporation, a manufacturer of integrated circuits and computers.

John D. Couch   Vice President and General Manager—Personnel Office Systems (age 34)

Mr. Couch joined the Company as Product Manager in October 1978 and was promoted to Vice President in April 1979. For more than five years prior to that time he held various engineering management positions at Hewlett-Packard Company, a manufacturer of business computers, during which time he was responsible for software development for the HP-3000 family of computers.

Albert A. Eisenstat   Vice President—Secretary and General Counsel (age 51)

Mr. Eisenstat joined the Company in July 1980 as Vice President and General Counsel and has also served as Secretary of the Company since September 1980. From December 1978 to July 1980 he was Senior Vice President of Bradford National Corporation, a computer services firm serving the banking, securities, and health care industries. From December 1974 through December 1978, he was Vice President and Corporate Counsel of Tymshare, Inc., an international computer time-sharing and services company. In both of these positions, he was responsible for legal and administrative duties.

Joseph A. Graziano   Vice President—Finance and Chief Financial Officer (age 38)

Mr. Graziano joined the Company in October 1981 as Vice President—Finance and Chief Financial Officer. From 1976 to 1981, he was employed at ROLM Corporation, a manufacturer of computer-controlled telephone systems and Mil-Spec computers, where he served as Treasurer from 1979 to 1981 and Assistant Treasurer from 1976 to 1979.

Frederick M. Hoar   Vice President—Communications (age 55)

Mr. Hoar joined the Company in July 1980 as Vice President—Communications. From March 1980 until his employment with the Company, he was Vice President—Public Affairs and Communications at Syntex Corporation, a pharmaceutical company. For more than five years prior to that time he was Vice President—Communications for Fairchild Camera & Instrument Corporation, a semiconductor manufacturer.

Wilfrid J. Houde   Vice President and General Manager—Personal Computer Systems (age 44)

Mr. Houde joined the Company in January 1979 as Director, Service and Operations. In April 1980, he was promoted to Director, Service, Operations, and Distribution. In April 1981, he was promoted to General Manager, Personal Computer Systems. In June 1981, he was promoted to Vice President and General Manager, Personal Computer Systems. Prior to his employment with the Company, he was Operations Manager, Computer Support at Hewlett-Packard Company for seven years.

Thomas J. Lawrence   Vice President and General Manager—Europe (age 47)

Mr. Lawrence joined the Company in August 1980 as Managing Director—Europe. In June 1981, he was promoted to Vice President and General Manager, Europe. From 1973 to 1980 he was employed at Intel Corporation, where he served as General Manager, Europe and Vice President of Intel International.

John Vennard   Vice President and General Manager—Peripherals (age 41)

Mr. Vennard joined the Company in June 1979 as Production Engineering Manager. In January 1979 he was promoted to General Manager—Peripherals. In June 1981 he was promoted to Vice President and General Manager—Peripherals. Prior to his employment with the Company, he held various technical management positions, including Director of Operations, at National Semiconductor Corporations.

Delbert W. Yocam   Vice President and General Manager—Manufacturing (age 46)

Mr. Yocam joined the Company in November 1979 as Director of Materials. In August 1981, he was promoted to Vice President and General Manager, Manufacturing. From May 1979 to November 1979 he was Line Material Manager for Fairchild Test Systems, a division of Fairchild Camera & Instrument Corporation. From May 1978 to May 1979, he was Staff Manager, Production Control and Planning at ITT Cannon Electric. From 1976 to 1978, he was Line Material Manager at Computer Automation, Inc.

Porter O. Crisp*   Board Member

Mr. Crisp is founding and managing partner of Venrock Associates, a limited partnership formed by the Rockefeller family to invest in technology-based enterprises. Elected to Apple's board of directors in October 1980, he also serves as a director of Crum and Forster, Eastern Airlines, Inc., Evans and Sutherland Computer Corporation, Itek Corporation, Thermo Electron Corporation, and a number of private companies.

Arthur Rock*   Board Member

Mr. Rock, one of the company's early investors, became a director of Apple in October 1980. Between 1969 and 1981 he was a general partner of Arthur Rock and Associates, venture capitalists, and for the past three years has been a limited partner of the San Francisco-based investment banking firm, Hambrecht and Quist. Mr. Rock also serves on the boards of Intel Corporation, Teledyne, Inc., and several privately held companies.

Philip S. Schlein*   Board Member

Mr. Schlein, chairman of the board and chief executive officer of Macy's California, became an Apple director in June 1979. He also serves as a director of R. H. Macy and Co., parent of Macy's California.

Henry E. Singleton*   Board Member

For 22 years Dr. Singleton has been chairman and chief executive officer of Teledyne, Inc., a diversified manufacturing company. He became a director of Apple in October 1978.

*Board of Directors.

CASE 8

Pabst Brewing Company

MARK KROLL
Sam Houston State University

JOHN MATHENY
General Electric Corporation

COMPANY HISTORY

The 139-year-old company that today is known as the Pabst Brewing Company was founded in Milwaukee in 1844, four years before Wisconsin became a state. A German immigrant, Jacob Best, and his four sons established the firm as Best and Company. In 1889, the stockholders of Best and Company voted to change the name of the brewery to the Pabst Brewing Company.

Pabst beer was awarded gold medals at the Philadelphia Centennial Exposition in 1876 and at the World's Fair in Paris in 1878. In 1893, at the Columbian Exposition in Chicago, Pabst won the highest award in competition with beers from all over the world. In that same year, sales topped 1 million barrels, making Pabst the largest brewer in the United States.

During Prohibition in the 1920s, Pabst, like other brewers, manufactured nonalcoholic products such as Pabst cheese, "near beer," tonic, malt syrup, and soft drinks. These products were distributed through Pabst's existing marketing operations. As Prohibition drew to a close, Pabst completed a merger with the Premier Malt Products Company of Peoria, Illinois. Harris Perlstein, president of Premier, was made president of Pabst. When the brewery resumed beer production, Perlstein steered Pabst's return to the prominent position that it had held prior to Prohibition.

With the acquisition of its Peoria plant, Pabst became a pioneer in the brewing of the same beer in separate geographical locations. The company opened its Newark, New Jersey, plant in 1945, and bought its Los Angeles Brewery in 1948, which made Pabst the first American brewer with plants from coast to coast.

In 1958, Pabst purchased another Milwaukee brewery, the Blatz Brewing Company. James C. Windham, president of Blatz at the time, was made president and chief executive officer of Pabst. In 1972 Windham was also elected chairman of the board.

At the time Windham assumed leadership of the company, Pabst's sales had been declining; the company ranked thirteenth in brewing industry sales. Under Windham's administration, however, Pabst was restored to prominence, becoming the third largest brewer in the nation. Production and sales of Pabst beer jumped from 1.9 million barrels in 1960 to 13.1 million barrels in 1973.

Today, after several consolidations and the acquisition of Olympia Brewing Company, Pabst has plant operations in Milwaukee, Wisconsin; Newark, New Jersey; Tampa, Florida; and Tumwater, Washington. In addition to Pabst Blue Ribbon beer, Pabst's products include Andeker, Jacob Best Premium Light, Olde English "800" Malt Liquor, Pabst Extra Light, Olympia beer brands, and Hamm's. The distinctive flavor characteristics that mark these individual brands are achieved through Pabst's continuing pledge, made over a century ago, to follow only the highest quality standards in the art of brewing.

THE BEER PRODUCT

Beer is a food product made from barley malt, hops, grain adjuncts, yeast, and water. The relatively small amount of alcohol in most beers results from the fermentation of barley malt and other cereal grains by yeast. Five major categories of beer are marketed by the major brewers:

Premium or Regular Beer

Sales in this category represent about 46.4% of total U.S. beer sales. This category includes Coors, Budweiser, Miller High Life, Schlitz, Olympia, Stroh's, Ranier, and Old Style.

Low-Calorie Beer

The introduction of Miller Lite in 1975 created this segment, which now accounts for about 18.1% of total beer sales in the United States. This category includes Bud Light, Miller Lite, Stroh's Light, Coors Light, and Old Milwaukee. Light beer sales have grown at an annual rate of 14 percent over the last two years, while total industry sales are up only 2 percent.

Super-Premium Beer

This segment comprises approximately 5.5 percent of the total sales volume of the U.S. beer industry. The growth rate of the super-premium category averaged 13.2 percent from 1975 to 1982 and is second only to the low-calorie category in percentage growth. The price of domestic super-premiums is generally twenty to forty cents per 6-pack greater than premiums. Brands in this category include Michelob, Lowenbrau, Herman Joseph's, and Henry Weinhard's.

Popular-Priced Beer

Beers in this category are priced lower than premium brand beers. Products in this segment include such beers as Busch, Hamm's, Burgermeister, Old Milwaukee, Blatz,

Buckhorn, and generic beers. More than half of Pabst Blue Ribbon is sold at popular prices. Popular-priced beer accounts for 23.8 percent of total beer sales in the United States. Malt liquors make up the remainder of U.S. production, with 3.1 percent of the total sales volume.

Imported Beer

Imported beer sales represented about 3.1 percent of the total beer sales in the U.S. in 1982. Between 1975 and 1982 imported beer sales grew at an annual rate of 19.2 percent. The dominant brands in this category are Heineken, Molson, Moosehead, and Beck's.

THE BEER INDUSTRY

Industry—1982 Status

There are forty-five companies currently brewing beer in the United States, and the industry today is highly competitive. The flurry of mergers, acquisitions, and reorganizations that beset this industry over the past few years has subsided—at least for the moment. Now the question is: Amidst all the maneuvering, who gained and who lost? The jury is still out on that one, but it seems safe to say that there are now just six serious contenders in the United States beer business: *Anheuser–Busch, Miller (a subsidiary of Philip Morris), Heileman, Coors, Pabst, and privately held Stroh.*

The "big six" beer producers are off and running in a race for market share that could determine who survives through the Eighties in an industry that is growing little, if at all. The basic problem is that the beer industry is mature, and demographic trends are working against all brewers. For the first time in years, the number of 18-to-24-year olds—who drink the most beer—declined in 1982. As the population continues to age in the decade ahead, the challenge for beer companies will be to attract new drinkers, while maintaining the loyalty of adults in the 25-to-49 age group.

The brewing industry grew at a compounded annual growth rate of about 3.0 percent from 1978 to 1981, but in 1982 it failed to grow for the first time in twenty-five years. However, some of the larger brewers have successfully developed licensed brewing contracts with various foreign brewers, and it appears that there may very well be a thirsty world out there waiting for American beer. Excluding any foreign sales, an expected compounded annual growth rate of 2.5 percent is possible throughout the remainder of the decade of the Eighties, as the nation's adult population is expected to grow by ten million between 1980 and 1985.

In terms of distribution, supermarkets and convenience stores hold 16 percent of all beer licenses, but sell 66 percent of all beer consumed; therefore, two-thirds of all beer sold in the United States is consumed in homes, not bars. Further, it is estimated that 20 percent of American beer drinkers, white- and blue-collar working men, consume 80 percent of all beer sold in the United States. Exhibit 1 provides volume and

Exhibit 1   U.S. brewing industry sales volume and share

BREWER	1983		1982		1981	
	M/BBLS	%SHARE	M/BBLS	%SHARE	M/BBLS	%SHARE
Anheuser–Busch	60.5	33.0	59.1	31.9	54.5	29.5
Miller	38.0	20.4	39.3	21.2	40.3	21.9
Stroh's	25.1	13.6	22.9	12.4	20.5	11.1
G. Heileman	17.5	9.5	14.5	7.8	14.0	7.6
Pabst	12.8	7.0	12.3	6.6	13.5	7.3
Coors	13.7	7.5	11.9	6.4	13.3	7.2
Top Six US Brewers	167.6	91.0	160.0	86.3	156.1	84.6
Other[a]	16.8	9.0	25.2	13.7	28.3	15.4
Total US Industry	184.4	100.0	185.2	100.0	184.4	100.0

Source: Various corporate stockholder reports

[a]Includes imports

market share figures for the six largest brewers for the years 1981, 1982, and 1983. Exhibit 2 reviews the profitability and sales growth for the six largest firms in 1982. Exhibit 3 provides operating data, balance sheets, and financial ratios for the six largest firms in the industry as of 1982. Exhibits 4, 5 and 6 provide more specific financial and operating performance for Pabst Brewing Company. Exhibit 4 reveals that Pabst lost $23,536,000 in 1981, and has experienced turbulent times since that year.

BATTLE FOR PABST

During the second half of 1980, Irwin Jacobs set in motion a takeover battle for Pabst that would ultimately prove to be one of the most dramatic in recent years. Before the battle concluded, several major brewing companies were drawn into the fray.

The Combatants
Irwin L. Jacobs   Mr. Jacobs is a Minneapolis entrepreneur who is known as "Irv the liquidator." Mr. Jacobs is no stranger to the brewing industry. In 1975 he paid $4.1 million for Minneapolis' Grain Belt Breweries. His attempt to manage the company was a dismal failure. While under his guidance, Grain Belt lost over $200,000 a month, and after ten months he liquidated the company at a $4.0 million profit. About $3.3 million of that profit was attributable to his having sold the rights of Grain Belt to G. Heileman Brewing Company of La Crosse, Wisconsin.
Paul Kalmanovitz   Mr. Kalmanovitz is a 77-year-old immigrant who arrived from Poland in 1926, lacking funds and formal schooling. He has built a brewing empire largely on once-popular regional beers—Falstaff, Ballantine, Narragansett, Lucky Lager,

Exhibit 2 Forbes—brewing industry yardsticks of management performance

| | PROFITABILITY | | | | | | | GROWTH | | | |
| | RETURN ON EQUITY | | | RETURN ON TOTAL CAPITAL | | | | SALES | | EARNINGS/SHARE | |
BREWERY	5-year average	5-year rank	last 12 months	5-year average	5-year rank	last 12 months	N/PROFIT MARGIN	5-year average	5-year rank	5-year average	5-year rank
G. Heileman	31.4%	1	27.7%	23.1%	1	19.1%	5.2%	28.6%	1	30.6%	1
Miller[a]	23.6%	2	22.9%	13.5%	2	12.1%	6.6%	20.3%	2	19.2%	3
Anheuser–											
Busch	19.4%	3	21.9%	11.3%	3	11.6%	6.3%	17.2%	3	20.1%	2
Coors	11.7%	4	8.9%	9.6%	4	7.5%	5.2%	7.2%	5	3.0%	4
Pabst	0.8%	5	0.3%	1.0%	6	0.6%	0.1%	4.5%	6	-38.6%	5
Stroh's[b]	N/A		N/A	N/A		N/A	N/A	N/A		N/A	
Alcoholic Beverage Medians	13.2%		10.0%	10.2%		7.3%	5.2%	8.8%		11.6%	
All-Industry Medians	15.9%		12.7%	11.0%		9.3%	3.4%	13.3%		12.3%	

Source: *Forbes*, January, 1983

[a]classified as tobacco company (Philip Morris)

[b]private company, not rated

Exhibit 3 U.S. brewing industry, 1982—selected financial data (in millions, except statistical data)

	ANHEUSER-BUSCH	MILLER	STROH'S	G. HEILEMAN	PABST	COORS
OPERATIONS:						
Net sales billed	4,576.6	9,101.6	1,530.0	870.8	785.6	915.3
Gross margin	1,244.9	3,682.3	N/A	246.6	117.6	256.3
Sales, general, and administrative expense	752.0	2,031.8	N/A	163.7	105.6	200.4
Operating margin	492.9	1,650.5	N/A	82.9	12.0	55.9
Net income	287.3	781.8	1.2	45.7	2.7	40.1
BALANCE SHEET:						
Inventories	307.8	3,068.5	N/A	70.4	63.5	118.7
Current assets	691.8	3,850.3	N/A	165.0	115.5	293.7
Plant and equip., net	2,988.9	4,194.9	N/A	167.5	228.7	705.8
Total assets	3,902.8	9,691.9	650.0	502.0	408.9	1,007.9
Current liabilities	646.0	1,613.8	N/A	97.9	90.4	120.0
Long-term debt	969.0	3,749.3	N/A	170.5	38.8	9.6
Total debt	2,376.2	6,029.0	N/A	307.9	154.6	224.7
Shareholders' equity	1,526.6	3,662.9	N/A	194.1	254.3	783.2
Capital expenditures	355.8	920.5	N/A	183.5	16.5	118.4
Working capital	45.8	2,236.5	N/A	67.1	38.8	173.7
Interest expense	89.2	267.2	N/A	4.2	3.6	2.5
No. shares outstanding	48.1	125.9	N/A	26.5	8.2	35.0
Market price per share	64.5	60.0	N/A	19.9	21.0	12.5
Cash dividends paid	65.8	301.5	2.5	10.6	3.3	10.5
KEY FINANCIAL RATINGS:						
Percent-Gross margin to sales	27.2	40.5	N/A	28.3	15.5	28.0
Percent-Operating margin to sales	10.8	18.1	N/A	9.5	1.6	6.1
Return on sales	6.3	8.6	0.1	5.2	0.4	4.4
Return on total assets	7.4	8.1	0.2	9.1	0.7	4.0
Return shareholders equity	18.8	21.3	N/A	23.5	1.1	5.1
Earnings per share	5.97	6.21	N/A	1.72	0.33	1.15
Current ratio	1.1	2.4	N/A	1.7	1.3	2.4
Quick ratio	0.6	0.5	N/A	1.0	0.6	1.5
Debt-to-equity ratio	1.6	1.6	N/A	1.6	0.6	0.3
Times interest earned	5.5	6.2	N/A	19.7	3.3	22.4
Total assets turnover	1.2	0.9	N/A	1.7	1.9	0.9
Price earnings ratio	10.8	9.7	N/A	11.5	63.7	10.9
Book value per share	31.74	29.09	N/A	7.32	31.07	22.38
Cash dividend/share	1.37	2.39	N/A	0.4	0.4	0.3
Sales per share	95.1	72.3	N/A	32.9	92.7	26.2

Exhibit 4   Pabst Brewing Company's three-year financial summary—operations

	1983	1982	1981
Barrels Sold	12,804,000	12,306,000	13,465,000
Sales	$799,988,000	$758,602,000	$811,523,000
Costs and expenses			
Costs of goods sold	543,552,000	531,608,000	509,324,000
Federal excise taxes	112,953,000	109,436,000	119,659,000
Marketing, general, and			
administrative expenses	129,743,000	105,610,000	105,746,000
	786,248,000	746,654,000	824,729,000
Operating income (loss)	13,740,000	11,948,000	(13,206,000)
Other income and (expense)			
Interest income	975,000	2,756,000	4,108,000
Interest expense	(9,950,000)	(3,567,000)	(1,965,000)
Plant closings and other			
dispositions	3,317,000	(3,241,000)	(39,791,000)
Miscellaneous—net	(612,000)	(3,600,000)	392,000
	(6,270,000)	(7,652,000)	(37,355,000)
Income (loss) before income taxes and equity in net loss of Olympia Brewing Co.	7,470,000	4,296,000	(50,561,000)
Provision (benefit) for income taxes:			
Current			
Federal	(2,393,000)	100,000	(7,800,000)
State	250,000	600,000	625,000
Deferred	5,243,000	425,000	(19,850,000)
	3,100,000	1,125,000	(27,025,000)
Income (loss) before equity in net loss of Olympia Brewing Company	4,370,000	3,171,000	(23,536,000)
Equity in net loss of Olympia Brewing Company	(765,000)	(478,000)	---
Net income (loss)-per average share: 1983–$.31; 1982–$.08; 1981–$(.72)	$ 3,605,000	$ 2,693,000	$ (23,536,000)

Regal, Jax, Pearl, and others—acquired and then tightly managed by Mr. Kalmanovitz. He slashes advertising budgets, breaking the cardinal rule within the industry of promoting heavily, and he then cuts prices to reflect the lower overhead, bidding for a constituency of price-conscious beer drinkers and old-time brand loyalists. Mr. Kalmanovitz has become known in the industry as its most prolific litigant—filing suits almost routinely when the acquisition road is rocky or when other problems crop up.

Exhibit 5   Pabst Brewing Company's five-year selected financial data
(In thousands except share amounts)

	1983	1982	1981	1980	1979	% CHANGE
Barrels Shipped	12,804	12,306	13,465	15,091	15,115	− 15.30
Sales	$799,988	$758,602	$811,523	$853,441	$785,043	− 2.00
Operating income (loss)	13,740	11,948	(13,206)	21,423	19,740	− 30.40
Equity in net loss of Olympia Brewing Co.	(765)	(478)	—	—	—	N.A.
Net Income (loss)	3,605	2,693	(23,536)	12,642	9,478	− 62.00
Net income (loss) per share	.31	.08	(.72)	.39	.28	+ 10.71
Cash dividends per share	$ —	$ .10	$ .10	$ .10	$ .10	− 100.00
Weighted average number of common shares outstanding	11,795	32,742	32,733	32,682	33,913	− 65.22
Depreciation and amortization	$ 20,549	$ 30,394	$ 32,110	$ 30,697	$ 30,006	− 31.52
Capital expenditures, including properties acquired under capital leases	12,027	16,533	40,569	28,574	31,620	− 62.00
At year end						
Total assets	243,915	408,939	404,045	430,334	410,172	− 40.53
Long-term liabilities	84,976	38,843	13,281	14,679	20,284	+ 318.93
Working capital	6,959	36,655	31,542	67,568	58,119	− 88.03
Stockholders' equity	37,003	254,255	254,835	281,432	272,059	− 86.40
Stockholders' equity per share	$ 5.97	$ 7.77	$ 7.78	$ 8.61	$ 8.32	− 28.25

William F. Smith, Jr.   Mr. Smith, who in October 1982 became Pabst's fourth chief executive in thirteen months, came over to Pabst from the Pittsburgh Brewing Company, producer of Iron City Beer. Mr. Smith is credited with saving the Pittsburgh brewery through his personal effort in talking strikers back to work after a seventeen-day walkout in 1978, and subsequently engineering a turnaround in circumstances similar to Pabst's. He is known as an aggressive executive with a strong sense of urgency, who is outwardly self-confident, a strong cost control manager, and a capable marketer.

Mr. Smith, who earned $70 thousand a year as head of the Pittsburgh Brewing Company, stands to earn three times that amount in direct compensation from Pabst. The Pabst assignment represents a return to the Milwaukee beer scene for Mr. Smith,

Exhibit 6   Pabst Brewing Company's consolidated balance sheet

	1983 (After Reorganization)	1982 (Before Reorganization)	1981
Cash	$ 5,406,000	$ 17,655,000	$ 7,861,000
Market securities	153,000	7,000,000	6,992,000
Accounts receivables	24,443,000	20,902,000	18,510,00
Inventories	63,796,000	63,512,000	79,716,000
Prepaid expenses and other current assets	3,051,000	4,252,000	15,064,000
Total current assets	96,849,000	113,321,000	128,143,000
Investment in Olympia Brewing Company	—	36,778,000	—
Properties held for sale	—	10,938,000	12,120,000
Intangible assets, less accumulated amortization	—	15,814,000	14,885,000
Notes receivable	7,388,000	2,134,000	—
Other	2,935,000	1,206,000	—
	10,323,000	66,870,00	27,005,000
Land	5,771,000	4,430,000	4,420,000
Buildings	52,302,000	81,843,000	77,992,000
Machinery and equipment	150,727,00	265,713,000	256,480,000
Construction in progress	1,749,000	6,745,00	11,522,00
Cooperage	36,525,000	38,392,000	38,553,000
	247,074,000	397,123,000	388,967,000
Less—accumulated depreciation	123,295,000	184,041,000	167,172,000
	123,779,000	213,082,000	221,795,000
Leased properties under capital leases	15,195,000	21,562,000	41,991,000
Less—accumulated depreciation	11,063,000	14,555,000	25,422,000
	4,132,000	7,007,000	16,569,000
Bottles and boxes	8,832,000	8,659,000	10,533,000
Total other assets	136,743,000	228,748,000	248,897,000
Total assets	$243,915,000	$408,939,000	$404,045,000
Accounts payable	54,143,000	45,905,000	45,974,000
Accrued wages and benefits	15,022,000	13,790,000	16,745,000
Federal excise and other taxes	10,189,000	6,803,000	7,082,000
Federal and state income taxes	8,970,000	654,000	136,000
Accrued and other current liabilities	$ —	$ 4,237,000	$ 819,000

who was a packaging executive at the Miller Brewing Company headquarters from 1973 to 1975. While in Pittsburgh he would often visit local bars, buying free beer for the customers. Now in Milwaukee, where Pabst remains the No. 1 seller, on weekends he loads a van with beer and distributes samples to tailgaters at local football games.

The motto that adorns the wall behind Smith's desk in his office at Pabst reads: "Show me a good loser and I'll show you a loser." Since coming to Pabst, Mr. Smith

Exhibit 6   Pabst Brewing Company's consolidated balance sheet (continued)

	1983 (After Reorganization)	1982 (Before Reorganiation)	1981
Current portion of long-term liabilities	$ 1,566,000	$ 5,277,000	$ 5,261,000
Accrued plant closing costs	—	—	19,120,000
	89,890,000	76,666,000	95,137,000
Liability to customers for returnable containers	14,595,000	13,700,000	15,742,000
Total current liabilities	104,485,000	90,366,000	110,879,000
Long-term debt	76,810,000	33,782,000	—
Obligations under capital leases	3,186,000	5,061,000	13,281,000
Other	4,980,000	—	—
Total long-term liabilities	84,976,000	38,843,000	13,281,000
Deferred income taxes	17,451,000	25,475,000	25,050,000
Common stock—no par value	39,073,000	9,726,000	9,726,000
Less—guaranteed employee stock ownership plan debt	(4,420,000)	—	—
	34,653,000	9,726,000	9,726,000
Less—treasury stock at cost	—	(20,620,000)	(20,620,000)
Retained earnings	2,350,000	265,149,000	265,729,000
Total shareholders' equity	37,003,000	254,255,000	254,835,000
Total liabilities and shareholders' equity	$243,915,000	$408,939,000	$404,045,000

has closed the Peoria Heights, Illinois, brewery, idling some 600 workers, as well as winning concessions from brewery workers at the Newark plant, a move that purportedly cut operating costs by about $4 million a year. In addition, he dismissed the company's top marketing officer, the vice-president in charge of sales, and Pabst's corporate secretary.

G. Heileman Brewing Company   Heileman's 47-year-old Chairman, Russell G. Cleary, has been ungraciously referred to as the "guerilla fighter" of the brewing industry. He has been described as a pricing and marketing wizard. The brewing industry's major thrust in the past decade has been elimination of the nation's small and medium brewers and a concentration of over half of the country's total beer market in the hands of just two companies, Anheuser-Busch and Miller. While other local and regional brewers have failed, Heileman's industry position has advanced from thirty-first in 1960, with revenues of $18.8 million, to fourth in 1982, with revenues in excess of $1 billion—quite an accomplishment in just twenty-two years.

G. Heileman is the fastest-growing beer company in the country, with a return on equity that has averaged 30.2 percent over the last five years—double the industry average. Mr. Cleary has achieved that record by acquiring at steep discounts the small regional plants the big companies had no use for, then gradually building up enough capacity to achieve economies of scale in materials purchasing and administration.

What's more, he did it mainly out of cash flow, while lowering debt gradually over the decade to a 27 percent debt-to-capital ratio, roughly the industry norm.

Mr. Cleary believes that the beer business is really a regional business. After acquiring Blatz Brewing Co., Jacob Schmidt Brewing Co., Rainier Brewing Co., and Drewery's Ltd. U.S.A, Heileman did not move in its existing brands. Instead, it continued to sell the products of those regional brewers. "If you look at the brewers below number two, you will see that they do not have uniform sales across the nation," says Cleary. "Each brand sells well in a particular area. If we were to buy Pabst or Schlitz or whoever, there would be no reason to try to sell the brands nationally. You just want to fish where the fish are."

C. Schmidt and Sons, Inc.   Schmidt is a 120-year-old privately held brewing company located in Philadelphia. Schmidt, which produces Rheingold, Knickerbocker, and Schmidt's beer, is the nation's tenth-largest brewer. Schmidt made an unsolicited bid to take control of the New York brewer, F. & M. Schaefer Corporation in 1978, but was foiled when Schaefer won an injunction barring the merger on antitrust grounds.

Gauging Schmidt's size and strength is difficult, but analysts put its annual revenue at about $192 million. Schmidt has a super image as a "popular-priced" brew, and has sought to shore up its market share with purchases of smaller brewers, most recently Philadelphia-based Ortlieb Brewing Company. Schmidt has concentrated its purchases and marketing efforts close to home and has established a very strong franchise in the Philadelphia area, with extremely high penetration in the on-premises (restaurant and bar taps) market.

Olympia Brewing Company   Olympia has been brewing beer from artesian springs located at their headquarters in Tumwater, Washington, since 1896. Olympia is the nation's eighth-largest brewer and controls about 3.2 percent of the total U.S. market. The company also owns the Theodore Hamm Brewing Co. and Lone Star Brewing Co., which gives Olympia plants and markets in St. Paul and San Antonio, respectively. Olympia continues to rely on the sale of its flagship brand and Olympia Gold, its entry in the light field, as well as Hamm's, Lone Star, and Buckhorn brands. According to the company, "Oly" Gold is the No. 1 light beer in the Pacific Northwest, No. 2 in Chicago, and No. 3 in the California market. The company lost $8.5 million on revenues of $393.4 million in 1981, lost $2.5 million on revenues of $325.9 million in 1982.

The Assault

In 1980, when Irwin Jacobs acquired 9.6 percent of Pabst common, he characterized his purchase to the skeptics as an investment in a well-managed company whose assets were undervalued by the market. Mr. Jacobs purchased his stake in Pabst for about $14 a share while the stock's book value at the time was approximately $33 a share, which would seem to indicate that "Irv" certainly had an eye for opportunity. When he acquired the approximately 800,000 shares of Pabst common and became the largest Pabst shareholder, Mr. Jacobs praised Pabst's management for their past exemplary performance in the face of unrelenting pressure from both the economy and the competition.

On July 2, 1981, Pabst's chairman and chief executive, Frank C. DeGuire, resigned under pressure. Mr. Jacobs demanded that he be elected chairman or vowed he would take the fight for control of the company to the shareholders. He also sought the resignation of four board members to make room for his own people. Mr. Jacobs felt the board did not own enough of the company's stock to make the kinds of tough decisions required for continued success in the highly competitive and quickly consolidating beer industry. However, Mr. Jacobs settled for a seat on the board, and the following week Pabst made a takeover bid for the ailing Jos. Schlitz Brewing Company. Pabst bid $588 million for Schlitz, topping an earlier offer by G. Heileman Brewing Company of $494 million. Analysts speculated that Mr. Jacobs was going to attempt a simultaneous liquidation of both companies. At the time, Pabst had little debt and $24 million in cash, while Schlitz had $120 million in debt, $326 million in equity, and $180 million in cash. Schlitz stock was worth $7 a share, compared to its market price of $15.

Ultimately, Pabst was forced to drop out of the bidding for Schlitz, while the Justice Department barred Heileman from acquiring Schlitz on the grounds that the combination would produce too heavy a concentration in the Midwest, and would therefore substantially lessen competition. Understandably, there was opposition to the merger from other brewers, most particularly from Anheuser-Busch and Miller, because the merger would have launched Heileman into their league. Less understandable was the opposition from the Reagan administration, whose antitrust enforcers had otherwise been receptive to the merging of much larger firms than Heileman and Schlitz.

During the same period, Stroh Brewing Co. had approached Schlitz. In April 1982 Stroh's acquired control of 67 percent of Schlitz common at $17 a share. Analysts agreed that Heileman's proposed takeover of Schlitz represented the best opportunity to significantly slow the growth of Anheuser-Busch and to make the industry more competitive.

Following Pabst's failure to successfully acquire Schlitz, director Jacobs resigned, but vowed to continue his campaign to gain control of Pabst. William F. Smith, Jr. was appointed president and chief executive officer at Pabst in October of 1981. Besides the ongoing battle with Jacobs, Pabst was engaged in an internal struggle brought about by sluggish sales and an anticipated loss of income for the year. It was feared that the firm would drop from its 1980 position of third in the industry to fifth in 1981.

In 1981, Mr. Jacobs teamed up with six associates, one of whom was Paul Kalmanovitz. This investor group controlled about 15 percent of Pabst. Mr. Jacobs declared that he had no plans to liquidate Pabst, but Mr. Smith was indisposed to let him try. Mr. Smith said that he owed his allegiance to the board that hired him and he intended to fight for the Pabst Brewing Company. Further, Mr. Smith said of Mr. Jacobs, "He's taking a lot of my time. I just wish I could get down to the job of selling beer." However, it was obvious what was driving Mr. Jacobs, as his investment in Pabst had cost him $20 million, and he had watched its value erode as Pabst's losses mounted.

On February 2, 1982, Pabst announced that it had reached an agreement in principle to acquire the Pittsburgh Brewing Company, a small but profitable regional brewer that produced Iron City and Iron City Light beers. Under the agreement, which was subject to the approval of Pittsburgh's shareholders, Pabst had agreed to pay, with its common stock, the equivalent of $7 a share for the 1.1 million shares outstanding.

On February 22, 1982, Pabst received an "unsolicited" cash merger proposal from C. Schmidt & Sons, Inc. Pabst said Schmidt proposed to buy its 8.18 million outstanding shares for $16 a share, or a total of $141 million. Schmidt's offer was only slightly above the stock's then current trading level. Pabst shares, which were sold over-the-counter, had closed the previous day at 14.25, up 1.124. On March 25, 1982, in their continued effort to merge with Pabst, C. Schmidt and Sons, Inc. increased their earlier offer of $16 a share to $20.50 a share, or a total of $168 million for all of Pabst's outstanding shares. In May 1982, C. Schmidt & Sons, Inc. sweetened its offer for Pabst to $25.50 per share, or a total of $208.7 million. The offer took the form of $20.50 per share in cash and $5 per share in debentures. In rejecting Schmidt's previous offers, Pabst had indicated that $25 a share in cash would be a fair price.

On December 10, 1982, the battle for Pabst escalated when Paul Kalmanovitz sued Pabst and Heileman for conspiracy. The suit charged that the defendants conspired to defraud Pabst shareholders, to injure Mr. Kalmanovitz's business, and to rig the offers in the bidding for Pabst control. The bidding was escalated when Mr. Kalmanovitz made a $32 per share offer for Pabst, which followed a new bid by Heileman at $29 a share.

Mr. Kalmanovitz denounced Heileman's alleged offer to him of $5 million if he agreed to drop his effort to acquire Pabst. At that time he was engaged in a partnership with Mr. Jacobs' investor group in an attempt to acquire Pabst. Subsequently, Mr. Jacobs' group pulled out of its agreement with Mr. Kalmanovitz to support Heileman's offer. Mr. Kalmanovitz stated that Mr. Jacobs "defected" to Heileman because Heileman paid Mr. Jacobs and his associates $7.5 million. He called the payment a "discriminatory premium over other Pabst shareholders." According to the suit, the Heileman bid violated federal law because the $5 million offer was not disclosed and the payment to Mr. Jacobs was "disguised" as a "litigation settlement." Mr. Kalmanovitz stated that the defendant's conduct was a "classic case of how insiders connive with covetous outsiders to frustrate competitive bidding and to fleece ordinary shareholders."

Pabst said that its board had noted that the Heileman offer would deliver more cash than the Kalmanovitz bid, $162.4 million compared with $132.8 million, even though Mr. Kalmanovitz's per-share offer was higher, $32 compared to $29. That was because Heileman had raised its target to 5.6 million shares and Mr. Kalmanovitz only wanted 4.2 million under the terms of his offer. However, both bidders were to complete their proposed mergers by swapping notes for the remaining Pabst shares outstanding. Heileman was to swap ten-year notes with a face value of $24 per share. Mr. Kalmanovitz was to swap three-year subordinated notes with a face value of $26 a share.

By December 23, 1982, Kalmanovitz raised his offer for 4.2 million shares of Pabst common from $32 each to $40. Mr. Kalmanovitz's opponent in the takeover fight, Heileman, had earlier increased its offer for Pabst to $32 a share to match Mr. Kalmanovitz's previous offer. Kalmanovitz increased to 18 percent from 15 percent the interest rate on subordinated notes that were to be swapped for all remaining shares if the merger was completed.

The Vote

G. Heileman Brewing Company eventually won the long battle for control of Pabst Brewing Company, despite an apparently higher offer from Mr. Paul Kalmanovitz. Heileman received 6,730,000 of Pabst's 8.2 million shares outstanding. Heileman accepted for payment 68 percent or 5.6 million shares as of Wednesday, midnight, December 22, 1982. Heileman's bid evidently won because investors feared that Kalmanovitz would be unable to accumulate the 4.15 million shares his offer required. If Heileman was able to secure the 5.6 million shares it sought, there would not be enough remaining outstanding Pabst's stock to meet Mr. Kalmanovitz's minimum. But if the offer from Kalmanovitz was higher, as it apparently was, why shareholders "feared" Kalmanovitz could not meet his minimum remains a mystery.

The New Pabst

The new management team at Pabst, led by William Smith, had spent the past twenty months beating back no less than seven takeover attempts—including multiple forays by Irwin Jacobs, Paul Kalmanovitz, and G. Heileman Brewing—and had completed a takeover of Olympia Brewing. But it was not accomplished without a cost. Pabst had to sell three of its seven breweries to Heileman, including one it acquired from Olympia, and had witnessed its planned acquisitions of Schlitz Brewing and Pittsburg Brewing fall apart.

The transactions that eventually allowed Pabst to retain its independence were so varied and tangled that to this day misconception persists. Subtleties of the transactions in which Heileman grabbed Pabst, removed its guts, and then gave back the empty shell had eluded most observers altogether. In fact, stock market investors had, at least initially, cast their vote for Pabst's management. Pabst's common shares, valued at $26 each for purposes of the March 18, 1983 merger with Olympia, had traded shortly after the merger for as high as $66.50. Initial buyers included a majority of Pabst's twenty-three officers and directors who had, at least at last count, purchased a total of 40,000 shares.

Unfortunately, while 1983 earnings per share of $.53 were a significant improvement over 1982 results, they were well below earnings forecasted. Throughout 1983, Pabst, structurally and financially drained from the takeover struggles, continued to lose market share to the larger brewers. While barrels sold rose slightly in 1983, the losses of plants to Heileman and the overwhelming advertising budgets of larger brewers resulted in Pabst's poor market share position in all of its markets, and especially in the Sun Belt. Current security analysts' estimates suggest that Pabst could lose one million barrels in sales in 1984 to the three largest brewers—Anheuser-Busch, Miller, and Heileman.

In order to hold current market share, Pabst spent a company record $63 million on advertising in 1983. In order to continue to hold market share even larger advertising expenditures will be required in 1984. Since domestic beer consumption is growing at only 1 percent a year, the three largest brewers are all targeting Pabst's markets, due to Pabst's diminished competitive capacity.

In late 1983, August U. Pabst, the great-grandson of the founder of the firm, resigned as executive vice-president. It was his conclusion that the only hope for Pabst was to acquire another large brewer in order to build market share instantly, or to be acquired by another brewer. However, the extremely weak financial condition of Pabst precluded any acquisitions, and the poor market share performance of Pabst's brands made the firm's acquisition at a price anything above its break-up value very doubtful.

William Smith was only a bit more optimistic at the beginning of 1984. While admitting that the firm was under extreme competitive pressures, he pointed to some bright spots. Barrelage had indeed risen in 1983 for the first time in several years. They still had four large, efficient plants located in the key Southeast, West Coast, and Midwest markets. Pabst had managed to improve production efficiency slightly. However, Smith had no illusions about the difficulties Pabst faced in the future. Could Pabst continue as a going concern? How could Pabst build market share in order to achieve economies of scale in both production and marketing? If Pabst could not continue, what was the most advantageous course of action from the shareholders' point of view?

REFERENCES

"Heileman Wins Pabst." *Business Week,* (January 10, 1983): 40.

Nelson-Horchler, Joani. "Showdown in the Sunbelt." *Industry Week* (June 13, 1983): 69–72.

Note: There are three excellent trade publications that contain additional information related to this case. They are: *Beverage World, Modern Brewing,* and *Beverage.*

CASE 9

Braniff
BOBBY G. BIZZELL
Stephen F. Austin State University

ROBERT L. ANDERSON
College of Charleston

The 1930 incorporation of Braniff Airways in Oklahoma was the genesis of what was to become the sixth-largest airline in the United States. Braniff Airways, Inc., operated as a small, somewhat obscure regional carrier until 1965. The major change was when Harding Lawrence became its president and director. In 1966, Lawrence and the Board of Directors began a diversification plan into areas other than air travel. They believed this move was to achieve long-range financial strength. The proposed incorporation of a holding company (Braniff International Corporation), in 1971 was a result of this diversification strategy. Braniff International Corporation (BIC) was conceived with no material assets or liabilities. In 1972 the BIC proposal was passed by the stockholders and subsequently approved by the Civil Aeronautics Board on November 28, 1983. At this time BIC merged with Braniff Airways, Inc., to form Braniff's principal line of business—a passenger and cargo airlines servicing major cities on an international basis.

Harding L. Lawrence received a Bachelor of Business degree from the University of Texas in 1942. He began his airline career with Pioneer Airlines in 1947. By 1955 he had obtained a law degree from South Texas College of Law (1949) and had risen to Vice-President of Sales of Pioneer Airlines. He held the same position with Continental Airlines until 1957, when he became Vice-President of Administration. In 1958 he was made Executive Vice-President, a position he retained until he left to join Braniff. In 1965 he resigned as a Continental director and as Executive Vice-President to take over the reins of Braniff as President and Chief Executive Officer.

Lawrence's tenure as President of Braniff was characterized by the flamboyance that became a part of Braniff's style. During this period Braniff was noted for the multiple colors of its planes, the striking uniforms of flight attendants, and its interesting and innovative advertising.

In 1968 Lawrence became Chairman of the Board of Braniff as well as President and Chief Executive Officer. He relinquished the title of President in 1977. He remained as Chairman until 1980, when he was replaced by John Casey.

For BIC the period from 1973 through 1978 was one of merging with a variety of subsidiaries which complemented Braniff. Among these subsidiaries was the Braniff International Hotels, which owned the popular Driskill Hotel and discotheque in Austin, Texas, and operated the private dining and housing facilities at Braniff's "world headquarters."

In 1972 Braniff Educational Systems, Inc. (BESI) was incorporated and then merged with BIC in 1973. The primary purpose of BESI was to provide airline career vocational training courses which were approved by the Texas Educational Agency and Veterans Administration.

In September 1973, Braniff International Resort Properties, Inc., was incorporated. This subsidiary was primarily involved in the sale of condominium units and resort properties.

Other subsidiaries include BIC Guardian Services and Braniff Realty. The combined revenue from all subsidiaries was less than 1 percent of BIC's total revenue. The primary revenue for BIC came from their flight activities. Braniff's corporate headquarters and principal hub for flight activities were located at the Dallas-Fort Worth

Source: The research and written case information were presented at a Case Research Symposium and were evaluated by the Case Research Association's Editorial Board. This case was prepared with the assistance of Mr. Kelly Palmer, as a basis for class discussion.

(DFW) Regional Airport. Braniff's other major hub cities included Denver, Houston, and Kansas City. Location and effective utilization of these hubs gave Braniff the ability to serve virtually all regions of the United States—the Southeast, the West Coast, the Eastern Seaboard, and Hawaii. In 1978, Braniff began to implement its expansion program and, by March 1979, service had expanded to 54 U.S. cities in 30 states including Washington, D.C. Three hundred fifty-eight thousand, nine hundred forty-two (358,942) average daily plane-miles were flown in December 1978. Leading flights in terms of revenue were DFW-New York, DFW-Chicago, DFW-Denver, Chicago-Houston, and DFW-Honolulu. In order to serve Alaska and Alberta, Braniff closed interchange agreements with two other airlines.

Internationally, Braniff expanded into cities in Latin America. This entry into Latin America was accomplished in the 1960s through a merger with Panagra. Braniff's expansion into South America left it as the leading U.S. flag airline in a number of cities and nations served in South America. During 1978, Braniff began daily non-stop flights to London. Service was also introduced to Frankfort and Brussels, as well as Seoul, Korea, and Hong Kong in the Far East.

Net income increased from $16 million in 1975 to $45 million in 1978. By December 1978, Braniff moved its new "world headquarters" to the west side of DFW.

Deregulation of the airline industry was brought about by the "Airline Deregulation Act of 1978" (Public Law 95–504). The act was designed to "encourage, develop, and attain an air transportation system which relies on competitive market forces to determine the quality, variety, and price of air services. . . ."

The basic premise of the act was to allow any carrier to serve any market for which the carrier is "fit, willing, and able" to serve. Congress felt the carrier could perform such transportation as was consistent with the public convenience and necessity.

If an airline elected to begin service on a route that was currently being served, the present airline could prevent the entry on certain conditions. Basically, the law prevented new service only if the company now providing the service could prove that the new service would endanger the public welfare. In addition, an airline could cut fares by fifty percent or raise the fares by five percent on any route in which they controlled less than seventy percent of traffic. Each airline could also claim one additional route per year in 1979, 1980, and 1981 without CAB approval.

The first phase of deregulation of the airlines industry went into effect in November 1978. Lawrence was opposed to deregulation because he felt it would be detrimental to the industry as a whole. Acting on his prognosis that Congress would deregulate—opening a "window" in which airlines could expand, and then reregulate—closing that window, Lawrence seemed to feel that whoever got out there and got their flagpoles stuck in as many places as possible would have grandfather rights and, therefore, would have expanded their airlines.[1]

After deregulation, and in just one day, Braniff added 16 cities and 32 routes. By December 1979, Braniff had added 18 new cities domestically and 8 new cities inter-

[1]Howard Putnam. Interview held at Braniff Headquarters, Dallas, Texas, June 8, 1983.

nationally—a 32% increase in seat miles. Lawrence's stated strategy was that expansion was essential to keep big airlines like American and United from swallowing Braniff.[2]

In order to service these new routes, Braniff ordered 41 new planes in December 1978 at a cost of over $925 million dollars. Lawrence had assumed that Congress would reregulate, and both fuel prices and the economy would remain stable. He was convinced Braniff had placed itself in a strong position for the 1980s.

As early as 1978 fuel prices began to rise. Braniff's annual report in 1978 stated, ". . . it is impossible to predict whether adequate fuel may be available in the future to operate services at levels approximately responsive to demands for Braniff's services," and, ". . . the cost of jet fuel in Latin America is considerably in excess of the average cost of jet fuel in the United States." Fuel costs rose from 40 cents per gallon in 1978 to 62 cents in 1979 and to 91 cents in 1980. Even with the above signs Braniff continued to expand. In 1979 and 1980 Braniff lost $44 million and $131 million, respectively. The South American routes, alone, were losing approximately $20 to $30 million a year.

As the recession deepened, passenger traffic declined 11% and interest rates soared. Braniff was under ever-increasing pressure from its thirty-nine private secured lenders. Flights were added to Florida and the Northwest in February, but in March Braniff suspended flights to Colorado Springs, Detroit, Jacksonville, and West Palm Beach. The private secured lenders agreed to defer until July 1, 1981, those debts due from February 1 through June 30, 1981. Braniff was able to sell 15 of its jets to American Airlines, reducing its fleet size and debt.

On the last day of 1980 Lawrence resigned and Braniff's Vice Chairman, John J. Casey, was installed as Chairman and President. Being an insider, Casey could perhaps see more, but not all, of the problems affecting Braniff. He attempted to streamline and simplify Braniff's organizational structure. Casey consolidated the senior executive positions into three areas: operations, finance, and marketing, each under an executive vice-president. Casey also began to reassign airline resources to more profitable routes, eliminating some of the unprofitable areas and routes. To help raise cash, Casey sold older aircraft. Casey also sacrificed his $200,000 plus salary in exchange for the employees' (Union's) agreement to take a 10% cut in pay—effective March 31, 1981—until profitability returned. This tactic alone saved Braniff $25 million in 1981. Five thousand employees were furloughed during Casey's reign, reducing the work force to 10,800 in 1981.[3]

Competition had become intense by 1980. American Airlines moved its corporate offices to DFW and proceeded to develop a hub centered at DFW to compete directly with Braniff. Casey had been with Braniff throughout the entire expansion and perhaps found it difficult to make some of the changes that had to be made. Casey called on Howard D. Putnam, President and Chief Executive Officer of Southwest Airlines, to attempt the now vital turnaround.

[2]Ibid.
[3]Ibid.

Exhibit 1 BIC and Braniff Airways officers—1980

The Senior Corporate officers in 1980 of Braniff International Corporation, the holding company whose principal asset includes all outstanding stock of Braniff Airways, Incorporated, included:

H. L. Lawrence	Chairman, Chief Executive Officer
Russell Thayer	President and COO
J. E. Riley	Senior Vice-President and General Counsel
E. E. Beckwith	Vice-President, Finance
D. J. Ethridge	Secretary
J. S. Holyfield	Treasurer

The Senior Corporate officers of Braniff Airways, Incorporated, as of 1980, included:

H. L. Lawrence	Chairman, Chief Executive Officer
Russell Thayer	President and COO
J. J. Casey	Vice-Chairman and Group Vice-President

Other corporate officers included nine Senior Vice-Presidents and 21 Vice-Presidents. In addition, there were approximately 15 staff Vice-Presidents.

Howard D. Putnam began his career in the airline industry as a baggage agent for Capital Airlines in Chicago, in 1955. In 1961 United Airlines absorbed Capital Airlines and Putnam moved to United. In 1966 he received an MBA in marketing from the University of Chicago.

Putnam was made Group Vice-President of United in 1976. He served as Group Vice-President until 1978, when he went to Southwest Airlines as President and Chief Executive Officer.

September 1981 was when Putnam left Southwest to become President, Chief Operating Officer, and member of the Board of Directors of Braniff International. He became Chief Executive Officer in January 1982 and Chairman of the Board in March 1982. He remained in these positions until June 10, 1983. Putnam's background at United had been in the marketing, sales, and services areas. Those experiences were utilized in developing a small, successful, entrepreneurial, intrastate carrier (Southwest Airlines) into a larger but even more productive (interstate) airline.[4] When Putnam, 44, became Braniff's Chief Executive Officer, he immediately began to make broad, sweeping changes. Realizing first that it was impossible to do this task alone, he brought with him M. Philip Guthrie to be his Executive Vice-President and his Chief Financial

---

[4]Howard Putnam, Address to Braniff International Lender's Meeting, Braniff Headquarters, Dallas, Texas, November 20, 1981.

Officer. Guthrie had held a similar position at Southwest Airlines while Putnam was Chief Executive Officer. The next step was to eliminate two entire levels of management and place more responsibility on fewer people. Approximately 18 vice-president positions were eliminated in the first four months. Putnam also streamlined and centralized decision making to expedite the process.[5]

When Putnam gained control he felt Braniff had an excellent route structure, an excellent fleet of jets, and an excellent facility at DFW. However, he met stiff resistance from the employees. Putnam and Guthrie had not expected the employees' attitude of "business as usual" in a period of such obvious financial distress. The employees actually felt there was an effective turnaround strategy in motion. Putnam was also surprised to learn that there was only 10 days of cash on hand. Instead of having a matter of months to turn Braniff around, they had only a few weeks. Braniff had been doing a billion dollars in revenue annually (about $3 million a day) and had 10 days of cash to operate a giant whose indebtedness was close to one billion dollars. In addition to these problems, Guthrie had determined that for every dollar generated in First Class, Braniff was losing $1.50.[6]

Putnam and Guthrie began to revamp scheduling and the fare structure in order to find a new niche for Braniff that was unique. They came up with the "Texas Class" fares and service concept.

Texas Class was Braniff's response to a variety of fares. Braniff had a total of 582 different fares. Putnam believed these could be simplified and better service provided to the flying public. He envisioned a new type of plane configuration with one class of service. The airline would offer service based upon "simplicity, quality, lower fares, friendliness, and timeliness." The result was an airline on the mainland with one type of aircraft—Boeing 727–200. Each plane had the same seating arrangement—146 seats in one class. Braniff would operate with a simple fare structure—fifteen fares covering all domestic routes flown. Two B747s continued in service to cover Honolulu and London service from DFW.

The purpose of these fares was aimed not only at the consumers, but also at generating increased revenue quickly. Braniff also had to come up with a financial restructuring plan by February 1, 1982, the end of the debt deferral period. They had to come up with a package that would convince the 39 lenders to continue to defer debt past February 1, 1982, leading toward a complete financial restructuring.

Braniff finally obtained the approvals for a debt deferral beyond February 1, 1982, on January 22, 1982. Braniff was given further debt deferral until October 1, 1982. However, a complete financial restructuring plan was to be submitted to the secured lenders by March 31, 1982, for their review. This was accomplished.

By Spring 1982, the rumors of a possible bankruptcy were spreading and affecting traffic. Some travelers and many travel agencies refused to buy Braniff tickets because of the rumored bankruptcy. Passenger traffic declined dramatically in April and May

---

[5]Howard Putnam. Interview held at Braniff Headquarters, Dallas, Texas, June 8, 1983.
[6]Ibid.

Exhibit 2 Prominent Braniff lenders

Lenders	Amount (in millions)	Loans to Other Airlines (in millions)	
Prudential Ins. Co.	$75.9	Western Airlines:	$ 82.5
		Pan American:	42.3
		Eastern	10.6
Aetna Life Ins. Co.	34.3	Continental:	17.0
		Pan Am:	10.3
		Western:	22.0
		Texas Int.:	14.1
Chase Manhattan	14.1	Continental:	141.0
		Eastern:	2.1
		Pan Am:	2.5
		Texas Int.:	10.5
		World Airways:	27.3
Citibank of New York	8.4	Republic:	97.2
		Western:	4.3
		Eastern:	2.1

Source: Aviation Week and Space Technology, May 24, 1982, p. 28.

1982. On Tuesday, May 11, 1982 after weeks of highly publicized cash shortages, Guthrie reported to Putnam that Braniff would not be able to meet its next payroll. Braniff was not even paying the debt service on what it owed, and it was still losing money. At 5 P.M., May 12, 1982, Braniff shut down all operations and terminated all but 200 employees. Braniff was filing for bankruptcy under Chapter 11 of the Federal Bankruptcy Code.[7]

INTERVIEW WITH HOWARD PUTNAM

Casewriter: It appears to an outsider that the strategy of Braniff at the time you came in was basically one of survival. Do you see that as being anything different?

Putnam: When I got here? Yes. I think the management that was here thought they had a real turnaround in place. We didn't think so, and the financial results did not indicate that. So, therefore, we went to Texas Class. But, whether you say survival or revival in turnaround may be a matter of semantics. When you're not even paying the debt service on what you owe, and still losing money, you've got severe problems.

Casewriter: Could you say that Braniff had done anything differently to adapt to what was going on in the external environment at the time with deregulation, rising fuel prices, increased competition?

[7]Ibid.

Exhibit 3 Braniff International Corporation's comparative balance sheets (000 omitted)

	Dec. 31, 1981	Dec. 31, 1980
Assets		
Current:		
Cash	$ 51,174	$ 19,799
Accounts Receivable	106,364	133,413
Inventory	32,891	35,047
Other Assets	9,808	9,531
Total Current Assets	200,237	197,790
Other Assets:		
Property & Equipment (net)	786,868	882,167
Other Assets	21,192	27,411
Total Other Assets	808,060	909,578
Total Assets	1,008,297	1,107,368
Liabilities		
Current Liabilities:		
Notes Payable	47,144	47,144
Debt Due	101,244	42,718
Accounts Payable	59,252	96,112
Cap. Lease Due	4,428	10,217
Accruals	101,487	69,865
Other Current Liabilities	91,522	74,976
Total Current Liabilities	405,077	341,032
Long-Term Liabilities:		
Senior Debt	438,980	488,600
Subordinate Debt	80,250	95,002
Capital Lease Obligations	71,782	69,473
Other Liabilities	67,184	11,738
Total Long-Term Liabilities:	685,196	664,813
Total Liabilities	1,063,273	1,005,845
Equity		
Preferred Stock	39,455	35,343
Common Stock	10,010	10,010
Capital Surplus	46,785	46,785
Retained Earnings	(151,226)	9,385
Total Equity	(54,976)	101,523
Total Liabilities and Equity	$1,008,297	$1,107,368

Exhibit 4   BIC and Braniff Airways' officers—1982

The Senior Corporate officers of Braniff International Corporation and Braniff Airways in 1982 included:

H. D. Putnam	Chairman, President and Chief Executive Officer
M. P. Guthrie	Executive Vice-President and Chief Financial Officer
W. E. Huskins, Jr.	Executive Vice-President, Operations

Putnam: The expansion was very hasty and very costly. They told people to go open new cities on 45 days' notice. When you walk into a city and try to get facilities, you sign long-term leases and then you run back and get unions to agree to sign a letter or contract in order to fly to, for example, Seoul, Korea, which you had never discussed before with the unions. You pay through the nose. All the seven months we were here prior to bankruptcy, we continued to pay the city of Atlanta nearly $80,000 a month for a gate and some office space which Braniff had signed a 40-year lease on in their great expansion. They served Atlanta less than a year, I believe, and withdrew. But the costs stayed in place. That's the problem we had all over. The domestic and international expansion was too traumatic, too rapid. Now, had not fuel costs gone up, had not the economy soured, had not a few other things happened, I wouldn't be here today and Harding Lawrence would be sitting here as the person who pulled off the world's greatest airline expansion. Unfortunately, that didn't happen. In the airline business, when you start to shrink the size of the plant, the revenue goes away very quickly. All you have to do is stop flying airplanes. But, the costs, like Atlanta, linger on forever. You can't just shrink it revenue-wise and survive if many of the costs remain in place.

Casewriter: Based on what you just said, why do you think it took the Braniff Board so long to take some action?

Putnam: I don't know. The only answer I can think of is that Harding had done an absolutely super job for many years and the Board had tremendous faith in him. But he was pretty much a one-man band. I think the lesson there would be another kind of case study that it's good to have a strong senior management team. And I don't believe you should ever, in this kind of a company, have one strong guy who can really run the whole show. If you go talking with the people I work with around here, we really don't operate that way. We tried to gather a small group, and we did, of about 10 senior management folks. And we shared the responsibility so that no one guy could ever be a dictator and drag the whole thing down the tube.

Casewriter: Do you feel comfortable making any other comments about any of the Braniff management when you got here?

Putnam: A couple of observations that I've already made publicly. Here was a company that was on the threshold of failure, but there was a certain amount of complacency that was hard for us to believe. We felt that we had a matter of months when we got here; it turned out that we had only weeks, because we didn't know that we only had 10 days of cash until the day we got here. That was not public information. We got a company that had been doing a billion dollars in revenue which you could divide by 365 and figure out what your revenue was a day. Roughly 3 million a day, and then we had 10 days of cash to operate this giant company, whose indebtedness at that time was close to one billion dollars. So, here we were coming in fired up ready to change the world in 48 hours and the people around here were kind of like "it's business as usual." It took me a while to figure it out. One problem area that we found, as an example, was budgets. Budgets were viewed as a license to spend, but we felt that we should tighten control over our expenditures. When we did find that somebody had spent $10,000 on something non-essential to survival, we would say "why?" "Oh, it was in the budget" was the response. So, we just decided to eliminate all budgets. Nobody had the authority to spend money on anything outside of day-to-day operating requirements unless Guthrie or I approved. But the bureaucracy was so thick even then that we were taking too long to get the word through. I told them that we were not going to eliminate jobs. We were going to eliminate levels of management in their entirety and we were going to increase responsibility on fewer people.

Casewriter: At the time you took over Braniff what did you feel were Braniff's strengths?

Putnam: Braniff had an excellent route structure. They had an excellent fleet of 727s/ 200s—the most modern in the airline industry. Average age was a little under 4 years old. They had an excellent facility here at DFW. They knew how to operate a hub-and-spoke operation.

Casewriter: Braniff was one of the first to get into this hub-and-spoke operation.

Putnam: Many airlines did it. Probably United did it in Chicago 20 years ago as the first one I really remember. Dallas was not a hub-and-spoke operation in years gone by because Texas had not grown at that point. But, what Braniff began to do years ago was to have frequency of service over a route vs. having one giant 747 going to Chicago twice a day. They would provide hourly service and they just kept building and building. It kept the costs down and kept the overhead low at that point in time. But after deregulation they got away from that strategy.

Casewriter: What, if any, resistance did you meet when you came in as President of Braniff?

Putnam: The idea of "We tried that before and it didn't work." We can't stop serving Montreal and Toronto. We just started serving Montreal and Toronto. But, you're losing $500,000 a month. Yes. But if we just had another three months, we think we could build it up. No, we're going to cut it off right now. Because we were fresh and new and we could see the broken doorsteps, the people who had been here and involved couldn't. Scheduling was very difficult. They had started down the track of having all one class airplanes for the short haul feeding into DFW but still having dual class, first class and coach, for people going to New York. Sounds logical except that productivity was going absolutely to hell. And every time an airplane got to Dallas, the customer had to get off and change and get on another plane. In hub and spoke, you want as many of your airplanes as possible to flow on through to the destination that is the most practical. So, we had to stop and revamp scheduling. A lot of resistance to that. I told them I wanted to see every airplane scheduled for (10) ten hours a day, and what cities we were were going to serve and what the frequency of service was. When you can show me that kind of schedule, then tell me how many airplanes are left over and where they're going. "We might need some aircraft for spares," they said. "We don't need any for spares," I said. "What if one breaks down?" "Then let her break down." We never had a spare airplane at Southwest. We flew them all up to 12 hours a day. That's how you make money. You don't have a spare Cadillac sitting in your garage in case yours breaks down.

Casewriter: Were you caught off guard with Mr. Casey leaving or was that expected?

Putnam: It was expected; when I came here I came as Chief Operating Officer. And shortly after getting here I saw that if you were going to do a turnaround you had to be the Chief Executive Officer to do it. You just couldn't share it with somebody else. You didn't have time. I later had both the presidency and the CEO title. John began to get bored. It was no longer fun to just be the chairman.

Casewriter: One of the things that you did that got a lot of publicity was the marketing strategy of the "two-for-one" tickets and the "Texas Class Fares." Do you think those were successful?

Putnam: Texas Class was absolutely the right strategy. I'll tell you about that. The two-for-one was not a good strategy. We knew it wasn't. We were starved for cash and we were trying to keep the doors open. Now, two-for-ones today are everywhere. You've got airlines doing two-for-ones all the time; so we set a new precedent in the airline industry. I don't care where you go, the two-for-one thing has become prevalent. In our case it was simply to generate cash. And the idea came from Tony Wainwright. He was the chairman of the Bloom Advertising Agency. He left the Southwest account and came with us here. I put him on the senior management committee even though he was an outsider. And when we got down into January and February (1982), we could see the dates when we would run out of cash, unless we did something dramatic. So we sat down one day and had a brainstorming session. How do we generate substantial new revenue? And Tony said, "You know, when I used to live in New York, there were Broadway shows on a light night or on a Saturday; we would have a 'two-for-one' sale. But you had to be hanging around the door in order to be able to get it. You couldn't buy it in advance. Otherwise everybody could do it." He said if we ran a surprise two-for-one sale, we'd bring in a bundle of cash. We did. We brought in over $20 million in a two-day period. It accomplished exactly what we wanted to do. But for the long term you can't do that and give away your profit.

Texas Class. Braniff couldn't continue having some airplanes in two classes and one class in the rest of the fleet. We had to get them all the same. We had to go one way or the other. We took a look first at the first class market and we saw that we were averaging four revenue passengers per flight in first class. Everybody said first class was always full. Sure it was. But it was all the crew members and employees riding up there for free. Phil Guthrie did a quick analysis himself and we learned that for every dollar of revenue in first class we were losing $1.50. We reflected on our experiences at South-

Exhibit 5   Braniff International Corporation's comparative income statement (000 omitted)

	Dec. 31, 1981	Dec. 31, 1980
Operating Revenues	$1,188,975	$1,452,130
Expenses:		
Flying Exp.	881,407	1,081,441
Maintenance	93,536	133,730
Nonairline Exp.	5,066	2,488
Sales and Advertising	172,785	198,906
Depreciation and Amort.	83,551	89,296
Gen. & Administrative Exp.	47,430	53,762
Operating Loss Equipment	94,800	107,493
Loss on Sale of EQ (gain)	(8,568)	(79,090)
Non-Operating Loss	7,871	15,079
Operating Income (Loss)	(94,103)	(43,482)
Interest Expenses	62,396	92,101
Income Taxes	—	(7,072)
Pfd. Dividends from Subsidiaries	4,112	2,925
Net Loss	$(160,611)	$(131,436)

west where we never had first class. Where we knew that people would enjoy frequency, dependability, some fun on the airplane, low fares and simple fares but with quality. That's what led us toward Texas Class. We had to find a niche for Braniff that was unique. Not just from the consumer's standpoint position, but from our secured lenders' standpoint. Remember, now, we had to come up with the financial restructuring by February 1, 1982, because that was when the debt deferral period ended. So, we had to put together a package for the lenders that would convince them that they ought to continue to defer debt because these folks had put something in place that was going to turn Braniff around. On November 4, 1981, we had a press conference downstairs. Texas Class was effective November 24, three weeks later. We simplified the fare structure from 568 different fares down to 15. We lowered the fares not by the 50% the media kept thinking we did, but when you compute your average yield, full fares and discount fares and so forth, and compared that to Texas Class, we took yield down around 12–15%. The public responded in the month of December 1981. We had a 60.7% load factor, the highest of any major airline in the airline industry.

Casewriter: When you got to the point that some financial restructuring was necessary, why did you choose Chapter 11 over some other option?

Putnam: We finally got the debt deferral for February 1, 1982, on January 22, only eight days before the deadline. What we got was a debt restructuring timetable. That then gave us until October 1, '82, for the final restructuring plan. When you have a billion

Exhibit 6   Braniff data

	Net Profit (Loss) in Millions	Long-Term Debt (Millions)	Available Seat Miles (Billion)	Passenger Load Level (%)	Break-Even Point (% of Load)
1977	$ 37	$221	15	50	47
1978	45	398	17	54	50
1979	(44)	668	24	56	60
1980	(131)	651	20	58	64
1981	(161)	591	16	56	63

dollars of indebtedness with 39 lenders and they all have to have 100% agreement on every item, it is almost an impossible task. The second step in that was that by March 31, we had to present to them a financial restructuring plan and then for the months of April, May, and June they would look at it. So, we presented it to them on March 31. It didn't generate an immediate response because now at that point we've already had the two-for-one sale. We've already had to defer employees' paychecks, half of it for a week period, so the concern was more with near-term survival.

Now, another alternative is to try to merge with somebody. Get somebody else to take you over. And we tried that. We tried every other airline we could think of and they didn't want to touch us because of the severity of the financial problems. So, you're really left with only two choices. Just let the status quo continue until creditors file for a Chapter 7 liquidation, or take the initiative and file under Chapter 11 so that you can preserve the assets and hopefully try to reorganize. That was why we chose Chapter 11. We made the decision that we would go into 11 voluntarily. That we would do it without telling anybody. We'd get all those airplanes home from South America and domestic flights to preserve the assets. Surprise was essential for a reorganization to occur under the protection of the federal bankruptcy statutes.

CASE 10

Kinder-Care Learning Centers, Inc.

DENNIS ALAN GUTHERY
American Graduate School of International Management, Glendale, Arizona

On July 14, 1983, Rob Hartley was returning to his office contemplating how he could "keep the momentum going." Rob, marketing director for Kinder-Care, had just participated in Kinder-Care's ground breaking ceremonies for its new 70,000 square foot corporate headquarters. On July 14, 1969, Kinder-Care Learning Centers, Inc., opened its first child care facility in Montgomery, Alabama. In fourteen short years it had become the industry leader in the dynamic field of child care services. The company now operated 800 pre-school and after school learning centers in 40 states and Canada, with 8,700 employees serving almost 70,000 children. Kinder-Care's rapid growth and ability to provide just the right services to its target markets had not gone unnoticed. The company had been featured in several national business magazine articles and had caught the eye of the investment community. Earlier in 1983 *Money* magazine had picked Kinder-Care as one of the best growth companies for the 1980s. With all this attention Rob felt even more responsible for developing the products and services necessary for Kinder-Care to reach its full potential.

THE BACKGROUND OF KINDER-CARE

Kinder-Care was conceived in 1968–69 by Perry Mendel, a Montgomery businessman. Mendel's idea was to start a child care franchising organization and use the same benefits of standardization that had made McDonalds and Holiday Inns giants in their industries. Mendel saw a trend of more and more women working outside the home and realized that this meant two things: a need for quality child-care and the ability to pay for that care through a second family income. While Mendel perceived the need he really wasn't convinced that his idea would work until he read a front page article in the *National Observer* on the economics of a proposed national day-care chain. "That was the clincher," Mendel recalls. "It was a good article. They gave out the pro forma numbers on what a day-care center could do and the numbers looked beautiful!"

Mendel sold the idea to eight friends who helped him raise $200,000 to start Kinder-Care Learning Centers, Inc. While he knew nothing about education or franchising, Perry Mendel did know about real estate financing and that has been one of the keys to Kinder-Care's success.

Mendel was the son of a Columbus, Georgia, restaurant owner. After WWII he went into the auto parts business in Birmingham with three brothers-in-law (the Aronovs). The firm grew and added a fabrication operation. The real success came when one of the Aronovs went into real estate development. The home building and mall

Source: Used by permission of Dennis Alan Guthery, Ph.D. and the Case Research Association. Distributed by the Case Research Association. All rights reserved to the author(s) and the Case Research Association. Permission to use the case should be obtained from the Case Research Association.

This case was written based on in-depth interviews with Kinder-Care executives and copyrighted Kinder-Care material. The case also includes some copyrighted material which was used in the company background section of the case. The author greatly appreciates permission granted from the following sources for reprinting excerpts of copyrighted material: Alexander Brown & Sons, *American Demographics, Forbes, Inc.*, Kinder-Care Learning Centers, Inc.

Original sources include: *Kinder-Care Learning Center, Inc.*, Alexander Brown & Sons Research, November 1982; "Demographic Forecasts," *American Demographics*, April 1982: 46–47; Geoffrey Smith, "Perry Mendel's Golden Diapers," *Forbes*, June 25, 1979: 67–69; *Kinder-Care's Standard Formula for Success*, John Halbrooks, Inc., October 1981: 84–86; SEC 10-K Report, Kinder-Care Learning Centers, Inc., November 1982.

development was attractive to Mendel and he began working in real estate full-time. Then the idea of Kinder-Care came along.

Mendel and his investors decided to hire a professional franchise selling organization to help them get started. After details of the franchising operation were worked out the group ran an ad in the *Wall Street Journal* with the headline "Join the Good Ship Lollipop." In spite of tremendous response to the ad, the decision was made to stop franchising after only seven months. Mendel calls the decision "the greatest decision we ever made!" He explains, "The people who thought they would love to be in the day-care business—an ex-teacher or an ex-minister who loves to take care of children—knew nothing about getting a building into existence, or finance. If we were going to have to arrange for all the financing, which is no mean trick, and get just 5% of gross revenues for all this effort, it didn't make sense."

Dick Grassgreen, a tax attorney, joined Kinder-Care in 1969 as chief operating officer and executive vice-president. He recalls the difficulty in obtaining financing. "We were developing a new industry. This wasn't shoes or steel. There was nothing to look at." The company did obtain a $3.75 million mortgage commitment from Eagle Savings Association, a Cincinnati bank. The loan was contingent on Kinder-Care's ability to show one dollar in net worth for every three dollars it drew in loans. This meant coming up with $1.25 million.

To raise the $1.25 million Mendel and Grassgreen decided to take Kinder-Care public. In late 1969 they decided to sell 40% equity for $2.8 million. During the registration period before the offering the company drew $800,000 in construction financing from Eagle Savings to develop new learning centers. Unfortunately, the 135-year-old underwriting firm chosen for the offering found itself in liquidity problems and merged with Bache. Bache refused to go along with the public offering because Kinder-Care was too small and still in the concept stage. A new underwriter was found but at this point the Securities and Exchange Commission issued a ruling that would severely hurt the company. It ruled that Kinder-Care would have to make a best efforts offering (an offering where the underwriter does not agree to place the entire amount) because of the commitment of some of the directors to purchase stock in the offering.

With no guarantee in the offering, $800,000 in construction loans, and $200,000 spent in preparing for the stock offering, the Kinder-Care group had to find a buyer for their company. Reluctantly, Kinder-Care was sold for $1.5 million in stock to Warner National Corporation, a Cincinnati real estate developer that had once owned Eagle Savings Association where Kinder-Care had its loan. Warner National provided Kinder-Care with $300,000 in capital and promised assistance for future growth. After a few months, Mendel and Grassgreen felt that Warner was neglecting Kinder-Care and putting its money into other ventures. Convinced that Kinder-Care would never grow unless it received more capital, they persuaded Warner National to let them take Kinder-Care public. After going public they renegotiated the merger contract and in May of 1973 the original Kinder-Care investors exchanged the Warner stock for Kinder-Care stock.

Kinder-Care broke away from Warner National in 1976. Mendel's group borrowed $2.25 million from banks and raised $2.25 million from 19 individuals to gain complete control. They were then stuck with the problem of how to pay off the bank loan. Taft Broadcasting, a Cincinnati based company, successfully negotiated with the Kinder-Care owners for a 20% minority position in exchange for paying the bank note.

In the late 1970s and early 1980s Kinder-Care had no problem in raising cash through bond and stock offerings. In 1982 the company sold $32 million in bonds and had a $25 million revolving credit line.

THE KINDER-CARE PHILOSOPHY

Perry Mendel's conception of what child care should be was radically different from what was being offered to the market in 1969. Day care was generally considered baby sitting. Small children were left with relatives or regular baby sitters. The older children who attended kindergartens were in class only 3 or 4 hours each day. After kindergarten they were picked up to pass the rest of the day with either a relative or a baby sitter.

Mendel's idea was to develop a day-long educational environment for children. The facility would have to be open in the mornings so that parents could drop the children off on their way to work. The facility would have to have a kitchen and serve nutritious meals. The day care program would have to be professionally developed to structure learning experiences for children of differing ages. The program would have to help the child develop physically, socially, and aesthetically. Different activities had to be planned throughout the day so that the child would not be bored before his parents picked him up after work. Finally, pick-up and delivery services would have to be provided for students with transportation problems. Kinder-Care's basic philosophy can be summarized by Exhibits 1 and 2.

THE KINDER-CARE FACILITY

A typical Kinder-Care center is a one-story, air conditioned building located on approximately one-half acre of land and constructed in accordance with a model design developed by Kinder-Care. The centers contain open classrooms and play areas and complete kitchen and bathroom facilities and can accommodate approximately 70 to 120 children. Each center is equipped with a variety of audio and visual aids, educational supplies, games, puzzles, toys, and indoor and outdoor play equipment. Each also has an open recreation area and, in most instances, an in-ground wading pool. In addition, centers have vehicles used for field trips and transporting children enrolled in Kinder-Care's after school program to and from their elementary schools. Kinder-Care carries general liability and property insurance as well as an accident insurance policy covering each child enrolled in its centers.

Exhibit 1 The fifteen goals of Kinder-Care's educational program

Through Kinder-Care's theme-related GOAL program each child will be provided the opportunities to:

1. Develop a healthy, positive self-image.
2. Develop communicative skills.
3. Develop self expression through creative media, dramatics, music, storytelling, block building and other forms of play.
4. Develop self-control, self-direction, and independence.
5. Develop social skills through group interaction.
6. Develop intellectually through a balance of teacher-directed and free choice activities.
7. Develop and strengthen auditory skills, visual acuity, and rhythm awareness.
8. Increase attention span and follow simple directions.
9. Practice thoughtful and courteous behavior.
10. Develop gross motor skills and manual dexterity.
11. Develop an awareness of physical fitness and good health habits.
12. Develop moral and aesthetic values.
13. Develop a respect for individual and cultural differences.
14. Experience a high degree of success through developmental activities.
15. Assume responsibility in given tasks.

Exhibit 2 GOAL: Educational program offered by Kinder-Care Learning Centers, Inc.

Kinder-Care's exclusive GOAL Program provides unlimited opportunities for the development of the TOTAL child. Our Program is oriented toward the gradual development of the child's social, emotional, physical, and intellectual needs. The Growth Opportunities for Achievement and Learning program combines three essential elements into one comprehensive program:

☐ a safe, healthy, developmentally sound environment

☐ well-trained caring adults

☐ a solid growth curriculum

Our child-oriented environment consists of classrooms which have been carefully designed and furnished to enhance the creative and developmental needs of young children. Each classroom is bright, happy, stimulating, and enriched by our Discovery Areas. The use of Discovery Areas within each classroom creates an environment that fosters socialization, satisfies curiosity, and allows many successful experiences. Each Discovery Area is enriched daily with materials and activities suitable to the child's interests and developmental levels of learning.

Each day provides a balance of quiet and active growth activities, participation in individual and group learning experiences, as well as time for eating, napping, outdoor play, occasional field trips, resource "guests," and "special" child-oriented events. Kinder-Care's coordinated concept of "the theme of the week" will provide the child with information and knowledge about the world in which he lives — animals, weather, seasons, transportation, health, safety, numbers, letters, manners, colors, shapes, sizes, just to name a few. Each classroom teacher is provided with weekly GOAL materials to use in preparation for classroom activities.

In addition, the pre-Kindergarten child will have the opportunity to participate in our pre-reading readiness program entitled *Happily Ever After*. This program offers pre-reading readiness activities through the magic, mystery, and excitement of classic selections of children's literature — *Little Red Riding Hood, The Three Bears, La Tortuga, The Elves and the Shoemaker, Jingles, Poems, and Rhymes, The Nightingale, The City Mouse and the Country Mouse, The Tug of War, Peter and the Wolf,* and *The ABC Book*.

The Kindergarten-aged child will participate in the highly respected *Beginning to Read, Write,* and *Listen* Program — a comprehensive, multi-sensory language arts and reading skills program designed for reading readiness. The program correlates reading, spelling, handwriting, auditory skills, language activities, and art projects in a solid reading/language arts program. This age child will also experience our activity-centered mathematics program — *Mathematics Their Way*. Through this program, the child will develop an understanding and insight into the patterns of mathematics through the use of concrete materials. The child will see relationships and interconnections in mathematics and will be able to deal flexibly with mathematical ideas and concepts. In addition, the Kindergarten-aged child will receive his/her own weekly copy of the well-regarded *Weekly Reader*. In our ongoing efforts to assure that the Kindergarten-aged child is prepared for entrance into the primary grades, Kinder-Care tests each Kindergarten child with the Metropolitan Readiness Test. This test is issued in the Spring of each year and serves as an additional tool with which to evaluate the child's progress.

Quarterly, during the academic year, all preschool children are issued Developmental Records. These Records serve to provide the parent and teaching staff with information relative to each child's interests, developmental levels, and achievements.

In addition to all of the above, our staff and parents alike are provided with additional materials to insure that communication between the Center, child and parent are maintained at the highest level. For example:

☐ What We Did Today Notes

☐ Kinder Calendar (published quarterly)

☐ Certificates of Completion (printed for both children and staff)

☐ 15 Goals of Kinder-Care's Educational Program

Kinder-Care's newest program, designed for school aged children, is entitled KLUBMATES — the after-school fun achievement club. The philosophy of the program stresses group and individual activities in which children will learn more about themselves and the world in which they live. Through the completion of activities in various areas of achievement, school aged children will have opportunities for discovery and the privilege of earning achievement badges.

Kinder-Care is very aware that the parent is the child's first and most important teacher. We wish to be the best support service to make learning not only beneficial, but fun!

In most centers children are given a hot breakfast, and in all centers children are given a mid-morning snack, a balanced hot lunch and a mid-afternoon snack, all prepared and served in the center in accordance with menus developed by Kinder-Care (Exhibit 3). Cots and blankets are provided for the children to take naps during rest periods.

Kinder-Care centers are open throughout the year, generally five days a week from 7:00 A.M. to 6:00 P.M. In a few areas, centers are open in the evening and on weekends. Children are usually enrolled on a weekly basis for either full-day or half-day sessions and are accepted, where capacity permits, on an hourly drop-in basis. Kinder-Care's current weekly charge for full-day service ranges from $32 to $65 per child, depending on the location of the center. Charges are payable weekly in advance.

Exhibit 3   "Our food service program—another Kinder-Care advantage!"

In addition to Kinder-Care's numerous programs and services available to our children and parents we are also responsible for providing meals and snacks daily. Every Kinder-Care Learning Center prepares and serves either a full or continental breakfast and a noon meal and two snacks every day.

Nutrition, being an important part of the overall Kinder-Care service, is vital to the development of the total child. Our daily menus are planned according to the nutritional requirements of young children as designated by each state. These menus are reviewed by Dr. Charles Radanovics, Director of Research and Development and Mr. Anthony Bartolotta, Director of Food Services, John Sexton and Company. Kinder-Care menus are served on a rotating 4 to 8 week basis and provide a significant percentage of the child's daily nutritional requirements. Some examples of Kinder-Care approved menus are as follows:

Typical Breakfast Menu	*Typical Lunch Menu*	*Typical Snack Menu*
Oatmeal	Meat Loaf	Saltines w/Cheese
Cheese Toast	Mashed Potatoes	Juice/Milk
Applesauce	Green Peas	
Milk	Bread w/margarine	
	Milk	
	Peach Slices	

Our food service personnel are trained in food preparation techniques, methods of presentation and service, food storage and other related areas. Also Kinder-Care provides its food service personnel with policies and procedures related to kitchen cleanliness, proper dishwashing techniques and other health and sanitation requirements. Every Kinder-Care kitchen is fully equipped with appliances, cooking utensils, and child-sized tableware to accommodate even the youngest appetite.

As you can see our daily food service program is just another part of the Kinder-Care Advantage — attractive and well-balanced meals, fully equipped kitchens and trained food service personnel. Our mealtimes and snack times provide opportunities for children to establish good eating habits and to enjoy nourishing meals in an environment that promotes socialization while eating together.

**LEARNING CENTER PERSONNEL, SALES, AND
OPERATIONS**

Personnel

Due to the relatively large number of centers and their geographic diversity, Kinder-Care has several levels of management. Ten to twelve Center Directors report to each District Manager. Regional Managers have about five District Managers under their supervision. There are also four Zone Managers, each supervising three to four Regional Managers. The Zone Managers report directly to the Vice-President of Operations located at corporate headquarters in Montgomery, Alabama. Management compensation is competitive with other service industries. With the company's projected growth, opportunities for career advancement are abundant.

Each center has a Director, Assistant Director, cook, and two to ten teachers depending on the center's size and local regulations. Teachers receive modest training and orientation when they are hired and thereafter receive printed materials directly from the educational specialists at headquarters detailing the curriculum to be followed during the upcoming week. Each zone has a Personnel and Training Manager who holds special seminars for teachers on new programs and acts as a liaison between the teachers and the program coordinator at headquarters. At present, 52% of the company's 9,000 employees, including teachers, are paid at or slightly above minimum wage.

About the low wage Kinder-Care pays, Grassgreen asserts, "Child care is pleasant work. The people who work in the centers like to be with children. They receive a strong sense of self-esteem from their work." Adds VP of Operations Eugene Montgomery who came to Kinder-Care from Burger Chef in 1980: "There's no comparison between the caliber of workers in fast foods and the people who work for Kinder-Care. In fast food, people are in it just for the money. In child care, there are other rewards."

Even so, the company suffers high turnover among employees. Pregnancy and spouse transfer are the major causes for resignations. Kinder-Care has rewarded high performers with advancement within the organization.

Sales

Kinder-Care relies heavily on word-of-mouth recommendation for new enrollment. In addition, it markets its services through local radio, television and newspaper advertising, direct mail, and Yellow Pages listings. Kinder-Care directs its advertising primarily toward the working mother, whose ability to work outside the home may depend on the availability of day care for her children. A large portion of Kinder-Care's advertising budget is spent in August, prior to Kinder-Care's fall enrollment period, with continued advertising throughout the year. In fiscal years 1981 and 1982, Kinder-Care spent approximately $1,245,000 and $1,356,000 on advertising, respectively.

Operating Controls and Procedures

Each week, center directors submit financial reports to Kinder-Care's home office and to the appropriate area and regional supervisors. These reports include, among other things, a breakdown of enrollment and tuition by age groups, a statement of prepaid tuitions, data on current enrollment and attendance, analysis of the staff-to-child ratios and salary and food costs, and a listing of all cash receipts. Kinder-Care's home office reviews each report and prepares combined records by zone, region, and for the company as a whole.

All funds received by each center are deposited in an account established by Kinder-Care in a local bank. All payroll and most other center expenses are paid directly by Kinder-Care's home office. Basic supplies are purchased for the centers through the home office. Direct expenditures by the centers are limited to miscellaneous operating expenses which are reimbursed by the home office by means of an imprest petty cash system.

KINDER-CARE'S GROWTH

Kinder-Care's growth in net earnings, operating revenues, and numbers of centers is summarized in Exhibit 4.

A significant portion of Kinder-Care's growth has been through acquisition. Of 747 centers operating on November 1, 1982, 238 had been acquired, including 112 in 1981, and 92 in 1980. On August 31, 1979, Kinder-Care acquired Mini-Skools Limited for 382,688 shares of common stock and $13,000,000 in cash and notes. Mini-Skools Limited operated 74 day care centers in the United States and 14 in Canada.

On August 1, 1980, Kinder-Care purchased Primary Learning Systems for a total consideration of $2,769,000 in cash and notes. Primary Learning Systems operated 31 day care centers in the states of Arizona and California and had two additional centers under construction in California.

On August 31, 1980, Kinder-Care acquired Living and Learning Centres, Inc. for $3,630,000 in cash and notes. Living and Learning Centres operated 48 centers and had two under construction.

From 1978 through 1982, new centers, including acquisitions, grew at an annual rate of 33%. Since no acquisitions are currently planned, new centers are expected to increase by approximately 15% per year for the next several years.

KINDER-CARE SERVICES

Klubmates

Klubmates is an after school and summer program for school age kids ages 6–12. Klubmates was a natural expansion from the preschool market. Children are picked up at their school and delivered to Kinder-Care Centers. As its name implies Klubmates tries to foster a club image along the same lines as Cub Scouts and Brownies. Klubmates

Exhibit 4 Kinder-Care Learning Centers, Inc.'s net earnings, operating revenues, and numbers of centers

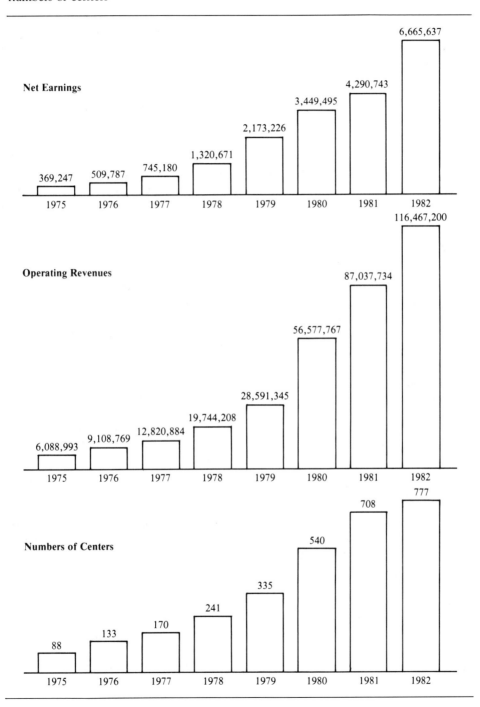

receive a membership card, an achievement book, 10 Klubmate badges (to be earned), and Klubmates T-shirt or totebag. The program has a $10 entry fee and after-school tuition runs about $20 each week. The program was initiated in 1982 and over 14,000 children were enrolled, far exceeding the company's expectations. The program operates year round.

Kinder Camp

Kinder Camp is the company's name for the summer program for pre-schoolers. It is activity oriented rather than strictly educationally oriented. Each week has a theme. Themes for the 1983 summer included: Little Theater, Camp-In, Mexican-Fiesta, Kinder-Care Circus, and Mystery Island, among others.

Kindustry

Kindustry is a cooperative effort of Kinder-Care and individual firms which offers employees a 20% deduction in Kinder-Care tuition for their children. It is a payroll deduction plan with the employer contributing 10% and Kinder-Care reducing tuition 10% for a total 20% deduction. The program was begun in April of 1981 and as of July 1983, 65 firms had signed Kindustry contracts. Due to the recessionary conditions the program has not been aggressively pursued by Kinder-Care. Two headquarters staff persons have been assigned to full-time Kindustry duties. A majority of the contracts signed have been with hospitals and insurance companies, both of which have female-dominated labor forces. In most cases the employees utilize any of the existing facilities. The hours are flexible with some hospital-oriented centers staying open all night if a minimum of 21 children are over-nighters. Three centers are in operation on the employer's premises: Connecticut General Life Insurance Company (Hartford, CT), Campbell Soup Company (Camden, NJ), and Disney World (Orlando, FL).

Kinder-Life

In June 1978 Kinder-Care Life Insurance Company was formed by Mendel and Grassgreen as part of their total package of services. C. Roger Slater was named president of the wholly owned subsidiary. Before joining Kinder-Life, Slater was the vice-president of an insurance company and had worked in insurance for 35 years. The insurance is sold in the Learning Center itself where customers come to the salesmen. The policy is available only to children enrolled in a Learning Center. The policy offered is a $5,000 modified whole life insurance policy. The policy carries lower premiums in the earlier years than level policies of the same face value. The company pays the first year's premium for all children enrolled. After the first year the parents must decide if they wish to continue the policy and pay the $10.50 semi-annual payment. At age 21 the premium increases to $30.50. A renewal rate of over 30% was achieved in each of the last three years. In 1983, Kinder-Life had approximately $23 million of life insurance in force. Income from Kinder-Life in 1983 is expected to be approximately $650,000. Many states have laws requiring out-of-state insurance companies to have 4–5 years of existence before they can be granted a license to sell insurance. Because Kinder-Life has now met this time requirement it has application to do business pending in over 20 states.

Kinderoo

Kinderoo is the trademark of Kinder-Care Learning Centers, Inc. The Kinderoo is a giant kangaroo. Kinder-Care employs four employees who wear the Kinderoo mascot apparel. These employees are in different geographic parts of the United States. They make frequent appearances in malls, hospitals, parades, and at Learning Centers. Their job is to be goodwill ambassadors for Kinder-Care.

Micro-Kids

Kinder-Care is running pilot computer programs in Montgomery, Houston, and Minneapolis. Pending success of the pilot program, computers may be introduced in Learning Centers nationwide.

THE CHILD CARE MARKET

Kinder-Care's primary target market has been middle-class households with children under 12 and with both adults bringing home paychecks. Most of the adults in this category are between the ages of 25–44. Tables 1 and 2 project the population of this age group through 1990. These projections, from *American Demographics,* indicate that families headed by people aged 25–34 will increase only 10%. However, the number of families headed by persons between the ages of 35–44 should increase 46%.

Alexander Brown & Sons Research estimates that chains control only 8% to 10% of the licensed day care industry. The 20,000 licensed day care centers are thought, in turn, to represent a small fraction of the total day care industry. Of the licensed centers, only 40% are profitable.

Within the industry Kinder-Care is the leader with 800 centers in operation. The next largest chain is La Petite Academy with approximately 375 centers. Three other chains are estimated to have approximately 125–130 centers each: Children's World, Mary Moppets Day Care School, and National Child Care. In addition to changing demographics and competition, two additional factors are important considerations in assessing the outlook for Kinder-Care. First, recent changes in federal income tax statutes have increased the tax incentive for child care, making such care more economical from the working parent's standpoint. The tax credit now ranges from 20% to 30% of certain child care expenses up to a maximum of $720 for the first child. For two or

Table 1 Families headed by persons 25–34, and unrelated individuals 25–34, by income (in thousands)

	1980	*1985*	*1990*
Families	14,200.2	15,366.6	15,616.7
Income (1982 dollars):			
less than $5,000	979.4	937.6	903.3
$5,000–9,999	1,035.0	947.7	837.0
$10,000–14,999	1,516.9	1,379.1	1,224.8
$15,000–24,999	3,906.0	3,710.0	3,395.6
$25,000–34,999	3,507.4	3,748.0	3,674.9
$35,000–49,999	2,442.0	3,340.8	3,769.1
$50,000–74,999	652.2	1,047.4	1,466.4
$75,000+	161.3	256.0	345.6
Unrelated individuals	5,913.1	8,008.4	9,457.4
Income (1982 dollars):			
less than $5,000	608.5	737.0	761.6
$5,000–9,999	994.7	1,127.8	1,161.7
$10,000–14,999	1,279.2	1,524.2	1,625.1
$15,000–24,999	2,022.2	2,763.8	3,210.7
$25,000–34,999	728.0	1,300.9	1,802.8
$35,000–49,999	207.9	415.3	670.9
$50,000–74,999	69.4	110.4	178.0
$75,000+	3.2	29.0	46.6

Source: American Demographics, April 1982, p. 47.

more children the maximum allowable credit has been increased from $800 to $1,440. The impact of this change can be more fully appreciated when it is considered that child care expenses average 10% of gross income for the working family. According to a Carnegie Corporation study, child care now is the fourth largest expenditure after housing, food, and taxes.

The second factor influencing the outlook for the industry is the trend toward including child care as a corporate benefit. In a 1982 Harris poll, 67% of corporate human resource executives expected child care to become a company benefit within the next five years. U.S. Secretary of Health and Human Services, Margaret M. Heckler, has stated that corporate child care programs will be the major fringe benefit of the 1980s and 1990s. Of the existing firms with such benefits, the corporation's share of the cost varies greatly. The higher the percentage picked up by the corporation, the greater the expectation that the benefit will be utilized. Campbell Soup picks up half of the day care expenses of its employees. The advantages of day care can have a tangible effect on performance. Intermedics, Inc., a Texas medical technology firm, is the largest day care center in the United States. Approximately 300 children are en-

Table 2 Families headed by persons 35–44, and unrelated individuals 35–44, by income (in thousands)

	1980	*1985*	*1990*
Families	12,367.2	15,305.6	18,026.4
Income (1982 dollars):			
less than $5,000	527.3	653.8	668.1
$5,000–9,999	716.7	749.3	756.5
$10,000–14,999	1,079.7	1,101.5	1,121.8
$15,000–24,999	2,816.4	2,954.4	3,096.9
$25,000–34,999	2,735.8	3,133.9	3,465.5
$35,000–49,999	2,684.5	3,544.1	4,257.3
$50,000–74,999	1,410.2	2,409.1	3,413.1
$75,000+	396.6	759.5	1,247.2
Unrelated Individuals	2,360.7	3,205.6	3,969.9
Income (1982 dollars):			
less than $5,000	301.1	378.6	406.9
$5,000–9,999	365.1	440.6	467.1
$10,000–14,999	414.8	508.1	567.8
$15,000–24,999	674.6	878.9	1,074.0
$25,000–34,999	358.7	528.3	720.3
$35,000–49,999	152.6	308.6	468.6
$50,000–74,999	62.2	114.0	178.1
$75,000+	31.6	48.5	87.1

Source: American Demographics, April 1982, p. 47.

rolled in the day care program, which costs parents $15 per week for each child. During the first year of operation the firm recorded a 23% decrease in employee turnover and 15,000 fewer work hours lost to absenteeism.

FINANCIAL INFORMATION

Kinder-Care Learning Centers are typically financed by local investors. The investors agree to build a Kinder-Care Center according to Kinder-Care construction department specifications. These specifications comply with all local and state codes and ordinances. Kinder-Care agrees to lease the building for 20 years with two 5-year options. Interest rates vary but many of the Learning Centers were built with 11% money. Typically, the investor would put up $50,000 and take out a mortgage for $150,000 at 11%. The investor would receive $24,000 annually in lease income. After approximately $16,500 in interest income he would net $7,500 or the equivalent of 15% pretax if a reduction of principal on the mortgage is included. That $7,500 is partially sheltered from tax by the closing costs and depreciation charges.

Kinder-Care is often able to go into a building with just the investment in equipment—usually $10,000 to $20,000. Mendel believes that one of the secrets of Kinder-Care's success has been the development of a sophisticated real estate department that can work with developers throughout the U.S.

Selected financial data are in Exhibits 5 and 6.

ROB HARTLEY

The dedication ceremony had provided Rob Hartley with another review of the company's trials and successes. Before finishing the reports on his desk Rob could not help but think about Kinder-Care's future and the role he would play in that future.

Hartley was dedicated to Perry Mendel's idea of providing a total package of services to Kinder-Care's target market. Rob knew that he had been brought into the organization to "make things happen." He had begun his corporate career with Sears but had left to go into franchising where he had become a millionaire before age 30. He had been instrumental in launching the highly successful Klubmates program. But with that program off the ground, he wondered if Mendel's ideas of catalog marketing might not be the area to investigate. Rob knew of many clubs, schools, and youth programs with a line of T-shirts, caps, jackets, and similar items available for their members through catalogs. Such items were not only a source of revenue but also of publicity.

Exhibit 5   Kinder-Care Learning Centers, Inc. summary of projections of earnings per share

	1981A[1]	1982A[1]	1983E[1]
Revenues (000)	$87,038	$116,467	$135,000
Pretax income (000)	$ 5,415	$ 8,297	$ 11,500
% of Revenues	6.2%	7.1%	8.5%
Income taxes (000)	$ 1,415	$ 2,160	$ 3,500
Tax rate	26.1%	26.0%	30.0%
Net income (Consol.) (000)	$ 4,000	$ 6,137	$ 8,000
Earnings from Unconsol.			
Subsidiary Kinder Life (000)	$ 291	$ 518	$ 650
Net income (000)	$ 4,291	$ 6,655	$ 8,650
Average shares outstanding (000)	9,630	10,130	10,250
Earnings per share	$.45	$.66	$.85
Number of Centers	708	757	857

[1] 1980–81 fiscal year ends approximately May 31. 1982 fiscal year ends approximately August 31.

Source: Annual reports and Alex. Brown & Sons estimates.

Exhibit 6   Selected financial data (dollar amounts in thousands, except per-share data)

	Fiscal Year Ended Sept. 3, 1982	Thirteen Weeks Ended August 28, 1981	Fiscal Year Ended			
			May 29, 1981	May 30, 1980	June 1, 1979	June 2, 1978
Operations						
Operating revenues	$116,467	$ 23,327	$ 87,038	$56,578	$28,591	$19,744
Operating income	14,180	(1,129)	10,663	8,586	3,990	2,779
Net earnings (loss)	6,655	(2,738)**	4,291	3,449	2,173	1,321
Working capital provided (used) by operations	12,127	(1,729)	9,274	7,199	4,092	2,697
Centers open at end of period	745	720	708	540	335	241
Licensed capacity at end of period	81,000	78,000	77,000	59,000	32,000	23,000
Financial data (at end of period)						
Working capital	$ 6,030	$ 3,966	$ 8,727	$ 3,271	$ 7,101	$ 1,309
Long-term debt	100,906	67,460	68,158	59,157	19,603	10,175
Stockholders' equity	37,830	31,977	34,665	18,812	7,307	5,413
Total assets	153,079	110,523	115,345	87,375	32,092	19,143
Per-share data*						
Net earnings (loss)	$ .66	$ (.27)**	$ .45	$ .44	$ .30	$ .19
Dividends	.08	.02	.072	.051	.038	.019
Book value	3.73	3.16	3.43	2.14	.99	.74
Financial statistics						
Current ratio	1.6	1.5	2.2	1.6	4.1	1.8
Long-term debt to equity ratio	2.7	2.1	2.0	3.1	2.7	1.9

* Adjusted for stock splits in 1977, 1978, 1980, and 1982.
** Including cumulative effect of accounting changes.
Source: Kinder-Care Learning Centers, Inc., Form 10-K, Nov. 24, 1982.

Another alternative might be to license the Kinderoo symbol for retail merchandise. The licensing of Snoopy and Garfield had been very successful. As with the catalog, not only royalties but also publicity would be generated.

A third area to explore was taking Kinder-Care overseas. Due to Rob's limited exposure to international business, he felt he would have to obtain the advice of an international consultant or marketing research firm to better evaluate this option. Rob looked at the reports on his desk and decided he would begin researching his options the first thing the next morning.

CASE 11

The Lincoln Electric Company, 1983

ARTHUR D. SHARPLIN
Northeast Louisiana University

INTRODUCTION

The Lincoln Electric Company is the world's largest manufacturer of welding machines and electrodes. Lincoln employs 2400 workers in two U.S. factories near Cleveland and approximately 600 in three factories located in other countries. This does not include the field sales force of more than 200 persons. It has been estimated that Lincoln's market share (for arc-welding equipment and supplies) is more than 40%.

The Lincoln incentive management plan has been well known for many years. Many college management texts make reference to the Lincoln plan as a model for achieving high worker productivity. Certainly, Lincoln has been a successful company according to the usual measures of success.

James F. Lincoln died in 1965 and there was some concern, even among employees, that the Lincoln system would fall into disarray, that profits would decline, and that year-end bonuses might be discontinued. Quite the contrary, eighteen years after Lincoln's death, the company appears stronger than ever. Each year, except the recession year 1982, has seen higher profits and bonuses. Employee morale and productivity remain high. Employee turnover is almost nonexistent except for retirements. Lincoln's market share is stable. Consistently high dividends continue on Lincoln's stock.

A HISTORICAL SKETCH

In 1895, after being "frozen out" of the depression-ravaged Elliott-Lincoln Company, a maker of Lincoln-designed electric motors, John C. Lincoln took out his second patent and began to manufacture his improved motor. He opened his new business, unincorporated, with $200 he had earned redesigning a motor for young Herbert Henry Dow, who later founded the Dow Chemical Company.

Started during an economic depression and cursed by a major fire after only one year in business, Lincoln's company grew, but hardly prospered, through its first quarter century. In 1906, John C. Lincoln incorporated his company and moved from his one-room, fourth-floor factory to a new three-story building he erected in east Cleveland. In his new factory, he expanded his work force to 30 and sales grew to over $50,000 a year. John Lincoln preferred being an engineer and inventor rather than a manager, though, and it was to be left to another Lincoln to manage the company through its years of success.

In 1907, after a bout with typhoid fever forced him from Ohio State University in his senior year, James F. Lincoln, John's younger brother, joined the fledgling company. In 1914 he became the active head of the firm, with the titles of General Manager and Vice President. John Lincoln, while he remained President of the company for some years, became more involved in other business ventures and in his work as an inventor.

One of James Lincoln's early actions as head of the firm was to ask the employees to elect representatives to a committee which would advise him on company operations. The Advisory Board has met with the chief executive officer twice monthly since that time. This was only the first of a series of innovative personnel policies which have, over the years, distinguished Lincoln Electric from its contemporaries.

The first year the Advisory Board was in existence, working hours were reduced from 55 per week, then standard, to 50 hours a week. In 1915, the company gave each employee a paid-up life insurance policy. A welding school, which continues today, was begun in 1917. In 1918, an employee bonus plan was attempted. It was not continued, but the idea was to resurface and become the backbone of the Lincoln Management System.

The Lincoln Electric Employees' Association was formed in 1919 to provide health benefits and social activities. This organization continues today and has assumed several additional functions over the years. In 1923, a piecework pay system was in effect, employees got two-week paid vacations each year, and wages were adjusted for changes in the Consumer Price Index. Approximately thirty percent of Lincoln's stock was set aside for key employees in 1914 when James F. Lincoln became General Manager and a stock purchase plan for all employees was begun in 1925.

The Board of Directors voted to start a suggestion system in 1929. The program is still in effect, but cash awards, a part of the early program, were discontinued several years ago. Now, suggestions are rewarded by additional "points," which affect year-end bonuses.

The legendary Lincoln bonus plan was proposed by the Advisory Board and accepted on a trial basis by James Lincoln in 1934. The first annual bonus amounted to about 25% of wages. There has been a bonus every year since then. The bonus plan has been a cornerstone of the Lincoln Management System and recent bonuses have approximated annual wages.

By 1944, Lincoln employees enjoyed a pension plan, a policy of promotion from within, and continuous employment. Base pay rates were determined by formal job evaluation and a merit rating system was in effect.

In the prologue of James F. Lincoln's last book, Charles G. Herbruck writes regarding the foregoing personnel innovations,

> They were not to buy good behavior. They were not efforts to increase profits. They were not antidotes to labor difficulties. They did not constitute a "do-gooder" program. They were expressions of mutual respect for each person's importance to the job to be done. All of these reflect the leadership of James Lincoln, under whom they were nurtured and propagated (Lincoln, 1961, p. 11).

By the start of World War II, Lincoln Electric was the world's largest manufacturer of arc-welding products. Sales of about $4,000,000 in 1934 had grown to $24,000,000 by 1941. Productivity per employee more than doubled during the same period.

During the War, Lincoln Electric prospered as never before. Despite challenges to Lincoln's profitability by the Navy's Price Review Board and to the tax deductibility of employee bonuses by the Internal Revenue Service, the company increased its profits and paid huge bonuses.

Certainly since 1935 and probably for several years before that, Lincoln productivity has been well above the average for similar companies. Lincoln claims levels of productivity more than twice those for other manufacturers from 1945 onward. Information available from outside sources tends to support these claims.

COMPANY PHILOSOPHY

James F. Lincoln was the son of a Congregational minister, and Christian principles were at the center of his business philosophy. The confidence that he had in the efficacy of Christ's teachings is illustrated by the following remark taken from one of his books:

> The Christian ethic should control our acts. If it did control our acts, the savings in cost of distribution would be tremendous. Advertising would be a contact of the expert consultant with the customer, in order to give the customer the best product available when all of the customer's needs are considered. Competition then would be in improving the quality of products and increasing efficiency in producing and distributing them; not in deception, as is now too customary. Pricing would reflect efficiency of production; it would not be a selling dodge that the customer may well be sorry he accepted. It would be proper for all concerned and rewarding for the ability used in producing the product.[1]

There is no indication that Lincoln attempted to evangelize his employees or customers—or the general public for that matter. The current Board chairman, Mr. Irrgang, and the President, Mr. Willis, do not even mention the Christian gospel in their

[1] James F. Lincoln, *A New Approach to Industrial Economics* (New York: The Devin Adair Co., 1961), p. 64.

recent speeches and interviews. The company motto, "The actual is limited, the possible is immense," is prominently displayed, but there is no display of religious slogans, and there is no company chapel.

Attitude Toward the Customer

James Lincoln saw the customer's needs as the *raison d'etre* for every company. "When any company has achieved success so that it is attractive as an investment," he wrote, "all money usually needed for expansion is supplied by the customer in retained earnings. It is obvious that the customer's interests, not the stockholder's, should come first."[2] In 1947 he said, "Care should be taken . . . not to rivet attention on profit. Between 'How much do I get?' and 'How do I make this better, cheaper, more useful?' the difference is fundamental and decisive."[3] Mr. Willis still ranks the customer as Lincoln's most important constituency. This is reflected in Lincoln's policy to "at all times price on the basis of cost and at all times keep pressure on our cost. . . ."[4] Lincoln's goal, often stated, is "to build a better and better product at a lower and lower price."[5] "It is obvious," James Lincoln said, "that the customer's interests should be the first goal of industry."[6]

Attitude Toward Stockholders

Stockholders are given last priority at Lincoln. This is a continuation of James Lincoln's philosophy: "The last group to be considered is the stockholders who own stock because they think it will be more profitable than investing money in any other way."[7] Concerning division of the largess produced by incentive management, Lincoln writes, "The absentee stockholder also will get his share, even if undeserved, out of the greatly increased profit that the efficiency produces."[8]

Attitude Toward Unionism

There has never been a serious effort to organize Lincoln employees. While James Lincoln criticized the labor movement for "selfishly attempting to better its position at the expense of the people it must serve,"[9] he still had kind words for union members. He excused abuses of union power as "the natural reactions of human beings to the

---

[2]Ibid., p. 119.

[3]"You Can't Tell What a Man Can Do—Until He has the Chance," *Reader's Digest*, January 1947, p. 94.

[4]George E. Willis' letter to author of 7 September 1978.

[5]Lincoln, 1961, p. 47.

[6]Ibid., p. 117.

[7]Ibid., p. 38.

[8]Ibid., p. 122.

[9]Ibid., p. 18.

abuses to which management has subjected them."[10] Lincoln's idea of the correct relationship between workers and managers is shown by this comment: "Labor and management are properly not warring camps; they are parts of one organization in which they must and should cooperate fully and happily."[11]

Beliefs and Assumptions About Employees

If fulfilling customer needs is the desired goal of business, then employee performance and productivity are the means by which this goal can best be achieved. It is the Lincoln attitude toward employees, reflected in the following quotations, which is credited by many with creating the record of success the company has experienced:

> The greatest fear of the worker, which is the same as the greatest fear of the industrialist in operating a company, is the lack of income . . . The industrial manager is very conscious of his company's need of uninterrupted income. He is completely oblivious, evidently, of the fact that the worker has the same need.[12]
>
> He is just as eager as any manager is to be part of a team that is properly organized and working for the advancement of our economy . . . He has no desire to make profits for those who do not hold up their end in production, as is true of absentee stockholders and inactive people in the company.[13]
>
> If money is to be used as an incentive, the program must provide that what is paid to the worker is what he has earned. The earnings of each must be in accordance with accomplishment.[14]
>
> Status is of great importance in all human relationships. The greatest incentive that money has, usually, is that it is a symbol of success . . . The resulting status is the real incentive . . . Money alone can be an incentive to the miser only.[15]
>
> There must be complete honesty and understanding between the hourly worker and management if high efficiency is to be obtained.[16]

LINCOLN'S BUSINESS

Arc-welding has been the standard joining method in the shipbuilding industry for decades. It is the predominant way of joining steel in the construction industry. Most industrial plants have their own welding shops for maintenance and construction. Manufacturers of tractors and all kinds of heavy equipment use arc-welding extensively in

[10]Ibid., p. 76.
[11]Ibid., p. 72.
[12]Ibid., p. 36.
[13]Ibid., p. 75.
[14]Ibid., p. 98.
[15]Ibid., p. 92.
[16]Ibid., p. 39.

the manufacturing process. Many hobbyists have their own welding machines and use them for making metal items such as patio furniture and barbeque pits. The popularity of welded sculpture as an art form is growing.

While advances in welding technology have been frequent, arc-welding products, in the main, have hardly changed except for Lincoln's Innershield process. This process, utilizing a self-shielded, flux cored electrode, has established new cost saving opportunities for construction and equipment fabrication. The most popular Lincoln electrode, the Fleetweld 5P, has been virtually the same since the 1930s. The most popular engine-driven welder in the world, the Lincoln SA-200, has been a gray-colored assembly including a four-cylinder continental "Red Seal" engine and a 200 ampere direct-current generator with two current-control knobs for at least three decades. A 1980 model SA-200 even weighs almost the same as the 1950 model, and it certainly is little changed in appearance.

Lincoln and its competitors now market a wide range of general purpose and specialty electrodes for welding mild steel, aluminum, cast iron, and stainless and special steels. Most of these electrodes are designed to meet the standards of the American Welding Society, a trade association. They are thus essentially the same as to size and composition from one manufacturer to another. Every electrode manufacturer has a limited number of unique products, but these typically constitute only a small percentage of total sales.

Lincoln's research and development expenditures have recently been less than one and one-half percent of sales. There is evidence that others spend several times as much as a percentage of sales.

Lincoln's share of the arc-welding products market appears to have been about forty percent for many years, and the welding products market has grown somewhat faster than the level of industry in general. The market is highly price-competitive, with variations in prices of standard products normally amounting to only a percent or two. Lincoln's products are sold directly by its engineering-oriented sales force and indirectly through its distributor organization. Advertising expenditures amount to less than one-fourth of one percent of sales, one-third as much as a major Lincoln competitor with whom the casewriter checked.

The other major welding process, flame-welding, has not been competitive with arc-welding since the 1930s. However, plasma-arc-welding, a relatively new process which uses a conducting stream of super heated gas (plasma) to confine the welding current to a small area, has made some inroads, especially in metal tubing manufacturing, in recent years. Major advances in technology which will produce an alternative superior to arc-welding within the next decade or so appear unlikely. Also, it seems likely that changes in the machines and techniques used in arc-welding will be evolutionary rather than revolutionary.

Products

The company is primarily engaged in the manufacture and sale of arc-welding products—electric welding machines and metal electrodes. Lincoln also produces electric motors ranging from one-half horsepower to 200 horsepower. Motors constitute about eight to ten percent of total sales.

The electric welding machines, some consisting of a transformer or motor and generator arrangement powered by commercial electricity and others consisting of an internal combustion engine and generator, are designed to produce from 30 to 1000 amperes of electrical power. This electrical current is used to melt a consumable metal electrode with the molten metal being transferred in a super hot spray to the metal joint being welded. Very high temperatures and hot sparks are produced, and operators usually must wear special eye and face protection and leather gloves, often along with leather aprons and sleeves.

Welding electrodes are of two basic types: (1) Coated "stick" electrodes, usually fourteen inches long and smaller than a pencil in diameter, which are held in a special insulated holder by the operator, who must manipulate the electrode in order to maintain a proper arc-width and pattern of deposition of the metal being transferred. Stick electrodes are packaged in six- to fifty-pound boxes. (2) Coiled wire, ranging in diameter from 0.035" to 0.219", which is designed to be fed continuously to the welding arc through a "gun" held by the operator or positioned by automatic positioning equipment. The wire is packaged in coils, reels, and drums weighing from fourteen to 1000 pounds.

MANUFACTURING OPERATIONS

Plant Locations

The main plant is in Euclid, Ohio, a suburb on Cleveland's east side. The layout of this plant is shown in Figure 1. There are no warehouses. Materials flow from the half-mile long dock on the north side of the plant through the production lines to a very limited storage and loading area on the south side. Materials used on each work station are stored as close as possible to the work station. The administration offices, near the center of the factory, are entirely functional. Not even the President's office is carpeted. A corridor below the main level provides access to the factory floor from the main entrance near the center of the plant.

A new plant, just opened in Mentor, Ohio, houses some of the electrode production operations, which were moved from the main plant. The main plant is currently being enlarged by 100,000 square feet and several innovative changes are being made in the manufacturing layout.

Manufacturing Processes

The electrode manufacturing process is highly capital intensive. Metal rods purchased from steel producers are drawn or extruded down to smaller diameters, cut to length and coated with pressed-powder "flux" for stick electrodes or plated with copper (for conductivity) and spun into coils or spools for wire. Some of Lincoln's wire, called

Figure 1 Factory layout

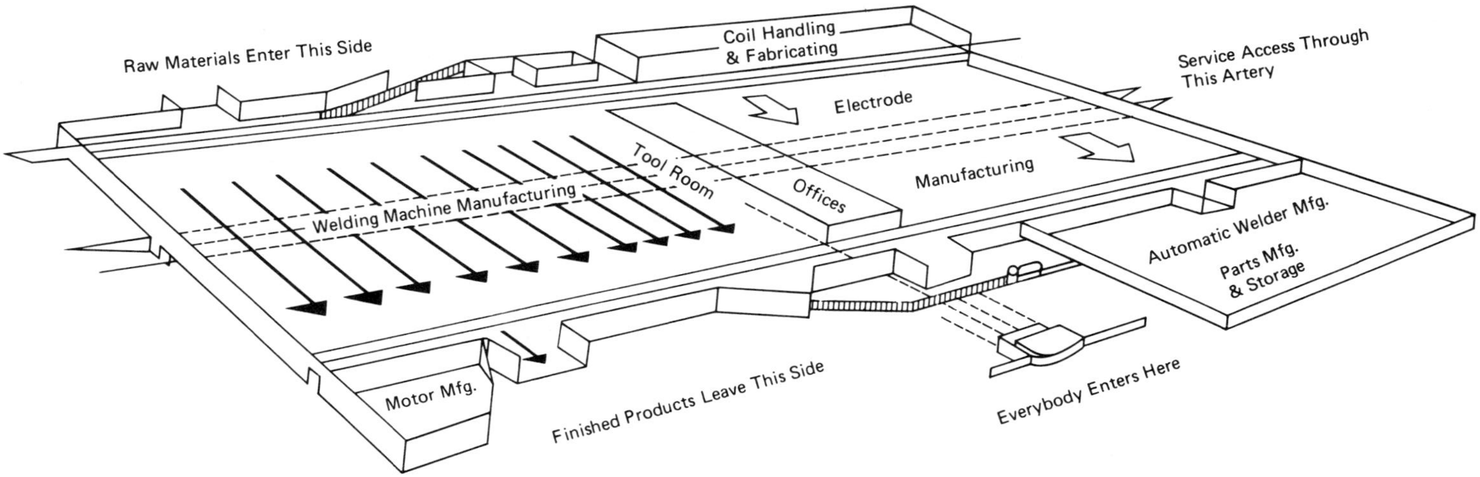

"Inner-shield," is hollow and filled with a material similar to that used to coat stick electrodes. Lincoln is highly secretive about its electrode production processes, and the casewriter was not given access to the details of those processes.

Welding machines and electric motors are made on a series of assembly lines. Gasoline and diesel engines are purchased partially assembled but practically all other components are made from basic industrial products, e.g., steel bars and sheets and bar copper conductor wire, in the Lincoln factory.

Individual components, such as gasoline tanks for engine-driven welders and steel shafts for motors and generators, are made by numerous small "factories within a factory." The shaft for a certain generator, for example, is made from a raw steel bar by one operator who uses five large machines, all running continuously. A saw cuts the bar to length, a digital lathe machines different sections to varying diameters, a special milling machine cuts a slot for the keyway, and so forth, until a finished shaft is produced. The operator moves the shafts from machine to machine and makes necessary adjustments.

Another operator punches, shapes and paints sheetmetal cowling parts. One assembles steel laminations onto a rotor shaft, then winds, insulates and tests the rotors. Finished components are moved by crane operators to the nearby assembly lines.

Worker Performance and Attitudes

Exceptional worker performance at Lincoln is a matter of record. The typical Lincoln employee earns about twice as much as other factory workers in the Cleveland area. Yet the labor cost per sales dollar at Lincoln, currently 23.5 cents, is well below industry averages.

Sales per Lincoln factory employee currently exceed $157,000. An observer at the factory quickly sees why this figure is so high. Each worker is proceeding busily and thoughtfully about his task. There is no idle chatter. Most workers take no coffee breaks. Many operate several machines and make a substantial component unaided. The supervisors, some with as many as 100 subordinates, are busy with planning and recordkeeping duties and hardly glance at the people they supervise. The manufacturing procedures appear efficient—no unnecessary steps, no wasted motions, no wasted materials. Finished components move smoothly to subsequent work stations.

Worker turnover at Lincoln is practically nonexistent except for retirements and departures by new employees.

ORGANIZATION STRUCTURE

Lincoln has never had a formal organization chart.[17] The object of this policy is to insure maximum flexibility. An open door policy is practiced throughout the company,

---

[17]Once, Harvard Business School researchers prepared an organization chart reflecting the below-mentioned implied relationships. The chart became available within the Lincoln organization, and present Lincoln management feels that it had a disruptive effect. Therefore, the casewriter was asked not to include any kind of organizational chart in this report.

and personnel are encouraged to take problems to the persons most capable of resolving them.

Perhaps because of the quality and enthusiasm of the Lincoln workforce, routine supervision is almost nonexistent. A typical production foreman, for example, supervises as many as 100 workers, a span-of-control which does not allow more than infrequent worker-supervisor interaction. Position titles and traditional flows of authority do imply something of an organizational structure, however. For example, the Vice-President, Sales, and the Vice-President, Electrode Division, report to the President, as do various staff assistants such as the Personnel Director and the Director of Purchasing. Using such implied relationships, it has been determined that production workers have two or, at most, three levels of supervision between themselves and the President.

PERSONNEL POLICIES

Recruitment and Selection

Every job opening at Lincoln is advertised internally on company bulletin boards and any employee can apply for any job so advertised. External hiring is done only for entry level positions. Selections for these jobs is done on the basis of personal interviews— there is no aptitude or psychological testing. Not even a high school diploma is required except for engineering and sales positions, which are filled by graduate engineers. A committee consisting of vice presidents and superintendents interviews candidates initially cleared by the Personnel Department. Final selection is made by the supervisor who has a job opening. Out of over 3500 applicants interviewed by the Personnel Department during a recent period fewer than 300 were hired.

Job Security

In 1958 Lincoln formalized its lifetime employment policy, which had already been in effect for many years. There have been no layoffs at Lincoln since World War II. Since 1958, every Lincoln worker with over one year's longevity has been guaranteed at least 30 hours per week, 49 weeks per year.

The policy has never been so severely tested as during the 1981–83 recession. As a manufacturer of capital goods, Lincoln's business is highly cyclical. In previous recessions Lincoln has been able to avoid major sales declines. However, 1982 sales were about one-third below those of 1981. Few companies could withstand such a sales decline and remain profitable. Yet, Lincoln not only earned profits, but no employee has been laid off, the usual year-end incentive bonuses were paid (averaging $15,600 per worker for 1982), and common shareholders continue to receive about the normal dividend (around $8 per share).

Performance Evaluations

Each supervisor formally evaluates his subordinates twice a year using the cards shown in Figure 2. The employee performance criteria, "quality," "dependability," "ideas and

Figure 2 Performance appraisal cards

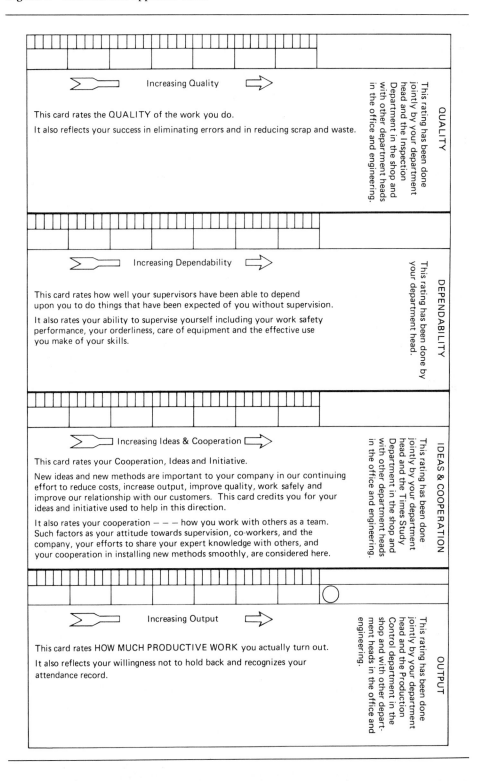

cooperation," and "output," are considered to be independent of each other. Marks on the cards are converted to numerical scores which are forced to average 100 for each evaluating supervisor. Individual merit rating scores normally range from 80 to 110. Any score over 110 requires a special letter to top management. These scores (over 110) are not considered in computing the required 100 point average for each evaluating supervisor. Suggestions for improvements often result in recommendations for exceptionally high performance scores. Supervisors discuss individual performance marks with the employees concerned. Each warranty claim on a Lincoln product is traced to the individual employee whose work caused the defect. The employee's performance score may be reduced by one point, or the worker may be required to repay the cost of servicing the warranty claim by working without pay.

Compensation

Basic wage levels for jobs at Lincoln are determined by a wage survey of similar jobs in the Cleveland area. These rates are adjusted quarterly in accordance with changes in the Cleveland Area Consumer Price Index. Insofar as possible, base wage rates are translated into piece rates. Practically all production workers and many others—for example, some forklift operators—are paid by piece rate. Once established, piece rates are never changed unless a substantive change in the way a job is done results from a source other than the worker doing the job. In December of each year, a portion of annual profits is distributed to employees as bonuses. Incentive bonuses since 1934 have averaged about the same as annual wages and somewhat more than after-tax profits. The average bonus for 1981 was about $21,000. Individual bonuses are exactly proportional to merit-rating scores. For example, assume incentive bonuses for the company total 110 percent of wages paid. A person whose performance score is 95 will receive a bonus of 1.045 (1.10×0.95) times annual wages.

Work Assignment

Management has authority to transfer workers and to switch between overtime and short time as required. Supervisors have undisputed authority to assign specific parts to individual workmen, who may have their own preferences due to variations in piece rates.

Employee Participation in Decision Making

When a manager speaks of participative management, he usually thinks of a relaxed, nonauthoritarian atmosphere. This is not the case at Lincoln. Formal authority is quite strong. "We're very authoritarian around here," says Mr. Willis. James F. Lincoln placed a good deal of stress on protecting management's authority. "Management in all successful departments of industry must have complete power," he said, ". . . Management is the coach who must be obeyed. The men, however, are the players who alone can win the game."[18] Despite this attitude, there are several ways in which employees participate in management at Lincoln.

Richard Sabo, Manager of Public Relations, relates job-enlargement to participation. "The most important participative technique that we use is giving more responsibility to employees." Mr. Sabo says, "We give a high school graduate more responsibility than other companies give their foremen." Lincoln puts limits on the degree of participation which is allowed, however. In Mr. Sabo's words,

> When you use "participation" put quotes around it. Because we believe that each person should participate only in those decisions he is most knowledgeable about. I don't think production employees should control the decisions of Bill Irrgang. They don't know as much as he does about the decisions he is involved in.

The Advisory Board, elected by the workers, meets with the Chairman and the President every two weeks to discuss ways of improving operations. This board has been in existence since 1914 and has contributed to many innovations. The incentive bonuses, for example, were first recommended by this committee. Every Lincoln employee has access to Advisory Board members, and answers to all Advisory Board suggestions are promised by the following meeting. Both Mr. Irrgang and Mr. Willis are quick to point out, though, that the Advisory Board only recommends actions. "They do not have direct authority," Mr. Irrgang says, "and when they bring up something that management thinks is not to the benefit of the company, it will be rejected."[19]

A suggestion program was instituted in 1929. At first, employees were awarded one-half of the first year's savings attributable to their suggestions. Now, however, the value of suggestions is reflected in performance evaluation scores, which determine individual incentive bonus amounts.

Training and Education

Production workers are given a short period of on-the-job training and then placed on a piecework pay system. Lincoln does not pay for off-site education. The idea behind this latter policy is that everyone cannot take advantage of such a program, and it is unfair to expend company funds for an advantage to which there is unequal access. Sales personnel are given on-the-job training in the plant followed by a period of work and training at one of the regional sales offices.

Fringe Benefits and Executive Perquisites

A medical plan and a company-paid retirement program have been in effect for many years. A plant cafeteria, operated on a break-even basis, serves meals at about sixty

---

[18]Lincoln, *Incentive Management* (Cleveland, OH: The Lincoln Electric Company, 1951), p. 228.

[19]Incentive Management in Action, *Assembly Engineering*, March 1967, p. 18.

percent of usual costs. An employee association, to which the company does not contribute, provides disability insurance and social and athletic activities. An employee stock ownership program, instituted in about 1925, and regular stock purchases have resulted in employee ownership of about fifty percent of Lincoln's stock.

As to executive perquisites, there are none—crowded, austere offices, no executive washrooms or lunchrooms, and no reserved parking spaces. Even the company President pays for his own meals and eats in the cafeteria.

FINANCIAL POLICIES

James F. Lincoln felt strongly that financing for company growth should come from within the company—through initial cash investments by the founders, through retention of earnings, and through stock purchases by those who work in the business. He saw the following advantages of this approach.[20]

1. Ownership of stock by employees strengthens team spirit. "If they are mutually anxious to make it succeed, the future of the company is bright."

2. Ownership of stock provides individual incentive because employees feel that they will benefit from company profitability.

3. "Ownership is educational." Owners-employees "will know how profits are made and lost; how success is won and lost . . . There are few socialists in the list of stockholders of the nation's industries."

4. "Capital available from within controls expansion." Unwarranted expansion will not occur, Lincoln believed, under his financing plan.

5. "The greatest advantage would be the development of the individual worker. Under the incentive of ownership, he would become a greater man."

6. "Stock ownership is one of the steps that can be taken that will make the worker feel that there is less of a gulf between him and the boss . . . Stock ownership will help the worker to recognize his responsibility in the game and the importance of victory."

Lincoln Electric Company uses a minimum of debt in its capital structure. There is no borrowing at all, with the debt being limited to current payables. Even the new $20 million plant in Mentor, Ohio, was financed totally from earnings.

The unusual pricing policy at Lincoln is succinctly stated by President Willis: "at all times price on the basis of cost and at all times keep pressure on our cost." This policy resulted in Lincoln's price for the most popular welding electrode then in use going from 16 cents a pound in 1929 to 4.7 cents in 1938. More recently, the SA-200 Welder, Lincoln's largest selling portable machine, decreased in price from 1958 through 1965. According to Dr. C. Jackson Grayson of the American Productivity Center in Houston, Texas, Lincoln's prices in general have increased only one-fifth as

[20]Lincoln, 1961, pp. 220–228.

fast as the Consumer Price Index since 1934. This has resulted in a welding products market in which Lincoln is the undisputed price leader for the products it manufactures. Not even the major Japanese manufacturers, such as Nippon Steel for welding electrodes and Asaka Transformer for welding machines, have been able to penetrate this market.

Huge cash balances are accumulated each year preparatory to paying the year-end bonuses. The bonuses totaled $55,718,000 for 1981 and about $41,000,000 for 1982. This money is invested in short-term U.S. government securities until needed. Financial statements are shown in Tables 1 and 2.

HOW WELL DOES LINCOLN SERVE ITS PUBLIC?

Lincoln Electric differs from most other companies in the importance it assigns to each of the groups it serves. Mr. Willis identifies these groups, in the order of priority Lincoln ascribes to them, as (1) customers, (2) employees, and (3) stockholders.

Certainly Lincoln customers have fared well over the years. Lincoln prices for welding machines and welding electrodes are acknowledged to be the lowest in the marketplace. Lincoln quality has consistently been so high that Lincoln "Fleetweld" electrodes and Lincoln SA-200 welders have been the standard in the pipeline and refinery construction industry, where price is hardly a criterion, for decades. The cost of field failures for Lincoln products was an amazing four one-hundredths of one percent in 1979. A Lincoln distributor in Monroe, Louisiana, says that he has sold several hundred of the popular AC-225 welders, and, though the machine is warranted for one year, he has never handled a warranty claim.

Perhaps best-served of all Lincoln constituencies have been the employees. Not the least of their benefits, of course, are the year-end bonuses, which effectively double an already average compensation level. The foregoing description of the personnel program further illustrates the desirability of a Lincoln job.

While stockholders were relegated to an inferior status by James F. Lincoln, they have done very well indeed. Recent dividends have exceeded $7 a share and earnings per share have exceeded $20. In January 1980, the price of restricted stock committed by Lincoln to employees was $117 a share. By February 4, 1983, the stated value, at which Lincoln will repurchase the stock if tendered, was $166. A check with the New York office of Merrill, Lynch, Pierce, Fenner and Smith on February 4, 1983 revealed an estimated price on Lincoln stock of $240 a share, with none being offered for sale. Technically, this price applies only to the unrestricted stock owned by the Lincoln family, a few other major holders, and employees who have purchased it on the open market, but it gives some idea of the value of Lincoln stock in general. The risk associated with Lincoln stock, a major determinant of stock value, is minimal because of the absence of debt in Lincoln's capital structure, because of an extremely stable earnings record, and because of Lincoln's practice of purchasing the restricted stock whenever employees offer it for sale.

Table 1 The Lincoln Electric Company, summary of balance sheet information ($000)

Assets	1977	1978	1979	1980	1981	1982
Cash	$ 2,203	$ 1,588	$ 2,261	$ 1,307	$ 3,603	$ 1,318
Govt. Securities & Certificates of Deposit	24,375	28,807	38,408	46,503	62,671	72,485
Notes & Accounts Receivable	34,093	38,786	41,598	42,424	41,521	26,239
Inventories (Life Basis)	28,449	35,916	37,640	35,533	45,541	38,157
Deferred Taxes & Prepayments	2,275	1,729	1,437	2,749	3,658	4,635
	$ 91,395	$106,826	$121,344	$128,516	$156,994	$142,834
Other Intangible Assets	14,172	19,420	19,164	19,723	21,424	22,116
Investments in Foreign Subs.	4,696	4,976	4,986	4,695	4,695	7,696
	$ 18,868	$ 24,396	$ 24,150	$ 24,418	$ 26,119	$ 29,812
Property, plant, equipment Land and Buildings (Net)	23,137	22,622	22,496	23,895	25,624	24,255
Machinery, Tools and Equipment (Net)	17,035	18,458	21,250	25,339	27,104	26,949
	$ 40,172	$ 41,080	$ 43,746	$ 49,234	$ 52,728	$ 51,204
Total Assets	$150,435	$172,302	$189,240	$202,168	$235,841	$223,850

Liabilities						
Accounts Payable	$ 9,891	$ 14,330	$ 16,590	$ 15,608	$ 14,868	$ 11,936
Accrued Wages	839	882	917	1,504	4,940	3,633
Taxes, Including Income Taxes	8,057	9,116	9,620	5,622	14,755	5,233
Dividends Payable	4,327	5,730	5,889	5,800	7,070	6,957
	$ 23,114	$ 30,058	$ 33,016	$ 28,534	$ 41,633	$ 27,759
Deferred Taxes and Other Long-Term Liabilities	—	—	—	$ 3,807	$ 4,557	$ 5,870
Shareholders' Equity Common Stock	4,479	286	280	276	272	268
Additional Paid-In Capital		4,216	4,143	2,641	501	1,862
Retained Earnings	122,842	137,742	151,801	166,910	188,878	188,091
	$127,321	$142,244	$156,224	$169,827	$189,651	$190,221
Total Liabilities & Shareholders' Equity	$150,435	$172,302	$189,240	$202,168	$235,841	$223,850

Table 2   The Lincoln Electric Company, summary of income statement information

	1977	1978	1979	1980	1981	1982
Income						
Net Sales	$276,947	$329,652	$373,789	$387,374	$450,387	$310,862
Other Income	5,768	7,931	11,397	13,817	18,454	18,049
	$282,715	$337,583	$385,186	$401,191	$468,841	$328,911
Costs and Expense						
Cost of Products Sold	$175,733	$210,208	$244,376	$260,671	$293,332	$212,674
General and Administrative Expense	23,821	28,126	33,699	37,753	42,656	37,128
Year-End Incentive Bonus	29,263	39,547	44,068	43,249	55,718	36,870
Payroll Taxes on Bonuses[a]	—	—	1,349[a]	1,251	1,544	1,847
Pension Expense	4,062	5,881	6,131	6,810	6,874	5,888
	$232,879	$283,762	$329,623	$349,734	$400,124	$294,407
Income Before Taxes	$ 49,836	$ 53,821	$ 55,563	$ 51,457	$ 68,717	$ 34,504
Provision for Taxes						
Federal	25,936	22,700	22,400	20,300	27,400	13,227
State and Local	—	3,573	3,165	3,072	3,885	2,497
	25,936	26,273	25,565	23,372	31,285	$ 15,724
Net Income	$ 23,900	$ 27,548	$ 29,998	$ 28,085	$ 37,432	$ 18,780
Eligible Employees (for Bonus)	2,431	2,533	2,611	2,637	2,684	2,634

[a]Payroll tax expense paid by The Lincoln Electric Company relating to year-end incentive bonus were distributed to Cost of Products Sold, Selling, Administrative and General Expenses prior to Year 1979.

A CONCLUDING COMMENT

It is easy to believe that the reason for Lincoln's success is the excellent attitude of Lincoln employees and their willingness to work harder, faster, and more intelligently than other industrial workers. However, Mr. Richard Sabo, Manager of Publicity and Educational Services at Lincoln, suggests that appropriate credit be given to Lincoln executives, whom he credits with carrying out the following policies:

1. Management has limited research, development and manufacturing to a standard product line designed to meet the major needs of the welding industry.

2. New products must be reviewed by manufacturing and all production costs verified before being approved by management.

3. Purchasing is challenged to not only procure materials at the lowest cost, but also to work closely with engineering and manufacturing to assure that the latest innovations are implemented.

4. Manufacturing supervision and all personnel are held accountable for reduction of scrap, energy conservation, and maintenance of product quality.

5. Production control, material handling, and methods engineering are closely supervised by top management.

6. Material and finished goods inventory control, accurate cost accounting and attention to sales cost, credit, and other financial areas have constantly reduced overhead and led to excellent profitability.

7. Management has made cost reduction a way of life at Lincoln, and definite programs are established in many areas, including traffic and shipping, where tremendous savings can result.

8. Management has established a sales department that is technically trained to reduce customer welding costs. This sales technique and other real customer services have eliminated nonessential frills and resulted in long-term benefits to all concerned.

9. Management has encouraged education, technical publishing, and long range programs that have resulted in industry growth, thereby assuring market potential for the Lincoln Electric Company.

CASE 12

New York Air
STEPHEN LYSONSKI
University of Rhode Island

On a recent morning Bernadette Riley, an executive for Riley Enterprises, headed out for one of her frequent trips to New York City. She took a taxi to Washington National Airport to catch an early flight. For years her routine had been to pay the $59 fare and board the Eastern Airlines Air Shuttle. Although the service on the Shuttle was impersonal and lacked the amenities of most flights, its hourly departures were dependable and did not require reserve seating.

This time, however, Ms. Riley was enticed by catchy radio and television commercials and newspaper reports—not to mention the $49 fare of a new airline. She

This case was prepared for class discussion and represents neither effective nor ineffective handling of an administrative situation.

From Comerford and Callaghan, *Strategic Management: Text, Tools, and Case for Business Policy* (Boston: Kent Publishing Company, 1985), pp. 469–487. © 1985 by Wadsworth, Inc. Reprinted by permission of Kent Publishing Company, a division of Wadsworth, Inc.

proceeded directly to a brightly colored sign with a "Big Apple" proclaiming "New York Air." The ticket agent cheerfully filled out her ticket and directed her to the concourse where the next flight was boarding. As Ms. Riley walked down the concourse to the boarding area, she could see her jet with a luscious red apple logo on the fuselage.

"Welcome to New York Air," said the flight attendant over the public address system. "We're going to try to make you feel at home so give us a shout if we can give you any assistance."

After soaring through the skies, the nonunion pilots flying the jet began the descent into New York's LaGuardia Airport. The fifty-five-minute flight seemed different than the routine excursions aboard the shuttle. Flight attendants enthusiastically served coffee, beverages, and pastries, and smiled good-naturedly at passengers. At the end of the flight, Ms. Riley was relaxed and cheerful. "I was amazed at the good will and no-hassle atmosphere aboard the flight," she commented. "When I fly on the Shuttle, everyone seems a lot more tense amid the hustle and bustle—even the flight attendants seem on edge." It was clear that Ms. Riley had lost her loyalty to the Eastern Shuttle.

As the passengers disembarked, nonunion service crews quickly unloaded the cargo at the space rented from United Airlines, so the plane could resume its flight to Boston.

THE EMERGENCE OF NEW YORK AIR

New York Air is an affiliate of Texas International Airlines, a Houston-based carrier that made waves in the industry when it attempted to acquire National Airlines by purchasing its stock in 1978. Although Texas International failed in the takeover attempt, it was rewarded handsomely after a bidding war developed between Pan American and Eastern for National's stock. When Texas International sold its shares of National, it suddenly acquired $36 million in after-tax profits. With these funds and an additional $89 million, Texas International decided to penetrate Eastern's foothold in the Northeast by launching New York Air.

The creation of New York Air marked the first time an established carrier had started a separate airline in a new service region. "It's almost as if Texas Air Corporation (the holding company established by Texas International) is setting up a franchise system," remarked airline analyst Michael Derchin of Oppenheimer and Company. "It's an interesting concept, setting up pockets of new service in various parts of the country and undercutting the incumbent carriers with low fares."[1] New York Air is a completely separate corporate entity from its parent company. Most New York Air executives, however, are also officials of Texas Air Corporation or Texas International, or both. The separate corporate status also caused New York Air some problems in obtaining slots at National Airport in Washington and forced it to go through the difficult and time-consuming process of obtaining CAB (Civil Aeronautics Board) and FAA (Federal Aviation Administration) certification.

---

[1]Roger Thurow, "New Approach to Expansion by Texas Air," *Wall Street Journal* (October 15, 1980).

New York Air began service on December 19, 1980, with ten daily weekday scheduled round-trip flights between New York's LaGuardia Airport and the Washington, D.C., National Airport (the busiest route in the nation). Management was overjoyed with the high level of demand. Credit for the immediate success of the program was given to Texas International's president, Frank Lorenzo. He was convinced that there was an unmet need for improved air service in the routes dominated by major carriers. In particular, the Eastern Air Shuttle reigned supreme with its virtual monopoly on the New York to Boston and Washington routes since American had cut back on its service between those cities almost twenty years before. Lorenzo's ambition for New York Air was not limited to the New York-Washington routes, though. He predicted, "Within a year or so, we expect New York Air to be in direct competition with many, if not most, of this country's largest airlines."

New York Air Versus Eastern's Shuttle

The importance of the Shuttle to Eastern Airlines was well known. As one Eastern official remarked, "The Shuttle is a very sizable proportion of our business and is very important to us."[2] The Washington-New York route was believed to represent about 5 percent of Eastern's total boardings, 1 percent of its system-wide revenue passenger miles, and 2.5 percent of its total revenues. Eastern claimed to fly 10,500 Shuttle passengers daily and one airline analyst estimated that the carrier has earned between $20,000,000 and $25,000,000 each year from its Shuttle routes.[3]

The crux of the struggle between the two carriers is New York Air's low-priced tickets versus the Eastern Shuttle's convenience. The stakes of this battle are enormous; more than 3 million passengers (about 90 percent of the air travelers between these two cities) fly the Shuttle.[4] Indeed it is viewed as an institution and "flying the Shuttle" has become a favored expression for air passengers in the Northeast.

James O'Donnell, the vice-president of marketing at New York Air, was confident that his company would be able to carve out a successful niche in Eastern's market. "We have a strong belief that the public loves and responds to competition," he asserted. O'Donnell maintained that the key ingredients of a successful formula were "price, destination, and frequency."[5] Nonetheless the destination and frequency components for the two carriers are virtually equivalent; the only variations are price and the amenities offered to the passengers. For example, compared with the $59 one-way fare between Washington and New York on Eastern, New York Air has a ceiling price of $49 and offers an off-peak fare of $29 for flights departing after 7 p.m. or on week-

---

[2]Michael Feazel, "Texas Air Confirms Plan for East Coast Service," *Aviation Week and Space Technology* (September 15, 1980).

[3]"N.Y. Air 'Deals' with Eastern," *Advertising Age* (January 12, 1981): 1.

[4]Tom Fiedler, "Eastern Patrons Tempted by Apples," *Providence Sunday Journal* (January 25, 1981): F-3.

[5]Ibid.

Exhibit 1   New York Air routes in 1981

Markets Entered in First Year	Fare Before New York Air	New York Air Fare Pleasure/Executive
New York–Washington	$ 60	$29/49
Boston–Washington	$108	$45/65
Cleveland–New York	$135	$45/65
Louisville–New York	$172	$69/89
Buffalo–New York	$ 69	$29/49
Detroit–New York	$128	$49/69
Cincinnati–New York	$176	$59/79
Boston–Orlando	$179	$79/99
Baltimore–Orlando	$139	$59/79
Cleveland–Orlando	$159	$89/109

Source: New York Air advertisement.

ends. Even a $29 standby fare has been introduced to attract travelers without reservations and to stimulate the market. Unlike Eastern, New York Air will reserve seats in advance and will not guarantee seating to everyone who arrives on time for a flight.

Airline officials expected that the low off-peak fares would attract the occasional traveler to visit New York City more frequently or to use New York Air in lieu of driving or going by train. As one Houston analyst said, "New York Air will be like a bus company that flies the skies instead of rolling down the highways. With their low fares, all they have to do is get cuter stewardesses than the competition and serve free drinks and they'll make money."[6]

Initial assessments of New York Air's impact on Eastern's Shuttle were mixed. Some industry officials maintained that the majority of travelers on the Shuttle's routes preferred the convenience of not having to make advance reservations and would not be tempted by the $10 difference in ticket prices on most flights. Some competitors were so pessimistic that they maintained New York Air would not last more than six months.[7]

After proving itself on the New York-Washington route, however, New York Air expanded quickly to provide service to other areas. For example, on February 15, 1981, it began service from New York City to Boston. See Exhibit 1 for the 1981 routes served by New York Air and the associated fares; Exhibit 2 indicates most of the cities other than New York which New York Air has been authorized to serve or which it has applied for authority to serve, the volume of passengers carried between metropolitan New York airports and each of those cities in 1979, and the ranking of the routes

[6]Thurow, "New Approach to Expansion."
[7]Feazel, "Texas Air Confirms Plan."

Exhibit 2   Characteristics of air routes originating in New York, 1981

	Nonstop Mileage from New York	Number of Annual Origin and Destination Passengers[b]	Ranking in Top 1000 CAB-Surveyed Domestic Routes by Number of Passengers[b]
Washington, D.C.[a]	·214	2,252,490	1
Boston, Mass.[a]	182	2,150,500	3
Chicago, Ill.	730	2,043,940	5
Detroit, Mich.[a]	499	884,430	11
Atlanta, Ga.	760	883,550	12
Pittsburgh, Pa.[a]	333	732,650	17
Cleveland, Ohio[a]	416	617,270	23
Buffalo/Niagara Falls, N.Y.[a]	289	554,730	28
St. Louis, Mo.	884	406,960	49
Rochester, N.Y.[a]	252	394,410	53
Cincinnati, Ohio[a]	583	297,090	88
Syracuse, N.Y.[a]	196	294,020	90
Charlotte, N.C.	543	286,280	92
Raleigh/Durham, N.C.	430	281,900	95
Columbus, Ohio[a]	476	264,550	105
Norfolk, Va.	295	244,440	112
Greensboro/High Point/ Winston-Salem, N.C.	460	231,790	120
Indianapolis, Ind.[a]	657	216,780	130
Baltimore, Md.	184	193,240	155
Richmond, Va.	292	181,830	174
Milwaukee, Wis.	735	178,940	180
Jacksonville, Fla.	834	177,550	181
Nashville, Tenn.	761	165,120	199
Dayton, Ohio[a]	547	154,350	215
Louisville, Ky.	655	150,150	220
Hartford, Conn.	100	146,830	229
Memphis, Tenn.	960	145,890	232
Providence, R.I.	141	129,140	259
Greenville/Spartanburg, S.C.	599	117,450	287
Albany, N.Y.[a]	135	113,720	299
Columbia, S.C.	616	100,460	351

[a]Indicates cities which New York Air has been authorized to serve.
[b]These data are derived from the CAB Origin–Destination Survey of Airline Passenger Traffic for the year 1979, which is based on CAB estimates from information supplied by interstate carriers.

between New York area airports and each of those cities among all domestic CAB-surveyed routes. It is evident that the routes that are served and may potentially be served are among the busiest in the nation. Consequently New York Air expects to encounter substantial competition not only from established carriers, but also from newly organized carriers.

The amenities offered by New York Air are in sharp contrast to those provided by the Shuttle, which does not serve coffee in the morning or cocktails at night. In-flight snacks, beverages, more personable flight attendants, and a "best of New York attitude" give a definite advantage to New York Air, according to O'Donnell. Above and beyond these features, O'Donnell suggests that, "We want to embody New York. We want to have flair, be a little bit cheeky and be very current in offering new kinds of fares, new kinds of deals."[8]

To emphasize its added services, New York Air's newspaper advertisements featured fictitious coupons for free drinks, snacks, and other amenities. The ads' headline told passengers to: "Take New York Air's coupons to the Eastern Shuttle and see what you probably won't get." The ads concluded with the statement: "These coupons are totally unnecessary on New York Air since the services are already provided as part of our New York flair."

New York Air Succeeds and Expands

Some observers were optimistic about New York Air's chances for success. For example, airline analyst Michael Derchin of Oppenheimer and Company said: "New York Air will bring 3 million new passengers into the market—all the train, bus, and car travelers. Half their traffic won't come out of Eastern's hide, it will come from Amtrack and Trailways."[9] He also stated: "If New York Air carves just a small niche in that market—and just a small niche is a lot—then Eastern can't sit back and do nothing."[10]

Exhibits 3, 4, 5, and 6 show the actual traffic stimulated by New York Air for several routes. These exhibits illustrate the daily passengers carried each way on specific routes for 1980 and 1981 and provide forecasted figures for 1981 passenger traffic if New York Air had not entered the route. In Exhibit 3, for example, the January 1981 forecasted traffic on the New York-Washington route was 2,904 passengers daily while the actual traffic was 3,778. The difference in these two figures suggests that New York Air's entry into this market resulted in a 30 percent increase in traffic as Exhibit 3 indicates.

Exhibit 7 shows New York Air's percentage of the market from month of inception on the routes for New York–Washington, D.C., New York–Boston, Boston–Washington, D.C., and New York–Cleveland. It is apparent from this exhibit that New York

---

[8]Fiedler, "Eastern Patrons Tempted."

[9]Beth Brophy, "East Coast Dog Fight," *Forbes* (November 24, 1980): 40.

[10]Ibid.

Exhibit 3   Actual and estimated traffic stimulation New York–Washington National

	Industry Daily Passengers Each Way			Year Over Year Percent Change in Traffic			Passengers	
	Actual 1980	1981 Forecast Without Stimulation	Actual 1981	Forecast 1981 Without NYA[a]	Actual 81 vs. 80	From Forecast Without Stimulation	Industry Increase from 81 Forecast	NYA Actual Carried
Jan	2,887	2,904	3,778	0.6	30.9	30.0	874	597
Feb	3,052	3,070	3,540	0.6	16.0	15.3	470	473
Mar	3,210	3,229	3,856	0.6	20.1	19.4	627	887
Apr	3,257	3,276	4,384	0.6	34.6	33.8	1,108	1,045
May	3,602	3,624	4,330	0.6	20.2	19.4	706	1,026
June	3,700	3,722	4,293	0.6	16.0	15.3	571	990
July	3,170	3,189	3,868	0.6	22.0	21.2	679	882

Eastern's Shuttle fare was $60 before New York Air's entry on December 19, 1980. New York Air's fares have averaged $40 since service began. This is estimated to be a 30% reduction in the average fare paid.
[a]Based on the average industry growth in the three months prior to New York Air's service.

Exhibit 4   Actual and estimated traffic stimulation, Boston–New York

	Industry Daily Passengers Each Way			Year Over Year Percent Change in Traffic			Passengers	
	Actual 1980	1981 Forecast Without Stimulation	Actual 1981	Forecast 1981 Without NYA[c]	Actual 81 vs. 80	From Forecast Without Stimulation	Industry Increase from 81 Forecast	NYA Actual Carried
Jan	2,953	3,119	3,119	5.6	5.6	5.6	—	—
Feb	3,149	3,086	3,518	(2.0)	11.7	13.9	432	585
Mar	3,286	3,220	3,639	(2.0)	10.7	13.0	419	691
Apr	3,405	3,337	4,149	(2.0)	21.9	24.3	812	855
May	3,327	3,260	4,027	(2.0)	21.0	23.5	767	715
June	3,354	3,483	4,302[a]	(2.0)	21.0	23.5	819	637
July	3,080	3,018	4,125[b]	(2.0)	33.9	36.6	1,107	618

Eastern's Shuttle fare was $56 before New York Air's entry on February 1. Since inception our average selling price has been about $37. It is estimated that this is a price reduction of about 30%.
[a]Includes 125 PAX/day for PE.
[b]Includes 290 PAX/day for PE.
[c]February–July forecast based on average growth in market for the three-month period prior to New York Air entry.

Exhibit 5   Actual and estimated traffic stimulation, Boston–Washington National

	Industry Daily Passengers Each Way			Year Over Year Percent Change in Traffic			Passengers	
	Actual 1980	1981 Forecast Without Stimulation	Actual 1981	Forecast 1981 Without NYA[a]	Actual 81 vs. 80	From Forecast Without Stimulation	Industry Increase from 81 Forecast	NYA Actual Carried
Jan	952	787	787	(17.3)	(17.3)	(17.3)	—	—
Feb	1,059	840	840	(20.7)	(20.7)	(20.7)	—	—
Mar	1,113	902	971	(19.0)	(12.8)	(7.6)	69	115
Apr	1,282	1,038	1,344	(19.0)	4.8	29.4	306	233
May	1,348	1,092	1,404	(19.0)	4.2	28.5	312	230
June	1,380	1,118	1,402	(19.0)	1.6	25.4	284	240
July	1,198	970	1,368	(19.0)	14.2	41.0	398	251

The coach fare was $108 prior to New York Air's entry into the market on March 15, 1981. New York Air introductory fare was $69 on all flights. An economy fare of $39 was introduced in April. The average fare in July was $45.82. The approximate fare reduction in July was 53%.

[a]January–February actuals. March–July calculated at average of January–February rate.

Exhibit 6   Actual and estimated traffic stimulation, Cleveland–New York

	Industry Daily Passengers Each Way			Year Over Year Percent Change in Traffic			Passengers	
	Actual 1980	1981 Forecast Without Stimulation	Actual 1981	Forecast 1981 Without NYA[a]	Actual 81 vs. 80	From Forecast Without Stimulation	Industry Increase from 81 Forecast	NYA Actual Carried
Jan	920	697	697	(24.3)	(24.3)	(24.3)	—	—
Feb	896	717	717	(20.0)	(20.0)	(20.0)	—	—
Mar	924	744	744	(19.5)	(19.5)	(19.5)	—	—
Apr	946	745	996	(21.3)	5.3	33.6	251	81
May	973	766	1,233	(21.3)	26.7	60.9	467	275
June	1,059	833	1,363	(21.3)	28.7	63.6	530	327
July	960	756	1,363	(21.3)	42.0	80.2	607	366

The coach fare was $135 prior to New York Air's entry on April 12, 1981. New York Air's July average fare was $50. It is estimated that this is a 57% reduction in the average fare paid prior to New York Air entry.

[a]Forecast for April–July based on the industry average growth in the three-month period prior to New York Air's service.

Exhibit 7   New York Air's percent share of market from month of inception

	Market Date of Entry			
	NYC–DCA *12/19/80*	*NYC–Bos* *2/1/81*	*Bos–DCA* *3/15/81*	*NYC–Clev.* *4/12/81*
Initial month	6.4%	16.6%	11.8%	8.3%
1st full month	15.8	18.9	17.3	22.3
2nd full month	16.6	20.6	16.3	23.9
3rd full month	23.0	17.6	17.1	24.2
4th full month	23.8	14.7	18.3	
5th full month	23.6	13.7		
6th full month	23.0			
7th full month	22.8			

Air has been successful in penetrating each of these markets; it commanded almost 25 percent of the New York–Washington market in the initial months of operation. Exhibit 8 illustrates passenger growth rates in short-haul high-density markets for 1981 versus 1980. On most of the routes examined in Exhibit 8, there were declines in passenger growth rates.

New York Air's entry into the Washington-New York market was a clear success. In response Eastern fought back with three marketing policy changes. First, it lowered its price to match Air's $29 weekend fare, limited to hours from noon Saturday to noon Sunday. Second, Eastern introduced another incentive to Shuttle passengers by offering each a 50 percent discount coupon for seats on Eastern's flights between New York and Los Angeles or San Francisco. This inducement was somewhat counteracted when New York Air offered to exchange the coupon for $15 cash to any New York Air ticket purchaser.

Exhibit 8   Passenger growth rates in short-haul high-density markets, 1981 versus 1980

	NYC–Ord	**Dtw–NYC[a]**	**Buf–NYC[b]**	**Buf–LGA**
Jan	(14.6)%	(3.0)%	(12.8)%	(12.7)%
Feb	(15.7)	(11.0)	(13.4)	(15.1)
Mar	(17.4)	(7.3)	(19.6)	(22.7)
Apr	(13.4)	3.6	(11.9)	(12.1)
May	(5.2)	(4.1)	1.7	(10.2)
June	(18.2)	(8.9)	9.0	(9.1)
July	(13.6)	(9.7)	18.9	(5.9)

[a]New York Air began service on September 20, 1981.
[b]New York Air began service on September 17, 1981; People's Express began May 1981.

Third, Eastern used advertising to defend its market. In its "Imagine Life Without Us" advertising campaign, Eastern disparaged New York Air's practice of wooing passengers with beverages and frills. The ads emphasized one important feature—dependability. "We know you want to get there quickly and without interruptions. So the Air Shuttle accommodates your needs and spares you the unnecessary fuss and bother," suggested one of the ads.[11]

Eastern's strategy was to emphasize the convenience and dependability of its Air Shuttle. Eastern Vice-President A. Russell Upshaw, who headed Shuttle operations, commented: "We have learned over the years that our passengers have told us they want one thing. They want to know that they can go to the airport, get on the airplane and get back the same way at the end of the day. You know that only the Air Shuttle flies every hour, on the hour, offers on-board ticketing and guarantees you a seat without reservations."[12] According to an Eastern survey, 83 percent of the Shuttle passengers were business executives whose companies pay for the travel. Hence Eastern officials felt that this factor made passengers less price conscious. Although Upshaw admitted that some passengers view the Shuttle as a "cattle car," June Farrell, Eastern's regional public relations director, maintained: "Our customers are like New York subway riders; they all moan and complain about the service, but they wouldn't want things any other way."[13]

New York Air has penetrated other routes besides the New York–Washington corridor with aggressive fare cutting. For example, one of their newspaper advertisements provided a $10 coupon for passengers who fly from or to Washington, D.C., on New York Air, and they used a two-tier price system for several routes. On the New York–Washington route for instance, pleasure flights cost $10 less than executive flights. Other New York Air advertisements claimed that the company "helped air travelers save over $50,000,000 in fares" in the first year of operation. Some routes' reductions were greater than 50 percent.

On April 12, 1981, the airline began service on the Cleveland–New York route. Another of its ads explained that New York Air was responsible for lowering the fares on this route by its competitor, United Airlines. The advertisement states: "Guess what could happen if we left Cleveland in United's friendly clutches? . . . What could happen is United could jack up the fare to New York right back to what it was, $135." United Airlines had to meet New York Air's $59 fare. New York Air almost seemed to welcome United's competition on this route. "When a carrier digs in and spends a lot of advertising dollars to promote low fares, they stimulate the market," says James O'Connell, vice-president for marketing at New York Air.[14] He estimates that since New York Air started competing last April, total New York–Cleveland air traffic has increased by 50 to 100 percent.

[11]Fiedler, "Eastern Patrons Tempted."

[12]Ibid.

[13]Ibid.

[14]John Curley, "Decontrol of Airlines Shifts Pricing from a Cost to a Competition Basis," *Wall Street Journal* (December 4, 1981).

Nevertheless New York Air is not impervious to competitive threats made by other airlines. "Rather than sit on the sidelines and watch New York Air invade their turf, the larger airlines have taken countermeasures," according to Bruce Cunningham, vice-president of planning at New York Air.[15] United Airlines, for example, has stopped writing tickets for New York Air and has dropped seat availability information from its Apollo reservation system, which is used by 3,700 travel agents. "It's not in our interests to be selling New York Air," states a United executive.[16] New York Air's vulnerability to the tactics of bigger airlines is a key concern for this fledgling venture. Cunningham stated that "it is a small thing for the major carriers to lose a little market share to us, while it is a veritable amputation when we lose our market share to them." He continued, "In Detroit, American Airlines matched dollar for dollar the fares of New York Air and even offered amenities that low-cost carriers couldn't offer."[17]

Established airlines have other ways of disrupting operations as well. Recently one new small airline was denied the use of basic airport equipment (even at a fee) that the dominant carrier at that terminal made available to all other airplanes using the airport.

Deregulation

The airline industry has undergone a major metamorphosis since October 1978, when Congress authorized the deregulation of the industry by enacting the Airline Deregulation Act.* This legislation ushered in dramatic changes in airline industry. Deregulation has given airlines almost total freedom to determine ticket prices and has made it possible for airlines to change fares at a day's notice. Now the carriers can raise fares by 30 percent or decrease them by 100 percent from the standard levels. Prior to deregulation rules established by the CAB required airlines to file proposed fare changes with the CAB thirty days in advance. The CAB placed a ceiling on fare increases of 5 percent and decreases to 50 percent from a "standard industry fare level" established for each route. In addition airlines have almost unlimited freedom to fly new routes.

The deregulated airline environment has brought about unrestrained competition and unprecedented opportunities for growth. Deregulation opened the skies to new entrants, unfettered by costly union contracts for their personnel or lease payments on terminal facilities. New airline fares reflect a classic example of a radical departure from traditional pricing strategy. Before deregulation pricing was determined by cost, but under deregulation pricing is based on competition. As John R. Zeeman, senior vice-president of marketing at United Airlines, has stated: "Pricing has gone from being a nonfactor to being one of the keys to an airline's success."[18] With the absence of regulations, airlines began to discount fares fiercely on popular routes to sell thousands of empty seats and compete with new low-cost carriers. For example, in the three quarters of 1981, about 65 percent of air flights were on discount fares as compared

[15]Personal interview with Bruce Cunningham, vice-president of planning at New York Air.

[16]"Are the Giants Unfair to Upstarts?" *Business Week* (July 13, 1981): 23–24.

[17]Interview with Cunningham.

*The deregulation act provides that the CAB's authority over fares will terminate on January 1, 1983.

[18]Curley, "Decontrol of Airlines."

with 45 percent in the same period of 1978. Moreover these discounts were at an average of 45 percent off full fare in contrast to the 35 percent average discount in 1978. Operating costs, such as rising fuel, labor, and other costs, still influence fares, however. The average price of a ticket has risen by 71 percent to $106 since 1978, while the consumer price index has increased only about 43 percent.[19]

Another striking effect of airline deregulation has been the unparalleled increase in the overall efficiency of the industry. Efficiencies were achieved through a host of methods. These included adding passenger seats to existing aircraft, route changes, and pricing experiments. Other cost savings were realized. According to Alfred Kahn, former chairman of the CAB, "Deregulation has exerted strong downward pressure on inflated wages; forced pilots to give up their 45-hour-per-month flying times and their demand for three pilots in cockpits designed for two; offered the flying public a much greater variety of price quality options; aligned fares on various routes more closely to the costs of serving them and, in many cases, given the public real bargains."[20] In effect the competitive forces unleashed by deregulation compelled airlines to capitalize on the opportunities born of deregulation.

THE AIR TRAFFIC CONTROLLER'S STRIKE

One of the most significant events interfering with New York Air's operations has been the strike by air traffic controllers. Slightly over 13,000 of the nation's 17,000 civilian air traffic controllers walked off their jobs on August 3, 1981 in a demand for improved benefits.*

New York Air was hard hit by this strike. Since existing and planned operations were concentrated predominantly at some of the twenty-two major airports most affected by the strike, New York Air has been compelled to alter routes significantly. The FAA denied New York Air some takeoff and landing rights (called slots) at airports where inadequate controller personnel forced a reduction in the number of planes that could land or take off. New York Air dropped service between New York and Boston and is presently using the planes to fly from Boston to Baltimore to Orlando and back. Moreover, to cope with the strike, New York Air also has instituted a 15 percent pay cut for management and has cut back its free on-board food and beverage service.

The strike had a major impact on New York Air's financial status. The airline, which was nearing break even before the strike, lost $4.9 million in the third quarter of 1981 on revenues of $18.3 million. In contrast New York Air had a net loss of $800,000 in the second quarter, half its net loss of $1.6 million in the first quarter. Operating loss was $900,000, revenues were $15.7 million, and expenses were $16.6 million, while the load factor† was 66.1 percent. A load factor of 70 percent was needed for break even. Financial information is provided in Exhibits 9–12.

[19]Ibid.

[20]Alfred Kahn, "Airline Deregulation: The Benefits of Marketplace Discipline," *Providence Journal* (March 11, 1982).

*President Reagan responded to this strike by firing the majority of the controllers who struck.

†Load factor is the percentage of available seats in the plane that are filled.

Exhibit 9 New York Airlines, Inc.'s condensed balance sheet

Assets	September 30, 1981 (Unaudited)	December 31, 1980
Current Assets		
Cash and cash items	$ 1,054,734	$ 8,763,862
Accounts and notes receivable	5,529,903	428,589
Inventories	675,697	464,193
Prepayments and other current assets	77,257	89,209
Total Current Assets	7,337,591	9,745,853
Property and Equipment, at Cost		
Flight equipment	20,756,509	1,429,987
Ground property and equipment	3,840,011	409,282
Less: Accumulated depreciation	(860,581)	(1,152)
Total Property and Equipment	23,735,939	1,838,117
Flight equipment under capitalized leases	21,889,425	—
Less: Accumulated depreciation	(182,888)	—
Total Property and Equipment Under Capital Leases—Net	21,706,537	—
Investments and Other Assets		
Restricted investments	1,671,806	—
Deferred preoperating costs—net	4,860,730	2,569,416
Other assets	759,185	304,623
Total Investments and Other Assets	7,291,721	2,874,039
Total Assets	$60,071,788	$14,458,009

Liabilities and Stockholders' Equity	September 30, 1981 (Unaudited)	December 31, 1980
Current Liabilities		
Current obligations under capital leases	$1,824,999	$ —
Payable to associated companies	1,456,801	1,561,231
Accounts payable	5,891,116	2,147,404
Other current liabilities	2,410,372	568,211
Advance ticket sales	1,148,418	83,865
Total Current Liabilities	12,731,706	4,360,711
Long-Term Debt	9,000,000	—
Other Noncurrent Liabilities	66,965	—
Obligations Under Capital Leases, Net of Current Portion	20,075,001	—
Stockholders' Equity		
Nonredeemable preferred stock—series A, $.01 par; 5,000,000 shares authorized; 2,500,000 shares outstanding stated at liquidating value	5,000,000	5,000,000
Common stock, $0.01 par; 10,000,000 shares authorized; shares issued 1981 —7,497,750 shares; 1980—5,737,750 shares	74,978	57,378
Additional paid-in capital, less notes receivable for common stock purchases of $314,460 and $602,880, respectively	20,590,158	5,246,268
Retained earnings (deficit)	(7,463,045)	(206,348)
Less: treasury stock, common, 2,650 shares—at cost	(3,975)	—
Total Stockholders' Equity	18,198,116	10,097,298
Total Liabilities and Stockholders' Equity	$60,071,788	$14,458,009

Exhibit 10 New York Airlines, Inc. condensed statement of changes in financial position for the nine months ended September 30, 1981 (unaudited)

Sources of Funds	
Net loss	$ (7,256,697)
Add: depreciation and amortization	1,671,503
Total from Operations	(5,585,194)
Net proceeds from sale of common stock	15,180,570
Proceeds from long-term debt	9,000,000
Payment of notes receivable related to common stock purchases	288,420
Increase in long-term obligations under capital lease	20,335,710
Total Sources	39,219,506
Applications of Funds	
Capital expenditures—Flight equipment	19,326,522
—Ground equipment	3,430,729
Noncurrent lease obligations transferred to current	260,709
Increase in preoperating and development costs	2,920,500
Increase in flight equipment under capital lease agreement	21,932,205
Restricted investments related to capital lease agreement	1,671,806
Dividends paid on preferred stock	107,500
Other, net	348,792
Total Applications	49,998,763
Decrease in Working Capital	$(10,779,257)
Changes in Components of Working Capital	
Cash and cash items	$ (7,709,128)
Notes receivable	34,000
Accounts receivable	5,067,314
Inventories	211,504
Prepayments and other assets	(11,952)
Total Current Assets	(2,408,262)
Current obligations under capital leases	1,824,999
Payable to associated companies	(104,430)
Accounts payable	3,743,712
Other current liabilities	1,842,161
Advance ticket sales	1,064,553
Total Current Liabilities	8,370,995
Decrease in Working Capital	$(10,779,257)

Exhibit 11 New York Airlines, Inc. condensed statement of operations (unaudited)

	Three Months Ended September 30, 1981	Nine Months Ended September 30, 1981
Operating Revenues		
Passenger	$18,239,234	$40,867,146
Other revenues	101,056	228,132
Total Operating Revenues	18,340,290	41,095,278
Expenses		
Flying Operations — Fuel	6,310,998	13,493,393
— Aircraft rental	1,964,135	4,957,623
— Other	706,802	1,463,587
Maintenance	1,328,829	3,536,220
Passenger service	1,278,481	2,673,796
Aircraft servicing	3,683,393	7,229,049
Traffic handling	1,069,543	2,321,775
Reservations and sales	2,751,719	5,576,521
Advertising and publicity	924,564	1,644,152
General and administrative	1,304,576	3,135,733
Depreciation and amortization	886,962	1,671,503
Transport related expense	0	4,395
Total Operating Expenses	22,210,002	47,707,747
Operating Gain (Loss)	(3,869,712)	(6,612,469)
Other Income (Expense)		
Interest income	252,880	1,009,689
Interest expense	(1,237,965)	(1,986,252)
Interest capitalized	0	332,843
Other income (expense)	520	(508)
Total Other Income (Expense)	(984,565)	(644,228)
Net Gain (Loss)	(4,854,277)	(7,256,697)
Less: preferred dividend requirements	(112,500)	(337,500)
Loss applicable to common shares	(4,966,777)	(7,594,197)
Loss per common share based on a weighted average number of common shares outstanding of 7,495,268 and 7,129,156, respectively	$(.66)	$(1.06)
Cash dividends declared per common share	$——	$——

Exhibit 12 New York Airlines, Inc. statement of stockholders' equity for the nine months ended September 30, 1981 (unaudited)

	Preferred Stock Series A		Common Stock		Additional Paid-in Capital	Retained Earnings (Deficit)	Common Stock in Treasury	
	Shares	Amount	Shares	Amount			Shares	Amount
Balance—December 31, 1980	2,500,000	$5,000,000	5,737,750	$57,378	$ 5,246,268	$ (206,348)	—	—
Common stock sold by means of a public offering			1,760,000	17,600	15,162,970			
Payments related to notes receivable for common stock purchases					288,420			
Preferred dividend declared					(107,500)			
Net loss for the period						(7,256,697)		
Purchase of treasury stock							(2,650)	$(3,975)
Balance—September 30, 1981	2,500,000	$5,000,000	7,497,750	$74,978	$20,590,158	$(7,463,045)	(2,650)	$(3,975)

Exhibit 13   Trend in domestic trunk industry traffic growth revenue passenger-miles, percent change versus prior year

	1980 vs. 1979	1981 vs. 1980		1980 vs. 1979	1981 vs. 1980
January	(0.5)%	(5.1)%	August	(11.3)%	(10.4)%
February	(1.3)	(11.5)	September	(13.6)	(2.0)
March	(7.2)	(13.7)	October	(10.1)	
April	(1.9)	(5.4)	November	(15.1)	
May	(4.5)	3.8	December	(5.3)	
June	(2.3)	(6.6)	Year	(6.9)	
July	(9.4)	(3.4)			

Parentheses indicate a decrease.

The effects of the strike have not been isolated to only New York Air. Peoples Express and prospective new airlines such as Columbia Air, Pacific Express, and Air Chicago have been negatively affected. The strike has also hurt older, established airlines, but diagnosing the effects on them is more difficult since these airlines have been facing more fundamental, long-term problems. These problems include an industry-wide recession causing a decline in passenger traffic and pricing and labor disputes stemming from the Airline Deregulation Act of 1978. For the major carriers, passenger traffic was down 5.6 percent in October 1981 and declined more than 8 percent in the first ten months of 1981.[21] On the whole it appears that the new, innovative airlines have suffered the most from the strike. According to one airline official.[22]

> What PATCO* is doing to carriers depends upon who you are where you are. . . . The airlines that need flexibility are in pain and those that need less flexibility are in less pain. The new airlines that have made their investment and are depending on a growth curve . . . and old airlines planning to restructure are in pain.

Some airline officials of the big carriers indicate privately that forced cutbacks at some airports have been a blessing in disguise. The rationale for this belief is that even with declining traffic caused by poor economic conditions (the trend in the domestic trunk industry is presented in Exhibit 13), major carriers would still not reduce the number of flights for competitive reasons. Therefore they would have wasted money by having flights with excess capacity. As a result personnel layoffs and grounding of some planes forced by the strike actually benefitted these airlines by lowering operating costs.

[21]Carole Shifrin, "Controllers' Strike Stacks Up Airlines," *Providence Sunday Journal* (December 13, 1981): J–7.
[22]Ibid.
*Professional Air Traffic Controllers Organization.

Many analysts had predicted that deep discounting would fade away if only because of government restrictions on capacity as a result of the strike. With fewer seats available, there would be less of a need for discounts, according to these analysts. In fact, discounting did not decline for the seven months after declaration of the strike.

Facilities, Services, and Employees

As a new carrier operating in a deregulated environment, New York Air has taken advantage of some money-saving practices. For example, certain services essential to the operations of New York Air are performed by independent contractors, including other airlines. Among these services are aircraft maintenance, baggage handling and ramp operations, and computer handling of reservation information. For example, ticket counters, check-in facilities (which are staffed by New York Air personnel), and access to gate positions and baggage areas at LaGuardia Airport are furnished to the company by Pan American World Airways under a short-term sublease. Ramp service, general baggage, and ground handling at LaGuardia are provided by United Airlines. At National Airport in Washington and Logan Airport in Boston, New York Air has arrangements with Northwest Airlines and Braniff Airways to supply ticket counter and check-in facilities, which are staffed by New York Air personnel. Moreover, these airlines also provide access to gate positions and baggage-handling makeup areas, and furnish ramp services and general baggage ground handling. So far counter and ticketing space, as well as gate and other facilities at LaGuardia, National, and Logan Airports, have been adequate to meet New York Air's immediate needs. This space is provided on a short-term basis by other airlines.

These service arrangements, which are common in the airline industry, have reduced New York Air's need for investment. However, the company is more dependent on others. Although the big carriers maintain that they provide all services to dependent airlines in good faith, the upstarts in the industry do not all agree with this claim. Full-service airlines can exercise their clout by tough bargaining on service contracts and withholding of airport cooperation of they wish to thwart new competition.

Because New York Air is a new company, it has not seen increases in employee wages and benefits that normally occur with increased seniority of employees. Another advantage of its labor force is that employees are not represented by labor unions. As a result the absence of union contracts allows the airline to cross-utilize employees for jobs other than those for which they were hired. Captains at New York Air are paid about $30,000 to start, well below the $75,000 that many Eastern pilots make. The salaries have upset the Airline Pilots Association, which has attacked New York Air in the courts, so far unsuccessfully. According to Cunningham, "With the general economic slowdown in the economy, hundreds of pilots are on furlough in the industry. One just has to mention a need for a pilot and many will appear."[23]

---

[23]Interview with Cunningham.

According to company sources:[24]

New York Air considers the motivation of its employees and their involvement in its business important corporate goals and it believes that high employee productivity is necessary to enable it to compete effectively on the basis of low fares. Accordingly, New York Air has sought to instill in its employees a sense of participation in the business of the company, is training them to perform a variety of work assignments and awarded a stock bonus to all nonofficer employees prior to the commencement of the company's operations.

Equipment

New York Air currently owns two and leases five DC-9 Series 30 aircraft and has arrangements to lease four additional planes of this type. The DC-9 series 30 is a twin-engine, two-pilot aircraft with a 120-passenger capacity, specifically designed for short-to-medium haul routes. On October 20, 1981, the company purchased three DC-9-30 aircraft, two of which it had already been operating under lease agreements, thereby increasing its fleet to twelve DC-9-30s. The company is also exploring the possibility of acquiring larger, more fuel-efficient aircraft such as the DC-9 Series 80 aircraft manufactured by McDonnell Douglas Corporation and the 757 aircraft manufactured by the Boeing Company. These twin-engine planes are operated by two pilots and are expected to produce significantly lower per-seat operating costs than the current aircraft used by New York Air. However, because of the significantly greater costs of these new aircraft, total ownership costs are likely to be substantially higher and the amount of financing required would be significantly greater than the financing for the DC-9 Series 30 aircraft.

NEW YORK AIR'S FUTURE

Despite New York Air's challenge to Eastern, officials at New York Air realize that Eastern will probably remain the dominant airline, given that the Air Shuttle has overcome previous challenges from other carriers such as American and Delta. These carriers expected to steal Air Shuttle regulars by offering gourmet snacks and drinks. They failed when they were unable to match Eastern's promise to guarantee all passengers a seat. Marketing Vice-President O'Donnell admits that, "Our objective isn't to knock Eastern out of the market. We want to see that market grow. We want to attract the person who would otherwise stay home, take a car, or use the train."[25]

At a recent meeting of New York executives, corporate officials expressed concern about the airline's future prospects. "There's no question that we'll mature," said one

[24]New York Air Common Stock Prospectus, February 20, 1981.
[25]Fiedler, "Eastern Patrons Tempted."

official, "but I don't think our costs will ever catch all the way up to those older carriers." He added: "Our biggest worry is that somebody new may sneak up on us with lower operating costs, more fuel-efficient aircraft, or greater financial resources than we have. We've got to defend our market share." Another executive shared the concern that, "We offer a service much like our competitors—the problem is how to make our product seem superior to the competitors'. What should we do?" One official summarized the problem as follows: "Look, if we don't keep our fares lower than our rivals, I just don't see a rosy future. The routes we are serving are among the busiest in the nation. If Eastern or any of our competitors makes big cuts in fares, we may have no choice but to follow suit. Can you imagine the adverse impact on our operating profits?"

CASE 13

Jefferson Enterprises: Small Business Conglomerate Style

ROBERT L. ANDERSON
College of Charleston

B. G. BIZZELL
Stephen F. Austin State University

Following World War Two, Charles Jefferson, a resident of Columbia, South Carolina, decided that he no longer wanted to work for someone else; therefore, he took his savings and money that he was able to borrow from friends and relatives and began a lumber business. Through hard work and astute management, Charles was able to develop a successful small business however, he decided that his business would never be large enough to compete with the really big lumber yards in Columbia, so in 1950 Charles began searching for a potentially more profitable business which would satisfy his desire to earn more money.

In 1952, Charles Jefferson sold his lumber business and bought a company that sold heating oil to residences and small commercial establishments. Again, Charles was

Source: The research and written case information were presented at a Case Research Symposium and were evaluated by the Case Research Association's Editorial Board. This case was prepared as a basis for class discussion.

able to increase the size and profitability of his oil business, and in the late 1950s he decided to invest his excess profits in other ventures. Over the next ten years or so, Charles bought a gas station near his oil company, a small grocery store in the same neighborhood, and several pieces of real estate, also in the same vicinity. The real estate that Charles purchased was both rental property, generally in good condition, and raw land.

Over the years Charles continued to invest in real estate and successfully operate his various businesses; however, his personal life was not so successful. Charles had a wife and eight children, but he also had a mistress with whom he spent considerable time. The affair was as discreet as affairs can be, but the relationship was made public upon Charles's death in 1975.

CONSEQUENCES OF CHARLES JEFFERSON'S DEATH

When Charles died, the mourning period in the Jefferson household was not excessive, but the reading of the will shocked the family and close relatives. Charles had bequeathed all his businesses and real estate, with the exception of his residence, to his mistress rather than to his wife or children. The legal problems created by this bequest were substantial and took many months and thousands of dollars to rectify.

The state of South Carolina has Dower Rights which require all property to be jointly owned by both husband and wife. All the property that Charles owned was also partially owned by his wife, so his mistress could not have clear title to any of it upon his death, but likewise neither could his wife. The attorneys for both parties met, conferred, offered, counter offered, and threatened lengthy court battles before settlement was finally achieved. At the end of negotiations, Mrs. Jefferson and her children agreed to purchase Charles's mistress's share of the properties and businesses at fair market value as determined by both attorneys and a professional real estate appraiser.

CREATION OF JEFFERSON ENTERPRISES

After the settlement of the will, Mrs. Jefferson and her children began the complicated and expensive process of repurchasing Mr. Jefferson's property and business. Decision making was difficult because three members of the Jefferson family who lived out of state had to be consulted on even trivial matters. The major decisions to be made pertained to the allocation of the property and business to family members and the location of funding sources to pay for the businesses and real estate. It was also necessary to keep the businesses operational while the financial matters were being settled.

Incorporation

During the two years following Charles Jefferson's death, things were not going well for the Jefferson family. With the exception of Mrs. Jefferson, no other family members were able to become involved in the day-to-day operations of the various businesses because of other commitments and responsibilities. The Jefferson offspring were either employed in other businesses and institutions or not interested in the "family" businesses. There was also disagreement about how much of the assets each family member was entitled to purchase or control. Therefore, in 1978 the family agreed to create a corporation.

The new corporation, Jefferson Enterprises, Inc., was established to purchase and operate the late Charles Jefferson's businesses and properties. The initial offering of one thousand shares of stock was evenly divided among the five Jefferson children who lived in South Carolina (the three children living out of state chose not to be part of the corporation). The articles of incorporation were standard, and each of the five children was made an officer in the corporation. The president of the corporation, David Jefferson, had other commitments, so the treasurer, Alice Jefferson, assumed the day-to-day responsibilities of the corporation. She was in fact the president or chief executive officer of Jefferson Enterprises, Inc.

The New CEO

Although not officially elected president of Jefferson Enterprises, Inc., Alice Jefferson became the principal, and often only, person involved with the daily operations of the company. For Alice, Jefferson Enterprises was an additional job, since she was employed full time as a high school math teacher (see Exhibit 1 for additional biographical information). Alice worked from 8 A.M. to 4 P.M. for the Columbia School District and from 5 P.M. to 11 P.M. for Jefferson Enterprises, Inc.

Corporate Operating Units

Between the time of incorporation and March 1983, Jefferson Enterprises, Inc., acquired all the assets owned by Charles Jefferson at the time of his death; however, not all of the property was owned by the corporation. Some of the Jefferson family members individually owned some pieces of real estate which they leased back to the company. The major assets and businesses of Jefferson Enterprises, Inc., include the following:

1. **National Oil Company.** This business, consisting of two fuel oil trucks and two twelve-thousand-gallon storage tanks, is the mainstay of the corporation.

2. **Rental Properties.** The corporation owns nine properties (see Exhibit 2) which are managed by the Block Company for an annual fee of $2,256.

3. **Nursing Home.** This non-operating nursing home was not owned by Charles Jefferson; however, it was bought by the corporation because it was located in the same area as the other properties. Alice Jefferson maintained that she acquired the nursing home because the price was $80,000 and the appraised value was $120,000.

Exhibit 1   Resume of Alice Jefferson

Name	Alice Jefferson
Address	1003 Maple Road
Phone	(803) 776-8261
Personal	Born: September 23, 1944 Single, no children U.S. citizen
Education	S.C. State College Orangeburg, South Carolina B.S. Mathematics 1967 M.E. Education 1977
	Completed SBA Seminar, 1978
	Licensed Insurance Agent for American Bankers Life, American Foundation Insurance Company, and First Commonwealth Insurance Company
	Practical experience from working in company when owned by father until present
Employment and business experience	1967–present. Teacher in the Columbia School System 1967–1971 and 1975–present. National Oil Company (part time)
	Duties include purchase orders, billings, bookkeeping, making payments to accounts payable, checking drivers' daily sales and receipts, using meter readings and metered tickets, inventory records, preparing monthly statements and sales report, and preparing suppliers' report.

Exhibit 2   Rental income per month

1145 Dunn Street	$ 200
1004 Maple Road	250
938 Maple Road	246
936 Maple Road	
Apt. A	197
Apt. B	197
Apt. C	197
Apt. D	197
932 Maple Road	250
1150 3rd. Ave.	150
Total	$1884

4. **Undeveloped Properties.** The corporation acquired several pieces of undeveloped property in the north and east sections of the city which had belonged to Charles Jefferson.

5. **B and F Gameroom.** This was the old gas station owned by Charles. It had been converted into a gameroom with two pool tables and three electronic games. Beer, but no liquor, is sold in the gameroom.

6. **Better Grocery Store.** This store is owned by Mrs. Jefferson and not the corporation, but when needed, profits from this business are used to cover other corporate losses.

JEFFERSON ENTERPRISES SINCE INCORPORATION

Although Alice Jefferson had devoted most of her "free" time to the corporation, it is evident that she has not operated it very profitably in the last few years (see Exhibits 3 and 4). Nevertheless, Alice is convinced that Jefferson Enterprises, Inc., could be

Exhibit 3   Income statements, 1980–1982

	1980	*1981*	*1982*
Revenue	$154,104	$146,062	$ 53,062
Cost of goods sold	96,923	93,480	17,510
Gross profit	$ 57,181	$ 52,582	$ 35,552
Expenses:			
Salaries	16,035	14,216	0
Payroll expenses	1,588	1,422	0
Maintenance and repairs	1,348	1,526	843
Advertising	377	270	47
Insurance	2,600	2,952	3,076
Utilities and telephone	9,173	8,913	8,624
Licenses and fees	327	593	306
Accounting and legal fees	2,845	1,659	1,872
Property tax	2,327	2,481	2,563
Depreciation	5,882	7,457	7,526
Interest	16,885	17,932	17,721
Casual labor	250	0	1,826
Rental expense	1,972	2,121	2,256
Other taxes	1,221	1,362	643
Freight and postage	360	220	46
Miscellaneous	180	342	150
Total expenses	$ 63,370	$ 63,466	$ 47,499
Net profit (loss)	$ (6,189)	$(10,884)	$(11,947)

Exhibit 4 Balance sheets, 1980–1982

	1980	1981	1982
Assets			
Cash in bank	$ 3,071	$ 2,460	$ 633
Accounts receivable	2,671	3,060	27
Inventories	9,745	7,394	1,233
Equipment	18,973	19,854	19,854
Improvements	4,689	0	6,231
Buildings	152,983	152,983	152,983
Land	8,500	8,500	8,500
Less reserve for depreciation	(14,572)	(22,024)	(27,136)
Total Assets	$186,060	$172,227	$162,325
Liabilities			
Notes to stockholders	15,189	15,189	15,189
Taxes payable	581	343	36
Notes payable	15,709	24,394	23,682
Mortgage payable	125,000	124,830	124,632
Other loans (personal)	0	5,600	0
Sales tax payable	636	301	267
Total Liabilities	$157,115	$170,657	$163,806
Net Worth			
Stock issued	1,000	1,000	1,000
Contributed capital	29,001	16,001	17,316
Retained earnings (deficit)	(1,056)	(15,431)	(19,797)
Total Liabilities and Net Worth	$186,060	$172,227	$162,325

turned around if she could count on other family members for active participation in the business. She is so sure that the company could be successful that she is considering leaving the school system and devoting all her time to Jefferson Enterprises.

Developments and Problems

A number of problems have arisen which were not anticipated, but could ruin Jefferson Enterprises, Inc., if not corrected. Alice has initiated action to try to solve the corporation's problems; however, she admits that she has not developed strategies to deal with all the problems. Some of the problems identified by Alice include the following:

1. **National Oil Company.** After incorporation, the oil company was badly neglected primarily because there was no one to manage it on a full-time basis. One of Alice's brothers was supposed to be responsible for the operations of the oil company; how-

ever, he lacked the management and financial skills to operate it successfully. Consequently, long-time customers began buying from other companies and suppliers became reluctant to make fuel oil deliveries to National Oil. When suppliers did sell to National, they did so on a strictly cash basis.

In December of 1981 National Oil ceased operations. The shut down was supposed to be temporary, but operations have still not been resumed. To make matters worse for the oil company, the bank holding the mortgage on National Oil's two trucks has threatened to repossess them if the missed payments are not made up immediately.

2. **Rental Properties.** The rental property owned by Jefferson Enterprises is part of the government's low-income rental property program. While this means that the government pays most of the rent for each occupied unit, it also means that the houses and apartments must meet certain size and structural requirements. To bring all the properties up to government standards, Alice hired a local contractor to make whatever repairs or modifications were necessary. The contractor overcharged Jefferson Enterprises, did not do some of the work he claimed to have completed, and used inferior materials wherever possible. Alice Jefferson has initiated legal proceedings against the contractor.

   Besides stipulating physical standards for the rental housing, the government also determines acceptable rents. Therefore, rents can be increased only when approved by a government representative; likewise, the amount of increase is also subject to governmental approval. Some of Jefferson Enterprises' properties are not commanding the rents they should, based on other properties in the neighborhood.

3. **B and F Gameroom.** Since its opening, the gameroom has not been properly serviced by Acme Games, the company which supplies the pool tables and electronic games. The installed games are not the ones currently popular with young people. For example, on several occasions customers have asked Alice to get Pac Man, Ms. Pac Man, or Donkey Kong, but she has been unable to convince Acme to install these games. Alice knows that many of her potential customers go to other nearby convenience stores in order to play the games unavailable at B and F Gameroom. Alice is looking for another game supplier.

4. **Vandalism and Drug Abuse.** Most of the properties and businesses owned by Jefferson Enterprises are located in a relatively high-crime area. When rental units are unoccupied for any length of time they are either damaged by vandals or used by drug users. The nursing home owned by the corporation has been especially hard hit. In addition to breaking windows in the building, vandals have stripped the building of anything valuable. The plumbing fixtures have been stolen, most of the panelling has disappeared, and even the copper pipes have been removed. It will be very expensive to rehabilitate the building and make it operational again.

Turnaround Strategies

Alice Jefferson has initiated or is contemplating a number of strategies which will possibly make Jefferson Enterprises, Inc., profitable again. She knows that not all of her actions will be successful, and she is painfully aware that time is not on her side. The following are some of Alice's possible strategies:

1. **Secure Bank Financing.** Jefferson Enterprises, Inc., will apply for a $25,000 Small Business Administration guaranteed loan to make National Oil operational. Alice is not sure whether the corporation will receive the money, and if it does, it may not be in time. All the supporting documentation (see Exhibits 5 through 9) has been submitted to the bank and Alice is awaiting its decision. Unfortunately, Jefferson Enterprises is caught in a "Catch 22" situation with the bank. The bank wants guaranteed customer contracts to make the loan more viable, but customers will not commit to National Oil until they are sure that the company will be operational in time to satisfy their needs.

2. **Apply for Minority Certification.** Alice has submitted a letter to the proper state authorities requesting that Jefferson Enterprises, Inc., be certified as a bona fide minority business. This certification will encourage more businesses, particularly those that are dependent on state and federal contracts, to become customers of National Oil Company.

Exhibit 5   Summary of loan application

Applicant	Jefferson Enterprises, Inc. 1003 Maple Road Columbia, South Carolina (803) 776-8261
Business	National Oil Company 1001 Maple Road Columbia, South Carolina (803) 771-7671
Type of business	Retail/wholesale fuel distributor
Size of business	Annual sales approximately $91,000
Use of funds	Lease/buy equipment and inventory
Ownership	Jefferson Enterprises, Inc.
Availability of funds from net worth outside of business	Alice Jefferson will contribute $8,000 from her retirement fund. She will maintain $1,500 for personal emergencies.

Exhibit 6   Loan request

Amount	$22,540 cash/line of credit
Terms	Four years with no prepayment penalties. First payment due four months after date of note.
Interest rate	Current rate (prime) and a reasonable risk factor.
Debt/equity ratio	$22,540/$8,000 = 2.82:1
Collateral	Trucks, inventory, and stock.
Other conditions	1. Borrower will assign life insurance in the amount of the loan and will keep it in force during the term of the loan.
	2. Borrower will provide annual financial statements to lender.
	3. $1,500 emergency fund will be maintained for short-term cash flow needs.
Purpose	The loan together with other funds will enable Jefferson Enterprises, Inc., to buy inventory, lease to buy existing trucks and equipment, make repairs to trucks and equipment, and provide working capital.

Exhibit 7   Use and source of funds

	Source of Funds		
Use of Funds	*Loan*	*Equity*	*Total*
Buy inventory	$15,836	$ 0	$15,836
Equipment	2,000	0	2,000
Business license	50	0	50
Start-up costs*	4,654	0	4,654
Working capital	0	8,000	8,000

* Repairs to trucks: 1 windshield, check brakes and tires. Repairs to equipment: repair inventory meters, add hose to diesel supply line.

3. **Rehabilitate the Nursing Home.** Alice has begun the long process of repairing the nursing home so that it will meet state specifications and can once again be used for its designed purpose.

4. **Locate a New Source for Electronic Games.** Replacing Acme Games may be difficult because it is the only company that rents both pool tables and games. Alice

Exhibit 8 Financial statement for Alice Jefferson as of October 15, 1982

Assets	
Cash on hand and in bank	$ 750
Partial interest in real estate	20,000
Automobile and personal property	10,000
Retirement fund	9,307
Interest in Jefferson Enterprises, Inc.	40,000
Total assets	$80,057
Liabilities	
Federal Credit Union	$ 5,000
Mastercard	2,000
Lowes	375
Total Liabilities	$ 7,375
Net Worth	$72,682
Total Liabilities and Net Worth	$80,057

will attempt to improve relations with the company in order to secure the needed games.

5. **Reduce Vandalism and Drug Abuse.** Alice has contacted the solicitor's office requesting additional police patrols in her neighborhood to reduce drug use and vandalism. Her requests have met with some success, as evidenced by the fact that police are more visible and Jefferson Enterprises' properties are not being damaged as frequently as in the past.

6. **Involve the Family in the Corporation.** For Alice, involving the other family members in the operations of Jefferson Enterprises, Inc., may be the most crucial and most difficult task she has to accomplish. It is obvious that Alice cannot run the corporation by herself, even if she were to do it on a full time basis; however, to date she has had no success involving other family members in the management of Jefferson Enterprises, Inc. Alice thinks that one of her brothers will manage National Oil Company if she can make it operational again, but she still needs more assistance from the rest of the family if Jefferson Enterprises is to become successful again.

Alice feels that she has been realistic in the identification of Jefferson Enterprises's problems, and she thinks that some or all of her possible solutions will enable the corporation to once again be profitable. Alice's difficulty now is selecting the order in which to implement her alternatives, and having some of the other corporate officers (her family members) assist her in the decision-making process.

Exhibit 9   Business plan

Name and address of business	National Oil Company 1001 Maple Road Columbia, South Carolina (803) 771-7671
History of business	National Oil Company was established in 1952 by Charles Jefferson. He successfully operated the business for more than twenty years. At one time, Mr. Jefferson had five trucks in operation. In 1978, three years after Mr. Jefferson's death, Jefferson Enterprises, Inc., was formed to operate the oil company. Due to waning interest and other responsibility, all family members except Alice Jefferson withdrew from active management of the oil company. Miss Jefferson was unable to operate the business on a part-time basis, and in 1982 the oil company was shut down because of a lack of customers and local suppliers.
Plan of operation with full-time management	Miss Jefferson, having worked in the business since a teenager, believes that with her full-time management this business, which is well known and respected in the community, can grow and prosper again. Miss Jefferson plans to resign from her teaching position. She is seeking minority business certification, and has compiled a list of potential business and residential customers.
Cost reduction	Miss Jefferson plans to competitively price her products in order to appeal to a large number of customers. Strict inventory controls will be initiated. Geographic area served will be divided into separate territories for each truck. Bulk deliveries will be made by suppliers or contracted haulers.
Market potential	The growth potential is substantial. Miss Jefferson will compete to service communities within her trade area that are not receiving full service from her competitors. In addition, there will be expansion of business contracts to include trucking firms, independent truckers, and users of diesel fuel such as construction companies.

CASE 14

Wall Drug Store, 1983

JAMES D. TAYLOR
ROBERT L. JOHNSON
PHILIP C. FISHER
University of South Dakota

The Wall Drug Store is a complex of retail shops located on the main street of Wall, South Dakota, population 770, owned and managed by the Hustead family of Wall. It includes a drug store, a soda fountain, two jewelry stores, two clothing stores, a restaurant with four dining rooms, a western art gallery, a bookstore, and shops selling rocks and fossils, camping and backpacking equipment, saddles and boots, as well as several souvenir shops. In 1983, a major expansion was underway which would add five more shops and a chapel. "The decision, as when you first wrote the case in 1974,[1] is, are we going ahead with our building program or not? That hasn't changed," announced Bill Hustead as he talked about his plans for Wall Drug. The tourist season was just beginning on June 1. The Spring had been cool and wet, and sales for the year to June 1 were down considerably from the previous year. Bill continued,

> We are still going ahead with the building program. The building program is not necessarily to make more money, but mainly it is to enlarge and enhance the store, so that it makes more of an impression on the traveling public. The church, the art gallery, the apothecary shop—we naturally feel these things will pay their way and make money, but the good part is, when the signs go down, we will have a place that people just won't miss. The place is so crazy, so different—it's the largest drugstore in the world; it may get in the *Guiness Book of Records* as the only drugstore with a church in it. People and writers will have a lot to talk about. We will continue to seek publicity. We will advertise in crazy places, we will have packets for writers and we will try to seek national and international publicity.

WALL DRUG HISTORY

Ted Hustead graduated from the University of Nebraska with a degree in pharmacy in 1929 at the age of 27. In December of 1931, Ted and his wife Dorothy bought the drug store in Wall, South Dakota, for $2,500. Dorothy and Ted and their four-year-old son

Source: This case prepared as the basis of class discussion.

[1]Professors James D. Taylor and Robert L. Johnson are co-authors of "Wall Drug Store," a case written in 1974.

Bill moved into living quarters in the back twenty feet of the store. Business was not good (the first month's receipts were $350) and prospects in Wall did not seem bright. Wall, South Dakota, in 1931, is described in the following selection from a book about the Wall Drug Store.

> Wall, then: a huddle of poor wooden buildings, many unpainted, housing some 300 desperate souls; a 19th century depot and wooden water tank; dirt (or mud) streets; few trees; a stop on the railroad, it wasn't even that on the highway. U.S. 16 and 14 went right on by, as did the tourists speeding between the Badlands and the Black Hills. There was nothing in Wall to stop for.[2]

Neither the drugstore nor the town of Wall prospered until Dorothy Hustead conceived the idea of placing a sign promising free ice water to anyone who would stop at their store. The sign read "Get a soda/Get a beer/Turn next corner/Just as near/To Highway 16 and 14/Free ice water/Wall Drug." Ted put the sign up and cars were turning off the highway to go to the drugstore before he got back. This turning point in the history of Wall Drug took place on a blazing hot Sunday afternoon in the summer of 1936.

The value of the signs was apparent and Ted began putting them up all along the highways leading to Wall. One sign read "Slow down the old hack/Wall Drug Corner/ Just across the railroad track." The attention-catching signs were a boom to the Wall Drug and the town of Wall prospered too. In an article in *Good Housekeeping* in 1951, the Hustead's signs were called "the most ingenious and irresistible system of signs ever derived."[3]

Just after World War II, a friend traveling across Europe for the Red Cross got the idea of putting up Wall Drug signs overseas. The idea caught on and soon South Dakota servicemen who were familiar with the signs back home began to carry small Wall Drug signs all over the world. Many wrote the store requesting signs. One sign appeared in Paris, proclaiming "Wall Drug Store 4,278 miles (6,951 kilometers)." Wall Drug signs have appeared in many places including the North and South Pole areas, the 38th parallel in Korea and on Vietnam jungle trails. The Husteads sent more than 200 signs to servicemen requesting them from Vietnam. These signs led to news stories and publicity which further increased the reputation of the store.

By 1958, there were about 3,000 signs displayed along highways in all 50 states, and two men and a truck were permanently assigned to service signs. Volunteers continue to put up signs. The store gives away 14,000 6 by 8 inch signs and 3,000 8 by 22 inch signs a year to people who request them. On the walls of the dining rooms at Wall Drug are displayed pictures from people who have placed signs in unusual places and photographed them for the Husteads.

[2]Jennings, Dana Close, *Free Ice Water: The Story of Wall Drug* (Aberdeen, South Dakota: North Plains Press, 1969), p. 26.

[3]Ibid., p. 42.

The signs attracted attention and shortly after World War II articles about Ted Hustead and Wall Drug began appearing in newspapers and magazines. In August, 1950, *Redbook Magazine* carried a story which was later condensed in October's *Readers Digest*. Since then, the number of newspapers and magazines carrying feature stories or referring to Wall Drug has increased greatly. In June of 1983, Wall Drug store files contained 543 clippings of stories about the store. The number by 10-year periods was as follows:[4]

1941–1950	19 articles
1951–1960	41
1961–1970	137
1971–1980	260
1981 through April 1983	59

The store and its sales have grown steadily since 1936. From 1931 until 1941 the store was in a rented building on the west side of Wall's Main Street. In 1941, the Husteads bought an old lodge hall in Wasta, S.D. (15 miles west of Wall) and moved it to a lot on the east side of the street in Wall. The building which had been used as a gymnasium in Wasta became the core around which the current store is built.

Tourist travel greatly increased after World War II and the signs brought so many people into Wall Drug that the Husteads claim they were embarrassed because the facilities were not large enough to service them. The store did not even have modern restrooms. Sales during this period grew to $200,000 annually.

In 1951, Bill Hustead, now a pharmacy graduate of South Dakota State University at Brookings, joined his parents in the store.

In 1953, Wall Drug was expanded into a former store room to the south. This became the Western Clothing Room. In 1954, they built an outside store on the south of the Western Clothing Room. This was accompanied by a 30% increase in business. In 1956, a self-service cafe was added on the north side of the store. In the early 1950s, sales were in the $300,000 per year range and by the early 1960s had climbed to $500,000.

In the early 1960s, Ted and his son Bill began seriously thinking of moving Wall Drug to the highway. The original Highway 16 ran by the north side of Wall, about two blocks from the store. It was later moved to run by the south side of Wall, about two blocks also from the drugstore. In the late 1950s and early 1960s, a new highway was built running by the south side of Wall paralleling the other highway. Ted and Bill Hustead were considering building an all-new Wall Drug along with a gasoline filling station alongside the new highway just where the interchange by Wall was located.

They decided to build the gasoline station first, and did so. It is called Wall Auto Livery. When the station was finished, they decided to hold up on the new store and then decided to continue expanding the old store in downtown Wall. This was a for-

---

[4]Twenty-seven clippings were undated.

tunate decision, since soon after that, the new interstate highway replaced the former new highway and the new interchange ran through the site of the proposed new Wall Drug.

In 1963, a new fireproof-construction coffee shop was added. In 1964, a new kitchen, again of fireproof construction, was added just in back of the cafe and main store. In 1964 and 1965, offices and the new pharmacy were opened on the second floor over the kitchen.

In 1968, the back dining room and backyard across the alley were added. This was followed in 1971 with the Art Gallery Dining Room.

By the late 1960s and early 1970s, annual sales volume went to $1,000,000.

In 1971, the Husteads bought the theater that bordered their store on the south. They ran it as a theater through 1972. In early 1973 they began construction of a new addition in the old theater location. This is called the "Mall." By the summer of 1973, the north part of the Mall was open for business. The south side was not ready yet. That year the Wall Drug grossed $1,600,000 which was an increase of about 20% over 1972. Bill believes the increase was due to their new Mall addition.

The development of the Mall represents a distinct change in the development of Wall Drug. All previous development had been financed out of retained earnings or short-term loans. In effect, each addition was paid for as it was built or added.

The Mall

The owners of Wall Drug broke with their previous method of expansion when they built the Mall by borrowing approximately $250,000 for 10 years to finance the Mall and part of 20 large new signs which stand 660 feet from the interstate highway.

During the last half of the 1960s and early 1970s, Bill Hustead had thought about and planned the concept of the Mall. The Mall was designed as a town within a large room. The main strolling mall was designed as a main street with each store or shop designed as a two-story frontier Western building. The Mall is thus like a recreated Western town. Inside the stores various woods are used in building and paneling. Such woods as pine from Custer, South Dakota, American black walnut, gumwood, hackberry, cedar, maple, and oak are among the various woods used. The store fronts are recreations of building fronts found in old photos of Western towns in the 1880s. Many photos, paintings, and prints line the walls. These shops stock products that are more expensive than the souvenir merchandise found in most other parts of the store. The shops are more like Western boutiques.

The northern part of the Mall was open for business shortly after July 10, 1973. In the fall of 1973, Bill was uncertain as to whether or not to open the south side. The Husteads perceived a threat to the tourist business in the 1974 season. They agonized over whether to finish the Mall and order the normal amount of inventory, or to hold up on the Mall and order conservatively. Among the conditions that seemed to threaten tourism were rising gasoline prices, periodic gasoline shortages in parts of the country, and trouble with American Indian Movement (AIM) at Wounded Knee and on the Pine Ridge Reservation. The more long-term threat to the businesses that depend on tourists, especially Wall Drug, was the highway beautification laws of the 1960s that threatened the removal of roadside advertising signs.

Bill finally decided in the winter of 1973 to prepare for a full tourist season, and therefore had the Mall finished and ordered a full inventory for the 1974 season.

The decisions the Husteads confronted in the fall and winter of 1973 marked the first time they had seriously considered any retrenchment in their 27 years of growth.

In May and June, the opening of the 1974 tourist season, there were nine shops in the Mall. Bill estimated in the winter of 1974 that the year would be a record breaker of $2 million. June, July and August sales were up 15 to 20%. September business was up 20 to 30%, October was up 40%, and November was a record setter for that month.

Bill gave the following reasons for the 1974 season:

1. Many other businesses bought light, Wall Drug bought heavy. Therefore, while others ran short, Wall Drug had merchandise towards the end of the summer.

2. Expensive items sold well in spite of the recession scare of the late 1974 period. Bill indicated that articles in Eastern merchandising journals indicated luxury items were doing well all over. Wall Drug had to reorder even into the fall on hot items, such as books, jewelry, and Western clothes.

3. Wall Drug had more goods and space than it ever had before, and each person was buying more.

4. There were more hunters than ever before in the fall. Signs on the highway advertising free donuts and coffee for hunters brought many in and they bought heavy.

5. Although visitations to Mt. Rushmore were down in the summer of 1974, Wall Drug sales were up. Why? Bill speculates that more people from South Dakota and bordering states took shorter trips this year, and thus went to the Black Hills. These people had likely been in the Black Hills before and had seen Mt. Rushmore on their first trip. However, these people like to pay another visit to Wall Drug to eat, see what has been added, and to shop.

In the fall of 1974, Wall Drug invested in more large signs to set 660 feet back from the interstate. By 1976, they had 29 of these signs. These were the only legal type signs that they could put up along the interstate, but by the spring of 1976, the language of the Highway Beautification Act was changed to put these signs outside the law also. Their signs (smaller ones) in neighboring states have been removed.

In 1975 and 1976, expansion continued with the addition of the Emporium, more dining area, and more restrooms at the north end of the store.

In 1978, the location of the Wall post office at the south end of the store beyond the Mall, which had previously been purchased, furnished expansion for the western clothing stores, boots and harness shop.

Currently, in 1983, there is further expansion under construction east of the Mall to the alley. The new area will feature a chapel modeled after a church built by Trappist Monks in Dubuque, Iowa, in 1850. Also featured will be a replica of the original Wall Drug Store, which will be called Hustead's Apothecary and will serve as the Drug Store Museum. The store will sell Caswell-Massey products from the store of that name in New York which is the oldest drugstore in the U.S. Other shops will be a western art gallery, a poster shop and western gift shop, and iron and pottery shop, and Hustead's Family Picture Gallery. The shops will be modeled after famous old western establishments. There will also be a new set of restrooms. In effect, the new addition will be an extension of the Mall.

STORE OPERATION

Wall is a small town of 770 people as of 1980. The economic base of the town is primarily built around the Wall Drug and is dependent on tourist business.

Wall is situated right on the edge of the Badlands and 52 miles east of Rapid City. For miles in either direction, people in autos have been teased and tantalized by Wall Drug Signs. Many have heard of the place through stories in the press, or have heard their parents or friends speak of the Wall Drug. In the summer of 1963, in a traffic count made on the highway going by Wall, 46% were eastbound and 54% were westbound. Of the eastbound traffic, 43% turned off at Wall. Of the westbound traffic, 44% turned off at Wall.

When people arrive at Wall (those westbound usually after driving 40 miles or more through the Badlands), they are greeted by the large Wall Drug sign on the interchange and an 80-foot-high, 50-ton statute of a dinosaur. The business district of Wall is two blocks long and is about three blocks to five blocks from the interchange. The town has eleven motels and a number of gasoline filling stations.

Cars from many states line the street in front of and several blocks on either side of the drugstore. Tabulation of state licenses from autos and campers parked in front of Wall Drug, June 1, 1983, at 12:00 noon are summarized as follows:

South Dakota (not local county)	20%
South Dakota, local county	22%
Balance of states and Canada	58%

Wall Drug is more than a store. It is a place of amusement, family entertainment, a gallery of the West, a gallery of South Dakota history, and a place that reflects the heritage of the West. Nostalgia addicts find Wall Drug particularly interesting. Children delight in the animated life-size cowboys singing, a tableau of an Indian camp, a stuffed bucking horse, a six-foot rabbit, a stuffed buffalo, old slot machines that pay out a souvenir coin for 25¢, statues of cowboys, dancehall girls and other characters of the old West, a coin-operated quick-draw game, and souvenirs by the roomful which make up part of the attractions.

The food is inexpensive and good, and although as many as 10,000 people might stream through on a typical day, the place is air conditioned and comfortable. The dining rooms are decorated with beautiful wood paneling, paintings of Western art are displayed, and Western music plays. One can dine on buffalo burgers, roast beef or steak, 5¢ coffee or select wine, and beer from the rustic, but beautiful, American walnut bar.

About one-fourth of the sales in Wall Drug is food, plus about 5% to 10% for beverages and soda fountain. (This varies with the weather.) About 10% to 15% is jewelry, 15% clothing and hats, 35% to 40% for souvenirs, and 5% to 10% for drugs, drug sundries, and prescriptions.

The store is manned by a crew of 201 people, 76 of whom are college girls and 25 are college boys who work there in the summer. Student help is housed in homes that have been bought and made into dormitory apartments. There is a modern swimming pool for their use, also. The clerks are trained to be courteous, informed, and pleasant.

Orders for the following summer season begin being placed in the preceding fall. Orders begin arriving in December, but most arrive in January, February, March, and April. Many large souvenir companies post-date their invoices until July and August. Each year brings new offerings from souvenir companies and other suppliers. Much of the purchasing is done by Bill, who admits he relies on trusted salespeople of their suppliers who advise him on purchasing. Many of these companies have supplied Wall Drug for 30 years or so. Wall Drug generally buys directly from the producers or importers, including photo supplies and clothing.

Years ago, much of what Wall Drug bought and sold was imported or made in the eastern part of the country. In recent years, much of the merchandise is being made regionally and locally. Indian reservations now have small production firms and individuals who make many handicrafts which are sold through Wall Drug. Examples of such firms are Sioux Pottery, Badlands Pottery, Sioux Moccasin, and Milk Camp Industries.

The Husteads rely a great deal on the department managers for buying assistance. The manager of the jewelry, for instance, will determine on the basis of last year's orders and her experience with customer reaction and demand, how much to order for the next season. All ordering is centered through Bill.

HIGHWAY BEAUTIFICATION AND PROMOTION

In the year 1965, Congress passed the Highway Beautification Act, which was designed to reduce the number of roadside signs. Anticipating the removal of the many Wall Drug advertising signs, Bill Hustead invested in new signs that were allowed under that legislation. These signs were to be placed no closer than 660 feet away from the road. To be read, these signs must be larger than the older signs, and cost close to $9,000 each. Now even these large signs are included in the laws for regulation or removal.

There has been slow compliance with this legislation by many states, including South Dakota, since many states in less populated areas have many tourist attractions, and find road signs the only practical way to advertise these attractions. Since the administration of President Reagan has been in office, there has been little enforcement of the sign legislation since there has been less money available for federal enforcement. There is new legislation being proposed by the Federal Highway Administration of the Department of Transportation as of 1983 that could have an impact on Wall Drug and other tourist dependent establishments.

Bill and Ted also decided that they must gain as much visibility and notoriety as possible, and to help achieve this, they began using advertising in unusual places. In the 1960s, Wall Drug began taking small ads in unlikely media such as the *International Herald Tribune,* and *The Village Voice,* in New York City's Greenwich Village, advertising 5¢ coffee and 49¢ breakfast as well as animal health remedies. This brought telephone calls and some letters of inquiry. It also brought an article in the *Voice* and probably attracted the attention of other media. On January 31, 1971 (Sunday), *The New York Times* carried an article about Wall Drug. This article may have led to Bill Hustead's appearance on Garry Moore's television program, "To Tell the Truth." In the year 1979, there were 75 articles in newspapers and magazines about Wall Drug. In the August 31, 1981, edition of *Time,* a full page article in the American Scene featured the store and the Husteads. Also, in 1981, Wall Drug was featured on NBC television's "Today Show" and Atlanta Cable "Winners."

For a while, the Wall Drug was advertised in the London city buses and subways, Paris Metro (subway) in the English language, and on the dock in Amsterdam where people board sight-seeing canal boats.

FINANCES

Exhibits 1 and 2 present summary income statements and balance sheets from 1973 through 1982. The Wall Auto Livery was consolidated into Wall Drug Store, Inc., in May 1975. Had this transition occurred prior to 1973, sales for 1973, 1974, and 1975 would have been about $192,000, $248,000, and $52,000 larger; and net profit would have been about $19,000 larger in 1973, and $21,000 larger in 1974, with a negligible effect in 1975. The value of the acquired net assets was about $180,000.

The company's growth and expansion has been financed primarily by retained earnings, temporarily supplemented at times with short-term borrowings. A major exception was a $250,000, ten-year installment loan in 1973, used to help finance the mall and some large signs located 660 feet from the highway. In 1975, this loan was prepaid through 1980. At the end of 1982, only $34,500 remained to be paid on this loan. Other long-term debt at the end of 1982 includes installment contracts for the purchase of real estate and a stock redemption agreement (occurring in 1979) for the purchase by the company of some Class B, non-voting stock. As indicated on the December 31, 1982 balance sheet, current maturities of long-term debt were $43,436. Of this amount, $34,496 is the final payment on the 1973 loan due in 1983.

Both the growth and the volatility of the business should be apparent from the income statements presented in Exhibit 1. Exhibit 3 presents the income statements as

Exhibit 1 Income statements (in 000's)

	1982	1981	1980	1979	1978	1977	1976	1975	1974	1973
Sales	4,733	4,821	3,970	3,552	4,125	3,777	3,464	2,679	1,991	1,607
Cost of sales	2,644	2,676	2,230	2,072	2,228	2,098	1,879	1,484	1,100	806
Gross profit	2,089	2,145	1,740	1,480	1,897	1,679	1,586	1,195	891	801
G + A expense	1,802	1,857	1,473	1,433	1,578	1,453	1,312	1,000	754	691
Income from operations	287	288	267	47	319	226	274	195	137	110
Other income expenses	36	81	43	−8	35	23	2	3	−8	−10
Income before tax	323	369	310	39	354	249	276	198	129	100
Tax	120	144	125	6	148	94	111	80	54	41
Net income	203	224	185	33	206	155	165	118	75	59

Exhibit 2 Balance sheets on December 31 (in 000's)

	1982	1981	1980	1979	1978	1977	1976	1975	1974	1973
Cash and short term invest.	$240	$282	$449	$.11	$82	$65	$51	$93	$145	$74
Inventories	631	547	369	403	338	276	249	248	174	144
Other current assets	60	57	53	99	51	58	50	32	26	26
Total current assets	$931	$886	$871	$513	$471	$399	$350	$373	$345	$244
Property, equipment	2907	2591	2380	2297	2230	1960	1739	1484	1234	1130
Accumulated depreciation	−1355	−1254	−1147	−1030	−906	−790	−674	−576	−496	−428
Other assets	24	25	27	53	55	33	29	31	34	34
Total assets	$2507	$2248	$2131	$1833	$1850	$1602	$1444	$1312	$1117	$980
Current maturities of LTD	$43	$40	$46	$8	$11	$5	$8	$7	$21	$20
Notes payable	0	0	0	68	20	0	0	5	70	20
Accounts payable	56	58	63	47	43	64	36	42	31	23
Accruals + other current liab.	252	244	310	124	232	167	178	193	136	110
Total current liab.	$351	$342	$419	$247	$306	$236	$222	$247	$258	$173
Long-term debt	191	149	179	238	133	130	133	136	222	244
Deferred tax	7	1								
Stockholder's equity	1958	1756	1533	1348	1411	1236	1089	929	637	563
Total liab. + equity	$2507	$2248	$2131	$1833	$1850	$1602	$1444	$1312	$1117	$980

Exhibit 3 Percent of sales statements

	1982	1981	1980	1979	1978	1977	1976	1975	1974	1973
Sales	100.0	100.0	100.0	100.0	100.0	100.0	100.0	100.0	100.0	100.0
Cost of sales	55.9	55.5	56.2	58.3	54.0	55.6	54.2	55.4	55.2	50.2
Gross profit	44.1	44.5	43.8	41.7	46.0	44.4	45.8	44.6	44.8	49.8
G + A expense	38.1	38.5	37.1	40.3	38.3	38.4	37.9	37.3	37.9	43.0
Income from operations	6.0	6.0	6.7	1.3	7.7	6.0	7.9	7.3	6.9	6.8
Other income expenses	.8	1.7	1.1	-.2	.9	.6	.1	.1	-.4	-.6
Income before tax	6.8	7.7	7.8	1.1	8.6	6.6	8.0	7.4	6.5	6.2
Tax	2.5	3.0	3.1	.2	3.6	2.5	3.2	3.0	2.7	2.5
Net income	4.3	4.7	4.7	.9	5.0	4.1	4.8	4.4	3.8	3.7

a percentage of sales. Exhibit 4 is an analysis of the rate of return on equity broken into the component parts using the format:

$$\frac{sales}{assets} \times \frac{gross~profit}{sales} \times \frac{operating~income}{gross~profit} \times \frac{net~income}{operating~income} \times \frac{assets}{equity} = \frac{net~income}{equity}$$

Between 1973 and 1982, prices, as measured by the Consumer Price Index, increased by about 115%. Percentage increases in some balance sheet and income accounts for Wall Drug over this period are:

Sales	163%
Total G. + A. expense	145
Net Income	159
Total assets	115
Equity	169

These percentages are based on combining Wall Auto Livery with Wall Drug in 1973 as if the merger occurring in 1975 has taken place.

Given below are percentage changes in some of the general and administrative expenses from 1976 through 1982:

Total G. + A.	37%
Utilities	137
Officers' salaries	2
Other salaries	42
Depreciation	5
Advertising	116
Profit sharing contribution	49

The items mentioned accounted for 77% of total general and administrative expenses in 1982 and 76% in 1976. These same items as percentages of sales were:

	1982	1976
Utilities	1.7%	1.0%
Officers' salaries	2.9	3.8
Other salaries	18.5	17.7
Depreciation	2.3	2.9
Advertising	2.1	1.3
Profit sharing contributions	2.0	1.8

Depreciation methods on various assets vary from straight line to 200% declining balance, and over lives of from 15 to 40 years for buildings and improvements to 5 to 10 years for equipment, furniture, and fixtures. Although not evaluated or recognized

Exhibit 4 Components of rate of return on equity

	1982	1981	1980	1979	1978	1977	1976	1975	1974	1973
$\dfrac{\text{Gross profit}}{\text{Sales}}$	.441	.445	.438	.417	.460	.444	.458	.446	.448	.498
$\dfrac{\text{Income from operations}}{\text{Gross profit}}$	.137	.134	.153	.032	.168	.135	.163	.163	.154	.137
$\dfrac{\text{Sales}}{\text{Assets}}$	1.89	2.14	1.86	1.94	2.23	2.36	2.40	2.04	1.78	1.64
$\dfrac{\text{Income from operations}}{\text{Assets}}$	.114	.128	.125	.026	.172	.141	.190	.148	.123	.112
$\dfrac{\text{Net income}}{\text{Income from operations}}$	.707	.778	.698	.702	.646	.686	.602	.605	.547	.536
$\dfrac{\text{Assets}}{\text{Equity}}$	1.28	1.28	1.39	1.36	1.31	1.30	1.33	1.41	1.75	1.74
$\dfrac{\text{Net income}}{\text{Equity}}$	.103	.128	.121	.025	.146	.126	.152	.126	.118	.105

on the financial statements, it is likely that some assets, such as the western art and the silver dollar bar, have appreciated.

STORE MANAGEMENT

Recruiting and training the seasonal workforce is a major task at Wall Drug. College students are recruited through college placement services. Training is of short duration but quite intense. Summer employees are tested on their knowledge of store operations and their ability to give information about the area to tourists.

Bill Hustead has commented:

> I really think that there isn't anything more difficult than running a business with 20 to 30 employees in the winter and then moving into a business with 180 to 200 employees, and you have to house a hundred of them and you have to supervise them, and train them. This lasts through June, July, and August; then the next year you start all over. It's kind of exciting and fun for the first 25 years but after 30 years you begin to think it's a tough racket.

The store had a permanent nucleus of 20 to 30 employees. While the business could operate with fewer employees during the winter, the Husteads believed that they needed the experienced employees to give stability to the operations in the summer. Permanent employees with seniority could get as much as six weeks' paid vacation. Commenting on this policy, Bill said:

> We probably go through the winter with more employees than we really need, but we give them time off in the winter because a seasonal business is so demanding. When the Fourth of July comes, you're working, when Memorial Day comes, you're working; when all those summer fun times come, you're working six days a week and it's quite a sacrifice. So, we try to be very generous with our paid vacations.

Dependence on seasonal tourists for the major portion of Wall Drug's business has inherent risks, and uncertainty over the future of the roadside signs, which have brought customers to the store for nearly 50 years, is a grave concern to the Husteads.

> We will try to have ideas to modify our outdoor advertising program to adapt to changes in the law which we are sure will be forthcoming. If they are drastic changes, they could put us out of business. If they nail it down so there isn't a sign on the interstate, that will do the job.

Asked about diversification as a hedge against this risk, Bill replied,

> We will try to diversify within our own community. By that I mean probably on our highway location in and around our Auto Livery. We have several hundred acres there (in sight of the interstate), and a motel and a modified drug store would be our last straw if we were wiped out in town.

The Husteads hoped to be able to create a fund to provide self-insurance for their dormitory houses. This fund would then also provide some measure of security from business risks as well.

Although over 80, Ted Hustead is still active in the management of the store, involved in everything from physical inspections of the premises to acting jointly with Bill in making policy decisions. Ted can frequently be seen on the grounds picking up litter. Dorothy, Ted's wife, comes to the store every day, summer and winter, helps with the banking, and spends from two to six hours each day on various chores. Bill's son Rick, 33, joined the store in 1980 and now shares in the management. Rick has a Master's degree in guidance and counseling and spent four years as a guidance counselor and teacher in high school. Rick also spent two years in the real estate business and one year in the fast food business before returning to Wall. During his school years, Rick spent ten seasons working in Wall Drug. His wife, Kathy, is a pharmacist and also works in the store.

Bill Hustead expressed his continuous concern with the future of Wall Drug in light of future action concerning roadside sign advertising. Can the store expansion continue; should diversification be attempted in the community; should diversification be considered in a way that will not be affected by the tourist? Will Wall Drug be able to continue to gain publicity as they have in the past to keep people aware of their "attraction" characteristics? The costs of doing business are rising, such as the increase in the cost of utilities, which is sizeable. How can they plan for a bad year or two given the increasing uncertainty in the tourist industry? With these thoughts in mind, the 1983 tourist season at Wall Drug was underway.

CASE 15

Wallace Women's College

RUDOLPH E. KOLETIC
University of Tampa

LAWRENCE R. JAUCH
Southern Illinois University—Carbondale

HISTORY

Founded in 1910, Wallace Women's College is a nonsectarian, suburban, private college for women located in a beautiful woodland setting of North Carolina. The nearest city is about five miles to the south with a population of about 500,000.

Note: This is a disguised case. That is, the facts in it are based on a real organization, but the names of the persons involved, the location, and the quantitative data have been changed because the organization under study requested it. It serves no useful purpose to try to determine which organization is the "real" organization.

The college was established primarily through a donation of 55 acres of land and $250,000 in cash from Jennifer Wallace, the widow of a prominent physician and a long-time advocate of women's suffrage and education.

Initially, the college was chartered to provide young women with a baccalaureate education in the liberal arts and sciences. Its basic goals were to foster an understanding and appreciation of the intellectual and cultural heritage of man, to cultivate in its students a love of the beautiful and the good, and to prepare its graduates to live in society with happiness for themselves and helpfulness to others.

In turn, these goals were subdivided into several somewhat more specific objectives:

1. To acquaint all students with the roles of language and of mathematics as a symbol of communication and discourse.

2. To develop in all students a synoptic understanding of the condition and concerns of man as they are presented through literature, history, and philosophy.

3. To offer all students the practical and empirical knowledge of the various disciplines upon which may be built a professional or civic career of service to others.

4. To encourage all students to explore concepts of aesthetic and ethical knowledge to develop for themselves standards of value by which to determine those objectives and those manifestations of behavior which are beautiful, good, and right.

By September 20, 1911, a two-story brick structure had been erected which housed administrative offices, classrooms, and a small library. At that time, the first entering class of 28 women was admitted with a faculty of 5, including the president and dean, both of whom taught on a part-time basis.

In the decades that followed, Wallace Women's College established an enviable reputation for the quality of its academic programs and the impressive careers of many of its alumnae. By the early 1940's the college community numbered 400 students and a full-time faculty of 30.

During the past twenty-five years, the President, Dr. Max Hegel, has provided the necessary leadership which permitted the college to grow and prosper. Although close to retirement age, Dr. Hegel continued to reflect the enthusiasm and interest in his responsibilities that have over the years earned him the respect and admiration of the public and college community.

THE MUSIC SCHOOL

In 1945, as a result of a capital bequest of $250,000 from the family of a retired member of the Philadelphia Symphony Orchestra, the college inaugurated the Pappelis School of Music. The instructional program was initially funded by interested civic leaders, local business, and patrons of the arts.

Although the school of music has always been an expensive area of instruction, Dr. Hegel has justified its continuation on the grounds that the music school has made significant contributions to the general purposes of Wallace Women's College. Its group performances and music recitals, which were always open to the public, have been extremely popular and well attended. In addition, many non-music majors with previous instrumental and vocal training were invited to audition and many were accepted into the school's symphony orchestra and choral group.

THE NURSING SCHOOL

In 1958, in response to a request from two community hospitals in the metropolitan area, the college established the Marianne Martin School of Nursing. During its early years, the nursing program received a major portion of its financial support through several Health, Education and Welfare grants, the last of which had expired in 1970. In much the same fashion as the Pappelis School of Music, the Marianne Martin Nursing School provided a new dimension to the college's curricula and a corresponding increase in student enrollment. The nursing program brought additional respect and recognition to Wallace Women's College through its service to the community. Its community influence was now quite obvious and its future appeared bright and viable.

THE TURNING POINT

During the early sixties the college's long-range plans began to reflect the pressures of an ever increasing enrollment pattern and a strong demand for student housing. In response to these demands, a dormitory was constructed in 1965 to house 500 women. In addition, classrooms and laboratories were expanded to accommodate 1,200 full-time students. This construction project was completed at a cost of $5,000,000 and was easily financed through the sale of long-term construction bonds. The annual rate of debt service for bond interest (3.375%) and principal approximated $285,000 and was projected to be well within the financial resources of the expanding college.

The nearby metropolitan area was not unaware of the nationwide crescendo of demands from high school graduates desiring further collegiate level of study at a modest cost. Plans were adopted for a community college and approved by the State legislature. In 1968, Metro Community College was founded offering several two-year programs of studies leading to an Associate degree in the arts and applied sciences.

During the late sixties and early seventies, the educational industry began to experience the growing pains of expansion programs born of the uncontrolled optimism of the earlier periods. The widespread "campus unrest" of the late sixties led to the introduction of courses which soon lost their appeal. The growing inflationary pressures of the early seventies brought about financial distress for small colleges and large universities alike.

Gradual increases in tuition, room and board fees necessitated by rising costs and lower enrollments were not enough to provide the revenue resources the college required. (See Exhibit 1.) During the past five years, the college has found its expenditures exceeding its revenue sources (Exhibit 2) and has been forced to borrow from the local banking industry to meet its current cash flow requirements, at exceedingly steep interest rates.

Exhibit 1   Student fees data

Year	Tuition	Room and Board
1975–76	1700	1100
1976–77	1800	1150
1977–78	1800	1200
1978–79	1950	1250
1979–80	1950	1300
1980–81	2000	1350
1981–82	2100	1450
1982–83	2200	1450
1983–84*	2350	1500

* Approved by the Board of Trustees, April 15, 1983.

Exhibit 2   Changes in current fund balance

Year	Surplus (Deficit) for the Year	Year-End Fund Balance
Balance 6/30/75		$ 30,000
1975–76	$ 40,000	$ 50,000
1976–77	15,000	75,000
1977–78	5,000	85,000
1978–79	(15,000)	65,000
1979–80	(55,000)	4,000
1980–81	(110,000)	(100,000)
1981–82	(80,000)	(180,000)
1982–83	(45,500)	(225,500)
1983–84*	(65,000)	(285,500)

* Projected.

THE PRESENT CRISIS

Responding to the current fiscal urgency experienced by Wallace Women's College, the Chairman of the Board of Trustees, Mr. Robert Trent, announced a full board meeting to be convened on June 15, 1983 at 2:00 P.M. The agenda for this meeting was as follows:

Academic

1. Grant tenure status to Dr. William Hook, assistant professor of history.

2. Approve Faculty Statutes, Sec. 4, Part 3, ref. Faculty Assembly.

Fiscal

1. Review current fiscal report 1982–83 (Exhibit 3).
2. Approve college operating budget for 7/1/83 to 6/30/84 (Exhibit 3).

On June 15, many of the twenty-five trustees began arriving earlier than usual and informal group discussion quickly turned to the fiscal problems of Wallace and what

Exhibit 3 Statement of current fund revenues, expenditures, and transfers for the year ended June 30, 1983

	1982–83			1983–84 Projected Plan
	Unre-stricted	Re-stricted	Total	
Revenues				
Educational and general:				
Tuition	$1,386,000		$1,386,000	$1,410,000
Gifts and grants	100,000	$70,000	170,000	200,000
Other	72,000	3,000	75,000	75,000
Total educational & general	$1,558,000	$73,000	$1,631,000	$1,685,000
Auxiliary enterprises:				
Residential and dining halls	435,000	—	435,000	450,000
Total revenues	$1,993,000	$73,000	$2,066,000	$2,135,000
Expenditures				
Educational and general:				
Instruction and departmental research	$ 535,000	$ 3,000	$ 538,000	$578,000
Library	72,000	—	72,000	80,000
Student services	100,000	—	100,000	105,000
Maintenance	142,000	—	142,000	140,000
General administration	130,000	—	130,000	125,000
Employee benefits	135,000	—	135,000	147,000
General institutional	100,000	—	100,000	100,000
Student aid	30,000	70,000	100,000	120,000
Debt retirement	120,000	—	120,000	120,000
Total educational & general	$1,364,000	$73,000	$1,437,000	$1,515,000
Auxiliary enterprises:				
Intercollegiate athletics	$ 34,500	—	$ 34,500	$ 35,000
Residence and dining halls	440,000	—	440,000	450,000
Debt retirement—residence halls	200,000	—	200,000	200,000
Total auxiliary enterprises	$ 674,500	—	$ 674,500	$685,000
Total expenditures	$2,038,500	$73,000	$2,111,500	2,200,000
Excess of expenditures over revenues	(45,500)	—	(45,500)	(65,000)

Note: 1982–83 financial operations were projected through June 30, 1983 as at May 31, 1983.

can be done about the rapidly deteriorating conditions. Promptly at 2:00 P.M. Mr. Trent called the meeting to order and extended a warm introductory welcome to several college officers. Among those present were Mr. Bart Basi, Treasurer; Dr. Helen Flack, Academic Dean; and Mrs. Robert Shine, Director of Admissions.

A motion was promptly introduced to defer discussion on the academic portion of the agenda until the fiscal reports had been received and discussed. This motion passed unanimously. The Treasurer, Mr. Basi, was called to review the fiscal state of affairs for 1982–83. Mr. Basi reported that the financial conditions of the college as projected through June 30, 1983 appeared to be more favorable than previously expected. He reminded the trustees that the original operating budget for 1982–83 had reflected a deficit of $95,000; however, due primarily to an unanticipated bequest of $50,000 from the estate of an alumna and some cutbacks in maintenance spending, it is now expected that the deficit for the year will approximate only $45,000.

Discussions concerning the current fiscal year were brief and concluded with a sigh of some relief that although the college will continue in a deficit mode it may not be as large as previously expected. Attention promptly turned to the projected budget plan for the new fiscal year beginning July 1, 1983. Mr. Basi pointed out that total revenues will be slightly higher than in the current period. Although a further decline of 5% in student enrollment is expected (Exhibit 4), higher tuition fees will more than make up the difference (Exhibit 5). Revenues from gifts and grants are also expected to increase . . . this cause for optimism was noted as a result of a new and intensified effort by Dr. Hegel and several local civic leaders to generate additional financial support from the local business community.

Expenditures were projected to increase very little except faculty salaries. An increase in student aid was requested in hopes of stabilizing student enrollment. Mr. Basi concluded his remarks by requesting the approval of the 1983–84 operating budget plan and optimistically assured that with increased student aid, stabilized enrollment can be achieved and that fiscal viability is possible.

Exhibit 4   Student enrollment data

Year	Commuter	Residence	Total
1975–76	400	500	900
1976–77	395	500	895
1977–78	390	490	880
1978–79	375	460	835
1979–80	360	440	800
1980–81	310	400	710
1981–82	310	365	675
1982–83	330	300	630
1983–84*	300	300	600

* Projected.

Exhibit 5 Revenue sources

| | | Room and Board | Gifts | | | |
Year	Tuition		Restrict-ed	Unre-stricted	Other	Total
1975–76	$1,530,000	$550,000	$ 70,000	$ 92,000	$95,000	$2,337,000
1976–77	1,611,000	575,000	65,000	80,000	91,000	2,422,000
1977–78	1,584,000	588,000	64,000	90,000	95,000	2,421,000
1978–79	1,628,250	575,000	66,000	50,000	84,000	2,403,250
1979–80	1,560,000	572,000	50,000	65,000	85,000	2,332,000
1980–81	1,420,000	540,000	49,000	40,000	80,000	2,129,000
1981–82	1,417,500	529,250	57,000	42,000	74,000	2,119,750
1982–83	1,386,000	435,000	70,000	100,000*	75,000	2,066,000
1983–84†	1,410,000	450,000	100,000	100,000	75,000	2,135,000

* Includes alumna bequest.
† Projected.

Mr. Trent opened the meeting to discussion of the report as submitted. "Mr. Chairman, may I have a brief moment to comment?" Mr. Harry Watson, Financial Vice President of Allegheny Packing Company and Vice Chairman of the Board, was recognized.

> Watson: Max, quite frankly I am apprehensive about the fiscal direction the institution is going and I am sure my consternation is shared by many of my colleagues on this Board. My background and experience is not in the academic world. . . . At times I suppose this becomes only too evident. . . . Nevertheless, I make no apologies. However, I *can* read a financial report and understand its meaning. I am a bottom line man. I am interested in responsible fiscal management and control . . . the bottom line is the measure of all these. We have experienced five deficit years and today we are being asked to approve still another. . . . This is not fiscal responsibility. I believe we have a good faculty and good academic programs. Yet our enrollment has dropped off over 30% in the last eight years. It can't be due solely to tuition increases. We've been very careful about raising tuition rates; besides, we're rather at or below every other private college in the State. We have 200 vacant rooms over in that dorm and our commuter students have dropped off 25%.
>
> As I see it, our primary product is instructional services. . . . Is there something wrong with it? Is there something we should be doing that we're not doing? Do we need to continue to support athletics?
>
> Take a look at the two reports we have here, Exhibits 6 and 7. The one on faculty distribution by program and the other on program enrollment. They tell us a great deal!

Exhibit 6 Faculty distribution by program, 1983–84

Faculty	Music	Nursing	Liberal Arts and Science	Total
Full time	4	4	22	30
Part time	10	5	5	20
Full-time equivalent*	8	6	24	38
Tenured	4	4	17	25
Percent tenured	100%	100%	77%	83%

* Percent of full time worked, whether an academic or fiscal year
contract. One way of computing FTE is:

9 months	1/7 = 0.11FTE	7/7 = 0.75FTE
12 months	1/9 = 0.11FTE	9/9 = 1.00FTE

Exhibit 7 Program enrollment

Year	Music	Nursing	Liberal Arts and Science	Total
1975–76	200	125	575	900
1976–77	200	120	575	895
1977–78	170	120	590	880
1978–79	150	100	585	835
1979–80	140	90	570	800
1980–81	130	90	490	710
1981–82	95	60	520	675
1982–83	85	55	490	630
1983–84*	75	50	475	600

* Projected.

Our overall student/faculty ratio is 16 to 1; the music school . . . let's
see . . . is 9 to 1, and the nursing school is 8 to 1. That's a pretty damn
good situation as far as the student getting close supervision of his work.

As far as the faculty goes, we've got 30 full-time faculty members earning,
on the average, $18,000 in salary plus fringe benefits. This national rating
scale I've got here for liberal arts colleges of our size puts us in the 60th
percentile on that score. I don't know how you did it, but you've got a
mighty good compensation package.

The remarks of John Folsum, board member and President of the Acme Container
Corporation, appeared to reflect the consensus of the majority of the Board.

Folsum: Mr. Chairman . . . as I sit here and study this report and listen to Bart (Basi) give his narration of the great white paper, it occurs to me that a number of warning signals continue to make themselves obvious . . . to be heard if you will . . . over and over again alerting each of us that all may not be right with the Wallace operation. Allow me to point out a few. Exhibit 8 shows declining enrollments and a deteriorating quality of the new student.

What does this mean? It must tell us something. . . . Is our tuition out of reach? . . . Are we continuing in the tradition of a women's college in spite of national trends? . . . Are our academic programs losing their appeal? I suppose I could go on and on about this but perhaps Mrs. Shine may wish to comment further on this subject a little later. Gifts and grants are falling off . . . except for this year's unexpected bequest we have no cause to be optimistic. I doubt very seriously that this community is prepared to witness the closing of this school without assisting in some way. I've been convinced for some time and have argued against the continuation of high-cost and low-interest programs and I, of course, got nowhere. How long, in the good name of this school, can we continue to guarantee life-time employment to our teachers when enrollment continues to drop? I believe we have another tenure decision to face later today. We are being forced to borrow just to keep our current ship afloat. . . . How long do we expect the banks to continue to extend this kind of credit?

We have $340,000 of quasi endowment funds. For those of you who may find difficulty with this term . . . Bart tells me it's funds set aside or their use restricted by the Board. Well, that is precisely what we did . . . Max, you recall when we placed these funds aside. . . . I believe it may have been in 1975. These were monies to be used in hopes of supporting some innovative academic programs if they should turn up. We may now be forced to use it just to pay off our accumulated bank loans. All these are

Exhibit 8 Comparative report on student enrollment and average freshmen SAT scores

Year	Enrollment	Average SAT Scores
1975–76	900	1025
1976–77	895	1025
1977–78	880	1020
1978–79	835	1017
1979–80	800	1015
1980–81	710	995
1981–82	675	980
1982–83	630	950
1983–84*	600	937

* Projected.

symptoms which characterize . . . pardon the expression . . . a very sick horse and what worries me is that the race is tomorrow! Maybe we should consider an accounting curriculum and possibly opening enrollment to men.

In response to the visible concerns of the Board, Mr. Hegel attempted to allay their fears and place into proper perspective the health of the institution as he visualized it to be.

> Hegel: The observations and remarks that have been made are well taken and under the circumstances understandable and I would be a fool to suggest that Wallace Women's College was without a problem. However, I believe I would do a great injustice and disservice to the institution if I were to fail to place these reports in their proper perspective and setting. . . . Wallace does have some difficult problems. . . . To deny this would be folly! However, these problems are not dissimilar to those being experienced by colleges and universities throughout the country. . . . Our problems are not unique. . . . Our institution is not immune to inflationary pressures. . . . We are not immune to the effects of changing life styles and academic goals of today's students. . . . We are not immune to the recessionary effects of the economy. . . . We are not immune to the expansion of the public tax-supported institutions that sell their services at a seventy-five percent discount and allow the taxpayer to subsidize the balance. In spite of all these pressures the college, in my judgement, has done reasonably well over the years.
> Wallace exists today because of its strengths, not its weaknesses. . . . Declining enrollment is a major concern to us all. . . . This problem is not necessarily beyond solution. However, I am firmly convinced that the institutional goals and objectives are sound and vibrant. I continue to support our educational philosophy which provides for an intellectual, cultural, and social environment that fulfills the needs and desires of the young woman today. Recent national reports suggest the continued need for institutions such as ours. . . . A recent campus survey of ours reported that 62% of the 405 Wallace students responding to the poll indicated that they are attending this college because of its programs that meet the unique requirements of young women. . . . Providing exclusively for young women *is a strength.*
> Our academic programs are stimulating and appropriate. . . . Under the capable leadership of Dr. Helen Flack our faculty have shown marked improvement in their professional competence. Currently 52% of our faculty have their earned doctorate. . . . This compares to only 25% in 1975–76. To achieve this splendid record, we were forced to grant tenure status to some faculty earlier than we may have otherwise been prepared to do. However, we have no regrets in this matter. The Middle States accreditation report of 1982–83 noted the caliber of faculty and the music program in particular. Although our library holdings are modestly deficient in some selected areas, our students do have the opportunity to use the Public Gen-

eral Library or the Metro Community Library . . . both only a short distance from our campus.

May I conclude by stating that I am strongly convinced that the strengths we have still form a solid foundation upon which we can continue to grow, prosper, and serve the community and its students. Although our fiscal program may need nourishment, our intellectual viability remains strong.

At the conclusion of Dr. Hegel's remarks, the Board unanimously agreed to defer action on the 1983–84 proposed operating budget until July 28, 1983. It was generally agreed that this would allow Dr. Hegel and his executive staff sufficient time in which to make whatever adjustments and modifications to the budget that appear necessary to restore fiscal responsibility to the college. The Board further encouraged the President that he attempt to achieve a "pay-as-you-go" posture for 1983–84; however, if this goal is unrealistic it certainly must be accomplished no later than the 1984–85 fiscal period. The Board also approved a motion to allow the institution to continue its operation during the month of July at current 1982–83 budgetary levels.

CASE 16

Super 8 Motels
E.J. GAINOK
Northern State College, Aberdeen, S.D.

Super 8 Motels, Inc. is a fast-growing chain of budget motels located in thirty-nine states and two Canadian provinces. Super 8 ranked fourth nationally in the economy lodging field, with 14,044 rooms in 227 motels as of October 1984. Key officers of the corporation are Dennis Brown, chairman of the board; Ronald J. Rivett, vice-chairman; Dennis Bale, vice-chairman and chief executive officer; and Loren D. Steele, president. These four individuals comprise the board of directors and sole stockholders of the corporation. Super 8 is headquartered in Aberdeen, South Dakota.

Super 8 Motels likes to think of its operation in terms of "Yesterday, Today, and Tomorrow." This "where have we been, where are we now, and where are we going" attitude is often found in fast-growing organizations. Since Super 8 is a relatively new organization, entrepreneurial spirit continues to be a driving force.

There is a trade publication called *Hotel and Motel Management* that most libraries in the United States carry. This is an excellent source for additional information related to this case. The top 50 economy motel chains are described in the April 1985 issue of this publication.

YESTERDAY

In 1972, attorney Dennis A. Brown and businessman Ronald J. Rivett formed a partnership to bring economy lodging to South Dakota. After two years of planning, the first Super 8 motel opened in Aberdeen in September 1974. It provided travelers a comfortable sleeping accommodation for $8.88. There were no conference rooms, no swimming pool, no restaurant, and only a functional lobby. This first Super 8 motel was built near the local Holiday Inn to attract overflow and cost-conscious travelers. In the mid-70s, bargain hunting and cost consciousness prevailed among both business and recreational travelers. (Super 8's 1984 lodging room price was $21.88 for a single room.)

Economy lodging, as we know it today, dates back to 1962. Prior to that year "Mom- and Pop" motels provided economy lodging with a variety of operations. The lodging industry is currently segmented into economy, midrange, and luxury motels. The first economy motel chain was Motel 6, which originated in California. Midrange motels such as Holiday and Ramada comprise the largest segment of the lodging industry. But they do not provide elaborate facilities, as do the Hyatt, Marriott, and Hilton luxury motels.

The number of economy motel rooms increased from 15,000 to 160,000 during the period 1968–1981. Economy rooms represent about 11 percent of all available lodging, and this share continues to increase annually. The basic concept of budget motels is often expanded to include lounges, restaurants, meeting rooms, pools, saunas, and game rooms. In spite of this, the general public continues to perceive the concept of the budget motel as consisting of guest rooms only. Suppliers of this type of lodging provide comfortable accommodations at a price well below (20–40 percent of) full-service lodging.

TODAY

As indicated in Exhibit 1, there were 257 Super 8 motels at the end of 1984, and another 243 inns planned for completion by 1990. Super 8 lays claim to being the fastest-growing motel chain in the country.

Super 8 is organized to operate its own units as well as assist owners in building and operating franchised motels. More than 90 percent of all Super 8 motels are owned by individual franchisees. The locations of the chain's motels are given in Exhibit 2. To purchase a franchise for a typical sixty-unit motel, an investor needs $90,000; $15,000 for the cost of the franchise and $75,000 for the initial payment for construction and motel furnishing. The chain charges its franchisees 4 percent royalty and 1 percent advertising fees, based on gross room revenue.

Super 8 attributes its rapid growth to several factors, including product, support services, motel developers, and locations. The management has adapted its concept of

Exhibit 1 Super 8 motel growth

Year	New Motels	Total Motels	Income
1974	1	1	(4 Percent of Gross Room Rent) (Company owned)
1975	3	4	(Company owned)
1976	9	13	$ 33,000
1977	20	33	83,000
1978	24	57	267,000
1979	14	71	447,000
1980	17	88	743,000
1981	22	110	1,081,000
1982	29	139	1,560,000
1983	48	187	2,220,000
1984	70	257	3,280,000 (estimated
1985–1990 (estimated)	243	500	$10,000,000 (estimated)

Exhibit 2 The locations of Super 8 motels

Alabama	1	Montana	14
Alaska	4	Nebraska	20
Arizona	6	Nevada	3
Arkansas	5	New Mexico	9
California	18	New York	10
Colorado	19	North Carolina	2
Connecticut	3	North Dakota	14
Florida	4	Ohio	3
Georgia	4	Oklahoma	3
Idaho	2	Oregon	1
Indiana	2	South Carolina	1
Iowa	15	South Dakota	24
Kansas	13	Tennessee	3
Kentucky	3	Texas	7
Louisiana	2	Utah	5
Maine	1	Virginia	2
Massachusetts	1	Washington	7
Michigan	6	Wisconsin	13
Minnesota	24	Wyoming	17
Missouri	17	Canada	2

Note: 67 of these were due to open soon after March 1, 1985. States with no Super 8 motels include Mississippi, West Virginia, Pennsylvania, Maryland, New Jersey, Rhode Island, Vermont, New Hampshire, and Hawaii.

economy lodging to particular markets. For example, the architectural differences required in South Florida and South Dakota were noted, and buildings (product) were then designed to meet the needs of the community while incorporating the standard ingredients in the Super 8 formula. Each room must meet the minimum size, have carpeting, bath/shower combinations, free color TV, direct dial telephones, blackout drapes, and approved furnishings. Super 8 provides support services that include a nationwide toll-free reservation system, marketing services, management training, a V.I.P. Club for guests, graphic arts support, and quality review through inspection of each motel every ninety days.

Super 8 Motels are developed primarily by existing franchisees (70 percent in 1984). Management likes to think that this reflects well on services provided by the franchisor. When considering locations, Super 8 has a product for virtually any community. Motels currently in the chain range in size from 30 to 192 rooms with the average being 65 rooms. This flexibility enables Super 8 to build in both rural communities and metropolitan locations. It also enables investors with limited funding to become motel owners.

Since Super 8 directs most of its marketing effort toward the frequent traveler, it attempts to assure that there will be no surprises. It is developing a guest profile, and identifying opportunities and threats that alert management to new wants and needs of guests. The goal is to assume that the customer receives what he or she expects—accommodations similar to those provided at the last Super 8 Motel where he or she was a guest.

Today there are fifteen economy motel chains with approximately 200,000 rooms. To coordinate activities more effectively, Super 8 recently constructed a national headquarters building in Aberdeen, staffed to develop two company-owned properties a month, to support independent franchise groups, and to help individual developers. As shown in Figure 1, the Super 8 corporation is organized functionally into four support groups: Associated Contractors Incorporated, which builds units; Hospitality Technology Incorporated, which markets telephone equipment to other businesses as well as motels; Midwest Motel Supply, which provides furniture, equipment, carpeting, and all types of supplies to Super 8 Motels; and Super 8 Management Incorporated, which provides management services to twenty-six motels, including the two company-owned units located in Aberdeen.

The headquarters facility also houses the Super 8 Superline Computerized Reservation System for all fifty states and Canada, and ties into a telex system for the Minotel chain for Americans traveling in Europe and for Europeans traveling in the U.S.A. Super 8's franchisees are advised that a 20 to 49 room unit will average 62 percent of expenses per rented room, a 50 to 79 unit motel will average 71 percent and 80 unit motels and over will average 67 percent. This figures out to costs of $11.79, $13.52, and $14.43 per room respectively for an average room price of $21.88 in 1984.

Aberdeen is a city of approximately 25,500 people serving northeast South Dakota's agricultural area in the north plains. Although the city is served by one major airline and two commuter lines, with transportation to Minneapolis, Fargo, and Den-

Figure 1 Super 8 Motels, Inc.

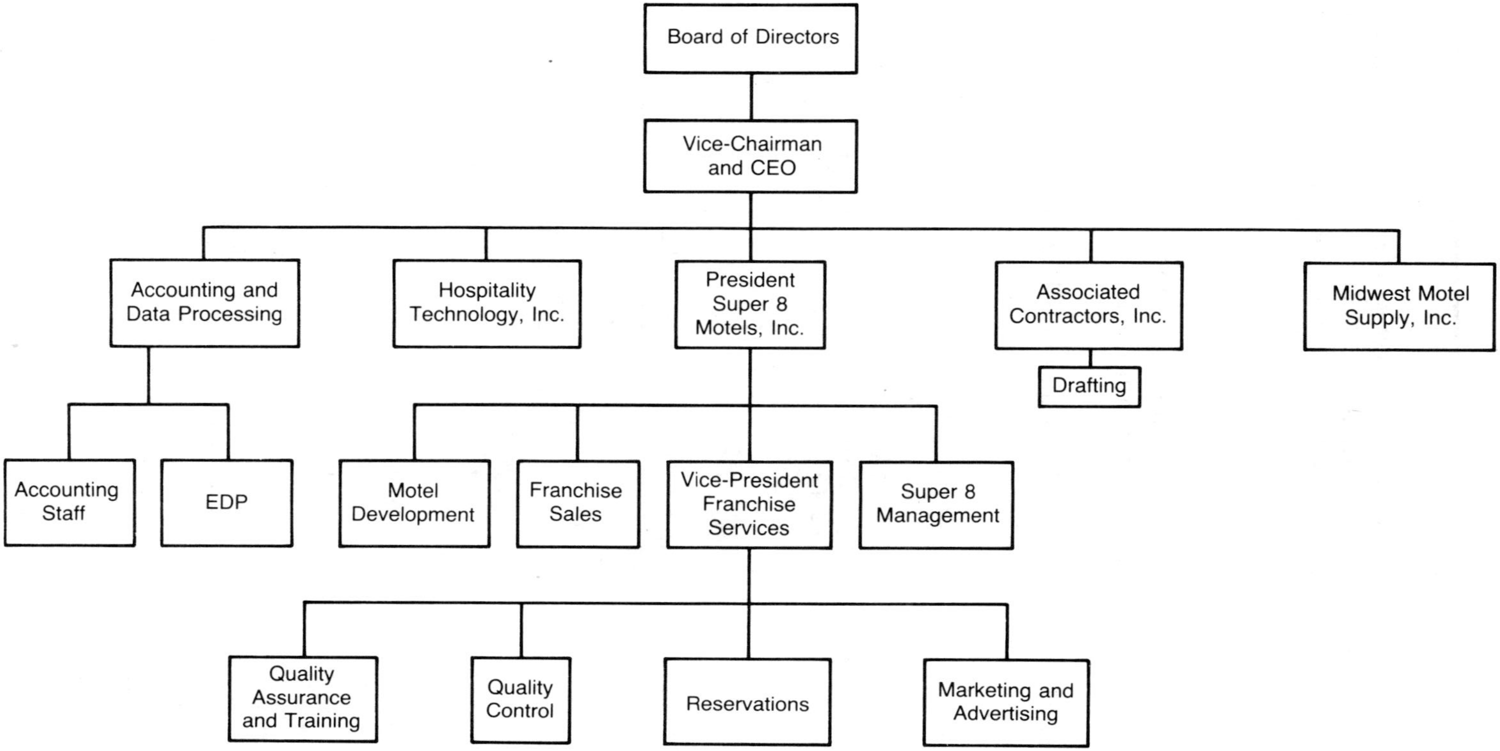

ver, this service does not meet Super 8's needs. Therefore, Super 8 recently expanded its aviation department to include three full-time pilots and three aircraft, which include a nine-passenger jet. Early in 1985, Super 8 purchased a small aviation company and now provides charter service to the public.

FINANCIAL CONDITIONS

Super 8's consolidated balance sheets for 1981, 1982, and 1983 are provided in Exhibit 3. Exhibit 4 gives consolidated statements of income for these years and 1984.

Exhibit 3 Super 8, Inc., and subsidiaries consolidated balance sheet (summarized)

| | Assets | | |
	1983	1982	1981
Current assets	$ 2,838,726	$1,518,456	$349,031
Investments	172,765	28,344	26,844
Property and equipment	13,024,838	1,435,302	224,297
Notes receivable	309,284	—	—
Cost in excess of			
purchased subsidiaries	1,451,590	—	—
Other assets	96,759	87,081	46,727
Total assets	$17,893,962	$3,069,183	$646,899

| | Liabilities and Equity | | |
	1983	1982	1981
Current liabilities	$ 3,812,048	$ 312,113	$244,782
Long-term debt	10,796,942	2,157,383	114,054
Deposits	85,000	58,000	22,500
*Equity			
Preferred stock	2,497,249	—	—
Common stock	1,000	1,000	1,000
Excess over par	25,108	25,108	25,108
Retained earnings	676,615	515,579	239,455
	$ 3,199,972	$ 541,687	$646,899
	$17,893,962	$3,069,183	$646,899

*Preferred stock—5,000,000 authorized
              2,497,249 issued and outstanding
Common stock—100,000,000 authorized
              100,000 issued and outstanding
              $.01 par value

Exhibit 4   Super 8 Motels, Inc., and subsidiaries consolidated statements of income, years ended December 31, 1984, 1983, 1982, and 1981

	1984	1983	1982	1981
Revenues				
Franchise fees:				
Initial	$1,191,000	$ 765,000	$ 319,000	$ 247,000
Recurring	2,979,617	2,034,465	1,560,674	1,081,251
Lodging	5,039,146	1,869,910		
Furnishings and supplies	4,856,465	1,514,665		
Telephone equipment	725,956	559,034		
Accounting fees	133,177	134,186	9,384	21,763
Rental income	146,790	112,079	54,846	65,961
Management fees	169,123	25,945		
Other income	554,674	226,699	32,276	85,354
Construction	8,438,835			
	24,234,783	7,241,983	1,976,180	1,501,329
Costs and expenses				
Administrative & general	4,067,375	2,915,742	1,510,999	•
Motel operations	2,635,576	944,634		
Furnishings and supplies	4,644,820	1,416,013	50,031	
Telephone equipment	625,038	562,110	37,496	
Interest	1,984,933	721,995	40,570	
Depreciation	1,149,235	513,944	83,960	
Amortization	71,675	31,131		
Construction	8,109,244			
	23,287,895	7,105,569	1,723,056	1,439,499
Income before income taxes	946,888	136,414	253,124	60,630
Income tax credits				
Current	40,400		(20,600)	11,400
Deferred	313,600	(24,622)	(2,400)	2,600
Provision in lieu of taxes	84,500			
	438,500	(24,622)	(23,000)	14,000
Income before extraordinary item	508,388			
Extraordinary item:				
Tax benefit from utilization				
of loss carryforward	84,500			
Net income	$592,888	$ 161,036	$ 276,124	$ 46,630

•Accounting system changed in 1982

TOMORROW

There is no doubt that Super 8 growth has been good. Since January 1976, one new Super 8 Motel has been opened every sixteen days, and projections are for new motels to open every six days in the future. Sustaining or increasing this level of operation is a monumental management task in terms of planning, organizing, staffing, motivating, and controlling. Management must coordinate activities involving three separate and distinct types of motel operations: (1) franchisees with only one small unit, (2) franchisees with two or more units, or authority over a state or region, and (3) corporation-owned units. Maintaining control as the organization grows is a primary concern of Super 8's management.

The corporate long-range plan is designed to make Super 8 the first national budget chain in all of the fifty states, with 500 motels by 1990. Super 8 plans to open new motels in small and medium-sized communities, as well as some in metropolitan areas.

COMPETITION

Motel 6, founded in 1963, was the first economy lodging chain. In 1963, a room at a Motel 6 cost just $6 a night. The room had a shower stall but no bath tub or TV. By 1984, more than 60 economy lodging chains were operating, with more than 2,400 properties and 250,000 rooms nationwide. The economy lodging segment has today segmented into three tiers:

The Upper Tier

This segment offers rooms at 20–25 percent less than the market-area average rate. Example chains are Dillon Inns, Drury Inns, Hampton Inns, La Quinta Motor Inns, Lexington Hotel Suites, Signature Inns, Skylight Inns, and Texan Inns.

The Middle Tier

This segment offers rooms at 30–40 percent less than the market-area average rate. Example chains are Red Roof Inns, Exel Inns, Thrifty Scot Motels, *Super 8 Motels*, Budgetel Inns, Comfort Inns, Econo Lodges, Knight's Inns, and Shoney's Inns.

The Lower Tier

This segment offers rooms at 50 percent below the market average. Motel 6 is the dominant chain in the lower tier. Motel 6 offers nationwide, year-round rates at all locations.

The top ten economy lodging chains in the United States are described in Exhibit 5.

Exhibit 5　The top ten economy lodging chains in the United States at the beginning of 1985

Chain Name	Ownership Structure	Number of Inns	Number of Rooms	Geographic Concentration
Day's Inn	Company owned/franchised	291	45,410	Eastern and Western United States
Motel 6	Company owned	394	43,881	Throughout United States
La Quinta Motor Inns	Company owned/franchised	157	19,545	Throughout United States
Econo Lodges	Franchised	233	17,561	Throughout United States
Super 8 Motels	Company owned/franchised	234	14,967	Throughout United States, Canada
Hospitality International (Master Host, Red Carpet, Scottish Inns)	Franchised	161	13,265	Eastern United States
Red Roof Inns	Company owned	123	13,161	Eastern United States
Comfort Inns (A division of Quality Inns)	Franchised	130	11,599	Throughout United States, Canada
Knights Inn	Company owned	60	6,594	Eastern United States
Affordable Inns (Regal 8)	Company owned/franchised	50	5,604	Eastern and Western United States

ISSUES, CONCERNS, AND STRATEGIES

As Super 8 enters the 1985–1990 era, a number of issues and concerns face the corporation's top management. It is important that Super 8 have a clear understanding of its internal strengths and weaknesses and its external opportunities and threats to effectively establish strategies, objectives, goals, and policies for the future. Some of the most important issues and concerns facing Super 8 are listed below:

1. Should Super 8 utilize equity financing, liability financing, or a combination of both to continue expansion? Is the objective of building 500 motels by 1990 viable? Can and should Super 8 continue to add a new motel every 6 days? (There were 216 hotel/motel failures in 1983 and 70 bankruptcies in the Summer of 1984). EPS-EBIT analysis could be performed to gain further insight into this question.

2. How many motels should the corporation own? What would be the best mix of corporate-owned and franchised units? Is Super 8's policy to have 10 percent of the motels company-owned a good one? How should Super 8 assist franchisees in financing? Using various scenarios, what are the profit contributions of franchise versus company-owned units?

3. What kind of organizational structure is needed to deal with Super 8's dispersed motels and the mix of corporate managers and franchisees? As the organization continues to grow, would a divisional structure by geographic area be more effective than the functional structure now being used? How would you redesign Super 8's structure to be more effective?

4. How can Super 8 maintain quality lodging at economy rates? Travelers staying at one Super 8 Motel expect the same accommodations at the next Super 8 Motel. How can Super 8 best minimize franchisees wishing to "milk" their business without realistic reinvestment, maintenance, and refurbishing?

5. Are Super 8 development objectives too optimistic? Will economy motel competition grow, remain stable, or decline? Will luxury and mid-range-priced motel chains see profitability in economy lodgings and attempt to move into this competitive arena?

6. Do Super 8's financial statements indicate a profitable future? Is the $15,000 initial franchise fee realistic? What about the 4 percent royalty and 1 percent advertising fees?

7. Super 8 Motels are normally located at sites near other motels and restaurants. Is this preferable to building restaurants at existing Super 8 Motels? Are choice sites at high prices worth the investment?

8. Should Super 8 Motels offer swimming pools, saunas, and other amenities found in mid-range and luxury motels/hotels? Should Super 8 offer gasoline at its motels? Could the firm do these things *and* continue rapid market development?

9. How important are controls for Super 8, Inc? What form should controls take in terms of inspections, reports, audits, and accounting procedures?

10. Should Super 8's headquarters be relocated somewhere besides Aberdeen, South Dakota? If so, where? Aberdeen presents travel complications, although these have been somewhat minimized due to the acquisition of three aircraft with assigned pilots.

11. Who are Super 8's key competitors and what are their strategies? How is Super 8 positioned in the ecomony lodging industry, in terms of price, location, convenience, service, and accommodations?

The Classic Car Club of America— 1984

MATTHEW C. SONFIELD
Hofstra University

THE "COLLECTOR CAR" HOBBY

The "collector car" hobby in the United States is a broad and wide-reaching activity involving a large number of Americans. Basically, a "collector car" is any automobile owned for purposes other than normal transportation. The most widely read collector car magazine, *Hemmings Motor News,* had a circulation of over 210,000 in March 1984, and its circulation has been steadily growing for many years. Thus, a figure of 250,000–300,000 would probably be a conservative estimate of the number of Americans engaged in this hobby.

"Collector car" is a loose term, ranging from turn-of-the-century "horseless carriages" to currently built but limited-production cars, such as Italian super sports cars and American convertibles. Naturally, owners of collector cars enjoy the company of other persons with similar interests, and thus a wide variety of car clubs exist, to suit almost any particular segment of this vast hobby. The largest of these clubs, the Antique Automobile Club of America, caters to owners of virtually all cars twenty-five years old or older, and in 1984 was close to achieving a membership level of 50,000.

HISTORY AND BACKGROUND

The Classic Car Club of America, Inc. (CCCA) was formed in 1952 by a small group of enthusiasts interested in luxury cars of the late 1920s and 1930s, and headquartered in Madison, New Jersey. A listing of certain high-priced, high-quality, and limited-production cars were designated as "Classic Cars," and the period 1925–1942 was chosen as the "Classic Era." The rationale was that cars built prior to 1925 had not yet reached technical maturity, and after World War II the quality of most so-called luxury cars had succumbed to the economic pressures of mass production.

Over the years, the list of CCCA-recognized Classics was modified and expanded, and the time period was extended to 1948 to include certain pre-WWII models that

There is an excellent trade publication entitled *Automobile News* that regularly contains articles relevant to this case.

continued in production for a few years after the war. While all cars included on the list were of considerably higher price and quality than mass-production cars of the era, there was also a wide variance in original price and quality of these recognized Classics. For example, a new 1930 Ford Model A (not a Classic) cost about $450. Two of the many CCCA-recognized Classics of that year were the Auburn Eight, priced as low as $1195, and the Duesenberg Model J, which sold in the $12,000–$14,000 range.

The Auburn, although a car of middle price and quality, is considered a Classic because its styling was exceptional at the time. The Duesenberg was the highest priced and most exotic American car of the era, carrying custom-built bodies and bought by an exclusive clientele of movie stars, playboys, and other super-rich personalities. Most Classics fell somewhere between these two extremes, with original prices in the $2000–5000 range. Exhibit 1 lists those cars recognized as Classics by the CCCA in 1984.

CCCA ACTIVITIES

When the CCCA's fiscal year ended on October 31, 1983, the club had 4,560 members, as indicated below:

Active (regular membership—1983 dues $25/yr)	3796
Associate (for spouses, no publications—$3/yr)	578
Life (one-time charge of $350, after 10 years)	142
Life Associate (spouse of Life—$35)	37
Honorary (famous car designers, etc.)	7
	4,560

CCCA members receive a variety of benefits from their membership. A magazine, *The Classic Car*, is published four times a year. High in quality, it features full-color photos of Classics on the front and back covers, and forty-eight pages of articles and black-and-white photos of Classics and CCCA activities within. A CCCA *Bulletin* is published eight times per year. The *Bulletin* contains club and hobby news, technical columns, and members' and commercial ads for Classic Cars, parts, and related items. Another publication is the club's *Handbook and Directory*, published annually. It contains the CCCA by-laws and judging rules, as well as a listing of current members and the Classic Cars they own.

The CCCA sponsors three national events each year. First, an Annual Meeting is held in January in a different location nationally each year. Second, a series of "Grand Classic" judging meets are held in July at a number of locations around the country. In 1983, 365 Classics were judged or exhibited at six different Grand Classics from coast to coast. At CCCA judging meets, cars are rated by a point system which takes into

Exhibit 1   CCCA recognized classic cars

A.C.	Farman*	Moon*
Adler*	Fiat*	Nash*
Alfa Romeo	Franklin*	Packard*
Alvis*	Frazer-Nash*	Peerless*
Amilcar*	Graham-Paige*	Peugeot*
Armstrong-Siddeley*	Hispano-Suiza	Pierce-Arrow
Aston Martin*	Horch	Railton*
Austro-Daimler	Hotchkiss*	Raymond Mays*
Auburn*	Hudson*	Renault*
Ballot*	Humber*	Reo*
Bentley	Invicta	Revere
Benz*	Isotta-Fraschini	Riley*
Blackhawk	Itala	Roamer*
B.M.W.*	Jaguar*	Rohr
Brewster*	Jensen*	Rolls-Royce
Brough Superior*	Jordan*	Ruxton
Bucciali	Julian*	Squire
Buick 90	Kissell*	S.S. Jaguar
Bugatti	Lanchester*	Stearns-Knight
Cadillac*	Lancia*	Stevens-Duryea
Chrysler*	Lagonda*	Steyr*
Cord	La Salle*	Studebaker*
Cunningham	Lincoln*	Stutz
Dagmar*	Lincoln Continental	Sunbeam*
Daimler*	Locomobile*	Talbot*
Darracq*	Marmon*	Talbot-Lago
Delage*	Maserati*	Tatra*
Delaunay Belleville*	Maybach	Triumph*
Delahaye*	McFarlan	Vauxhall*
Doble	Mercedes	Voisin
Dorris	Mercedes-Benz*	Wills Ste Claire*
Duesenberg	Mercer	Willys-Knight
du Pont	M.G.*	
Excelsior*	Minerva*	

*Indicates that only certain models of this make are considered Classic and/or post-WW II models require individual approval from the club for Classic status.

account the authenticity of restoration and the general condition of the car, both cosmetically and mechanically.

Third, the club sponsors one or more "Classic CARavans" each summer in various parts of the U.S.A. and Canada. The CARavan is a tour in which more than 100 Classics join together in a week-long planned itinerary.

Figure 1 Classic Car Club of America—organization chart

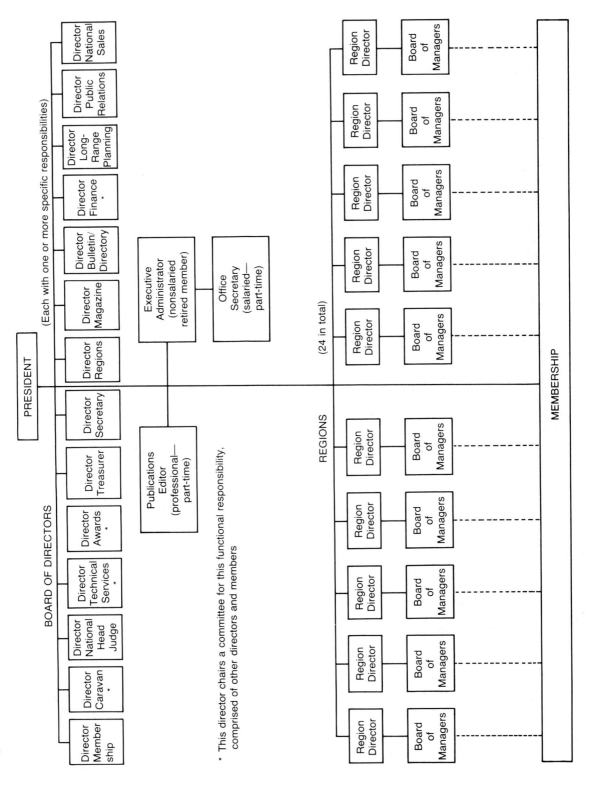

PRESIDENT

BOARD OF DIRECTORS

(Each with one or more specific responsibilities)

Director Member ship

Director Caravan *

Director National Head Judge

Director Technical Services *

Director Awards *

Director Treasurer

Director Secretary

Director Regions

Director Magazine

Director Bulletin/ Directory

Director Finance *

Director Long-Range Planning

Director Public Relations

Director National Sales

Publications Editor (professional—part-time)

Executive Administrator (nonsalaried retired member)

Office Secretary (salaried—part-time)

REGIONS (24 in total)

Region Director — Board of Managers

MEMBERSHIP

* This director chairs a committee for this functional responsibility, comprised of other directors and members

The CCCA has technical advisors available to assist members. The club makes available for sale to members certain club-related products, such as hats and ties with a Classic Car design.

CCCA ORGANIZATION

The club is managed by a fifteen-person board of directors, with president, vice-presidents, treasurer, and secretary. All are club-member volunteers (from all over the U.S.A.) who have shown a willingness and ability to help run the CCCA. Club officers are elected by the total membership to three-year terms of office. They are not reimbursed for their expenses, which include attending monthly board meetings, most of which are held in Madison, N.J. The only paid employees of the club are a part-time secretary and the publications editor. An organization chart of the CCCA is shown in Figure 1.

In addition to belonging to the National CCCA, the majority of members also pay dues and belong to a local CCCA Region. In 1984, there were twenty-four regions throughout the U.S.A., as shown in Figure 2. Each region sponsors a variety of local

Figure 2   Map showing boundaries of regions of Classic Car Club of America

activities and publishes its own magazine or newsletter for members. Many of the regions derive revenues from the sale of Classic Car replacement parts or service items to members of the national club.

CURRENT PROBLEMS FACING CCCA

Although the CCCA's officers and directors believe the club to be strong, both financially and in its value to its members, a variety of concerns about the future exist. As indicated in the financial statements provided in Exhibit 2, the CCCA experienced a negative cash flow for fiscal 1983.

Another concern is the effect of inflation upon the club's ability to maintain its current level of service and benefits to the membership. In particular, the costs of publications and office administration have risen considerably in recent years. The board of directors has responded by raising dues several times. The directors recognize that certain cost increases are unavoidable, and that raising dues too high will result in a loss of members.

One way to overcome the problem of expenses is to increase the number of members, thus creating greater revenues for the club. The directors know that many Classic owners do not belong to the CCCA. While CCCA members owned about 6500–7000 Classics in 1983, no one really knows how many Classics and owners are not in the club. Club efforts in recent years to increase membership have been targeted at Classic-owning non-CCCA individuals. Letters have been sent to past members who failed to renew their CCCA membership (about 5 percent to 10 percent each year). Also, regional officers have contacted local non-CCCA members known to own Classics. In addition, several articles about CCCA activities as well as some advertisements have been placed in old-car hobby magazines.

Some CCCA members do not own Classics, but most do, because much of the pleasure of belonging to the club derives from participating in the various activities with a Classic Car. Thus, the primary focus of CCCA's new membership efforts has been on persons currently owning a Classic.

Yet, unless the listing of recognized Classics is expanded, the number of Classics in existence is fixed, and with it, by and large, is the number of Classic owners. There are varying opinions within the CCCA on whether to expand the current listing of Classics. While there is some debate over adding further makes and models within the current 1925–1948 era, the main controversy concerns whether or not to add cars built after 1948. The prices of Classics vary greatly, depending upon the make of car, its condition, and type of body.

A minority of members who favor post-1948 expansion make several arguments. They say that some high-quality cars were built after 1948 and these should be considered "Classic." Furthermore, they argue that the club is currently not attracting young members (only 20 percent of CCCA members are under forty-five), because younger people are less able to afford the cost of a Classic. They are also unable to "identify"

Exhibit 2   CCCA financial statements

	FY 1983	FY 1982	FY 1981
Receipts			
Active dues (dues received for current fiscal year)	$47950	$43900	$41199
Prepaid active dues (received for next fiscal year)	54975	47370	33440
Associate dues ($3.00/yr '83, '82, '81)	972	978	801
Prepaid associate dues (for next fiscal year)	1227	762	648
Life membership ('83: $350; '82 & '81: $250)	7310	5375	6775
Publications (back issue, individual copy sales)	3429	3472	4202
Bulletin advertising	3663	3396	1459
Magazine advertising	3567	1658	2752
Awards (payments from members for judging meets and meetings)	5240	5091	5230
CARavan (current years)	5300	5646	5900
CARavan (prepaid for next fiscal year)	6360	1500	1550
National sales items (badges, jewelry, clothing)	5235	4045	609
Interest earned	10416	8750	9957
Regional insurance (reimbursements from regions)	1100	1550	1300
Misc. and foreign exchange	887	2330	322
Total receipts	$157631	$135823	$116144
Assets			
Bank balance	$ 5356	$ 1891	$ 5485
Investments (at cost; notes, C.D.'s, money market funds)	96566	88997	85236
(includes life membership fund)	(37245)	(29800)	(24255)
Liabilities			
None			
Disbursements			
Bulletin	$ 18961	$ 17036	$ 13739
Magazine	57123	42099	33756
Directory	16181	9277	9237
Awards (judging, meetings, trophies, etc.)	8888	9648	10025
General administration	8786	7573	10843
Office (salaries, rent, utilities, etc.)	28573	21824	16934
CARavan	5069	5564	4252
National sales items	1710	4123	126
Membership (recruitment)	5670	3401	1619
Regional insurance	1600	1177	1279
Regional relations	454	462	431
Computer services	3678	3611	8011
Misc. and foreign exchange	2562	1972	1142
Total disbursements	$159255	$127767	$111394
Surplus	$(− 1624)	$ +8056	$ +4750

Notes to Financial Statements:
Cash basis reporting.
Security transactions not included.
Other assets not included (furniture, fixtures, sales items, trophies, deposits, etc.)

with a 1925–1948 car, as they can with a car of the 1950s or 1960s. Many current CCCA members own Classics because of nostalgia for the cars of their youth.

Most members of the board of directors, along with a clear majority of the membership, argue against expansion of the list of Classics past 1948. The primary argument is that a Classic Car is more than just a high-quality luxury car. Rather, it is the product of a "Classic Era," when the truly wealthy lived a separate life-style from the rest of the population, and when an elite group of auto makers and custom body craftsmen were willing and able to produce cars to meet this upper-class life-style. By the end of World War II, social upheavals ended this life-style. Economic pressures closed down custom body builders and most of the independent luxury-car makers. The remaining luxury cars generally became bigger and heavier versions of other cars made by multiline manufacturers. While a few truly special car models were made after 1948, the quantities produced were small. The addition of these cars to the list would bring in few new members to the CCCA.

Beyond concerns about the future financial strength of the club, there is concern about the use of Classics and the nature of CCCA activities. The value of Classics has risen significantly over the years. In 1952, when the club was founded, most people viewed Classics as simply "old cars," and they could generally be bought for a few hundred to a few thousand dollars. Today, Classics are viewed as a major investment item, with professional dealers and auctions being a significant factor in the marketplace. While some less exotic and unrestored Classic models can be found for under $10,000, most sell for $10,000–$75,000, and the best Classics (convertible models with custom bodies, twelve- and sixteen-cylinder engines, etc.) can sell for $100,000 and more.

Judging meets have become very serious events, with high scores adding significantly to a Classic's sales value. Thus, many top-scoring Classics are now hardly driven at all, and are trailered to and from judging meets. While most Classic owners still enjoy driving their cars, the emphasis in the club is definitely moving from the driving to the judging, and this upsets many CCCA members.

Another concern of some members involves possible future gasoline shortages in the U.S. If such a shortage arose, how would the public view Classic Cars and the old car hobby in general? Would the ownership and driving of cars for nontransportation purposes be considered unpatriotic or antisocial?

MEMBERSHIP SURVEY

In response to the various concerns, the CCCA board established a long-range planning committee to study issues about the future of the club. The committee was charged with making recommendations to the board. In late 1983, a membership questionnaire was developed and sent to all members along with their 1984 membership renewal material. The response rate was excellent—about 75 percent of the club's members returned a completed questionnaire with their 1984 dues. Exhibit 3 presents this questionnaire and a tabulation of quantifiable responses.

Exhibit 3 Classic Car Club of America membership questionnaire

Please help your National Board of Directors guide the CCCA in the path that you desire by completing this questionnaire and returning it with your membership renewal.

1. I have been a member of the CCCA
   ☐ less than 2 years ☐ 2–5 years ☐ 5–10 years ☐ more than 10 years
       11%   20%   18%   51%

2. I live in the _____ region (or state if there is no region)

3. My age is ☐ under 25 ☐ 25–34 ☐ 35–44 ☐ 45–54 ☐ 55–64 ☐ 65 and over
              1%   3%   17%   30%   28%   22%

4. I am a member of a CCCA Region ☐ yes ☐ no
                                     69%   31%

   If not, why not? _____

5. I have attended
   64% ☐ One or more Grand Classics
   19% ☐ One or more National CCCA CARavans
   24% ☐ One or more Annual Meetings
   52% ☐ One or more Regional Events

6. I belong to _____ (how many) other car clubs.

	0	1	2	3	4	5	6	7	8	9	10& +
	9%	19%	23%	17%	12%	7%	5%	2%	2%	1%	3%

I am more active in some of these clubs than I am in the CCCA. ☐ yes ☐ no
                                                    44% 56%

   If "yes," why? _____

7. Compared to other car clubs, the CCCA is
   ☐ the best ☐ better than most ☐ average ☐ poor
      31%   47%   21%   1%

8. Compared to other car clubs, the value I receive for my CCCA dues is
   ☐ the best ☐ better than most ☐ average ☐ poor
      27%   40%   31%   3%

9. Overall, I rate _"THE CLASSIC CAR"_ magazine ☐ excellent ☐ good ☐ fair ☐ poor
                                     74%   24%   1%   0%

10. Overall, I rate the _"CCCA BULLETIN"_ ☐ excellent ☐ good ☐ fair ☐ poor
                                   35%   51%   13%   1%

Exhibit 3 (Continued)

11. In "*THE CLASSIC CAR*," the types of articles I enjoy most are:

Rate each: 3 = enjoy a great amount   2 = enjoy a fair amount   1 = enjoy a little   0 = do not enjoy

2.3	Grand Classic articles	2.4	Articles on classic car designers
1.5	Annual Meeting articles	2.7	Car photos from the Classic Era
2.1	CARavan articles	2.3	Reprints from classic era publications
2.7	Stories and photos of members' cars	1.5	Book reviews
2.8	Historic articles on classic cars or coachbuilders	1.6	Articles on regional events
2.4	Technical articles	1.3	Articles on non-CCCA car events
2.5	Restoration articles	1.7	Classic car humor
2.4	Articles on car collections or car museums	1.8	Letters to the editor

Other: _____

12. I would prefer

    28% ☐ to continue to have the *HANDBOOK-DIRECTORY* published every year
    72% ☐ to have it published every other year if a significant savings to the club would result

13. Currently the club's By-Laws require that 7 candidates run each year for election to 5 open National Board positions. While this gives the membership a choice in their voting, it also means that the two least-known candidates generally lose and will not seek election to the Board again.

    I think it is important to continue the system of 7 candidates for 5 positions.   ☐ yes   ☐ no

                                                                                              64%   36%

14. With regard to the CCCA's listing of recognized Classic Cars,

    69% ☐ I basically think the current listing is good
    28% ☐ I think the listing should be expanded
    3% ☐ I think the listing should be reduced

    Comments: _____

15. With regard to the CCCA 100-point judging system,

    86% ☐ I basically think the current system is good
    14% ☐ I think the system could be improved

    If so, how: _____

16. Overall, I would rate the Grand Classics as
☐ excellent ☐ good ☐ fair ☐ poor ☐ don't know
50% 30% 2% 1% 17%

17. Overall, I would rate the Annual Meetings as
☐ excellent ☐ good ☐ fair ☐ poor ☐ don't know
15% 22% 5% 0% 59%

18. Overall, I would rate the CARavans as
☐ excellent ☐ good ☐ fair ☐ poor ☐ don't know
28% 16% 2% 0% 54%

19. I think the CCCA should have additional National Judging Meets. ☐ yes ☐ no
23% 77%

If "yes," what type? _____

20. I think the CCCA could be improved by:

_____

_____

_____

_____

_____

Other comments: _____

_____

_____

_____

_____

_____

_____

Thank you for your assistance.

Some common themes were repeated:

- A concern about trailered cars and professionally restored cars competing with other Classics in judging.
- Too much emphasis in the CCCA on judging, and not enough emphasis on driving. A focus on cosmetics rather than mechanics.
- To attract younger members, the club must expand the listing of Classics beyond 1948.
- "The _____(which I happen to own) should be recognized as a Classic. It is as fine a car as the _____, which is recognized by the CCCA as a Classic."
- The CCCA should not dilute the meaning of "Classic." Hold fast to the 1925–1948 limits.

FUTURE DIRECTION OF CCCA

In 1984, the CCCA board of directors was studying these and other issues. Board members knew that they could not ignore the problems of rising costs. The directors' response must go beyond raising dues. While the survey clarified some of the opinions of members, the board did not view this survey as a mandate to follow the majority preference in every question area.

As they met for their monthly meeting, the fifteen officers and directors of the CCCA asked themselves the following questions:

1. How should we deal with rising costs to the club?
2. What should be our policy with regard to future dues increases?
3. Should we reduce the number and quality of CCCA services?
4. Is expansion of the listing of recognized Classic Cars desirable?
5. What are alternative ways to increase membership in the club?
6. How can younger people be attracted to the CCCA?
7. Are there other sources of revenue for the club?
8. Were important questions not included in the 1983 membership survey that should be included in a future survey?
9. Are there other long-range issues or concerns that the club has not yet addressed?

Bevell's True Value Hardware, Inc.

FREDERICK C. HAAS
Virginia Commonwealth University

INTRODUCTION

Bevell's True Value Hardware is a well-established small business in Blackstone, Virginia. Bevell's broad and varied product line serves a wide spectrum of customers. The business provides full-time employment for twelve persons and part-time work for seven additional employees. Bevell's president is Mr. Robert Daniels, an energetic, even-tempered man who is respected and liked by both employees and customers.

Since 1980, Bevell's has enjoyed consistent growth in dollar sales. The business has modernized facilities and excellent customer loyalty. Recent refinancing of debt greatly improved the firm's cash flow. Some of Bevell's problems include an obsolete warehouse, slow-growth population in the Blackstone area, heavy competition from many local retailers, slow-moving inventory items due to seasonal demand, and changing customer preferences.

PRODUCT LINE SALES

Bevell's Hardware is a franchise of the Cotter Company. In addition to supplying True Value products, the Cotter Company provides legal advice, store layout planning, market surveys, store performance evaluations, uniforms (for lease or purchase), insurance, trucks (for lease only), and cars and equipment.

Bevell's carries several thousand items, grouped into nine categories. These product categories provide the following contributions to Bevell's total sales:

1. Hardware   15–20%
2. Housewares   3–5% (seasonal)
3. Paint   3%
4. Plumbing supplies   10%
5. Electrical supplies 10%
6. Tools   5%
7. Lawn and garden   10–12% (seasonal)
8. Sporting goods/toys 0–2% (seasonal)
9. Building supplies   40–50% (anything *not* in the main showroom)

ORGANIZATION AND PERSONNEL

Bevell's workforce has been quite stable. Employee turnover has been very low. There is a waiting list of experienced applicants from which the store could select new employees as needed. Most of Bevell's employees have several years experience selling hardware products. Regular customers know Bevell's employees on a first-name basis. Bevell's organizational structure is shown in Figure 1.

A brief experience profile of full-time employees is provided in Exhibit 1. Bevell's pay scale and employee benefits are competitive with those of other employers in the community. There is no union at the store and little union representation in the Blackstone area. Both store and warehouse employees show a strong career-oriented attitude about their jobs.

ADVERTISING AND SELLING

Bevell's advertising expenditures have averaged 1.6 percent of sales yearly for the past five years. About 29 percent of these expenditures have gone to mass mailings, 36

Figure 1   Organization chart, Bevell's True Value Hardware, Inc., January 1984

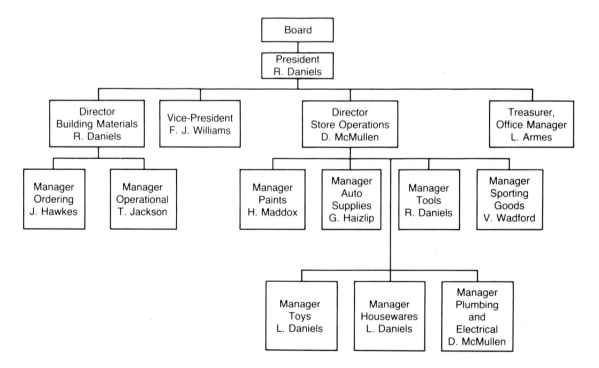

Exhibit 1   Employee experience profiles

Name	Age	Profile
Robert Daniels	44	President. Owned and managed rental real estate properties and several fast food establishments before assuming the presidency of Bevell's Hardware.
Bell Alder	66	Semiretired—works two days/wk
Laura Armes	30	Twelve years experience at Bevell's Hardware
Paul Black	55	Twenty years experience at Bevell's Hardware—runs detached warehouse
Lynn Daniels	39	Thoroughly familiar with Bevell's Hardware (President's wife) and develops media advertising, housewares, and toys
Gary Haizlip	20	Two years at Bevell's Hardware
James Hawkes	65	Thirty years at Bevell's Hardware
Thomas Jackson	30	Three years at Bevell's Hardware
Herbert Maddox	28	Seven to eight years at Bevell's Hardware
Dewey McMullen	50	Ten years experience hardware, 5 to 6 years at Bevell's Hardware
Mary Slaw	55	Thirty plus years experience in other hardware stores, one year at Bevell's Hardware
Vickie Wadford	30	Experienced Ace Hardware prior to joining Bevell's Hardware
Barbara Wampler	45	Five years at Bevell's Hardware—works in billings and customer accounts

percent to radio and TV spot advertising, 25 percent to newspaper ads, and 10 percent to miscellaneous advertising such as promotional contests. Advertising is concentrated primarily in the Blackstone area, where over 50 percent of Bevell's repeat customers reside. Some advertising is directed to other residents of Nottoway County, which comprise another 20–25 percent of Bevell's repeat customers.

Bevell's sends a True Value-produced publication to regular customers. Newspaper ads are placed primarily in *The Courier–Record*. A heavy seasonal emphasis is placed on spot radio and TV ads, usually featuring one high-ticket item during the period of heavy demand.

Bevell's showroom is designed for customer self-service. Small items are stocked on shelves, in bins, and on racks at selected points in the store. Regular customers familiar with the store often serve themselves. Payment can be made by cash, check, or credit card. Recording cash registers provide a record of sales by inventory category (hardware, paint, or building supplies, for example) on a paper tape printout. These registers are not linked to a computer and do not serve any function in inventory control or replenishment. Customers can charge purchases by having the salesperson prepare a charge ticket in duplicate.

Customers needing sales help are serviced by any Bevell's employee. However, for a special need, the salesperson responsible for that area usually is consulted. Bulky or heavy items, such as power tools and lumber, are loaded by employees at the warehouse onto a Bevell's delivery truck or the customer's automobile or pick-up truck.

STORE AND WAREHOUSE FACILITIES

Bevell's Hardware occupies three buildings and an outside storage yard for materials that could not be damaged by exposure to the weather. The layout of these buildings is shown in Figure 2. A description of the buildings follows:

Store

One-story cement block building having 11,900 square feet and opening on two streets. Used for sales area and office administration, plus some storage of small fast-selling items.

Figure 2   Layout of Bevell's Hardware buildings

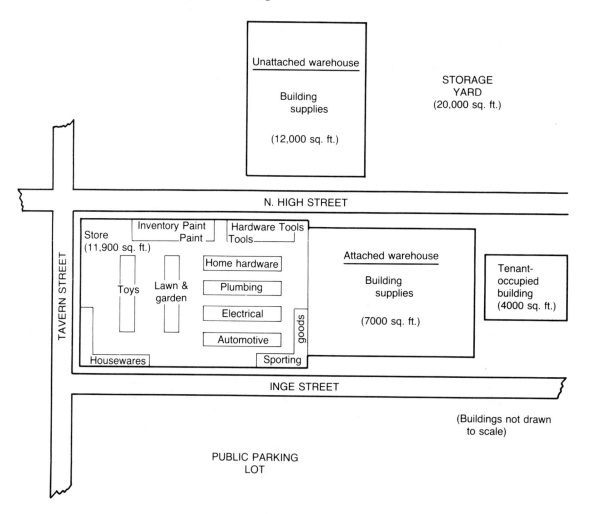

Attached Warehouse

A steel-trussed, framed and sheathed, concrete-floored building with a 25-foot ceiling. Floor is designed for heavy vehicles. Used for storage and display of bulky building materials.

Unattached Warehouse

An old wooden building having 12,000 square feet on main level plus a 3000-square-foot balcony, a 4,000-square-foot cellar, and several shed roofs attached to its exterior walls. Used for storage and display of bulky building materials.

Outside Yard Storage

Yard storage (20,000 square feet) for building materials that are not subject to weather damage.

FINANCIAL DETAILS

A certified public accountant in Blackstone performs accounting services for Bevell's Hardware. During fiscal 1984, this service was computerized. A four-digit identification number was assigned to all charge customers. This numbering system helped to compile charges in billing and to credit account payments. Locating and/or grouping customers for various purposes (such as promotional mailings) also could be done using this control number.

A representation of Bevell's historical financial data is shown on the balance sheet in Exhibit 2 and on the income statement in Exhibit 3. Note that an important financial rearrangement was made during fiscal 1983 when Bevell's purchased the buildings and furnishings it had previously been leasing. The cost to purchase these facilities was as follows:

Land	$30,000.00
Store building and warehouses	$160,000.00
Furnishings and equipment	$2,500.00

As part of the purchase program, an additional $82,500.00 was borrowed for renovation of existing facilities and for construction of a new warehouse to replace an obsolete one. The purchase was financed by issuing $275,000 in Industrial Development bonds through the Industrial Development Authority of the Town of Blackstone. The bonds were purchased by Citizens Bank and Trust Company of Blackstone. They carried 8-1/2 percent interest and required 240 monthly payments of $2,386.51 from June 28, 1983 until May 28, 2003. Purchase of the facilities gave Bevell's Hardware a fixed monthly bond payment (instead of monthly lease payments) totaling $1,916.67, plus 3 percent of gross sales over $1 million. This represented a substantial decrease in total cash outflow.

Exhibit 2   Bevell's True Value Hardware, Inc. balance sheet

	1983	1982	1981	1980[1]	1979
ASSETS					
Current Assets					
Cash in bank/on hand	$ 91,879	$ 92,389	$ 79,384	$ 61,694	$ 44,003
Accounts receivable	175,156	190,427	137,863	187,907	68,032
Notes and loans receivable	4,152	4,324	165,571	10,999	104,255
Inventory	249,909	202,030	212,712	206,065	231,841
Prepaid expenses	5,738	1,376	2,851	2,521	1,786
Total current assets	526,834	490,546	598,381	469,186	449,917
Long Term					
Buildings, equipment, vehicles	284,165	8,573	11,489	7,711	2,100
Other assets	97,943	138,979	1,159	602	1,477
Total assets	908,942	638,098	611,029	477,499	453,494
LIABILITIES AND EQUITY					
Current Liabilities					
Accounts payable	141,407	107,858	160,225	153,744	83,502
Notes and loans payable	109,567	138,812	53,440	12,203	58,093
Accrued expenses	—	1,321	1,637	1,182	17,740
Taxes due	50,339	46,288	26,436	20,353	7,425
Mortgage payments due	5,476	—	—	—	—
Total current liabilities	306,789	294,279	241,738	187,082	166,760
Long Term Debt[2]					
Mortgage notes and other notes payable	269,524	100,000	175,000	175,000	225,000
Total liabilities	576,313	394,279	416,738	362,082	391,760
Stockholders' Equity					
Capital stock	1,000	1,000	1,000	1,000	1,000
Retained earnings	331,629	242,819	193,291	114,417	60,734
Total equity	332,629	243,819	194,291	115,417	61,734
Total liability and equity	$908,942	$638,098	$611,029	$477,499	$453,494

[1]Year ending was changed from July 31 to April 20 during fiscal year 1980. The 1980 financial data is based on only three quarters.

[2]Buildings and equipment which the business had been leasing were purchased during the 1983 fiscal year.

MARKET AREA SERVED

The 1980 Census indicated that Blackstone's population of 3,624 was 30.4 percent white females, 26.9 percent white males, 24.0 percent black females, and 18.7 percent black males. Over 84 percent of Blackstone's residents were native Virginians; 39 percent were high school graduates and 12.6 percent had completed four or more years of college study. The median family income for Blackstone's residents in 1979 was $14,769, while the per capita income was $5,400. Although 65.9 percent of males over

Exhibit 3 Bevell's True Value Hardware, Inc. income statement

	1983	1982	1981	1980[1]	1979
Sales (Net)	$1,435,549	$1,390,573	$1,322,779	$913,636	$1,113,581
Cost of Goods Sold					
Beginning inventory	202,030	212,712	206,065	231,841	199,934
Purchases	1,059,551	1,025,494	1,027,883	666,437	869,869
Freight and related expenses	34,144	19,497	17,303	10,197	14,351
Ending inventory	(249,909)	(202,030)	(212,712)	(206,065)	(231,841)
Total charges	1,045,816	1,055,673	1,038,539	702,410	852,313
Gross profit	389,733	334,900	284,240	211,226	261,268
Deduct Operating Expenses					
Warehouse and store	43,900	78,636	35,299	29,938	38,193
General and administration	62,750	81,966	40,853	24,736	35,695
Selling	164,666	158,292	133,177	93,870	134,252
Total operating expenses	271,316	318,894	209,329	148,544	208,140
Profit (loss) from OPNS	118,417	16,006	74,911	62,682	53,138
Other income	58,474	61,892	43,164	26,395	31,300
Total	176,891	77,898	118,075	89,077	84,428
Interest expense[2]	24,328	10,000	17,500	17,500	22,500
Income (before tax)	152,563	67,898	100,575	71,577	61,928
Fed. income tax	63,753	18,370	21,701	17,894	16,235
Net income (loss)	88,810	49,528	78,874	53,683	45,693
Retained earnings beginning	242,819	193,291	114,417	60,734	15,041
Retained earnings ending	331,629	242,819	193,291	114,417	60,734
Earnings per share	$ 888	$ 495	$ 789	$ 537	$ 457

[1]Year ending was changed from July 31 to April 20 during fiscal 1980. The 1980 financial data is based on only three quarters.
[2]Buildings and equipment which the business had been leasing were purchased during the 1983 fiscal year.

16 years of age and 43.8 percent of females were in the labor force, 20.1 percent of all families had no working members. In Blackstone, 20.6 percent of all families were classified as having a 1979 income below the poverty level. A map of Blackstone showing Bevell's location is provided in Figure 3.

Figure 3   Location of Bevell's Hardware

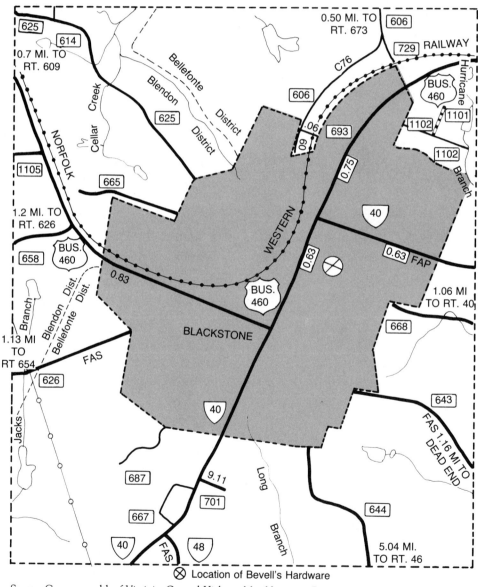

⊗ Location of Bevell's Hardware

Source: Commonwealth of Virginia, General Highway Map Nottoway County

Exhibit 4   Population projections for Bevell's market areas

County	Year 1980	Year 1985	Year 1990	Year 1995	Year 2000
Nottoway	14,666	14,600	15,000	15,100	15,300
Amelia	8,405	8,700	9,200	9,500	9,900
Brunswick	15,652	16,100	16,100	16,200	16,200
Cumberland	7,881	8,300	9,300	9,700	10,400
Dinwiddie	22,602	22,800	23,600	23,900	24,200
Lunenburg	12,124	12,200	12,500	12,600	12,800
Prince Edward	16,456	17,200	17,900	18,400	18,900
Nottoway & Surrounding Counties TOTAL	97,786	99,900	103,600	105,400	107,700
5-Year Increase Totals		+2,114	+3,700	+1,800	+2,300
20-Year Increase Totals					+9,914

Source: Virginia Population Projections, Dept. of Planning and Budget Report (June 1983): 11, 12.

The 1980 Census indicated a Nottoway County population of 14,666, of whom over 84 percent were native Virginians. Of all county residents aged twenty-five or older, 38.9 percent were high school graduates and 8.8 percent had completed four or more years of college study. Further, 68.7 percent of all males and 45.6 percent of all females over sixteen years of age were in the labor force. However, 14.4 percent of all families residing in the county had no working member.

Nottoway County has some industrial base of small factories that make shoes, furniture, clothing, and various other products, but it is highly dependent on farming for its economic base. Beef and dairy cattle, pigs, sheep, chickens, and other animals are raised. Crop farming includes tobacco, sorghum, various kinds of hay and grain, and a variety of vegetables. Trees are grown and sold as logs for use in making paper. A population projection of Nottoway and surrounding counties (provided in Exhibit 4) shows Bevell's potential market area as experiencing very slow growth.

COMPETING STORES

In competing with other retail stores, Bevell's Hardware offers a central location, wider variety of products, and generally more competitive prices. Bevell's competitors are described in Exhibit 5. Note that there is not a mass retailer such as K-Mart or Wal-Mart in Blackstone. Bevell's major competitor is Kenbridge Mfg. and Supply Company. Kenbridge carries all of Bevell's product categories in greater or lesser variety. Kenbridge is located eleven miles southwest of Blackstone. Mr. Daniels believes Bevell's Hardware and Kenbridge Supply compete in the territory lying between them. However, both Bevell's and Kenbridge have great difficulty in shipping (selling) past each

Exhibit 5   Competitive businesses

Business	Competing Lines
Rose's Variety Store	Housewares
	Hardware
	Electrical supplies
	Paint and sundries
	Toys
Dollar General Store	Electrical supplies
	Paint and sundries
	Sporting goods
	Housewares
Western Auto	All of Bevell's categories except building supplies
Sears Catalog	All of Bevell's categories except building supplies
Eppes Supply	Primarily automotive supplies
United Motor Parts	Hand tools
	Automotive supplies
Wards Catalog	All of Bevell's categories except building supplies
Sheffield TV and Appliance	TVs and appliances
Blackstone Fuel and Supply Co.	Hand tools
	Paints and sundries
	Lawn and garden
	Lawn/saddlery
Pennington Aluminum Products	Building materials
	All doors and windows
Planters Southern States	All of Bevell's categories except building supplies
Sheffield Furniture	Floor coverings
Janet's Nook	Arts and crafts
Freeman Auto Parts	Hand tools
	Automotive supplies

other geographically. This applies primarily to building supplies and heavy items that require delivery by one of Bevell's or Kenbridge's large flat bed trucks.

PAST AND PRESENT OPERATING STRATEGIES

When asked to explain the steady and rapid sales growth of Bevell's Hardware during the six years he has been its president, Mr. Daniels cited several factors that promoted profitable sales.

- Sufficient inventory that is reviewed and upgraded continually
- Purchase of inventory at the best cost

- Freedom given to department managers to experiment with inventories and sales techniques
- Emphasis on tie-in sales
- Emphasis on seasonals

Under Daniels' direction, Bevell's Hardware has carried an inventory averaging 15–16 percent of sales. Some items, such as power tools and gasoline-powered gardening tools, are displayed and demonstrated for customers. Daniels believes that many hardware and building-supply-item sales are lost whenever customers have to wait for delivery, because resulting construction delays are costly to contractors.

Mr. Daniels describes inventory purchases as being from three sources. First, Bevell's Hardware could buy direct from any manufacturer whenever the price was excellent. Second, they could buy through Cotter True Value relays, a computer-based method for placing mixed-item, various-quantity orders. Third, they could buy from the Cotter True Value warehouse stock. Direct purchase is the least costly source, while purchase from the True Value warehouse is most costly. Mr. Daniels' target was to average one third of inventory purchases from each of these sources.

Tie-in sales are a heavily emphasized technique at Bevell's, especially in building materials. For example, purchase of wall paneling usually results in the purchase of nails, glue, moldings, and tools to aid the installation. Drop-ceiling panels and insulation create substantial tie-in sales, as does the sale of numerous other items.

Another sales strategy was to focus on heavy promotion of seasonal items, including preplanned inventory buildup, in-store promotions used in advertising, and direct selling.

LOOKING TOWARD THE FUTURE

For 1984 through 1987, Mr. Daniels plans to focus on improving his present location rather than branching out to other sites, even though he is aware of the limited growth potential in the town and county. Daniels believes that the time and resources needed to locate and purchase another business and integrate it into Bevell's Hardware, or to establish another branch site, could be better spent developing the present location, where he plans to expand in several selected building supply, hardware, and houseware product lines. He believes this expansion could produce annual sales increases for the next five years.

Mr. Daniels is considering refurbishing the front of Bevell's Hardware at a cost of $50,000. He also plans to replace the warehouse at a cost of $300,000. Daniels would like to add a small engine repair service at Bevell's. He would like to improve Bevell's management policies and marketing practices. Perhaps most of all, Daniels would like someone with expertise in strategic management to assist him in formulating and implementing strategies for the future. The survival and profitability of this small business largely depends upon effective strategic decisions being made now.

CASE 19

Dick's Place, Inc.

FREDERICK C. HAAS
Virginia Commonwealth University

INTRODUCTION

The door to Bill Paulette's office swung open and was closed again quickly as his business partner, Bob Borum, entered and sat down.

"Thanks for keeping out the heat," said Paulette, without looking up from his paper work. The company's books were open on the desk before him.

"No need to remind me," replied Borum, with a laugh. "I've been in here before when your air conditioner was broken."

Indeed, getting away from the heat was a major consideration on this July day. The temperature outside was ninety-five degrees, and the shop was just down the short hallway from the office. Tire recapping, with its pressurized molds filled with hot rubber, was not the sort of work for those who liked to stay cool.

"At least I haven't had to spend much time in the plant today," said Paulette. "In fact, I've been spending more time than usual at the desk instead of waiting on customers the last few days. I've been thinking about the recapping plant here. The place is driving some of the men nuts."

"I know," said Borum. "I used to work here. When you've recapped a number of tires, you have to roll 'em up the ramp and stack 'em in a particular area by size. Then, when a customer buys a tire, we have to go up there, sometimes dig it out of a stack, then roll it down again."

"It wastes time, and it's hard work, especially in this heat," nodded Paulette. "Well, I suppose I might as well tell you, I've been thinking about what it might cost to replace this old building."

"That would be great. But wouldn't we have to borrow some more money? Interest rates are pretty high now."

"Sure they are. On the other hand, if we don't move now, they could be even higher in six months. I just feel that we've got to have a more efficient operation if we're going to compete with the national chains."

"Speaking of chains, did you know a new Firestone place is going to move into J.C. Penney's old building at the mall up on Route 60? I thought we'd have a little less competition in that area when Penney's got out of the auto service business, but it doesn't look that way."

HISTORY OF THE BUSINESS

"Dick" was Mr. Richard A. Johns, Jr., who founded the business in 1941 as a wayside service station in Amelia County, Virginia. His total investment had been $360.00. Two years later, Dick's Place relocated to U.S. Route 360 and became a truck stop. In 1955, Dick's Place moved into a building designed better for tire recapping and sales. In 1965, the building was destroyed by a fire, but Mr. Johns reopened the business in Richmond, Virginia in 1972.

In 1976, Robert Borum and William Paulette purchased Dick's Place. They persuaded Mr. Johns to accept a note for a major portion of the purchase price. Most of Dick's Place employees were happy to stay on under the new management; in fact, Borum and Paulette considered their loyal and customer-oriented work force as one of their greatest intangible assets. Dick's Place opened a new facility in Blackstone, Virginia in 1980. The Richmond operation moved to a new building in 1984. Both of these expansion moves had been financed through a lease-back arrangement.

NATURE OF THE BUSINESS

As shown in Figure 1, Dick's Place is located in Richmond, Amelia, and Blackstone, Virginia. An organizational chart of Dick's Place is given in Figure 2. Revenues from the business are derived from the following sources:

Truck tire sales	50 percent
Truck tire recapping	20 percent
Passenger car tire sales	15 percent
Passenger car tire recapping	15 percent

At the Amelia location, purchasing and billing averaged about 900 transactions per month. This business is handled by an office staff of three. Unlike the Blackstone and Richmond facilities, Dick's Place owns the building in Amelia.

The Blackstone facility is a relatively small two-bay operation, managed by James Paulette, the president's brother. The Richmond facility consists of a four-bay service area and a large storage room for tire inventory. This operation is managed by Mr. Borum, the co-owner.

Along with recapped tires, all Dick's Place locations carry a major brand of new tire, Armstrong. The company competes with dealers selling many other brands, including Bridgestone, Cooper, Dunlop, Firestone, General, B.F. Goodrich, Goodyear, and Michelin. Dick's Place does not keep any brand of tire in stock except Armstrong. Through newspaper and local radio, Dick's Place advertises to a large portion of central Virginia. Customers come from a number of counties, including Brunswick, Charlotte, Cumberland, Lunenburg, Nottoway, and Prince Edward.

Figure 1   Location of Dick's Place facilities

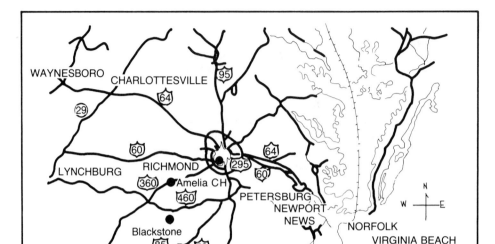

Figure 2   Dick's Place organization chart

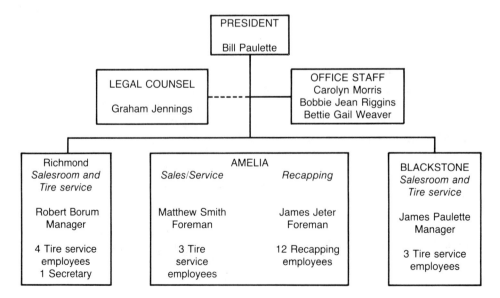

Table 1   Population projections for locations of Dick's Place sales facilities

County	Base Year 1980	Year 1985	Year 1990	Year 1995	Year 2000
Amelia	8,405	8,700	9,200	9,500	9,900
Nottoway	14,666	14,600	15,000	15,100	15,300
Richmond SMSA[1]	630,015	679,157[2]	728,300	769,500[2]	810,700
Totals	653,086	702,457	752,500	794,100	835,900
10-Year Cumulative Growth			15.2%		11.08%
20-Year Cumulative Growth					27.99%

[1]Richmond SMSA includes the City of Richmond and Henrico County and Chesterfield County (where Dick's Place facility is located).

[2]Value was obtained by extrapolation.

Dick's Place is represented in the Richmond Yellow Pages by a two-line listing. There are over eighty listings for competing new-tire dealers, and thirty more for tire recappers. Richmond has a population of about 630,000. As shown in Table 1, Richmond is expected to increase in population to 810,700 by the year 2000.

THE TIRE RECAPPING BUSINESS

Statistics show that retail tire sales and recap sales are countercyclical. In good times, when disposable income is higher, people tend to buy new tires; when times are tighter, recap sales tend to pick up. Sales of new tires generate a steady supply of reusable tire bodies at Dick's Place.

Before recapping a tire, the old tire body is inspected with a special tool to find broken cords or other damage. Bodies that pass this step are buffed to ready them for a new rubber cap, and then reinspected for damage that may previously have been hidden. In the recapping process itself, a tire body is inflated on a Probitread Machine, which applies a coating of heated rubber under precise computer control. Next the tire is "cured" in a heated mold under pressure. The completed retread is finished by removing small rubber spikes left by the mold, and the recap is then placed in inventory. Some tires are brought in for recapping by customers, and these, of course, are not inventoried.

Economics of the truck tire business virtually guarantee a continuing demand for retreads. A new tire for an over-the-road hauler lists for about $280.00, plus a federal excise tax of $29.75 (which has risen from $12.20 in 1983). A complete new set of tires for a truck-and-trailer rig with eighteen wheels would cost about $6,000. Recapped tires for this same vehicle would cost less than $1,200 and there is no excise tax.

Not all tire bodies are strong enough for recapping. The recapping process produces tons of rubber scrap in the form of small black particles. This form of trash is not welcome at the local county landfill because rubber does not deteriorate with age. Therefore, Dick's Place pays a fee for each tire and load of scrap taken to the dump. Occasionally, Dick's Place gets a call from somebody who wants a ditch filled, a purpose for which old tires are admirably suited.

THE FUTURE

President Paulette recently conducted some market research and determined that people are keeping their cars longer: average vehicle age is now 4.7 years. The average car is driven 17,498 miles per year. The trade journal *Tires and Treads Forever* reports that the average life for all tires is 28,500 miles; radials last about 38,000 miles; two out of five tires sold are radials, and the trend toward radials is increasing.

Within a thirty-mile radius of Richmond, there are 400,000 cars and trucks registered with the Division of Motor Vehicles. Nottoway County, which includes Blackstone, has 10,750 vehicles, and Amelia County has 6,600.

Exhibit 1 Dick's Place—balance sheet

Assets	1984	1983	1982	1981
Current assets				
Cash	$ 247,371	$ 231,373	$108,962	$189,750
Accounts receivable—Trade	375,550	389,495	352,925	287,235
Inventory	247,287	244,475	238,572	239,448
Prepaid taxes	35,176	—	21,403	22,107
Total current assets	$ 905,384	$ 865,343	$721,862	$738,540
Property, plant and equipment				
Land	$ 116,142	$ 70,000	$ 70,000	$ 70,000
Building	303,563	48,505	48,505	48,505
Equipment and furniture	300,698	274,550	251,152	245,903
Vehicles	75,535	66,621	50,087	67,561
Leasehold improvement	18,241	18,242	18,242	18,242
	$ 814,179	$ 477,918	$437,986	$450,211
Less: Accumulated depreciation	337,236	267,952	229,895	221,218
Net property, plant and equipment	$ 476,943	$ 209,966	$208,091	$228,993
Other Assets				
Employee savings account	$ —	$ —	$ 10,675	$ —
Loans receivable—Employees	10,348	12,639	16,840	10,676
Loans receivable—Other	40,006	35,126	32,645	—
Total other assets	$ 50,354	$ 47,765	$ 60,160	$ 10,676
Total assets	$1,432,681	$1,123,074	$990,113	$978,209

Liabilities & Stockholders' Equity	1984	1983	1982	1981
Current liabilities				
Accounts payable—Trade	$ 449,458	$ 337,639	$348,263	$268,980
Current portion of long-term liabilities	51,899	43,250	38,923	61,702
Accrued salaries and wages	49,450	97,602	27,419	33,100
Employee savings plan	—	—	5,456	—
Payroll taxes accrued and withheld	1,874	989	1,199	611
Sales and excise taxes payable	5,947	6,637	7,372	7,113
Income taxes payable	—	37,644	—	22,786
Total current liabilities	$ 558,628	$ 523,761	$428,632	$394,292
Long-term liabilities				
Notes payable—R. A. Johns, Jr.	$ 461,274	$ 199,706	$220,261	$239,346
Notes payable—Bank	17,878	38,990	57,358	73,340
Loans payable—Stockholders	—	3,259	15,259	15,259
	$ 479,152	$ 241,955	$292,878	$327,945
Less: Current portion (above)	51,899	43,250	38,923	35,067
Long-term liabilities	$ 427,253	$ 198,705	$253,955	$292,878
Total liabilities	$ 985,881	$ 722,466	$682,587	$687,170
Stockholders' equity				
Common stock outstanding	$ 7,500	$ 7,500	$ 7,500	$ 7,500
Additional paid-in capital	67,500	67,500	67,500	67,500
Retained earnings	403,555	357,364	264,282	247,795
	$ 478,555	$ 432,364	$339,282	$322,795
Less: Treasury stock (at cost)	31,755	31,756	31,756	31,756
Total stockholders' equity	$ 446,800	$ 400,608	$307,526	$291,039
Total liabilities and stockholders' equity	$1,432,681	$1,123,074	$990,113	$978,209

Because of the price differential between recaps and new tires, and because truck traffic in general is increasing, Mr. Paulette anticipates a 30 percent rise in his truck tire recapping business in 1985.

Conversely, he expects a 25 percent drop in passenger car tire recapping, partly because consumer income is up, and partly because of a recent drop in the federal excise tax on new passenger car tires. The decrease has been five cents per pound, or about two dollars per tire.

Despite the competition, Borum and Paulette are pleased with Dick's Place's location in Richmond, because U.S. Route 360 carries a heavy volume of truck traffic and brings thousands of commuters past the business each day.

Examination of the company's financial statements in Exhibits 1 and 2 show a dramatic decrease in net income in 1984. Borum and Paulette are concerned about the future of Dick's Place. They would like to hire someone with expertise in strategic management to assist them in formulating and implementing strategies for the future.

Exhibit 2 Dick's Place income statement

	1984	1983	1982	1981
Sales	$2,738,048	$2,575,354	$2,669,256	$2,340,000
Cost of goods sold	1,840,522	1,691,031	1,862,688	1,524,255
Gross profit	$ 897,526	884,323	806,568	816,145
Operating Expenses				
Salaries and wages	$ 499,587	$ 517,185	$ 465,192	$ 407,693
Advertising, entertainment and promotion	17,607	12,431	7,991	10,939
Bad debts—Net	9,218	(5,072)	34,727	47,264
Bank discounts	1,601	1,793	1,587	—
Collection fees	1,021	1,308	629	209
Depreciation and amortization	74,522	48,281	41,517	33,306
Donations	7,752	5,982	2,000	399
Dues and subscriptions	1,041	837	908	215
Employee savings plan	—	6,155	6,535	7,065
Employee group insurance	10,203	7,585	6,330	7,545
Insurance	22,893	20,302	20,435	19,842
Legal accounting	4,370	2,600	4,265	5,327
Office supplies and postage	7,597	6,512	9,093	8,532
Rent	64,019	43,063	44,609	42,088
Taxes and licenses	50,237	38,229	39,120	32,429
Telephone	9,784	8,796	9,227	8,864
Uniform service	2,335	4,129	3,876	3,915
Utilities	49,527	41,034	46,098	38,483
Vehicle expenses	27,516	17,659	32,244	35,552
Total operating expenses	$ 860,830	$ 778,809	$ 776,384	$ 709,667
Income from operations	$ 39,696	$ 105,514	$ 30,184	$ 106,478
Other Income				
Gain on sale of property and equipment	$ 643	$ 1,175	$ 8,994	$ 6,577
Interest and discounts	36,699	36,975	2,882	3,095
Rent	15,345	14,079	5,400	5,400
Total other income	$ 52,687	$ 52,229	$ 17,276	$ 15,072
	$ 89,383	$ 157,743	$ 47,460	$ 121,550
Other Expense				
Interest	36,106	22,415	28,484	24,562
Income before income taxes	$ 53,277	$ 135,328	$ 18,976	$ 96,988
Provision for income taxes	7,084	42,247	2,489	22,786
Net income	$ 46,193	$ 93,081	$ 16,487	$ 74,202

Specifically, Borum and Paulette recognize the need for a comprehensive internal and external audit of the business. New management, marketing, and finance policies may be needed. *Pro forma* statements for 1985, 1986, and 1987 must be developed to determine appropriate objectives and goals for Dick's Place.

CONCLUSION

"As a matter of fact," continued Mr. Paulette, "Firestone has a big ad in this morning's paper announcing the opening. The big boys have all that T.V. advertising behind them, too, not to mention the free training, accounting, and legal support. I was reminded of *that* when I was signing another $200 check to Jennings yesterday."

"I suppose you're right about the need to be more efficient here at the plant," agreed Bob Borum, after a thoughtful pause. "And things could get worse. But our timing could be wrong. Let's kick this thing around for awhile before we jump into that much debt. You know, Bill, it's the plant that's our big problem, even more than these offices or this showroom. Maybe we should just build a new recapping building."

"That's a good point, Bob. And here's another angle. Maybe we should go ahead now on another Richmond tire sales and service outlet, or maybe one in some other place, perhaps Petersburg or Fredericksburg."

CASE 20

Western Nursery, Inc.

LYNDA L. GOULET
University of Northern Iowa

PETER G. GOULET
University of Northern Iowa

INTRODUCTION

Western Nursery, located in northern California, raises grapevines and fruit and nut trees for sale to commercial farmers and to other nurseries. The business was incorporated in 1973 by Edward Vincent and his son-in-law, Steven Wood.

Mr. Vincent retired in 1973 from his previous career as a manager at Greene Nursery, a few miles away. Greene Nursery sells a variety of evergreen and deciduous trees and shrubs, flowers, and lawn and garden supplies for residential and commercial landscaping. At Greene, Mr. Vincent was responsible for purchasing and plant care, including the application of chemicals for disease and pest control, and the pruning and transplanting of plants.

Steve Wood served in the armed forces after high school, then returned to college, graduating in June, 1973, with a degree in Agricultural Economics. He was instrumental in persuading his father-in-law to start the business. Mr. Vincent and his wife owned the seven acres of land on which their home was situated, and a double-wide mobile home that Steve Wood and his family rented from them. Five of the acres, valued at $4,000, were transferred to Western Nursery upon its incorporation. Several prefabricated structures, financed with a bank loan of $10,000, were subsequently erected on the land. (This loan was retired in 1978.) Mr. Vincent and Steve Wood paid $15,000 in cash as initial capital for the start-up of business.

In 1974, Steve Wood arranged to lease fifteen acres of land from a nearby farm, purchased 50,000 rootstocks for grafting fruit trees, and reached agreements with local farmers to obtain 25,000 grapevine cuttings and budwood from ten varieties of fruit trees. One full-time employee, Bill Taylor, was hired as a field supervisor. Western Nursery had its first crop of trees and vines under cultivation in 1974.

Western Nursery has 1,100,000 trees and 500,000 grapevines in various stages of cultivation on 145 acres of rented land in 1984. A year-round labor force of ten laborers, two field supervisors, and an operations manager (Bill Taylor) are employed. Exhibit 1 summarizes Western Nursery's capital position in 1973 and 1983.

Exhibit 1 Balance sheet data, Western Nursery

Opening Balance Sheet, 1973			
Cash	$15,000	Short-term debt	$ 0
Buildings	10,000	Long-term debt	10,000
Land	4,000	Common stock	1,000
	$29,000	Paid-in capital	18,000
			$29,000
Year-End Balance Sheet			
December 31, 1983			
Cash	$ 6,400	Accounts payable	$ 2,100
Accounts receivable	2,800	Long-term debt	0
Supplies	15,400	Common stock	1,000
Equipment	61,000	Paid-in capital	18,000
Buildings	10,000	Retained earnings	50,300
Accumulated depreciation	(28,200)		$71,400
Land	4,000		
	$71,400		

OPERATIONS

Grapevine Production

Although there are over 8,000 varieties of grapes in the world, only about two dozen varieties are grown in any appreciable quantity. In 1983, Western Nursery cultivated five popular varieties. Grapevines are started from cuttings obtained from mature vines known to produce superior fruit. Western has an arrangement with several viticulturists in the county to take cuttings in early spring. There is no cost, other than Western's labor cost, as the vines must be heavily pruned every season. These cuttings are then planted by hand, at a density of about 15,000 plants per acre. Essentially, a hole is poked in the soil and the cutting is inserted. With practice, a worker can average one plant per minute.

Grapevine cuttings root quite easily and are ready for sale the next January. They are mechanically harvested and hand-packaged into sets of 100 plants each. These rooted cuttings are planted in a vineyard at a rate of approximately 500–600 plants per acre. They should not be permitted to develop fruit for the first two years.

Rootstock Production

All fruit and nut trees grown at Western Nursery are grafted onto one of six varieties of rootstock by a technique called *budding*. Budding consists of cutting a bud from a mature tree of a desired variety, slitting the bark of the rootstock plant, inserting the bud beneath the bark, and securing the grafted bud in place, using a wrapping. After the bud is firmly established, the rootstock plant above the bud is removed so that all subsequent growth of the plant is forced through the grafted bud. Grafting produces clones, identical to the original budwood tree. This process is necessary to the propogation of certain fruit and nut trees, because the species do not root easily on their own.

Rootstock varieties are developed to grow well in given soil conditions and to resist disease. Rootstock seeds are mechanically planted in March (for yearling trees), in June (for June bud nut trees), and in July (for June bud fruit trees). June bud rootstock is planted at a density of 12,000 plants per acre, whereas yearling rootstock is planted at a rate of 8,000 per acre. About 500,000 rootstocks are started at Western Nursery each year. The rootstock seedlings are budded after nine months for June buds and after a year and a half for yearlings. All rootstock plants grown at Western are intermediate goods, used only for the production of other products.

June Bud Production

The June bud is Western's most important product category. About 400,000 June buds of nearly 200 varieties of fruit and nut trees are produced each year. These include varieties of apple, pear, peach, cherry, apricot, nectarine, plum, almond, and walnut trees. June buds are trees that are budded in the spring on less-than-year-old rootstock, to be sold twelve to fifteen months later. An experienced worker can bud about one plant per minute. June bud plants are dug by machine and hand-packaged into sets of

25 plants each. Such trees will not reach bearing age for six or seven years after transplanting in the buyer's orchard. Fewer than 15 percent of Western's June bud sales are to nurseries; most are sold to orchardists.

Yearling Production

Yearling trees are produced in a manner similar to that of June buds. The main difference is that the rootstock is more than one year old before it is budded. As a result, yearlings reach bearing age a year sooner. Approximately 20 percent of yearling sales are to nurseries; the rest are sold to orchardists. (Refer to the production schedule in Figure 1 to see the timing of the production cycles for all Western's plants).

Figure 1 Planting and harvesting schedule—March 1982 through March 1985

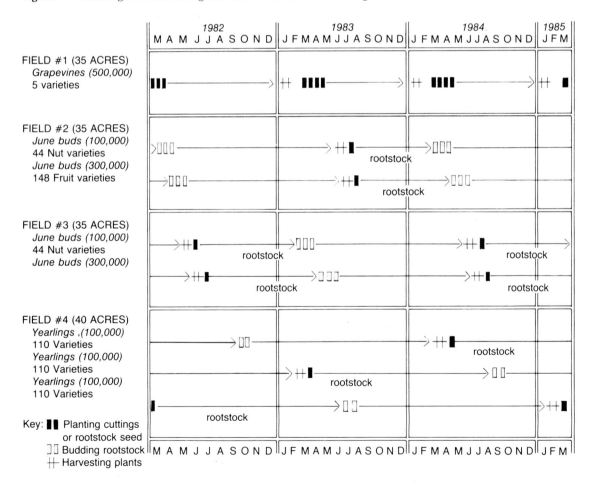

RESOURCES

Land

Western Nursery's office building, storage sheds, and packing shed are located on the five acres of owned land. Western currently rents four fields at an average price of $80 per acre per year. Western's production is allocated to the land as follows: 35 acres for grapevines, 40 acres for yearlings, and two fields of 35 acres each for June buds. These leases are currently being renegotiated by Western. Steve Wood has been assured that the rent will be held at the current rate for at least five more years, with the total lease term offered at ten years. Recently, however, a farmer has offered to sell 125 acres to the nursery for $1400 per acre, a price substantially below the current market value. The terms of the proposed sale involve a land contract with 20 percent down, 9 percent interest on the unpaid balance annually, a twenty-year payment schedule, with the principal balance due as a balloon payment after ten years. Steve Wood believes renting has the primary advantage of permitting Western to rotate its fields. The major disadvantage of renting is that fields may be physically separated, making field supervision more difficult.

Plant Resources

Western grows many varieties of each type of fruit and nut tree. For example, the nursery has twenty-one varieties of apple trees under cultivation. There are several reasons for this. Some varieties of a fruit are appropriate for a specific use (eating fresh, canning, baking, drying, or freezing); some require specific climatic and soil conditions for proper growth. Certain varieties ripen sooner than others, permitting a more or less continuous harvest season if several varieties are combined in an orchard. Some varieties require cross-pollination by one or more other varieties. Particular rootstocks result in different tree sizes which, in turn, permit different densities of plantings, lend themselves to varying degrees of mechanized harvesting and maintenance, and result in different investments and yields per acre for the farmer. New varieties are developed frequently that seek to improve climatic adaptability; to improve insect or disease resistance; or to solve specific horticultural, marketing, or processing problems.

Obtaining the cuttings for grapevines presents little difficulty for Western Nursery. This is not the case for the nearly 200 varieties of budwood (trees from which the buds are cut for grafting purposes). Many of the fruit varieties for the June bud plants must be obtained under a license arrangement (for a fee). Further, the nearest sources for many varieties of fruit and nut budwood required by Western are located over 100 miles from Western's premises. Typically, two crews of three to five laborers each (one headed by Bill Taylor, the other by Steve Wood) will drive to one budwood location in the morning, proceed to a second location in the afternoon, returning to Western late in the day. The branches cut from the selected budwood are then used to bud the rootstock the following day. One branch provides about a dozen buds.

Labor Resources

Western's employment fluctuates throughout the year, with spring being the busiest season. In 1983 as many as thirty-three field workers were employed in early March. New employees are first assigned to cultivating the grapevines. When this task is completed, the workers are moved to the budding of fruit trees. By late summer, the size of the workforce has shrunk by 50 percent through attrition. Western rewards all remaining workers with a 10¢-per-hour raise. In October, ten workers are retained for the winter to harvest the grapevine cuttings and yearlings and bud nut trees in the early spring. Western can thereby adjust its average wage rate downward by retaining more of its newer workers with lower wage rates.

Bill Taylor maintains that experience is not very critical after a point—the tediousness of the work overcomes any real benefits from experience. Most of the field work at Western requires a great deal of bending and kneeling. The workweek is long, up to fifty-six hours per week. The labor is nonunion. Wages equal those paid to other comparable agricultural field workers in the area. Most of the labor force is Mexican, as is one of the field supervisors. The two field supervisors each receive a salary of $200 per week. Additional information regarding workforce strength and allocation is found in Exhibit 2.

Exhibit 2   1983 labor summary

Time Period and Work Description	Hours Worked	Labor Cost
January to Early February (5 weeks)		
10 laborers from 1982 @ $2.80/hour avg.	2600	$ 7280
Management—Taylor, 2 field supervisors		
Tasks—Mechanized digging of 500,000 grapevines; preparation of soil for 1983 grapevines, packaging of vines, filling orders, and deliveries.		
Early February to Mid-March (6 weeks)		
10 laborers @ $2.80/hour avg.	2850	7980
Management—Taylor; 2 field supervisors for first 4 weeks		
Tasks—Mechanized digging of 100,000 yearlings, preparation of soil for rootstock planting, sowing of rootstock seed for yearlings, packaging, filling orders, and delivery.		
Late March to Early May (7 weeks)		
9 laborers @ $2.90/hour avg.	3150	9140
Management—Taylor; Wood for 2 weeks		
Tasks—Cut budwood for nut varieties; graft 100,000 June bud nut plants.		

Early March to Early May (9 weeks)
23 new laborers @ $2.40/hour.   11200 $ 26880
Management—2 field supervisors

Tasks—Obtain grapevine cuttings; plant 500,000 grapevine cuttings.

Early May to Mid-June (6 weeks)
9 laborers @ $2.90/hour avg.   2825   8190
23 laborers @ $2.40/hour   7500   18000
Management—Wood, Taylor, 2 field supervisors

Tasks—Cut budwood for fruit varieties; graft 300,000 June bud fruit plants.

Mid-June to Late July (5 weeks)
8 laborers @ $2.90/hour avg.   2225   6450
18 laborers @ $2.40/hour   4950   11880
Management—Taylor, 2 supervisors

Tasks—Mechanized digging of 400,000 June buds, preparation of soil for rootstock planting, sowing of rootstock seed for June buds, packaging, filling orders, and delivery

Late July to Early September (6 weeks)
6 laborers @ $3.00/hour avg.   1700   5100
9 laborers @ $2.50/hour   2575   6440
Management—Taylor, 2 supervisors

Tasks—General plant and soil care.

Early September to Early October (5 weeks)
6 laborers @ $3.00/hour avg.   1500   4500
9 laborers @ $2.50/hour   2225   5560
Management—Wood, Taylor, 2 supervisors

Tasks—Cut budwood for yearling varieties; graft 100,000 yearlings.

Early October to End of Year (12 weeks)
10 laborers @ $2.80/hour avg.   5075   14200
Management—Taylor, 2 supervisors

Tasks—General plant and soil care.

Totals   50375 $131600

SALES

Promotion, Advertising, and Pricing

In 1983, Steve Wood assumed complete responsibility for sales. During the year he has increased the percentage of sales made to commercial growers (orchardists and viticulturists) from 75 percent to nearly 88 percent. Excluding wholesale sales to other nurseries, approximately 70 percent of Western's sales are to repeat customers.

Western's advertising consists of direct mailings to potential customers and newspaper advertising in the adjacent four-county area. Direct mail advertisements are sent twice a year to 1500 farmers. An early spring mailing includes a postcard requesting the previous year's customers to estimate the number and variety of trees for which they require replacements. (It is industry practice for nurseries to guarantee their stock for one season. Trees that do not survive are replaced in accordance with a set policy).

A fall mailing campaign requests that prospective customers telephone Western to arrange an appointment for the sales manager to visit their farm and discuss planting needs. As a result of this mailing, Steve spends most of his time between October and March on the road. Newspaper advertisements describe the more popular varieties and mention that discounts are available for contract orders and quantity purchases. A summary of available discounts follows. Discounts for wholesale sales are standard in the area (the same terms are offered to Western).

Discount Terms	Client Category
50%	Replacements
40%	Wholesale customers
25%	Co-op customers
20%	Contract sales
up to 15%	Negotiated for quantity

Although the prices offered by Western and its competitors are almost identical, there is a great deal of price competition through the offering of "bonus" discounts. Many nurseries throughout the season offer such promotional discounts on varieties that are overstocked. Steve Wood refuses to do so, based on previous bad experiences with this practice. Local customers who had purchased plants at a higher price in the early part of the season became irritated when they discovered their friends had paid lower prices later for the same varieties.

Western offers free delivery in the adjacent four-county area. Western grants thirty-day credit terms on its sales. It does add a 1 percent per month finance charge to all balances outstanding over thirty days.

Contract Sales and Demand Estimation

In order to satisfy the demands of its customers and avoid overstocking problems, Western must make reasonable estimates of demand for each variety—one year in advance for June buds and a year and a half for yearlings. The penalty for overestimating demand is that any plant that can't be sold is burned at the end of the selling season. Trees and cuttings that have been dug up and packaged do not transplant successfully after three months. If demand is underestimated, either additional stock must be purchased from other nurseries to complete orders or sales are lost to the competition.

Contract sales are intended to avoid the problems of miscalculating the demand for specific plant varieties. The present proportion of each plant category sold on contract is: June buds, 30 percent, yearlings, 25 percent, and grapevines, 15 percent. To obtain maximum selectivity, the orchardist must place the order before the rootstock is planted. In this way, the orchardist may choose the best rootstock for the particular farm and the variety of plant to be grafted as well. A contract sale is subject to cancellation or change only by mutual consent and at no loss to the nursery. A contract order requires a deposit of 20 percent at the time the order is placed, with the balance to be paid within thirty days of delivery.

Sales Philosophy

Western Nursery has attempted to look at fruit and nut tree cultivation from the viewpoint of the farmer (orchardist or viticulturist). Farmers are naturally most concerned with the potential profitability of their orchards or vineyards. Most look to nurseries for advice concerning the particular varieties that would be most profitable to grow. Steve feels many (competitive) nurseries use this as an opportunity to rid themselves of plants that are overstocked. Western avoids such practices, as Steve feels they could generate bad customer relations. Western's policy is to refuse to make specific recommendations. Instead, Steve prefers to discuss the pros and cons of several varieties with the farmer and to leave the final decision to the customer.

In spite of his policy, Steve is troubled by the way in which farmers make their plant-purchase decisions. They tend to want to buy those varieties that produce fruit or nuts in great demand at the time of planting. What they fail to consider is: when bearing age is finally reached for these trees, there is likely to be an oversupply of the produce, causing prices to fall. Western's policy is to attempt to alert farmers to this situation and to try to persuade them to plant the varieties that will grow best on their land, regardless of prevailing market conditions.

Competitive Considerations

Western's competition derives from three sources. A large, publicly held nursery is located about seventy-five miles to the south. Although one of the largest nurseries in the state, it has only a limited effect on Western because most of its sales are ornamental plants. A second competitor, a commercial fruit and nut tree nursery, is located 100 miles to the southwest. Although that nursery sells throughout the state and is larger than Western, it concentrates on the more populated counties south of its location. The chief competition is a nursery in the next county with a sales volume similar to Western's. However, this competitor does not do much actual growing. Instead, most of its stock is purchased from other nurseries. This competitor does employ a sales force that travels statewide.

Western's local market share is strong for most of its product lines. It has 85 percent of local grapevine sales, 60 percent of June bud fruit tree sales, 40 percent of June bud nut tree sales, and 25 percent of yearling sales. Statewide, Western has about a 5 percent share of the grapevine market and smaller shares for the other products.

ADMINISTRATION

Personnel

Ed Vincent gradually has been withdrawing from the full-time management of the firm. He is no longer involved in sales but does all the purchasing and oversees the maintenance of equipment. Steve does all the sales and advertising, heads one of the two crews that obtain budwood, and oversees the entire operation. Both men receive annual salaries of $30,000.

Bill Taylor receives a salary of $18,000. He reports directly to Steve and is responsible for hiring laborers and directing the field supervisors. According to Steve, Bill is sufficiently experienced in soil treatment and plant cultivation to make most of the chemical application decisions by himself. However, he is reluctant to do so. Potentially the source of this difficulty can be traced to Mr. Vincent's retirement from sales. Given additional free time, Mr. Vincent frequently meddles in the field operations. On several occasions, he countermanded Bill's instructions to field staff concerning some aspect of plant care.

In the office, there is one clerical worker and a receptionist who also performs various clerical chores. She is Mary Vincent, Ed Vincent's sister, and is known as the local gossip who spends a good deal of time on the phone. Steve believes the situation has worsened recently, since his sales calls have left her largely unsupervised. Mr Vincent considers telephone privileges a fringe benefit, since her salary is rather low at $6000.

There is one other person in the office, Ted Asken. Ted is a high school graduate with some junior college training in accounting. Steve hopes to persuade Ted to pursue additional business training in night school, so eventually he can be given a number of managerial duties in purchasing, costing, and inventory control. Mr. Vincent has stated emphatically that Ted could spend as much time as he liked costing products, but should stay clear of anything relating to inventory and purchasing.

An organization chart summarizing the key personnel and their responsibilities is shown as Figure 2.

Financial Policies

Western follows a policy of incurring no debt and takes all discounts available for prompt payment of accounts. Steve follows up personally on all overdue accounts receivable, and has sued on three occasions. Whenever short-term loans are needed, either Steve or Mr. Vincent provides personal funds at a rate of 6 percent interest. Steve felt that since the company owns little land, and the inventory is considered poor collateral by banks, the firm has few resources to secure loans from traditional sources.

In the years since Western Nursery was incorporated, it has paid no dividends, using all earnings to finance growth. Total earnings retained to date amount to about

Figure 2 Western Nursery's organization chart

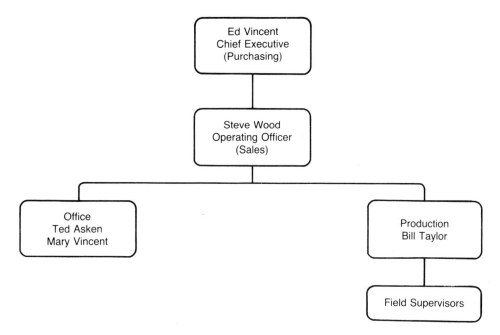

$50,000. Steve and Mr. Vincent are reluctant to issue additional stock at the present time, as Steve desires to have his son follow in his footsteps.

Insurance coverage on nursery stock is marginal at best and prohibitively expensive, except for traditional crop-hail coverage. If a disease or pest outbreak were to occur, two years' growth of June bud plants and three years' growth of yearlings could be destroyed. Frost damage to new cuttings could also be a setback, but would be relatively less damaging.

The financial results for 1983 are presented in Exhibit 3. Net income in that year was a record for the firm. In the first three years of operation, Western operated at an overall loss of about $5000. Through 1982, average profits were about $6750 per year. For the last three years, the basic production volume and cost structures have been similar to those experienced in 1983.

Note in Exhibit 1 that there are very few items in Western's balance sheet. This is because of a lack of inventory at the end of the season, and the firm's policies concerning accounts payable and receivable. The inventory of plants in the ground, still in the growth process, is assigned no value because it is unsalable and highly subject to damage and loss.

To estimate product costs and help determine prices, it was Ted's idea to keep track of the time that Steve, Bill, and the field supervisors spent on various products.

Exhibit 3   Western Nursery's income statement for year ending December 31, 1983

Gross Sales[1]

Grapevines (407,300 plants)	$101,800	
June buds—nuts (74,700 plants)	71,000	
June buds—fruit (236,200 plants)	200,800	
Yearlings (45,600)	68,400	
		$442,000

Less—Discounts

Grapevines	$ 11,200	
June buds—nuts	10,400	
June buds—fruits	35,800	
Yearlings	10,600	
		(68,000)
Net Sales		$374,000

Operating Expenses

Salaried personnel	$112,800	
Field labor	131,600	
Land rent	11,600	
Property taxes	1,800	
Utilities[2]	7,100	
Insurance and state taxes	6,500	
Office supplies	5,200	
Depreciation	6,100	
Advertising	8,600	
Purchased plants, licenses[3]	18,900	
Repairs	2,300	
Field supplies, packing	10,400	
Gasoline	6,900	
Chemicals	26,700	
		356,500
Income before tax		$ 17,500
Income tax		3,000
Net income		$ 14,500

[1]Does not include extra plants provided free on large-quantity orders.

[2]Two-thirds of utility cost is for irrigation.

[3]Primarily royalties on licensed June bud fruits

This was the reason for constructing the 1983 labor summary table shown as Exhibit 2. Further, Ted and Steve agreed that, to create a better cost system for the products, some overhead items should be allocated in proportion to the acreage under cultivation. These items included field supplies, machinery repair, chemicals, gasoline, crop irrigation, land rental, and field labor for general plant and soil care. They could not decide how other overhead costs should be allocated.

OTHER STRATEGIC CONSIDERATIONS

Quality

Both Steve and Bill contend that none of Western's competitors have any better quality plants; some having much lower quality. In the past, quality was not as important to the customer as price, especially for varieties in high demand. However, both men feel that orchardists are becoming more quality-conscious. To help ensure quality and satisfaction, Bill Taylor personally inspects every order that is shipped, to make certain the roots have been adequately protected from excessive drying. The plants are stored in moist sawdust after packaging and sprayed with a fungicide. In addition, Western has a policy of including five extra plants for every 1000 ordered.

The quality of propogated plants depends on both the rootstock and the budwood. If any of the budwood is diseased, the disease will be transmitted to the new tree, but will not be apparent until the tree reaches bearing age. Steve uses plant pathologists at the California Department of Agriculture to test his budwood for viral infections. Steve first identifies the best-producing orchard for a given variety within a 150-mile radius, then obtains permission or license rights to cut buds. Next he takes sample branches from the orchard to the laboratory for testing. Finally, those trees that are shown to be disease-free are identified on a map of the orchard. When crews are sent to collect budwood, the map is used to identify those trees that are acceptable for cutting.

Products

Western licenses twenty-three patented varieties of fruit trees. Steve is attempting to develop new strains, though the time he can devote to this task is now limited since Mr. Vincent has withdrawn from sales. Steve has several varieties under development, but as yet has not obtained patents for any of them. One of the problems associated with such R & D is the long test period, up to ten years, required to establish the characteristics of the new tree. Though every new strain is patentable, the useful life of a patent is limited by the constant development of new varieties.

Western cannot compete in the area of controlled experimentation with the very large nurseries. For example, a firm in Michigan where Steve once worked has over 1000 acres of orchards that are working laboratories. These orchards are used to develop new nursery products and improve nursery production practices. Other areas of research undertaken by this firm include frost control techniques, rootstock development, pollination testing, chemically induced plant growth regulation, and packaging protection.

Expansion Considerations

Steve Wood and Mr. Vincent have allowed their operation to stabilize during the last few years. With Ed's gradual retirement on the horizon, Steve is concerned about the prospect of new sales growth. He feels he will be unable to cope with any new growth, should it take place under these circumstances, because he needs to be involved in both sales and operations. Because he feels it is most important that he keep a tight rein on operations, Steve has considered hiring a salesperson. Such a person could typically expect to be paid a 20 percent commission. Based on this, Steve feels that to earn a good living the salesperson would have to increase sales about 20 percent. Steve is concerned because he is unsure of the firm's ability to expand production accordingly.

To avoid hiring sales personnel, Steve has taken steps to increase local referrals. He has induced Mr. Vincent to buy all of Western's chemical needs from local dealers instead of taking volume discounts from regional suppliers. Several new customers had mentioned that they had been referred to Western by a local farm chemical dealer.

Future Directions

It was January 1984 when Steve asked Ted to try to develop a new price list for the coming season. He asked Ted to use his new costs as a basis for these prices, Ted found he was faced with a number of questions that needed answering. What was the product mix going to be for the coming year? Was Steve going to hire a new salesperson? Had Steve made any decision concerning the land purchase? Ted also looked at last year's expenses and profits and wondered why they planned to burn all those plants again this year. It seemed to him that someone should want them. He also needed to know if Steve planned to place the same emphasis on contract sales for the coming season. Ted realized that some major strategic decisions needed to be made for Western Nursery. He also believed the firm's marketing and management policies needed to be reexamined. Ted was registered to take Business Policy during the coming semester and he hoped to learn some concepts and techniques that could be employed at Western Nursery.

CASE 21

Jensen Oil
Lynda L. Goulet
Peter G. Goulet
Saul Diamond
University of Northern Iowa

HISTORY AND PRESENT STATUS

Jensen Oil Company, located in Eastport, Iowa, is a wholesale distributor and retailer of bulk petroleum and related products. All Jensen Oil's properties are located in a single county that has a total population of approximately 30,000. Jensen Oil owns two facilities that consist of above-ground steel storage tanks for bulk petroleum products—one in Eastport and the other in Riverton.

Jensen Oil was founded by Benton Jensen in 1936 in Eastport, Iowa. The firm has been associated with the Mobil Oil Corporation for thirty years. In 1971, the business was incorporated as a Subchapter S corporation. At that time, Jack Donovan, an employee of the firm since the end of World War II, purchased a 20 percent share in the enterprise.

In the late 1960s, Jensen Oil expanded from its original location in Eastport by adding bulk facilities in Riverton and Rock City. Both of these locations were smaller operations than the main location, carrying a limited line of higher-turnover gasolines and fuel oils. The Riverton and Rock City locations utilize leased land. Their purpose was to reduce the time and cost of delivery to areas in the northern and southwestern parts of the county.

In late 1979 Mr. Jensen died suddenly and his 80 percent ownership interest transferred to his heirs. The heirs agreed to sell all of their interests to Mr. Donovan for $200,000. This was estimated to be 80 percent of the book value of owners' equity at the time of Jensen's death. Mr. Donovan secured a ten-year, $200,000 SBA-guaranteed loan for the firm, carrying a 15 percent rate of interest. He then personally used the cash to pay the heirs. (Note the balance sheet entry of an account receivable, rather than a note receivable from Donovan, since 1980).

June 1980 ended Mr. Donovan's first year as sole owner of Jensen Oil. The year 1980 was also the last year in which government controls on gasoline and fuel oil prices were in effect. (These controls had been established in the 1970s after the world oil crisis.) The years 1981 through 1983 were characterized by higher oil prices and moderate declines in fuel oil sales. With decontrol of prices, many residential fuel oil users switched to less expensive heating sources, such as natural gas. In response to such changes, Mr. Donovan closed his 40,000-gallon-capacity Rock City facility in March 1982. Several of the storage tanks were moved to the other locations. Rock City is now serviced primarily from Riverton, fifteen miles to the southwest, and from Eastport, ten miles to the east.

The Eastport bulk terminal now has a total capacity of 120,000 gallons from eight storage tanks. The Riverton plant has a 70,000 gallon capacity and five tanks. However, the Riverton plant must be relocated within six months due to a termination of the firm's lease on the existing site. The relocation will require purchase of a new parcel of land for $6000, rezoning of the parcel, construction of a dike for safety purposes, concrete work for placement of the storage tanks, removal of the tanks at the existing site, and installation at the new site. The total estimated cost of the relocation, excluding land purchase, is $5000. Property taxes are estimated to be $100 annually, compared to the current rental cost of $200 per month.

MANAGEMENT

Jack Donovan began working for Jensen Oil in the 1940s. He assumed the firm's bookkeeping duties upon its incorporation and continues to perform that task. However, once a year a CPA is employed to prepare financial and tax statements. Mr. Donovan periodically reviews salaries and gives raises according to employee performance, but in line with wages offered by similar businesses in the area. He is a member of the state Oil Jobber Association and the National Federation of Independent Businesses.

Mr. Donovan believes that a major determinant of a business's success is the employees. He feels that service is the critical factor for ensuring lasting customer satisfaction. As a result, service is extended to customers in several ways: providing information and technical expertise; offering new products as they become available; giving better-than-Mobil warranty service; extending extra credit under certain conditions; and making spot deliveries to farmers.

Jensen Oil offers its three employees and owner a group health insurance plan and a life insurance plan, but no pension plan. The Riverton location employs a salesman who also owns the local Mobil service station. His responsibilities to Jensen Oil include acquiring and servicing customers, making deliveries of bulk petroleum products with a tank wagon, and maintaining the bulk storage tanks. He receives a straight commission of 2 cents per gallon sold. This commission rate represents a $0.25 per gallon increase, effective since June, 1982.

The Rock City area is serviced by a part-time sales and delivery man who also draws social security benefits. He uses the Riverton tank truck and makes his deliveries in the evenings and on Saturdays. This man has been with the firm since 1968, and is paid a monthly salary of $275. The third employee is an hourly paid delivery man, servicing the Eastport area. The Eastport facility is operated by Mr. Donovan, who makes deliveries occasionally during busy periods.

Mr. Donovan is considering relinquishing the corporation's Subchapter S status. Under Subchapter S, all of Mr. Donovan's salary, bonuses, and the business net income is taxed as personal income. Mr. Donovan's personal marginal tax bracket is 45 percent, as he and his wife have substantial income unrelated to Jensen Oil. As a regular corporation, dividends would be double-taxed. Mr. Donovan was not overly concerned with this double-taxation, since shortly before Mr. Jensen's death he had succeeded in persuading Jensen to reduce the dividend payout to themselves, retaining the funds for replacing worn-out equipment and for future expansion. Donovan also recognized that at the end of the fiscal year he could increase his salary and/or give himself a bonus (rather than declare any dividends). Bonuses and salary increases, however, must be reasonable according to IRS guidelines of compensation paid to employees and officers in similar industries, for similar asset-sized firms. Comparative compensation figures for firms in the oil jobber industry were between $20,000 and $30,000 in recent years.

PRODUCTS AND CUSTOMERS

Jensen Oil carries five different classes of products—gasolines, fuel oils, lubricating oils, tires, and batteries—which it sells at both the wholesale and retail levels. Sales of fuel oils tend to be highly seasonal, while gasoline sales are fairly uniform throughout the year. Farm usage of diesel fuels peaks in the fall and spring, while home heating oil demand begins in September and declines in April. Gasolines are sold to five Mobil service stations in Jensen's sales area, down from eight in 1980. Kerosene is sold to Jensen's customers on a self-service basis, rather than being delivered. In recent years, diesel fuel has increasingly replaced gasoline for Jensen's farm customers.

Almost all of the tires supplied to dealers by Jensen are Mobil tires, primarily because of the incentive plan offered by Mobil. Since there is a great deal of local competition in tires, Jensen Oil is considering dropping this product line. Lubricating oils are sold primarily in drums or cases of quart cans to gas stations, farmers, and local industrial manufacturers for factory machinery. A full line of Mobil batteries for cars and trucks is sold to local service stations. Table 1 shows the product mix and prices for gasolines and fuel oils in recent years.

Jensen Oil has about 300 accounts, which are subdivided into four categories: retail, commercial, home heating, and farm. Retail accounts are represented by the service stations. There are twenty implement and feed stores that comprise the commercial accounts. Additional sales are made to some sixty home heating accounts in rural areas and to 200 farmers. The home heating accounts have declined by almost 30 percent since 1980.

There are no guidelines for credit approval, or procedures for collection of accounts. However, Mr. Donovan knows almost all the firm's customers personally and believes such experience is sufficient in determining their ability to pay. He is especially

Table 1 Sales volume and prices 1980–1983

	1980		1981		1982		1983	
	Sales	*Price*	*Sales*	*Price*	*Sales*	*Price*	*Sales*	*Price*
Products	*m gal*	*¢/gal*	*m gal*	*¢/gal*	*m gal*	*¢/gal*	*m gal*	*¢/gal*
Gasolines								
Regular	920	88.7	940	118.1	860	133.4	715	120.9
No lead	230	94.6	260	122.7	245	138.4	245	125.9
Gasohol	100	90.7	125	120.1	105	135.9	110	124.4
Fuel Oils								
Diesel	260	83.7	270	116.1	265	130.7	270	120.7
Kerosene	50	108.8	50	120.4	55	132.9	60	142.2
Heating	140	77.7	135	108.6	130	122.9	125	112.9
Furnace	50	72.6	50	102.6	50	115.9	45	102.9
Total	1750		1830		1710		1570	

Sales in Thousands (m) of Gallons
Prices in Cents Per Gallon

sensitive to the needs of the farmers, given the seasonal nature of their cash flows. There are no discounts for early payment. Collection efforts consist of phone calls or personal contact with customers whose accounts are overdue. Statements are sent on an irregular basis.

Collection of most farm accounts is facilitated by government policies toward farmers. Users of gasoline for agricultural purposes get a tax refund from the state when fuel is purchased. However, to qualify for a timely refund, farmers must pay suppliers within ninety days of purchase invoice date and obtain a sales receipt. Failure to do so defers the refund until year end. Diesel fuel for farmers is not taxed.

Mr. Donovan is concerned about the current high level of accounts receivable. Slow and irregular collections have made it difficult to anticipate monthly cash flows. Service station accounts normally pay within thirty days and present no real problems. Farm accounts are more problematic. As of June 30, 1983, over $50,000 of the accounts receivable balance was questionable. Two accounts totaling $35,000 were in bankruptcy and another $17,000 account was being collected in $100-per-month installments with no interest charge. Mr. Donovan estimated that, as a creditor, he might receive as much as fifty cents on the dollar from the pending bankruptcies. Exhibit 1 summarizes the age structure of Jensen's accounts receivable.

COSTS, PRICING AND PROMOTION

Prior to 1981, Jensen Oil's gasoline prices could not exceed ceiling prices set by the government. Gasoline was classified as either "farm" or "dealer" and maximum markups differed, depending upon the classification: sixteen and one-tenth cents per gallon maximum markup for farm gas and seven and seven-tenths cents for dealer gas. In 1980, Jensen Oil sold approximately 30 percent of its gasolines and diesel fuel to farmers, with a markup of ten cents per gallon. Dealer gasolines were marked up six cents per gallon. The markups on Jensen Oil's other products included the following: eleven cents per gallon for heater oil; ten cents per gallon for furnace oil; ten cents per gallon for diesel fuel; ten cents per gallon for kerosene; and a 15 percent markup on all tires, batteries, and lubricating oils.

After decontrol, Mr. Donovan continued to utilize the same practices until competitive pressure caused him to alter his pricing practices. Average markups, net of excise taxes, on gasolines and fuel oils dropped to six and eight-tenths cents per gallon

Exhibit 1   June 30, 1983, age of accounts receivable

Current accounts	43%
Between 30 and 60 days	25%
Between 60 and 90 days	8%
Between 90 and 120 days	3%
Over 120 days	21%

in 1983 from seven and one-half cents per gallon in 1980. However, Jensen Oil's sales of gasoline and diesel fuel to farmers increased to 35 percent of total sales by 1983.

A summary of the selling prices and purchase costs for the fuel portion of Jensen's sales is shown in Exhibit 2. In response to competitive pressures that compressed fuel margins through the period, Mr. Donovan increased the markups on tires, batteries, and lubricating oils to 20 percent in 1982. There was one exception to the fuel price and margin trends in the period. Specifically, increased demand for kerosene permitted increased margins on this product in 1983.

Jensen Oil relies primarily on word-of-mouth advertising. Fall and spring newspaper advertising is used to promote lubricating oils. Mr. Donovan places advertisements in *Farm Futures*, a quarterly publication consisting of articles of interest to farmers. Donovan pays $120 per year for 150 copies, which are mailed to customers and prospective customers of his choosing. Other promotions include brochures, left by deliverymen, that advertise oil specials, annual gift calendars, and Christmas turkeys given to each of Jensen Oil's twenty-five retail and commercial accounts.

LOCAL COMPETITION AND THE OIL JOBBER INDUSTRY

Jensen Oil competes with four other oil jobbers in the area: Able Oil, selling Texaco products; Baker Oil with Standard products, Charlie Oil with Sinclair products, and Farmer's Co-op, selling unbranded products. Oil jobbers obtain their petroleum products from one or more intermediate storage facilities called terminals. Most of these terminals are owned by major oil refiners (Mobil, Gulf, Sunoco, etc.). Some independent wholesalers also own terminals, obtaining their supplies from one or more of the oil refiners. Petroleum products are either "branded" or "unbranded." Branded products are purchased from a major refiner, such as Mobil Oil, and advertised as such. Recently, trends in the industry are toward fewer independent terminals and increased brand-name advertising emphasis.

Oil jobbers purchase supplies from large terminals, providing storage and distribution services for their local areas. Jobbers can purchase and sell both branded and unbranded petroleum products, but trademark laws restrict sales made to branded service stations to the displayed brand. Other buyers may be served with unbranded products, provided the jobber does not represent such product to be affiliated with the major oil refiner.

Oil jobbers' total share of the U.S. motor fuel market has been slowly growing, from a 40 percent share in the 1970s to almost a 50 percent share in the 1980s. Jensen Oil has the leading share of its local market based on gallons of motor fuel sold in fiscal 1983. (Refer to Table 2.)

According to the U.S. Department of Energy, 1982 demand for motor fuel averaged about 435 gallons per person. In Jensen Oil's market area, consumption is significantly lower for highway use and higher for nonhighway uses. Overall, the local consumption rate is 80% of the national average.

Exhibit 2   Jensen Oil's income statements

| | For the Fiscal Years Ended June 30 | | | |
	1980	1981	1982	1983
Sales:				
Tires, etc.	$ 275,300	$ 279,150	$ 265,600	$ 228,000
Gas/fuel oil	1,541,750	2,150,250	2,265,750	1,909,100
− Excise tax	(139,250)	(151,900)	(208,750)	(202,500)
Net sales	1,677,800	2,277,500	2,322,600	1,934,600
− Cost of sales	1,474,750	2,060,050	2,160,250	1,804,350
Gross profit	203,050	217,450	162,350	130,250
Operating Expenses				
Commissions	17,200	17,950	15,750	14,650
Wages	11,850	11,850	12,350	12,650
Salary	12,000	12,000	14,000	14,000
Rent	9,350	9,350	8,600	6,200
Truck operation	11,400	11,900	11,650	10,950
Insurance	8,550	9,700	9,500	8,050
Bad debts	7,800	8,150	7,600	10,250
Interest	0	30,000	28,500	26,800
Depreciation	2,900	4,950	4,300	4,150
Maintenance/repair	4,700	4,250	8,600	3,900
Utilities	5,100	5,350	5,500	5,200
Miscellaneous	6,900	6,650	6,000	5,100
Total operating expenses	97,750	132,100	132,350	121,900
Income from operations	$ 105,300	$ 85,350	$ 30,000	$ 8,350
Dividends	10,000	8,000	3,000	0
Cost of Sales:				
Beginning Inventory				
Tires, batteries, oils	14,000	29,600	27,300	33,450
Fuels	48,500	156,250	189,900	165,800
	62,500	185,850	217,200	199,250
Purchases				
Tires, batteries, oils	255,000	240,450	227,500	201,650
Fuels	1,343,100	1,850,950	1,914,800	1,609,400
	1,598,100	2,091,400	2,142,300	1,811,050
Available	1,660,600	2,277,250	2,359,500	2,010,300
Ending Inventory				
Tires, batteries, oils	29,600	27,300	33,450	45,100
Fuels	156,250	189,900	165,800	160,850
	185,850	217,200	199,250	205,950
Cost of sales	1,474,750	2,060,050	2,160,250	1,804,350
Per gallon of fuels:				
Avg. sale price	88.1¢	117.5¢	132.5¢	121.6¢
Avg. purchase cost excl. tax	72.6¢	101.7¢	113.3¢	101.9¢

Table 2   Comparison of local market shares for motor fuel jobber market

	1980		1983	
	Sales Volume	*Market Share*	*Sales Volume*	*Market Share*
Jensen Oil	1.51 mil	29.5%	1.34 mil	28.9%
Able Oil	1.10 mil	21.5%	1.22 mil	26.3%
Baker Oil	1.21 mil	23.6%	.98 mil	21.1%
Charlie Oil	.72 mil	14.1%	.51 mil	11.0%
Farmers' Co-op	.58 mil	11.3%	.59 mil	12.7%
Total gallons	5.12 mil		4.64 mil	

ALTERNATIVE STRATEGIES

Trends in consumption and competition during the early 1980s pressured Jensen Oil's net profit margin. As Mr. Donovan looked at the latest income figures, as well as the general trends in the industry, he became convinced that the best way to increase Jensen's profitability was to increase volume. He has identified several alternative strategies that would achieve this end.

With deregulation, oil refiners have been permitted to cancel contracts with oil jobbers. Oil jobbers with low-volume sales are likely to be targets of such activity, because major refiners feel they can improve margins and lower inventory investments by eliminating large numbers of small customers. Mr. Donovan anticipates that two oil jobbers north of his territory with a combined volume of less than 500,000 gallons of gasolines and fuel oils may no longer be served directly by Mobil after December 1983. Were this to happen, Jensen Oil could act as a "subjobber," providing these firms with their needed supplies.

In the subjobber capacity, Jensen Oil could make a one cent profit per gallon sold, less any additional expenses the firm would incur in servicing those two large accounts. Oil supplies would be transported from Mobil terminals directly to those firms, rather than be delivered first to Jensen Oil. However, Jensen Oil would be billed directly for these shipments. No doubt the other local oil jobbers would attempt to win those two accounts for themselves, but Donovan believes he would have the obvious edge, since his firm carries the same branded products.

Further, Mr. Donovan had been contemplating acquiring one or both of these firms as a means of expanding his markets. Mr. Donovan hoped the uncertainty of this situation and prospects of narrower margins would act as a stimulus for these firms to favor merging with Jensen Oil. He believed the outright purchase of either firm would be improbable due to his outstanding SBA loan. Donovan anticipated being able to give a minor share of Jensen Oil stock to each firm, retaining the owners as partners and managers of their existing businesses. Mr. Donovan had ascertained that profit margins of these two small firms had recently been about the same as Jensen Oil's.

A third alternative strategy involved attempting to increase penetration in the southeastern part of the county, in a town called Woodville. Donovan felt this area was not being served adequately by any oil jobbers at the present time, because fewer inhabitants and numerous gravel roads resulted in higher servicing costs. The Woodville area has a population of about 3000 people, with a total usage of gasolines and fuel oils of about 1,000,000 gallons per year. Mr. Donovan believed it would be possible to capture 40 percent of this total market, as no other oil jobbers have facilities within twenty miles of the community. Setting up an operation of the type needed to service the Woodville area would require some additional facilities and the hiring of additional personnel as described:

Four storage tanks (10,000 gal. each)	$12,000
Installation	3,000
Tank truck for deliveries	18,000
Rent, insurance, bad debts, misc.	5,700
Costs for gallons sold:	
Truck operation and maintenance	1¢/gal
Delivery/salesperson (retired)	2¢/gal

Expansion of the Eastport location was a fourth alternative being considered by Mr. Donovan. If a part-time office worker were hired, Donovan could devote more personal time to sales. Under such circumstances, Mr. Donovan felt he could regain some lost sales in the Rock City area, which amounted to almost 125,000 gallons or 40 percent of Jensen's former sales level in that area. Able Oil and the Farmers' Co-op had both benefited when Jensen Oil closed its Rock City facility.

Additional sales were potentially available in Franklin, located in the adjacent county about twelve miles to the east of Jensen's Eastport facility. A new bridge under construction was expected to be completed by spring of 1984 and would make easier delivery across the river that divided the counties. The old bridge had restricted truck traffic since the mid-1970s, making sales to this area uneconomical. Mr. Donovan anticipated that 150,000 gallons in gasoline and fuel oil sales could be achieved, with 250,000 gallons as a probable upper limit. To sell more than this upper limit would require the establishment of a bulk facility across the river.

Donovan believed an expansion of the Eastport location to serve Franklin and Rock City would require an investment in another truck and two more storage tanks, plus their installation. New fixed costs would include $5000 for the office worker, $4.50 per hour for an additional driver, and $3000 for other costs. New variable costs would be one cent per gallon sold for truck costs. However, the part-time Rock City delivery man, working out of Riverton, would be dismissed.

Mr. Donovan had one misgiving concerning the Eastport expansion. He felt such expansion might preclude his opening a facility in Franklin similar to the one contemplated for Woodville. If he did not expand Eastport, however, he was not certain he could justify a greater sales effort in Rock City without incurring most of the costs ascribed to the expansion.

CONCLUSION

Before the winter season began, Mr. Donovan knew he needed to relocate the Riverton facility and make some strategic decisions. He was not pleased with Jensen Oil's current performance and recognized that some action had to be taken to improve it. (Exhibit 3 gives Jensen Oil's balance sheet for fiscal years 1980 through 1983.) He realized that Jensen Oil needed a formal organizational chart and some specific objectives, goals, and policies for the future. Mr. Donovan contemplated what new marketing, management, finance, and production practices would be needed as Jensen Oil continued to grow.

Exhibit 3   Jensen Oil's balance sheets

| | For the Fiscal Years Ended June 30 | | | |
	1980	1981	1982	1983
Assets				
Cash	$ 12,600	$ 6,100	$ 7,350	$ 10,300
Accounts receivable	169,400	246,150	298,350	316,250
Inventory[1]	185,850	217,200	199,250	205,950
Loan[2]	200,000	175,000	150,000	125,000
Total current	567,850	644,450	654,950	657,500
Net fixed assets	9,000	27,100	22,800	18,650
Total assets	576,850	671,550	677,750	676,150
Credits				
Accounts payable	$ 21,150	47,100	33,850	36,250
Accrued excise tax payable	10,400	11,650	15,450	16,100
LTD—current	9,850	11,350	13,000	15,000
	41,400	70,100	62,300	67,350
SBA loan	190,150	178,800	165,800	150,800
Total debt	231,550	248,900	228,100	218,150
Capital stock	50,000	50,000	50,000	50,000
Paid-in-capital	200,000	200,000	200,000	200,000
Earned surplus	95,300	172,650	199,650	208,000
Total equity	345,300	422,650	449,650	458,000
Total capital	576,850	671,550	677,750	676,150

[1]Gallons of fuels in inventory   180,000g   170,000g   150,000g   160,000g
1979—80,000g
[2]Personal loan to Donovan to pay heirs.

CASE 22

Star Manufacturing, Inc.
Trouble at Al Tech

PETER G. GOULET
University of Northern Iowa

LYNDA L. GOULET
University of Northern Iowa

The year 1983 will be critical for the Al Tech Division of Star Manufacturing, Inc. Al Tech has just reopened after a two-week shutdown for the Christmas holidays. Russell (Rusty) Wainscott, general manager of Al Tech, is returning to work after a four-month convalescence from injuries suffered in an auto accident. In Rusty's absence, George Hayes was assigned by Star as acting manager of the division. George's performance as acting manager earned him a promotion to vice-president of strategic planning for Star. In this capacity he was to develop and implement a strategic planning process for Star and supervise and coordinate planning activities of the various divisions of the firm.

HISTORY OF STAR MANUFACTURING, INC.

Star Manufacturing was founded in Baltimore, Maryland, in the mid-1940s. The company initially produced only industrial refrigeration systems. In 1968, Star acquired Missouri Compressor, Inc., the chief supplier of compressors used in Star's refrigeration systems. Missouri Compressor, located in St. Louis, survived in an industry dominated by large firms by making small quantities of custom-designed, high-quality, high-efficiency compressors. In spite of recent innovations by its larger competitors, Missouri Compressor retains a good reputation and holds a respectable position in the industry.

Shortly after acquiring Missouri Compressor, Star acquired Allied Stampings Company, a small, custom producer of metal stampings. This firm was a key supplier to Missouri Compressor and to firms manufacturing industrial, automotive, and construction equipment in the St. Louis area. This unit is now called the Metal Stampings Division.

In 1976, Star was approached by a major air conditioning manufacturer to build some components for a new line of low-cost, high-efficiency air conditioning systems for the manufactured housing market. For a number of reasons, the air conditioning manufacturer decided that this product did not fit its image, and subsequently sold all its facilities to Star. This became the Air Conditioning Division of Star Manufacturing, Inc.

Star's latest acquisition, Al Tech, was consummated to provide the firm with additional access to the manufactured housing industry and to lower existing product costs. A summary of Star's key product markets served is shown in Figure 1. Exhibits 1, 2, and 3 summarize Star's recent financial results, both consolidated and by division.

Figure 1 Key product markets served—Star Manufacturing, Inc.

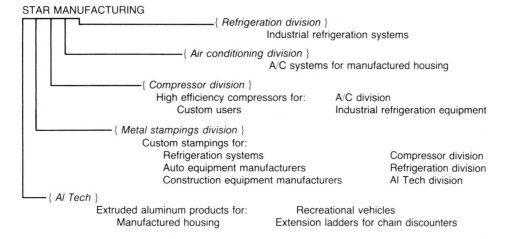

STAR MANUFACTURING

- { *Refrigeration division* }
  - Industrial refrigeration systems
- { *Air conditioning division* }
  - A/C systems for manufactured housing
- { *Compressor division* }
  - High efficiency compressors for: A/C division
  - Custom users   Industrial refrigeration equipment
- { *Metal stampings division* }
  - Custom stampings for:
    - Refrigeration systems   Compressor division
    - Auto equipment manufacturers   Refrigeration division
    - Construction equipment manufacturers   Al Tech division
- { *Al Tech* }
  - Extruded aluminum products for: Recreational vehicles
  - Manufactured housing   Extension ladders for chain discounters

Exhibit 1 Star Manufacturing, Inc.'s comparative income statements, year ending 1982

	Divisions					Corporation
	Al Tech	Metal Stampings	Industrial Refrigeration	Air Conditioning	Missouri Compressor	Star Manufacturing
			In $000			
Net sales	13887	18136	72653	8267	22465	135408
− Cost of goods sold	− 10832	− 13239	− 45045	− 5456	− 15052	− 89624
Gross profit	3055	4897	27608	2811	7413	45784
− Operating expenses	− 2500	− 3475	− 17437	− 1736	− 4942	− 30090
Operating profit	555	1422	10171	1075	2471	15694
Other income	130	185	1346	0	580	2241
− Interest	− 225	− 146	− 794	− 186	− 316	− 1667
Income before taxes	460	1461	10723	889	2735	16268
− Taxes	− 214	− 669	− 5061	− 415	− 1277	− 7637
Net income	246	792	5662	474	1458	8632
Average shares outstanding						2236
Earnings per share						$3.86
Dividends						3354

Exhibit 2   Star Manufacturing, Inc.'s comparative balance sheets, year ending 1982

| | Divisions | | | | | Corporation |
	Al Tech	Metal Stampings	Industrial Refrigeration	Air Conditioning	Missouri Compressor	Star Manufacturing
			In $000			
Assets						
Cash and marketable securities	448	550	4036	344	1152	6530
Accounts receivable	1712	2519	11718	1302	4239	21490
Inventory	3086	2667	15136	2147	5349	28385
Other assets	122	236	1876	86	0	2320
Total C/A	5368	5972	32767	3880	10740	58725
Fixed assets	3315	2834	15073	2067	3907	27195
− Accum. depreciation	−1326	−1502	−7778	−475	−1797	−12878
Intangibles	2000	2500	0	0	3500	8000
− Accum. amoritization	−200	−625	0	0	−1750	−2575
Net F/A	3789	3207	7295	1591	3860	19742
TOTAL ASSETS	9157	9178	40062	5471	14599	78467
Liabilities and Equity						
Notes payable	250	350	1400	180	865	3045
Accts. payable	2472	1836	9465	682	2271	16725
Taxes payable	45	183	1435	124	377	2164
Accr. liabilities	63	112	1268	47	268	1758
Total C/L	2830	2481	13568	1033	3781	23692
L.T. debt	1400	734	4500	1200	1475	9309
Total debt	4230	3215	18068	2233	5256	33001
Common stock	250	100	1000	100	500	1950
Paid-in capital	750	1400	2500	2000	1500	8150
Retained earnings	3927	4463	18494	1138	7343	35366
Total equity	4927	5963	21994	3238	9343	45466
TOTAL LIABILITIES AND EQUITY	9157	9178	40062	5471	14599	78467

Exhibit 3   Star Manufacturing, Inc.'s miscellaneous financial data, year ending 1982

	Divisions					Corporation
	Al Tech	Metal Stampings	Industrial Refrigeration	Air Conditioning	Missouri Compressor	Star Manufacturing
			Figures in $000			
Sales	13887	18136	72653	8267	22465	135408
Net income	246	792	5662	474	1458	8632
Average Annual Compound Growth— 5-Year (Actual)						
Sales (%)	6.17	6.45	8.76	24.00	6.53	8.39
Income (%)	7.35	10.87	11.35	12.65	10.25	11.05
Industry Ratios						
Sales growth	10.91	9.84	10.66	11.29	8.13	7.00
Income growth	13.64	12.30	12.79	15.01	10.81	8.40
Performance Compared to Plan (Actual/Plan)						
Sales	.93	.92	1.02	.85	1.05	.98
Income	.33	.88	1.06	.82	1.03	1.00
Selected Industry Ratios						
Current ratio	2.12	2.71				2.36
Quick ratio	0.97	1.40				1.04
Sales/inventory	5.37	7.12				6.59
Gross margin	29.02%	26.46%				31.70%
Coll. period	45.45	50.80				66.00
Fixed asset turnover	7.22x	6.15x				6.11x
Net margin	5.06%	5.37%				7.30%
Total debt/Total assets	.46	0.31				0.45
Total asset turnover	1.79x	1.92x				1.25x
ROI (TA)	9.06%	10.31%				9.12%
Times interest earned	9.27x	20.65x				11.66x
% FA depreciated	52.85%	58.60%				46.60%

In 1978, as a result of the Al Tech acquisition, Star effected a corporate reorganization to improve efficiency throughout the organization. The original business line—industrial refrigeration equipment—was separated from the corporate level. Figure 2 is an organization chart of the corporation. The chart reflects the recent appointment of George Hayes.

Three vice-presidents and the CEO now comprise the Executive Committee of Star Manufacturing. This committee meets regularly to discuss corporate policy matters. One of the first issues on the agenda for the Executive Committee is the preparation of

Figure 2   Divisional organization, Star Manufacturing Inc.

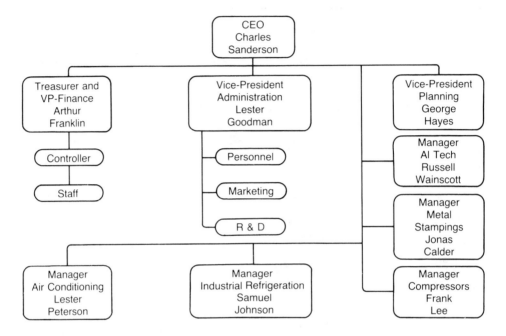

a revised set of corporate objectives and a revised mission statement. George Hayes has been assigned the task of drafting a set of proposed objectives for the group to consider at its January meeting.

AL TECH'S PRODUCTS, OPERATIONS, AND FACILITIES

Current Products

The Al Tech Division of Star manufactures a number of products for the manufactured housing (MH) and recreational vehicles (RV) industries. Its key product is a line of aluminum windows for use in MH and RV units. The line includes three basic types of windows: awning windows, horizontal sliding windows, and vertical sliding windows. In addition, Al Tech makes matching screens and storm windows to sell with its main product lines in the same markets.

The awning window is used primarily in RVs and lower-priced MH units. An awning window and its complete trim package costs about $15. The average MH unit contains about twelve windows. Sliding windows are somewhat higher in price and generally more deluxe than awning windows. Vertical sliders are used in higher-valued MH units to give an appearance closer to that of conventional housing. To complement the window lines and to add variety, a few fixed light (picture window) units are made by Al Tech. The division also produces a line of aluminum patio doors that are similar in appearance and operation to their conventional housing counterparts. The patio doors are sold both to the MH and RV markets.

All of Al Tech's windows are similar to aluminum windows used in conventional houses. However, they are not usable in conventional applications as currently designed because MH and RV walls are thinner. Al Tech has an experimental-design window for the conventional market, but so far only one shipment has been made—to a large condominium developer.

The final major product made by Al Tech is an aluminum extension ladder designed to sell as a private brand in chain discount stores. The product is well made and built to compete in the medium-quality price range. The product has done well and has provided Al Tech's management with valuable experience in dealing with chain store marketing channels.

Table 1 gives additional product and customer information for the Al Tech Division.

Table 1   Product and customer data, Al Tech Division

Product Mix, 1982

Product	Percent Contribution to Sales	Income	Average Unit Price
Awning windows	30.8	4.6	$ 9.25
Horizontal sliders	11.6	3.5	12.00
Vertical sliders	19.4	8.6	12.00
Trim/screen (wood)	6.4	2.0	2.00
Storm/screen	8.8	4.3	5.00
Patio doors	12.5	28.4	104.00
Ladders	10.5	48.6	56.00

Customer Mix, 1982

Product	Sales Contribution Percent To RVs	To MHs
Awning windows	45.0	55.0
Horizontal sliders	28.0	72.0
Vertical sliders	0.0	98.0[1]
Trim/screen (wood)	40.0	60.0
Storm/screen	18.0	82.9
Patio doors	29.0	70.0[1]

[1]Remaining percentages sold to condominium contractor.

Manufacturing Operations

Al Tech has two extrusion presses for making parts for its windows and ladders. One of these presses is rated at 1400 tons and the other at 1800 tons. The smaller press has the capacity to run 2,400,000 pounds of aluminum per shift, per year, and is currently operating at 75 percent of capacity on two shifts. (A shift is 250 work days of eight hours each). The large press can run 3,400,000 pounds per shift, per year, and is operating on one shift at 70 percent of capacity. Though both machines are currently operating below capacity, there is no way to remedy this situation by reducing the second shift on the small press or shutting down one of the presses, because certain parts cannot be made on both presses.

An aluminum extrusion press operates on much the same principle as a common cookie press, forcing a heated aluminum ingot through a cylindrical hole against a hardened steel profile die. Approximately 15 percent of the metal weight run through an extrusion press is scrap, consisting primarily of butt ends and lineal extrusions that do not run properly. Larger, heavier shapes like ladder parts and patio door frames run more easily with lower scrap rates. Such parts also run more pounds per hour on the average, which reduces unit labor cost. An extrusion press takes a crew of five to seven to run efficiently. These jobs are fairly skilled because the machine is very complex.

Window and accessory product lines are composed of extruded aluminum frames, glass, extruded plastic seals, and miscellaneous die-cast and stamped hardware such as cranks, operators, locks, and hinges. Al Tech manufactures its own aluminum extrusions and purchases the rest of its parts. A few of the stampings are purchased from the Metal Stampings Division of Star.

Al Tech's window assembly processes require moderate skills and fairly expensive tooling for punch or brake presses. The aluminum storm and screen units made by the firm are much simpler to build, as are the wood frames used for awning window screens. The firm's patio doors are made in much the same way as its sliding windows. The ladders contain basically two types of parts, which are cut to length and fastened in a large press through a process called *swedging*, which fixes the rails into side frame parts.

Al Tech's products are all made in one plant in its midwestern location. The plant is owned, as is the equipment. The main fixed assets are the two extrusion presses, both of which were purchased used. The firm purchases all of its major inputs—aluminum, glass, and plastic—from large firms like Reynolds and Goodyear. A typical awning window contains an average of five pounds of aluminum compared to four pounds for the typical sliding window. Storm windows and screens have approximately one pound of aluminum per unit. Patio doors and ladders contain twenty-five and twenty-four pounds of aluminum, respectively.

In 1982, aluminum was purchased in billet form for an average price of $.55 per pound. Additionally, Al Tech purchased billets made from remelted scrap at an average price of $.15 per pound. The price of aluminum billets is volatile and related to both domestic and international economies.

Al Tech's labor force is unionized by a local of the United Auto Workers. This is a residual from a time when Al Tech supplied lighting to the auto industry. The firm has had reasonable labor relations in the past, having experienced only two labor strikes in the last twenty years. The presence of a UAW local union forces Al Tech to pay the highest wages of anyone in its industry segment.

Painting Facility

The new painting facility at Al Tech is a modern electrostatic spraying system designed to coat lineal aluminum extrusions up to twenty feet long. It is currently one of the highest-capacity systems in the U.S., with the capacity to process about 256 lineal feet of extrusions, weighing a total of eighty-five pounds, each minute. The assembly line operates an average of fifty minutes each hour.

Operation of the paint facility requires a crew of six people at its current operating level of 60 percent capacity. The crew size increases somewhat smoothly with nine people required at 90 percent or more of capacity. The base labor rate for the paint crew is $6.00 per hour per person plus 30 percent of salary for fringe benefits. In addition to the crew, a paint operator is needed at $8.00 an hour plus fringes, as well as a supervisor at $20,000 per year plus fringes. Other major costs of the operation are paint and utilities. Gas and electricity, plus miscellaneous supplies, cost roughly $20,000 per million pounds painted. Paint is more difficult to estimate because the amount of total surface area in the extrusions varies widely by shape. An estimate for the coating material is about $.015 per pound. Finally, there is about $100,000 in additional fixed costs associated with the operation annually. Open market prices for painted extrusions range from $.15 to $.22 per pound, depending on the weight and complexity of the piece.

RECENT EVENTS AT AL TECH

When Al Tech closed for the Christmas Holidays, George Hayes prepared a report for corporate management, summarizing his activities as acting general manager of Al Tech. George's report identified major issues pending in the division, giving Rusty a formal baseline from which to act at his return. George's report characterized a number of important events and issues, which are described below.

By November 1982, Al Tech's new aluminum painting facility was operational. George reported that the installation of equipment had gone smoothly. Unfortunately, he also had to report that the new painting facility was operating only one day per week during the last four weeks of operation in 1982, a level of output far below profit plan forecasts.

George felt there were several reasons for the lack of usage of the paint line. First, the recession in the housing sector of the economy and the continued presence of high interest rates had definitely hurt the sales of Al Tech's key customers. Further, use of the facility for contract painting did not materialize as planned. George felt this was a result of overoptimistic forecasting and failure of salespersons to make a concerted effort to obtain contract work. In addition, initial resistance to Al Tech as a supplier was unexpectedly high due to lack of experience with the process. Finally, George felt that a part of the difficulty stemmed from the attitude and actions of Stu Carter, Al Tech's sales manager.

Stu Carter apparently was having a great deal of difficulty accepting the implications of changes occurring in the manufactured-housing industry. After great growth in the sixties and early seventies, the industry's shipments dropped from a high of 575,000 in 1972 to 212,000 in 1975. Since that time, annual shipments of manufactured housing units have averaged about 250,000 units. No steady growth has since been established.

Al Tech had committed nearly a million dollars to its new paint facility to raise profit margins in its manufactured housing product lines. The facility was also to provide the firm with some new-product prospects to help provide a cushion against depressed demand in the MH and RV product segments. Stu Carter had repeatedly shown that he was unwilling to consider these new directions seriously and had done nothing to develop sales outside of the traditional products. In fact, Carter had even gone so far as to instruct his sales personnel not to call on any customers except the ones he assigned. Further, because sales were depressed in the traditional product lines, Stu had used widespread price cuts in an attempt to hit his sales targets. This had a significant negative impact on profit margins. George wanted to discharge Stu in mid-November but felt that it would be an inappropriate action for him to take, given his position as acting manager.

George's Actions As Acting Manager

As George saw the events of fall 1982 unfold, and as he examined Al Tech's financial statements, he began to see the need for quick action. Though he recognized his role as a caretaker at Al Tech, he also recognized the need to take action to get the division back on track.

The first step George took was to develop a plan for reorganization of the Al Tech division. Anticipating expanded sales outside the MH and RV markets and a greater variety of products, George formulated a plan for the gradual emergence of a matrix organization. His initial step was to divide the sales and design departments into two distinct subunits: housing products and other products. George's proposal intended that as the "other product" category began to grow, these departments, as well as production, would require separate managers.

The move to a new organization was prompted by two factors. Chain stores that carried Al Tech's ladder line had expressed a strong interest in carrying additional products from the firm. Also, George realized that for any new product lines to be promoted adequately, there would have to be a dedicated sales force to do the job. George's matrix type organization chart for the Al Tech Division is given in Figure 3.

George also formed a committee consisting of representatives from the accounting, design, and sales departments. The committee was given the task of researching new markets and new products for Al Tech. The committee's report was to be completed by February 1, 1983. Stu Carter was specifically excluded from this research effort be-

Figure 3   Organization chart—Al Tech division

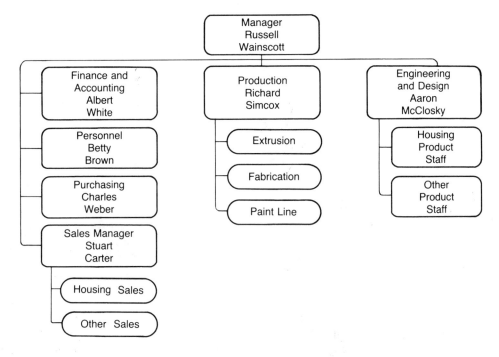

cause George felt it would be too disruptive for him to participate. The report was to be submitted to Rusty Wainscott, as well as to corporate headquarters.

Finally, George had two meetings with corporate management during the month of December, where all these issues were discussed, along with problems at the other divisions. It was becoming apparent that many of Star's market environments were changing and that closer management of the planning process was going to be required. It was becoming clearer that Star, though it had the opportunity to take advantage of interdivisional synergy, was not now doing so. Top management agreed that George's proposed changes were needed.

EXECUTIVE COMMITTEE MEETING

On January 17, the Executive Committee at Star met to consider a revised set of corporate objectives proposed by George Hayes. The committee spent all day discussing the matter and concluded by adopting the objectives enumerated in Exhibit 4. As a result of this session, profit planning targets were finalized and sent to the division managers. The group felt that these targets should be an incentive for managers to achieve their goals, so the group met again on the 20th and devised an incentive plan for division managers. This plan was studied and implemented immediately. The plan is described in Exhibit 5, the memo to Russell Wainscott.

Exhibit 4   Corporate objectives, Star Manufacturing, Inc., January, 1983

Corporate Mission

Star Manufacturing, Incorporated's mission is to become an integrated manufacturer of high quality, competitively priced products for industrial and consumer markets. The firm places special emphasis on expanding its existing experience as a supplier to the industrial refrigeration and housing markets, to design, build, and market innovative consumer products aimed at the improvement of overall environmental comfort.

Corporate Objectives

- To provide a stimulating and open environment where its employees may develop to their maximum productive capacity.
- To earn a fair return for the firm's shareholders. Specifically, the corporation wishes to earn an overall return on its assets of 12 to 15 percent and a return on shareholders' investment of 22 to 25 percent.
- The firm would like to grow substantially in the next ten years, at which time it will realize total sales of $500,000,000. This growth will be achieved through internal growth and a policy of selective acquisition, to the extent that suitable, well-managed, candidates can be located to provide the firm with synergy coincident with its mission. This growth will be financed with internally generated funds, the judicious use of creditor capital, and the issuance of new common stock whenever appropriate.

Exhibit 5   Memo to Russell Wainscott from George Hayes

Memo to: Russell Wainscott, division manager, Al Tech Division, Star Manufacturing, Inc.

From: George Hayes, vice-president, planning, Star Manufacturing, Inc.

Date: January 30, 1983

As a result of the reformulation of our corporate objectives, we have restructured our profit plan targets and instituted a new incentive plan for division managers. The new objectives are enclosed with this memo. The new plan calls for each manager to be evaluated on the basis of his ability to achieve the ROI targeted for his division. A bonus of up to 50 percent of base salary will be paid for performance above this target. For each one-half of 1 percent of capital your return exceeds this target you will receive a bonus of 5 percent of your base salary. The target for the Al Tech Division has been set at a 9 percent return on total assets. From now on, this target will be assigned during the regular profit planning cycle about the end of November.

(Signed) George Hayes

RESEARCH COMMITTEE REPORT

On February 8, 1983, George Hayes and Charles Sanderson received copies of the research report George had commissioned in the previous fall. The report was forwarded to Star by Rusty Wainscott, who also included a memo from Stu Carter, since it was also related to the new-product question. Both the body of the report and the Carter memo are reproduced in Exhibit 6.

Exhibit 6   Committee report; Carter memo

Memo to: Rusty Wainscott
From: Ad Hoc Committee on Product Development
Date: February 4, 1983
The basic condition of Al Tech at present is not as good as corporate management would like. The paint room will be operating at about 30 percent of capacity by next month. The extrusion lines are still at the same level as in the last quarter. With the current shift arrangement, we have about 2.2 million pounds of unused capacity. Adding another shift on the large press would add another 3.4 million pounds. Profit for 1982 was about 33 percent of plan. The question obviously is "What can we do to fill up some of the unused capacity and raise profits?" Our suggestions appear below.

- The current recession has raised the level of competition in the MH and RV segments of our business, causing a general depression in the prices in those markets. Our feeling is that the typical awning window ought to sell for $10, versus the current average price of $9.25. Similarly, sliders ought to sell for about $13.00 average price instead of the current $12.00 average.

- To improve the performance of the painting facility, we need to raise the level of activity. We currently paint 75 percent of our RV sliders, 50 percent of our RV awning windows, 60 percent of our MH sliders, 20 percent of our MH awnings, and 35 percent of all patio doors. The rest of our scheduled capacity utilization is made up of contract painting jobs recently acquired. It should be realistically possible to raise the level of penetration on painted RV awnings and painted MH sliders to 75 percent. Other improvements in penetration by painted products are much less certain. Painted windows can be sold for an average price of $.75 to $1.00 more than a comparable mill-finish unit, over and above any other possible price adjustments. Finally, we feel it will be possible to scrounge about 50,000 to 100,000 pounds a month in contract paint business. A concerted effort might produce up to 250,000 a month if one or two large customers could be located.

- Accelerated development of a new sliding window for the conventional housing market might result in sales of 25,000 to 50,000 units in the first year or two. The product, which is about 25 percent heavier than current models, could be sold through lumber yards or chain stores for the Do-It-Yourself (DIY) market. In this market, as many as 250,000–500,000 units could be sold annually after five years. This product should wholesale at $15 to $18 in mill finish and $20 painted. The price could be higher with an optional storm/screen unit. Sears and other big retailers sell this kind of thing now and charge an arm and a leg for it. We could be quite competitive.

- We could also sell a redesigned patio door to the DIY market in a painted or mill-finish version. This market is not likely to be as large, but this is really a big-ticket item, retailing for as much as $300–$500.

- Along with patio doors, we could look at designing a shower door to sell to current customers as well as the conventional market. There is some well-established competition here, especially from some of the integrated aluminum companies, some of whom are our suppliers. These doors are almost all anodized, which would be expensive if our runs are small.

- Our last idea is to develop a line of painted trim moldings for the MH and RV markets. We used to make this product, but dropped it for a number of reasons, including prices and inventory headaches.

For the time we had, this is all we could come up with. If you want us to do anything further, please let us know.
(Signed by committee)

Memo to: Rusty Wainscott
From: Stu Carter
Date: Feb. 1, 1983
A couple of days ago, I heard one of my salespeople talking to Al White about some report. I did a little snooping and found out that you put some people on a fishing expedition looking for some new-product ideas. You must know that I am more than a little upset that you didn't consult me on this. I don't know what they told you, but I have a dynamite idea of my own I've been working on for quite a while. We've got to get into the picture frame business! We're not just going to make them—we're going to set up franchise stores all over the country.

Last week I just happened by this do-it-yourself frame shop over on East Street. They have a nice little gold mine there. You can get them to frame your picture or you can do it yourself. It's just like building one of our storms. We could get into this racket easily. We've got all the stuff; all we've got to do is set people up as franchisees. We supply materials (forever), training, equipment, and the use of our name. I've got the name all worked out—*I've Been Framed.* I've got a sign designer working on the logo already. I've also met with our lawyer to get him going on an air-tight franchise agreement.

Don't do anything until you talk to me about this. We might even have to set up another paint room if this takes off. These guys charge around $6.00 a foot retail for anodized lineals. We can make that stuff for about $.30–$.40 anodized! Wow! Three years in this and we'll be running Star instead of the other way around.
(Signed) Stu

REACTIONS AT HEADQUARTERS

When the research report and memo were received at Star, there was some fairly swift reaction. Charles Sanderson, the CEO, read the report and immediately sent a memo to George Hayes to request further information. Mr. Sanderson wished to know the following:

1. What is the nature of the DIY market?
   Are any of the research committee's products good entry points to this market? Which ones?
   How do alternatives for this market affect capacity utilization?

2. What is the price elasticity for the window product lines?

3. What are the prospects for interdivisional synergy between Al Tech and Star's other divisions?
   Can the sales or design departments help with this issue?

Sanderson felt the committee report answered a number of questions and raised others. He wanted George to study the situation and report back by the first week in March.

In response to the request of the CEO for more information, George Hayes prepared a lengthy report covering the basic points addressed in the CEO's request. The essence of that report follows:

The DIY Market

- Growing quickly—tripled in ten years.

- 60 percent of home improvement customers are DIY purchasers.

- DIY is substitute for leisure time.

- Saves money—instead of using leisure to earn money to pay for labor, save tax on income and save labor cost.

- Typical DIY customer—baby boomer who owns home.

- Estimated 70 percent of twenty-two million DIY customers might demand products being considered by Al Tech.

- DIY requires high skills in some cases, or very well-designed products and accompanying instructions. Products must be idiot-proof. Al Tech working on design for self-leveling patio door.

- Difficult marketing channel-will require study. Chain stores, hardware, discount lumber yards, home improvement stores, regular chain discount stores (K-Mart).

Price Elasticity of Window Products

Difficult to assess. *S&P Industry Reports* on MH market in late 1982, reports many favorable trends in industry. Key factors are continuing rises in housing costs and high interest rates. Restrictive zoning also gradually easing.

Interdivisional Synergy

- Star currently buys 500,000 pounds of extrusions from outside of firm.
  Most outside work can be done by Al Tech.
  Will require $30,000 in new dies.

- Redesign of some of Star's products could result in need to run 1.5 to 2.0 million pounds at Al Tech.
  Extrusions would replace other types of parts.

- Total ultimate savings equivalent of 5 to 10 cents per pound on 1.5 to 2.0 million pounds in two years.

- There would be significant, presently unknown tooling costs.

CASE 23

Kitty's Knitting & Fabric Shoppe
TIMOTHY R. MILLER
University of Wisconsin—Parkside

HISTORY

Kitty's Knitting and Fabric Shoppe is a small business that was founded on February 2, 1982 by Karen (Kitty) Sayre. Kitty's Knitting was initially an exclusive distributor of electronic knitting machines in Racine, Wisconsin. After three years in operation, the business has expanded to include the sale of crafts, craft supplies, knitting machines, and other related items.

Her interest in knitting led Kitty Sayre to attend various educational seminars on knitting-machine operations. An acquired expertise in knitting-machine operations and a perceived demand, led Sayre to open a small retailing operation specializing in knitting machines and related supplies. Sayre was granted a $30,000 loan from a local bank for inventory and working capital. No long-run objectives, other than to make a profit, were ever established.

Kitty Sayre's business policies were influenced heavily by relatives, friends, competitors, sales representatives, and even magazines. Kitty had no formal business education and no experience. She relied heavily on the advice of others. In her opinion, the business should have turned into a profitable organization in two years. Kitty alone performed all the bookkeeping, purchasing, sales, and maintenance of the business.

In July of 1982, Kitty Sayre began to increase her product lines. She added sewing machines, fabrics, and fabric patterns to the existing product line of knitting machines, patterns, yarns, and consignments. Kitty soon acquired a larger selection of calico print fabrics than any of her competitors. She hoped that such increases in product lines would boost sales during her effort to find a profitable line.

Store hours at Kitty's Knitting & Fabric Shoppe are Monday through Saturday from 10:00 A.M. to 6:00 P.M. Occasionally, Kitty would open on a Sunday, unannounced, to gain exposure and increase weekly sales. Sunday openings never exceeded three or four times a year, and were never previously advertised.

Advertising was one of Kitty's largest expenses. Virtually all mediums had been used, but a local paper containing classified advertisements generated the most sales. This form of advertising was also the most inexpensive.

This case was prepared under the direction of William G. Ferko and the University of Wisconsin—Parkside, as the basis for class discussion, rather than to illustrate either effective or ineffective handling of a management situation.

In order to obtain the help she needed, Kitty Sayre joined several local organizations. First, she joined "Old Main Street Association," then "Sixth Street Association," and finally "Downtown Association." Each of these attempts to gain assistance in running a small business proved to be fruitless, partly due to her belief that money was the primary reason for slumping sales. These organizations could not provide the financial help needed.

In July 1983, Sayre received another $20,000 bank loan for the purpose of turning Kitty's Knitting and Fabric Shoppe around. Product lines were again expanded, as needles, crafts, and more patterns were purchased and targeted at the home sewer. Lower prices and less trendy items were emphasized. Also, during July 1983, Sayre moved from the initial low-to-middle-income south side store to a similar neighborhood on the north side of town. The new location was rent-free, with only an agreement to pay for all utilities.

Shortly after the move, with sales levels sporadic and a negative cash flow, advertising levels were drastically reduced. Despite this, product lines were again expanded to include unrelated product lines such as greeting cards, an expensive photocopy machine service, and even cosmetics. In January 1984, with sales at the lowest levels ever, Sayre relocated her business again. This move was in response to a local newspaper's study identifying the need for a craft shop downtown. Rent would be much higher, but the survey indicated that the downtown area was in need of a fabric and craft store. (Kitty's Knitting and Fabric Shoppe's 1983 sales percentages are provided in Exhibit 1, its 1983 expense percentages in Exhibit 2.) Daily sales for January 1983 are shown in Figure 1.

With the latest move, Sayre was situated on a street adjacent to the main strip in the heart of downtown. She was surrounded by many types of businesses, such as taverns, a flower shop, a karate school, a shoe repairer, and two vacant store fronts. Her business now faced heavy car traffic on a busy one-way street, but with little foot traffic because of the low-income area and limited parking. Seldom would shoppers make the effort to walk three blocks off the main strip to enter this area.

Exhibit 1   Kitty's sales percentages (1983)

Fabrics and patterns	24.3%
Knitting and sewing machines	19.3%
Crafts	13.1%
Yarns	11.2%
Notions	8.7%
Consignment	8.0%
Books	8.0%
Other	7.4%
TOTAL SALES PERCENTAGES	100.0%

Exhibit 2   Kitty's expense percentages (1983)

Interest	27.7%
Depreciation	19.0%
Utilities	16.7%
Advertising	8.2%
Miscellaneous	8.2%
Legal fees	8.2%
Insurance	4.0%
Lease payments	3.0%
Other	5.1%
TOTAL EXPENSE PERCENTAGES	100.0%

Figure 1   Kitty's daily sales

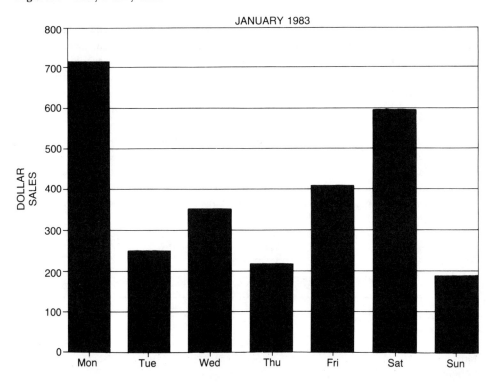

Along with the move downtown, Sayre felt a name change was in order. Therefore, in January 1984, Kitty's Knitting and Fabric Shoppe formally changed to Kitty's Craft Centre. The name change was aimed at targeting a wider selection of customers. Sayre again increased her product line to include a large inventory of

Figure 2 Kitty's store layout

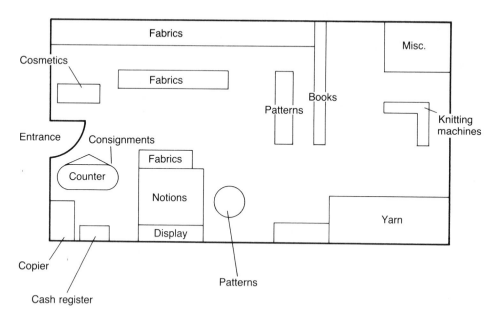

unrelated books, mostly paperbacks purchased from a local bookstore filing bankruptcy, along with additional notions and craft-related items. (Kitty's store layout is shown in Figure 2.)

The name change did motivate customers to search for and enter the store, but most left disappointed. Misleading advertising, describing the store as a huge fabric discount house, was also tried. Although this strategy did bring many into the store, they left angry or disappointed. Nearly all revenue was generated from repeat customers. This revenue was not enough to meet expenses.

During the first quarter of 1984, Kitty's Craft Centre became delinquent with suppliers and creditors. Utilities, accounts payable on inventory, and rent were all overdue. Overburdened with work, and with ordering on a C.O.D. basis only, Sayre lost her enthusiasm for the business. Store hours became irregular, but further financial help was sought from various leaders, banking institutions, local business organizations, a congressman, and the Small Business Administration. Due either to the status of her business or the paperwork involved with the applications for aid, all efforts were unsuccessful.

A local attorney recommended filing for bankruptcy under Chapter 13. Sayre attempted to file, but was unable to meet all the requirements and was later rejected. Sayre is confident she can turn her business around, given another $25,000 to invest in other product lines.

COMPETITION

Competition with Kitty's Craft Centre is intense. A total of twenty-three other retailers in Racine, Wisconsin supply virtually identical product lines, and most of them have specialized in one area (Exhibit 3). Almost all of this competition is located in other areas within the city. Only one other craft store is located near Kitty's. Approximately six knitting or fabric shops are situated in the middle of town, and a few fabric or craft stores are west and north of town. The remaining competitors are on the rapidly expanding southwest edge of town. A new mall just opened on the southwest side of town

Exhibit 3   Kitty's Competitors

Knitting

- The Little Knit Shop (south of town)
- Calico, Canvas, and Colors (west side)
- The Unique (midtown)
- The Needle Worker, Ltd. (north side)
- Fashion Knit Boutique (midtown)
- Corner Needlecraft (south of town)
- Love-in Homemade Gifts and Crafts (midtown)
- Stitch'N Knit'N (south of town)

Crafts

- Craft Villa (downtown)
- Creative Sewing (west side)
- Gary's Uptown Hobby Center (midtown)
- Swiss Village Arts & Crafts (south of town)
- Vi's Creations (west of town)

Fabrics

- Brooks Upholstery & Fabrics (west side)
- Fritsche's Sewing Center (midtown)
- Furr by Us Factory Outlet (south of town)
- Minnesota Fabrics (south side)
- Phildar Yarn Shop (southwest side)
- Cloth Horse (north side)
- Material Things (north of town)
- Jo-Ann Fabrics (south side)
- Stretch & Sew Fabric Center (west side)
- Northwest Fabrics (south sidc)

and another is scheduled to open in fall 1984. Kitty's Craft Centre is located in the nondeveloping, rapidly decaying downtown area.

Of the twenty-three competitors, Sayre was able to name only six, and may not have been aware of the others. Due to the store's downtown location, it has a difficult time competing with larger, more efficient retailing outlets.

FINANCE

As a result of slumping sales, it was not possible for Kitty's Craft Centre to employ a bookkeeper or an accountant. This resulted in insufficient records on itemized product sales, itemized costs, profit percentages, and even the routine preparation of proper financial statements. Due to insufficient record keeping, data was not available for a proper financial analysis. Nonetheless, the records that are available indicate serious financial weaknesses. The business' 1982 and 1983 balance sheets are provided in Exhibit 4 and Exhibit 5.

Exhibit 4 Kitty's Knitting & Fabric Shoppe's balance sheet—July 31, 1982

ASSETS		LIABILITIES	
Cash	(−407.62)	Accrued expenses	2,152.97
Inventory	38,561.10	Accounts payable	12,232.63
Land contract	70,000.00	Loan payable—bank	28,000.00
Total Assets	$108,153.48	Land contract	61,065.85
		Loan payable—relative	3,000.00
		Owner equity	1,702.03
		Total Liabilities & Net Worth	$108,153.48

Prepared without audit from the books of Karen Sayre by J. M. Knors 9/24/82

Exhibit 5 Kitty's Knitting & Fabric Shoppe's balance sheet—March 31, 1983

ASSETS		LIABILITIES	
Cash	(2,165.41)	Accrued expenses	4197.52
Inventory	25,934.58	Accounts payable	11,616.05
Total Assets	$23,769.17	Loan payable—bank	28,000.00
		Loan payable—family	7,000.00
		Loan payable—J. Sayre	12,386.45
		Owner equity	(39,430.85)
		Total Liabilities & Net Worth	$23,769.17

Prepared without audit from the books of Karen Sayre by J.M. Knors 5/25/83

BANKRUPTCY

Up until Chapter 13 was formally rejected, and for some time after that, Sayre was completely relieved from the daily burden of creditors attempting to collect. Under bankruptcy provisions, collectors are forbidden by law to harass creditors filing bankruptcy. Two other forms of bankruptcy, Chapter 7 Liquidation, and Chapter 11 Business Reorganization, had not been considered by Kitty Sayre.

Federal Bankruptcy Code has two purposes; the first is to provide for an even-handed treatment of creditors, and the second is to provide overburdened debtors with a fresh start. Under Chapter 7 a person may voluntarily petition to convert nonexempt assets into cash, and to distribute this cash as provided under the Bankruptcy Code. The purpose is to grant the honest debtor a discharge from most remaining debts.

The purpose of Chapter 11, on the other hand, is to allow financially troubled firms to stay in business while undergoing financial rehabilitation. The firm is reorganized by negotiation between debtor and creditors for a plan of adjustment of debts. This plan may change management, or even liquidate the firm, but continuation of the business is the typical goal. Most corporations, partnerships, or individuals eligible for Chapter 7 are also eligible for Chapter 11. In either case, trustees are appointed to collect, liquidate, and distribute the estate for those filing.

STRATEGY

Kitty's Craft Centre was primarily interested in making a profit by specializing in the fabric and craft items not carried by any one competitor. While Sayre was the exclusive distributor for knitting machines in the Racine area, some customers traveled from as far as Northern Illinois for these machines. Demographically, customers included all types of people, both men and women. Although no formal target market was ever established, the product lines primarily aimed at middle-aged housewives who were interested in crafts and in saving money by making clothes.

Although Karen Sayre never established a specific pricing policy, 50 to 100 percent markup was common on most items. Sayre on occasion did some competitive price checking, but this was never a routine practice. Prices would not be lowered to meet the competition and prices of outdated patterns would not be lowered. In many cases, competitors were altogether ignored.

A typical knitting machine sold for $700 to $1500. With each machine sold, many hours of additional instruction were required, at no additional charge. Occasionally, Sayre would offer classes for advanced knitting instruction for a nominal fee, but attendance was usually poor. No financing or layaway package was available for those not able to afford the machine. Any repairs had to be sent back to the manufacturer.

Market research for Kitty's Craft Centre was based strictly on the random observation of competitors and on articles in magazines and newspapers. All forms of advertising were used at one time or another, including cable television, radio, newspapers, and mailed circulars. (Advertising in a weekly newspaper, distributed free to all local residents, was successful.) Advertising became very expensive and at times exceeded one-half of the total monthly expenses. All advertising was eventually eliminated. During periods of financial difficulties, barter was resorted to in fulfillment of obligations to creditors.

With a sole proprietorship such as this, and with no other management, bookkeepers, or clerical employees, daily tactical functions became overwhelming. All planning ceased to exist and was replaced with constant day-to-day crisis situations. All objectives turned from profit orientation to "raise enough money to pay the rent." Store maintenance ceased and control over inventory and product layout subsided. With such financial difficulties and lack of managerial expertise, sales continued to fall as 1985 approached. Phone services were discontinued and other utilities were sometimes being disconnected.

FUTURE

Although bankruptcy may still be implemented, Sayre is sure that success is still possible. She is determined to continue operation of the business. Although financial matters are foremost in mind, Sayre is considering the courses of action outlined in Exhibit 6. Kitty would like someone with expertise in strategic management to assist her in making critical decisions about her business. Some of Kitty's Craft Centre's strengths, weaknesses, opportunities, and threats are given in Exhibit 7.

Exhibit 6   Alternative strategies for Kitty's Craft Centre

- Bankruptcy (Chapter 7, Chapter 11)
- A move to a new location
- Specialization
- Incorporation
- Obtaining operational and managerial advice from retired businesspeople's organizations
- Promotion through sidewalk sales, church bazaars, craft/art fairs
- Mission determination
- Stocking and selling only profitable lines
- Target market identification
- Advertising to reach target market
- Determining short- and long-run objectives, planning, and strategies
- Changes in store layout
- Hiring store manager
- Restructuring debt
- Hiring bookkeeper
- Purchasing insurance
- Financing through venture capitalists

Exhibit 7   Key internal and external factors facing Kitty's Craft Centre

Strengths
Determination
Good selection of fabrics
Handmade quality products at reasonable
  prices
One of the few vendors in the area selling
  knitting machines
Substantial amount of repeat customers
Good window displays

Opportunities
Incorporation
Change of location
Sell-off of inventory
Help from retired businesspeople's
  organizations
Expansion of market to include northern
  Illinois with price-competitive knitting
  machines
Exploitation of the expanding market for
  calico fabric
Chapter 11 bankruptcy

Threats
Creditors, default
Obsolescence or spoilage of inventory
Tax audit
Damage due to theft or fire (no insurance)
Eviction
Utility cut-off
Repossession of stock
Delayed renovation of downtown area

Weaknesses
Limited parking
Location
Poor financial services
Poor inventory turnover
Absence of record keeping and performance
  tracking
Too much work for one person
Frequent location changes
Ineffective advertising
Poor store layout
Disorganized displays
No pricing strategies
Cash-only ordering
No previous business experience
No inventory control
Poor rapport with creditors
Lack of planning
No objectives
Cyclical industry
No insurance
Obsolete inventory
Indecisiveness
Uninformed about target market

CASE 24

The Flying Tiger Line: The World's Largest All-Cargo Airline

TERESA AVILA
Ball State University

INTRODUCTION

The 1980s have witnessed an era of rapid growth and diversification for both the air-freight carrier Flying Tiger and its parent corporation, Tiger International. Flying Tiger Line is unique. It is the only all-cargo airline that operates throughout the world as well as the United States. It flies 25 percent of the world's 747 freighters, the efficiency of which in transoceanic cargo operations is unparalleled.

The Flying Tiger Line is not a newcomer to adversity. Its feisty beginnings in 1945 are indicative of the organization's strength and tenacity. The company was founded just before V-J Day by World War II ace, Robert W. Prescott. Prescott was a veteran of Claire Chennault's famed Flying Tigers, an American volunteer group whose pilots inspired a degree of terror among the Japanese.

On March 3, 1978, Robert W. Prescott died at his home in Palm Springs. The Flying Tigers had come a long way from their modest beginnings in a two-car garage in Long Beach.

Prior to 1982, Flying Tigers operated primarily on an airport-to-airport basis, but today door-to-door operations comprise the fastest-growing part of the company. O'Hare International Airport in Chicago is Flying Tiger's principal hub for door-to-door services.

FUNCTIONAL-AREA STRATEGIES

Marketing

Tiger began operations with one basic strategy in mind: to provide customers with the quality of service they desire at a reasonable price, flying virtually any cargo, anywhere, anytime. Nearly forty-five years later, the company continues to operate on that principle. As customer demand increases and becomes more sophisticated, the Flying Tigers have expanded routes and improved their quality and breadth of services. This has meant more departures, greater capacity, and improved customer service.

Note: *Flight International* and *Aviation Weekly* are two excellent publications that contain additional information relevant to this case.

According to company marketing research efforts, service elements remain the most important factors that determine the freight carrier or forwarder a shipper will choose. Most specifically, door-to-door time, pick-up and delivery service, tracing ability, claims processing, customer service, and price were found to be significant shipper decision variables. Contrary to Tiger philosophy, competitors in many air cargo markets typically advocate the importance of price.

In response to increased competition since deregulation of air freight in 1978, Flying Tiger has introduced a guaranteed door-to-door delivery and airport-to-airport service provided to forwarder customers. The company also offers second- and third-day delivery options. The Flying Tigers now are redefining their market to include retail customers.

The Flying Tigers formerly conducted commercial passenger charters and limited-schedule service under the name of Metro International Airways. In 1983 the company disposed of its three Boeing 747 passenger aircraft and terminated those operations. Total charter and passenger operations generated revenues of $98,981,000 in 1981, $109,513,000 in 1982, 66,644,000 in 1983, and $42,605,000 in 1984, of which commercial cargo charter operations were $63,894,000 in 1981, $53,157,000 in 1982, $50,272,000 in 1983, and all revenues in 1984.

Flying Tiger maintains a policy of value-of-service pricing based on its market segmentation strategy. This concept can be used to price service above fully allocated costs where there is little competition, and below fully allocated costs to develop a new market or reduce excess capacity. In either case, both costs and competition can be carefully balanced.

The airfreight industry is divided on the ideal pricing philosophy. The crux of the disagreement rests on differing perceptions of the price elasticity of demand and the ability of passenger airlines to transport belly freight on the basis of marginal costs. In the long run, it is generally acknowledged that freight rates must relate fairly closely to costs to insure survival. The business of Flying Tigers is seasonal in nature, with the highest revenues of the year normally being recorded in the third and fourth quarters.

Manufacturing/Operations

As of March 1, 1984, Flying Tigers' operating fleet consisted of eleven DC-8-63, six DC-8-61, seven Boeing 747-100F, ten Boeing 747-200F, one Boeing 747-273C and four Boeing 727-100 aircraft. These planes service Flying Tigers' domestic, transpacific and transatlantic scheduled routes, Military Airlift Command and commercial charters. The transpacific route system, historically the company's most profitable market, remained strong during 1983. Revenues on this route increased by 45 percent, due primarily to higher volume.

The transatlantic market had an 8 percent decrease in revenue ton miles, which in part was the result of Flying Tigers revising its marketing approach in that market.

In 1983, the Flying Tigers reduced flight frequency across the Atlantic by 50 percent and established two European hubs, one located in London and one in Frankfurt. A European trucking network replaced previous scheduled flights. The purpose of this measure was two-fold. First, costs were reduced on already unprofitable European flights, and second, the Flying Tigers were able to redeploy aircraft in more profitable markets. In 1983, those markets were Asia and Australia.

Flying Tigers have long been a proponent of the hub concept popularized by Federal Express. The airline's major hubs are located in Chicago and Los Angeles, with secondary hubs in Detroit, Cleveland, and Anchorage, and Narita, a city in Japan, serves as the company's Pacific hub. The hub concept provides for scheduling flexibility by consolidating traffic from numerous thin markets, and increases scheduling reliability. Hubs do, however, increase costs each time an aircraft sets down to transfer loads.

Flying Tiger has taken active steps in the beginning of the 1980s toward more efficient operations, through a resizing of its airfleet and an expansion of ground facilities. New and modernized terminals are designed to improve service by reducing aircraft and freight handling time and allowing more competitive schedules.

Other efficiency measures include working to achieve the maximum utilization of its aircraft fleet by increasing flight time and higher load factors, as seen in the redeployment of aircraft from the Atlantic to Asian routes. Besides providing access to expanding markets, the Pacific operations also allow for a more efficient utilization of Tigers' operating fleet through an increase in actual operating time.

Charter operations also improve aircraft utilization, primarily as a result of the nature of the charter business. Charter volume is greater on weekends when cargo operations are slowest, and it can be used to fill in excess capacity during slow times.

The Flying Tiger Line has a commitment to operating fuel-efficient aircraft. Although financial constraints in recent years have restricted expenditures for fleet improvements and have even required the selling of many aircraft, fuel efficiency still remains a priority for the organization.

Another significant aspect of Flying Tiger's operating strategy is the combination of aircraft and over-the-road trucking for pick-up and delivery services. Trucking facilities are available to the airline through its parent company, Tiger International, but Flying Tiger has also engaged in interline agreements with other surface carriers.

Innovation

While spirit and determination have been synonymous with Flying Tigers since their beginning, innovation has played an equally important role in the company's growth. After its certification in 1949, the Flying Tigers began the first "economy" passenger travel by offering coast-to-coast service for just $99. This move forced big airlines to offer two-class service.

Working directly with a manufacturer, Flying Tiger also designed special convertible passenger seating that could be folded and stored in a plane's "belly" when flying cargo. The company also developed the first high-density seating, increasing passenger capacity to 100.

The Flying Tiger line has long been known for its innovative cargo, flying military and civilian passenger missions as well as a diverse spectrum of four-legged animals, food, and insects. Early charters included football teams like the Hollywood Bears, and troops and supplies during the Korean conflict. The company set records in the early years for the largest and fastest movement of commercial airfreight.

More recent creative efforts have been directed toward market segmentation and fleet development. Innovation in containerization and distribution services has been a particular interest of Tiger International, the parent company, hence of Flying Tiger as well. In the words of Robert W. Prescott, "We're unique, so let's not imitate. Imitation lets you catch up to the guy ahead . . . but never lets you pass."

Financial Profile

Despite its unparalled growth to become the largest cargo carrier in the world, Tiger has had relatively little success maintaining financial stability. The late 1970s and 1980s have seen an increase in revenues from $457,611,000 in 1979 to $1,171,017,000 in 1984. Yet Flying Tiger's bottom line reflected pretax losses of $10 million, $23 million, $73 million, and $67.5 million, in 1980, 1981, 1982 and 1983 respectively. Flying Tiger's pretax income in 1984 was a positive $60.7 million.

From a deficit of $200,000 in its first year of operation, the Flying Tigers struggled for survival amidst a tenuous competitive environment. Deregulation of air cargo in late 1977 provided a broad scope of opportunities for the growing airline. To position itself to take advantage of these opportunities, Flying Tiger began rapid-route and fleet growth requiring substantial capital investment. To support this growth, additional personnel and ground handling equipment were also added.

In 1980, the company acquired Seaboard World Airlines for $400 million, in order to complement its existing operations and to penetrate the north Atlantic market. But 1981 saw the company's financial position severely damaged by excessive interest rates persisting into a deep business recession. Additionally, the costly expansion into European markets suffered from unforeseen overcapacity and severe price-cutting actions by competitors. Domestic profitability was hampered by the effects of deregulation, high interest rates, high fuel costs, and the recession, all of which prevailed through 1983. Consolidated financial statements are included in Exhibit 1 with segment data following in Exhibit 2.

In order to combat a worsening financial position, Tiger began measures in 1982 toward both reducing costs and improving revenues. The company cut costs through staff reductions, salary cuts and freezes, and general operating efficiencies. To improve revenue, door-to-door service was instituted and traffic diverted from the unprofitable Atlantic to growing Pacific markets. Excess cash was raised in 1982 through the sale of aircraft to United Parcel Service.

On December 30, 1983, the Flying Tigers were able to negotiate agreements with private lenders concerning debts on which the company was in default. Approximately $588 million of indebtedness was waived or suspended and a new $45 million credit facility was provided for within the restructuring agreement. The deferred amounts will be payable in twenty quarterly installments of $2,398,000, beginning on July 2, 1985. The "new credit facility" is a revolving loan plan with amounts outstanding at June 30, 1985 convertible into a five-year term loan. Additional provisions concerning interest and a pledging of assets were also included in the agreement. The net effect of the plan was to improve cash flow. The Flying Tigers continue, however, to have high debt-service cost in light of projected cash flow and earnings.

In February of 1984, Flying Tiger went public through a debt/equity swap and is traded on the over-the-counter market. Tiger International continues, however, to own over 90 percent of Flying Tiger stock. This maneuver reduces the airline's public debt and is expected to save cash during 1984.

MANAGEMENT AND PERSONNEL

Strong and innovative leadership, such as that provided by Flying Tiger's founder, Robert Prescott, has been the molding force behind the airline. Prescott had a dream that was worth fighting for and without his initiative, drive, and determination, the dream would not have been able to survive the turbulence of the airfreight industry. Wayne M. Hoffman, current president and chairman of the board at Flying Tiger, has continued Prescott's tradition of strong leadership.

Flying Tiger appears to promote its managers from within the organization and has always attracted strong and ambitious personalities. In the words of the airline's founder, "Whether or not Tigers like to be called people, people seem to like being called Tigers. More than anything else, for whatever reasons, the airline has always attracted unusual personalities—men and women with more than the normal amount of imagination, energy, ingenuity . . . and guts."

Flying Tiger management has consistently pursued its mission to be the most innovative, efficient, customer-oriented transportation company in the world, through its development as a worldwide airfreight carrier. The organization has typically attracted young managers and has chosen to train them in a variety of transportation modes. The organization's dedicated and flexible employees are one of its major assets. Despite a brief eighteen-day strike in the summer of 1979, employee relationships have been favorable. The strike by 1850 mechanics, traffic agents, and ramp service personnel halted operations between August 24 and September 11, 1979. The return to service was prompt, however, and employee attitudes remained positive.

As with any airline, employee costs represent a significant portion of operating expenses at Flying Tiger. Cost-cutting measures in 1982 and 1983 resulted in reductions in personnel, salary, and benefits. Tiger's headquarters staff was reduced by 43 percent and Flying Tiger employees accepted wage and work-rule changes.

Exhibit 1   Tiger International, Inc. and subsidiaries' consolidated balance sheet and statement of operations

Consolidated balance sheet	For the Years Ended December 31		
	1984	1983	1982
Assets	(in 000)		
Current Assets			
Cash and short-term investments	$ 158,803	$ 42,604	$ 64,904
Receivables, net	168,271	188,096	176,932
Inventories	17,029	24,526	70,875
Prepaid expenses and other	12,266	9,430	44,488
Total current assets	356,369	264,656	357,199
Investment in finance leases	—	—	76,278
Property, Plant and Equipment			
Equipment used in operations	819,830	970,943	2,261,253
Buildings and leasehold improvements	53,951	88,690	143,837
Shop and terminal facilities and other	73,501	81,715	116,627
Construction in process	2,581	28,884	41,704
	949,863	1,170,232	2,563,421
Less accumulated depreciation and amortization	353,181	401,327	798,761
	596,682	768,905	1,764,660
Other Assets			
Investments, other receivables and deposits	16,405	20,951	88,117
Net assets, exclusive of certain obligations, of discontinued operations	—	—	70,545
Cost in excess of fair value of acquired businesses, net	57,272	59,254	83,820
	73,677	80,205	242,482
Total Assets	1,026,728	1,113,766	2,440,619
Liabilities and Stockholders' Equity			
Current Liabilities			
Short-term borrowings	132,151	—	20,000
Current portion of long-term obligations	58,864	48,997	116,834
Accounts payable and accrued liabilities	182,946	205,610	261,207
Total current liabilities	373,961	254,607	398,041
Long-Term Obligations			
Notes payable and equipment obligations	326,538	399,521	1,151,358
Subordinated debt	27,281	29,086	76,061
Capital lease obligations	249,239	263,285	399,843
	603,058	691,892	1,627,262
Deferred Credits			
Deferred income taxes and tax credits	1,417	3,299	71,326
Reserve for discontinued operations	—	31,261	—
Other	43,705	48,171	55,237
	45,122	82,731	126,563
Commitments			
Minority Preferred Stock Subject to Mandatory Redemption	2,626	—	5,587
Stockholders' Equity			
Common stock, $1 par value			

	For the Years Ended December 31		
	1984	1983	1982
Authorized—50,000,000 and 35,000,000 shares	21,711	20,508	17,035
Additional paid-in capital	256,311	250,998	219,257
Retained earnings (deficit)	(273,566)	(184,626)	48,557
	4,456	86,880	284,849
Less treasury stock, at cost (192,608 and 166,835 shares)	2,495	2,344	1,683
Total stockholders' equity	1,961	84,536	283,166
Total liabilities and stockholders' equity	$1,026,728	$1,113,766	$2,440,619

Consolidated statement of operations

	(in 000 except per share data)		
Revenues			
Operating revenues	$1,209,890	$1,056,868	$ 945,861
Costs and Expenses			
Costs of operations	875,525	806,508	775,737
Selling, general, and administrative	160,762	171,390	139,577
Depreciation and amortization	65,880	73,034	75,428
	1,102,167	1,050,932	990,742
Income (loss) from operations	107,723	5,936	(44,881)
Other income (expense)			
Gain on sale of equipment	16,591	3,909	4,792
Interest expense	(78,847)	(86,894)	(103,162)
Interest capitalized	986	2,095	5,168
Other	2,652	(10,034)	26,362
	(58,618)	(90,924)	(66,840)
Income (Loss) from continuing operations before income taxes	49,105	(84,988)	(111,721)
Income tax provision (benefit)	4,900	—	(47,900)
Income (Loss) from Continuing Operations	44,205	(84,988)	(63,821)
Discontinued operations			
Loss from operations of discontinued businesses, less applicable tax benefit of $(4,900), $-0- and $(14,300)	(14,878)	(99,448)	(52,402)
Provision for loss on disposal of discontinued operations	(118,267)	(58,196)	(20,000)
	(133,145)	(157,644)	(72,402)
Loss Before Extraordinary Gain	(88,940)	(242,632)	(136,223)
Extraordinary Gain	—	19,792	—
Net Loss	$ (88,940)	$ (222,840)	$ (136,223)
Income (loss) per share			
— Continuing operations	$ 2.05	$ (4.71)	$ (3.77)
— Discontinued operations	(6.18)	(8.73)	(4.27)
	(4.13)	(13.44)	(8.04)
— Extraordinary Gain	—	1.10	—
Loss Per Share	$ (4.13)	$ (12.34)	$ (8.04)
Shares used in computation of income (loss) per share	21,518	18,050	16,936

Source: Tiger International's 1984 Form 10K, 25–27.

Exhibit 2 Segment data

	Revenues	Pretax Results Before Interest Expense	Interest Expense Net	Pretax Income (Loss)	Identifiable Assets	Capital Expenditures	Depreciation and Amortization Expense
				(In $000)			
1984							
Air cargo (Flying Tigers)	$1,171,017	$ 125,638	$ 64,855	$ 60,783	$ 978,494	$ 46,097	$ 64,274
Trucking	39,453	2,923	5	2,918	30,307	1,503	1,268
Other	(580)	(1,595)	13,001	(14,596)	17,927	9	338
Continuing operations	1,209,890	126,966	77,861	49,105	1,026,728	47,609	65,880
Discontinued operations	191,255	(125,106)	12,939	(138,045)	—	1,005	9,124
	$1,401,145	$ 1,860	$ 90,800	$ (88,940)	$1,026,728	$ 48,614	$ 75,004
1983							
Air cargo (Flying Tigers)	$1,019,832	$ 7,086	$ 74,603	$ (67,517)	$ 987,119	$ 23,254	$ 71,419
Trucking	42,932	1,034	11	1,023	28,110	622	1,409
Other	(5,896)	(8,309)	10,185	(18,494)	9,167	205	206
Continuing operations	1,056,868	(189)	84,799	(84,988)	1,024,396	24,081	73,034
Discontinued operations	391,288	(57,973)	99,671	(157,644)	89,370	31,018	69,018
	$1,448,156	$ (58,162)	$184,470	$(242,632)	$1,113,766	$ 55,099	$142,052
1982							
Air cargo (Flying Tigers)	$ 905,496	$ (1,519)	$ 71,070	$ (72,589)	$1,043,630	$ 58,325	$ 74,036
Trucking	47,012	2,178	62	2,116	30,617	1,239	1,397
Other	(6,647)	(14,386)	26,862	(41,248)	66,230	150	(5)
Continuing operations	945,861	(13,727)	97,994	(111,721)	1,140,477	59,714	75,428
Discontinued operations	589,117	14,703	101,405	(86,702)	1,300,142	79,352	82,372
	$1,534,978	$ 976	$199,399	$(198,423)	$2,440,619	$139,066	$157,800

Source: Tiger International's 1984 Form 10K, p. 34.

"Other" includes parent company and corporate intercompany elimination items.

EXTERNAL ENVIRONMENT

Industry

The airfreight industry is a disparate mix of companies. Major participants in the long-haul portion of the industry include major airlines and all-cargo carriers. Remaining traffic is accounted for by charters, air-taxi and commuter carriers, and airfreight forwarders. Exhibit 3 shows the division of industry traffic and revenues.

Operations of the major market participants have been marginally profitable at best, due to a number of factors. The reasons most often cited include lack of appropriate aircraft, an inflexible pricing system, intense competition, fuel prices, overly optimistic growth projections, and the powerful position of airfreight forwarders.

Some barriers to entry exist in the airfreight industry due to the availability and price of appropriate aircraft. In order for a new entrant to compete most effectively against existing all-cargo scheduled airlines, a massive investment is necessary, with small promise of return. Deregulation of the industry has encouraged increased competition in both price and service, and has allowed for increasing market segmentation.

Threats to the Industry and Problems

Given the tenuous profit position of the airfreight industry, it is very susceptible to adverse environmental variables, both present and future. There has been a recent reduction in jet fuel prices due to oversupply, but fuel considerations remain a significant threat to the industry. In fact, Douglass Aircraft, in a 1982 "Outlook for the Eighties," projects an upward trend in energy prices throughout the 1990s. This increases pressure toward fuel efficiency and increases future operating costs for air and ground operations.

The open entry, overexpansion, and cutthroat competition promoted by deregulation is a threat to the industry. Competitive and uncooperative actions between participants in the airfreight market do little to insure the industry's viability vis-a-vis other modes of freight transportation. What is lacking is a coordination of efforts for the promotion of the industry as a whole.

The cyclical nature of freight transportation is also problematic. Recent recession and high interest rates spell trouble for capital-intensive airfreighters. Other economic factors including inflation, subsidized foreign airlines, mergers, take-overs, labor disputes (unions), foreign trade imbalances, curtailment of export-import bank financing, and foreign currency translation are also important determinants of continued industry success.

Environmental concerns may also alter future freight operations. "Q" day (Quiet Day), scheduled for January 1, 1985, mandates operators to comply with part 36 stage 3 noise level requirements. This could entail aircraft replacement, modification, or abandonment of service in some areas. Additionally, many airports are considering the imposition of nighttime curfews. This would severely hamper the service options of shippers and freighters who rely on overnight prime-time service.

Exhibit 3 World airline freight traffic and revenues—1982–84 (excludes mail)

Airline	Estimated 1983 FTKs* (000)	% Change vs. 1982	Forecast % Change in 1984	Estimated 1983 Freight Revenue (000)	% Change vs. 1982	Forecast % Change in 1984	% of Total Revenues Derived from Freight		
							1982	1983	1984
Aer Lingus	48,500	0.0	25.0	$ 37,022	11.0	7.5	n.a.	n.a.	n.a.
Aeromexico	57,010	10.8	(13.0)	16,927	n.a.	(15.9)	5.7	5.6	4.3
Air Canada	511,231	12.9	10.0	132,400	2.8	15.0	12.4	12.0	12.0
Air France	2,001,800	18.2	5.9	469,441	20.2	14.4	19.2	19.5	19.6
Air Illinois	16	0.0	1.0	125	(17.0)	1.0	n.a.	n.a.	n.a.
Air Inter	17,658	2.0	0.6	10,599	18.8	8.2	1.9	2.0	2.0
Air Malawi	9,671	18.0	20.0	4,000	6.0	20.0	24.0	15.0	20.0
American	741,849	7.4	n.a.	230,274	(4.8)	n.a.	8.0	7.8	n.a.
Ansett	58,958	1.5	5.0	n.a.	n.a.	n.a.	n.a.	n.a.	n.a.
Braathens SAFE	2,813	(4.4)	3.0	4,850	11.8	7.0	5.0	5.0	5.0
British Airways	900,000	9.0	5.0	234,300	9.0	9.0	8.0	8.0	8.0
Cathay Pacific	1,300,000	25.0	15.0	n.a.	35.0	15.0	18.0	22.0	25.0
China Airlines	407,000	39.7	10.0	121,000	29.6	5.0	19.0	30.0	31.0
Comair	n.a.	20.0	n.a.	200	47.0	n.a.	1.0	1.0	1.0
Czechoslovak	14,000	2.0	3.0	n.a.	n.a.	n.a.	n.a.	n.a.	n.a.
Eastern Provincial	3,019	n.a.	n.a.	3,158	n.a.	n.a.	n.a.	n.a.	n.a.
Finnair	73,970	21.0	15.0	33,000	20.0	15.0	9.5	11.0	11.5
Flying Tigers	2,475,000	18.0	(2.0)	888,500	20.0	12.0	100.0	100.0	100.0
Frontier	n.a.	n.a.	n.a.	n.a.	n.a.	n.a.	5.0	n.a.	n.a.
Garuda	169,845	(2.0)	(10.0)	54,268	(17.0)	1.0	9.9	8.9	7.6
Golden Pacific	13	45.9	40.0	83	68.9	50.0	5.0	7.0	10.0
Horizon	n.a.	139.0	75.0	1,500	117.0	100.0	n.a.	n.a.	n.a.
Icelandair	23,011	24.4	0.0	7,871	(1.9)	0.0	6.7	6.2	6.7
Imperial	n.a.	40.4	35.0	301	46.0	40.0	2.0	2.0	4.0
Indian	76,340	15.0	15.0	28,489	12.0	10.0	5.8	6.0	6.0

Airline								
Japan Air Lines	2,257,000	12.9	6.0	609,700	8.8	4.0	18.0	18.0	18.0
Kenya Airways	32,517	22.0	10.0	6,500	20.0	15.0	8.0	12.0	13.0
KLM	n.a.	n.a.	n.a.	n.a.	n.a.	n.a.	n.a.	17.0	n.a.
Kuwait Airways	119,198	7.1	n.a.	43,408	(2.1)	n.a.	11.9	12.0	n.a.
LAB	12,500	(3.0)	13.0	4,708	(48.0)	10.0	9.0	7.0	10.0
Ladeco	7,100	0.0	4.0	3,273	4.0	n.a.	9.0	8.5	9.0
Lufthansa	1,946,400	21.2	n.a.	553,700	9.4	9.8	19.4	19.6	19.8
Martinair	375,000	44.0	10.0	55,000	57.0	10.0	34.0	50.0	60.0
Merpati	70,951	9.2	18.0	27,269	7.0	9.0	8.0	10.0	15.0
Northwest Territorial	2,549	22.0	15.0	15,000	0.0	20.0	60.0	60.0	65.0
Ozark	6,300	16.0	0.0	9,000	5.0	0.0	2.0	n.a.	n.a.
Philippine	241,777	42.0	n.a.	85,400	32.0	10.0	n.a.	n.a.	n.a.
Piedmont	19,710	35.0	37.0	29,800	25.0	25.0	4.5	5.0	5.0
PSA	14,926	13.0	12.0	10,041	13.0	14.0	n.a.	n.a.	n.a.
Qantas	470,000	4.0	3.0	153,000	8.0	6.0	15.0	16.0	16.0
Republic	84,691	25.6	4.3	56,116	0.0	4.1	3.5	4.0	n.a.
Rocky Mountain	54	55.0	n.a.	850	30.0	n.a.	7.0	7.0	7.0
Royal Brunei	5,059	4.0	n.a.	n.a.	n.a.	n.a.	n.a.	n.a.	n.a.
Sabena	487,645	2.0	(5.0)	127,349	5.0	(3.0)	24.9	24.1	22.8
SAS	396,000	(2.0)	(4.0)	160,000	12.0	3.0	15.0	14.0	15.0
SATA	379	4.1	3.0	n.a.	49.0	17.0	4.4	5.8	5.5
Saudia	425,740	20.6	8.0	201,495	11.6	7.8	11.8	10.1	9.9
Southwest	n.a.	15.0	15.0	11,000	20.0	0.0	n.a.	n.a.	n.a.
Summit	35,027	4.0	28.0	23,431	9.0	33.0	83.0	87.0	88.0
Swissair	540,000	17.0	5.0	180,000	1.0	5.0	13.0	13.0	13.0
TAP-Air Portugal	93,600	(4.3)	5.1	29,656	10.0	58.0	12.0	13.0	13.0
TWA	540,000	16.0	4.0	111,000	2.0	6.0	5.0	5.0	5.0
USAir	16,330	8.6	n.a.	24,000	6.4	n.a.	4.0	4.0	n.a
Total/average	17,092,157	16.0	4.9	$4,809,004	11.2	9.1	13.5	14.1	15.7

*Freight Ton-Kilometers

The regulatory environment surrounding the industry is also subject to change. The Civil Aeronautics Board's authority over airfreight carriage is subject to a sunset provision effective at the end of 1984. This may mean a shift of authority to another governmental entity with a different perspective on industry operations. Such a shift could mean a boom or a hindrance to freighters, as regulatory policy may well be altered in the midst of already tenuous circumstances.

Changing Trends

Despite the somewhat ominous problems and threats to be dealt with by the airfreight industry, recent projections show an optimistic outlook for the future. The steady growth in multinational business and exportation should expand the market. Technological improvements in aircraft design, warehousing, ground operations, and containerization show promise for significant cost reduction in the future. The potential for more intensive intermodal combination is also gaining respect among carriers, and is indicative of a changing attitude in the transportation industry. Specialization by mode of service may not be the way of the future.

Recent years have seen a plea for cooperation between competitors both in rate setting and in advertising. Price competition has been blamed to a large extent for marginal profitability in the industry. Airfreight experts generally agree that an agreement between carriers is vitally needed. Cooperative advertising efforts are also seen as necessary to develop the market potential for air shipments.

Competitors

The number of competitors in Flying Tiger's domestic markets has rapidly increased. This competition is a result of new market entrants and increased traffic from previous competitors. Additionally, current international aviation policies of the Reagan administration have increased the number of foreign competitors serving the U.S. domestic market. Many foreign competitors are subsidized by their governments, and have compounded rate crunches experienced by U.S. carriers.

Previously, Flying Tiger's competitors were the major airlines, other all-cargo operators, charter carriers, and smaller air-taxi and commuter carriers. Recently, air freight forwarders, which have comprised a significant portion of Flying Tiger's airport-to-airport business, are becoming increasingly independent and are buying or chartering their own aircraft. These corporations, such as Emery Air Freight Corp. and Airborne Freight Corp., are now Flying Tiger's major competitors in the domestic door-to-door market.

Charter carriers have also demonstrated that they are a significant force to be reckoned with. This group has significantly stimulated industry growth by flying cargoes that had previously not been carried by air (e.g., monkeys, insects) providing low-cost airfreight service, and meeting the demand scheduled carriers were unwilling or unable to fulfill. Their comparative advantage is flexibility. Supplemental carriers (charter carriers) are able to quickly adjust capacity to fluctuations in demand. They can also more easily access markets not easily reached by all-cargo carriers.

Commuter carriers too, are of growing importance in the air cargo market. Prior to deregulation, C.A.B. regulations limited the size of operating aircraft of commuter carriers, hence restricting their ability to compete in various markets. With freedom to obtain certification for larger fleets and routes, these airlines will be equipped to compete with larger carriers. (See Exhibit 4.)

A significant threat also exists from air couriers who have typically concentrated on small package delivery. Should firms such as Federal Express expand their expertise to larger cargoes, the industry may find itself in turmoil.

The passenger airlines that served many points exclusively prior to deregulation, reduced cargo services in response to post-deregulation competition. Due to the volatile nature of the passenger market, many airlines chose to concentrate managerial and financial resources on emerging problems in that sector. In the two years following deregulation, the domestic trunk carriers' share of the domestic cargo market fell from 76 to 68 percent. In the next ten to twenty years, however, the amount of air cargo being carried in passenger aircraft is expected to substantially increase. Exhibit 5 details current U.S. airline participation in major markets.

COMPETITOR PROFILES

Lufthansa

Deutsche Lufthansa is the biggest cargo carrier in Europe and one of Flying Tiger's major competitors in the North Atlantic. The company began service in 1955 with a fleet of leased aircraft. As of 1981, the airline provided service to most continents with a fleet of 95 aircraft, two all-freighters and seven B747 combination passenger/freighter planes. Unlike Flying Tiger, Lufthansa has found the passenger/cargo combination profitable. The airline believes the trend toward large belly carrying will continue, estimating that 50 percent of its cargo will eventually be carried in this way.

Emery

Emery Worldwide is indicative of the new type of domestic competitor Flying Tiger faces. As a freight forwarder and former customer, Emery is not only taking its own business away from Flying Tiger, but other business as well. If the trend continues, this could prove to severely hamper Flying Tiger's domestic market.

Emery Air Freight began in 1946 with $250,000 in seed capital and a very simple business plan. The years that followed saw the company expand to a $500,000,000 business with no additional debt. According to John C. Emery, Jr., chairman, the key to Emery's early success was flexibility in adapting to the market and customer demands.

Exhibit 4 U.S. small regional/commuter carrier traffic—January 1984

Airline	ATW Rank	Fees	% Change vs. '83	Load Factor	ATW Rank	RPMs	% Change vs. '83	ATW Rank	Freight (lbs.)	% Change vs. '83	ATW Rank	Mail (lbs.)	% Change vs. '83
Air Kentucky	13	6,678	12.7	36.5	14	951,947	8.8	12	5,927	3.0	3	8,542	n.a.
Air North	4	15,213	35.0	41.9	2	2,876,405	23.2	20	1,457	n.a.	4	8,337	n.a.
Air Sedona	37	87	24.0	46.2	31	8,326	23.0	—	—	—	—	—	—
Air Vermont	16	5,484	200.8	n.a.	—	n.a.	n.a.	—	n.a.	n.a.	—	—	—
American Central	8	11,830	92.1	n.a.	4	2,603,332	97.1	—	n.a.	—	—	—	—
Atlantis	15	6,194	20.8	n.a.	—	n.a.	n.a.	14	3,703	(45.1)	7	2,014	n.a.
BAS	32	1,025	31.0	45.0	24	154,501	33.0	21	362	145.0	—	—	—
Big Sky	21	4,186	29.2	41.8	13	957,009	19.6	5	31,423	14.2	—	—	—
Chaparral	9	11,715	27.1	n.a.	5	2,410,000	41.9	9	16,507	(12.8)	6	6,263	110.6
Chautauqua[1]	3	15,268	6.6	n.a.	—	n.a.	n.a.	—	n.a.	n.a.	—	—	—
Christman	27	2,640	112.1	17.9	18	480,713	101.8	22	188	283.7	—	—	—
Colgan	28	2,451	(3.7)	n.a.	—	n.a.	n.a.	—	n.a.	n.a.	—	—	—
Crown[1]	5	14,747	11.6	44.1	11	1,197,327	13.2	10	16,330	(8.8)	5	6,969	59.1
Cumberland	29	2,450	15.5	n.a.	21	299,130	(8.9)	3	67,334	(8.5)	8	275	n.a.
Direct Air	36	169	(2.9)	21.1	30	23,491	(2.9)	16	2,272	n.a.	—	—	—
Flacher Bros.[1]	1	16,004	33.7	41.0	7	1,723,432	41.0	8	18,516	32.6	1	24,571	65.2
Golden Pacific	31	1,181	93.3	25.4	25	140,648	93.0	6	22,580	522.0	—	—	—
Great American	18	5,325	(13.2)	75.4	1	3,212,150	(13.6)	—	—	—	—	—	—
Gull Air	2	15,609	185.3	59.0	12	1,058,150	301.1	1	204,487	30.0	2	14,431	17.0
Harbor	30	1,251	(3.2)	48.1	27	72,558	(4.9)	18	1,768	84.6	—	—	—
Jetstream Int'l.	23	3,935	46.3	n.a.	—	n.a.	n.a.	—	n.a.	n.a.	—	—	—
Las Vegas	33	529	(25.4)	n.a.	23	169,372	(29.9)	—	—	—	—	—	—
Marco Island	25	3,838	5.6	n.a.	20	356,943	5.6	19	1,521	n.a.	—	—	—

NewAir	11	10,174	60.7	n.a.	10	1,396,830	52.0	—	—	—	—
Pacific Coast	10	10,343	80.1	59.7	6	2,261,116	67.1	—	—	—	—
Pocono[1]	7	13,196	64.9	47.8	8	1,704,295	79.3	11	11,280	124.1	—
Scenic	26	3,447	(23.7)	74.0	17	620,460	(26.3)	—	n.a.	n.a.	—
Serno	35	208	35.1	29.9	29	29,120	35.1	17	1,896	33.5	—
Sky West	6	13,529	22.2	n.a.	3	2,675,691	27.5	2	124,785	(3.1)	—
Sunaire	20	4,757	30.4	n.a.	22	199,794	30.3	13	4,202	n.a.	—
Sunbird	19	5,166	(3.3)	30.7	16	637,050	(22.1)	—	—	—	—
Sun West	22	3,939	50.4	44.1	15	781,448	35.6	7	21,855	47.6	—
Tennessee Airways	24	3,887	0.8	n.a.	—	n.a.	n.a.	—	n.a.	n.a.	—
Trans-Central	14	6,339	82.3	26.0	9	1,562,303	74.7	15	3,652	643.8	—
Valley	34	360	31.4	37.9	28	60,074	26.5	—	—	—	—
Virgin Island Seaplane	12	9,571	19.2	70.5	19	412,572	23.9	4	31,955	0.3	—
Wings West	17	5,483	(2.8)	38.4	26	93,211	(2.8)	—	—	—	—
Totals		237,938	33.5			31,129,598	30.6		594,000	13.4	71,402
											51.1

U.S. Cargo Commuter Carrier Traffic

Airline	ATW Rank	Freight (lbs.)	% Change vs. '83
Blackhawk	5	165,000	48.5
Combs	1	2,072,179	n.a.
Emerald	3	1,195,200	(31.5)
Mountain Air Cargo	2	1,989,279	10.9
Saber	4	419,918	105.9
Totals		5,841,576	(33.5)

[1] Allegheny Commuter

Exhibit 5   Freight traffic, January 1984 versus 1983 (U.S. airlines)

Rank	Airline	Freight Ton-Kilometers		% Change
		1984 (000)	1983 (000)	
Transatlantic				
7	Air Florida	480	580	(17.25)
6	American	2,905	—	—
8	Capitol	197	89	121.34
4	Delta	3,824	2,367	61.55
1	Flying Tigers	43,655	57,978	(24.71)
5	Northwest	3,140	9,052	(65.32)
2	Pan Am	29,623	27,753	6.73
3	TWA	25,857	16,701	54.82
9	World	85	785	(69.18)
	Total	109,766	115,305	
Latin America				
9	Air Florida	3	5	(50.00)
4	American	1,752	3,013	(41.88)
7	Capitol	214	3	—
8	Continental	32	82	(60.98)
5	Delta	485	472	2.75
3	Eastern	3,732	2,606	43.20
2	Flying Tigers	5,663	3,036	83.29
1	Pan Am	8,100	9,070	(10.70)
6	Western	270	269	0.37
	Total	20,151	18,556	
Transpacific				
5	Continental	4,306	4,647	(7.34)
1	Flying Tigers	101,920	68,048	49.77
2	Northwest	54,874	33,944	61.66
3	Pan Am	17,867	15,120	18.16
4	United	6,279	—	—
	Total	185,246	121,759	

Mr. Emery's management style has been strictly entrepreneurial, although the eighties have seen the development of a long-range corporate plan to organize the firm's future growth. Emery made a conscious effort to segment its market by transit time, and developed five service dimensions in keeping with these segments.

Reliability has always been a priority for Emery and ground and operating equipment is developed for that end. Another important element in Emery's success has been its blue-ribbon board of directors. The board combines individuals with aircraft management experience, financial expertise, an oil man, a representative of manufacturing and business, and an academician to help the company address its future.

Korean Airlines

Korean Air Lines has grown into one of the world's major intercontinental airlines. With its operating fleet of four 747fs and two 707fs, KAL now maintains the largest freighter fleet in Asia. Since 1969, the firm has increased its cargo tonnage by an average of 35 percent annually to 1.2 billion freight tonnage-kilometers in 1983. This rapid growth is in large part due to the accompanying growth in Korea's export industry (Korea's GNP was over $66 billion in 1982 with a growth rate of 7.5 percent per year in the preceding decade). Cargo represented 23.6 percent of KAL'S operating revenues in 1982, while charter service accounted for 1.1 percent and mail carriage an additional 0.7 percent.

Choong Hoon Cho, Chairman of KAL, has defined the company's policy in the following manner: "We proceed on a step-by-step basis—slowly, steadily, and cautiously." This deliberate process has also been described as "making haste slowly," as the company pursues a strategy of growth through consolidation rather than rapid or drastic expansion. The eighties will also represent a shift in or development of corporate policies at KAL. The airline intends to upgrade its employees through re-education and training, and to revamp its image. (A KAL passenger DC-9 was shot down by the Russians in 1984.)

CUSTOMERS: FREIGHT FORWARDERS

Flying Tiger's domestic and international customers are cargo agents, freight forwarders, and direct shippers.

In international markets, freight forwarders provide nine basic services to shippers:

1. Advice to customers on transportation mode
2. Advice on packing problems (containers, etc.)
3. Customs clearance
4. Transportation insurance coverage
5. Advice on warehousing and distribution
6. Supervision of the movement of goods
7. Provision of carriers' and forwarders' documents
8. Choice of carrier and contractual obligations
9. Compliance with trade regulations and letter of credit instructions

There has historically been a great deal of dissatisfaction between freight forwarders and carriers. This is especially unfortunate due to the fact that forwarders tender a great deal of freight business to airlines. The high volume and large loads resulting from forwarders' business provide carriers with a steady and dependable income stream. Freight forwarders insist, however, on overnight freighter service while cargo carriers, such as Flying Tiger, believe that need is exaggerated and overly costly. That is, carriers contend that a large percentage of shippers need only second-day delivery. As a result of this issue, many forwarders have purchased or chartered their own aircraft to enable them to provide the service level they feel to be most appropriate.

A further area of discord between these two groups is the wholesaler/retailer controversy. An increasing number of airlines are expanding their services to include direct dealings with shippers. Forwarders resent the airlines' invasion of their retailing function and the airlines have refused to be forced into a strictly wholesaling role. As a result, the two groups are competitors in one instance and business associates in another.

Important freight forwarders such as Emery have been disappointed with Flying Tiger's service and reliability. John C. Emery, Jr. contends that his company's pleas for expanded service fell on deaf ears. "They'd say our shipment had gone, and twenty-four hours later it was still on the dock," reports Robert G. Brazier, president of Airborne Freight Corp., another airfreight forwarder that has since purchased its own planes. Other concerns about Flying Tiger's efficiency have rested on late flights, particularly in new markets, and delays due to missed connections.

Approximately 16 percent of Flying Tiger's business in 1981, 17 percent in 1982, and 12 percent in 1983 was performed for the United States Government through the Military Airlift Command for the U.S. Post Office. Contracts for the MAC are awarded annually, based on airlines participation in CRAF (Civilian Reserve Air Fleet). All of the Flying Tiger operating fleet is committed to CRAF. MAC contracts contain standard provisions that make them subject to negotiation and termination at the will of the U.S. Government. Revenues from MAC charters were $114,984,000 in 1982, $84,274,000 in 1983, and $104,411,000 in 1984.

Substitute Products

The most obvious substitute for air transportation in domestic markets is surface transportation modes such as pipelines, rail, and trucking. In some domestic and most international markets, shipping is also a substitute service. Airfreight has always had an undeniable advantage, however, due to its flexibility and speed. For some products, time is of the essence in shipment and the additional cost of airfreight becomes a minor decision variable. When the costs associated with a loss of timeliness are not fully known by the shipper, surface transportation modes may be chosen. Air cargo rates are some five times higher than competitive surface rates.

In small-package delivery, particularly mail carriage, other substitutes have become increasingly important. Advanced data transmission and communication equipment provide shippers with an alternative to top priority mail. Not only would the ability to transmit time-sensitive information decrease reliance on air transport, but might one day make it obsolete. This would reduce Flying Tiger's postal business significantly, but would have a lesser effect on the company's overall operations. Flying Tiger's average shipment weighs 150 pounds, indicating the company's greater reliance on comparatively large shipments.

ISSUES AND PROBLEMS

- An internal weakness facing the Flying Tiger line is its financial stability. Flying Tiger maintains a higher cost structure than its competitors; it is suffering from overcapacity and the repercussions of a too-rapid expansion program.
- An external threat facing the Flying Tigers is the changing competitive environment. Small package carriers, such as Federal Express, are using DC-10's in their operations. With a distribution network in place and a proven reputation, these carriers are positioned to gain immediate market share. Passenger carriers are also updating their fleets by replacing small jets with wide-body planes to improve costs per passenger mile. These wide-bodied aircraft improve freight carriage capacity and efficiency. Charter flights are also increasing in popularity and market share.
- The migration of large customers to competitors, as seen in changes in the freight forwarding business, is also an area of great concern for the Flying Tigers.
- Flying Tiger's service reputation is a problem for future success. Despite efforts to improve operational efficiency, customer complaints remain. Little marketing effort has been directed at researching and solving customer-service problems.
- A possible strategy for the Flying Tiger Line is to segment its currently diverse market by shipment size, transit time, geography, customer size, or line of business. This could replace the current strategy of flying anything, anywhere, anytime. While the airline offers differing service levels through alternative transit times, it has not made a commitment to specialization.
- Although the firm has recently abandoned passenger carriage, perhaps such service should be reinstated in order to stabilize operating revenues and to compete more effectively with major airlines. Further, while in apparent conflict with current operating strategy, the Flying Tiger line might choose to allocate resources strictly to passenger transportation, despite past dedication to airfreight.
- The area of charter operations also provides a potential opportunity for Tiger. A healthy profit might be realized through successful marketing in this arena. This might open up additional opportunities through exclusive contracts with manufacturers or other business enterprises.
- In order to thwart the effects of product substitution, the firm might also pursue an interest in the data transmission field. Additionally, Flying Tigers might engage in backward or forward integration, perhaps through the purchase of a freight forwarder or airparts supplier or manufacturer.
- Less-developed countries are expected to show significantly higher rates of growth than other areas in the coming years. Perhaps business in new geographic areas should be more actively pursued.

REFERENCES

1. Carron, Andrew S. *Transition to a Free Market: Deregulation of the Air Cargo Industry.* Washington: The Brookings Institution, 1981.

2. *Conference Proceedings of the Eleventh International Forum for Air Cargo P-116.* Pennsylvania: Publishers Choice Book Mfg. Co., 1982.

3. Loving, Ruch, Jr. "A Tiger with Air Cargo by the Tail." *Fortune* (June 19, 1981).

4. Merwin, John. "The Gunfighters." *Forbes* (September 27, 1982).

5. "Steinberg Stalks Tiger." *Business Week* (April 29, 1985), 36.

6. Taneja, Nawal K. *The U.S. Airfreight Industry.* Lexington, Mass.: D.C. Heath and Company, 1979.

7. "Tiger Gives Steinberg a Seat." *Business Week* (May 6, 1985), 54.

8. "Tiger's Heavy Load of Trouble." *Business Week* (May 24, 1982).

CASE 25

Cessna Aircraft Corporation

NANCY MARLOW
Eastern Illinois University

FRED DAVID
Mississippi State University

INTRODUCTION

Man's dream of flying is as old as man himself; throughout history men have attempted to bring that dream to reality. As a result of studying birds in flight, man's earliest attempts to fly were with bird-like wings. Balloons were man's approximation of the airborne qualities of clouds. Leonardo da Vinci worked hard, long, and unsuccessfully to learn the mechanical principles of flight. In spite of his lack of success, da Vinci's work provided the basis for future development of the propeller, the fabric-covered airplane, and the parachute.

Most accounts of aviation's history begin on December 17, 1903, just outside Kitty Hawk, North Carolina, where Orville Wright was the first man to fly a heavier-than-air machine under its own power. His twelve-second flight went a distance of 120 feet. On that same day and in the same aircraft, Orville's brother Wilbur made a flight that

Note: *Flight International* and *Aviation Week* are excellent trade publications to find additional information relevant to this case.

lasted fifty-nine seconds and covered 852 feet. Many of history's heroes are also aviation's heroes. Edward Rickenbacker, Amelia Earhart, Charles Lindbergh, Richard Byrd, Roald Amundsen, and Wiley Post are only a few of the well-known names associated with aviation. The heroes continue with the astronauts of the space program.

From its inception in 1927, Cessna Aircraft Corporation has grown from a one-man operation to a multimillion-dollar organization. Cessna is the major manufacturer of general aviation aircraft in the United States. Cessna's headquarters are located in Wichita, Kansas. Prior to 1981, Cessna enjoyed a history of outstanding success. However, between 1981 and 1984, sales and profits declined rapidly. Today, Cessna is struggling to survive. The company lost $18 million in 1983 alone. This case focuses on Cessna Aircraft's problems, concerns, and future.

HISTORY

Cessna Aircraft Company was incorporated on September 7, 1927, but the company's actual beginnings can be traced to earlier events. On February 11, 1911, Clyde V. Cessna, an Enid, Oklahoma car dealer, discovered his fascination with airplanes and flying at the Moisant International Aviation Air Circus in Oklahoma City. Clyde purchased and assembled a Bleriot airplane in which he installed his own water-cooled engine. Clyde Cessna taught himself to fly and began test flying the airplane. In June 1911, Mr. Cessna recorded his first successful flight and landing.

The years that followed were busy for Clyde Cessna. From 1912 through 1915, he spent the winters modifying airplanes. Each summer and fall he performed aerial exhibitions in Kansas and Oklahoma. In the fall of 1916, an automobile manufacturer in Wichita let Clyde use his production facility in exchange for painting the name of the company's new car, the Jones-Six, on the bottom wing of Cessna's new plane.

The outbreak of World War I ended Clyde Cessna's flying until 1925, when he, Walter Beech, and Lloyd Stearman founded the Travel Air Manufacturing Company. Unfortunately, Mr. Beech and Mr. Cessna had different ideas regarding airplane designs. Beech preferred biplanes and Cessna was convinced that monoplanes were the way of the future. These differences led to Cessna's resignation from Travel Air.

In a small shop in Wichita, Cessna designed a strutless monoplane. On September 8, 1927, he and Victor Roos organized the Cessna–Roos Company. Cessna's first factory, a 50- by 100-foot building, was constructed for $35,000 in December of 1927, the same month that Roos left the company. When Roos departed, Cessna–Roos became known as the Cessna Aircraft Company.

As the United States approached World War II, Cessna Aircraft increased production to accommodate large military orders for training aircraft and troop/cargo gliders. In order to meet this increased demand, Cessna constructed another plant sixty miles northwest of Wichita. In its history, Cessna has won the Army–Navy "E" (for effort) Award five times.

With the end of World War II, Cessna returned to commercial production of two-seater light planes, in anticipation of a postwar boom in aviation. However, the anticipated boom was never realized, and the market for two-seater planes became saturated. Therefore, Cessna turned its production efforts to four- and five-seat models.

The decades of the 1950s and 1960s were productive for Cessna. Cessna introduced the Skyhawk, the most popular airplane in history, and the Skylane, the most popular high-performance single-engine plane of the decade. During 1960, Cessna acquired a 49 percent interest in Reims Aviation, S.A. in France, and purchased McCauley Industrial Corporation, a manufacturer of propellers and other aircraft parts. McCauley still operates as a division of Cessna today. Cessna's 50,000th plane was produced in 1963.

Cessna continued to be a leader in the general aviation industry in the 1970s. During this decade, more than 1,100 Cessna Pilot Centers were opened across the nation. Cessna introduced its Citation, the world's leading business jet. The company was virtually unaffected by the recession of 1973–74.

The 1980s have not been so kind to Cessna. After achieving sales of over $1 billion and a market share of 54 percent in 1980, the company experienced declining sales and profits in 1981, 1982, and 1983. Cessna ended fiscal 1983 with a net operating loss of $18.8 million. The company hopes to broaden its market in 1984 by introducing a new version of its P210 pressurized single piston aircraft. Relatively inexpensive, this aircraft is targeted to recreational flyers and small businessmen. Exhibit 1 highlights Cessna's accomplishments from its first airplane through the reintroduction of the P210 in 1984.

Exhibit 1   Cessna milestones

1911	Clyde Cessna builds and flies his first airplane.
1927	The Cessna Aircraft Company is formed on September 8.
1928	Cessna produces the first full-cantilever-wing light airplane to go into production in this country.
1936	For the third time, the Detroit News names the Airmaster the world's most efficient airplane, awarding the trophy to Cessna permanently.
1940	Production begins on the Bobcat, Cessna's first twin-engine plane.
1943	Cessna builds more than 750 gliders, capable of carrying thirteen troops plus equipment, for the Army Air Force.
1944	Nearly 5400 Bobcat twins produced since introduction in 1940.
1946	Cessna returns to commercial production with the Models 120 and 140.
1946	Cessna's Fluid Power Division begins delivery of hydraulic power components to farm implement manufacturers.
1947	Production begins on the 5-place Models 190 and 195, Cessna's first all-metal airplanes.
1948	Cessna enters the 4-place airplane market with the Model 170.
1949	Cessna converts to metal-covered wings on the Models 120, 140, and 170.
1954	Introduction of the 310, Cessna's first business twin.
1954	Production of the T-37 Air Force jet trainer begins.
1956	Introduction of the Cessna Skyhawk, to become the most popular airplane in history.
1956	Introduction of the Cessna Skylane, to become the most popular high-performance single.
1959	Cessna purchases the Aircraft Radio Corporation as a wholly owned subsidiary.

1960	Cessna affiliates with Reims Aviation, S.A., Reims, France.
1960	Cessna acquires McCauley, manufacturer of propellers and other aircraft components.
1963	Cessna produces its 50,000th airplane, a Skyhawk.
1965	Deliveries begin of the Model 411, Cessna's first cabin-class business airplane.
1965	Cessna announces the first turbocharged single-engine airplane, a Turbo Centurion.
1965	Cessna's new agricultural airplane, the Ag Wagon is introduced.
1967	The 75,000th Cessna airplane is delivered, a Skymaster.
1967	Cessna leads the industry in multiengine deliveries and total aircraft deliveries.
1967	Introduction of the Model 421 Golden Eagle, the first general aviation aircraft to combine cabin pressurization with a turbocharging system.
1968	The 1,000th T-37 jet trainer is delivered to the U.S. Air Force. Production of the new A-37B twin-jet attack aircraft begins.
1969	Introduction of the Aerobat adds a new dimension to flying through precision aerobatics.
1969	The Model 414 is introduced as Cessna's second pressurized business twin.
1970	A nationwide network of Cessna Pilot Centers is inaugurated, featuring the exclusive Cessna Integrated Flight Training System.
1971	Introduction of the Cessna Citation, to become the world's leading business jet.
1972	The Model 340 is introduced to expand Cessna's pressurized twin market.
1975	Cessna delivers the 1,000th Golden Eagle.
1975	Cessna produces its 100,000th single-engine airplane.
1976	Deliveries begin on the all-new Titan, Cessna's largest piston-engine aircraft for business, commuter, and cargo use.
1976	Cessna announces initial design of the Citation III.
1977	Development begins of the Skylane RG, a retractable-gear version of the Skylane.
1977	Introduction of the Pressurized Centurion, the world's only pressurized single-engine piston airplane in production.
1977	First deliveries are made of the Conquest, Cessna's entry in the propjet market.
1978	First deliveries of the Citation II are made.
1978	Cessna leads the industry with the availability of weather radar on single-engine aircraft.
1978	The Ag Husky is introduced as the only turbocharged agricultural airplane in the world.
1978	Cessna refines and improves the most popular two-place training aircraft, and gives it a new name— The 152.
1979	The Turbo Centurion and Pressurized Centurion are certified for flight into icing, the only production singles to achieve this capability.
1979	Introduction of the Cutlass RG, to become the most popular retractable-gear airplane in its first year of production.
1980	Introduction of the Stationair 8—the only piston-powered 8-place single in production.
1980	Cessna sales top $1 billion for the first time.
1980	Cessna achieves an all-time high market share of 54 percent.
1980	Introduction of the Corsair propjet.
1981	First deliveries of the all-new Crusader twin.
1982	The 1,000th Citation is delivered.
1982	Introduction of the Citation III intercontinental business jet.
1984	Sale of ARC Avionics to Sperry-Rand.
1984	Introduction of improved P210.

Source: Company Reports

CESSNA'S PRODUCT LINE IN 1984

Cessna specializes in the design and production of light commercial aircraft for business, personal, and military use. The company also develops and produces a broad line of airborne navigation and communication equipment, including propellers, wheels, and brakes. Cessna manufactures hydraulic power systems for agricultural, construction, and light industrial uses.

Cessna's most recent products include the Caravan I, the Caravan II, the pressurized Centurion, the Citation S/II, the Navy Citation, and the Citation III. The Caravan I, a utility aircraft, made its first flight in December 1982. It is a single-engine propjet with a 14-passenger load capacity. The Caravan I can be equipped with wheels, floats, or skis to allow effective operation on a variety of surfaces. Federal Express purchased thirty of these aircraft to go into service in December 1984. The Caravan II, first introduced in Paris, is a twin-engine propjet utility aircraft. It is designed primarily for distribution in countries where aviation gasoline is scarce or expensive. The Caravan II's turbine engines use jet fuel. The pressurized Centurion was first introduced in 1978 and is the only pressurized single-engine airplane in the world. An improved Centurion model is scheduled for delivery in 1984.

Cessna's Citation business jets have been popular. Citation II was introduced in 1978 and became a top-selling plane. The Citation S/II, a refinement of the Citation II, is designed to fly faster, go farther, and carry a larger load. The Navy Citation is also a refinement of the Citation II. In addition to improvements of the Citation S/II, the Navy Citation offers improved high-speed handling at low altitudes, plus better acceleration, climb rate, and speed. The Citation III is Cessna's newest and most advanced intercontinental business jet. The company has a backlog of orders for this plane. (The first Citation III was purchased by professional golfer Arnold Palmer.)

In the 1980s, Cessna has followed a strategy of product development. Even when total sales declined 22 percent in 1982 and then 37 percent more in 1983, Cessna allocated resources primarily to support a product development strategy.

COMPETITION

Between 1979 and 1983, Cessna Aircraft Corporation accounted for about 51 percent of the general aviation industry's total unit output. The general aviation industry does not include military or commercial aircraft, but rather is comprised of personal and business planes. Cessna's major competitors are Piper Aircraft Corporation, Gates Learjet Corporation, and Beech Aircraft Corporation, which share the remainder of the market. Piper Aircraft Corporation is a subsidiary of Lear Siegler, a producer of electronic and automotive parts, farm equipment, and material-handling systems. Piper lost $38.5 million during fiscal year 1983.

Gates Learjet Corporation manufactures business jet aircraft, produces avionics equipment, and services its aircraft; almost 65 percent of Gates Learjet stock is owned by Gates Rubber Company. Gates Learjet accounted for 13 percent of total general aviation dollar sales in 1983, whereas Cessna accounted for 25 percent.

Beech Aircraft Corporation was founded in 1932 by Walter H. Beech, one-time partner of Clyde Cessna. Beech Aircraft is a wholly owned subsidiary of Raytheon Company. Raytheon, a *Fortune* 100 company, operates in five areas: electronics, aircraft products, major appliances, energy services, and other (which includes textbook publishing, field engineering, and construction). Like Cessna, Beech Aircraft and Gates Learjet have home offices in Wichita.

THE MARKET

The market for general aviation planes declined 41 percent in 1983. Cessna is "hoping" for an economic recovery in the aviation industry and cites several favorable signs pointing toward this recovery. First, many other industries are recovering, especially the automobile industry. Second, interest rates are stable, although not as low as desired. Third, aviation fuel prices, although high, are stable, and fuel is readily available. Fourth, the number of general aviation flights has increased. Finally, the used aircraft market has strengthened, especially for jets.

In spite of favorable indications and projections, aviation industry sales have remained low. Dealers are reluctant to stock new airplanes without a retail contract, due to previous losses, large inventories, and high interest rates. In addition, dealers have been forced to reduce their sales staffs to offset high inventory costs. One of the highest priorities for Cessna in 1984 is to encourage dealers to invest in sales personnel and marketing expenditures to allow more aggressive promotion of new aircraft.

Cessna is confident that aircraft sales will increase in 1985. The April 20, 1984, edition of the *Value Line Investment Survey* projects strong capital gains potential for Cessna stock in the next five years. This potential is based on the predicted recovery of the general aviation industry, which could come about as businesses increase their capital spending and buy small planes for use at airports not serviced by commercial airlines.

SALES

Cessna Aircraft Corporation builds more airplanes than all other general aviation manufacturers combined. However, Cessna's sales decreased from $1.06 billion to $534 million between 1981 and 1983; profits fell from $60 million to a negative $18 million; the number of employees fell from 14,838 to 7,657; and the number of shareholders declined from 13,503 to 11,900. A continued deterioration of sales in all segments of general aviation produced Cessna's first annual loss, ever, in 1983.

During fiscal 1983, Cessna delivered 1034 aircraft and accessory equipment for total sales of $524 million. Note in Exhibit 2 that 828 single-engine planes were sold in 1983 compared to 206 multiengine planes. In August of 1983, President and Chairman Russell Meyer said, "It should be obvious by now that the general aviation industry is not participating in the economic recovery that is being reported in some areas."

Although the volume for almost every Cessna product was lower in 1983 than in 1982, the multiengine business was proportionately higher than the single-engine busi-

Exhibit 2   Cessna commercial aircraft sales in units, through September 30, 1983

	1977	1978	1979	1980	1981	1982	1983
SINGLE ENGINE MODELS							
150/A150	429						
F150/FRA150 (Reims Aviation)	108	4					
152/A152	1522	1918	1268	887	634	265	165
F152/FRA152 (Reims Aviation)	19	110	142	142	79	52	16
172 Skyhawk	1711	1810	1621	1022	939	319	191
F/172 Skyhawk (Reims Aviation)	151	123	144	137	83	62	18
Cutlass						8	18
Hawk XP	598	213	254	155	40	3	
Reims Hawk XP	27	15	24	8	5	5	
117/Cardinal	122	69	1				
Reims Rocket	19						
Cardinal RG	189	96					
Reims Cardinal RG	19	4					
Cutlass RG			185	486	271	107	44
182/Skylane	826	596	660	425	294	196	81
Reims 182/Skylane	39	34	35	29	11		
182 Skylane RG	82	660	558	340	156	90	44
Reims 182 Skylane RG		18	23	13	19		
Skywagon 180	123	117	108	51	31	1	
Skywagon 185	264	226	242	200	156	65	20
Ag Wagon	36	33	35	15	8		
Ag Carryall	12	3	13	2			
Ag Pickup							
Ag Truck	269	152	89	63	49	32	20
Ag Husky		27	114	110	80	37	15
Super Skylane 206							
Skywagon 206							
Stationair 206	480						
Stationair 6	101	560	714	559	451	188	103
Skywagon 207	48						
Stationair 7	6	75	66	1			
Stationair 8			10	95	54	33	10
210/Centurion	719	710	688	437	371	173	62
Pressurized 210/Centurion		158	261	192	104	43	21
SUBTOTALS	7919	7731	7255	5369	3835	1679	828
MULTIENGINE MODELS							
Skymaster	42	80	38	38			4
Reims Skymaster	6	1		1			
Pressurized Skymaster	28	25	23	19			
Reims Pressurized Skymaster	5	2					
310	225	199	199	112	27	1	

T303/Crusader Skyknight					31	131	49
335			11	34	17	2	1
340	174	160	200	129	72	26	19
401							
402	60	82	167	126	117	27	16
404/Titan	92	76	56	89	41	24	
411							
414/Chancellor	59	129	154	122	79	28	9
421/Golden Eagle	148	129	115	125	100	21	26
Corsair/Conquest I				7	100	38	26
Conquest II	4	69	42	77	65	39	14
Citation	8						
Citation I	69	49	61	43	67	27	9
Citation II		38	79	102	129	97	22
Citation III							11
SUBTOTALS	920	1039	1145	1024	895	461	206
GRAND TOTALS	8839	8770	8400	6393	4680	2140	1034

ness. In 1982 and 1983, multiengine planes accounted for 65 percent and 67 percent of Cessna's aircraft sales, respectively. Those percentages are projected to reach 80 percent in 1984.

Overseas deliveries of Cessna aircraft decreased to 294 in 1983, compared to 735 in 1982, 1428 in 1981, and 1782 in 1980. In 1982, Cessna's export sales were 25 percent of the total, whereas in 1983 they were only 19 percent. According to Russell Roth, senior vice-president of finance, the reduction has been caused by restrictive import practices in many countries, a strong dollar, and a slow economic recovery in foreign countries.

FINANCE

Cessna's income statements and balance sheets for 1981, 1982, 1983, and 1984 are given in Exhibit 3 and Exhibit 4 respectively. In 1983, Cessna suffered a net loss, issued $100 million in 8 percent convertible bonds, and sold 500,000 shares of common stock to General Dynamics.

ORGANIZATION

During 1983, there had been some major changes among the top corporate officers of Cessna. R. W. Van Sant was elected president and Russell Meyer, Jr. assumed sole responsibility as Cessna's chairman of the board. Van Sant joined Cessna after twenty-six years with John Deere Farm Equipment Company as vice-president of engineering

Exhibit 3 Consolidated statement of operations and earnings reinvested in business

Years ended September 30	1984	1983	1982	1981
Sales and other income:				
Sales	$693,586,278	$524,395,393	$831,527,765	$1,060,097,076
Earnings of finance subsidiaries, before income taxes thereon	19,770,674	24,632,474	23,284,405	21,809,937
Other income, principally interest	5,317,877	9,272,178	6,459,658	7,277,493
	718,674,829	558,300,045	861,271,828	1,089,184,506
Costs and expenses:				
Manufacturing and engineering costs	622,117,150	465,700,628	673,613,560	837,720,335
Depreciation	12,155,397	12,638,512	11,913,423	9,899,501
Sales and administrative expenses	104,777,021	111,367,050	130,972,607	106,465,341
Interest	11,314,853	6,039,141	9,912,424	16,433,107
	750,364,421	595,745,331	826,412,014	970,518,284
Earnings (loss) before provision for income taxes	(31,689,592)	(37,445,286)	34,859,814	118,666,222
Provision for income taxes, including finance subsidiaries				
Current	(27,604,000)	(19,874,000)	21,587,000	59,284,000
Deferred	(5,035,000)	1,274,000	(4,805,000)	(1,184,000)
	(32,639,000)	(18,600,000)	16,782,000	58,100,000
Net earnings (loss)	949,408	(18,845,286)	18,077,814	60,566,222
Earnings reinvested in business at beginning of year	—	263,466,376	256,889,030	207,758,059
	—	244,621,090	274,966,844	268,324,281
Cash dividends on common stock				
$.40 per share (1982 – $.60 per share, 1981 – $.60 per share)	—	7,663,420	11,500,468	11,435,251
Earnings reinvested in business at end of year	—	$236,957,670	$263,466,376	$ 256,889,030
Net earnings (loss) per share of common stock	$.05	$(.98)	$.94	$3.19

Source: Cessna's 1984 Annual Report, p. 16.

Exhibit 4 Consolidated statement of financial position

Years ended September 30	1984	1983	1982	1981
ASSETS				
Current assets:				
Cash and commercial paper	$ 3,294,836	$ 53,046,744	$ 1,888,666	$ 12,505,810
Notes and accounts receivable:				
Trade	42,614,857	32,324,990	29,473,918	38,593,743
Finance subsidiaries	17,279,000	18,513,315	12,775,304	42,802,271
	59,893,857	50,838,305	42,249,222	81,396,014
Refundable income taxes	27,642,472	22,973,000	—	—
Inventories	232,047,244	220,021,418	252,898,143	300,195,351
Deferred income tax benefits	30,750,026	43,183,826	29,954,000	18,143,000
Prepaid expenses	1,013,481	1,097,255	2,325,122	672,215
Total current assets	354,641,916	391,160,548	329,315,153	412,912,390
Investments in unconsolidated companies				
Finance subsidiaries	144,901,113	134,093,439	120,551,965	117,944,853
Other subsidiaries and affiliate	3,950,087	3,950,087	3,250,087	3,250,087
	148,851,200	138,043,526	123,802,052	121,194,940
Property, plant, and equipment—at cost				
Land	1,173,647	1,173,647	1,173,647	1,145,847
Buildings and improvements	86,574,355	86,756,733	85,573,293	83,219,997
Machinery and equipment	120,178,958	129,186,319	124,342,810	106,060,661
	207,926,960	217,116,699	211,089,750	190,426,505
Less accumulated depreciation and amortization	125,255,131	124,186,638	112,058,698	99,644,945
	82,671,829	92,930,061	99,031,052	90,781,560
Deferred tooling	77,328,149	68,022,065	52,102,325	30,548,970
Other assets	10,751,139	8,630,685	7,608,385	2,203,575
	$674,244,233	$698,786,885	$611,858,967	$657,641,435
LIABILITIES AND STOCKHOLDERS' EQUITY				
Current liabilities:				
Short-term debt	$ —	$ —	$ 14,000,000	$ —
Accounts payable	43,977,969	35,630,635	31,314,617	44,937,502
Customer deposits	48,095,098	86,095,655	56,688,934	76,339,508
Income taxes	4,787,365	2,878,087	1,895,597	33,363,050
Accrued and other liabilities	16,905,901	91,914,224	97,646,041	101,082,400
Long-term debt due within one year	3,210,000	4,290,000	4,487,500	6,572,500
Total current liabilities	206,976,333	220,808,601	206,032,689	262,294,960
Deferred income tax	10,650,000	25,031,000	24,405,000	20,641,000

Years ended September 30	1984	1983	1982	1981
LIABILITIES AND STOCKHOLDERS' EQUITY (continued)				
Long-term debt due after one year				
5.95% notes payable	$ 1,600,000	$ 2,750,000	$ 3,900,000	$ 5,050,000
9.5% notes payable	14,625,000	16,250,000	17,875,000	19,500,000
Other notes payable	3,600,000	3,700,000	4,800,000	1,112,500*
Capitalized lease obligations	2,130,000	2,465,000	2,880,000	3,280,000
8% convertible subordinated debentures	100,000,000	100,000,000	—	185,000
	121,955,000	125,165,000	29,455,000	29,127,500
Contingent liabilities				
Stockholders' equity				
Preferred stock, $1 par value, 3,000,000 shares authorized, none issued				
Common stock, $1 par value, 44,000,000 shares authorized, 19,760,196 shares issued. (1983—19,245,916 shares)	19,760,196	19,245,916	19,223,506	19,202,552
Paid-in surplus	89,243,536	76,771,021	76,016,069	75,681,928
Earnings reinvested in business	230,084,876	236,957,670	263,466,376	256,889,030
	339,088,608	332,974,607	358,705,951	351,773,510
Less:				
Treasury stock at cost, 77,569 shares (1983—59,322 shares)	1,330,201	1,093,257	1,241,442	—
Restricted stock plan deferred compensation	3,095,507	4,099,066	5,498,231	6,195,535
	334,662,900	327,782,284	351,966,278	345,577,975
	$674,244,233	$698,786,885	$611,858,967	$657,641,435

Source: Cessna's 1984 Annual Report, pp. 14–15.

*6.5% mortgage note

and manufacturing services. Another change was in the office of senior vice-president of Finance, where Robert P. Bauer was replaced by Russell R. Roth. Roth joined Cessna after having been vice-president and controller of the Bendix Automotive Group. A list of Cessna's corporate officers is provided below:

Russell W. Meyer, Jr.	Chairman of the board
R. W. Van Sant	President
Brian E. Barents	Senior vice-president, Aircraft Marketing
Russell R. Roth	Senior vice-president, Finance
John E. Moore	Senior vice-president, Personnel and Community Relations
Pierre Clostermann	Vice-president
Homer G. Nester	Vice-president, controller and treasurer
David R. Edwards	Secretary

Because of the size of Cessna's operation, it is impossible for one group of individuals to oversee the entire organization. For this reason, Cessna is divided into nine divisions, each headed by a vice-president or general manager. The divisions and the locations of their main offices are given as follows:

Fluid Power Division	Hutchinson, Kansas
McCauley Accessory Division	Dayton, Ohio
Pawnee Aircraft Division	Wichita, Kansas
Wallace Aircraft Division	Wichita, Kansas
Citation Marketing Division	Wichita, Kansas
Conquer Marketing Division	Wichita, Kansas
Piston Aircraft Marketing Division	Wichita, Kansas
International Marketing Division	Wichita, Kansas
Product Support Division	Wichita, Kansas

A new position, Product Support Manager for Federal Express, was added to Cessna's Product Support Division as a result of the recent sale of 30 Caravan I aircraft to Federal Express. Reid Jewett filled this position and will organize and administer Cessna's program to train flight crews and maintenance technicians for Federal Express.

RESEARCH AND DEVELOPMENT

In 1983, Cessna's research and development expenditures declined to $45.2 million, a 13.6 percent decrease from 1982. This total represented 8.6 percent of Cessna's total sales. To put this percentage into perspective, R&D expense to sales ratios for competing companies in 1983 are given below:

McDonnell Douglas	3.7%
Gates Learjet	2.0%
Northrop	8.2%
Boeing	3.9%
General Dynamics	2.2%

Cessna and General Dynamics Corporation have recently entered into a joint technology program. General Dynamics, builder of the F-16, has long been interested in general aviation. In fact, they had approached both Beech Aircraft and Gates Learjet about merger or acquisition possibilities. In exchange for $12.7 million, General Dynamics received 500,000 shares of Cessna's stock, which amounts to about 2.8 percent of the company's total shares. In addition, David S. Lewis, chairman of General Dynamics, has become a member of Cessna's board of directors. Meyer, chairman of Cessna, has said that this joint project is not an indication of a merger between the two companies. The technology program includes research and development in the areas of composite structures, aerodynamics, and flight control systems for high-performance aircraft. These new technologies are being applied to Cessna's Citation, Conquest, and Caravan lines.

1984 SUMMARY

As fiscal year 1984 came to an end, Cessna reported the following year-end results:

1. We delivered 922 aircraft worth $603 million in fiscal 1984, down in units from 1,371 in 1983, but up in dollar volume from $453 million.
2. Turbine aircraft revenues increased 64 percent from $254 million in 1983 to $417 million in 1984.
3. Citation deliveries reached 96, compared to 73 last year, and included 47 Citation III's, compared to 11 a year ago.
4. Piston aircraft deliveries declined to 786 from 1,238 last year.
5. Export shipments declined in 1984 to 160 piston and turbine aircraft worth $89 million, compared to 294 airplanes worth $93 million exported in 1983.
6. Research and development expenditures were about 8 percent of gross revenues in 1984, totaling $57 million.
7. The Pawnee and Wallace Aircraft Divisions were merged to form a single Aircraft Division.
8. The company and its employees reached a new thirty-eight-month labor agreement.
9. Net earnings for 1984 were $949,048.
10. Cessna's average number of employees increased to 8,645 in 1984, compared to 7,657 in 1983.

FUTURE STRATEGY

Cessna plans to implement a new marketing strategy, centered around a leasing package. This package will offer a one-year, zero-interest loan to purchasers of single-engine aircraft. This program is designed to create new business for both its Citation business jets and turboprops. The jet package will include a customized plane, two pilots, maintenance services, a hangar, office space, and landing expenses for a fixed $36,500 per month over five years, excluding fuel. This will be considerably less than purchasing a $1.7 million jet and paying associated expenses over five years. Cessna is able to offer this package because it, not the lessee, will get the depreciation and tax credits.

Cessna plans to reduce its inventory requirements for dealers and offer a learn-to-fly program. The learn-to-fly program is intended to lure business people into learning to fly. Usually, aircraft purchasers are brand-loyal to the plane in which they learned to fly.

Cessna has entered into a joint venture with Sperry Rand Corporation. This venture is associated with the 1984 sale of Cessna's ARC Avionics Division to Sperry. ARC's sales volume was restricted because the division could sell only to Cessna's own aircraft. ARC produces electronic devices for use in general aviation. These products complement Sperry's product line of similar equipment for larger military and commercial aircraft. Together, Cessna and Sperry plan to develop an engine instrument, a crew advisory system, and a flight management system. These items are to be produced by Sperry and installed in Cessna's planes.

To improve its operations in 1985, Cessna must take advantage of external opportunities, avoid environmental threats, capitalize on its own strengths, and overcome its internal weaknesses. As Mr. Meyer, chairman, and Mr. Van Sant, president, discuss Cessna's future, some special concerns come to mind:

1. Should Cessna divest of other divisions to raise needed capital? Which ones and why?

2. Should Cessna diversify into aviation services, such as air cargo and air mail? Why?

3. Unlike its major competitors (Piper, Gates Learjet, and Beech), Cessna is not controlled by a larger company. Should Cessna offer itself for sale to General Dynamics or Sperry Rand? How much is Cessna worth?

4. Should Cessna improve its marketing and distribution practices?

5. In addition to the learn-to-fly and leasing programs, what other strategy-implementation approaches could benefit Cessna?

6. Why isn't the general aviation industry participating in the economic recovery? Will it rebound in the future?

SUGGESTED READINGS

"Cessna's Current Workforce of 9300 Down Sharply from Peak of 21,200 in December 1979." *Wall Street Journal* (March 1, 1984): 6.

"Cessna Lost $18.8 Million on Sales of $524.4 Million in Fiscal Year 1983, Ended September 30, 1983." *Aviation Week* (October 31, 1983): 26.

"Cessna Must 'Lower the Cost of Flying.'" *Flight International* (February 25, 1984): 504.

"Cessna: Relying on Its Big Planes, New Sales Tactics, and Austerity." *Business Week* (October 11, 1982): 95–98.

"Cessna Shuts Down Every Line." *Flight International* (August 20, 1983): 470.

"Cessna to Jointly Develop Flight Management Systems with Sperry." *Wall Street Journal* (October 24, 1983): 62.

"Cessna to Suspend Production of Piston Aircraft at Pawnee Division for Three Months." *Wall Street Journal* (March 1, 1984): 6.

"Cessna Will Be 2.8% Acquired by General Dynamics for $12.7 Million." *Aviation Week* (November 14, 1983): 34.

"Cessna Wins Contract for 30 Turboprop Aircraft from Federal Express." *Aviation Week* (December 12, 1983): 27.

"Cessna Wins US Navy Trainer Contest." *Flight International* (June 4, 1983): 1618.

Mayborn, Mitch, and Bob Pickett. *Cessna Guidebook.* Dallas, Texas: Flying Enterprise Publications, 1973.

CASE 26

Bicycles Unlimited

VICTOR R. RIOS
Virginia Polytechnic Institute and State University

LARRY D. ALEXANDER
Virginia Polytechnic Institute and State University

INTRODUCTION

When Dwight Young opened Bicycles Unlimited in 1980, his father wanted him to have a partner or use a consultant in the business. However, Dwight admitted that he was possessive and wanted to do everything himself. As he recalled, "I wanted to live or die by my own efforts. In hindsight I wish I had at least let my father's friend set up books for me and show me how to keep them."

Dwight Young opened his bicycle shop with a $4,300 loan from his father and $500 worth of tools he had accumulated. The bike shop was the only one in Cliffville, Tennessee. Dwight initially sold Fuji bicycles, a wide selection of parts and accessories, and a variety of used bicycles. His business was open from 9:00 a.m. to 7:00 p.m. Monday through Saturday, with two exceptions—he stayed open until 9:00 p.m. on Friday, but closed at 3:00 p.m. on Wednesday to go for a weekday bike ride.

Dwight Young was born in Cliffville, a city of 14,000 people, but was raised ten miles away in Kermit, a city of 9,000. (A map of Cliffville and the surrounding area is shown in Figure 1.) He attended Cliffville College, a school of some 5,000 students, and was only one class short of a B.S. degree in liberal arts. Dwight hoped to go back and finish his degree, but he didn't have time to do so now. He had previously worked three years as a bicycle mechanic, a parts wholesaler, a sales representative, and a store manager.

Since the store opened, Dwight has worked at least 58 hours a week. He takes out $200 a month for expenses and believes that his income is approximately $4,000 a year. Since opening Bicycles Unlimited, Dwight's home had been the basement of his business. It is March 1984 now and Dwight is starting to feel burned out with the many hours of work, modest living conditions, and low income.

Initial work on this case was done by Patrick S. Herrity and Laura E. Collins in a small business management class at Virginia Tech.

Figure 1 Map of Grantstown and surrounding area

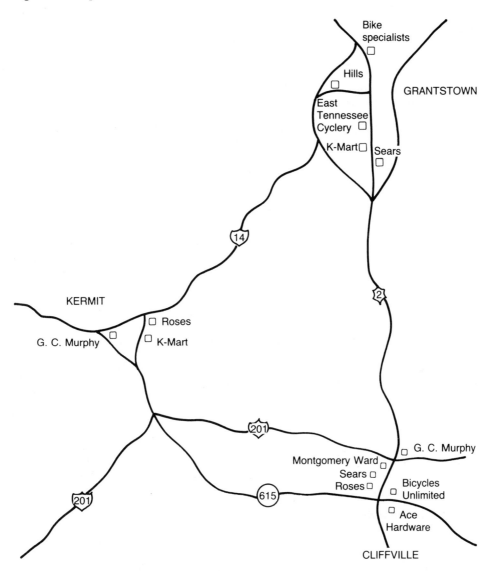

BICYCLES UNLIMITED'S FUNCTIONAL AREAS

Operations

Dwight Young's business consists primarily of selling new and used bicycles and doing repairs on bicycles. Young has approximately twenty new and forty used bikes for sale.

New bikes range in price from $129 to $429, while used bikes average selling for $100 each. Young recently dropped his Fuji brand of bicycles because he could not repay the $5,000 he owed Fuji for bicycles and parts.

In order to give customers more to choose from, Young decided to carry the Miyata line of bicycles.

Bicycles Unlimited takes in used bikes as trade-ins and reconditions them for resale. One problem associated with taking trade-ins is that the shop is encumbered with a large inventory. However, Young considers used bikes to be a good value. As he says:

> It is nice to carry used bikes because many people come in and don't know exactly what they want. I feel that a used bike is a good bargain and worth the money. A lot of times, people can get a much better bike for their money with a used bike than by buying a brand new one.

Although he has a variety of used bicycles, Young tends to shy away from taking department store bicycles such as Huffy and Murray. He considers these brands generally more trouble than they are worth.

The largest proportion of Young's revenues comes from repairing bicycles. Since Bicycles Unlimited is the only bike repair shop in Cliffville, it has something of a monopoly on the repair business. Dwight charges $12 an hour for repair work. He commented:

> When a person brings a bike in, that's when I really explain how a bike functions and point out any little problems with the bike. It is then that I do a real sales job. However, I don't try to sell a repair that isn't needed.

Young takes enormous pride in his work. He does some occasional ski tuning and works on wheelchairs for the Red Cross. He likes to fix anything. He once even fixed a bongo drum.

Marketing

Bicycles Unlimited primarily sells high-quality, medium-priced bicycles. It appears from the price of the bicycles that Dwight's target market is the serious cyclist, but this is not the case. Dwight says:

> I am after anybody and everybody, not just the serious cyclist. I am happy to sell a bicycle to somebody who wants to use it for recreation, not necessarily just for training. What I try to make people understand is that quality pays off in the long run, . . . even if you have to pay a little more for it in the beginning. I really feel that what I offer is of much better value than anything in department stores.

Although Cliffville is a college town, less than one-half of Bicycles Unlimited's sales are to students and faculty. When the business first opened, however, nearly two-thirds of all sales were made to this group.

Young says "you have to be very careful with advertising because you could spend a lot more than you could get out of it." Dwight admits that he does almost no advertising. Outside of the Yellow Pages, the only ad he was running in early 1984 was a small one for fully reconditioned used bikes, in the classified ads of the Eastern Tennessee section of the *Knoxville Gazette and Times.* However, as soon as he reconditions some more bikes, he plans to expand his advertising. In the past, Fuji had paid for 50 percent of the shop's advertising expenses on any ad that mentioned its brand name exclusively. This advertising support was of course dropped, when the Fuji line was dropped.

Bicycles Unlimited tries to undercut the prices charged by two Grantstown bicycle specialty shops; however, prices in all three shops are above those in retail chains. Young regrets that there is not a lot of money to be made in bicycles. The markup on a new bicycle is only 40 percent. The margin on bicycle parts, however, is much greater. "I thank God every day for nails and tacks and pieces of glass," says Young. Two examples of the markup on bicycle parts help illustrate this point: he charges $7.00 for a new bicycle tire that costs only $2.79, and a tire gauge that sells for $5.00 actually costs only $1.60. (No standard markup is used for parts. Dwight admits that he figures the margin by a seat-of-the-pants estimate.)

Finance/Accounting

Young believes that roughly 45 percent of his income comes from bicycle sales, 45 percent from parts, and 10 percent from labor charges. His bicycle sales consist of approximately one-half new and one-half used bikes. Sales figures for 1983 are shown in Exhibit 1.

Bicycles Unlimited has never had any type of bookkeeping system, but does keep track of monthly sales. Young admits that he lacks the personal knowledge to set up and the time to maintain a complicated bookkeeping system. He feels that the labor-intensive nature of his business prevents him from doing all the administrative tasks that probably should be done. Instead, only scattered accounts-payable records are kept. Dwight never has filed either federal or Tennessee state income tax returns, since he really does not know whether the business has ever made a profit. He plans to file amended returns, but doubts that he will owe much of anything.

Bicycles Unlimited extends credit, but records often fail to show the balance due, the amount paid, the debtor's phone number, or even the debtor's name. Dwight reasoned, "When you are in the rush of business, it's hard to keep track of all that stuff." Although he does keep track of all money that comes across the register, he says improvements are needed in his credit policy.

The shop's total debt currently is approximately $10,000, of which $5,000 is owed to Fuji, $2,000 is owed to Miyata, and the rest is spread among various creditors. Dwight admits that he does not have a good picture of his debt situation.

Exhibit 1   Bicycles Unlimited's sales figures for 1983

MONTH	SALES
January	$1,984.00
February	$2,707.28
March	$7,039.14
April	$6,121.31
May	$6,221.12
June	$7,137.56
July	$7,124.24
August	$6,302.84
September	$8,565.93
October	$4,507.08
November	$3,336.06
December	$4,375.84

Human Resources

College students are hired on a part-time basis to do a small amount of sales and repair work. These employees are paid on a commission basis only, which usually amounts to less than minimum wage. Typically, one-third of what a customer is charged goes to the employee. Some difficulty has been encountered in scheduling help and there exists a moderate employee turnover problem. Young is not happy with the quality of workers hired, especially the local college students. He says, "Students are fine, except none of them really make a commitment to the business. It's like they will help you for a few months, but their highest priority is the next party they are going to."

In February of 1984, Young placed an advertisement in the Eastern Tennessee section of the *Knoxville Gazette and Times* for someone to take over his bookwork and be an assistant to him. He also put an advertisement in the placement office at Cliffville College and East Tennessee State University for the same position. Although he does not know what kind of salary he can offer that person, he plans to pay at least minimum wage. However, he realizes that a salary of $5 to $6 an hour is more attractive. In order to compensate for the low salary, Young says the most important thing he has to offer is an opportunity to open another store in Grantstown or Knoxville, a city sixty-eight miles away with approximately 182,000 people.

Purchasing/Inventory Control

Bicycles Unlimited has a card system to keep track of inventory. Dwight keeps a physical inventory of bicycles. However, items sold or received to the parts inventory are not posted on an ongoing basis. Furthermore, there is no formal reorder system. Young purchases in large quantities to obtain quantity discounts, in some cases regardless of his need or ability to pay. In total, Young has a $20,000 investment in bicycles and parts. The large inventory of used bicycles takes up floor space and tends to detract from the display of new bicycles. Young typically spends a lot of time ordering parts. This is partially due to the fact that he uses fifteen to twenty different suppliers. Dwight has never made any formal study to determine which suppliers offer the most in terms of price, reorder minimums, delivery time, purchase discounts, and other terms of sale.

THE EXTERNAL ENVIRONMENT

The Bicycle Industry

The U.S. bicycle industry was hit hard by the economic downturn in 1981–1983. Some manufacturers held the opinion that the downturn in sales was due to reduced consumer spending and had little to do with long-term consumer bicycle demand. Some analysts predict that bicycle sales should experience a recovery in 1984 and beyond, since consumers' incomes seem to be strengthening and they would be more willing to spend money on consumer durables.

Bicycles are primarily sold by two different types of stores—major retailers and bicycle specialty shops. Approximately 75 percent of all bicycles are sold by large national and regional retailers. Small, individually owned shops specializing in bicycles sell the remaining 25 percent. In 1982, unit sales of bicycles declined 23.6 percent from 8,900,000 bicycles sold in 1981. Domestic bicycle sales accounted for 5,200,000 units of the total, and imports accounted for 1,600,000. Some industry projections for 1983 and beyond suggest that imports will continue to increase. Exhibit 2 shows imported bicycles by country and major world region as a percentage of total imports. Taiwan is the clear leader among nations exporting bicycles to the U.S.

Many domestic manufacturers have complained that Taiwan and the Republic of Korea are dumping government-subsidized bicycles on the U.S. market. The Bicycle Manufacturers Association's investigation found that both of these charges are true. The B.M.A. is expected to reach a decision in 1984 on whether legal action should be initiated to stop the unfair practices of Taiwan and the Republic of Korea.

Domestic bicycle manufacturers in 1983 include Huffy, Murray, Roadmaster, Schwinn, Columbia, and Ross, along with a group of specialty manufacturers. Market research conducted by Murray in 1982 determined that Huffy is the largest bicycle manufacturer, with approximately a 36 percent market share. Murray is a close second with a 33 percent market share, while the other domestic manufacturers together comprise the remaining 31 percent of the market.

Lightweight bicycles, which are still the best-selling bike category, accounted for 53 percent of the 1982 market. The B.M.A. defines these bikes as any diamond-frame or mixte-frame, multispeed model with at least 24-inch diameter wheels. Although these bicycles are sold primarily to teenagers and young adults, this market segment is benefiting from an increasing number of adults who want bicycles for transportation and exercise.

Exhibit 2   Imported bicycles—percent of imports by country and region

	1970	1982
Orient	30.2%	89.6%
Taiwan	2.8	62.6
Japan	27.2	19.6
Korea	0.2	7.4
Europe	59.1%	7.5%
France	2.6	4.4
Poland	1.6	2.4
United Kingdom	19.3	—
Austria	19.3	0.2
West Germany	16.3	0.1
Italy	—	0.4
Other Nations	10.7%	2.9%
	100 %	100 %

Source: *Murray Ohio, 1982 Annual Report,* p. 5.

The category of bicycles experiencing the fastest growth is the BMX (bicycle motocross) bike. These models accounted for 37 percent of all bicycle sales in 1982, which represented a phenomenal increase in recent years. The Bicycle Manufacturers Association projects that BMX bicycle sales will probably account for 40 percent of all sales in 1983. The BMX is primarily a youth bicycle sold in the 20-inch wheel size. There exists a significant growth in the sport of BMX racing, which started in Southern California and is sponsored by local Y.M.C.A.s and Boy's Clubs. BMX racing regularly appears today on television, in magazines, and in movies.

BICYCLE MANUFACTURERS

Huffy

Huffy, located in Miamisburg, Ohio, is the largest manufacturer of bicycles in the U.S., with approximately 36 percent of all domestic manufacturers' unit shipments. While bicycles are a major product line for Huffy, it also sells basketball backboards and goals, exercise equipment, and fishing products. Huffy had net sales of $222,345,000 and profits of $3,055,000 for fiscal year 1982. Huffy's products are sold primarily to national retail chains, regional retailers, and sporting goods distributors and dealers. In 1982, over 76 percent of Huffy's bicycles were produced under the Huffy brand and sold to over 300 national and regional retailers. Huffy also manufactures and sells bicycles to customers who want their own private label to market. Larry Cain, Huffy's bicycle marketing manager, believes that building bicycles for the youth market presents many challenges. As he puts it:

> Everything has to be built just right, from the kid-sized pedals and handle grips to the frame. Also the machines must be safe, durable, and adjustable, so that the bikes can grow with the young riders. Even the chain guards are fully enclosed.

Huffy's new line of bicycles for both boys and girls has earned the Good Housekeeping Seal of Approval.

Murray

Murray Ohio Manufacturing Company, which, surprisingly, is located in Brentwood, Tennessee, had sales of $288,642,000 and profits of $5,093,000 in 1982. Murray Ohio manufactures one out of every three bicycles produced in the United States. Bicycles and accessories account for 40 percent of the total sales and 28 percent of the total operating profits for the firm. Competitive pricing pressures from foreign producers has reduced Murray's profits in recent years.

Murray sells bicycles mainly to national and regional full-line retail chains in the United States. This line of bicycles includes all types and sizes for both the youth and adult markets. The Murray line accounts for 49 percent of total company sales. In addition, Murray is the world's largest producer of private-label bicycles. The BMX series of bicycles, particularly the X20, is a very profitable product for Murray. In order to promote this youth-oriented bicycle, Murray has established its own BMX racing team and sponsors the World Cup BMX race in Knoxville.

In January 1983, the Los Angeles Olympic Organizing Committee announced that bicycles produced by Murray Ohio would bear the official symbol of the 1984 Olympic Games under an exclusive agreement. In conjunction with its Olympic promotions, Murray plans to sponsor a lightweight bicycle racing team. Murray recently introduced a new modified lightweight bicycle line that was supported by an extensive television advertising campaign.

COMPETITION IN CLIFFVILLE

Bicycles Unlimited's competition in Cliffville includes department stores, catalog stores, and a hardware store located across the street. A summary of Bicycles Unlimited's competitors in Cliffville is shown in Exhibit 3. In general, local competition offers cheaper, but lower-quality bicycles. Dwight Young feels that if people really want quality bicycles, they will not go to a department store or a hardware store. He does concede, however, that price is a major factor for many first-time bicycle purchasers. Second-time bike purchasers are more likely to purchase a higher-quality bicycle from a specialty bike shop.

Exhibit 3 Bicycles Unlimited's competition in Cliffville

	Bicycles Unlimited	Roses	G. C. Murphy	Sears	Montgomery Ward	Ace Hardware
Location	Cliffville	Cliffville and Kermit	Cliffville and Kermit	Cliffville and Grantstown	Cliffville	Cliffville
Distance from Bicycles Unlimited	n/a	0.8 mile in Cliffville, 10 miles in Kermit	1.5 mile in Cliffville, 10 miles in Kermit	0.6 mile in Cliffville, 16 in Grantstown	0.7 mile	Across the street
Types of Bikes Sold	Primarily adult	Adult and Children's	Adult and Children's	Adult and Children's	Adult and Children's	Adult and Children's
Primary Brands Sold	Fuji and Miyata	Huffy	Murray	Sears	Montgomery Ward	Murray
Price Range for Adult Bikes	$129 to $429	$110 to $130	$117 to $131	$99 to $259	$99 to $159	$124 to $159
Used Bikes	40	None	None	None	None	None
Repair Shop	Yes	No	No	Takes work to Johnson's Repair Shop	Takes work to various shops	Takes work to Bicycles Unlimited
Labor Rate	$12/hour	n/a	n/a	n/a	n/a	n/a
Layaway Plan	Flexible, no set plan	$1 down, 10% every week, 5 weeks to pay balance	10% down, 10 weeks to pay; $1 fee	None	No down payment; 30 days to pay balance	Optional payment plan; 90 days to pay balance

Roses

Roses has two stores that compete with Bicycles Unlimited. They are located in Cliff-ville and Kermit. Roses carries mainly BMX bicycles and some small children's bikes with training wheels. Most of the bikes are made by Huffy, and the rest by Murray, Hedstrom, and Roadmaster. Roses' BMX bikes are priced from $78 to $130, while small children's bikes range from $53 to $75. Roses also carries a number of 3-speed and 10-speed bicycles, ranging from $110 to $130. Roses charges a $10 fee to put bikes together.

Sears

A Sears catalog store is located less than a mile away in Cliffville and another one is in Grantstown. Bicycles are sold only through the catalog, with no store display models being available at these two locations. Sears-brand bikes are priced from $99 to $259 for the adult bikes and $79 to $199 for the BMX type. Sears also carries small children's bikes with training wheels, and tricycles, ranging in price from $40 to $90. They also sell a three-wheeled bike made by Hedstrom, and a tandem bike, each around $260. Delivery time on Sears bikes is normally three days. If any problems develop while the bike is still under warranty it is sent to Johnson's Repair Shop, across the river in Cliffville.

Ace Hardware

Ace Hardware, located across the street from Bicycles Unlimited, has six adult and six children's bikes for sale. The adult bikes range in price from $124 to $159, while children's bikes sell for $84 to $149. All of Ace Hardware's bikes are made by Murray. Whenever a repair is needed on a bike, it is sent across the street to Bicycles Unlimited.

COMPETITION IN NEARBY CITIES

The other main competitors to Bicycles Unlimited, that are located in nearby Kermit and Grantstown, are summarized in Exhibit 4. While Kermit has only department stores, Grantstown has two bike specialty shops, department stores, and another Sears catalog store. Grantstown is the largest town in this tri-city area, with a population of 25,000, including a student population of about 4,000 from Grantstown Community College, a two-year junior college.

Bike Specialists

Bike Specialists, located in Grantstown, Tennessee, approximately sixteen miles from Bicycles Unlimited, is one of two bike shops in Wilmington County that directly compete with Bicycles Unlimited. Bike Specialists primarily carry lightweight adult bicycles

Exhibit 4   Bicycles Unlimited's competition in nearby cities

	Bike Specialists	East Tennessee Cyclery	K-Mart	Hills
Location	Grantstown	Grantstown	Grantstown and Kermit	Grantstown
Distance from Bicycles Unlimited	16 miles	16 miles	16 miles in Grantstown 10 miles in Kermit	10 miles
Types of Bikes Sold	Adult and Children's	Primarily Adult	Adult and Children's	Adult and Children's
Primary Brands Sold	Shogun & Jetter	Schwinn and Trek	Murray	Murray and Huffy
Price Range for Adult Bikes	$140 to $465	$154 to $400	$110 to $130	$100 to $128
Used Bikes	14	20	None	None
Repair Shop	Yes	Yes	No	No
Labor Rate	$12/hour	$16/hour	n/a	n/a
Layaway Plan	20% down, flexible payment plan	20% down, pay balance in 60–90 days	$1 fee, 10% down, 60 days to pay balance	$1 fee, 10% down, 10% payment every week

with 10, 12, and 18 speeds, and with prices from $140 to $465. The adult new bikes include Shogun, Jetter, Ross, and Univega. The shop also carries several models of the recently popular mountain bike, a type of BMX bike for adults. It features straight handlebars and ten or more gears, along with fat, knobby tires. Besides new bikes, Bike Specialists also has a limited inventory of about twenty used bikes, priced from $25 to $125. All bike prices include assembly. Bike Specialists also carries about ten different types of children's bikes. These are primarily BMX bicycles plus two models with training wheels. The children's bicycles, made exclusively by Jetter, range in price from $100 to $175. They are considered to be of higher quality than Huffy or Murray bikes.

Bike Specialists has its own repair facility and charges $12 an hour for labor. The owner feels this labor rate is quite low, considering the industry average is around $18 an hour. Every new bike sold has a lifetime guarantee on any defect, but used bikes have only a thirty-day guarantee.

East Tennessee Cyclery

East Tennessee Cyclery, also located in Grantstown, is the other bike specialty shop in this somewhat rural county. It sells primarily adult bikes manufactured by Schwinn and

Trek, priced from $154 to $400. It also sells a few children's bikes by Schwinn, ranging from $109 to $121. Like Bicycles Unlimited and Bike Specialists, East Tennessee Cyclery has its own repair shop. It charges $16 an hour for repair work. The owner plans to increase the labor charge as soon as Bike Specialists, his nearby competitor, raises its rate.

K-Mart

K-Mart has two stores that compete with Bicycles Unlimited, one ten miles away in Kermit and one in Grantstown. The Grantstown store carries over twice as many bicycles as the somewhat closer Kermit store. Virtually all the bicycles sold by K-Mart are made by Murray, with a few made by Huffy. K-Mart carries BMX and adult 10-speed bikes, children's bikes with training wheels, and tricycles. The BMX bikes are priced from $76 to $100 and the children's bikes start around $66. The adult bikes are primarily 10-speeds, with only a few 3-speeds, ranging from $110 to $130. All prices are for unassembled bicycles. K-Mart charges a $10 fee to assemble any bike. The Grantstown K-Mart store has been using Bike Specialists to assemble its bikes. K-Mart does no repairs on its own bicycles except for minor ones. If a bicycle is returned with a defect within thirty days, the store either fixes it or gives the customer a new bike. After thirty days, the bike is sent back to the manufacturer.

ISSUES FACING BICYCLES UNLIMITED

Bicycle conditions around Cliffville and the immediate area are not the best for cycling due to hilly terrain, narrow roads, and few sidewalks. An established bus system in Grantstown limits the number of student cyclists, since the system is convenient for commuting to and from Grantstown Community College. Furthermore, many off-campus students at Cliffville College drive their cars or walk rather than ride bicycles. Weather conditions in the area also prevent many from riding bicycles. Spring and fall usually means either rain or high winds. In the winter there are periods of ice, snow, and bitter cold. Furthermore, the area is plagued with amazing temperature swings, with little notice.

Dwight Young has problems with potential new suppliers. Young's $5,000 outstanding debt to Fuji carries an 18% interest charge. Fuji has refused to deal with him anymore. When contacted by potential suppliers, Fuji gives Dwight a bad reference. The situation is making it very difficult for Dwight to get bicycles from any suppliers.

In early 1984, Discount Appliance Store in Cliffville started giving away a free bike with other purchases. If a customer purchased a television, stereo, or something else for as little as $150, he could get a free bike. These bicycles were 27-inch adult bikes with 12 speeds, and seemed to be of average quality. It remains to be seen how long this new development might be in effect, or what impact it might have on Bicycles Unlimited's sales.

FUTURE DIRECTIONS FOR THE FIRM

Up to now, Dwight Young has concentrated on one basic category of bicycles, 10- and 12-speed adult bicycles. Young's narrow product/market focus is probably hindering him from pursuing other opportunities. The BMX market looks particularly interesting, since it has been experiencing the fastest growth of any market segment. The new mountain bike is another opportunity for Bicycles Unlimited. There has been a rise in the popularity of these bicycles in the last few years. Mountain bikes are compatible with the hilly terrain and numerous paved and dirt backroads. All three major cities in the county are above 1,500 foot elevation. The Great Smoky Mountains are only 75 miles to the southwest.

Governmental actions may provide a boost in sales for bike dealers. The United States Environmental Protection Agency (EPA) has released a videotape entitled, "Bicycling to Work." The tape encourages people to use bicycles to reduce urban air pollution. Other advantages pointed out by the EPA include reduced energy consumption, space and time savings, health improvements, and money savings.

Young is considering opening a new store in a larger area such as Grantstown. He also thought about opening a store in metropolitan Knoxville.

In March of 1984, Dwight finally hired someone to assist him and to start maintaining accurate bookkeeping records. The new assistant will soon graduate with a degree in business. She is presently taking business policy and has offered to prepare a detailed strategic management analysis for Dwight. Dwight says he looks forward to receiving the analysis. Only time will tell whether having an assistant will work out for Bicycles Unlimited.

REFERENCES

Anonymous. "Huffy Kiddie Bikes Earn Good Housekeeping Seal." *Bicycle Business Journal* 38, no. 2 (February 1984): 18.

Huffy Corporation. *1982 Corporate Annual Report*, p. 5.

"Leisure Time" (Basic Analysis). *Standard and Poor's Industry Surveys* (October 13, 1983): 27–28.

CASE 27

The Harley-Davidson Motor Co., Inc.

ROBERT D. GODDARD
Appalachian State University

To some people the term "Hog" is as clear as mud. But to the thousands of Harley-Davidson owners who affectionately refer to their motorcycles as Hogs, there is no confusion.

A Harley-Davidson is not fat. It doesn't eat you out of house and home. And by achieving 47 to 54 mpg on the highway, it's definitely not a gas hog.

A Harley-Davidson is not cheap either. And we don't turn them out like popcorn. We never have. There is a lot of careful hand work. A lot of meticulous assembly and constant quality control.

We put more into a Harley. So you get more out of your Harley. You get more every time you ride down the street. And you get more down the road, when it comes time to sell. Just check the want ads in your paper. You'll see. A Harley may be called a hog. But don't be confused. There's no better place to put your money. *Motorcycles: By the people. For the people.*

HISTORY AND BACKGROUND

The story of Harley-Davidson begins in 1901, when two young men conceived the idea of propelling a bicycle by means of a gasoline motor. By fitting a motor into a cycle frame and driving the rear wheel, all of the drudgery would be taken out of bicycling. Bill Harley and Arthur Davidson collaborated in a basement workshop in an attempt to bring their dream to reality.

Bringing that dream to reality required more expertise than Bill, a draftsman, and Arthur, a pattern maker, possessed, so they called for help. Walter Davidson, Arthur's brother and a skilled machinist, responded to the two friends' offer of a ride on their new motorcycle, if he would only come to Milwaukee. The only problem was, Walter would have to help build the machine first! A third Davidson brother, William, joined the trio, and together the four devoted much time to the project. Valuable mechanical advice and assistance was given by Ole Evinrude, who founded the famous outboard motor company.

Note: Two excellent trade publications that contain other articles relevant to this case are *American Machinist* and *American Metal Market*.

After experimenting with various designs, it was 1903 when the group felt they had a motorcycle good enough for production. They built a wooden shed and hand-lettered the words "Harley-Davidson Motor Company" on the door. The first production model was a 405cc single-cylinder engine, mounted in a bicycle-type frame, with a belt driving the rear wheel. There was no transmission and no clutch; the machine was pushed and pedaled to start. Top speed was, for that time, an outstanding 45 miles per hour.

From that first rather crude model, Harley-Davidson began producing a series of well-engineered machines. The company grew at a remarkable rate. In 1907, a total of about 150 machines were produced. In 1909, Harley introduced an 880cc V-twin motorcycle (two cylinders arranged in a "V" configuration). Improved in subsequent years, the classic V-twin was destined to become a Harley-Davidson trademark.

In 1915, Harley introduced a very advanced machine, the Model 11F. This motorcycle featured a 61-cubic-inch (1000cc) engine with overhead valves, electric or acetylene lighting, three-speed transmission with clutch, and chain drive. The introduction of this machine marked the beginning of the modern motorcycle, and it continued in production for the next ten years. By 1917, about 18,000 Harley motorcycles were being produced annually. In 1922, Harley's first 74-cubic-inch (1213cc) motorcycle was designed for pulling the then-popular two-person sidecar. By 1934, the big V-twin was the only engine type being offered by Harley-Davidson.

Probably the largest motorcycle ever sold to the public, at least up to that time, was introduced in 1936. It was the massive 80-cubic-inch (1311cc) side-valve V-twin. Simultaneously, Harley unveiled the 61-cubic-inch (1000cc) Model 61–E, which became very popular with the buying public. During World War II, Harley produced some 88,000 machines for the war effort. These motorcycles saw duty on all of the battle fronts, including Africa, Europe, and the Pacific islands. They were rugged, durable machines, and became almost as commonplace as the ubiquitous "Jeep."

When Americans came marching home after WWII, Harley was ready for the transportation demands of ex-GI's with the new 74-cubic-inch, overhead-valve V-twin. The first change in Harley-Davidson suspensions in 40 years was announced in 1949, with the introduction of the Hydra-Glide telescopic front fork. By 1953, the hand shifter and foot-operated clutch had given way to the now-standard hand-operated clutch/foot shifter.

Harley-Davidson had been family-owned since 1901, but the company went public in 1965. Then in 1969, AMF, Inc., which makes leisure and industrial products, acquired Harley-Davidson. With the infusion of some $60 million into the business, production tripled to about 50,000 vehicles per year. The motorcycle industry was expanding, and Harley-Davidson controlled the big-bike market, consisting of cycles with engines of 1,000cc and larger. Harley has lost market share in the big bike segment, as indicated in Table 1.

Harley-Davidson is today the sole surviving American motorcycle producer in an industry that once included such famous names as Cleveland, Crocker, Cyclone, Excelsior, E.R. Thomas, Henderson, Indian, Merkel, Minnesota, Pierce, Pope, Reading,

Table 1 Harley-Davidson motorcycles percent of new registrations (1,000cc and larger)

Year	Percent
1974	100
1975	74
1976	63
1977	49
1978	42
1979	40
1980	34
1981	35

Source: R. L. Polk & Co.

Standard, Thor, and Yale. Over 145 manufacturers of motorcycles have come and gone from the American scene; only Harley-Davidson remains. But the future of Harley-Davidson is now in doubt.

COMPETITION

Prior to 1975, Harley-Davidson enjoyed a competition-free market niche. The British motorcycle industry, strong until about 1955, was now all but nonexistent. Triumph was the sole survivor, as famous names such as Norton, BSA, Enfield, and others had disappeared. German competition was from BMW, the automobile/motorcycle manufacturer catering to the specialized sport-touring market. Laverda, Moto Guzzi, Benelli, and Ducati were Italian firms still competing in the world-wide market, but the numbers of these expensive machines being imported was miniscule.

However, a major effort by the so-called "Big Four" was being mounted from the East. The Japanese manufacturers, Honda, Kawasaki, Suzuki, and Yamaha, who had confined their efforts to smaller-engined motorcycles, decided to attack Harley-Davidson on its own ground; the big-bike market. Japanese manufacturers had come to dominate the small-machine market, long vacated by Harley-Davidson, by offering quality, variety, and low prices. Their cheaper bikes were converting college kids and other people who might have had second thoughts about being seen on a Harley.

For years, Harley-Davidson had been synonymous with a heavy, powerful, noisy, "macho" sort of bike, which was hard to handle, leaked oil, broke down frequently, and required constant attention. As one former Harley "hog" owner put it, "This bike is not for wimps and little kids. This bike is for driving through brick walls." Harley-Davidson's reputation is changing, both through improved technology and more effective advertising. Advertising copy such as the following has benefitted the company.

We think motorcycles should be dependable, serviceable, and durable. Not disposable.

That is our philosophy. Our motorcycles are shining examples of it. Each one is based on our belief in simplicity of design. That is what makes them durable. And that makes them valuable, every time you ride and when it comes time to sell. If you've ever checked the want ads, you know.

Another reason Harley-Davidson motorcycles hold their value is because we've held our ground. We've stuck to the basic ideas set forth by our founders 80 years ago. True, our motorcycles have become more sophisticated. But not more complicated. Even today, most of the routine maintenance can be handled by the rider himself.

Further evidence of commitment to our philosophy is our V-Twin engine design. By today's standards, one of its most remarkable qualities is that it can be rebuilt—many times over. The number of classic and antique Harleys in showroom condition attests to that fact.

Ask any of those owners if they think a motorcycle should be disposable. They'll all agree that it is a great idea for things like baby diapers. But any respectable motorcycle is a far cry from that. *Motorcycles. By the people. For the people.*

AMF stayed too long with slow, costly hand-machining of its motors while the Japanese geared up for low-cost volume production. AMF did not respond fast enough to the first entry by a Japanese manufacturer in the big-bike market, dominated by the "hogs." The Honda Gold Wing first appeared on the market in 1975 with a host of innovations. It quickly set the standard for the "dressed-up" touring market—"hog" country.

In 1977, Harley-Davidson filed a brief with the U.S. Treasury Department to support a petition for the imposition of anti-dumping duties against Japanese competitors. The brief alleged that Honda, Kawasaki, Suzuki, and Yamaha were selling their motorcycles in the United States at much cheaper prices than they charged in Japan or Europe. While the Treasury Department agreed with the arguments presented by Harley-Davidson, they ruled that the dumping margins were very thin, and didn't warrant retaliation.

RECENT PROBLEMS

During 1980, Harley's operating profit declined to $12.3 million from $13.3 million in 1979. Sales, however, rose to $289.5 million from $247.3 million in 1979. Earnings were forecasted to drop further in 1981, to $10 million, while sales were expected to drop 5 percent to $275 million. Profit margins were 5.4 percent in 1979, 4.2 percent in 1980, and were projected at 3.6 percent for 1981. Sales of all motorcycles fell from a high of about one million new registrations in 1977 to 838,000 in 1980.

In 1981, Honda and Yamaha introduced V-twin motorcycles that were Harley look-alikes. These cycles had modern technical innovations such as shaft-drive, water cooling, and improved suspensions. They were better made, and were priced on the average some $1,500 less than comparable Harley models. AMF had managed to increase unit sales, but had not invested enough in new tooling. As one *Cycle World* tester put it, "Not long ago some of the hardware found on Harley-Davidsons looked as if it were hammered out of iron ore by rock-wielding natives along the shores of the Milwaukee River."

In March 1981, AMF, Inc. signed a letter of intent to sell the Harley-Davidson division to a group of Harley's current management, led by Vaughn L. Beals, Jr., an AMF vice-president and Motorcycle Products group executive. The price paid for the Harley division was estimated at between $75 million and $80 million, later revised down to $65 million. Willie Davidson and John Davidson, grandsons of the founder, were also part of the management group, although John Davidson retired shortly after the sale was consummated.

The new owners were very aware of the problems facing the new Harley-Davidson Motor Company, but things quickly deteriorated further for the company. The new Japanese V-twins, introduced in 1981, quickly won an estimated 19.4 percent share of the heavyweight V-engine market in 1982. That was just a hint of the troubles that were to follow.

THE MARKET GLUT

With the recession of 1981–1983 in full swing, and with Japanese production running at record levels, a 1½ to 2-year inventory of unsold Harley and Japanese motorcycles started filling warehouses and distribution centers. Phil Schilling, Editor of *Cycle* magazine, said, ". . . an unbelievable, unprecedented number of new Japanese motorcycles has stockpiled in this country. Glut understates the case, and should prosperity return tomorrow to the economy as a whole, motorcycling would still be in a hell of a mess."[1] Schilling further stated, "Don't underestimate the gravity of the situation. This unsold inventory is the central controlling fact of life and death in the motorcycle market today. It's highly unlikely that any Japanese motorcycle subsidiary in the United States made a profit on its motorcycle operations in 1982. Furthermore, until those warehouses are cleared, it's hard to foresee any profitable year on U.S. operations."[2]

With this background, Harley-Davidson filed a Section 201 petition with the International Trade Commission (ITC), claiming that competition from low-priced Japanese imports was the greatest cause of Harley's current financial problems. Harley asked the ITC to put tariffs on all heavyweight (over 700cc) motorcycles and motorcycle powertrains imported into the United States.

In January, 1983, after considering the arguments from both sides, the U.S. International Trade Commission recommended to President Reagan that the duty on heavy motorcycles be increased from 4.4 percent to 49.4 percent to help Harley-Davidson regain sales. In an attempt to head off final action, Japanese motorcycle manufacturers

1. P. Schilling, "Crisis," *Cycle* (May 1983): 8.
2. Ibid., 38.

offered Harley technical assistance, to the tune of some $20 million. Harley turned down the offer, gambling that President Reagan, in an election year, would act favorably on the ITC's recommendation.

On April 1, 1983, the Office of the United States Trade Representative, Executive Office of the President, released the following statement:

> President Reagan decided to proclaim a duty increase and tariff-rate quotas on heavyweight motorcycles (engines over 700cc) imported into the United States, effective within fifteen days, U.S. Trade Representative Bill Brock announced today.
>
> The President's action, taken under the Trade Act of 1974, increases tariffs on completed heavyweight motorcycles by 45 percent *ad valorem* in the first year, declining to 35, 20, 15, and 10 percent above scheduled rates in subsequent years. It also sets five-year tariff-rate quotas at 5000 units (increasing yearly to 6000, 7000, 8500, and 10,000) for imports of motorcycles manufactured in West Germany, and 4000 units (increasing 1000 yearly for five years) for imports from all other countries. In order to treat Japan fairly, a tariff-rate quota of 6000 units (increasing 1000 yearly) for imports from Japan will be established. The additional duties will apply to all quantities above the tariff-rate quotas.
>
> Announcing the action, Ambassador Brock said the President's determination follows a report by the U.S. International Trade Commission (USITC) on the results of its investigation of a petition filed under Section 201 by Harley-Davidson Motor Company, Inc., and Harley-Davidson York, Inc. Harley-Davidson has petitioned for relief from imports of heavyweight motorcycles and power train subassemblies. The USITC found that imports of heavyweight motorcycles, but not subassemblies, were imported in such numbers as to threaten the U.S. motorcycle industry with serious injury.
>
> U.S. imports of heavyweight motorcycles rose from 153,506 units (222 million dollars) in 1977 to 202,329 units (440 million dollars) in 1981, while inventories quadrupled from 53,400 to 205,400 units between 1977 and 1982.
>
> Ambassador Brock said that the level of relief recommended by the USITC is needed to reduce the threat of injury from excessive imports during the period that Harley-Davidson is undertaking its trade adjustment program designed to improve its international competitiveness. Ambassador Brock explained further that the tariff-rate quotas were established to maintain an openness of the U.S. market for the small volume producers of heavyweight motorcycles imported from countries that pose no threat of injury to the U.S. industry.

On Saturday, April 2, 1983, President Ronald Reagan approved recommendations by the International Trade Commission (ITC) to implement a tariff structure designed to limit the appeal of large-displacement motorcycle imports. This ruling raised the existing 4.4 percent tariff an *additional* 45 percent in 1983 on imported motorcycles having engine displacement of over 700 cubic centimeters. The duty will be lowered in each of the next four years according to the following schedule:

1984—39.4 percent
1985—24.4 percent
1986—19.4 percent
1987—14.4 percent

Additionally, the first 6,000 Japanese motorcycles of over 700cc displacement imported in 1983 are exempt from the added duty. After 1983, the number of large-displacement motorcycles imported into the U.S. without the added tariff will increase by 1,000 units per year.

According to one source, the American consumer is being asked to pay once more for the mismanagement of an American firm. Larry Works, Editor of *Cycle Guide* magazine, says that the motorcycle industry changed over the past twenty years, and Harley-Davidson failed to change with the industry. The market size expanded greatly over that time period, and Harley got caught up in the wave of market expansion. Harley did not respond to the needs of this growing, changing market. The company was content to produce the same basic product, aimed at a small segment that had always purchased the "hog." When the market finally stabilized, Harley's customers, the blue-collar workers, were caught up in the midst of the recession. They were not purchasing new motorcycles, and Harley-Davidson had nothing to offer in the other market segments.

FUTURE PLANS AND OUTLOOK

The 1984 lineup of Harley-Davidson products includes fifteen models, with prices ranging from $4,599 to $12,299. Without the resources to invest heavily in new technology, Harley is taking an evolutionary approach to product development. The heart of the "new" Harley is the redesigned 45-degree, 80-cubic-inch Evolution Engine. The so-called "Blockhead" engine represents five years and 750,000 road miles in testing and development. Work on this new engine began in 1978, and was based on a study of warranty claims and service problems reported on Harley's existing engines. Five new Harley-Davidson models are powered by the new Blockhead engine, while the rest use the familiar Shovelhead and Sportster engines.

Chairman Beals knows that simply having a new engine will not be enough. During a press trip to Harley-Davidson's test facility in Talledega, Alabama, and to an assembly plant in York, Pennsylvania (reported in *Cycle World* magazine, November 1983) writers were impressed with the commitment to quality exhibited by Harley workers and management alike.

Harley's new advertising campaign includes a new twist; they are actually encouraging prospective Harley buyers to take a test ride on new Harleys. As Beals told the press, "We're stressing test rides for 1984, because people can't believe the difference in modern Harley-Davidsons."[3] The following advertising copy reveals this new strategy:

> Pictured here is Mr. Chuck Irwin, the founder and ex-president of the Suzuki owners group, with his new motorcycle, the 1984 Harley-Davidson FXRT Sport Glide.
>
> Last summer he challenged Harley-Davidson to a direct comparison of the new Harley FXRT and the Suzuki GS 1100G.
>
> For 3,000 miles he rode, testing our new V2 Evolution engine, our new antidive suspension and our new wind tunnel designed fairing. He tested the new braking, the ride and the handling. He watched the new V-Twin for oil leaks. And there were none. He watched for maintenance problems. And there were none.
>
> In an 8-page letter to the Suzuki Owners Group, he reported the Truth with all the zeal of a new convert. "The FXRT is a quick vehicle . . . long and ultra stable, rock steady . . . mirror glass smoothness . . . enhanced by air assisted suspension on both ends . . . ."
>
> Chuck Irwin bought the new Harley FXRT to replace his GS 1100. He resigned his position as president of the Suzuki Owners' Club. His conclusion to the Suzuki faithful was simply, "I rode the machine with an open mind . . . have you?"
>
> Now it's your turn.
>
> Take a free, no-obligation test ride on the new FXRT Sport Glide and the other New Harleys at your participating Harley-Davidson dealer.
>
> We figure the best way to sell you on the New Harleys is to put you on The New Harleys. And let you ride.
>
> Special Introductory Offer. Buy a new FXRT Sport Glide before June 1, 1984 and your participating dealer will give you a free matching Tour Pak, AM/FM/cassette with antenna, gauge kit, luggage rack and fairing pockets—nearly a $900 retail value—free. *The new Harleys. Ride one.*

Additionally, Harley-Davidson has entered into an agreement with Ford Motor Credit Company to offer financing to purchasers of Harley motorcycles. Harley's 700 U.S. dealerships and all Ford Credit's branch offices now offer this financing.[4]

Harley-Davidson was, at one time, the largest supplier of police motorcycles in the United States. After eleven years of not receiving the California Highway Patrol (CHP) motorcycle business, the company announced recently that Harley won the CHP account by underbidding Kawasaki. The CHP purchased 131 specially equipped Harley motorcycles in 1984, after having thoroughly tested performance, handling, and reliability of competing bikes.[5] The Los Angeles Police Department, which has a larger motorcycle fleet than does the CHP, is considering Harley-Davidson as a potential

---

3. "Harley-Davidson: What's in Store for '84," *Cycle World* (November 1983): 51–53.

4. "Harley Financing Offered by Ford," *Cycle World* (April 1984): 34.

5. "Harley Wins CHP Business," *Cycle World* (April 1984): 32.

supplier. Harley motorcycles have an established reputation of holding their value, as indicated in the following advertising copy:

> Harley-Davidson motorcycles hold their value. If you haven't checked the want ads, you'd better.
>
> You might say that Harleys cost more to begin with. In most cases you're right. And in most cases they're worth more when you want to sell.
>
> One reason, Harleys cost more to build. Because we put more into them. There's a lot of careful hand work. A lot of meticulous assembly and constant quality control.
>
> Here's what we mean. Take a look at any Harley-Davidson gas tank. Look at the deep, rich paint that will wax up brilliantly for years. Well that is only the half of it. If you look inside the tank, you'll see that it is painted, too. Fact is, gas causes tanks to rust. Every motorcycle knows that, but we do something about it. And we charge a little extra for it. Across the board, we're proud to say that there are a lot of those little extras. And that's what makes up the difference in our purchase price. It also makes up a big difference at trade-in time.
>
> So don't write off a Harley-Davidson because it costs too much. You may end up writing off a lot more if you don't buy one. *Motorcycles. By the people. For the people.*

Suzuki and Yahama have no U.S. production facilities and are hurt by the ITC ruling. Two of the three Suzuki street bikes are 1100cc machines, affected directly by the import tariff. Suzuki prices ranged from $3099 to $4785. Yamaha offers seven street models for 1984, ranging in price from $2399 to $8299 for the top-of-the-line Venture Royale. The Royale features a 1198cc engine, saddlebags, travel trunk, a computer leveling air suspension system with on-board microprocessor and air compressor, an AM/FM stereo tuner, auto-reverse cassette deck with 12-watt amplifier, and cruise control.

Kawasaki, with a manufacturing facility in Lincoln, Nebraska, is in better position to cope with the ITC ruling than either Suzuki or Yamaha. With ten models, ranging in price from $2799 to $8299, Kawasaki covers the street-bike market well. Most of Kawasaki's large-displacement motorcycles are produced in the Lincoln facility, thus avoiding the extra tariffs. Additionally, a pair of 700cc bikes have been introduced that slide under the lower limits of motorcycles affected by the ITC ruling.

And that leaves Honda. With the largest share of the American market, Honda covers the street-bike market with seventeen separate models, ranging from the smallest (125cc) to the heavyweights (1200cc). With a production facility in Marysville, Ohio, and five new models displacing just under 700cc, Honda was the quickest Japanese manufacturer to react to the ITC ruling.[6] Honda's new model lineup should do nothing to hurt its market share domination as shown in Table 2 for 1983.

6. Model information and prices from: "Catalog of Street and Touring Motorcycles," *Cycle '84 Street and Touring Guide* 42–46, 67–80.

Table 2   Honda's market share domination, 1983

Company	Market Share
Honda	57.49%
Yamaha	16.55
Suzuki	13.29
Kawasaki	7.99
Harley	3.29
BMW	0.67

Source: R. L. Polk & Co. Reported in *Cycle World* (August 1983): 28.

All is not peaches and cream for the Japanese motorcycle industry, however. According to a report in *Cycle Guide* magazine, Japanese production dropped in 1982 for the first time since 1979, and more importantly, exports dropped by a full 18.1 percent. For the fiscal year ending April 30, 1983, Yamaha, the hardest hit of the Japanese manufacturers, reportedly lost $97 million, shifted 17,500 employees out of the motorcycle division into other Yamaha divisions, and laid off 3,500 workers.[7]

As a result of overproduction coupled with the effects of the recession, 1984 was the time to get the deal of a lifetime on a new motorcycle, according to *Rider* magazine.[8] With inventories at all-time record highs, Japanese manufacturers are cutting the prices on "new" 1981, 1982, and 1983 motorcycles drastically.

7. "Hard Cash," *Cycle Guide* (February 1984): 31.
8. "Bargain Bikes," *Rider* (January 1984): 50–53.

DISCUSSION QUESTIONS

1. Since Harley-Davidson represents a 'drop in the bucket' in terms of its importance in the American industrial picture, what do you think prompted President Reagan to approve the recommendations of the International Trade Commission? Was the President acting solely to protect Harley-Davidson, or was he using the Harley appeal to send another sort of message to Japan?

2. What impact does the ITC action have on the American motorcycle purchaser in the short run? In the long run?

3. Since Honda and Kawasaki have American production facilities in place and operating, do you think that they will increase their relative market shares?

4. What other reactions, by Yamaha and Suzuki, as well as Honda and Kawasaki, do you predict?

5. Can Harley-Davidson survive, given this period of "breathing room" by the ITC ruling?

6. What strategies should Harley-Davidson pursue to increase its share of the large-displacement motorcycle market?

7. Should Harley-Davidson introduce motorcycles to compete with Japanese manufacturers in the *other* market segments? Other geographic areas?

8. Should Harley-Davidson diversify? If yes, into what new areas?

SUGGESTED READINGS

"A Second Chance for Harley 'Hogs.'" *American Machinist* (July 1983): 75.

Crier, P. "Harley-Davidson Asks for Protection from Japanese Imports." *The Christian Science Monitor* (September 9, 1982): 10.

Farnsworth, C. "Reagan Aid Backs Harley." *The New York Times* (April 1, 1983): D1, D12.

The Harley-Davidson Story. Milwaukee, Wis.: The Harley-Davidson Motor Co. (undated).

Hayes, G. "The Harley-Davidson Story." *Rider* (October 1982): 35, 75–77.

Holusha, J. "Harley-Davidson Maps Growth." *The New York Times* (March 14, 1983): 30, 32.

Kitchen, S. "Thunder Road." *Forbes* (July 18, 1983): 92–93.

Kolbenschlag, Michael. "Harley-Davidson Takes Lessons from Arch-Rivals' Handbook." *International Management* (February 1985): 46–48.

Schilling, P. "Crisis." *Cycle* (May 1983): 8, 38, 68, 93.

Shannon, D. "Economy Puts the Brakes on Motorcycle Sales." *The New York Times* (April 11, 1982).

CASE 28

Bristol–Myers Company

FRED DAVID
Auburn University

MIRIAM MAIER
BOB AHUJA
Mississippi State University

INTRODUCTION

Every day millions of Americans use products such as Ban antiperspirant, Enfamil infant formula, Miss Clairol, Excedrin, Sea Breeze moisture lotion, Vitalis, Nice 'n Easy, Datril, Congesprin, Drano, Windex, Final Net hairspray, True-to-Light makeup mirrors, Crazy Curl styling wands, Loving Care, Mr. Muscle, Endust, Keri Lotion, and Renuzit air fresheners. What do these products have in common? They are all manufactured by the Bristol–Myers Company. Bristol–Myers manufactures hundreds of other products too, many of which are leaders in their area. It's product Platinol is often considered to be the most effective anticancer drug available and Desyrel has become the third most widely prescribed antidepressant drug.

Bristol–Myers' worldwide sales in 1984 increased 7 percent to $4,189,400,000, and its net income increased 16 percent to $472,374,000. The company's employees number around 36,500. Approximately 65 percent of Bristol–Myers' net sales and 73 percent of its operating profits are derived from the drug industry. This industry is fiercely competitive and includes such firms as Eli Lilly, Merck, Pfizer, Abbott Laboratories, A.H. Robins, G.D. Searle, Squibb, SmithKline Beckman, American Home Products, Johnson & Johnson, and Upjohn. The drug industry is currently undergoing some radical changes that represent major opportunities and threats for pharmaceutical companies such as Bristol—Myers.

THE DRUG INDUSTRY

Current Situation

The United States is a world leader in prescription and over-the-counter (OTC) drugs. The United States accounts for about 24 percent of the world's total shipments of legal drugs, valued at approximately $74 billion. From 1981 to 1984, the net profit of the drug industry as a whole increased from 10.9 percent of sales to 13.5 percent. This increased profitability was the result of a continued trend toward higher prices of prescription drugs, with an average increase of 7.5 percent in 1984 over 1983.

A substantial portion of pharmaceutical companies' total revenues is devoted to applied and basic research for the development of new products. The average cost of developing a new drug from conception to introduction is $80 million. The drug industry's research and development expenditures reached $3.5 billion in 1984, an increase of 15 percent from 1983. Funding by U.S. companies of R&D outside the United States is increasing at a rate of 17 percent a year. The U.S. share of world R&D spending fell from 60 percent in 1964 to about 25 percent in 1984.

Some of the major U.S. drug companies realized 40 to 50 percent of their sales from foreign subsidiaries. Since 1979, the increasing strength of the dollar has depressed the profits of these firms, although recently some foreign currencies have strengthened, which gives a boost to U.S. earnings. Since American drug companies have established a reputation for product safety and quality, the pharmaceutical industry has maintained a positive balance of trade. The value of exports of pharmaceuticals was an estimated $2.7 billion in 1984, an increase of 6.5 percent, while imports rose to $1.8 billion, up 35 percent.

The Pharmaceutical Segment

The drug industry is divided into three segments: the biologicals segment (SIC 2831), the medicinals and botanicals segment (SIC 2833), and the pharmaceutical preparations segment (SIC 2834). The pharmaceutical preparations segment most directly affects Bristol—Myers. According to the *U.S. Industrial Outlook*, the value of shipments by pharmaceutical companies was $23.7 billion in 1984, up 3.1 percent over 1983 after adjusting for price increases. Prescription drugs account for about 65 percent of this total. Average prices of prescriptions have been increasing considerably faster than prices for all nondurables.

A factor in the increase in pharmaceutical revenues is an increase in generic drug sales. Generics are the therapeutic chemical equivalents of drug products on which the patents have expired. The value of shipments of generic products made up about 35 percent of the total value of prescription drugs sold in 1984, compared to 15 percent in 1981. Consumer interest in generics and direct sales is growing. Mail-order catalog sales have been escalating, especially among the aged. Savings of more than 50 percent are reported on many generic prescription drugs.

Two-thirds of all doctors' visits result in a prescription, with 30 percent of these visits resulting in four or more prescriptions. Women receive 60 percent of all drugs prescribed in the United States. Senior citizens average eleven prescriptions a year, which amounts to almost one-third of all prescribed drugs purchased. Prescriptions for chronic ailments such as arthritis, heart and circulatory ailments, and asthma constitute 58 percent of all drugs dispensed. Cardiovascular drug sales climbed rapidly to a volume 18 percent higher in 1983 than in 1982. It is estimated that the value of these prescriptions rose moderately to about $1.58 billion in 1983, up from $1.46 billion in 1982.

Higher prices for prescription drugs and an increasing number of drugs being switched to OTC status are two factors that are having a negative effect on sales volume in the drug industry. Prescription drug prices increased 12.8 percent a year between 1981 and 1983. Due to a trend towards more self-medication, more promotional education of consumers, new multisymptom products, and more drugs being switched from prescription status, sales of OTC drugs increased 11 percent in 1983 to $5.5 billion. Since 1977, twenty-five prescription drugs were changed to OTC status. The most rapid OTC growth has been in vitamins, self-diagnosis kits, contact lens solutions, skin treatments, cough medicines, and cold preparations. In 1984, OTC companies will make 6,000 products under 60,000 different brand names. Consumer education in the use of OTC drugs is improving every year.

Antibiotic drugs are surging ahead due to an influx of new products and an increase in the number of surgical operations. Japanese firms are particularly strong in the $1.6 billion worldwide market for antibiotics. As a result, U.S. companies are obtaining rights to market new antibiotics that are developed and manufactured in Japan. Food and Drug Administration clearances for new pharmaceutical compounds have slowed dramatically. Only fourteen new drugs were approved by the FDA for marketing in the United States in 1984, versus 14 in 1983, twenty-eight in 1982, and twenty-seven in 1981.

Concerns for 1985

In the mid-1980s, the drug industry and Bristol–Myers face a number of other potential opportunities and threats. The ethics of direct advertising of prescription drugs to consumers and the proposed extension of patents on various drug products are concerns. Also, there is an indication that short-term profit objectives are being overly emphasized, as prices on prescription drugs continue to increase. In addition, a strong dollar abroad translates into foreign currency exchange losses for U.S. multinational companies. Rising competition from less expensive generic substitutes presents a serious challenge for domestic drug makers. There exists a growing trend toward foreign drug companies establishing bases of operations in the United States, and American companies establishing operations abroad. The following excerpt is taken from the *U.S. Industrial Outlook—1984:*

> The pharmaceutical industry cannot continue to raise prices as they did from 1979 through 1983. The long-term outlook would indicate an eventual decline in profitability, unless drug companies can increase the number of new product introductions. A National Academy of Engineering report says the U.S. drug industry is losing its world leadership role because fewer new drugs are under development. To combat this, U.S. firms are becoming more internationalized. More emphasis is being placed on basic research. Biotechnology and genetic engineering will play a key role in this expansion. Worldwide sales of pharmaceuticals, estimated at $66 billion in 1980, is expected to climb to $100 billion by 1990.

The rising use of generic drug substitutes is likely to reduce the profits of drug companies in the mid-1980s. The use of generic substitutes for brand-name drugs will accelerate in the coming years as a result of government moves to contain spiraling health-care costs, greater patient and physician awareness of the economy of generic drugs, and the expiration of patents on several major brand-name drugs during the next five years.

COMPANY HISTORY

The Bristol-Myers Company was incorporated in New York on June 9, 1900, as an outgrowth of Clinton Pharmaceutical Company, which was formed in 1887. The company has made a number of important acquisitions since the 1950s. For example, in 1959 Bristol-Myers acquired Clairol; it acquired Mead Johnson in 1967, Carmen Curlers, Westwood Pharmaceuticals, and Renuzit Home Products in 1969, Pelton & Crane and Ellen Kaye Cosmetics in 1971, and Sea Breeze Laboratories in 1979. Bristol-Myers has become a major producer and distributor of pharmaceutical and medical products, nonprescription health products, toiletries and beauty aids, and household products. The company currently manufactures products in thirty-six major locations around the world. Twenty-four of these facilities are located in the United States and Puerto Rico. The remaining twelve facilities are located in Brazil, Canada, Denmark, England, France, Italy, Japan, and the Philippines.

Bristol-Myers' foreign facilities are used not only for manufacturing, but also for research, administration, storage, and distribution. Domestic facilities accounted for 75 percent of sales and 41 percent of operating profits in 1984, while foreign facilities represented 25 percent of sales and 59 percent of operating profits. Additional information regarding Bristol-Myers' domestic versus foreign operations is provided in Exhibit 1.

Exhibit 1 Bristol–Myers' domestic and foreign operations

Geographic Areas	Net Sales			Profit (in $ millions)			Year-End Assets		
	1984	1983	1982	1984	1983	1982	1984	1983	1982
United States	$3,148.8	$2,889.3	$2,587.6	$592.9	$535.0	$440.0	$1,553.4	$1,380.8	$1,280.7
Europe, Mid-East and Africa	462.9	471.9	484.3	80.5	98.4	83.5	333.0	324.7	316.9
Other Western Hemisphere	439.4	439.0	445.5	87.9	68.1	83.3	252.5	248.0	277.2
Pacific	362.1	334.7	293.4	56.1	43.4	44.1	268.4	276.3	253.7
Inter-area eliminations	(223.8)	(217.9)	(210.9)	(8.7)	2.4	6.0	(114.0)	(120.7)	(112.3)
Net sales, operating profit and assets	$4,189.4	$3,917.0	$3,599.9	808.7	747.3	656.9	2,293.3	2,109.1	2,016.2
Unallocated expenses and other assets				(28.2)	(55.8)	(50.8)	955.3	898.2	740.0
Earnings before income taxes and total assets				$780.5	$691.5	$606.1	$3,248.6	$3,007.3	$2,756.2

Source: Bristol-Myers' *Annual Report*, 1984, p. 53.

BRISTOL–MYERS' INDUSTRY SEGMENTS

Bristol–Myers' principal products are grouped into the following four industry segments: pharmaceutical and medical products, nonprescription health products, toiletries and beauty aids, and household products. The nonprescription health products segment reported the highest 1984 sales and earnings growth of any of the divisions, with sales exceeding $1.1 billion for the first time. Although all four segments experienced growth in 1984, the nondrug segments (toiletries and beauty aids and household products) grew much more slowly than the drug segments. Bristol-Myers' sales, profits, and year-end assets by segment are presented in Exhibit 2. Location of he company's manufacturing facilities by segment is given in Exhibit 3.

Pharmaceutical and Medical Products

In 1984, the pharmaceutical and medical products segment of Bristol-Myers remained the largest and most profitable division, contributing 38 percent of net sales and 43 percent of operating profit. The major contributors to this growth were two anticancer drugs, Vepesid and Platinol; an antidepressant, Desyrel; and orthopedic and surgical products. Sales of a wide range of anticancer drugs were up 20 percent to over $200 million in 1984; sales of Desyrel doubled; and orthopedic and surgical products recorded sales gains of better than 20 percent. Sales of antibiotics, the segment's largest product group, declined some in 1984, principally due to the exchange rates on foreign sales.

Bristol-Myers' strong position in pharmaceuticals is partly due to significant advances in a number of therapeutic areas. Late in 1983, Bristol Laboratories, a subsidiary company of Bristol–Myers, received approval to market Vepesid for use in the treatment of refractory testicular cancer. Platinol, another Bristol Laboratories product that is used in the treatment of bladder, testicular, and ovarian cancers, has become the nation's leading chemotherapeutic agent since its introduction into the market in 1982. Bristol Laboratories' exclusive license to market this drug was extended through 1988 by the FDA. In return, the company has made a commitment to reduce Platinol's price by 30 percent over the course of the extended period of exclusivity. Other leading products manufactured by Bristol Laboratories are Ultracef, an oral antibiotic, and Bufferin with Codeine #3.

Another product that helped to strengthen the pharmaceutical and medical products division was Mead-Johnson's successful antidepressant, Desyrel. Desyrel has become the third most widely prescribed antidepressant in less than two years. Toward the end of 1983, Mead-Johnson's Buspar was recommended for approval by the FDA's Psychopharmacologic Drug Advisory Committee as safe and effective in the treatment of anxiety. Special interest has been shown in Buspar because, unlike the widely used benzodiazepines, it is not addictive and does not interact negatively with alcohol. In September of 1983, the company acquired an exclusive license from the Danish Eer-rosan Group to develop and market femoxetine, a second antidepressant.

In 1984, Bristol-Myers filed a New-Drug Application for Enkaid, a medicine that in clinical trials has demonstrated the ability to reduce or abolish arrhythmias. Also in

Exhibit 2 Bristol–Myers' sales, profits, and assets by segment in 1982, 1983, and 1984

Industry Segments	Net Sales			Profit			Year-End Assets		
				(in $ millions)					
	1984	1983	1982	1984	1983	1982	1984	1983	1982
Pharmaceutical and medical products	$1,586.6	$1,505.0	$1,360.2	$336.3	$318.7	$294.8	$1,209.3	$1,065.5	$1,021.0
Nonprescription health products	1,555.7	1,038.5	920.7	232.5	227.2	173.3	439.1	454.1	421.7
Toiletries and beauty aids	1,020.9	986.4	963.2	182.9	148.5	140.2	507.1	457.0	452.5
Household products	426.0	387.0	355.7	57.0	52.9	48.6	137.8	132.5	121.0
Intersegment and other sales	.2	.1	.1						
Net sales, operating profit, and assets	$4,189.4	$3,917.0	$3,599.9	$808.7	$747.3	$656.9	$2,293.3	$2,109.1	$2,016.2

Source: Bristol-Myers' *Annual Report, 1984*, p. 53.

Exhibit 3   The number and location of Bristol–Myers' major manufacturing facilities by segment

	U.S. and Puerto Rico	Other Countries	Total
Pharmaceutical and medical products	10	6	16
Nonprescription health products	7	2	9
Toiletries and beauty aids	5	3	8
Household products	6	3	9
	28	14	42
Less: Facilities shared by two segments	4	2	6
	24	12	36

Source: Bristol–Myers' Form 10K, 1983, p. 5.

1984, the National Heart, Lung, and Blood Institute announced the findings of a ten-year study confirming that a cholesterol-lowering diet combined with drug treatment, can cut high blood cholesterol levels. The drug used in the study was cholestyramine, which is marketed by Bristol-Myers under the brand name Questran.

Other factors contributed to the increase in sales and profits of the pharmaceuticals and medical products division: the increased worldwide use of Zimmer knee and hip replacements; the acquisition of The Jobst Institute, which broadened Bristol-Myers' technological base and provided the company with expertise in vascular surgery and burn care; and the acquisition of the Medical Engineering Corporation in 1982, providing the company with entry into the surgical specialties of urology and plastic surgery.

Nonprescription Health Products

The second largest segment of Bristol–Myers, the nonprescription health products segment, reported a sales and earnings growth of 11 percent and 2 percent respectively in 1984. Eighty percent of the sales increase for the segment in 1984 was due to the combined performance of analgesics and nutritional products. Bristol–Myers' worldwide sales of nutritionals approached $700 million in 1984, up 7 percent from 1982. In 1983, Improved Formulation Enfamil was successfully launched by Mead-Johnson. Mead-Johnson also added Trauma Cal to its adult line of nutritionals. (This is a nutritional product designed for the specific needs of burn and trauma patients.)

Bristol-Myers' analgesics and cough/cold products account for about 19 percent of this $1.3 billion market. Bufferin and Excedrin together make Bristol-Myers the biggest seller of aspirin-based pain killers. Sales of these two products in 1983 increased 21 percent and 10 percent respectively. However, Bristol-Myers failed to really capitalize on the 1982 Tylenol events. When seven people died from cyanide-laced capsules in

1982, millions of Tylenol bottles were destroyed or recalled. However, Johnson & Johnson's Tylenol rebounded strongly in 1983, gaining a 31 percent market share of the pain relief market.

Several other developments are likely to have an impact on Bristol-Myers' future. One is the FDA's requirement that all drugs have tamper-resistant packages after February 5, 1983. Another is a move to market nonprescription forms of ibuprofen when its original patent runs out, and Bristol-Myers' response to the move. The company recently signed a joint venture with Upjohn Company to be the sole distributor of its nonprescription form of ibuprofen, which is being marketed under the name Nuprin. This drug is a prescription arthritis medicine being sold by Upjohn under the brand name Motrin. The Bristol-Upjohn deal is viewed as a plus for both companies. It gives Bristol-Myers a bigger share in the analgesics market and relieves Upjohn of the burden of marketing this product. The pact with Upjohn also gives Bristol-Myers ammunition to fight its longtime adversary, American Home Products (AHP). AHP markets two ibuprofens, Anacin and Advil.

Toiletries and Beauty Aids

The third largest segment of Bristol-Myers is the toiletries and beauty aids segment, which is made up of hair coloring and hair care preparations, deodorants and antiperspirants, and beauty appliances. The domestic sales of hair coloring products, including Miss Clairol, reported record sales growth in 1983. Leading Clairol products include Kindness instant hairsetters, True-to-Light makeup mirrors, Crazy Curl styling wands, The Foot Fixer, Son of a Gun hairdryer, and the Clairol Custom CareSetter product line. There was also an improvement in the sales of antiperspirants and all the facial care products. This segment reported a 23 percent increase in operating profit in 1984, principally from shampoos, antiperspirants, and the newly acquired Infusium line of hair care products.

Household Products

The smallest segment of Bristol-Myers is the Household Products Division, which contributed 10 percent of company sales and 7 percent of operating profits in 1984. Growth in this division was due largely to the successful introduction of Renuzit Fresh 'n' Dry, an aerosol home deodorant. The division markets household cleaning and laundry products, including Endust, Behold, Twinkle, Mr. Muscle, Windex, Vanish, O-Cedar, Drano, Fleecy, and Javex. Procter and Gamble is the division's major competitor.

ADVERTISING AND R&D

The markets in which Bristol-Myers competes are broad-based and very competitive. The principal bases of competition are quality, service, price, and product performance. Bristol-Myers' pharmaceutical and medical products are promoted nationally and internationally in medical journals and directly to the medical profession. The company's other products are promoted on a national and international basis through the use of television, radio, print media, couponing, consumer offers, and in-store displays.

In 1984, Bristol-Myers spent $743.8 million on advertising and promotion of its products, compared to $651.4 million in 1983. This increase in spending reflects aggressive advertising efforts to support major product lines and new brands in the consumer-packaged goods business. A major part of Bristol-Myers' advertising focus in 1983 and 1984 is a multimillion dollar network TV campaign for Nuprin. It is hoped that this media blitz will help strengthen the company's position in the analgesics market.

Bristol-Myers continues its strong financial commitment to long-term growth in research and development of new products and markets. R&D expenditures in 1984 increased to $212.4 million, more than doubling since 1978, with nearly 75 percent of these expenditures devoted to the discovery and development of pharmaceutical drugs. The company's total R&D expenditures in 1983 and 1982 were $185.3 million and $161.0 million respectively.

BRISTOL-MYERS' TOP COMPETITORS

Selected financial information on Bristol-Myers' major competitors is given in Exhibit 4. Note that the company's profit margin during the first quarter of 1984 is tenth out of twenty-two pharmaceutical competitors. The company considers its two major competitors to be American Home Products and Johnson & Johnson.

American Home Products

American Home Products is a well-diversified producer of consumer products in four major lines of business: prescription drugs, packaged drugs, food products and housewares, and household products. Nearly every American home contains products manufactured by American Home, including Anacin, Dristan, Preparation H, Woolite,

Exhibit 4 The drug companies' performances in 1984

Company	(in thousands)		Number of Employees
	Sales	Net Income	
Johnson & Johnson	$6,124,500	$514,500	72
American Home Products	4,804,299	682,082	47
Bristol–Myers	4,189,400	472,374	36
Pfizer	3,854,500	507,900	39
Eli Lilly	3,109,200	490,200	29
Merck	3,559,665	492,967	35
SmithKline Beckman	2,949,200	503,600	30
Warner–Lambert	3,166,657	223,887	41
Upjohn	2,179,060	173,272	23

Easy-Off oven cleaner, Black Flag insecticides, Gulden's mustard, Chef Boy-Ar-Dee pasta products, and Ecko pots and pans. AHP is one of the largest prescription drug manufacturers in the world, with sales of $4.8 billion in 1984, profits of $682 million, and a 32.7 percent return on stockholders' equity.

American Home is a very tightly managed company, renowned for using every dollar to its fullest extent. It trains people well, drives them hard, and loses some of them to competitors who offer better working conditions. American Home has been pinching pennies and accumulating profits since it was incorporated in 1926. When it bought Anacin in 1930, the product was just a pain killer that was promoted to dentists. AHP turned it into one of the nation's best-selling over-the-counter analgesics, until Tylenol took over first place in 1976. AHP transformed a sunburn ointment into Preparation H and gained control of the hemorrhoid market.

Prescription drugs and medical supplies contributed about 48 percent of AHP's sales and 63 percent of operating profits. Perhaps American Home's greatest strength is its use of advertising. According to a recent issue of *Business Marketing*, AHP spent $2,344,974 million on advertising in 1983. Historically, AHP's weak area has been research and development, but the company spent $161 million on R&D in 1983 and opened two new research facilities.

A problem facing American Home Products is the patent expiration on three of its mainline ethical drugs: Ativan, Serax, and Inderal. Competitors are developing generic equivalents to these drugs. Another problem facing AHP is trying to find a buyer for its housewares division. If AHP can find a buyer, divestiture of this division would generate capital for needed acquisitions in the health care field. According to financial experts, American Home Products will continue to be a tough competitor for Bristol-Myers in the foreseeable future.

Johnson & Johnson

A second major competitor of Bristol-Myers is Johnson & Johnson. J&J is best known to consumers for such products as Band-Aids, Baby Shampoo, and Baby Powder, but J&J holds powerful and profitable franchises in hospital supplies and prescription drugs. Since 1973, J&J's earnings growth has averaged 13 percent annually. In 1984, about 55 percent of the company's $6 billion in sales and much of its $514 million in earnings came from products that are No. 1 in their markets. The company's revitalization of Tylenol after the 1982 cyanide deaths, its repositioning of Baby Shampoo for the adult market, and its emergence as No. 2 in infant's toys exemplifies a legendary marketing dominance. Since 1980, J&J has acquired twenty-five companies in promising high-technology markets ranging from special lenses and surgical lasers to magnetic resonance scanners for diagnostic imaging.

The $1.2 billion combined sales of its four pharmaceutical divisions made J&J the fifth largest drug company in the United States in 1983. More than 40 percent of its R&D spending, which last year totaled $405 million or 6.8 percent of sales, went to pharmaceuticals. Nearly 60 percent of J&J's sales come from products that did not exist in 1978. J&J's facilities are located in forty-nine countries around the world. Foreign operations account for about 43 percent of J&J's sales and 52 percent of operating profit.

FINANCIAL POSITION

In 1984, Bristol-Myers continued its long history of improved sales and earnings. The acceleration in sales growth in 1984 resulted from balanced growth in established products, strong performances from new product lines, and recent acquisitions. The strong exchange value of the dollar in 1984 reduced total company sales. Increased unit volume played a larger part in the sales growth in 1984 than in 1983.

Bristol-Myers' net earnings in 1984 were $472 million, which was 16 percent greater than the prior year. Earnings per share in 1984 were $3.45, up from $3.00 in 1983. Bristol-Myers' income statements and balance sheets for the period 1981 to 1984 are given in Exhibit 5 and Exhibit 6 respectively.

Exhibit 5   Bristol—Myers' income statement and statement of retained earnings

Year Ended December 31	1984	1983	1982	1981
	\multicolumn — (in $ millions except per share amounts)			
Earnings				
Net sales	$4,189.4	$3,917.0	$3,599.9	$3,496.7
Expenses:				
Cost of products sold	1,409.1	1,385.8	1,299.0	1,327.7
Marketing, selling, and administrative	1,104.3	1,048.8	1,003.0	949.0
Advertising and product promotion	743.8	651.4	567.1	555.3
Research and development	212.4	185.3	161.0	144.0
Other	(60.7)	(45.8)	(36.3)	(31.2)
	3,408.9	3,225.5	2,993.8	2,944.8
Earnings before income taxes	780.5	691.5	606.1	551.9
Provision for income taxes	308.1	283.5	257.4	246.1
Net earnings	$ 472.4	$ 408.0	$ 348.7	$ 305.8
Earnings per common share	$ 3.45	$ 3.00	$ 2.59	$ 2.29
Retained Earnings				
Retained earnings, January 1	$1,890.0	$1,640.6	$1,429.5	$1,243.8
Net earnings	472.4	408.0	348.7	305.8
	2,362.4	2,048.6	1,778.2	1,549.6
Less dividends:				
Common stock	205.2	157.9	136.3	117.8
Preferred stock	.5	.7	1.3	2.3
	205.7	158.6	137.6	120.1
Retained earnings, December 31	$2,156.7	$1,890.0	$1,640.6	$1,429.5

Source: Bristol—Myers, *1984 Annual Report*, p. 47.

Exhibit 6   Bristol–Myers' balance sheets

December 31,	1984	1983	1982	1981
		(in $ millions)		
Assets				
Current assets:				
Cash and time deposits	$ 215.6	$ 122.2	$ 220.0	$ 212.5
Marketable securities				
(at cost which approximates market)	543.8	621.2	391.6	216.8
Accounts receivable (less reserves):	612.9	598.6	559.0	571.5
Other receivables	65.3	59.9	72.5	83.4
Inventories	592.8	551.0	559.1	565.3
Prepaid expenses	64.7	65.1	66.6	52.1
Prepaid taxes	74.4	82.9	72.9	68.2
Total current assets	2,169.5	2,100.9	1,941.7	1,769.8
Property, plant and equipment—net	791.1	701.7	653.6	581.8
Other assets	140.2	85.7	70.5	54.4
Excess of cost over net tangible assets				
received in business acquisitions	147.8	119.0	90.4	82.5
	$3,248.6	$3,007.3	$2,756.2	$2,488.5
Liabilities				
Current liabilities:				
Short-term borrowings	$ 172.8	$ 156.8	$ 167.8	$ 156.6
Accounts payable	201.1	185.1	191.5	178.1
Accrued expenses	324.9	326.4	292.8	264.6
U.S. and foreign income taxes payable	163.0	201.3	180.9	144.7
Total current liabilities	861.8	869.6	833.0	744.0
Other liabilities	137.7	133.4	95.3	77.8
Long-term debt	103.2	96.4	113.5	102.2
Total liabilities	1,102.7	1,099.4	1,041.8	924.0
Stockholders' Equity				
Preferred stock, nonredeemable	.2	.3	.4	1.0
Common stock	137.4	136.4	67.6	66.5
Capital in excess of par value of stock	44.3	30.8	85.2	68.6
Cumulative translation adjustments	(191.6)	(148.5)	(78.3)	—
Retained earnings	2,156.7	1,890.0	1,640.6	1,429.5
	2,147.0	1,909.0	1,715.5	1,565.6
Less cost of treasury stock—				
96,756 common shares in 1984	1.1	1.1	1.1	1.1
Total stockholders' equity	2,145.9	1,907.9	1,714.4	1,564.5
	$3,248.6	$3,007.3	$2,756.2	$2,488.5

Source: Bristol–Myers, *1984 Annual Report*, p. 48.

FUTURE OUTLOOK

Increasing demand for Bristol-Myers' new drugs, coupled with further gains in established pharmaceutical, nutritional, and consumer product lines, are positive factors for this organization in the mid-1980s. Already strongly positioned in the anticancer field with Platinol and Vepesid, Bristol-Myers plans to develop more drugs to treat disorders of the central nervous system and cardiovascular system.

Many areas of concern currently face Bristol-Myers, such as the prices of prescription drugs, the change in the Medicare reimbursement rules, the entry of foreign competitors into domestic markets, the strengthening OTC drugs, and the value of the dollar in world markets. Some critics say Bristol-Myers is not well-positioned to take advantage of changing demographic trends in this country. As the baby-boom generation gets older, there is an increasing demand for products that relate to their health care problems. Also, the number of Americans over age seventy is increasing dramatically each year. Bristol-Myers must develop strategies to take advantage of these trends.

Bristol-Myers' top management is in the process of establishing strategies, objectives, goals and policies for the mid-1980s. What would be your specific recommendations to the company's Chief Executive Officer, Mr. Richard L. Gelb? Mr. Gelb, age 59, has been Bristol-Myers' CEO since January 1972.

REFERENCES

"Bristol–Myers Bucks the Odds in Search of a Blockbuster Drug." *Business Week* (October 29, 1984), pp. 136, 140.

Bristol-Myers Co., 1984 Annual Report.

Bristol-Myers, Securities and Exchange Commission Form 10-K, 1983.

"Changing a Corporate Culture: Can Johnson & Johnson Go from Band-Aids to High Tech?" *Business Week* (May 14, 1984): 130–38.

Fraker, Susan. "American Home Products Battles the Doubters." *Fortune* (July 25, 1983): 59–64.

Freeman, Laurie. "Nuprin Breaks Ad Campaign." *Advertising Age* (April 2, 1984): 1.

Giges, Nancy. "Bristol-Myers Touts Easy-Open Tops." *Advertising Age* (January 31, 1983): 10.

Giges, Nancy. "New Analgesic Lures J&J and Bristol–Myers." *Advertising Age* (July 9, 1984): 62.

Johnson & Johnson, 1984 Annual Report.

"New Looks at Three Group 2 Stocks." *The Outlook* (May 2, 1984): 793.

"Personal Goods." *Industry Week* (March 19, 1984): 39.

Sanger, Elizabeth. "Just What the Doctor Ordered." *Barron's* (December 19, 1983): 13.

"The Fortune 500 of the Largest U.S. Corporations." *Fortune* (April 29, 1985): 266–285.

Waldhole, Michael. "Bristol-Myers Signs Pact with Upjohn to Market Nonprescription Pain Drug." *Wall Street Journal* (March 29, 1984): 7.

CASE 29

Lomas & Nettleton Financial Corporation

FRED DAVID
Auburn University

JIMMY MOSS
Sam Houston State University

> Home is where we keep our prized possessions, the objects we value most.
> Walk into any home, and in the things around you, you will find the pride
> and joy of the people who live there: an heirloom that represents the con-
> tinuity of generations; an antique hutch that displays the family's orderliness
> as well as its china; a brass clock on the mantel, keeping time.

This quotation is from Lomas & Nettleton's 1984 Annual Report. As a mortgage
banker, Lomas & Nettleton is helping home ownership to become accessible to a wid-
ening number of Americans.

During the period 1974 to 1984, Lomas & Nettleton's revenues increased from
$54 million to $239 million and net income moved from $1.6 million to $34 million.
Even during the housing slump of 1981 and 1982, L&N increased its earnings 16 percent and 32 percent respectively. Fiscal 1984 was the best year in the history of Lomas
& Nettleton Financial Corporation.

Despite past successes, L&N is not without problems. The Dallas-based company
is being challenged directly by Norwest Corp. In 1983, Norwest's revenues jumped 66
percent and the firm's president, David W. Beal, stated publicly that Norwest intends
to soon surpass L&N as the leading mortgage banking firm in the United States. In
addition to Norwest, such Wall Street titans as Merrill Lynch, Aetna Life & Casualty,
E.F. Hutton, American Express, and Citicorp are entering L&N's field of mortgage
banking. Some experts say that L&N must diversify to survive in the late 1980s; L&N's
past efforts to diversify into areas such as real estate development and venture capital
have failed.

HISTORY

John Lomas founded the Lomas & Nettleton Company in 1894 in New Haven, Connecticut. In 1963, Lomas & Nettleton was acquired by Wallace Investments, Inc.,

which changed its name in 1965 to Lomas & Nettleton Financial Corporation. L&N acquired the servicing portfolio of T.J. Bettes in 1968, making it the nation's largest mortgage banking operation. L&N has acquired a number of mortgage companies since that time, as indicated in Exhibit 1.

SERVICES

Mortgage banking involves originating real estate loans and selling them to institutional lenders. This activity forms the core of L&N's operations. Revenues from mortgage banking come primarily from loan administration, mortgage production, mortgage warehousing, mortgage trading, and insurance operations. At year end 1984, L&N represented 970 institutional investors, such as life insurance companies, savings and loan associations, pension and profit-sharing funds, and commercial banks. L&N is the largest mortgage servicer for the Federal National Mortgage Association and currently is the largest issuer of securities backed by the guarantee of the Government National Mortgage Association.

L&N obtains applications for mortgage loans principally through established contacts with real estate developers, brokers, and builders. Through its mortgage banking

Exhibit 1   A history of Lomas & Nettleton Financial Corporation

1894	L&N was founded in New Haven, Connecticut.
1963	Wallace Investments, Inc. purchased the L&N.
1965	Wallace Investments Inc. changed its name to the Lomas and Nettleton Financial Corp.
1968	L&N acquired the servicing portfolio of T.J. Bettes Co.
1969	L&N Mortgage Investors, a real estate investment trust, was formed.
1970	L&N acquired United Mortgage Servicing Corp. in Virginia, providing a base of operations in the Southeast.
1971	L&N acquired the Northwest Mortgage, Inc. in the state of Washington, providing a base of operations in the Northwest.
1972	L&N acquired the Kardon Investment Co. in Pennsylvania, providing a base of operations in the Northeast.
1979	L&N acquired the portfolio of National Homes Acceptance Corp. in Indiana and the Great Lakes Mortgage Corp. of Chicago. These acquisitions established L&N as the first truly national mortgage banking operation.
1981	L&N formed Lomas & Nettleton Housing Corp., a real estate investment trust located in Maryland.
1982	L&N purchased Vista Mortgage Realty, Inc. and formed a joint venture with Oppenheimer & Co. to own and operate Advance Mortgage Corp.
1983	L&N formed the Lomas & Nettleton Securities Corp. to provide relocation financial services and act as a broker-dealer.

Source: New Employee Orientation Program. Dallas, Texas; Lomas and Nettleton Financial Group, 1982.

activity, the company provides long-term financing for home buyers and developers of commercial projects such as apartment complexes, office buildings, shopping centers, and industrial facilities. L&N markets these long-term mortgage investments to other institutions.

L&N originates short-term construction loans through Lomas & Nettleton Mortgage Investors, Lomas & Nettleton Housing Corporation, and Lomas & Nettleton Management Company. Short-term loans are provided to home builders and to commercial developers. Special projects that are often financed include the acquisition of land, the development of streets, the installation of sewer systems, and the construction of residential and commercial housing projects.

L&N has invested a large part of its funds in new, multifamily rental projects in major metropolitan areas. These projects are built by and owned jointly with experienced real estate developers. L&N's investment philosophy has been to invest almost exclusively in new projects, and the company does not assume any construction risk. Rather, L&N issues a commitment to the developer for the lesser of a predetermined amount or his cost in the project. The developer then obtains construction financing from another financial source, which underwrites timely completion of the project within a stated budget. Only after satisfactory completion of the project in accordance with approved plans and specifications does the company fund the investment.

L&N has two life insurance subsidiaries, Mayflower National Life Insurance Company and Lomas Financial Security Insurance Company. These institutions provide credit life, mortgage redemption, accident and health insurance, and life insurance. L&N is also engaged in the business of developing real estate for sale to others, principally to professional real estate builders and to institutional investors. To date, this activity has been limited to the acquisition, development, and sale of tracts of land located in the Dallas–Fort Worth metroplex and in Houston, two of the country's fastest-growing areas.

OFFICES AND SUBSIDIARIES

Lomas & Nettleton's headquarters are located in Dallas, Texas. The seven regional offices of L&N and their respective locations are:

Regional Office	Location
Northeast	Philadelphia, Pennsylvania
Southeast	Virginia Beach, Virginia
Central	Dallas, Texas
Arizona	Phoenix, Arizona
West	Panorama City, California
Northwest	Seattle, Washington
Mideast	West Lafayette, Indiana

The company has 174 offices located in forty-two states, but services loans in all fifty states and the District of Columbia. The regions and locations of the L&N's offices are shown in Exhibit 2. Note on the U.S. map that L&N has more offices in California, Florida, Texas, Virginia, Illinois and Pennsylvania than in the other states. It has no offices in New York, New Jersey, Delaware, New Hampshire, Rhode Island, Hawaii, Kentucky, and Iowa.

SERVICING AND SALES

The growth of L&N's servicing portfolio from 1967 to the present is shown in Exhibit 3. Note that L&N's portfolio in 1984 is just over $18 billion. This total represents more than a fourfold increase since 1973, even though the total number of loans declined in six of the eleven years. A breakdown of L&N's current portfolio, by the seven regions, is shown in Exhibit 4. L&N's three largest regions in terms of mortgage loans

Exhibit 2   The location of L&N's offices in 1983

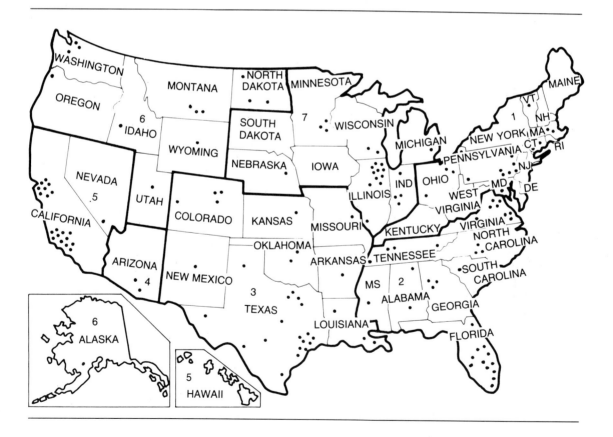

Exhibit 3 Summary of growth of L&N's servicing portfolio

Fiscal Year Ended June 30	Portfolio Principal Balance (in $000)	Number of Loans	Average Loan Balance	Loan Administration Income* (in $000)
1967	$ 784,736	59,279	$13,238	$ 3,998
1968	816,168	61,047	13,370	4,255
1969	2,256,293	190,263	11,859	12,052
1970	2,256,016	192,376	11,727	12,385
1971	3,267,279	264,513	12,352	16,344
1972	4,124,230	323,235	12,759	19,780
1973	4,411,655	331,702	13,300	23,093
1974	4,602,630	329,352	13,975	23,614
1975	4,814,845	328,937	14,638	24,419
1976	5,298,445	335,422	15,796	26,613
1977	5,625,555	335,790	16,753	29,304
1978	6,174,025	331,297	18,635	31,400
1979	6,708,477	327,839	20,463	33,578
1980	10,842,425	492,373	22,224	52,365
1981	11,588,771	492,158	23,547	58,942
1982	12,075,037	488,675	24,710	62,643
1983	17,763,000	676,500	26,258	94,012
1984	18,253,387	657,164	27,776	106,818

*Includes related insurance, data processing, and bond servicing revenues.

Exhibit 4 L&N's servicing portfolio by geographic region

Region	Number of Loans	Percent	Dollar Value of Loans	Percent
Northeast	110,525	16	2,674,495	15
Southeast	143,283	21	3,377,967	19
Central	127,832	19	3,953,283	22
Arizona	32,351	5	910,725	5
West	101,197	15	2,481,582	14
Northwest	35,061	5	1,165,666	7
Midwest	126,203	19	3,198,848	18
	676,452	100	17,762,566	100

and principal amounts are the Southeast, Central, and Midwest. Its largest concentration of activities is in Texas, California, Illinois, Florida, Pennsylvania, and Virginia.

COMPETITION

L&N's two major competitors in the mortgage banking field are Norwest Mortgage, Inc., and Manufacturers Hanover Mortgage, Inc. Norwest's net income for 1982, 1983, and 1984 was $89.1 million, $125.2 million, and $69.5 million. Norwest has 2,100 clients compared to L&N's 1,010. The top ten competitors in the mortgage banking industry are given in Exhibit 5.

More and more companies are either expanding their services or entering the mortgage banking field. This represents both a threat and an opportunity to L&N. The threat is increased competitiveness from many different types and sizes of firms, while the opportunity is that L&N could diversify into other areas of business. Savings and loan companies were the largest holder of commercial mortgages in the United States in 1983, with commercial banks and life insurance companies also having a larger share of this market than mortgage banking companies. Increased competition is making the mortgage banking business more complex and risky.

FINANCIAL INFORMATION

L&N is organized into six segments: mortgage banking, short-term lending, investments, real estate development, life insurance, and other. A breakdown of the company's sales revenues, operating profits, and identifiable assets by segment for 1981 through 1984 is shown in Exhibit 6. L&N's income statements and balance sheets for

Exhibit 5   The ten largest mortgage banking companies in the United States in 1983

Company	Mortgage Volume in $	Number of Mortgages
Lomas & Nettleton Financial Corp.	17,762,566,000	676,452
Norwest Mortgage Inc.	9,636,133,117	155,485
Manufacturers Hanover Mortgage Corp.	9,026,360,000	270,122
Fleet Mortgage Corp.	7,749,252,000	183,955
Weyerhaeuser Mortgage Co.	6,637,000,000	233,614
Suburban Coastal Corp.	5,987,000,000	117,818
Colonial Mortgage Service Co.	5,932,684,292	158,295
Kissel Co.	5,912,443,479	221,569
Ralph C. Sutro Co.	5,601,000,000	131,518
Cameron Brown Co.	5,097,629,000	141,772

Source: *American Banker* (October 17, 1983): 26. See the May 7, 1984 issue for an update on this information.

Exhibit 6 Revenues and operating profit by major segments (in $000)

	1984		1983		1982		1981	
	Dollars	Percent	Dollars	Percent	Dollars	Percent	Dollars	Percent
Revenues:								
Mortgage banking	171,064	71	159,174	77	93,360	70	84,331	70
Short-term lending	28,480	12	16,874	8	18,684	14	23,606	19
Investments	7,076	3	5,500	3	6,604	5	5,058	4
Real estate development	15,504	6	10,839	5	9,834	7	3,377	3
Life insurance	16,582	7	12,418	6	3,036	2	2,965	2
Other	1,256	1	734	1	2,358	2	1,784	2
Total	239,962	100	205,539	100	133,876	100	121,121	100
Operating Profits:								
Mortgage banking	44,030	59	43,542	72	23,761	55	23,854	58
Short-term lending	12,054	16	4,012	7	5,114	12	11,475	28
Investment	6,063	8	2,248	4	3,051	7	1,925	5
Real estate development	6,993	10	8,243	14	8,726	21	2,925	7
Life insurance	5,181	7	3,344	5	938	2	367	.8
Other	120	0	(747)	(2)	1,273	3	819	1.2
Total	74,441	100	60,642	100	42,863	100	41,365	100
Identifiable Assets:								
Mortgage banking	660,102	66	758,716	75	550,887	70	462,318	74
Short-term lending	195,141	19	102,612	10	117,850	15	101,035	16
Investments	30,709	3	34,396	3	32,687	4	32,991	5
Real estate development	70,192	7	68,937	7	54,986	7	14,244	2
Life insurance	40,588	4	30,272	3	9,108	1	8,649	1
Other	10,655	1	17,345	2	27,404	3	10,950	2
Total	1,007,387	100	1,012,278	100	792,912	100	630,187	100

Exhibit 7   Statement of consolidated income, Lomas & Nettleton Financial Corporation and subsidiaries

| | Year Ended June 30 | | | |
	1984	1983	1982	1981
Revenues:				
Mortgage banking	$171,064,000	$159,174,000	$ 93,360,000	$ 84,331,000
Interest and financing charges	23,778,000	12,818,000	14,996,000	19,961,000
Investments	7,076,000	5,500,000	6,604,000	5,058,000
Management fees	4,702,000	4,056,000	3,688,000	3,645,000
Real estate development	15,504,000	10,839,000	9,834,000	3,377,000
Life insurance	16,582,000	12,418,000	3,036,000	2,965,000
Other	1,256,000	734,000	2,358,000	1,784,000
	239,962,000	205,539,000	133,876,000	121,121,000
Expenses:				
Mortgage banking	127,034,000	115,632,000	69,598,000	60,477,000
Related to management fees	3,461,000	3,253,000	2,910,000	2,731,000
Real estate development	8,511,000	1,634,000	1,108,000	452,000
Life insurance	11,401,000	9,074,000	2,098,000	2,598,000
Other operating expenses	1,136,000	974,000	839,000	964,000
Interest on long-term debt	27,284,000	12,558,000	6,128,000	7,381,000
Other interest	5,063,000	12,480,000	14,460,000	12,533,000
General and administrative	9,217,000	7,592,000	5,414,000	4,865,000
State income and franchise taxes	1,763,000	1,191,000	1,010,000	789,000
Provision for possible losses	500,000	1,850,000	—	—
	195,370,000	166,238,000	103,565,000	92,790,000
Income before federal income taxes	44,592,000	39,301,000	30,311,000	28,331,000
Federal income taxes:				
Current	5,075,000	12,045,000	7,580,000	10,221,000
Deferred (credit)	5,181,000	(225,000)	1,816,000	59,000
	10,256,000	11,820,000	9,396,000	10,280,000
Net income	$ 34,336,000	$ 27,481,000	$ 20,915,000	$ 18,051,000

these fiscal years are given in Exhibit 7 and Exhibit 8 respectively. The Statement of Consolidated Changes in Financial Position that is given in Exhibit 9 reveals L&N's sources and application of funds for fiscal 1981 through 1984.

ORGANIZATION

The chairman and chief executive officer of Lomas & Nettleton Financial Corporation is Jess Hay. L&N has a thirteen-member board of directors. As illustrated in the company's organizational chart (Exhibit 10), Ted Enloe is president and chief operating officer of the short-term lending and investment division, and James M. Wooten is

Exhibit 8 Consolidated balance sheet, Lomas & Nettleton Financial Corporation and subsidiaries

	June 30			
	1984	1983	1982	1981
Assets				
Cash	$ 11,763,000	$ 9,523,000	$ 11,016,000	$ 14,421,385
First mortgage loans held for sale	325,017,000	482,425,000	334,162,000	267,598,168
Notes and accounts receivable	246,721,000	185,132,000	155,773,000	122,118,276
Investments	232,151,000	180,920,000	179,914,000	146,968,734
Foreclosed real estate and investment in related entity holding foreclosed properties	12,060,000	12,868,000	18,239,000	10,029,489
	490,932,000	378,920,000	353,926,000	279,116,499
Less allowance for possible losses	(3,994,000)	(5,482,000)	(2,582,000)	(3,658,818)
	486,938,000	373,438,000	351,344,000	275,457,681
Fixed assets—at cost	71,672,000	25,010,000	23,861,000	16,148,973
Prepaid expenses and other assets	23,562,000	22,150,000	26,676,000	4,995,309
Cost of purchased future servicing income	77,181,000	88,144,000	34,863,000	40,457,825
Mortgage servicing contracts and goodwill	11,254,000	11,588,000	10,990,000	11,107,475
	1,007,387,000	1,012,278,000	792,912,000	630,186,816
Escrow, agency and fiduciary funds (segregated in separate bank accounts and excluded from corporate assets and liabilities)	356,241,000	371,191,000	223,140,000	243,046,968
Liabilities and Stockholders' Equity				
Notes payable	462,041,000	573,291,000	584,536,000	436,776,228
Accounts payable and accrued expenses	28,175,000	45,637,000	25,316,000	16,275,369
Insurance reserves	10,320,000	6,541,000	1,287,000	—
Federal income taxes payable	4,639,000	9,485,000	1,653,000	2,067,422
Deferred federal income taxes	8,334,000	2,881,000	3,105,000	849,618
Minority interest in consolidated subsidiary	1,756,000	1,698,000	—	—
Term notes payable	206,534,000	122,407,000	36,009,000	39,006,000
Subordinated note and			17,500,000	20,000,000
convertible debentures	122,804,000		5,928,000	9,265,000
convertible subordinated debentures —due in 2008	122,804,000		—	—
Stockholders' Equity				
Common stock	35,874,000	17,820,000	17,187,000	16,799,728
Other paid-in capital	74,577,000	73,157,000	67,757,000	64,516,325
Retained earnings	85,746,000	83,797,000	67,957,000	56,915,183
Unrealized loss on marketable equity securities (deduction)	(4,116,000)	(112,000)	(6,038,000)	(3,060,000)
Treasury stock (deduction)	(29,297,000)	(29,285,000)	(29,285,000)	(29,224,057)
	162,784,000	145,377,000	117,578,000	105,947,179
	$1,007,387,000	$1,012,278,000	$792,912,000	$630,186,816
Liability for escrow, agency and fiduciary funds	$ 356,241,000	$ 371,191,000	$223,140,000	$243,046,968

Exhibit 9   Statement of consolidated changes in financial position, Lomas & Nettleton Financial Corporation and subsidiaries

| | Year Ended June 30 | | | |
	1984	1983	1982	1981
Cash at beginnng of year	$ 9,523,000	$ 11,016,000	$ 14,421,000	$ 14,347,000
Source of Funds:				
From operations:				
Net income	34,336,000	27,481,000	20,915,000	18,051,000
Add (deduct) items not involving receipt or outlay of funds:				
Depreciation	4,855,000	4,227,000	2,544,000	1,781,000
Provision for possible losses	500,000	1,850,000	—	—
Amortization of cost of purchased future servicing income, mortgage servicing contracts, and goodwill	11,544,000	15,078,000	6,599,000	6,854,000
Other	5,779,000	(274,000)	3,848,000	1,441,000
	57,014,000	48,362,000	33,906,000	28,127,000
Collection of notes receivable	186,890,000	125,852,000	61,075,000	184,064,000
Notes receivable transferred to foreclosed real estate	916,000	3,575,000	10,502,000	1,558,000
Sales of first mortgage loans	1,865,966,000	1,841,158,000	874,230,000	868,738,000
Sales of investments	102,502,000	50,794,000	45,672,000	23,580,000
Sales of foreclosed real estate	6,675,000	18,406,000	4,346,000	5,645,000
Borrowing on term notes	100,000,000	68,000,000	—	—
Issuance of 9¾% debentures	—	110,000,000	—	—
Increase (decrease) in federal income taxes	—	6,893,000	26,000	(3,031,000)
Increase in accounts payable and other liabilities	—	6,255,000	10,328,000	669,000
Additions to capital	1,584,000	6,032,000	3,628,000	29,497,000
Total funds available	2,331,070,000	2,296,343,000	1,058,134,000	1,153,194,000
Application of Funds:				
Advances on notes receivable	248,585,000	141,252,000	99,789,000	99,162,000
Origination of first mortgage loans	1,708,558,000	1,966,894,000	940,793,000	938,419,000
Additions to fixed assets	48,595,000	3,985,000	10,256,000	11,828,000
Purchases of investments	141,590,000	33,713,000	82,816,000	37,066,000
Additions to foreclosed real estate	6,813,000	10,281,000	13,025,000	2,669,000
Increase in accounts receivable, prepaid expenses, and other assets	19,528,000	4,588,000	28,542,000	1,350,000
Cost of purchased future servicing income and goodwill	1,604,000	2,728,000	887,000	542,000

	1984	1983	1982	1981
		Year Ended June 30		
Purchase of acquired companies:				
Future servicing income	—	65,358,000	—	—
Other assets net of liabilities	5,375,000	4,028,000	6,796,000	—
Conversion or cancellation of				
debentures	1,052,000	4,572,000	3,337,000	29,159,000
Decrease (increase) in notes payable	123,098,000	37,780,000	(149,058,000)	10,468,000
Treasury share acquired	—	—	62,000	—
Cash dividends paid	14,509,000	11,641,000	9,873,000	8,110,000
Total funds applied	2,319,307,000	2,286,820,000	1,047,118,000	1,138,773,000
Cash at end of year	$ 11,763,000	$ 9,523,000	$ 11,016,000	$ 14,421,000

president and chief operating officer of the mortgage banking division. Assisting Ted Enloe are the executive vice-presidents in charge of development, underwriting, and loan administration.

The Employee Participation Idea Council (EPIC) of L&N was established in 1982 to allow the company's 2,800 employees to participate more in management decisions. L&N's EPIC is actually a program of quality circles where teams discuss work-related problems and possible solutions. The EPIC's major objectives are to reduce unit cost, improve work quality, and increase levels of service. Through the EPIC, employees are learning to analyze problems and compile data to support their recommendations to management.

SPECIAL CONCERNS AND OUTLOOK FOR 1985

Jess Hay would like for L&N to evolve into a more diversified financial services company, while remaining specialists in mortgage banking. In the highly cyclical housing environment, this type of strategy is expected to provide stable long-term growth for the company. L&N expects revenues to increase by 13 percent and net income to increase by at least 15 percent in 1985. These projections are based on the belief that prime interest rates will remain favorable in 1985. L&N expects housing starts and business investments in structures to rise in 1985. Based on these forecasts, L&N's mortgage loans and commercial investments should increase by $10 million in 1985 for L&N.

Despite optimistic projections, Jess Hay ponders over basic questions about L&N's future. Should L&N seek to acquire other mortgage banking companies? Should L&N expand into states such as New York where it currently has no offices? Should L&N diversify more into insurance or related areas? Should L&N diversify into commercial banking? What effect will continued deregulation of the financial industry have on L&N? How can L&N compete more effectively in the mortgage banking industry? How

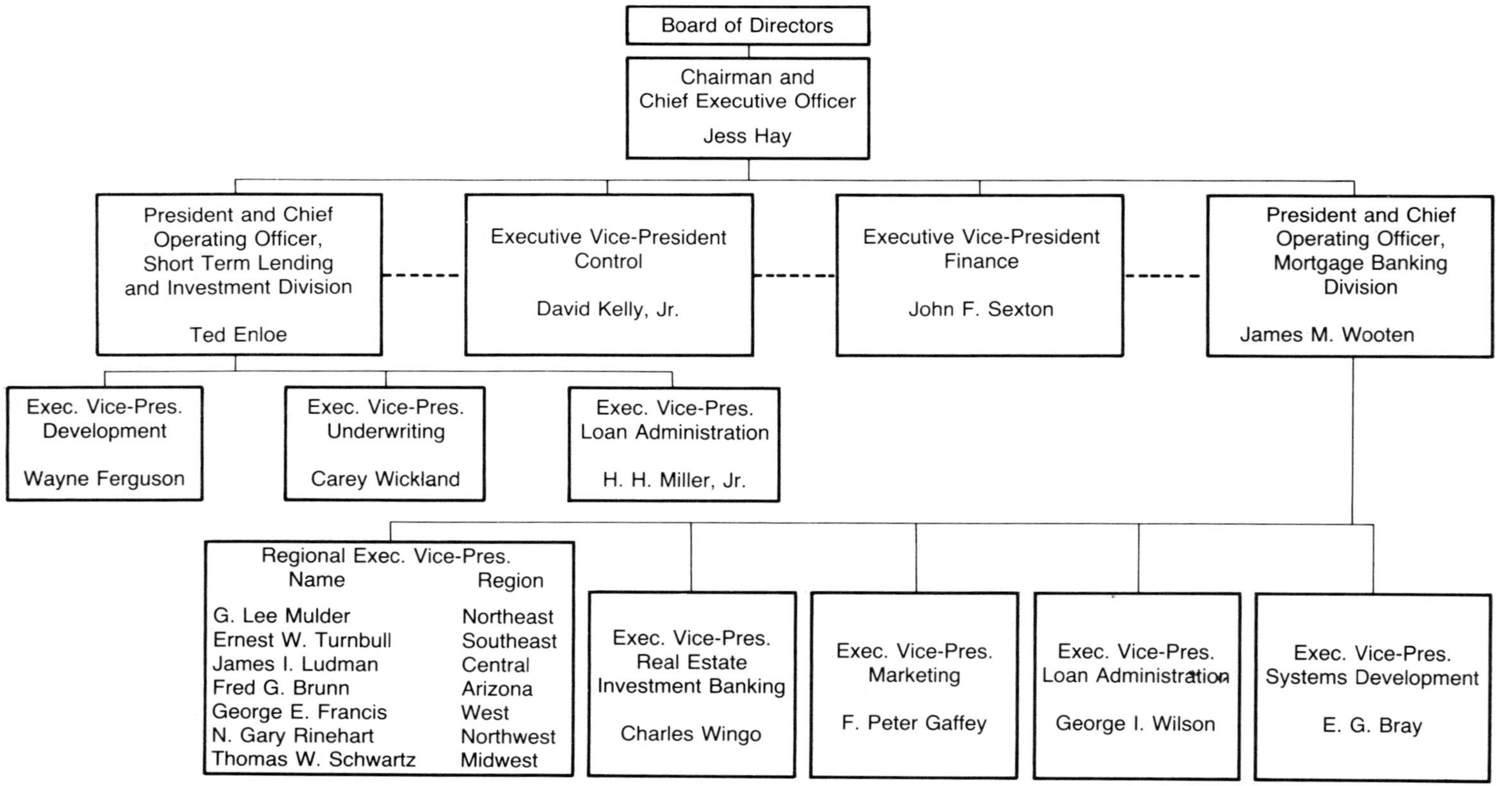

Exhibit 10 Lomas & Nettleton Financial Corporation's organizational chart

can L&N reverse its declining trend in short-term lending activity? If interest rates climb and inflation increases, what effect will this have on L&N? What contingency plans should L&N prepare? What are Norwest's strategies for 1985?

SUGGESTED READINGS

"Commercial Mortgages: Now It's a Buyer's Market." *Business Week* (July 4, 1983): 73.

Hicks, Kenneth J. "Top 300 Mortgage Firms Post Record Rise." *American Banker* (October 17, 1983): 6, 26.

Holmes, Peter A. "Surge in Consumer Spending, Business Investment, and Jobs." *Nation's Business* (January 1984): 20–25.

"Lomas & Nettleton Forms Unit." *Wall Street Journal* (May 5, 1983): 41.

"Lomas & Nettleton Says It Agreed to Buy Vista Mortgage Realty." *Wall Street Journal* (December 29, 1981): 3.

"Lomas & Nettleton: Still Taking Risks to Stay No. 1 in Mortgage Banking." *Business Week* (November 21, 1983): 80–84.

CASE 30

The Limited, Inc.

JILL AUSTIN
Middle Tennessee State University

FRED DAVID
Auburn University

INTRODUCTION

"I was convinced that the highest margins were in sportswear and my father was equally convinced you needed a full line to attract customers." This argument between father and son led young Leslie Wexner to try to prove his point. Wexner opened the first Limited Store in August 1963. During fiscal 1983, total sales of The Limited reached $1.1 billion. As of March 1984, The Limited, Inc. was comprised of five retail store divisions: The Limited (523 stores), Lane Bryant (244 stores), Sizes Unlimited (84 stores), Limited Express (76 stores), and Victoria's Secret (17 stores).

Note: Some other excellent articles about The Limited can be found in the following issues of *Business Week*: (5-13-85, p. 32; 2-25-85, p. 78; 2-18-85, p. 66; 7-30-84, p. 38; 6-4-84, p. 38; 5-14-84, p. 45).

Leslie Wexner's merchandising strategy has made The Limited successful. Instead of offering a wide variety of fashionable clothing, the stores offer a limited assortment of women's clothes and classic outfits in large quantities and in a variety of colors. The company operates Brylane and Victoria's Secret, two mail order divisions, and Mast Industries, a production procurement company. The Limited, Inc., headquartered in Columbus, Ohio, has grown to become the largest women's apparel specialty store and mail order retailer in the United States.

In mid-1984, The Limited, Inc. is planning to purchase Carter Hawley Hale Stores, Inc. Carter Hawley consists of ten divisions: Broadway Southern California, Broadway–Southwest, Emporium Capwell Company, John Wanamaker, Thalhimer Bros., Inc., Weinstock's, Neiman–Marcus, Bergdorf Goodman, Inc., Holt, Renfrew & Co., Ltd., Walden Book Company, Inc., and Contempo Casuals. Carter Hawley Hale is trying to prevent being taken over by The Limited. This case focuses on The Limited's takeover attempt and the potential strategy-implementation problems that could result.

HISTORY

In 1963, Leslie Wexner borrowed $10,000 from an aunt and a bank to open The Limited's first store. During its first year in operation, this store achieved sales of $157,000. Wexner believed that providing quality fashionable sportswear at medium prices would lead to success, so he opened other Limited stores. By the late 1970s, The Limited began diversifying its product line. Mast Industries was acquired in 1978. Limited Express stores were opened in 1981. Lane Bryant, Roamans, and Victoria's Secret were acquired in 1982. Also in 1982, the Limited Credit Corporation was formed and The Limited, Inc. was listed for the first time on the New York Stock Exchange.

The year 1983 was good for The Limited. Sales increased to $1.1 billion and net income rose to $70.9 million. Long-term debt was reduced during the year from $74 million to $22 million. One hundred twelve new stores were opened, increasing the total number to 937 stores. Property was purchased for a new distribution and freight center. New store designs were developed for Lane Bryant, Victoria's Secret, and Sizes Unlimited. Critics warn, however, that The Limited is expanding and growing too rapidly. Bess Gallanis, a Chicago-based free-lance writer, reveals the following information about The Limited:

> The uniqueness of The Limited's ability to gather fashion trends and have merchandise in the store quickly lies in its private labels. In the 1950s, private labeling was the rule, at a time when shoppers were loyal to a department store. The store's own label created an identity, which attracted and defined its customer by taste and price. Private labeling is again emerging as a major retailing trend as consumers shift toward boutique shopping in search of a unique identity at a reasonable price. Each of The Limited's three labels, Hunter's Run, Cassidy, and The Limited, has its own, separate

identity. The Limited seldom uses outside consultants and has only toyed with advertising in twenty years. There was a time when every detail was attended to by Leslie Wexner, and he still keeps his fingers in nearly all pies. The Limited is always experimenting with merchandise mix in each store. By monitoring weekly sales and inventory data, management determines store price points and predicts the next look.[1]

CURRENT BUSINESS STRUCTURE

The Limited is organized into seven major operating divisions: Limited Stores, Limited Express, Lane Bryant, Sizes Unlimited, Victoria's Secret, Brylane Mail Order, and Mast Industries. Nearly all of The Limited's stores are located in leased facilities. These leases generally have no renewal options and expire at various dates between fiscal 1984 and the year 2003.

Limited Stores

Limited stores form the flagship division of this organization. Originally, merchandise in Limited stores was targeted at women between the ages of sixteen and thirty-five. Because of the aging American population, Limited stores have shifted their orientation to women in the twenty-five to forty-four age group. Stores of this division specialize in the sale of medium-priced fashion clothing. The merchandise assortment includes skirts, blouses, sweaters, shirts, pants, coats, suits, dresses, and accessories. Limited stores are wholly company owned and managed. The 523 Limited stores are located across the United States in regional shopping centers or malls. Only a few stores are in downtown locations.

Limited Express Stores

Wexner began to experiment with the Limited Express concept as an expansion possibility. Limited Express is a "Neon-lit high-tech" store that sells a unique assortment of popular-priced sportswear. These fashions are the latest in American and international styles. Limited Express stores are designed to appeal to women between the ages of fifteen and twenty-five, but store managers have found that these fashions also appeal to women over age twenty-five. There are seventy Limited Express stores operating today. These stores are located in regional shopping malls in California and the Midwest. Expansion plans call for more Limited Express stores to be opened in Southern California, midwest, and southwest markets. An average Limited Express store has 2,000 square feet of selling space, compared to the typical Limited store, which averages 4,000 square feet.

[1]Bess Gallanis, "Smart Marketing," *Advertising Age* (July 25, 1983): 10.

Lane Bryant Stores

The Limited, Inc. acquired Lane Bryant in 1982. Lane Bryant had been in operation for eighty years and was actually larger than The Limited at the time of purchase. Lane Bryant's market is primarily women between thirty and fifty years of age. The store specializes in the sale of medium-priced clothing for the "special-sized woman." The merchandise assortment includes blouses, shirts, sweaters, skirts, pants, coats, suits, dresses, intimate apparel, and accessories. Nearly all of the Lane Bryant stores are located in regional shopping centers. Wexner began expansion of Lane Bryant in 1983 and has targeted almost five hundred shopping malls that presently have Limited stores to be future bases for Lane Bryant outlets. Since about 14 percent of American women sixteen or older wear Lane Bryant-sized clothing, Wexner believes this division has excellent growth potential. Lane Bryant stores typically contain 6,000 square feet of merchandising space.

Brylane Mail Ordering

The Brylane mail-order division is the nation's leading catalog retailer of women's special-sized clothing. Four catalogs are published annually and each is directed toward a special-sized customer. The catalogs include Lane Bryant, Roaman's, Tall Collection, and Nancy's Choice. Brylane will circulate over eighty-five million mailing pieces in 1984. This division of The Limited, Inc. maintains a distribution center in Indianapolis, Indiana, where all mail orders are received and shipped.

Victoria's Secret Stores

The Victoria's Secret stores specialize in the sale of European and American designer lingerie. The store sells high-quality lingerie with prices ranging from $5 to $2,000. This division focuses on women aged twenty-five to forty-five, but gifts purchased by men account for a significant portion of the total sales. There are sixteen Victoria's Secret stores, all of which are located in regional shopping centers in southern California. The stores are decorated as Victorian parlors. Victoria's secret publishes a mail-order catalog four times per year. On the average, Victorian parlors have 1,200 square feet of selling space.

Sizes Unlimited

The Sizes Unlimited division operates eighty-five Smart Size or Sizes Unlimited stores, selling special-sized, name-brand women's clothing at low and budget prices. Smart Size and Sizes Unlimited stores target mainly to women over age twenty-five. The merchandise assortment includes blouses, shirts, sweaters, skirts, pants, coats, suits, dresses, intimate apparel, and accessories. These stores are located in smaller shopping centers in the East and Midwest.

Mast Industries

The business of the Mast Industries division is to import women's clothing from around the world and to wholesale this merchandise to The Limited's stores and other companies. Mast Industries arranges for foreign manufacturers to produce clothing for U.S. companies that want to supplement their product lines. Mast specializes in high-quality products that are produced at low costs. Much of the merchandise imported by Mast is marked with one of The Limited's own three labels: Hunter's Run, Cassidy, or The Limited. Hunter's Run clothing is classic or "preppy" sportswear including polo type shirts, cotton chino pants, skirts, sweaters, and belts. The Cassidy label is used for suits and dresses designed for work or dress-up occasions. The Limited label is used for fashion-forward clothing that represents new styles. Leslie Wexner believes that having its own brands allows The Limited to keep merchandise inventory current and unique.

DISTRIBUTION FACILITIES

The Limited, Inc. operates a national distribution center in Columbus, Ohio. The center has a capacity to handle 1,200 retail stores. Sixty-seven percent of the U.S. population is located within a five-hundred-mile radius of Columbus, so Wexner feels this is an ideal location for a distribution center. Another advantage of the Columbus location is its nearness to New York City, the port where incoming merchandise produced in foreign countries is received by Mast Industries.

All merchandise arriving in New York is shipped directly to the distribution center for allocation among The Limited's stores. A computerized distribution system aids distributors in their selections for each store's inventory. This system allows The Limited to monitor inventory levels, the merchandise mix, and sales patterns at each store, so that appropriate adjustments can be made as needed. In 1984, The Limited started construction of a second distribution center at the site of the existing center. The new center will increase the distribution capacity of The Limited, Inc. to 3,000 retail stores.

COMPETITION

The retail sale of women's clothing is a very competitive business. Competitors of The Limited include nationally, regionally, and locally owned department stores, specialty stores, and mail-order catalog businesses. Some of The Limited's major competitors are Marshall Field, Carson Pirie Scott, May Department Stores, Boston Stores, Gimbel's, Dayton Hudson Stores, Carter Hawley Hale Stores, Peck and Peck, Paul Harris, Virginia Crabtree, The Body Shop, Sizes 5, 7, 9, Round Robin, Talbots, Ormonds, Lots to Love, Castner Knott, Stewart's, McRae's, Red Rooster, Sears, and J.C. Penney. Two national chains, Brooks Fashion Stores and U.S. Shoe, are perhaps The Limited's major competitors.

Brooks Fashion Stores

Brooks Fashion Stores, Inc. is a chain of women's apparel stores. There were 476 Brooks stores in thirty-eight states at the end of fiscal 1983. During 1983, Brooks opened fifty new stores, entered the Kansas market for the first time, acquired the sixteen-store Alcroe Association Chain in California, and increased sales by 18 percent to $211.5 million. Selected financial information on Brooks is give in Exhibit 1.

Brooks stores appeal to younger women in the same age group as Limited Express and also to working women from the age group targeted by the Limited stores. However, in 1980 Brooks acquired the T. Edwards chain of women's specialty stores, which appeals to the twenty-five to forty-year-old customer. T. Edwards appears to be much like The Limited, Inc. in its appeal, price ranges, and styles. The T. Edwards Company is more fashion-forward than Brooks. By the end of fiscal 1983, there were twenty-four T. Edwards stores in operation. Brooks store management plans to open about ninety more Brooks and T. Edwards stores in 1984.

Exhibit 1 Financial information for Brooks Fashion Stores

Highlights	Fiscal 1983	Fiscal 1982	Percentage Change
Net sales (000)	$211,540	$179,146	18.1
Income before taxes (000)	$ 12,445	$ 13,056	(4.7)
Net income (000)	$ 7,205	$ 7,826	(7.9)
Per share	$ 1.25	$ 1.35	(7.4)
Net return on sales	3.41%	4.37%	—
Working capital (000)	$ 24,920	$ 24,048	3.6
Current ratio	2.0:1	2.3:1	—
Total assets (000)	$ 90,546	$ 77,011	17.6
Stockholders' equity (000)	$ 59,830	$ 54,440	9.9
Equity per share	$ 10.42	$ 9.48	9.9
Return on average equity	12.6%	15.1%	—
Net common shares outstanding (000)	5,745	5,745	—
Stores open at fiscal year end	500	453	10.4

Source: Brooks Fashion Sores, Inc., 1983 Annual Report.

U.S. Shoe

At the beginning of 1984, U.S. Shoe Corporation operated 552 Casual Corner stores. Casual Corner attempts to appeal to fashion-conscious working women, as do the Limited Stores. Casual Corner stores are usually located in major shopping centers. U.S. Shoe operates other clothing specialty stores that compete with subsidiaries of The Limited, Inc. For example, Ups'n Downs is designed for the fourteen to twenty-one-year-old woman, much like The Limited Express. U.S. Shoe operates 154 Ups'n Downs stores.

During 1983, retail tests of a new women's apparel store called Career Image were conducted in seven shopping malls. These stores carry the same items as Casual Corner, but are about 2,500 square feet compared to 4,500 square feet of most Casual Corner stores. The test was successful and about forty Career Image stores should be in operation by the end of 1984.

U.S. Shoe sells intimate apparel through mail order in their "Intimique" catalog. Gains in sales and earnings for 1983 were reported by almost all of U.S. Shoe's specialty store divisions. Casual Corner sales increased by 16 percent over 1982 levels. U.S. Shoe's women's apparel divisions had sales of $523 million in 1983, up from $424 million in 1982. Exhibit 2 reveals U.S. Shoe's plans for opening new women's apparel stores.

Department Stores

Competition from department stores is increasing. J.C. Penney now sells designer brands and has a brand much like The Limited's Hunter's Run called Hunt Club. Sears also is becoming more competitive, especially with its Cheryl Tiegs Collection. Both

Exhibit 2 The number of women's apparel stores (U.S. Shoe Corporation)

	January 1983	January 1984	Estimated January 1985
Casual Corner	516	552	588
Ups'n Downs	117	154	214
Caren Charles	22	46	75
Career Image	—	7	37
August Max	28	28	34
Petite Sophisticate	—	15	23
T. H. Moody	11	16	18
Total	694	818	989

Source: U.S. Shoe Corporation, 1983 Annual Report, p. 7.

of these stores operate major mail-order businesses. It appears that competition for The Limited, Inc. is practically every store that sells women's fashions in the United States, and especially those located in shopping malls.

PROMOTION

Leslie Wexner does not believe that advertising is effective for shopping center retailers. When Lane Bryant was acquired, one of the first actions taken was to cut its $7 million annual advertising budget. Historically, The Limited has advertised on the radio with slogans like "Look to The Limited" and "For the Styles of Your Life." However, the company now advertises only on the tabloids distributed at malls. The Limited relies on the high traffic of malls to draw customers and the company is willing to pay in mall rent what other companies pay in advertising.

FINANCIAL CONDITION

The Limited's income statements and balance sheets for three years ending January 1984 are provided in Exhibit 3 and Exhibit 4 respectively. These statements reveal increasing levels for sales, income, assets, liabilities, and shareholders' equity. A consolidated statement of The Limited's shareholders' equity is given in Exhibit 5. The Limited's rapid growth in number of stores over the last five years is evidenced in Exhibit 6.

Exhibit 3   The Limited's income statements

	Jan. 1984	Jan. 1983	Jan. 1982
	(in $000 except per share amounts)		
Net sales	$1,085,890	$721,394	$364,900
Cost of goods sold, occupancy and buying costs	758,274	512,020	255,654
Gross income	327,616	209,374	109,246
General, administrative, and store-operating expenses	192,239	138,431	70,860
Operating income	135,377	70,943	38,386
Interest expense	(10,248)	(11,756)	(1,864)
Other income, net	9,810	1,405	1,964
Income before income taxes	134,939	60,592	38,486
Provision for income taxes	64,000	27,000	16,100
Net income	$ 70,939	$ 33,592	$ 22,386
Net income per share	$ 1.18	$ .57	$ .40

Source: The Limited, Inc., 1983 Annual Report.

Exhibit 4   The Limited's balance sheets

	Jan. 1984	Jan. 1983 (in $000)	Jan. 1982
ASSETS			
Current Assets			
Cash and equivalents	$ 1,282	$ 5,489	$ 11,326
Accounts receivable	44,201	19,040	7,832
Inventories	115,608	94,910	37,453
Prepayments and other	8,339	5,563	1,855
Total current assets	169,430	125,002	58,466
Property and equipment, at cost	261,815	223,274	117,110
Less—Accumulated depreciation and amortization	81,473	55,412	36,109
Net property and equipment	180,342	167,862	81,001
Investment in limited credit corporation	13,730	12,359	—
Other assets	13,894	15,169	3,191
Total assets	377,396	320,392	142,658
LIABILITIES AND SHAREHOLDERS' EQUITY			
Current Liabilities			
Accounts payable	65,134	62,987	22,847
Accrued expenses	42,224	25,966	7,880
Income taxes payable	7,801	1,979	4,011
Deferred income taxes	14,140	11,183	—
Total current liabilities	129,299	102,115	34,738
Long-term debt	21,763	74,411	16,571
Deferred income taxes	33,758	21,288	8,199
Commitments			
Shareholders' equity			
Common stock, $.50 par value (100,000,000 shares authorized)	29,590	14,608	1,376
Paid-in capital	18,088	12,267	8,254
Retained earnings	144,898	95,703	73,520
Total shareholders' equity	192,576	122,578	83,150
Total liabilities and shareholders' equity	$377,396	$320,392	$142,658

Source: The Limited, Inc. *1982 and 1983 Annual Reports*

CARTER HAWLEY HALE TAKEOVER ATTEMPT

On April 4, 1984, Leslie Wexner submitted an offer to buy Carter Hawley Hale Stores, Inc. for $1.1 billion. The Limited's offer was to purchase 20,300,000 shares of Carter Hawley Hale stock at $30 per share. Carter Hawley Hale, a Los Angeles-based company, is made up of 124 department stores, 117 specialty shops, and 841 bookstores.

Exhibit 5   Consolidated statement of shareholders' equity

	Number of Shares Outstanding	Common Stock (in 000)		Retained Earnings
		Par Value	Paid-in Capital	
Balance, Jan. 31, 1981	13,517	$ 169	$ 6,744	$ 53,180
Balance, Jan. 30, 1982	13,755	1,376	8,254	73,520
Balance, Jan. 29, 1983	29,216	14,608	12,267	95,703
Balance, Jan. 28, 1984	59,180	29,590	18,088	144,898

Source: The Limited, Inc., *1983 Annual Report*, p. 30.

Exhibit 6   The Limited, Inc.'s growth in stores

Fiscal Year	Stores at Beginning of Year	Stores Opened or Acquired During Year	Stores Closed During Year	Stores at Ending of Year
1979	258	51	-0-	309
1980	309	43	-0-	352
1981	352	78	-0-	430
1982	430	395	-0-	825
1983	825	116	4	937

Source: The Limited, Inc. Form 10-K, p. 3.

The operating divisions of Carter Hawley Hale are described as follows:

Broadway operates fifty stores in southern California, Arizona, New Mexico, and Nevada. These stores offer a complete assortment of men's, women's and children's apparel and accessories, furniture, appliances, and home furnishings of medium to higher quality.

Emporium Capwell Co. operates twenty-one department stores in northern California. Emporium offers complete assortments of apparel, accessories, furniture, appliances, and home furnishings.

John Wanamaker operates sixteen full-line department stores, in Pennsylvania (twelve), New York (one), New Jersey (two), and Delaware (one).

Thalhimer Bros., Inc. sells women's, men's, and children's apparel and accessories, home furnishings, and other items through twenty-five stores in Virginia,

South Carolina, and North Carolina. Thalhimer's headquarters are in Richmond, Virginia.

Weinstock's operates twelve department stores in the central valley of California, eight in Nevada, and three in Utah. Weinstock's central office and warehouse are in Sacramento, California.

Neiman–Marcus operates nineteen specialty stores in Texas, six in Georgia, one in Missouri, two in Illinois, two in California, four in Washington, D.C., and a single store in both New York and Nevada. Neiman–Marcus sells apparel, accessories, and gifts for men, women, and children. Neiman–Marcus also operates a mail-order business. This division's headquarters and warehouse are in Dallas.

Bergdorf Goodman is a fashion apparel and accessories store on Fifth Avenue in New York City.

Holt, Renfrew & Co., Ltd. sells quality furs and women's, men's and children's apparel through sixteen stores located in Canada.

The Walden Book Co., Inc. sells books thru 845 retail stores and nine leased departments.

Contempo Casuals operates eighty-seven women's sportswear stores, mainly in southern California.

The Limited had already started accumulating Carter Hawley Hale stock and owned about 700,000 shares at the time of its offer. The Limited plans to borrow $609 million to buy Carter Hawley. Since Carter Hawley Hale's long-term debt is estimated at $530 million, this acquisition would cause the Limited's debt to rise to $1.16 billion and its debt-to-equity ratio would rise to 1.25 to 1. Carter Hawley Hale has filed suit in federal court to stop The Limited's takeover attempt, claiming that The Limited failed to disclose information about potential antitrust problems.

General Cinema Corporation, a large theater and soft drink company, has attempted to stop The Limited's takeover attempt by acquiring $300 million of Carter Hawley Hale's preferred stock. The stock, convertible to common stock in one year, will allow General Cinema to obtain 22 percent voting rights. In addition, Carter Hawley Hale has begun buying some of its own shares to counteract the Limited's takeover plans. Over six trading days, Carter Hawley Hale acquired 17.9 million of its own shares at an average price of $26. The Securities and Exchange Commission ruled that the Carter Hawley Hale purchase of its own stock is a tender offer of its own and should have been registered with the SEC. The SEC has filed a suit in federal court to force Carter Hawley Hale to distribute enough shares to stockholders to bring the total number of shares outstanding to the level before the company began purchasing its own stock.

In April 1984, Carter Hawley Hale gave General Cinema a six-month option to purchase their Walden Books division for $285 million, but General Cinema decided not to follow through with the purchase. Carter Hawley Hale then decided to sell its Walden Books division to K-Mart Corporation for $295 million.

Exhibit 7   A financial history of Carter Hawley Hale, Inc.

	1980	1981	1982	1983	1984*
Gross Revenues					
(in $ millions)	2,408.0	2,632.9	2,870.7	3,054.8	3,632.7
Operational profit margin (%)	9.9	10.8	5.4	5.4	5.2
Return on equity (%)	11.9	9.3	7.0	7.1	8.7
Net income (in $ millions)	69.7	58.1	44.8	49.0	67.5
Working capital (in $ millions)	347.2	382.0	341.8	345.4	376.6
Shares (in thousands)	25,192	26,540	28,920	31,890	35,341
Earning per share ($)	2.67	2.11	1.55	1.55	1.93
Dividend per share ($)	1.08	1.15	1.21	1.22	1.22
Dividend payment (%)	40	55	78	79	63
Price range	20.63–14.63	23–14.88	20.88–14.25	17.25–10.5	24.75–15.13
P/E ratio	6.6	9.0	11.3	9.0	10.3
Average yield	6.1	6.1	6.9	8.8	6.1

*Fiscal year ends in January.

Although problems with The Limited's takeover attempt have arisen for the moment, Leslie Wexner plans eventually to control the Los Angeles-based retailer. Wexner says, "I'm a patient man. Only history will tell whether we've been determined or stubborn." So right now, The Limited, Inc. is waiting. They hope that legal and financial pressures on Carter Hawley Hale will make possible a new tender offer at a lower price. In a recent interview, Wexner stated that The Limited could sell its 700,000 shares or continue to buy stock and eventually gain control. He says, "What you've got now is a siege, as opposed to an active battle." Selected financial information on Carter Hawley Hale is provided in Exhibit 7.

FUTURE OUTLOOK

According to Leslie Wexner, the main desire of The Limited, Inc. is to satisfy customer needs. He feels many changes in company operations are needed, as customers' needs change. Wexner believes there is opportunity to expand the retailing divisions to 3,000 stores. He says he sees The Limited "as a confederation of specialized businesses." Wexner would like to have more outside buyers for the clothing produced and imported by Mast Industries. He would like to streamline the operation of all divisions so that the company's profitability will increase. Future possibilities exist for expanding catalog sales, entering foreign markets, expanding the number of domestic stores, and acquiring Carter Hawley.

Wexner believes that all his retail operations, even Mast Industries, can support a catalog. However, like all organizations, The Limited, Inc. does not have unlimited resources and cannot pursue all the strategic alternatives that currently face the firm. Critics warn that the company's debt ratios are already too high. Jerome Chazen, executive vice-president for sales at Liz Claiborne Inc., a Limited supplier says, "The whole success of The Limited is based on a tremendous amount of expertise in a relatively narrow field. Whether that is transferable to a department store is the question."[2]

[2] "The Tough Fight Limited Is Picking," *Business Week* (April 16, 1984): 57.

QUESTIONS FOR DISCUSSION

1. What are the advantages and disadvantages of The Limited, Inc. acquiring Carter Hawley Hale Stores, Inc? Do the advantages outweigh the disadvantages? Is the $1.1 billion offer reasonable?

2. Is Wexner allowing The Limited, Inc. to expand too rapidly? Is the company becoming too diversified?

3. Should The Limited advertise? Why? How much? In what media?

4. How could The Limited, Inc. compete more effectively with other women's retail clothing stores?

5. What are The Limited's market positioning strategies? Are they effective?

6. What are The Limited's market segmentation strategies? How could they be improved?

7. Should The Limited issue stock, incur debt, or use some combination of stock and debt to acquire Carter Hawley Hale? Use EPS/EBIT analysis to make this decision.

8. What are your recommendations for The Limited, Inc. at this point? Show what impact these recommendations will have on the company by preparing *pro forma* financial statements for 1984.

9. Explain how a firm can be taken over by another, even when top management of the acquired firm does not support the takeover. What strategy implementation problems could this cause for the acquiring firm?

REFERENCES

Alter, Jennifer. "Limited Puts Lane Bryant on Special Diet." *Advertising Age* (August 1982): 4–6, 18.

"Carter Hawley's White Knight May Be an Invading Army." *Business Week* (April 30, 1984): 46.

Fatehi-sedeh, K. and B.G. Shin. "The Growing Phenomenon of Corporate Takeovers: How Target Companies Can Defend Themselves." *Managerial Planning* (January–February, 1984): 39–42.

Gallanis, Bess. "I See Undervalued Assets." *Forbes* (August 2, 1982): 45.

Gallanis, Bess. "Smart Marketing Is a Specialty." *Advertising Age* (July 25, 1983): M10–M11.

Johnson, A. "How To Measure Your Company's Value." *Nation's Business* (April 1983): 68, 70.

Metz, Tim. "SEC Investigates Insider Trading on Takeover Bids." *Wall Street Journal* (July 23, 1984): 2.

Rodnick, R. "Getting the Right Price for Your Firm." *Nation's Business* (March 1984): 70, 71.

Sansweet, S.J. "Carter Hawley To Sell Walden Book Unit to K-Mart: General Cinema Ends Option." *Wall Street Journal* (July 23, 1984): 2.

Solomon, Jolie B. "Limited Ends Its Offer for Carter Hawley but Says Control of Retailer Is Still a Goal." *Wall Street Journal* (May 22, 1982): 5.

"The Tough Fight Limited Is Picking." *Business Week* (April 16, 1984): 57.

CASE 31

Tri-City Area Scanner Cooperative, Inc.

RAJ A. PADMARAJ
Bowling Green State University

Computerized tomography scanners provide a three-dimensional image of the human body. A traditional X-ray gives only a two-dimensional view of the body, so CT-scanners are much more effective. They also are much more expensive.

Mr. Thompson, chairperson of the ad hoc committee on CT (Computerized Tomography) scanner acquisition and the other members of the committee must decide whether to recommend the purchase of one whole-body CT-scanner for all three of the Tri-City hospitals. The CT-scanner ad hoc committee was formed in 1983 to find a way to make the services of a whole-body CT-scanner available to patients in Tri-City and the surrounding areas. The committee traveled to other hospitals in the region and acquired several estimates including cost and operational data regarding the CT-scanner. Prolonged discussions and consultations with hospital administrators, doctors, and other interested parties are nearly complete. This is a major strategic decision for these hospitals. This case summarizes all the available information. Mr. Thompson and members of the committee are now ready to make their recommendation.

BACKGROUND INFORMATION

The three hospitals in Tri-City—Lakeshore, General, and St. Vincent—have never before organized or combined their efforts to develop any program of this type. A few years earlier, attempts made by a senior administrator of one of the hospitals to eliminate duplication in certain surgical services met with very limited success. But escalating hospital costs in recent years appear to have subdued the opposition to hospitals' active cooperation, especially in the area of cost containment.

Radiation therapy, one of the three accepted methods of treating cancer, is presently offered by both Lakeshore and General hospitals. The other two methods, chemotherapy and surgery, are also available. In addition, Lakeshore operates a school of Radiologic Technology, which offers a two-year program and a Tumor Registry service for follow-up research and medical education on malignancies. No other hospital in Windsor County, where these three hospitals are located, offers acute care service for

Copyright © 1984 by the author. Presented at the Midwest Case Writers' Association Meeting, Valparaiso, July 13–14, 1984. The author acknowledges Mr. Puffenberger's help in the collection and the processing of data.

An excellent trade publication entitled *Healthcare Financial Management* regularly publishes articles relevant to this case.

area patients. In short, these three hospitals are solely responsible for planning and meeting total health care and treatment needs of the surrounding community.

NEED FOR A CT-SCANNER

Medical Analysis

At present, there are no CT-scanner services available either in Windsor County or in the neighboring counties of Dennison, Georgia, or Chesop. High initial costs associated with a CT-scanner (Exhibit 1) and uncertainty associated with cost recovery have delayed the hospitals in acquiring a scanner. No hospital wanted to go at it alone because the burden of economic failure was too high. With 14.7 percent unemployment, it was doubtful whether the local community would rescue any hospital in a financial bind.

Exhibit 1   Program costs and financing

The costs of the proposed project are estimated as follows:

	To Be Spent In	
	1984	1983
General Electric 8800 CT/T Scanning System	$ 755,000	
Radiation therapy equipment	21,400	$ 18,600
Film processor	15,000	
Emergency backup system	6,000	
Office equipment and furnishings	10,000	
Leasehold improvements, remodeling	133,000	
Electrical transformer	5,000	
One-time professional fees	24,800	30,000
Contingency	36,000	
	$1,000,000	48,600

The specific assumptions for the financing of the tax-exempt bonds are listed as follows:

1. The interest rate on the bonds will be no more than 80 percent of the floating prime rate. It is assumed that the average interest rate will be 11 percent or approximately 80 percent of the current 13.75 percent prime rate.

2. The bonds are to be issued on August 1, 1984.

3. Principal payments will be made semiannually in ten equal installments of $100,000 over a period of five years, commencing on February 1, 1985 and concluding on August 1, 1989.

4. Interest payments will be made quarterly, based on the principal balance existing on the bonds at the beginning of the period commencing November 1, 1984 and concluding August 1, 1989.

5. The three hospitals have a beginning equity of $105,000 at the end of 1983.

Nevertheless, the need for a body scanner in the area was quite high. Cancer mortality statistics provided by the Health Planning Association (HPA) studies indicated that cancer was the second leading cause of deaths in Tri-City and the surrounding areas. The average mortality rate (deaths per 100,000 population) for the area was 175.62, which was 2 percent above the state average and 5 percent above the national average. Trend analysis of deaths in the area paints a much gloomier picture. The mortality rates for malignant neoplasms have been increasing over the past seven years. A goal of HPA was to reduce the cancer mortality rate in the area.

The survival rates for common cancers are greatly improved if they are detected and treated in the early stages of development. Based upon the available technical information, CT-scanners detect malignant neoplasms earlier than any other diagnostic procedure, including X-rays, and increase the chances of patients' recovery. It is therefore reasonable to believe that the availability of a CT-scanner for patients' use would help achieve the HPA goal of arresting or slowing down the rate of growth of cancer mortality in the area through earlier detection and treatment. In addition, the availability of technologically advanced medical equipment could attract additional and better qualified medical personnel to the area.

Mrs. Stranan, a member of the ad hoc committee, a sociology instructor at the local community college, and a prominent member of the community, summed up the feelings of many of the area residents when she stated that the community area hospitals have a moral obligation to provide the most modern medical services to local area patients. According to Mrs. Stranan, no costs were too high when it came to saving lives; therefore, she indicated that she would fully support a joint acquisition of the scanner by the area hospitals. Mr. Paul Goenka, a local industrialist and another member of the committee, was not sure the scanner or any other medical services should be provided at *any* cost. While he believed strongly in the sanctity of human life, he wondered whether there is any cost limit at which the family or society should reconsider the decision to prolong a human life through medical means.

Exhibit 2 Service area population

	1970	1980	Percent Change 1970–1980	Projected 1985	Percent Change 1980–1985
Primary Service Area					
Windsor County	75,909	80,506	6.1	82,662	2.7
Secondary Service Area					
Dennison County	37,099	37,409	0.8	37,532	0.3
Georgia County	60,983	62,230	2.0	62,678	0.7
Chesop County	49,587	49,798	0.4	49,754	(0.1)
Total Secondary	147,669	149,437	1.2	149,964	0.4
Total Primary and Secondary	223,578	229,943	2.8	232,626	1.2

Area Analysis

There are no CT-scanners in any of the four counties of Windsor, Dennison, Georgia, and Chesop. Consequently, patients needing CT-scanner services must travel seventy miles to the cities of Radner to the east, Diskey to the south, or Carmen to the west. If a CT-scanner were to be located in the Tri-City area, patients would have to travel only twelve to fifteen miles at the most (Exhibits 2 and 3).

Exhibit 3   Area hospital statistics, 1983

	Number of Acute Care Beds	Number of Admissions
Primary Service Area		
Windsor County		
Lakeshore Hospital	134	4,901
General Hospital	166	6,269*
St. Vincent's Hospital	209	7,770
Total Primary Service Area	509	18,940
Secondary Service Area		
Dennison County		
Dennison Lakeshore Hospital	94	2,882
Georgia County		
Lakeshore Hospital of Georgia County	180*	7,242*
Georgia General Hospital	68*	1,997*
Chesop County		
Chesop Lakeshore Hospital	112*	4,374*
County General Hospital	74	2,818
Total Secondary Service Area	528	19,313
Total Primary and Secondary Service Areas	1,037	38,253

*Source: *AHA Guide to the Health Care Field,* various editions. Other data from hospital records.

	Number of Radiology Procedures		
	Diagnostic X-Ray Procedures	Diagnostic Ultrasound Procedures	Diagnostic Radionuclide Procedures
General Hospital	24,422	465	1,786
St. Vincent's Hospital	35,360	234	4,461
Lakeshore Hospital	27,785	408	1,116
Total	87,567	1,107	7,363

Source: Hospitals' records.

At present, 71 percent of patients in the three Tri-City hospitals come from Windsor County, covering a geographic area of approximately 300 square miles. The secondary service area, covering approximately 1,000 square miles, consists of Chesop County to the east, Georgia County to the south, and Dennison County to the west and north. These counties provide about 24 percent of the total hospitals' admissions (Exhibit 4).

ORGANIZATIONAL STRUCTURE AND LOCATION

The ad hoc committee initially wrestled with deciding what type of organizational format was needed to undertake the project. It was not clear to the committee whether such a service-oriented collective investment should be undertaken under a cooperative format or as a business corporation. But the committee was clear on one thing. The joint acquisition of a scanner must result in eliminating duplication and minimizing costs to patients in the area. In addition, the format should facilitate quick approval of the certificate of need that must be submitted to the State Department of Health for approval. The certificate of need program was instituted by several states primarily to try to control escalating health costs by eliminating duplication of equipment purchases in the same geographic area. After considerable discussion the committee decided to adopt a cooperative format.

The committee also had to decide on the scanner location within the Tri-City area. Although locating the scanner in any one of the three member hospitals would save some money on building and related costs, the committee did not want to displease the other two member hospitals. A large shopping center located in the center of the city and possessing the requisite parking space was chosen for the scanner location. The shopping center location was ideal because it was within two miles of the member hospitals. Moreover, space needs of the project (about 1,600 square feet) were readily available for lease.

Exhibit 4   Patient origin, Tri-City Hospitals

	Percent of Admissions
Windsor County	
Tri-City	55
Other Windsor County	16
Total Primary Service Area	71
Dennison County	6
Georgia County	12
Chesop County	6
Total Secondary Service Area	24
All other areas	5
Total All Areas	100

ESTIMATED REVENUES AND EXPENSES

Revenues and Fees

Information provided by the Blue Cross/Blue Shield Company allowed a rate structure to be established. These rates were based on rates charged at other CT-scanner installations.

Head Scan $210.00

Head Scan with Contrast $220.00

Body Scan $245.00

Body Scan with Contrast $250.00

It was estimated that an average charge for a CT-scan would be approximately $220. This average was expected to increase by about 5–7 percent a year over the next four-year period. Any additional charges for hospitalized patients would be billed to the respective hospital, and similar charges for nonhospitalized patients would be billed to referring physicians or patients. Professional fees for supervision and interpretation of CT-scanning examinations would be privately billed by the physician to the patient or his or her insurer.

Provisions for losses on noncollectible patient accounts and charity write-offs were assumed to be approximately 4 percent of total operating revenues. This percentage was based upon a detailed analysis of each hospital's patient revenues after they were categorized by financial class and source of payment.

Staffing Requirements

Staffing requirements were based upon existing staffing patterns at other CT-scanner installations. It was determined that two full-time (2,080 hours per year) radiologic technicians, a full-time clerical assistant, and an executive director would be permanently needed to run the facility. For the year 1984 however, each technician will work approximately 1,000 hours per year. A part-time radiologic technician will be added in the beginning of the third year and will work approximately 910 hours per year. A provision for an administrative salary expense of $1,000 per month for the executive director (honorarium) should also be included in the staffing budget. Forecasted salaries and wages were based upon wage rates in effect for similar job descriptions in Tri-City area hospitals ($4.50 per hour for clerical personnel and $16 per hour for radiologic technicians for 1984) and were assumed to increase by 6–7 percent annually during the forecast period. However, no change in the amount of honorarium paid was anticipated during the four-year period.

Other Benefits and Fees

The estimated fringe benefits included FICA, medical and hospitalization insurance, group life insurance, workers' compensation, and pension contributions. Fringe benefit expenses and annual increases were based upon health care industry trends. These expenses were assumed to approximate 15 percent of total salaries and wages, excluding administrative salary expense.

Professional fees, primarily for accounting and legal services, were estimated to be $8,000 per year based upon services to be rendered and on existing arrangements with the member hospitals. These fees were expected to remain constant through the four-year period except for a 9 percent annual inflation increase. In addition, professional fees for planning, consulting and legal work of $24,800 during the first year and $30,000 during the second year will be incurred.

Supplies and Lease Expenses

Supplies (mainly forms for patient billing and transcription, films, and CT tube replacement) were projected to be $7,860 for the first year and respectively $29,960, $46,680 and $50,880 for the second, third and fourth years. These estimates were based upon information of current and assumed changes in price levels, as provided by representatives of the supplier company and the executive director.

Maintenance contract and tube replacements were estimated at approximately $9,520, $80,150, $160,360 and $174,790 for the four years. The lease arrangement for the forecast period includes utilization of 1,600 square feet of space at $3.50 per square foot a year, with no annual increases. To allow ample time to make necessary improvements to the facility, the lease will commence on April 1 of the first year.

Miscellaneous Expenses

Utility, janitorial and other miscellaneous expenses (mainly insurance) were estimated to be $11,280 for the first year and $20,250, $22,360 and $24,680 for the second through fourth years. Estimates of utility expenses were based on the projected area utility rates, which in turn were based upon the estimated consumption levels as well as potential rate increases. Rate increases were assumed to average 12 percent per year during the forecast period. Estimates of a maintenance contract for janitorial services and insurance expenses were based upon current price agreements and on discussions with insurance carriers. Annual inflation increases of 9 percent were assumed during the forecast period.

Patients' billing and transcription expenses were estimated to be $4,560, $17,390, $27,080 and $29,520 for the four years.

Depreciation charges for the years 1984 through 1987 were estimated to be $69,250, $166,200, $166,200 and $166,200 and leasehold improvement amortization for the years were calculated at $11,080, $26,600, $26,600 and $26,600.

FORECASTED UTILIZATION

The HPA document entitled "Project Review Manual Criteria, Radiology Service— CT-scanning (Nonreplacement Applications)," provides guidelines for establishing a

CT-scanner in a hospital. The guidelines state that an applicant for a CT-scanner, in order to be considered as financially viable, shall offer diagnostic X-ray examination services, diagnostic ultrasound scanning services, and diagnostic radionuclide imaging services as well as currently performing 30,000 diagnostic X-ray examinations. The three Tri-City member hospitals performed 87,567 X-ray examinations in 1983. Additionally, in the publication *Modern Healthcare* (September 1980) it was noted that of the hospitals with 500 beds or more, 99 percent had CT-scanners; and 75 percent of hospitals with 400 or more beds had the same equipment. The three Tri-City hospitals have a total bed complement of 509 beds. The secondary service area hospitals have an additional 528 beds. Assuming only 50 percent of these secondary service area beds (and thereby service area patients) were to use the Tri-City CT-scanner, it appears that the need was clearly present for a CT-scanner installation.

Manufacturers of CT-scanners have also developed a methodology for determining potential CT utilization over a period of time. The General Electric's Leonard Need Methodology appeared to predict the usage rate very well. Specifically, the Second Regional Program Plan for Computed Tomographic (CT) Scanning Services prepared by the CT-scanning monitoring committee for the executive committee and board of directors of the Central New York Health Systems Agency, Inc., in February 1980 states:

> By January, 1980, over 100 hospitals had been processed through the Leonard Methodology. In these applications, the model appeared to predict actual performance within 10 percent of actual levels. It should be noted that the model predicts performance with full-body, latest-generation scanners.

Exhibit 5 contains data relating to the CT-scanner utilization. The estimated usage rate was based on several assumptions: (1) contrast material would be utilized in approximately 70 percent of the total head and body scans, (2) head scans would comprise approximately 60 percent of total scans, and (3) no additional CT-scanners would be installed in the surrounding service area in the next four years.

Exhibit 5   Estimated utilization

Years Ending December 31	Head Scans			Body Scans			Total Number of Procedures
	Without Contrast	With Contrast	Total	Without Contrast	With Contrast	Total	
1984	150	350	500	90	210	300	800
1985	300	1,380	1,680	340	780	1,120	2,800
1986	720	1,680	2,400	480	1,120	1,600	4,000
1987	720	1,680	2,400	480	1,120	1,600	4,000

Note: The annual estimated utilization figures are based on the estimates given by a consultant to the committee. The consultant gave three sets of figures for three different states of economy—high, medium, and low—but the committee selected only the low estimates, which are given here.

CT-SCANNER RECOMMENDATION

The chairperson and the members of the committee must now decide what recommendation to make to the member hospitals, and more importantly, to the patients in the area. There was little disagreement among members concerning need due to the high incidence of cancer in the area and the need for early diagnosis and treatment. Although forming an ad hoc committee to study the feasibility of acquiring a CT-scanner was a step in the right direction, it was not clear whether the three hospitals would give up their independence and agree to share the scanner facility under a cooperative or any other organizational format.

The Committee must address some special concerns in making its recommendation. For example, what if forecasted utilization rates fail to materialize? What impact would the failure of a joint investment have on the general financial health of each of the hospitals? Specifically, do these area hospitals have sufficient financial reserves or income-generating ability to service the debt? Would the city government or local communities come to their rescue in the event of financial failure? Even if it was assumed that the hospitals could jointly finance the project by borrowing, and service the debt with ease, how should the committee evaluate the scanner acquisition decision? These hospitals are not-for-profit organizations. Should the committee use the standard capital budgeting techniques of payback, and internal rate of return (IRR) criteria or use a predetermined discount rate to determine the project's acceptability? What discount rate is appropriate? What if the payback is longer than four years? What if traditional capital budgeting approaches indicate rejection of the scanner acquisition? Are the hospitals then morally bound to provide the latest medical services to area patients even at the risk of bankruptcy or financial insecurity?

The committee's task is to review all these possibilities and make specific recommendations concerning the scanner acquisition. The committee would like to utilize strategic planning concepts and techniques in making its decision.

CASE 32

Mary Kay Cosmetics, Inc.

FRED DAVID
Auburn University

KATIE KEMP
Livingston University

INTRODUCTION

"Aerodynamically, the bumblebee shouldn't be able to fly," says Mary Kay. "But the bumblebee doesn't know it, so it goes on flying anyway." A gold and diamond-studded bumblebee pin is Mary Kay's favorite award for the hundreds of female sales executives who are flying to success. The analogy lies in the fact that against such giants as Avon and Revlon, this Dallas-based firm should not be able to fly—to compete in the saturated cosmetics industry. However, like the bumblebee, Mary Kay saleswomen do not know this and many continue to fly anyway.

For the years 1972–1983, net sales at Mary Kay increased from $17 million to over $323 million. Net income for the same period increased from $2.5 million to over $36 million. However, Mary Kay's sales and profits leveled off in 1983 and then declined dramatically in 1984. One might ask what factors have contributed to Mary Kay's past success? More importantly, what should Mary Kay do now to regain its competitive position?

THE COSMETICS INDUSTRY

The personal care products industry had enjoyed steady growth for two decades, largely as a result of women entering or reentering the work force. However, in 1982, industry sales flattened and even declined a bit in certain product areas. A recessionary period might be expected to have this effect on nonessentials such as cosmetics, toiletries, and fragrances. But even when the economy began to improve in 1983, the industry continued to suffer.

All product areas were not affected by the industry trend. Skin-care products maintained solid growth during the early 1980s. Industry analysts were predicting continued growth because of the heightened need for products designed to manage aging skin, as the average age of females in the population increased. Customers seemed to turn away from medium-priced products during the period. Industry analysts reported that consumers were buying either more expensive goods or switching to generic, low-priced products. For example, luxury brands such as Chesebrough–Pond's Erno Laslo, on the one hand, and Noxell Corporation's low-priced Cover Girl on the other, were successful in 1983. However, midpriced products in the cosmetics industry experienced a decline in sales and profits during the early 1980s.

Some of the reasons for the decline were apparent. A tightening economy caused consumers to reduce in-home inventories of personal-care items. The rate at which women were entering the work force declined. And there was a leveling in the population growth rate of twenty-five to forty-four-year-old women, who had typically been the heaviest users of cosmetics.

Avon Products and Mary Kay, the two big names in direct selling of personal care products, had an additional problem during this period. Both companies depend heavily on recruiting new independent representatives in order to grow, and declines in recruitment as well as high rates of turnover resulted in lost customers and sales. The problem seemed to stem from two major contributing factors: (1) the nation's declining unemployment rate, and (2) a significant increase in the number of direct sales companies. The increasing employment rate reduced both the amount of time available for direct selling and the number of new recruits interested in selling. Industry analysts expect some improvement in cosmetic sales in the mid-1980s—if the economic recovery continues.

COMPANY HISTORY

Mary Kay Cosmetics, Inc. was founded in Dallas, Texas in 1963 by Mary Kay Ash, chairman of the board, and her son, Richard R. Rogers, president. Mary Kay had previously had successful careers with Stanley Home Products and World Gift Company, both direct-sales companies. She resigned from her position as World Gift's national training director after a policy dispute. As a way of venting frustration, she decided to write down everything she knew about direct sales—the good and the bad. She ended up with a long list of problems that women in business have. Mary Kay dreamed of starting a company that could give women an unlimited opportunity for success.

Mary Kay had used an excellent skin cream produced locally by the granddaughter of a tanner. She bought the old tanner's formula and used it as the original basis for her skin-care line. Armed with the idea that there was opportunity in the cosmetics industry for personalized, professional instruction in the proper use of skin-care and makeup products, Mary Kay Cosmetics began operations on Friday, the 13th of September, 1963. The original sales force was made up of ten hand-picked Beauty Consultants trained personally by Mrs. Ash. The firm had a total capital base of $5,000 and one shelf of cosmetics.

The venture represented the best of the ideas Mary Kay had gathered over the years. From Stanley Home Products she borrowed the house-party technique, except that the "party" was limited to no more than six participants. Other innovative ideas employed included the highest commissions paid in the direct-sales field. No fixed territories were assigned, and she instituted a system of incentives for recruiting new salespeople. Products were packaged in pink and gold, and pink continues to be an identifying characteristic of Mary Kay products.

Mary Kay has described her success as "gradual, based on the fact that I give women the ultimate chance to do whatever they are smart enough to do. I believe you can praise people to success." Her personal touch in the company has proven to be a big asset. For example, she personally designs a birthday card to be sent to each of the independent consultants each year; she learns associates' names and rarely gets one wrong; she personally signs correspondence; and she does not allow any form of prejudice in the organization.

The first year of operation closed with $198,000 in retail sales; the second with $800,000. By the end of the 1960s, the small regional company was generating sales of approximately $6 million. During the 1970s, Mary Kay concentrated on geographic expansion with the opening of four major distribution centers in Los Angeles, Atlanta, Chicago, and Piscataway, New Jersey. The sales organization grew to approximately 70,000 beauty consultants and 1,400 sales directors. Mary Kay products were distributed in every state in the United States and throughout Canada and Australia.

In 1980, Mary Kay began operations in Argentina. In a spectacular era of growth, Mary Kay grew from 44,000 consultants in 1978 to 194,586 in 1983. The company's net sales increased from $53.7 million to over $323 million during the same period, with profits growing from $4.8 million to over $36.6 million. However, Mary Kay's rate of growth in sales and profits came almost to a halt in 1982 and 1983. Then, during 1984, Mary Kay experienced an 8 percent decline in net income and a 14 percent decline in sales. The number of beauty consultants dropped to 151,615.

ORGANIZATION/THE MANAGEMENT TEAM

Mary Kay is a "participative management organization" in that everyone is responsible for the quality of the product. The atmosphere of the company is very relaxed; the chairman of the board is known as Mary Kay instead of Mrs. Ash. The organization of the firm consists of upper management personnel, national sales directors, sales directors, and beauty consultants. A policy of promotion from within exists in the company. An organizational chart of Mary Kay Cosmetics, Inc. is provided in Exhibit 1.

CORPORATE PHILOSOPHY

Mary Kay Cosmetics, Inc. is in the business of producing and marketing cosmetics. Sales are by independent beauty consultants and sales directors, trained to service the need of the individual consumer for skin care and makeup instruction. Purchasers of Mary Kay "try before buying" through participation in demonstrations given in the privacy of their homes in the United States, Australia, Canada, and Argentina. The firm bases its operations on four principles: proven products, a commitment to quality,

Exhibit 1 Mary Kay Cosmetics, Inc.'s organizational chart

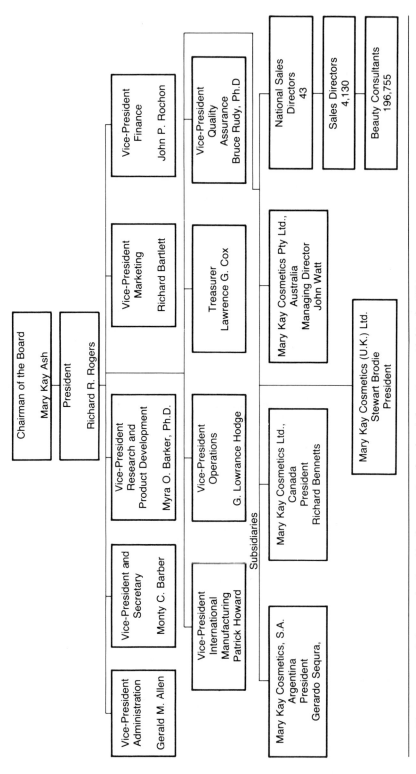

Note: This organizational chart was developed by the case writers based on information provided in the 1984 *Annual Report*, pp. 31, 32.

personalized service and instruction, and a marketing plan through which proficient independent beauty consultants achieve success by recruiting and building their own sales organizations. The corporate mission for the 1980s is to be the finest teaching-oriented skin care organization in the world. Mrs. Ash's personal philosophy—God first, family second, career third, and the Golden Rule—serves as the basis for the corporation's philosophy. (Note: A copy of Mary Kay's mission statement is given in Chapter 3.)

PRODUCT LINE

Mary Kay has a product line consisting of glamour items, toiletries, fragrances, hair-care products and a line of skin- and body-care products. A basic skin-care program, consisting of five products, accounts for approximately 50 percent of the company's annual sales volume. Mary Kay's Five Steps to Beauty—cleanse, stimulate, freshen, moisturize, and protect—include scientifically based products for virtually every type of healthy skin.

Mary Kay offers special products and services at special times of the year. For example, skin screen products are offered in the summer, special moisturizers to prevent dry skin are offered in the winter, and a selection of holiday limited-edition fragrance gift items are offered during holiday seasons. In the fall and spring, Mary Kay issues its biannual *Fashion Forecast*, featuring timely new glamour products in the latest fashion shades. Mary Kay also offers a line of men's skin-care and fragrance products, which account for one to two percent of annual sales.

Mary Kay's product line is purposely limited. In the last five years the number of regular line items has grown less than 10 percent. As a result, the company has been able to establish manufacturing efficiencies in terms of economies of scale, length of manufacturing runs, and automated processing and purchasing. In addition, consultants are able to be totally familiar with the entire line. They also are able to keep adequate stocks of inventory because of the limited product line and can deliver purchases to the customer at the point of sale. Over the past few years, Mary Kay has introduced hair-care products and expanded the number of skin-care products; in 1983 the Company introduced four body-care products. Several products were deleted in conjunction with these additions, leaving the total number in the product line at approximately fifty. Average prices of products increased 10 percent in 1982, 7 percent in 1983, and 4 percent in 1984. Exhibit 2 provides a listing of Mary Kay's basic product offerings and their 1984 prices. A breakdown of Mary Kay's sales by product type is provided in Exhibit 3.

More than 80 percent of Mary Kay's research and development budget goes to improving and testing the existing product line to ensure that products are manufactured to the highest quality standards and are packaged for the strongest market appeal. The company offers a money-back guarantee with each product sold. Mary Kay's laboratories are staffed with teams of experts in cosmetic chemistry, dermatology, physiol-

Exhibit 2 Mary Kay Cosmetics, Inc.'s price list

ITEM	PRICE	✓
Complete Collection (Personalized)	*	
Basic Skin Care plus Basic Glamour	$81.00	
Basic Skin Care	43.00	
Basic Skin Care Replacement Items	*	
CLEANSE		
Cleansing Cream Formula 1, 4 oz.	7.00	
Cleansing Cream Formula 2, 4 oz.	7.00	
Cleanser Formula 3, 3.75 oz.	7.00	
STIMULATE		
Magic Masque Formula 1, 4 Oz.	8.50	
Magic Masque Formula 2, 4 oz.	8.50	
FRESHEN		
Skin Freshener Formula 1, 6.75 oz.	8.50	
Skin Freshener Formula 2, 6.75 oz.	8.50	
MOISTURIZE		
Night Cream Formula 1, 4 oz.	12.50	
Night Cream Fromula 2, 4 oz.	12.50	
Moisturizer, 2.8 oz.	12.50	
PROTECT		
Day Radiance Formula 1, .5 oz.	6.50	
Day Radiance Formula 2, 1 oz.	6.50	
☐ Porcelain Ivory ☐ Sunlit Beige		
☐ Misty Ivory ☐ Desert Bronze		
☐ Creamy Ivory ☐ Burnished Bronze		
☐ Sheer Beige ☐ Deep Bronze		
☐ Natural Beige ☐ White		
☐ Rose Beige ☐ Yellow		
☐ Honey Beige		
GLAMOUR COLLECTION		
Blush Rouge	4.50	
Blusher	9.00	
☐ Pinks ☐ Berries		
☐ Peaches		
Translucent Pressed Powder	9.00	
☐ Sheer Ivory ☐ Soft Topaz		

ITEM	PRICE	✓
Eyebrow Pencil	$ 4.00	
☐ Soft Black ☐ Light Brown		
☐ Brown ☐ Blonde		
Eyeliner	6.00	
☐ Black ☐ Brown		
Conditioning Mascara	6.00	
☐ Black ☐ Brown		
Waterproof Mascara	6.00	
☐ Black ☐ Brown		
Lip and Eye Compact	17.50	
(With lip palette, eye palette, and 2 brushes)		
Lip Compact	15.50	
(With 2 lip palettes and a lip brush)		
Eye Compact	15.50	
(With 2 eye palettes and an eye brush)		
Retractable Lip or Eye Brush	2.00	
Glamour Blending Brush	2.00	
Lip or Eye Palette Refill	5.00	
Great Fashion™ Lip Color Shade Selections:		
☐ Reds ☐ Roses		
☐ Corals ☐ Spices		
☐ Russets ☐ Plums		
Great Fashion™ Eye Shadow Shade Selections:		
☐ Greens ☐ Browns		
☐ Blues ☐ Highlighters		
☐ Plums		
Lip Liner Pencils	4.50	
☐ Golden Raisin ☐ Red Currant		
Eye Defining Pencils	4.50	
☐ Sable ☐ Navy		
☐ Slate ☐ Grape		
Lip Gloss	5.00	

ALL PRICES ARE SUGGESTED RETAIL. ADD SALES TAX WHERE APPLICABLE. Mary Kay, Intrigue, Angelfire, Avenir, Mr. K, ReVeur, Exquisite, Day Radiance and Magic Masque are registered trademarks of Mary Kay Cosmetics, Inc.

ITEM	PRICE	✓
SPECIALIZED SKIN CARE		
Moisturizer, 2.8 oz.	$12.50	
Hand Cream, 2.8 oz.	6.00	
Facial/Under Makeup Sun Screen, 2.7 Oz.	7.50	
BODY CARE		
Cleansing Gel, 8 oz.	7.50	
Buffing Cream, 6 oz.	8.00	
Moisturizing Lotion, 8 oz.	7.00	
Sun Screening Lotion, 6 oz.	9.00	
BASIC HAIR CARE		
Shampoo for Normal/Dry Hair, 8 oz.	5.00	
Shampoo for Oily Hair, 8 oz.	5.00	
Protein Conditioner, 8 oz.	7.00	
Intense Conditioner, 3 oz.	8.00	
Non-Aerosol Hair Spray, 8 oz.	5.00	
FRAGRANCE BOUTIQUE		
Avenir Spray Cologne, 2 oz.	16.00	
Angelfire Spray Cologne, 1.75 oz.	14.00	
Intrigue Spray Cologne, 1.75 oz.	12.00	
Exquisite Body Lotion, 8 oz.	7.00	
MEN'S PRODUCTS		
Mr. K Skin Care System	37.50	
Cleanser, 2.7 oz.	5.00	
Mask, 2.6 oz.	7.50	
Toner, 2.6 oz.	5.50	
Moisture Balm, 2.5 oz.	12.00	
Sun Screen, 2.7 oz.	7.50	
Tamerisk™ Cologne, 4 oz.	16.50	
ReVeur After Shave Cologne, 3.75 oz.	12.00	
Mr. K Cologne, 3.75 oz.	11.00	
Mr. K Lotion, 3.4 oz.	5.00	

*Price varies from $150.50–$157.00 according to your Specialized Skin Care needs.

Source: Mary Kay Cosmetics, Inc. 1984 sales literature.

Exhibit 3   Analysis of sales by product type

		1979	1980	1981	1982	1983	1984
Skin care products for women		49%	52%	49%	46%	44%	46%
Skin care products for men		1	2	1	1	1	1
Makeup items		26	22	26	26	30	28
Toiletry items for women		10	10	10	12	11	11
Toiletry items for men		2	2	2	2	2	2
Hair care		2	2	2	2	2	2
Accessories		10	10	10	11	10	10
	Total	100%	100%	100%	100%	100%	100%

Source: Mary Kay Cosmetics, Inc., *1984 Annual Report*, p. 23.

ogy, biochemistry, toxicology, microbiology, analytical chemistry, process technology and package engineering. Mary Kay is an industry leader in two research areas: 1) biophysical properties of the skin, which encompass such factors as skin elasticity and moisturization and 2) anatomical and structural qualities of the skin. Much of the research is conducted in cooperation with academic institutions and the American Academy of Dermatology.

MARKETING/PROMOTION

Mary Kay's total market includes women, and to some extent men, from the United States, Canada, Australia, and Argentina. While marketing efforts are certainly not limited to any age person, a specifically targeted group includes women eighteen to thirty-four years of age.

According to some analysts, 90 percent of all women in the United States are aware of the Mary Kay brand of cosmetics. This degree of awareness has been enhanced by the vast amount of publicity the company receives. Mrs. Ash has appeared on several television talk shows such as *60 Minutes, The Phil Donahue Show, Today, Good Morning America,* and *Late Night with David Letterman.* Her success story, as well as the company's, has been told in periodicals such as *The Saturday Evening Post* and *Reader's Digest.* News magazines and newspapers across the United States give Mary Kay Cosmetics, Inc. a considerable amount of coverage.

Mrs. Ash's autobiography, published in 1981, resulted in more publicity and greater brand awareness for the company. *The Mary Kay Guide to Beauty* was published in 1983 in conjunction with the firm's twentieth anniversary. It was on best-seller lists for several weeks and was a featured selection of the Book of the Month Club. The company's beauty consultants use the book as a recruiting aid and as a supplement to their teaching efforts.

Mary Kay has historically depended a great deal on word-of-mouth advertising through its consultants, rather than spending amounts typical of the industry on television, magazine, and newspaper advertising. However, turnover is a significant factor in any direct-sales organization and 120,000 Mary Kay salespeople were fired or left the company during 1982. This represented an 80 percent turnover rate. When a salesperson quits, there is the likelihood that customers will be lost. Accordingly, Mary Kay has recently turned to television to attract customers.

In 1983, a television advertising campaign costing over $6 million was instituted to promote the cosmetics, advise past and future customers that Mary Kay sales directors are listed in the Yellow Pages, and to boost the company's image. The theme of the campaign was, "Because every skin is different, you need skin care that's different. You need Mary Kay." The idea was also used in Mary Kay's magazine advertisements. For example, an ad in the March 8, 1983 issue of *Woman's Day* (p. 26) used the above-mentioned theme as a headline and included a picture of three women of varying ages and complexions. The advertisement read as follows:

> The very things that make your skin unique make it necessary to care for your skin a special way. Factors such as your age and hormone balance. Your environment and exposure to the sun. As well as your skin's natural oil production and moisture-retention ability. Together, they make your skin unlike any other.
>
> Mary Kay is specially formulated for your individual skin type. While all skins have the same basic needs, every skin has special needs, too. After years of research, a variety of Mary Kay skin care products has been scientifically formulated to bring out the vibrant qualities of your skin. Whether it's dry. Normal. Or oily.
>
> We don't just tell you about skin care. We teach you. At Mary Kay, we believe the best way to learn about skin care is through personal instruction. That's why you'll work closely with a professional Mary Kay Beauty Consultant. You'll learn about Mary Kay's Five Steps to Beauty, a total skin care system based on products that work together to make your skin naturally radiant.
>
> Every woman wants to look as good as she can. So it makes sense to start caring for your skin as soon as you can. And stay with it.
>
> The right beauty regimen with the right products is the closest thing yet to keeping your youthful look. That's why the more you care about your skin, the more you need Mary Kay.

THE MARY KAY SALES FORCE

The Mary Kay sales force consists of four major levels of independent contractors: beauty consultants, sales directors, senior sales directors, and national sales directors. Everyone in the sales force starts as a beauty consultant, and promotions are based entirely on performance.

A typical Mary Kay consultant is a woman between twenty-five and forty-four years of age, a little above middle income, with some college background. Mary Kay's sales force experiences an average 80 percent turnover per year; this figure compares with a 150+ percent annual turnover rate at Avon. Rogers estimates that only about 60,000 of the 195,000 consultants are actively productive. As indicated in Exhibit 4, the average annual productivity of Mary Kay's salespeople has been erratic, declining from $1,757 to $1,603 between 1982 and 1984.

The job of a beauty consultant is two-fold: (1) sell products and (2) recruit new consultants, and the salesperson's compensation reflects both of these duties. New consultants are trained on the job by their recruiter, and no previous selling experience is required. The initial investment and risk associated with becoming a Mary Kay consultant are relatively low. Requirements include the purchase of a Beauty Consultant Showcase ($80) and an adequate inventory of fifteen basic products. Recruits are advised not to take any sales revenues as profit until a minimum of $2,000 wholesale has been ordered. The national average for sales at a Mary Kay beauty show (party) is $130. Therefore, the consultant must reinvest revenues from approximately fifteen shows before actually showing a profit.

When a beauty consultant decides to permanently terminate her association with Mary Kay, the company will buy back all inventory at 90 percent of the wholesale price paid. She may, however, temporarily become "inactive" and choose not to return her inventory. An example of the recruiting materials used by consultants when introducing Mary Kay to prospective salespersons is provided in Exhibit 5.

According to Dick Bartlett, vice-president of marketing, the major point of difference between Mary Kay and competitors is that Mary Kay's compensation and promotion program is one of the most generous in the direct-selling industry. Consultants buy Mary Kay products at discounts ranging from 40 percent of the retail selling price on a minimum $200 order up to 50 percent on an order over $1000.

Exhibit 4   Consultants' productivity—1979 to 1984

	Average Number of Consultants	Average Annual Productivity	Net Sales (in $000)
1984	173,101	$1,603	$277,500
1983	195,671	1,655	323,758
1982	173,137	1,757	304,275
1981	134,831	1,745	235,296
1980	94,983	1,758	166,938
1979	57,989	1,576	91,400

Source: Mary Kay Cosmetics, Inc., *1984 Annual Report,* p. 21.

Exhibit 5 Mary Kay's recruiting/commission schedule

I'd Like to Share
The Opportunity With You

There Are Five Ways to Earn Money in Your Mary Kay Career!

1. Beauty shows
   (50% . . . the highest direct sales commission paid in the United States. An average show is approximately $85–$100).
   • Attendance ranges from 3–6 people.
   • A beauty show with driving time is approximately 3 hours. (You may choose to call them Skin Care Classes—much more professional.)

2. Reorders (50%)
   • Our product is consumable like sugar or bread, so reorders become a large part of our income.
   • An average customer (using the five steps to beauty and a few glamour items) will reorder approximately $40–$80 within a year.
   • A part-time consultant building and taking care of only 100 customers will see approximately $4,000–$8000 retail sales within a year in this area of income.

3. Dovetail
   • (15% . . . when unable to hold a show another consultant will hold it and pay this dovetail fee to the consultant who actually booked the show.)
   • This area of income gives us the freedom to put our family before our business.
   • This area of income also gives us the opportunity to double book.

4. Recruiting
   • This is paid directly from the company in the form of a bonus check. It is never taken out of the new recruit's pocket.
   • This will continue for as long as the recruit and the recruiter are active with Mary Kay Cosmetics.
     4% . . . 1, 2, 3, 4, qualified recruits
     5% . . . 5 qualified recruits
     6% . . . 6 qualified recruits
     7% . . . 7 qualified recruits
     8% . . . 8 or more qualified recruits

5. Directorship
   • 13% director commission is paid to the unit director from the company based upon the unit's monthly wholesale production. It comes in the form of a bonus check . . . never taken from the consultant's pocket.
   • To become a director, these qualifications must be met: (1) six months service with Mary Kay Cosmetics, (2) $6000 in retail sales over nine months, and (3) twelve qualified recruits.

IMPORTANT FACTS YOU WILL WANT TO KNOW: NO QUOTAS, NO TERRITORIES, LOTS OF TRAINING!!

1. Tax benefits
   - Automobile costs–25 cents per mile.
   - House payment or rental—a portion for a separate room as an office.
   - Utilities—a portion to heat and light that office.
   - Telephone—a portion of base and all Mary Kay long distance calls.
   - Entertainment—when relating to Mary Kay.
   - Vacations—can do business anywhere.
   - Babysitter.
   - Office supplies, etc.

2. Investment
   - $75 beauty case that is tax deductible.

3. Inventory—You decide
   It's a proven fact that when having on the spot delivery, sales are higher, all of the education of teaching skin care is retained, and it makes our career much easier!
   If you choose to start with inventory, you will decide how much you want to start with.

   Buy back guarantee: If for some unforeseen reason, the consultant must terminate her association with Mary Kay Cosmetics, she can return her unused products to Mary Kay, and she will be reimbursed 90% of what she paid for the merchandise.

Mary Kay's beauty consultants receive a commission based on the wholesale prices of products purchased by other beauty consultants whom they personally have recruited. This recruiting commission schedule is as follows:

Number of Recruits	Percent of Recruit's Wholesale Order
4 or less consultants (whether or not active recruits)	4
5 Active consultants	5
6 Active consultants	6
7 Active consultants	7
8 or more Active consultants	8

Mary Kay's commissions provide an incentive for consultants to recruit as well as sell. There are no territories to limit where a beauty consultant may sell or recruit. To remain "active," a consultant must place a minimum order of $120 wholesale every three months.

The qualifications for directorship are six months service with Mary Kay, $6,000 in retail sales over a nine-month period, and twelve qualified recruits. Sales directors receive a commission on their total unit's wholesale purchases. The commission schedule is as follows:

Monthly Wholesale Production	Commission
$ 0.00 - $ 2,999.99	9%
$ 3,000.00 - $ 4,999.99	10%
$ 5,000.00 - $ 7,999.99	11%
$ 8,000.00 - $11,999.99	12%
$12,000.00 or more	13%

Sales directors can receive additional compensation and awards that include a $100–$400 bonus each month based on (1) total unit wholesale purchases or (2) the number of new qualified recruits in the unit. If a unit makes $36,000 in wholesale sales in each of two consecutive quarters, the sales director receives a pink Cadillac.

To qualify as a senior sales director, an individual must have motivated one of her recruits to fulfill all the requirements for sales director. In addition, she must have demonstrated consistently high personal sales. A senior sales director receives a 4 percent commission on the wholesale value of products sold by her sponsored sales director's unit, combined with all her own compensation as a sales director.

Becoming a national sales director is the highest level of achievement in the sales force at Mary Kay. All national sales director promotions are at the company's discretion, but the minimum requirements include the motivation of at least ten of the consultants in her group to become sales directors with a varying number of those ten developing new units. The compensation of a national sales director includes 3 to 7 percent of the wholesale value of products sold by her first-line units (units developed from her original unit) and two percent of the combined monthly wholesale volume of associated second-line units.

In an annual three-day seminar held in Dallas, Texas, Mary Kay's top salespeople are recognized and rewarded for their accomplishments. Rewards include 14K gold and diamond bumblebee pins with emerald eyes; mink coats; diamond rings and necklaces; all-expense-paid trips; $5,000 shopping sprees in Neiman–Marcus; and the use of a pink Cadillac, Buick Regal, or Oldsmobile Firenza. Mary Kay calls this their VIP Program. On December 31, 1984, 1700 beauty consultants were awarded the use of an Oldsmobile Firenza.

A LOOK AT MARY KAY'S TOP COMPETITORS

Avon

Although it is considered the leader in the cosmetics industry, Avon has fallen on hard times. As indicated in Exhibit 6, Avon's profit margin dropped 16 percent between 1982 and 1983. The company currently has 1.28 billion representatives around the world. Avon representatives are not as richly compensated as Mary Kay consultants.

Exhibit 6   Financial performances of selected personal care products companies in 1984 (in $000)

Company	Sales	Net Income	Number of Employees
Avon Products	$3,143,300	$181,700	38
Revlon	2,399,205	112,098	30
Gillette	2,288,600	159,300	31
Chesebrough–Ponds	1,857,330	119,529	25
International Flavors and Fragrances	476,000	69,242	3

Note: All five of these competitors are Fortune 500 firms.

Diminished productivity lies at the heart of Avon's problems. Customer service has headed downward since 1979 and increases in dollar sales per representative have lagged behind inflation. Another factor contributing to Avon's problems are difficulties with direct sales of their noncosmetic product lines. Sales for gifts, decorative items, and costume jewelry have all declined. Avon's target market is the lower and middle income level consumer.

Estee Lauder

Estee Lauder's target market is the middle- and upper-income-level woman. With the success of its Clinique product line and its new Night Repair lotion, Estee Lauder may now have the largest share of the $2.6 billion skin-care segment of the cosmetics business. Part of the Lauder success has been in their keen insights about people, products, and consumer trends. Estee Lauder has an estimated $1 billion in annual sales. The Company focuses primarily on more affluent women who shop in department stores. Estee Lauder is number one in the United States in department store cosmetic sales.

Revlon

Revlon experienced a significant decline in earnings in 1981. Revlon Chairman, Michel C. Bergerac, attributed this decrease to the rapid rise in the value of the dollar, which reduced the company's income overseas. Thirty-six percent of Revlon's sales are in foreign countries. As shown in Exhibit 6, Revlon is larger than Mary Kay, but not as large as Avon.

Whatever the major reasons for its slump in sales, Revlon will have to devise new strategies to survive in the 1980s. One plan is to introduce a $3.50 shampoo called Hair's Daily Requirement. A $25 million campaign is planned for 1984, which Revlon officials call "the biggest launch in the company's history." This introduction is projected to help put some life back into Revlon's sales, which rose less than 1 percent in the first nine months of 1983.

Exhibit 7   Consolidated balance sheets (December 31, 1981–1984)

	1984	1983	1982	1981
ASSETS				
Current assets:				
Cash and equivalents	$ 40,914,000	$ 26,831,000	$ 35,697,000	$ 7,953,000
Accounts and note receivable	1,116,000	1,765,000	1,010,000	2,715,000
Inventories:				
Raw materials	9,115,000	10,578,000	11,171,000	8,888,000
Finished goods	16,473,000	25,312,000	19,558,000	18,193,000
	25,588,000	35,890,000	30,729,000	27,081,000
Deferred income tax benefits	6,364,000	5,779,000	4,999,000	2,948,000
Other current assets	1,675,000	2,372,000	2,392,000	1,213,000
Total current assets	75,657,000	72,637,000	74,827,000	41,910,000
Property, plant, and equipment, at cost:				
Land	15,577,000	24,460,000	19,313,000	12,298,000
Buildings and improvements	46,919,000	31,316,000	28,293,000	23,869,000
Furniture, fixtures, and equipment	63,008,000	51,714,000	36,916,000	28,299,000
Construction in progress	24,864,000	20,923,000	7,783,000	4,829,000
	150,368,000	128,413,000	92,305,000	69,295,000
Less accumulated depreciation	29,350,000	21,008,000	15,044,000	10,519,000
	121,018,000	107,405,000	77,261,000	58,776,000
Other assets	879,000	641,000	369,000	290,000
	$197,554,000	$180,683,000	$152,457,000	$100,976,000
Note receivable	20,000,000			
	$217,554,000			
LIABILITIES AND STOCKHOLDERS' EQUITY				
Current liabilities:				
Note payable to bank	$ 535,000	$ 1,596,000	$ 1,110,000	$ 1,260,000
Accounts payable	12,214,000	12,061,000	10,704,000	8,061,000
Accrued liabilities	22,985,000	22,301,000	22,602,000	16,659,000
Income taxes	1,343,000	-0-	8,798,000	5,712,000
Deferred sales	934,000	1,879,000	4,662,000	1,321,000
Current portion on long-term debt	20,000	1,018,000	1,000,000	1,058,000
Total current liabilities	38,031,000	38,855,000	48,876,000	34,071,000
Long-term debt	3,826,000	3,915,000	4,669,000	2,366,000
Deferred income taxes	11,951,000	6,188,000	3,596,000	2,587,000
Stockholders' equity	163,746,000	131,725,000	95,316,000	61,952,000
	$217,554,000	$180,683,000	$152,457,000	$100,976,000

Source: Mary Kay Cosmetics, Inc. *Annual Report, 1984,* p. 25.

FINANCIAL INFORMATION

Mary Kay's 1984 financial statements reflect the disappointing performance of the firm during the year. While sales and earnings for 1983 established new company records, profit margins decreased from 1982's levels. Mary Kay's consolidated balance sheets for 1981, 1982, 1983, and 1984 are given in Exhibit 7. Mary Kay's income statements for 1981 through 1984 are provided in Exhibit 8. Net sales declined 14 percent in 1984. Net income declined 8 percent in 1984. Financial information by geographical area is presented in Exhibit 9.

FUTURE OUTLOOK FOR MARY KAY

What does the future hold for Mary Kay Cosmetics, Inc.? Leading company executives emphasize that future sales growth will depend primarily on the beauty consultant. Current statistics indicate that 30 percent of Mary Kay's consultants generate about 70 percent of its business. Furthermore, the supply of sales recruits could eventually run out. Therefore, management is increasingly concerned with raising the productivity and number of beauty consultants.

Mary Kay established a goal in 1980 of achieving sales exceeding $800 million a year during the decade of the 1980s and to become recognized as the leading teaching-oriented skin care company in the world. However, Mary Kay today is struggling to

Exhibit 8   Consolidated statements of income (years ended December 31, 1984, 1983, 1982, and 1981)

	1984	1983	1982	1981
Net sales	$277,500,000	$323,758,000	$304,275,000	$235,296,000
Cost of sales	79,867,000	88,960,000	87,807,000	71,100,000
Selling, general and administrative expenses	156,202,000	168,757,000	154,104,000	120,880,000
Operating income	41,431,000	66,041,000	62,364,000	43,316,000
Gain on sale of land	15,047,000	—	—	—
Interest and other income, net	3,802,000	3,734,000	2,763,000	1,485,000
Interest expense	5,273,000	2,886,000	1,284,000	1,014,000
Income before income taxes	55,007,000	66,889,000	63,843,000	43,787,000
Provision for income taxes	21,226,000	30,235,000	28,471,000	19,632,000
Net income	$ 33,781,000	$ 36,654,000	$ 35,372,000	$ 24,155,000
Net income per common and common equivalent share	$1.12	$1.22	$1.18	$ .82
Average common and common equivalent shares	30,230,000	30,138,000	29,894,000	29,324,000
Cash dividends per share		.12	.11	.10

Source: Mary Kay Cosmetics, Inc. *Annual Report, 1984.*

Exhibit 9   Domestic and foreign operations

	1984	1983	1982	1981
Net Sales	(in $000)			
United States				
To consultants	$254,751	$295,333	$277,681	$208,463
Interarea	1,747	2,771	2,623	6,503
	256,498	298,104	280,304	214,966
Canada	14,420	21,895	21,356	19,994
Other areas	8,329	6,530	5,238	6,839
Eliminations	(1,747)	(2,771)	(2,623)	(6,503)
Total net sales	$277,500	$323,758	$304,275	$235,296
Geographic Area Profits				
United States	$ 36,616	$ 59,602	$ 60,211	$ 42,534
Canada	1,147	3,891	3,347	752
Other areas	(558)	223	(576)	(411)
Eliminations and corporate items	17,802	3,173	861	912
Total income before income taxes	$ 55,007	$ 66,889	$ 63,843	$ 43,787
Identifiable Assets				
United States	$211,678	$172,557	$144,642	$ 94,242
Canada	6,420	7,675	7,021	5,133
Other areas	6,010	3,892	3,600	5,098
Eliminations and corporate items	(6,554)	(3,441)	(2,806)	(3,497)
Total assets	$217,554	$180,683	$152,457	$100,976

Source: Mary Kay Cosmetics, Inc. *Annual Report, 1984.*

reverse recent declines in sales and profits. The firm's top managers recognize the need to identify and take advantage of external opportunities and to avoid potential external threats. What seems more important now is to utilize the firm's internal strengths to overcome its weaknesses. Mr. Rogers and company executives are considering a number of proposals for attaining company goals. Some of their thoughts include:

1. Should we broaden our product lines to include deodorants and nail care products?
2. Should we expand into other overseas markets? Which markets would be most attractive?
3. Should we complete construction of the new production facility and corporate warehouse in Dallas?
4. How can we develop an effective customer retention program?
5. Should we change our advertising strategy? In what ways?
6. How can we develop an effective direct mail program?

7. Should we increase our recruiting commissions? How much?

8. Should we attempt to diversify by acquiring a women's clothing store chain, such as The Limited, Inc.

9. Should sales bonuses for our sales directors be increased? How much?

10. Should we change our requirements for directorship? In what ways?

11. Should we begin marketing the Mary Kay name on clothes, sporting goods, or related types of products?

12. Should we attempt to acquire one of the other ailing cosmetic firms? Which one and for how much?

Mrs. Ash is enthusiastic as ever about Mary Kay's future. She says: "We have only 4 percent of the total retail cosmetics market. The way I see it, 96 percent of the people in the U.S. are using the wrong product."

REFERENCES

"Avon, You've Looked Better." *Sales and Marketing Management* (April 5, 1982): 52–57.

"Corporate Scoreboard—Personal Care Products Industry Outlook." *Business Week* (March 21, 1984): 20–63.

"Direct's Sleeker Sell." *Advertising Age* (March 1, 1982): 18.

"For Avon, Everything Depends on Recruiting." *Financial World* (December 31, 1983): 28–29.

"Lauder's Success Formula: Instinct, Timing, and Research." *Business Week* (September 26, 1983): 122–124.

"Mary Kay Cosmetics: Looking Beyond Direct Sales to Keep the Party Going." *Business Week* (March 28, 1983): 130.

"Mary Kay Finds Incentives That Pay Off." *Chemical Week* (May 13, 1981): 50–51.

"Mary Kay, Jafra Show Dramatic Growth." *Advertising Age* (August 23, 1982): 22.

"Mary Kay's Plan To Go Private." *Business Week* (June 17, 1985): 44.

"Mary Kay's Sweet Smell of Success." *Reader's Digest* (November, 1978): 17–20.

"Revlon: A Painful Case of Slow Growth and Fading Glamour." *Business Week* (April 12, 1982): 116–120.

"Revving Up Revlon." *Financial World* (November 15, 1980): 31–33.

"Up and Down Wall Street." *Barron's* (June 8, 1981): 45–46.

CASE 33

Winnebago Industries, Incorporated

FRED DAVID
Auburn University

JANET DOLAN
Pfeiffer College

INTRODUCTION

Saving money is nice, but it isn't the real reason people travel in a motor home. Motor homing is just plain fun. Motor homers are an adventurous lot. They like to go, see, and do. According to reservations made through *Wheeler's RV Resort and Campground Guide,* Florida residents have recently replaced Californians as the most active campers. New Yorkers are third on the "most on the go" list. Most recreational vehicle (RV) owners say they not only save money when camping, but they "get the feel for where they are" by not having to stop for restaurants and bathrooms. Motor homers stop when there is really something to see and do. They often spend the summers where it is cool and the winters where it is warm.

Although once the undisputed leader in the motor home industry, Winnebago Industries is now struggling to maintain third place behind two major competitors—Fleetwood Enterprises and Coachmen Industries. This business policy case describes why Winnebago faltered in the late 1970s, how the company has rebounded in the early 1980s, and what the firm plans to do in the mid and late 1980s. This case provides sufficient information to analyze Winnebago's present strategies and to establish future objectives, strategies, goals, and policies for the company.

HISTORY

Winnebago Industries was founded in 1958 in Forest City, Iowa. Winnebago experienced phenomenal growth during the 1960s, but this came to an abrupt end in 1970. That year was marked by a recession, and Winnebago saw its stock plummet nearly 60 percent before recovering. The OPEC oil embargo hit in 1973 and 1974 and had disastrous effects on Winnebago. The company's net income averaged less than 1 percent of sales between 1973 and 1978. Despite a record level of sales of $229 million in 1978, Winnebago's sales dropped to $92 million in 1979. The company was nearly forced into bankruptcy in 1980 when net income was a negative $13.5 million.

A dissatisfied board of directors called John K. Hanson out of retirement in March of 1979, reelecting him chairman of the board and president of Winnebago. (Hanson had founded the company twenty-one years earlier.) To resolve Winnebago's problems, Hanson concentrated on four basic areas: First, he reduced the number of Winnebago employees from 4,000 to 800 in less than nine months. Second, he completely retired Winnebago's $18.5 million short-term debt within fourteen months. Third, he initiated the development of propane conversion systems for motor homes, which allow users to power their vehicles with less costly propane, eliminating worries about the supply and cost of gasoline. Fourth, he pioneered the development of a lightweight, fuel-efficient motor home powered by a revolutionary heavy-duty diesel engine. Fifth, Hanson took the following actions to reduce Winnebago's production capacity:

1. He sold the 131,000-square-foot plant in Riverside, California.
2. He terminated the lease for the 66,000-square-foot van conversion plant in Asheville, North Carolina.
3. He closed the north plant complex in Forest City.
4. He leased to the 3M Company the 185,000-square-foot shipout building that comprised the south plant complex in Forest City.
5. He consolidated all component assembly operations into one main production plant in Forest City.

As conditions improved, employment at Winnebago increased from 800 at the beginning of 1980, to 950 at the beginning of 1981, and then to 1,400 by May 1981. During this year, Winnebago introduced a fuel-efficient, lightweight, aerodynamically designed line of motor homes. In 1982, Winnebago entered into an agreement with five manufacturers to allow use of the Winnebago name on products ranging from camping equipment to outdoor clothing. Winnebago declared its first cash dividend on common stock, ten cents per share, in October of 1982.

In 1983, Winnebago introduced a new family of front-wheel-drive vehicles, powered by Renault diesel engines. Sales of $239 million in 1983 set an all-time record, and the number of Winnebago employees was up to 2,200 by the end of the year. On August 10, 1983, John Hanson was inducted into the Recreational Vehicle/Motor Home Hall of Fame in South Bend, Indiana. In 1984, Winnebago Industries won an award for the outstanding company turnaround in 1983. Net earnings in 1984 totaled $27,817,000 or $1.10 a share, up 77 percent over net earnings of $15,737,000 in 1983. Sales in fiscal 1984 were up 72 percent over the record sales level in 1983.

WINNEBAGO'S CURRENT PRODUCT LINE

The three principal kinds of recreation vehicles manufactured by Winnebago in fiscal 1984 are Type A motor homes, Type C motor homes, and van conversions. Type A and Type C motor homes are marketed under the Winnebago and Itasca brand names and sold through a network of 382 dealers in the United States and Canada. In 1984,

92 automobile dealers in the United States market Winnebago's front-wheel-drive van conversions. Some of these dealers are also motor home dealers.

Type A motor homes are constructed on a chassis that already has the engine and drive components. An example of the Type A motor home is the 1984 Chieftain, which is available in a range of lengths from the 22-foot unit to the luxurious 33-footer. The 33-foot Chieftain offers a shower, a four-burner with oven, a large refrigerator, two double beds and bunks, and rich carpet throughout. Winnebago is expanding on the Type A motor homes in 1984 by introducing a series of larger vehicles. Beginning at 31 feet, the Elandan and the Windcruiser are examples. These vehicles are built on a Chevrolet chassis with a 454-cubic-inch engine. The price is just under $46,000.

Type C motor homes are constructed on a van chassis in which the driver's compartment is accessible from the living area. Type C motor homes are compact, simple to drive, and priced less that $23,000. An example Type C motor home is the Minnie Winnie. This vehicle is available in 20- and 24-foot lengths. Other Type C motor homes are Winnebago's LeSharo and the Phasar, which were introduced in late 1983. The LeSharo is a 20-foot motor home with a two-liter diesel engine that gets 22 miles per gallon on the highway. This vehicle offers six-foot head room, a shower, a stove, a sink, a refrigerator, and two double beds. The LeSharo and Phasar motor homes are currently marketed to the 35–44-year age group.

The third group of recreational vehicles manufactured by Winnebago are the van conversions. These vehicles are actually conventional vans manufactured by Ford, GMC, Chrysler, and AMC, custom-tailored by Winnebago with special interiors, exteriors, additional windows, and vents. An example van conversion is the Centauri, which retails for under $20,000. At 19 feet and 7 inches, it is the largest van conversion available. On a 3,000 mile test trip, it recently averaged 24.11 miles per gallon.

Winnebago's unit sales of recreation vehicles are given in Exhibit 1.

Exhibit 1   Winnebago's unit sales of recreation vehicles

Year Ended (1)	August 25, 1984	August 27, 1983	August 38, 1982	August 29, 1981	August 30, 1980	August 25, 1979
Motor Homes						
Type A	9,528	5,818	4,068	4,198	3,173	7,690
Type C	4,911	2,747	1,574	1,983	1,169	4,167
Total	14,439	8,565	5,642	6,181	4,342	11,857
Vans and Van Conversions	1,837	1,479	1,001	452	961	2,507

Source: Winnebago's *1984 Annual Report*, p. 7.

(1) The fiscal year ended August 30, 1980 contained 53 weeks: all other years in table contained 52 weeks.

Exhibit 2   Winnebago's net sales by major product line

Year Ended (1)	($ in thousands)					
	August 25, 1984	August 27, 1983	August 28, 1982	August 29, 1981	August 30, 1980	August 25, 1979
Motor Homes	$ 376,733	$ 207,933	$ 129,578	$ 122,619	$ 73,643	$ 188,318
	91.6%	86.9%	88.4%	85.7%	80.1%	87.7%
Other Recreation Vehicle Sales (2)	$ 21,281	$ 18,077	$ 9,993	$ 10,457	$ 11,344	$ 20,291
	5.2%	7,6%	6.8%	7.3%	12.3%	9.5%
Total Recreation Vehicle Sales	$ 398,014	$ 226,010	$ 139,571	$ 133,076	$ 84,987	$ 208,609
	96.8%	94.5%	95.2%	93.0%	92.4%	97.2%
Non-Recreation Vehicle Sales (3)	$ 12,960	$ 13,255	$ 7,054	$ 9,973	$ 6,952	$ 5,984
	3.2%	5.5%	4.8%	7.0%	7.6%	2.8%
Total Sales	$ 410,974	$ 239,265	$ 146,625	$ 143,049	$ 91,939	$ 214,593
	100.0%	100.0%	100.0%	100.0%	100.0%	100.0%

Source: Winnebago's *1984 Annual Report*, p. 6.

(1) The fiscal year ended August 30, 1980 contained 53 weeks; all other years in table contained 52 weeks.

(2) Primarily vans, van conversions, and recreation-vehicle-related parts and service.

(3) Principally sales of extruded aluminum, specially designed trams, commercial vehicles, bus chassis, and a wide range of component products for other manufacturers.

In addition to recreational vehicles, Winnebago makes travel trailers that are pulled by cars, pickup trucks, and vans. Also, Winnebago manufactures draperies, chairs, tables, metal stampings, aluminum products, commercial vehicles, and various plastic and fiberglass products. The New Ventures Division of Winnebago has projects that include a vehicle for handicapped or elderly persons, and trams. A tram is a vehicle that has a seating capacity of 274 persons and is designed for rapid loading and unloading. Universal Studios has ordered twenty-eight trams to be produced at a total cost of $9,000,000. Winnebago's net sales by major product line are given in Exhibit 2.

THE WINNEBAGO LOGO

Use of the Winnebago name is in great demand. Eighty percent of all Americans recognize the Winnebago name. Nine licensees currently pay royalties to the company for using the name on a range of products from camping equipment to clothing. Recent announcement copy for various products marketed under the Winnebago name is shown in Exhibit 3. There are presently 2,000 retail outlets that carry one or more Winnebago-name products. Five major licensees of Winnebago products are given in Exhibit 4.

Exhibit 3   A recent Winnebago announcement

New Winnebagos fit in suitcase

Some of the newest Winnebagos fit in a suitcase. Others *are* suitcases.

Winnebago Industries recently unveiled a complete line of Winnebago brand camping gear, sportswear, footwear and soft-sided luggage.

The new products carry the Winnebago name, but are made and distributed by licensed manufacturers. The product lineup includes a wide variety of camping equipment, from stoves, lanterns, and grills to sleeping bags, air mattresses, tents, and screenhouses. There are also portable toilets, coolers, and picnic jugs.

The sportswear includes casual men's wear such as slacks, shorts, shirts, vests, and jackets, plus knit scarves, gloves, socks, and hats for the whole family.

Rounding out the new Winnebago lineup are Winnebago boots, shoes, marine flotation devices, backpacks, sports bags, and travel bags.

Source: *Winnebago Rolling Review,* Vol. 1, No. 1, p. 10.

Exhibit 4   Winnebago's licensees

Licensee	Products
Outdoor Venture Corporation Steins, Kentucky	Cabin tents, screen rooms, dome tents, and sleeping bags
Century Tool and Manufacturing Co. Cherry Valley, Illinois	Propane stoves, barbecues, and lanterns
CSA, Inc. Foxboro, Massachusetts	Backpacks, sportsbags, and travel bags
Taurus International, Inc. Wayne, New Jersey	Cotton, rubberized air mattresses
Oxford Industries, Inc. Atlanta, Georgia	Lines of men's rugged outdoor apparel, including shirts, sweaters, slacks, and jackets

PRODUCTION FACILITIES

Winnebago has production facilities in Forest City, Iowa, where it occupies 2.5 million square feet of roofed buildings. Forest City has a population of 4,500 and is nestled among thousands of acres of cornfields. During fiscal 1984, Winnebago expanded its operations beyond Forest City. Specifically, the company opened a sewing plant employing twenty-five persons in Lorimer, Iowa. In addition, a fiberglass parts plant was opened in Hampton, Iowa, employing 125 people. A third expansion was recently announced for a sewing operation in Juarez, Mexico to employ twenty-five people.

These expansions are part of a long-range strategy to move labor-intensive operations out of Forest City. Eighty percent of all components that go into a Winnebago product are made by Winnebago.

Winnebago uses computer technology to design all of its motor homes. Regarding computer technology, the following article appeared in the *Winnebago Rolling Review* (Vol. 1, No. 1, p. 1).:

> Just like the automotive industry, Winnebago Industries is using computers to improve their products. Winnebago Industries' new Computer Aided Design System (CAD) is unique to the motor home industry. Thanks to CAD, Winnebago designers can "draw" a new motor home directly on a TV screen. Working with the image on the screen, the computer can be directed to move walls, alter the floor plan, make it longer or shorter, or change the entire styling. The computer can show what the motor home would look like from the outside or from the inside out. It can even peel away the outer skin to reveal the support members underneath—and then move them a hundredth of an inch in any direction. Winnebago designers are proud of their CAD, and they are tight-lipped about the new models CAD is creating.

Winnebago has four 1,000-foot assembly lines for its motor homes. As a motor home flows down the assembly line and is completed, quality control is carefully monitored. Units are randomly taken from the assembly line for a more thorough examination. The performance of each RV is tested before it is delivered to a dealer's lot. Winnebago has a very effective three-year-old quality circle program. One of every five employees is a member of a quality circle group.

COMPETITORS

Winnebago's two major competitors in the motor home industry are Fleetwood Enterprises and Coachmen Industries. These two companies' sales in 1984 were $1,420 million and $521 million, respectively. Fleetwood and Coachmen's net profit margin in 1984 was 4.5 percent and 2.7 percent respectively. An article in *Business Week* (January 16, 1984), reads:

> Fuel shortages and soaring gasoline prices in 1979, plus high interest rates, wiped out about half of the RV manufacturers and dealers by 1982. But industry shipments raced ahead by 40 percent in the first nine months of 1983, to 277,200 units. Coachmen intends to seize sales in the booming $2.9 billion (wholesale) RV market by dazzling the customer with variety. Industry leader Fleetwood Enterprises, which sells nearly 20 percent of the RV units in the U.S., aims for the mass market with midprice models ranging from $5,600 to $48,000. Well-known Winnebago Industries tries to entice first-time buyers with novel designs such as a small motor home that can double as a van.

Fleetwood

Fueled by increasing disposable income, Fleetwood's motor home and travel trailer revenues advanced 75 percent in fiscal 1984. Fleetwood's manufactured housing shipments jumped in fiscal 1984 to 53,040 units, comprising 37 percent of total company sales. The company's aggressive marketing of low-priced mobile homes was a major factor. Selected financial statistics on Fleetwood are given in Exhibit 5.

Coachmen

Headquartered in Elkhart, Indiana, Coachmen's net sales increased from $478 million to $521 million in 1984 over 1983, while net income declined from $23 million to $14 million. New developments at Coachmen in 1984 include formation of a credit life insurance company to write insurance through the firm's dealers, and formation of a travel insurance motor club. The motor club will provide tow service on breakdowns, certain repairs, bail bonds, etc. Coachmen has announced plans to expand its recreational vehicle manufacturing facilities into western regions of the United States, and

Exhibit 5 Selected financial statistics on Fleetwood Enterprises (in $000)

	Manufactured Housing	Recreational Vehicles	Other Operations	General Corporate	Total
Sales					
1984	$517,792	$899,405	$3,221	$ —	$1,420,418
1983	343,008	513,811	1,206	—	858,025
1982	232,026	348,292	1,114	—	581,432
1981	206,064	220,429	1,128	—	427,621
Operating Profit (Loss)					
1984	15,492	101,228	3,439	(8,257)	111,902
1983	9,826	47,926	172	(7,129)	50,795
1982	(167)	18,248	459	(4,590)	13,950
1981	(211)	(281)	(389)	(3,207)	(3,310)
Assets					
1984	54,538	154,622	7,848	151,370	368,378
1983	47,172	98,986	5,149	131,313	282,620
1982	40,634	78,799	4,692	64,668	188,793
1981	47,716	68,937	4,444	48,368	169,465
Capital expenditures					
1984	8,155	9,919	1,643	1,545	21,262
1983	2,837	2,776	2,406	798	8,817
1982	1,598	4,352	719	735	7,404
1981	1,656	572	1,220	1,772	5,220

Source: Fleetwood Enterprises' *1984 Annual Report.*

has purchased a manufacturing facility in Mt. Angel, Oregon, and a similar facility in southern California. Coachmen manufactures a full line of RVs in multiplant facilities located in Indiana, Michigan, Georgia, Pennsylvania, Texas, and Oregon. Products are marketed through more than 1500 dealers in 49 states and five provinces of Canada.

Thomas Corson, Coachmen's chairman and founder, recently stated publicly that his company plans to catch up with Fleetwood by 1988. Corson plans to inch his firm's 13 percent market share up 1 percent or 2 percent each year. Coachmen's major brand names are All American, Camper's Pride, Coach-Lite, Consolidated Leisure, Cross-country, Fan, Frolic, Kenco, Lux, Marlette, Midas, Nite-N-Day, Pathfinder, Shadow, Shasta, Sportscoach, Techniglas, and Viking. In 1984, Coachmen became the first RV company to utilize national network television. Commericals featured the company's logo mascot Pete, a Dalmatian that appears on every Coachmen RV. Selected financial statistics on Coachmen Industries are given in Exhibit 6.

FINANCIAL INFORMATION

Winnebago's consolidated income statements and balance sheets for 1981, 1982, 1983, and 1984 are given in Exhibit 7 and Exhibit 8 respectively. Note that Winnebago's

Exhibit 6 Coachmen's sales by product from 1979 to 1984 (in $000)

	1979		1980		1981		1982		1983		1984	
Recreational Vehicles												
Motor Homes	$ 63,260	35%	$ 32,678	26%	$ 63,500	31%	$ 90,626	34%	$255,281	54%	$297,122	57%
Travel Trailers	$ 59,252	33%	47,103	38%	57,612	28%	64,622	24%	83,138	17%	78,190	15%
Camping Trailers	$ 7,433	4%	7,886	6%	11,713	6%	10,679	4%	11,697	2%	10,425	2%
Truck Campers	$ 3,001	2%	1,649	1%	2,104	1%	2,799	1%	3,193	1%	5,212	1%
Parts and Accessories	$ 38,869	21%	27,663	22%	35,307	17%	48,521	18%	69,282	14%	88,617	17%
Manufactured Housing	—	—	—	—	22,098	10%	33,138	13%	45,052	9%	41,702	8%
Other Operations	8,113	5%	8,574	7%	14,545	7%	14,955	6%	11,099	3%	—	—
Total Sales	$179,928	100%	$125,553	100%	$206,879	100%	$265,340	100%	$478,742	100%	$521,268	100%

Source: Coachmen Industries, Inc., *Annual Report, 1984,* p. 1.

Exhibit 7   Winnebago's consolidated income statements
(in $000, except per share data)

Year ended	August 25, 1984	August 27, 1983	August 28, 1982	August 29, 1981
Net sales	$410,974	$239,265	$146,625	$143,049
Cost of goods sold	345,685	203,375	127,098	126,266
Gross profit	65,289	35,890	19,527	10,783
Operating expenses:				
Selling and delivery expenses, net	15,182	7,699	7,152	3,882
General and administrative expenses	10,425	8,747	6,984	7,886
Total operating expenses	25,607	16,446	14,136	11,768
Operating income	39,682	19,444	5,391	5,015
Financial (income) expenses, net	(2,501)	(5,558)	(3,815)	(2,987)
Income before income taxes and items shown below	42,183	25,002	9,242	8,000
Provision for federal and state income taxes	18,016	10,247	2,752	4,028
Income before items shown below	24,167	14,755	6,490	3,974
Equity in income of unconsolidated subsidiaries before extraordinary item	3,650	982	1,360	649
Income before extraordinary item	27,817	15,737	7,850	4,623
Extraordinary item—reduction in federal and state income taxes due to net operating loss carry forwards utilized	—	—	2,285	4,053
Net income	$ 27,817	$15,737	$10,135	$ 8,676
Income per common share:				
Income before extraordinary share	$ 1.10	$ .63	$ .31	$ .19
Extraordinary item	—	—	.09	.16
Net income	$ 1.10	$ .63	$ .40	$ .35
Weighted average number of shares in common stock (in thousands)	25,397	25,171	25,039	24,988

Source: Winnebago Industries, Inc. *Annual Report, 1984,* p. 10.

sales were up 72 percent in 1984 over 1983. Winnebago's research and development expenses charged to operations for fiscal 1984, 1983, 1982, and 1981 were approximately $1,923,000, $729,000, $1,350,000, and $990,000, respectively. Coachmen's R&D expenditures in 1983 were $648,000.

FUTURE PLANS, PROBLEMS, AND CONCERNS

Winnebago recently signed a temporary agreement with U–Haul to test-market the rental of motor homes. The test market took place mostly in the southern and western United States. The two companies could not come to terms for a more permanent

Exhibit 8   Winnebago's consolidated balance sheets (in $000)

Year Ended	August 25, 1984	August 27, 1983	August 28, 1982	August 29, 1981
Assets				
Current Assets				
Cash and marketable securities	$ 25,155	$ 45,463	$ 24,474	$23,756
Receivables, less allowance for doubtful accounts	23,436	24,136	8,010	8,527
Income tax refund receivable	2,029	4,772	—	—
Rental motor homes and trailers at cost less accumulated depreciation of $479	—	—	7,692	—
Inventories	44,144	28,717	24,735	19,727
Prepaid expenses	1,790	1,536	1,585	1,841
Deferred income tax charges	2,671	2,593	1,987	463
Total current assets	103,225	107,217	68,483	54,314
Investments				
Investments in unconsolidated subsidiaries, at equity in net assets	47,372	9,498	8,517	15,398
Property and Equipment, at cost,				
Land	1,296	1,299	1,311	1,306
Buildings	25,627	23,438	22,552	22,552
Machinery and equipment	40,955	32,583	28,845	22,483
Transportation equipment	4,394	4,181	4,160	1,574
	72,272	61,401	56,868	47,915
Less accumulated depreciation	34,495	31,094	27,920	26,287
Other assets	2,564	2,991	2,120	2,090
	$190,938	$150,013	$108,068	$93,430
Liabilities and Stockholders' Equity				
Current Liabilities				
Notes payable, Winnebago Acceptance Corporation unsecured, due on demand, 12%	—	$ 11,085	$ 4,461	$ —
Current maturities of long-term debt	3,877	5,752	—	—
Accounts payable, trade	35,237	17,687	12,420	11,015
Accrued expenses:				
Property and payroll taxes	1,344	1,246	986	1,023
Insurance	1,341	1,028	1,031	1,295
Profit sharing and bonus	3,131	2,265	1,778	1,578
Other	4,058	4,035	2,059	2,468
Income taxes payable	5,694	1,026	605	2,512
Provision for liability on product warranties	3,682	2,531	1,768	2,201
Total current liabilities	58,364	46,655	25,108	22,092
Long-term debt	121	3,715		
Deferred compensation	1,005	—	—	—
Deferred income tax credits	8,461	3,181	1,728	463

Exhibit 8   (continued)

Year Ended	August 25, 1984	August 27, 1983	August 28, 1982	August 29, 1981
Stockholders' Equity				
Capital stock, common, par value $.50; authorized 60,000,000 shares; issued 24,436,000 and 25,320,000 shares	12,718	12,660	12,627	12,626
Additional paid-in capital	25,186	23,997	22,433	22,330
Reinvested earnings	85,083	59,805	46,580	36,445
	122,987	96,462	81,640	71,401
Less treasury stock (204,000 shares at cost)	—	—	408	526
	122,987	96,462	81,232	70,875
	$190,938	$150,013	$108,068	$93,430

Source: Winnebago Industries, Inc. *Annual Report, 1984*, p. 8 and 9.

agreement and talks broke off. However, Winnebago says that it is considering other rental agencies to handle this type of venture. The identity of these companies has not been disclosed.

Winnebago and Anheuser–Busch are working together on the development of a new fleet of promotional vehicles. These vehicles will have a large red "Budweiser" on the side and will have special paint jobs, public address systems, beer taps, mirrored rear windows, and a spare tire cover that will resemble a beer bottle cap. Winnebago is considering developing this type of arrangement with other companies.

In the future it may become necessary for Winnebago to build other production facilities to serve local markets. The California, New York, and Florida markets are simply a long way from Forest city, Iowa. Furthermore, foreign markets are virtually untapped by producers of recreational motor vehicles. A possible strategy for Winnebago in the mid and late 1980s could therefore be market development into foreign countries.

There exist a number of other concerns that occupy the minds of Winnebago's top managers. For example, the company is experiencing some problems with its dealers' ability to service the new Renault engines and even to carry the new, smaller RVs. Also, the company could be severely crippled if another fuel crisis occurs. Finally, the company is concerned about the dramatic gains enjoyed by Fleetwood and Coachmen in recent years. Winnebago hates being number three in an industry it once dominated.

REFERENCES

Coachmen's 1984 *Annual Report*.

Fleetwood's 1984 *Annual Report*.

Gissen, J. "Good Times in Forest City." *Business Week* (February 13, 1984): 66.

Winnebago's 1984 *Annual Report*.

Daktronics, Inc.

PHIL FISHER
University of South Dakota

CHARLES ROEGIERS
University of South Dakota

Daktronics, Inc. was founded in 1968 by Dr. Aelred (Al) Kurtenbach and Dr. Duane Sander, who were then members of the electrical engineering faculty of South Dakota State University in Brookings, South Dakota. Kurtenbach and Sander set up operations in a converted garage, originally intending to manufacture biomedical instruments. In November of 1983, Daktronics moved into a 36,000-square-foot plant on the outskirts of Brookings. This brought their total space to 64,000 square feet. Their sales in the previous year had been $6.4 million from the manufacture of athletic scoreboards, electronic message centers, time and temperature signs, voting display systems, and other custom electronic display systems.

Al Kurtenbach, Daktronics' president, commented on the nature of the company's products.

> Our products are computer-driven, large information displays. We have a new communications medium that is not yet understood, even by information people. We are in the information business with a new medium that will be used wherever people gather.

COMPANY HISTORY

Al Kurtenbach and Duane Sander, both native South Dakotans, became friends while undergraduates studying electrical engineering at the South Dakota School of Mines and Technology. After graduation in 1961, Kurtenbach earned a masters degree from the University of Nebraska. He received a Ph.D. from Purdue University in 1968 in Electrical Engineering. That same year he returned to South Dakota to join the faculty at South Dakota State University. In the meantime, Sander had completed graduate work at Iowa State University and had already joined the South Dakota State University faculty.

This case was presented at the Midwest Case Writers Association Workshop in 1984.

Reflecting on that period Kurtenbach commented:

> That was back in the so-called go-go sixties, with emerging high technology companies. Although the term *high tech* wasn't used so much then, the market was hotter that it is now. I came through that when I was at Purdue University. Some of my friends were starting companies and it seemed that we could do the same thing here.

Starting with the conviction that they could design products, Dr. Kurtenbach and Dr. Sander in 1968 organized a stock offering through the S.E.C. and began selling stock to private citizens in Brookings. This effort continued over two years and raised nearly $200,000.

The company's first product was an electronic thermometer, but enough capital had not been raised to market it successfully. This was a radically different product from the traditional mercury thermometer and would have required a substantial marketing effort. Potential customers would not purchase a prototype, but wanted to see a finished production-run product.

Kurtenbach and Sander then began searching for products that they could produce and market with the capital they had raised. Two products came to their attention about the same time; these were voting display systems for state legislatures, and wrestling scoreboards. Both products were electronic display systems.

During 1969 Kurtenbach and Sander discussed the requirements of voting display systems with leaders in the South Dakota legislature and with legislative leaders in Colorado as well. Then, in June of 1970, the State of Utah advertised for bids on a voting display system for the Utah legislature. Kurtenbach and Sander submitted a bid on the project. Their price was based on bids submitted by other companies on an unsuccessful bidding held in Utah two years before. Daktronics was the low bidder this time, and despite their lack of manufacturing experience, they were awarded the contract on the basis of their design expertise. They successfully filled that contract and made another sale that same year to the State of Montana. By 1983, thirty-two state legislatures used Daktronics voting display systems.

The need for scoreboards designed specifically for wrestling meets was discovered through Kurtenbach's interest in the sport and his contact with the University's wrestling coach, Warren Williamson. Williamson helped Kurtenbach and Sander identify the necessary product features and set up demonstrations of the Daktronics prototype at regional and national wrestling meets in 1970 and 1971. The floor-level, portable product was a clear improvement over basketball scoreboards that had typically been used at wrestling meets. Exposure at wrestling meets brought Kurtenbach into contact with wrestling coaches across the country and produced immediate sales. In 1983, Daktronics offered a full line of athletic scoreboards, and this product line was their sales leader.

Although they considered themselves to be in the electronic controls business, Kurtenbach and Sander extended their product line into other types of display devices. They developed a full line of athletic scoreboards. Time and temperature signs were brought out in 1971; commercial message displays were produced in 1972; custom scoreboards for large stadiums and arenas were added to the line in the late Seventies.

Dr. Kurtenbach resigned his faculty position in 1973 to devote full attention to the company. Dr. Sander remained on the faculty, but continued to serve on the Daktronics Board of Directors and had an important influence on company policy. Commenting on this arrangement, Sander said, "I like teaching better than I do this sort of work (managing). I like to have my fingers in it, but I really don't think you can run the show with two leaders. Al is really the brains and the salesman. I've given more moral support than anything—I've been there when he'd like someone to bounce an idea off of. I've still got a lot of monetary risk involved in the company. If Al were not the president, I'd be much more involved. I trust what he is doing because I saw him when we were starting. I understand that he won't let the company go down. He will put out a superhuman effort to make it successful."

Daktronics' exposure to the market for athletic scoreboards got a boost when the company received a contract to supply all scoreboards for the 1980 Winter Olympics at Lake Placid, N.Y. Although fulfilling this contract severely strained the personnel resources of the company, Kurtenbach believed that the long-term effect had been beneficial to Daktronics' status in the market.

In 1978, Daktronics designed a control system for a wastewater treatment plant in Brookings. This project required a great deal of design time and resulted in a very advanced and elaborate system. Installation was completed in 1980. In spite of the success of the project from a technical standpoint, a combination of factors: decline of federal support for such projects, the large number of competitors in the field, and the growth of Daktronics' display business, led to a decision not to actively pursue sales in this technology.

The wastewater treatment project and a lack of effective internal controls were cited by company officials as causes of a financial crisis in 1980 that led one large bank to withdraw its participation in Daktronics financing. However, Daktronic's principal bank, located in Brookings, continued to provide lending to the company. Kurtenbach said of this, "We have a good partnership with the local banker, who has ridden up and down with us, staying with us even when the balance sheet . . ."

Improved cost controls and increasing sales in 1981, 1982 and 1983 had placed the company on a firmer financial base, and Daktronics' managers were confident of future growth in their markets.

Exhibits 1, 2, and 3 provide financial information.

ORGANIZATION AND MANAGEMENT

After a 1982 management consultant's study found that 29 people were reporting to Al Kurtenbach, Daktronics was organized into three major areas: sales, engineering, and manufacturing. Jim Morgan, vice-president for engineering, was a student of Kurtenbach's at South Dakota State and had been employed by Daktronics since its inception.

Exhibit 1   Daktronics, Inc. and subsidiaries' consolidated balance sheets—April 30, 1983 and 1982

ASSETS	1983	1982
CURRENT ASSETS:		
Cash and short-term investments	$ 40,985	$ 19,988
Accounts receivable, less allowance for doubtful accounts of $73,000 and $31,000, respectively	884,351	649,872
Current maturities of long-term notes and contracts receivable	103,560	77,752
Inventories	1,198,906	1,002,376
Costs and estimated earnings in excess of billings on uncompleted contracts	337,398	224,237
Prepaid expenses	31,101	43,756
Deferred income tax benefits	65,000	—
Total current assets	2,661,301	2,017,981
LONG-TERM RECEIVABLES AND OTHER ASSETS:		
Notes and contracts receivable, less current maturities	459,723	241,920
Deferred income tax benefits	—	22,000
Other	23,341	16,255
Total long-term receivables and other assets	483,064	280,175
PROPERTY AND EQUIPMENT:		
Land	88,681	88,681
Building	361,209	360,329
Machinery and equipment	331,476	311,694
Transportation equipment	75,678	69,228
Office furniture and equipment	80,462	61,681
Construction in progress	13,000	—
Less—Accumulated depreciation	(349,966)	(260,658)
Total property and equipment	605,540	630,955
	$3,749,905	$2,929,111
LIABILITIES AND STOCKHOLDERS' INVESTMENT		
CURRENT LIABILITIES:		
Cash overdraft	$ —	$ 101,176
Notes payable to bank	385,000	406,000
Current maturities of long-term debt	194,888	171,886
Accounts payable	468,271	333,645
Customer deposits	222,067	142,025
Accrued liabilities	290,108	228,860
Accrued product warranties	188,352	109,267
Income taxes payable	69,303	90,000
Total current liabilities	1,835,989	1,582,859
LONG-TERM DEBT, less current maturities	812,500	740,605
DEFERRED TAX LIABILITY	96,000	—
Total liabilities	$2,744,489	$2,323,464

COMMITMENTS AND CONTINGENCIES

STOCKHOLDERS' INVESTMENT:

Common stock, $1 par; 1,000,000 shares authorized; 64,707 and 57,518 shares issued and outstanding in 1983 and 1982, respectively	$ 64,707	$ 57,518
Subscribed common stock	3,866	3,566
Additional paid-in capital	340,432	276,069
Retained earnings	634,751	295,095
Less—Common stock subscriptions receivable	(38,340)	(26,601)
Total stockholders' investment	1,005,416	605,647
	$3,749,905	$2,929,111

Source: Daktronics, Inc. *Annual Report, 1983.*

Exhibit 2 Daktronics, Inc. and subsidiaries' consolidated statements of operations for the years ended April 30, 1983 and 1982

	1983	1982
NET SALES	$6,395,023	$4,690,736
COST OF GOODS SOLD:	3,839,493	2,878,275
Gross profit	2,555,530	1,812,461
Gross margin	40.0%	38.6%
OPERATING EXPENSES:		
Selling	$1,329,550	$ 890,955
General and administrative	392,654	458,921
Product design and development	228,855	57,420
Total operating expenses	1,951,059	1,407,296
Operating income	604,471	405,165
OTHER INCOME (EXPENSE):		
Interest expense	(155,025)	(177,563)
Interest income	79,307	76,396
Other	25,903	16,487
Total other income (expense)	(49,815)	(84,680)
Income before income taxes	554,656	320,485
PROVISION FOR INCOME TAXES	215,000	86,715
NET INCOME	$ 339,656	$ 233,770
EARNINGS PER SHARE	$5.70	$4.35

Source: Daktronics, Inc. *Annual Report, 1983.*

Exhibit 3   Key financial and operating figures for the years ending April 30, 1978–1983

Year	Net Sales ($000)	Net Profit After Taxes ($000)	Total Assets ($000)	Total Stockholder Equity ($000)	Retained Earnings ($000)	Number of Employees
1978	1954	109	1356	175	(33)	N/A
1979	2701	5	2137	192	(28)	108
1980	3449	(196)	2457	10	(224)	96
1981	4059	295	2591	311	61	100
1982	4691	234	2929	606	295	101
1983	6395	340	3750	1005	635	120

Source: Daktronics, Inc. *Annual Report, 1983.*

Joe Fuks, manufacturing manager, and Frank Kurtenbach, the sales manager, had joined Daktronics in 1978 and 1979 respectively. Frank Kurtenbach, Al's brother, had been a coach and educator before coming to Daktronics. (See Exhibit 4 for an organizational chart.)

The office of president was supported by an administrative staff of fourteen people organized into personnel, accounting, purchasing, and production and inventory control. The production and inventory control position was new in 1983 and had just been filled by Bob Mock, a returning Brookings native with several years of experience in production and inventory control.

Generally, reorganization of the company was considered an improvement, but one that still required time and effort to perfect. As one manager put it, "We really lacked a chain of command for a long time. I don't think it's mastered here yet; lines of communication tend to be very fluid." While most long-time Daktronics employees apparently believe that growth of the company has made a more formal structure necessary, acceptance of the changes are mixed with some expressions of regret. One employee, commenting on the transitions that have taken place, said, "We are still a family-type organization in some respects, but we aren't in others."

Kurtenbach holds monthly employee meetings in the company lunchrooms. These meetings, typically one session for administrative, engineering, and marketing personnel, and one session for manufacturing personnel, include all employees and are used to keep employees informed of the status of the company and important developments such as a new sales contracts. Blueprint drawings of custom scoreboards and large displays are hanging on the walls of the lunchroom in the manufacturing complex; these are drawings of products currently being manufactured. On-site pictures of recently installed products decorate bulletin boards in both buildings.

Exhibit 4   Daktronics, Inc. 1983 partial organization chart

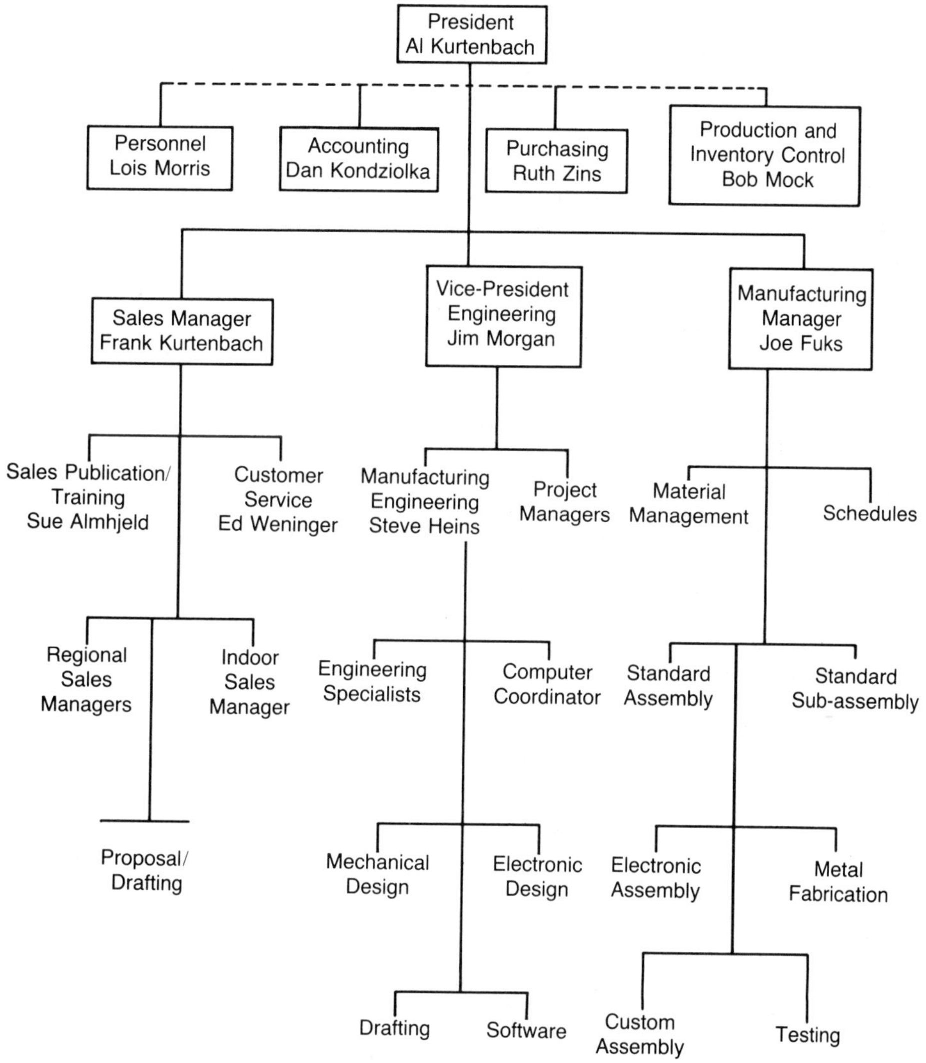

Kurtenbach described his approach to leadership:

Here at Daktronics we use the waterboy style of leadership. We've got to help everybody and support them. That's how we lead. Whenever I get someone that leans to the sergeant style of leadership, I have to work with that person to get him to understand how we do things.

Comments from his managers supported Kurtenbach's description.

> "Al is a very good teacher. He takes the time to sit down with you so you learn."
> "Dr. Kurtenbach uses more of the soft sell approach; he explains the why of things."
> "He is liked by everyone. He's very people-oriented. Why, we call OSHA and those types in every year to look us over."

Sander made it clear, however, that while Kurtenbach prefers a supportive role, he expects and gets high performance from his employees. "He is not only persuasive, he is very forceful. If things aren't going right, if some employees are not working up to their capabilities or the requirements of the job, he's very forthright in telling them that and getting straight before we are in serious trouble."

PLANNING

In 1983, Daktronics was in the process of formalizing its long-range planning. According to Kurtenbach:

> Up to now, long-term planning has been mostly in my head. I could stay on top of both product and market development, but we are at the point now where that is outdated. Strategic and business plans are going to be on paper.

To assist in the planning process, Kurtenbach established two committees in the fall of 1983. One was a marketing committee made up of Al Kurtenbach; Jim Morgan; Frank Kurtenbach; Ed Weninger, customer service manager; Sue Almhjeld, publication and training manager, an account executive from Daktronics' ad agency, and engineers directly involved in current product development. This committee was instituted to assure that product development and market development were coordinated and carried on simultaneously.

All new products or product-enhancement projects are to be submitted to the marketing committee for review before formal work can begin on them. Requests for product development have to state the purpose of the development, its key features, the estimated market for the product, a marketing strategy, and a proposed method of distribution. After preliminary approval is given, engineering will develop a schedule and budget for the committee's review and final approval.

Daktronics is also developing a Marketing/Sales Profile for each existing product. This profile would define the product's market, its marketing philosophy and strategy, its marketing budget, the method of selling, and its annual sales budget.

The second committee is a manufacturing committee. This committee is composed of Kurtenbach, Joe Fuks, Jim Morgan, Bob Mock, and Steve Heins, the manufacturing engineer. Its purpose is to look at long-range productivity improvements through the use of new equipment, improvements in product design, and changes in production methods.

MARKETS

Daktronics defines its product as advertising and information media that can be used wherever large numbers of people pass or gather. Athletic events, sports arenas, race tracks, and well-traveled roads or streets are places where Daktronics' displays can effectively convey a message. Electronic displays have several advantages over other types of message displays: (1) Visibility: Displays using incandescent lights can display messages that are visible at distances of a mile or more; (2) Visual impact: Moving messages, animation, and different colors attract viewers' attention; (3) Flexibility: A single electronic display can be used to send many messages.

Daktronics' largest volume of sales has been in electronic scoreboards, but the greatest opportunities for the future are thought to be message displays for on-premises advertising by truck stops, supermarkets, or other retail establishments, and for electronic billboards purchased by advertising companies. Instead of having a single advertising message for each billboard, outdoor advertisers can use the electronic display for several advertisements at each site. The typical use is to run five- to seven-second messages in sequence that are repeated every four or five minutes. Development in these markets has been impeded by the much larger capital investment required for electronic displays (approximately six times the cost of a conventional billboard) and sign ordinances in some municipalities. Moreover, Daktronics' managers believe that outdoor advertising companies do not really understand the possibilities of the electronic display media. More progress has been made with advertising executives at television stations who have a greater understanding of the use of media with a short time span of impact. They can use electronic billboards as a way of expanding their advertising media.

Daktronics has made some limited sales in foreign markets. Its primary channel to overseas markets is a U.S.-based export agent, although it has dealers in Hong Kong and Germany. The 1983 exchange rate is unfavorable to U.S. exporters, and Daktronics' executives believe they need more favorable rates to expect much expansion of foreign sales.

Daktronics' products can be acquired in one of three ways. Outright purchases account for the greatest volume of sales. Lease-buy-back arrangements are used primarily by banks for time and temperature signs. Banks loan Daktronics the amount of purchase and then make lease payments at 1 percent above the interest rate on the loan. The third method is contracts for advertising. With contracts for advertising, Daktronics retains ownership of the display, usually a large stadium scoreboard, and then acquires long-term contracts from advertisers for use of the display. Approximately two-thirds of Daktronics' notes receivable are from advertising contracts and the other third from contracts on time and temperature signs.

SALES AND DISTRIBUTION

Daktronics groups its products into four different types, each requiring a different marketing approach, including different channels of distribution. These product groupings are: (1) all standard athletic scoreboards; (2) information display products, including time and temperature signs and commercial message centers; (3) custom scoreboards for large arenas and stadiums; and (4) voting display systems.

Standard scoreboards are sold to a nationwide dealer network. Daktronics has divided the United States into five regions and has a fairly extensive dealer network, supported by a regional sales manager and inside sales representatives in three of these regions. In the South and Far West, a more limited number of dealers receive only inside support. Daktronics is developing dealers in these two areas, mostly sporting equipment dealers who are given exclusive territories limited to customer types that the dealers can effectively service. To illustrate, Daktronics might have three dealers in the same area, one selling to new construction, one selling in the replacement market, and a third selling aquatic scoreboards to swim clubs.

Standard scoreboards are sold primarily to high schools, at retail prices ranging from $1500 to $15,000, and Daktronics' 1982 factory sales of standard scoreboards were $1.3 million. Frank Kurtenbach estimates that the total market for this product line is about $10 million. The market for standard scoreboards is mature, with fairly constant sales levels. Most of Daktronics' competitors in this market have been in the business for many years. The largest is Fair-Play Scoreboards of Des Moines, Iowa, with estimated sales of $5 million in standard and custom scoreboards. Nevco Scoreboard Company of Greenville, Illinois, and Naden Industries of Webster City, Iowa, are smaller, long-time standard scoreboard manufacturers. A new entry in the market is Colorado Time of Loveland, Colorado, which is making some inroads with low-priced products. Gross margins for standard scoreboards are the lowest of Daktronics' product lines and are declining, but the product line is profitable.

Information displays are sold through separate dealers, primarily sign companies, in four of the five regions. In the southern region, Daktronics sells through an agent who has a trained sales force of twelve people. The agent, who had sold for a competitor, works on a commission basis, with Daktronics providing support in developing proposals. Regional sales managers provide support to dealers in three of the regions.

Information displays include time and temperature signs that are sold primarily to banks and savings and loan companies, and large message centers sold as advertising media to a wide variety of commercial users. Prices range from $3,000 to $8,000 for time and temperature signs, and up to $200,000 for the largest message centers. This is a rapidly growing market, and Daktronics' managers are not confident that they can estimate total market sales. Daktronics' sales in 1982 were $1 million and sales were running at double that rate in 1983. Competitors in this market are much larger, with Panasonic, a division of Matsushita Electric Industrial Co. Ltd. of Japan, being the largest. American Sign and Indicator (AS&I) of Spokane, Washington is believed to be the sales leader in this area, with $41 million in sales of displays and custom scoreboards. White Way Sign and Maintenance Co. of Chicago is a strong competitor in the upper Midwest. While sales estimates for White Way are not available, its assets and number of employees are believed to be about the same as Daktronics'.

Custom scoreboards are installed in stadiums and sports arenas where college and professional teams play. These scoreboards are designed to meet the specifications of the stadium or arena, and are sold by inside plant specialists. Terms for installation of custom scoreboards are negotiated. The terms vary, and occasionally the manufacturer retains ownership of the scoreboard. Sales revenues come from long-term contracts for advertising, with larger colleges and professional teams often receiving a share of the revenues. Contracts on custom scoreboards range from $50,000 to $500,000. Daktronics' sales in this market were $2.8 million in 1982 and were expected to exceed $3 million in 1983. Gross margins in the market are the highest of Daktronics' product lines. Frank Kurtenbach estimates that the total market for custom scoreboards exceeds $30 million; scoreboard contracts for the 1984 Olympics alone were $13 million. Competitors in this field are large display companies, Panasonic, A. S. & I., and White Way, as well as Fair-Play Scoreboards.

Daktronics has experienced success in competing for contracts in collegiate stadiums and arenas. Both Al and Frank Kurtenbach have been college varsity athletes and feel they know how to work with college athletic directors. Daktronics scoreboards have been placed in the Cotton Bowl and in stadiums and arenas at Clemson University, the University of Georgia, Kansas State University, the University of Minnesota, and the University of Houston, as well as at many smaller colleges and universities. Sales to professional teams have been smaller, but Daktronics has made some inroads with sales of an auxiliary scoreboard at Soldiers Field in Chicago, a 128-foot-long scoreboard in the Boston Gardens, and baseball scoreboards to minor league teams. Daktronics also sold and installed a large multisport scoreboard at the U.S. Olympic Training Center at Colorado Springs, Colorado.

Voting display systems are sold directly to state legislatures and legislative bodies of large city and county governments. Because of the limited number of customers, sales of these products vary significantly from year to year. While most are sold through a competitive bidding process, personal selling to legislative leaders is also required. Al Kurtenbach took a leading role in this.

> I think it's important for the guy who runs the company to get involved in selling. Presidents who go out and get involved in the presentation give the customer confidence.

Voting display systems are sold and installed for prices ranging from $250,000 to $500,000. In recent years Daktronics has achieved a dominant position in this market, with 75 percent of total sales. Daktronics' sales of voting display systems in 1982 were $800,000.

ADVERTISING AND PROMOTION

Daktronics' chief advertising and promotion efforts are in direct mailing and convention displays. Direct mailings are made to public school officials, collegiate athletic directors, arena managers, banks, savings and loan institutions, supermarkets, grain elevators, public officials, and other groups. Inquiries that result from these mailings are forwarded to the appropriate dealer in the area. Daktronics maintains a file on each lead and the results of the dealer follow-up. Inquiries from areas where no dealer has yet been established are followed up by telephone from inside sales representatives. In 1983, Daktronics received about 100 leads each week.

Strong, well-informed, and loyal dealers are a high priority for Daktronics. The Sales Publication and Training Department, headed by Sue Almhjeld, provides dealers with illustrated literature on the product line and provides a variety of training opportunities. Training seminars for dealers are held in Brookings. This provides dealers with information on topics from special product information to general management issues and gives dealers an opportunity to see the plant and meet Daktronics' managers.

In 1982, Daktronics made appearances at forty-seven conventions. Frank Kurtenbach had a leading role in this effort, overseeing shipping and setup, and making contacts. The types of conventions attended include those for coaches, shopping-mall managers, and truck stop operators. As with direct mailings, convention activities are directed toward getting dealer leads.

Daktronics does some magazine advertising, but has reduced this as a proportion of their promotion effort. Ads are placed primarily in trade journals.

CUSTOMER SERVICE

Daktronics' customer-service department has responsibility for installation and repair of most Daktronics products. Customer service provides supervision at most installations, except for voting display systems and the most complex custom installations, which are installed by engineering. The actual electrical and lifting work is typically subcontracted to local electricians and crane operators. On custom installations, operator training and software are an important part of the support provided. Animated sequences particularly require a library of software, which Daktronics makes available to the user.

Post-installation repairs are made free of charge during the warranty period, after which customers select from a variety of five different service contracts. Daktronics subcontracts to local technicians who perform first and second line maintenance. Factory representatives are sent out if local subcontractors cannot handle the problem. This is required for less than 1 percent of service calls. Subcontractors are typically T.V., air conditioning, or two-way radio technicians trained by Daktronics.

Ed Weninger, customer service manager, explains Daktronics' customer service philosophy:

> If Daktronics has a customer, we want that customer to be satisfied. We work with dealers, but feel strongly that customers should be satisfied, so we will bypass the dealer if the end user can't get satisfaction. Our phone number is in the product manual. My biggest fear is that a piece of equip-

ment is down someplace, with a customer frustrated, and I don't know about it.

The customer service department maintains an inventory of replacement parts. Daktronics has an exchange program whereby defective subassemblies are returned to the company in exchange for good ones. The defective subassemblies are repaired and returned to the customer-service inventory.

The customer service department is a profit center within Daktronics. Revenues come from service contracts and repair charges. Warranty work is charged to a warranty account at cost and provides no internal profit. The department has succeeded in making its budgeted profit in recent years, providing 7.1 percent of Daktronics' gross profit on 5.1 percent of sales.

MANUFACTURING

Manufacturing at Daktronics consists primarily of metal fabrication and assembly of purchased components. Products are designed to make use of standard subassemblies. Various scoreboards and information displays are constructed from different configurations of standard subassemblies.

In November, 1983, manufacturing operations moved into a new 36,000-square-foot steel building constructed adjacent to the old plant. This new facility was financed with $710,000 in industrial development bonds issued by the city of Brookings; it provides adequate space for expansion of capacity and permits storage of finished standard subassemblies. Currently, Daktronics is able to ship orders six weeks after receipt, which is comparable with competitors. The ability to store finished subassemblies, while increasing Daktronics working capital needs, reduces shipping time to two weeks on standard scoreboards and information displays. It also allows smoother, more efficient scheduling. Standard sports scoreboards are completed for inventory and stocked during their season.

Until recently, manufacturing schedules and priorities at Daktronics had been based upon shipping schedules and were done on a short-term basis. Getting the order out on time had been the first priority. This resulted in the need for constant communication and adjustments among various manufacturing departments. The new production control manager, Bob Mock, is moving toward a scheduling system that will improve manufacturing efficiency, sometimes adjusting shipping schedules to accommodate work loads in the various departments. Joe Fuks, the manufacturing manager, describes the changes as having moved manufacturing from a job shop technology to a batch production technology.

Another area where progress is being made is engineering support for manufacturing. Tom Weber, a production supervisor who has been with Daktronics for eight years, remarks that "Designing used to be done right on the floor. We are better organized now. Of course we didn't have the volume that we do now."

Standard methods and standard times for various operations are being developed and used as a basis for production scheduling and control. Mock believes that the manufacturing process in some departments needs improvement. With regard to possible opposition to efforts to standardize production methods, Mock says:

> The process must be efficient and standard methods are needed, but you have to have a peoples' program, something to make people believe they are part of the team. We will try to involve manufacturing people in manufacturing changes. We've worked closely with supervisors about changes and got their feedback . . . They must be a part of the change.

Efforts to standardize production methods have met with some skepticism, but there has been little negativism toward changes. He points out that the Daktronics manufacturing work force is very young, and many employees have no other manufacturing work experience. Thus, there is a certain "show-me" attitude present, but also a willingness to accept changes that work.

There are complaints from some departments that work standards are being set too high. Specific areas cited as needing improvements are upgrading machinery, reducing rework, and delegating authority. Several manufacturing people believe that Kurtenbach puts an emphasis on sales that comes at the expense of manufacturing efficiency. One frequently mentioned problem is the practice of making last minute scheduling changes. One supervisor commented, "The philosophy here is the customer is first, no matter what. We do what it takes to get it out the door, even if it means overtime or causing part shortages." Another says, "He's been away from this and doesn't get the opportunity to get in here that much."

ENGINEERING

One factor that had motivated Kurtenbach and Sander to locate Daktronics in Brookings was the ability of graduate engineers to work at their profession. Jim Morgan and some of his department heads are long-time Daktronics employees. They and most of the engineering staff are graduates of South Dakota State University. Al Kurtenbach says:

> Our major strength is location. We have a strong educational base here. I'm able to get the top people in South Dakota and they're as good as the top people anyplace. We can hire people at a better rate because they have a better life here. There are few hassles.

Daktronics displays use three basic light sources. Incandescent bulbs are most commonly used. They are inexpensive, and have the greatest visibility. They also use more power and have a shorter life than other devices. For scoreboards, these are not serious drawbacks because the lights are actually used very few hours. Light-emitting diodes (L.E.D.'s) use less power and have a longer life, but are less visible, and are suitable for indoor use only. The newest technology, reflected light, consists of discs that are rotated to expose either a reflective or black surface to a light source. The light source could be the sun, or floodlights provided in the display. These devices are considered to have a very long lifetime and are power-efficient. They are more expensive, however, and do not have high visibility in all locations.

Daktronics recently developed the reflected light display that is technically superior to others presently on the market. This system moves discs faster than competitors' models. Daktronics managers believe this will be the technology of choice for time and temperature signs or other continuous displays with a high level of audience interest.

Engineering initiates new product developments at Daktronics. A marketing committee review and a new set of formal product-development procedures require engineers to do a more in-depth market analysis of product ideas than had previously been required.

Large scale custom scoreboards and message centers are placed under the control of project managers in the engineering department. Project managers coordinate the design, manufacture, and installation of these products. Engineering is responsible for development of software for animation and other complex displays, and for initial operator training.

In 1983, Daktronics engineers were developing a four-color display system and evaluating technologies and markets for additions to the product line. Daktronics currently has 35 employees in engineering (compared to 33 in sales and 48 in manufacturing) reflecting the company's commitment to technological change. Daktronics is involved in evaluating possibilities of technology developed elsewhere, as well as creating innovations internally.

Manufacturing engineering is a fairly recent development within engineering. This activity is carried on by Steve Heins, who was hired in 1982. Heins is responsible for establishing manufacturing methods for new and existing products. Heins does the economic analysis of capital budget requests.

BUDGETING AND FINANCIAL CONTROL

Daktronics develops financial plans on an annual basis. Sales forecasts by product line are converted to manpower and cost-of-sales budgets. Until 1983, manpower needs were determined by "gut feel." Daktronics is currently installing a Materials Requirement Planning (MRP) program, which will allow computerized production planning, projecting material and manpower requirements based on sales forecasts. Manufacturing and engineering overhead budgets are based on historical data and computed as percentages of budgeted direct labor. Money specifically budgeted for product development is based on a market and product development plan. The marketing budget is based on a percentage of sales, while the administrative budget is based on historical trends.

Previously budgeting has been performed by Al Kurtenbach and the accounting manager, Dan Kondziolka. However, the planning procedure being developed in 1983 involves all top managers in the budgeting process. Requests for capital expenditures for equipment are made for a three-year period. These requests are analyzed for payback by Steve Heins. Currently, projects are approved only if the payback period is two years or less. Don Kondziolka says of this procedure, "We are going to start taking a more mathematical approach." He noted that approval of these requests is also constrained by "what Al thinks is reasonable."

Cost control is maintained by a job-cost accounting system. Department managers receive a weekly report by job. Cost reporting at the company level is done on a monthly basis. Custom products budgets are under the control of the project manager and evaluated at the end of the project. Projects are typically completed in ninety days or less. Al Kurtenbach also holds monthly meetings with project managers to review the progress of each custom project.

Presently (1983), only payroll and inventory control are computerized. Kondziolka hopes to automate accounting to provide management with more current information. When asked about the state of cost control at Daktronics in 1983, he said, "Over the past two years, we've integrated engineering and manufacturing through better documents and tighter procedures, but engineering gets behind and manufacturing problems result!"

Daktronics is governed by a board of directors consisting of Kurtenbach and Sander and five residents of Brookings, who either represent local investors or were selected because of specific expertise. Kurtenbach and Sander own slightly less than 30 percent of the stock, the rest being held by approximately 135 stockholders, most of them local citizens. Daktronics has never paid a dividend, and as yet there is no real market in Daktronics stock. Daktronics has an employee stock purchase plan, and as of April 30, 1983 there were options outstanding for 3,866 shares, exercisable at $11.50 per share.

COMPETITIVE POSITION

No company competes with Daktronics in all product lines. Competitors are typically scoreboard companies or sign companies that have expanded into electronic information displays. Recently, two of Daktronics major competitors in the information display market, American Sign and Integrated Systems Engineering, have been acquired by the Brae Company. Brae, characterized as a communication conglomerate, topped *Inc.* magazine's 1983 list of fast-growing small companies. Although Daktronics' executives do not know what plans Brae has for these recent acquisitions, they feel that the two acquired companies have very different approaches to the business and that their consolidation will be difficult, creating opportunities for Daktronics. The agency handling Daktronics information displays in the South has formerly been associated with one of these competitors.

Daktronics managers believe their product is technically superior to the competition in most lines. Sales manager Frank Kurtenbach explains, "We are known as a pretty technical company with fairly high prices. In some product lines, Daktronics prices are competitive. The use of standard subassemblies makes our price on standard information displays very competitive. A stronger technical and manufacturing component also gives us some price advantage in the relatively small market for electronic timers for swim meets."

Joe Fuks is more emphatic: "The talent in this company will lead us to be one of the dominant companies in this profession. We will be darn good competition with Matsushita. We've got two or three firsts in reflective lights; I think we are on the cutting edge of this whole business." Joe Fuks also says Daktronics' product line is a strength. "Fairplay and A. S. & I. are our really tough competitors, but we span a much broader range than they do in the product line, and I think we will prevail."

When asked about competitive weaknesses, Daktronics managers made the following comments:

> Frank Kurtenbach—Management ability . . . the problem is getting off the phone while ten people are standing around. We need to back off and teach and observe. There is too much of doing it ourselves; too much stuff on our desks.
>
> Don Kondziolka—We need a better handle on manpower requirements—there are too many people employed. We've also got a poor handle on inventory and purchasing procedures. Our inventory levels are too high.
>
> Duane Sander—I'm not sure we have figured out how to project sales and our cost of sales. We've never been able to come very close. I think that's partly because of some very optimistic thoughts on Al's part. I'm not going to say that's all wrong, because we've been successful.
>
> Al Kurtenbach—I still want to get up to 3M's profit on sales. Those guys can put out 10 percent after-tax profit on sales. If that huge company can do it, I don't see why a small company can't do it. We're more flexible. We're not there yet, but I'm going to make that somehow. Because there are only a few ways to grow, and from within seems to be a good approach.

DISCUSSION QUESTIONS

1. Evaluate Daktronics' current position and identify its strengths and weaknesses.

2. What do you think of Al Kurtenbach's definition of Daktronics products and how would you evaluate Daktronics current strategy in terms of markets, products, and management?

3. What is your assessment of the direction Daktronics is taking? What pitfalls do you see?

4. Assess the role Al Kurtenbach plays in Daktronics today.

5. What recommendations do you have for Daktronics?

Subject Index

Name Index

Company Index